INTERNATIONAL ENVIRONMENTAL LAW

Third Edition

**Alexandre Kiss
and Dinah Shelton**

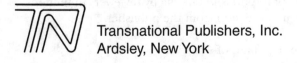

Transnational Publishers, Inc.
Ardsley, New York

Published and distributed by *Transnational Publishers, Inc.*
Ardsley Park
Science and Technology Center
410 Saw Mill River Road
Ardsley, NY 10502

Phone: 914-693-5100
Fax: 914-693-4430
E-mail: info@transnationalpubs.com
Web: www.transnationalpubs.com

Library of Congress Cataloging-in-Publication Data

Kiss, Alexandre Charles, 1925–
    International environmental law / Alexandre Kiss and
Dinah Shelton.–3rd ed.
        p. cm.
    Includes bibliographical references and index.
    ISBN 1-57105-309-3
        1. Environmental law, International.   I. Shelton, Dinah.
    II. Title.

K3585.K57 2003
344.04'6–dc22

                                                    2003065053

Coventry University

To see the World in a Grain of Sand
And a Heaven in a Wild Flower
Hold Infinity in the Palm of your Hand
And Eternity in an Hour

William Blake, Auguries of Innocence

AUTHORS' PREFACE

The field of international environmental law has rapidly expanded in recent decades to encompass many issues of fundamental concern to international law scholars and practitioners, environmental lawyers, public officials and civil society. To serve these various audiences, this treatise introduces the major international legal rules, institutions, and procedures concerned with protecting the environment. The book discusses the theory, objectives, and historical evolution of international environmental law, as well as the principles of general international law that are particularly important in the environmental field. The text reviews the norms applicable to each sector or milieu of the environment, as well as developments concerning sources of environmental harm, such as chemicals, toxic waste and global warming. It further describes and analyzes the move towards integrated protection and ecosystem management, as well as efforts to include environmental considerations in other international legal regimes.

The first edition of the book was published in 1991, before the landmark United Nations Conference on Environment and Development, held in Rio de Janeiro in June 1992. The second edition included developments that took place in the subsequent five years. Now, a decade after the Rio Conference and with the conclusion of the World Summit on Sustainable Development, held in Johannesburg, South Africa, in September 2002, the third edition looks at global and regional legal measures adopted through the end of July 2003.

Agenda 21, the Program of Action adopted at the Rio Conference, created widespread hope for improving environmental conditions throughout the world. The anticipated progress has been slow in coming. The United Nations University and the Institute of Advanced Studies provided a sobering overview of the global environment in their report to the World Summit on Sustainable Development:

> There are at least 1.1 billion people who still lack access to safe drinking water and 2.4 billion who lack adequate sanitation. Two-thirds of the world's population will live in 'water-stressed' areas by the year 2025. In some cases groundwater levels are falling by one to three meters each year. 75 percent of the world's energy is being produced by burning fossil fuels, increasing CO_2 emission levels by 1 percent each year, despite reduction targets being established

since the adoption of the United Nations Framework Convention on Climate Change. The fourteen hottest years since 1860, when systematic measuring began, have all occurred in the past two decades. More than 8 percent of children in developing countries still die before the age of five, and in some of the poorest countries, one in five children die before their first birthday. More than 113 million school-age children in developing countries are not in school, over 60 percent of them girls. About 815 million people in the world are undernourished. Hunger in South Asia, where it is most prevalent, is declining, while in Africa, about one-third of the population is undernourished and the numbers are increasing. In many developing countries, poor health conditions prevail as a result of contaminated water, poor sanitation, severe indoor air pollution, malaria and other infectious diseases, and the spread of HIV/AIDS. The loss of 2.5 percent of forests globally each year, along with the threat of extinction of 24 percent of mammals and 12 percent of birds, leads experts to the estimation that we are losing one major drug every two years, whilst only one percent of the world's tropical plants have been screened for potential pharmaceutical application. If this current development continues, biodiversity will be threatened on up to 74 percent of the land area by 2032.[1]

In this growing environmental crisis, international environmental law and policy take on added urgency and there is evident need to place environmental considerations at the center of social and economic issues. In addition, international institutions and civil society need to play an increasing role in developing international obligations and monitoring compliance with them.

The potential for law and policy to improve the environment can be seen in some of the positive developments of recent years. Water quality has generally improved in developed countries. The 2002 report on Bathing Water Quality in the European Union[2] found 97 percent of coastal sites across Europe now comply with the EC Directive on Bathing Water Quality[3] while 100 percent of the freshwater sites in the United Kingdom meet the standard. After decades of absence, salmon have returned to the Rhine River. European forests that were dying 20 years ago due to environmental stresses are again healthy and expanding. In other regions of the world,

---

[1]   United Nations University/Institute of Advanced Studies, *International Sustainable Development Governance* 8 (Aug. 2002).

[2]   European Commission, Report on Bathing Water Quality, May 29, 2002.

[3]   EEC Directive Concerning the Quality of Bathing Water, 76/160/EEC, O.J. L 31 (5/2/76).

species once threatened or endangered have recovered. These successes, however, are largely overshadowed by the scope of the current problems.

In taking needed action, states and other actors are increasingly mainstreaming or integrating environmental protection into other subject areas of international regulation, such as human rights, armed conflict, and trade. The expansion and maturing of international environmental law is also reflected in the large number of treaties adopted in the past two decades, the development of customary international norms, and the increasing utilization of international dispute settlement mechanisms to address environmental problems.

Without analyzing in detail each of the hundreds of agreements and other normative instruments in the field, this volume attempts a comprehensive overview of the development of international environmental law, its current status and emerging trends. The book is divided into three parts. Part I examines the structure, basic concepts, and institutions of international environmental law. The second part turns to the regulation of each environmental sector or milieu (soil, water, air, living organisms) and the sources of environmental harm. Part III concerns integrated approaches to environmental protection, such as ecosystem management, and the mainstreaming of environmental issues into the international legal regimes of human rights, armed conflict, and international economic law. Due to the increased availability of primary texts, no international instrument is reproduced herein. Print and electronic resources are indicated in the bibliographies that follow each chapter.

We hope the book will prove a useful resource not only for those persons studying and actively involved in environmental protection, but also those who have a general interest in the subject. It is important to thank the University of Notre Dame for research leave time in the spring 2003 and the summer grants that enabled this revision to be completed in a timely manner. We are also grateful to Elizabeth Renton for her careful proofreading of the manuscript.

TABLE OF CONTENTS

PART III. INCLUSIVE ENVIRONMENTAL PROTECTION

(handwritten margin notes: "procedural ①" next to B.; "greening ②" next to C.; "new right ③" next to D.)

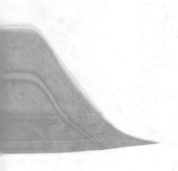

LIST OF ABBREVIATIONS

AJIL	American Journal of International Law
ASEAN	Association of Southeast Asian Nations
ATCM	Antarctic Treaty Consultative Meeting
ATCP	Antarctic Treaty Consultative Parties
A.T.S.	Antarctic Treaty System
B.F.S.P.	British and Foreign State Papers
CBD	Convention on Biological Diversity
CCAMLR	Convention on the Conservation of Antarctic Marine Living Resources
CCPR	Covenant on Civil and Political Rights
CDM	Clean development mechanism
CFC	Chlorofluorocarbons
CIEL	Center for International Environmental Law
CITES	Convention on International Trade in Endangered Species
Cmd.	United Kingdom Command Papers
CMS	Convention on the Conservation of Migratory Species of Wild Animals
COLO. J. INT'L ENVTL. L. & POL'Y	Colorado Journal of International Environmental Law and Policy
COP	Conference of the Parties
CSD	Commission on Sustainable Development
CTE	World Trade Organization Committee on Trade and Environment
C.T.S.	Canadian Treaty Series
DSB	Dispute Settlement Body of WTO
ECOL. L.Q.	Ecology Law Quarterly
ECOSOC	United Nations Economic and Social Council
EC	European Community
ECJ	European Court of Justice
EEZ	Exclusive Economic Zone
EIA	Environmental Impact Assessment
EMEP	Cooperative Program for Monitoring and Evaluation of LRTAP in Europe
EMuT	International Law: Multilateral Agreements
ENVTL. L.	Environmental Law

E.P.L.	Environmental Policy and Law
E.T.S.	European Treaty Series
EU	European Union
Eur. CT. H.R.	European Court of Human Rights
E.Y.B.	European Yearbook
FAO	Food and Agriculture Organization
GATT	General Agreement on Tariffs and Trade
GEF	Global Environment Facility
GEMS	Global Environment Monitoring System
GEO. INT'L ENVTL. L. REV.	Georgetown International Environmental Law Review
GHG	Greenhouse gases
HARV. ENVTL. L. REV.	Harvard Environmental Law Review
IAEA	International Atomic Energy Agency
IBRD	International Bank for Reconstruction and Development
I.C.J.	International Court of Justice Reports
ICRC	International Committee of the Red Cross
ICZM	Integrated coastal zone management
IDA	International Development Association
IFC	International Finance Corporation
ILC	International Law Commission
I.L.M.	International Legal Materials
ILO	International Labor Organization
IMF	International Monetary Fund
IMCO	International Maritime Consultative Organization
IMO	International Maritime Organization
IPCC	Intergovernmental Panel on Climate Change
IRPTC	International Register of Potentially Toxic Chemicals
ITLOS	International Tribunal on the Law of the Sea
ITTA	International Tropical Timber Agreement
IUCN	World Conservation Union
IWC	International Whaling Commission
JI	Joint implementation
J.O.R.F.	Journal officiel de la République française
Kiss	Selected Multilateral Treaties in the Field of the Environment (1983)
LMO	Living modified organism
L.N.T.S.	League of Nations Treaty Series
LRTAP	Convention on Long-Range Transboundary Air Pollution

MARPOL	International Convention on the Prevention of Pollution by Ships
MEA	multilateral environmental agreement
MICH. L. REV.	Michigan Law Review
MIGA	Multilateral Investment Guarantee Agency
MOP	Meeting of the Parties
MOU	Memorandum of understanding
NAFTA	North American Free Trade Agreement
NAT. RES. J.	Natural Resources Journal
NETH. Y.B. INT'L L.	Netherlands Yearbook of International Law
NGO	Non-governmental organization
N.Y.L.S. J. INT'L & COMP. L.	New York Law School Journal of International and Comparative Law
N.Y.U. INT'L & COMP. L.J.	New York University International and Comparative Law Journal
O.J.	Official Journal of the European Communities
OAS	Organization of American States
OAU	Organization of African Unity
ODS	ozone depleting substance
OECD	Organization for Economic Cooperation and Development
OSCE	Organization for Security and Cooperation in Europe
PCBs	polychlorinated biphenyls
PIC	Prior informed consent
POPs	persistant organic pollutants
RECIEL	Review of European Community and International Environmental Law
RGDIP	Revue générale du droit international public
S. CAL. L. REV.	University of Southern California Law Review
Stat.	Statute
TEU	Treaty on European Union
T.I.A.S.	U.S. Treaties and Other International Agreements
TOMAS	Tropospheric Ozone Management Areas
U. COLO. L. REV.	University of Colorado Law Review
U.K.T.S.	United Kingdom Treaty Series
UNCC	United Nations Compensation Commission
UNCED	United Nations Conference on Environment and Development
UNCLOS	United Nations Convention on the Law of the Sea
UNCTAD	United Nations Conference on Trade and Development

UNDP	United Nations Development Program
UNECE	United Nations Economic Commission for Europe
UNEP	United Nations Environment Program
UNESCO	United Nations Educational, Scientific and Cultural Organization
UNFCCC	United Nations Framework Convention on Climate Change
U.N.GAOR	United Nations General Assembly Official Records
UNIDO	United Nations Industrial Development Organization
UNITAR	United Nations Institute for Training and Research
U.N.RIAA	United Nations Reports of International Arbitral Awards
U.N.T.S.	United Nations Treaty Series
U.S.T.	United States Treaty Series
VA. J. INT'L L.	Virginia Journal of International Law
VOCs	Volatile organic compounds
WESTON	BURNS WESTON, INTERNATIONAL LAW AND WORLD ORDER: BASIC DOCUMENTS
WHO	World Health Organization
WMO	World Meteorological Organization
WSSD	World Summit on Sustainable Development
WTO	World Trade Organization
WWF	Worldwide Fund for Nature
YALE J. INT'L L.	Yale Journal of International Law
Y.B. I.L.C.	Yearbook of the International Law Commission

CHRONOLOGICAL TABLE OF TREATIES AND OTHER INTERNATIONAL INSTRUMENTS

30 May 1814	Treaty of Paris, Fr.-Gr. Brit., 63 Consol. T.S. 193 (1814); 74
29 November 1868	Declaration of St. Petersburg Renouncing the Use, in Time of War, of Explosive Projectiles, AJIL 1 (Supp.) 95; 735
13 July 1878	Treaty of Berlin between Great Britain, Austria-Hungary, France, Italy, Germany, Russia and Turkey, 3 Martens 2d 449; 74.
19 May 1900	Convention for the Preservation of Wild Animals, Birds and Fish in Africa, 188 Parry 418; 39, 366
19 March 1902	Convention for the Protection of Birds Useful to Agriculture (Paris), 30 Martens (2d) 686; 102 B.F.S.P. 969; 39, 355, 426–27
21 May 1906	United States-Mexico Convention Concerning the Equitable Distribution of the Waters of the Rio Grande for Irrigation Purposes, UN DOC/ST/ LEG/Ser. 8/12, at 232; 34 Stat. 2953, T.S. 455; 9 Bevans 924; 488
18 October 1907	Convention (No. IV) Respecting the Laws and Customs of War on Land (The Hague), 36 Stat. 2277; T.S. No. 539; 74, 734, 735, 736
11 January 1909	Treaty between the United States and Great Britain Respecting Boundary Waters Between the United States and Canada (Washington), 36 Stat. 2448, T.S. No. 548; 12 Bevans 319; 4 AJIL 239 (1920 Supp.); 40, 147, 475, 572, 642
7 February 1911	Treaty for the Preservation and Protection of the Fur Seals (Washington), 104 B.F.S.P. 175; 40, 415, 640
22 March 1923	U.S.-Great Britain Convention for the Preservation of the Halibut Fishery (Washington D.C.); 404
17 June 1925	Geneva Protocol for the Prohibition of the Use in War of Asphyxiating, Poisonous or Other Gases and of Bacteriological Methods of Warfare (Geneva), 26 U.S.T. 571; T.I.A.S. No. 8061; 14 I.L.M. 49 (1975); 735, 737

24 April 1978	Protocol Concerning Regional Cooperation in Combating Pollution by Oil and Other Harmful Substances in Cases of Emergency, 17 I.L.M. 526 (1978); 504, 537, 547
19 May 1978	UNEP, Principles of Conduct in the Field of the Environment for the Guidance of States in the Conservation and Harmonious Utilization of Natural Resources Shared by Two or More States, U.N. Doc. UNEP/1G 12/2 (1978); 17 I.L.M. 1097 (1978); 5 WESTON V.B.8; 54, 94, 192, 639–40
30 June 1978	Convention Relating to the Status of the River Gambia, Natural Resources/Water Series No. 134 ST/ESA/141 (1984) at 39; 477
3 July 1978	Treaty for Amazonian Cooperation (Brasilia), 17 I.L.M. 1045 (1978); 370
21 September 1978	OECD Recommendation for Strengthening International Cooperation on Environmental Protection in Transfrontier Regions, C(78)77(Final); 17 I.L.M. 1530 (1978); 198
22 November 1978	United States-Canada Agreement on Great Lakes Water Quality with Annexes, 30 U.S.T. 1383, T.I.A.S. 9257. Amended October 16, 1983; T.I.A.S. 10798; 40, 147, 193, 467, 475–76
8 May 1979	OECD Recommendation C(79)115 on Environment and Tourism; 93
23 June 1979	Convention on the Conservation of Migratory Species of Wild Animals (Bonn), 19 I.L.M. 15 (1980); Kiss 500; 5 WESTON V.H.11; 17, 33, 50, 72, 89, 220, 234, 236, 362–65, 376, 417
19 September 1979	Convention on the Conservation of European Wildlife and Natural Habitats (Bern), E.T.S. 104; U.K.T.S. 56 (1982); Cmd. 8738; Kiss 509; 17, 19, 33, 53, 83, 104, 128, 221, 234, 307, 371–74, 438
13 November 1979	Convention on Long-Range Transboundary Air Pollution (Geneva), U.K.T.S. 57 (1983), Cmd. 9034; T.I.A.S. No. 10541; 18 I.L.M. 1442 (1979); Kiss 519; 5 WESTON V.E.3; 44–5, 78, 95, 99, 176, 190, 199, 200–01, 226, 227, 233, 270, 319, 556, 564–70, 619
5 December 1979	Agreement Governing the Activities of States on the Moon and Other Celestial Bodies, G.A. Res. 34/68; U.N. GAOR Supp. No. 46 at 77, U.N. Doc. A/34/46; 18 I.L.M. 1434 (1979); 5 WESTON V.E.23; 616
20 December 1979	Convention for the Conservation and Management of the Vicuña, Lima, EMuT 979:94; 425

11 December 1992   Regional Agreement on the Transboundary
                        Movement of Hazardous Waste (Panama), EMuT
                        992:91; 51, 611

12 December 1992   Treaty on Sharing of the Ganges Waters at Farakka
                        Between Bangladesh and India, 36 I.L.M. 519 (1997);
                        EMuT 992:91; 478

17 December 1992   North American Free Trade Agreement (Washington,
                        8 and 17 Dec.; 11 and 17 Dec., Ottawa; 14 and 17 Dec.
                        Mexico City); 32 I.L.M. 289; 32 I.L.M. 605 (1993); 59,
                        63, 790–93

21 December 1992   Central European Free Trade Agreement (Krakow),
                        34 I.L.M. 3 (1995); 795

22 December 1992   G.A. Res. 47/191creating the Commission on
                        Sustainable Development, 5 WESTON V.A.7; 96, 107,
                        112

22 December 1992   G.A. Res. 47/443, Decision on Large-scale Pelagic
                        Driftnet Fishing and its Impact on the Living Marine
                        Resources of the World's Oceans and Seas; 107

13 January 1993   Convention on the Prohibition of the Development,
                        Production, Stockpiling and Use of Chemical Weapons
                        and on their Destruction (Paris), 32 I.L.M. 800
                        (1993); 59, 308, 739–40

26 March 1993   Agreement on Joint Activities in Addressing the
                        Aral Sea and the Zone around the Sea Crisis,
                        Improving the Environment, and Ensuring the
                        Social and Economic Development of the Aral Sea
                        Region, UNEP/DEWA/DPDL/RS.02/4; 641

7 April 1993   Hungary-Slovak Republic Special Agreement for
                        Submission to the International Court of Justice of
                        the Differences Between them Concerning the
                        Gabcíkovo-Nagymaros Project (Brussels), 32 I.L.M.
                        1293 (1993); 482–83

10 May 1993   Convention for the Conservation of Southern
                        Bluefin Tuna (Canberra); 406

16 June 1993   Agreement Establishing the South Pacific Regional
                        Environment Program (SPREP), EMuT 993:45

21 June 1993   Convention on Civil Liability for Damage Resulting
                        From Activities Dangerous to the Environment
                        (Lugano), 32 I.L.M.1228 ((1993); EMuT 993:19; 3,
                        262, 286, 294–97, 631

1 July 1993   Memorandum of Understanding concerning
                        Conservation Measures for the Siberian Crane; 364,
                        365

TABLE OF EUROPEAN UNION LAW

Treaties

18 April 1951	Treaty Establishing the European Coal and Steel Community (Paris), 261 U.N.T.S. 140; U.K.T.S. 16 (1979); Cmd. 7461, 158 B.F.S.P. 630; 132
25 March 1957	Treaty Establishing the European Economic Community (Rome) 298 U.N.T.S. 11; U.K.T.S. 15 (1979); Cmd. 7480; 24, 25, 132
25 March 1957	Treaty Establishing the European Atomic Energy Community (Euratom) (Rome) 298 U.N.T.S. 167; U.K.T.S. 15 (1979); Cmd. 7480; 132
27 September 1968	Convention on Jurisdiction and Enforcement of Judgments in Civil and Commercial Matters (Brussels), O.J. L 304/77 1978; EC 46 (1978); Cmd. 7395; 8 I.L.M. 229 (1969); 279
17 February 1986	Single European Act, EC 12 (1986); Cmd. 9758; U.K.T.S. 31 (1988); Cmd. 372; 25 I.L.M. 506 (1986); 134, 213
7 February 1992	Treaty on European Union (Maastricht), EMuT 992:11; 31 I.L.M. 247 (1992); 87, 134, 207, 213
2 October 1997	Treaty of Amsterdam amending the Treaty on European Union, Consolidated Versions O.J. C 32 (12/24/02); 94, 134–139, 204, 210

Regulations, Directives, and Decisions

18 March 1967	Directive Relating to the Classification, Packaging and Labelling of Dangerous Substances, 67/548/EEC O.J. No. L 196 of 8/16/67. Amended: Mar. 13, 1969 (O.J. L 68 of 3/19/69); Mar. 6, 1970 (O.J. L 59 of 3/14/70); Mar. 22, 1971 (O.J. L 74 of 3/29/71); May 21, 1973 (O.J. L 167 of 6/25/73); June 24, 1975 (O.J. L 183 of 7/14/75); and Sept. 18, 1979, (O.J. L 98 of 7/22/78); 3, 250, 598
22 November 1973	Directive Relating to Detergents, 73/404/EEC, O.J. 347 (1973); 133

TABLE OF CASES

INTRODUCTION

International environmental law is complex and vast, comprising hundreds of global and regional norms that aim to protect the earth's living and non-living elements and its ecological processes. This relatively recent body of law emerged from growing public awareness, informed by warnings of scientists, that our planet is endangered by the activities of an ever-increasing number of humans, by invasive technology, and by rapid consumption of the earth's resources. Environmental degradation is evident in the pollution of rivers and lakes, black tides along the coasts, and poisonous fog and smog in the cities of nearly all countries. Other problems stem from endemic poverty, including desertification and the creation of immense urban areas. Throughout the world, humans are causing the unprecedented extinction of biological resources.

Global change, including internationalization of markets and the emergence of transnational civil society presents new challenges and new opportunities. While globalization of communications makes possible more rapid knowledge of the existence and scope of environmental problems, global movements of persons and products are accompanied by the introduction of alien species and the spread of new pollutants and disease vectors. Over-consumption in wealthy countries threatens to exhaust living and non-living resources while producing greenhouse gas emissions that impact the global climate. New problems resulting from technological advances are constantly being identified, such as the risks of genetically-modified organisms, the environmental impacts of industrial fish- and crustacean-farming and endocrine disruption in various species, including humans, due to the introduction of unprocessed pharmaceuticals in wastewater. As a consequence, there is a constant need to develop and when necessary revise the international and national legal framework responding to these challenges.

Concern for conserving aspects of the environment has long been evident. National laws enacted in the Middle Ages aimed to combat a specific pollutant such as smoke or to protect a particular forest or a body of water.[1] International agreements have been adopted for over a century. The first

---

[1]   In 1306, an ordinance of Edward I prohibited the use of coal in open furnaces in London. Other early laws can be found in Belgium, France, and the Netherlands. *See* C.A. COLLIARD, LA POLLUTION ATMOSPHERIQUE EN DROIT FRANCAIS ET EN DROIT COMPARÉ, at 22, 90, 101, 139 (1976).

agreements aimed at improving the status of endangered species of domesticated or wild flora or fauna: for example, the 1900 Convention for the
Protection of Wild Animals, Birds and Fish in Africa, the 1902 Convention
"for the protection of birds useful to agriculture"[2] and a 1911 treaty protecting fur seals. These instruments approached the subject primarily from
a utilitarian perspective that sought to maximize economic exploitation of
the designated species.[3]

Concepts about nature changed fundamentally near the end of the
1960s. Under growing pressure from international public opinion, governments began to demonstrate concern over the general state of the environment and introduced legislation to combat pollution of inland waters,
ocean, and air, and to safeguard certain cities or areas. Simultaneously, they
established special administrative organs, ministries or environmental agencies, to preserve more effectively the quality of life of their citizens. Developments in international environmental law paralleled this evolution within
states.

A. Concept and Scope of the "Environment" and "Environmental Law"

A legal definition of the "environment" is important to delineate the scope
of the subject, determine the application of legal rules, and establish the
extent of liability when harm occurs. The English-language term "environment" is borrowed from an ancient French word "environner," meaning to
encircle. Most languages had to borrow or invent new terms when concern
emerged about the potential destruction of natural resources and processes
on which life depends.[4] A program of UNESCO[5] uses the term "biosphere"
to designate the part of the universe where, according to present knowledge, all life is concentrated. *Webster's Dictionary* begins with a general definition of the environment, reflecting the original French meaning: "the
circumstances, objects, or conditions by which one is surrounded."[6] It con-

---

    [2]   For further discussion of these instruments, *see* Chapter 8 on protec-
tion of living organisms and ecosystems.

    [3]   The history of international environmental law is discussed in more
detail in Chapter 2.

    [4]   New words have emerged in many languages to express the concept of
the environment: "Umwelt" (German), "milieu" (Dutch), "medio ambiente"
(Spanish), "meio ambiente" (Portuguese), "Al'biah" (Arabic), "okruzhauchhaia
sreda" (Russian) and "kankyo" (Japanese).

    [5]   UNESCO, Man Belongs to the Earth: UNESCO's Man and the Bios-
phere Program (1988).

    [6]   "Environment" defined in *Webster's Ninth New Collegiate Dictionary* (1983).

tinues with a more precise meaning: "the complex of physical, chemical, and biotic factors (such as climate, soil, and living things) that act upon an organism or an ecological community and ultimately determine its form and survival" to which it adds "the aggregate of social and cultural conditions that influence the life of an individual or community." The last definition is very broad and brings problems such as traffic congestion, crime, and noise within the field of environmental protection.

In law, "environment" can refer to a limited area or encompass the entire planet, including the atmosphere and stratosphere. International legal instruments generally define "environment" broadly. A text of the European Community includes "water, air and land and their inter-relationship as well as relationships between them and any living organism."[7] The Espoo Convention on Environmental Impact Assessment in a Transboundary Context[8] and the European Convention on Civil Liability for Damage Resulting from Activities Dangerous to the Environment[9] contain comprehensive definitions. The latter provides:

> For the purpose of this Convention . . .
> "Environment" includes:
> — natural resources both abiotic and biotic, such as air, water, soil, fauna and flora and the interaction between the same factors;
> — property which forms part of the cultural heritage; and
> — the characteristic aspects of the landscape.

Thus, the man-made environment, including structures and landscapes, can be considered a part of the environment to be protected. The International Court of Justice defines the environment to include a social dimension, stating that "the environment is not an abstraction, but represents the living space, the quality of life, and the very health of human beings, including generations unborn."[10]

Broad definitions and the fact that all human activities have an impact on the environment make it difficult to establish the limits of environmental law as an independent legal field; indeed they imply the integration of environmental protection into all areas of law and policy. Environmental law springs from the understanding that the environment determines the form and survival of each organism and community; thus national, regional, and international efforts must be taken to ensure the continued viability of

---

7   Article 2, Council Directive of June 27, 1967, O.J. L 196 (7/16/67).
8   Espoo, Feb. 25, 1991.
9   Lugano, June 21, 1993.
10   *Legality of the Threat or Use of Nuclear Weapons*, Advisory Opinion, 1996 I.C.J. Rep. 241–42, para. 29.

the planet and the sustainability of its myriad species, through holistic approaches such as integrated or ecosystem protection.

The breadth of the definitions entails that in some cases law and policy will respond to environmental deterioration produced by natural events, such as volcanic eruptions, as well as those caused by human intervention. Even though law cannot affect the natural processes causing environmental changes, law can and does regulate human behavior, including behavior in response to natural disasters. Thus, the fact of a natural disaster does not modify a state's international legal duty to notify and cooperate with other states in response to an environmental emergency.

Due to the inevitable environmental impact of human actions, rules having other objectives sometimes provide indirect protection and can have great ecological importance. Early international conventions concerning fishing, for example, were enacted primarily to allocate marine living resources and to assure their management in order to protect local economies and prevent conflicts between fishermen of different nationalities. These objectives, based upon the goal of sustainable exploitation of living resources, nonetheless have had beneficial environmental impact, permitting the maintenance and renewal of stocks.

Environmental protection is sometimes advanced through rules adopted with another motivation. The severe ecological consequences of marine accidents such as the 1988 grounding of the Alaskan oil tanker *Exxon Valdez*, the 1999 breakup of the tanker *Erica*, and the similar disaster caused by the *Prestige* in 2002, demonstrated the importance of international maritime rules, including those governing the construction of ships and training of vessel crews. Similarly, norms that standardize the performance of internal combustion engines, originally adopted in order to facilitate international trade, have supported clean technology that have led to a reduction in engine noise and the emission of noxious gases.

In its own domain, environmental law prescribes and prohibits by so-called "command and control" mechanisms, adopts economic incentives and disincentives, and creates management tools. Economic measures such as taxes on pollution emissions or on fuel, subsidies for clean technology, financial benefits for persons who manage their land in an ecologically-sound way, tradable permits for pollution, eco-auditing, and eco-labels generally require legal instruments. Public authorities similarly must organize and ensure the functioning of environmental management for units larger than individual business or government enterprises.

B. The Necessity of International Law

The need and desire to protect the environment presents a challenge for international law because it is now widely recognized that many environmental problems are transboundary, regional or global in scope. The 1968

European Water Charter, one of the first modern international instruments relating to the environment, articulated a fundamental principle at the beginning of the ecological era: water knows no boundaries. Experience and observation since then have made it obvious that neither the ocean, nor the atmosphere, nor living resources in general know political boundaries. Any significant impact on the environment can produce effects outside national territory, as evidenced by the consequences of long-range transboundary air pollution,[11] the widespread impact of ozone-depleting substances, and global climate change resulting from the emission of greenhouse gases.

Economic factors play a role as well in internationalizing efforts to safeguard the environment. A state that enacts environmental measures must count the increased costs that are borne by its economy. In the long term, "green" investments are advantageous, because it is more costly and in some cases impossible to repair environmental damage by, for example, cleaning up rivers or groundwater, rehabilitating the countryside, or reintroducing wildlife species. In the short term, however, environmental protection costs are borne by the producers, consumers or public authorities of the enacting state. The national economy feels the consequences, because the costs usually are reflected in the export prices of national products and services. The state that protects its environment thus risks a competitive disadvantage in the marketplace unless international legal measures harmonize the environmental protection requirements for all competitors.

Controlling the international transfer of polluting products, wastes, installations and environmentally-harmful activities also requires international cooperation and the adoption of common standards. In some instances, there is a risk that activities prohibited or regulated by one country will move into a state whose legislation or enforcement is less rigorous. The latter often are developing countries which accept the risks involved in order to welcome less expensive or otherwise unavailable foreign products and investment. Widely-reported deaths due to the use of exported pesticides banned in the country of origin, as well as industrial catastrophes such as the 1984 disaster in Bhopal, India, which killed 2,500 people and injured thousands of others,[12] demonstrate the very real dangers that exist. International agreements based on prior informed consent of the importing

---

[11]   In the 1980s an estimated 50 percent of atmospheric acidity deposited in eastern Canadian aquatic and terrestrial ecosystems was "imported" from the United States, with levels in some areas exceeding 80 percent. John M. Sibley, *A Canadian Perspective on the North American Acid Rain Problem,* 4 N.Y.L.S. J. INT'L & COMP. L. 529–30 (1983). The 1990 U.S. Clean Air Act Amendments and the 1991 U.S.-Canada Bilateral Agreement on Air Quality took steps to remedy the problem. *See US-Canada Air Quality Progress Report,* 2–3 (2000).

[12]   See Marc Galanter, *Bhopals Past and Present: The Changing Legal Response to Mass Disaster,* 10 WINDSOR Y.B. OF ACCESS TO JUSTICE 151 (1990).

states[13] or a ban on the transfer of certain substances[14] address some of these problems, but these efforts may be challenged as incompatible with international policies that emphasize free trade and investment.[15] Unilateral measures to block environmentally-harmful products already have run afoul of the obligations contained in the General Agreement on Tariffs and Trade, as interpreted by the organs of the World Trade Organization.

Finally, the dimensions of some existing phenomena require regional or global action: desertification, reduction of the world genetic heritage, ozone-depletion, global warming—the catalogue lengthens as our understanding of the biosphere's life-supporting systems and processes improves. It has become clear that worldwide rules are necessary to protect the biosphere, including the ozone layer, migratory species, habitats and ecosystems, and areas outside national jurisdiction.

International regulation thus becomes a basic guarantee of environmental protection. Standard-setting, the primary purpose of which is to prevent environmental harm, is insufficient by itself to assure effective environmental protection. An indispensable corollary to international regulation is the creation of supervisory institutions and the maintenance of cooperation between states, especially where continuity of action is necessary. Finally, international law must ensure compliance and provide redress for harm to those injured. The following chapters in Part I discuss the foundations and sources of international environmental law, its history, the general principles of law applicable today, implementation techniques and procedures, the international institutional framework and civil society, and, finally, compliance and enforcement.

BIBLIOGRAPHY

BIRNIE, P. & BOYLE, A., INTERNATIONAL LAW AND THE ENVIRONMENT (2d ed. 2002).

BROWN, L. et al. STATE OF THE WORLD 1997 (1997).

CALDWELL, L., INTERNATIONAL ENVIRONMENTAL POLICY: FROM THE TWENTIETH TO THE TWENTY-FIRST CENTURY (1996).

---

[13] *See, e.g.*, Convention on the Prior Informed Consent Procedure for Certain Hazardous Chemicals and Pesticides in International Trade (Sept. 10, 1998); Protocol on Biosafety to the Convention on Biological Diversity (Montreal, Jan. 29, 2000).

[14] *See, e.g.*, Montreal Protocol on Substances that Deplete the Ozone Layer (Sept. 16, 1987); Convention on the Ban of the Import into Africa and the Control of Transboundary Movement and Management of Hazardous Wastes Within Africa (Bamako, Jan. 29, 1991).

[15] *See* Chapter 17.

CAMPBELL, D. & STEWART, M. eds., INTERNATIONAL ENVIRONMENTAL LAW AND REGULATIONS (1996).

DEMKO, G. & YOUNG, O., GLOBAL ENVIRONMENTAL CHANGE AND INTERNATIONAL GOVERNANCE (1993).

HOHMANN, H. ed., BASIC DOCUMENTS OF INTERNATIONAL ENVIRONMENTAL LAW (1992).

HOOG, G. & STEINMETZ, A. eds., INTERNATIONAL CONVENTIONS ON PROTECTION OF HUMANITY AND ENVIRONMENT (1993).

NANDA, V., INTERNATIONAL ENVIRONMENTAL LAW AND POLICY (1995).

PALMER, G., ENVIRONMENT: THE INTERNATIONAL CHALLENGE (1995).

RUSTER, B. & SIMMA, B. eds., INTERNATIONAL PROTECTION OF THE ENVIRONMENT (1975–1983, 1989–).

SANDS, PH., TARASOFSKY, R. & WEISS, M. eds., DOCUMENTS IN INTERNATIONAL ENVIRONMENTAL LAW (1995–).

SANDS, PH., PRINCIPLES OF INTERNATIONAL ENVIRONMENTAL LAW (2d ed. 2003).

SINGH, G., ENVIRONMENTAL LAW: INTERNATIONAL AND NATIONAL PERSPECTIVES (1995).

VOGLER, J. & IMBER, M. eds., THE ENVIRONMENT AND INTERNATIONAL RELATIONS (1996).

WEISS, E., SZASZ, P. & MAGRAW, D., eds., INTERNATIONAL ENVIRONMENTAL LAW: BASIC INSTRUMENTS AND REFERENCES (1992).

PART I

STRUCTURE AND BASIC CONCEPTS

CHAPTER 1

FOUNDATIONS OF INTERNATIONAL ENVIRONMENTAL LAW

International environmental law aims to protect the biosphere from major deterioration that could endanger its present or future functioning. This objective provokes the fundamental questions: Why protect the biosphere and for whose benefit? Who has legal obligations in this field and on what bases do such obligations exist? The present chapter addresses these questions, as well as the characteristics of international environmental law deriving from scientific, economic, political and legal realities. It begins with an overview of the religious, ethical and philosophical foundations of environmental protection.

A. Religion and Philosophy

Religious and philosophical concepts are crucial to understanding the views of nature and humankind's relationship to it that form the bases of environmental law. These views have ranged from exploitive and dominating to holistic and cognizant of the intrinsic value of nature; they are relevant to understanding current law and to creating new approaches to environmental protection.

1. Religious Sources

Religious texts provide some conceptual foundations of environmental protection.[1] In Judeo-Christian religious traditions, two contrasting approaches can be found. A view prevalent in the past claimed human supremacy and ownership over all creation based on the "dominion" given humans in the first of the Creation stories in Genesis.[2] More recent interpretations argue

---

1   For an overview of the Judeo-Christian sacred texts, see D. Shelton, *Nature in the Bible, in* MAN AND THE ENVIRONMENT: ESSAYS IN HONOR OF ALEXANDRE KISS 63 (1998).

2   "Be fruitful, and multiply, and replenish the earth, and subdue it; and have dominion over the fish of the sea, and over the fowl of the air, and over every living thing that moveth upon the earth." (Gen. 1:28).

that the relevant passage does not grant ownership to humans,[3] but rather establishes human power over other creatures and the right to beneficial use of them, imposing a type of guardianship or a trust. It does not include the right to waste or destroy that which belongs to the Creator.[4] Certain passages clearly indicate that humans do not own the earth and its resources. The Psalms proclaim, for example, that "the earth is the Lord's and the fullness thereof; the world, and they that dwell therein. For He hath founded it upon the seas, and established it upon the floods."[5] The Biblical story of the flood includes a command to Noah to save all creatures, "to keep seed alive upon the face of the earth"[6] and ends with a Covenant between God and man "and every living creature . . . for perpetual generations."[7] Jewish law provided for conservation of birds,[8] protection of trees during wartime,[9] and regulated the disposal of human waste.[10]

In the *Summa Theologica*, Thomas Aquinas argues that man's dominion over nature includes a competence to use and manage the world's resources,

---

[3]   *Cf.* "for the earth is the Lord's and the fullness thereof" (I Cor. 10:26). In speaking of the desolation of Egypt, God says "the river is mine and I have made it." (Ezek. 29:9).

[4]   In Revelation, the 24 elders worship God by saying "Thou art worthy, O Lord, to receive glory and honour and power: for thou hast created all things, and for thy pleasure they are and were created." All things being created for God's pleasure, humans err in extinguishing any of them. In Revelation the angels are commanded not to hurt the earth, the sea, the grass of the earth, nor any green thing including any tree. (Rev. 7:3, 9:4) Only humans are marked and judged, at which judgment God will "destroy them which destroy the earth." (Rev. 11:18).

[5]   Psalm 89:11–12. Other Psalms contain similar messages: "The heavens are thine, the earth also is thine; as for the world and the fullness thereof, thou has founded them. The north and the south thou hast created them." (Psalm 24:1–2); "The sea is his, and he made it: and his hands formed the dry land. O come, let us worship and bow down: let us kneel before the Lord our maker." (Psalm 95:5).

[6]   Genesis 7:2–3.

[7]   Genesis 9:10–13.

[8]   "Those coming upon a bird's nest either in a tree or on the ground may not take the mother bird, although the eggs and the young may be taken." (Deut. 22:6–7).

[9]   "When thou shalt besiege a city a long time, in making war against it to take it, thou shalt not destroy the trees thereof by forcing an axe against them: for thou mayest eat of them, and thou shalt not cut them down (for the tree of the field is man's life) to employ them in siege." (Deut. 20:19).

[10]   Places outside camps were to be established for human waste. "And thou shalt have a paddle upon thy weapon; and it shall be, when thou wilt ease thyself abroad, thou shalt dig therewith, and shalt turn back and cover that which cometh from thee." (Deut. 23:13)

not selfishly, but in the interests of all, being ready to help others in case of necessity.[11] Individual title is seen as imposing a responsibility and a trust. In an address on January 1, 1990, the World Day of Peace, Pope John Paul II stated: "In our day, there is a growing awareness that world peace is threatened not only by the arms race, regional conflicts and continued injustices among peoples and nations, but also by a lack of due respect for nature, by the plundering of natural resources and by a progressive decline in the quality of life."[12]

In 1983, Muslim experts undertook a study of the relationship between Islam and environmental protection. The results underscored that

> Islam presents a way of life that encompasses an overall view of the universe, life, man and the interrelationships existing between them and also combines conviction, belief, legislation and enforcement of this legislation.[13]

Humans are seen as forming part of the universe, whose elements are complementary to one another in an integrated whole, but humankind has a special relationship to the other parts of nature, a relationship of utilization and development. The basic principle of the biosphere is that:

> God's wisdom has ordained to grant man inheritance on earth. Therefore, in addition to being part of the earth and part of the universe, man is also the executor of God's injunctions and commands. And as such he is a mere manager of the earth and not a proprietor; a beneficiary and not a disposer or ordainer. Man has been granted inheritance to manage and utilize the earth for his benefit, and for the fulfillment of his interests. He therefore has to keep, maintain and preserve it honestly, and has to act within the limits dictated by honesty.[14]

In this perspective, each generation is entitled to use nature to the extent that it does not disrupt or upset the interests of future generations. Islamic

---

[11] THOMAS AQUINAS, 30 SUMMA THEOLOGICA 2a2ae, 66, 2 (Blackfriars, 1975). The commentary notes that this "contains the nub of the teaching that individuals should be only trustees and stewards of the world's resources—and, presumably, on behalf of future generations of the human race as well as of the living." *Id.* at 69, n. f.

[12] Quoted in *Environment and the World of Work*, Report of the Director-General of the ILO, at 4 (1990).

[13] *Islamic Principles for the Conservation of the Natural Environment*, IUCN Environmental Policy and Law Paper No. 20 at 9 (1983).

[14] *Id.* at 45.

principles thus envisage the protection and the conservation of basic natural elements, making protection, conservation and development of the environment and natural resources a mandatory religious duty of every Muslim.[15] Any deliberate or intentional damage to the natural environment and resources is forbidden. In conclusion the study proposes Islamic legislative rules to serve as the foundation of procedures and measures necessary for the protection and conservation of the environment.

Ancient Buddhist chronicles, dating to the third century B.C. record a sermon on Buddhism in which the son of the Emperor Asoka of India stated that "the birds of the air and the beasts have as equal a right to live and move about in any part of the land as thou. The land belongs to the people and all living beings; thou art only the guardian of it."[16] Subsequently, the Emperor initiated a legal system which continued to exist into the 18th century providing sanctuaries for wild animals.

The religious beliefs of indigenous peoples also contain precepts on respect for all life and impose duties on individuals and the community to avoid waste or harm.[17] According to one commentator, "indigenous peoples unanimously emphasize the spiritual nature of their relationship with the land or earth, which is basic to their existence and to their beliefs, customs, traditions, and culture."[18]

2. Utilitarianism

Many early treaties had a utilitarian or anthropocentric orientation based on the centrality of human dominance and humankind's unlimited right to exploit nature, found in some religious doctrines and philosophy. Utilitarianism grounds environmental protection on the well-being of humans, seeing nature primarily or only as a means to enhance the quality of human life and the satisfaction of human needs. Some environmental agreements thus stressed the protection of resources "useful" to man and the destruction of non-useful living creatures. Early environmental laws also tended to focus on pollution, because of its impact on human health, and only later addressed issues of endangered species and protection of biological diversity.

---

[15] *Id.* at 20.

[16] *The Mahavamsa, or the Great Chronicle of Ceylon*, Chap. 14, quoted in I.C.J., Case Concerning the Gabçikovo-Nagymaros Project (Hungary/Slovakia), Sep. Op. of Judge C. Weeremantry, n. 44.

[17] *See* J. Callicott, *Traditional American Indian and Western European Attitudes Toward Nature: An Overview*, 4 Envtl. Ethics 293 (1982); J. Hughes, American Indian Ecology (1983).

[18] Hannum, H., *New Developments in Indigenous Rights*, 18 Va. J. Int'l L. 649, 666 (1988).

One of the central texts of international environmental law, the 1992 Rio Declaration on Environment and Development, reflects a utilitarian approach, attempting to merge the goal of economic development with environmental protection. Its first principle proclaims that "[h]uman beings are at the center of concerns for sustainable development. They are entitled to a healthy and productive life in harmony with nature." This approach was further reinforced by the Political Declaration of the World Summit on Sustainable Development (WSSD) which emphasizes the importance of economic and social development, especially combating poverty.

The healthy life mentioned in the Rio Declaration has long been recognized in international and domestic legal texts and has served as a basis for environmental protection. It has taken on renewed force with the focus, *inter alia* by the WSSD and the World Health Organization, on providing every individual with sufficient water of adequate quality by 2012.

3. Equity

Environmental ethicists construct environmental protection around concepts of equity and justice, as seen in three sets of relationships: among existing persons, between present and future generations, and between humans and other species.[19]

a.   Intra-Generational Equity

The first ethical requirement is to assure justice among existing human beings. Beyond the fundamental protections of human rights, discussed in Chapter 15, states and the international community must fairly allocate and regulate scarce resources to ensure that the benefits of environmental resources, the costs associated with protecting them, and any degradation that occurs (*i.e.*, all the benefits and burdens) are equitably shared by all members of society. In this regard, environmental justice is an application of the principles of distributive justice as it seeks to reconcile competing social and economic policies in order to obtain equitable sharing of resources.[20]

---

[19]   *See* K. BOSSELMAN, WHEN TWO WORLD'S COLLIDE: SOCIETY AND ECOLOGY (1995); C. STONE, THE GNAT IS OLDER THAN MAN: GLOBAL ENVIRONMENT AND THE HUMAN AGENDA (1993); R. NASH, THE RIGHTS OF NATURE: A HISTORY OF ENVIRONMENTAL ETHICS (1989).

[20]   *See also* the discussions of human rights in Chapter 15, common but differentiated responsibilities in Chapter 3 and sustainable development in Chapter 2.

b.   Inter-Generational Equity: Rights of Future Generations

Humanity's concern with long-term human survival underlies legal and social norms and may be grounded in a genetic or biological imperative.[21] Interest in survival of the human species requires that "humanity" be seen to include not only present but also future generations.[22] Concern for future generations can thus be seen as implicit in all that touches environmental protection and the preservation of natural resources, reflected in the requirement that development be sustainable. One of the first expressions of inter-generational equity is found in Jomo Kenyatta's book *Facing Mount Kenya:*

> A man is the owner of his land. . . . But insofar as there are other people of his own flesh and blood who depend on that land for their daily bread, he is not the owner, but the partner, or at the most a trustee for the others. Since the land is held in trust for the unborn as well as for the living, and since it represents his partnership in the common life of generations, he will not lightly take it upon himself to dispose of it.

International environmental texts have referred to the need to conserve the natural heritage of humankind for the benefit of present and future generations, at least since the International Convention for the Regulation of Whaling (Dec. 2, 1946). Principle 2 of the 1972 Stockholm Declaration on the Human Environment endorsed a concern with future generations, stating:

> The natural resources of the earth, including the air, water, and flora and fauna and especially representative samples of natural ecosystems, must be safeguarded for the benefit of present and future generations through careful planning or management, as appropriate.[23]

The same year, the UNESCO World Heritage Convention included a reference to future generations.[24] Particularly significant is Article 3 (1) of the

---

[21]   *See* M. Gruter, *The Origins of Legal Behavior,* J. Social Biol. Struct. 43 (1979); Sociobiology and Human Politics (E. White ed., 1981); Law, Biology & Culture (M. Gruter & P. Bohannan eds., 1983).

[22]   For further elaboration, *see* Edith Brown Weiss, In Fairness to Future Generations (1988).

[23]   Principle 2, Stockholm Declaration on the Human Environment, U.N. Doc. A/CONF.48/14/Rev.1 (U.N. Pub. E.73.II.A.14) (1973); 11 I.L.M. 1416 (1972).

[24]   Other recent texts mentioning future generations include the 1973

Framework Convention on Climate Change which declares that "[t]he parties should protect the climate system for the benefit of present and future generations of humankind."[25] At the same time, Principle 3 of the Rio Declaration on Environment and Development links concern for future generations with the right to development, declaring: "The right to development must be fulfilled so as to equitably meet developmental and environmental needs of present and future generations."

On the basis of these treaty provisions, declarations, and resolutions, it is possible to conclude that each generation may benefit from and develop the natural and cultural patrimony inherited from previous generations, but then must pass it on to future generations in no worse condition than it was received. This is not a completely satisfactory approach, however, over the long term. It is not clear how the same amount of space, wilderness, clean water, and biological diversity can be guaranteed to endless generations of increasingly larger numbers of individuals. It is also impossible to anticipate the preferences of future generations.

Concretely, the rights of future humanity may be encompassed in the concept of sustainable development, deemed to include the attainment of economic, social and cultural rights. The realization of such rights requires the availability of natural resources over an indefinite period of time and includes not only material resources that are essential to the survival of humankind and those that serve to enrich it, but also ecosystems, life-support processes, and biological diversity. The enjoyment of cultural rights necessarily includes the conservation of basic elements of civilization, including wild flora and fauna, landscapes and natural sites. This broad interpretation of economic, social and cultural rights reflects the interests of present and future humanity.

Convention on International Trade in Endangered Species of Wild Fauna and Flora; 1976 Convention for the Mediterranean Sea; 1976 Convention on the Conservation of Nature in the South Pacific; 1976 Convention on the Prohibition of Military or Any Other Hostile Use of Environmental Modification Techniques; 1978 Kuwait Regional Convention; 1979 Convention on the Conservation of European Wildlife and Natural Habitats; 1979 Convention on the Conservation of Migratory Species of Wild Animals; 1983 Convention for the Wider Caribbean Region; 1985 ASEAN Agreement on the Conservation of Nature and Natural Resources; 1992 Convention on Biological Diversity; 1992 U.N. Framework Convention on Climate Change; 1994 U.N. Convention to Combat Desertification; and 1997 United Nations Convention on the Law of the Non-Navigable Uses of International Watercourses. The same concept appears in United Nations General Assembly resolutions. *See, e.g.*, Protection of global climate for present and future generations of mankind, G.A. Res. 43/53, Dec. 6, 1988, U.N. Doc. A/Res/43/53, Jan. 27, 1989.

[25]   EMuT 992:42.

A recognition of the rights of future generations also raises the problems of defining a generation and means of implementing such rights. The concept of a generation is not clear. Based on average life expectancy and reproductive patterns, the time-span of a human generation has been taken to be 30 years, but there are significant differences in both of these elements between individuals and between industrialized and developing countries. In fact, there are no distinct generations, because at each moment hundreds of human beings are born and die, with the result that some six billion people of all ages co-exist. In law, therefore, it is perhaps more logical to speak of future humanity, rather than future generations, as the holder of rights, and to recognize humanity, including its present and future members, as a collective legal person. National and international law already recognize various entities as legal persons, from the state and other levels of government to corporations. The same capacity could be afforded humanity as a whole, although this does raise the problem of who might represent it.

International instruments provide little guidance on representation and implementation of the rights of future humanity, but domestic legal systems offer some guidance, notably in the Philippine Supreme Court decision *Minors Oposa v. Secretary of the Department of Environment and Natural Resources.*[26] Thirty-five minors, represented by their parents and an association, sought an order requiring the government to discontinue existing timber licenses and restraining it from issuing new licenses. Their petition was based on the allegation that deforestation was causing environmental damage. The Court ruled that the plaintiffs had standing to represent their as yet unborn progeny and that they had adequately asserted a right to a balanced and healthy ecology. It also declared that "the minors' assertion of their right to a sound environment constitutes, at the same time, the performance of their obligation to ensure the protection of that right for the generations to come." The decision provides an example of how rights of future generations might be enforced in practice. Internationally, the task of ensuring the rights of future humanity could be conferred upon an independent international authority, such as an international environmental agency or ombudsman.

c.   Inter-Species Equity

Inter-species equity emerges from and enhances respect for the intrinsic value of nature independently of its utility to humans. It posits a non-hierarchical view of human relations with other species. Precursors of this concept can be seen in those constitutions, laws, and international instruments that require the humane treatment of living creatures.[27] At the beginning

---

26   33 I.L.M. 168 (1994).

27   *See, e.g.*, Art. 32 of the Constitution of the German Land of Thuringen,

of the 1970s, some theorists suggested that the legal personality of certain components of the environment, such as trees or animals, could be recognized.[28] However, legal systems have difficulty integrating such solutions because the systems are created by humans to serve human interests. Movements for recognition of "animal or biotic rights" are increasingly evident, however, motivated by ethical considerations and concern about the continued decline of biological diversity at an alarming rate.[29] The comprehensive philosophical world views encompassed by the "deep ecology" and the animal rights movements could imply profound changes in law and policy.

The preamble of the 1979 Bern Convention on the Conservation of European Wildlife and Natural Habitats was one of the first to express a basis of environmental protection in the intrinsic value of nature:

> Recognizing that wild flora and fauna constitute a natural heritage of aesthetic, scientific, cultural, recreational, economic, and intrinsic value that needs to be preserved and handed on to future generations.[30]

The text demonstrates an integrated approach: the natural heritage presents a certain number of qualities important for humanity, but these do not diminish nature's inherent value. The contracting parties to the 1992 Convention on Biological Diversity similarly profess that they are "[c]onscious of the intrinsic value of biological diversity and of the ecological, genetic, social, economic, scientific, educational, cultural, recreational and aesthetic values of biological diversity and its components."[31] Given the

---

"Animals are to be respected as living beings and fellow creatures. They will be protected from treatment inappropriate to the species and from avoidable suffering." International and national legal texts have long protected species from inhumane treatment. See the 1968 European Convention on the Protection of Animals during International Transport, EmuT 968:92 and the 1979 Convention on the Conservation of European Wildlife and Natural Habitats, E.T.S. 104.

[28] C. Stone, *Should Trees Have Standing? Towards Legal Rights for Natural Objects*, 45 S. CAL. L. REV. (1974); C. Stone, *Should Trees Have Standing Revisited: How Far Will Law and Morals Reach? A Pluralist Perspective*, 59 S. CAL L. REV. 1 (1985).

[29] *See* D. Favre, *Wildlife Rights: The Ever-Widening Circle*, 9 ENVTL. L. 279 (1979); A. D'Amato & S. Chopra, *Whales: Their Emerging Right to Life*, 85 AJIL 21 (1991).

[30] Preamble, para. 3, Convention on the Conservation of European Wildlife and Natural Habitats (Bern, Sept. 19, 1979).

[31] Preamble, para. 1, Convention on Biological Diversity (Rio de Janeiro, June 5, 1992). Other international treaties that take into account the intrinsic value of nature include the 1980 Convention for the Conservation of Antarctic Marine Living Resources, the 1991 Protocol to the Antarctic Treaty on

lack of legal status for components of the environment despite recognition of their intrinsic and independent value, an integrated approach best creates a foundation for environmental protection. The first phrases of the preamble of the World Charter for Nature set out such an approach:

> Mankind is a part of nature and life depends on the uninterrupted functioning of natural systems which ensure the supply of energy and nutrients[.]

The intrinsic value of the biosphere is not rejected but is integrated with an understanding that humans make up part of the universe and cannot exist without conservation of the biosphere and the ecosystems comprising it. In this perspective all components of the environment have a value not only in their short-term utility to humans, as the earlier exclusively utilitarian approach would have it, but also as indispensable elements of an interrelated system which must be protected.[32] While the aim of human survival remains anthropocentric, humans are not viewed as apart from or above the natural universe, but as a linked and interdependent part of it. It follows that because all parts of the natural web are linked, they must all be protected and conserved. It is in this sense that "intrinsic value" may be understood.[33]

In conclusion, it may be noted that the religious and philosophical conceptions upon which environmental protection may be based imply individual responsibility, whether for the benefit of other persons, of future generations, of other species, or of the processes and life-support systems of the biosphere. Principle 1 of the Stockholm Declaration expresses this duty, proclaiming that "man bears a solemn responsibility to protect and improve the environment for present and future generations."

Environmental Protection, and the 1973 CITES Convention. The Draft IUCN Covenant on Environment and Development declares as a fundamental principle (Art. 2) that "[n]ature as a whole warrants respect; every form of life is unique and is to be safeguarded independent of its value to humanity."

[32]   *See* L. Tribe, *Ways not to Think About Plastic Trees: New Foundations for Environmental Law*, 83 YALE L.J. 1315 (1974).

[33]   There are no doubt other philosophical and ethical foundations to the conservation movement, some of which may lead to conflicting approaches. Similar problems exist in other areas of the law. During the drafting of the Universal Declaration of Human Rights, Jacques Maritain confessed that agreement could be reached on a catalogue of human rights so long as no attempt was made to agree on *why* human rights should be protected.

B. Science

Environmental law has several characteristics deriving from the need to take into consideration the "laws of nature" basic to biology, chemistry and physics. Few legal disciplines require the same consideration of scientific knowledge. Most areas of law attempt to regulate variable and often unpredictable human interrelationships. In contrast, environmental law uses science to predict and regulate the consequences of human behavior on natural phenomena.

The need for environmental law to take into consideration the "laws of nature" inevitably leads to an interdisciplinary approach to environmental problems. Law-makers and jurists must rely upon and utilize scientific expertise. Scientists themselves must share knowledge. In efforts to understand global climate change, for example, atmospheric scientists trained in meteorology and chemistry produce climate change models, but biologists and ecologists are needed to analyze the impact of these changes on biotopes and ecological systems.

Environmental law and policy also must take into account the interdependence of different sectors of the environment. Ocean pollution taints the shore, as recognized in the 1982 United Nations Convention on the Law of the Sea (UNCLOS) and a number of regional instruments.[34] In turn, a large proportion of marine pollution derives from land-based sources. Atmospheric pollution also can affect the earth and imperil forests and buildings. The 1992 UN Framework Convention on Climate Change recognizes that climate change due to emissions of certain gases into the air can have significant deleterious effects on the composition, resilience or productivity of natural and managed ecosystems, on the operation of socio-economic systems, and on human health and welfare.[35] Freshwaters receive a large part of their pollution from the soil, whose pollutants may seep into the underground water table. Obviously, all pollutants endanger biodiversity. Such interrelationships necessarily have international consequences, because the transfer of pollution from one milieu to another will frequently result in transboundary impacts. International instruments, notably UNCLOS, stress the need to avoid substituting injury or risk to one sector of the environment with injury to another and of replacing one type of pollution with another.[36]

---

[34] United Nations Convention on the Law of the Sea (Montego Bay, Dec. 10, 1982), Art. 211 (hereinafter UNCLOS). The regional seas conventions are discussed in Chapter 11.

[35] New York, May 9, 1992, Art. 1(1).

[36] UNCLOS, Art. 195.

Another scientific reality with which environmental law and policy must grapple is the lack of scientific certainty about many aspects of the physical world. Although there is unprecedented scientific knowledge available today, no one knows the ecological processes over the five billion year history of the earth with sufficient detail and understanding to be able to predict all the consequences and causal relationships of various human interventions and activities. Debates over the impact of anthropogenic greenhouse gases on global warming are but one aspect of this uncertainty.[37] Even the concept of "balance of nature," *i.e.*, that nature generally remains in a state of stable equilibrium, has been challenged by some studies which see nature ruled by flux and perpetual disturbances.[38]

Scientific uncertainty thus often attends issues of the nature and scope of the adverse environmental impacts of human activities. Exacerbating the uncertainty, damage often is measurable only years after the causative actions have occurred. Given this situation, questions arise over how to develop environmental policy and how to allocate risk between the present and the future. Many decisions cannot await scientific certainty, assuming something approaching certainty can ever be achieved. Therefore, debate centers on whether a policy should be adopted to assume harmful consequences will occur unless activities or products are proven safe or whether to take a less cautious approach, knowing that many environmental processes and changes may be irreversible and ultimately life-threatening.[39] The technique of risk assessment, discussed in Chapter 6D, attempts to evaluate the probability and magnitude of harm from a given activity or substance.

---

[37]   While most scientists predict severe ecological disruption from global warming attributable to unchecked pollution, others reach different conclusions or find that the data are insufficient to reach any conclusions. One study concluded that more than half the global temperature increases of recent years are due to warm ocean currents known as El Nino, but acknowledged that it is not known whether the currents themselves are affected by the rise in carbon dioxide, methane, and other heat-trapping gases. *See generally* D. Bazelon, *Science and Uncertainty: A Jurist's View*, 5 HARV. ENVTL. L. REV. 209 (1981).

[38]   William K. Stevens, *Scientists Rethinking Balance of Nature*, San Francisco *Chronicle*, July 31, 1990, A5.

[39]   On occasion, scientific uncertainty has been invoked as a reason for refusing to take costly environmental action. One author notes that the United States as a recipient of acid rain exported from Mexico does not debate the scientific certainty of the causal link between pollutants and acid rain damage. However, when the United States is exporting similar pollutants towards Canada, scientific uncertainty is cited as a reason to delay adopting measures. *See* Jutta Brunnee, ACID RAIN AND OZONE LAYER DEPLETION: LAW AND REGULATION (1988). The United States government has also refused to ratify the 1997 Kyoto Protocol on Climate Change based upon its claims of scientific uncertainty about anthropogenic global climate change

In addition to uncertainty and irreversibility, environmental law must recognize the fact that the environment is dynamic and constantly evolving. This characteristic requires flexible laws and policies that are capable of rapid alteration in response to new circumstances. At the same time, and perhaps paradoxically, the legal framework must look long term in its efforts to maintain life and the ecological balance in an unseeable future.

Finally, as early as 1962 Rachel Carson demonstrated that the combined effect of substances can be very different than the environmental impact of each substance released separately.[40] A chemical innocuous in isolation may be polluting or even highly toxic when combined with other substances in the environment. Industrial emissions, for example, change their characteristics in the atmosphere, creating acid rain. Synergistic interactions have been observed in mixtures of up to 20 or more chemicals, with some effects 10,000 times more harmful that would be expected from adding the toxicities of the individual chemicals.[41] The need for precaution and an integrated or holistic approach thus emerges from the science of ecology.

C. Economics

The current economic system presents numerous challenges to environmental protection. First, if the earth's resource base is considered as a whole, the structure and functioning of the marketplace can produce what has long been referred to as the "tragedy of the commons."[42] In addition, the emphasis on free trade in goods and services in the international economic system raises problems of competitive disadvantage and opposition to trade barriers resulting from regulations to protect the environment. Finally, the North-South disparity in economic development and resources creates difficulties for the traditional legal technique of imposing uniform norms and standards through international agreements.

The tragedy of the commons is a consequence of the market of supply and demand, a fundamental principle of liberal economic theory. In an open market, the pressure of demand leads to higher prices as goods become scarce. Prices that are too high deter further purchasers leading to a fall in demand. For many environmental amenities, however, the market system does not work because such resources are considered "public goods"

---

[40] RACHEL CARSON, SILENT SPRING 195–196 (1962).

[41] D. HUNTER, J. SALZMAN, & D. ZAELKE, INTERNATIONAL ENVIRONMENTAL LAW AND POLICY 22 (2d ed. 2002).

[42] *See* Garrett Hardin, *Tragedy of the Commons*, 168 SCIENCE 243 (1968). The article describes a common pasture in which everyone in a village has unlimited grazing rights for sheep. It is to each person's advantage in the short run to maximize the grazing of her or his own sheep. Within a short time, the pasture is destroyed through over-grazing.

that are free and in principle shared by all. No one legally can prevent another from using air. The lack of a market for public goods means that no price rise signals scarcity due to, *inter alia*, environmental degradation. Each consumer continues to maximize use until the resource is exhausted. The consequences of this system are perhaps most apparent in regard to exhaustible living resources, such as fish. Unregulated fishing on the high seas leads each vessel to try to obtain the maximum possible catch, leading fisheries to "crash."[43]

The same profit motivation likewise produces environmental degradation from pollution. The harmful introduction of substances into the environment results from each person deciding that her or his short-term advantage involves discharging pollutants into the commons rather than bearing the cost of purifying emissions before release. If the sole objective of the market is to maximize the wealth of each individual, a system of open and non-regulated access to the commons will invariably result in environmental degradation. The environmental law response has been to formulate the "polluter pays" principle that converts the economic externalities of commons degradation into costs for the polluter.[44]

The second economic issue is competitive disadvantage: a state taking measures to protect the environment must count the increased costs which are borne by its economy. Distortions are especially felt in an interstate system founded on free trade. The former European Economic Community, now incorporated in the European Union, initially based its environmental protection measures on Article 100 of the Treaty of Rome, which promoted the approximation of national legislation that has a direct effect on

---

[43]   *See* FAO, THE STATE OF WORLD FISHERIES AND AQUACULTURE 2002 (stating that about 47 percent of the main stocks or species groups are fully exploited and are therefore producing catches that have reached, or are very close to, their maximum sustainable limits. Thus, nearly half of world marine stocks offer no reasonable expectations for further expansion. Another 18 percent of stocks or species groups are reported as overexploited. Prospects for expansion or increased production from these stocks are negligible, and there is an increasing likelihood that stocks will decline further and catches will decrease, unless remedial management action is taken to reduce overfishing conditions. The remaining 10 percent of stocks have become significantly depleted, or are recovering from depletion and are far less productive than they used to be, or than they could be if management can return them to the higher abundance levels commensurate with their pre-depletion catch levels.)

[44]   According to Principle 16 of the Rio Declaration on Environment and Development, "[n]ational authorities should endeavor to promote the internalization of environmental costs and the use of economic instruments, taking into account the approach that the polluter should, in principle, bear the cost of pollution, with due regard to the public interest and without distorting international trade and investment."

the establishment or functioning of the common market. The purpose of approximation is "to eliminate disparities between the legislative or administrative provisions of the Member States which distort the conditions of competition in the Common Market."[45] The preoccupation with conditions of competition is evident also in the work of the Organization of Economic Cooperation and Development (OECD)[46] and the environmental side agreement to the North American Free Trade Agreement (NAFTA). The latter calls for cooperation to better conserve, protect, and enhance the environment, while avoiding the creation of trade distortions or new trade barriers.[47] Chapter 17 describes the current efforts to protect the environment in the context of the international market.

Thirdly, the solidarity imposed by global problems necessitates better cooperation between industrialized and developing countries, North and South. The collaboration of both groups is required to safeguard the planet's environment. Full collaboration involves assisting poor countries to face the burden of implementing environmental measures that serve to safeguard the biosphere as a whole. In addition, it is now understood that global poverty threatens human existence through its impact on the environment. The result is an increased emphasis on partnership and mutuality in multilateral environmental protection, as well as on the interrelationship of environmental protection and development.[48]

While these economic challenges are complex and difficult, the field of economics offers possible means to quantify the value of the environment to society, important when decisions are based on a cost-benefit analysis. Direct valuation can compute the revenues generated by products extracted from nature, including food, medicine, petroleum and minerals. Indirect methods of estimating substitute markets may measure ecosystem services, which are probably of even greater value. These include the value of coral reefs in protecting shorelines from storm surges and mangroves services in slowing erosion and preventing siltation of coastal waters. Soil provides important ecological services by purifying groundwater and supporting agriculture, honeybees contribute through pollination. Harder to measure are the life-supporting services provided by the ozone layer, for example, or Antarctica's contribution to regulating the global climate. Even less quantifiable are such aspects as the aesthetic enjoyment of landscapes

---

[45]   Art. 101(1), Treaty Establishing the European Economic Community (Rome, Mar. 25, 1957). For further discussion *see infra*, Chapter 4.

[46]   *See* Chapter 4.

[47]   North American Agreement on Environmental Cooperation (Sept. 13, 1993), Art. 1.

[48]   *See, e.g.*, the results of the World Summit on Sustainable Development, discussed in Chapter 2F.

and the inherent contribution of each species to the ecosystem in which it lives.[49] Nonetheless, various initiatives are attempting to provide better valuation of the environment. The United Nations Statistical Office released a handbook in 1993 setting forth a System of Environmental and Economic Accounting (SEEA). It includes environmental functions and natural resources as assets of production and records depletion of a resource as capital depreciation. The World Bank uses SEEAs in its economic analyses. Some economists suggest an alternative method to directly value the ecological functions that serve to meet human needs from subsistence to identity and freedom, rather than measuring production and consumption.[50] Finally, the development of an Environmental Sustainability Index provides a basis for assessing the ability of states to meet the environmental needs of their society in a sustainable manner. The ESI looks at core indicators based on a larger set of underlying variables. It measures five key components of environmental sustainability: natural systems; environmental stresses and risks; human exposure and risks (vulnerability to harm); societal capacity to respond to environmental challenges; and transboundary equity issues (contributions to harm and to solutions of environmental problems).

D. International Law

International law, as traditionally defined, governed relations among juridically equal states, once considered the sole subjects of international law. International law has regulated interstate relations through rules based on the consent of states reflected in the adoption of treaties and the development of customary international law through state practice viewed as obligatory (*opinio juris*). While the contours of this classic system remain intact, it has undergone fundamental changes in the past half century. International environmental law is both a product of and in part a cause of this transformation that affects the processes of law-making and the role of consent as well concepts of sovereignty. Many aspects of modern international environmental law are linked to the concepts of the common concern of humanity and common heritage of mankind.

---

[49]   For discussions about valuing ecological services, *see* G. DALY ed., NATURE'S SERVICES: SOCIETAL DEPENDENCE ON NATURAL ECOSYSTEMS (1997); D. CLARK & D. DOWNES, WHAT PRICE BIODIVERSITY? (CIEL, 1995); ROBERT COSTANZA et al., AN INTRODUCTION TO ECOLOGICAL ECONOMICS (1997).

[50]   *See* ROBERT COSTANZA ed., ECOLOGICAL ECONOMICS (1991).

1. Sovereignty

State sovereignty, one of the oldest principles of international law, means that each state has exclusive jurisdiction within its territory to adopt laws and enforce them, administer the territory, and judge disputes that arise therein. The sovereign rights of states include exclusive jurisdiction over their resources.[51] Principle 21 of the Stockholm Declaration explicitly applies this principle to environmental matters by affirming that "[s]tates have, in accordance with the Charter of the United Nations and the principles of international law, the sovereign right to exploit their own resources pursuant to their own environmental policies. . . ." The same formulation has been reproduced in other binding and non-binding international instruments. Principle 2 of the Rio Declaration uses the same wording, but enlarges its scope by referring to "environmental *and developmental* policies," reflecting the focus of the Rio Conference on both environment and development.

A tension between traditional notions of state sovereignty and environmental concerns can be seen in the evolution of legal texts regarding permanent sovereignty over natural resources. Early formulations mainly focused on rights of states over these resources, responding to concerns about neo-colonialism and economic development. The Stockholm Declaration was the first international document to balance state sovereignty with "the responsibility to ensure that activities within their jurisdiction or control do not cause damage to the environment of other States or of areas beyond the limits of national jurisdiction." The formulation is repeated in the Rio Declaration and in the Convention on Biological Diversity and other international texts. Repetition of the principle, its invocation in state practice and its widespread acceptance, led the International Court of Justice to declare that "the general obligation of States to ensure that activities within their jurisdiction and control respect the environment of other States or of areas beyond national control is now part of the corpus of international law relating to the environment."[52] More expansively, Article 192 of the 1982 Convention on the Law of the Sea provides: "States have the obligation to protect and preserve the marine environment." This formulation clearly includes areas within national jurisdiction even where harm has no impact outside those limits.

Some environmental issues raise serious problems for the application of state sovereignty, since the environment knows no boundary. Migratory species of wild animals, birds, and fish as well as pollution of oceans, rivers,

---

[51]   A. Kiss & D. Shelton, *Systems Analysis of International Law: A Methodological Inquiry*, 1986 NETH. Y.B. INT'L L. 45.

[52]   *Legality of the Threat or Use of Nuclear Weapons*, Advisory Opinion, 1996 I.C.J. Rep. 241–42, para. 29.

lakes and the air, do not stop at the limits of territorial jurisdiction. Such situations can lead to conflicts between sovereign rights which can only be solved by international law. Treaties to which a state becomes a contracting party limit its sovereignty, but such limitations are self-imposed. Each state is now involved in a large web of international treaty obligations concerning environmental protection that must be executed on its territory, including agreements to protect species of wild fauna and flora, prohibit the dumping of harmful substances into rivers, lakes or the sea, and prevent atmospheric pollution by constraints imposed upon industries. The general trend toward integrated protection of the environment requires that states exercise broad control over activities which can harm the environment and this necessarily limits their freedom of action.

2. Cooperation

An obligation to cooperate with other states derives from the very essence of general international law, and finds reflection in the existence and proliferation of international institutions. In the field of environmental protection, international cooperation is necessary to conserve the environment in its totality, as much for states within their territorial jurisdiction as for areas outside territorial limits. The general need to cooperate to conserve the environment is expressed in several texts, starting with Principle 24 of the Stockholm Declaration:

> International matters concerning the protection and improvement of the environment should be handled in a cooperative spirit by all countries, big and small, on an equal footing. Cooperation through multilateral or bilateral arrangements or other appropriate means is essential to effectively control, prevent, reduce and eliminate adverse environmental effects resulting from activities conducted in all spheres, in such a way that due account is taken of the sovereignty and interests of all states.

The UN General Assembly reaffirmed the same principle in Resolution 2995 (XXVII) of December 15, 1972, and in the 1982 World Charter for Nature. According to the latter instrument, states shall cooperate in the conservation of nature through common activities and other relevant actions, including information exchanges and consultations. They must also establish standards for products and manufacturing processes that may have adverse effects on the environment, as well as methods to assess these effects. The Rio Declaration on Environment and Development is also largely based on the principle of cooperation, in particular between industrialized and developing countries.

The principle of cooperation underlies most treaty obligations. Nevertheless, several texts make it explicit, such as Article 197 of the 1982 Convention on the Law of the Sea:

> States shall cooperate on a global basis and, as appropriate, on a regional basis, directly or through competent international organizations, in formulating and elaborating international rules, standards and recommended practices and procedures consistent with this Convention, for the protection and preservation of the marine environment, taking into account characteristic regional features.

An example of regional cooperation is provided by the Memorandum of Understanding between Kenya, Tanzania and Uganda for Co-operation on Environment Management.[53] Its aim is the development and harmonization of national framework environmental laws on environmental impact assessment, management of non-hazardous and hazardous wastes, toxic and hazardous chemicals, wildlife and forest resources, laws for the management of the Lake Victoria ecosystem and formulation of environmental standards. Cooperation shall include continued consultations, capacity building and networking on environmental policies, laws and strategies, undertaking joint programs and the development and implementation of environmentally sound principles, agreements, instruments and strategies for environment and natural resources management. The MOU provides for the establishment of an Interim Sectoral Committee for the three states as well as interim national focal points.

Different legal instruments specify the fields of international cooperation. According to Principle 5 of the Rio Declaration all states and peoples shall cooperate in the essential task of eradicating poverty as an indispensable requirement for sustainable development. In 1995, during the World Summit for Social Development, 117 Heads of State agreed to an integrated approach to poverty eradication based on the concept of partnership, within societies as well as between developed and developing countries.

The concept of partnership emerged during preparations for the Rio Conference as an expression of closer and more systematic cooperation. Principle 27 of the Rio Declaration adds that cooperation shall be conducted in good faith and shall include further development of international law in the field of sustainable development. The 2002 World Summit on Sustainable Development extended the concept of partnership to encompass non-state actors as well as states. The Johannesburg Declaration on Sustainable Development recognizes that sustainable development requires a long-term perspective and "stable partnerships with all major groups"

---

[53] Nairobi, Oct. 22, 1998.

(Para. 23). The Johannesburg Plan of Implementation also calls for enhanced partnerships between governmental and non-governmental actors, including all major groups.

The Rio Declaration also insists on cooperation to strengthen endogenous capacity-building for sustainable development, by improving scientific understanding through exchange of scientific and technological knowledge, and by enhancing the development, adaptation, diffusion and transfer of technologies, including new and innovative technologies (Principle 9). Similar clauses related to the transfer of knowledge, information, and technology form an important part of most global environmental treaties. Article 4(5) of the 1992 Framework Convention on Climate Change, for example, provides that the developed country parties shall take all practicable steps to promote, facilitate and finance, as appropriate, the transfer of, or access to, environmentally sound technologies and know-how, in particular to developing countries. They also are to support the development and enhancement of endogenous capacities and technologies of developing countries.

Another designated area of international cooperation in the Rio Declaration is in regard to the relocation and transfer to other states of any activities and substances that cause severe environmental degradation or are found to be harmful to human health. Principle 14 requires, *inter alia*, that if a state chooses to ban or restrict the importation of hazardous substances or the relocation of hazardous activities, the ban or restriction should be respected by other states. The 1989 Basel Convention on the Control of Transboundary Movements of Hazardous Wastes and their Disposal[54] supports this principle.

Cooperation also is needed for the rational and equitable use of shared resources, such as transboundary watercourses and international lakes. Another essential part of cooperation is providing financial assistance to countries to enable them to comply with their obligations, especially in the relations between industrialized and developing countries. Article 20(2) of the 1992 Convention on Biological Diversity and Articles 20 and 21 of the Convention to Combat Desertification in those Countries Experiencing Serious Drought and/or Desertification, Particularly in Africa[55] provide that the developed country parties shall provide new and additional financial resources to developing or affected country parties.

Finally, the order on provisional measures issued December 3, 2001, by the International Tribunal on the Law of the Sea in the *Mox Case* (Ireland v. United Kingdom) makes concrete the duty of states to consult and cooperate. Ireland invoked Article 123 of the United Nations Convention on the Law of the Sea (UNCLOS), concerning enclosed or semi-enclosed seas,

---

[54]   Mar. 22, 1989.

[55]   June 17, 1994.

which requires states to cooperate in exercising their rights and performing their duties. Ireland also relied upon Article 206 which requires assessment of the potential effects of planned activities that may cause substantial pollution or significant and harmful changes to the environment. The Court enunciated in paragraph 82 of its order that the duty to cooperate is a fundamental principle in the prevention of pollution of the marine environment, according UNCLOS Part XII, and in general international law and that rights arise therefrom which the tribunal may consider appropriate to preserve under Article 290 of the Convention (on provisional measures). Judge Wolfrum's separate opinion questioned whether the customary international obligation to cooperate for environmental protection creates corresponding legal rights but he did find that UNCLOS creates a legally protected right to cooperation for its contracting parties.

3. Common Concern of Humanity

The cohesion of every society and community is based upon and maintained by a value system such as a common religion, philosophy, ideology or ethics. The system may demand respect for the human person, propriety, patriotism, respect for cultural values, or adherence to a particular social order. The protection of such fundamental values is generally recognized as a common concern of the community and is ensured through law, especially constitutional law.

The common concern of a society thus leads to the creation of a legal system whose rules impose duties on society as a whole and on each individual member of the community. Almost all national constitutions proclaim fundamental human rights and freedoms and require the government to respect and ensure those rights. Increasingly, similar provisions are included to secure environmental protection. Article 66 of the 1976 Portuguese Constitution is illustrative. It proclaims an obligation on the state through its agencies to prevent and control pollution and its effects and harmful forms of erosion, to organize territorial space so as to establish biologically balanced landscapes and to create and develop natural parks and reserves. As a counterpart, the Constitution recognizes that all persons have the right to a human, healthy and ecologically-balanced environment and the duty to protect it. The national regulatory system is built upon this foundation.

International law lacks a constitutional text and central authority to determine the common concern of all humanity because states individually and jointly draft and adopt legal regulations governing international relations. During the second half of the 20th century states aimed to create a universal political organization to maintain international peace and security and improve the well-being of all humanity. This ambitious effort could only proceed by defining domains of common concern. The international recognition of human rights and fundamental freedoms constituted a first step of paramount importance in developing the concept of an international community built upon the fundamental values of humanity. Similarly, knowledge that the biosphere is the only known place in the universe where life is possible led to the emergence of another universal value, protection of the human environment as a common concern of humanity. The global environment, an interdependent ecological system, can only be protected at the global level, making it a common concern for all humanity. Transboundary and domestic environmental issues that cannot be managed effectively by national or regional efforts also are common concerns. The modalities of protection and preservation are formulated in law and policy and enforced by national and international institutions.

A large number of international instruments recognize the common concern of humanity. The term "common interest" appeared early in international treaties concerning the exploitation of natural resources. The 1946 International Convention for the Regulation of Whaling recognizes in its preamble the "interest of the world in safeguarding for future generations the great natural resources represented by the whale stocks" and that it is in the common interest to achieve the optimum level of whale stocks as rapidly as possible.[56] The depletion of fish resources, which began as a local problem, took on much larger dimensions in the second half of the 20th century. States then recognized that it was in their common interest to take conservation measures. The 1952 Tokyo Convention for the High Seas Fisheries of the North Pacific Ocean expresses the conviction of the parties that it will best serve the common interest of mankind, as well as the interests of the contracting parties, to ensure the maximum sustained productivity of the fishery resources of the North Pacific Ocean[57]

A major step in international recognition of the common concern of humanity was conclusion of the 1959 Antarctic Treaty.[58] Its preamble affirms that "it is in the interest of all mankind that Antarctica shall continue forever to be used exclusively for peaceful purposes." Article IX authorizes the adoption of measures for the preservation and conservation of living resources in Antarctica "in furtherance of the principles and objectives of the Treaty." The Antarctic Treaty system further developed with adoption of the Canberra Convention on the Conservation of Antarctic Marine Living Resources (CCAMLR) which made express reference to the "interest of all mankind to preserve the waters surrounding the Antarctic continent for peaceful purposes only."[59] The most recent addition to the Antarctic Treaty

---

56   Washington, Dec. 2, 1946.
57   May 9, 1952.
58   Washington, Dec. 1, 1959.
59   May 20, 1980, preamble. *See also* Daniel Vignes, *Protection of the Antarctic Marine Fauna and Flora, The Canberra Convention and the Commission Set up by It,*

system, the 1991 Madrid Protocol on Environmental Protection to the Antarctic Treaty[60] achieved full recognition of the common interest. Its preamble expresses the conviction that the development of a comprehensive regime for the protection of the Antarctic environment and dependent and associated ecosystems is in the interest of mankind as a whole and for this purpose it denominates Antarctica a nature reserve, devoted to peace and science.[61]

Such evolution must be seen as reflecting awareness of the general depletion of natural resources and of the threats to the environment, awareness that is increasing the pressure to adopt broad measures in the interest of present and future generations. Even before the 1972 Stockholm Conference, the 1968 African Convention on the Conservation of Nature and Natural Resources had expressed the desire of the contracting states to undertake individual and joint action for the conservation, utilization and development of natural resources by establishing and maintaining their rational utilization for the present and future welfare of mankind.[62] With the words "future welfare" the temporal dimension of the common interest of humanity has appeared.

Other international environmental treaties similarly recognize the common concern of mankind. The 1979 Bonn Convention on the Conservation of Migratory Species of Wild Animals recognizes in its preamble that "wild animals in their innumerable forms are an irreplaceable part of the earth's natural system which must be conserved for the good of mankind. . . . [E]ach generation of man holds the resources of the earth for future generations and has an obligation to ensure that this legacy is conserved and, where utilized, is used wisely."[63] The Convention on the Conservation of European Wildlife and Natural Habitats, adopted several months after the Bonn Convention joins the concepts of general interest and future humanity by recognizing that wild flora and fauna constitute a natural heritage that "needs to be handed on to future generations."[64] Similarly, the World Charter for Nature states that the preservation of species and of ecosystems

---

in INTERNATIONAL LAW FOR ANTARCTICA 159 (F. FRANCIONI & T. SCOVAZZI eds., 1996).

[60]   Oct. 4, 1991. *See also* Laura Pineschi, *The Madrid Protocol on the Protection of the Antarctic Environment and its Effectiveness, in* FRANCIONI & SCOVAZZI *op. cit.*, 261.

[61]   *See also* the U.N. General Assembly Resolution on the Question of Antarctica, Dec. 6, 1991, G.A. Res. 46/41, U.N. GAOR, 46th Sess. Supp. No 49, at 83, U.N. Doc. A/46/49 (1992) which implicitly expresses that Antarctica constitutes a common concern for all the states.

[62]   Algiers, Sept. 15, 1968.

[63]   June 23, 1979.

[64]   Bern, Sept. 19, 1979.

should be ensured "for the benefit of present and future generations."[65]
The World Charter opened the door for the 1992 Convention on Biological
Diversity which explicitly proclaims the principle of common concern of
humanity[66] by stating "the importance of biological diversity for evolution
and for maintaining life sustaining systems in the biosphere," and by "affirming that the conservation of biological diversity is a common concern of
humankind. . . ." The Framework Convention on Climate Change similarly
affirms in the first paragraph of its preamble that "change in the Earth's climate and its adverse effects are a common concern of humankind."

The inclusion of smaller areas in the common concern is seen in the
Paris Convention for the Protection of the Marine Environment of the
North-East Atlantic, adopted several months after the Convention on
Biological Diversity. It recognizes that "the marine environment and the
fauna and flora which it supports are of vital importance to all nations."[67]
More recently, the UN Convention to Combat Desertification in those
Countries Experiencing Serious Drought and/or Desertification, Particularly in Africa refers to "the urgent concern of the international community, including states and international organizations, about the adverse
impacts of desertification and drought," although only some parts of the
world are directly concerned.[68]

As within states, the common concern, *l'intérêt général*, is a general concept which does not connote specific rules and obligations, but establishes
the general basis for the concerned community to act. The conventions
cited imply a global responsibility to conserve disappearing or diminishing
wild fauna and flora, ecosystems, and natural resources in general in danger. Language to this effect can be found in the October 30, 1980 resolution of the UN General Assembly on the draft World Charter for Nature,
which asserts the "supreme importance of protecting natural systems, maintaining the balance and quality of nature and conserving natural resources,
in the interests of present and future generations."[69]

The right and duty of the international community to act in matters of
common concern must be balanced with respect for national sovereignty.
States retain sovereignty subject to the requirements of international law
developed to ensure the common interest. Other domains of international
law, including trade and diplomatic relations, are instrumental to achiev-

---

[65]   Oct. 28, 1982; Res. 37/7, U.N. Doc. A/37/51.

[66]   *See* on the replacement of the concept of "common heritage of mankind"
by "common concern," N. Schrijver, Sovereignty over Natural Resources, Balancing Rights and Duties 246, 389 (1997).

[67]   Sept. 22, 1992.

[68]   Paris, June 17, 1994.

[69]   G.A. Res. 35/7 on the Draft World Charter for Nature, U.N. GAOR, 35th
Sess., Supp. No. 48 at 15; U.N. Doc. A/35/7, Nov. 5, 1980; 20 I.L.M. 462 (1981).

ing this common interest of humanity. They do not constitute in themselves the ultimate goals of international society but are means to improve the social and economic well-being of humanity as a whole. The terms of the United Nations Charter indicate that international peace and security must be coupled with economic and social advancement of all peoples and individuals in order to ensure overall advancement of humanity. Respect for human rights, economic development and environmental protection have been unified in the concept of sustainable development as a common concern of humanity.

4. Common Heritage of Mankind

The common heritage of mankind is a concept that emerged at the end of the 1960s to challenge older concepts of *res nullius* and *res communis* in legal approaches to common resources. *Res nullius,* which in most systems included wild animals and plants, belong to no one and can be freely used and appropriated when taken or captured. The concept of *res communis* implies the reverse, common ownership that precludes individual appropriation but allows common use of the resources, *e.g.,* navigation on the high seas. The concept of common heritage of mankind is distinct from both earlier concepts, in part because of its inclusion of the word "heritage," connoting a temporal aspect in the communal safeguarding of areas incapable of national appropriation. Special legal regimes have been created for the deep seabed and its subsoil,[70] Antarctica, the Moon, the geostationary orbit of satellites, and areas, sites and monuments that form essential parts of the cultural heritage of humanity.

The nature of the common heritage is a form of trust whose principal aims are exclusive use for peaceful purposes, rational utilization in a spirit of conservation, good management or wise use, and transmission to future generations. Benefits of the common heritage may be shared in the present through equitable allocation of revenue, but this is not the essential feature of the concept. Benefit-sharing can also mean sharing scientific knowledge acquired in common heritage areas, like Antarctica or the Moon, or sharing use, as with cultural heritage or the orbit of geostationary satellites.

Whether the trustee is the international community through the intermediary of an international body or one or more states acting on the community's behalf is a policy decision. The common heritage of mankind can be administered by a special authority, like the International Seabed Authority created by the 1982 Convention on the Law of the Sea, amended by agreement in 1994. It also can be administered in common by a group

---

70   *See* U.N. Division for Ocean Affairs and the Law of the Sea, The Law of the Sea, Concept of the Common Heritage of Mankind (1996).

of states, as in Antarctica. Finally, it can remain under state sovereignty and be administered by individual states under the supervision of an international body, as with the cultural and natural heritage designated by the 1972 UNESCO Convention for the Protection of the World's Cultural and Natural Heritage. The last example shows that, in contrast to the concept of *res communis*, the common heritage of mankind can remain under national sovereignty, like protected cultural areas in Egypt or nature reserves in Kenya, and even can be owned by private persons.

During the drafting of the Convention on Biological Diversity, some states criticized the concept of common heritage of mankind. States having rich biological diversity opposed considering such resources as parts of the common heritage of mankind, the benefit of which should be shared with others. These views demonstrated a lack of understanding of the concept of common heritage, which does not necessarily include the present sharing of material benefit. The Convention on Biological Diversity, by entrusting the contracting states with the conservation and sustainable use of biological diversity on their territories (Arts. 6–10), incorporates the main elements of the concept of common heritage.

E. Conclusions

The foundations of international environmental law presented here can be summarized by highlighting several key characteristics. Policies emerge from religious and philosophical beliefs but also must be based on scientific and economic realities that require an integrated and interdisciplinary approach. At the international level, the emergence of environmental protection as a common interest of humanity alters the traditional role of state sovereignty. A lack of reciprocity in most environmental obligations necessitates new forms of law-making, compliance techniques and enforcement. Other consequences, to be discussed further, include the importance of participation by non-state actors and management of environmental resources at all levels of governance. One approach that brings together many of these ideas is the notion of subsidiarity. Subsidiarity means making decisions and implementing them at the lowest effective level of government or other organization. Each higher level of governance is subsidiary to the level below it, serving as a safety net when problems cannot be resolved. In addition to EU use of this as a fundamental principle, the European Landscape Convention (Florence, October 20, 2000) includes the principle in Article 4: "Each Party shall implement this Convention, in particular Articles 5 and 6, according to its own division of powers, in conformity with its constitutional principles and administrative arrangements, and respecting the principle of subsidiarity, taking into account the European Charter of Local Self-government. Without derogating from the provisions of this Convention, each Party shall harmonize the implementation of this Convention with its own policies." This idea also seems woven throughout the entire United Nations Desertification Convention.

BIBLIOGRAPHY

Bodansky, D. *Scientific Uncertainty and the Precautionary Principle*, 33 ENVIRONMENT 4 (1991).

BOSSELMAN, K., WHEN TWO WORLD'S COLLIDE: SOCIETY AND ECOLOGY (1995).

Cole, L., *Remedies for Environmental Racism: A View from the Field*, 90 MICH. L. REV. 1991 (1992).

Collin, R., *Environmental Equity: A Law and Planning Approach to Environmental Racism*, 11 VA. ENVTL. L.J. 495 (1992).

COSTANZA, R. ed., ECOLOGICAL ECONOMICS (1991).

COWARD, H., POPULATION, CONSUMPTION AND THE ENVIRONMENT: RELIGIOUS AND SECULAR RESPONSES (1995).

DALY, H. & TOWNSEND, K. eds., VALUING THE EARTH: ECONOMICS, ECOLOGY, ETHICS (1993).

DALY, H., ELEMENTS OF ENVIRONMENTAL MACROECONOMICS (1993).

DES JARDINS, J.R., ENVIRONMENTAL ETHICS (1993).

EHRLICH, P., THE POPULATION BOMB (1968).

FREESTONE, D., THE PRECAUTIONARY PRINCIPLE IN INTERNATIONAL ENVIRONMENTAL LAW (1996).

GORE, A., EARTH IN THE BALANCE (1992).

GRIFO, F. & ROSENTHAL, J. eds., FATAL SYNERGISMS: INTERACTIONS BETWEEN INFECTIOUS DISEASES, HUMAN POPULATION GROWTH AND LOSS OF BIODIVERSITY (1997).

Jacobsen, J., *Population, Consumption and Environmental Degradation: Problems and Solutions*, 8 COLO. J. INT'L ENVTL. L. & POL'Y 255 (1995).

LOMBORG, B., THE SCEPTICAL ENVIRONMENTALIST: THE REAL STATE OF THE ENVIRONMENT (2001).

Mohai, P. & Bryant, B., *Environmental Injustice: Weighing Race and Class as Factors in the Distribution of Environmental Hazards*, 63 U. COLO. L. REV. 921 (1992).

Naess, A., *The Deep Ecological Movement: Some Philosophical Aspects*, 8 PHIL. INQUIRY 10 (1986).

NORGAARD, R.B., SUSTAINABILITY AND THE ECONOMICS OF ASSURING ASSETS FOR FUTURE GENERATIONS (1992).

Norton, B., *Environmental Ethics and the Rights of Future Generations*, 4 ENVTL. ETHICS 19 (1982).

PASSMORE, J., MAN'S RESPONSIBILITY FOR NATURE: ECOLOGICAL PROBLEMS AND WESTERN TRADITION (1974).

PIERCE, C., PEOPLE, PENGUINS AND PLASTIC TREES (1986).

Sagoff, M., *On Preserving the Natural Environment*, 84 YALE L.J. 205 (1974).

SCHUMACHER, E.F., SMALL IS BEAUTIFUL: ECONOMICS AS IF PEOPLE MAT-
TERED (1973).

Stone, C., *Should Trees Have Standing?—Toward Legal Rights for Natural Objects*,
45 S. CAL. L. REV. 450 (1972).

STONE, C., THE GNAT IS OLDER THAN MAN: GLOBAL ENVIRONMENT AND
HUMAN AGENDA (1993).

TOBIAS, M. ed., DEEP ECOLOGY: AN ANTHOLOGY (1985).

UNEP, POVERTY AND THE ENVIRONMENT (1995).

CHAPTER 2

ORIGIN AND EVOLUTION OF INTERNATIONAL ENVIRONMENTAL LAW

The present ecological era began at the end of the 1960s, after post-World War II reconstruction led to unprecedented global economic development. This development was unequal, accentuating differences in wealth between countries of the Northern and Southern hemispheres as well as within countries. It also required unprecedented use of exhaustible natural resources such as clean water, air, flora and fauna, and minerals. As it became clear that limited resources would ultimately become incapable of satisfying the various needs of industrial and developing countries, public opinion increasingly demanded action to protect the quantity and quality of the components of the environment.

During preceding centuries, sporadic efforts were made to remedy specific local forms of pollution or nuisances, such as smoke, noise, and water pollution. The first international agreements appeared in the 19th century with the conclusion of international fishing treaties and agreements to protect various plant species, but their primary purpose was to sustain the harvesting of economically valuable species. Genuine measures of environmental protection appeared only during the second half of the 20th century. A brief glance at the period prior to the development of modern international environmental law indicates the significance of current international legal norms.

A.   International Environmental Law before the Stockholm Conference

The 1902 Convention for the Protection of Birds Useful to Agriculture[1] was the first global convention to enter into force for the protection of designated species of wildlife.[2] Its very title reveals the perspective of those who adopted it. The Convention concerned *useful* birds, especially insectivores,

---

[1]   International Convention for the Protection of Birds Useful to Agriculture (Paris, Mar. 19, 1902).

[2]   An even earlier Convention for the Preservation of Wild Animals, Birds and Fish in Africa (May 19, 1900), never entered into force. It was motivated by the desire to halt the massacre of diverse animal species deemed useful or inof-

and was aimed primarily at enhancing agricultural production. Annex 2 numbered among "non-useful birds" the majority of hunting birds, including some eagles and falcons which are strictly protected today. The criterion was short-term utility, the immediate usefulness of protected species. The role of other birds in ecosystems, particularly hunters of small rodents, was completely ignored. The same utilitarianism characterizes the 1911 United States-Great Britain Treaty Relating to the Preservation and Protection of Fur Seals,[3] and the subsequent Washington Convention joining each of these states with Japan and Russia.[4] However, these early treaties also called for national quotas and regulating international trade in objects produced from seal hunting, both progressive techniques.

Several early boundary waters treaties contain measures against water pollution. The 1909 agreement respecting boundary waters between the United States and Canada[5] was considered a model. It is still in force and was expanded during the 1970s.[6] This treaty instituted a mixed commission which continues play a role in pollution control.[7]

Some genuinely ecological approaches emerged in the 1930s, with the adoption of two regional instruments that can be seen as precursors to present-day environmental concepts. First, the 1933 London Convention Relative to the Preservation of Fauna and Flora in their Natural State, applied to an Africa then largely colonized. It excluded from its scope the metropolitan areas of the colonial powers.[8] Within the territories to which it applied, however, it provided for the creation of national parks and strict protection for some species of wild animals. It also included measures regulating the export of hunting trophies and banned certain methods of hunting. The Convention remained fundamentally utilitarian, however, adopting these measures in part for the purpose of preserving big game hunting (Art. 4(2)); it also specifically called for measures to be taken to domesticate wild

---

fensive to man. The treaty simultaneously encouraged the destruction of creatures deemed harmful to human interests, including lions, leopards, crocodiles, and poisonous snakes.

   [3]   Treaty for the Preservation and Protection of the Fur Seals (Washington, D.C., Feb. 7, 1911).

   [4]   Interim Convention on Conservation of North Pacific Fur Seals (Washington, Feb. 9, 1957).

   [5]   Washington, Jan. 11, 1909.

   [6]   *See* United States-Canada Agreement relating to the Establishment of Joint Pollution Contingency Plans for Spills of Oil and Other Noxious Substances (June 19, 1974); United States-Canada Agreement on Great Lakes Water Quality with Annexes (Nov. 22, 1978), amended Oct. 16, 1983, T.I.A.S. No. 10798.

   [7]   *See* Chapter 10D for a discussion of the Mixed Commission.

   [8]   Convention Relative to the Preservation of Fauna and Flora in their Natural State, Art. 1 (London, Nov. 8, 1933).

animals susceptible of economic utilization (Art. 7(8)) and allowed additional measures to be taken to protect species of animals or plants "which by general admission are useful to man or of special scientific interest." (Art. 8(4)). The second instrument, the Convention on Nature Protection and Wildlife Preservation in the Western Hemisphere,[9] also envisages the establishment of reserves and the protection of wild animals and plants, especially migratory birds; however, the main provisions of the Convention are more general and less restrictive than those of the London agreement.

Between the two world wars, states entered into a growing number of boundary water agreements that included provisions on the problem of water pollution. These efforts continued after World War II, especially in Central and Eastern Europe. Some states, like the former Yugoslavia, concluded a network of bilateral agreements to regulate the utilization of waters through the creation of international commissions. In 1950, Belgium, France and Luxembourg concluded the first treaty entirely dedicated to countering freshwater pollution, one part of which created a tripartite standing committee to tackle the problem.[10] Similar treaties followed for the Mosel (1956),[11] Lake Constance (1960),[12] Lake Leman (1962),[13] and the Rhine (1963).[14] Although in the majority of cases these treaties established international commissions, they did not set water quality standards nor adopt norms against pollution.

Efforts to combat marine pollution appeared during the 1950s. The 1954 London Convention for the Prevention of the Pollution of the Sea by Oil[15] was the first rather tentative step in this direction. The Convention was later modified and reinforced, then replaced in 1973 by a much more detailed and effective convention.[16] New technologies, in particular the utilization of nuclear energy, led to further international regulation. A 1963

---

[9]   Convention on Nature Protection and Wildlife Preservation in the Western Hemisphere (Washington D.C., Oct. 12, 1940).

[10]   Protocol to Establish a Tripartite Standing Committee on Polluted Waters (Brussels, Apr. 8, 1950).

[11]   Convention on the Canalization of the Mosel (Luxembourg, Oct. 27, 1956).

[12]   Agreement on the Protection of Lake Constance against Pollution (Steckborn, Oct. 27, 1960).

[13]   Convention between France and Switzerland Concerning the Protection of Lake Leman against Pollution (Paris, Nov. 16, 1962).

[14]   Agreement concerning the International Commission for the Protection of the Rhine against Pollution (Bern, Apr. 29, 1963).

[15]   International Convention for the Prevention of Pollution of the Sea by Oil (London, May 12, 1954).

[16]   International Convention for the Prevention of Pollution by Ships (London, Nov. 2, 1973).

treaty addressed military use of radioactive materials, banning nuclear weapons testing in the atmosphere, in outer space and under water.[17]

During this period, environmental concerns increasingly appeared in general international legal texts. The 1959 Antarctic Treaty forbid all nuclear activity on the sixth continent and also envisaged the adoption of measures to protect animals and plants.[18] Two of the four 1958 conventions relating to the law of the sea prohibited ocean pollution by oil or pipelines and by radioactive waste, as well as damage to the marine environment caused by drilling operations on the continental shelf.[19] A third convention was entirely dedicated to fishing and the conservation of marine living resources.[20] For the other commons area, the 1967 Treaty on Principles Governing the Exploration and Use of Outer Space declared that states should avoid contamination as well as harmful modifications of the earth through the introduction of extraterrestrial substances.[21]

Thus, incrementally, the first elements emerged of an international code for the protection of the environment. International jurisprudence contributed by introducing the fundamental principles which dominate the law of transfrontier pollution. The *Trail Smelter* arbitration of March 11, 1941,[22] affirmed that no state has the right to use its territory or permit it to be used to cause serious damage by emissions to the territory of another state or to the property of persons found there. In 1949, the International Court of Justice, in the *Corfu Channel* case, affirmed that no state may utilize its territory contrary to the rights of other states.[23] Finally, in the *Lake*

---

[17] Treaty Banning Nuclear Weapons in the Atmosphere, in Outer Space, and Underwater (Moscow, Aug. 5, 1963).

[18] The Antarctic Treaty (Washington, D.C., Dec. 1, 1959).

[19] Convention on the High Seas, Arts. 24–25 (Geneva, Apr. 29, 1958); Convention on the Continental Shelf, Art. 5(7) (Geneva, Apr. 29, 1958).

[20] Convention on Fishing and Conservation of the Living Resources of the High Seas (Geneva, Apr. 29, 1958).

[21] Treaty on Principles Governing the Activities of States in the Exploration and Use of Outer Space, Including the Moon and Other Celestial Bodies, Art. IX (Jan. 27, 1967).

[22] Arbitral Award in the *Trail Smelter Case*, (Mar. 11, 1941), 3 U.N. RIAA 1905.

[23] *Corfu Channel Case* (U.K. v. Albania) (Apr. 3, 1949), Merits, 1949 I.C.J. Rep. 4.

Lanoux decision of November 19, 1956,[24] the arbitral panel alluded to the invasion of the rights of states that may result from pollution of boundary waters. These precedents furnished the first legal principles from which present environmental law has evolved.

At the end of the 1960s, scientific studies raised general public awareness of dangers threatening the biosphere.[25] The resulting mobilization of public opinion was unprecedented in two ways. First, it was a grass roots phenomenon, only later finding a power base when several governments officially adopted environmental policies. Second, the movement was transnational from the beginning. The global grass roots efforts emerged from a changing philosophical and ethical consensus, incorporating new individual and social values in reaction to the post-war "consumer society." Rejecting traditional ideologies to the degree that they were seen as materialistic, the ecological movement spanned all political factions and political parties. In consequence, many environmental laws were adopted unanimously by national legislatures.

These factors explain the brevity of time it took for international organizations to recognize the emergence of a new problem. The United Nations Economic Commission for Europe,[26] for example, made studies beginning in 1956 about pollution of inland waters and later the dumping of wastes. The year 1968 was the turning point, however, with the United Nations, the Council of Europe and the Organization of African Unity all taking decisive steps.

The Council of Europe adopted the first general environmental texts approved by an international organization: a Declaration on Air Pollution Control,[27] and the European Water Charter, proclaimed May 6, 1968.[28] Today the principles they affirm appear obvious. At that time, however, even the fact that water and air cross boundaries was not generally grasped. During the same year, the Council of Europe also adopted the first European regional environmental treaty: the European Agreement on the Restriction of the Use of Certain Detergents in Washing and Cleaning Products.[29]

---

[24]   *Lake Lanoux Case* (France v. Spain) (Nov. 19, 1957), 12 U.N. RIAA 281 (1957).

[25]   Rachel Carson's classic THE SILENT SPRING (1962) is often credited with bringing environmental concerns to public awareness.

[26]   *See* Chapter 4C.1.d.

[27]   Res. 60(4) of Mar. 8, 1968, Committee of Ministers, Council of Europe.

[28]   Published as a separate sheet, without number.

[29]   European Agreement on the Restriction of the Use of Certain Detergents in Washing and Cleaning Products (Brussels, Sept. 16, 1968).

Africa produced the second major initiative despite a widely-held view in the region that environmental deterioration was due to industrial pollution and was thus primarily a problem of the northern hemisphere. On September 15, 1968, the heads of states and governments of the Organization of African Unity signed an African Convention on the Conservation of Nature and Natural Resources,[30] replacing the 1933 London Convention. The African Convention is a model of comprehensiveness: it concerns the conservation and utilization of soil, water, plant and animal resources, virtually the entire environment. This breadth of objectives means that certain provisions in the Convention announce only general principles, but those that concern the conservation of plant and animal resources adopt precise rules, including the creation of reserves, regulation of hunting, capturing and fishing and protection of specific species. Two important environmental innovations appear in the African Convention: the recognized need to protect the habitat of endangered species as well as the species itself, and the proclaimed special responsibility of the state whose territory is the sole locale of a rare species.[31]

B. The Stockholm Conference on the Human Environment

The United Nations joined the actions of 1968 directed at protecting the environment when the General Assembly convoked a world conference on the human environment to be held in Stockholm in 1972.[32] This decision gave rise to intense and diverse activity, particularly within inter-governmental organizations whose mandate could extend to environmental problems. Numerous national and international non-governmental environmental organizations and various governments also engaged in considerable preparatory work.

Ecological catastrophes such as the 1967 "black tides" off the coasts of France, England and Belgium, caused by the grounding of the oil tanker *Torrey Canyon*, and realization that the environment increasingly was threatened, incited governments to take action immediately, without waiting for the Stockholm meeting. These efforts focused on international cooperation to counter marine oil pollution through measures of prevention and establishment of liability. Several steps also were taken to conserve wild animals, notably conclusion of the 1971 Ramsar Convention on Wetlands of

---

[30]   African Convention on the Conservation of Nature and Natural Resources (Algiers, Sept. 15, 1968), revised July 21, 2003.

[31]   Art. VIII(1).

[32]   G.A. Res. 2398 (XXIII), Dec. 3, 1968.

International Importance[33] and the 1972 London Convention for the Conservation of Antarctic Seals.[34]

While these actions responded to some of the urgent environmental problems, ambitious preparations for the Stockholm Conference continued, based on the work of a special committee of 27 states advising the United Nations Secretary General. When the Stockholm meeting took place June 5–16, 1972, it brought together some 6,000 persons, including delegations from 113 states, representatives of every major inter-governmental organization, 700 observers sent by 400 non-governmental organizations, invited individuals, and approximately 1,500 journalists.

The inclusiveness helped the Conference achieve an internationally recognized significance. The importance of the Conference also derives from the texts adopted during a closing plenary session, notably the Declaration on the Human Environment,[35] adopted by acclamation, an "Action Plan" containing 109 recommendations and a long resolution on institutional and financial implementation within the United Nations.

The Stockholm Declaration on the Human Environment begins with the statement that man is at once the creature and molder of his environment; the natural element and the man-made are essential to human well-being and to the full enjoyment of basic human rights, including the right to life. Protecting the human environment is also viewed as a major issue for economic development. The Declaration recognizes that the natural growth of world population continuously poses problems for preserving the environment, but expresses a conviction that with social progress and the evolution of production, science, and technology, human ability to improve the environment strengthens each day.

The principles contained in the second part of the Declaration translate the preambular concepts into more concrete language, while reflecting the various political preoccupations of the meeting's participants. The first principle, for example, affirms the fundamental human right to liberty, equality and adequate conditions of life in an environment of a quality that permits a life of dignity and well-being, adding that man bears a solemn responsibility to protect and improve the environment for present and future generations. The principle concludes by condemning apartheid, racial segregation and discrimination, colonialism, and other forms of

---

[33] Feb. 2, 1971. The initial aim of the Ramsar Convention was to protect the habitat of migratory waterbirds.

[34] June 1, 1972.

[35] Stockholm Declaration on the Human Environment (June 16, 1972).

oppression and foreign domination. Significantly, Principle 1 establishes the fundamental link between environmental protection and human rights despite the conflation of ideas and themes.

Principles 2 to 7 constitute the heart of the Declaration. They proclaim that the natural resources of the globe are not only oil and minerals, but also air, water, earth, plants and animals as well as representative samples of natural ecosystems. These should be preserved in the interest of present and future generations. Man has a particular responsibility to safeguard the heritage of wildlife and its habitats. Renewable resources must maintain their ability to replenish themselves and non-renewable resources should not be wasted. In all cases the Declaration emphasizes the necessity of adequate resource management. This section concludes by calling for a halt to the production of toxic wastes or other matter that cannot be absorbed by the environment and in particular for a prevention of marine pollution.

Principles 8 to 25 address implementation of environmental protection. Four provisions concern the particular situation of developing countries. After stating that economic and social development is indispensable if an environment favorable to the existence and work of man is to be sought, Principle 9 affirms that the best means to remedy underdevelopment is to enhance financial and technical assistance. National environmental policies should assist the potential progress of poorer countries and they should be accorded supplementary international assistance. Principles 10 to 12 concern international trade and economic consequences of environmental protection, particularly for developing countries. Principle 10 provides that the stability of prices and an adequate remuneration for primary products and goods is essential for the management of the environment. Principles 13 to 15 underline the necessity of integrated, coordinated and rational development planning. Demographic issues produced a simple recommendation in Principle 16 in favor of policies which respect fundamental human rights and are judged adequate by the governments concerned. Principles 18–20 mention other instruments of environmental policy: recourse to science and technology, exchange of information, and finally, teaching and information about environmental matters.

The last group of principles, 21 to 26, is of particular interest in the development of international law. Principle 21 is generally recognized today as expressing a basic norm of customary international environmental law:

> States have, in accordance with the Charter of the United Nations and the principles of international law, the sovereign right to exploit their own resources pursuant to their own environmental policies, and the responsibility to ensure that the activities within their jurisdiction or control do not cause damage to the environment of other states or of areas beyond the limits of national jurisdiction.

The Declaration further affirms that states should cooperate to develop international law regarding liability and compensation for victims of pollution and other environmental damage produced outside their boundaries (Principle 22). They should define criteria and norms in environmental matters, taking into consideration the system of values prevailing in each country, in particular in developing countries (Principle 23). States should cooperate to protect and improve the environment and ensure that international organizations play a coordinated, effective and dynamic role in this field (Principles 24–25). The final principle condemns nuclear weapons and all other means of mass destruction.

The "Action Plan for the Human Environment,"[36] another major outcome of the Stockholm Conference, does not always follow an operational order but can be regrouped around three themes: a global environmental assessment program, environmental management activities, and supporting measures. The assessment program, christened "Earthwatch," includes evaluation and review, research, monitoring and information exchanges. Understandably, international cooperation is given an important place.

The chapter on environmental management, which concerns both human establishments and natural resources, contains most of the provisions concerning pollution. The Plan addresses the problem of dumping toxic or dangerous substances, elaboration of norms to limit noise, control of contaminants in food, and measures for controlling pollution. The Plan's authors give particular attention to protection of the marine environment, understandable in light of the fact that preparations for the Third United Nations Conference on the Law of the Sea had already begun. Finally, the Plan addresses wildlife and natural spaces, with the accent again strongly placed on international cooperation through conclusion of treaties, coordinated action by governments, and exchange of information on national legislation. The text stresses the importance of planning, including the development of international plans of action.

Measures of support contained in the Stockholm Action Plan focus on information and public education as well as training of specialists in environmental matters. They include institutional aspects, in effect providing that anticipated actions should be coordinated at the international level. For this, the Plan recommends creation of a central organ to be charged with environmental matters. In addition, the Action Plan recommends a division of duties among specialized agencies of the United Nations (FAO, WHO, UNESCO, etc.) and among regional organizations. On the basis of the recommendations of the Stockholm Conference, in part found in the Action Plan, in part in independent texts, the United Nations General

---

[36] U.N. Doc. A/Conf.48/14, July 3, 1972, at 10.

Assembly in 1972 created a specialized subsidiary organ, the United Nations Environment Program (UNEP).[37]

C. From Stockholm to Rio

The Stockholm Conference had immense value in drawing attention to the problem of environmental deterioration and methods to prevent or remedy it. The Conference was global both in its planetary conception of the environment, and in its view of institutional structures and world policies. It was also global in addressing all the major environmental themes of the time.

The vision of Stockholm and its implications characterize the subsequent evolution of environmental law until the Rio Conference. International environmental law substantially increased in the two decades after Stockholm. The dominant approach of the 1970s concentrated on protecting specific sectors of the environment: oceans, inland waters, atmosphere, outer space, wild plants and animals. The United Nations reaffirmed and developed the general principles of the Stockholm Declaration in 1982 when the General Assembly adopted the World Charter for Nature.

During the 1980s, it became increasingly evident that a sectoral approach was insufficient to address environmental deterioration because generally it failed to regulate the causes or sources of harm that could affect more than one or several sectors. Thus, a second approach, which aimed to regulate sources and risks of harm, became a common complement to sectoral regulation. This eventually led to common management of shared resources and an ecosystem approach. Finally, global problems emerged that required comprehensive cooperation among all states, such as climate change and the loss of biological diversity.

1. Global Instruments

The Stockholm Conference had a major impact on legal developments in several fields of international law. First, the negotiations at the United Nations Conference on the Law of the Sea which began in 1972, produced the United Nations Convention on the Law of the Sea (UNCLOS)[38] in 1982 after ten years of work. UNCLOS encompasses the grand themes of marine environmental protection, giving a general legal framework to formerly disparate regulations. UNCLOS reaffirms and details global and regional regulations to combat certain aspects of marine environmental injury, such as vessel-source and land-based pollution and pollution caused by dumping of

---

[37]   *See* Chapter 4C.1.a. for a discussion of UNEP.

[38]   Montego Bay, Dec. 10, 1982. For a detailed discussion of the environmental aspects of UNCLOS, *see* Chapter 11.

wastes and other matter. UNCLOS also adopted significant new rules, in particular the fundamentally important principle that states have a general obligation to protect and preserve the marine environment.[39] The obligation encompasses the totality of the marine environment, even areas under the jurisdiction of the state itself.

Several weeks before the adoption of UNCLOS, the United Nations General Assembly solemnly proclaimed the World Charter for Nature.[40] The Charter contains a preamble and 24 articles. The preamble expresses fundamental concepts: mankind itself is part of nature, civilization is rooted in nature, every form of life is unique and merits respect regardless of its worth to man. Thus, all human conduct that could affect nature is to be guided and judged according to the proclaimed principles.

The principles themselves state that nature shall be respected and its essential processes shall not be impaired, the genetic viability of the earth shall not be compromised, and the population levels of all life forms, wild and domesticated, shall be at least sufficient for their survival. In addition, special protection shall be afforded to the unique areas of the globe, both land and sea. Ecosystems and organisms as well as other natural resources shall be managed to achieve and maintain their optimum sustainable productivity and continuity.

The Charter envisages the integration of nature conservation into social and economic development planning and implementation, taking into consideration the long-term capacity of natural systems to ensure the subsistence and settlement of human populations. Nearly half of the principles concern application of the Charter and foresee incorporation of its principles in the law and practice of each state, the broadest dissemination possible of knowledge of nature and efforts to increase that knowledge, as well as monitoring of the status of nature. Funds, programs and administrative structures necessary to achieve the objective of conserving nature should be provided.

The principles of the World Charter for Nature were not elaborated in a binding legal instrument, but they have influenced the direction of international environmental law, particularly in regard to the principle of sustainable development. Moreover, they have been incorporated in conventions such as the 1985 South-East Asian Agreement on the Conservation of Nature and its Resources,[41] and in some national laws.

---

[39] Art. 192, UNCLOS.

[40] World Charter for Nature, Oct. 28, 1982, G.A. Res. 37/7, 37 U.N. GAOR Supp. (No. 51), at 17; U.N. Doc. A/37/51 (1982). For the legislative history and a commentary on the Charter by the European Council for Environmental Law, *see* THE WORLD CHARTER FOR NATURE (1986).

[41] Kuala Lumpur, July 9, 1985.

Noteworthy conventions on nature protection were concluded even prior to the World Charter for Nature. Three of them, the 1971 Ramsar Convention on Conservation of Wetlands of International Importance,[42] the fundamentally important UNESCO Convention on the Protection of the World Cultural and Natural Heritage,[43] and the 1979 Bonn Convention on the Conservation of Migratory Species of Wild Animals,[44] envisage the protection of nature in designated natural zones. The fourth treaty, the 1973 Washington Convention on International Trade in Endangered Species of Wild Fauna and Flora,[45] tackles the protection of species by regulating the particular threat posed by trade in endangered plants and animals.

Following the Stockholm Conference, new problems emerged that had not been perceived earlier, such as long-range air pollution and depletion of the ozone layer. The global Vienna Convention, adopted March 22, 1985 and the 1987 Montreal Protocol[46] created an effective international system to reduce emissions of ozone-depleting substances. The compliance mechanisms they introduced have become a model for other environmental treaties. The unprecedented nuclear catastrophe at Chernobyl, April 26, 1986, similarly raised awareness of another new problem. It led to the almost immediate adoption of two conventions, the first of which requires rapid notification of nuclear accidents, the second of which covers assistance in the case of a nuclear accident or radiological emergency.[47]

The regulation of other potential sources of environmental harm became more common. Toxic or dangerous products and processes that threaten most or all parts of the environment must be regulated during their whole lifetime. This "cradle to grave" approach means that regulations should apply to production, transport, marketing, and waste elimination. The regulation of production is a highly technical issue which has to be solved by applying different methods to different groups of products. UNEP has established an International Register of Potentially Toxic Chemicals containing detailed information on substances of international importance. It may be consulted by those responsible for health and environmental protection in different countries. The Convention on the Control of Trans-

---

[42]   Ramsar, Feb. 2, 1971.

[43]   Nov. 23, 1972.

[44]   Bonn, June 23, 1979.

[45]   Washington, Mar. 3, 1973.

[46]   Convention for the Protection of the Ozone Layer (Vienna, Mar. 22, 1985); Montreal Protocol, Sept. 16, 1987.

[47]   Convention on Early Notification of a Nuclear Accident and Convention on Assistance in the Case of a Nuclear Accident or Radiological Emergency (Vienna, Sept. 26, 1986).

boundary Movements of Hazardous Wastes and their Disposal[48] and regional treaties on the topic concluded for Africa,[49] Central America[50] and the South Pacific[51] contributed significantly to this development.

Stockholm also stimulated institutions concerned with other fields of international law to consider environmental issues. New rules were included in instruments concerned with international law, including human rights,[52] humanitarian law,[53] and economic law.[54] Article 30 of the Charter of Economic Rights and Duties of States, adopted by the United Nations General Assembly in 1974,[55] proclaims that the protection, preservation and management of the environment for present and future generations is the responsibility of all states; they should strive to halt any detrimental policies in environmental matters and develop programs conforming to this responsibility. More generally, on October 30, 1980, the United Nations General Assembly proclaimed the responsibility of states for the preservation of nature in the interest of present and future generations.[56]

Building on its 1980 resolution, the General Assembly voted in 1983 to create the World Commission on Environment and Development, an independent body linked to but outside the United Nations system and later more commonly known as the Brundtland Commission.[57] Its mandate was to examine critical environment and development issues and to formulate realistic proposals for dealing with them; to propose new forms of international cooperation on these issues to influence policies in the direction of needed changes; and to raise the levels of understanding and commitment to action of individuals, organizations, businesses and governments. The conclusions of the Brundtland Report stressed the need for an integrated approach to development policies and projects which, if environmentally sound, should lead to sustainable economic development in both developed and developing countries. The report emphasized the need to give higher priority to anticipating and preventing problems. It defined "sustainable development" as development that meets present and future environment and development objectives and concluded that without an equitable sharing of the costs and benefits of environmental protection within and

---

[48]   Basel, Mar. 22, 1989.

[49]   Bamako, Jan. 29, 1991.

[50]   Panama, Dec. 11, 1992.

[51]   Waigani, Sept. 16, 1995.

[52]   *See* Chapter 15.

[53]   *See* Chapter 16.

[54]   *See* Chapter 17.

[55]   G.A. Res. 3281 (XXIX), Dec. 12, 1974, U.N. GAOR, 29th Sess., Supp. No. 31, U.N. Doc. A/9631, at 50.

[56]   G.A. Res. 35/7; 20 I.L.M. 462 (1981).

[57]   *See* OUR COMMON FUTURE (1987).

between countries neither social justice nor sustainable development can be achieved. The Brundtland Report led the United Nations to convene a second global conference on the environment, held in 1992 in Rio de Janeiro, under the title United Nations Conference on Environment and Development (UNCED). The very name of the conference reflected a change of approach from that of the Stockholm Conference on the Human Environment.

2. Regional Instruments

At the regional level, equally important evolution occurred. The same year as the Stockholm Conference, the Conference of Heads of State and Governments of the European Economic Community met in Paris and adopted a Declaration stating that economic expansion is not an end in itself, but that the quality of life should be improved, with particular attention given to intangible values and to protecting the environment.[58] The Community adopted its first Action Program on the Environment the following year. It declared that economic activities could no longer be imagined in the absence of an effective campaign to combat pollution and nuisance and to protect the environment.[59] Both quantitatively and substantively, the EC has taken particularly important action in the environmental field, principally but not exclusively against pollutants and nuisances. The EC Programs of Action have led to the elaboration of a veritable "Corpus Juris" now comprising more than 200 texts, the majority of which are obligatory for the member states. In addition, the EC regularly participates in actions directed by other institutions or in other forums, including the negotiation of global and regional environmental treaties.

In 1975, at the conclusion of the Helsinki Conference on Security and Cooperation in Europe,[60] all European countries, Canada and the United States adopted a Final Act that contained an entire chapter on cooperation in the environmental field. The declaration envisaged international studies of environmental problems, increased effectiveness of national and international measures, in particular procedures for evaluating environmental accidents, and efforts to reconcile or harmonize environmental policies and legislation. The chosen institutional structure was the United Nations Economic Commission for Europe. In 1979, the Geneva Convention on Long Range Transboundary Air Pollution was adopted within this frame-

---

[58] EC Commission, 6th General Report 8 (1972).

[59] First Action Program on the Environment, O.J. 1983, No. C 112. *See also* Chapter 4.

[60] Helsinki, Aug. 1, 1975.

work.[61] Subsequent protocols have created a general system to regulate the emissions of air pollutants.

The importance of regional institutions to international environmental law was demonstrated by the major role played by the Nordic Council in concluding the 1974 Nordic Convention on the Protection of the Environment,[62] considered a model on the subject of environmental cooperation between neighboring states and an inspiration for OECD's principles on transfrontier environment cooperation. Also within Europe, the Council of Europe specialized in actions for the protection of nature, elaborating the 1979 Bern Convention on the Conservation of Wildlife and Natural Habitats in Europe.

Global institutions also undertake actions concerning specific regions of the world. UNEP has drafted a series of conventions concerning regional seas, sometimes in collaboration with other institutions such as the Food and Agriculture Organization. Treaty systems now exist for more than a dozen maritime and coastal zones of the world, most of them adopted under UNEP auspices: the Mediterranean (Barcelona, 1976), the Persian Gulf (Kuwait, 1978), Western and Central Africa (Abidjan 1981), East Africa (Nairobi, 1985), the South-East Pacific (Lima, 1981), the Red Sea and Gulf of Aden (Jeddah, 1982), the Wider Caribbean (Cartagena, 1983), the South Pacific (Noumea, 1986), Black Sea (Bucharest, 1992), North-East Atlantic (Paris, 1992), the Baltic Sea (Helsinki, 1992) and the North-East Pacific (Antigua, 2002).[63]

Regional regulations, like those adopted on the global level, address sources of harm as well as environmental milieu. OECD adopted recommendations concerning methods of assessing the potential environmental effects of activities. Regional transport of dangerous or toxic materials became regulated by separate international conventions relating to rail, road, and river transport. The EC regulated the marketing of chemical products, mainly by harmonizing the classification, packaging and handling of dangerous substances. The OECD and the European Union also adopted regulations governing specific hazardous substances, such as mercury and phytopharmaceutical products. Cooperation to prevent industrial accidents or to minimize their effects also progressed, in particular through EC directives and a 1992 Convention on the Transboundary Effects of Industrial Accidents drafted in the framework of the UN Economic Commission for Europe.

---

[61] Geneva, Nov. 13, 1979.

[62] Stockholm, Feb. 19, 1974.

[63] *See* Chapter 11.

3. Customary International Law

A few principles of customary law concerning environmental relations among states emerged during the period following the Stockholm Conference. Some of them were formulated first within the OECD, then adopted by the United Nations Environment Program as part of the "Principles of conduct in the field of the environment for the guidance of States in the conservation and harmonious utilization of natural resources shared by two or more states." Approved by UNEP's Governing Council May 19, 1978, the Principles on Shared Resources reiterate Stockholm Principle 21 in recognizing the sovereign right of states to exploit their own resources coupled with an obligation to ensure that the activities undertaken within the limits of their jurisdiction or under their control do not damage the environment in other states. The UNEP Principles also express the obligation of states to notify the latter of plans which can be expected to affect significantly their environment, to enter into consultations with them, and to inform and cooperate in the case of unforeseen situations which could cause harmful effects to the environment. The measures also guarantee equality of access for non-residents to administrative and legal procedures in the state originating the harmful conduct, and non-discrimination in the application of national legislation to polluters, whatever the place of the harmful effects.

D. The United Nations Conference on Environment and Development

UNCED emerged from the Brundtland Report. The UN General Assembly resolution accepting the Report[64] convened a world conference on environment and development to be held in Brazil in 1992. To achieve this, it created a preparatory committee (PREPCOM) open to all United Nations member states, members states of specialized agencies, and accredited observers.

The three PREPCOM sessions negotiated legal, institutional and financial questions. The initial goal was to proclaim an Earth Charter, *i.e.*, principles containing general environmental obligations of states. After very difficult negotiations, the idea was abandoned in favor of adopting a declaration of principles, a compromise between the developing countries (Group of 77) who sought only political commitments, and industrialized countries, mainly OECD member states, who insisted on legal norms. In addition, there were competing views on the Declaration's contents: the industrialized countries considered it essential to include principles on public information and participation, precaution, and the polluter pays prin-

---

[64]   G.A. Res. 44/228, Dec. 22, 1989.

ciple, while developing countries demanded inclusion of the rights to development, poverty alleviation, and recognition of common but differentiated responsibilities.

The debate over institutions centered on the necessity of creating new organs as opposed to revitalizing and restructuring existing bodies. The delay in raising this issue limited the degree of innovation possible. Ultimately, the participating states agreed to create a Commission on Sustainable Development under the authority of the UN Economic and Social Council. The question of its composition and functioning was left to the UN General Assembly.[65]

UNCED met in Rio de Janeiro from June 3 to 14, 1992. One hundred seventy-two states (all but six members of the United Nations) were represented by close to 10,000 participants, including 116 heads of state and government; Japan alone sent 300 delegates. One thousand four hundred non-governmental organizations were accredited as well as nearly 9,000 journalists.

Five texts emerged from the meeting. Two conventions, drafted and adopted before the Conference, were opened for signature at Rio: the UN Framework Convention on Climate Change and the Convention on Biological Diversity. The Conference also adopted a declaration whose title reflects the difficulties of reaching agreement on it: Non-legally binding authoritative statement of principles for a global consensus on the management, conservation and sustainable development of all types of forests.[66]

Two texts adopted at UNCED have a general scope: the Declaration on Environment and Development and an action program called Agenda 21. The Declaration, a short statement of 27 principles, has a composite character which its legislative history can explain. It reaffirms the Stockholm Declaration of 1972 on which it seeks to build, but its approach and philosophy are very different. The central concept is sustainable development, as defined by the Brundtland Report, which integrates development and environmental protection. Principle 4 is important in this regard: it affirms that in order to achieve sustainable development, environmental protection shall constitute an integral part of the development process and cannot be considered in isolation from it.

Such views also are reflected in Principle 1, whose anthropocentric approach can be contrasted with the Stockholm Declaration and the World Charter for Nature: "Human beings are at the center of concerns for sustainable development. They are entitled to a healthy and productive life in harmony with nature."

The Rio Declaration contains several principles of an unambiguous, if general, legal character. It reinforces some existing principles and proclaims

---

65   *See* Chapter 4C.1.b.
66   *See* Chapter 8F.2.a.

new ones. The first category includes Principle 2, which concerns the trans-boundary effects of activities. It is similar to Principle 21 of the Stockholm Declaration, but adds the word "developmental." Other legal norms can be found in Principle 10, affirming rights of public information, participation, and remedies, Principle 13, which calls for the development of liability rules, and Principles 18 and 19 which require notifying other states about emergencies and projects that may affect their environment. The formulation of then-emerging principles includes the precautionary principle (Principle 15), the "polluter pays" principle that requires internalization of environmental costs (Principle 16) and the general requirement of environmental impact assessment (Principle 17). Principle 11 stresses the importance of enacting effective environmental legislation, although it notes that standards applied by some countries may not be appropriate to others because of the economic and social costs involved.

Other principles are more in the nature of policy guidelines, although the line between law and policy is not always clear. A distinction can be made between three groups of policy provisions. The first group expresses concern for development: Principle 3 aims at the eradication of poverty, Principle 6 claims special priority for the needs of developing countries, and Principle 9 relates to the strengthening of endogenous capacity-building for sustainable development by improving scientific understanding. All these provisions use the term "shall," while the other groups of policy principles substitute "should" for "shall."

A second group of principles addresses the world economic order. Principle 7 proclaims common but differentiated responsibilities, including the special responsibility of developed countries "in view of the pressures their societies place on the global environment." Principle 8 adds that states should reduce and eliminate unsustainable patterns of production and consumption and promote demographic policies. Although it is not made explicit, the first part of this principle mainly concerns industrialized states, while the second part concerns situations in developing countries. Economic aspects are treated in Principle 12 which advocates a "supportive and open economic system" and international consensus, and condemns discriminatory trade measures or disguised restrictions on international trade, as well as unilateral actions. Finally, Principle 14 aims to discourage or prevent the relocation and transfer to other states of activities and substances that cause severe environmental degradation or are harmful to human health.

A last group of principles concerns public participation. Principle 10 recognizes for individuals the rights to information, to participation and to remedies in environmental matters. Principles 20 to 22 stress the importance of the participation of women, youth and indigenous peoples, but the terms used show that these provisions are more guidelines than legal norms.

The second general document adopted by the Rio Conference is Agenda 21, a program of action consisting of forty chapters with 115 specific topics contained in 800 pages. There are four main parts:

- socio-economic dimensions (*e.g.*, habitats, health, demography, consumption and production patterns);
- conservation and resource management (*e.g.*, atmosphere, forest, water, waste, chemical products);
- strengthening the role of non-governmental organizations and other social groups such as trade unions, women, youth;
- measures of implementation (*e.g.*, financing, institutions).

Legally, the chapters concerning different sectors such as the atmosphere (chapter 9), biological diversity (chapter 15), the oceans (chapter 17), and freshwater resources (chapter 18), as well as discussion of specific problems such as biotechnology (chapter 15), toxic chemicals (chapter 19), and waste (chapters 20–22) are of particular interest. Additionally, two chapters are dedicated to international institutional arrangements (chapter 38) and international legal instruments and mechanisms (chapter 39).

The chapter on international legal instruments has implications for international law in general because it designates specific means that should be used to develop international environmental law, both in substance and in procedure. It insists on particular norms such as the legal aspects of sustainable development and on the adoption of environmental standards. It calls for the integration of environment and development policies in international treaties and emphasizes the participation in and the contribution of all countries to the further elaboration of international environmental law in the context of sustainable development. It refers to the relationship between existing national instruments and relevant social and economic agreements and calls for improvement in the efficacy of international environmental law, in particular by procedures and mechanisms to promote and review the implementation of treaties, such as efficient and practical reporting systems.

Agenda 21 pays particular attention to national legislation. It makes frequent reference to national laws, measures, plans, programs, and standards. Chapter 8, Integrating Environment and Development in Decision-Making, advocates the use of legal and economic instruments for planning and management, seeking incorporation of efficiency criteria in decisions. It recognizes the importance of laws and regulations suited to country-specific conditions for transforming environment and development policies into action, adding that not only "command-and-control" methods should be used, but also a normative framework for economic planning and market instruments. Such methods can also be useful for the implementation of obligations resulting from international treaties.

Governments should regularly assess the laws and regulations enacted and the related institutional or administrative machinery with a view to rendering them effective; integrated strategies should be developed to maximize compliance with law and regulations relating to sustainable development. Finally,

> Governments and legislators (. . .) should establish judicial and administrative procedures for legal redress and remedy of actions affecting environment and development that may be unlawful or infringe on rights under the law, and should provide access to individuals, groups and organizations with a recognized legal interest.

In sum, the Rio documents join environmental protection and economic development in the concept of sustainable development. All components of society are called upon to participate towards the achievement of this goal.

Although at first some contested the importance of the Rio Conference legal texts, the two Conventions and the Declaration represent milestones in international environmental law. Several principles of the Declaration, such as public participation, the prior assessment of environmental impacts, precaution, notification of emergencies, and prior information and consultation on projects potentially affecting the environment of other states, have been included in numerous binding and non-binding international instruments since Rio and constitute emerging customary law rules.

E. From Rio to Johannesburg

In the aftermath of Rio, virtually every major international convention concerning multilateral cooperation includes environmental protection as one of the goals of the states parties. Areas of international law that developed during earlier periods are now evolving in new directions because of insistence that they take into account environmental considerations. The result is an infusion of environmental norms into nearly every branch of international law.

In the area of trade relationships,[67] the 1994 Charter Establishing the World Trade Organization[68] and regional free trade agreements mention environmental cooperation as an aim. Examples of regional economic agreements that call for respect for the environment include the: 1992 Treaty Establishing the South African Development Community;[69] 1993

---

[67] *See further* Chapter 17.

[68] Marrakesh, Apr. 14, 1994.

[69] Windhoek, Aug, 17, 1992.

Treaty Establishing a Common Market for Eastern and Southern Africa;[70] 1992 Agreement on the North American Free Trade Area; [71] 1994 Tropical Timber Agreement[72] and 1994 European Energy Charter,[73] call for respect for the environment. The Treaty on European Union concluded before Rio affirmed the importance of environmental protection. Its provisions indicate that some of the Rio Declaration principles already enjoyed international support.

Human rights law and humanitarian law also show the impact of international environmental law.[74] The human rights community increasingly views environmental protection as an appropriate part of the human rights agenda. Institutions from the UN Human Rights Commission to the World Health Organization and the International Committee of the Red Cross have dealt with environmental concerns in recent years and are likely to continue their efforts. The humanitarian protections afforded during periods of armed conflict have become increasingly important as technology offers destructive forces of unprecedented scope. The Rio Declaration, Principle 24, declares that warfare is inherently destructive of sustainable development. States are to respect international law providing for the environment in times of armed conflict and cooperate in its further development, as necessary. The IAEA General Conference adopted a resolution on September 21, 1990 recognizing that attacks or threats of attack on nuclear facilities devoted to peaceful purposes could jeopardize the development of nuclear energy, affirmed the importance and reliability of its safeguard procedures, and emphasized the need for the Security Council to act immediately should such a threat or attack occur.[75] The Security Council itself affirmed the liability of Iraq for environmental harm resulting from its invasion of Kuwait.

Weapons systems are internationally regulated if they cause indiscriminate effects or excessive injuries. Chemical and nuclear weapons and anti-personnel land mines, in particular, have been targeted by the international community. A Convention on the Prohibition of the Development, Production, Stockpiling and Use of Chemical Weapons and on their Destruction was signed in Paris, January 13, 1993. In 1996, the conference of state parties to the Convention on Prohibitions or Restrictions on the Use of Certain Conventional Weapons adopted a protocol on the use of mines, booby-traps and other devices.[76] Finally, the Convention on the Prohibition of the Use,

---

70   Kampala, Nov. 5, 1993.

71   Washington D.C., Ottawa, Mexico City, Dec. 17, 1992.

72   Jan. 26, 1994.

73   Dec. 17, 1994.

74   *See further* Chapters 15 and 16.

75   IAEA GC (XXXIV)RES/533 (Sept. 21, 1990).

76   Protocol II to the Convention on Prohibitions on the Use of Certain

Stockpiling, Production and Transfer of Anti-Personnel Mines and on Their Destruction,[77] mentions the environment, although its purpose is to end the casualties caused by land mines.

Other emerging issues in international environmental law stem from the continual necessity to anticipate the consequences of new technologies, especially to avoid potentially disastrous consequences of some of humanity's ingenuity. On September 20, 1994, the IAEA adopted a Convention on Nuclear Safety that obliges all contracting parties to establish and maintain a legislative and regulatory framework to govern the safety of nuclear installations. Biotechnology also is emerging as a major topic for environmental protection. The need to promote biosafety has centered on two related issues: first, the handling of living modified organisms (LMOs) in the laboratory in order to protect workers and prevent the accidental liberation of such organisms into the surrounding ecosystem ("contained use"); second, the need for regulatory systems to govern the deliberate release of LMOs into the environment for testing or commercial purposes. The OECD has issued recommendations concerning the deliberate release of LMOs into the environment during field testing. The EC issued recently revised directives that provide a lengthy series of control procedures both for laboratory research and for the release of LMOs. States parties to the Convention on Biological Diversity adopted a protocol on biosafety on January 29, 2000, after years of negotiations.

The importance of controlling substances which can harm the environment necessitates an active role for states engaged in international trade. As early as the 1973 Washington Convention on International Trade in Endangered Species of Wild Fauna and Flora, states parties introduced a double authorization procedure by the exporting and the importing states. The technique is a fundamental part of the 1989 Basel Convention on the Control of Transboundary Movements of Hazardous Wastes and Their Disposal and the 1991 Bamako Convention on the Ban of the Import into Africa and the Control of Transboundary Movement and Management of Hazardous Wastes within Africa. It has been further developed by the 1998 Rotterdam Convention on the Prior Informed Consent Procedure for Certain Hazardous Chemicals and Pesticides in International Trade and by the 2000 Cartagena Protocol on Biosafety to the Convention on Biological Diversity. Such procedures allow states parties to determine the goods and substances they accept to be introduced into their environments, with the aim of making the treaty regimes more effective.

One can thus affirm that there is increased recognition of the international and multidimensional character of environmental problems and

---

Conventional Weapons which may be Deemed to be Excessively Injurious or to have Indiscriminate Effects (Geneva, May 3, 1996).

[77]   Oslo, Sept. 18, 1997.

potential remedies for them. Most states now accept that global efforts are required to solve many aspects of environmental deterioration, such as ocean pollution, depletion of stratospheric ozone, the greenhouse effect, and threats to biodiversity. Such problems especially require cooperation between industrialized and developing countries. The June 17, 1994, International Convention to Combat Desertification in Those Countries Experiencing Serious Drought and/or Desertification, particularly in Africa is one of the most significant results of such cooperation, strongly reflecting the concept of common but differentiated responsibilities. In addition, it takes the principle of cooperation and melds it with the right of public participation, emphasizing the need for all levels of governance and civil society to be involved in actions to combat desertification.

Concern for ecosystems has broadened and deepened as well, due to integrated approaches to safeguarding the planet's environment. The earlier sectoral aim of protecting wild fauna and flora is now incorporated in the comprehensive goal of maintaining biological diversity. This expanded and integrated vision includes efforts to reverse the trend towards monocultural agriculture and stockbreeding, as well as to combat the abuse of pesticides and fertilizers. The latter problem is addressed through the technique of prior informed consent in the Convention on the Prior Informed Consent Procedure for Certain Hazardous Chemicals and Pesticides in International Trade.[78] An integrated approach also appears in recent instruments addressing the environmental protection of large ecosystems: Antarctica (Madrid Protocol of 1991), the Alps (Salzburg Convention of 1991 and its Protocols), and the Arctic region (1996 Declaration).

The same trend can be seen in the shift to protecting freshwater resources as hydrographic units rather than as individual watercourses. The unity of water resources in a hydrographic basin and a consequent ecosystem approach to regulating such resources is now generally accepted. The 1987 Agreement on the Action Plan for the Environmentally Sound Management of the Common Zambezi River System[79] was one of the first to adopt a holistic approach to water resources management through the entire river system. The UN Convention on the Non-navigational Uses of International Watercourses[80] which unified the international legal status of surface and subsurface water, hastened recognition of the need to regulate freshwaters within the entire catchment basin, mainly a regional task. The problem ahead is to organize the shared management of water resources by those who are concerned.

---

[78] Rotterdam, Sept. 10, 1998.

[79] Harare, May 28, 1987, *available at* <http://faolex.fao.org/docs/texts/bot15888.doc>.

[80] New York, May 21, 1997.

The crucial role of economic and other non-state actors in environmental protection became increasingly recognized during this period. Representatives of public opinion emerged as powerful new actors in the international law-making process during the preparations for the Rio Conference and in the negotiation of treaties. They have contributed to the elaboration of a legal regime for the global environment by participating in the meetings as observers, bringing and dispatching information and even taking part in the drafting of important international agreements, assisting official state delegations and on occasion, being included in them. Enterprises have become more responsive to public pressure, insurance requirements, and often developed environmental consciousness. Parallel to this evolution, states and inter-governmental organizations have utilized more and more innovative economic incentives in environmental protection, such as labeling, standardization, environmental auditing, use of the best available techniques and environmental practices.

With the proliferation of international environmental instruments, there is an inevitable overlap in goals and subject areas. Some relatively comprehensive conventions, like the 1992 Convention on Biological Diversity, address the entire range of human activities in an effort to protect natural systems. Other agreements are more specialized, directed either at particular activities or particular areas or species. Global and regional agreements may reinforce each other on the same or similar issues. Rarely does a convention specifically indicate its relationship to other agreements. The Convention on Biological Diversity is one of the few instances where a hierarchy is established; it provides in Article 22 that the CBD shall not affect the rights and obligations of any contracting party deriving from any existing international agreement *except where the exercise of those rights and obligations would cause a serious damage or threat to biological diversity.* It adds that the Convention is to be implemented consistent with the rights and obligations of states under the law of the sea. Difficult issues may arise when there is a dispute over a bilateral treaty and one state is a party to the Biodiversity Convention but the other state is not.

The June 29, 1994, Danube Convention mandates that states parties adapt existing bilateral or multilateral agreements or other arrangements where necessary to eliminate contradictions with the basic principles of the Convention. The June 17, 1999, Protocol on Water and Health to the 1992 Convention on Transboundary Watercourses extends the application of the Espoo Convention on Environmental Impact Assessment in a Transboundary Context to any waters within the scope of the Protocol. The Protocol covers surface and ground waters, estuaries, coastal waters used for recreation, aquaculture or shellfish, enclosed bathing waters, and wastewater. Article 4(6) calls for environmental impact and risk assessment prior to any action that may have a significant impact on the environment of any waters within the scope of the Protocol. For that purpose, compliance with requirements of the Espoo Convention "shall satisfy the requirement" in respect of the proposed action.

The 1992 North American Free Trade Agreement, in Article 104 and Annex 104.1, provides that in the event of any inconsistency between the Agreement and the obligations set out in named environmental agreements, the latter obligations prevail. These choice of law provisions are a new trend in international law and reflect the importance given to environmental protection. If the preemption of treaty obligations by environmental norms becomes widely accepted, this could be the beginning of recognition that core environmental obligations constitute fundamental norms of international law.

One avenue to resolve conflicts in international obligations is through the jurisprudence of the International Court of Justice (ICJ) and other international tribunals. The ICJ established a chamber for environmental matters in 1993 and since then it has given several opinions and judgments in which it has recognized the importance of environment protection. None of the matters were heard in the chamber. In the 1996 *Nuclear Weapons* advisory opinion and the 1997 *Gabčikovo-Nagymaros* judgment, the Court affirmed that the duty not to cause transboundary environmental harm is an obligation of general international law.

The multiplication of instruments of international environmental law and of actors also raises the problem of compliance with international environmental commitments. Old and new techniques are attempted in order to ensure the implementation of obligations in this field.

F. The World Summit on Sustainable Development

In the decade after the Rio Conference, environmental concerns encountered increasing competition on the international agenda from economic globalization, an emphasis on free trade, and the development crises of poor countries. As one example, the Doha Declaration of the World Trade Organization, adopted by a Ministerial Meeting on November 14, 2001, appears to give priority to WTO norms in addressing the relationship between existing free trade rules and the trade obligations set out in multilateral environmental agreements. As another and more visible example, the United Nations convened a conference to mark the tenth anniversary of the Rio meeting, but failed to mention the environment in its name. Instead, it was convened as the World Summit on Sustainable Development.

Between August 26 and September 4, 2002, the representatives of more than 190 countries met in Johannesburg, South Africa, in order to "reaffirm commitment to the Rio Principles, the full implementation of Agenda

21 and the Programme for the Further Implementation of Agenda 21."[81]
At the end of the conference the participating governments adopted a
Declaration on Sustainable Development affirming their will to "assume a
collective responsibility to advance and strengthen the interdependent and
mutually reinforcing pillars of sustainable development—economic development, social development and environmental protection—at local,
national, regional and global levels."[82] While recognizing that "the global
environment continues to suffer," and acknowledging the loss of biodiversity, the depletion of fish stocks, the progress of desertification, the evident
adverse effects of climate change as well as pollution of the air, of water
and of the sea,[83] the Declaration mainly focuses on development and
poverty eradication, especially in the poorest countries. Despite proposals
advocating the creation of a specialized global institution for environmental protection, the Declaration less ambitiously supports the leadership role
of the UN and proposes more effective, democratic and accountable international and multilateral institutions to achieve the goals of sustainable
development.[84]

A lengthy Plan of Implementation provides concrete suggestions of
measures to implement the Declaration. The Plan mentions the principle
of common but differentiated responsibilities and declares that "(p)overty
eradication, changing unsustainable patterns of production and consumption, and protecting and managing the natural resource base of economic
and social development are overarching objectives of and essential requirements for sustainable development."[85]

The economic pillar dominates the two texts. Care for environmental
protection appears in Part III of the Plan which advocates changing unsustainable patterns of consumption and production towards sustainability
within the carrying capacity of ecosystems, de-linking economic growth and
environmental degradation and reducing resource degradation, pollution
and waste. It also recommends application of the polluter-pays principle,
increasing eco-efficiency, the use of cleaner production programs, enhancing corporate environmental responsibility, environmental management
systems, the use of economic instruments and of environmental impact
assessment procedures.[86] The text also calls for sustainable energy production and use, for an integrated approach to policy-making for transport ser-

---

[81]   Plan of Implementation of the World Summit on Sustainable
Development, A/CONF.199/CRP.7, 1.

[82]   A.CONF./L.6/Rev.2, para 5.

[83]   Para. 13.

[84]   Paras. 27 and 28.

[85]   A/CONF.199/CRP.7, para 2.

[86]   Paras. 11–18.

vices, and for sound management of chemicals and of hazardous wastes.[87]
Part IV of the Plan on Protecting and Managing the Natural Resource Base
of Economic and Social Development is particularly important for environmental protection, although its legal content is rather weak. Given the
threatening shortage of freshwater, the text proposes to mobilize international and domestic financial resources at all levels, transfer technology and
support capacity-building for water and sanitation infrastructure and services development. It also calls for developing water management resources
and water efficiency plans by 2005.[88]

The Plan contains lengthy discussions of issues related to oceans, seas,
islands and coastal areas. It invites states to ratify or accede to and implement existing international treaties to achieve sustainable fisheries, in particular by maintaining or restoring stocks to levels that can produce the
maximum sustainable yield not later than 2015.[89]

Paragraphs 36 and 37 address the atmosphere and despite the refusal
of the U.S. to proceed with ratification of the Kyoto Protocol to the
UNFCCC, they confirm the determination of governments to ensure the
entry into force of the Protocol and to embark on the required reduction
of emissions of greenhouse gases.

The Plan devotes only one paragraph to biodiversity. It invites the governments to comply with the Convention on Biological Diversity and to
achieve by 2010 a significant reduction in the current rate of loss of biological diversity, adding that such effort will require the provision of new
and additional financial resources to developing countries.[90] The problems
of forests are similarly treated.[91]

Remaining parts of the Plan of Implementation concern sustainable
development in a globalizing world, health and sustainable development,
small island developing states, Africa and other regional initiatives. Part IX,
on Means of Implementation, gives financial and trade aspects a major role,
but some recommendations concern access to and development, transfer
and diffusion of environmentally sound technologies.[92] While the recommendations on education only speak of sustainable development, one paragraph proposes to ensure access, at the national level, to environmental
information and judicial and administrative proceedings in environmental
matters, as well as public participation in decision-making.

---

[87]   Paras. 19–22.
[88]   Paras. 24–28.
[89]   Paras. 29–35.
[90]   Para. 42.
[91]   Para. 43.
[92]   Para. 99.

The section on institutional development proposes to strengthen collaboration within and between the UN system, international financial institutions, the Global Environment Facility and the WTO, mainly in the perspective of sustainable development. A short paragraph at the end of the Plan invites partnerships between governmental and non-governmental actors, including all major groups, as well as volunteer groups, on programs and activities for the achievement of sustainable development at all levels.[93]

In sum, economic development, international trade and corporations—many of which are more powerful than small states—prevailed. Major economic actors are encouraged to create "partnerships" for enhancing sustainable development. The rules of WTO are given a high political status, while environmental law is relegated to second place. An opportunity to further discuss the link between human rights and environmental protection was missed.

For the future it must be noted that the instruments adopted at the World Summit did not affect the validity of Agenda 21 which continues to govern the environmental program of international institutions and remains a general guideline for governments, regional and local authorities as well as for non-state actors. Indeed, the WSSD reaffirms the texts adopted at Rio and calls for priority attention to two matters: the implementation of and compliance with international environmental agreements by contracting states and the coordination among the secretariats of multilateral environmental agreements.[94]

BIBLIOGRAPHY

Biermann, F., *Common Concern of Humankind: The Emergence of a New Concept of International Environmental Law*, 34 ARCHIV DES VÖLKERRECHTS 426 (1996).

CAMPIGLIO, L., et al. eds., THE ENVIRONMENT AFTER RIO: INTERNATIONAL LAW AND ECONOMICS (1993).

CARSON, R., THE SILENT SPRING (1962).

Sohn, L., *The Stockholm Declaration on the Human Environment*, 14 HARV. INT'L L.J. 423 (1973).

SHABECOFF, P., A NEW NAME FOR PEACE: INTERNATIONAL ENVIRONMENTALISM: SUSTAINABLE DEVELOPMENT AND DEMOCRACY (1996).

SULLIVAN, F., THE EARTH SUMMIT AGREEMENTS: A GUIDE AND ASSESSMENT (1993).

---

[93]   Para. 151.

[94]   *See* the Report of the Executive Director of UNEP to the Governing Council, Dec. 16, 2002, UNEP/GC.22/4.

Symposium, United Nations Conference on Environment and Development, 4(1) COLO. J. INT'L ENVTL. L. & POL'Y. (1993).

WORLD COMMISSION ON ENVIRONMENT AND DEVELOPMENT, OUR COMMON FUTURE (1987).

CHAPTER 3

THE SOURCES OF INTERNATIONAL ENVIRONMENTAL LAW

In response to the challenge of safeguarding the biosphere, the international legal system has elaborated rules to protect the environment both within and outside the limits of state jurisdiction. Despite the rapid emergence of these rules, international environmental law has developed some common features that differ from characteristics of other international regimes. In particular, state practice respecting treaties has modified to take into account the needs of the environment. In addition, the use of so-called "soft law" is especially prevalent in international environmental law. Soft law can mean formally non-binding expressions of commitment, such as the Stockholm and Rio Declarations, or it can refer to general directions or guidelines in treaties. These and other aspects of environmental law-making are described in this chapter.

Traditional international law identifies its sources in Article 38(1) of the Statute of the International Court of Justice, initially drafted in 1920 for the predecessor Permanent Court of International Justice. Although applying only to the Court, Article 38 represents the authoritative listing of processes that states identified at the time as capable of creating rules binding on them; it remains to date the only such listing. It sets out in order general or specialized international conventions (treaties), international custom as evidence of a general practice accepted as law, general principles of law recognized by civilized nations, and, as subsidiary sources, international judicial decisions and doctrine. This enumeration is the accepted minimum, but does not reflect either the current international practice or the diverse activities that can contribute to the development of a new rule of law. In particular, it omits all texts, other than treaties, that are adopted by international organizations, although they play more than a nominal role in the formation of international law in general and environmental law in particular.

This chapter first will review environmental norms derived from the traditional sources of international law, then turn to rules stemming from acts of international organizations and conferences. Finally, it considers the development of codes and other norms by non-state actors, which can influence the content of international environmental law.

A. International Conventions

The first source of international environmental law is "conventional norms,"
which now number more than one thousand in this field, although many
agreements contain only a few provisions concerning the environment.[1]
Article 2.1(a) of the 1969 Vienna Convention on the Law of Treaties[2]
defines a "treaty" as "an international agreement concluded between States
in written form and governed by international law, whether embodied in a
single instrument or in two or more related instruments and whatever its
particular designation." This definition omits all international agreements
to which inter-governmental or non-governmental organizations are parties
as well as agreements concluded by internal agencies not entitled to bind
the state, for example port authorities or customs offices. Yet, all these entities increasingly enter into agreements intending to cooperate under agreed
norms for environmental protection.

The geographic coverage of environmental treaties varies widely. Some
instruments contain norms regulating the entire international community.
Article 35(3) of Protocol I to the 1949 Geneva Conventions Relative to
Protecting Victims of International Armed Conflicts, for example, prohibits
all states in such conflicts from employing methods or means of warfare
which are intended, or may be expected to cause widespread, long-term and
severe damage to the natural environment.[3] The London conventions of
1972 and 1973 concerning pollution of the high seas[4] and the CITES regulation of trade in endangered species[5] similarly address global problems.
In fact, a broad global framework of international law has been established
for the four "traditional" sectors of the environment: water, soil, atmosphere
and biological diversity.

---

[1]   The 1967 Outer Space Treaty, for example, contains only one relevant
provision, Art. IX, which relates to protecting the earth against pollution from
outer space and, in turn, protecting outer space from earth-source contamination: ". . . States Parties to the Treaty shall pursue studies of outer space, including the moon and other celestial bodies, and conduct exploration of them so as
to avoid their harmful contamination and also adverse changes in the environment of the Earth resulting from the introduction of extraterrestrial matter and,
where necessary, shall adopt appropriate measures for this purpose." Art. IX,
Treaty on Principles Governing the Activities of States in the Exploration and
Use of Outer Space, including the Moon and Other Celestial Bodies (Jan. 27,
1967). A large number of treaties concerning boundary waters similarly contain
one or a few provisions on water pollution.

[2]   Vienna Convention on the Law of Treaties (May 23, 1969).

[3]   *See* Chapter 16A.

[4]   *See infra* Chapter 11E.1 and E.5.

[5]   *See infra* Chapter 8D.1.a.

Principles and norms adopted for the whole community of nations often are more effective when implemented and enforced regionally, as has been experienced in the field of human rights. UNEP aims at regional application of international environmental law through conventions for different maritime regions around the globe, including the Mediterranean, Persian Gulf, West Africa, South-East Pacific, Red Sea, Gulf of Aden, Caribbean, and East Africa.[6] These conventions rely on the same principles and generally adopt the same norms, often incorporating those previously articulated in global instruments, including some not yet in force. The regional approach is motivated by the similarity of the geography and environment among neighboring states bordering regional seas and is enhanced in many cases by like economic, cultural, and political conditions. At the same time, the agreements can and do take into consideration the different ecological conditions in the regional seas.

Apart from UNEP's systematic regional seas program, specific environmental problems of geographically-limited areas usually are better regulated by the small number of affected states. Efforts to combat pollution of rivers and lakes and the depletion of regionally-endemic species of plants or animals have benefitted from organizations such as the Council of Europe or the OECD, which frequently initiate the development of conventional solutions to these problems among their member states. In addition, the trend towards ecosystem protection allows a holistic approach to the problems of a single geophysical space.

Despite their variety in subject matter and geographic scope, environmental treaties have common characteristics, use similar legal techniques, and often are interrelated. The main features they share are: (1) an absence of reciprocity of obligations, (2) interrelated or cross-referenced provisions from one instrument to another, (3) framework agreements, (4) frequent interim application, (5) the creation of new institutions or the utilization of already existing ones to promote continuous cooperation, (6) innovative compliance and non-compliance procedures and (7) simplified means of modification or amendment.

1. The Nature of Obligations

Each international environmental agreement contains legally binding rules, although such engagements may differ considerably from most traditional norms, for in many treaties there are few precise duties created. Instead, the provisions indicate areas of cooperation, and, in some cases, the means states parties should adopt to achieve the goals of the treaty. Environmental treaties often invade traditional spheres of government activities by requiring

---

6   *See* Chapter 11D.

states to limit pollution emissions, establish licensing systems, regulate and monitor waste disposal, control the export and import of endangered species and hazardous products, and enact penal legislation. Such treaties usually set forth the obligations in general terms, however, and require completion through internal legislative or executive action. For countries like the United States that distinguish between self-executing and non-self-executing treaties—those capable of immediate judicial application and those that require implementing measures—such treaties fall within the latter category,[7] although it is more common to find treaties containing a mixture of self-executing and non-self-executing obligations. Thus, individual treaty provisions must be analyzed, rather than the agreement as a whole.

Non-self-executing provisions of treaties encompass an obligation on the part of states to enact the necessary legislation or regulations. The 1979 Bonn Convention on the Conservation of Migratory Species of Wild Animals,[8] for example, requires that states in the migratory areas of animals listed in Convention Annex I forbid the taking of any of these animals.[9] States also may be called upon to designate or create organs to be entrusted with certain functions, such as maintaining contacts with the authorities of other states parties,[10] or issuing licenses or authorizations for regulated activities.[11] Of particular interest are treaty provisions that oblige states parties to enact and enforce penal sanctions against persons who violate their terms. For example, Article 8 of CITES provides:

1. The Parties shall take appropriate measures to enforce the provisions of the present Convention and to prohibit trade in specimens in violation thereof. These shall include measures:

   a) to penalize trade in, or possession of such specimens, or both; and

   b) to provide for the confiscation or return to the State of export of such specimens.[12]

---

[7] For the distinction between self-executing and non-self-executing treaties in U.S. courts, *see Foster v. Nielson*, 27 U.S. (2 Pet.) 253, 314 (1829). This structure also resembles a type of domestic French legislation, known as "lois-cadre." Such a law establishes legislative goals and principles, leaving to the executive the duty to take the necessary implementing measures. *See* Law No. 76-676 relating to Nature Protection, Dalloz 1976.308.

[8] June 23, 1979.

[9] Art. 3(5).

[10] Nordic Convention for Environmental Protection (Feb. 19, 1974), Art. 4.

[11] Convention on International Trade in Endangered Species of Wild Fauna and Flora, Art. 9 (Washington, Mar. 3, 1973).

[12] Similarly, Art. 4 of the International Convention for the Prevention of

An increasing trend with respect to international environmental treaties is their cross-referencing of other international instruments. Recent marine environment treaties, for example, often cite the rules of MARPOL or UNCLOS, sometimes incorporating their rules by reference. This can result in extending the legal effect of these instruments to states that have not ratified them but which ratify the later texts. The Convention on the Protection of the Black Sea against Pollution[13] states that the Contracting Parties are

> taking into account the relevant provisions of the Convention on Prevention of Marine Pollution by Dumping of Wastes and Other Matter of 1972 as amended; the International Convention on Prevention of Pollution from Ships of 1973 as modified by the Protocol of 1978 relating thereto as amended; the Convention on Control of Transboundary Movement of Hazardous Wastes and Their Disposal of 1989 and the International Convention on Oil Pollution Preparedness, Response and Cooperation of 1990.

In some cases, specific treaties or provisions may be affirmed as customary international law. The preamble of the Convention for the Protection of the Marine Environment of the North-East Atlantic,[14] for example, refers to "the relevant provisions of customary international law reflected in Part XII of the UN Law of the Sea Convention and, in particular, Art. 197 on global and regional cooperation for the protection and preservation of the marine environment."

Some treaties even incorporate "soft law" texts. The Sept. 14, 1992, Namibia-South Africa Agreement on the Establishment of a Permanent Water Commission provides that the parties have agreed to the text "wishing to consolidate their existing friendly relations by promoting regional water resource development on the basis of the rules relating to the uses of the waters of international rivers approved in 1966 at Helsinki by the 52nd Conference of the International Law Association."

The cumulating of instruments through repeated cross-referencing can be seen as a movement toward consolidation of a global environmental code.

The principle of reciprocity, characterized in Roman law by the adage *do ut des* seeks a legal equilibrium between the obligations accepted by one

---

Pollution from Ships (MARPOL) London, Nov. 2, 1973, requires states parties to prohibit and sanction any violation of the requirements of the Convention and to bring proceedings against any ship which commits a violation, or furnish evidence to the state administering the ship. The penalties adopted by the state "shall be adequate in severity to discharge violations of the present Convention and shall be equally severe irrespective of where the violations occur."

[13]   Apr. 21, 1992.

[14]   Paris, Sept. 22, 1992.

state and the advantages it obtains from the other contracting party or parties. Treaties of commerce, treaties of alliance, instruments regulating diplomatic and consular relations, indeed nearly all conventions of the 19th century, were governed by the principle of reciprocity. Exceptions to this construct existed, however, even during the dominant period of positivist international law prior to the First World War. Conventions began to establish rules of general obligation, including freedom of navigation on international rivers and canals, prohibition of slave trading,[15] protection of religious liberty,[16] and restrictions on the means and methods of warfare.[17] States subscribing to these treaties accepted their obligations without receiving any demonstrable, immediate advantage.

Other exceptions to the principle of reciprocity emerged after World War I, primarily in international labor conventions.[18] Suppressing phenomena such as exploitation of child labor or inhuman and dangerous conditions of work appealed in a systematic fashion to the international community. Immediately following World War II, non-reciprocal obligations enlarged still further to include the international protection of human rights,[19] regulations on the use of Antarctica and its surrounding seas, codes governing activities in outer space and on celestial bodies, and reaffirmation of freedom of the high seas with an obligation to respect its biological resources.

Rules of international environmental law, adopted in the common interest of humanity, generally do not bring immediate advantages to contracting states when their objective is to protect species of wild plant and

---

[15]   Treaty of Paris, May 30, 1814.

[16]   In 1878, Western powers agreed at the Berlin Congress that the Balkan States would be recognized only under the condition that they did not impose any religious disabilities on their subjects. Treaty of Berlin, July 13, 1878. *See* L. SOHN & T. BUERGENTHAL, INTERNATIONAL PROTECTION OF HUMAN RIGHTS at 143–92 (1973).

[17]   Conventions to protect medical personnel, wounded and sick combatants and to restrict certain means of warfare were adopted in 1864 (Geneva), 1899 and 1907 (The Hague). *See* P. BOISSIER, HISTORY OF THE INTERNATIONAL COMMITTEE OF THE RED CROSS: FROM SOLFERINO TO TSUSHIMA (1985).

[18]   Since 1919, the International Labor Organization has engaged in standard-setting and supervision of international labor standards. *See* C.W. JENKS, HUMAN RIGHTS AND INTERNATIONAL LABOR STANDARDS (1960). Recent summaries of the work of the ILO can be found in the Report of the Director-General to the 77th International Labor Conference (1990) and the Report of the Committee of Experts on the Application of Conventions and Recommendations (Report III, Part 4A) (1990). On the ILO and the Environment, *see infra* Chapter 4, C.8.

[19]   There is extensive literature on international human rights law. For an introduction, *see* T. BUERGENTHAL, D. SHELTON & D. STEWART, INTERNATIONAL HUMAN RIGHTS (2002).

animal life, the oceans, the air, the soil, and the countryside. Even treaties concluded among a small number of states generally lack reciprocity. For example, states upstream on a river are not in the same situation as those downstream. For coastal states, the general direction of winds and ocean currents may cut against the equality of the parties and diminish the importance of reciprocity.

Describing these developments, some international jurists have posited the existence in international law of "treaty-laws," distinguished from "treaty-contracts." The distinction may have meaning in the sense that "treaty-laws" are concluded in the common interest of humanity, while "treaty-contracts" are based on the principle of reciprocity. In its *Advisory Opinion on Reservations to the Convention on Genocide*, the International Court of Justice distinguished conventions adopted in the common interest from those based on reciprocal rights. States parties to conventions in the former category

> do not have any interests of their own; they merely have, one and all, a common interest, namely, the accomplishment of those high purposes which are the *raison d'être* of the convention. Consequently, in a convention of this type one cannot speak of individual advantages or disadvantages to states, or of the maintenance of a perfect contractual balance between rights and duties. The high ideals which inspired the convention provide, by virtue of the common will of the parties, the foundation and measure of all its provisions.[20]

In municipal law, a similar distinction is made between public law legislated in the general interest and private contract law based on consensual offer, acceptance, and consideration. Most importantly, properly enacted public laws apply whether or not a particular individual disagrees with the substance of the norm. The roles of reciprocity and of consent become altered in the shift from contract to legislation.

Common interests shared by the international community may be protected as obligations *erga omnes*. In the *Case of Barcelona Traction, Light and Power Company, Limited*[21] the International Court of Justice recognized the distinction between reciprocal and regulatory norms:

> [A]n essential distinction should be drawn between the obligations of a State towards the international community as a whole, and those arising vis-a-vis another State in the field of diplomatic protection. By their very nature the former are the concern of all

---

[20]   1951 I.C.J. Rep. 15

[21]   *Barcelona Traction, Light and Power Company, Limited* (New Application: 1962) (Belgium v. Spain, Second Phase) 1970 I.J.C. Rep. 4, 32.

States. In view of the importance of the rights involved, all States can be held to have a legal interest in their protection; they are obligations *erga omnes*.

The Court included in the category of obligations *erga omnes* the international laws prohibiting aggression, genocide, slavery and racial discrimination. More recently, the International Court of Justice has cited with approval the view of the International Law Commission that safeguarding the earth's ecological balance has come to be considered an essential interest of all states, to protect the international community as a whole.[22] This factor, plus the absence of reciprocity, characterizes much of international environmental law. Thus, many of the codified norms and customary standards in the environmental field may be viewed as obligations *erga omnes*.

International environmental obligations also differ from most international law in calling upon the state to regulate the behavior of non-state actors which are the source of most harm to the environment. The obligations must be implemented in national law to control non-state actors within the state's territory and jurisdiction. In contrast, treaties to establish diplomatic relations, or to lower trade barriers, generally impact the state and its agents only. Human rights law also primarily applies to the conduct of state authorities.

Another characteristic of international environmental agreements is the abandonment of the traditional identity of rights and obligations among states parties. Principle 7 of the Rio Declaration proclaims that

> States shall cooperate in a spirit of global partnership to conserve, protect and restore the health and integrity of the Earth's ecosystem. In view of the different contributions to global environmental degradation, States have common but differentiated responsibilities. The developed countries acknowledge the responsibility that they bear in the international pursuit of sustainable development in view of the pressures their societies place on the global environment and of the technologies and financial resources they command.

Principle 8 adds that states should reduce and eliminate unsustainable patterns of production and consumption and promote appropriate demographic policies, implicitly referring both to industrialized states and to developing ones.

---

[22] *Case Concerning the Gabčikovo-Nagymaros Project* (Hungary/Slovakia), 1996 I.C.J Rep. 7, para. 53, citing the International Law Commission, Commentary to Art. 33 of the Draft Articles on the International Responsibility of States, *See* Y.B. I.L.C., Part 2, at 39, para. 14 (1980).

The character of differentiated responsibility refers to general legal and political obligations rather than the formal concept of state responsibility which is the consequence of harm caused another or a violation of law. The acceptance by an industrialized state of its differentiated responsibility results in increased participation in the effort to enhance sustainable development. Nonetheless, there have been links made between fulfillment by one group of their responsibilities and reciprocal compliance by the other group of states.

The concept of common but differentiated responsibility has been incorporated in all global environmental conventions adopted since the end of the 1980s. In addition, the 1989 Basel Convention on the Control of Transboundary Movements of Hazardous Wastes and Their Disposal (Art.10(2)), the 1987 Montreal Protocol on the Protection of the Ozone Layer as amended in 1992, the 1992 Convention on Biological Diversity (Arts. 16, 20, and 21), and the 1992 UN Framework Convention on Climate Change all provide for transfer of technology or for financial assistance. The last instrument illustrates the differentiation by making a distinction between three categories of states:

(a) The developed country parties are to take the lead in combating climate change and the adverse effects thereof (Art. 3(1)). They shall provide new and additional financial resources to meet the agreed full costs incurred by developing country parties in complying with their obligations (Art. 4(3)). They also shall assist the developing country parties that are particularly vulnerable to the effects of climate change in meeting costs of adaptation to those adverse effects (Art. 4(4)). They shall facilitate the transfer of environmentally sound technology and know-how to developing countries (Art. 4(5)).

(b) Formerly communist countries of Central and Eastern Europe[23] are considered to be undergoing a process of political and economic transition and are granted some flexibility to enhance their ability to address climate change (Art. 4(6)).

(c) Developing countries are to receive financial assistance and benefit from the transfer of technology. They have more time to make their initial communication on the measures they have taken to implement the convention and the least-developed parties may make their reports at their discretion.

The 1994 Convention to Combat Desertification in those Countries Experiencing Serious Drought and/or Desertification, particularly in Africa[24] contains the most detailed provisions on the obligations of devel-

---

23   Central Asian republics that were part of the Soviet Union are grouped with developing country parties.
24   Paris, June 17, 1994.

oped country parties. They should mobilize substantial financial resources, including new and additional funding from the Global Environment Facility in order to support the implementation of programs to combat desertification and mitigate the effects of drought (Arts. 21, 22).

Two remaining characteristics of international environmental agreements are significant. The first is the deliberate reference to non-party states in many such treaties. To the extent that international environmental agreements impact international trade, it is necessary to include measures to discourage free-riders or provide incentives to compliance. CITES and the Montreal Protocol, for example, seek to influence the behavior of non-parties by requiring parties to restrict imports from them unless they effectively comply with the provisions of the agreement. The Antarctic Treaty also contains an obligation on states parties to see that "no one" acts inconsistent with the principles of the treaty (Art. X).

Finally, many environmental agreements and larger law-making treaties such as UNCLOS prohibit reservations, requiring states to accept them in their entirety. This is understandable in treaties that codify customary international law, which is binding independently of the treaty, but most environmental agreements cannot claim to be codifications of customary law. Instead, the absence of reservations may reflect the give and take of a multilateral negotiating process where decisions are based upon consensus and bargains. The process would unravel if states could pick and choose their obligations after the fact.

2. Framework Agreements

Since the beginning of the 1970s an increasing number of international treaties have been adopted by procedures that include several phases. The technique of "framework conventions" means that a convention of general scope is adopted, proclaiming basic principles on which consent can be achieved. The parties foresee the elaboration of additional protocols containing more detailed obligations.

This method first was used in regional seas agreements, beginning with the 1976 Convention for the Protection of the Mediterranean Sea against Pollution.[25] Regional seas conventions state the basic principles which the contracting parties are to apply. Detailed regulations are set forth in additional protocols, some of which are signed at the same time as the principal instrument. Others are elaborated later. Most regional seas treaty systems include development plans for the concerned region.

In a different realm, the 1979 Geneva Convention on Long-Range Transboundary Air Pollution created a legal structure for subsequent nego-

---

[25]   Barcelona, Feb. 16, 1976.

tiations. The Convention has been completed by a series of protocols establishing the detailed content of the general obligation contained in the main treaty. The 1985 Convention for the Protection of the Ozone Layer[26] and the Montreal Protocol followed this pattern as well. Among UNCED texts, the Framework Convention on Climate Change adopted the approach.

Framework agreements have the advantage that a consensus on basic principles and on the need for action which will follow generally is easier to reach than on the details of the action itself, which often have a technical character. Further negotiations can elucidate these measures with the cooperation of scientists, representatives of economic interests, and civil society. New elements can be incorporated as well, as exemplified by the Montreal Protocol on the Protection of the Ozone Layer which reflects the discovery of the ozone "hole" above Antarctica after the Vienna Convention was adopted. Such changes in knowledge and even basic concepts make framework treaties particularly well-adapted to the needs of environmental protection.

3. Interim Application

Several international environmental agreements respond to urgent problems that must be confronted in the shortest possible time. Taking this into account, negotiating states have adopted the technique of approving interim application of the agreements pending their entry into force. This technique was used with the 1998 FAO Convention on Prior Informed Consent and the August 4, 1995, Agreement for the Implementation of the Provisions of UNCLOS relating to the Conservation and Management of Straddling Fish Stocks and Highly Migratory Fish Stocks, Article 41.[27]

4. Mechanisms and Organs of Cooperation

The previous considerations inevitably lead to a need for permanent international organs of cooperation among states parties to environmental treaties. Fifty years ago the *Trail Smelter* arbitration, the first case of transfrontier pollution and a principal source of customary international law in this field, concluded that the two contending states should cooperate to

---

[26] Vienna, Mar. 22, 1985.

[27] Art. 41(1) provides: "This Agreement shall be applied provisionally by a State or entity which consents to its provisional application by so notifying the depositary in writing. Such provisional application shall become effective from the date of receipt of the notification." Art. 41(2) adds that provisional application terminates upon entry into force of the agreement or upon notification by the state that it intends to terminate provisional application.

jointly examine questions concerning damage caused by the smelter's air pollution. Today, the importance of acquiring new knowledge, disseminating information and observing the biosphere makes international cooperation even more necessary and, clearly, permanent. It is not surprising, therefore, that most environmental protection treaties contain institutional provisions, granting varied powers and competence to international organs. Sometimes new functions are confided to organs of already-existing international organizations. The MARPOL Convention, for example, gives the International Maritime Organization (IMO) competence to receive information from governments on action taken regarding any violation of the Convention by a ship,[28] obtain reports on incidents involving harmful substances,[29] as well as details of laws, procedures, and national authorities concerned with implementation of the Convention,[30] and the results of investigations on polluting accidents.[31] IMO also plays a role in the administration of the Convention, in the amendment procedure, and in the promotion of technical cooperation.[32] These numerous functions can be regrouped under three headings: managing the Convention, gathering and diffusing information, and supervising enforcement of the Convention's norms by states parties.

Authority also may be confided to new organizations created by environmental treaties to serve the special needs of the agreement, particularly in the field of regional or sub-regional cooperation.[33] Throughout the world, dozens of Conferences of the Parties (COPs) or international commissions have been created to assure permanent cooperation among contracting parties to treaties concerning *e.g.*, inland waters,[34] the oceans,[35] and the protection of wildlife.[36] As a general rule these organizations are lightly structured; many do not have permanent secretariats or the secretariat functions are handled by another existing inter-governmental or non-governmental organization.[37]

---

[28]   Arts. 4(3) and 6(4).

[29]   Art. 8.

[30]   Art. 11.

[31]   Art. 12.

[32]   Arts. 13–19.

[33]   *See* Chapter 4D for further discussion.

[34]   The International Commission for Protection of the Rhine against Pollution, created by the Bern Convention of Apr. 29, 1963.

[35]   The 1974 Helsinki Convention on the Protection of the Baltic Sea Area created a commission.

[36]   An International Commission and a Scientific Committee were created by the 1980 Canberra Convention on the Conservation of Antarctic Marine Living Resources.

[37]   UNEP is often invested with the secretariat function of the regional seas conventions, *e.g.*, Barcelona Convention of Feb. 16, 1976, Art. 13; Abidjan

5. Compliance Procedures

A fundamental obligation of international law is that treaties must be observed and their obligations performed in good faith.[38] Generally, each state party to a treaty monitors whether or not other states parties comply with the requirements of the agreement. This approach remains basic to environmental agreements, but such conventions often establish international supervisory mechanisms in addition.

A treaty may also delegate supervision to specific states. UNCLOS Article 218 provides, for example, that when a ship voluntarily enters a port or offshore installation, the port state can investigate and, where the evidence warrants, institute proceedings regarding any discharge from that vessel outside the state's internal waters, territorial sea or exclusive economic zone in violation of applicable international rules and standards established through the competent international organization or general diplomatic conference. The Basel Convention on Transboundary Movement of Hazardous Wastes delegates supervision generally: each party suspecting a breach is to inform the Secretariat and the offending party. The Secretariat, in turn, informs other parties.

Procedures that override state jurisdiction are rare. As discussed in Chapter 7B.1, the most accepted supervisory technique remains a state reporting system that obliges treaty parties to address periodic reports to an organ established or designated by the treaty, indicating the implementing measures which they have taken. Article 16 of the African Convention on the Conservation of Nature and Natural Resources[39] designated the Organization of African Unity as the organ to which states should address the texts of laws, decrees, regulations and instructions in force in their territories and aimed at ensuring the application of the Convention. They also had to report on the results obtained in applying the Convention's terms. In addition, on request, they were to provide all information required to permit review of matters treated by the Convention.

International conventions seeking to proclaim and establish the common interest of humanity, distinguished by the restricted role of reciprocity in their provisions, pose particular problems of enforcement. In an international society without institutional strength, bilateral reciprocity has provided an essential guarantee of respect for obligations undertaken, due to the implicit threat of sanctions imposed in the event obligations are breached. With an agreement that contains reciprocal rights and duties, a

---

Convention of Mar. 23, 1981, Art. 16; Cartegena Convention of Mar. 24, 1983, Art. 15.

[38]   Convention on the Law of Treaties (Vienna, May 23, 1969), Art. 26; U.K.T.S. No. 58 (1980); Cmd. 7964; 8 I.L.M. 679 (1969); 63 AJIL 875 (1969).

[39]   Algiers, Sept. 15, 1968, revised 2003.

state violating the treaty rights of another state risks losing benefits under the same agreement. Such results are inconceivable in a conventional system aimed at the common interest: violation of human rights by one state cannot be sanctioned by another state engaging in similar violations. It is the same for international environmental law: norms against pollution of the sea or the air cannot be enforced by reciprocal pollution. Enforcement must be by other means, especially by international control mechanisms that supervise the implementation of international environmental law by states.

Recent experience shows that compliance with multilateral environmental agreements and even non-binding norms is best ensured at the international level when there is institutional support. Many international environmental agreements create their own institutional framework rather than relying on existing international organs, as discussed in Chapter 4F. Over time, the states drafting international environmental agreements have created a now widely-used pattern of institutions. As agreements proliferate, so do the institutions and the compliance mechanisms. Increasingly, communities of scientists, government officials, and non-governmental organizations are involved. The proliferation of international institutions shows no signs of decreasing, leading to problems of coordination and possible conflict between their roles and norms.

As a rule, the costs of international administration (secretariat, meetings, programs) are financed by contributions of states parties, either voluntary or agreed at each meeting of the Conference for a fixed subsequent period.

6. *Adaptation and Evolution of Obligations*

One of the principal needs of environmental law, both internal and international, is to adapt to changes in conditions or knowledge altering the requirements of environmental protection. The state of the environment may change rapidly. Marine or river pollution may increase due to the appearance of new substances or new means of production or consumption, or a species of wildlife may risk extinction due to new threats which develop before international rules can be adopted or existing rules amended. In a recent case the ICJ has recognized that as a supplemental means of interpreting treaties, nothing in the Vienna Convention prevents the Court "from taking into account the present-day state of scientific knowledge."[40]

Knowledge of the biosphere, its deterioration, renewal and the effects of pollution, evolves quickly. Most authorities viewed atmospheric pollution

---

[40]   ICJ, *Case Concerning Kasilili/Sedudu Island (Botswana v. Namibia)* (Dec. 13, 1999), 1999 I.C.J. Rep. 98.

as a local phenomenon until, during the 1970s, acidity in the lakes of Scandinavia showed that long-range damage could occur. After 1980, the destruction of forests demonstrated that sulfur dioxide (SO_2) was not the only agent responsible for atmospheric pollution, because nitrogen oxide (NO_2) emitted from automobiles may also play a major role in causing damage. Subsequently, discovery that the stratospheric ozone layer is damaged added yet another element to the problem of protecting the atmosphere from pollution. Thus, international action to address one problem necessarily evolved and changed directions during the space of a dozen years.

It must be questioned how law which is based upon predictability and the constancy of rules can respond to these changing directions and the needs of environmental protection. In addition to using the technique of framework conventions, states have developed an effective response by drafting treaties that establish stable general obligations but also add flexible provisions, especially those prescribing technical norms. The latter may designate the specific products that cannot be dumped or discharged in a given area or may identify the endangered species needing additional protection. The general obligations are set forth in the treaty, which remains stable, while the detailed listing of products or species is reserved to annexes that can be modified easily without amending the principal treaty. The annexes form an integral part of the treaty and thus the modification procedure must be expressly included in the treaty's provisions.

Agreements of this type include the 1979 Bern Convention on the Conservation of European Wildlife and Natural Habitats.[41] Its Article 16 allows for amendment of the treaty according to generally recognized international rules codified in Articles 39 and 40 of the Vienna Convention on the Law of Treaties. In other words, any amendment must be accepted by all the contracting parties according to their internal constitutional requirements. In contrast, the treaty's annexes listing protected species may be modified pursuant to the procedure set forth in Article 17 which allows changes to be proposed by a permanent Committee established by the Convention. Proposals are communicated to the contracting parties and at the expiration of three months each modification enters into force for all states that have not filed objections.

Other treaties establish different flexible procedures. Formal approval rather than tacit acceptance is required by Article 9 of the 1972 London Convention for the Conservation of Antarctic Seals.[42] Another variation provides for formal approval followed by automatic entry into force after a certain period of time for states that have not voiced opposition, foreseen by Article 15 of the London Convention on the Prevention of Marine Pollution

---

[41]   Sept. 19, 1979.
[42]   June 1, 1972.

by Dumping of Wastes and Other Matter.[43] States thus must opt out of obligations, rather than having the task of expressing their approval and agreement to be bound. These treaties thus establish a bifurcated modification process, in which the structural parts of the treaties are subject to traditional, rather difficult, amendment processes, while the technical details may be altered quickly and less formally, in many cases requiring states to affirmatively opt out of any changes made.

B. Customary International Law

To speak of rules of customary international law in a field as new as that of international environmental law may appear surprising. Nonetheless, it is possible to discern among current norms "evidence of a general practice, accepted as law," even though only a short period of time has elapsed.

The UN Conference on the Law of the Sea, which met between 1973 and 1982, adopted one of the most important of modern international treaties. During the long process of its elaboration by states of the world, a certain number of existing rules were codified, but there also arose a consensus on several new norms. On the basis of this consensus an international practice formed, even before adoption of the treaty. This was particularly the case with the creation of the "exclusive economic zone," now codified in Part V of the Convention.[44] During the negotiations, it was clearly recognized that coastal states have sovereign rights for the purpose of conserving and managing living and non-living natural resources and have jurisdiction to preserve the marine environment.[45] It also became accepted that coastal state jurisdiction to legislate regarding ships in innocent passage through the territorial sea includes measures to conserve marine biological resources and preserve the marine environment and to prevent, reduce and control marine pollution.[46]

Other rules of customary international law can be observed emerging and at different stages in their evolution. The formulation of non-binding principles undoubtedly plays an important role in this process. Another factor is the repetition of specific rules in numerous international texts. Third, it is possible that the process of formulating a rule that may or may not have been applied by different states creates a rather rapid consensus which leads to general acceptance of the rule in state practice. The follow-up to the nuclear accident at Chernobyl illustrates this development. Although the Soviet government evacuated nearly 50,000 persons in the days immediately

---

[43] Dec. 29, 1972.

[44] Arts. 55–75.

[45] Art. 56(a).

[46] Art. 21.

following the incident, it failed to inform other states until much later and did not give a complete explanation of the event until a specially organized meeting of the International Atomic Energy Agency took place between August 25 and 29, 1986. One of the general principles that had emerged from repeated conventional requirements was the duty of a state to urgently notify other states at risk of having their environment adversely affected by any situation or any event. The non-application of this principle by the USSR after Chernobyl made it necessary to formulate the norm in more detail, based on the parallel conventional provisions. Thus, 58 states signed an agreement in Vienna on early notification of a nuclear accident and the treaty entered into force with unusual speed one month later. As its title indicates, it requires states to give notification without delay of any nuclear accident which will or might lead to radioactive consequences for another state.[47] The information to be transmitted is specified in the Convention.[48] The speed of codification of this rule can only be explained by the circumstances and by the recognition of a prior international duty to notify.

Several other customary rules of international environmental law have emerged or are emerging in state practice. In particular, no state may cause or allow its territory to be used to cause damage to the environment of other states. This norm first arose in international jurisprudence and was formulated in Principle 21 of the Stockholm Declaration before being adopted and reaffirmed in numerous other binding and non-binding international instruments. The duty to cooperate, announced by Principle 24 of the Stockholm Declaration, also appears to have acquired this status, as well as reflecting a fundamental norm of the entire United Nations system. Other principles may be cited which form the core of an international common law of the environment.[49] In sum, it is possible to speak of a body of customary international environmental law composed of fundamental principles underlying the entire system and applicable to all environmental subjects.

The number of treaties and other international instruments reproducing the same legal norms concerning the environment continues to grow. UNCED contributed greatly to this evolution. The work of the International Law Commission shows that the repetition of the same norms in numerous international instruments can be considered as giving birth to new customary rules. In this regard, it is worth noting that several international instruments have declared that Part XII of UNCLOS, relating to protection of the marine environment, is part of customary international law, even prior to the entry into force of the Convention in 1994.

---

[47] Vienna, Sept. 26, 1986, Art. 1.

[48] Art. 5.

[49] *See* Chapter 5.

C. General Principles of Law

The third source of international law provoked much discussion in scholarly writings, particularly between the two world wars. The underlying concept seeks to identify those principles that are common to the major legal systems of the world, if not to all of them. The global proliferation of national norms concerning the environment, whose number may exceed 30,000, will no doubt permit discovery of numerous such rules after a period of consolidation. Nonetheless, even now certain principles may be considered as an established part of the common law of environmental protection. Many of them originate from the inter-penetration of legal rules at all levels of governance from the global to the municipal. Laws and policies adopted at the global, regional, and national levels influence each other. Initiatives begun at one level of governance often lead to similar approaches being adopted in other legal orders. A few examples demonstrate this widespread practice.

The 1941 arbitral decision resolving a long-standing dispute between the United States and Canada over air pollution originating in a Canadian smelter found no applicable international law on the topic and turned to norms articulated in the case law of federal states—the United States and Switzerland, in particular—to establish the principle that states have a duty not to cause significant transboundary air pollution. Principle 21 of the Stockholm Declaration made this a general obligation not to cause transboundary environmental harm. The Rio Declaration reiterated the duty and it has been incorporated since then into numerous environmental treaties and other texts.

International norms similarly can formulate new principles that pass into regional and national laws. Most states traditionally had few rules protecting wildlife, which was freely available for capture, killing, or other use. From hunting safaris in Africa to whaling on the open seas and plant collectors in Latin America, unregulated access was the general rule. Many of the norms that now protect wildlife developed first in international agreements to protect migratory species and resources of the commons. The international regulations were incorporated into the national law of states parties to treaties and influenced other states. Even now, the Convention on Biological Diversity is more protective of flora and fauna than the laws of most states and will require additional national measures.

Substantive obligations are not the only aspect of environmental law that has benefitted from the mutual influence of national, regional and international law. The tools and techniques to implement environmental law also reflect the trend towards borrowing from the experience of different levels of governance. The environmental impact assessment procedure (EIA), for example, was first mandated in the United States at the end of the 1960s in the State of Michigan. Its aim was and remains to ensure that

adequate and early information is obtained on the likely environmental consequences of development projects and on possible alternatives and measures to mitigate harm. United States legislation adopted the EIA as national
law in 1969, following which it was introduced into the laws of many other
countries. It became part of regional law initially with the 1978 Kuwait
Regional Convention for Co-operation on the Protection of the Marine
Environment from Pollution.[50] From the regional seas agreements, it was
introduced at the global level in UNCLOS Art. 206, which proclaims the
principle of assessment of potential effects of environment-harming activities. Several years later, a Directive of the European Communities obliged
member states to adopt national EIA legislation by July 1988. In 1991, the
EIA procedure became the subject of a specific agreement drafted by the
UN Economic Commission for Europe: the Convention on Environmental
Impact Assessment in a Transboundary Context.[51] The procedure is the cor-
nerstone of another 1991 agreement, the Madrid Protocol to the Antarctic
Treaty on Environmental Protection.[52] It also appears in the 1992 UN
Framework Convention on Climate Change.[53]

In sum, the EIA, having started as the law of a component unit of a federal state, was progressively adopted at the federal level, then by other countries and by regional organizations and regional treaty systems. Finally it
became a major part of global environmental regulation, proposed to countries whose domestic legislation has not adopted it as yet.

Another example traverses the legal orders in the opposite direction,
showing the effects international law and policy can have on national law.
Principle 15 of the 1992 Rio Declaration formulated the precautionary
approach, according to which lack of full scientific certainty shall not be
used as a reason for postponing measures to prevent environmental degradation where there are threats of serious or irreversible damage. During the
same period, the precautionary principle appeared in regional texts as well,
e.g., in the 1991 Bamako Convention on the Ban of the Import into Africa
and the Control of Transboundary Movement and Management of
Hazardous Wastes within Africa[54] and the Treaty on European Union.[55] It
spread rapidly during the following years in regional seas treaties, such as
those concerning the Baltic Sea area and the North-East Atlantic.[56] The
legal system of different countries also adopted it either by introducing it
into laws or regulations or by applying it in judicial decisions.[57]

---

[50] Apr. 24, 1978.
[51] Espoo, Feb. 25, 1991.
[52] Madrid, Oct. 4, 1991.
[53] Art. 4(1)(f).
[54] Jan. 29, 1991, Art. 4(3)(f).
[55] Art. 130R, para 2.
[56] Helsinki, Apr. 9, 1992; Paris, Sept. 22, 1992. See Chapter 11D.
[57] *See, e.g.*, the judgment of the Supreme Court of India handed down on

As these examples demonstrate, the various levels of the legal order interact as initiatives move among them to provide models for action, adapting and evolving as necessary. Certain principles, techniques and practices are or could be extended from one level to others providing dynamic and creative solutions to environmental problems.

D. Judicial Decisions and Doctrine

Although the Statute of the International Court of Justice refers to jurisprudence as a subsidiary source for determining rules of law, judgments and advisory opinions of the World Court and arbitral or other international tribunals are quite important in fact. These decisions often are considered as the affirmation or the revelation of customary international rules. The arbitral judgment of March 11, 1941, in the *Trail Smelter* case is considered as having laid the foundations of international environmental law, at least regarding transfrontier pollution. Confirmed by a more general principle enunciated in the *Corfu Channel* case[58] and referred to in the 1956 *Lake Lanoux* arbitration in the context of transfrontier water pollution,[59] the announced rule undoubtedly forms part of positive international law today.

Scholarly writings in international environmental law continue to expand rapidly in quantity and improve in quality. While books entirely devoted to international environmental law remained exceptional until the end of the 1980s, a mass of articles began appearing after the1972 Stockholm Conference. Other significant sources are the legal texts adopted by scientific and professional associations, such as the 1979 Athens resolution of the International Law Institute on pollution of rivers and lakes in international law,[60] and the numerous texts of the International Law Association, including the Helsinki rules on the uses of the waters of international rivers (1966),[61] principles concerning land-based marine pollution (1972),[62] the relations between international water resources and other natural resources and the environment (1980),[63] and transfrontier pollution in general (1980).[64]

August 28, 1996 in *Vellore Citizens' Welfare Forum v. Union of India and Others* and the decision of the French high administrative court, the Conseil d'Etat of Sept. 25, 1998 in *Association Greenpeace France*.

[58]   I.C.J., Apr. 3, 1949 ("No state may utilize its territory contrary to the rights of other States").

[59]   12 U.N. RIAA 285, at 303.

[60]   ANNUAIRE FRANÇAIS DE DROIT INTERNATIONAL 1233 (1979).

[61]   ILA, The Helsinki Rules with Commentaries (1967). *See* E.J. MANIER, THE PRESENT STATE OF INTERNATIONAL WATER RESOURCES LAW, ILA, 1873–1973; THE PRESENT STATE OF INTERNATIONAL LAW 131 (1973).

[62]   ILA, Report of the 55th Conference, New York, 1972, at 97, 98.

[63]   ILA, Report of the 59th Conference, Belgrade, 1980, at 373.

[64]   *Id.* at 531.

E. Other Sources of Obligation

International practice indicates that instruments that are not treaties and thus not formally binding nonetheless serve several important roles in the development of international environmental law.

First, states can avoid serious domestic legal or political obstacles to treaty ratification by adopting common rules of conduct in non-binding form. The negotiating period of such instruments generally is shorter and because the texts are not subject to national ratification, they can take instant effect.

Second, states feel less constrained about accepting norms and goals that are not legally binding,[65] especially where their capacity to comply is not certain.

Third, non-legally binding instruments may be more appropriate to the substance under consideration than formal agreements. Examples are action plans outlining desirable approaches or orientations, rather than commitments that may be difficult to negotiate and fulfill when contracting parties are at different stages of development.

Fourth, the negotiation of non-binding instruments more easily allows the participation of international institutions and of non-state actors in the process of creating and complying with environmental rules. IUCN prepared the first draft of the World Charter for Nature which was sent out by the UN General Assembly to the member states for comments and later adopted and solemnly proclaimed on October 28, 1982.[66] NGOs also participated in the adoption and continue to be involved in monitoring memoranda of understanding complementing the 1979 Bonn Convention on the Conservation of Migratory Species of Wild Animals.

Finally, resolutions and similar non-binding instruments may be used where there is uncertainty about the scope of the problem or the appropriate solution. The codes of good practices and guides relating to safety of nuclear facilities adopted by the International Atomic Energy Agency indicate how soft law regulations evolve with the development of knowledge in a given domain. Recommended measures adopted under the Antarctic

---

65   The participation in the Memorandum of Understanding related to the Siberian Crane, a formally non-binding instrument, drafted under the 1979 Bonn Convention on the Conservation of Migratory Species of Wild Animals is particularly high: seven out of the nine known range states accepted it, including four states which are not parties to the Bonn Convention. Similarly, another soft law instrument, the Memorandum of Understanding concerning Conservation Measures for the Slender-billed Curlew was signed by 17 range states out of 30. Only six of these are party to the Bonn Convention.

66   G.A. Res. 37/7, 37 U.N. GAOR, Supp (No 51) at 17; U.N. Doc. A/37/51 (1982).

Treaty by the Consultative Parties[67] show that governments are more willing to be innovative when the text is not legally binding.

In sum, soft law rules have the necessary flexibility to enable the international community to progress in the new domain, especially for approaching problems which are new for international co-operation, such as the conservation of biological diversity or the control of movements of hazardous substances.

Compliance with formally non-binding norms varies for several reasons. One of the factors affecting compliance is the authority of the text on which the instruments are based. In becoming parties to the Antarctic Treaty, states bind themselves to carry out the Treaty's purposes and principles. Recommendations that become effective in accordance with Article IX of the Treaty are "measures in furtherance of the principles and objectives of the Treaty" and thus have a high degree of authority. Legitimacy also can be conferred on non-binding texts by the fact that they have been adopted with an overwhelming majority or by consensus by an inter-governmental institution or under the aegis of such a body.

The legitimacy of the adoptive process of a recommended measure and the perceived fairness of the norm also favor compliance: the adoption of the 1989 Convention for the Prohibition of Fishing with Long Driftnets in the South Pacific[68] was a major incentive for the resolutions of the UN General Assembly[69] generally prohibiting this means of fishing as part of a much larger effort to address concerns over the environment and resource implications at a time when the concept of sustainable development became influential.

Scientific evidence and media publicity can enhance compliance with non-binding instruments by rasing public awareness of a problem and the need for it to be addressed. Meetings of the Parties to the 1987 Montreal Protocol on Substances that Deplete the Ozone Layer successively adjusted their obligations to accelerate the phasing out of ozone-depleting substances. This upward revision was the consequence of a Declaration adopted in Helsinki in May 1989 where 82 countries calling for a complete CFC phase-out by the end of the century.

Incentives enhance compliance, from technical and financial assistance for institutional strengthening and specialized training to improve the capacity and infrastructure of developing countries, to the sharing of experience. At the opposite extreme, the absence of enforcement measures, sanctions for non-compliance, and mechanisms for dispute resolution obvi-

---

[67]   Antarctic Treaty, Washington, Dec. 1, 1959, Art. IX(1)(f).

[68]   Wellington, Nov. 24, 1989.

[69]   Resolutions on Large-Scale Pelagic Driftnet Fishing and its Impact on the Living Marine Resources of the World's Oceans and Seas, Dec. 22, 1989, Dec. 21, 1990; and Dec. 20, 1991. *See* Chapter 11.

ously are not conducive to enhancing compliance among reluctant states. The development of legal rules concerning driftnet fishing shows, however, that monitoring compliance with non-binding texts constitutes a useful tool for exercising pressure upon states, especially when monitoring is ensured not only by individual states but by inter-governmental organizations and independent NGOs.

1. Resolutions and Decisions of International Organizations

One of the principal characteristics of international organizations is that very few have the power to adopt legally binding texts. Only three have such power among all the organizations which are concerned with matters of environmental protection. Thus, since their beginning in the 19th century, international organizations have adopted non-binding resolutions addressed to member states. This procedure has taken on increased importance over the years, particularly for new fields of international regulation such as environmental protection. Recommendations and declarations of principles of conferences such as Stockholm or meetings of the United Nations Environmental Program (Vancouver 1976, Mar del Plata 1977, Nairobi 1978) have had great impact on the evolution of international environmental law. Moreover, the multiplication of inter-governmental organizations has considerably augmented the number and diversity of non-binding texts because they are the principal means of expression for most organizations. With many resolutions adopted by consensus and implemented and invoked in practice, it may be argued that they constitute a now-recognized source of international law not foreseen by the Statute of the International Court of Justice, or a new technique for creating international juridical norms. This technique is particularly effective in establishing law for new fields where rapid decisions are needed, like human rights, exploration and exploitation of outer space and the deep sea-bed, and environmental law.

The Security Council of the United Nations, by virtue of its peace-keeping functions and other roles conferred on it, is one of the few organizations that can adopt binding decisions. Its actions in regard to environmental destruction in the Persian Gulf in the aftermath of the Iraqi invasion of Kuwait indicate a heightened concern for environmental protection during armed conflict.[70] In addition, according to Article 5 of the Convention on the Prohibition of Military or Any Other Hostile Use of Environmental Modification Techniques,[71] each state party that has reason to believe another state party is violating its obligations can file a complaint with the Security Council. The latter may undertake an inquiry with the

---

70   *See* Chapter 16.
71   Geneva, Dec. 10, 1976.

power to decide that the state bringing the complaint has been or might be harmed due to a violation of the Convention. However, the consequences of such a decision are not discussed. No doubt they would include application of Articles 36 and 37 of the United Nations Charter, which recommend dispute-settlement procedures.

The Organization for Economic Cooperation and Development (OECD) has wider competence in the field of environmental protection. In order to achieve its objectives, this organization of market-economy industrial states can take decisions which, unless otherwise stated, bind all its members.[72] The nature of this organization as an agency of study and consultation, however, means that in practice binding environmental decisions are infrequent. When taken, they generally treat narrow, technical subjects, such as the exchange of information on polychlorinated biphenyls (PCBs),[73] the mutual acceptance of data in the assessment of chemicals,[74] and the institution of a multilateral organ for consultation and surveillance of marine dumping of radioactive waste.[75]

The reverse is true of the European Union, which is invested with the power to adopt two kinds of measures binding on its members: "regulations" obligatory in all their elements and directly applicable in all member states, and "directives" which require each state to achieve a given result but leave the means and methods to individual state control.[76] Numerous texts having an obligatory character have been adopted, generally in the form of directives, concerning water and air pollution, dumping, and protection of wild animal species. These directives allow member states to jointly regulate environmental matters within the Community.[77]

Resolutions issuing from conferences or international organizations are often in the form of directive recommendations or declarations of principles.

Directive recommendations form the bulk of acts by which inter-governmental organizations address themselves to member states. The importance of such recommendations derives from the law of international organizations. In joining an international institution, member states freely accept the obligations contained in the organization's constituting instrument, which is often drafted in general or abstract terms. One of the functions of the organization's component organs is to explicate and detail the obligations of member states in concrete cases. Resolutions adopted by the

---

[72]   Art. 5(a), Convention on the Organization for Economic Co-operation and Development, 12 U.S.T. 1928.

[73]   Decision C(73)1, Feb. 13, 1973.

[74]   Decision C(81)30, May 12, 1981.

[75]   Decision C(77)115, July 22, 1977.

[76]   Art. 189, Treaty of Rome.

[77]   EC texts are collected in W.E. BURHENNE, ENVIRONMENTAL LAW OF THE EUROPEAN COMMUNITIES.

organs competent to speak on behalf of the organization serve to interpret and apply the general rules. Although not formally obligatory, the recommendations constitute authoritative interpretations and guidelines addressed to members states who should and generally do give them considerable deference.

Directive recommendations concerning environmental protection have played an important role in the activities of most inter-governmental organizations and in the general development of international environmental law. The UN General Assembly has adopted resolutions on global climate change, Antarctica, driftnet fishing, sustainable development, and, indeed, nearly all the subjects of international concern. On the regional level, the OECD has adopted recommendations on such subjects as hazardous products,[78] transfrontier pollution,[79] tourism,[80] waste management,[81] the relationship between the environment and economy,[82] the management of natural resources,[83] and the management of coastal zones.[84]

Declarations of principles differ from directive recommendations in that they do not envisage precise action to be undertaken, but they may fix general guidelines for states to follow and they may exercise considerable influence on the development of subsequent legal rules.[85] Another function of principles is to set forth a fundamental societal consensus on the underlying rationale for a body of law. In this respect, principles serve one of the fundamental objectives of any legal system, which is to recognize and formulate the emergence of new social values recognized as essential within the society. At the international level, this can be achieved through declarations adopted and proclaimed by global organizations or international conferences.

Principles are widely used in international environmental law, perhaps more than in any other field of international law. All the major soft law texts contain principles that are then taken up, defined and given concrete

---

[78] *E.g.*, Recommendation C(73)172, Sept. 19, 1973, Measures to Reduce all Man-made Emissions of Mercury to the Environment.

[79] Recommendation C(74)224, Nov. 14, 1974; Principles Concerning Transfrontier Pollution, 14 I.L.M. 234 (1975).

[80] Recommendation C(79)115, Environment and Tourism, May 8, 1979.

[81] Recommendation of C(76)155, Sept. 28, 1976, A Comprehensive Waste Management Policy.

[82] Recommendation C(72)128, May 26, 1972, Guiding Principles concerning International Economic Aspects of Environmental Policies.

[83] *E.g.*, Recommendation C(78)4, Apr. 5, 1978, Water Management Policies and Instruments.

[84] Recommendation C(76)161, Oct. 12, 1976, Principles Concerning Coastal Management.

[85] *See generally* NICOLAS DE SADELEER, ENVIRONMENTAL PRINCIPLES: FROM POLITICAL SLOGANS TO LEGAL RULES (2002).

meaning in international treaties and jurisprudence. The 1997 EU Treaty Title XVI sets out the principles meant to guide European policy on the environment, principles that shape secondary legislation in the EC. Article 174(2) provides that EC environmental policy shall be based on the precautionary principle and on the principles that preventive action should be taken, that environmental damage should as a priority be rectified at source and that the polluter should pay.

The concept of principle and the juridical value, if any, of a principle change from one legal system to another with varying definitions and application of principles. Principles can be descriptive and indicate the essential characteristics of legal institutions, designate fundamental legal norms, or fill gaps in positive law by assigning a value to rules not yet contained in formal legal instruments, although they are considered important. Principles can be foundational (equality and legal certainty) or technical (proportionality). They may appear in constitutions and basic laws, as in European continental legal traditions, or they may be of judicial construction. According to some, a principle provides the general orientation and direction to which positive law must conform, a rationale for the law, without itself constituting a binding norm. Another definition of a principle is a rule of indeterminate conduct where the degree of abstraction is so great that it is not possible to deduce obligations with a degree of certainty, thus leaving a wide margin of appreciation or discretion to the actor.[86]

Most environmental principles proclaimed in declarations have reappeared in one form or another in conventional texts, in the mandate given to international institutions, and in the practice of states. The influence of the principles contained in the Stockholm Declaration, the World Charter for Nature, and the 1992 Rio Declaration on Environment and Development is undeniable. Other declarations of principles have directly led to the creation of obligatory norms, including the European Water Charter,[87] the 1974 OECD recommendation containing principles relative to transfrontier pollution,[88] and the 1978 UNEP statement of principles of conduct in the field of environment for the guidance of states in the conservation and harmonious utilization of natural resources shared by two or more states.[89] Finally, even where declarations of principles are not directly transformed into binding rules, they may serve to guide states in adopting legislation. Without the Stockholm Declaration, it is likely that national environmental laws would have been fewer and weaker.

---

[86]   *Id.* at 309.
[87]   May 6, 1968.
[88]   Nov. 14, 1974.
[89]   UNEP/IG.12/2, May 19, 1978.

2. Decisions of COPs/MOPs

The Vienna Convention on the Law of Treaties makes clear that the states parties to international agreements may interpret the agreement or define its terms through subsequent state practice.[90] The policy-making conferences or meetings of the parties that are created by MEAs are increasingly adopting interpretive decisions, recommendations and guidelines for action. The decisions and recommendations can have considerable juridical value when they express the common understanding of the states parties concerning the norms and obligations contained in the agreement. The Agreed Measures adopted by the Antarctic Treaty Consultative Parties constitute a veritable code of conduct for all activities in the Antarctic region and themselves are supplemented by decisions and resolutions of more hortatory value. During the 1960s alone, some 74 agreed measures were adopted. Similarly, the Ramsar, CBD, and CITES meetings have produced numerous and lengthy guidelines, recommendations and decisions, such as the Bonn Guidelines on Access to Genetic Resources and Fair and Equitable Sharing of the Benefits Arising out of their Utilization, adopted by the sixth conference of the parties to the Convention on Biological Diversity, discussed further in Chapter 8D.1.a.

3. Action Plans and Programs

While directive recommendations are addressed to states members of an international organization, programs of action often are aimed at the organizations which draft them, setting forth the activities to be undertaken within a given period of time. The European Community, for example, has adopted programs of action for successive four-year periods since 1973. Similarly, the IUCN in 1980 proposed its global program of action, the "World Conservation Strategy."

Treaties normally require states parties to undertake or refrain from specific conduct, but the nature of environmental problems often makes it impossible to define the exact content of obligations, especially when long-range pollution or long-term problems are addressed. The result is more programmatic, even vague obligations. The 1979 Geneva Convention on Long-Range Transboundary Air Pollution,[91] for example, concerns pollution "at a distance where it is generally not possible to distinguish the source or sources of emission."[92] Rather than fix precise duties, the obligations of states parties are to cooperate in the field of research and to implement a

---

[90] Vienna Convention, Art. 31.
[91] Nov. 13, 1979.
[92] Art. 1(b).

common program of continuous observation and evaluation of long range air pollution.[93] States parties also agree to elaborate policies and strategies to combat the dumping of pollutants into the atmosphere. The Paris Convention to Combat Desertification in those Countries Experiencing Serious Drought and/or Desertification, particularly in Africa[94] provide for action programs at the national, sub-regional and regional levels to be supported by inter-governmental and non-governmental bodies.

Treaties referring to action programs may be completed by more precise obligations for contracting parties through the conclusion of additional protocols to the original text. The 1979 Geneva Convention on Long-Range Transboundary Air Pollution, for example, has been supplemented by a series of protocols that give greater precision to the obligations of its states parties.[95] Similar arrangements exist for many of the regional seas treaties.[96]

The first well-known action plan is no doubt the Action Plan for the Human Environment, adopted by the 1972 Stockholm Conference on the Human Environment. The text is composed of 109 recommendations, sometimes addressed to governments, sometimes to international organizations, sometimes to both. It contains not only an indication of actions to be taken, but also directive recommendations. It has served, in fact, as the basis for a large number of international measures taken since its adoption, including the global environmental assessment plan (Earthwatch) to survey the state of the environment. It also has been the foundation of global conventions, studies sponsored by various inter-governmental organizations, and UNEP's regional seas program begun in 1974. Agenda 21, adopted by the 1992 Rio Conference, succeeded to it as a global program for sustainable development. It added to each chapter an evaluation of the cost of the proposed measures.

The role of non-binding texts expanded in the follow-up to UNCED. The UN General Assembly created the Commission on Sustainable Development (CSD) on Dec. 22, 1992 "in order to ensure the effective follow-up of the Conference" and "to examine the progress of the implementation of Agenda 21 at the national, regional and international levels, fully guided by the principles of the Rio Declaration on Environment and Development." Thus, an institution created by a non-binding General Assembly resolution reviews state compliance with two other non-binding international instruments.

The periodic reporting procedure foreseen for the CSD is a technique widely used in monitoring state compliance with international legal oblig-

---

[93]   Arts. 8 and 9.

[94]   June 17, 1994, Arts. 9, 15.

[95]   Such Protocols were adopted in Geneva, Sept. 28, 1984; in Helsinki, July 8, 1985; in Sofia, Oct. 31, 1988; and in Oslo, June 14, 1994.

[96]   *See* Chapter 11D.

ations, but until now has been based upon treaty provisions obliging states to file reports. The CSD, however, seeks information based upon "the commitments" and "agreed objectives" contained in Agenda 21, including those related to the provision of financial resources and transfer of technology. The import of these provisions is to further blur the line between binding and non-binding international instruments.

4. Standardization

International norms may be developed not only by states, but by organizations in which private actors are dominant. The standards developed may apply directly to private organizations, or to states. The International Organization for Standardization is one such organization. It is a federation of over 100 national standardization bodies, one from each represented country. It was formed in 1946 to harmonize technical requirements and standards. Each national body establishes the composition of its delegations, which should include a mix of producer, consumer and other relevant interests. It often includes government officials. International meetings adopt the standards. By the late 1980s the standards included a global standard for quality control management, one source of emerging environmental management standards. Other inputs came from corporate codes of conduct. Similar, sometimes competing, environmental management standards developed in Europe and in national law.

Environmental management standards require the company management to define the organization's environmental policy and ensure that it is appropriate to the nature, scale and environmental impacts of its activities. Each registered facility must commit to continual improvement, to comply with relevant laws, and to the prevention of pollution. The commitment must be publicly available and the organization must set up procedures to identify the environmental effects of its activities, create and maintain procedures to document these activities, identify individual responsibilities, train appropriate personnel, and prepare an emergency response plan. These activities must be periodically monitored and corrective action taken in cases of noncompliance. Environmental audits, whether internal or external, are required.

5. Codes of Conduct

A growing number of guidelines or codes of conduct have been developed within industry, including the World Industry Council for the Environment, the FAO International Code of Conduct on the Distribution and Use of Pesticides, the Responsible Care Initiative of the Chemical Manufacturers

Association, the CERES/Valdez Principles, the ICC Business Charter on Sustainable Development, and the Royal Dutch/Shell Group Statement of General Business Principles. The latter enunciates a duty "to conduct business as responsible corporate members of society, observing applicable laws of the countries in which they operate giving due regard to safety and environmental standards and societal aspirations." Point 7 states that Shell shall conduct its activities to take account of health and safety and to give proper regard to the conservation of the environment, complying with the requirements of relevant legislation and promoting measures for the protection of health, safety and the environment. Such measures pertain to the safety of operations, product safety, prevention of air, water and soil pollution and precautions to minimize damage from accidents.

Private regulation may constrain behavior by exercising a moral or practical (sanctioning) influence as effective as that of law. Breach of private codes may be evidence of malpractice or negligence, providing a relatively inexpensive means of evaluating conduct in case of a dispute. On the other hand, private codes may involve monopolistic professional regulation that is contrary to the public interest, less precise than legislation, and with standards below those that would be adopted through the normal law-making process. Where standards are stringent, the code may be ignored unless there is strong public pressure for compliance. The 1990 Valdez Principles on corporate environmental conduct, now known as the CERES Principles, may be debated within these terms. The Valdez Principles were adopted by the Coalition for Environmentally Responsible Economies, a group of investors and environmental organizations. The intent was to create corporate self-governance "that will maintain business practices consistent with the goals of sustaining our fragile environment for future generations, within a culture that respects all life and honors its independence."[97]

Whether they are strong or weak, non-state codes may become *de facto* minimum requirements for non-state actors. Corporate codes of conduct, industry standards, guidelines, recommendations, backed by informal or formal pressures, sometimes may effectively regulate the conduct of the community. Where norms are drafted by one community to regulate another, the results may be less pronounced, although the expertise and disinterestedness of the drafters may make the rules influential. The authority and legitimacy of the body adopting a normative text is no doubt important to the impact of the standards adopted. Both may be enhanced when the target community participates in the formulation of the norm. Although self-regulation may be self-serving and produce minimal constraints, it is

---

[97]   The Social Investment Forum, CERES Project, Valdez Principles Statement of Intent (Sept. 7, 1989) *quoted in* Daniel H. Pink, *The Valdez Principles: Is What's Good for America Good for General Motors?*, 8 YALE L. & POL'Y REV. 180 at 186 (1990). *See also* Valerie Ann Zondorak, *A New Face in Corporate Environmental Responsibility: The Valdez Principles*, 18 B.C. ENVTL. AFF. L. REV. 457 (1991).

also likely to produce a high degree of compliance. A process that is not wholly self-regulatory, but which allows meaningful participation of the regulated community and other interested communities may be most effective.

6. State/Private Contracts

Negotiated agreements between government and industry can serve to implement environmental standards. The existence of transboundary contracts between public and private bodies should be noted. On August 21, 1991, the Municipality of Rotterdam and the German Association of Chemical Industries concluded a contract to improve water quality and to reduce contaminated mud in the Rotterdam harbor. The so-called "Rhine Contract" ensures that certain categories of listed substances shall be reduced by 2010. The Association issues reports on the achieved reduction of the substances in the waste water. Rotterdam submits a report on the quality improvement of the harbor and the reduction in mud every two years. Significantly, according to Article 3 of the contract Rotterdam waived any prior claims to compensation that it might have had against the subscribing companies. In case of non-performance by the companies, Rotterdam can withdraw from the contract after three months notice.

F. Conclusions

An increasing number of concepts, principles and norms appear repeatedly in national, regional and global instruments, usually following an initial formulation in a non-binding instrument. Principles such as public participation, EIA, notification of environmental emergencies, prevention, precaution and polluter pays are examples of principles that have been incorporated into treaties and given greater specificity. In many cases this can result in greater agreed specification, such as when the same definition of a term appears from one treaty to another.[98] In some instances, however, the effort to detail obligations leads to divergences from one instrument or region to another. For example, the duty not to cause transboundary harm has been variously qualified as "significant" "measurable" "serious" or "appreciable" harm. As with the institutional proliferation discussed in Chapter 4, normative proliferation leads to a need for coordination and reconciliation of obligations.

---

[98] *See, e.g.*, the definition of pollution in the 1974 OECD Principles Concerning Transfrontier Pollution, Art. 1 of the 1979 Convention on Long-Range Transboundary Air Pollution, Art. 1(4) of UNCLOS and Art. 1(c) of the 1992 Paris Convention for the Protection of the Marine Environment of the North-East Atlantic.

BIBLIOGRAPHY

BENEDICK, R. OZONE DIPLOMACY (rev. ed. 1998).

Bodansky, D., *Customary (and Not So Customary) International Environmental Law*, 3 IND. J. GLOBAL LEGAL STUDIES 105 (1995).

Brown, E.D., *The Conventional Law of the Environment*, 13 NAT. RES. J. (1973).

Brownlie, I., *A Survey of International Customary Rules of Environmental Protection*, 13 NAT. RES. J. 179 (1973).

Charney, J., *Universal International Law*, 87 AJIL 529 (1993).

Dupuy, P., *Soft Law and the International Law of the Environment*, 12 MICH. J. INT'L L. 420 (1991).

DUPUY, R.-J., THE FUTURE INTERNATIONAL LAW OF THE ENVIRONMENT (1985).

EBBESSON, J., COMPATIBILITY OF INTERNATIONAL AND NATIONAL ENVIRONMENTAL LAW (1996).

JEWELL, T. & STEELE, J. eds., LAW IN ENVIRONMENTAL DECISION-MAKING— NATIONAL, EUROPEAN AND INTERNATIONAL PERSPECTIVES (1998).

JOYNER, C., ed., THE UNITED NATIONS AND INTERNATIONAL LAW (1997).

KRAMER, L., CASEBOOK ON EU ENVIRONMENTAL LAW (2002).

Mcgraw, D.B., *Legal Treatment of Developing Countries: Differential, Contextual and Absolute Norms*, 1 COLO. J. INT'L ENVTL. L. & POL'Y 69 (1990).

Nanda, V.P., *Trends in International Environmental Law*, 20 CAL W. INT'L L.J. 187–205 (1989–90).

Palmer, G., *New Ways to Make International Environmental Law*, 86 AJIL 259 (1992).

Robinson, N.A., *Emerging International Environmental Law*, 17 STAN. J. INT'L L. 229 (1981).

SADELER, N. DE, ENVIRONMENTAL PRINCIPLES (2002)

Sand, P., *UNCED and the Development of International Environmental Law*, 3 Y.B. INT'L ENVT'L. L. 3 (1992).

SHELTON, D. ed., COMMITMENT AND COMPLIANCE: THE ROLE OF NON-BINDING NORMS IN THE INTERNATIONAL LEGAL SYSTEM (1999).

SUSSKIND, L. ed., INTERNATIONAL ENVIRONMENTAL TREATY-MAKING (1992).

Szasz, P., *International Norm-making, in* WEISS, E.B. ed., ENVIRONMENTAL CHANGE IN INTERNATIONAL LAW (1995).

CHAPTER 4

INTERNATIONAL INSTITUTIONS AND CIVIL SOCIETY

Protecting the environment poses problems of considerable qualitative and quantitative variety that necessitate action by international institutions. Global and regional intergovernmental and non-governmental organizations participated from the beginning in the development and implementation of international environmental law. No single institution is in charge or coordinates the many activities. In addition the complexity of environmental problems has demanded the entry and participation of new actors in international law, including economic entities, scientific and professional associations, and the general network of civil society. In addition the functions of organizations have expanded in response to demands for management of environmental problems of the global commons and shared resources.

Principle 25 of the Stockholm Declaration expressed the participating states' desire for cooperative action with international institutions: "States shall ensure that international organizations play a coordinated, efficient and dynamic role for the protection and improvement of the environment." Agenda 21, adopted at the 1992 Rio Conference on Environment and Development, recognized that additional financial resources would be required to strengthen the capacities of international institutions to implement their responsibilities in the field of environmental protection. The Conference also called for the creation of a high-level UN commission to ensure and monitor the implementation of Agenda 21. Implementing this recommendation, the UN General Assembly created the Commission on Sustainable Development, discussed *infra*.

The 2002 World Summit on Sustainable Development (WSSD), while reaffirming Agenda 21, proposed new tasks in its Program of Action. The question of whether environmental governance[1] should be centralized

---

[1]   The term governance, now common in international policy, can be defined as the rational organization of society in order to achieve the objectives emerging from its common concerns. It is based on material, economic, historical and cultural foundations and needs. Governance includes the creation and the functioning of institutions and of norms at various levels from the local to the global. It also should determine the place and role of non-state actors and of stakeholders in public life. A particular aspect of governance is the designation and organization of basic services ensuring personal security, the supply of energy, food, transport systems, health, education, the conservation and

gained considerable attention prior to the WSSD. The issue of an international environmental agency was first raised at the Stockholm Conference but rejected because it was thought existing organizations would be reluctant to transfer their authority to such a body. Again in 1992, governments decided against a single entity, choosing instead to maintain the United Nations Environment Programme (UNEP) while creating the Commission on Sustainable Development. The notion of a World Environment Organization was advocated once more at Johannesburg, but governments continued to support UNEP as the "principal United Nations body in the field of the environment." In the end, no new institution emerged from the meeting.

The role of international institutions is important for several reasons. First, as noted earlier, scientists and policy-makers are far from having complete knowledge about the environment, its current and potential deterioration, and the measures which should be adopted. During the more than three decades since the Stockholm Conference, new issues have arisen needing relatively quick and coordinated attention, from the depletion of the stratospheric ozone layer, to deforestation, desertification, global climate change, and the loss of biological diversity. Rapid evolution in knowledge makes necessary permanent assessment of the environment, in most cases on an international level or in cooperation with researchers from other countries. In this regard international organizations are indispensable, because effective assessment requires coordinated environmental monitoring to fully obtain and evaluate information on global environmental trends.

Second, elaboration of and adherence to international norms and standards are indispensable to prevent deterioration of the environment. By itself, however, entry into force of standards usually does not and cannot ensure resolution of the problems addressed. Evolution of the state of the environment and knowledge of it requires virtually constant revisions of the rules, adapting existing instruments and their application. In addition, there must be mechanisms to supervise application of the rules. These tasks also demand sustained cooperation and an institutional framework.

What is known about the environment also suggests that the solution to environmental problems lies in the management of natural resources. To be efficient, such management must be international and continuously

---

management of natural resources. Art. 2 (2) of EC Reg. 2371/2002 on the Conservation and Sustainable Exploitation of Fisheries Resources under the Common Fisheries Policy contains the following principles of good governance: "(a) clear definition of responsibilities at the Community, national and local levels; (b) a decision-making process based on sound scientific advice which delivers timely results; (c) broad involvement of stakeholders at all stages of the policy from conception to implementation; (d) consistence with other Community policies, in particular with environmental, social, regional, development, health and consumer protection policies. EC Reg. No 2371/2002, Dec. 20, 2002; O.J. L 358 (12/31/02).

supervised. For this, as well, international organizations are crucial. Finally, international organizations representing the common interests of mankind can best integrate and respond to the interdependent issues of environmental quality, development, product control and energy resource management.

These various tasks and the importance of developing international environmental law necessitate a continuity of cooperative structure that can be assured only by permanent institutions. The proliferation of environmental agreements has resulted in increased duties for existing international organizations and the creation of new institutions charged with supervising implementation of international environmental obligations. Most of the major multilateral conventions establish a governing structure, generally consisting of a conference or meeting of the parties, a secretariat, and often a scientific and other subsidiary committees. While these institutions have taken on considerable importance, problems of coordination and duplication have been exacerbated, particularly among United Nations organs. The present chapter highlights these issues in providing an overview of global and regional institutions concerned with environmental protection.

A. Functions

There are many structural and functional parallels among international institutions that lead to similar and sometimes overlapping activities regarding the environment.

1) *Research* plays a particularly important role in the activities of international organizations. While they rarely carry out their own scientific research, organizations often undertake comparative legal studies of national or international measures prior to drafting international treaties, recommendations, directives, and model laws. In this regard the work of the FAO and the OECD can be cited. Where research programs do require scientific analysis, the member states generally undertake the research with international organizations assuring coordination of the tasks delegated to one or more states and disseminating the results. In certain cases, institutions like the EC Commission may give financial assistance or may conclude research contracts with experts or groups, as is done by UNESCO and the OECD.

2) *Exchange of information* based on national and international studies, research and projects is another important aspect of cooperation within international organizations. All international organizations concerned with environmental protection, *i.e.* nearly all of them, collect and exchange information with and among member states.

Some international organizations also prepare a synthesis of information received. The synthesis may concern a given problem, such as reports prepared by the United Nations Economic Commission for Europe, or may address the whole state of the environment, as does the annual report of the United Nations Environment Program.

3) *Regulatory functions* are often exercised by international organizations. Various bodies adopt new norms for members states, either recommendations or, more rarely, obligatory decisions or draft treaties. Many binding texts follow a common path before being adopted as international instruments, *i.e.*, elaboration by a group of experts followed by submission to a diplomatic conference, without this necessarily leading to adherence by every member state.[2] Another means of standard-setting may occur when an environmental agreement creates its own supervisory or executive organ. In such instances, the organ is often given responsibility for elaborating rules for implementation or application of the treaty or for modification of existing norms, sometimes contained in detailed appendices. When such power is conferred, participating states generally maintain their right to object to the changes and thus to withhold acceptance of them. Some regulatory regimes develop considerable complexity, as is the case with the Ozone treaty and its Montreal Protocol.

4) *Supervising implementation* of the norms generally does not extend to coercive action, such as policing the high seas to catch polluters, but such power may be granted either to the organization or, more commonly, to its member states. The use of such coercive measures may be increasing in respect to common resources. Article 24 of the 1980 Canberra Convention on the Conservation of Antarctic Marine Living Resources establishes an international system of "observation and inspection." The 1995 UN Convention on Straddling Stocks[3] also provides for boarding, inspecting, and even potential seizure of vessels illegally fishing in regulated high seas fishing areas. Supervision is much more common, however, through review by designated international organs of periodic state reports about national implementation of international norms.

---

[2]   An example is the 1979 Bern Convention on Protection of Wildlife and Nature in Europe, developed within the Council of Europe and discussed in Chapter 8D.2.c.

[3]   The full title is Agreement for the Implementation of the Provisions of the United Nations Convention on the Law of the Sea of Dec. 10, 1982 Relating to the Conservation and Management of Straddling Fish Stocks and Highly Migratory Fish Stocks (Aug. 4, 1995). *See* Chapter 8F.1.a.

5) *Management of natural resources* by an international organization is no doubt the most ambitious measure of international cooperation in the field of environmental protection. Article V(2) of the 1957 Interim Convention on the Conservation of North-Pacific Fur Seals confers on its Commission power to recommend to states parties appropriate measures concerning the size, sex, and age of the seals taken each year. There is also a management system for mineral resource activities on the deep seabed created by Chapter XI of the 1982 Law of the Sea Convention, in which protection of the marine environment holds a high place. Shared natural resources are in fact increasingly coming under international management agreements, such as those governing international fisheries and freshwaters. Management of fish stocks is often ensured by international bodies created by treaties, such as the 2000 Convention on the Conservation and Management of Highly Migratory Fish Stocks in the Western and Central Pacific.[4] The ultimate outcome of this development is the emergence and general application of an ecosystem approach.

B. Division of Tasks

Efforts to protect the environment touch most activities of public agencies and institutions. As a result, many national and international organizations are engaged in studies or actions aimed at protecting the biosphere, generating concerns about efficiency and conflicting norms or policies. The first and obvious limitation imposed on the activities of international organizations is the scope of the powers and functions granted each one; thus, the World Health Organization's mandate extends to problems affecting human health, the International Maritime Organization (IMO) is concerned with ocean pollution, and the Food and Agriculture Organization addresses problems of water and soil. At the same time, the treaty mandates of international organizations are often written in broad terms and permit many subject areas and powers to be implied. The FAO considers fisheries within its food mandate, for which it must cooperate with UNEP and the IMO, and also regulates pesticides and other hazardous chemicals. Coordination of the activities of international organizations with eachother and with the growing number of treaty bodies established by international environmental agreements is increasingly essential. The problem is similar to that faced by national governments in determining whether to grant an agency or organ primary responsibility and large power over all aspects of environmental protection or whether a specific agency should only

---

4   For further discussion, *see* Chapter 8F.1.a.

coordinate the many and varied activities of other organs that are concerned with specific aspects of the problem. In the international field only the last solution is possible in the absence of a global environmental authority.

Another criterion is geographic. Certain environmental questions can be dealt with either on a global level, essentially by institutions within the United Nations system, or on a regional basis by regional organizations, or, finally, on a subregional level, where a few states are concerned with the solution to a concrete problem of limited geographic scope. The latter include the pollution of a watercourse or a lake, protected areas in a border zone, and the protection of endemic species of wild fauna or flora. The principle of subsidiarity, applied within the European Union, may be generalized to express a preference for decision-making at the lowest effective level of governance. Decisions made at a local level may be more likely to take account of local conditions and allow the participation of those directly affected. While the principle of subsidiarity will decentralize much decision-making, the requirement of effectiveness in resolving a problem will still require many regional and global regulations.

There follows a survey of the principal international organizations concerned with environmental questions.[5] The primary focus is on the legal aspects of the organizations' environmental activities.

C. Global Organizations

As a result of growing knowledge about the widespread detrimental impacts of human activities, many environmental problems are recognized to affect the entire biosphere. Such issues must be addressed on a global level by United Nations organs and its specialized agencies.[6] Several global non-governmental organizations also undertake important activities in the field; two of these, the World Conservation Union (IUCN) and the World Wide Fund for Nature (WWF), are discussed in this chapter.

1. United Nations

The United Nations became actively involved in general environmental matters in 1968 when the General Assembly, upon a proposal by the Economic and Social Council, recommended convening what became the Stockholm Conference on the Human Environment.[7] The General Assembly has made other major initiatives in the field of environmental protection since convening the Stockholm Conference. It created a special subsidiary organ, the

---

5   International financial institutions are also discussed in Chapter 17.
6   Treaty bodies also exist at the global level; they are reviewed in section F.
7   G.A. Res. 2398 (XXIII), Dec. 3, 1968.

United Nations Environment Program (UNEP),[8] adopted the World Charter for Nature,[9] set up the Brundtland Commission, and established the Commission on Sustainable Development.[10] It also convened the 1992 Rio Conference and the 2002 World Summit on Sustainable Development. It has adopted important treaties such as the 1997 UN Convention on the Law of the Non-Navigational Uses of International Watercourses. Finally, the General Assembly regularly recommends measures on urgent subjects, such as its series of resolutions concerning "large-scale pelagic drift-net fishing; unauthorized fishing in zones of national jurisdiction; and fisheries by-catch and discards." The resolutions include calls for minimizing pollution, waste, discards, catch by lost or abandoned gear, catch of non-target species and impacts on associated or dependent species.[11] In 1997 the United Nations General Assembly held a special session on progress achieved towards meeting objectives of the Earth Summit, which adopted a program for further implementation of Agenda 21.

As a consequence of the Gulf War, the UN Security Council adopted a series of resolutions concerning the occupation of Kuwait by Iraq. In Resolution 687 (1991) the Security Council affirmed that Iraq ". . . is liable under international law for any direct loss, damage, including environmental damage and the depletion of natural resources. . . ." It also established a UN Compensation Commission in April 1991 to hear claims of environmental damage and depletion of natural resources caused by military activities.[12]

a. United Nations Environment Program (UNEP)

The United Nations General Assembly created UNEP as a subsidiary body following the Stockholm Conference. UNEP's secretariat is the central organ of action and coordination for environmental matters within the United Nations system as well as for regional organizations outside the

---

[8]   G.A. Res. 2995 on Institutional and Financial Arrangements for International Environmental Co-operation (establishing UNEP), Dec. 15, 1972.

[9]   G.A. Res. 37/7, Oct. 28, 1982.

[10]   G.A. Res. 47/49 on Institutional Arrangement to Follow up the UN Conference on Environment and Development (creating the Commission on Sustainable Development), Dec. 22, 1992; 5 WESTON V.A.7.

[11]   *See e.g.,* G.A. Decision on Large-scale Pelagic Driftnet Fishing and its Impact on the Living Marine Resources of the World's Oceans and Seas, U.N. Resolutions 44/207 (Dec. 22, 1989), 45/197 (Dec. 21, 1990), 46/215 (Dec. 20,1991), 47/443 (Dec. 22, 1992), 48/445 (Dec. 21, 1993), 49/436 (Dec. 19, 1994), 50/25 (Dec. 5, 1995), 51/36 (Dec. 9, 1996), 52/29 (Nov. 26, 1997), 53/33 (Jan. 6, 1999). For further discussion, *see* Chapter 8F.1.a.

[12]   *See* Chapter 16.

United Nations. Its role is generally that of a catalyst for action by other institutions. It studies environmental problems and elaborates programs, but implementation is undertaken by the United Nations as a whole, with the aid, if appropriate, of regional governmental and non-governmental organizations as well as individual states. Specific projects are encouraged by utilizing the Environment Fund[13] to contribute to the cost of the program or operation. Persuasion, based on information relating to environmental threats, is another means of stimulating action.

UNEP has a Governing Council composed of the representatives of 58 states selected geographically and elected by the UN General Assembly. UNEP's Governing Council meets once every two years and reports to the General Assembly through the Economic and Social Council. The UN Secretary-General appoints the Executive Director of UNEP, who heads the staff, 60 percent of whom are based at the headquarters in Nairobi. UNEP also has regional bureaus in Geneva, Bangkok, Mexico, Bahrain and New York as well as a liaison office in Washington, D.C. Specialized units have been created for certain problems; for example, a Bureau of Industry in Paris and a coordinating unit for the Caribbean in Kingston, Jamaica. One of UNEP's most important functions is to provide the secretariat of multilateral environmental conventions, including the 1973 Washington Convention on the International Trade of Endangered Species, the 1979 Bonn Convention on the Conservation of Migratory Species of Wild Animals, the ozone treaties of Vienna (1985) and Montreal (1987), the 1989 Basel Convention on Transboundary Movements of Hazardous Wastes, the 1992 Convention on Biodiversity, and the 1994 Convention on Desertification. UNEP activities thus have global dimensions and include a large range of tasks.

UNEP's working method largely consists of programming, with most actions involving three successive stages. First, UNEP gathers information on environmental problems and existing efforts to solve them. Based on this information, it each year chooses particular subjects and integrates them into a report on the state of the environment presented to the Governing Council at its following session. The second stage consists of defining the objectives and strategies to achieve, through undertaking particular actions. A program for the environment is presented to interested international organizations, governmental or non-governmental, as well as to governments. Finally, in a third phase, activities are chosen to receive support from the Environment Fund, priority being given to actions that can stimulate or coordinate other activities.

---

[13]   The operational financing of UNEP comes from the general United Nations budget but specific UNEP actions are financed by the Environment Fund, established by G.A. Res. 2997(XXVII). States make voluntary contributions, which vary considerably over time, to the Fund.

The areas of UNEP action form six sometimes closely-linked groups: (1) human establishments; (2) human and environmental health; (3) terrestrial ecosystems; (4) oceans; (5) environment and development; and (6) natural disasters. Altogether, UNEP undertook over 1,000 projects during its first 15 years, most of which did not directly concern the development of environmental law.

UNEP's most important actions fall within the three categories foreseen by the Stockholm Action Plan: environmental assessment, management and supporting measures. The Stockholm Conference gave the name *Earthwatch* to assessment of the global environment, encompassing continuous monitoring, research, exchange of information and examination of data concerning the environment. *Earthwatch* includes coordination of national installations and services and international financing without, however, creating a well-defined institutional framework. Currently, monitoring and exchange of information fall within the mandate of the Global Environmental Monitoring System (GEMS). The principal tasks delegated to organizations that participate in *Earthwatch* are the monitoring of renewable resources, *inter alia* by the United Nations Economic Commission for Africa, monitoring of climate and the ozone layer by the World Meteoro iklogical Organization, of health by the World Health Organization, and studies of air quality, oceans and the world biogeochemical carbon cycle. A data base on world resources has been instituted within the context of *Earthwatch*.

UNEP also created an international information system on the environment, INFOTERRA, in 1977. INFOTERRA puts national and international establishments in contact with experts, establishes links between thousands of cooperating institutions, both users and suppliers of information, and furnishes on request copies of basic documents supplied by countries and United Nations organs. In a related activity, UNEP gathers and disseminates data on chemical substances that can cause accidents or harm the environment. This action led to the creation of a Geneva-based International Register of Potentially Toxic Chemicals. A network of correspondents operates a world data bank for the exchange of information, particularly necessary for countries lacking the resources to undertake their own often expensive chemical analyses of substances. Descriptive entries exist for hundreds of substances, containing information on their physical and chemical characteristics, methods of utilization, concentrations in the environment, and effects and toxicity for man and the environment. These entries can be obtained through the Information Service of IRPTC. A legal listing, aimed at protecting against risks caused by registered chemicals, contains information on national and international regulations and recommendations. Assistance also is given countries wishing to establish national registers. UNEP's information system is largely accessible through the Internet.

UNEP's mandate on management of the environment includes the regulation of human activities that have any measurable impact on the environment and has led it to play a major role in the development of international environmental law. First, UNEP developed a program on regional seas. The program has drafted treaties and action plans for different maritime regions of the world in order to combat pollution and contribute to the best management of the environment as a whole in the regulated areas.[14]

Second, in 1982 UNEP adopted its Montevideo Program for the development of international environmental law. The Program provided a framework for most of UNEP's normative activities and led to the creation of a special unit dedicated to promoting environmental law. The Environmental Law Unit prepares draft treaties which are reviewed and revised by ad hoc expert working groups. Drafts are then submitted to the Governing Council for debate and adoption or UNEP may convene a diplomatic conference to adopt the text, as it did with the 1985 Vienna Convention for the Protection of the Ozone Layer and the 1987 Montreal Protocol on Substances that Deplete the Ozone Layer. Over the last 25 years more than 40 multilateral environmental treaties have been negotiated under UNEP's guidance, including, *inter alia*, the 1973 Washington Convention on the International Trade in Endangered Species, the 1989 Basel Convention on the Control of Transboundary Movements of Hazardous Wastes, the 1992 Convention on Biological Diversity; the 1994 Paris Convention to Combat Desertification in those Countries Experiencing Serious Drought and/or Desertification particularly in Africa, as well as the regional seas treaty systems. In cooperation with FAO, UNEP facilitated the development of the 1998 Convention on the Prior Informed Consent Procedure for Certain Hazardous Chemicals and Pesticides in International Trade. It provided substantive support and expertise for the development of sub-regional treaties such as the Agreement on the Action Plan for the Environmentally Sound Management of the Common Zambezi River System and for the Lusaka Agreement on Cooperative Enforcement Operations Directed at Illegal Trade in Fauna and Flora.

UNEP has been active also in the development of non-binding instruments in the field of the environment. The Governing Council of UNEP or inter-governmental meetings convened by UNEP adopted such instruments as the Principles of Conduct in the Field of the Environment for the Guidance of States in the Conservation and Harmonious Utilization of Natural Resources Shared by Two or More States; the Conclusions of the Study of Legal Aspects concerning the Environment Related to Offshore Mining and Drilling within the Limits of National Jurisdiction; the Montreal Guidelines for the Protection of the Marine Environment against Pollution from Land-Based Sources; the Cairo Guidelines and Principles for the

---

[14]   *See* Chapter 11.

Environmentally Sound Management of Hazardous Wastes; the Goals and Principles of Environmental Impact Assessment; the London Guidelines for the Exchange of Information on Chemicals in International Trade; the Code of Ethics on the International Trade in Chemicals; the Global Program of Action for the Protection of the Marine Environment from Land-based Activities; and the International Technical Guidelines for Safety in Biotechnology.

Following UNCED, Agenda 21 added a new dimension to UNEP's lead role in the progressive development of international environmental law, placing its mandate within the context of sustainable development. By Decision 187/25 (1993) the Governing Council adopted the Program for the Periodic Development and Periodic Review of Environmental Law for the 1990s, commonly referred to as "Montevideo II." It included issues such as effective state participation, implementation of international law, adequacy of existing international instruments, dispute avoidance and settlement, and mechanisms for the prevention and redress of environmental damage. It also addressed liability and compensation for environmental damage from military activities, and the development of regimes for the conservation, management and sustainable development of soils and forests.

With the expiration of Montevideo II, UNEP's Governing Council adopted a Program for the Development and Periodic Review of Environmental Law for the first Decade of the Twenty-First Century (Montevideo III, February 2001). For this period, the main themes are compliance with multilateral environmental agreements (MEAs) and the proliferation of environmental agreements, which many observers see as interrelated topics. By Decision 21/27 the Governing Council requested UNEP to prepare guidelines on compliance with MEAs as well as on capacity-building and effective national enforcement.[15] In respect to the second theme, Decision 21/21 (February 9, 2001) on "International Environmental Governance," established an Open-ended Inter-Governmental Group of Ministers to undertake a "comprehensive policy-oriented assessment of existing institutional weaknesses as well as future needs and options for strengthened international environmental governance." Working Group II of this Ministerial body is concerned with improving coordination and coherence between multilateral environmental agreements (MEAs) and enhancing coordination across the UN system.[16]

---

[15]   The Guidelines were prepared and adopted by the Council in February 2002. Chapter I aims at enhancing compliance with MEAs throughout the process of adopting international agreements. Chapter II addresses national enforcement and international cooperation to combat violations of national laws implementing international agreements.

[16]   31 E.P.L. 124, 194, 260, 266, 271 (2001).

Finally, UNEP assists governments of developing countries with drafting national environmental laws and with training judges[17] on the enforcement of international environmental norms. Through its activities, UNEP has exerted a marked influence on the development of environmental protection throughout the world.

b. Commission on Sustainable Development

The United Nations General Assembly created the Commission on Sustainable Development (CSD) as a functional commission of the Economic and Social Council (ECOSOC) following UNCED.[18] The CSD is composed of 53 UN member states serving three-year terms. Its activities are funded through the UN's regular budget. Patterned explicitly after the work of the United Nations Human Rights Commission, the CSD examines the progress in implementing Agenda 21 at the national, regional and international levels, explicitly guided by the principles of the Rio Declaration. The Commission monitors the integration of environmental and developmental goals throughout the United Nations system, coordinates inter-governmental decision-making on environment and development and makes recommendations on any new arrangements needed to advance sustainable development. It receives reports from organs, organizations, programs and institutions, as well as information provided by governments in the form of periodic communications, and information provided by non-governmental organizations. It specifically reviews progress in state implementation of the financial commitments contained in Agenda 21. It may make recommendations through ECOSOC to the General Assembly.

At its first full session, held in New York in June 1993, the Commission adopted six resolutions outlining some of the mechanisms to monitor the implementation of Agenda 21. It established two ad hoc inter-sessional expert groups, one to assist in monitoring requirements, availability and adequacy of financial resources, and related issues such as debt relief and terms of trade, and the other to assist in reviewing progress achieved in promoting the transfer of environmentally-sound technologies, cooperation and capacity-building.

The CSD adopted a framework program for nine areas. Five of these are considered on an annual basis: critical elements of sustainability, such as poverty and changing consumption patterns; financial resources and mechanisms; education, science, and transfer of environmentally sound

---

[17]   UNITAR, the United Nations Institute for Training and Research, has also conducted numerous training programs in international environmental law directed at government officials including judges.

[18]   G.A., Res. 47/191, Dec. 22, 1992; 5 WESTON V.A.7.

technologies; decision-making structures; and roles of major groups. On a three-year cycle, the Commission considers health, human settlements and freshwater; toxic chemicals and hazardous wastes; land, desertification, forests and biodiversity; and atmosphere, oceans and all kinds of seas. The decisions taken have suggested to some that economic development has been the Commission's priority, with environmental problems subordinated: *e.g.*, problems of the oceans and the atmosphere, the greatest resources of the earth, were relegated to triennial consideration beginning in 1996. When the Commission was criticized for not maintaining a balance in its work, it decided at its sixth session, in 1998, to take up the issue of freshwater and of strategic approaches to freshwater management as a sectoral theme.[19]

The CSD meets annually for a period of two to three weeks and has received substantive and technical services from the Department of Economic and Social Affairs/Division for Sustainable Development. More than 1,000 NGOs are accredited by the CSD, the highest level of involvement in any UN Commission. Recent CSD sessions have sought to create a general dialogue between governments and major non-governmental groups on actions concerning a sector, such as agriculture or industry, and to identify measures that can contribute to sustainable development. Despite these efforts, criticism of the CSD continues to grow as its impact has been minimal in the ten years since it was established. The broad mandate given by the comprehensive Agenda 21 is part of the problem, as is the fact that many of the issues considered by the CSD are also addressed in other fora. Some accuse the CSD of becoming an avenue of complaint or reconsideration for governments unhappy with the decisions or outcomes of discussions in meetings of environmental treaty bodies.[20] The result may be increasing fragmentation or disagreement over priorities and necessary actions.

c. International Law Commission

The 34 member International Law Commission, established by the United Nations General Assembly,[21] was created for the codification and progressive development of international law. Within its mandate it has considered issues of international environmental law since its early work on the law of the sea.[22] A survey of its work program in 1971 reflected emerging ecological views, stating that greater attention would have to be paid in the future to problems of protecting the environment.[23] Entering the 1990s, a large

---

[19]   28/3-4 EPL110 (1998).

[20]   UNU/IAS Report at 25.

[21]   G.A. Res. 174(II), Nov. 21, 1947.

[22]   *See* S.C. McCaffrey, *The Work of the International Law Commission Relating to the Environment*, 11 ECOL. L.Q. 189 (1983).

[23]   A/CN.4/245, II-2 Y.B. I.L.C. 1100 (1971).

number of subjects on the agenda of the ILC directly involved the development and codification of international environmental law.

First, in 1996, the Commission adopted the text of a Draft Code of Crimes Against the Peace and Security of Mankind, Article 20 of which states:

> Any of the following war crimes constitutes a crime against the peace and security of mankind when committed in a systematic manner or on a large scale . . . (g) in the case of armed conflict, using methods or means of warfare not justified by military necessity with the intent to cause widespread, long-term and severe damage to the natural environment and thereby gravely prejudice the health or survival of the population where such damage occurs.

The following year, the Commission submitted to the UN General Assembly a draft Convention on the Non-Navigational Uses of International Watercourses. The General Assembly adopted the draft on May 21, 1997.[24] In 2001 the ILC completed work on its articles on the law of state responsibility and presented its draft to the General Assembly.[25] The ILC has long distinguished the issue of state responsibility for wrongful conduct from the issue of international liability for injurious consequences arising out of acts not prohibited by international law.[26] The major focus of the latter study, which started in 1978, has turned to transboundary environmental harm. In 2001, the ILC completed Draft articles on Prevention of Transboundary Harm from Hazardous Activities.[27] The General Assembly requested the ILC to resume consideration of the liability aspects of the topic "bearing in mind the interrelationship between prevention and liability, and taking into account the developments in international law and comments by Governments." [28] The ILC draft on prevention of harm recommends that a convention be adopted on the topic, something not done in the articles on state responsibility.

---

[24]   U.N. Doc. A/51/869; 36 I.L.M. 700 (1997).

[25]   Draft Articles on Responsibility of States for Internationally Wrongful Acts, in Report of the International Law Commission on the Work of Its 53d Session, U.N. GAOR, 56th Sess., Supp. No. 10, at 45, U.N. Doc. A/56/10 (2001), approved by the General Assembly in G.A. Res. 56/83 (Dec. 12, 2001). For a history of the ILC's work and commentary on the articles, *see* James Crawford, The ILC's Articles on State Responsibility (2002).

[26]   International Law Commission, A/CN.4/450, Apr. 5, 1993.

[27]   *See* Report of the ILC, United Nations 53d Sess., at 370 (2001), U.N. Doc. A/56/10 (2001).

[28]   G.A. Res. 56/82, Dec. 12, 2001.

d.   United Nations Economic Commission for Europe (UNECE)

The Economic and Social Council of the United Nations created the Economic Commission for Europe in 1947, in the perspective of post-war European reconstruction. Since the 1950s, UNECE has been active in questions concerning the environment, even though this was not its initial aim. It supplies governments with analyses and economic, technological and statistical information. Its method of work is to assemble experts, prepare and publish analyses and statistics and organize exchanges of technical information. In appropriate cases it elaborates texts announcing action principles or draft conventions. The UNECE then submits such drafts to diplomatic conferences for adoption.

The UNECE first addressed an environmental problem in 1956 when its committee on transportation considered the issue of water pollution during its work on inland navigable waterways. Over time, other committees similarly faced questions of environmental deterioration. In 1963, the committee on coal production took up the issue of air pollution by coal factories, after which the committee on electric energy became interested in pollution caused by heating plants and thermal pollution of inland waters. In 1967, it looked at environmental protection for the first time in a larger perspective, leading to a 1969 decision that inter-governmental cooperation in the environmental field should constitute one of the four principal objectives of the organization's overall waste program.

The Committee on Environmental Policy plays a key role within UNECE as do the Ministers of Environment who regularly meet in the framework of the Ministerial Conferences on Environment for Europe. The Conference of 1995, held in Sofia, adopted a Pan-European Biological and Landscape Strategy which envisages five-year action plans to provide a framework for a common European response to the Convention on Biodiversity. The Strategy entrusts the Committee on Environmental Policy with specific tasks to assess and report on progress made in the implementation of an Environmental Program for Europe.

International conventions elaborated within UNECE have made important contributions to the development of environmental law. One of the first environmental agreements adopted by UNECE, in 1958, concerned uniform standards and recognition of standards for equipment and parts for motor vehicles and included, in an annex, norms concerning polluting gasoline emissions. Another 1958 agreement, relating to international road transport of dangerous merchandise, acted to prevent soil and water pollution. The most important conventions drafted in the context of the UNECE are the 1979 Convention on Long-Range Transboundary Air Pollution and its Protocols, the 1991 Convention on Environmental Impact Assessment in a Transboundary Context, the 1992 Convention on Transboundary Effects of Industrial Accidents, the 1992 Convention on the

Protection and Use of Transboundary Watercourses and International Lakes, the 1998 Convention on Access to Information, Public Participation in Decision-Making and Access to Justice in Environmental Matters; and the 2003 Carpathian Mountain Agreement.

e.   Other UN Bodies

Another institutional child of UNCED is the High Level Advisory Board on Sustainable Development. The 21 members were appointed in July 1993 by the UN Secretary-General. The Board formulates policy proposals and identifies emerging issues for the attention of relevant intergovernmental bodies, particularly the Commission on Sustainable Development and the Economic and Social Council. Many of its members are environmental experts. The UN also created an Inter-Agency Committee on Sustainable Development, made up of nine members, representing UNEP, FAO, IAEA, ILO, UNDP, UNESCO, WHO, WMO, and the World Bank.[29] Established in October 1992, it is one of the main bodies concerned with implementing Agenda 21, ensuring cooperation and coordination within the United Nations. It is charged with allocating competence and tasks within the system, as well as with evaluating financial and material needs. It is the link between technical UN working groups and agency heads. Its role is to prepare policy recommendations to improve cooperation and coordination among different UN organs.

Other organs of the United Nations are increasingly concerned with environmental issues as it becomes integrated throughout the system. The Human Rights Commission and the Sub-Commission on Prevention of Discrimination and Protection of Minorities have been occupied with environmental issues since the late 1980s. In 1988 the Sub-Commission first considered the relationship between the environment and human rights, taking up the issue of the movement of toxic and dangerous products and wastes. It adopted a resolution referring to the right of all peoples to life and the right of future generations to enjoy their environmental heritage. It called for a ban on the export of toxic and dangerous wastes and a global convention on that subject. As discussed in detail in Chapter 15, the Commission and Sub-Commission have added to their agendas topics related to human rights and the environment, appointing special rapporteurs to undertake a study of the relationship of human rights and the environment, the impact on human rights of international movements of toxic and hazardous substances, the right to food, and the right to water.

---

[29]   Res. 47/191, para. 25.

Finally, the work of the United Nations Development Program is increasingly concerned with environmental issues. Created in 1965 to administer technical assistance for developing countries, it has now incorporated principles of sustainable development throughout its program. In response to Agenda 21, UNDP created the Sustainable Energy and Environment Division which consolidated into one office all the operations at UNDP headquarters with responsibility for environmental issues. The mandate of the Division is "to help developing countries successfully design and carry out programs which integrate the protection and regeneration of the environment and the use of natural resources to reduce poverty, generate sustainable livelihoods, and advance the status of women." The Division therefore seeks to ensure that all aspects of UNDP's activities are considered from an environmental perspective.

2. UNESCO

The mandate of the United Nations Educational, Scientific and Cultural Organization may appear rather far from matters concerned with the environment. However, influenced by public opinion interested in ecological problems, UNESCO launched the Man and Biosphere Program (M.A.B.) in 1970, commissioning a study on the interactions between man and the environment. Fourteen principal themes were included in the framework of this project, including the impact of human activities on different sectors of the environment and the conservation of natural areas and the genetic resources they contain. A "world bank" of biosphere reserves was proposed and adopted. Each of these reserves both conserves and utilizes resources, including characteristic examples of ecosystems and human habitats. One of the objectives of the biosphere reserves is to establish management models of space and water, combining the satisfaction of human needs with the necessities of conservation. By 2003, some 425 sites have been recognized as biosphere reserves in 95 countries. UNESCO has incorporated the World Network of Biosphere Reserves into two non-binding instruments adopted in 1995: the Seville Strategy and the Statutory Framework.

UNESCO also has elaborated two major global conventions, the Ramsar Convention on Wetlands of International Importance and the 1972 World Cultural and Natural Heritage Convention. As of March 2003, over 730 items were on the World Heritage list established by the second Convention, including more than 144 natural and 17 mixed natural and cultural sites. Other UNESCO treaties touch on environmental issues, such as the 2002 Convention on Underwater Cultural Heritage and the 1954 Convention for the Protection of Cultural Property in the Event of Armed Conflict.

3. Food and Agriculture Organization (FAO)

According to its statute, signed October 16, 1945, the mission of the FAO is to promote investment in agriculture, promote better soil and water management, improve yields of crops and livestock, incite the transfer of technology to, and the development of agricultural research in, developing countries. It is not surprising, therefore, to find it concerned with the conservation of natural resources. The mandate of the FAO Commission on Plant Genetic Resources, for example, includes all components of biodiversity of relevance to food and agriculture, including animal, plant, forestry and fishery genetic resources.[30]

The FAO has contributed significantly to the development of international environmental law. Even before the Stockholm Conference it adopted measures to protect fisheries and plants from environmental harm. Later it drafted the 1981 World Soil Charter[31] and the 1985 International Code of Conduct on the Distribution and Use of Pesticides. More recently, it elaborated the 1993 Agreement to Promote Compliance with International Conservation and Management Measures by Fishing Vessels on the High Seas[32] and on November 3, 2001, completed and opened for signature the International Treaty on Plant Genetic Resources for Food and Agriculture. It also has participated in drafting numerous international texts, for example the 1976 Barcelona Convention for the Protection of the Mediterranean, and its Protocols, the 1987 London Guidelines for the Exchange of Information on Chemicals in International Trade, the 1995 Code of Conduct for Responsible Fisheries prepared by the Committee on Fisheries and approved by the FAO Conference (Resolution 4/95), and the 1998 Convention on the Prior Consent Procedure for Certain Hazardous Chemicals and Pesticides in International Trade. Often, it cooperates with UNEP in the drafting or updating of such texts. The Codex Alimentarius establishing food standards is the result of cooperation between FAO and WHO.

The FAO is the source of legislation in numerous countries, above all developing ones, regarding agriculture, forests, fishing, and soil conservation, subjects closely linked to environmental protection. For this purpose the FAO publishes a series of legislative studies that contain national and international legal texts, for example on the law of water, fishing regulations, and evaluations of the environmental impact of agricultural development. Food security is a major issue and in 1996 the FAO issued Legislative Study No. 59, entitled The Legal Framework for Food Security.

The working methods of FAO enhance the role of environmental considerations in FAO projects. On the one hand, states or parties are assisted

---

[30]   Resolution 3/95 of the FAO Conference.
[31]   FAO Doc. C81/27, Oct. 1981, *reprinted in* 8 E.P.L. 63 (1982).
[32]   33 I.L.M. 968 (1994).

by the collection and dissemination of information, by the opinions of experts, by training courses and by the implementation of pilot projects. On the other hand, FAO supports the integrated development of agriculture, including monitoring of soil, inventory of water resources, development of hydrographic basins, and implementation of particularly adapted agricultural systems. An example of the work of FAO's legal office is the technical assistance provided to the Lake Chad Basin Commission. The office prepared a draft agreement on water utilization and conservation in the Lake Chad Basin. Article IV of the draft requires states to take every reasonable measure to ensure the conservation of the water resources of the Basin, to maintain their natural flow and quality, to prevent their misuse, waste or pollution, and to plan and implement projects conducive to the integrated development of the Basin.[33]

In 1996, the FAO created three new sub-regional offices as part of a restructuring and decentralization, designating them for the Pacific Islands, as part of the larger regional office for Asia and the Pacific, the Caribbean, and North Africa. The principal duty of the offices is to assist countries in the region to reinforce their agricultural sectors.

4. World Health Organization (WHO)

Obviously, the principal mandate of the World Health Organization, created July 22, 1946, is international cooperation in the interests of human health. By virtue of Article 2 of its Constitution, WHO has, in particular, the task of seeking to eliminate epidemic, endemic and other illnesses and improve housing and hospitals. All these objectives are linked to environmental protection. As a result, WHO collects and disseminates information, publishes manuals and guides, furnishes technical assistance and organizes courses and seminars, establishes centers for information, conducts research, and monitors particular pollutants harmful to health.

WHO developed a Global Strategy for Health and Environment as a response to Agenda 21. Implementation of the Strategy is guided by action plans for WHO's programs, including the Program for the Promotion of Environmental Health and the Program for the Promotion of Chemical Safety. The problem of the supply of drinking water is a crucial issue of concern to WHO and it requires a favorable environmental context. WHO has established a Community Water Supply and Sanitation Unit to monitor and report on progress in improving health in this sector. It also has drafted Guidelines for Drinking Water Quality. WHO has a Food Safety Program concerned with protecting human health from unsafe or potentially unsafe food through the prevention of health hazards associated with biological

---

[33] International Law Commission, U.N. Doc. A/CN.4/412 Add 1, at 30.

and chemical contamination and additives. WHO with FAO established the Codex Alimentarius Commission to implement joint FAO/WHO Food Standards Program. Its current membership represents over 98 percent of the world's population. The Prevention of Environmental Pollution Unit of WHO's Division of Environmental Health provides support to member states in the development of national programs for control of environmental health hazards, whether chemical, physical, or biological and monitors environmental quality and human exposure.

In the field of law, WHO has established binding and non-binding health standards. On December 8, 1989, a WHO regional conference of ministers of health and environment concluded a European Charter on the Environment and Health.[34] The Charter, recognizing that a clean and harmonious environment exercises a beneficial influence on health and well-being, provides that every individual is entitled to an environment conducive to the highest attainable level of health and well-being, to information and consultation on the state of the environment and on plans, decisions and activities likely to affect both the environment and health, and to participation in the decision-making process. In turn every individual has a responsibility to contribute to the protection of the environment, in the interests of his or her own health and the health of others. The Charter adopts as a preferred approach "prevention is better than cure," application of which requires that new policies, technologies and initiatives should be adopted only after prior assessment demonstrating that they will have no negative impact on the environment and health. The Charter also provides that environmental standards should be constantly revised in light of new knowledge relating to the environment and health as well as new economic conditions. Further, it is necessary to apply the "polluter-pays" principle, whereby any public or private entity causing or likely to cause damage to the environment is financially responsible for preventive or restorative measures. To implement these principles, the Charter calls for clearly defined responsibility, adoption and application of norms, standards, and strategies based upon the best scientific evidence, and elaboration of emergency plans regarding environmental accidents.

In 2003 the WHO sponsored an Anti-Tobacco Convention which, although its principal aim is health, has obvious consequences for air pollution, particularly in contained environments. The WHO also collects, edits, and disseminates information, particularly through the trimestrial publication "International Digest of Health Legislation."

---

[34] WHO Doc. ICP/RUD 113/Conf.Doc./1, *reprinted in* 20 E.P.L. 57 (1990).

5. World Meteorological Organization (WMO)

Created in 1947, WMO aims to establish a system of monitoring and rapid exchange of meteorological information, standardize observations, encourage applications of meteorological science, including prediction and modification of weather, and encourage and coordinate research. These activities permit the observation of pollution and its persistence in the atmosphere. In addition, WMO is clearly placed to assess reduction in the stratospheric ozone layer and its consequences. Overall WMO is particularly equipped to undertake global monitoring. It actively participated in the creation of a world system of continuous monitoring of the environment (GEMS), contributing greatly to the field of environmental protection. The legal office of WMO has contributed to the elaboration of international instruments on artificial weather modification, protection of the ozone layer, and long range atmospheric pollution.

6. International Atomic Energy Agency (IAEA)

The IAEA was created in 1956 in order to hasten and increase "the contribution of atomic energy to peace, health and prosperity in the entire world." Its functions also include the task of establishing and overseeing implementation of norms designed to protect health and reduce to a minimum the dangers to which persons and property are exposed from radiation. Thus, for projects which the Agency assists or for any other arrangement where interested parties invite the Agency to apply its standards, the Agency seeks to ensure that the projects conform to its norms and it can require application of any safety measures it prescribes.

As discussed in more detail in Chapter 13D, the Agency adopts norms for nuclear safety and codes of proper procedure which it proposes to member states, including radioactive waste management. It has adopted guidelines for monitoring and preventing radiological contamination of personnel and the environment, safe handling and the transport of radioactive materials, treatment and disposal of radioactive wastes, and containment and safety of nuclear power plants. In 1961, it published a regulation on transportation of radioactive materials which has been revised several times. In 1984 it proposed directives for the conclusion of arrangements between member states for mutual emergency assistance in case of nuclear accident or radioactive crisis. However, not all nuclear states have fully implemented these directives, which as recommendations are not legally binding. In fact, only one of the recommended arrangements was signed, providing for mutual assistance between the Nordic countries in case of accidents implying radioactive damage.[35]

---

[35]   IAEA Doc. INFCIRC/310.

After the Chernobyl nuclear accident of April 26, 1986,[36] IAEA was asked to examine the consequences of Chernobyl and furnish the framework necessary to elaborate international standards regarding future accidents having international implications. Two international conventions, one on Early Notification of a Nuclear Accident, the other on Assistance in the Case of Nuclear Accident or Radiological Emergency were adopted September 26, 1986, by the IAEA general conference meeting in extraordinary session. The organization continues to be involved in standard-setting and in verification of nuclear safeguards. The latter role has become particularly important with concerns about international terrorism.

7. International Maritime Organization (IMO)

In 1948 states meeting at an international conference in Geneva agreed to establish an institution for the regulation of international commercial navigation. The founding treaty entered into force in 1958 and the new organization, originally called the International Maritime Consultative Organization, met for the first time the following year. IMO's first important responsibility was safety at sea and it adopted a number of legal instruments on this topic, most importantly, the 1960 International Convention for the Safety of Life at Sea (SOLAS).[37] By the late 1960s, however, the increasing amount of oil being transported by sea in ever-larger oil tankers became a particular concern, especially after a number of major tanker accidents.

IMO has introduced a series of measures designed to prevent accidents and to minimize marine pollution due to oil. It also has tackled the environmental threats caused by routine operations such as the cleaning of oil cargo tanks and the disposal of engine room wastes—a bigger menace than accidents in terms of tonnage. Measures introduced by IMO are concerned with the safety of containers, bulk cargoes, liquefied gas tankers and other ship types. Special attention has been paid to ship crews, including the adoption of a convention on standards of training, certification and watch-keeping.

---

[36]   *See infra* Chapter 13D.2.

[37]   June 17, 1960, replaced Nov. 1, 1974. The first version of the SOLAS Convention was adopted in 1914, in response to the Titanic disaster, the second in 1929, the third in 1948 and the fourth in 1960. The 1960 Convention was the first major task for IMO after the Organization's creation and was adopted to modernize regulations and keep pace with technical developments in the shipping industry. The IMO intended to adopt periodic amendments to maintain the Convention, but in practice the amendments procedure proved to be very slow. As a result, a completely new Convention was adopted in 1974 which included not only the amendments agreed up until that date but a new amendment procedure—the tacit acceptance procedure—designed to ensure that changes could be made within a specified (and acceptably short) period of time.

IMO's mandate includes establishing a system to ensure redress for those who suffer financially as a result of pollution. It adopted treaties in 1969 and 1971 to enable victims of oil pollution to obtain compensation simply and quickly, later followed by conventions on liability and compensation for other shipping hazards.

The IMO has benefitted from technological advances that allowed major improvements to the maritime distress system. In the 1970s it initiated a global search and rescue system and began use of the International Mobile Satellite Organization (INMARSAT) which greatly improved radio and other ship communications. In 1992 the Global Maritime Distress and Safety System became operative. With it, a ship in distress anywhere in the world can be guaranteed assistance even if its crew does not have time to radio for help, because the distress signal is transmitted automatically.

The adoption of maritime legislation is still IMO's most visible responsibility. The Organization has sponsored approximately 40 conventions and protocols, most of which have been amended on several occasions to ensure that they keep up with changes in world shipping. The most important treaties for environmental protection are the 1954 Convention for the Prevention of Pollution of the Sea by Oil (OILPOL); the 1972 Convention on the Prevention of Marine Pollution by Dumping of Wastes and Other Matter; the 1993/78 Convention for the Prevention of Pollution by Ships (MARPOL); the 1969 Convention Relating to Intervention on the High Seas in Cases of Oil Pollution Casualties; the 1990 Convention on Oil Pollution Preparedness, Responses and Co-operation; the 1969 Convention on Civil Liability for Oil Pollution Damage; the 1971 Convention on the Establishment of an International Fund for Compensation for Oil Pollution Damage; the 1971 Convention relating to Civil Liability in the Field of Maritime Carriage of Nuclear Materials; the 1976 Convention on Limitation of Liability for Maritime Claims; the 1996 Convention on Liability and Compensation for Damage in connection with the Carriage of Hazardous and Noxious Substances by Sea.[38]

IMO has created a Marine Environment Protection Committee that discusses the on-going issues of revising MARPOL annexes and other environmental problems such as harmful aquatic organisms in ballast water. The question of IMO's constitutional competence has arisen with the adoption of the Global Program of Action for the Protection of the Marine Environment from Land-Based Activities (GPA). UN General Assembly Resolution 51/189, on Institutional Arrangements for the Implementation of the GPA, adopted in December 1996, called upon the IMO to develop a clearing-house mechanism for oils and litter in the marine environment that originate from land-based sources. The IMO Assembly responded that the IMO had a mandate to prevent marine pollution from sea-based sources only and

---

38   For a discussion of these agreements, *see* Chapter 11.

that the subject matter of the request lay outside its constitutional responsibilities. When no voluntary resources were provided by member states, the Assembly concluded that the IMO should not undertake the work.

8. International Labor Organization (ILO)

The ILO has a constitutional mandate to assist countries in improving the working environment. Since 1919 ILO has devoted a significant proportion of its efforts in that direction, especially through standard-setting activities. The extensive list of ILO instruments that concern occupational safety and health include the Working Environment (Air Pollution, Noise and Vibration) Convention (No. 148) and Recommendation (No. 156)(1977) as well as the Safety and Health in Construction Convention (No. 167) and Recommendation (No. 175), adopted in June 1988. The ILO also adopted conventions on indigenous peoples (1989), chemicals in the workplace (1990), and agricultural work (2002), which contain provisions directly concerned with environmental protection. On January 17, 1995, ILO signed a Memorandum of Understanding Concerning Establishment of the Inter-Organization Program for the Social Management of Chemicals which created a framework for coordinating chemicals-related policies and activities with UNEP, the FAO, the WHO, the UN Industrial Development Organization, and OECD.[39] An action program on the use of chemicals at work was completed in 1996, involving assistance in designing and implementing national programs for the environmentally sound management of hazardous chemicals and their waste in five countries. An ILO technical working group has been established to elaborate a set of harmonized hazard communication tools, such as labeling, chemical safety data sheets and training. The ILO also contributed to the elaboration of the FAO convention on prior informed consent and has worked with the IMO on maritime standards.[40]

In 1994, the ILO launched an Inter-Departmental Project on Environment and the World of Work. Since that time, environmental issues have become integrated in all programs and activities of the organization in keeping with the goals set by Agenda 21. In addition to standard-setting activities, ILO aims to promote and support efforts at the international, regional and national levels to reduce occupational accidents and diseases and to

---

[39] *See* 34 I.L.M. 1311 (1995). The MOU was revised in 1996 to add ethical considerations as an integral part of the IPCS's work.

[40] In 1996, the ILO held a maritime session that adopted three new international conventions, three recommendations and a Protocol to the Merchant Shipping (Minimum Standards) Convention No. 147. The major focus of Convention 147 is accident prevention and a key feature is port state control.

improve the working environment. The Occupational Safety and Health Branch within the Working Conditions and Environment Department has prepared a draft code to prevent major hazards, a training manual on the use of chemicals at work, and dissemination of information.

9. International Civil Aviation Organization (ICAO)

The first nuisance the public experienced from civil aviation was aircraft noise and ICAO initially focused its efforts on securing quieter aircraft. ICAO also insists on the importance of compatible land-use planning and control, in order to avoid offsetting the gains of reduced engine noise with further residential developments around airports.

In the early 1980s, in response to concerns regarding air quality in the vicinity of airports, ICAO established standards to control aircraft engine emissions through an engine certification scheme. These standards, contained in Volume II of Annex 16 to the Convention on International Civil Aviation, establish limits for emissions of oxides of nitrogen (NOx), carbon monoxide, and unburned hydrocarbons from new engines during an aircraft's landing and take-off. The NOx standards were tightened in 1993 by 20 percent. Recent concerns about climate change, depletion of the ozone layer, and long-range air pollution have led to questions about the contribution of aircraft and space shuttle launch emissions to these problems. ICAO coordinates its activities on these issues with other UN bodies, but scientific information is lacking on aviation's impact on the global atmosphere. The development of a new emissions parameter that would take into account technical performances, climb and cruise emissions, new communications, navigation, surveillance and air traffic management could be an effective means to reduce fuel burning and avoiding unnecessary emissions.

10. World Trade Organization (WTO)

After World War II, the international community first envisaged an international organization governed by a comprehensive code governing all aspects of trade. Negotiations for the organization did not succeed but produced a General Agreement on Tariffs and Trade in 1947.[41] The GATT evolved as a set of normative standards and eventually developed some institutional elements through a series of eight multilateral rounds of negotiations. The last round of negotiations, known as the Uruguay Round, ended in December 1994 and led to formation of the World Trade Organization on January 1, 1995.

---

[41]   *In force* Jan. 1948.

The Agreement Establishing the WTO, signed in Marrakesh, incorporates the original GATT and adds new undertakings on five main subject matters that have impacts on environmental protection. They are the Agreement on Technical Barriers to Trade, Agreement on Sanitary and Phytosanitary Measures, Agreement on Subsidies and Countervailing Measures, Agreement on Trade-Related Aspects of Intellectual Property, and General Agreement on Trade in Services. States joining the WTO undertake to comply with all these agreements. The WTO Dispute Settlement Understanding is another important feature of the organization; it establishes procedures for resolving trade disputes and creates a Dispute Settlement Body consisting of panels and an Appellate Body. The WTO also has a Committee on Trade and the Environment (CTE) whose mandate is to identify the trade-related aspects of environmental measures and, if necessary, to make recommendations for modification of the rules of the multilateral trading system or attempt to resolve problems of policy coordination while upholding the principles of the multilateral trading system. In particular the CTE looks at the relationship between the trade rules and the use of trade measures for environmental purposes; the use of environmental charges and taxes, and environmental standards for packaging, labeling and recycling; the effect of environmental measures on developing country's market access and the environmental benefits of removing trade restrictions and distortions.

D. Regional Organizations

Almost all regional organizations have become engaged in activities in the environmental field. Organizations within Europe have the most comprehensive regulation, for several reasons. First, the process of political and legal integration is most developed in Europe. Second, Europe is very densely populated and highly industrialized, leading to greater risks of pollution. Finally, cooperation in environmental matters is facilitated by the homogeneity of economic structures and the similarity of political conceptions.

"European organizations" includes entities that are very different from one another. Pan-European organizations such as the Organization for Security and Cooperation in Europe (OSCE) are not exclusively European.[42] Similarly, all Western and Central European countries are members of the

---

[42]   The OSCE consists of 55 member countries of Europe and North America and includes the states of the Caucasus and Central Asia.

Organization for Economic Cooperation and Development (OECD) but it also has as members the United States, Canada, Mexico, Japan, Korea, Australia, and New Zealand.[43] The 45 member states of the Council of Europe now range from Iceland to Russia and Turkey. Some members of the Council of Europe also form the European Union. The United Nations Economic Commission for Europe could also be included here, but as a UN entity is discussed above.[44]

The first section discusses the Council of Europe, the OECD, the European Union, and the OSCE. The work of organizations in other regions follows: the Organization of American States (OAS), the African Union, and the organizations of Asia and the South Pacific. Finally, mention will be made of the increasingly important sub-regional and bilateral institutions.

1. Council of Europe

The oldest of the existing European institutions, the Council of Europe, was created in London May 5, 1949, and is based in Strasbourg. Today it consists of 45 states, nearly all the European countries except parts of the former Yugoslavia and the Asian republics of the former Soviet Union. The Council of Europe has sufficiently broad jurisdiction to address environmental issues, because Article 1 of its statute permits it to consider all regional questions except those relating to national defense. Its broad competence is not accompanied by equally expansive powers, however. The Committee of Ministers, its executive organ, can only adopt recommendations addressed to member states. The other principal organ, the Parliamentary Assembly, has few powers but carries considerable weight with European public opinion. In fact, Assembly debates and the resolutions it addresses to the Committee of Ministers largely reflect European political consensus and often set forth solutions which are adopted subsequently either at the European or national level.

Even prior to Stockholm, the Council of Europe took action and adopted several basic texts proclaiming principles to protect the environment. In 1962 the Council created a European Committee for the Protection of Nature and Natural Resources. Since that time, nature conservation has remained one of the principal concerns of the Council. Between 1968–1974, the Council adopted numerous declaratory texts, including the European Water Charter (1968), the Declaration of Principles on Air Pollution Control (1968), and the European Soil Charter (1972). In

---

43 T.I.A.S. No. 4891, *entered into force* Sept. 30, 1961.
44 *See* Chapter 4C.1.d.

addition the European Conference of Local Authorities, created at the initiative of the Parliamentary Assembly, adopted in 1970 a European Declaration regarding Conservation of Nature. The same year, a conference meeting to celebrate the European Year of Nature Conservation proclaimed a Declaration on the Management of the Natural Environment in Europe. The Council actively participated in the elaboration and adoption, in 1995, of the Pan-European Biological and Landscape Diversity Strategy and serves as its Secretariat and coordinator. In addition, it is responsible for several action themes of the Strategy, such as the establishment of the Pan-European Ecological Network and the Protection of Threatened Species.

The Council of Europe has concluded a considerable number of environmental treaties since its initial effort to conclude the European Agreement on the Restriction of the Use of Certain Detergents in Washing and Cleaning Products, signed September 16, 1968. The Council has adopted the Convention for the Protection of Animals during International Transport[45] and the Bern Convention on the Conservation of European Wildlife and Natural Habitats of September 19, 1979. The latter, a particularly important contribution in this field, created a permanent supervisory committee which functions within the Council of Europe. In addition, the Council of Europe drafted and adopted the 1993 Lugano Convention on Civil Liability for Damage Resulting from Activities Dangerous to the Environment, the 1998 Convention on the Protection of the Environment through Criminal Law, and the 2000 European Landscape Convention.

Among its numerous other environmental activities, the Council of Europe promotes transnational cooperation. Its efforts have produced a European Outline Convention on Transfrontier Cooperation between Territorial Communities or Authorities, adopted in Madrid on May 21, 1980. The Convention explicitly designates environmental protection and mutual assistance in case of accidents among the topics which may be the object of joint action between local or territorial authorities from different states. The Convention annexes model agreements on such questions as mutual transfrontier urban development and protection of nature, water and air.

The Council of Europe first began activities relating to regional planning at the 1970 European Conference of Ministers Responsible for Regional Planning, held in Bonn. In January 2002, the Committee of Ministers of the Council of Europe adopted Recommendation Rec(2002)1 on the guiding principles for sustainable spatial development of the European continent. In this context, the Guiding Principles recommend to member states to take account of the needs of all who presently live in Europe's regions without jeopardizing the fundamental rights and development prospects of future generations. The objectives of the Principles

---

[45]   Paris, Dec. 13, 1968.

include the conservation, enhancement and management of landscapes and of the natural, cultural and landscape heritage, as well as environmental protection, resource management and risk prevention. The text especially stresses the need to reduce environmental damage and enhance and protect natural resources and the cultural heritage.

Finally, the European Court of Human Rights, established by the European Convention on Human Rights, under the auspices of the Council of Europe, hears and decides cases alleging violations of human rights linked to environmental harm.[46]

2. *Organization for Economic Cooperation and Development (OECD)*

The OECD, successor to the former Organization for European Economic Cooperation, was founded in 1948 to administer the Marshall Plan and took its current form in 1960. It consists of all Western and Central European countries, Australia, Canada, Japan, Korea, Mexico, New Zealand, and the United States. The Commission of the European Community participates in the work of the organization.

The executive organ of OECD is a Council composed of the representatives of members states. In addition, the OECD secretariat is particularly important because OECD is primarily an organ of study and economic reflection, responsible for making an inventory of resources, analyzing and elaborating measures for the future.[47] OECD can take decisions that are obligatory for all the member states who participate in their adoption, not including states which abstain. Resolutions adopted by the Council are obligatory for the organization itself. Recommendations addressed to the member states are not binding, but do reflect the general views and intentions of the governments which vote in favor of them.

OECD activities have a sufficiently broad scope to include issues of environmental protection. As a result, in 1970 OECD created a Committee on the Environment to take over the work of some 20 other committees. Its purpose is to aid the governments of OECD member states to define their policies in regard to environmental problems, taking into account pertinent information, especially economic and scientific, and to reconcile their environmental policies with economic and social development. The Committee also is entitled to review the state of the environment in member countries. Reports on the environmental performances of OECD countries are regularly published.

---

46   *See* Chapter 15.

47   OECD has published several of its studies: Problems of Transfrontier Pollution, 1974; Legal Aspects of Transfrontier Pollution, 1977; OECD and the Environment, 1986.

In 1991, with the creation of the Joint Session on Trade and Environment Experts the OECD became the first international organization to examine, on a regular basis, the integration of trade and environmental policies.

OECD has made major contributions to the development of international environmental law. OECD recommendations, sometimes accompanied by declarations of principles, formulated the first legal definition of pollution and enunciated the basic standards applicable to transfrontier pollution. It also enunciated the obligation to inform and consult, to notify of emergency situations, the principle of equality of access between residents and non-residents, non-discrimination in the application of legislative rules, and the polluter-pays principle. Moreover, OECD has adopted precise regulations concerning some types of air and water pollution. Its standard-setting has been decisive in the regulation of chemical substances as well as toxic and dangerous wastes, including radioactive wastes.

In recent action, OECD drafted for transmission by its governments voluntary principles and standards for responsible business conduct.[48] Section V of the text affirms that enterprises should take due account of the need to protect the environment and recommends good environmental management, communication with the public and the adoption of preventive and precautionary approaches. Thus, despite its essentially economic focus, OECD has been a pioneer in international environmental law.

3. *Organization for Security and Cooperation in Europe (OSCE)*

The OSCE has 55 participating states and thus can claim to be the largest existing regional security organization. Its area includes continental Europe, the Caucasus, Central Asia, and North America, and it cooperates with Mediterranean and Asian partners. The OSCE thus brings together the Euro-Atlantic and the Euro-Asian communities "from Vancouver to Vladivostok." It succeeded to the Conference on Security and Cooperation in Europe,[49] more widely known as the Helsinki Conference, which has met regularly since the first session of all Western, Central and Eastern European states, together with the United States and the Soviet Union, opened in Helsinki in 1973.[50] The Helsinki Final Act adopted at the close of the

---

48   Guidelines for Multinational Enterprises, June 27, 2000; 40 I.L.M. 237 (2000).

49   The 1994 participating states changed the name of the body from the Conference on Security and Cooperation in Europe to the Organization for Security and Cooperation in Europe.

50   The first follow-up meetings were held in Belgrade (1977–78); Madrid (1980–83); Vienna (1989) and Copenhagen (1990).

Conference on August 1, 1975, contained a section specifically devoted to the environment. The process emphasizes cooperation, based on a conviction stated at the outset that many environmental problems, particularly in Europe, can be solved effectively through close international cooperation.

The OSCE approach to security is comprehensive and cooperative. It deals with a wide range of issues, including environmental security, because it sees the various aspects of security as interconnected and interdependent. A continuous effort is made by the OSCE participating states to enhance the complementarity of the various dimensions of security. The Organization is thus active in all phases of the conflict cycle, from early warning and conflict prevention to conflict management and post-conflict rehabilitation.

The OSCE has no legal status as a formal organization under international law and its decisions are politically but not legally binding. Nevertheless, it possesses most of the normal attributes of an international organization: standing decision-making bodies, permanent headquarters and institutions, permanent staff, regular financial resources and field offices. Most of its instruments, decisions and commitments are framed in legal language and their interpretation requires an understanding of the principles of international law and of the standard techniques of the law of treaties.

The OSCE's economic dimension involves monitoring economic and environmental developments among participating states, with the aim of alerting them to any threat of conflict; and facilitating the formulation of economic and environmental policies and initiatives to promote security in the OSCE area, particularly in participating states that are involved in a process of transition. During the CSCE era three meetings focused specifically on economic, scientific and environmental issues, beginning with a Meeting on the Protection of the Environment held in Sofia in 1989. A Charter for European Security, adopted in Istanbul on November 19, 1999, addressed the economic and environmental dimensions of OSCE's common response to the challenges it faces. Recalling the risk to security from environmental degradation and the depletion of natural resources, the Declaration stresses that economic liberty, social justice and environmental responsibility are indispensable for prosperity. Affirming the intention of the signatories to "help build vibrant civil societies" it proclaims adhesion to the 1998 Aarhus Convention on Access to Information, Public Participation in Decision-Making and Access to Justice in Environmental Matters.

4. European Union (EU)

A distinction is often made between the preceding organizations, which are generally organizations of cooperation, and the European Union, a unique agent of economic and political integration. The European Union benefits

from a true transfer of sovereignty from member states which have abandoned in its favor some of their national powers. It begins to approach a
federal state in its attributes and powers.

The European Union, originally consisting of six Western European
countries and scheduled to expand to 25 states, began as a set of three economic communities, which merged into a single entity that was transformed
into the Union. The main institutions of the European Union are the
Council of the European Union, the European Commission, the European
Parliament and the European Court of Justice. The legal instruments that
progressively integrated the member states also gradually strengthened the
provisions concerning the environment. The 1951 Paris Treaty creating the
European Coal and Steel Community, the 1957 Treaty of Rome establishing the European Economic Community and the 1957 Euratom Treaty initially had no mention of environmental matters. The first initiative was a
political decision taken outside the statutory organs of the Communities.
The heads of state or government of the then-nine member countries, meeting in Paris October 19–20, 1972, adopted a declaration proclaiming the
need to improve the quality of life, paying particular attention to nonma-
terial values and to protection of the environment. The declaration called
for development of an environmental policy and invited the Community
institutions to establish, before July 31, 1973, an action program setting
forth a precise calendar.

The Commission elaborated a Program of Action of the European
Communities on the Environment to cover the years 1974–1976[51] and other
action plans followed. On July 22, 2002, the Parliament and the Council
adopted the Sixth Community Environment Action Program to apply for
the ten years following its adoption. It aims to promote the process of integrating environmental concerns into all Community policies and activities,
incorporate new ways of working with the market, and involve citizens,
enterprises and other stakeholders in order to induce necessary changes in
both production and public and private consumption patterns that influence negatively the state of the environment. It recognizes that economic
globalization means that environmental action is increasingly needed at
international level. The key environmental priorities to be addressed by the
Community are climate change, nature and biodiversity, health and quality
of life, and natural resources and waste.[52]

Article 100 of the Rome Treaty provided the initial legal basis for action.
It authorized the European Economic Community to adopt directives[53] for

---

[51]   O.J. C 112 (12/2073).
[52]   Decision No. 1600/2002/EC, O.J. L. 242 (9/10/02).
[53]   Directives, the only form of instrument authorized by Article 100, bind
every member state to achieve the stated result, but leave to national authorities the choice of means. Regulations, obligatory in all their elements and

the approximation of legislative and administrative provisions that had a direct impact on the establishment or the functioning of the Common Market, particularly when disparities among the provisions distorted conditions of competition in the Common Market. Article 235 of the EEC treaty also could be used as it permitted action by the Community when necessary to achieve one of the aims in the functioning of the Common Market.

The Community adopted over 100 legal texts under this regime. Environmental measures dating from this period based exclusively on Article 100 include directives concerning the lead content of petrol,[54] detergents,[55] and the permissible sound level and exhaust system of motorcycles.[56] The European Court of Justice confirmed the appropriateness of legislative reliance on Article 100 in a decision in which the validity of Directive 75/716, relating to the maximum sulphur content of liquid fuel was at issue. The judgment reflects an understanding of the potential for competitive disadvantage from environmental protection measures:

> It is by no means ruled out that provisions on the environment may be based upon Article 100 of the Treaty. Provisions which are made necessary by considerations relating to the environment and health may be a burden upon undertakings to which they apply and if there is no harmonization of national provisions on the matter, competition may be appreciably distorted.[57]

Most of the Community's environmental legislation during this period is based, however, both on Article 100 and Article 235, including the directives on pollution caused by certain dangerous substances discharged into the aquatic environment of the Community;[58] combating of air pollution from industrial plants;[59] the major accident hazards of certain industrial plants;[60] and regulation of toxic and dangerous waste.[61]

The joint use of both Articles 100 and 235 for environmental protection was confirmed by the Court of Justice in a decision that marks the first time the Court recognized environmental protection as one of the Community's

---

directly applicable in every member state, are adopted in the field of environmental protection generally when the provisions concern external trade of the Communities, for example, banning the importation of certain hazardous substances.

[54] Directive 85/210, O.J. L 96/25.
[55] Directive 73/404, O.J. L 347/51.
[56] Directive 78/1015, O.J. L 349/21.
[57] Case 92/79 *Commission v. Italy* (1980) E.C.R. 1115.
[58] Directive 76/464, O.J. L 129/23 (1976).
[59] Directive 84/360, O.J. L 188/20 (1984).
[60] Directive 82/501, O.J. L 230/1 (1982).
[61] Directive 78/319, O.J. L 84/43 (1978).

essential objectives. It was an important step for the further development of Community action in this field. In the case, concerning the validity of a directive on the disposal of waste oils, the Court held:

> In the first place it should be observed that the principle of free-dom of trade is not to be viewed in absolute terms but is subject to certain limits justified by the objectives of general interest pursued by the Community, provided that the rights in question are not sub-stantively impaired. There is no reason to conclude that the directive has exceeded those limits. The directive must be seen in the perspective of environmental protection, which is one of the Community's essential objective.[62]

During this period the EC became a contracting party to the major international treaties on nature protection and biological diversity, includ-ing CITES,[63] the Bonn Convention on Migratory Species,[64] and the Bern Convention on the Conservation of European Wildlife and Natural Habitats.[65] It also adopted directives of general scope relating to the assess-ment of the effects of certain public and private projects on the environ-ment,[66] integrated pollution prevention and control, the freedom of access to information on the environment,[67] and to eco-labeling.[68]

An important change in the action of the EC in the field of environ-mental protection resulted from the adoption, on February 27, 1986, of the Single European Act (SEA), which superseded the original founding treaties. The SEA instrument settled the issue of Community competence in respect to environmental protection. Later the SEA was replaced by the Maastricht Treaty on European Union (TEU) of February 7, 1992 which was modified in turn by the Treaty of Amsterdam adopted on October 2, 1997. The latter amended some provisions of the TEU and renumbered them. The following discussion refers to the consolidated text approved in Amsterdam.[69]

---

[62]   Case 240/83, ABDHU (1985) E.C.R. 531.
[63]   Regulation 3626/82 Dec. 3, 1982, O.J. L. 384 (12/31/82).
[64]   O.J. L 210 (7/19/82).
[65]   O.J. L 38 (2/10/82).
[66]   Directives 85/337, O.J. L. 175 (7/7/85) and 97/11, O.J. L. 5 (3/13/97).
[67]   Directive 90/313, O.J. L. 158 (6/21/90).
[68]   Regulation 880/92, O.J. L. 58 (2/27/97).
[69]   Maastricht, Feb. 7, 1992, EMuT, 992:11; EU Consolidated Versions of the Treaty of European Union and the Treaty Establishing the European Community, O.J. C 32 (12/24/02).

The TEU includes provisions designed specifically to confirm the Community's task in developing a Community environmental policy. TEU Article 3 sets forth the objectives of the EU and includes a policy in the field of environmental protection. Article 174(2) adds that the Community policy on the environment shall aim at a high level of protection taking into account the diversity of situations in the various regions of the Community. Further details can be found in Articles 174 to 176. Article 174(1) designates the four aims of the Community policy: (1) preserving, protecting and improving the quality of the environment, (2) protecting human health, (3) prudent and rational utilization of natural resources, and (4) prompting measures at international level to deal with regional or worldwide environmental problems.

Article 174(2) proclaims that the Community's environmental policy shall be based on the precautionary principle and on the principles that preventive action should be taken, that environmental damage should as a priority be rectified at source and that the polluter should pay. According to Article 174(3), in preparing its policy on the environment, the Community shall take account of available scientific and technical data; environmental conditions in the various regions of the Community; the potential benefits and costs of action or lack of action; the economic and social development of the Community as a whole and the balanced development of its regions (Art. 174(3)).

Problems may arise in reconciling the conditions which must be taken into account on the one hand and the basic principles proclaimed by Article 174(1) on the other. The precautionary principle implies that there can be lack of full scientific certainty, which means that taking account of available scientific and technical data will not always afford a solution. Similarly, the "polluter pays principle" should be reconciled with the economic and social development of the Community and, in particular, with the balanced development of its regions. The latter could imply the appropriateness of subsidies in order to help polluters suppress or minimize the pollution they cause. Article 175(5) may help. It provides that without prejudice to the principle that the polluter should pay, if a measure based on a decision of the Council taken in conformity with the usual procedure involves costs deemed disproportionate for the public authorities of a member state, the Council shall, in the act adopting that measure, lay down appropriate provisions in the form of either temporary derogations and/or financial support from a special fund of EC.

While the TEU confers specific powers upon the Community in the field of environmental protection, it also establishes limits on those powers. In particular:

(a) Such powers are to be exercised only if the Community's environmental objectives can be attained better at the Community level than at the level of the individual Member States. This flows from the principle of subsidiarity, one of the basic principles of the Community.[70]

(b) According to Article 174(2), harmonization measures for environmental protection shall include, where appropriate, a safeguard clause allowing member states to take provisional measures, for non-economic environmental reasons, subject to a Community inspection procedure.

(c) The protective measures adopted pursuant to the environmental principles proclaimed by the Treaty do not prevent any member state from maintaining or introducing more stringent protective measures. Such measures must be compatible with the Treaty and be notified to the Commission (Art. 176). Concerns about the impact of environmental measures on free trade are evident and arise not only inside the European Community but also in the large context of globalization.

(d) Finally, while Article 174(4) recognizes the capacity and the authority of the Community to conclude arrangements with non-member states or other international institutions in the field of environmental protection, it also affirms that such authority does not deprive the Member States of the right to negotiate in international bodies and to conclude international agreements.

Further limitations are found in a Protocol on the application of the principles of subsidiarity and proportionality of the Treaty of Amsterdam. It requires the EC to justify the relevance of its proposals with regard to the principle of subsidiarity and take due account of the need for any burden, whether financial or administrative, imposed upon government or industry.[71] EC action cannot go beyond what is necessary to achieve the objectives of the Treaty, must be as simple as possible, and leave as much scope for national decisions as possible. Framework directives are preferred over detailed measures.

The Council is the only institution that directly represents the governments of the member states. The Council consists of a "representative of each Member State at ministerial level, authorized to commit the government of

---

[70] According to Article 3B of the Amsterdam Treaty "In areas which do not fall within its exclusive competence, the Community shall take action, in accordance with the principle of subsidiarity, only if and in so far as the objectives of the proposed action cannot be sufficiently achieved by the Member States and can therefore, by reason of the scale or effects of the proposed action, be better achieved by the Community."

[71] Protocol on the application of the principles of subsidiarity and proportionality, Treaty of Amsterdam, Protocols annexed to the Treaty establishing the European Community, consolidated version, O.J. C 340 (11/10/97).

that Member State" (TEU, Art. 146). The ministers who meet are specialists, chosen by their government according to the issue which is discussed. The environment ministers meet regularly two or three times a year as the Council of Ministers. The most important acts which the Council adopts are regulations and directives. In both cases the Council adopts such texts after submission of a proposal by the Commission and required consultations. The Council acts either upon unanimous or weighed majority vote.

The Commission has 20 members chosen by agreement of the governments of the member states. There are one or two members from each of them. Commissioners act in the Community's interest and not on behalf of their individual States. The Commission is appointed by unanimous agreement of the member states for a five-year term and can only be removed by vote of censure from the European Parliament. The two principal functions of the Commission are to propose Community policy to implement the treaties and to provide for the administration of the Community. In regard to the first activity, the Commission prepares, discusses, and adopts preliminary drafts of proposed standards for submission to the Council.

The second main function is foreseen by TEU Article 211 which provides that the Commission must "ensure that the provisions of the Treaty and the measures taken by the institutions pursuant thereto are applied." The latter authority is exclusive and may not be delegated to any other organ or institution. In supervising implementation of the Treaty and of other Community obligations, the Commission acts where it finds a Treaty infringement, first by sending a formal note, then by delivering a "reasoned opinion." Subsequently, if further action is needed, the Commission may bring a judicial proceeding against the involved member state or entity. It also can take other measures, when, *e.g.*, a member state does not incorporate or apply Community rules, by warning it that other members states could take sanctions against it.

The European Parliament has 626 members directly elected by the people of the member states and serving for a period of five years. Members of the European Parliament do not sit by nationality but according to political affiliation. The Parliament participates in the formulation of EC Law and the Community budget as well as in monitoring the activities of the European Commission and Council. The Parliament has set up a special committee on environmental questions, public health, and consumer protection. Its main influence on legislation lies in its right to be consulted, its right to move amendments and its power to delay legislation by withholding its opinion until the Commission responds to its proposed amendments. When the Council has transmitted to Parliament a Common or Interim Position it adopted and Parliament initially rejects or amends it, the Council must convene a "Conciliation Committee" to negotiate a compromise. Within specified time limits, the Council representatives and the parliamentary representatives must attempt to negotiate a common position.

Once achieved, the Council and Parliament vote on the Committee proposal, by qualified and absolute majorities, respectively. Unless approved by both, the proposal lapses. If the Committee fails to achieve a common proposal, the Council may go forward with its draft unless the Parliament rejects it by absolute majority.

Once a regulation or directive is adopted, the European Court of Justice ensures correct interpretation and application of its provisions. The Court is composed of 15 judges and eight advocates-general, the former organized in chambers of three, five or seven judges. There is one judge sitting for each member state. The advocates-general are also nominated by member states. The Court has jurisdiction to settle disputes within the Community and to award damages. It may review the validity of acts of the Council or the Commission and give judgments on actions by member states, the Council or the Commission when it is alleged that there has been legal incompetence, errors of substantial form, infringement of the treaties or abuse of power. Any individual or company may appeal a decision addressed to it, or an act which, although in the form of a regulation or decision addressed to another person, is of direct and individual concern.

In 1988 a Court of First Instance was set up, consisting of 15 judges nominated by member states. Its jurisdiction extends to direct actions brought by natural or legal persons, whether for annulment or damages. Appeals may be taken to the European Court of Justice, but only on points of law.

Two bodies of consultative character can play a role in the legislative process of the EC. The Economic and Social Committee ensures the involvement of all economic and social groups in the development of the EC: it represents employers, workers and various interest groups from agriculture, transportation, the professions and consumers. Its members are appointed by the Council. A Committee of the Regions represents regional and local communities, its members are equally appointed by the Council.

The Council created a European Environmental Agency by Regulation adopted on May 7, 1990. Its main objective is to provide technical and scientific support to the Community and member states regarding environmental protection. Unlike other organs of the Community, the Agency is open to non-member countries who share the environmental concerns of the member states. The Agency is directed by a management board consisting of one representative of each member state and two representatives from the Commission. In addition, the European Parliament designates two "scientific personalities" to the Board. The Agency, the functions of which are mainly non-political, is based in Copenhagen.

During its existence of almost half a century the EC has developed comprehensive legislation in environmental matters. Following the general trend in domestic as well as in international environmental legislation, its policy shifted from indirect approaches towards distinct measures aiming at the protection of water, or of air or of wildlife. During the 1990s the EC demonstrated a general trend towards integrated protection. Most human activities which can have an impact on the environment thus enter the scope of EC environmental legislation. At the same time economic aspects of the proposed measures as well as the generally proclaimed need for sustainable development are increasingly taken into account. The proposed European Charter of Fundamental Rights and Freedoms of the European Union, which falls short of proclaiming a human right to environment, expresses well this trend. Its Article 37 affirms that "a high level of environmental protection and the improvement of the quality of the environment must be integrated into the policies of the Union and ensured in accordance with the principle of sustainable development."

5. Organization of American States (OAS)

The OAS is the oldest regional political organization in the world, dating back to the First International Conference of American States held in Washington D.C. in 1890. Today the OAS is made up of 33 states of the Western Hemisphere.[72] Although the OAS Charter does not mention the environment and, as amended, places heavy emphasis on economic development,[73] the Organization has long undertaken environmental activities, particularly concerning nature protection.

The Eighth International Conference of American States, meeting in Lima, Peru, in December 1938, recommended the establishment of a committee of experts to study problems relating to nature and wildlife in the American republics and called for preparation of a draft convention for nature and wildlife protection.[74] The Executive Council of the Pan American

---

[72] Antigua and Barbuda, Argentina, The Bahamas, Barbados, Bolivia, Brazil, Canada, Chile, Colombia, Costa Rica, Cuba, Dominica, Dominican Republic, Ecuador, El Salvador, Grenada, Guatemala, Haiti, Honduras, Jamaica, Mexico, Nicaragua, Panama, Paraguay, Peru, St. Kitts and Nevis, Saint Lucia, Saint Vincent and the Grenadines, Suriname, Trinidad and Tobago, the United States, Uruguay and Venezuela.

[73] Chapter VII, added by the Protocol of Cartagena de Indias in 1985, calls upon member states to cooperate for integral development. Article 32 refers to development of a more just economic and social order as a primary responsibility of each country. The basic development goals are listed in Article 33 without reference to the environment. Charter of the Organization of American States, Apr. 30, 1948; 119 U.N.T.S. 3; 2 U.S.T. 2416; T.I.A.S. No. 2361; *amended* Feb. 27, 1967, 721 U.N.T.S. 326; 21 U.S.T. 607; T.I.A.S. No. 6847; *amended* Dec. 5, 1985, O.A.S.T.S. 1-D; OEA/Ser.A/2 Rev. 2.

[74] Resolution XXVIII: Protection of Nature and Wildlife, Eighth International Conference of American States (Dec. 1938).

Union (today the Permanent Council of the OAS) convened the recommended meeting of experts which prepared the Convention on Nature Protection and Wildlife Preservation in the Western Hemisphere.[75] The Convention was adopted in Washington June 4, 1940. States parties agree to adopt certain measures of mutual cooperation to preserve nature by establishing parks, reserves and protected areas and to take all steps necessary to administer and conserve wildlife and nature and to protect threatened species. The OAS Secretariat is depository of the Convention.

Since enactment of the 1940 Convention, the OAS has convened several inter-American meetings on environmental protection, including the 1965 Mar Del Plata Conference on Problems Related to the Conservation of Renewable Natural Resources of the Continent. Several sub-regional multilateral agreements and numerous bilateral treaties also have been concluded. Since 1977 the Secretariat has been instrumental in encouraging oil spill contingency planning in the wider Caribbean region, leading to adoption of the First Protocol of the Cartagena Convention for the Protection of the Marine Environment.

In 1988, the Inter-American Juridical Committee (IJC) called for creation of an Inter-American System of Nature Conservation.[76] The IJC resolution recommended the creation of a permanent inter-American mechanism utilizing the existing institutions of the OAS to identify environmental problems common to the countries of the Americas, link the numerous multilateral and bilateral agreements that cover various geographic and subject areas, and coordinate efforts to optimize regional management of natural resources. Because of this broad focus, the IJC recommended the creation of a "system" and not the adoption of a "treaty." The General Assembly considered the report and instructed the Secretariat to conduct a multidisciplinary study aimed at creating the proposed system.[77]

The Secretariat study was completed in November 1989 and presented to the Permanent Council of the OAS.[78] The study analyzes the Americas' natural and developmental features and reviews prior regional action. It then discusses the objectives, functions, alternative structures and courses of action necessary to establish the Inter-American System of Nature Conservation. The alternatives considered are (1) adoption of a convention; (2) adoption of a program of action and the subsequent establishment of a permanent commission, and (3) creation of a technical office to implement the 1940 Convention. In June 1990, the OAS General Assembly instructed the Permanent Council as a priority matter to establish a special

---

[75] 161 U.N.T.S. 193; 56 Stat. 1354; T.S. No. 981; 3 Bevans 630.
[76] AG/doc.2282/88.
[77] AG/RES.948 (XVIII-0/88).
[78] OEA/Ser.G, CP/doc.2036/89, Nov. 3, 1989.

working group to review the Secretariat study and present its conclusions and recommendations by December 31, 1990.

The Working Group report proposes establishment of the first OAS environmental program of action and subsequent establishment of a permanent commission on the environment. It does not recommend adoption of a new regional convention, at least at first. There is concern that the process of drafting a new agreement could delay effective measures which are currently needed. In addition, the lack of political will among some states in the region, reflected in a few key OAS officials, might prevent adoption of effective conventional norms. The reality is that in spite of increased environmental damage from air, water and soil pollution, and the particular impact of acid rain on archaeological ruins, most national and regional efforts are consumed by poverty and debt. The developing countries of the Western Hemisphere have an outstanding debt which is greater than that of Africa or Asia. The program of action thus will be forced to consider implementation of environmental protection within an economic context very different from that of the EC.

In June 1996, the OAS created a Unit of Sustainable Development and Environment within the Office of the Secretary General. It is the principal entity within the General Secretariat responsible for matters directly related to sustainable development and the environment and for providing technical and administrative support to the Organization's efforts to become the principal inter-American forum for formulating regional policy in this field. The Unit has four basic functions: (1) to provide support, in the areas of its expertise, to the fora and organs of the OAS, and to participate in the pertinent technical dialogue in hemispheric and subregional conferences, workshops, and seminars; (2) to formulate and selectively execute technical cooperation projects within its field of technical competence, including the integrated development of water resources, especially international river basins; sustainable development of border areas; coastal-zone management; biodiversity and conservation; environmental management in emerging trade corridors and the mitigation of natural disasters; (3) to facilitate the exchange of information related to sustainable development and environment in the region; and (4) to support efforts to promote coordination and cooperation among agencies in the pursuit of goals established by the member states of the OAS. The Unit of Sustainable Development and Environment has undertaken major projects in the region and within the OAS Secretariat has been assigned the primary responsibility for the follow-up of the Summit on Sustainable Development, which took place in Bolivia in December 1996.

An important step forward was made with the Declaration of Santa Cruz de la Sierra and the Plan of Action for the Sustainable Development of the Americas adopted by the Heads of State and Government of the American States on December 9, 1996. The declaration is based on the Rio

Declaration and on Agenda 21. The signatories confirm their intention to assess the environmental impacts of their policies, strategies, programs and projects nationally and in the framework of international agreements, to ensure that adverse environmental effects are identified, prevented, minimized or mitigated as appropriate. They intend to enhance the progress of international environmental law and promote the reform and modernization of national laws, as appropriate, to reflect sustainable development concepts. Accordingly, the Plan of Action lists a series of initiatives which the governments pledge to take concerning fields such as sustainable agriculture and forests, water resources and coastal areas management, mining, and energy production.

6. South Pacific Regional Organizations

The South Pacific region contains about 10,000 small islands scattered through a hemispheric ocean. The region may contain major sources of non-renewable resources and is the largest source of renewable marine living resources. It is also an area which has been harmed by nuclear tests and is further threatened by the dumping of radioactive waste. Another important concern is the prevention or mitigation of the greenhouse effect. In this context, there are two regional organizations which separately and cooperatively have elaborated legal instruments to protect the vast Pacific territory.

The South Pacific Commission, created in 1947 by Australia, France, the Netherlands, New Zealand, the United Kingdom, and the United States, now has nine participating states, with the addition of Fiji, Nauru, Papua New Guinea and Western Samoa.[79] Only 2 percent of the 30 million square kilometers within the mandate of this region consists of land.

The Commission is a consultative and advisory body which studies, formulates and recommends measures regarding, *inter alia*, fisheries and forestry. The Commission is composed of two Commissioners appointed by each of the member states. Within the Commission each state votes once for itself and once for each territory it administers. The South Pacific Conference which regularly meets is an advisory body to the Commission,

---

[79]   The 1947 Agreement has been amended by the Agreement Extending the Territorial Scope of the South Pacific Commission (Nov. 7, 1951); Agreement relating to the Frequency of Sessions of the South Pacific Commission (Apr. 5, 1954); Agreement Amending the Agreement Establishing the South Pacific Commission (Oct. 6, 1964); and Annex to the Agreement Establishing the South Pacific Commission. Annex II, Proceedings of the 35th Session of the South Pacific Commission (1972). For a discussion of South Pacific regional organizations, *see* B. Cicin-Sain & R.W. Knecht, *The Emergence of a Regional Ocean Regime in the South Pacific*, 16 Ecol. L.Q. 171 (1989).

representing each state and territory within the geographic scope of the Commission.

Although the Commission and Conference were originally established to promote economic development, environmental issues have become increasingly important. As a result, the Commission launched a Special Project on Conservation of Nature and Natural Resources in July 1974, working with IUCN and UNEP. The project resulted in the 1976 Convention on Conservation of Nature in the South Pacific (Apia) and the Comprehensive Environmental Management Program.

In 1971, another Pacific group was formed, the South Pacific Forum. Without formal structure or permanent secretariat, the Forum of 15 states[80] meets annually in different capitals throughout the region.

Both the South Pacific Commission and the Forum have been involved in adopting recent instruments concerning the Pacific region. Based on a suggestion of the South Pacific Commission, a coordinating body began work with UNEP in 1980 to prepare a regional Conference on the Human Environment in the South Pacific, held in 1982. Part of UNEP's regional seas program, the Conference adopted a South Pacific Declaration on Natural Resources and the Environment, an action plan for resource management, and an agreement on administrative and financial arrangements to implement the action plan.

After four years of work on the action plan known as the South Pacific Regional Environment Program, a 1986 conference in Noumea adopted the Convention for the Protection of the Natural Resources and Environment of the South Pacific Region[81] and two protocols, one relating to pollution emergencies and the other the prevention of pollution by dumping. Administration of the Convention and protocols is assigned to the South Pacific Commission.

On the issue of nuclear testing and dumping of radioactive wastes, the South Pacific Forum has taken the lead. Australia introduced the idea of a Pacific nuclear-free zone at the 14th meeting of the Forum in 1983. The 15 Forum in 1984 adopted the proposal leading to the South Pacific Nuclear Free Zone Treaty, signed in Raratonga, Cook Islands, August 6, 1985.[82] The Treaty of Raratonga prohibits the testing, manufacture, acquisition and stationing of nuclear weapons in the territory of the states parties, as well as the dumping of nuclear wastes at sea.[83]

---

[80] Australia, the Cook Islands, the Federated States of Micronesia, Fiji, Kiribati, Marshall Islands, Nauru, New Zealand, Niue, Papua New Guinea, Solomon Islands, Tonga, Tuvalu, Vanuatu, and Western Samoa.

[81] Noumea, Nov. 25, 1986; 26 I.L.M. 38.

[82] 24 I.L.M. 1440 (1985).

[83] Arts. 3, 5, 6–7. The geographic scope of the Inter-American Treaty for the Prohibition of Nuclear Weapons in Latin America, known as the Treaty of

Another concern of the South Pacific states is the depletion of fishing stocks due to unregulated driftnet fishing. During 1989 the South Pacific Forum and South Pacific Conference met to develop a response to the problem. In November 1989, 20 Pacific states and territories met and adopted a Convention for the Prohibition of Fishing with Long Driftnets in the South Pacific.[84] Two protocols containing implementation and enforcement measures were adopted on October 20, 1990.[85] Protocol I is open to countries which fish in the South Pacific region, while Protocol II is open to all Pacific rim states.

On the other side of the Pacific, Peru, Ecuador, Chile and Colombia are members of the South Pacific Permanent Commission. Created in 1954,[86] the Commission acts with regard to common interests in the states' exclusive economic zones and also takes common action to protect the marine environment from pollution. In 1987, the Ministers of Foreign Affairs of the four countries declared the Commission to be the appropriate regional organization to implement measures required by UNCLOS regarding conservation and utilization of marine living resources.

7. Organization of African Unity/African Union

The OAU, established in large part to stimulate the end of colonialism in Africa, considered environmental concerns from the time it was founded. Africa is home to extraordinary wildlife. The OAU took action to protect this resource through the conclusion of the 1968 African Convention on the Conservation of Nature and Natural Resources.[87] The Convention called on states parties to protect natural resources by all necessary measures to ensure conservation, utilization and development in the bests interests of the people. Article IX called for regulation of trade in certain species. The Convention was revised and updated in July 2003, as discussed in Chapter 8.D.2.

Tlatelolco extends outwards to meet the area covered by the Raratonga Treaty. The two treaties plus the Antarctic Treaty make the entire area of the South Pacific a nuclear-free zone. However, the Treaty of Tlatelolco does not prohibit the dumping of nuclear wastes within the area it covers. Treaty for the Prohibition of Nuclear Weapons in Latin America (Feb. 14, 1967).

84   Wellington, Nov. 24, 1989.

85   *Id.* at 1462.

86   The South Pacific Permanent Commission was created by agreement between Chile, Ecuador, and Peru at the Second Conference on the Exploitation and Conservation of Marine Resources of the South Pacific, Dec. 4, 1954, in Lima, Peru. *Law and Regulations on the Regime of the Territorial Sea*, U.N. Doc. ST/LEG/SER.B/6, U.N. Sales No. 1957.v.2 (1957). Colombia became a member in 1979.

87   Sept. 15, 1968.

In 1964, the OAU adopted a Declaration on the Denuclearization of Africa. Three decades later, in 1996, in cooperation with the United Nations and the IAEA, it adopted the Treaty of Pelindaba[88] establishing an African Nuclear Weapons Free Zone. Article 1 establishes the zone as comprising the African continent, island state members of the OAU and islands considered by the OAU to be part of Africa. The Treaty bans nuclear testing and regulates the dumping of radioactive wastes within the zone. In a more general agreement concerning wastes, the best known of the African agreements on pollution is the Bamako Convention on the Ban of Import Into Africa and the Control of Transboundary Movement and Management of Hazardous Wastes Within Africa,[89] signed by all 51 members of the OAU. The Convention generally bans the import of hazardous waste generated outside Africa, calling unauthorized and illegal dumping a crime against the African continent.

Taking an innovative approach to environmental protection, the 1981 African Charter on Human and Peoples Rights, adopted under the auspices of the OAU, was the first international human rights instrument to include the right "to a general satisfactory environment" among its guarantees.

Despite its successes and contributions to the development of international environmental law, the OAU has not maintained environmental protection as a high priority, as reflected in the new Charter of the African Union which fails to mention the environment. This lack of emphasis may be due in part to concern for economic development in the world's poorest region, but also may reflect a shift towards sub-regional and ecosystem approaches seen in the Congo Basin initiative, the 1994 Lusaka Agreement on criminal enforcement of wildlife treaties in East Africa, and the Southern African Center for Ivory Marketing.

E. Sub-Regional and Bilateral Organizations

Sub-regional and bilateral treaties that are partly or wholly devoted to environmental protection frequently establish permanent agencies to assure equitable sharing and efficient utilization of resources. Generally their features are similar to those of other international organizations: governmental participation, permanent secretariats or organs, specified functions and powers. The number of such treaties is extremely high: for water resources alone there are perhaps 600 international treaties concerning over 200 river basins shared by two or more states.[90] Examples of bilateral

---

[88]   Apr. 11, 1996; G.A. Res. A/50/426.

[89]   Bamako, Jan. 29, 1991.

[90]   *See* J. Linnerooth, *The Danube River Basin: Negotiating Settlements to Transboundary Environmental Issues*, 30 NAT. RES. J. 629 (1990).

and sub-regional agencies are discussed in various chapters, especially those concerning the protection of inland waters, atmospheric pollution, and integrated protection.

In Africa the Niger River Commission was created in 1964 between the nine riparian countries to promote and coordinate all matters related to exploitation of the basin resources. Its functions were expanded in 1980 when it became the Niger River Authority. It now insures an integrated developmental program for all Niger basin water resource activities.[91] The functions of the Authority include collecting, centralizing, standardizing, disseminating and exchanging data, coordinating and considering plans and projects, making recommendations, monitoring research and works of member states, and formulating coordinated plans.[92] Article 4 of the 1963 agreement[93] requires riparian states to closely cooperate with regard to the study and execution of any project likely to have an appreciable effect on features of the river, its tributaries and sub-tributaries, including the sanitary conditions of their waters and the biological characteristics of their fauna and flora. To achieve this cooperation, the riparian states agree to inform the Commission at the earliest stage, of all studies and works upon which they propose to embark and to abstain from carrying out any works likely to pollute the waters, or any modification likely to affect biological characteristics of its fauna and flora without adequate notice to and consultation with the Commission.[94]

On a bilateral level, numerous boundary commissions exist which exercise jurisdiction over shared natural resources.[95] For example, the United

---

[91] Convention creating the Niger Basin Authority, Nov. 21, 1980, *reprinted in U.N. Treaties Concerning the Utilization of International Water Courses for Other Purposes than Navigation*, 13 Nat. Res. Water Ser. 56, U.N. Sales No. E/F.84.II A.7.

[92] Other African Commissions include the Senegal River Basin Management Organization, created in 1972, the Lake Chad Basin Commission and the Organization for the Development of the Gambia River Basin. In Asia, there is a Committee for the Lower Mekong River and the Permanent Indus Commission, established in 1960. For a description of these Commissions, *see* Dante Caponera, *Patterns of Cooperation in International Water Law: Principles and Institutions, in* TRANSBOUNDARY RESOURCES LAW 19 (L. TECLAFF & A. UTTON eds.).

[93] Niamey Act regarding Navigation and Economic Cooperation between the States of the Niger Basin (Oct. 26, 1963).

[94] Niamey Agreement concerning the River Niger Commission and the Navigation and Transport on the River Niger, Art. 12 (Nov. 25, 1964).

[95] In addition to those discussed, there are bilateral commissions established between Argentina-Paraguay, Agreement Concerning a Study on the Parana River, June 15, 1971, OEA Rios y Lagos Internacinales 5119 (1971); Ecuador-Peru, Agreement on the Use of Binational Basins Puyango-Tumbes and Catamayo Chire, Sept. 27, 1971, 385 Registro Oficial (Ecuador) 1 (1972); Finland-Sweden, Treaty Concerning Frontier Waters; 825 U.N.T.S. 191; Finland-

States and Mexico created an International Boundary Commission in 1889 to examine and settle boundary demarcation disputes. This Commission was replaced and its functions expanded in 1944 upon adoption of the Water Utilization Treaty,[96] which established the International Boundary and Water Commission (IBWC). It is responsible for the application of the treaty, the regulation and exercise of the rights and obligations which the two governments assume under the treaty and the settlement of all disputes between the parties. However, the Commission is authorized to act as an arbitral tribunal to settle disputes only with the permission of both nations, which seldom occurs; thus the Commission acts primarily as an administrative body. The IBWC is composed of two national sections of technical engineers and legal advisors. Each section reports directly to its nation's foreign office for policy guidance. Since 1944, the IBWC has primarily been concerned with construction of flood control and municipal sewage treatment works along the border, including joint waterway management projects. The treaty contains no substantive obligations or principles for water quality protection and the role of the Commission has been limited; however, recent agreements have expanded its functions.

The U.S. and Canada also set up an International Joint Commission under the terms of the 1909 treaty for the protection of boundary waters between the two countries. The Commission is composed of six members, three named by each government. It takes its decisions by majority vote. The Commission's jurisdiction consists of a power of prior authorization for certain works, a function of consultation or inquiry, and even an arbitral role for disputes which the states agree to submit to it. However, to date the latter power has never been utilized. In practice, the most important function of the Joint Commission has been to serve as a consultative organ. Its action led to the conclusion of the November 22, 1978, agreement on water quality in the Great Lakes. In addition, the Canada-United States Agreement on Air Quality (Ottawa, March 13, 1991), establishes a bilateral Air Quality Committee composed of an equal number of members representing each party. The Committee reviews progress made in the implementation of the agreement, including general and specific objectives; prepares and submits to the parties a progress report every two years; and refers each progress report to the International Joint Commission for action. The Air Quality Committee releases the progress report to the public after its submission to

---

U.S.S.R., Treaty Concerning Frontier Watercourses, Apr. 2, 1964; 537 U.N.T.S. and nearly all Central and Eastern European States. *See* Caponera, *supra* note 92, at 19.

    [96]   Treaty Relating to the Utilization of Waters of the Colorado and Tijuana Rivers and of the Rio Grande, Feb. 3, 1944; 59 Stat. 1219; T.S. No. 994; 3 U.N.T.S. 313. *See also* Chapter 10D.2.

the parties. The pre-existing International Joint Commission may hold hearings on the progress reports, but shall in any case, invite comments on the reports and synthesize these for the parties. The synthesis is also released to the public after its submission to the Parties.

Finally, the environmental side agreement of the North American Free Trade Agreement set up a Commission on Environmental Cooperation (CEC), consisting of one high-level representative from each of the three parties.[97] It also creates a 15-member Joint Public Advisory Committee, with equal national representation. The CEC Secretariat reports regularly to the commission on the state of the environment in the three countries and on efforts to make improvements, particularly in enforcement of each country's own environmental standards. The public as well as governmental and non-governmental organizations may file complaints that such standards are not being applied. If the Secretariat decides that complaints show a "consistent pattern of failure" of enforcement, it can require a response from the government involved and submit a report to the commission. If the dispute is not settled within 60 days, the Commission by two-thirds vote will appoint a five-member panel, drawn from a roster of 45 environmental experts to conduct public hearings.

The panel can call for the government involved to submit an action plan to fix the problem. To enforce its decisions, the panel can impose fines on the offending government. If the fines are not paid, the other parties may impose sanctions of pre-NAFTA tariffs.

F. Institutions Established by Multilateral Environmental Conventions

A common feature of multilateral environmental agreements can be observed in the institutional structures and procedures they establish. The pattern of institutions includes a plenary Conference or Meeting of the Parties (COP or MOP), a secretariat, and scientific committees or other subsidiary commissions. Article 7(2) of the Framework Convention on Climate Change is typical in providing the mandate for its COP: "The Conference of the Parties, as the supreme body of this Convention, shall keep under regular review the implementation of the Convention and any related legal instruments that the Conference of the Parties may adopt, and shall make, within its mandate, the decisions necessary to promote the effective implementation of the Convention." Article 7 goes on to grant a number of specific powers to the COP: periodically examine the Convention and institutions to keep them current; promote and facilitate the exchange of information on and coordinate implementation of the Convention by par-

---

[97] Canada-Mexico-United States: *North American Agreement on Environmental Cooperation*, Sept. 8–14, 1993. See Chapter 17E.2.

ties; promote development and refinement of scientific methodologies relevant to the Convention; undertake compliance review; adopt and publish reports on implementation; mobilize financial resources; establish subsidiary bodies and review their reports; adopt rules of procedure for all bodies; seek and utilize appropriate services and cooperate with other international organizations and non-governmental bodies; and "exercise such other functions as are required for the achievement of the objective of the Convention as well as all other functions assigned to it under the Convention."

Treaty organs thus serve as compliance monitoring bodies, but also act in a quasi-legislative capacity, making decisions, interpreting the principal agreement, and adopting recommendations, plans of action, amendments and protocols to achieve the goals of the instrument. They set the policy for most treaty regimes, act as information clearing-houses, and promote scientific research. It is these bodies that maintain the flexibility and responsiveness of international environmental treaties and they are thus of crucial importance to the effectiveness of the agreements.

The crucial function of reviewing implementation of a convention is normally conducted by discussing reports submitted by states parties as well as other public information concerning measures that the contracting parties have taken in order to ensure the effectiveness of the provisions of the agreement. In some cases COPs discuss information provided by NGOs or even individuals. COPs can adopt recommendations for the guidance of all the contracting parties and in some cases address recommendations to individual states parties.

Several conventions invest their COPs with the power to adopt amendments to the convention according to a special procedure, allowing the convention to be adapted to new circumstances to enhance its effectiveness. In addition the COP often may draft and adopt additional protocols; this function may constitute one of the most important contributions of COPs to achieving the goals of the concerned treaty. The role of the 1987 Montreal Protocol in the implementation of the 1985 Vienna Ozone Convention is the most developed example. The Kyoto Protocol could initiate a similar process concerning climate change. The Kyoto Protocol makes it possible to progress towards the implementation of the principles of the UN FCCC by requiring certain countries to meet quantified emission limitation and reduction commitments with respect to six greenhouse gases. When such protocols are adopted, the instruments can have separate plenary bodies, as is the case with the Conference of the Parties of the Vienna Ozone Convention and the separate Meeting of the Parties of the Montreal Protocol.

The meetings of COPs are often open to participants other than representatives of the contracting parties and the trend is towards greater openness. This is an important feature to ensure the transparency of the work of COPs and cooperation with inter-governmental bodies as well as with non-state actors. The 1989 Basel Convention on Transboundary Movement of

Hazardous Wastes is particularly progressive in this regard; it foresees that the UN, its specialized agencies, as well as states not party to the Convention may participate as observers at COP meetings. Any other body or agency, whether international or national, governmental or non-governmental, such as industry associations, that are qualified in the matter of hazardous wastes or other wastes, and having given notice of their interest in attending the COP can participate as observer unless one-third of the states parties objects. Other COPs also admit observers: more than 200 governmental and non-governmental organizations were represented in Kyoto in 1997.

COPs usually create subsidiary bodies to ensure the functioning of the treaty between sessions and to facilitate state implementation of the Convention. The most developed body in the latter respect is the Montreal Protocol's Implementation Committee of the Non-Compliance Procedure. Scientific bodies are particularly important in environmental protection and they have a key role in many treaty regimes. The Biodiversity Convention, for example, has a Subsidiary Body on Scientific, Technical and Technological Advice (SBSTTA) whose members meet annually to draft proposals for adoption by the COP. Each party to the Convention may designate a governmental representative, but the representative must have expertise in one or more of the relevant fields. The SBSTTA has drafted many important guidelines that the COPs have adopted, such as on access to genetic resources, and on integrated coastal management. Similar bodies exist for the Ramsar Convention (Scientific and Technical Review Panel), the Antarctic Treaty System (Scientific Council on Antarctic Research), CITES, the UNESCO World Heritage Convention, and others.

Secretariats, in most cases either designated or created by the basic Convention, assist the COPs. Their services may be provided by existing international bodies like UNEP which provides the secretariat for the Convention on Biological Diversity, CITES and the Basel Convention. The ozone treaties refer to other international bodies such as UNDP, the World Bank, WMO, and GEF. More frequently, however, environmental agreements establish their own secretariat, sometimes after a transitory period. Secretariats can play an important role in supporting the implementation of the relevant conventions by collecting national reports on compliance by domestic authorities. In some cases they can also accept information on compliance submitted by other governments, NGOs and/or individuals. They transmit to the COP such reports and information but sometimes they elaborate a synthesis of the national reports and information on implementation.

Sometimes a secretariat, such as that of the Convention on Biological Diversity, can act as an information clearing-house. In the ozone treaty system, the secretariat receives data reported by the parties on production, imports and exports of each substance controlled by the Montreal Protocol, analyses the data and submits a report to the Implementation Committee and to the Meeting of the Parties. It also can initiate the non-compliance procedure of the Montreal Protocol by transmitting the information with the corroborating data to the Implementation Committee.

Secretariats may assist states parties to implement the Convention. The secretariat of the Convention on Biological Diversity, for example, facilitates technology and information transfer and the development of cross-border projects, and in certain cases works to enhance the capacity of officials regarding implementation. The secretariat of the Basel Convention on Hazardous Wastes contributes to capacity-building and development of appropriate legislation by states in order to prevent and monitor illegal traffic. For this purpose, the secretariat has compiled existing national legislation of contracting parties and drawn up a draft model law on the management of hazardous wastes and other wastes and their disposal. It also has prepared a manual for the implementation of the Convention and a number of technical guidelines on related issues for the practical management of wastes. The UNEP-administered secretariat for CITES has published Guidelines for Legislation to Implement CITES. It undertakes technical assistance and analysis of national implementing legislation.

Capacity-building also can be enhanced by regional workshops organized by convention secretariats or by UNEP or UNITAR, in consultation with governments. Voluntary contributions from contracting parties may allow the reimbursement of expenses for participating representatives from developing countries or countries in transition. In 1994, UNEP opened an International Environmental Technology Center (IETC) whose main function is to facilitate the transfer of environmentally sound technologies to developing countries and countries with economies in transition.

COPs/MOPs also can facilitate compliance by creating financial bodies. The Multilateral Fund was established by a decision of the Second Meeting of the Parties to the Montreal Protocol (London, June 1990) and began operation in 1991. The main objective of the Multilateral Fund is to assist developing country parties to the Montreal Protocol whose annual per capita consumption and production of ozone depleting substances (ODS) is less than 0.3 kg to comply with the control measures of the Protocol. Currently, 130 of the 175 parties to the Montreal Protocol meet these criteria. They are referred to as Article 5 countries. Contributions to the Multilateral Fund from the industrialized countries, or non-Article 5 countries, are assessed according to the United Nations scale of assessment. The Fund has been replenished four times: U.S. $240 million (1991–1993), U.S. $455 million (1994–1996), and U.S. $466 million (1997–1999), and U.S. $440 million (2000–2002). As of July 2001 the contributions made to the Multilateral Fund by some 32 industrialized countries amounted to U.S. $1.3 billion.

The Fund is managed by an Executive Committee assisted by the Fund Secretariat. Projects and activities supported by the Fund are implemented by four international implementing agencies. Responsibility for overseeing the operation of the Fund rests with an Executive Committee, comprising seven members each from Article 5 and non-Article 5 countries. The term of office of the Executive Committee is one calendar year. The Chair and Vice-Chair of the Executive Committee alternate each year between the two groups. The functions of the Committee include developing operational policies, criteria for project eligibility, and other guidelines and administrative arrangements, monitoring the implementation of these policies, approving implementing agencies' business plans and work programs, approving expenditures for investment projects and other activities, allocating and disbursing resources, and monitoring and evaluating performance. The Executive Committee holds three meetings per year, each of three days duration. The meetings are preceded by two day meetings of the Executive Committee's two standing Sub-Committees on Monitoring, Evaluation and Finance and on Project Review, which are held in parallel.

The Fund Secretariat was established in 1991 in Montreal, Canada. It assists the Executive Committee in the discharge of its functions. Its activities include: development of the three-year plan and budget and a system for fund disbursement; management of the business planning cycle of the Multilateral Fund; monitoring the expenditures and activities of the implementing agencies; preparation of policy papers and other documents; review and assessment of investment projects, country programs and the business plans and work programs of the implementing agencies; liaison between the Committee, governments and implementing agencies; and servicing meetings of the Executive Committee. Monitoring and evaluation were added to the secretariat's functions by the Executive Committee in May 1997.

UNEP, UNDP, the World Bank and the United Nations Industrial Development Organization (UNIDO) have contractual agreements with the Executive Committee to assist Article 5 countries by preparing country programs, feasibility studies and project proposals, providing technical assistance for project development and implementation, as well as information dissemination. Additionally, several developed countries provide similar assistance on a bilateral basis. With the assistance of these four implementing agencies as well as the bilateral agencies, recipient enterprises prepare project proposals and ODS phase-out related activities which are reviewed by the Fund secretariat and considered by the Executive Committee.

The proliferation of environmental agreements and new treaty bodies combined with the generalized attention to environmental matters within international organizations result in a vast array of international entities working on similar issues, raising the problem of coordination and cooperative action. While by no means resolved, several actions have been taken to increase coordination. The secretariats of some treaty bodies have concluded Memoranda of Understanding to provide mutual assistance. In some instances, state-adopted Memoranda of Understanding invite inter-governmental and non-governmental organizations to become signatories (*e.g.*, MOUs concluded under the Bonn Convention on Migratory Species). The Ramsar secretariat has been particularly proactive in seeking cooperation with other treaty bodies like the secretariat of the Convention on Biological Diversity.

In other actions, the complex problems raised by hazardous substances in international trade led to the establishment of an Inter-Organizational Programme for the Sound Management of Chemicals (IOMC), whose participating members are the WHO, ILO, UNEP, FAO, UNIDO, OECD and UNITAR. Particular areas of coordination include harmonizing the classification of chemicals, information exchange on toxic chemicals and chemical risks, pollutant release and transfer registers, and chemical accident prevention and response. The General Assembly also has acted, creating by General Assembly Resolution 53/242 an overarching Environmental Management Group that includes specialized agencies, funds and programs of the UN system and the secretariats of MEAs.

G. International Financial Institutions

The legal instruments creating international financial institutions do not mention environmental protection but it has become an issue in their lending policies. Today, nearly all international financial institutions support sustainable development and condition funding of development projects on respect for the environment. Since the beginning of the 1990s most of them have created specific procedures for selecting environmentally-friendly projects and also have instituted mechanisms to revise projects considered as not respecting environmental conditions.

1. World Bank

The World Bank and the International Monetary Fund were created in 1944 to assist in the reconstruction of Europe and Asia after the Second World War, although the Bank has since turned its attention to the economic problems of developing countries. The IMF works closely with the Bank on economic policy, but is more concerned with financial markets and stability than with development and poverty. The Bank is founded on Articles of Agreement supplemented with by-laws approved by the member states. A Board of Governors meets once a year to set policy for the Bank while ongoing operations are handled by a 24-member Board of Executive Directors that meets weekly. The Bank President acts as the Chair of the Board of Executive Directors. Voting in the Bank is weighted and based upon financial shares that correspond in large part to the global economic rank of the member state. The seven largest industrial states (G-7) hold about 45 percent of the voting shares at the Bank. Generally, however, decisions are taken by consensus.

The World Bank Group is comprised of five associated institutions: the International Bank for Reconstruction and Development, the International Development Association, the International Finance Corporation, the Multilateral Investment Guarantee Agency, and the International Center for the Settlement of Investment Disputes. The Group uses financial instruments to promote sustainable development, including by loan arrangements, long-term low-interest concessional credits and grants made to the poorest countries, partial risk guarantees, and private sector debt and equity.[98] The Bank also acts as implementing agency for the GEF, the Montreal Protocol Multilateral Fund, the Rain Forest Trust Fund, the Prototype Carbon Fund and the Critical Ecosystem Partnership Fund.

The Bank's Articles of Agreement do not mention the environment. During the past decade, however, the World Bank has addressed social and environmental issues through the development of ten "Safeguard Policies" and through the work of the Inspection Panel established in 1993. In doing so, the Bank recognized the connection between economic issues and environmental degradation. In 1998 the Bank decided to reorganize its Operational Manual around related themes. Ten key environmental social and legal policies were grouped together, covering Environmental Assessment (OP 4.01, January 1999), Natural Habitats (OP 4.04, September 1995), Forestry (OP 4.36 September 1993), Pest Management (OP 4.09, December 1998), Involuntary Resettlement (OP 4.12, December 2001), Indigenous Peoples (OD 4.20, September 1991), Cultural Property (OP 11.03, September 1986), Safety of Dams (OP 4.37, September 1996), International Waterways (OP 7.50, October 1994), and Projects in Disputed Areas (OP 7.60, November 1994). Disclosure of Information applies to all ten safeguard policies according to the new Disclosure Policy which came into effect in January 2002. During the 1980s, environmental concerns also were integrated into the World Bank's activities through establishing an environmental department in all four of the regional divisions of the Bank.

Bank lending for environmental projects has grown substantially in recent years. During 1996, the Bank issued $1.63 billion in loans and credits for 20 environmental projects. By the end of 1997, the Bank's active projects involving improvement in environmental management stood at

---

98   IBRD and IDA provide loans for public-sector projects, with IDA providing concessional or low-cost loans to the poorest countries, while IBRD provides loans to other developing countries and to countries in transition. The IFC finances private sector projects and MIGA provides insurance against the risks of loss private investors face in developing countries.

approximately $12.3 billion for 184 projects in 62 countries.[99] In addition to funding environmental projects, the Bank provides technical and legal environmental assistance to developing countries, in particular by helping in the development of Country Environmental Strategies and planning coordinated responses to address regional environmental problems, mainly in Central and Eastern Europe.

The World Bank established the Inspection Panel in 1993 because of growing concerns about the accountability of it and other international development agencies in supporting projects and programs. The Panel is an independent investigatory body receiving and investigating complaints issuing from those in the territory of a borrower whose rights or interests have been adversely affect by the Bank's failure to comply with its policies and procedures in the design, appraisal and implementation of a Bank-financed project. The Panel may investigate complaints upon authorization by the Bank Board of Executive Directors, and assess to what extent the Bank has complied with its standards. At the first stage, the Panel registers the request and asks Management to respond to the concerns expressed in it. The Panel then assesses whether or not the request meets the eligibility requirements, in particular, whether *prima facie* the Bank has engaged in a serious violation of its operational policies and procedures resulting or likely to result in material and adverse harm to those making the request and to which Management has failed to respond adequately. On the basis of this assessment, the Panel recommends to the Executive Directors whether or not to authorize an investigation. If authorized, the Panel investigates the merits and reaches findings. The process can result in a remedial action plan requiring management to take actions in response to Bank failures.

In its first five years, the Panel received 17 requests for inspection. Two were outside the mandate; of the 15 remaining, 13 concerned infrastructure, environmental and land reform projects, while two related to adjustment operations. The Panel recommended investigation in six cases but was only authorized to investigate two matters. In four other cases, a type of friendly settlement under Panel verification was reached.

Two outside reviews have led to clarifications and changes in the operation of the Inspection Panel. The first review, done in 1996, focused on procedure. The Second Inspection Panel Review, completed in 1999,[100] added to and revised the 1996 conclusions. The results clarify that the initial (admissibility) stage of the procedure must focus on assertions of non-compliance and resulting potential or material harm; it is not a decision on the merits involving a true finding of harm. The issue of non-compliance is

---

[99]   Report on the World Bank, *in* 1997 Y.B. INT'L ENVTL. L. 570, 571.

[100]   Conclusions of the Second Review of the World Bank Inspection Panel, 39 I.L.M. 243 (2000). See further, Chapter 7B.3. For Bank EIA procedures, see Chapter 5C.3.a.

antecedent to the issue of harm and supports the notion of the Inspection Panel as a mechanism of accountability rather than a true remedial procedure. Other aspects of the conclusions similarly focus on the Panel's role to monitor the Bank non-compliance with its own policies and procedures.

The 1999 review of the panel paid particular attention to the relatively small number of full reviews that had been undertaken by the Panel. The 1999 Clarifications prevent management from short-cutting the procedure. The Clarifications make clear that the Board will authorize an investigation the Panel recommends without making any judgment on the merits and without discussion except in relation to "technical eligibility criteria" or admissibility requirements. The latter define "affected party" to mean two or more persons with common interests in the borrower's territory. In addition they require: that the request allege a serious violation by the Bank of its operational policies and procedures resulting in or likely to have a material adverse effect on the requesting party; that the matter be submitted to Management without adequate response; that the matter not relate to procurement and that the related loan not be closed or substantially disbursed. The matter also must be a new matter or raise new evidence or circumstances. The Panel when established is authorized to collect all pertinent bank records, interview bank staff, the requesters and others in the territory who may be able to provide information about the issue. The 1999 clarifications emphasize the non-judicial function of the Panel and its absence of authority to interpret the legal instruments involved in the request. If issues of interpretation arise, the Panel is to seek the advice of the Legal Department.

Efforts to extend the Inspection Panel to private sector funding were opposed by the relevant institutions (IFC/MIGA) who instead appointed a Compliance Adviser/Ombudsman with different terms of reference, a more flexible confidential procedure and emphasis on mitigating damage. The cooperation of the Bank and the private International Finance Corporation means that in some instances both procedures may apply to a single project, *e.g.*, the Chad/Cameroon Pipeline and the Bujagali Hydropower Project in Uganda.

2. Global Environment Facility (GEF)

The Global Environment Facility is the primary mechanism providing developing countries with "new and additional grants and concessional funding to meet the agreed full incremental cost of measures to achieve global benefits," as required by various global environmental agreements.[101]

---

[101] *See Instrument for the Establishment of the Restructured Global Environment Facility* (1994), 33 I.L.M. 1273 (1994).

In particular, funding is intended to address four environmental issues: climate change, stratospheric ozone depletion, loss of biological diversity and pollution of international waters. The costs of activities relating to land degradation, particularly desertification and deforestation, are also eligible for funding "insofar as they achieve global environmental benefits by protecting the global environment in the four focal areas." The GEF operates as the interim financial mechanism under the Climate Change Convention, the Convention on Biological Diversity, and the POPs Convention.

GEF, launched in 1991 for a three-year pilot phase with an initial sum of $1.2 billion,[102] was restructured and made permanent in 1994. It is governed by an Assembly, a Council and a Secretariat. The Assembly consists of representatives of 160 countries; it meets every three years to review and revise the GEF's general policy and operations. The Council consists of 32 members representing constituency groups; it has primary authority for developing, adopting and evaluating the operational policies and programs for GEF-financed activities. It also reviews, approves and monitors the implementing agencies' work program. The Secretariat is located at the World Bank which provides administrative support, but the GEF is supposed to be functionally independent. The World Bank, the United Nations Environment Program (UNEP) and the United Nations Development Program (UNDP) are the GEF's "Implementing Agencies." They are accountable to the Council for their GEF-funded activities. The World Bank administers the funds, while UNDP funds institution-building, training, and other technical assistance projects. UNEP ensures consistency with international environmental agreements, funds a small number of research projects related to GEF issues and supports the independent Scientific and Technical Advisory Panel.

3. *International Finance Corporation (IFC)*

The International Finance Corporation is the private sector part of the World Bank Group, providing loans to private companies for projects in developing countries. Established in 1956, IFC is the largest multilateral source of loan and equity financing for private sector projects in the developing world. It promotes sustainable private sector development primarily by: (1) financing private sector projects located in the developing world; (2) helping private companies in the developing world mobilize financing in international financial markets; (3) providing advice and technical assistance to businesses and governments. IFC has 175 member countries, which collectively determine its policies and approve investments. To join IFC, a

---

102 World Bank, Mar. 14, 1991. By 1999, GEF grants totaled $2.7 billion. *See* <http://www.gefweb.org>.

country must first be a member of the World Bank. IFC's corporate powers are vested in its Board of Governors, to which member countries appoint representatives. IFC's share capital, which is paid in, is provided by its member countries, and voting is in proportion to the number of shares held. IFC's authorized capital is $2.45 billion. Statement of Capital Stock and Voting Power. The Board of Governors delegates many of its powers to the Board of Directors, which is composed of the Executive Directors of the IBRD, and which represents IFC's member countries. The Board of Directors reviews all projects. The President of the World Bank Group also serves as IFC's president. Although IFC coordinates its activities in many areas with the other institutions in the World Bank Group, IFC generally operates independently as it is legally and financially autonomous with its own Articles of Agreement, share capital, management and staff. IFC monitors the environmental and social performance of projects in its investment portfolio. Project monitoring usually occurs in one or more of the following ways: (1) review of annual monitoring reports prepared by the project company (in a format agreed by IFC); (2) supervision missions carried out by the Investment Department and the Environment and Social Development Department; and/or (3) project site visits by staff of the Environment and Social Development Department. The frequency of the site visits depend on the environmental and social complexity of a project. The IFC published, in September 1993, a document providing guidance to its staff in conducting an environmental review of proposed projects.[103] This document is discussed in Chapter 6C.3.b.

4. *European Bank for Reconstruction and Development (EBRD)*

The European Bank for Reconstruction and Development was established in 1991 when communism was crumbling in central and eastern Europe and ex-soviet countries needed support to nurture a new private sector. The EBRD has used investment to help build market economies and democracies in 27 countries from central Europe to central Asia. The EBRD is owned by 60 countries and two intergovernmental institutions. Despite its public sector shareholders, it invests mainly in private enterprises, usually together with commercial partners. It provides project financing for banks, industries and businesses, both new ventures and investments in existing companies. It also works with publicly owned companies, to support privatization, restructuring state-owned firms and improvement of municipal services. The Bank uses its close relationship with governments in the region to promote policies that will bolster the business environment. The mandate of the EBRD stipulates that it must only work in countries that are com-

---

[103] *Environmental Analysis and Review of Projects,* Sept. 8, 1993.

mitted to democratic principles. All the powers of the EBRD are vested in the Board of Governors, to which each member appoints a governor, generally the minister of finance or an equivalent. The Board of Governors delegates most powers to the Board of Directors, which is responsible for the direction of EBRD's general operations and policies.

Respect for the environment is attached to all EBRD investments. An Environmental Policy document[104] details the commitment contained in the Founding Agreement for the "promotion of environmentally sound and sustainable development." The 1996 Environmental Policy and Procedures was revised in order to reaffirm and strengthen the commitment and to enhance good governance. The policy requires that all projects financed by the Bank be designed to be environmentally sound. In addition, projects with specific environmental objectives can be financed by any of the Banking Department's business sector groups. Projects with specific environmental aims include energy efficiency credit lines and waste water treatment facilities. Environmental benefits may also result from funded technology upgrades which improve environmental efficiency. Banking teams with a specific environmental role are Municipal and Environmental Infrastructure and Energy Efficiency. The EBRD also has a Nuclear Safety Department.

5.   *European Bank of Investment*

The European Investment Bank (EIB), the financing institution of the European Union, was created by the Treaty of Rome. The EIB's mission is to further the objectives of the European Union by providing long-term finance for specific capital projects. The Bank funds long-term development projects outside the Union, in the ACP countries, in the Mediterranean region and in Central and Eastern Europe. The EIB grants loans mainly from the proceeds of its borrowings, which, together with "own funds" (paid-in capital and reserves), constitute its resources. The Bank's departments: (1) evaluate, appraise and finance projects; (2) raise resources on the capital markets and manage the treasury; (3) assess and manage risks attaching to EIB operations, carry out necessary economic or financial background studies. As an organ of the EU, the EIB acts in conformity with the environmental legislation of the EC, including the requirement of environmental impact assessments prepared by the borrowers. It also functions in cooperation with other EU institutions, mainly the EC Commission.

---

[104]   See the *Principles of Action* adopted by the EBRD in Mar. 1992, document ML 057.

6.   Inter-American Development Bank

The Inter-American Development Bank Group is the main source of multilateral financing for economic, social and institutional development in Latin America and the Caribbean. The IDB Group includes three institutions: (1) the Inter-American Development Bank, which supports economic and social development and regional integration in Latin America and the Caribbean, mainly through lending to public institutions and also funds some private projects, typically in infrastructure and capital markets development; (2) the Inter-American Investment Corporation, a multilateral financial organization that promotes economic development in Latin America and the Caribbean by financing small and medium-scale private companies and (4) the Multilateral Investment Fund, an autonomous fund managed by the IDB. It supports private sector development, mainly in the microenterprise sector.

The Inter-American Development Bank first adopted a document on Environmental Policy in 1979. Today, its operational standards and guidelines as well as decisions of its Board require that all operations financed by the Bank be environmentally and socially sustainable. The focal point of environmental quality and social impact management within the Bank is the Committee on Environment and Social Impact (CESI) which attempts to address the root causes of environmental deterioration and the institutional framework that determines the success of measures to prevent and mitigate harm. Project review includes, e.g., the promotion of adequate environmental regulatory and management frameworks; the adoption of environmental protection, management, mitigation and enhancement measures in specific operations; indigenous rights and community development issues; involuntary resettlement matters; and issues of social impact and sustainability.

7.   African Development Bank

The African Development Bank Group is a multinational development bank supported by 77 nations (member countries) from Africa, North and South America, Europe and Asia. Established in 1964, its mission is to promote economic and social development through loans, equity investments, and technical assistance. Headquartered in Abidjan, Cote d Ivoire, the Bank Group consists of three institutions: the African Development Bank [ADB], the African Development Fund [ADF], the Nigeria Trust Fund [NTF]. The Board of Directors of the African Development Bank adopted an Environment Policy Paper in 1990, with the overall objective of ensuring environmental viability of investment projects in the Bank Group's Operation Program. The Environmental Policy Paper aimed to assess the state of the environment in the continent and assist Regional Member Countries in identifying major environmental issues; to present environmental policies for each of the sectors of the ADB Group project and non-project lending programs; to present recommendations for the implementation of environmental policies and the use of appropriate environmental assessment procedures in the project cycle; to assist Regional Member Countries in developing national environmental policies, legislative framework and institutions involved with environmental and natural resources management. In 1991, the Bank initiated action for the preparation of Environmental Assessment Guidelines and environmental assessment procedures which were finalized in 1992. The guidelines are based on the principles that environmental assessment procedures should be linked as much as possible with existing procedures in the Bank Group and that loans and project officers will identify further action to be taken at the earliest stage. The Board of Governors of the African Development Bank adopted a new "Group Vision" in 1999 after extensive consultations with all stakeholders. In order to operationalize this Vision, the Boards of Directors approved a new organizational structure that became effective January 1, 2002, and approved the Bank's First Strategic Plan for the Period 2003–2007.

8. Asian Development Bank

The Asian Development Bank is a multilateral development finance institution dedicated to reducing poverty in Asia and the Pacific. Established in 1966, it is owned by 62 members, mostly from the region. The headquarters is in Manila, but there are 24 other offices around the world, including 16 resident missions in Asia, a regional mission for the Pacific in Vanuatu, a country office in the Philippines, and representative offices in Frankfurt for Europe, Tokyo for Japan, and Washington, DC for North America. ADB is a non-profit financial institution that engages in mostly public sector lending for development purposes in its developing member countries. Its clients are its member governments, who are also its shareholders.

Over the years, ADB's environment agenda has evolved from impact mitigation to impact prevention, and has expanded to cover environmental integration in its country operations, and sector and macro policy work, along with targeted interventions in loan projects to achieve direct environmental benefits. ADB's decision in 1999 to make poverty reduction its overarching objective shifted the focus of its environment program towards supporting this aim. In addition to targeting interventions to achieve direct environmental benefits in loan projects and programs, ADB mainstreams environmental considerations in country operational strategy studies, sector policies, and into its loan and investment projects and programs.

In addition to addressing country-specific environmental problems, ADB undertakes activities on environmental issues common to several developing country members at regional and subregional levels in cooperation with bilateral funding agencies and international organizations. Transboundary environmental issues addressed through ADB technical assistance included climate change, acid rain in northeast Asia, and the impact of atmospheric haze brought about by forest fires in the countries of the Association of Southeast Asian Nations (ASEAN). The ASEAN Regional Strategy for Haze Prevention and Mitigation was achieved through ADB assistance.

In addition to the specific practices described above, several international lending institutions have established formal channels through which local communities, organizations and other groups, and, in special cases members of the Board of Directors, can request independent review or "inspection" of the bank's role in specific bank-financed projects.[105]

The environmental practices of international financial institutions display several general trends. The first is the creation of special procedures for introducing environmental conditions in the banks' decision-making processes. Such procedures always involve the prior assessment of potential environmental impacts of planned activities, a factor that has become important in selecting projects for funding. In some cases the environmental impact is understood in a large manner, taking into account the broad environmental and social effects. The legislative and institutional capacity of the borrowing state to fulfil the environmental conditions of the loan generally are considered as well. Information to and the participation of local groups and NGOs at different stages of the procedure are always required. The importance of the intervention of local groups and of NGOs is also reflected in the possibility afforded them to ask for the review of a decision they consider as contrary to environmental protection. The special procedures that the financial institutions have established for this purpose generally combine expertise and independence.

H.   Non-Governmental Organizations and Civil Society

During much of international legal history, states were considered as the sole subjects of international law, leaving other entities without legal competence and with few roles to play. A transformation of the international system occurred in the 20th century with the emergence of non-state actors, from the international organizations described in the preceding sections to non-governmental organizations, multinational companies, and individual participants. The role of transnational civil society has been particularly important in the evolution of international environmental law.

---

[105]   See the World Bank rules governing the inspection panels adopted on Aug. 19, 1994; the Asian Development Bank Inspection Procedures approved by the Board of Directors on October 9, 1996, and for the Inter-American Development Bank the document on Independent Investigation Mechanism.

1. The Role of NGOs

Non-governmental organizations formed to advance the interests of their members have long existed[106] but their numbers have grown considerably along with their ability to participate in international events. An estimated 275,000 NGOs operate in the United Kingdom alone.[107] Environmental groups emerged due to frustration with governments' lack of initiative to address the extent of environmental degradation, while the communications revolution has made it possible to connect the global community efficiently and inexpensively. In the past two decades, environmental NGOs have developed scientific expertise and lobbying skills that allow them to effectively participate in negotiations for environmental agreements. Some of the environmental NGOs have become well-known for their work on a global basis: IUCN, Friends of the Earth, Greenpeace International, and the World Wide Fund for Nature (WWF). Thousands more work nationally or transnationally, sometimes on single issues and at other times with broad mandates. Because of their importance, the Brundtland Commission recommended that governments establish official consultation with NGOs to share information, strategies and resources, and to permit meaningful participation in all aspects of environmental matters.

Many NGO's act within international institutions, seeking to influence international decision-making, as well as within states, where they promote positive environmental policies. They represent their members in advancing their common values. Like individual members of the public, NGOs may compile data, seek to influence legislation, intervene in decisions on licensing or permitting projects, and monitor compliance with environmental laws. With these roles and because of their greater means, expertise, and organized efforts, NGOs often can effectively assert public rights of information and participation. They have a variety of assets, including access to funds, ability to attract media attention, and the ability to acquire, communicate and disseminate expert information. Most importantly, they possess a legitimacy and transnationalism that gives them influence and permits them to push the transparency of international institutions as they frame issues, build communities, and set examples, at their best becoming moral agents of change. Increasingly, too, they have become aware of their own needs for transparency and are becoming more public about funding sources, membership and other governance issues.

The strength of NGOs is often necessary to counterbalance powerful

---

[106] *See* Lyman C. White, International Non-Governmental Organizations: Their Purposes, Methods and Accomplishments (1951).

[107] *See* Lester M. Salamon, *The Rights of the Non-Profit Sector*, 75 Foreign Affairs 109, 111 (1994).

business interests,[108] but the industry itself can contribute to the implementation of international environmental law, as is discussed in more detail in Chapter 17. Chemical companies supported the ozone regime by rapidly developing chemical alternatives to ozone-depleting substances. The insurance sector has undertaken advanced research on climate change and supported action to curb greenhouse gas emissions. Representatives of the tourist industry have participated in consultative meetings of the Antarctic Treaty system.

To strengthen the international role of NGOs, Agenda 21 called on the UN system, including international finance and development agencies, and all intergovernmental organizations and forums, in consultation with NGOs, to take measures to:

(a) Review and report on ways of enhancing existing procedures and mechanisms by which NGOs contribute to policy design, decision-making, implementation and evaluation at the individual agency level, in inter-agency discussions and in UN conferences;

(b) On the basis of subparagraph (a) above, enhance existing or, where they do not exist, establish mechanisms and procedures within each agency to draw on the expertise and views of NGOs in policy and program design, implementation and evaluation;

. . .

(d) design open and effective means of achieving the participation of NGOs in the processes established to review and evaluate the implementation of Agenda 21 at all levels; and

. . .

(g) provide access for NGOs to accurate and timely data and information to promote the effectiveness of their programs and activities and their roles in support of sustainable development.[109]

A Decision of the EC of March 1, 2002 defines the role of NGOs by laying down a Community action program promoting NGOs that are primarily active in the field of environmental protection. It recognizes that NGOs are essential to coordinate and channel to the EC Commission information and views on the new and emerging perspectives, which cannot be, or are not being, fully dealt with at the state or a subordinate level. In addition, NGOs have good understanding of public concerns on the environment

---

[108] As part of the private sector, business groups may also form NGOs. At COP-7 of the Framework Convention on Climate Change, held in Marrakesh at the end of 2001, the overwhelming majority of accredited NGOs represented the energy sector, coal and steel producers, the chemical industry, and other business interests.

[109] Agenda 21, Chapter 27.9.

and thus promote these views and can channel them back to the EC Commission.[110]

Many NGOs obtain formal status in international institutions. Article 71 of the UN Charter provides that the Economic and Social Council may extend "consultative status" to international NGOs that satisfy criteria established by the United Nations. Such status entitles an NGO to access to UN meetings and conferences, and, in some instances, the right to intervene orally and submit written statements. NGOs were prominent at the Stockholm and Rio Conferences. At UNCED, some 1,500 NGOs were accredited to attend formal meetings and some informal meetings. They were permitted to lobby, present documents and meet among themselves. NGOs also have been present at negotiations for the Kyoto Protocol and similar international agreements and have been afforded widespread observer status in international environmental treaties.[111] They increasingly have a role in launching international inquiries.[112]

Several recent environmental agreements recognize a formal role for NGOs. The Convention for the Protection of the Marine Environment of the North-East Atlantic (September 22, 1992) granted observer status to NGOs along with non-party states and inter-governmental organizations. Article 4.1 of the Framework Convention on Climate Change (June 4, 1992) provides that all parties shall "promote and cooperate in education, training and public awareness related to climate change and encourage the widest participation in this process, including that of non-governmental organizations." Article 7.2.1 addresses the issue of supervising the implementation of the Convention by the Conference of the Parties and states that it shall "seek and utilize, where appropriate, the services and cooperation of, and information provided by, competent international organizations and inter-governmental and non-governmental bodies." The Convention on International Trade in Endangered Species of Wild Fauna and Flora (Washington, March 3, 1973), Article 11(7), similarly provides them a role. The Montreal Protocol (September 16, 1987) establishes a relatively open process for NGOs. It states that

> Any body or agency, whether national or international, governmental or non-governmental, qualified in fields relating to the protection of the ozone layer which has informed the secretariat of its

---

[110] Decision No. 466/2002/EC, Mar. 1, 2002, O.J. L. 75 (3/16/02).

[111] *See, e.g.*, Convention on Biological Diversity, Art. 23(5); Convention for the Protection of the Marine Environment of the North East Atlantic, Sept. 22, 1992.

[112] *See, e.g.*, the discussion of the World Bank Inspection Panel and NAAEC in Chapters 4 and 17.

wish to be represented at a meeting of the Parties as an observer may be admitted unless at least one third of the parties present object. (Article 11.5).

The rules of procedure of the Executive Committee for the Multilateral Fund established by the Protocol provide for notification to qualified NGOs of meetings where they may participate as observers without the right to vote, upon invitation of the Chairman and if there is no objection from Committee members present. The language of the 1992 Biodiversity Convention is nearly identical to that of the Montreal Protocol. The UN Desertification Convention (June 17, 1994) speaks in its preamble of "the special role of non-governmental organizations and other major groups in programs to combat desertification and mitigate the effects of drought." Finally, during the drafting of the 1998 Rotterdam Convention on Prior Informed Consent, a number of representatives strongly advocated that the Chemical Review Committee should be open not only to the participation of observers from Governments, but to international organizations and non-governmental organizations. In the end, the adopted treaty allows such participation unless one-third of the parties objects.

In August 1989, the World Bank adopted Operational Directive 14.7 "Involving Non-governmental Organizations in Bank-Supported Activities." This allows the Bank to consult NGO assessments of official development programs and confirms them as a source of information on intended beneficiaries. NGOs also may serve as consultants or sources of information and monitor a project.

Agenda 21 encourages the United Nations Commission on Sustainable Development to be open to NGO participation. Resolution 47/191 specified that arrangements for NGO accreditation and participation in the CSD should take into account both the established rules of procedure of ECOSOC and its functional commissions, as well as relevant decisions and rules of UNCED and Agenda 21, chapter 38. All ECOSOC-accredited NGOs may designate authorized representatives to be present at and observe meetings of the Commission and its subsidiary organs. NGOs may at their own expense make written presentations to the Commission and its subsidiary organs. NGOs may be given opportunity to address the meetings, but have no formal negotiating role in the work of the Commission and its subsidiary organs. NGO participation at CSD is now the highest of all the UN bodies.

In addition to their formal role, NGOs act outside institutions to mobilize public opinion, exposing environmental harm and setting environmental agendas. Globalization may enhance the power of NGOs to mobilize effective consumer actions. The response to Royal Dutch Shell's proposal to scuttle the Brent Star oil rig is an example. Although Shell had received all appropriate domestic and international approvals to abandon the rig on the ocean floor, Greenpeace launched a consumer boycott of Shell gasoline to oppose the plan. Within weeks, Shell's sales in Germany were down 30 percent and Shell reversed its decision.[113]

Non-governmental organizations may draft or develop norms either for their own governance, or for submission to states for adoption. NGOs also perform monitoring, information gathering and other functions related to compliance with binding and non-binding norms. In practice, most non-binding international norms—indeed most binding international norms—are not drafted by one type of international actor independently of all others but, instead, are adopted through a complex interplay of state and non-state actors. The relatively homogenous character of the international order at the beginning of the last century has given way to an international system comprised of a highly diverse and enlarged group of states, international institutions, and non-state actors. All of them increasingly take part in making and applying national and international norms. Today, purely inter-state development of norms is probably non-existent in most fields of international law. It is also rare to find purely private standard-setting. The modes of interaction between state and non-state actors may be particularly important to achieving compliance with soft law norms, as a participatory process enhances the legitimacy and authority of the norms adopted.

The important role of NGOs in the development of and compliance with international norms and standards is indicated by several examples. IUCN was instrumental in elaborating and pressing for UN adoption of the World Charter for Nature. The International Law Association adopted the 1966 Helsinki Rules on the Uses of the Waters of International Rivers that provided the basis for several treaties on international waterways, such as the agreement between Namibia and South Africa to establish a permanent water commission.[114]

An NGO sometimes serves as the secretariat for an inter-governmental treaty, *e.g.,* IUCN in regard to the 1971 Ramsar Convention on Wetlands of International Importance. Other non-governmental bodies serve as expert bodies in treaty administration, such as the Scientific Committee on Antarctic Research of the International Council of Scientific Unions in regard to the Antarctic Treaty system. On occasion, NGOs may take on an official role in regard to monitoring and compliance. Unofficially, most of

---

[113] *See* Tony Paterson, *North Sea Shell Game: Greenpeace's Campaign Against Oil Multinational Royal Dutch Shell,* THE EUROPEAN June 30–July 6, 1995. According to reports, Shell subsequently sought to consult with Greenpeace over the decommissioning of oil rigs. *See Shell Discusses Future of Brent Spar with Greenpeace,* EUR. ENV'T, Jan. 23, 1996.

[114] Agreement between the Government of the Republic of Namibia and the Government of the Republic of South Africa on the Establishment of a Permanent Water Commission, done at Noordoewer, Sept. 14, 1992. *See also* Chapter 4E.

them serve as "watchdogs" in the process of adoption and implementation of international environmental law.

The role of NGOs is expanding, as are their members. During the negotiations for the Kyoto Protocol more than 200 NGOs were accredited as observers. The expanded functions of NGOs can be seen in the Rules of Procedure of the Permanent Committee of the Bern Convention. It authorizes oral declarations and written submissions by NGOs; their propositions may be the subject of a vote if requested by a delegation (Art. 9 Rules of Procedure). Going further, the Mediterranean Commission on Sustainable Development, created in 1995, comprises 36 delegates, of which 21 represent states and 15 come from environmental NGOs. They sit on a basis of equality. It is, however, only a consultative organization in which there is no vote.

Given their expanded functions, NGOs sometimes form alliances among themselves and with inter-governmental organizations to help implement international environmental law. In the early 1980s, the World Wide Fund for Nature, IUCN and UNEP formed the World Conservation Monitoring Center to collect and provide information services on conservation and sustainable use of biological resources. The Monitoring Center now provides data management services for the CITES Secretariat, the World Heritage Convention, the Convention on Biological Diversity, the Convention on Migratory Species and the Ramsar Convention. Centralizing conservation data allows the Center to work with the secretariats of the five major biodiversity treaties to harmonize reporting and management of information.

Finally, NGOs may be able to participate in dispute settlement procedures, either as parties, or as *amicus curiae*. In the U.S. shrimp/turtle case at the World Trade Organization, NGO briefs were attached as exhibits to the U.S. submission, but a revised version of one of the briefs was submitted independently by a group of NGOs and was accepted by the panel, despite protests of some governments.

2.   *World Conservation Union (IUCN)*

The World Conservation Union (formerly the International Union for the Conservation of Nature and Natural Resources) [115] was created in 1948 at the initiative of the French government. IUCN has the unique quality of being a non-governmental organization made up of conservation groups, states and other public law entities. In 1990, IUCN was composed of 62 states, 108 public law entities, such as universities and research institutes, and more than 400 non-governmental organizations, most of which are national but including at least 30 international organizations. In all, approximately 117

---

[115]   IUCN changed its name in 1988 on the 40th anniversary of its creation.

countries are represented either by official organs or otherwise. The objectives of the Union are to evaluate the status of renewable natural resources and their evolution, to encourage the preparation of conservation measures, and education about conservation, and to provide information to members of IUCN and different groups which collaborate with the Union. Among the work assigned the organization is consultation with governments and different institutions in regard to conservation, collection and analysis of information and its diffusion among members and affiliates, elaboration of measures of conservation to propose to governments, provision of technical support in regard to treaties to be adopted or already concluded in the field, and encouragement of research into and application of new techniques relating to conservation.

The structures of IUCN strongly resemble those of inter-governmental organizations. A General Assembly of the members meets once every three years. A Council elected by the Assembly examines the execution of the program and between meetings a secretariat works in the name of the Union. One unusual aspect of IUCN is the importance to its work of six commissions, coming from its 3,000 volunteer experts. A commission on environmental policy and law is responsible for questions of environmental law.

The activities of IUCN include recommendations to governments. Since 1980 IUCN has repeatedly published a World Conservation Strategy which has been highly influential. It is addressed to public authorities and encourages them to integrate conservation of living resources in their development policies, because the latter will not be lasting unless they are founded on the conservation of renewable resources. The accent is put on action to resolve priority problems such as depletion of agricultural land, erosion, deforestation, desertification, climate modification, extinction of living species, reduction of the genetic heritage, and pollution. The Strategy states the principal conditions necessary to resolve these problems and proposes effective means to attain the objectives of (1) maintaining essential ecological processes and systems supporting life; (2) preservation of genetic diversity; and (3) sustainable utilization of species and ecosystems.

In the field of law, the World Conservation Strategy sets forth an ambitious series of international legal measures. These cover conservation of tropical forests and arid regions as well as conservation of the high seas, the atmosphere and Antarctica. There also are included regional strategies to improve conservation of living resources shared by several states, particularly in seas and international river basins.

Several publications sustain the World Strategy. The Red Data Books describe threatened species of mammals, amphibians, reptiles, invertebrates, plants and papilionides. In addition, each year a list of threatened species is published along with a list of national parks and protected areas. Finally, a monthly bulletin gives information on the major ecological problems, the activities of IUCN and particularly on the implementation by different states of the World Conservation Strategy.

The Union has played an essential role in the elaboration of some half dozen of the major international conventions relating to the conservation of nature and natural resources, such as the 1968/2003 African Convention, the 1973 Convention on Trade in Endangered Species (CITES), and the 1979 Convention on Conservation of Migratory Species. The IUCN also prepared the first draft of the 1982 World Charter for Nature and, since the end of the 1980s, has worked on elaborating a comprehensive Covenant on Environment and Development. Finally, the legal office of IUCN, located in Bonn, has a virtually complete collection in its library of international instruments, acts of international organizations, national legislation, and other documents concerning environmental law, as well as hundreds of secondary sources on the subject.

3.   World Wide Fund for Nature (WWF)

This international non-governmental organization is well known throughout the world from its emblem, the endangered giant panda. Its objective is to collect, manage and dispense funds for the global conservation of the natural environment of animals, plants, countryside, water, soil, air and other natural resources. A letter dated December 6, 1960, from London businessman Victor Stolan to Sir Julian Huxley, first director general of UNESCO, proposed creating WWF. Stolan suggested establishing a program of environmental protection through a global campaign with the mobilization of large financial support.

The WWF, officially created in September 1961, is a private foundation with its headquarters located at Gland, Switzerland since 1979. It maintains close links with the IUCN. Besides the normal institutional organs—administrative council, executive committee, director general—WWF has the unusual feature of an International Council composed of 23 representatives of national organizations, most from industrialized countries, but also from India, Malaysia, and Pakistan. These representatives play a prominent role in the activities of the WWF, notably in collecting funds for conservation.

WWF finances operations of conservation throughout the world. Funds are allocated to different projects for maintaining and protecting tropical forests, wetlands, savannas, and the marine environment. Part of the operations are done in collaboration with inter-governmental organizations like UNEP, especially for implementing and financing joint programs. However, the principal partners of WWF are international non-governmental organizations, primarily IUCN. WWF and IUCN annually draft a common strategy, taking decisions on certain programs in common. IUCN then directs the scientific aspects while WWF administers the financial side. Certain common programs of the two organizations produce published results, such as the Red Data Books.

In international legal actions, WWF supports the application of existing norms. It is particularly interested in the effective implementation of CITES, the 1979 Bonn Migratory Species Convention, and the 1971 Ramsar Convention. WWF also has played an important role in the elaboration and implementation of the IUCN World Conservation Strategy.

WWF was one of the pioneering entities in exchanging a reduction in the debt of developing countries for greater environmental protection. In 1984, Dr. Thomas Lovejoy III of the World Wildlife Fund suggested encouraging environmental protection through debt-for-nature swaps. During 1987–88, WWF entered into and implemented such exchanges with Costa Rica, Ecuador and the Philippines. The first agreement with Ecuador retired $1 million in exchange for support for local environmental groups and greater protection for undeveloped lands.[116] Despite some expressions of concern from a few developing countries about conditionality and loss of sovereignty, the efforts of WWF in this regard appear to have strengthened local environmental protection.

Finally, in certain exceptional cases, WWF has supported legal action against projects judged to be particularly devastating for the environment. It intervened, for example, in a case concerning the construction of a hydroelectric dam on the Danube near Hainbourg in Austria, which would have caused the destruction of an ancient forest unique in Europe. Austria abandoned the project following two decisions of the Austrian High Court in January 1985 and September 1986.[117] WWF also intervened in the 1990s, in the Danube Dam dispute between Hungary and Slovakia, making proposals for environmentally friendly solutions.

4. Civil Society

The communications revolution that introduced faxes, the Internet, and electronic mail has allowed environmental activism to move beyond formal NGOs to create grass-roots networks and campaigns that may be limited to a single project or may form around a larger issue. This dynamic process can result in powerful movements that force governments to consider public opinion beyond their borders, creating change in many parts of the world.[118] The notion of an international civil society is now widely recognized[119] and seen

---

116   See, T. Hamlin, *Debt-For-Nature Swaps: A New Strategy for Protecting Environmental Interests in Developing Nations*, 16 Ecol. L.Q. 1065 (1989).

117   WWF News, No. 43, Sept. Oct. 1986.

118   *See* Jessica Tuchman Matthews, *Power Shift*, Foreign Affairs 50 (1997).

119   *See, e.g.*, J. Smith, *Global Civil Society*, 42 Am. Behavioral Scientist 93 (1998).

as a process of directly channeling public participation to private actors in policy-making and implementation. Political discourse across borders helps shape common interests and the identities of societies. The interaction also lends legitimacy and increases accountability when compared to many traditional decision-making processes and structures.

BIBLIOGRAPHY

Are International Institutions Doing Their Job? 90 ASIL Proc. 224 (1996).

BARTLETT, R.V., KURIAN, P.A. & MALIK, M. eds., INTERNATIONAL ORGANIZATIONS AND ENVIRONMENTAL POLICY (1995).

Bodansky, D., *The Legitimacy of International Governance: A Coming Challenge for International Environmental Law*, 93 AJIL 614 (1999).

DRUESNE, G., DROIT ET POLITIQUES DE LA COMMUNAUTE ET DE L'UNION EUROPEENNES (1995).

GUNTHUR, KONRAD ET AL. eds., SUSTAINABLE DEVELOPMENT AND GOOD GOVERNANCE (1995).

GOLUB, J., SOVEREIGNTY AND SUBSIDIARITY IN EU ENVIRONMENTAL POLICY (1996).

HAAS, PETER ET AL eds., INSTITUTIONS FOR THE EARTH—SOURCES OF EFFECTIVE ENVIRONMENTAL PROTECTION (1993).

HOLLINS, S. & MACRORY, R., A SOURCE BOOK OF EUROPEAN COMMUNITY ENVIRONMENTAL LAW (1995).

KEOHANE R. ET AL., INSTITUTIONS FOR THE EARTH (1993).

KIMBALL, L.A., FORGING INTERNATIONAL AGREEMENT: STRENGTHENING INTER-GOVERNMENTAL INSTITUTIONS FOR ENVIRONMENT AND DEVELOPMENT (1992).

KRAMER, L, CASEBOOK ON EU ENVIRONMENTAL LAW (2002).

MALJEAN-DUBOIS, S. & MEHDI, ROSTANE, LES NATIONS UNIES ET LA PROTECTION DE L'ENVIRONNEMENT: LA PROMOTION D'UN DEVELOPPEMENT DURABLE (1999).

Palmer, G., *New Ways to Make International Environmental Law*, 86 AJIL 259 (1992).

POTTER, D., NGOS AND ENVIRONMENTAL POLICIES: ASIA AND AFRICA (1996).

ROLEN, M., SJOBERG, H. & SVEDIN, U. eds., INTERNATIONAL GOVERNANCE ON ENVIRONMENTAL ISSUES (1997).

Sands, Ph., *The Role of Environmental NGOs in International Environmental Law*, 2 DEVELOPMENT 28 (1992).

SCOVAZZI, T., THE PROTECTION OF THE ENVIRONMENT IN A CONTEXT OF REGIONAL ECONOMIC INTEGRATION (2001).

SHIHATA, I. THE WORLD BANK INSPECTION PANEL (1994).

Turlock, A.D., *The Role of Non-governmental Organizations in the Development of International Environmental Law*, 68 CHI-KENT L. REV. 61 (1992).

UNEP, *UNEP's New Way Forward* (1995).

WERKSMAN, J. ed., GREENING INTERNATIONAL INSTITUTIONS (1996).

World Bank, *Making Development Sustainable: the World Bank Group and the Environment* (1994).

INTERNET SITES

Commission on Sustainable Development
<http://www.un.org/dpcds/dsd/csd.htm>

Council of Europe
<http://www.coe.int/>

FAO
<http://www.fao.org/>

Global Environment Facility
<http://www.gefweb.com/>

IAEA
<http://www.iaea.org/>

ILO
<http://www.ilo.org/>

International Law Commission
<http://www.geneva.ch/ilc.htm>

International Maritime Organization
<http://www.imo.org/>

IUCN
<http://www.iucn.org/>

NAFTA CEC
<http://www.cec.org/>

OECD
<http://www.oecd.org/>

Organization of African Unity
<http://www.rapide-pana.com/demo/oau>

Organization of American States
<http://www.oas.org/>

UNDP
<http://www.undp.org/>

UNESCO
<http://www.unesco.org/>

UNEP
<http://www.unep.ch/>

U.S.-Canada International Joint Commission
<http://www.ijc.org/>

WHO
<http://www.who.org/>

WMO
<http://www.wmo.org/>

World Bank
<http://www.worldbank.org/>

World Wide Fund for Nature
<http://www.wwf.org/>

CHAPTER 5

CUSTOMARY INTERNATIONAL LAW AND PRINCIPLES

Customary international law, general principles of law, and normative instruments have advanced a kind of a common law of the environment. Norms and principles have emerged to become widely accepted and repeated consistently in treaties and national laws concerned with environmental protection. New norms and principles are in the process of formation as international environmental law evolves to meet new challenges.

International law first faced issues of environmental protection in the context of bilateral disputes resulting from transfrontier pollution. The international community subsequently realized that environmental problems are not so limited and that approaching environmental protection through rules designed to resolve bilateral problems would provide only limited solutions or might serve only to transfer the environmental harm elsewhere.

The integrated nature of the biosphere signifies that international rules must be concerned with the environment within states, even when harmful activities produce no obvious detrimental effects outside the territory. International law also must protect areas that are outside national jurisdiction, including the high seas and sea-bed, the atmosphere of the commons, Antarctica, outer space, and the moon. In sum, general concepts and rules are necessary to guide states in environmental matters. Article 192 of the UN Convention on the Law of the Sea first expressed this requirement by affirming that "[s]tates have the general obligation to protect and preserve the marine environment." Underlying this duty are broad legal concepts that express the major characteristics of international environmental law. These concepts, as well as others that are emerging, play an important role in IUCN's attempted codification of international environmental law, the Draft International Covenant on Environment and Development.[1]

This chapter assesses the common law of the environment, from its rules concerning transfrontier pollution to the general principles that have emerged to govern environmental protection in all its dimensions.

---

[1]   IUCN, Draft Covenant on Environment and Development (2003).

A. The Regulation of Transfrontier Pollution

1. *Definition of Transfrontier Pollution*

To understand the scope and limitations of international norms on transfrontier pollution, both "pollution" and "transfrontier" require definition.
States first agreed on the meaning of pollution in a recommendation
adopted after several revisions by the OECD Council on November 14,
1974.[2] The same definition has since appeared, with minor modifications,
in all major texts concerning pollution.[3]

> pollution means the introduction by man, directly or indirectly, of
> substances or energy into the environment resulting in deleterious
> effects of such a nature as to endanger human health, harm living
> resources and ecosystems, and impair or interfere with amenities
> and other legitimate uses of the environment.

Several aspects of the definition are notable. First, pollution can result
only from human activities; naturally occurring events such as lightning,
floods, and earthquakes are excluded. Of course, pollution-causing natural
events triggered by human conduct, such as a flood of contaminated water
caused by upland deforestation, may fall within its terms. The reverse chain
of events, where pollution results from human activities set in motion
through natural events—a chemical factory that burns because it is struck
by lightning or radioactive fallout from a nuclear installation damaged due
to an earthquake—may at least trigger the duty to inform those who might
suffer harm from the pollution. The reference to "substances or energy"
means that not only solid, liquid or gaseous material objects, but also noise,
vibrations, heat, and radiation can be considered pollution.

The clauses concerning the introduction of pollution "directly or indirectly" "into the environment" pose the difficult problem of delimiting the
environment. Most international texts seem to suggest that "environment"
means areas outside industrial installations and habitations.[4] Thus, the

---

[2]   Council Recommendation C(74)219, Nov. 14, 1974.

[3]   *See, e.g.,* Art. 2(a) of the 1976 Convention for the Protection of the
Mediterranean Sea against Pollution (Feb. 16, 1976); Art. 1, EC Council Directive
concerning Pollution caused by Certain Dangerous Substances Discharged in
the Aquatic Environment of the Community, O.J. L 129 (5/18/76); Art. 1,
Geneva Convention on Long-Range Transboundary Air Pollution (Nov. 13
1979); and Art. 1(1)(4) United Nations Convention on the Law of the Sea (Dec.
10, 1982).

[4]   However, recent ILO efforts have extended international concern over
environmental pollution into the workplace. *See* Chapter 4. The World Bank

"introduction" of pollutants from the discharge of liquid waste, dumping of solid waste, emission of air pollutants or of dust, is the act through which such substances are directly placed in the natural milieu. Indirect introduction covers situations where an intermediary element occurs between the original human act and the arrival of polluting substances in the environment. For example, discharge of pollutants into a sewage system that directly leads into a watercourse or the sea would be within the definition.[5]

The requirement of "deleterious effects" raises the problem of determining the proper threshold and criteria for labeling a substance or act polluting, because all human activity alters the environment to some extent. The definition requires that the activity attain a requisite level of importance in light of the stated relevant consequences: endangerment of human health and harm to resources. Many international texts refer to "significant" environmental impact.[6] Although the term significant generally is not defined, it would clearly exclude *de minimis* damage.[7] The phrase "of such

---

and related institutions have given broad interpretation to the environmental matters with which they are concerned, encompassing issues "pertaining to the natural and social conditions surrounding all organisms, particularly mankind, and including future generations." Actions affecting the environment include not only pollution but also waste of resources and "despoiling of mankind's aesthetic and cultural heritage." WORLD BANK, ENVIRONMENTAL POLICIES AND PROCEDURES, 1–2 (1984).

    5   This is very important for the definition of land-based marine pollution.

    6   *See, e.g.*, G.A. Res. 2995 (XXVII) of Dec. 15, 1972 concerning cooperation between states in the field of the environment, U.N. GAOR Supp. No. 30, at 42 (1973); Art. 7, Mexico-United States Agreement to Cooperate in the Solution of Environmental Problems in the Border Area, 23 I.L.M. 1025 (Aug. 14, 1983); Art. 6, OECD Principles Concerning Transfrontier Pollution, Council Recommendation C(74)224, Nov. 14, 1974; Art. 21 (2) of the UN Convention on the Law of the Non-Navigational Uses of International Watercourses (May 21, 1997), speaks of "significant harm to other watercourse States or to their environment, including harm to human health or safety, to the use of the waters for any beneficial purpose or to the living resources of the watercourse." Other instruments use terms such as "appreciable," "measurable," "serious" or "substantial."

    7   According to the ILC Special Rapporteur on liability for transboundary harm, some discussions in the ILC have suggested that "significant" harm is more than *de minimis*, "negligible," "detectable," or "appreciable" but need not be at the level of "serious" or "substantial." Further, the harm must lead to real detrimental effects on such aspects as human health, industry, property, the environment or agriculture in other states, measured by factual and objective standards. Pemmaraju Sreenivasa Rao, First Report on the Legal Regime for Allocation of Loss in Case of Transboundary Harm Arising out of Hazardous Activities, International Law Commission, 55th Sess., May 5–June 6 and July 7–Aug. 8, 2003, U.N. Doc. A/CN.4/531, Mar. 21, 2003, *citing* 2 Y.B. I.L.C. (Part Two) (1996); U.N. Doc. A/51/10, annex I, paras. (4) and (5) of the commentary to Art. 2.

a nature as to endanger" greatly enlarges the scope of the definition by including risk or possible risk of damage. The phrase "to endanger" signifies the risk and "of such a nature" adds to it a second more comprehensive element. Applying these terms, an industrial installation may be deemed dangerous because of its inherently risky nature as well as because of its activities at any particular time. The definition thus encompasses the notion of ultra-hazardous activities and recalls various national laws requiring prior authorization for dangerous installations.[8]

"Human health" is designated as the primary reason to combat pollution. This anthropocentric approach is reinforced in protecting human "amenities" and "other legitimate uses of the environment" from interference. "Impair or interfere with amenities" can cover aesthetic nuisances such as pollution of lake waters or beaches, or harming tourist activities through deterioration of sites by smoke or waste. Even the reference to "living resources" shows that other creatures are envisaged in light of their service to humans. "Other legitimate uses of the environment" are sometimes specified in other conventions, including the 1982 UN Convention on the Law of the Sea, which speaks of "hindrances to marine activities, including fishing and other legitimate uses of the sea.[9]

"Ecosystem" may be understood as the totality of the physical-chemical environment and the living things which populate it,[10] characterized as a system by the dynamic relations of its constituting elements and processes. Pollutants act to disturb these relations and such processes as the water cycle and the biological food chain.

The term "transfrontier" may be understood to refer to spatial or territorial limits. The narrow range of early pollutants meant that concern about transboundary pollution initially extended to a zone only 15–20 miles on each side of an international border.[11] This led to a mistaken identification of the border region with "transfrontier" pollution, when in fact many pollutants, especially those transported by air, have their origin and impact in areas separated by considerable distances. The better foundation for legal regulation is the phenomenon of pollution itself and not the place

---

8   *E.g.*, French Law, July 19, 1976, which defines the activities requiring prior authorization because of their dangerous or polluting character. *See* M. PRIEUR, DROIT DE L'ENVIRONNEMENT 578 (1985).

9   UNCLOS Art. 1(4). *See* the similar definition in the Convention for Cooperation in the Protection and Sustainable Development of the Marine and Coastal Environment of the Northern Pacific (Antigua, Feb. 18, 2002).

10   F. RAMADE, ELEMENTS D'ECOLOGIE APPLIQUÉE (1982), p. 425.

11   Bilateral agreements on transfrontier pollution continue to establish geographic limits to their application. For example, the 1983 Mexico-United States Agreement to Cooperate in the Solution of Environmental Problems in the Border Area defines the border area as "the area situated 100 kilometers on either side of the inland and maritime boundaries." 23 I.L.M. 1025 (1983).

of origin or where the harmful effects are produced. A second OECD recommendation, this one relating to the implementation of a regime of equality of access and nondiscrimination in matters of transfrontier pollution,[12] reflects this broader approach:

> "Transfrontier pollution" means any intentional or unintentional pollution whose physical origin is subject to, and situated wholly or in part within the area under the national jurisdiction of one country and which has effects in the area under the national jurisdiction of another country.

The 1979 Geneva Convention on Long-Range Transboundary Air Pollution also refers to "any intentional or unintentional pollution whose physical origin is subject to, and situated wholly or in part within the area under, the national jurisdiction of one country and which has effects in the area under the national jurisdiction of another country." However, it further defines "long-range transboundary air pollution" as "air pollution whose physical origin is situated wholly or in part within the area under the national jurisdiction of one state and which has adverse effects in the area under the jurisdiction on another state at such a distance that it is not generally possible to distinguish the contribution of individual emission sources or groups of sources."

It should be noted that the above definitions of the transfrontier phenomena still require the presence of two states, although the causative agent may be outside the territorial limits of the responsible state as long as it is "subject to" the state's jurisdiction. These and similar provisions may be thought to exclude pollution within a single state or pollution within zones that are not part of any state's territory: the high seas and superadjacent airspace, Antarctica, and outer space. The limitation necessitated general rules to govern the entire environment.

2. Historic Approaches

Traditional international law respects each state's exclusive jurisdiction over its territory. Yet, acts which originate on the territory of one state may cause damage or infringe upon the sovereignty of another state, giving rise to conflict between the rights of the two states. The conflict can be looked at from two perspectives: that of the state on whose territory the pollution originates and that of the state whose territory is affected by the pollution. The pol-

---

12   Annex, Council Recommendation for the Implementation of a Regime of Equal Right of Access and Non-Discrimination in Relation to Transfrontier Pollution, C(77)28(Final), May 17, 1977.

luter state might argue the theory of absolute state sovereignty, but this approach has been repudiated in a world where states are increasingly obliged to cooperate. It is therefore necessary to search for more useful international legal principles.

a. Claims of Absolute Sovereignty

The claim of absolute sovereignty is identified with the "Harmon Doctrine," named for a 19th century United States Attorney General. In 1895, during a conflict between the United States and Mexico, Harmon expressed his official opinion through the State Department that the Mexican government had no right to protest water pollution in the boundary Rio Grande River, which lowered water quality in Mexico and damaged Mexican agriculture. Harmon contended that the rules, principles, and precedents of international law imposed no obligation or responsibility on the United States to protect Mexico from pollution and therefore any harm to Mexico was a political rather than a legal question.[13] Doctrine and international practice are virtually unanimous in condemning this extreme view of state sovereignty, which offers no legal solutions capable of reconciling the rights of two opposing and equal states, especially when the conflict is over use of a shared natural resource.

b. Abuse of Rights

The doctrine of abuse of rights recognizes the exclusive territorial jurisdiction of the polluting state, but subordinates the exercise of jurisdiction to a superior rule of international law which forbids sovereignty to be wielded in an abusive manner. Abuse of rights means the arbitrary exercise of a right, *i.e.*, the absence of an acceptable motivation for action when the activity prejudices another state. It can also be applied to acts whose benefits are negligible when compared to the harmful consequences produced in another state. Taking a concrete example, if dumping chemicals from an installation of relatively small importance would pollute an international watercourse and thereby deprive another state of its source of drinking water, the state on whose territory the installation is located should deny permission for the dumping. An agreement between Finland and Sweden concerning boundary waters incorporates this concept:

> Where the construction would result in a substantial deterioration
> in the living conditions of the population or cause a permanent

---

13   21 Op. Att'y Gen. 274, at 280–83 (1895).

change in natural conditions such as might entail substantially diminished comfort for people living in the vicinity or a significant nature conservancy loss or where significant public interests would be otherwise prejudiced, the construction shall be permitted only if it is of particular importance for the economy or for the locality or from some other public standpoint.[14]

This principle requires balancing the interests of the two states and respecting proportionality in conduct.[15] The OECD Principles on Transfrontier Pollution explicitly refer in the introduction to "a fair balance of the rights and obligations among countries concerned by transfrontier pollution"[16] and subsequently state that "countries should seek, as far as possible, an equitable balance of their rights and obligations as regards the zones concerned by transfrontier pollution."[17]

Today it is generally accepted that the principle forbidding abuse of right, whose origin lies in Roman law (*sic utere iure tuo ut alterum no laedas*) and which exists in all legal systems, forms part of international law. Treaties and judicial decisions apply the abuse of right principle to transfrontier pollution.[18] According to Article 5(1) of the UN Convention on the Law of the Non-Navigational Uses of International Watercourses:[19]

Watercourse States shall in their respective territories utilize an international watercourse in an equitable and reasonable manner. In particular, an international watercourse shall be used and developed by watercourse States with a view to attaining optimal and sustainable utilization thereof and benefits therefrom, taking into account the interests of the watercourse States concerned, consistent with adequate protection of the watercourse.

---

14   Art. 3(2), Agreement Concerning Frontier Rivers between Finland and Sweden (Sept. 16, 1971).

15   The legal principles drafted by the panel of independent experts for the Brundtland Commission reflect this concept. *See* Art. 12, at 28.

16   OECD, Principles Concerning Transfrontier Pollution, C(74)224, Nov. 14, 1974, Introduction.

17   *Id.*

18   As early as 1911, in reference to international watercourses, the Institute of International Law stated that neither state bounded by a river may "on its own territory, utilize or allow the utilization of the water in such a way as seriously to interfere with its utilization by the other State or by individuals, corporations, etc., thereof." J. BROWN SCOTT, RESOLUTIONS OF THE INSTITUTE OF INTERNATIONAL LAW DEALING WITH THE LAW OF NATIONS 169 (1916).

19   New York, May 21, 1997.

The widespread adoption of the concept of equitable utilization in treaty law and state practice could be deemed to create a specific rule of international law directly forbidding significant transfrontier pollution, without further recourse to the theory of abuse of right, if transfrontier pollution is viewed as inherently inequitable. Thus, an autonomous norm prohibiting transfrontier pollution may emerge from the doctrine of abuse of right. However, before addressing this, it is important to examine the problem of transfrontier pollution from the point of view of the state whose territory suffers injury from the pollution.

c. The Right to Be Free from Transfrontier Pollution

The "receiving" state has the same right to exclusive territorial jurisdiction as does the polluting state. In principle, because it has the right to have its territory respected, it should remain free from outside intervention. In particular, it is not obliged to accept damage to its environment due to acts taking place on the territory of other states. This right is no less absolute than that of the polluting state to utilize its own territory.

The need to reconcile the rights of the two states is evident. The International Court of Justice, in its judgment in the 1949 *Corfu Channel* case, announced a fundamental principle of general international law. The Court referred to "every State's obligation not to allow knowingly its territory to be used contrary to the rights of other states."[20] The same year as this decision, the United Nations Survey of International Law concluded that there is "general recognition of the rule that a State must not permit the use of its territory for purposes injurious to the interests of other States in a manner contrary to international law."[21] Within this framework several international precedents directly address the issue of transfrontier pollution.

The earliest case is the well-known arbitral decision between the United States and Canada[22] resulting from the activities of a Canadian smelter of zinc and lead ores, located in Trail, British Colombia. From the beginning of its operations in 1896, American farmers suffered damage due to emissions of sulphur dioxide by the plant. In 1903, the record year, these emissions exceeded 10,000 tons a month. In 1930, 300 to 350 tons of sulphur, in addition to other chemical residues, poured into the air. Initially, the smelter company paid indemnities to those suffering from the pollution, either following American court procedures or as a result of bilateral accords. In 1925, the case was reopened after the smelter added two 409-

---

[20]   1949 I.C.J. Rep., 22.
[21]   U.N. Doc. A/CN.4/1/Rev.1 (U.N. Pub. 1948. V.1(1)), at 34 (1949).
[22]   1931–1941, 3 U.N. RIAA 1905.

foot stacks to the plant to increase production, resulting in greater pollution. An association of injured persons was formed in order to obtain general damages in the place of individual recoveries. In 1927, the United States government officially took up the case and presented a claim to the government of Canada. After various efforts to settle the case by other means, the two governments submitted the matter to arbitration, signing a Convention to this effect April 15, 1935.[23]

The Convention settled the issue of responsibility. Its first article obligated the Canadian government to pay the United States government $350,000 to settle damage claims arising out of smelter activity before January 1, 1932. For periods after this date, the arbitral commission was asked to respond to four questions:

(1) Did the Trail Smelter cause damage after January 1, 1932, and if so, what indemnity should be paid as a consequence?

(2) If the first question is answered affirmatively, should the Trail Smelter be required to refrain from causing damage in the State of Washington in the future, and if so, to what extent?

(3) In light of the preceding question, what measures or regime, if any, should be adopted or maintained by the Trail Smelter?

(4) What indemnity or compensation should be paid on account of the decision of the arbitral tribunal?

In an interim decision, dated April 16, 1938, the arbitral tribunal responded to the first question concerning damage caused by the Trail Smelter since January 1, 1932. For the period between that date and October 1, 1937, the tribunal awarded $78,000 for damage to cleared and uncleared land.[24] The tribunal also decided that the Trail Smelter should be subject to a temporary regime to continue until October 1, 1940, including abstention from causing damage and installation of equipment to control pollution.

The final decision of the arbitral tribunal, issued March 11, 1941, detailed the facts and topographical, meteorological, and economic conditions of the region subjected to pollution. On the merits, it applied the principle of *res judicata*, calling it "an essential and settled rule of international law" and thus refused to review its previous opinion concerning

---

23   Convention for the Settlement of Difficulties arising from Operations of Smelter at Trail, B.C. (Ottawa, Apr. 15, 1935); 162 L.N.T.S. 73; 49 Stat. 3245, T.S. No. 893; 6 Bevans 60; C.T.S. 1935, No. 20; 30 AJIL 163 (Supp.).

24   The United States had presented claims for $1,849,156.16, including harm to (1) cleared and uncleared land and improvements, (2) livestock, (3) property in Newport, (4) infringement of United States sovereignty, (5) unpaid interest and (6) business losses. With interest the total came to $2,100,011.17. Only the first claim was accepted. The tribunal found that the language of the compromise precluded it from considering harm to United States sovereignty.

damage occurring before October 1, 1937. It also refused to allow an indemnity to the United States government for damage to crops, trees or otherwise during the following period, judging that the government had failed to provide sufficient evidence.

On the question of whether or to what extent the Trail Smelter must refrain from causing damage on the American territory, the tribunal defined the applicable principles in referring to Article IV of the arbitration Convention. It decided that it should take into consideration not only international law and practice but the law and practice existing in federal states. It deemed United States and Swiss law to confer on their constituent units rights analogous to those of states under international law. The arbitrators found the air pollution law of the United States in dealing with the quasi-sovereign rights of the states of the union conformed to the general rules of international law while providing more detail.

On the international plane, the tribunal asserted a general duty on the part of a state to protect other states from injurious acts by individuals within its jurisdiction. It also noted the difficulty of determining what constitutes an injurious act. In this regard it referred to two decisions of the Federal Court of Switzerland concerning the Cantons of Soleure and Argovia related to a military shooting range which endangered the border between the two cantons. Despite claims for absolute prohibition of the harmful activity, the Court concluded, and this tribunal agreed, that precautions taken by a state should be the same as those it would take to protect its own inhabitants.

The arbitral tribunal discovered no international precedent concerning pollution of the atmosphere or water, but found guidance in decisions of the United States Supreme Court that concerned both sectors. Several are cited, in particular an air pollution decision concerning Georgia and the Tennessee Copper Co. and Ducktown Sulphur, Copper and Iron Co. Ltd.[25] The Tribunal quoted approvingly a judgment of the U.S. Supreme Court for the proposition that a state has an interest in all the earth and air within its domain, and that it is a fair and reasonable demand that the air over its territory should not be polluted on a grand scale by sulphurous acid gas by acts of persons beyond its control. Thus,

> [t]he Tribunal, therefore, finds that the above decisions, taken as
> a whole, constitute an adequate basis for its conclusions, namely,
> that, under the principles of international law, as well as of the law
> of the United States, no State has the right to use or permit the use

---

[25]   *State of Georgia v. Tennessee Copper Company and Ducktown Sulphur, Copper and Iron Company, Ltd.*, 206 U.S. 230 (1907). The Tribunal also cited *Missouri v. Illinois*, 200 U.S. 496 (1906); *Kansas v. Colorado*, 185 U.S. 125 (1902); and *New York v. New Jersey*, 256 U.S. 296 (1921).

of its territory in such a manner as to cause injury by fumes in or to the territory of another or the properties or persons therein, when the case is of serious consequence and the injury is established by clear and convincing evidence.[26]

For the arbitral tribunal, Canada's liability for the Trail Smelter derived from its duty to ensure that the Smelter's activities conform to the obligations that international law places on each state. The Trail Smelter itself should refrain from causing damage by emission of fumes on the territory of the State of Washington. The damage which did occur should be repaired by the government, in conformity with Article XI of the arbitral Convention.

The third question posed to the tribunal concerned the future, asking what measures or what regime should be adopted or maintained by Canada. In responding, the tribunal elaborated a complete system based on studies previously made on its initiative and setting out control measures. The latter included the right to inspect the installations of the Smelter and to visit each property which allegedly suffered damage because of pollution. Notably, the regulatory scheme by its own terms allowed modification or suspension conforming to the decisions of a scientific commission to be constituted. The regime thus foreseen was aimed at eliminating future damage on U.S. territory by air pollution from Canada. Should the Smelter fail to conform to the order given it to refrain from causing further damage, the tribunal, in response to the fourth question regarding future damages, approved the principle of indemnity, leaving the extent and amount to agreement between the governments involved.

It is difficult to overestimate the importance of the *Trail Smelter* arbitration.[27] The arbitral Convention itself constitutes a noteworthy precedent, insofar as it announces two principles. First, it recognized the responsibility of a state for acts of pollution having their origin on its territory and causing damage on the territory of other states, even if the polluting acts are not imputable to the state itself or its organs. Thus, the state may be responsible for not enacting necessary legislation, for not enforcing its laws against those within its jurisdiction or control, for not preventing or terminating an illegal activity, or for not sanctioning the person responsible for it. Second, the Convention transcends international responsibility to resolve the conflict before it, aiming towards a common regulation of the issue. The judgment itself affirms the existence of a rule of international law forbidding transfrontier pollution, a fact of fundamental importance. The

---

26   3 U.N. RIAA 1938, 1965.

27   The case continues to be invoked. In 1972, Canada referred to the judgment when an oil spill in Washington polluted beaches in British Colombia. 11 CAN. Y.B. INT'L L. 333–34 (1973).

Tribunal also elaborated a framework for the future, perhaps exceeding its mandate, in recognizing the necessity of further cooperation between the interested states. In requiring regulation, the judgment identifies what is now seen as a general requirement of environmental law: the rules adopted should be flexible and adaptable according to the evolution of the situation and knowledge of it.

The enlightened approach of the *Trail Smelter* arbitrators is also seen in the last sentence of the decision, which sums up a fundamental aspect of international environmental law: "The Tribunal expresses the strong hope that any investigations which the Governments may undertake in the future, in connection with the matters dealt with in this decision, shall be conducted jointly."

Some 15 years after the *Trail Smelter* award, the *Lake Lanoux* arbitral decision[28] also alluded to the problem of transfrontier pollution in holding that France could use the waters of the lake for French public works, restoring the waters to the River Carol which crosses the Spanish frontier to join the Segre River. No water pollution was alleged, but the arbitral tribunal nonetheless addressed the matter:

> It could have been argued that the works would bring about a definitive pollution of the waters of the Carol or that the returned waters would have a chemical composition or a temperature or some other characteristic which could injure Spanish interests. Spain could then have claimed that her rights had been impaired in violation of the Additional Act.[29]

The Tribunal later indicated the consequences which would occur from such pollution:

> Thus, while admittedly there is a rule prohibiting the upper riparian State from altering the waters of a river in circumstances calculated to do serious injury to the lower riparian State, such a principle has no application to the present case, since it was agreed by the Tribunal . . . that the French project did not alter the waters of the Carol.[30]

---

28   Lake Lanoux Arbitration (France-Spain), Arbitral Tribunal (1957), 12 U.N. RIAA 281. An English translation of the award appears in 2 Y.B. I.L.C., Part Two, at 194–99 (1974); U.N. Doc. A/5409, paras. 1055–1068; 53 AJIL 156–71 (1959); and I.L.R., at 101–42 (1957).

29   12 U.N. RIAA 303.

30   2 Y.B. I.L.C. Part Two, at 197 (1974); U.N. Doc. A/5409, para. 1066.

A pollution case which arose in the Netherlands in 1974 should be added to this international jurisprudence. Twelve million tons of salt were dumped each year into the river during this time, most of it from potassium mines in Alsace, France, making the production of drinking water extremely expensive and adding to the constant problem of combating salt water infiltration into Dutch agricultural fields. Diplomatic efforts to resolve the problem failed. A Dutch association, "Reinwater," intervened in a case brought in Rotterdam by a grower who claimed damages from the Alsatian company for his salt-damaged crops.

The Rotterdam court addressed the merits of the case in several decisions. The first, issued in 1979,[31] held that Dutch courts should apply international law which is part of Dutch law. Finding no treaty between France and the Netherlands containing an applicable rule and no relevant rule of customary international law, it referred to general principles of law, according to Article 38(1)(c) of the Statute of the International Court of Justice. It cited the *Trail Smelter* decision as a case of abuse of right, a general principle of law. After it was established by clear and convincing evidence that the grower's damage was caused by the dumping of salt, the Court found the dumping constituted a violation of the abuse of right principle. Thus, the defendant could owe reparations to the victim, but the Tribunal demanded evidence on several points, including the nature of the damages, what part of the Rhine was used by growers who claimed injury, and the effect of chlorides on plants.

On the basis of a subsequently prepared expert report, a second decision was rendered in 1983[32] holding the mines responsible for an average of 37.5 percent of the salt transported by the Rhine to the Netherlands. The Tribunal therefore concluded that the dumping of salt by the Mines de Potasse was contrary to its obligations and illegal.

The second Rotterdam judgment developed the international law considerations reviewed in the first decision. In its view, international custom did not forbid the dumping of wastes in an international waterway. However, international law did recognize the principle that an upstream country's rights to utilize the waters require that it take into account the equitable uses of downstream states. In addition, states must respect the principle announced in the *Trail Smelter* arbitration which forbids causing damage to the territory or inhabitants of another state, confirmed in the *Lake Lanoux* arbitration. The prohibition against utilizing a right to the detriment of another is equally applicable to common usages of an international waterway.

---

31   *Handelskwekerij G.-J. Bier B.V., Stichting Reinwater c. Mines de potasse d'Alsace* S.A. (in Dutch only).

32   Rotterdam Tribunal, *Handelskwekerij G.-J. Bier et autres v. Mines de Potasse d'Alsace*, Dec. 16, 1983; 15 Neth. Y.B. Int'l L. 1984.

The two judgments were upheld by the Hague Court of Appeal in 1986. However, the Court moved away from international law, deciding that international law applies only in relations between states, and thus the only ground for judging the case was internal Dutch law. It still held the Mines de Potasse negligent and therefore liable for failing to take into consideration the damage resulting downstream from their dumping of salt into the Rhine.[33] This negligence resulted in their liability. The case was finally settled in 1988, with the Mines de Potasse agreeing to pay the plaintiffs 11,250,000 French francs (approximately $2,000,000).

These cases reflect a trend towards liability for transfrontier pollution. The second judgment of the Rotterdam Tribunal referred to the evolution in the law during the preceding decade. Today it seems possible to affirm that specific rules of international law forbid, or at least regulate, transfrontier pollution. To this must be added a body of principles, more or less emerging, which derive partly from the prohibition, partly from the necessity to cooperate, affirmed by the *Trail Smelter* arbitral tribunal.

3. *Current Norms*

a. Respect for the Environment of Other States and Commons Areas

Case law precedents and the application of general rules of international law have led to development of the fundamental norm of international environmental law concerning transfrontier pollution. The 1972 Stockholm Declaration formulated it in Principle 21 as follows:

> States have, in accordance with the Charter of the United Nations and the principles of international law, the sovereign right to exploit their own resources pursuant to their own environmental policies, and the responsibility to ensure that activities within their jurisdiction or control do not cause damage to the environment of other States or of areas beyond the limits of national jurisdiction.

The rule was reiterated in Principle 2 of the 1992 Rio Declaration, adding the adjective "developmental" between the words "environmental" and "policies" and was again confirmed in the 2002 World Summit on Sustainable Development.

---

[33]   Judgment of Sept. 10, 1986. The Potassium Mines lodged a further appeal. On September 23, 1988, the Supreme Court of the Netherlands denied the appeal, indicating that transboundary pollution is not a matter of international law. It applied the Dutch law of nuisance, where the gravity of the harm inflicted and the weighing of interests are the central issues.

The norm contains two elements. One, it reaffirms the sovereign right of states over their natural resources, pronounced in numerous declarations of the General Assembly[34] as well as international instruments relating to the protection of human rights.[35] However, the allusion to national environmental policies gives a more ecological color to this norm, inviting states to develop a coherent policy for environmental protection. The addition of the term "developmental" in the Rio Declaration corresponds to the emergence of the concept of sustainable development.

In its second aspect, Principle 21 affirms the duty of states "to ensure" that activities within their jurisdiction or control do not cause damage to the environment of other states. In the first place, this means that states are responsible not only for their own activities, but also that they have a due diligence obligation to regulate all public and private activities within their jurisdiction or control. This implies a duty to regulate activities that could harm the environment of other states or areas outside the limits of their jurisdiction. In numerous countries this regime takes the form of a licensing of installations which could prejudice the environment.[36] Second, states should apply the same rules not only in places where they exercise territorial competence ("within their jurisdiction"), that is on land, in the territorial sea, on the continental shelf and within the exclusive economic zone, but everywhere they exercise "control." In other words, the obligation exists for ships, airplanes and spacecraft having the nationality of the state, as well

---

[34]   *E.g.*, Permanent Sovereignty over Natural Resources, G.A. Res. 1803 (XVII), Dec. 14, 1962; The New International Economic Order, G.A. Res. 3201 (S-VI), May 1, 1974; Charter of Economic Rights and Duties of States, G.A. Res. 3281(XXIX), Dec. 12, 1974, U.N. GAOR 29th Sess., Supp. No. 31 (A/9631), at 50. *See also* N. SCHRIVER, SOVEREIGNTY OVER NATURAL RESOURCES, BALANCING RIGHTS AND DUTIES 231–51 (1997).

[35]   *E.g.*, common Art. 1, United Nations Covenants on Civil and Political Rights, 999 U.N.T.S. 171, and Economic, Social, and Cultural Rights, 993 U.N.T.S. 3 (Dec. 16, 1966); Art. 21, 1981 African Charter on Human and Peoples' Rights, 7 HUM. RTS. L.J. 403 (1986); 21 I.L.M. 58 (1982).

[36]   In the United States, both the Clean Water Act, 33 U.S.C. § 1251–76, and the Clean Air Act, 42 U.S.C. §§ 7401–7642, apply to transfrontier pollution on condition of reciprocity where there is reason to believe that pollution is occurring that endangers the health or welfare of persons in a foreign state. Hearings may be held with the participation of the foreign country that may be adversely affected by the pollution. Another form of regulation is found in an Executive Order on Environmental Effects Abroad of Major Federal Actions, which requires federal agencies to take into consideration environmental impact statements and relevant international environmental studies when approving major federal actions significantly affecting the environment of the global commons outside the jurisdiction of any nation. U.S. Exec. Order No. 12114, Jan. 4, 1979, Section 3–4, 44 Fed. Reg. 1957 (1979).

as for missions to Antarctica, troops stationed in foreign territories, and any occupied or dependent territories.

Principle 21 fundamentally derives from the obligations that states assume towards the international community. Thus, the duty to not cause damage to the environment exists not only towards other states, but also towards the "areas beyond the limits of national jurisdiction:" the high seas and the airspace above them, the deep sea-bed, outer space, the Moon and other celestial bodies, and Antarctica. In part, it is the control over activities in these regions that engages the obligations of states, together with the duty to combat any pollution coming directly from their territory that affects these regions.

Principle 21 of the Stockholm Declaration, although part of a non-binding text, is nonetheless recognized as a rule of customary international law. It has been reaffirmed in declarations adopted by the United Nations, including the Charter of Economic Rights and Duties of States and the World Charter for Nature, and has been adopted by other international organizations and conferences.[37] Its content is inserted in the Convention on the Law of the Sea[38] as well as in Article 20 of the ASEAN Convention on the Conservation of Nature and Natural Resources.[39] The 1979 Geneva Convention on Long Range Transboundary Air Pollution reproduces Principle 21 of the Stockholm Conference stating that the Principle "expresses the common conviction that States have" on this matter. Principle 21 as restated in the 1992 Rio Declaration also appears in the preamble of the 1992 UN Framework Convention on Climate Change and Article 3 of the Convention on Biological Diversity, to which virtually all the states of the world are contracting parties. Finally, the International Court of Justice recognized in an advisory opinion that "[t]he existence of the general obligation of states to ensure that activities within their jurisdiction and control respect the environment of other states or of areas beyond national control is now part of the corpus of international law relating to the environment."[40] This statement was repeated in the judgment concerning the *Gabčikovo-Nagymaros Project*, in which the Court also "recall[ed] that it has recently had occasion to stress . . . the great significance that it attaches to respect for the environment, not only for states but also for the whole of mankind."[41]

---

[37]   *See, e.g.*, Preliminary Declaration of a Program of Action of the European Communities in respect to the Environment, O.J. C 112/1, (12/30/73); Final Act, Conference on Security and Cooperation in Europe, Helsinki, Aug. 1976.

[38]   UNCLOS Art. 194(2).

[39]   ASEAN Agreement on the Conservation of Nature and Natural Resources (Kuala Lumpur, July 9, 1985); 15 E.P.L. 64 (1985).

[40]   *Legality of the Threat or Use of Nuclear Weapons*, Advisory Opinion, 1996 I.C.J. Rep. 241–42, para 29.

[41]   Sept. 25, 1997, para. 53.

In 2001, after many years of debate and drafting, the UN International Law Commission completed a set of draft articles on prevention of significant transboundary harm from hazardous activities. The General Assembly reviewed the articles and asked the ILC to continue work on the topic of international liability.[42]

b.   Notification of Imminent Harm

The common law of the environment requires states to immediately inform other states likely to be affected by any sudden situation or event that could cause harm to their environment and to provide those states with all pertinent information. The foundation of this rule appears in general international law. In the *Corfu Channel* case, the International Court of Justice held that Albania, in the interest of navigation in general, had a duty to make known the existence of a mine field in Albanian territorial waters and to alert warships of the British navy at the moment when they approached imminent danger from the mines. This obligation, said the Court, derives from certain general and well-known principles, including elementary considerations of humanity.[43] On the basis of analogous considerations a duty is imposed to alert states of any serious transboundary risk to their environment.[44]

Several non-binding texts affirm the duty to notify, beginning with OECD's Principles concerning Transfrontier Pollution,[45] later developed by OECD in a decision on the exchange of information concerning accidents capable of causing transfrontier damage.[46] This decision requires members to exchange information, consult to prevent accidents causing transfrontier damage, and reduce damage caused. Practical measures in Annex I include arrangements or agreements on the means of exchanging information on hazardous installations and hazardous substances, defined in appendices.

---

[42]   *See* Report of the ILC, United Nations 53d Sess, at 370 (2001); U.N. Doc. A/56/10 (2001).

[43]   1949 I.J.C. Rep. at 22.

[44]   Comment (e) to section 601 of the Third Restatement of Foreign Relations Law of the United States, finds within the general environmental responsibilities of states an obligation to warn another state promptly of any situation that may cause significant pollution damage in that state.

[45]   Principle 9, OECD, "Principles Concerning Transfrontier Pollution," C(74)224 (Nov. 14, 1974): "Countries should promptly warn other potentially affected countries of any situation which may cause any sudden increase in the level of pollution in areas outside the country of origin of pollution, and take all appropriate steps to reduce the effects of any such sudden increase."

[46]   C(88)84(Final), July 8, 1988.

A particularly complete formulation is contained in the 1978 UNEP Principles on Shared Resources:

> States have a duty urgently to inform other states which may be affected:
>
> (a) Of any emergency situation arising from the utilization of a shared natural resource which might cause sudden harmful effects on their environment;
>
> (b) Of any sudden grave natural events related to a shared natural resource which may affect the environment of such states.[47]

While the notion of "shared natural resource" is difficult to define, boundary waters or contiguous seas and air to a certain distance can be considered as included.

The duty to notify is expressed even in regard to remote sensing. Principle 10 of a resolution adopted June 13, 1986, by the UN Committee on Peaceful Uses of Outer Space, provides that states conducting remote sensing activities should transmit to the states concerned any information they acquire indicating harmful environmental phenomena on earth.[48]

The customary duty to notify of environmental crises has developed in a general fashion and is spelled out more concretely in numerous international treaties. UNCLOS Article 198 sums up the provisions contained in various conventions relating to marine pollution, both in general and in regard to regional seas.[49]

> When a State becomes aware of cases in which the marine environment is in imminent danger of being damaged or has been damaged by pollution, it shall immediately notify other States it deems likely to be affected by such damage, as well as the competent international organizations.

Articles 4 and 5 of the 1990 London Convention on Oil Pollution Preparedness, Response and Co-operation[50] develop this obligation by organizing procedures of information. Principle 18 of the Rio Declaration formulates the same obligation in the following way: "States shall immedi-

---

47   Principle 9(1), of the 1978 UNEP Principles of Conduct in the Field of the Enviroment for the Guidance of States in the Conservation and Harmonious Utilization of Natural Resources Shared by Two or More States.

48   June 13, 1986, 25 I.L.M. 1334 (1986).

49   For example, *see* Art. 5, Agreement for Cooperation in Dealing with Pollution of the North Sea by Oil (June 9, 1969); Art. 8, International Convention for the Prevention of Pollution from Ships (Nov. 2, 1973); and the series of agreements concerning regional seas concluded under the auspices of UNEP.

50   Nov. 30, 1990, EMuT 990:88.

ately notify other States of any natural disasters or other emergencies that are likely to produce sudden harmful effects on the environment of those States."

The duty to notify is often inserted in treaties relating to rivers. It is included, for example, in Article 11 of the Convention for the Protection of the Rhine Against Chemical Pollution, which also established an international alert system.[51] It must be noted, however, that this system did not perform well during the November 1, 1986 Sandoz factory chemical spill near Basel, Switzerland, which caused serious pollution of the Rhine.[52] The system has since been reviewed and corrected.[53] The model in this regard is Article 14 of the 1992 Helsinki Convention on the Protection and Use of Transboundary Watercourses and International Lakes:[54]

> The Riparian States shall without delay inform each other about any critical situation that may have transboundary impact. The Riparian Parties shall set up, where appropriate, and operate coordinated or joint communication, warning and alarm systems with the aim of obtaining and transmitting information. These systems shall operate on the basis of compatible data transmission and treatment procedures and facilities to be agreed upon by the Riparian Parties. The Riparian Parties shall inform each other about competent authorities or points of contact designated for this purpose.[55]

Finally, Article 28 of the UN Convention on the Law of the Non-Navigational Uses of International Watercourses requires states parties to notify without delay and by the most expeditious means available, potentially affected states and competent international organizations of any emergency originating within its territory.[56]

Provisions on notification are also included in more general agreements, as exemplified by Article 20(d) of the ASEAN Convention on the

---

51   Art. 11, Bonn Convention on Protection of the Rhine (Dec. 3, 1976). A duty to notify of pollution emergencies is also contained in Arts. 6(1)(i) and 10 of the 1978 Great Lakes Water Quality Agreement between Canada and the United States. For a listing of other agreements, *see* WCED ENVIRONMENTAL PROTECTION AND SUSTAINABLE DEVELOPMENT 117–19 (1986).

52   *See* Aaron Schwabach, *The Sandoz Spill: The Failure of International Law to Protect the Rhine from Pollution*, 16 ECOL. L.Q. 443 (1989).

53   *See* Chapter 10.

54   Helsinki, Mar. 17, 1992; EmuT 992:22.

55   Art. 16 of the Convention on Cooperation for the Protection and Sustainable Use of the Danube River (Sofia, June 29, 1994), can be considered as a further development of this provision.

56   New York, May 21, 1997.

Conservation of Nature and Natural Resources,[57] Article 10 of the 1992 Helsinki Convention on Transboundary Effects of Industrial Accidents,[58] Article 15(2)(b) of the Madrid Protocol on Environmental Protection to the Antarctic Treaty,[59] and Article 14(1)(d) of the Convention on Biological Diversity.[60] Similarly, the duty to notify is found in several bilateral conventions regarding environmental disasters along shared borders[61] and in numerous agreements concerning nuclear accidents.[62] Among the latter, particular attention is due the Vienna Convention on Early Notification in the Case of Nuclear Accident or Radiological Emergency.[63] Article 2 requires that each state on whose territory a nuclear accident occurs notify other states which are or could be physically affected, of the accident, its nature, the moment when it occurred and its exact location. It thus must rapidly furnish available relevant information in order to limit as much as possible the radioactive consequences to the exposed state or states. In another response, IAEA and WMO announced on February 26, 1988, the development of a worldwide early warning network which would alert states of the possibility of pollution resulting from a nuclear power plant accident.[64]

c.   Assistance in Emergencies

It is less clear that there is a legal obligation to assist a state in an environmental emergency. In its Declaration of Principles on Transfrontier Pollution, OECD couples the duty to warn with a principle that for incidents that could result in transfrontier pollution, "countries should assist each other, whenever necessary, in order to . . . minimize, and if possible eliminate, the effects of such incidents, and should develop contingency plans to this end."[65]

---

[57]   Kuala Lumpur, July 9, 1985.

[58]   Helsinki, Mar. 17,1992.

[59]   Madrid, Oct. 4, 1991.

[60]   Rio de Janeiro, June 5, 1992.

[61]   *See* the German-French Agreement of September 20, 1973, *Bulletin d'information du Gouvernement fédéral allemand,* No. 115, at 1141 (Sept. 21, 1973).

[62]   Such agreements sometimes extend to nuclear weapons. *See, e.g.,* the 1978 agreement between France and the Soviet Union regarding prevention of accidental or unauthorized use of nuclear weapons. The treaty requires each state to notify the other party immediately "of any accidental occurrence or any other unexplained incident that could lead to the explosion of one of their nuclear weapons which may have harmful effect on the other party." 1036 U.N.T.S. 299.

[63]   IAEA INFCIRC 335; 25 I.L.M. 1370 (1986).

[64]   Int'l Envt. Rep. 161, Mar. 3, 1988.

[65]   Principle 10, Nov. 14, 1974.

A general duty of assistance, or, at least of cooperation, has been inserted in the majority of conventional provisions establishing an obligation to notify. However, notification does not *per se* necessitate a special procedure, although it can be useful to establish communications systems and know which authorities of the foreign state should be alerted. In contrast, assistance usually implies operations on the territory of a foreign state and necessitates specific arrangements between the states requesting and supplying assistance. States may hesitate because assistance, while sometimes necessary, is also inherently more intrusive. UNCLOS Article 199 summarizes the situation well, foreseeing that in case of imminent risk of damage or of actual damage from pollution to the marine environment

> . . . States in the areas affected, in accordance with their capabilities, and the competent international organizations shall cooperate, to the extent possible, in eliminating the effects of pollution and preventing or minimizing the damage. To this end, States shall jointly develop and promote contingency plans for responding to pollution incidents in the marine environment.

The 1990 International Convention on Oil Pollution Preparedness, Response and Cooperation[66] provides that upon the request of any party affected by oil pollution, the parties will cooperate according to their capabilities and the availability of relevant resources, by providing advisory services, technical support, and equipment for the purpose of responding to the incident. An annex to the Convention concerns the reimbursement of costs of assistance.

A growing number of contingency arrangements do exist. The earliest of these agreements aimed at providing emergency assistance and mutual cooperation in combating oil spills or nuclear accidents, such as the Nordic Mutual Emergency Assistance Agreement in Connection with Radiation Accidents,[67] the International Convention Relating to Intervention on the High Seas in Case of Oil Pollution Casualties,[68] and the Bonn Agreement for Cooperation in Dealing with Pollution of the North Sea by Oil.[69]

In many cases, common emergency plans have been elaborated on a bilateral basis. For example, a common emergency plan is in effect between Canada and Denmark concerning ocean pollution caused by ships, annexed to their Agreement on Cooperation Relating to the Marine Environment (August 6, 1983).[70] A 1977 agreement between France and Germany

---

66 London, Nov. 30, 1990; 30 I.L.M. 733 (1991)
67 Oct. 17, 1963; 525 U.N.T.S. 75.
68 Nov. 29, 1969.
69 June 9, 1969.
70 23 I.L.M. 269 (1984).

provides for mutual assistance in case of catastrophe or serious accidents. The 1990 International Convention on Oil Pollution Preparedness, Response and Co-operation provides that the parties will cooperate and provide advisory services, technical support and equipment for the purpose of responding to an oil pollution accident, when the severity of such incident so justifies, upon the request of any party affected or likely to be affected.[71] Eight of the UNEP regional seas treaty systems include protocols on emergencies and provide for cooperation in cases of grave and imminent danger to the marine environment and the establishment in this regard of joint contingency plans.[72]

Generally, cooperation arrangements should detail action required prior to any accident and action to be taken in case of an accident. Prior action consists of exchanges of information regarding the competent organs which should be notified, the plans or national programs applicable in case of an emergency, and the applicable legal rules. The information may include the means available to combat the consequences of any accident, the means of communication, and the relevant measures concerning security. The surveillance of specified zones can be organized, as is seen in the Bonn Agreement for Cooperation in Dealing with Pollution of the North Sea by Oil[73] and in the 1990 Cooperation Agreement for the Protection of the Coasts and Waters of the North-East Atlantic against Pollution.[74]

For action during emergencies, plans should focus on the organization of assistance and the scope and division of authority. Material aspects must not be ignored, including arrangements for financing of assistance and customs formalities concerning the border passage for aid personnel and supplies. The 1990 Lisbon Agreement concerning Cooperation for the North East Atlantic provides for the establishment of an International Center with the aim of assisting the parties to react swiftly and effectively to pollution accidents[75]

After the Chernobyl accident, along with the convention on early notification, a second treaty was concluded focusing on assistance in the case of a nuclear accident or radiological emergency.[76] Due to the complexity of the subject, the measures adopted were in the nature of a framework treaty necessitating further agreements between states. Article 1 requires only that the states parties cooperate "to facilitate assistance," without truly imposing

---

[71]   Art. 7, London Convention, Nov. 30, 1990.

[72]   *See* P. SANDS, PRINCIPLES OF INTERNATIONAL ENVIRONMENTAL LAW 337 (1995).

[73]   June 9, 1969.

[74]   Lisbon, Oct. 17, 1990.

[75]   Arts. 18–21. Annex 2 to the Agreement defines the functions of the Center.

[76]   Convention on Assistance in the Case of a Nuclear Accident or Radiological Emergency (Vienna, Sept. 26, 1986).

an obligation to assist a state which is the victim of significant environmental deterioration because of nuclear accident or radioactive emergency.

Treaties relating to inland waters also provide for mutual assistance. According to Article 15 of the 1992 Helsinki Convention on the Protection and Use of Transboundary Watercourses and Lakes[77] riparian states party shall provide mutual assistance upon request and establish procedures for doing so. These should address issues such as the direction, control, coordination and supervision of assistance, the existence of local facilities and services, the facilitation of border-crossing formalities, the indemnization and/or compensation of the assisting party and/or of its personnel and the methods of reimbursing assistance services. The UN Convention on the Law of the Non-Navigational Uses of International Watercourses[78] also prescribes the joint development of contingency plans for responding to emergencies, in cooperation, where appropriate, with other potentially affected states and competent international organizations.

d. Advance Notification and Consultation

Apart from emergency situations where urgent notification and possibly assistance is required, a state that plans to undertake or authorize activities capable of having significant impact on the environment of another state must inform the latter and should transmit to it the pertinent details of the project, to the extent that no national legislation or applicable international treaty prohibits such transmission. The 1992 Rio Declaration formulates the obligation as follows: "States shall provide prior and timely notification and relevant information to potentially affected States on activities that may have a significant adverse transboundary environmental effect and shall consult with those States at an early stage and in good faith."

The requirement of prior notification of projects that could cause transfrontier pollution was first included in bilateral treaties, notably concerning the construction of nuclear installations.[79] It is also included in many watercourse agreements. A series of non-binding texts also proclaim the norm, after an initial setback at the Stockholm Conference where consensus could not be achieved due to disagreement among Latin American states. The obligation is included in a 1973 resolution of the United

---

[77] Mar. 17, 1992. Art. 17 of the Convention on Cooperation for the Protection and Sustainable Use of the Danube River (Sofia, June 9, 1994) reproduces this provision.

[78] New York, May 21, 1997, Art. 28(3) and (4).

[79] *See, e.g.*, the French-Belgian agreement on protection from radioactivity concerning construction of the nuclear power station at Ardennes, Sept. 26, 1966, Art. 2.

Nations[80] and in Article 3 of the Charter of Economic Rights and Duties of States. It is most developed in a series of OECD resolutions, beginning with Title E of the 1974 Principles concerning Transfrontier Pollution.[81] Several OECD texts insist on the transmission of information to persons who risk being exposed to the harmful consequences of a project.[82]

The duty to consult often accompanies the duty to inform.[83] Principle 6 of the 1978 UNEP Principles of Conduct in the Field of the Environment for the Guidance of States in the Conservation and Harmonious Utilization of Natural Resources Shared by Two or More States is particularly explicit in this regard. It stresses the necessity to notify in advance the other state or states of the pertinent details of plans to initiate activities which can reasonably be expected to significantly affect the environment in the territory of the other state or states, and upon request of the other state or states, to enter into consultations concerning the above-mentioned plans.

The number of international treaties requiring prior notification increased during the 1970s and the first half of the 1980s. The agreements mainly concern air pollution or water pollution, but the norm can also be found in more general instruments like the Nordic Environmental Protection Convention[84] which effectively integrates the territories of the con-

---

[80]   G.A. Res. 3139(XXVIII), Dec. 13, 1973.

[81]   Title E, Art. 6, provides that "prior to the initiation in a country of works or undertakings which might create a significant risk of transfrontier pollution, this country should provide early information to other countries which are or may be affected. It should provide these countries with relevant information and data, the transmission of which is not prohibited by legislative provisions or prescriptions or applicable international conventions, and should invite their comments." Council Recommendation C(74)224, Nov. 14, 1974.

[82]   OECD, Implementation of a Regime of Equal Right of Access and Non-Discrimination in Relation to Transfrontier Pollution, Recommendation C(77)28(Final), May 17, 1977, part C; Strengthening International Cooperation on Environmental Protection of Transfrontier Regions, Recommendation C(78)77(Final) of Sept. 21, 1978, para. 3.

[83]   In the 1974 OECD Principles Concerning Transfrontier Pollution, the Title E obligation to provide information is coupled with a duty to consult: "7. Countries should enter into consultation on an existing or foreseeable transfrontier pollution problem at the request of a country which is or may be directly affected and should diligently pursue such consultations on this particular problem over a reasonable period of time." In addition, Article 8 provides that countries should refrain from carrying out projects or activities which might create a significant risk of transfrontier pollution until they have informed and provided a reasonable amount of time for diligent consultation with countries which are or may be affected. Such consultations "held in the best spirit of cooperation and good neighborliness" should not entail unreasonable delay or impediments to the activities or projects.

[84]   Stockholm, Feb. 19, 1974.

tracting parties in regard to the authorization of environmentally-harmful activities; any activity that could cause harm in another state is equated with a nuisance in the state where the activity is carried out. Other conventions of the same period include a more modestly drafted duty to inform. The regional Kuwait Convention on the Protection of the Marine Environment from Pollution[85] provides in Article 11 for the dissemination of information containing an evaluation of the possible effects of planned activities on the environment. Similarly, Article 20 of the ASEAN Agreement on the Conservation of Nature and Natural Resources[86] provides that the contracting parties will notify in advance the other contracting parties of the pertinent details of proposed activities which "can reasonably be expected to have" significant impact outside the limits of their national jurisdiction. Article 20 also provides for consultation on a project or activity at the request of a state whose environment could be affected by it. States parties to the 1979 Geneva Convention on Long-Range Transboundary Air Pollution are required to institute exchanges of information not so much on specific activities as on national policies and industrial development in general and the effects that changes in these areas could produce regarding long-range air pollution.[87]

In a bilateral example, the 1980 United States-Canada air quality agreement includes a rather detailed commitment to continue and expand the long-standing practice of advance notification and consultations on proposed actions involving a significant or potential risk of causing or increasing transboundary air pollution, including: (a) proposed major industrial development or other actions which may cause significant increases in transboundary air pollution; and (b) proposed changes of policy, regulations or practices which may significantly affect transboundary air pollution.[88]

In the 1990s the same norm appeared almost regularly in treaties relating to transboundary issues, generally linked with an environmental impact assessment procedure. The entire Helsinki Convention on Environmental Impact Assessment in a Transboundary Context[89] is based upon the obligation to notify other states of proposed activities which are listed in Appendix I to the Convention. Appendix III sets general criteria to assist in the determination of the environmental significance of activities not

---

[85]   Kuwait, Apr. 24, 1978.

[86]   Kuala Lumpur, July 9, 1985.

[87]   Arts. 4 and 8, Geneva Convention on Long-Range Transboundary Air Pollution (Nov. 13, 1979). A similar obligation is found in the 1980 Memorandum of Intent between Canada and the U.S. concerning Transboundary Air Pollution.

[88]   Memorandum of Intent between Canada and the U.S. Concerning Transboundary Air Pollution, Aug. 5, 1980.

[89]   Espoo, Feb. 25, 1991.

listed in Appendix I. Article 5 and Appendix II specify the information to be transmitted.

The related obligation to enter into consultations signifies that the state which is the potential polluter must be willing to discuss the information which it has forwarded to the potentially-affected state, which in turn may make observations concerning the project. However, the observations need not be fully accepted by the state which proposes to act; otherwise the potentially-affected state would have an effective veto over planned projects.

Part III of the 1997 UN Convention on the Law of the Non-Navigational Uses of International Watercourses[90] describes in detail the procedure to be applied. Watercourse states are to exchange information and consult each other and, if necessary, negotiate on the possible effects of planned measures on the condition of an international watercourse. This includes timely notification concerning planned measures with possible adverse effects. The notified state has a period of six months to answer, but the period can be extended in exceptional cases for another six months. During this period the planned measures shall not be implemented without the consent of the notified state. If a notified state finds that implementation of the planned measures would be inconsistent with the norm of equitable and reasonable utilization, the reply to notification shall include a documented explanation in this regard. If the notified state does not reply within the period applicable, the notifying state may proceed with the implementation of the planned measures. If the notification is made, the concerned states shall enter into consultations and, if necessary negotiations, conducted in good faith with a view to arriving at an equitable resolution of the situation. Special procedures are provided for the absence of notification and for the event that the implementation of planned measures is of the utmost urgency in order to protect public health, public safety or other equally important interests.

The procedure of information and consultation has been applied in a different context in the Protocol Concerning Mediterranean Specially Protected Areas.[91] Article 6 provides that when one contracting party proposes to create a protected zone contiguous to the frontier or limits of a zone of national jurisdiction of another party, the competent authorities of the two shall consult to arrive at an agreement on the measures to take and, among other things, examine the possibility for the second state to create a corresponding protected zone or to adopt any other appropriate measure.

In the end, the obligation to inform and to consult is a product of the obligation to cooperate for improving the protection of the environment. This is evidenced in Article 5 of the 1979 Geneva Convention on Long-

---

[90] New York, May 21, 1997, Arts. 11–19.
[91] Geneva, Apr. 3, 1982.

Range Transboundary Pollution, which provides for consultations between any state affected by long-range transboundary air pollution or exposed to a significant risk of such pollution and the state on whose territory and within whose jurisdiction a substantial part of such pollution is created because of existing or proposed activities.

e.   Equality of Access to Administrative or Judicial Procedures

This norm emerged principally in non-binding international texts[92] and in some judicial opinions. It specifies that if the activities taking place within the limits of jurisdiction or control of one state cause or threaten deterioration to the environment of another state, the residents of the latter who are or risk being affected should have access to administrative or judicial procedures in the state causing the environmental harm, under the same conditions as the residents of the latter state. If the persons residing elsewhere have already suffered damage, the same remedies should be available to them as to residents of the country. This includes application of the same substantive law and the same measures of compensation as are available to persons injured within the polluting state's territory. Throughout these procedures, nonresidents are entitled to the same treatment as residents.[93]

Equality of access concerns not only the nationals of the state that experiences transfrontier pollution, but all those inhabiting its territory, even if they possess another nationality. There are, however, particular problems concerning non-profit organizations, principally nature protection associations, which do not always have access to procedures and remedies. An OECD Council recommendation on equality of access regarding transfrontier pollution[94] proposes that when the national law of a state permits such entities to engage in actions for the furtherance of their environmental purposes, the country should also permit the same actions by comparable groups domiciled in the country threatened with harm.

The norm of equality of access contains four elements: informing non-residents, allowing their participation in decision-making procedures,

---

[92]   *See, e.g.*, OECD Recommendation C(76)55(Final), May 11, 1976 on Equal Right of Access in Relation to Transfrontier Pollution.

[93]   National laws sometimes implement this norm on a basis of reciprocity. *See* the U.S. Comprehensive Environmental Response, Compensation and Liability Act of 1980 (CERCLA), 42 U.S.C. § 9601. CERCLA provides that a foreign claimant may assert a claim to the same extent as a United States claimant if there is a treaty or executive agreement with the foreign country involved, or if the Secretary of State certifies that such country provides a comparable remedy for United States claimants. § 42 U.S.C. Sec. 9611(1).

[94]   C(76)55(Final), May 11, 1976.

permitting the possibility of appeal in case of inadequate application of relevant rules during the procedures, and providing remedies in case of damage.

Information is required on projects, activities and new developments which could engender a risk of damage to the environment of non-residents. Also, access to information that the competent national authorities make available to interested local persons may be included. This aspect of transfrontier cooperation obviously resembles the interstate duty to inform of projects that could cause transfrontier pollution.

According to a 1977 OECD recommendation, the authorities of the country of origin should take appropriate measures to provide persons exposed to a significant risk of transfrontier pollution with sufficient information to enable them to exercise their rights in a timely manner. This information should be equivalent to that provided in the country of origin in cases of comparable domestic pollution. However, it is also provided that exposed countries should designate one or more authorities who have the duty to receive this information and to disseminate it.[95]

The participation of non-residents implies that they have the right to make oral or written observations or to manifest their opinion in any other manner under the same conditions as residents.[96] Where existing procedures in the state of origin have not been respected, non-residents should have at their disposition the same remedies as residents.

Finally, the right of non-residents to demand compensation for damage they have suffered due to transfrontier pollution is undoubtedly the most accepted norm of equality of access. Leaving aside questions of jurisdiction, the statutes and case law of various countries recognize the right of nonresidents to claim damages.[97]

Early texts such as the OECD Recommendation of 1974 concerning Transfrontier Pollution[98] and the 1977 Recommendation on Implementation of a Regime of Equal Right of Access in Relation to Transfrontier Pollution, as well as Principle 13 of the UNEP principles relating to shared resources, contain a separate rule on non-discrimination. According to this

---

[95]	OECD Council Recommendation C(77)28(Final), May 17, 1977.

[96]	*See* M. Bothe, *Note*, Bundesverwaltungsgericht, FRG, Judgment, Dec. 17, 1986, REV. JUR. ENVT. 188 (1988).

[97]	*E.g.*, the 1977 OECD recommendation for implementation of equal access and nondiscrimination was accepted by the United States and Canadian Bar Associations. In the absence of a treaty, a private Joint Working Group from the two countries prepared a draft Uniform Transfrontier Pollution Reciprocal Access Act, subsequently incorporated into the state and provincial laws of Colorado (Colo. Rev. Stat. § 13–1.5.101 (1984)), Montana (Mont. Code Ann. § 75-16-101 (1987)), New Jersey (N.J. Stat. Ann. 2A:58A-1 (1984)), Wisconsin (Wis. Stat. Ann. § 144.995 (1987)), Manitoba (Man. Stat. 1985, ch.11), and Ontario (Ont. Stat. 35 Eliz.II, c.10 (1986)).

[98]	Principle 4.

norm a state may not discriminate in its legislation according to the source of environmental harm, by applying its laws less rigorously to activities which produce harmful effects only outside the territorial limits.

Some treaty provisions support the existence of a norm of non-discrimination which is separate from the principle of equality of access. According to Article 227 of UNCLOS, when exercising their rights and performing their duties under Part XII of the Convention, which relates to the marine environment, states shall not discriminate in form or in fact against vessels of another state. Article 32 of the 1997 UN Convention on the Law of Non-Navigational Uses of International Watercourses however, makes no distinction between the two:

> Unless the watercourse States concerned have agreed otherwise for the protection of the interests of persons, natural or juridical, who have suffered or are under a serious threat of suffering significant transboundary harm as a result of activities related to an international watercourse, a watercourse State shall not discriminate on the basis of nationality or residence or place where the injury occurred, in granting to such persons, in accordance with its legal system, access to judicial or other procedures, or a right to claim compensation or other relief in respect of significant harm caused by such activities carried on in its territory.

B. General Legal Principles

Principles are widely used in international environmental law, perhaps more than in any other field of international law. Principles can indicate the essential characteristics of legal institutions, designate fundamental legal norms, or fill gaps in positive law by assigning a value to rules considered important although they are not yet formally set in legal instruments. Principles can be foundational (*e.g.*, equality and legal certainty) or technical (*e.g.*, proportionality). They may appear in constitutions and basic laws or they may be of judicial construction. According to some, a principle provides the general orientation and direction to which positive law must conform, a rationale for the law, without itself constituting a binding norm. Principles can also be defined as "rules of indeterminate content," having a degree of abstraction so great that it is not possible to deduce obligations from them with a degree of certainty. Principles as such therefore can be defined and applied in varying, even competing ways. Even the concept of "principle" and the juridical value, if any, of a principle change from one legal system to another.[99]

---

99   *See* Nicolas de Sadeleer, Environmental Principles: From Political Slogans to Legal Rules (2002).

All the major non-binding normative instruments contain principles, taken up, defined and given concrete meaning in international treaties and jurisprudence. The Treaty of European Union, Title XVI, sets out the principles meant to guide policy on the environment, principles that shape legislation in the EU. Article 174(2) provides that EC environmental policy shall be based on "the precautionary principle and on the principles that preventive action should be taken, that environmental damage should as a priority be rectified at source and that the polluter should pay."

It is precisely the complexity of many environmental issues that makes specific regulation so difficult at the international level and why principles play such an important role in setting forth the general approach of anticipation rather than reaction. The anticipatory model is necessary because "our understanding of the environment is no longer able to keep pace with our ability to modify it."[100] Prevention thus leads to precaution.

1. Prevention

Experience and scientific expertise demonstrate that prevention must be the Golden Rule for the environment, for both ecological and economic reasons. It is frequently impossible to remedy environmental injury: the extinction of a species of fauna or flora, erosion, and the dumping of persistent pollutants into the sea create irreversible situations. Even when harm is remediable, the costs of rehabilitation are often prohibitive. The duty of prevention also clearly emerges from the international responsibility not to cause significant damage to the environment extra-territorially, but the preventive principle seeks to avoid harm irrespective of whether or not there are transboundary impacts.

The requirement of prevention is complex owing to the number and diversity of the legal instruments in which it occurs. It can perhaps better be considered an overarching aim that gives rise to a multitude of legal mechanisms, including prior assessment of environmental harm, licensing or authorizations, that set out the conditions for operation and the consequences for violation of the conditions. Emission limits and other product or process standards, the use of best available techniques (BAT) and similar techniques can all be seen as applications of the principle of prevention. The preventive approach also can involve the elaboration and adoption of strategies and policies.

The primary obligation that flows from the principle of prevention is prior assessment of potentially harmful activities.[101] Since the failure to exer-

---

[100] *Id.*

[101] This duty is expressed in the Rio texts: Principle 17, Chapter 22 of Agenda 21, Art. 8(h) of the Statement on Forests, and Art. 14(1)(a) and (b) of

cise due diligence to prevent significant transboundary harm can lead to international responsibility, it may be considered that properly done environmental impact assessments can serve as one standard for determining whether or not due diligence was exercised. Preventive mechanisms also include monitoring, notification, and exchange of information, all of which are general obligations in nearly all environmental agreements. The International Tribunal for the Law of the Sea, in the MOX case, considered the duty to cooperate in exchanging information concerning environmental risks a "fundamental principle in the prevention of pollution of the marine environment" under UNCLOS and general international law. Obligations to conduct environmental impact assessments are also found in the 1991 Espoo Convention on Environmental Impact Assessment in a Transboundary Context,[102] the 1992 Convention on Transboundary Effects of Industrial Accidents,[103] and the 1993 North American Agreement on Environmental Co-operation.[104]

The duty of prevention extends to combating the introduction of exogenous species into an ecosystem. The 1976 Convention on Conservation of Nature in the South Pacific[105] provides that the contracting parties must carefully examine the consequences of such introduction (Art. 5(4)). More stringently, Article 22 of the UN Convention on the Law of the Non-Navigational Uses of International Watercourses[106] requires watercourse states to "take all measures necessary to prevent the introduction of species, alien or new, into an international watercourse which may have effects detrimental to the ecosystem of the watercourse resulting in significant harm to other watercourse States."

In fact, the objective of almost all international environmental instruments is to prevent environmental deterioration, whether they concern pollution of the sea, inland waters, the atmosphere or the protection of living resources. Only a few international texts use other approaches, such as the traditional principle of state responsibility or direct compensation of the victims.

The preventive approach requires each state to exercise "due diligence," which means to act reasonably and in good faith and to regulate

---

the Biodiversity Convention treat both the national and international aspects of the issue. *See also* Art. 206 Convention on the Law of the Sea (Dec. 10, 1982) ("When states have reasonable grounds for believing that planned activities under their jurisdiction or control may cause substantial pollution of or significant and harmful changes to the marine environment, they shall, as far as practicable, assess the potential effects of such activities on the marine environment and shall communicate reports of the results of such assessments.")

[102]   Espoo, Feb. 25, 1991.
[103]   Helsinki, Mar. 17, 1992, Annexes IV and V.
[104]   Sept. 13, 1993, Art. 2(1)(e).
[105]   Apia, June 12, 1976.
[106]   New York May 21, 1997.

public and private activities subject to its jurisdiction or control that are possibly harmful to any part of the environment. The principle does not impose an absolute duty to prevent all harm, but rather an obligation on each state to prohibit activities that could cause significant harm to the environment, for instance the dumping of toxic wastes into an international lake. The state should also regulate to minimize the detrimental consequences of permissible activities, by imposing limits, for example, on the discharges of sulphur dioxide (SO^2) in the atmosphere.

The concept of prevention is partly linked to the notion of deterrence and the idea that disincentives such as penalties and civil liability will cause actors to take greater care in their behavior to avoid the increased costs. To the extent that the activity causing the harm is lawful, resulting, *e.g.*, from societal choice to destroy habitats by deliberate conversion of land to other uses, there is no liability. Little empirical work has been done, but there is some evidence for the preventive effect of a liability regime. One study examined the relationship between the imposition of strict liability for environmental damages and emissions of toxic chemicals into the environment and found that "strict liability has little obvious effect on annual emission levels."[107] As a matter of economic analysis, in a perfect market those responsible for harm would be expected to invest in prevention when the cost of prevention is likely to avoid damage that would be more costly to restore than to prevent. The market is not perfect, however, in part because of the complexity of regulation. For example, prevention may require new equipment that tax regulations demand be capitalized and depreciated over time, while the costs of restoration can be deducted immediately as expenses, giving an economic incentive for the latter. Permit requirements may make changes to installations more difficult and costly, even if the result is greater prevention. The uncertainty of harm, its scale or likelihood may also contribute to a decision that the costs of prevention are greater than the potential costs of liability.

2. Precaution

The proclamation of the precautionary principle can be considered one of the most important provisions in the Rio Declaration. Principle 15 provides:

> In order to protect the environment, the precautionary principle
> shall be widely applied by States according to their capabilities.
> Where there are threats of serious or irreversible damage, lack of

---

[107]   D. Austin & A. Alberini, *An Analysis of the Preventive Effect of Environmental Liability: Environmental Liability, Location and Emissions Substitution: Evidence from the Toxic Release Inventory* (Resources for the Future, Washington D.C. 2001).

full scientific certainty shall not be used as a reason for postponing cost effective measures to prevent environmental degradation.

Formulations of the precautionary principle are relatively recent. The term first appeared in international environmental law in a declaration adopted by a conference on the North Sea in 1987. In 1990, the ministers of the 34 member states of UNECE and the representative of the EC adopted the Bergen Declaration which included a broad formulation of the precautionary principle foreshadowing the Rio text.[108] Since then, the precautionary principle has appeared in almost all international instruments related to environmental protection.[109]

Precaution is also one of the bases of the European Union's environmental policy according to the 1992 Maastricht Treaty,[110] but the term is not

---

[108] "In order to achieve sustainable development, policies must be based on the precautionary principle. Environmental measures must anticipate, prevent and attack the causes of environmental degradation. Where there are threats of serious or irreversible damage, lack of full scientific certainty should not be used as a reason for postponing measures to prevent environmental degradation." Bergen Declaration, Principle 7, May 15, 1990; 20 E.P.L. 200 (1990).

[109] *See, e.g.,* the Bamako Convention on the Ban of the Import of Hazardous Wastes into Africa and on the Control of their Transboundary Movements within Africa, Art. 4(3)(f) (Jan. 29, 1991); Helsinki Convention on the Protection of the Marine Environment of the Baltic Sea, Art. 3(2) (Apr. 9, 1992); Framework Convention on Climate Change, Art. 4(1)(f); Convention on Biological Diversity, Preamble (June 5, 1992); Amendments to the Protocol for the Protection of the Mediterranean Sea against Pollution from Land-Based Sources, Preamble (Syracuse, Mar. 7, 1996); Protocol to the 1979 Convention on Long-Range Transboundary Air Pollution to Abate Acidification, Eutrophication and Ground-Level Ozone (Gothenburg, Nov. 30, 1999); the Cartagena Protocol on Biosafety (Jan. 29, 2000); Convention on the Conservation and Management of Highly Migratory Fish Stocks in the Western and Central Pacific Ocean (Honolulu, Sept. 5, 2000); Convention on the Conservation and Management of Fishery Resources in the South-East Atlantic Ocean (Apr. 20, 2001); the Stockholm Convention on Persistent Organic Pollutants (May 22, 2001); and the European Energy Charter Treaty, Art. 19(1) (Lisbon, Dec. 17, 1994); Agreement on the Conservation of Albatrosses and Petrels, Art. II(3) (Cape Town, Feb. 2, 2001) and the Convention for Cooperation in the Protection and Sustainable Development of the Marine and Coastal Environment of the Northeast Pacific (Antigua, Feb. 18, 2002); ASEAN Agreement on Transboundary Haze Pollution (Kuala Lumpur, June 10, 2002).

[110] "Community policy on the environment shall aim at a high level of protection. . . . It shall be based on the precautionary principle and on the principles that preventive action should be taken, that environmental damage should as a priority be rectified at source . . ." Other regional instruments that include the precautionary principle are: Amendments to the Protocol for the Protection

defined by the treaty. In February 2000, the European Commission produced a Communication to inform all EC institutions and member states of the manner in which the Commission intends to apply the principle when faced with risks of environmental harm.[111] Seeking a common position on the application of the principle, the Communication describes precaution as a risk management tool which is part of a risk analysis framework rather than an overall guide to implementation. Precautionary action should only be taken after experts prepare an objective quantitative risk assessment. "The implementation of an approach based on the precautionary principle should start with a scientific evaluation, as complete as possible, and where possible, identifying at each stage the degree of scientific uncertainty."[112] It is thus a temporary measure pending further scientific information. The Communication mentions the need to incorporate qualitative as well as quantitative scientific evidence, acknowledging that protection of human health and the environment should have priority over economic concerns. It also encourages a transparent and open decision-making process with the participation of all interested parties as early as possible. According to the Communication, the determination of what constitutes an "acceptable" level of risk is eminently a political responsibility and that the Commission thus has the right to fix levels of protection of the environment, within the limits of proportionality and non-discrimination, cost-benefit analysis and review. The Council endorsed the broad lines of the Communication during the Nice Summit in December 2000.

The European Court of Justice (ECJ) has adopted the precautionary principle, particularly in respect to environmental risks that pose dangers to human health. The Court held that the Commission had not committed manifest error when banning the export of beef during the so-called "mad cow" crisis.[113] The ECJ said: "At the time when the contested decision was adopted, there was great uncertainty as to the risks posed by live animals,

---

of the Mediterranean Sea against Pollution from Land-Based Sources, Preamble (Syracuse, Mar. 7, 1996); Protocol to the 1979 Convention on Long-Range Transboundary Air Pollution to Abate Acidification, Eutrophication and Ground-Level Ozone (Gothenburg, Nov. 30, 1999); Convention on the Conservation and Management of Fishery Resources in the South-East Atlantic Ocean (Apr. 20, 2001); Convention on the Conservation and Management of Highly Migratory Fish Stocks in the Western and Central Pacific Ocean (Honolulu, Sept. 5, 2000); and the ASEAN Agreement on Transboundary Haze Pollution (Kuala Lumpur, June 10, 2002).

[111]   *See* Communication from the Commission on the Precautionary Principle (COM(2000)1).

[112]   *Id.* para. 4

[113]   Case C 180/96 P, United Kingdom v. Commission, [1996] ECR I-3903, para. 93; Case T-76/96 R, National Farmers' Union (NFU), [1996] ECR II-815, para. 88.

bovine meat and derived products. Where there is uncertainty as to the existence or extent of risks to human health, the institutions may take protective measures without having to await the reality and seriousness of those risks to become fully apparent."[114] In the European Free Trade Association case, the Court held that proper application of the precautionary principle presupposes an identification of potentially negative consequences and a comprehensive evaluation of the risk based upon the most recent scientific information.[115] Where the insufficient, inconclusive or imprecise nature of the conclusions make it impossible to determine risk or hazard with any certainty, but the likelihood of harm persists, the precautionary principle would justify taking restrictive measures. The criteria are: "Such restrictive measures must be non-discriminatory and objective, and must be applied within the framework of a policy based on the best available scientific knowledge at any given time. The precautionary principle can never justify the adoption of arbitrary decisions, and the pursuit of the objective of 'zero risk' only in the most exceptional circumstances."[116]

Concrete application of the precautionary principle is often found in treaties for the management of living resources, especially those concerning fishing. The 1995 Agreement for the Implementation of the Provisions of the UN Convention on the Law of the Sea of December 10, 1982, Relating to the Conservation and Management of Fish Stocks and Highly Migratory Fish Stocks[117] declares that states shall apply the precautionary principle (Art. 5(c)). Article 6 adds that such application includes the precautionary approach to conservation, management and exploitation of straddling fish stocks and highly migratory fish stocks, *inter alia*, by improving decision-making in this field, by taking into account uncertainties relating to the size and productivity of the stocks, by developing knowledge, by not exceeding reference points, by enhanced monitoring and by adopting, if necessary, emergency measures. Similarly, the Convention on the Conservation and Management of Highly Migratory Fish Stocks in the Western and Central Pacific Ocean (Honolulu, September 5, 2000) provides that the Commission created by this instrument shall apply the precautionary approach (Art. 5(c)). EC Regulation 2371/2002 of December 2002 on the Conservation and Sustainable Exploitation of Fisheries Resources under the Common Fisheries Policy also foresees that the Community "shall apply the

---

114 *Id.* para. 63. *See also* Case T-199/96, Bergaderm, [1998] ECR II-2305; Case T-79-99P, Alpharma, [1999] ECR II-2027; Case C-514/99, France v. Commission, [2000] ECR I-4705. Marismas de Santona, Case C-355/90, Commission v. Spain, [1993] ECR I-6159, para. 28; Armand Mondiet, Case C-405/92, [1993] ECR I-6176, paras. 31–36.

115 Case E-3/00, EFTA Surveillance Authority v. Norway, paras. 16, 21.

116 Para. 2.3.

117 Aug. 4, 1995.

precautionary approach in taking measures designed to protect and conserve living aquatic resources, to provide for their sustainable exploitation and to minimize the impact of fishing activities on marine ecosystems" (Art. 2(1)).[118]

The 2000 Cartagena Biosafety Protocol to the Convention on Biological Diversity is based upon the precautionary principle. It is contained in Article 1 on the objectives of the Protocol which refers explicitly to Rio Principle 15. Articles 10 and 11 contain the key provisions on the principle. Article 10(6) says that "lack of scientific certainty due to insufficient relevant information and knowledge regarding the extent of the potential adverse effects of an LMO shall not prevent the party from taking a decision on the LMO in order to avoid or minimize such potential adverse effects." Article 11 uses similar language. Thus a country may reject an import even in the absence of scientific certainty that it will potentially cause harm. These provisions are broader than Rio Principle 15 because they lack reference to "serious or irreversible damage" or to cost-effectiveness.

The precautionary approach is included in the Regulations on Prospecting and Exploration for Polymetallic Nodules (Mining Code) which the International Seabed Authority approved on July 13, 2000: "In order to ensure effective protection for the marine environment from harmful effects which may arise from activities in the Area, the Authority and sponsoring States shall apply a precautionary approach, as reflected in Principle 15 of the Rio Declaration, to such activities. The Legal and Technical Commission shall make recommendations to the Council on the implementation of this paragraph."[119] The Recommendations for the Guidance of Contractors for the Assessment of Possible Environmental Impacts Arising from Exploration for Polymetallic Nodules in the Area, approved by the Legal and Technical Commission of the ISBA adopts this approach as well.[120]

In litigation outside the European Union, international tribunals have appeared reluctant to use the precautionary principle despite its inclusion in nearly all recent environmental agreements. In the *Gabçikovo Case*, the International Court of Justice court did not accept Hungary's argument that a state of necessity could arise from application of the precautionary principle.[121]

---

[118]   Other EC instruments use the term "precautionary principle" which appears in the Amsterdam Convention on the European Union. EC practice considers that the two expressions are equivalent. The variations in terminology may also reflect a degree of uncertainty or controversy surrounding the contents and requirements of the principle. Notably, the 1991 Bamako Convention calls precaution both a principle and an approach.

[119]   Document ISBA/6/A/18, Oct. 4, 2000, Reg. 31, para. 2.

[120]   Document ISBA/7/LTC/1/Rev.1, July 10, 2001.

[121]   *See* 1997 Judgment, paras. 54–56.

In a case involving nuclear testing in French Polynesia, the European Commission on Human Rights also sought more than a demonstration of potential risk of harm. The applicants had to show "reasonable and convincing indications of the probability of the occurrence of a violation that personally concerned [the applicant]; mere suspicions or conjectures are in this respect insufficient."[122] The Commission added a reference to precaution, however, saying that "[a] claim must demonstrate in a defensible and detailed manner that owing to failure by the authorities to take sufficient precautions, the probability that damage will occur is high enough that it constitutes a [human rights] violation, provided that the repercussions of the act in question are not too remote."[123]

Within the WTO and GATT, dispute settlement panels have agreed that in cases where it is not possible to conduct a proper risk assessment,[124] Article 5(7) of the Sanitary and Phytosanitary (SPS) Agreement allows members to adopt and maintain a provisional or precautionary SPS measure. According to the GATT Panel and Appellate Body, this provision incorporates the precautionary principle to a limited extent, when four cumulative criteria are met: (1) the relevant scientific information must be insufficient; (2) the measure should be adopted on the basis of available pertinent information; (3) the member must seek to obtain the additional information necessary for a more objective assessment of risk;[125] (4) the member must review the measure accordingly within a reasonable period of time established on a case by case basis depending on the specific circumstances, including the difficulty of obtaining additional information needed for review and the characteristics of the SPS measure.[126] At the same time, the WTO has expressed skepticism about whether the precautionary principle or approach has become customary international law.[127]

In the 1999 *Southern Bluefin Tuna Case*, the International Tribunal on the Law of the Sea (ITLOS) seemed to view the precautionary principle more favorably than does the WTO or other tribunals. ITLOS could not conclusively assess the scientific evidence regarding the provisional measures

---

[122]   Report of Dec. 4, 1995, *re* Application No. 28204–95.

[123]   *Id.*

[124]   On risk assessment, *see* Chapter 6.

[125]   Japan Varietals, Measures Affecting Agricultural Products, WTO Doc. WT/DS76/AB/R (Feb 22, 1999), para. 92.

[126]   *Id.* para. 93.

[127]   In 1997 the *Beef Hormones Case*, the Appellate Body observed that: "The precautionary principle is regarded by some as having crystallized into a general principle of customary international environmental law. Whether it is widely accepted by Members as a principle of general or customary international law appears less than clear. We consider, however, that it is unnecessary and probably imprudent, for the Appellate Body in this appeal to take a position on this important, but abstract, question." Para. 123.

sought by New Zealand and indeed, the latter requested the measures on the basis of the precautionary principle, pending a final settlement of the case. ITLOS found that in the face of scientific uncertainty regarding the measures, action should be taken as a measure of urgency to avert further deterioration of the tuna stock. In its consideratum, the Tribunal said that in its view, "the parties should in the circumstances act with prudence and caution to ensure that effective conservation measures are taken to prevent serious harm to the stock of southern bluefin tuna."[128] It prescribed a limitation to experimental fishing to avoid possible damage to the stock. In the MOX plant case, ITLOS responded Irish demands for provisional measures on the basis of the precautionary principle. Ireland argued that the latter required Britain to prove no harm. Using again the terms "prudence and caution," the Tribunal rejected the request for provisional measures but called on the parties to cooperate in exchanging information concerning risks or effects of the operation of the plant and devising ways to deal with them, as appropriate.[129]

In general, the precautionary principle can be considered as the most developed form of prevention which remains the general basis for environmental protection measures. Precaution means preparing for potential, uncertain even hypothetical threats, when there is no irrefutable proof that damage will occur. It is prevention based on probabilities or contingencies but it cannot involve eliminating all claimed risks, even those without any basis, such as astrological predictions or psychic visions. Precaution particularly applies when the consequences of non-action could be serious. The problems of irreversibility and scientific uncertainty are thus brought into international law. Policy-makers must consider the circumstances of a given situation and decide which scientific opinion is based upon the most credible evidence and most reliable scientific methodology. Such a development expands the important role of scientists in the protection of the environment: decision-makers must adopt measures based upon a general knowledge of the environment and the problems its protection raises. Like in all environmental matters, the public must support the decision. The role of scientists thus includes a general environmental education of the public as well as of those who take the formal decision.

3. "Polluter Pays" Principle

The polluter pays principle seeks to impose the costs of environmental harm on the party responsible for the pollution. This principle was set out

---

[128] ITLOS, Southern Bluefin Tuna Case (Australia and New Zealand v. Japan), Order of Aug. 27, 1999, para. 77.

[129] ITLOS, MOX Plant Case (Ireland v. U.K.), Order No. 10 of Dec. 3, 2001, para. 84, *reprinted in* 41 I.L.M. 405 (2002).

by the OECD as an economic principle and as the most efficient way of allocating costs of pollution prevention and control measures introduced by the public authorities in member countries. It is intended to encourage rational use of scarce environmental resources and to avoid distortions in international trade and investment.

The Rio Declaration includes it in rather abstract terms stating in Principle 16 that

> National authorities should endeavor to promote the internalization of environmental costs and the use of economic instruments, taking into account the approach that the polluter should, in principle, bear the cost of pollution, with regard to the public interest and without distorting international trade and investment.

Prior to UNCED, the polluter pays requirement was included in different EC documents such as the 1986 Single European Act,[130] the 1992 Maastricht Treaty (Art.130R(2)) and in the successive Programs of Action on the Environment. The Convention on the Protection of the Marine Environment of the Baltic Sea Area[131] states the principle as an obligatory norm, while the 1992 Helsinki Convention on the Protection and Use of Transboundary Watercourses and International Lakes[132] includes it as a guiding principle.

On the global level, the International Convention on Oil Pollution Preparedness, Response and Cooperation[133] states in its preamble that the polluter pays principle is "a general principle of international environmental law." More recent examples of reference to it are found in the Amendments to the Protocol for the Protection of the Mediterranean Sea against Pollution from Land-Based Sources,[134] and the Stockholm Convention on Persistent Organic Pollutants.[135]

The content of the polluter pays principle can be seen in the 1992 Convention for the Protection of the Marine Environment of the North-East Atlantic.[136] According to Article 2(2)(b) "[t]he contracting parties shall apply: . . .the polluter pays principle, by virtue of which the costs of pollution prevention, control and reduction measures are to be borne by the polluter." This can be interpreted in different ways depending upon the extent of prevention and control and whether compensation for damage is

---

130 Feb. 17, 1986.
131 Helsinki, Apr. 9, 1992, Art. 3(4).
132 Mar. 17, 1992, Art. 2(5).
133 London, Nov. 30, 1990, Preamble.
134 Syracuse, Mar. 7, 1996, Preamble.
135 Stockholm, May 22, 2001.
136 Paris, Sept. 22, 1992.

included in the definition of reduction. Further, the very concept of the "polluter" can vary, from the producer of merchandise to the consumer who uses it and who pays the higher price resulting from anti-pollution production measures. International practice thus far, mainly that of the EC, seems to aim at eliminating public subsidies for pollution abatement by companies.

In fact, pollution control costs can be borne either by the community, by those who pollute, or by consumers. Community assumption of the costs can be demonstrated using the example of an industry that discharges pollutants into a river. There are at least three possibilities: (1) the river can remain polluted and rendered unsuitable for certain downstream activities, causing the downstream community to suffer an economic loss; (2) the downstream community can build an adequate water treatment plant at its own cost; (3) the polluter may receive public subsidies for controlling the pollution. In all these hypotheses, the affected community bears the cost of the pollution and of the measures designed to eliminate it or to mitigate its effects. The polluter pays principle avoids this result by obliging the polluter to bear the costs of pollution control, to "internalize" them. In most cases the enterprise will in fact incorporate the costs in the price of the products and pass them on to the consumer.

"Polluter pays" thus is a method for internalizing externalities. Those who benefit from air made cleaner have a positive externality if they do not pay for the cleanup. Where air is fouled by producer who bears no cost it is a negative externality; those who buy the product also are free riders if the fouling is not reflected in the price of the goods. Internalization requires that all the environmental costs be borne by the producer/consumer instead of the community as a whole. Prices will reflect the full cost if regulatory standards require or if taxes on the production or product correspond to the true cost of environmental damage. Coase's theorem posits an alternative, that from an economic perspective it is just as efficient to allow the victim of pollution a right to compensation as it is to recognize the polluter's right to pollute.[137] In this view, both the polluter and the victim compete for the same limited natural resource, and there is no a priori right to prefer one over the other. If each is ready to pay for use of a resource, they will be inclined to conclude a transaction to reduce pollution in order to reach optimal economic efficiency. So, it is most efficient to attribute ownership rights over natural resources. If the polluter holds a right to pollute, the victims must pay for cessation or reduction of the activity. Conversely the polluter will have to compensate any party suffering from pollution. This rejects the intervention of public authorities in favor of free negotiation. It only works, however, where the rights of the parties are clearly defined, information is complete and there are few if any transaction costs.

---

[137]   See R. Coase, *The Problem of Social Cost*, 3 J.L. & Econ. 1 (1960).

This rarely happens. Further, this ignores the role of prevention and the common interests in natural resources, now and in the future.

The polluter pays principle can be applied most easily in a geographic region subject to uniform environmental law, such as within a state or in the European Union. In fact, the polluter pays principle has been well-defined in EU law. An EC Council recommendation of November 7, 1974 defined "polluter" as "someone who directly or indirectly damages the environment or who creates conditions leading to such damage." The breadth of the definition has been criticized because it can apply to automobile drivers, farmers, factory owners and community sewage treatment plants. The recommendation provides alternatives if identifying the polluter proves impossible or too difficult, and hence arbitrary, because the pollution arises from several simultaneous causes, (cumulative pollution), or from several consecutive causes. In such instances, the pollution-abatement cost should be borne at the point and by the legal or administrative means which offer the best solution administratively, economically, and environmentally. Thus, in the case of pollution "chains," costs should be charged at the point at which the number of economic operators is least and control is easiest or at the point where the most effective contribution is made towards improving the environment, and where distortions to competition are avoided.

Polluters should pay for the cost of pollution control measures, such as the construction and operation of anti-pollution installations, investment in anti-pollution equipment and new processes, so that a necessary environmental quality objective is achieved. An important application of the principle is found in an EC Directive of December 6, 1984, on the control within the European Community of the transfrontier shipment of hazardous waste. It instructs the member states to impose the costs of waste control on the holder of the waste and/or on prior holders or the waste generator. Also, Article 9 of EC Directive 2000/60 on water requires member states to take account of the principle of recovery of the costs of water services, including environmental and resource costs. Water pricing policies by 2010 are to provide adequate incentives for the efficient use of water resources. In sum, the polluter pays principle has to be taken into account by all the EC institutions and the European Court of Justice (ECJ) must ensure respect for the principle in the cases it decides.

In fact the ECJ applied the principle in the *Standley Case*,[138] when a British High Court asked for a preliminary ruling on Directive 91/676/EEC of December 12, 1991, concerning the protection of waters against pollution caused by nitrates from agricultural sources. Farmers argued that the directive violated the polluter pays principle because they were asked to bear the cost of reducing the concentration of nitrates into waters, below

---

[138] C-293/97, Standley and Others, judgment of Apr. 29, 1999, [1999] ECR I-2603.

the threshold level set, even though agriculture is only one source of nitrates. According to the ECJ, however: "the Directive does not mean that farmers must take on burdens for the elimination of pollution to which they have not contributed; . . . the Member States are to take account of the other sources of pollution when implementing the Directive and, having regard to the circumstances, are not to impose on farmers costs of eliminating pollution that are unnecessary. Viewed in that light, the polluter pays principle reflects the principle of proportionality."[139]

The global economic system does not similarly impose the polluter pays principle, although it permits a state to apply it. In the *U.S. Superfund Case*, the EC argued before GATT that a U.S. tax on certain chemicals was not eligible for border tax adjustment because the regime would only finance environmental programs of benefit to U.S. producers. Since the U.S. production was causing pollution in North America, the EC said that the polluter pays principle required the U.S. to tax domestic products only. The Panel found that since the tax was directly imposed on products, it was eligible for border tax adjustment independent of its purpose. According to the panel GATT rules on tax adjustment "give the contracting party . . . the possibility to follow the polluter-pays principle, but they do not oblige it to do so."[140]

4. Sustainable Development

Since the end of the 1980s the term sustainable development has dominated international activities in the field of environmental protection. It was defined in the 1987 Report of the World Commission on Environment and Development as "development that meets the needs of the present without compromising the ability of future generations to meet their own needs." The Report identified the critical objectives of sustainable development:

— reviving growth but changing its quality;
— meeting essential needs for jobs, food, energy, water and sanitation;
— ensuring a sustainable level of population;
— conserving and enhancing the resource base;
— reorienting technology and managing risk; and
— merging environment and economics in decision-making.[141]

Principle 4 of the Rio Declaration states that "in order to achieve sustainable development, environmental protection shall constitute an integral part of the development process and cannot be considered in isolation

---

[139]   *Id.* at paras. 51–2.
[140]   GATT BISD 34S/136 (1987).
[141]   WCED, Our Common Future 43 (1987).

from it." Building on this provision, the IUCN Draft Covenant on Environment and Development insists on the integration of environment and development. Development policies should aim at the eradication of poverty, the general improvement of economic, social and cultural conditions, the conservation of biological diversity, and the maintenance of essential ecological processes and life-support systems. Environmental conservation should be treated as an integral part of the planning and implementation of activities at all stages and at all levels, giving full and equal consideration to environmental, economic, social and cultural factors. To this end, states should conduct regular national reviews of environmental and developmental policies and plans, enact effective laws and regulations which use, where appropriate, economic instruments and establish and strengthen institutional structures and procedures to fully integrate environmental and developmental issues in all spheres of decision-making.

Also necessary are approaches that take into account long-term strategies and that include the use of environmental and social impact assessment, risk analysis, cost-benefit analysis and natural resources accounting. The integration of environmental, social and economic policies also requires transparency and broad public participation in governmental decision-making.

As its title shows, the Johannesburg World Summit on Sustainable Development focused on this concept with particular emphasis on eradicating poverty. During the same year, a new attempt to define sustainable development appeared in Article 3(1)(a) of the Convention for Cooperation in the Protection and Sustainable Development of the Marine and Coastal Environment of the Northeast Pacific:[142]

> For the purpose of this Convention sustainable development means the process of progressive change in the quality of life of human beings, which places it as the center and primordial subject of development, by means of economic growth with social equity and the transformation of methods of production and consumption patterns, and which is sustained in the ecological balance and vital support of the region. This process implies respect for regional, national and local ethnic and cultural diversity, and full participation of people in peaceful coexistence and in harmony with nature, without prejudice to and ensuring the quality of life of future generations.

The concept of "environmental services" has also become linked with sustainable development. According to the 2002 Antigua Convention it means the services provided by the functions of nature itself, such as the

---

[142] Antigua, Feb. 18, 2002.

protection of soil by trees, the natural filtration and purification of water, and the protection of habitat for biodiversity (Art. 3(1)(c)).

The 70th Conference of the International Law Association, held in New Delhi, India, April 2–6, 2002, adopted Resolution 3/2002, the New Delhi Declaration of Principles of International Law Relating to Sustainable Development. It expresses the view that sustainable development involves a comprehensive and integrated approach to economic, social and political processes, aiming at the sustainable use of natural resources of the Earth and the protection of the environment. It firmly asserts that the realization of all human rights is central to the pursuit of sustainable development. The Declaration adopts seven principles of sustainable development: (1) the duty of states to ensure sustainable use of natural resources; (2) the principle of equity and the eradication of poverty; (3) the principle of common but differentiated responsibilities; (4) the principle of the precautionary approach to human health, natural resources and ecosystems; (5) the principle of public participation and access to information and justice; (6) the principle of good governance;[143] and (7) the principle of integration and interrelationship, in particular in relation to human rights and social, economic and environmental objectives.

5. Protection, Preservation and Conservation

General international legal norms for the protection of the environment continue to emerge. For the most part, these norms appear piecemeal but regularly in texts and in international practice. They apply within the territory of states whether or not there are transfrontier environmental impacts or consequences in zones outside national jurisdiction.[144]

---

[143]   This principle commits states and international organizations: (a) to adopt democratic and transparent decision-making procedures and financial accountability; (b) to take effective measures to combat official or other corruption; (c) to respect due process in their procedures and to observe the rule of law and human rights; and (d) to implement a public procurement approach according to the WTO Code on Public Procurement. It adds that civil society and non-governmental organizations have a right to good governance by states and international organizations, but that non-state actors should also be subject to internal democratic governance and to effective accountability. Good governance requires full respect for the principles of the 1992 Rio Declaration on Environment and Development as well as the full participation of women in all levels of decision-making. Good governance also calls for corporate social responsibility and socially responsible investments as conditions for the existence of a global market aimed at a fair distribution of wealth among and within communities.

[144]   The U.S. Restatement of Foreign Affairs Law, § 601, refers to the oblig-

The most fundamental norm to appear is the obligation of all states to conserve the environment and the earth's natural resources. It designates a specific objective in the framework of interstate cooperation. Although all international environmental instruments have this aim, clear statements of the duty are rare. Article 192 of the UN Convention on the Law of the Sea, however, explicitly proclaims the duty of states to protect and preserve the marine environment. Article 20 of the 1997 UN Convention on the Non-Navigational Uses of International Watercourses[145] affirms the same duty for international freshwater. The 1992 Convention on Biological Diversity lists the measures which should be taken to ensure conservation and sustainable use of biological resources, while the 1992 Framework Convention on Climate Change declares, in Article 3(1), that the parties should protect the climate system.

There is no treaty definition of the terms "protect," "preserve" or "conserve." The first two terms are used in Article 192 of the Convention on the Law of the Sea, suggesting that their meaning differs. Protection can be seen as abstaining from harmful activities and taking affirmative measures to ensure that environmental deterioration does not occur.[146] Increasingly, the concept of protection includes comprehensive ecological planning and management, with substantive regulations, procedures, and institutions on a national scale. Preservation could be considered as including long-time perspectives which take into account the rights and interests of future generations for whom natural resources should be safeguarded.[147] The term "conserve" or "conservation" has a narrower scope, but falls under the heading of protection. It generally is used in the field of living resources and is based upon the status quo, mainly demanding maintenance of the conditions necessary for continued resource existence. The IUCN World Conservation Strategy demonstrates the conservation principle in establishing as its objectives: (1) maintaining essential ecological processes and life-support systems; (2) preserving genetic diversity; and (3) achieving sustainable utilization of species and ecosystems.

When applied to exploited species of flora and fauna, conservation often meant establishing "optimal sustainable yields," signifying exploitation

---

ation of states "to conform to generally accepted international rules and standards for the prevention, reduction, and control of injury to the environment of another state or of areas beyond the limits of national jurisdiction."

[145] New York May 21, 1997.

[146] The American Heritage Dictionary defines "protect" as "to keep from being damaged, attacked, stolen, or injured; guard."

[147] The American Heritage Dictionary defines "preserve" as "to maintain in safety from injury, peril, or harm; protect," and adds "to keep in perfect or unaltered condition; maintain unchanged." In relation to food it has the meaning of preparing for future use, supporting the implication that it refers to more long-term approaches.

of the resource without exceeding the limits that guarantee its renewal and thus its sustainability. In recent texts "conservation" has been supplemented or replaced by reference to "sustainable development," assuring the ongoing productivity of exploitable natural resources and conserving all species of fauna and flora. A relatively recent and related concept is the "favorable state of conservation," based not on the idea of exploitation or of yield but on that of maintaining living resources.

Terms such as "essential ecological processes," "genetic diversity" and even "sustainable development" are abstract and new, making it difficult for a state to comply with its legal obligations without the close collaboration of several scientific disciplines. The legal principles adopted by the World Commission on Environment and Development provide details on some terminology. They provide that states shall:

(a) maintain ecosystems and related ecological processes essential for the functioning of the biosphere in all its diversity, in particular those important for food production, health and other aspects of human survival and sustainable development;

(b) maintain maximum biological diversity by ensuring the survival and promoting the conservation in their natural habitat of all species of fauna and flora, in particular those which are rare, endemic or endangered;

(c) observe, in the exploitation of living natural resources and ecosystems, the principle of optimum sustainable yield.[148]

The same concerns are evident in various international conventions aimed at protecting living species threatened with extinction and those concerned with the natural heritage. One of the earliest such international instruments is the Ramsar Convention on Wetlands of International Importance.[149] Article 2(6) speaks of the responsibility of each contracting party for the conservation, management, and wise use of migratory stocks of waterfowl, notably in designating wetlands in its territory which should receive a special protection. More extensive duties exist in the UNESCO Convention Concerning the Protection of the World Cultural and Natural Heritage.[150] Article 4 of this treaty proclaims the obligation of states to ensure the identification, protection, conservation, presentation and transmission to future generations of the cultural and natural heritage which is situated on its territory. Similarly, the preamble to the 1979 Bonn Migratory Species Convention recognizes that states are and must be the protectors of the migratory species of wild animals that live within the limits of their national jurisdiction or which cross these boundaries.[151]

---

[148]   *Id.*

[149]   Ramsar, Feb. 2, 1971.

[150]   Nov, 23, 1972.

[151]   Bonn, June 23, 1979.

On the regional level such provisions appear even more frequently. The 1976 Convention on the Conservation of Nature in the South Pacific contains numerous expressions of the duty to protect the environment, without explicitly speaking of the responsibility of states. The 1979 Bern Convention on the Conservation of European Wildlife and Natural Habitats leaves few doubts about the obligation to preserve and transmit to future generations the natural heritage of wild plant and animal species. Finally, the 1985 ASEAN Convention on the Conservation of Nature and Natural Resources recognizes the importance of natural resources for present and future generations and imposes clear duties on the South-East Asian states parties. All these formulations make clear that one of the foundations of all environmental law, protecting the interests of future generations, is a primary motivation for conserving nature and natural resources.

Monitoring the state of the environment is a corollary of the duty of conservation. Logically, measures of conservation cannot be taken without knowledge of the environmental conditions nor can the impact of certain activities be evaluated. Principle 19 of the World Charter for Nature recommends monitoring in all sectors of the environment for all forms of environmental deterioration, not only by states, but also by international organizations, individuals and groups. The status of natural processes, ecosystems and species shall be closely monitored to enable early detection of degradation or threat, ensure timely intervention and facilitate the evaluation of conservation policies and methods.

Permanent monitoring and international cooperation are closely linked in several international conventions, especially those concerning regional seas. Thus, Article 10 of the 1976 Convention for the Protection of the Mediterranean Sea Against Pollution provides for the institution by contracting states, in close cooperation with competent international organizations, of complementary or common continuous monitoring systems against pollution in the Mediterranean Sea.[152] Similarly, in international treaties relating to conservation of wildlife, states frequently undertake to furnish information concerning the status of protected species or their activities aimed at conserving or managing specific species.[153]

Public information and participation, although generally seen as a matter of internal law, play a particularly important role in regard to the

---

[152] *See also* Art. 10(1), Kuwait Regional Convention for Cooperation in Combating Pollution by Oil and other Harmful Substances in Cases of Emergency (Apr. 24, 1978); Art. 14, Convention for Cooperation in the Protection and Development of the Marine and Coastal Environment of the West and Central African Region (Mar. 23, 1981); and Art. 10, Regional Convention for the Conservation of the Red Sea and of the Gulf of Aden Environment (Feb. 14, 1982).

[153] *E.g.*, Art. 20 of the 1980 Convention on the Conservation of Antarctic Marine Living Resources.

obligations of states to protect the global environment. As discussed in detail in Chapter 15, this role consists of pressing for legal norms and for enforcement of existing rules. Nearly all recent environmental agreements insist on the need for and right to public information and participation in environmental matters.

C. Conclusions

Taken as a whole, the common law of the environment is rapidly developing to include a general obligation to protect and conserve the global environment. Recent environmental agreements demonstrate the widespread acceptance of this notion and the principles discussed above. The Framework Convention on the Protection and Sustainable Development of the Carpathians, adopted in Kiev on May 22, 2003, provides an example in its Article 2. The objective of the treaty is articulated as "the protection and sustainable development of the Carpathians with a view to, *inter alia*, improving quality of life, strengthening local economies and communities, and the conservation of natural values and cultural heritage." In order to achieve the stated objectives, Article 2(2) provides that the parties are to utilize the principles of precaution and prevention; the polluter pays principle; public participation and stakeholder involvement; transboundary cooperation; integrated planning and management of land and water resources; a programmatic approach; and the ecosystem approach. The integrated and ecosystem approaches reflect the on-going evolution of international environmental law and are discussed in Chapter 14.

BIBLIOGRAPHY

Adede, A. *United Nations Efforts toward the Development of an Environmental Code of Conduct for States Concerning Harmonious Utilization of Shared Natural Resources*, 43 ALBANY L. REV. 485 (1979).

Bramsen, C., *Transnational Pollution and International Law*, 42 NORDISK TIDSSKRIFT FOR INT'L RET. 153 (1972).

NOLLKAEMPER, A., THE LEGAL REGIME FOR TRANSBOUNDARY WATER POLLUTION: BETWEEN DISCRETION AND CONSTRAINT (1993).

OECD, LEGAL ASPECTS OF TRANSFRONTIER POLLUTION (1977).

OECD, TRANSFRONTIER POLLUTION AND THE ROLE OF STATES (1981).

Partan, D.G., *The "Duty to Inform" in International Environmental Law*, 6 BU INT'L L.J. 1–149 (1988).

Schroth, P.W., *Public Participation in Environmental Decision-making: A Comparative Perspective*, 14 FORUM 352–68 (1978).

Stein, R.E., *OECD Guiding Principles on Transfrontier Pollution*, 6 GA. J. INT'L & COMP. L. 245–58 (1976).

WCED, ENVIRONMENTAL PROTECTION AND SUSTAINABLE DEVELOPMENT: LEGAL PRINCIPLES AND RECOMMENDATIONS (Experts Group On Environmental Law, World Commission on Environment and Development (1986).

Williams, S.A., *Public International Law Governing Transboundary Pollution*, 13 U. QUEENS L.J. 112–37 (1984).

CHAPTER 6

IMPLEMENTING INTERNATIONAL ENVIRONMENTAL LAW: TECHNIQUES AND PROCEDURES

A. Introduction

International environmental instruments often suggest or mandate the use of specified techniques and procedures to achieve the aims of the agreement. While most instruments call for the adoption of legislation or regulation, some also detail the specific content of the measures to be taken[1] and others permit or recommend particular techniques.[2]

The variety, complexity and acceptance of these legal mechanisms have increased in recent years through the mutual influence of national and international environmental law. International environmental agreements today usually require states parties to adopt environmental impact or risk assessment procedures, licensing, and monitoring. Environmental auditing, product labeling, use of best available techniques and practices, and prior informed consent also commonly appear in global and regional instruments. States often enact and implement several techniques and procedures simultaneously, in response to treaty mandates as well as to particular threats to the environment, national and local conditions, traditions and cultural norms, and the economic situation specific to each country. This chapter will discuss the legal techniques and procedures that commonly appear in international environmental instruments.

---

[1]   UNCLOS (Dec. 10, 1982), Art. 210 requires states parties to adopt laws and regulations to prevent, reduce and control pollution of the marine environment by dumping. The third paragraph of the article specifies that the measures "shall ensure that dumping is not carried out without the permission of the competent authorities" of the state.

[2]   UNCLOS Art. 62, for example, allows that the laws and regulations of a state party concerning fishing in the EEZ "may relate" to licensing of fishermen and fishing vessels, payment of fees, setting fishing quotas and seasons, and similar measures.

Environmental agreements and national laws often regulate a single environmental milieu, *e.g.*, water,[3] air,[4] soil,[5] biological diversity,[6] due to the particular environmental problems facing a given area, political or economic priorities, or the ease of achieving consensus on a specific environmental issue. A more comprehensive approach seeks integrated pollution prevention and control, *i.e.*, protection against pollution of all natural systems necessary to support the biosphere. The 1994 United Nations Convention to Combat Desertification in those Countries Experiencing Serious Drought and/or Desertification, Particularly in Africa requires states parties to adopt an integrated approach addressing the physical, biological and socio-economic aspects of the processes of desertification and drought (Art. 4(2)(a)). Other international agreements mandate broad national action plans, with targets and timetables.[7]

Texts calling for integrated pollution prevention and control exist also on the regional level, in the European Union and the OECD. An OECD Council Recommendation of January 31, 1991 expresses the purpose of integrated pollution prevention and control: to prevent or minimize the risk of harm to the environment as a whole, recognizing the integrated nature of the environment by taking account of the effects of substances or activities on all environmental media.

The focus of "integrated pollution prevention and control" is thus on eliminating or at least reducing the input of each polluting substance, noting its origin and geographic target. Integrated pollution prevention and control involves a "cradle to grave" approach that considers the whole life cycle of substances and products, anticipates the effects of substances and activities on all environmental media, minimizes the quantity and harmfulness of waste, uses a single method such as risk assessment for estimating and comparing environmental problems, and involves complementary use of objectives and limits. Certain policies are essential to an effective integrated approach. They include sustainable development, clean technologies, and use of less harmful substances. In addition, it requires application

---

[3]   UNCLOS, ECE Transboundary Watercourses Convention (Mar. 17, 1992), UN Convention on the Law of the Non-Navigational Uses of International Watercourses (May 21, 1997).

[4]   Convention on Long-Range Transboundary Air Pollution (Nov. 13, 1979) and the Protocols thereto; Vienna Convention on the Ozone Layer (Mar. 22, 1985) and the Montreal Protocol (Sept. 16, 1987); Climate Change Convention (May 9, 1992).

[5]   FAO Soil Charter (Nov. 25, 1981), the European Soil Charter (May 30, 1972) and the Desertification Convention (Oct. 14, 1994).

[6]   Convention on Biological Diversity (June 5, 1992).

[7]   *E.g.*, Montreal Protocol (Sept. 16, 1987); Climate Change Convention (May 9, 1992); Biological Diversity Convention (June 5, 1992). *See also* Agenda 21 and Principle 3 of the Forest Principles (1992).

of the precautionary principle and public information and participation during the evaluation of the effects of new substances and proposed activities.

B. Regulatory Measures

The duty to prevent environmental harm implies the application of measures to avoid harm and reduce or eliminate the risk of harm. Many international agreements require or suggest the adoption of implementing laws and regulations and specify measures such as those discussed below. Overall, states must make efforts to prevent environmental damage that is foreseeable through the normal operations of an activity or the use of a product and mitigate or prevent accidental transboundary harm. International law also is concerned with environmental protection within states, due to the inherently integrated nature of the environment and its problems. Laws and regulations generally should apply to all activities and products within the state, whether of foreign or domestic origin, to comply with international trade rules.

Recent treaties often contain a general obligation to apply the best available technology (BAT) or use the best practicable means.[8] This requirement can be seen as deriving in part from the customary international obligation of "due diligence" to prevent environmental harm. In determining whether a particular technology is the best available, several factors are to be taken into account, including the nature and volume of the pollution and the economic feasibility of the technology in question.

Several international texts define best available technology or related terms. The Convention on the Protection and Use of Transboundary Watercourses and International Lakes (Helsinki, March 17, 1992) defines "best available technology" in Annex I as:

> the latest stage of development of processes, facilities or methods
> of operation which indicate the practical suitability of a particular
> measure for limiting discharges, emissions and waste.

---

8   *See e.g.*, Art. 2(3)(b), Convention for the Protection of the Marine Environment of the North-East Atlantic (Sept. 22, 1992); Art. 3(3), Convention on the Protection of the Baltic Environment (Apr. 9, 1992); Art. 3(1)(f), UNECE Convention on the Protection and Use of Transboundary Watercourses and International Lakes (Mar. 17, 1992); Art. 194(1), UNCLOS (Dec. 10, 1982); Art. 6, 1979 Convention on Long-Range Transboundary Air Pollution (Nov. 13, 1979) and Art. 2(2) of its 1988 Protocol; and Amendments to the Protocol for the Protection of the Mediterranean Sea against Pollution from Land-Based Sources, Annex IV (Mar. 7, 1996).

The 1992 Convention for the Protection of the Marine Environment in the North-East Atlantic defines the similar term "best available techniques" as

> the latest stage of development (state of the art) of processes, of facilities or of methods of operation which indicate the practical suitability of a particular measure for limiting discharges, emissions and waste.

The same instrument defines the term "best environmental practice" as the application of the most appropriate combination of environmental control measures and strategies ranging from education and information to establishing a system of licensing. Other treaties use related terms. The Convention on the Protection of the Elbe calls on the contracting parties to develop work programs providing proposals for the application of state of the art techniques for the reduction of emissions and reduction of pollution (Art. 1(3)). UNCLOS requires states to take measures to prevent, reduce and control marine pollution using for this purpose the best practicable means at their disposal.[9]

To aid states in determining what is the best available technology, techniques or practices, some international agreements specify the criteria to which special consideration shall be given. These include: comparable processes, technological advances and changes, economic feasibility, time limitations, the nature and volume of the discharges and effluents concerned, low and non-waste technology. The Stockholm Convention on Persistent Organic Pollutants[10] (POPs), in its Annex C Part V on unintentional production of POPs, provides general guidance on best available techniques and best environmental practices. It describes general measures to prevent the formation and release of its listed chemicals, such as using low-waste technology and less hazardous substances, promoting the recovery and recycling of waste, improving waste management programs, adopting preventive maintenance programs and avoiding the use of certain substances.

Public authorities may require activities within their jurisdiction to apply the best available technology or techniques and verify its application through authorization, permits, licenses and monitoring, or through other administrative or judicial enforcement.

---

   9   *See also* the regional seas agreements, *e.g.*, Convention for the Protection, Management and Development of the Marine and Coastal Environment of the Eastern African Region, Art. 4 (June 21, 1985); Convention for the Protection and Development of the Marine Environment of the Wider Caribbean Region, Art. 4 (Mar. 24, 1983), Convention for the Protection of the Natural Resources and Environment of the South Pacific Region, Art. 5 (Nov. 24, 1986).
   10   May 22, 2001.

1. Standard-Setting

International agreements sometimes call on states parties to establish standards for products and processes that impact the environment. Standards are prescriptive norms that govern products or processes or set limits on the amount of pollutants or emissions produced. Four categories of standards may be distinguished according to the subjects they regulate.

a. Process Standards

Process standards specify design requirements or operating procedures applicable to fixed installations such as factories or may designate permissible means and methods of activities like hunting or fishing. Sometimes, a particular production process or technique is imposed on operations, such as the installation of purification or filtration systems in production facilities. International process standards include the requirement that hazardous waste be incinerated (1991 Antarctic Environment Protocol), the ban on driftnet fishing (1989 Driftnet Convention), and operating procedures for biotechnology (EC Directives).

Process standards often are used to regulate the operations of hazardous activities posing a risk of accidents or other dangers. The 1987 Montreal Protocol on the Ozone Layer calls on states parties to determine the feasibility of banning or restricting the import from non-state parties of products produced with, but not containing, ozone-depleting substances. UNCLOS requires states parties to adopt measures to prevent pollution from installations and devices used in exploration or exploitation of the natural resources of the sea-bed, in particular measures to prevent accidents and emergencies, including regulation of the operation and manning of such installations or devices (Art. 194(3)(c)).

As discussed in Chapter 17, process standards that apply to imported products pose particular problems in respect to their compatibility with the international trading regime set up under GATT and the WTO.

b. Product Standards

Product standards are used for items that are created or manufactured for sale or distribution. Such standards may regulate:

- The physical or chemical composition of items such as pharmaceuticals or detergents. Examples include regulations that control the sulphur content of fuels or list substances whose presence is forbidden in certain products, for instance, mercury in pesticides.

- The technical performance of products, such as maximum levels of pollutant or noise emissions from motor vehicles, or specifications of required product components such as catalytic converters.
- The handling, presentation and packaging of products, particularly those that are toxic. Packaging regulations may focus on waste minimization and safety. Labeling requirements are used to ensure that consumers are aware of the contents and permissible uses of products. In addition, the "green label" is increasingly used to identify environmentally-safe products. Labeling is discussed further in the context of legislated market incentives to environmental protection. While most product standards are based on normal uses of the product, labeling requirements often aim to avoid accidental environmental harm through misuse, spills, or improper disposal of the product.

For economic reasons, product standards usually are adopted for an entire industry. In general, standards for new products are drafted to reflect the best available pollution control technology, in some cases requiring a percentage reduction of pollutants emitted in comparison with older sources. International product standards include the 1991 Amendments to MARPOL 73/78 requiring construction of new oil tankers with "double hulls," the ban on trade in products containing ozone-depleting substances (1987 Montreal Protocol, Art. 4(3) as amended), and the requirement to provide unleaded fuel for motor vehicles (1988 Sofia Protocol to the 1979 Convention on Long-Range Transboundary Air Pollution, Art. 4).

c.   Emission Standards

Emission standards specify the quantity or concentration of pollutants that can be emitted in discharges from a specific source. As a general rule, emission standards apply to fixed installations, such as factories or homes; mobile sources of pollution are more often regulated by product standards. Emission standards establish obligations of result, leaving to the polluter the free choice of means to conform to the norm

Often the environmental sector of the discharge, *e.g.*, groundwater, air, soil, is a variant factor. Emission standards may also vary according to the number of polluters and the capacity of the sector to absorb pollutants. Different standards may be imposed in response to particular climatic conditions, for example persistent fog or inversion layers. Emission standards are the type of standard most commonly required by international agreements and are mandated by the Protocols to the 1979 Convention on Long-Range Transboundary Air Pollution, the 1985 ASEAN Agreement on the Conservation of Nature and Natural Resources, the regional seas agreements, the Rhine Conventions on Chemicals and Chloridies, MARPOL, and the Climate Change Convention.

Emission standards are often applied to protect a specific environmental resource. The Convention for the Protection of the Marine Environment in the North-East Atlantic (Paris, September 22, 1992) partly uses this approach. Annex I states that the parties shall strictly authorize or regulate point source discharges from land-based sources to the maritime area and releases into water or air which reach and may affect the maritime area, implementing relevant decisions of the PARCOM Commission foreseen by the agreement. The Commission plans for the reduction and phasing out of hazardous substances and for the reduction of inputs of nutrients from urban, municipal, industrial and other sources.

Emission standards are based on several assumptions. First, that a certain level of some contaminants will not produce any undesirable effect, second, that there is a finite capacity of each environment to accommodate substances without unacceptable consequences (the assimilative capacity) and, third, that the assimilative capacity can be quantified, apportioned to each actor and utilized. Each of these assumptions has been questioned because in all cases chemicals discharged into the environment are likely to lead to statistically significant deterioration. Pollution occurs when the effects of the contamination on biological systems can be measured. Emission standards most often reflect a political decision about the amount of pollution that is deemed acceptable. Reflecting these concerns, the 1991 Bamako Convention on Waste in Africa is rare in opposing emissions standards based on assumptions about assimilative capacity, calling instead for application of clean production methods (Art. 3(3)(f)).

d. Quality Standards

Quality standards fix the maximum allowable level of pollution in an environmental sector or target during normal periods. A quality standard may set the level of mercury permissible in rivers, the level of sulfur dioxide in the air, or noise level of airplanes in the proximity of residential areas. Quality standards often vary according to the particular use made of the environmental resource. For example, different water quality standards may be set for drinking water and waters used for bathing and fishing. Quality standards also can vary in geographic scope, covering national or regional zones, or a particular resource, such as a river or lake, but each quality standard establishes base norms against which compliance or deviance is measured. The 1992 UN Convention on the Protection and Use of Transboundary Watercourses and International Lakes calls on each party to define, where appropriate, water-quality objectives and to adopt water-quality criteria, setting forth guidelines for this purpose in Annex III. Some bilateral and regional agreements on freshwaters and air foresee or mandate water-quality objectives.

2. Restrictions and Prohibitions

If an activity, product or process presents a risk of environmental harm, strict measures can be imposed in an effort to reduce or eliminate the harm. When the likelihood of risk is too great, the measure may call for a total product or process ban. The numbers and types of restrictions are almost unlimited, but certain ones are commonly used.

a. Limits or Bans

Environmental instruments call for restricting or banning hazardous products, processes or activities.[11] Controlled substances or activities frequently are named in easily-amended lists appended to the regulation. Such lists permit individualizing situations and give the regulation some flexibility. Lists also avoid too much technical detail being included in the basic legislative or regulatory text. The use of lists is very common in combating pollution by dumping of wastes, discharge of hazardous substances during normal operations, and the protection of wild flora and fauna, especially endangered species.

Lists have been widely employed in protocols to environmental treaties, beginning with the Convention on the Prevention of Marine Pollution by Dumping of Wastes and Other Matter (London, Dec. 29, 1972). The model of "black" and "grey" lists it establishes was subsequently employed in UNEP regional seas agreements for controlling land-based sources of pollution.[12] Substances are classified and limits established on the basis of their toxicity, persistence, and bioaccumulation.

Critics of the listing approach claim that its utility is limited because it is inherently responsive to previously identified problems, is often based upon uncertain dose-response relationships, and is not specific or flexible enough to be truly protective. Several hundred new substances are introduced each year and may cause considerable harm before their environmental impacts are known, especially given the possibilities of transformation of pollutants coming into contact with others after release.

---

[11]   *See, e.g.,* Convention and Montreal Protocol on the Ozone Layer (Mar. 22, 1985, Sept. 16, 1987); Convention on the Prevention of Marine Pollution by Dumping of Wastes (Dec. 29, 1972); Antarctic Treaty (Dec. 1, 1959) and Environmental Protocol (Oct. 4, 1991); Sofia Protocol to the 1979 Convention on Long-Range Transboundary Air Pollution concerning the Control of Emissions of Nitrogen Oxides (Oct. 31, 1988).

[12]   *See e.g.,* Protocol for the Protection of the Mediterranean Sea Against Pollution from Land-based Sources (May 17, 1980).

Setting legal limits for the acceptable concentration of substances requires a judgment on the amount of damage which is acceptable as a consequence of human activities and how much the population is willing to pay for reducing or lowering the risks of such damage.

Recent work has sought to estimate the "lowest-observed-effect level" and "no-observed-effect level." The first is defined as the lowest test dose at which the response is significantly different from the control group. The second is the dose at which the difference with the control group is not statistically significant. Both are highly dependent upon the size and conditions of the test populations and on the effects being monitored. A safety factor may then be added. Similar concepts are the "critical loads" and "critical levels" of pollutant concentrations, as developed in the context of the 1979 Convention on Long-Range Transboundary Air Pollution. Critical load is defined in Article 1(7) of its NOx Protocol as "a quantitative estimate of the exposure to one or more pollutants below which significant harmful effects on specified sensitive elements of the environment do not occur according to present knowledge." Article 1(8) of the Volatile Organic Compounds (VOC) Protocol defines the related notion of critical level: "concentrations of pollutants in the atmosphere for a specified exposure time below which direct adverse effects on receptors, such as human beings, plants, ecosystems or materials do no occur according to present knowledge."

Lists of polluting substances whose discharge is prohibited or submitted to prior authorization raise practical problems in enforcement. A substance such as mercury or cadmium usually is discharged in the environment as a component of many different compounds rather than in its pure form. Implementing the 1976 Conventions related to the Protection of the Rhine against Pollution by Chemicals and by chlorides required an investigation into the use of most of the listed substances and it was estimated that the number of listed substances and materials had to be multiplied by hundreds. As a result, some conventions have moved to "reverse listing," specifying in annexes those substances or activities that are permitted rather than those that are prohibited. The 1989 Basel Convention on Transboundary Movements of Hazardous Wastes adopted this approach, prohibiting all discharges except those which are explicitly authorized in individual cases. Its annexes list categories of wastes not only according to constituent substances and materials, but also according to the generating activities (*e.g.*, clinical wastes, wastes from the production, formulation and use of organic solvents) and hazardous characteristics (*e.g.*, explosive, flammable, poisonous). The 1992 Convention on Protection of the Baltic Marine Environment also uses reverse listing. The precautionary approach suggests that the method of reverse listing is justified, because it requires those seeking to act or to release a new substance or product to prove that it will cause no significant harm.

b.   Taking and Trade Measures

Treaties for the protection of biological diversity frequently mandate the use of trade restrictions or require the imposition of limits on taking specimens of protected living or non-living resources.[13] The types of restrictions vary and include:

Hunting and Collecting Restrictions. Hunting and collecting restrictions are used to protect biological diversity by prohibiting non-selective means of killing or capturing specimens of wildlife. The 1979 Bern Convention on the Conservation of European Wildlife and Natural Habitats includes a special Appendix listing hunting means prohibited for mammals and for birds.

More generally, protective measures may restrict injury to and destruction or taking of some or all wild plants and animals. The revised African Convention on the Conservation of Nature and Natural Resources requires adoption of adequate legislation to regulate hunting, capture and fishing, and to prohibit certain means of hunting and fishing.[14] Annexes specify measures to be taken regarding threatened or endangered species, which benefit from the most stringent protective legal measures.

Migratory species are also subject to special protection by treaties such as the 1979 Bonn Convention on the Conservation of Migratory Species of Wild Animals, which is aimed at all states through which such species transit and in which they spend part of their lives. States parties to the Bonn Convention are obliged to ban or regulate the taking of these animals in cases where the conservation status of such animals—the sum of influences on their long-term distribution and abundance—is unfavorable.

Taking restrictions and prohibitions may apply to non-living as well as living resources, although they are imposed more frequently for flora and fauna. Principle 5 of the Stockholm Declaration states that "the non-renewable resources of the earth must be employed in such a way as to guard against the danger of their future exhaustion and to ensure that benefits from such employment are shared by all mankind." International agree-

---

[13]   *See, e.g.,* CITES (Mar. 3, 1973), the Basel (Mar. 22, 1989) and Bamako (Jan. 29, 1991) Conventions on Hazardous Waste; the Montreal Protocol (Sept. 16, 1987), the Regional Seas Agreements concerning Protected Areas and Wild Fauna and Flora, MARPOL (Feb. 17, 1978), the International Convention for the Regulation of Whaling (Dec. 2, 1946), UNCLOS Arts. 61–65, 119 (Dec. 10, 1982), and the Convention on the Conservation of Migratory Species of Wild Animals (June 23, 1979).

[14]   Maputo, July 11, 2003, Art. 9. *See also* the ASEAN Convention on the Conservation of Nature and Natural Resources (July 9, 1985), Art.4(2), the Convention on Nature Protection and Wild-Life Preservation in the Western Hemisphere (Oct 12, 1940), and the Convention on Biological Diversity (June 5, 1992), Art.8.

ments regulate the taking of non-living resources in international commons areas (the deep sea-bed, Antarctica and outer space), and to shared fresh-water resources. Within states, the 1994 Desertification Convention calls for long-term integrated strategies that focus on improved productivity of land and the rehabilitation, conservation and sustainable management of land and water resources (Art.2(2)).

Import/export restrictions, both temporary suspensions and permanent, are commonly utilized for the protection of wild flora and fauna. The 1973 Convention on International Trade in Endangered Species of Wild Fauna and Flora (CITES), for example, uses trade restrictions and trade bans as means of protecting threatened and endangered species. The Convention lists in a first appendix all species threatened with extinction that are or may be affected by trade. Trade in these species is virtually prohibited, requir-ing prior grant and presentation of export and import permits issued under stringent conditions. Two additional appendices list those species that may become threatened with extinction unless trade is regulated. The EC has issued additional regulations banning the importation of cetacean and fur seal products.

Trade regulations also are used to prohibit or regulate transport and dumping of toxic and dangerous wastes. The Basel Convention of 1989 reg-ulates the transfer of toxic or dangerous wastes and particularly requires informed consent of the countries concerned prior to any transfer.

c. Land Use Regulation

The Convention on Biological Diversity, the regional seas protocols on spe-cially protected areas, and other global and regional nature protection agreements call for land use regulation. Land use controls play a major role in environmental law for both urban and rural areas, through zoning, phys-ical planning, and the creating of protected areas. Zoning helps distribute activities harmful to the environment in order to limit potential damage and allows application of different legal rules from zone to zone for more effective protection. The broader approach of physical planning merges provisions for infrastructure and town and country planning in order to integrate conservation of the environment into social and economic devel-opment.[15] Generally, once a planning scheme for the relevant land and water areas is approved by the state or local government, special procedures must be used to obtain exceptions. Regional planning procedures may clas-sify a city, a region or the entire territory of a country into broad land use

---

[15] *See* Chapter 10, Agenda 21 (1992). *See also* Art. 3(1), Ramsar Conven-tion (Feb. 2, 1971); Art. 6(b) Biological Diversity Convention (June 5, 1992); Art. 12 of the ASEAN Agreement (July 9, 1985).

categories such as residential, industrial, agricultural, forest, or nature conservation. Designated geographical areas may be given special legal protection for purposes such as health care or nature conservation, including national parks, reserves, and sanctuaries.

Land use planning and zoning regulations are normally expressed in negative terms, as prohibitions or restrictions on any undesirable utilization or change in utilization of the area. Modern planning also may encourage and promote economic land uses that are considered beneficial or compatible with environmental objectives and special land use management plans. Because of the evolution of environmental protection schemes and the numerous levels of government involved, land use regulations can become extremely complex.

Protected Areas. International environmental instruments require states parties to set aside areas for specific management and the *in situ* conservation of biological diversity as well as to protect monuments and sites of outstanding importance for geological, physiographical, paleontological or other scientific reasons, or for aesthetic purposes.[16] There are many kinds of protected areas and flexibility is necessary to design appropriate ones to ensure their effectiveness in conserving biological diversity. "Buffer zones" are special areas surrounding protected areas, designed to preserve them from harmful outside influences. Activities which do not have adverse effects on the protected area may be allowed to continue. "Interconnected corridors," created through land use regulations or private contracts and other incentives, are necessary to allow genetic exchanges to occur between protected areas. If the gene flow is impeded, protected areas soon lose a part of their biological diversity. Corridors can be linear, such as along river banks if natural vegetation is maintained, or may consist of strings or patches of natural vegetation from which animals (and plants) can move. Effective use of protected areas requires development and application of comprehensive conservation and management plans.

C. Environmental Impact Assessment

Environmental impact assessment (EIA) is a procedure that seeks to ensure the acquisition of adequate and early information on likely environmental consequences of development projects, on possible alternatives, and on

---

16   Biological Diversity Convention (June 5, 1992); Convention on Nature Protection and Wild-life Preservation in the Western Hemisphere (Oct. 12, 1940); African Convention on the Conservation of Nature and Natural Resources (Sept. 15, 1968); ASEAN Agreement on the Conservation of Nature and Natural Resources (July 9, 1985); Ramsar Convention on Wetlands of International Importance (1971); World Heritage Convention (Feb. 2, 1972); and the Convention on Migratory Species of Wild Animals (Sept. 19, 1979).

measures to mitigate harm. It is generally a prerequisite to decisions to undertake or to authorize designated construction, processes or activities. EIA procedure requires that a developer or business owner submit a written document to a designated agency or decision-making body, describing the probable or possible future environmental impact of the intended action. The procedure may be integrated into licensing schemes or land use planning.

Throughout the 1970s and early 1980s, international agreements began imposing EIA requirements that were increasingly broad in their scope and detailed in their requirements and provisions. At present environmental impact assessment is singularly important in both domestic and international environmental law. International instruments commonly provide that states should not undertake or authorize activities without prior consideration, at an early stage, of their environmental effects.[17]

Some of the early EIA provisions were written into regional seas agreements, beginning with the 1978 Kuwait Regional Convention for Cooperation on the Protection of the Marine Environment from Pollution. Article 11 says that each contracting state shall endeavor to include an assessment of the potential environmental effects in any planning activity entailing projects within its territory, particularly in the coastal areas, which may cause significant risks of pollution in the Sea Area. "Significant risks" is not defined. The Sea Area includes the high seas, the territorial seas, and the exclusive economic zones within the limits fixed by the Convention.[18]

An obligation to assess activities risking significant harm also is found in the 1982 United Nations Convention on the Law of the Sea (UNCLOS) in Article 206:

When states have reasonable grounds for believing that planned activities under their jurisdiction or control may cause substantial pollution of or significant and harmful changes to the marine

---

[17] Espoo Convention (Feb. 25, 1991); Art. 14(1)(a), Biological Diversity Convention (June 5, 1982); Art. 4(1)(f), Climate Change Convention (May 9, 1992); Art. 206, UNCLOS (Dec. 10, 1982); Art. I, Kuwait Regional Convention (Apr. 24, 1978); Art. 13, West and Central African Marine Environment Convention (Mar. 23, 1981); Art. 10, South-East Pacific Marine Environment Convention (Nov. 20, 1981); Art. 14, ASEAN Agreement (July 9, 1985); Preamble, Amendments to the Protocol for the Protection of the Mediterranean Sea against Pollution from Land-Based Sources, (Syracuse, Mar. 7, 1996); Art. III(3), Agreement on the Conservation of Albatrosses and Petrels (Feb. 2, 2001). *See also* Principle 17 of the Rio Declaration (1992) and Principle 11 of the World Charter for Nature (Oct. 28, 1982).

[18] *See also* the Convention on the Protection of Nature in the South Pacific (June 12, 1976).

environment, they shall, as far as practicable, assess the potential effects of such activities on the marine environment and shall communicate reports of the results of such assessments. . . .

This obligation clearly applies to any part of the marine environment, including marine waters under national jurisdiction.[19] Similarly, Article 4 of the United Nations Framework Convention on Climate Change (1992) calls for using EIAs as a tool to minimize adverse effects on the environment. Principle 17 of the Rio Declaration more generally extends the rule of prior assessment of potentially harmful activities to include activities whose impacts are felt solely within a state. Chapter 22 of Agenda 21 similarly proclaims the necessity to assess the environmental impact of certain planned activities. Article 14(1)(a) and (b) of the Biodiversity Convention concerns both the national and international aspects of the issue.

Environmental impact assessment is required in a transboundary context by the Espoo Convention (February 25, 1991). The treaty requires that states parties establish an environmental impact assessment procedure with regard to listed activities that are "likely to cause significant adverse transboundary impact." Impact is defined to mean any effect caused by a proposed activity on the environment, including human health and safety, flora, fauna, soil, air, water, climate, landscape and historical monuments or other physical structures or the interaction among these factors; it also includes effects on cultural heritage or socioeconomic conditions resulting from alterations to those factors. For these activities, the party of origin must prepare an EIA.

The list of 17 activities subject to the EIA requirement includes crude oil refineries, thermal and nuclear power stations, treatment, storage and disposal of radioactive waste, smelting, asbestos factories, chemical installations, road and rail construction, oil and gas pipelines, ports, toxic and dangerous waste disposal, large dams and reservoirs, groundwater abstraction, pulp and paper manufacturing, major mining, offshore oil production, storage of petroleum and chemicals, and major deforestation. Non-listed activities may be subject to the Convention requirements if the party of origin and the affected party or parties agree.

To determine the significance of the activity to the environment, criteria are provided in Appendix III of the treaty: size, location, and effects, including those giving rise to serious effects on humans or on valued species

---

[19]   The Montreal Guidelines for the Protection of the Marine Environment Against Pollution from Land-Based Sources (1985) is similarly broad: "States should assess the potential effects/impacts, of proposed major projects under their jurisdiction or control, particularly in coastal areas, which may cause pollution from land-based sources, so that appropriate measures may be taken to prevent or mitigate such pollution" (Art. 12).

or organisms, those which threaten the existing or potential use of an affected area and those causing additional loading which cannot be sustained by the carrying capacity of the environment.

The Espoo Convention sets out in detail the procedural and substantive requirements of an environmental impact assessment. First, any proposed, listed activity likely to cause significant adverse transboundary impact shall be notified to any potentially affected Party as early as possible. The latter has the right to participate in the environmental impact assessment procedure if it wishes. The public in the affected area—both inside the country of origin and in other states—also has the right to be informed of and to participate in the assessment procedure.

The environmental impact assessment documentation submitted by the originator must contain at a minimum:

1. a description of the proposed activity and its purpose;
2. a statement of the reasonable alternatives including a no-action alternative;
3. information on the environment likely to be significantly affected and alternative sites;
4. the potential environmental impact of the proposed activity and its alternatives and an estimation of its significance;
5. a description of mitigation measures to keep adverse environmental impact to a minimum;
6. an explanation of predictive methods and underlying assumptions as well as the relevant environmental data used;
7. an identification of gaps in knowledge and uncertainties encountered in compiling the required information;
8. where appropriate, an outline for monitoring and management programs and plans for post-project analysis; and
9. a non-technical summary, including a visual presentation.

Article 6(1) delineates the manner in which a final decision should be reached, requiring the party of origin to take "due account" of the environmental impact assessment documentation, as well as the comments thereon received, and the outcome of the consultations as referred to in Article 5. The party of origin should consider possible alternatives to the proposed activity and measures to mitigate significant adverse impacts. Once the final decision is reached, the party of origin must notify the affected party of the decision, along with the considerations which form its basis. Finally, Article 6 anticipates the situation where new information is obtained which was not available when the final decision was made, but before work on the project has begun. In this situation, Article 6(3) requires the parties to consult to determine if the decision should be revised.

The last step in the procedure is post-project analysis, an important innovation of the Convention. Article 7(1) states that the concerned parties should determine what manner of post-project analysis needs to occur, suggesting surveillance of the project as a preferred method. If either the party of origin or the concerned party determines that there is a significant adverse transboundary impact, the parties then consult to determine what measures should be taken to eliminate the adverse impact. This includes monitoring compliance with the conditions of approval of the activity and the effectiveness of mitigation measures, as well as verification of past predictions in order to utilize the results in regard to future activities of the same type.

The Espoo Convention was amended at the second meeting of the parties, held on February 27, 2001, in Sofia, in order to clarify that the public entitled to participate in procedures under Articles 2(6) and 3(8) of the Convention, includes civil society and, in particular, non-governmental organizations. The amendment also allows states situated outside the UNECE region to become parties to the Convention.

A second international agreement providing a model for EIAs is the Madrid Protocol on Environmental Protection of the Antarctic (October 4, 1991). Article 3 sets forth the general environmental principles which apply to all Antarctic activities, while Article 8 and Annex I detail the requirements for prior impact assessment. All activities for which advance notice is required under the Antarctic Treaty, pursuant to scientific research programs, tourism and all other governmental and non-governmental activities in the Treaty area, shall be subject to national assessment "in the planning processes leading to decisions" to undertake them and when there is any proposed change in the activities.

The need for an EIA depends on whether the activity has: (a) less than a minor or transitory impact; (b) a minor or transitory impact; or (c) more than a minor or transitory impact. If the impact is found to have less than a minor or transitory impact it may proceed forthwith. In every other case there must be Initial Environmental Evaluation (IEE) which shall include sufficient details to assess whether the activity may have more than a minor or transitory impact. If the IEE indicates that no more than such minor impact is likely, the activity may proceed, but appropriate procedures, including monitoring must be put into place. In cases where more than a minor impact is indicated, a Comprehensive Environmental Evaluation must be undertaken, with procedures for public comments and consideration by the Committee for Environmental Protection.

The Comprehensive Environmental Evaluation (CEE) is governed by the provisions of Annex I Article 3.[20] Once a draft of the CEE is complete,

---

[20]   Art. 3(2) lists the information that should be included in the Comprehensive Environmental Evaluation:

    (a) a description of the proposed activity including its purpose, location, duration, and intensity, and possible alternatives to the activity, includit is made publicly available and circulated to all parties for 90 days in order to allow comment. The final CEE should include any comments which are made during the 90-day period. Article 4 requires that decisions on the proposed activity be based on the CEE.

Other provisions of the Treaty require monitoring the impacts of any activity that proceeds after the CEE is considered (Annex I, Art. 5), and annually circulating to the parties, the Committee, and the public any information about any Initial Assessments and other information obtained as a result of the assessment process (Annex I, Art. 6). The Treaty also contains an emergency provision in Annex I, Article 7 that allows parties to bypass the EIA process in the case of certain emergencies, provided notice is later circulated describing the emergency actions which were taken.

No final decision may be taken to proceed with the proposed activity until a Consultative Meeting has had an opportunity to consider the Evaluation and comments, for a period of up to 15 months. A final Evaluation, on which any decision to proceed must be based, is then prepared and must be made public for 60 days before activity can begin.

---

  ing the alternatives of not proceeding, and the consequences of those alternatives;

(b) a description of the initial environmental reference state with which predicted changes are to be compared and a prediction of the future environmental reference state in the absence of the proposed activity;

(c) a description of the methods and data used to forecast the impacts of the proposed activity;

(d) estimation of the nature, extent, duration, and intensity of the likely direct impacts of the proposed activity;

(e) consideration of possible indirect or second order impacts of the proposed activity;

(f) consideration of cumulative impacts of the proposed activity in the light of existing activities and other known planned activities;

(g) identification of measures, including monitoring programs, that could be taken to minimize or mitigate impacts of the proposed activity and to detect unforeseen impacts and that could provide early warning of any adverse effects of the activity as well as deal promptly and effectively with accidents;

(h) identification of unavoidable impacts of the proposed activity;

(i) consideration of the effects of the proposed activity on the conduct of scientific research and on other existing uses and values;

(j) an identification of gaps in knowledge and uncertainties encountered in compiling the information required under this paragraph;

(k) a non-technical summary of the information provided under this paragraph; and

(l) the name and address of the person or organization which prepared the Comprehensive Environmental Evaluation and the address to which comments thereon should be directed.

1.   Criteria and Procedures

As the examples indicate, not every proposed activity is subject to assessment, only those that may be or are likely to cause a stated level of harm to the environment. The threshold differs in the many treaty references to EIA, with some referring to "measurable" effects, others "appreciable" or "significant" harm. The most frequently stated formulation requires a comprehensive EIA where the extent, nature, or location of a proposed activity is such that it is likely to significantly affect the environment.[21] The Espoo Convention requires an EIA for all activities which could cause "significant adverse transboundary harm." The procedure to determine whether an EIA is necessary in the 1991 Environmental Protocol to the Antarctica Treaty refers to assessing the "possible impacts" of activities "on the Antarctic environment and dependent and associated ecosystems."[22] Article 14 of the 1985 ASEAN Convention on the Conservation of Nature and Natural Resources provides that all proposed activities which "could have significant effects on the natural environment" are to be evaluated before they are adopted and the results of this evaluation taken into account in the decision-making process. The obligation applies without regard to the place where the effects on the environment might take place.

The requirement to conduct EIAs may be based upon

(a) lists of categories of activities that by their nature are likely to have significant effects;[23]
(b) lists of areas that are of special importance or sensitivity (such as national parks); the impact of any activity within or affecting such areas must be assessed;[24]
(c) lists of categories of resources or environmental problems which are of special concern;
(d) an initial environmental evaluation of all activities, a quick and informal assessment to determine whether the effects are likely to be significant;
(e) defined and listed criteria which make an impact "significant."

Consultation and dissemination of information to the public are important objectives of EIAs. For example, the 1986 Convention for the Pro-

---

[21]   Rio Declaration, Principle 17; Espoo Convention, Art. 2(2) (Feb. 25, 1991); ASEAN Agreement, Art. 14(1) (July 5, 1985); Agreement on the Caribbean Marine Environment, Art. 12(2) (Mar. 24, 1983).

[22]   1991 Madrid Protocol to the Antarctic Treaty, Art. 3(2)(c).

[23]   EC Council Directive on the assessment of the effects of certain public and private projects on the environment (June 27, 1985).

[24]   Art. 1(2) of Appendix III of the Espoo Convention (Feb. 25, 1991).

tection of the Natural Resources and Environment of the South Pacific Region, Article 16(3), requires that the information gathered in the assessment be shared with the public and affected parties. In Africa, the Memorandum of Understanding of October 22, 1998, between Kenya, Tanzania and Uganda[25] contains the agreement of the three states to develop technical guides and regulations on environmental impact assessment procedures, including enabling public participation at all stages of the process and to enact corresponding legislation (Art. 14). The Convention on Biological Diversity (1992) also emphasizes public participation as a goal of environmental assessment in Article 14(1)(a), and includes a notification and consultation requirement in Article 14(1)(c). Additionally, each contracting party is required to "ensure that the environmental consequences of [their] programmes and policies that are likely to have significant adverse impacts on biological diversity are duly taken into account" (Art. 14(1)(b)). This Convention also requires assessment of national *policies* as well as of proposed projects. In Article 14(1)(d), the Convention contains emergency clauses, typically found in the more comprehensive EIA regimes, which allow immediate emergency action when there is grave danger to biological diversity.

2. European Community Law

Within Europe, Directive 85/337/EEC of June 27, 1985,[26] obliged EC member states to have national EIA legislation by July 1988. Some non-member European states have developed legislation based on the EC Directive which has a very broad scope, requiring assessment, prior to consent being given, of the effects of those public and private projects likely to have significant impact on the environment due to the nature, size or location of the project. Assessment must be made of both the direct and indirect effects of a project on (1) human beings, fauna and flora; (2) soil, water, air, climate, and landscape; (3) the interactions between the factors mentioned in (1) and (2); and (4) material assets and the cultural heritage. Member states retain power to exempt a specific project from the assessment requirement in exceptional cases, but must inform the Commission. The Directive (Annex I) and some national laws list classes of projects that require impact assessments, thus presuming that they risk substantial environmental impact. The Directive also lists in Annex II the classes of projects subject to an assessment procedure if national law deems it necessary.

The EIA is integrated into the procedure introduced by Directive 96/61/EC of September 24, 1996 concerning Integrated Pollution

---

25   Nairobi, Oct. 22, 1998.
26   Community Directive 85/337 of June 27, 1985, O.J. L 175 (7/5/85).

Prevention and Control. This instrument establishes a system of permits for new installations listed in an annex to the directive, such as energy industries, production and processing of metals, mineral and chemical industrial plants, and waste management. An application to the competent authority for a permit must include a description of the major elements of an EIA (Art. 6), but the requirement may be fulfilled by submitting information obtained in accordance with the 1985 EIA Directive or other information produced in response to legislation fulfilling the requirements of the new directive.

3. Procedures of International Financial Institutions

a. World Bank

In October 1991 the World Bank issued an Operational Manual including Operational Directives[27] that describe its procedure of environmental assessment during project preparation and before appraisal, closely linked to a feasibility study of the project. The environmental assessment covers project-specific and other environmental impacts in the area influenced by the project. Its purpose is to ensure that the project options under consideration are environmentally sound and sustainable.[28] All environmental consequences should be recognized early in the project cycle and taken into account in project selection, siting, planning and design. The environmental assessment should also identify ways of improving projects, by preventing, minimizing or compensating for adverse environmental impacts.

The Operational Directive distinguishes types of environmental assessment: project-specific, regional, and sectoral, where similar but significant development activities are planned for a localized area, for sector investment loans and loans through intermediaries, emergency recovery projects, and larger issues such as ozone depletion or pollution of international waters. The preparation of the environmental assessment is the responsibility of the borrower, but the Bank's task manager assists and monitors the project and screens it in order to determine the nature and extent of the environmental work required. After the screening the project is assigned in one of three categories:

> Category A: A full environmental assessment is required;
> Category B: Environmental analysis is required, but not a full one;
> Category C: No environmental assessment is required.

---

[27]   OD 4.01. *See* Chapter 4G.1.
[28]   Guidance on sustainability is provided in OMS 2.36, *Environmental Aspects of Bank Work.*

The Operational Directive includes checklists of potential issues for an environmental assessment. It also proposes outlines and models for the assessment and prescriptions for the assessment and the screening procedures.

The Bank expects the borrower to ensure coordination among government agencies and to take the views of affected groups and local NGOs.[29] It also requires the borrower to provide relevant information to affected groups and local NGOs and to hold meaningful consultations with them. The environmental assessment should form part of the overall feasibility study or project preparation and be submitted to the Bank which decides on the loan.

b. International Finance Corporation

The International Finance Corporation (IFC) published in September 1993 a document providing guidance to its staff in conducting an environmental review of proposed projects.[30] This document is similar in many respects to the World Bank's OD 4.01 (Environmental Assessment) and has identical goals, but there are some significant differences between the two texts. The procedure of the International Finance Corporation addresses project sponsors who approach the institution much later in the project development cycle, often after feasibility studies, site selection, and preliminary design work have been completed. In such cases, the sponsor may be required to do the environmental analysis concurrently with the appraisal of other aspects of the project. Thus, IFC's procedure is designed for flexibility, to accommodate projects brought to the IFC in various stages of development. The IFC also does not require the project sponsor to consult with local interested parties and affected groups during the preparation of the environmental assessment or to make the draft EA publicly available for review and comment, including release to relevant national agencies and institutions.

c. Regional Banks

The Environmental Policy document of the European Bank for Reconstruction and Development (EBRD) requires that all of its investment and technical cooperation activities undergo environmental appraisal as part of an overall financial, economic, legal and technical due diligence. The environmental appraisal must be initiated at an early stage. The Bank determines the type of appraisal needed and provides guidance on how it should

---

[29]   *See* OD 14.70 *Involving Non-governmental Organizations in Bank-Supported Activities.*

[30]   *Environmental Analysis and Review of Projects,* Sept. 8, 1993.

be conducted,[31] but the Project Sponsor is responsible for providing sufficient environmental information to the Bank, by preparing an environmental action plan that forms part of the legal documents of the Bank's
investment. On behalf of the Bank, an Operation Leader has the overall
responsibility for the environmental aspects of the operation. Together with
the Office of the General Counsel, the Operation Leader incorporates environmental requirements in legal documentation.

The environmental appraisal by EBRD includes not only prior environmental impact assessment, but also an environmental audit which identifies past or present concerns and potential environmental and health and
safety risks and liabilities associated with the project. A generic environmental audit protocol for manufacturing facilities and specific question-
naires for various sectors have been developed by the Bank.

The European Bank of Investment, an organ of the European Union,[32]
it acts in conformity with the environmental legislation of the EC and thus
applies Directive 85/337 relating to the environmental impact assessment.
The Bank takes an active part in identifying the potential risks of projects
and the necessary or appropriate mitigation measures. The borrower must
prepare an environmental impact assessment which must be combined with
public consultation. When screening the project, the Bank can require the
insertion in the loan contract of appropriate provisions for guaranteeing
environmental protection. The Bank also can intervene as a consultant in
environmental issues and fund the identification and the preparation of
projects improving the environment.

The Inter-American Development Bank's review procedures apply to
all Bank operations, including sector loans, investment loans, technical
cooperations, small projects, private sector operations and any major refor-
mulation of those operations. The Committee on Environmental and Social
Impact relies on the Bank's Country Environmental Strategy, when available, an environmental and social impact brief and, in specific cases, on an
environmental and social report. The environmental and social impact
brief, required only for projects above U.S. $3,000,000, establishes the envi-
ronmental assessment requirements to be met in preparing the project and
identifies the environmental quality and social impact issues that must be
resolved to ensure that the project is viable and eligible for Bank support.
The evaluation stage includes an environmental impact assessment pre-

---

[31]   *See* the *Principles of Action* adopted by the EBRD in March 1992, document ML057.
[32]   *See* Chapter 4G.

pared, as a rule, by the borrower or the project sponsor, who has to take into account recommendations contained in the environmental and social impact brief. In addition to the usual elements, the EIA must include a record of the process and a summary of the results of consultations with affected groups; monitoring, reporting and evaluation requirements during the execution of the operation and thereafter; a description and when possible quantification of the environmental and social benefits as well as of the costs of any unmitigated environmental and social impacts. The data and information thus gathered are analyzed and the Project Team prepares an environmental and social impact report which is the Bank's final impact statement after review and discussion by the CESI. The draft loan contract contains the recommended environmental quality and social impact management measures. After approval, the full environmental and social impact report is made available to the public. For projects that include environmental quality and social impact management components or conditions, regular project reporting is required.

The African Development Bank carried out environmental screening during the identification of projects that need further attention due to their impacts on the environment. The Environmental Assessment Guidelines compare this initial environmental examination to an early warning system. It determines whether a project will be assigned to a category requiring detailed field review and an environmental impact assessment, specific measures or changes in the project design, or no environmental assessment. It also determines whether the selected project site is located in an environmentally sensitive area, characterized by ecosystems with high species diversity, by the presence of endangered or endemic species, or the presence of unique historical or archeological sites. The impact assessment should envisage, if necessary, mitigating measures and should take into consideration the priorities and concerns of the local population, by working in close consultation with NGOs and local institutions at all stages of the project cycle.

Once the project is approved, the Bank undertakes environmental monitoring to ensure that the planned mitigating measures are implemented and that legal standards for pollutants are not exceeded, and to provide early warning of environmental damage. After project completion, the actual impacts of project operations, the accuracy of the predictions, the effectiveness of the mitigating measures and the functioning of the established monitoring program are determined and evaluated through auditing.

Finally, the Asian Development Bank's Office of the Environment categorizes all projects listed in country operational program papers according to their type, location, sensitivity and the nature and magnitude of their potential impact and availability of cost-effective mitigation measures. If a significant impact is expected, an EIA or an initial environmental examination is required for the project, according to the importance of the impact. When an impact assessment is mandated, the procedure starts with the submission of a summary environmental assessment by the Projects department to the Board. The full EIA should be made available to a member of the Board upon request. The Bank requires the borrower to take the views of affected groups and local NGOs into account in the preparation of environmental assessment reports. The assessment reports may also be made available to them. Specific rules govern program loans, sector loans and private sector operations.

For all projects that can have a potential impact on the environment, the project staff should carry out an initial environmental examination. On the return of the fact-finding mission, the report is reviewed and the terms of reference for the special study or EIA are prepared with the active assistance of the Office for the environment. The loan fact-finding mission analyzes the results of the assessment and identifies probable additional environmental concerns not addressed in the study or resulting from changes in project scope. Towards the end of each calendar year a report is published listing all projects requiring specific environmental treatment during the implementation phase.

A review mission is dispatched periodically to discuss with concerned executing agencies the implementation of environmental mitigation measures agreed upon by both the borrower and the Bank. It verifies that environmental safeguards built into the project design are satisfactorily implemented during the construction and the operation of the project. At the end of the operations a project completion report should include a general assessment of any significant environmental impact experienced during project implementation.

In addition to the specific practices described above, several international lending institutions have established formal channels through which local communities, organizations and other groups, and, in special cases members of the Board of Directors, can request independent review or "inspection" of the bank's role in specific bank-financed projects.[33] These are discussed in Chapter 7.

Finally, a series of global and regional agreements require environmental impact assessment for exploitation of the non-living marine resources. On the global level, the Legal and Technical Commission of the International Seabed Authority established under UNCLOS approved in

2001 Recommendations for the Guidance of Contractors for the Assessment of Possible Environmental Impacts Arising from the Exploration for Polymetallic Nodules in the Area. Under the recommendations and Regulation 38 of the Mining Code on which they are based, two lists indicate activities for which EIAs are and are not required to be prepared by potential operators in the Area. Regional seas agreements for the Mediterranean and Persian Gulf similarly establish requirements that impact assessment be done before activities may be permitted. The details of the requirements are discussed in Chapter 11.

D. Risk Assessment

The concept of risk is a predominant factor of modern environmental law. Risk means the possibility or likelihood of adverse consequences from a given action. All human actions involve some risk and interaction with nature itself features risks. Managing and reducing risk is a basic objective of many governmental policies, legislation and regulation. Activities posing certain known risks are highly regulated: industrial activities; airline, rail, and automobile transportation, products containing mercury or lead.

The concept of risk is inherently uncertain, however, because if a given result is certain or it is impossible there is no risk. It is a question of the probabilities in between these two extremes. Ignorance can pose the greatest risks, *e.g.*, not knowing that asbestos causes mesothelioma cancers, or that CFCs deplete the ozone layer. The first goal thus is to understand what is known and not known about the impacts of substances and actions. Risk assessment is thus a specific application of the precautionary principle,[34] because it attempts to evaluate the probabilities of various harms resulting from a proposed activity. From a legal perspective, once a *prima facie* case is made that a risk exists, the burden may be placed on the polluter to minimize or eliminate the risk.[35]

---

[33] *See* the World Bank rules governing the inspection panels adopted on Aug. 19, 1994; the Asian Development Bank Inspection Procedures approved by the Board of Directors on Oct. 9, 1996 and for the Inter-American Development Bank the document on Independent Investigation Mechanism (no date is available).

[34] *See* Art. 3(3), Climate Change Convention (May 9, 1992) (states should adopt policies that are "comprehensive, cover all relevant sources, sinks and reservoirs of greenhouse gases and . . . comprise all economic sectors").

[35] *See* the Prior Justification Procedure adopted by the Oslo Commission. OSCOM Decision 89/1. EC law applies the same approach in prohibiting the

The criteria for assessing the need to regulate risk involve the probability and magnitude of harm. For many industrial activities both the likelihood and the nature of harm are well understood. Other risks can only be estimated because there is no prior human experience with them: LMOs, ozone depletion, anthropogenic climate change, and endocrine disrupting substances, for example, are all governed by uncertainty about the quantity and quality of risk associated with them, i.e., the likelihood of harm, the geographic range of the harm, and the character of damage (duration, reversibility, etc.). The reliability of any prediction will be affected by the complexity of the problem and the number of factors it is necessary to take into account.

Once the factors are assessed, policy-makers must determine the acceptable level of risk, knowing that zero risk is an impossibility if actions are allowed to proceed. Some legal definitions speak of the "likely" or "evident" risks, based on technical knowledge of "serious or irreversible" harm. Proportionate measures may be required to avoid the harm. Other legal instruments set the threshold for responsive action at harms that are "non-negligible," "appreciable" or "significant."

When policy-makers or societies differ about the appropriate level of risk, providing information may be the primary legal obligation imposed. The Cartagena Biosafety Protocol requires that risk be assessed prior to the first intentional transboundary movement of an LMO for intentional introduction into the environment of the importing country. The treaty then leaves it to the importing state to decide whether or not to accept the risk. Risk assessment and informed consent thus form the heart of the Protocol's regulatory process. Article 15 establishes the basic obligation to carry out risk assessment in a scientifically sound manner, in accordance with Annex III and taking into account recognized risk assessment techniques and risks to human health. Developing countries may encounter difficulties complying with this obligation due to lack of scientific data, technical bases, financial resources or biological experts. The Protocol accepts that these factors

---

introduction of new substances on the market until they have been proven to be safe. Art. 7 of Directive 67/548/EEC on the Approximation of the Laws, Regulations and Administrative Provisions of the Member States Relating to the Classification, Packaging, and Labeling of Dangerous Substances, O.J. L 96/1 (1967), amended, *inter alia*, by Directive 93/21/EEC, O.J. L 110/20 (1993). See also Regulation 793/93 of March 23, 1993, and Regulation 1488/94 on risk assessment.

may require the party of import to shift the costs of risk assessment to the notifying party, an application of the principle of common but differentiated responsibilities. Article 16 of the Protocol requires parties to establish and maintain a system to control the risks identified through the assessment procedure.

The application of risk assessment to products in international trade implicates the international trading regime. WTO cases show that panels require the identification of real risks as a *sine qua non* for trade barriers to be compatible with the GATT/WTO regime and especially with bans permitted by the Sanitary and Phytosanitary (SPS) Agreement. In various cases, the dispute settlement panels and the Appellate Body have established the contours of a GATT-acceptable risk assessment procedure: (1) risk assessments should set out both the prevailing view and opinions taking a divergent view; (2) there is no requirement to establish a minimum threshold level of risk and states may set zero risk as the level it will accept; (3) risk must be ascertainable and not theoretical, but ascertainable potential is enough; (4) the criteria used by the state must include all risks and their origin with a degree of specificity. Perhaps most importantly, there must be a rational or objective relationship between the SPS measure and the scientific evidence.[36]

In cases where it is not possible to conduct a proper risk assessment, Article 5(7) of the SPS Agreement allows members to adopt and maintain a provisional SPS measure. According to WTO Panels and the Appellate Body, this provision incorporates the precautionary principle to a limited extent, when four cumulative criteria are met: (1) the relevant scientific information must be insufficient; (2) the measure should be adopted on the basis of available pertinent information; (3) the member must seek to obtain the additional information necessary for a more objective assessment of risk; (4) the member must review the measure accordingly within a reasonable period of time established on a case by case basis depending on the specific circumstances, including the difficulty of obtaining additional information needed for review and the characteristics of the SPS measure.

Environmental agreements require states to act once there is a "likelihood of" or a "reasonable concern for" harm.[37] Cost/benefit analysis is not

---

[36] *See, e.g.,* Australian Measures Affecting the Importation of Salmon, WTO Doc. WT/DS18/AB/R (Oct. 20, 1998); Japan—Varietals, Measures Affecting Agricultural Products, WTO Doc. WT/DS76/AB/R (Feb. 22, 1999).

[37] *See* Art. 4(3), Convention on the Ban of Import into Africa and the Control of Transboundary Movement and Management of Hazardous Wastes within Africa (Jan. 29, 1991); Art. 2(5), Convention on the Protection and Use

included in the treaty formulations; for example, states are not allowed to consider the costs of regulation in determining whether transboundary water pollution is likely to cause significant adverse transboundary effects and thus crosses the threshold where action is required. However, in practice, states often weigh the benefits of the proposed activity against the magnitude and probability of occurrence of the risks identified, in determining what actions to take. States must still assess how serious a given risk is in relation to other risks and allocate resources accordingly. Consideration may be given to extended latency periods that may exist between exposure and effects, with potential cumulative impacts, and irreversibility of harm. As a result, abatement may be required of relatively remote dangers.

Risk assessment thus addresses the issues of scientific uncertainty in a procedural manner, documenting each part of a process that is accessible or transparent to all key parties. There are several key steps, beginning with hazard identification (the possible consequences of the proposed action) and risk characterization (estimating he magnitude and distribution of risks based on assessments of the qualities of the substance or action under review and the extent and nature of exposure). Alternatives to the action must be identified and compared as must risk management strategies, on the basis of costs, technical and administrative feasibility, and distributive consequences. Once a risk management strategy is chosen, it must be implemented, reviewed and, if necessary adjusted.

E. Strategic Environmental Evaluation

Strategic Environmental Evaluation (SEE) or strategic environmental assessment (SEA) is an advanced form of impact assessment procedure that was developed by the World Bank. It is a comprehensive and integrated process for evaluating environmental plans, policies and programs along with the social and economic impacts of a project early in the decision-making. The process can and should be adapted to the specific circumstances of different regions. Some of the characteristics of a SEE are:

- Its perspective is more general than that of an EIA, not targeting a specific project but rather a broader sector of human activities and developing general guidelines for the sector (*e.g.*, transport, energy, poverty reduction);
- It should influence the macro level of decision-making to develop policies that could become law in the future;

---

of Transboundary Watercourses and International Lakes (Mar. 17, 1992); Art. 3(2), Convention on the Protection of the Baltic Sea Area (Apr. 9, 1992); Art. 3(3), United Nations Framework Convention on Climate Change (May 9, 1992).

- It should easily adapt to different activities and projects in the sector for which it is elaborated and allow for combination with programs and policies for other sectors;
- SEE normally includes consultation with the potential stakeholders on a long-term basis, including individuals, NGOs, indigenous or local communities;
- SEE sector guidelines can be cost effective in evaluating future projects, especially in the public domain.

Within Europe, the EC adopted a Directive on strategic environmental assessment.[38] The Directive is supplementary to existing EIA requirements. It calls for adequate transboundary consultations where the implementation of a plan or program being prepared in one member state is likely to have significant effects on the environment of another member state. Significant is not defined, but Annex II sets out criteria for determining the likely significance of effects. Consultations and their results are deemed part of the assessment, which also includes preparation of an environmental report, taking it into account, and the provision of information on the decision (Art. 2(b)). Articles 6 and 7 further detail the requirements of consultations and their importance.

About the same time as the EC adopted its directive, the second Meeting of the Parties to the Espoo Convention, held Feb. 26–27, 2001, established a working group to develop a protocol on strategic environmental assessment. The Protocol on Strategic Environmental Assessment (SEA) to the UNECE Convention on Environmental Impact Assessment in a Transboundary Context was adopted in Kiev May 23, 2003. The Protocol clearly differentiates between assessment of two kinds of decision-making instruments: plans and programs (Arts. 12, 14) and policies and legislation (Art. 13). The assessment of plans and programs is binding, while for policies and legislation it is only recommended. On the whole the Protocol follows the EC SEA Directive that is based on project-related environmental impact assessment. Annex IV lists elements to be contained in the environmental report which must be made publicly available. Article 12 also requires the results of monitoring to be made available to the public. Article 13 on strategic environmental assessment of policies and legislation includes a substantive obligation to consider and integrate environmental and health policies into proposed policies and legislation. Its drafting is, however, weak and only requires the parties to "endeavor to ensure . . . to the extent appropriate . . ." the assessment of such policies and legislation. Significantly, the Protocol addresses health consequences in the same way as the environmental effects of planned activities. It requires health effects

---

[38]   EC Directive 2001/42 of June 27, 2001, O.J. L 197 (7/21/01) on the Assessment of the Effects of Certain Plans and Programs on the Environment.

to be examined together with environmental effects, which is an important step toward the integration of the two major concerns.

The SEE process corresponds to the three pillars of sustainable development—the social, the economic, and the environmental dimensions—developed by the WSSD. As such, it is likely to be influential at the international level in future law and policy. It also should be noted, finally, that EIA, risk assessment and SEE are not mutually exclusive. Indeed, the Framework Convention on the Protection and Sustainable Development of the Carpathians (Kiev, May 22, 2003) requires its parties to apply, where necessary, "risk assessments, environmental impact assessments, and strategic environmental assessments, taking into account the specificities of the Carpathian mountain ecosystems, and shall consult on projects of transboundary character in the Carpathians, and assess their environmental impact, in order to avoid transboundary harmful effects." (Art. 12(1)).

F.   Licensing and Permitting

One of the most widely used techniques to prevent environmental harm is government authorization through permits, certification, or licensing.[39] Each activity or establishment considered environmentally hazardous is defined or listed and made subject to formal licensing procedures. Another purpose of licensing or permitting is to ensure the sustainable use of environmental resources. In addition to laws containing general licensing measures, it is common to find norms that regulate directly or indirectly only specific aspects of environmental protection, such as air pollution, drinking water, noise, chemicals, and taking of wildlife. In this regard, hazardous installations such as nuclear plants, mines, natural gas or petroleum works are likely to have more stringent licensing requirements.

1.   Purpose and Goals

Most licensing controls are not designed to eliminate all pollution or risk, but rather to control serious pollution and to reduce its level as much as

---

[39]   *See, e.g.*, the Oslo Convention for the Prevention of Marine Pollution by Dumping from Ships and Aircraft (Feb. 15, 1972); the Paris Convention for the Prevention of Marine Pollution from Land-Based Sources (June 4, 1974); the Bonn Convention on Protection of the Rhine against Chemical Pollution (Dec. 3, 1976); CITES (Mar. 3, 1973); the Basel (Mar. 22, 1989); and Bamako (Jan. 29, 1991) Conventions on Hazardous Waste, the London Dumping Convention (Dec. 20, 1972), MARPOL (Feb. 17, 1978); UNCLOS (Dec. 10, 1982); the regional seas agreements; the Whaling Convention (Dec. 2, 1946); the Antarctic Treaty (Dec. 1, 1959); and the African (Sept. 15, 1968) and ASEAN (July 9, 1985) Agreements on Conservation of Nature and Natural Resources.

possible. Pollution-control licenses represent a middle ground between unregulated industrial practices and absolute prohibition. As such, they provide an alternative to zoning as a means to site installations and allow experimentation through the granting of temporary licenses. Where environmentally-hazardous products are present, such as industrial chemicals, pesticides or pharmaceuticals, authorizations may be required at each step for the manufacture, use, marketing, importation or exportation of the product. Taking permits allow the government to regulate the numbers of wild plants or animals that may be appropriate for private use.

The requirement that installations acquire a license is often given broad application. Most licensing systems operate on the basis of a list, or an inventory of activities necessitating a license because of their foreseeable potential harm to the environment. These lists may constitute part of the law or be contained in a supplementary legal instrument, as in the Annexes to the 1972 London Dumping Convention. Most laws make no distinction between profit-making and non-profit-making enterprises, except as to public bodies where they often exempt military operations. Retroactivity is also a problem because in principle laws are not given retroactive effect, but exemption for existing installations arguably grants them a *de facto* subsidy. The gradual trend favors requiring licenses for the continued operation of preexisting facilities.

An essential condition for initial and continuing authorization is compliance with certain environmental standards. These conditions are reviewed at least once every four years and require, for example, use of the best available techniques; compliance with obligations under national or international law relating to environmental protection; compliance with limits or requirements and achievement of quality standards or objectives prescribed by legislation; imposition of emission limits; and a requirement of advance notification of any proposed change in the operations of the activity or process.

Conditions often are based upon environmental impact assessments whose preparation may be incorporated into the licensing process and form part of the decision for or against issuing the license. In many cases, particularly in regard to chemicals and pharmaceuticals, elaborate testing procedures according to accepted laboratory practices serve the same purpose and may replace environmental impact assessments.

2. Procedures

Initial control consists of an examination of the installations and an assessment of the foreseeable results of their operations; licensed activities generally also are subject to measures of ongoing special supervision. The existence of several different licensing systems may result in similar functions being confided to different bodies in respect to the same installation.

In practice, several licenses may be required for a single project, but in some cases multiple license applications may be merged. Provision then is made for a more detailed investigation, incorporating the procedures of the different licensing systems. The decision is based on information supplied by the applicant and, in most cases, an environmental impact assessment. In general, the costs of the procedure are borne by the public authorities, but in some cases, costs are paid by the applicant.

Community Directive 85/337/EEC plays a significant role in licensing procedures in Europe. It provides in Article 6 that any demand for authorization of a public or private project which could have effect on the environment, as well as information received on this subject, should be made public. States also should ensure that opportunity is given to concerned members of the public to express an opinion before the project is approved. States members should establish the means to provide this information and allow consultation. The particular characteristics of the projects or sites concerned may determine what sector of the public is affected, control the location where the information can be consulted and establish the particular methods of information (poster, newspapers, displays). States also may determine the manner according to which the public should be consulted, whether it is by written submission, public inquiry or other, and fix the appropriate time limits for the various stages of the procedure.

Once the inquiry is closed, the authority may grant a license, if appropriate with conditions, give partial or temporary authorization, or refuse a license entirely. If the license is refused, there may be grounds for appeal to a judicial body for review of the decision. In most cases, there are both time limits and restrictions on who may take the appeal.

International requirements for licensing are increasing, part of the strong trend toward transparency attending the movement and use of substances, products and activities which might have a negative impact on the environment. In international trade, the delivery of *export* licenses and permits are often subject to the prior authorization of the *importing* state. Such consent is required by the 1989 Basel Convention on the Control of Transboundary Movements of Hazardous Wastes. The 1998 Convention on Prior Informed Consent, derived from non-binding principles established by UNEP and FAO, extends the system of double authorization to hazardous substances and products others than wastes. It also represents a step towards inter-state recognition of national permits. Such a practice is already found in the acceptance by other states of flag state certification that marine vessels conform to international legal standards. The 1977 International Convention for the Safety of Fishing Vessels was one of the first to establish that certificates issued by one party according to the provisions of the Convention shall be accepted by other parties as having the same validity as one issued by them (Art. 4). In 1989, the OECD similarly mandated the mutual recognition of data on chemical hazards provided by states that assure that test data have been generated in accordance with good laboratory practices.

G. Prior Informed Consent

Like environmental impact assessment, prior informed consent (PIC) is a procedural mechanism utilized in advance of activities in order to avoid potential conflict and reduce the risks of environmental or social harm. Prior informed consent requires obtaining and disseminating the decisions of importing countries on whether they wish to receive shipments of restricted or banned products after they have been fully informed about the hazards posed by the products. In most instances, the product to which the procedure applies are those that pose serious or irreversible risks to health or the environment. The procedure also applies, however, to mediate access to a state's biological resources, in order to obtain disclosure of potential benefits arising from the access.

The importance of PIC was recognized as early as 1983 in General Assembly resolution 37/137 which states:

> Products that have been banned from domestic consumption and/or sale because they have been judged to endanger health and the environment should be sold abroad by companies, corporations or individuals only when a request for such products is received from an importing country or when the consumption of such products is officially permitted in the exporting country.[40]

In 1989 the FAO Conference introduced the principle of prior informed consent when amending the International Code of Conduct on the Distribution and Use of Pesticides. The Governing Council of UNEP also adopted it for incorporation in the London Guidelines for the Exchange of Information on Chemicals in International Trade.[41] A 1992 MOU between the two organizations led to guidelines on the PIC principle. In 1994 and 1995, the two organizations agreed on the need for a legally binding instrument for the application of the PIC procedure for certain hazardous chemicals and pesticides in international trade. The Convention was adopted in Rotterdam in 1998.

UNEP's London Guidelines for the Exchange of Information on Chemicals in International Trade (1987) defines prior informed consent as

---

[40]   G.A. Res. 37/137 para. 1 (1983).
[41]   UNEP/GC.14/17, annex IV.

the principle that international shipment of a chemical that is banned or severely restricted in order to protect human health or the environment should not proceed without the agreement, where such agreement exists, or contrary to the decision, or the designated national authority in the importing country.

Three global environmental agreements rely on a form of prior informed consent: the Convention on Transboundary Movements of Hazardous Wastes;[42] the Convention on Prior Informed Consent Procedure for Certain Hazardous Chemicals and Pesticides in International Trade;[43] and the Biosafety Protocol[44] to the 1992 Convention on Biological Diversity (CBD). The CBD itself calls for access to genetic resources on agreed terms and requires that such access be subject to the prior informed consent of the provider country of such resources. (Art. 15(5)). UNCLOS suggests a similar procedure for scientific research within a state's exclusive economic zone, specifying that foreign vessels obtain prior state consent.

The modalities of the PIC process as applied to access to genetic resources were elaborated through the Bonn Guidelines adopted by Decision VI/24 of the sixth Conference of the Parties April 2002. The Guidelines set forth basic principles of a prior informed consent system for access to genetic resources. They set forth that the system should include: (1) legal certainty and clarity; (2) accessibility, in that access to genetic resources should be facilitated at minimum cost; (3) transparency: restrictions on access to genetic resources should be transparent, based on legal grounds, and not run counter to the objectives of the Convention; and (4) consent of the relevant competent national authority(ies) in the provider country and the consent of relevant stakeholders, such as indigenous and local communities should be obtained as appropriate and according to domestic law.

The 1998 Rotterdam Convention has a broad scope, requiring prior informed consent for any product or substance subject to final regulatory action, so that it includes chemicals refused permission to enter the market as well as those which have been withdrawn or banned. All information on such substances is channeled through the secretariat (UNEP/FAO) to a subsidiary body, the Chemicals Review Committee. The final listing decision rests with the Conference of the Parties which takes such decisions by consensus. Unlike the Basel and Cartagena agreements, the Rotterdam Convention does not require shipments made without consent to be taken back by the exporting state. The Cartagena agreement is unique among the treaties in requiring a risk assessment as part of the process.

---

[42]   Basel, Mar. 22, 1989.
[43]   Rotterdam, Sept. 10, 1998.
[44]   Montreal, Jan. 29, 2000.

H. Economic Measures

As an alternative to the regulatory approach, some international instruments recommend that states make efforts to influence the decisions of individual state and non-state actors who choose their activities by comparing the benefits and costs of the available and perceived options. Decisions can be influenced by limiting the options, altering the cost and/or benefits or altering the priorities and significance agents attach to environmental change (preferences). Economic measures can act as incentives or disincentives to behavior. Yet a third approach relies on education, information, and training, as well as social pressure, negotiation and moral arguments.

Economists in general see pollution as an externality that leads to an inefficient or sub-optimal allocation of scarce resources. Corrective devices are necessary to establish an optimal solution, one that maximizes the benefits to society. Polluters need to be confronted with a tax or charge equal to the marginal external costs or damage of their pollution in order to induce them to take account of the full social costs of their activities. Alternatively, an environmental agency could issue permits for emissions, the total number of which equals the optimal emission level, and allow sources to bid for them. Another market device sets the overall pollution limits and allows emission rights to be traded.

The use of economic measures is an application of the polluter pays principle. International environmental texts show a trend towards use of economic instruments and market mechanisms for environmental protection. Principle 16 of the Rio Declaration calls on national authorities to promote the internalization of environmental costs and the use of economic instruments, taking into account the approach that the polluter should, in principle, bear the cost of pollution, "with due regard to the public interest and without distorting international trade and investment." Agenda 21 also calls for the effective use of economic instruments, as does the Convention on Biological Diversity, in which the parties undertake to provide financial support and incentives for national activities intended to achive the objectives of the Convention.

Most international instruments do not attempt to define what is meant by "economic instruments," but instead enumerate the major categories considered relevant. The OECD addressed the subject of economic instruments in a general regulation on their use in environmental policy, adopted January 31, 1991.[45] The regulation recommends that member countries make greater and more consistent use of economic instruments, such as charges and taxes, marketable permits, deposit-refund systems, and financial assistance, to complement other policy instruments, on both national

---

[45]   OECD Council Regulation on the Use of Economic Instruments in Environmental Policy (Jan. 31, 1991).

and international levels. An Annex provides guidelines for the use of economic instruments, establishing five sets of criteria:

- Environmental effectiveness, determined by the ability of polluters to react to the incentives provided;
- Economic efficiency, achieved by an optimal allocation of resources. It implies that the economic cost of complying with environmental requirements is minimized;
- Equity in regard to the distributive consequences;
- Administrative feasibility and cost, including the ease and cost of monitoring given the existing legal and institutional arrangements;
- Acceptability. "It is of crucial importance that target groups be informed and consulted on the economic instruments imposed on them. In general, the success of any (economic) instrument requires certainty and stability over time with respect to their basic elements."

Economic incentives can either (1) coerce or apply disincentives; (2) provide incentives or; (3) allow participants to negotiate the level of benefits they receive by providing, *e.g.*, tradable emissions. The first group includes "governmental interventions which impose a net burden or disadvantage on economic agents for the purpose of inducing environment-friendly behavior."[46] Incentives can be applied not only internally, but internationally to encourage participation in a multilateral treaty regime. The 1987 Montreal Protocol on Substances that Deplete the Ozone Layer, for example, granted a ten-year implementation period to developing countries and EC members were allowed to aggregate their national consumption limits. On a national level, economic incentives not only include direct investment subsidies, but preferential loans, accelerated depreciation allowances, tax differentials, tax exemptions, credits and other promotional measures. Often such measures aim to include the cost of environmental damage, as well as the cost of raw materials, production, marketing, etc., in the price of a product. Even the concept of "product" changes, as the consumption of fresh air and clean water becomes priced and polluters pay, through fees or taxes, for causing deterioration to these resources. Some of the most widely used economic measures are discussed below.

1. Taxation

Charges are the "price" paid for pollution, a disincentive to environmentally damaging behavior. Polluters have to pay for their implicit claim on environ-

---

46   Peter Sand, *International Economic Instruments for Sustainable Development: Sticks, Carrots and Games*, 36 INDIAN J. INT'L L. 8(1996).

mental services. This enters into their cost/benefit analysis, but because environmental charges and taxes set an artificial price on pollution their actual impact on behavior is uncertain. Charges also may have a revenue-raising impact, intended for collective treatment, rather then being high enough to be a disincentive. Taxes can finance environmental investments and provide incentives to reduce pollution and waste. The state must monitor and if necessary correct the tax rate in order to ensure the goal is achieved.

Effluent charges are charges that are levied according to the quantity and/or quality of discharge of polluting substances into the environment. Emissions charges may take the form of user charges, payments for the costs of collective or public treatment of effluent. Tariffs may be uniform or may differ according to the amount of effluent treated.

Product charges are levied on products that are polluting in the manufacturing or in the consumption phase or that are obsolete and for which a disposal system is introduced. The charges can be based on some characteristic of the product (mercury content) or the product itself (paint). Tax differentiation is one aspect, leading to more favorable prices for environmentally friendly products.

Tax differentiation may result in subsidizing a relatively clean product by introducing a product charge on a polluting substitute. The differentiation results in more favorable prices for clean products.

User charges are payments, either at a uniform rate or based on amounts involved, for the costs of collective treatment of wastes.

Administrative charges are control and authorization fees, paid for government services, such as the registration of chemicals or for implementation and enforcement of certain regulations.

Taxes on polluting industries or products are a common mechanism used to induce environmental improvement. Though opposed by industry, many countries have enacted some form of environmental tax or other fiscal incentives. This is in line with the generally accepted "polluter pays" principle. Both the United Nations and the OECD are in favor of greater use being made of environmental taxes and charges.

Revenues from collected taxes usually go into the general fund from which government expenditures are financed. Earmarking introduces inefficiencies and constraints. If environmental taxes are earmarked for expenditure on environmental investments, the level of those investments will be dictated by the tax revenues or the tax rates will be dictated by the abatement expenditure requirements and will not be estimates of the environmental damage. On the other hand, earmarking may increase political support for environmental taxes. Moreover, environmental taxes can be seen as charges for the use of specific environmental services and the revenues appropriately used to maintain the quality of the same services. Earmarking also can play an important role in funding environmental protection in a declining economy.

2. Loans

In some countries, government financial assistance and incentives, taking the form of low-interest loans, aid the construction and operation of more environmentally-safe installations and recycling systems. International instruments do not often refer to loans, but speak of grants and "concessional" access to funds.[47]

3. Insurance

Governments can impose an obligation on those whose activities present a risk for the environment to be insured against any responsibility for damage to third parties, the state, or the local authorities which may result from an ecological accident. Some multilateral treaties include provisions that require the maintenance of insurance or other financial security for the payment of damages in the case of liability. These are often found in agreements imposing strict liability on hazardous activities, *e.g.*, the 1962 Convention on the Liability of Operators of Nuclear Ships; the 1963 Vienna Convention on Civil Liability for Nuclear Damage; the 1960 Convention on Third Party Liability in the Field of Nuclear Energy; the 1969 International Convention on Civil Liability for Oil Pollution Damage; and the 1993 Convention on Civil Liability for Damage Resulting from Activities Dangerous to the Environment.

Insurance can have a positive influence on the behavior of companies by putting pressure on them to act in an environmentally sound way; insurance companies may exercise influence to avoid high payouts for environmental accidents. In the same way, investor concerns may impact on company behavior.

The law and practices governing insurance coverage of pollution-related claims vary from one jurisdiction to another. However, a general principle is that insurance only covers fortuitous events. Therefore, if damage results from pollution caused by deliberate acts or omissions of the insured, there usually is no coverage.

Disputes over the application of exceptions, especially over broad interpretations of "accidental pollution" clauses, led to the introduction of pollution exclusion in the 1980s, completely eliminating coverage for pollution, whether or not the source was sudden and accidental. As an alternative, the insurance industry began offering, on a limited basis, Environmental Impairment Liability (EIL) coverage at premiums several times higher than the average policy. Coverage is narrowly drawn, often excluding the cleanup

---

[47]   Convention on Biological Diversity (June 5, 1992) and Framework Convention on Climate Change (May 9, 1992).

of hazardous waste dump sites and including only gradual escape of pollutants from the insured's own property. In addition, policies typically cover tangible property loss or damage, but exclude such consequences as loss of use of a facility caused by toxic air pollution in the area. Several environmental regulatory programs require insurance coverage as a precondition to licensing or issuance of required permits. In some cases, letters of credit, trust funds or solvency tests may be substituted for insurance.

In recent years, insurance companies in several countries have formed pools. These pools underwrite new, relatively unknown pollution risks under a controlled regime of environmental legislation. Unlike earlier policies, there is a tendency to extend coverage to gradual pollution risk. Generally, there is no coverage for expenses incurred for the restoration and reconstruction of the insured's operating equipment or installation grounds.

4. Grants and Subsidies

Environmental funds, which have been created in several countries, often directly finance environmental protection. Subsidies can include fiscal measures such as reduced taxes on anti-pollution activities, accelerated depreciation allowances, and favorable interest rates for anti-pollution investments. Such subsidies should not create significant distortions in international trade and investment. Subsidies to new polluting installations are generally prohibited. However, public authorities may aid research and development for the purpose of stimulating experimentation with new pollution control technologies, and development of new pollution abatement equipment. They also may subsidize anti-pollution investment in the framework of regional, industrial, social, agricultural and scientific policies, or whenever new environmental protection measures would create serious economic dislocations.

Subsidies are a particular problem when dealing with exploitation of living resources. Among the issues on the agenda of the Doha round of trade negotiations are subsidies, tariffs and access to fisheries resources. During discussions of the WTO Committee on Trade and Environment in 1997–98, governments disagreed over the impact of subsidies on the status of fish stocks and whether subsidies should be singled out for special treatment. Several major countries argued that subsidies have a negative impact from a conservation standpoint. Other participants disagreed and argued that fisheries management should be dealt with in a comprehensive manner. In 1999 some twenty countries expressed support for an Icelandic proposal for a WTO agreement on subsidy removal in the fisheries sector. In preparation for the 1999 multilateral trade round, states calling themselves "Friends of the Fish" (Australia, Iceland, New Zealand, Peru, Philippines and United States) formed a group to promote conservation and sustainability of fish stocks. Jurisdiction became an issue, with some states arguing for return of the matter to the FAO. The Friends of the Fish sought to obtain an agreement to form a negotiating group on fisheries subsidies, but debate continued without achieving a result throughout the next year. In the meantime, various organizations studied the impact of subsidies on overfishing. The OECD confirmed that subsidies contributed to overfishing and overexploitation in several regions of the world, although many other factors influence the health of fish stocks.

In late 2000, FAO convened an Expert Consultation on Economic Incentives and Responsible Fishing which reviewed and reported on the impacts of subsidies on fishery resources and on trade. Subsidies can allow the expansion of fishing fleets by, *e.g.*, supporting the building of new, larger ships or allowing purchase of new equipment; or it can simply hinder the reduction of fleets by supporting economically unsustainable capacity. Subsidies have the effect of slowing the exit of capital from the fishing industry even when it is in difficulty because of overcapacity and declining catches.[48]

Resolving the problem is difficult in part because it is not easy to determine what is a subsidy. It may be considered, for example, that states who pay foreign countries to cover any significant part of the effective costs of access to a foreign fishery are in effect subsidizing the entry of their fishing fleet. Such indirect subsidies are imbedded in international fishing access agreements through an agreed level of compensation for distant water fishing fleets to have a specific level of access to a fishery. From the perspective of conservation, the problem is that access is sometimes granted to already fully exploited or even over-exploited fisheries. Japan has argued that the negative impacts of subsidies "can be minimized if appropriate management and conservation measures are taken."[49] One economic model suggests that as long as the Total Allowable Catch does not change, subsidies have minimal impact. The subsidy simply transfers resources among industry. The problem is that for most fisheries, especially high seas ones, there is no established Total Allowable Catch. Due to the conservation problems raised by various mechanisms that have the effect of subsidizing fishing fleets, the Doha round of negotiations of GATT/WTO parties placed the matter on its agenda.

Virtually every major fishing state has used a decommissioning scheme over the past three decades to reduce overcapacity in its fishing fleet. The

---

[48]   For further information on fishing subsidies, *see* APEC FISHERIES WORKING GROUP, STUDY INTO THE NATURE AND EXTENT OF SUBSIDIES IN THE FISHERIES SECTOR OF APEC MEMBER ECONOMIES (2000); FAO, GOVERNMENT FINANCIAL TRANSFERS TO FISHING INDUSTRIES IN OECD (2000); FAO, REPORT OF THE EXPERT CONSULTATION ON ECONOMIC INCENTIVES AND RESPONSIBLE FISHERIES (2001). OECD, TRANSITION TO RESPONSIBLE FISHERIES: ECONOMIC AND POLICY IMPLICATIONS (2000).

[49]   *See* GARETH PORTER, FISHERIES AND THE ENVIRONMENT (UNEP, 2001).

question of whether these can be considered as environmental subsidies given a special status within a fisheries subsidies regime remains open. Many states strongly assert that aid to decommission fishing vessels should be considered a benefit to the industry and the environment, because by reducing the fishing fleet, it in all likelihood reduces the total catch and improves profits for those who continue to fish. Transfers aimed at capacity reduction, combined with other conservation measures, can reduce pressures on fish stocks. But unless those who remain are discouraged from expanding vessel capacity or utilizing more efficient gear to take more fish, the result can be at best neutral. Indeed, decommissioning can be overwhelmed by "input stuffing" to expand take among those who remain in the industry. With decommissioning, the value of a license becomes more valuable to those who remain, making vessels more valuable and stimulating increased investment in fishing capacity. Decommissioning funds may be used to buy bigger, faster and better equipped vessels. Some decommissioned vessels simply reappear as reflagged ships. Some stricter measures have been taken, such as limits on "days at sea" or prohibitions on re-entry of decommissioned vessels. The problem is to ensure that the "catching power" of a vessel does not increase to equal or surpass the loss occasioned by decommissioning.

5. Negotiable Permits and Joint Implementation

A system of negotiable permits, sometimes referred to as "bubbles," fixes total amount of pollution permissible within an area. Each company is required to obtain an emission permit from local authorities conforming to emission standards. Companies investing in processes that reduce pollution may exchange or sell their permits to other companies located in the same geographic area. Emissions trading allows discharges to operate under a multi-source emission limit and trade is allowed in permits adding up to that limit. Resource extraction concessions also can be traded.

The idea underlying tradeable permits is to leave the decisions on allocating permission to pollute and actual pollution behavior to the market. The initial distribution of permitted levels may be based on historic levels of emissions, which raises the question of how market allocation can be controlled so that regionally disproportionate distribution of pollution does not arise and present an unacceptable risk of harm to those in that area. In the case of carcinogens for which safe concentration levels cannot be determined, even very low levels may be unacceptable and a tradeable permit system inappropriate.

Tradeable permits may provoke objections if the system is not coupled with requirements to use and maintain the best available technology. A periodic devaluation or phasing out of tradable permits may be appropriate with incentives for technological innovations.

Joint implementation is related to the idea of negotiable permits. It allows industrialized countries to meet their obligations by financing or undertaking activities in other countries. Many states and scholars favor joint implementation for addressing anthropogenic climate change, where the issue lends itself to global trading markets for pollution because reduction in carbon dioxide emissions anywhere in the world should produce a positive effect in mitigating climate change. Due to this, the EU obtained in the 1997 Kyoto Protocol the right to meet its obligations under the UN Framework Convention on Climate Change as a bloc, in effect creating a "bubble" over Europe.

Article 4(2) of the Climate Change Convention also endorses the general concept of joint implementation. It provides that, for the purpose of meeting its commitments, any developed country may transfer to or acquire from any other developed party "emission reduction units" for projects aimed at reducing emissions or enhancing anthropogenic removals by sinks of greenhouse gases in any sector of the economy. Such emissions trading can only be counted towards meeting a states' commitments if the emissions reduction or removal is greater than would otherwise occur. In other words, the acquisition of emission reduction units should be supplemental to domestic actions for the purposes of meeting commitments under Article 3. A developed country may authorize legal entities to participate, under its responsibility, in actions leading to the generation, transfer or acquisition of emission reduction units (Art. 6(3)).

The argument in favor of such trading is that it lowers the overall cost of reducing emissions and may increase the amount of abatement that can be achieved. Those who are concerned about this technique focus on the technical difficulty of assessing the climate benefits resulting from joint implementation because assessment requires estimating the amount of greenhouse gas emissions that would have occurred in the absence of the joint implementation project or activity. It will be difficult, if not impossible, to accurately measure, monitor and verify actual benefits. In addition, some countries fear that joint implementation will distort development in favor of projects that "count" for climate change and that they will not receive a fair price, including transfer of technology, for their carbon offset actions. On a theoretical level, it may be questioned whether joint implementation violates the polluter pays principle by allowing polluters to continue their activities without paying full costs. In spite of these concerns, some countries have actively sought joint implementation projects and have benefitted therefrom.

6. Deposits

Another market mechanism is mandatory deposits on glass, plastic or metal containers to encourage their return or recycling. Deposit/refund systems add a surcharge to the price of potentially polluting products. The surcharge is refunded when the product or residual is returned to a collection agent.

7. Labeling

Labeling requirements are not new; they have been used to detail the nutritional content of foods, the proper use and hazards of cleaning products, and the dangers of cigarettes. However, broader environmental concerns recently have led to adapting the use of labels to promote environmentally "friendly" products. The "ecolabel" is an increasingly popular incentive to environmental protection. It is part of a gradual trend away from "end of the pipe" reactive solutions, which can be extremely costly, toward identifying and avoiding environmental problems before they occur. Environmental labeling programs constitute an economic instrument promoting pro-environmental purchasing on the side of the public and a precautionary approach on the side of industry.

Environmental labeling can involve regulations that insist upon accurate reporting of all the contents and dangers involved in a product. International instruments concerned with hazardous substances and products often call for adequate labeling of the dangers involved in the use of the substance or product. These instruments include the London Guidelines for the Exchange of Information on Chemicals in International Trade and the FAO Code of Conduct on the Distribution and Use of Pesticides. MARPOL, Annex III requires adequate labeling of harmful substances carried by sea.

The second method involves a public or private body awarding positive labels to inform consumers that the products are less destructive of the environment than similar competitive products, based on a holistic, overall judgment of the product's environmental quality. As such, it differs from "negative" labels that warn of particular dangers, and specific matters such as the use of recycled materials.

Labeling programs are very difficult to administer due to the need to comprehensively assess the entire life-cycle of the product, provide financing and establish product categories and criteria. However, their use continues to spread. The EC adopted Regulation 880/92 on March 22, 1992[50] to create a Community system for awarding the ecology label, based on voluntary participation of manufacturers. The determination of product groups and ecological criteria is ensured by the Commission, assisted by a committee composed of representatives from the member states. Initially, the regulation will not apply to food, beverages and pharmaceutical products.

---

[50] O.J. L 99/1 (4/11/92).

In conclusion, like all forms of environmental regulation, economic incentives must be studied to evaluate their effectiveness in protecting the environment. Effectiveness requires analysis of the changes of producer and/or consumer behavior and the costs of the measures taken. Some procedures may have only small effect while being administratively cumbersome and thus do not meet the requirements of efficiency or effectiveness. On the other hand, efforts at environmental protection also can provide a degree of economic growth.

I.   Monitoring and Surveillance

The implementation, as well as the formulation, of environmental laws and policies must be based on the collection of reliable information and on its continuous assessment. The techniques adopted in international and national environmental laws to ensure this are surveillance, reporting, and monitoring. International environmental instruments generally require the acquisition of data through surveillance, mainly a scientific activity, on which further action such as monitoring may be based.[51] Surveillance includes taking samples of the affected environments. It can be done by individual enterprises, by associations or by local or national authorities. Once the information is gathered, it must be assembled, organized and analyzed by an appropriate agency or institution to which the information is sent. It is common to find environmental laws requiring reporting by enterprises or state institutions.

Monitoring is the continuous assessment of information, comparing it to mandated parameters. The 1992 OSPAR Convention, Annex IV, Article 1 defines monitoring as the "repeated measurement" of three separate, but related, factors: (a) the quality of the environment and each of its compartments; (b) activities or natural and anthropogenic inputs which may affect the quality of the environment; (c) the effects of such activities.

Monitoring is a necessary foundation for giving effect to all environmental obligations. Generally, the monitoring organ can intervene based on reports and other means of surveillance that make it possible to assess the effectiveness of legislation or action taken. Monitoring provides constant feedback for decision-making, from long-term protection to rapid guidance in emergency situations. To ensure progress, the effectiveness of surveillance and monitoring must itself be monitored and assessed.

---

51   *See, e.g.*, UN Straddling Stocks Convention (Aug. 4, 1995); the Convention on Biological Diversity (June 5, 1992); the Climate Change Convention (May 9, 1992); the regional seas agreements, MARPOL (Feb. 17, 1978); UNCLOS (Dec. 10, 1982); and the Rhine Chemicals Convention (Dec. 3, 1976).

Principle 19 of the World Charter for Nature recommends that states, international organizations, and private actors monitor all sectors of the environment for all forms of environmental deterioration "to enable early detection of degradation or threat, ensure timely intervention and facilitate the evaluation of conservation policies and methods." Some international agreements contain explicit surveillance and monitoring obligations. The United Nations Convention on the Law of the Sea in Art. 204 mandates that states shall

consistent with the rights of other states, endeavor, as far as practicable, directly or through the competent international organizations, to observe, measure, evaluate and analyze, by recognized scientific methods, the risks or effects of pollution of the marine environment.

2. In particular, states shall keep under surveillance the effects of any activities which they permit or in which they engage in order to determine wither these activities are likely to pollute the marine environment.

Notably, this obligation extends to all areas of the marine environment.

Permanent monitoring and international cooperation are also required by other international conventions, including the regional seas agreements and those governing the dumping of wastes at sea, international watercourses, ozone-depleting substances, air pollution, climate change, biological diversity, fisheries, and desertification. Article 7 of the Convention on Biological Diversity is an example:

Each Contracting Party shall, as far as possible and as appropriate, in particular for purposes of Articles 8 to 10 [*in situ* and *ex situ* conservation]:

(a) Identify components of biological diversity important for its conservation and sustainable use having regard to the indicative list of categories set down in Annex I;
(b) Monitor, through sampling and other techniques, the components of biological diversity identified pursuant to sub-paragraph (a) above, paying particular attention to those requiring urgent conservation measures and those which offer the greatest potential for sustainable use;
(c) Identify processes and categories of activities which have or are likely to have significant adverse impacts on the conservation and sustainable use of biological diversity, and monitor their effects through sampling and other techniques; and

(d) Maintain and organize, by any mechanism, data derived from identification and monitoring activities pursuant to subparagraphs (a), (b) and (c) above.

The 1979 Convention on Long-Range Transboundary Air Pollution contains one of the most detailed monitoring systems. It establishes a cooperative program for the monitoring and evaluation of the long-range transmission of air pollutants in Europe (EMEP), to monitor sulphur dioxide and related substances and to develop and use comparable or standardized monitoring procedures, and establish monitoring stations as part of an international program (Art. 9). A 1984 Protocol provides for long-term financing of EMEP.

Monitoring or inspection of record books is required by treaties relating to the carriage of oil, carriage by sea of hazardous substances, imported species and goods, worker health, air quality of the working environment, the composition of waste to be dumped, discharge of harmful substances, and fisheries conservation levels. In some circumstances UNCLOS allows the physical inspection of foreign vessels as do many Memoranda of Understanding on Port State Control. Monitoring systems have been established by several international organizations and the use of monitoring to identify trends and patterns is now well-established.

J. Environmental Management and Audits

The environmental audit or independent review, sometimes referred to as the eco-audit, has come to serve two purposes. First, it is a legislative control mechanism of growing popularity. Second, it is a device of importance to business in sales, acquisitions and other transactions involving assets, where the risk of liability for environmental non-compliance can be a crucial element in negotiations and contracts. It differs from environmental monitoring because it is not a continuous process, but an overall evaluation at a specific moment.

With increasingly complex technology, company structures and environmental regulations, it is sometimes difficult for management and authorities to remain fully informed about the environmental consequences of company operations. This can result in hidden problems, leading to accidents as well as to violation of environmental laws and regulations. Environmental management and auditing is the systematic investigation of the procedures and work methods of a company or institution, as they are relevant to its environmental responsibilities. It is designed to determine to what degree these procedures and methods are consistent with legal regulations and generally-accepted practices. Both the 1991 Espoo Convention on Environmental Impact Assessment in a Transboundary Context and EC regulations refer to environmental audits.

The main elements of the environmental audit are the introduction of a systematic approach by companies to setting environmental standards; self-assessment by companies of their performance; an independent body to audit companies; and companies' right to use a certified statement of their participation in the scheme. The regulation includes criteria for accrediting environmental verifiers and a listing of their functions.

Eco-auditing can be part of the legal-administrative procedure for decision-making or part of the role of the judiciary. There can be parliamentary commissions of inquiry or studies by non-governmental environmental organizations, which play an important review role. Often research is undertaken by independent experts in the field. Environmental audits add an element of external quality control to the administrative system.

In 1993, the EC adopted an Eco-Management and Audit Scheme (EMAS).[52] EMAS is intended to be a management tool to encourage companies to apply high standards of environmental management and to evaluate the environmental impact of their activities. Although it is voluntary, participating companies must conform to the requirements of the Regulation's Annex I. The Annex requires the company policy to be in writing, to be regularly reviewed, in particular in the light of environmental audits, to be revised if necessary, and to be publicly available. Company policy must aim to provide for compliance with all relevant environmental requirements and to continually improve environmental performance. The company policy is also to include specific environmental objectives to be achieved over defined time-scales.

Annex II sets forth the requirements of environmental auditing, referencing other international standards including those of the International Standards Organization (ISO). The objectives of each audit, which must take place at least once every three years, must include assessing the management systems in place and determining compliance with relevant environmental regulatory requirements. Environmental audits, including on-site discussions, inspections and reviews, must be performed by independent persons with appropriate knowledge of the sectors and fields audited. Written audit reports are submitted to the top company management and culminate in the preparation and implementation of a plan of appropriate corrective action. Appropriate mechanisms must be in place and in operation to ensure follow-up to the audit.

A 2001 Recommendation contains guidance on the EMAS environment statement intended to assist organizations in producing the environmental statement required by the scheme. It identifies issues to be considered in preparing the statement. Its Annex III stresses that significant environmental aspects must be at the center of attention of an organization's

---

[52]   Council Regulation No. 1836/93 June 29, 1993 allowing voluntary participation by companies in the industrial sector in a Community eco-management and audit scheme, O.J. L 168/1 (7/10/93).

environmental management system. The organization must evaluate and improve its environmental performance by setting objectives and targets maintaining an ongoing review process.[53]

Apart from its function as a regulatory mechanism, environmental audits form a growing part of business transactions. Purchasers of businesses may seek to have environmental representations and warranties, or a determination whether they will be assuming liabilities for environmental damage. This can involve physical inspection of property and assets, including any disposal site used in the processes carried out on the property; examination of documents, including all operating licenses and permissions; and physical and scientific analysis of processes, by-products, and waste streams. Specific investigation usually is made for any signs of past environmental misconduct that would lead to a claim for liability for environmental damage in the future. The results of the audit can govern the nature and extent of protection built into the contract covering acquisition of the company or asset.

K. Conclusions

While the techniques designed to promote sustainable development including environmental protection are many and varied, all depend upon some degree of legal regulation. While law in and of itself is not sufficient to ensure improvement, good laws and effective institutions contribute to security and provide incentives to environmental protection. Despite the variations in international agreements and national strategies and legal systems, certain common issues arise in deciding upon adoption of specific techniques. First, the law should be predictable, understandable and enforceable, adopted with the participation of relevant stakeholders. Rules should concern access to and management of public goods and natural resources. At the same time, regulatory obstacles can increase costs and create disincentives to compliance. It is also important to attempt to coordinate various agencies and departments concerned with different aspects of legal regulation. In this regard, methods of integrated and ecosystem protection, discussed in Chapter 14, can be especially useful. Finally, a strong judiciary can not only enforce the law, but ensure access to justice for communities and individuals seeking to protect their environmental rights, powers and responsibilities.

---

[53] Recommendation of Sept. 2, 2001 on guidance for the implementation of Regulation (EC) No 761/2001 of the European Parliament and of the Council, O.J. L. 247 (9/17/01).

BIBLIOGRAPHY

BOYLE, A., & FREESTONE, D. eds., INTERNATIONAL LAW AND SUSTAINABLE DEVELOPMENT—PAST ACHIEVEMENTS AND FUTURE CHALLENGES (1999).

FREESTONE, D., THE BURDEN OF PROOF IN NATURAL RESOURCES LEGISLATION: SOME CRITICAL ISSUES FOR FISHERIES LAW (1998).

FREESTONE, D. & HEY, E., THE PRECAUTIONARY PRINCIPLE AND INTERNATIONAL LAW: THE CHALLENGE OF IMPLEMENTATION (1996).

HELFER, L.R., INTELLECTUAL PROPERTY RIGHTS IN PLANT VARIETIES: AN OVERVIEW OF OPTIONS FOR NATIONAL GOVERNMENTS (FAO, 2002).

GLOWKA, L., THE ROLE OF LAW IN REALISING THE POTENTIAL AND AVOIDING THE RISKS OF MODERN BIOTECHNOLOGY: SELECTED ISSUES OF RELEVANCE TO FOOD AND AGRICULTURE (2002).

CHAPTER 7

COMPLIANCE AND DISPUTE SETTLEMENT

International environmental law is largely a system to coordinate national legal responses to unsustainable behavior by state and non-state actors. The proliferation of international environmental agreements arouses concern over the extent to which states can and do implement and comply with the multitude of obligations imposed by such instruments. The potential for competitive advantage through non-compliance, due to the incremental costs of environmental protection, requires a credible monitoring system to deter free-riders. The greater the cost of compliance, the greater the disincentive to comply. There is also an incentive to violate or refrain from joining some agreements as they become more effective. This is the case, in particular, with agreements that call for a ban on production or trade in substances for which there is a market. Increased compliance leads to greater scarcity which drives up the price of the substance. The potential for profit increases the incentive to holdout or violate the agreement.

International environmental law thus places emphasis on national measures of enforcement, complemented by international compliance and enforcement procedures, from state reporting to judicial proceedings based on state responsibility. The number and variety of mechanisms created to supervise national implementation compliance have increased steadily. As in other fields of international law, the progress of states in meeting treaty obligations is monitored largely through international institutions.

Prevention is the Golden Rule for the environment, both for ecological and economic reasons. It is frequently impossible to remedy environmental injury and even if the damage is reparable, the costs of rehabilitation may be prohibitive.[1] Moreover, prevention cannot be assured solely by reliance on the principle of state responsibility, because there are significant procedural hurdles to obtaining a remedy for breaches of international

---

[1]   Damage to the French coastline from the Amoco Cadiz oil spill was estimated at $2.2 billion. The need for preventive measures increases the use of equitable judicial remedies. As the U.S. Supreme Court noted in *Amoco Production Co. v. Village of Gambell, Alaska,* 107 S. Ct. 1396 (1987): "Environmental injury, by its nature, can seldom be adequately remedied by money damages and is often permanent or at least of long duration, i.e., irreparable. If such injury is sufficiently likely, therefore, the balance of harms will usually favor the issuance of an injunction to protect the environment."

law, as well as problems of proving causation and injury. These factors, plus relatively low damage awards, indicate that in the present state of international law, imposition of liability cannot be relied upon as the primary means of halting environmental harm. Instead, treaty regimes focus on other means to enforce international obligations.

A. National Enforcement of International Environmental Norms

International environmental law requires implementation and enforcement at the national level. Treaties and other agreements call on states to take appropriate action in domestic legal systems to enforce the laws they enact pursuant to international obligations. UNCLOS, for example, requires states parties to enforce their laws and regulations and take the other measures necessary to implement applicable international rules and standards (Arts. 213-220). In particular, flag states of ships violating international norms are to take enforcement actions, including conducting an immediate investigation and, where appropriate, instituting proceedings. Penalties are required to be adequate in severity to discourage violations wherever they occur (Art. 217(8)).

National remedies should be provided as well for transboundary environmental harm. Procedures can include administrative remedies, civil actions and criminal prosecution of persons who violate norms and standards of environmental law. Some treaty obligations specify particular national measures, such as a civil liability regime to hold liable the polluter or "the operator or owner of a facility."[2] If no remedies are available or the remedies provided are inadequate, the case may become an inter-state dispute engaging state responsibility or liability.

1. Administrative Procedures

The breach of a statutory environmental duty, even without measurable harm, can result in sanctions or remedies, just as infraction of speeding laws can result in a traffic citation and fine even if no accident occurs. Proceedings usually can be initiated either by the authorities, concerned individuals or companies, or by associations. In some states, administrative procedures of a quasi-judicial character are the primary means of enforcing environmental laws. Environmental laws also may permit agencies to impose fines on violators.

---

[2] Convention on the Marine Environment of the South-East Pacific (Nov. 20, 1981), Art. 11; Nuclear Liability Convention (July 29, 1960), Art. II; Oil Pollution Civil Liability Convention (Nov. 29, 1969), Art. III.

The range of remedies may include fines, confiscation of machinery and tools, closure of the installation, prohibitions on exercise of a profession or activity, and depriving a company or individual of the right of public competition. There also exists an obligation to restore the environment that can be undertaken by the state and charged to the company if the latter fails to carry out its duty. Other sanctions may include a denial of government contracts or blacklisting of harmful products. Lending institutions may refuse loans or other benefits to projects failing to meet environmental standards or those scheduled for establishment in areas not attaining quality objectives. For example, the European Investment Bank may reject projects for areas not attaining EC air quality objectives.

2. Civil Liability

Despite efforts to prevent pollution and protect the environment, human activities and accidents give rise to environmental damage. In order to deter harmful acts and remedy damage as fully as possible, legal consequences attach to those acts that cause injury. International agreements and domestic law may refer liability issues for determination between the actor and the injured parties, or may provide for both inter-state and private actions. The increasingly accepted solution is to transfer the question from the inter-state level to the inter-personal level, that is from public to private international law where the polluter and victim are brought directly before the competent domestic authorities. A transnational element is present in all these cases, creating potential jurisdictional problems. It is not surprising, therefore, that states have sought to overcome the difficulties by prior agreement, concluding treaties or adopting other international texts to resolve at least some of the problems.

Civil liability refers to the liability of any legal or natural person under rules of national law adopted pursuant to international treaty obligations which establish harmonized minimum national standards. Several treaties establish rules on civil liability for environmental or related damage. These regimes usually have developed in regard to specific activities, such as nuclear installations and oil transport. Recent regional treaties in Europe apply more generally to industrial operations. Civil liability agreements generally define the activities or substances and the harm covered, channel liability, establish a standard of care and exceptions, set limitations on the amount of liability, and provide for enforcement of judgments. In addition, most include a provision for mandatory insurance or other financial guarantees.

The concept of liability generally implies that damage or harm has occurred to something. Normally, civil actions are commenced by those who have suffered harm to themselves or their property. They seek to halt further damage and repair that which has been done. Liability is most often imposed on the principal owner or manager of a polluting enterprise. Remedies can be sought if the damage results from the breach of law and the damage is not too remote from the wrongful action. Some national laws permit consumers or even those with no direct injury to sue. While the international law of strict liability is less developed than is national law, the concept applies in most of the treaties concerned with hazardous activities and substances. In civil liability, as in state responsibility, the fundamental problems are to establish causation, identify the polluter, and prove damage. To these difficulties are added three issues particular to the field of private international law: jurisdiction, choice of law and execution of judgments.

a.   Adjudicative Jurisdiction

Adjudicative jurisdiction can exist in the state where the pollution occurs or the state where the polluter is found. As a general rule, private international law favors jurisdiction in the defendant's domicile, sometimes under principles of *forum non conveniens*.[3] Several factors support this approach: the accused is able to defend itself in local tribunals, the evidence of harmful activity is more readily available, witnesses more easily may be called, and execution of a judgment in favor of the plaintiff will be more easily enforced. Conversely, it can be argued that the victim of the pollution should have the benefit of local courts to obtain compensation, especially because evidence of damage is more readily available in plaintiff's domicile where experts can evaluate and establish the scope of injury. Moreover, the innocent victim should not have to bear the additional expenses of litigation in a foreign country. Whatever solution is taken, the basic principle applies of equality of access and equal treatment of aliens and nationals.

State practice has evolved in this field. German courts have accepted cases brought by resident victims against non-resident defendants since 1957, when the Sarrebrucken Court of Appeal permitted suit by a German

---

[3]   In United States federal courts and most state courts, there is a presumption in favor of plaintiff's choice of forum which the defendant must overcome by showing that the chosen forum would be unnecessarily burdensome. *Piper Aircraft Co. v. Reyno*, 454 U.S. 235, 102 S. Ct. 252, 70 L. Ed. 2d 419 (1981) at n. 19. In various cases, often involving international litigation, the United States Supreme Court has stated that a plaintiff's choice of forum should rarely be disturbed. *Piper Aircraft v. Reyno*, *supra*; *Gulf Oil v. Gilbert*, 330 U.S. 501, 67 S. Ct. 839, 91 L. Ed. 1055 (1947); *Koster v. Lumbermens Mut. Case. Co.*, 330 U.S. 518, 67 S. Ct. 828, 91 L. Ed. 1067 (1947). *See also Macedo v. Boeing Co.*, 693 F.2d 683 (7th Cir. 1982) (reversing dismissal that would require resort to foreign forum) and *In re Union Carbide Corp. Gas Plant Disaster at Bhopal, India in December 1984*, 809 F.2d 195 (2d Cir. 1987) (upholding dismissal on *forum non conveniens* grounds).

restaurateur located on the German side of the Mosel against a French power station in Lorraine for damage caused by smoke and dust.[4] The plaintiff complained that the smoke had destroyed his gardens, made his houses unrentable and rendered his outdoor terrace unusable. The Court applied French law and awarded damages. However, there was no guarantee that the judgment would be enforced in France. The parties had to rely on comity and French cooperation due to the lack of an international text requiring mutual recognition of judgments.

Subsequently, EC countries adopted a Convention concerning Jurisdiction and the Enforcement of Judgments in Civil and Commercial Matters (the "1968 Brussels Convention").[5] Unfortunately, the Convention did not settle the jurisdictional issue. According to Article 3, the contracting parties agree that a defendant can be sued in tort before the courts of the place where the harmful event occurred, but in reality the harmful event could be deemed to occur in the place where the wrongful act is committed or the place where the harm is suffered. The first interpretation gives jurisdiction to courts in the state where the polluter acts; the second interpretation favors the state of the victim.

Several tribunals deciding claims based on environmental damage have utilized the Brussels Convention, with conflicting results. A trial court in Freiburg, Germany, awarding damages on a complaint by German farmers against a French chemical factory, held that jurisdiction lies in the court of the place where the damage is felt.[6] In contrast, a Rotterdam court, in a Rhine pollution case, initially held it had no jurisdiction because the action had to be brought where the polluting acts originated.[7] On appeal, plaintiffs argued that interpretation of the jurisdictional clause in the treaty should be referred to the European Court of Justice.[8] The appellate court agreed and submitted the question for determination. The European Court of Justice judgment of November 30, 1976, supported the plaintiffs.[9] The Court declined to adopt a preference for one jurisdiction over another, finding

---

[4]   *Poro v. Houilleres du Bassin de Lorraine,* 11 Oberlandesgericht (OLG) Saarbrucken 752 (1958), summarized at 1973 R.C.A.D.I. 161.

[5]   European Convention on Jurisdiction and the Enforcement of Judgments in Civil and Commercial Matters (Brussels, Sept. 27, 1968), 8 I.L.M. 229 (1968), amended in 1978, 21 O.J. L 304 (1977); 18 I.L.M. 81(1979).

[6]   Unpublished opinion, 1975.

[7]   *See Handelskwkerij G.J. Bier et al. v. Mines de Potasse d'Alsace S.A.* (Rotterdam municipal court, 6th chamber, Judgment of May 12, 1975); 1976 Rev. Jur. Env. 71.

[8]   The amendments to the Brussels Convention, adopted by Protocol, conferred jurisdiction on the European Court of Justice to interpret the terms of the Brussels agreement.

[9]   *G.J. Bier v. Mines de Potasse,* Judgment No. 21/76, 1976 Com. Mkt Rep. 7816.

too close a link between the two elements of liability (wrongful polluting activities, subsequent damages suffered). In the Court's view, the circumstances of every transboundary pollution case give rise to factors of proof and procedure which support the jurisdiction of both courts. According to the Court, the authors of the Convention deliberately created the ambiguity in Article 3, no doubt having in mind the interests of the injured party, for whom it is advantageous to be able to choose the best forum. Moreover, the nature of the wrong in question, international pollution, might require the choice of forum be left to the plaintiff. Thus, the provision should be read to encompass both locations. This meant that the Dutch plaintiffs could choose freely to bring the case either before Dutch or before French courts.[10]

b.   Choice of Law

Choice of law in the demand for compensation is determined, of course, by the court with jurisdiction. Generally, tribunals apply local law, but public policy concerns and the principle of non-discrimination may affect the choice. The latter rule requires that in no case may the plaintiff's complaint be judged according to rules less favorable than those which would be used to judge the matter in the state where the activities took place. This norm is included in Article 3(2) the 1974 Nordic Environmental Protection Convention and should lead judges to apply foreign law when its substance is more favorable than local law. German courts have chosen to apply the law most favorable to the victim in two cases involving transfrontier pollution coming from France to cause harm to German plaintiffs. Each time the more favorable French law was applied.[11]

c.   Assessing Damages

Providing compensation for environmental harm requires a consideration of the amount of damage that has occurred. The concept of harm to the

---

[10]   Following the Rhine case, the first application of the European Court judgment on jurisdiction was by the Tribunal of Bastia (France). In its December 8, 1976, judgment the tribunal upheld its jurisdiction to decide a complaint by Bastia fishermen against the Italian company Montedison, based on the dumping of sludge into the Mediterranean causing harm to the fishing off Corsica. The decision was upheld on appeal February 28, 1977. The appellate judgement expressly referred to the decision of the European Court of Justice. 8 REV. JUR. ENV. 331 (1977).

[11]   The *Poro* plaintiff sought and was awarded damages for business losses which were not recoverable under German law, but were permitted by the French Civil Code. *Poro v. Houilleres du Bassin de Lorraine, Sarrebrucken, supra* note 4.

environment is often viewed as a property concept, where economic value is placed on the lost or damaged object. This may include market value, loss of income, and damage to moral, aesthetic and scientific interests. The economic approach poses problems for protection of species of wild fauna and flora that are not exploited and thus have no market value, as well as for ecosystems or landscapes the economic value of which cannot be assessed. Evaluating the economic value of the intangible aspects of the environment, such as biological diversity, balanced ecosystems, and environmental services, is difficult. The situation is similar for areas that are under common ownership, and even more for those areas that are for common use but not capable of ownership, such as the high seas and outer space. Measurement or evaluation of harm for the purpose of damage awards also involves important questions of the threshold or *de minimis* level of harm, proximity of harm, especially for long-term, long-distance, multiple-authored actions and, finally, the possible irreversibility of the harm caused. The last issue is something that is thus far largely ignored in law.

One of the most difficult issues in environmental litigation is the scope of damage. The key question is whether damage extends beyond persons and properties to include damage to the environment itself. Increasingly, relevant civil liability conventions are addressing damage to the environment but generally limit recovery to the cost of reasonable measures of reinstatement and the costs of preventive measures. The UNECE Task Force on Responsibility and Liability regarding Transboundary Water Pollution has proposed a definition of damage that includes "detrimental changes in ecosystems." For this there may be awarded the equivalent cost of reasonable measures of reinstatement actually undertaken and further damages exceeding those provided for under the first measure, *i.e.*, there may be substitute damages where reinstatement is impossible because of the irremediable nature of the harm.[12]

The *Amoco Cadiz* case illustrates the current problems in the civil liability regime, especially in regard to the assessment of damages. The Amoco Cadiz tanker ran aground on March 16, 1978, due to damage to its navigational equipment. The accident occurred two miles from the small port of Portsall on the coast of Brittany. During the following three weeks, nearly all the 219,617 tons of crude oil cargo as well as its fuel, together totaling nearly 230,000 tons of oil, escaped into the sea creating an oil slick 18 miles wide and eight miles long. Part of the oil evaporated, another part broke down by natural means, but the rest filtered to the sea-bed or reached the coastline, creating ecological disaster.

---

[12]   *See* Alfred Rest, *New Tendencies in Environmental Responsibility/Liability Law: The Work of the UNECE Task Force on Responsiblity and Liability regarding Transboundary Water Pollution*, 21 E.P.L. 137 (1991).

Three hundred seventy five kilometers of coast were polluted by 50–60,000 tons of oil. Of this, 15–20,000 tons were cleaned up by volunteers and the military. In the affected zone, in the sea and on the coast, a total of 30 percent of the animal life and 5 percent of the plant life was destroyed. Approximately 20,000 birds died, the shellfish industry suffered damage, and the fishermen lost 45–60 days of fishing. There was also indirect damage, notably to tourism.

In 1983, multiple lawsuits filed in the United States were consolidated in the United States District Court for the Northern District of Illinois. The claimants included the French government, various French administrative departments, numerous towns, businesses, associations, individuals, and the insurers of the cargo. The defendant Amoco parties included Astilleros Espanoles, the Spanish company that designed and constructed the Amoco Cadiz; Amoco Transport Company, the Liberian company which was the registered owner of the ship and whose principal place of business was in Bermuda; Standard Oil Company, the owner of Amoco Transport Company, incorporated in Indiana, with its principal office in Illinois; Amoco International Oil Company, also owned by Standard Oil, incorporated in Delaware; Bugsier Reederei und Bergungs A.G., the German salvage tug company that sought to assist the Amoco Cadiz; and the American Bureau of Shipping, which approved the design of the supertanker.

Normally, the pollution victims would have been able to bring an action in a French court for damages under the Brussels Liability Convention, discussed below, which France had ratified. However, their damages substantially exceeded the limits of 77 million francs which would have been due under the original Liability Convention formula. According to estimates prepared at the time, the cleanup alone cost some 450 million francs, the damage caused to fish and shellfish was 140 million, and the losses caused by the reduction in tourism were more than 400 million. In these circumstances the victims sought to escape the limits of the Liability Convention by taking the case to the United States courts because the United States is not a party to the Liability Convention. The complaint sought $2.2 billion damages for environmental harm suffered due to the negligence of the companies in the construction, maintenance, and operations of the Amoco Cadiz.

In a judgment of April 18, 1984, the Court determined it had jurisdiction over the action and that United States law would apply, finding that local law was not proved to be different from French law which should govern because of the place of the harm.[13] The Court seemingly ignored the

---

[13]   Elsewhere in the opinion the Court does seem to recognize that ratification of the Liability Convention by France creates differences in substantive law: "The [Liability Convention] is the law of France and not the United States; it thus does not apply. . ." 20 Env't Rep. Case (BNA) at 2076.

fact that France was a party to the Liability Convention and the latter thus formed part of French law. Of course, the Court could have reached the same result by conceding the difference in law and concluding that United States law should apply for policy reasons or on an interest analysis.

This ruling was sufficient to escape the limits of the Brussels Convention, which would have limited the liability of Amoco to under $20 million. If the Convention had been applied, the provisions of Article 9, according to which no claim may be presented except before the tribunal of the state victim of the pollution, would likely have required dismissal of the action. Even if this were not the case, choice of French law including the Liability Convention would have bolstered Amoco's arguments for dismissal on grounds of *forum non conveniens.*

On the merits, the court held liable Standard Oil and its two subsidiaries.[14] Amoco International Oil Company, the American corporation responsible for the organization and administration of transportation for all of Standard Oil, was found negligent in its obligation to maintain the Amoco Cadiz in a state of navigability. In particular, there was a negligent breakdown in the steering mechanism of the tanker which was one of the immediate causes of the grounding of the tanker and the resulting damage. Moreover, the crew of the tanker was not sufficiently trained to maintain, utilize, inspect and repair the steering system, a supplementary cause of the grounding. Finally, the company using the Amoco Cadiz was negligent in leaving the ship without any backup steering system and without any other means of controlling the direction of the ship in case of failure. There was no limitation set on liability for any of the defendants.

Four years later the court examined in detail the question of damages, awarding the plaintiffs $85.2 million. The court's 435-page opinion[15] addressed the claims made by France, the harmed cities and towns, individuals, farmers, fishermen and environmental protection groups,[16] discussing several categories of damages:

1. Cleanup operations by public employees. The court accepted the claim for costs of the cleanup to the extent that public employees, including elected officials and the military, took time from their regular duties or put in overtime to assist. Travel costs incurred in the cleanup were also reimbursed. The time of volunteers was not

---

[14]   The plaintiffs failed to show the required gross negligence or willful misconduct necessary to hold the German salvage tug company liable. The Spanish design and construction company defaulted.

[15]   *In re Oil Spill by Amoco Cadiz off the Coast of France on March 16, 1978,* No. MDL376 (N.D. Ill. 1988), 1988 U.S.Dist. LEXIS 16832.

[16]   The various claimants initially demanded $2.2 billion in damages. *See* BUSINESS INSURANCE, Apr. 30, 1984, at 1. *Final Cost of Amoco Cadiz,* 14 MAR. POLLUTION BULL. 12 (1983).

compensated because their efforts were donated, but the proven costs of transportation, food and lodging could be claimed.

2. Gifts made by local communities in money or goods to volunteers or military officials were found to be inappropriate for inclusion in the damage claim, being in the nature of recognition of and gratitude for the services rendered.

3. Costs of material and equipment purchased for the cleanup. The court allowed recovery, less the residual value of purchased items, provided the acquisition was reasonable and the equipment was, in fact, used during the cleanup and that a residual value could be proven. As for previously-owned equipment, depending on the evidence the claimants were found entitled to recover either the difference between the value of the equipment before its use commenced and the value thereafter, or a reasonable rental value for the equipment during the term of its use.

4. Costs of using public buildings. The damage suffered by buildings during the cleanup operations was compensated and reimbursement was awarded for the extra costs arising from use of the buildings during the cleanup, such as increased water, power, and telephone usage.

5. Coastline and harbor restoration. The expenses for these purposes were included.

6. Lost enjoyment. The court applied French law and rejected this claim, which it viewed as a claim for damage to the quality of life and public services.

7. Loss of reputation and public image of the towns. This claim assumed that tourists who would normally have visited the communes for vacation and other recreational purposes went elsewhere due to deterioration of the beaches. The court rejected the claim, finding that it was more precisely covered and measurable in individual claims brought by hotels, restaurants, campgrounds and other businesses.

8. Individual claims. The court accepted some of the numerous individual claims, applying as a general rule the loss of income for one year. A claim by the Departmental Union of Family Associations was rejected as tenuous and not grounded in French law.

9. Ecological harm. This part of the decision was awaited with the greatest interest and it produced the greatest disappointment. The court did not award damages for injury to the biomass, the totality of life in the sea and on the bottom in the affected zone, deeming the matter complex, attenuated, speculative and based on a chain of assumptions. The court also found it did not have to reach this issue, because the damage was to *res nullius* and no one had standing to claim compensation. French arguments that the state could assert a legal interest in protecting the maritime public domain were found

unpersuasive. In addition, the court decided that damage caused to the ecosystems already had been fully recognized in the claims of fishermen and fishing associations, based on the reduction in their catches and their resultant profits. In respect to French governmental programs to restore the ecosystems, the Court allowed only expenses incurred to reintroduce species that suffered from the pollution and its consequences, finding that if the initial experiments were useful, the program should not be financed further by the defendants.

Ecologists, in particular, deplored the judge's failure to attach importance to the deterioration of ecosystems. An opportunity was lost to progress towards solving the difficult problem of evaluating ecological damage, that is, damage to the environment itself apart from any harm suffered by those who exploit its resources.

d.　Execution of Foreign Judgments

Execution of foreign judgments in tort matters is not guaranteed absent treaty protection, although the state of the polluter may consent to respect the judgment on the basis of comity. Uncertainty on this question may induce plaintiffs to choose the courts of the state where the polluter is found rather than their own national courts.

Within the EC, the question is regulated by Article 31 of the 1968 Brussels Convention, according to which the decisions rendered in one contracting state may be executed in another contracting state on request of any interested party. This guarantee of the execution of judgments complements the European Court of Justice decision permitting victims of transfrontier pollution to choose the jurisdiction to which to bring cases by ensuring that even judgments rendered in local courts will be effective in the state of the polluter.

e.　Treaty Regimes of Liability and Compensation

Given the myriad uncertainties and risks of litigation, a plaintiff could become involved in a legal steeplechase where one hurdle after another must be overcome in order to receive compensation for environmental harm. States have agreed on special procedures in an effort to reduce the hurdles in fields where the effects of environmental harm may be the most serious: *e.g.,* the transportation of hazardous substances by sea and the production and use of nuclear energy.

Current treaties on civil liability number about one dozen, nearly all of them concerned with one type of hazardous activity (nuclear energy generation, oil transport). Only the regional Lugano Convention on Civil Liability for Damages Resulting from the Exercise of Activities Dangerous for the Environment applies to all harmful activities. Apart from it, there are several conventions on marine pollution from shipping and on nuclear damage, and one each on pollution from offshore oil and gas exploitation; carriage of dangerous goods by various means of transport, and transboundary movements of hazardous wastes.

i. Marine Oil Pollution

Marine oil pollution, in particular compensation for environmental injury caused by it, is regulated by an entire system based on the 1969 International Convention on Civil Liability for Oil Pollution as modified in 1971, 1976,1984 and 1992.[17] To this must be added the 1971 Convention on the Establishment of an International Fund for Compensation for Oil Pollution Damage, also modified by the Protocols. The 1969 Convention establishes the liability of the owner of a ship[18] for pollution damage caused by oil escaping from the ship as a result of an incident on the territory of a party and covers preventive measures to minimize such damage. Other marine liability conventions include the 1976 International Convention on Civil Liability for Oil Pollution Damage Resulting from the Exploration for or Exploitation of Submarine Mineral Resources,[19] the 1996 Convention on Carriage of Hazardous and Noxious Substances,[20] and the 2001 Convention

---

[17]   In contrast to the treaty system, some states, notably the U.S., have held out and enacted national legislation with much higher limits of liability, including some contexts in which liability is unlimited. *See* Oil Pollution Act of 1990, Public Law 101–380, enacted following the Exxon Valdez disaster of 1989.

[18]   The owner of the ship is not responsible if he can prove that the damage resulted from an act of war, hostilities, civil war, insurrection or a natural phenomenon of an exceptional, inevitable and irresistible character. The same is true if the damage results from an act or omission of a third party done with intent to cause damage or results from the negligence or other wrongful act of any government or other authority responsible for the maintenance of lights or other navigational aids.

[19]   Dec. 17, 1976. Due to dissatisfaction with limits of liability, there are no ratifications as of 2003.

[20]   May 3, 1996. The HNS treaty system of liability is similar to the 1992 oil pollution agreement, imposing strict liability for damage caused. It has a wide definition of hazardous and noxious substances, excluding nuclear materials. Insurance is required and liability is limited on a sliding scale depending on the size of the ship. A second tier of compensation applies when a shipowner is not liable because the incident falls within the treaty's exceptions or the owner has no reason to know of the nature of the substances being transported, or where the claim exceeds the liability limits. A fund is created, financed by levies on the importation of HNS cargoes.

on Civil Liability for Bunker Oil Pollution Damage.[21]

The 1992 Protocol defines pollution as "loss or damage caused outside the ship carrying oil by contamination resulting from the escape or discharge of oil from the ship, wherever such escape or discharge may occur, and includes the cost of preventive measures and further loss or damage caused by preventive measures." While the Convention applies to incidents wherever occurring, Article 3 of the 1992 Protocol specifies that the Convention covers only damage suffered in the territory, the territorial sea or the EEZ of a contracting state. The Convention also applies to preventive measures, wherever taken, to prevent or minimize such damage. The 1992 Liability Protocol makes clear that this includes environmental harm. It states that compensation for impairment of the environment other than loss of profit from such impairment shall be limited to costs of reasonable measures of reinstatement actually undertaken or to be undertaken.[22] The owner may limit liability except in case of actual fault and must maintain insurance or other financial security to cover its liability.

The structure of oil pollution liability was extended to other hazardous substances in 1996 with the adoption of the International Convention on Liability and Compensation for Damage in Connection with the Carriage of Hazardous and Noxious Substances at Sea (HNS Convention).[23] The treaty covers claims for damage arising from the carriage of such substances at sea, *i.e.*, that period during which the substances are on the ship or ship's equipment. Article 1(6) of the HNS Convention defines damage to include, in addition to loss of life or personal injury or the loss of or damage to property, loss or damage by contamination of the environment caused by hazardous and noxious substances, provided that compensation for impairment

---

[21] International Convention on Civil Liability for Bunker Oil Pollution Damage (Mar. 23, 2001), IMO Doc LEG/CONF.12/DC/1, *available at* <http://www.imo.org>.

[22] Art. 8(2) of the Antarctic Mineral Resource Activities Convention also provides for strict liability for damages "in the event that there has been no restoration to the *status quo ante*." The Council of Europe rules on compensation for damage caused to the environment include among the definitions given in Rule 2: (9) "'Measures of reinstatement' means any appropriate and reasonable measures aiming to reinstate or restore damaged or destroyed natural resources or where appropriate or reasonable to introduce the equivalent of these resources into the environment." In all cases, restoring the environment to its *status quo ante* is the preferred remedy and this is especially true where it is difficult to assess the harm and the corresponding compensation. Only when restoration is not possible would it then be necessary to measure the damages.

[23] May 3, 1996, LEG/CONF.10/8/2 (May 9, 1996). For a similar strict liability regime, see the earlier Convention on Civil Liability for Damage Caused During Carriage of Dangerous Goods by Road, Rail and Inland Navigation Vessels of October 10, 1989.

of the environment other than loss of profit from such impairment shall be limited to the costs of reasonable measures of reinstatement actually undertaken or to be undertaken, and the costs of preventive measures and further loss or damage caused by preventive measures.

The marine pollution system balances strict liability with limitations on liability. The Protocol to amend the Convention on Limitation of Liability for Maritime Claims,[24] Article 2(2), established a ceiling defined by IMF special withdrawal rights.[25] The Protocol differentiates between claims for loss of life or personal injury in respect of which the minimum limit is 2 million Units of Account. That limit increases with the tonnage of the involved ship. In respect of any other claim the minimum is 1 million which is augmented following the same method (Art. 6). For states which are not members of the IMF the corresponding amounts are respectively 30 million and 15 million monetary units (Art. 8(2)).

Any claim for compensation for pollution damage may be brought directly against the insurer or other persons providing financial security for the owner's liability for pollution damage (Art. 7(8)). When an action is brought, in order to benefit from the limitation on liability, the owner must deposit the total sum representing the limit of his liability with the court or other authority with jurisdiction, either by direct deposit of the sum or by producing a bank guarantee or another guarantee considered adequate by the legislation and national authority of the state. If liability is found, the fund is then distributed among the claimants in proportion to their established claims.[26] The owner of a ship registered in a contracting state and carrying more than 2000 tons of oil in bulk as cargo must maintain insurance or other financial guarantee of compensation in case of liability for pollution damage. An insurance or guarantee certificate must be issued to each ship by the appropriate national authority and contracting states are obliged to prevent a ship from trading unless the appropriate certificate has been issued. Each state must recognize the certificates issued by other contracting states.

Before its amendments, the 1969 Convention threatened to become obsolete because the damages ceiling was far too low to compensate for the harm that could occur. As a result, a 1971 Convention established an International Fund for Compensation for Oil Pollution Damage. Basing itself on the 1969 Convention, this treaty also has been modified by protocols, the last of which, in 1984, brought about important changes in the system. The aim of the International Fund is to assure payment of compensation for pollution damage to the extent that protection afforded by the Liability Convention proves insufficient. The Convention applies to pollution dam-

---

[24]   May 2, 1996.

[25]   Protocol Art. 2(2).

[26]   Arts. 5(3) and 5(4).

age caused on the territory of a state, in its territorial waters and its exclusive economic zone. Damages are defined in Article 3 to include measures taken to prevent or minimize pollution damage.

The Fund is required by Article 4 to pay compensation to any person suffering pollution damage if the person is unable to obtain full and adequate compensation for the damage under the terms of the Liability Convention, either because no liability arises under the treaty, because the owner is financially incapable of payment, or because the damage exceeds the owner's liability under the Convention. However, the total amount of damages that the Fund will pay is limited, also, to 135 million Special Drawing Rights. This ceiling can be raised to 200 million for certain polluting accidents.[27]

The Fund is an international organization, made up of a General Assembly composed of all contracting states, an independent secretariat headed by a Director, and an Executive Committee. The latter consists of one-third of the members of the Assembly, elected by the latter taking into account an equitable geographical distribution ensuring adequate representation of contracting states particularly exposed to the risks of oil pollution and those having large tanker fleets. Contributions to the Fund are made by any person who has received total quantities of oil in excess of 150,000 tons during the prior calendar year.[28] The amount of the contributions is fixed by the Assembly for each of these persons on the basis of a sum fixed by ton of oil.

The system has been active. Hundreds of claims have been brought against shipowners and the Fund and between 1971 and 2000, the Fund has paid out nearly 300 million British pounds sterling with respect to 102 incidents.[29] The system also continues to evolve. In October 2001, the IMO Assembly approved a draft protocol to the Fund Convention on Compensation for Oil Pollution Damage. It follows concerns about the failure to secure full and timely compensation following serious oil pollution incidents such as that involving the *Erica* in 1999. The protocol creates an optional third tier level of compensation above the prior conventions.

Environmental damage or threat of damage to the coastline or a related interest may raise maritime claims and lead to the arrest of a ship. The 1999 International Convention on Arrest of Ships[30] allows and regulates such arrest by the state within whose jurisdiction the ship is found, irrespective of the flag the ship is flying (Art. 8). A ship may be arrested or released only under the authority of a court of the state party in which the arrest is

---

[27] Art. 4(4)(c).

[28] Art. 10.

[29] *See* International Oil Pollution Compensation Fund, Annual Report for 2000, 37–40.

[30] Geneva, Mar. 12, 1999.

effectuated (Art. 2). Maritime claims can include compensation for environmental damage, measures taken to prevent, minimize, or remove such damage, costs of reasonable measures of reinstatement of the environment undertaken or to be undertaken, and loss incurred or likely to be incurred by third parties in connection with such damage. The courts of the state in which an arrest has been effected shall have jurisdiction to determine the merits of the case (Art. 7).

The 2001 International Convention on Civil Liability for Bunker Oil Pollution Damage is the latest of the IMO Conventions on civil liability for marine pollution. About 14 million tons of oil are carried as fuel by vessels that are not transporting oil as cargo. These vessels are responsible for the majority of oil spills but are not covered by the 1971/1992 Civil Liability Convention. Hence the new treaty, which acts like the tanker treaties.

In contrast to earlier conventions dealing with damage caused by the cargo of relatively small and well-defined categories of vessels, the Bunker Convention potentially applies to all ships, defined as "any seagoing vessel and seaborne craft whatsoever." Bunker oil means "any hydrocarbon mineral oil, including lubricating oil, used or intended to be used for the operation or propulsion of the ship, and any residues of such oil." The definition of "pollution damage" is identical to that of the 1992 Convention on Civil Liability. It is also subject to the same limitation in that it does not cover damage to the environment in itself, but only clean-up costs and the loss of profit suffered by victims such as fishermen and local industries dependant on ocean resources and the tourist trade. Actions for compensation may only be brought in the courts of the states where damage was suffered. Ships must carry certificates attesting to their financial security and claims for compensation may be made directly against the insurer or other provider of financial security.

Unlike other treaties, the Bunker Oil Convention does not channel liability to a single person but defines ship owner to include others who have joint and several liability. However, only the registered owner of a ship over 1,000 gross tonnage is required to provide financial security. The regulation of mutual liability is left to national law. Article 6 provides that the ship owner may limit liability "under any applicable national or international regime," such as the 1976 Convention on Limitation of Liability for Maritime Claims.[31] Under this convention, the limits of liability are on a sliding scale depending on the size of the ship. A 1996 protocol, not in force at the beginning of 2003 will raise the limits. In any case, the reference to national and international law means a lack of uniformity in liability limits for oil spills from non-tanker vessels. While it was proposed to exclude from liability any person taking reasonable measures to prevent or minimize the

---

[31]   16 I.L.M. 606 (1977),

effects of oil pollution, no agreement was reached to include such a provision. Instead, the conference recommended legal provisions for such persons in domestic laws.[32]

ii. Nuclear Operations

The three nuclear liability treaties adopted in the 1960s concern civilian uses. Their aim is partly to protect potential victims and partly to insulate nuclear industry from devastating claims. The first agreement, the 1960 Convention on Third Party Liability in the Field of Nuclear Energy (Paris Convention) is a regional agreement concluded in the context of OECD. It was intended to provide unified rules for adequate and equitable compensation while still supporting development of nuclear energy. The Paris Convention has obtained only 14 ratifications, less than half the OCED member states. Non-members may ratify but only one has done so. There are no known transnational claims brought to date based on the Paris Convention, although some national claims[33] are based on legislation implementing the Paris Convention. The Paris Convention was enhanced in 1963 with a Supplementary Convention (Brussels).[34]

The Paris Convention is linked to the second agreement, the Vienna Convention on Civil Liability for Nuclear Damage of 1963, by a Joint Protocol adopted in 1988 and the 1997 Protocol to Amend the 1963 Vienna Convention on Civil Liability for Nuclear Damage. These conventions are based on civil liability and share the following main principles:

— Liability is channeled exclusively to the operators of the nuclear installations;
— Liability of the operator is absolute, *i.e.*, the operator is held liable irrespective of fault;
— Liability is limited in amount. Under the Vienna Convention, it may be limited to not less than U.S. $ 5 million (value in gold on April 29, 1963), but an upper ceiling is not fixed. The Paris Convention sets a maximum liability of 15 million Special Drawing Rights (SDRs) provided that the installation state may provide for a greater or lesser

---

[32]   *See* IMO Resolution on the Protection of Persons Taking Measures to Prevent or Minimize the Effects of Oil Pollution, IMO/LEG/CONF.12/18.

[33]   *E.g., Merliun v. British Nuclear Fuels*, (1990) 3 All ER 711.

[34]   The Supplementary Convention allows compensation beyond the liability limits of the Paris Convention. All claims must be brought in the state where the incident occurred if there is one and if not then the territory of the installation or the operator. Claims must normally be brought within ten years of the date of the incident and awards are enforceable in any state party. Eleven states are parties to the supplementary convention.

amount but not below 5 million SDRs taking into account the availability of insurance coverage. The Brussels Supplementary Convention established additional funding beyond the amount available under the Paris Convention up to a total of 300 million SDRs, consisting of contributions by the installation state and contracting parties;
— Liability is limited in time. Compensation rights are extinguished under both Conventions if an action is not brought within ten years from the date of the nuclear incident. Longer periods are permissible if, under the law of the installation state, the liability of the operator is covered by financial security. National law may establish a shorter time limit, but not less than two years (the Paris Convention) or three years (the Vienna Convention) from the date the claimant knew or ought to have known of the damage and the operator liable;
— The operator must maintain insurance of other financial security for an amount corresponding to his liability; if such security is insufficient, the installation state is obliged to make up the difference up to the limit of the operator's liability;
— Jurisdiction over actions lies exclusively with the courts of the contracting party in whose territory the nuclear incident occurred;
— A guarantee of non-discrimination respecting victims on the grounds of nationality, domicile or residence.

Following the Chernobyl accident, the IAEA initiated work on all aspects of nuclear liability with a view to improving the basic conventions and establishing a comprehensive liability regime. In 1988, as a result of joint efforts by the IAEA and OECD/NEA, the Joint Protocol Relating to the Application of the Vienna Convention and the Paris Convention was adopted. The Joint Protocol established a link between the Conventions combining them into one expanded liability regime. Parties to the Joint Protocol are treated as though they were parties to both Conventions and a choice of law rule is provided to determine which of the two Conventions should apply to the exclusion of the other in respect of the same incident.

The 1997 Protocol[35] set the possible limit of the operator's liability at not less than 300 million Special Drawing Rights (SDRs) (equivalent to U.S. $400 million). The Convention on Supplementary Compensation defines additional amounts to be provided through contributions by States Parties on the basis of installed nuclear capacity and the UN rate of assessment.[36] The Convention is open for adherence regardless of whether the state is

---

[35] Two instruments were in fact signed: the Protocol to Amend the Vienna Convention, *reprinted in* 36 I.L.M. 1462 (1997) and a Convention on Supplementary Compensation for Nuclear Damage, *reprinted in* 36 I.L.M. 1473 (1997).

[36] Vienna, Sept. 12, 1997.

party to any existing nuclear liability conventions or has nuclear installations on its territories. The Protocol redefines nuclear damage to include the concept of environmental damage and preventive measures, extends the geographical scope of the Vienna Convention, and extends the period during which claims may be brought for loss of life and personal injury. It also provides for jurisdiction of coastal states over actions baed on nuclear damage during maritime transport.

Finally, the 1971 Convention relating to Civil Liability in the Field of Maritime Carriage of Nuclear Material[37] provides that the shipowner is liable if the shipowner committed or omitted to do an act with intent to cause damage.

iii. Hazardous Wastes

A Protocol on Liability and Compensation for Damage resulting from Transboundary Movements of Hazardous Wastes and their Disposal[38] has further developed the regime of civil liability for environmental damage. Its purpose is to provide a comprehensive regime for liability and for adequate and prompt compensation for damage resulting from transboundary waste movements, including illegal traffic. It defines damage broadly to include not only loss of life or personal injury and loss of or damage to property, but also loss of income directly deriving from an economic interest in any use of the environment incurred as a result of impairment of the environment. It also includes recovery of the costs of measures of reinstatement of the impaired environment, limited to the costs of measures actually taken or to be undertaken and the costs of preventive measures, including any loss or damage caused by such measures. Preventive measures are defined as any reasonable measures taken by any person in response to an incident to prevent, minimize, or mitigate loss or damage, or to affect environmental clean-up (Art. 2 (2)). The Protocol applies to damage due to an incident occurring during a transboundary movement of hazardous wastes and other wastes and their disposal, including illegal traffic, in particular in relation to movements destined for disposal operations specified in Annex IV of the 1989 Basel Convention (Art. 3). Similar to other treaties related to environmental liability, the Basel Protocol imposes strict liability on, first, the person who provides notification of a proposed transboundary movement according to Article 6 of the Basel Convention, and, thereafter, the disposer of the wastes. Liability for damage is subject to financial limits specified in Article 12(1) and Annex B to the Protocol. During the ten year period of liability, those potentially liable shall establish and

---

37 11 I.L.M. 277 (1972).

38 Basel, Dec. 10, 1999.

maintain insurance or other financial guarantees (Art. 14). Liability limits are removed if the responsible person causes or contributes to causing damage by failure to comply with the provisions implementing the Basel Convention, or due to wrongful intentional, reckless or negligent acts or omissions. (Arts. 5 and 12(2)). Any person in operational control of hazardous wastes and other wastes at the time of an incident shall take all reasonable measures to mitigate damage arising therefrom (Art. 6).

The Protocol imposes upon the Contracting Parties the obligation to adopt the legislative, regulatory and administrative measures necessary to implement the Protocol and to inform the Secretariat of the Protocol of the measures it has taken (Art. 10). For the rest, the Protocol shall not affect the rights and obligations of the contracting parties under the rules of general international law with respect to state responsibility (Art. 16). The competent jurisdictions are the courts of the state where the damage was suffered or the incident occurred or the defendant has his habitual residence or has his principal place of business (Art. 17). All matters of substance or procedure regarding claims before the competent court shall be governed by the law of that court (Art. 19). Enforceable judgments thus handed down shall be mutually recognized and enforced (Art. 21).

iv. The Lugano Convention

A regional model for civil liability is the Lugano Convention on Civil Liability for Damages Resulting from the Exercise of Activities Dangerous for the Environment (June 21, 1993). It establishes general standards for indemnification of those injured by hazardous activities and products. The Convention broadly imposes responsibility on all persons and companies and the state and all agencies exercising control over dangerous activities, irrespective of the place of the harm. However, if the damage occurs in a non-contracting state, the Convention permits reservations to be filed demanding reciprocity of remedies.

The Convention applies to dangerous activities and substances, including living modified organisms. The quality of dangerousness is largely based upon assessment of the risk of harm to man, the environment or property. Nuclear damage is excluded if the incident is regulated by the Paris Convention on Civil Liability of 1960 or by the Vienna Convention of 1963 with its amendments, or by national legislation at least as favorable to the plaintiffs as the Conventions. Workplace accidents covered by social security and automobile accidents in places inaccessible to the public as well as assimilated to other activities within the installation also are excluded.

In addition to compensation for death, bodily harm, and injury to property other than that found on the site or within the installation where the dangerous activity has taken place, recovery can be had for environmental

harm,[39] limited to the costs of reasonable measures taken to restore or reha-
bilitate the environment to its prior state. Recovery is also possible for the
costs of mitigating measures and any losses or damage caused by such measures after an incident or event. The maximum amount of liability may be
fixed by local law, which should also insist upon adequate insurance coverage taking into account the risks associated with the activity.

Anyone who is in control of a dangerous activity is responsible for damages caused by that activity.[40] The problem of multiple or long-term sources
is solved imposing joint responsibility and by placing the burden of proof
on the various persons who were in control of the activity or activities to
prove they were not responsible. In cases where the activity has ceased when
the damage occurs, the last person in control will be liable unless he can
show that the causative event took place before he was in control.

Liability is not imposed if damage occurs as a result of armed conflict,
a natural disaster, an intentional act of a third party, a state command, "pollution of a level acceptable having regard to the relevant local circumstances," or if the activity was taken for the benefit of the person damaged,
to the extent it was reasonable for the latter to be exposed to the risks of
the dangerous activity, or if the injured party was at fault.

From the perspective of the plaintiff, there are several favorable provisions. Article 10 provides that in examining the proof of causality, a judge
in any case falling within the terms of the Convention should take into
account the probable risk of damage inherent in the dangerous activity in
question. Moreover, the statute of limitations is rather long. According to
Article 18, actions should be brought within five years of the date on which
the plaintiff knew or reasonably should have known of the damage and of
the identity of the person in control. No action may be brought more than
30 years after the causative event or the last in a series of causative events.
For waste disposal sites, the final date is 30 years from the closure of the site.
Article 20 permits the action to be filed either in the courts of a state party
where the damage occurred, where the dangerous activity took place, or
where the defendant has its permanent residence.

Injunctive relief may be sought by environmental associations in the
courts where the dangerous activity takes place, on conditions set by internal law. States may declare at signature, ratification, or accession that this

---

39   For these purposes, environment is broadly defined to include biotic
and abiotic natural resources, such as air, water, soil, fauna and flora, the
interaction between them, cultural property and characteristic aspects of the
countryside.

40   States parties may reserve to the basic principle of liability, to the extent
of allowing the defendant to escape liability if it can show that the state of scientific and technical knowledge at the moment of the incident was insufficient
to indicate the dangerous properties of the substance or the organism.

possibility will be open to non-governmental organizations based in other states parties. Environmental groups may demand prohibition of any illegal dangerous activity threatening serious environmental harm as well as injunctions against the person in control of a dangerous activity, in order to require preventive or remedial actions be taken. Where remedial action is sought, the courts of the state where the action should be taken also have jurisdiction over the case. Public authorities have the right to intervene when environmental groups bring actions. Article 19 is explicitly subject to reservations.

All judgments rendered by a tribunal with jurisdiction according to the Convention are entitled to be recognized in other states parties unless they are contrary to public order, the defendant was not properly notified of the action in time to prepare a defense, or if the decision is irreconcilable with a decision rendered between the same parties (*res judicata*).

In sum, several common traits are found in the liability agreements:

a. Identification of the polluter is assured through a presumption which channels responsibility. Thus, in case of damage, the responsibility automatically is imputed to the exploiter or the ship owner.

b. The system of liability is settled by imposing strict liability for damage, but specifying a limited set of excuses.

c. Jurisdictional competence is determined by designating the proper forum, in some cases that of the plaintiff, in other cases that of the polluter or in permitting the victim the free choice of tribunal.

d. Time limits are imposed. The Lugano Convention makes it three years from the date of knowledge or the time when the plaintiff reasonably should have known of the damage and the identity of the operator. An absolute bar to suit is imposed after 30 years.

e. Liability limits are coupled with mandatory insurance requirements.

f. The execution of judgments is assured.

Civil liability and compensation procedures require that there be identifiable victims with standing to bring an action, something that may not exist in all cases of all environmental harm, for example that caused on the high seas, Antarctica, or outer space. Damage in these places risks escaping protection if no specific norms are adopted, making regulation and international cooperation to implement and supervise enforcement of the rules essential. Within the Antarctic system, efforts to conclude a liability Annex to the 1991 Madrid Protocol have been unsuccessful until 2003, and efforts have turned to reaching a more limited agreement on environmental emergencies, as a step towards complying with Protocol Article 16. The emergency regime would establish rules on liability for the failure to provide for response action as well as rules related to the prevention of damage, contingency planning and response action. There is broad support for imposing liability on an operator for the costs of response action taken by other parties to the protocol and payments to an environmental fund if such action has not been taken by the operator.

It must be noted, in conclusion, that only four of the 11 major liability treaties are in force because many states oppose the limits on liability that these agreements contain. The Lugano Convention has not been ratified by any state to date. The fact of certain holdout states in turn discourages others from accepting what becomes an unequal burden-sharing. While limited liability derives from maritime law existing for several centuries in recognition of the value of maritime transport and the extant dangers, some see it as an unwarranted subsidy at the expense of other interests and as undermining the polluter pays principle.[41] Those favoring limited liability respond that unlimited damage awards could drive responsible shipowners out of business.[42] It is also argued that unlimited liability will mean maritime transport will become uninsurable. In fact, liability limits have been set in large part according to insurance industry indications, rather than degree of risk and needs of victims. The problems are political and practical rather than principled.

3. Penal Law

The function of penal law is to protect the most important values of society, by creating and enforcing penalties, including those involving deprivation of liberty. Increasingly, national law is imposing criminal liability on those who pollute and perform other acts damaging to the environment.

In most states, not only the company, but also directors and other senior managers may be held responsible. Normally, a company will be guilty of an offense if the offense-relevant conduct involves instructions or other acts of a "directing mind" of the company. Conversely, the director's position as a directing mind will not always produce criminal liability on his part, but may do so.

A resolution adopted by the UN Economic and Social Council[43] insists on the importance of environmental criminal law and, *inter alia*, recommends that states seriously consider enacting legislation prohibiting and sanctioning the export of products that have been banned from domestic use, as well as the production and import of specific dangerous materials, unless sufficient precautionary measures can be taken in respect of their

---

[41]   *See* G. Gauci, *Limitation of Liability in Maritime Law: An Anachronism?* 19 MARINE POL'Y 65 (1995).

[42]   *See* Robin R. Churchill, *Facilitating (Transnational) Civil Liability Litigation for Environmental Damage by Means of Treaties: Problems and Progress,* 12 Y.B. INT'L ENVTL. L. 1, 35–36 (2001).

[43]   Based on a recommendation of the Commission on Crime Prevention and Criminal Justice, Third Session, Vienna, Apr. 26–May 6, 1994; 24 E.P.L. 286 (1994).

use, treatment or disposal in their countries. It also recommends giving support to the idea of imposing criminal or non-criminal fines or other measures on corporations.

There are elements of environmental offenses that distinguish them from other areas of criminal law. Most criminal law is based on a direct individual relationship between a perpetrator and a victim who has been harmed. Environmental protection can involve perpetrators and victims who can only be identified statistically where harm results from long-term multiple causes. To regulate, two possibilities exist. The first is to assume the existence of danger or harm to public interests that are traditionally protected by penal law, such as life, health and property. The other is to develop new offenses against the environment, protecting independent natural elements without requiring an element of provable harm to specific victims. Both approaches can be found in existing provisions of penal law.

Penal sanctions can range from fines for petty offenses to imprisonment for more serious offenses. Criminal liability may be primary, accomplice, or conspiracy. In many countries, accomplice liability is imposed on those who give help, support, or assistance to a person committing an offense, or who incite, encourage, or counsel such a person. The lesser offense of conspiracy involves a decision by two or more parties to perpetrate an unlawful act.

Several existing international agreements call for penalties adequate to deter violations. UNCLOS, the Paris Convention for the Prevention of Land-Based Pollution, and the Basel Convention on Transboundary Movement of Hazardous Wastes require contracting parties to ensure compliance by taking appropriate measures to not only prevent but to punish conduct in contravention of the provisions of the agreement. The 1991 Bamako Convention on Waste Trade in Africa goes further in requiring that the penalties be sufficiently high to both punish and deter illegal traffic. The 1994 Lusaka Agreement on Cooperative Enforcement Operations directed at Illegal Trade in Wild Fauna and Flora supplements earlier provisions regarding the illegality of such trade by requiring states parties to investigate and prosecute such cases.

The Council of Europe adopted on November 4, 1998, the first treaty specifically devoted to criminalizing acts causing or likely to cause environmental damage, the Convention on the Protection of the Environment through Criminal Law.[44] The provisions call for administrative sanctions for less serious offenses, while serious, intentional offenses should result in imprisonment or fines and may call for reinstatement of the environment (Art. 6) or confiscation of profits (Art. 7). The text also calls for criminalizing acts that "endanger" the environment by creating a significant risk of serious harm. Article 2 lists categories of intentional offenses that the states

---

[44]　Convention on the Protection of the Environment through Criminal Law (Strasbourg, Nov. 4, 1998); E.T.S. No. 172.

parties must declare criminal both as to the principals and those aiding and abetting the commission of the offenses:

— release of substances or ionizing radiation into air, soil, or water which causes death or serious injury to any person or creates a significant risk of causing death or serious injury;

— unlawful release of substances or ionizing radiation into air, soil, or water which causes or is likely to cause their lasting deterioration or death or serious injury to any person or substantial damage to protected monuments, other protected objects, property, animals, or plants;

— unlawful disposal, treatment, storage, transport, export or import of hazardous waste which causes or is likely to cause death or serious injury to any person or substantial damage to the quality of air, soil, water, animals, or plants and unlawful operation of a plant in which a dangerous activity is carried out presenting the same risks;

— unlawful manufacture, treatment, storage, use, transport, export, or import of nuclear materials or other hazardous radioactive substances which causes or is likely to cause death or serious injury to any person or substantial damage to the quality of air, soil, water, animals, or plants.

States also should criminalize these offenses when committed with gross negligence. Lesser offenses are defined in Article 4 and include unlawfully discharging less dangerous substances or ionizing radiation, causing noise, disposing of wastes, operation of a plant, handling of radioactive substances or hazardous chemicals, causing detrimental changes to protected areas, and interference with protected wild flora and fauna.

Jurisdiction over offenses can be based on territory, flag, and nationality. Corporate liability does not exclude individual liability (Art. 9) and states parties should cooperate in investigations and judicial proceedings. States parties also may file declarations at any time permitting environmental non-governmental organizations to participate in criminal proceedings (Art. 11).

Following the example of the Council of Europe, the EC adopted a Framework Decision on January 27, 2003[45] inviting member states to establish criminal jurisdiction with respect to environmental offenses. One of the aims is to avoid physical or legal persons escaping prosecution by the simple fact that the offence was not committed in the territory of a state.

For both intentional and negligent offenses, states should take the necessary measures to criminalize under domestic law pollution causing the death or serious injury to any person, unlawful pollution causing substantial damage to any person or to protected monuments, property, animals

---

[45]   O.J. L 29 (2/5/03).

or plants, unlawful disposal and handling of waste, unlawful operation of a plant or of nuclear materials causing serious damage. Unlawful trade in ozone-depleting substances shall also be considered as a criminal offense as well as the unlawful possession of or trading in protected wild fauna and flora species or parts thereof, when they are threatened with extinction. These provisions should assist in compliance with international treaty obligations.

Corporate or entity liability is included in Article 6, which specifies the liability of legal persons for conduct committed for their benefit by any person in a leading position, acting either individually or as part of an organ of the entity. The proposed sanctions include disqualifying the entity from industrial or commercial activities, placing it under judicial supervision or ordering it to cease operations.

Each member state shall take the necessary measures to establish its jurisdiction with regard to offenses committed fully or in part in its territory, even if the effects of the offense occur elsewhere. Jurisdiction also extends on board a ship or an aircraft registered in the state or flying its flag, to legal persons with a registered office in its territory or to the state's nationals, if the offense is punishable under criminal law where it was committed or if the place where it was committed does not fall under any territorial jurisdiction. These rules should have a major impact on the international protection of the environment if properly enforced. Member states of the EC shall adopt the measures necessary to comply with the provisions of the Framework Decision before January 27, 2007.

Effective enforcement of criminal law may require international cooperation, particularly when the offenses concern illicit trade. Recognizing this, 12 of the 13 member states of the Southern African Development Community (SADC)[46] adopted a Protocol on Wildlife Conservation and Law Enforcement[47] which aims to ensure regional conservation and sustainable use of wildlife and the enforcement of wildlife conservation laws. As all the contracting states are members of the International Criminal Police Organization (Interpol), enforcement measures include coordinating the designated Interpol National Central Bureaus. The Bureaus exchange information concerning the illegal taking of, and trade in, wildlife and wildlife products, coordinate efforts to apprehend illegal traders and takers and to recover and dispose of illegal wildlife products. The Bureaus may request from each other any assistance or information which may be required to locate, apprehend or extradite an individual charged with violating the wildlife laws of a state party. States parties are to provide all available data on the location and movement of illegal takers and traders and the location of routes for illegal transfrontier trafficking in wildlife and

---

[46]   Windhoek, Aug. 17, 1992.
[47]   Maputo, Aug. 13, 1999.

wildlife products.[48] Institutional arrangements provide for the establishment of different committees and of a Wildlife Sector Technical Coordinating Unit. The Protocol is unusual in foreseeing that sanctions can be imposed against any state party that persistently fails, without good reason, to fulfil its obligations assumed under the Protocol or that implements policies which undermine the treaty's objectives and principles.[49] The contracting states also recognize that compliance with wildlife conservation laws depends on the perceptions and development needs of people living with wildlife. The Convention thus affirms that regional management of wildlife products will promote awareness of the socio-economic value of wildlife and enable equitable distribution of the benefits derived from the sustainable use of it. The parties signal their intention to promote "community based wildlife management," allowing a community or group of communities to receive the benefits from managing wildlife. The Protocol also aims at ensuring cooperation at the national level among government authorities, non-governmental organizations and the private sector.

In conclusion, principles of international environmental law and more precise obligations found in international agreements give guidance to states in their drafting of national and local environmental laws and procedures. The array of techniques and procedures discussed serves to direct the implementation of international norms and standards; the actual techniques and procedures adopted in each legal system will reflect local priorities and conditions as well as international law. Careful choices and legal drafting will assist in making law an effective tool to protect and preserve the environment.

B. International Compliance Mechanisms

International environmental agreements often include provisions pertaining to monitoring, implementation review, compliance verification, and non-compliance mechanisms. It is increasingly clear that the effectiveness of such procedures and institutions should be evaluated to determine whether they require reform and harmonization. It is also important to evaluate the underlying normative framework of each agreement to understand whether, if fully implemented, it is capable of producing the desired improvement in the status of the environment. Good compliance with rules that do not go beyond existing practice or that represent an inadequate goal will not prevent further environmental deterioration.

Environmental problems often require long-term solutions, making supervision of international agreements difficult. Scientific uncertainty or

---

[48]   Art. 9.

[49]   Art. 12.

political disagreement over the required solutions can lead to international environmental obligations that are vague and indeterminate, constituting obligations of comportment rather than of result. An example is found in framework conventions that establish broad guidelines which are difficult to evaluate. If the nature of the norm has an impact on compliance review, according to one view, the less precise the obligation, the more important the review.[50]

The process is dynamic and on-going, requiring periodic review of national laws to implement agreed goals that shift over time. The 2001 Protocol to the Convention on Long-Range Transboundary Air Pollution on Persistent Organic Pollutants expresses the need for constant updating of laws and policies. Annex V, paragraph 4 notes that "Experience with new plants incorporating low-emission techniques, as well as with retrofitting of existing plants, is constantly growing. The regular elaboration and amendment of the annex will therefore be necessary. Best available techniques (BAT) identified for new plants can usually be applied to existing plants provided there is an adequate transition period and they are adapted."

International environmental law places great emphasis on mechanisms and procedures that are non-coercive or non-contentious. The objective is to prevent any violation of an environmental norm and to assure respect and promotion of it. Control mechanisms are considered primarily as forums for observing the behavior of the parties and only secondly as a means of resolving conflicts through discussion and negotiation. They are considerably different from the judicial institutions and procedures that have developed in other fields of international law.

1. *Reporting Obligations*

International environmental agreements rely heavily on reporting by states parties in order to monitor implementation. The most accepted supervisory technique in international law generally, it obliges states parties to a treaty to address periodic reports to an organ established or designated by the treaty, indicating the implementing measures they have taken. It also applies within international organizations in regard to some non-binding instruments. The Commission on Sustainable Development created following UNCED examines the progress in implementing Agenda 21 largely through review of periodic state reports, along with information provided by non-governmental organizations.

Most environmental agreements expressly require parties to report certain information to the international organization designated by the agree-

---

[50]   J. Charpentier, *Le contrôle par les organisations internationales de l'exécution des obligations des Etats, in* 182 RCADI [1983-IV] 172.

ment. States parties are required to report, for example, on national measures to halt trade in endangered species (CITES, Art. VII),[51] to reduce greenhouse gas emission (Framework Convention on Climate Change, Art. 12) and levels of ozone-depleting substances (Montreal Protocol, Art. 7),[52] to conserve biological diversity (Convention on Biological Diversity, Art. 26), to control transboundary movements of hazardous wastes (Basel Convention)[53] and to halt marine dumping (1972 Convention on the Prevention of Marine Pollution by Dumping of Wastes and Other Matter).[54] Article 12 of the Climate Change Convention is indicative. It requires each state party to conduct a national inventory, in this case containing estimates of the party's greenhouse gas emissions and removals by sinks. The inventories are to be developed, periodically updated, published and made available to the Conference of the Parties. The 1997 Kyoto Protocol supplements this obligation in Article 8, setting out a system of implementation review based on expert review teams. It also sets up a means of establishing guidelines for the review.

As the 1992 Climate Change Convention illustrates, the text of the treaty sets forth the general reporting requirements. These are usually supplemented by guidelines drafted by the international body. The 1992 Convention on Biological Diversity states that "[e]ach Contracting Party shall, at intervals to be determined by the Conference of the Parties, present to the Conference of the Parties, reports on measures which it has taken for the implementation of the provisions of this Convention and their effectiveness in meeting the objectives of this Convention." Further standards or guidelines establish the periodicity of the reports, the contents of

---

51   CITES (Mar. 3, 1973) requires that each state keep records of all transactions involving protected species, including the types of permits authorized, and file annual reports with the Secretariat. Art. VII(6) and (7). With such reports the Secretariat and the parties can determine the volume of trade in a given species as well as monitor the quantity and type of permits granted.

52   The Montreal Protocol on the Ozone Layer (Sept. 16, 1987) contains precise reporting requirements relating to annual production and imports and exports of controlled substances. Art. 7 requires that parties notify the Secretariat of any allowed transfer of production between parties and of any addition to calculated production levels allowed by the Protocol. With this data the Secretariat and the parties may determine that other parties are meeting their consumption level under the defined baselines.

53   The Basel Convention (Mar. 22, 1989) on hazardous wastes requires parties to report annually information relating to the amount and types of wastes governed by the convention which are exported and imported. Information is required on disposal operations and efforts to reduce the amount of waste subject to transboundary movements.

54   The MARPOL Convention (Nov. 2, 1973) also requires the communication of information, including a statistical report, on an IMO-prepared standardized form, of penalties imposed for infringement of the Convention Art. 11.

the reports, and the procedures to be followed in submitting and reviewing the reports. The information to be submitted may include the texts of relevant laws or regulations, statistical data on matters covered by the agreement (*e.g.*, production, imports and exports, consumption, numbers of permits issued), decisions taken by national authorities, scientific reports, and enforcement actions.

A major issue in designing reporting systems concerns the methods for critically examining the contents of state reports and the question of follow-up. Experience indicates that the role of non-governmental organizations is often crucial to the effectiveness of the procedure. NGOs may comment on or supplement information given by states about compliance with international obligations. Agenda 21, chapter 39 suggests a formal role for NGOs in committees of control, given their expertise and concrete knowledge. Recent conventions institute scientific and technical committees independent of the parties and such committees also may have a role in the review of compliance reports.[55] The UNESCO World Heritage Convention (Nov. 23, 1972) and the Ramsar Convention (Feb. 2, 1971) allow verification of the information furnished by the state reports.

Regional agreements also require reporting. Article 29 of the revised African Convention on the Conservation of Nature and Natural Resources[56] is particularly complete. It specifies as follows:

> 1. The Parties shall present, through the Secretariat, to the Conference of the Parties reports on the measures adopted by them in the implementation of this Convention and the results thereof in applying its provisions in such form and at such intervals as the Conference of the Parties may determine. This presentation shall be accompanied by the comments of the Secretariat, in particular regarding failure to report, adequacy of the report and of the measures described therein.
>
> 2. The Parties shall supply the Secretariat with:
> a)   the texts of laws, decrees, regulations and instructions in force which are intended to ensure the implementation of this Convention;
> b)   any other information that may be necessary to provide complete documentation on matters dealt with by this Convention;
> c)   the names of the agencies or coordinating institutions empowered to be focal points in matters under this Convention; and

---

[55]   *See, e.g.*, Madrid Protocol on Antarctica (Oct. 4, 1991); Convention on Biological Diversity (June 5, 1992); Framework Convention on Climate Change (May 9, 1992).

[56]   Maputo, July 21, 2003.

d) information on bilateral or multilateral agreements relating to
     the environment and natural resources to which they are parties.

A United Nations study setting forth the objectives of international
reporting procedures,[57] although undertaken in the context of human
rights reporting, conveys that the procedure should ensure that states parties undertake a comprehensive initial review of national legislation, administrative rules, and procedures and practices either before or soon after
ratification and regularly monitor the actual situation with respect to each
of the obligations, to become aware of the extent to which the various duties
are, or are not, being fulfilled. The reporting procedure itself should provide a basis for the elaboration of clearly stated and carefully targeted policies, including the establishment of priorities that reflect the provisions of
the treaty in question. It also should facilitate public scrutiny of relevant
government policies, encouraging the involvement of various sectors of society in the formulation, implementation, and review of national policies. On
the international level, the procedure should provide a basis for the state
party as well as the supervisory body effectively to evaluate the progress
made in the realization of the obligations contained in the treaty, giving the
state party a better understanding of the problems and shortcomings
encountered in its efforts to comply. Among the states parties, the procedure can facilitate the exchange of information and develop a better understanding of the common problems faced.

One may be skeptical of the effectiveness of reporting systems, expect-
ing that states will be less than forthcoming about problems and defects.
Even the fact of having to write a report is useful, however, and exercises an
influence on state behavior. Often state reports are discussed in the supervisory organs where independent experts or representatives of other states
can address questions to or request information from the state authoring
the report.[58] The strength of the system is both psychological and political.
States may not always protect the environment as they should, but they seek
to maintain a good reputation in this field where public opinion is particularly sensitive. Thus, they make efforts to avoid or mitigate damage that
could result in condemnation or criticism during review of their reports.

---

[57]   *Report of the 3d Session of the UN Committee on Economic, Social and Cultural
Rights*, E/1989/22, Annex III.

[58]   For example, under CITES (Mar. 3, 1973), the Secretariat is empowered
to study reports of the parties and request any information it deems necessary to
ensure the implementation of the convention and to focus the attention of the
parties on any pertinent matter. Art. XII, 2(d) and (e). In addition the Secretariat
may notify a party directly if it believes that the Convention is not being effectively
implemented and the party is obliged to respond. Art. X.

In addition to assisting in determining treaty compliance, reporting requirements serve to provide information on whether the objectives of the agreement are being met or whether new policies need be developed or amendments proposed. Effective reporting systems depend, however, upon the willingness and capacity of parties to gather and report data accurately and objectively, and on the existence of well-resourced secretariats that can process the information into accessible formats in order to track the implementation process.

The proliferation of reporting obligations raises a problem of capacity and overburdening of states parties. Many states have fallen behind in reporting, making supervision of implementation difficult. The 1992 Biodiversity Convention and the Convention on Climate Change attempt to respond to this problem by making financial resources available to developing countries to meet the incremental costs of fulfilling their reporting obligations. Consolidation of reporting obligations also could ease the burden, allowing states to file a single report with core environmental data, to which specific information relevant to the particular instrument could be added.

2. Verification and Non-Compliance Procedures

International environmental agreements and international organizations have established a variety of innovative compliance verification procedures to supplement or substitute for reporting procedures. Some regional organizations are undertaking full compliance review. OECD, for example, has engaged in independent review of the environmental performance of each of its 29 member states. It publishes a country report, together with recommendations for improvement. Treaties that link the environment with other issues or provide financial benefits, *e.g.*, NAFTA (1993) and the UNESCO World Heritage Convention (November 23, 1972), can stimulate compliance by the threat of withdrawing benefits.

The implementation of the Ramsar Convention on Wetlands of International Importance especially as Waterfowl Habitat (February 2, 1971) is enhanced by a Monitoring Procedure created to address specific problems that may arise in maintaining the ecological character of a designated wetland of international importance. The Monitoring Procedure may take the form of a mission to the contracting party concerned, with the consent of that state. The mission generally is composed of one secretariat representative and two international experts with expertise appropriate to the technical circumstances. The mission undertakes field visits and holds office-based discussions with local experts and government representatives. A detailed report, with recommendations for action, then is compiled and submitted to the government concerned.

A different method is established in the Bern Convention on the Conservation of European Wildlife and Natural Habitats (September 19, 1979). To improve compliance, a special supervisory procedure has been set up using "case files." The procedure may be initiated by a complaint of non-compliance from a state party, an NGO, or an individual. The Secretariat of the Convention refers the complaint to the relevant party for details and clarification. The latter should answer within a reasonable period of time. After the response, the Secretariat decides whether the case should be placed on the agenda of the Standing Committee, which by consensus after discussions can open a case file and make recommendations. If any doubt or difficulties arise regarding implementation measures, on-the-spot appraisals by an independent expert also are possible with the consent of the concerned parties.

A common method of supervision is through the delegation of specific monitoring powers to the states parties. Coastal states, for example, may exercise prescriptive and enforcement jurisdiction over vessel-source pollution that affects their internal waters and territorial seas. Port state jurisdiction is perhaps even more common. Under MARPOL, port and coastal states have a responsibility to detect violations and the right to inspect vessels in their ports and offshore terminals. If a ship reveals significant violations then the ship may be held in port until the repairs are made. UNCLOS Article 218 provides that when a ship voluntarily enters a port or offshore installation, the coastal state can investigate and, where the evidence warrants, institute proceedings regarding any discharge from that vessel outside the internal waters, territorial sea or exclusive economic zone of that state in violation of applicable international rules and standards established through the competent international organization or general diplomatic conference. UNCLOS Article 220(6) also provides authority for a coastal state to detain foreign ships and institute legal proceedings for violation of international rules concerning the prevention, reduction or control of pollution from vessels if that violation causes "major damage or threat of major damage to the coastline or related interests of the coastal state" or to any resources of its territorial sea or exclusive economic zone.

Some treaties, particularly those involving resource use in the commons areas, specify monitoring by designated observers. The Antarctic Treaty system has used this method of supervising compliance with obligations since it began. Supplementing the original mandate, the Canberra Convention on Conservation of Antarctic Marine Living Resources (CCAMLR, May 20, 1980) includes procedures relating to on-site visits to and inspections of ships operating in the applicable zone. The inspections are undertaken by observers and inspectors designated by members of an international

Commission established by the Convention.[59] The August 4, 1995, Agreement for the Implementation of the Provisions of the UN Convention to the Conservation and Management of Straddling Fish Stocks and Highly Migratory Fish Stocks delegates to parties in regional fishing agreements the power to monitor the activities of other parties fishing in the region. Any member state may board and inspect fishing vessels flying the flag of another state. Inspectors may inspect the vessel itself and its license, gear, equipment, records, facilities, fish and fish products, and any relevant documents needed to verify compliance. Similar provisions are found in the Convention on Antarctic Marine Living Resources and the February 11, 1992, Convention for the Conservation of Anadromous Stocks in the North Pacific Ocean. Physical inspection may unnecessary to monitor compliance with many of these obligations. Remote sensing from satellites can monitor national emissions of specific pollutants, the loss of forest resources and the activities of fishing vessels.

Verification is a central part of the Chemical Weapons Convention (January 13, 1993). Even states parties with no chemical weapons to destroy must comply with the verification measures. The CWC creates the Organization for the Prohibition of Chemical Weapons (OPCW) an independent international body to monitor CWC states parties and ensure that their activities comply with the CWC. The Technical Secretariat, consisting of a Director-General appointed for a four-year term as well as inspectors and other personnel, carries out the CWC verification measures which include on-site inspections.

Many non-compliance procedures instituted by international environmental agreements aim to provide assistance to the defaulting state. In the Montreal Protocol to the Ozone Convention, for example, a party that cannot meet its obligations may report its compliance problems to the Implementation Committee.[60] In addition, any party or parties that has concerns about another party's implementation of its obligations under the Protocol may communicate the concerns in writing, supported by corroborating information, to the secretariat.

The Implementation Committee can request further information or, upon the invitation of the party concerned, can gather information on site. At the end of the procedure, the Committee reports to the Meeting of the Parties. Any recommendation it considers appropriate can be included in the report, which is made available to the parties six weeks before the meeting. The Meeting of the Parties may decide upon steps to bring about full compliance with the Protocol. Any state involved in a matter under consideration by the Implementation Committee cannot take part in the

---

[59]   May 20, 1980.

[60]   Ozone Convention, Mar. 22, 1985; Montreal Protocol, Sept. 16, 1987. The Implementation Committee consists of ten parties elected by the Meeting of the Parties for two years, based on equitable geographical distribution.

elaboration and adoption of recommendations concerning it. The parties subject to the procedure must subsequently inform the Meeting of the Parties of the measures they have taken in response to the report.

Annex V of Decision IV/18 contains an indicative list of measures that might be taken by the Meeting of the Parties in respect of non-compliance with the Protocol. The first consists in providing assistance, for, *e.g.*, the collection and reporting of data, technology transfer, financing, information transfer and training. At the second level "cautions" or warnings are issued. The third level involves the suspension of specific rights and privileges under the Protocol. Such rights and privileges can concern industrial rationalization, production, consumption, trade, transfer of technology, financial mechanisms and industrial arrangements.

In May 1995, the Russian Federation, Belarus, Bulgaria, Poland and Ukraine, in a joint statement, expressed concern about their capability to be in full compliance with the obligations under the Protocol in 1996, due to the severe situation of their economies. The Implementation Committee took this statement as a submission under the non-compliance procedure of the Protocol. After consultations a draft decision was submitted to the Meeting of the Parties.[61] The report noted that the Russian Federation was in compliance with its obligations under the Montreal Protocol in 1995 but would likely not be in non-compliance in 1996. The draft decision recommended that international assistance should be considered in consultation with the relevant Montreal Protocol Secretariats and the Implementation Committee. It said that the Russian Federation should submit annual reports on progress in phasing out ozone depleting substances in line with the schedule included in its submission to the parties. Disbursement of the international assistance should be contingent on the settlement of problems related to the reporting requirements and the action of the Russian Federation.[62] It is worth noting that the decision concerning the Russian Federation was adopted without its consent and may indicate the limits of the non-compliance procedure.

The Kyoto Protocol compliance regime was developed pursuant to Article 18 of the Climate Change Convention (May 9, 1992) by the Conference of the Parties (COP) serving as the meeting of the parties (MOP) to the Protocol. A Joint Working Group elaborated a draft regime on compliance which COP-7 approved in 2001 as part of the Marakesh Accords. The objective of the regime is to "facilitate, promote and enforce compliance with the commitments under the Protocol."[63] The Marrakech Accords contain an innovative, unprecedented compliance mechanism. It foresees

---

[61]   26 E.P.L. 68 (1996).

[62]   Draft Decision VII/16. *See* 26 E.P.L. 120 (1996).

[63]   Art. 1, Annex on Procedures and Mechanisms relating to Compliance under the Kyoto Protocol, COP 7 of the Climate Change Convention, Document FCCC/CP/2001/L.21.

a Compliance Committee with two branches, a facilitative branch and an enforcement branch. The facilitative branch supports efforts by parties to comply. The enforcement branch is to monitor compliance with the most important obligations. The enforcement branch has several tools available to bring about compliance: a party may be prohibited from selling under the emissions trading regime and for every ton of emissions by which a party exceeds its target, 1.3 tons will be deducted from its assigned among for the subsequent commitment period. The party will be required to submit a compliance action plan for review by the committee. An appeals procedure provides for a review of decisions by the UNFCCC Conference of the Parties serving as the Protocol's Meeting of the Parties. During the procedure, the decisions by the Compliance Committee remain in force. Overturning the decision requires a three-fourth's majority of the COP/MOP. Both branches of the Committee are composed of ten members, one each from the five regions, one small island developing state and two from Annex I and two from non-Annex 1 countries. A double majority vote is required for decisions: three-fourths of all members including a simple majority of Annex I and non-Annex I countries.

While the compliance procedure was not adopted as an amendment to the Kyoto Protocol and thus is not legally binding as part of the treaty, it has the advantage of being applicable to all parties to the protocol upon adoption.

The UNFCCC parties also agreed to establish three new funds to promote compliance by developing countries, two under the UNFCCC and one under the Kyoto Protocol. Decision 7/CP.7 creates "a special climate change fund" complementary to GEF funding to provide finances for the adaptation to technology transfer, and the mitigation of greenhouse gases. In addition to, countries that are heavily dependent on the export of fossil fuels shall be encouraged and assisted in diversifying their economies. The second fund is reserved for the least developed countries to assist financially in the preparation of national programs. Third, an adaptation fund under the Kyoto Protocol is financed by voluntary contributions and by a share of 2 percent of proceeds from certified emissions reductions generated by the clean development mechanism under Article 12 of the Kyoto Protocol.[64] It marks the first time that a levy is foreseen on business transactions to finance environmental and developmental activities.

On a regional level, NAFTA's Environmental Side Agreement, the North American Agreement on Environmental Cooperation (NAAEC, September 13, 1993)) created a trilateral commission to investigate and report on allegations of a consistent pattern of lack of enforcement of environmental laws and agreements. NAAEC is designed to complement the existing environmental provisions of NAFTA. It creates a mechanism that allow individuals and non-governmental organizations to make submissions

---

[64]	*See* Decisions 10/CP.7 and 17/CP.7.

alleging that a state party is failing to effectively enforce its environmental law (Article 14 Submissions on Enforcement Matters). The procedure is not designed to provide a remedy for individual environmental harm; instead, its purpose is to enlist the public to help ensure that the parties abide by their obligation to enforce their respective environmental laws. Anyone residing or established in North America can bring a submission. The identity of the submitter must be established, although privacy and confidentiality can be protected, and the party must have been given prior notice of the matters alleged in the submission. Sufficient facts must be alleged to allow the Secretariat to review the submission.

The Secretariat determines if the submission merits making a request for a response from a party based on criteria in Article 14(2). The secretariat should decide whether:

(a) the submission alleges harm to the person or organization making the submission;

(b) the submission, alone or in combination with other submissions, raises matters whose further study in this process would advance the goals of the NAAEC;

(c) private remedies available under the law of the party concerned have been pursued; and

(d) the submission is drawn exclusively from mass media reports.

A complaint must aim at promoting enforcement rather than at harassing industry.[65] According to Article 14, the Secretariat will solicit a response from a party if the complaint raises matters whose further study in the process would advance the goals of the Agreement. The party must provide a response, which may consist of responding to the complaint, referring the matter to relevant judicial proceedings, or advising that private remedies are available. The Secretariat may dismiss the submission on the basis of the response or may recommend to the Council the creation of a Factual Record of the submission and the response. The Council must approve the recommendation by a two-thirds vote, after which the Secretariat is authorized to create the Factual Record (Art. 15(2)). In preparing the Factual Record, the Secretariat is mandated to consider information furnished by a party and any relevant technical, scientific or other information that is (a) publicly available; (b) submitted by interested non-governmental organizations or persons; (c) submitted by the Joint Public Advisory Committee; or (d) developed by the Secretariat or by independent experts. No judgment issues nor are remedies directly afforded.

Since NAAEC came into force on January 1, 1994, the Secretariat has received 40 submissions from NGOs and private persons and prepared five Factual Records, three involving Mexico, and one each for Canada and the

---

[65]   NAAEC, Art. 14(1)(d).

United States. The first of the Factual Records prepared on Mexico is typical. It was based on a submission filed by Mexican environmental groups alleging that the government had failed to enforce its environmental law by not requiring the preparation of an environmental impact assessment in connection with a port and related works on the island of Cozumel near the Paraiso coral reef. The submission was accompanied by extensive factual documentation. Among the points raised in response, Mexico challenged the jurisdiction of the CEC because the acts complained of occurred prior to NAAEC's entry into force and because the submitters had not alleged that they suffered any harm. The Secretariat adopted the notion of "continuing effects," well known in human rights jurisprudence, and decided that the submission was admissible in regard to lack of enforcement that continued after the January 1, 1994, date the treaty entered into force. The Secretariat took a broad view on the issue of standing, rejecting the argument that national tests for standing should be applied to the international procedure. While the Secretariat noted that the submitters "may not have alleged the particularized, individual harm required to acquire legal standing to bring suit in some civil proceedings" in domestic courts, it found that the matter should go forward given "the specially public nature of marine resources." It found that the submitters' concerns were within the "spirit and intent" of the NAAEC. Looking at the submission as a whole, the Secretariat affirmed that the object and purpose of the Agreement is the overriding consideration in deciding on whether or not to recommend the preparation of a Factual Record. The Council concurred and ordered the preparation of the Record.

The Council approved Guidelines for Submissions on Enforcement Matters under Articles 14 and 15 of NAAEC October 13, 1995, and revised them by Council Res. 99–06 on June 28, 1999, in order to improve transparency and fairness consistent with the Agreement. Council Res. 01–06 of June 29, 2001, further amended Section 10.2 of the Guidelines in order to provide a more speedy and open process. The provision now specifies that five days after the Secretariat notifies the Council of its opinion that a factual record is needed, both the notice and the Secretariat's reasoning will be placed in the public registry. If the Council decides not to authorize the preparation of a factual record, the reasons for that decision will be made public. The NAAEC registry contains summary information of all proceedings so that any interested non-governmental organization or person, as well as the JPAC, may follow the status of any given submission during the submission process envisaged under Articles 14 and 15 of the Agreement. The registry is accessible to the public. In addition the Secretariat maintains a file on each submission at its headquarters in Montreal that is available for public access, inspection and photocopying, subject to confidentiality requirements.[66]

---

[66]   Information on activities of the North American Commission on

The Canada-Chile Environmental Side Agreement, very similar to NAFTA's side agreement, led to the creation of the Canada-Chile Commission for Environmental Cooperation. The main objectives are to strengthen environmental cooperation and ensure effective enforcement of environmental laws and regulations. Like the NAFTA side agreement it allows citizens and non-governmental organizations to file submissions if one of the participating countries fails to effectively enforce its environmental legislation.

The Convention on the North East Atlantic (September 22, 1992) contains other types of non-compliance procedures. The Commission it establishes has the duty to review the condition of the marine area, the effectiveness of the measures being adopted and the need for any additional or different measures and to supervise the implementation of the Convention as a whole (Art. 10(2)). The contracting parties report to the Commission at regular intervals on the legal, regulatory, or other measures taken by them to implement the provisions of the Convention and decisions and recommendations of the Commission, as well as on their effectiveness. They also shall report on measures taken to prevent and punish conduct in contravention of those provisions (Art. 22). The Commission assesses the conformity of national measures with the obligations under the Convention. When appropriate, it decides upon and calls for steps to bring about full compliance including measures to assist a state to carry out its obligations (Art. 23). The impact of this procedure may be increased by the presence of observers at the meetings of the Commission. Any non-party state and any international governmental or non-governmental organization can be admitted as an observer by unanimous vote of the Commission. Such observers may present any information or reports relevant to the objectives of the Convention (Art. 11).[67]

Customary international law traditionally allowed the use of proportional countermeasures and some other forms of self-help in response to an illegal act by another state. Such a system does not work well in its classic form in the field of environmental law. A state cannot reasonably respond to another state's illegal environmental harm by similarly injuring its own environment. In this regard, environmental obligations are similar to humanitarian obligations which the Vienna Convention on the Law of Treaties excepts from the system of counter-measures.

Environmental Cooperation and on citizen submissions is *available at* <http://www.cec.org>.

[67] *See,* E. Hey, T. Ijlstra & A. Nollkaemper, *The 1992 Paris Convention for the Protection of the Marine Environment of the North-East Atlantic: A Critical Analysis,* 8 INT'L J. MARINE AND COASTAL L. 1–49. The text of the Convention is annexed, *id.* at 50–76.

A different and often unilateral approach to non-compliance links environmental protection and trade. It is a controversial approach to non-compliance, as is reflected in the Rio Declaration, Principle 12, which says that "unilateral actions to deal with environmental challenges outside the jurisdiction of the importing country should be avoided." Yet, trade sanctions are used by some states in an attempt to enforce international environmental norms. U.S. law bans the importation of shrimp products caught by methods that endanger turtles and took action to bar the importation of tuna caught by methods that excessively killed dolphins. The primary controversy is over measures that seek to protect resources located outside the jurisdiction of the country imposing the restriction. As discussed herein and in Chapter 17, World Trade Organization dispute settlement panels have condemned most unilateral trade sanctions when they concern the environment outside national jurisdiction. The issue of multilateral trade measures also must be considered.

3.   *World Bank Inspection Panels*

After criticism of its support for major environmentally damaging projects, such as the construction of a dam and reservoir in Java between 1985 and 1993 and the Sardar Sarovar dam in India, the World Bank began to play an increasing role in the field of the international protection of the environment. The World Bank established its Inspection Panel in 1993 because of growing concerns about the accountability of it and other international development agencies in supporting projects and programs. The Panel is an independent investigatory body receiving complaints issuing from those in the territory of a borrower whose rights or interests have been adversely affected by the Bank's failure to comply with its own policies and procedures in the design, appraisal and implementation of a Bank-financed project. The Panel may investigate complaints upon authorization by the Bank's Board of Executive Directors, and assess to what extent the Bank has complied with its standards. At the first stage, the Panel registers the request and asks Management to respond to the concerns expressed in it. The Panel then assesses whether or not the request for inspection meets the eligibility requirements, in particular, whether *prima facie* the Bank has engaged in a serious violation of its operational policies and procedures resulting or likely to result in material and adverse harm to those making the request and to which Management has failed to respond adequately. On the basis of this assessment, the Panel recommends to the Executive Directors whether or not to authorize an investigation. If authorized, the Panel investigates the merits and reaches findings. The process can result in a remedial action plan requiring management to take actions in response to Bank failures.

In its first five years, the Panel received 17 requests for inspection. Two were outside the mandate; of the 15 remaining, 13 concerned infrastructure, environmental and land reform projects, while two related to adjustment operations. The Panel recommended investigation in six cases but was only authorized to investigate two matters. In four other cases, a type of friendly settlement was reached to be verified by the Panel.

Two outside reviews have led to clarifications and changes in the operation of the Inspection Panel. The first review, done in 1996, focused on procedure. The Second Inspection Panel Review, completed in 1999, added to and revised the 1996 conclusions.[68] The results clarify that the initial (admissibility) stage of the procedure must focus on assertions of non-compliance and resulting potential or material harm; it is not a decision on the merits involving a true finding of harm. The issue of non-compliance is antecedent to the issue of harm and supports the notion of the Inspection Panel as a mechanism of accountability rather than a true remedial procedure. Other aspects of the conclusions similarly focus on the Panel's role to monitor the Bank's non-compliance with its own policies and procedures.

Other Banks have developed similar procedures with some minor differences. At the World Bank the panel consists of three members, while the Inspection Committee of the Asian Bank comprises six members of the board, including four regional members. The Inter-American Development Bank maintains a permanent roaster of ten investigators to exercise an independent investigation mechanism triggered by requests for investigation.

Requests for inspection of bank-financed projects generally can be made by communities, organizations or other groups residing in the borrowing country where the project is being implemented or is proposed to be implemented (Asian Bank, Inter-American Bank) or in another member country adjacent to that country if the group is affected by the project (Asian Bank). Requesters need not have independent legal status (Asian Bank). The World Bank's Panel can receive requests from groups of at least two persons.

The request must describe the project and explain how the rules, procedures and the agreed provisions of the bank have been violated (World Bank). It must present reasonable evidence that the rights or interests of the requesting party have been or are likely to be directly, materially and adversely affected by an action or omission of the Bank (World Bank, Asian Bank, Inter-American Bank). A request for inspection must assert that the Bank has failed, in formulating, processing or implementing a project, to follow its operational policies or procedures (World Bank, Asian Bank, Inter-American Bank) and the failure was brought to the attention of the Bank's management, which failed within a determined period to demonstrate that

---

[68] Conclusions of the Second Review of the World Bank Inspection Panel, 39 I.L.M. 243 (2000).

the Bank had followed, or was taking adequate steps to follow, its operational policies and procedures (Asian Bank).

The inspection process starts with a written complaint to the President of the Bank (World Bank, Asian Bank). In the mechanism of the Asian Bank the management responds to the complaint, but if the complaining party is unsatisfied with this response, it can make a written request to the Committee for an inspection of the project. The Committee will recommend to the Board whether an inspection is warranted. If the Board authorizes an inspection, it will select a panel of experts from the Roster to inspect the project and make a report to the Committee. The World Bank's procedure provides that the panel recommends within 21 days whether or not to proceed to an inspection. The procedure of the Inter-American Bank prescribes that the request for investigation is forwarded to the President who recommends to the Board whether or not to proceed to an investigation. If such investigation is recommended, the Board of Executive Directors names a three-person panel from the permanent roster. The investigation report of the Panel shall address all relevant facts and shall conclude with findings on the Bank's compliance with all its relevant operational policies and norms. On the basis of such investigations, the Board of Executive Directors shall determine what preventive or corrective action, if any, should be taken.

At the conclusion of the Asian Bank procedure, the Board takes a decision which can ask for changes in the scope or implementation of an approved project. Any remedial changes in project scope or implementation are processed in accordance with standard Bank procedures and the relevant legal documents. At the World Bank, the Panel adopts conclusions to be submitted to the Management, which addresses recommendations to the Board. The final decision is taken by the Bank Council. In all the procedures, the conclusions and decisions taken by the Banks generally are made available to the public.

C. State Responsibility and Liability

Environmental harm occurs through intentional or negligent acts and as the consequence of an accident. In order to sanction and remedy wrongful conduct, law must determine appropriate enforcement actions and remedies. Legal systems must also decide who should bear the loss when accidental harm occurs. In making such determinations, those drafting and enforcing norms have to address such questions as the degree or amount and kind of harm that may lead to legal action, who is entitled to instigate the action, before what forum or tribunal, and what appropriate orders, sanctions, or compensation may be foreseen. International action is generally inter-state, based on doctrines of state responsibility or liability. State responsibility requires a state that breaches an international obligation to repair harm caused to another state. This responsibility based on fault may be distinguished from imposition of liability for the deleterious effects of lawful acts, that is, without fault. In environmental law, the latter concept can be seen as an application of the polluter pays principle, requiring that the operator or actor who benefits from a lawful activity bear the risk of loss when harm is done to others.

The legal consequences of environmental harm encompass both state responsibility for breaches of international law and liability for harm resulting from an activity permitted under international law, that is, strict or absolute liability over activities attributable to the state. Responsibility is thus a question of duty while liability addresses the allocation of risk.[69] The terms are not always consistently used. UNCLOS distinguishes the two terms in Article 139, seemingly describing liability as the consequence of a failure of state responsibility:

> 1. States Parties shall have the responsibility to ensure that activities in the Area, whether carried out by States Parties, or state enterprises or natural or juridical persons which possess the nationality of States Parties or are effectively controlled by them or their nationals, shall be carried out in conformity with this Part . . .

> 2. Without prejudice to the rules of international law and Annex III, Art. 22, damage caused by the failure of a State Party or international organization to carry out its responsibilities under this Part shall entail liability; States Parties or international organizations acting together shall bear joint and several liability.

A similar distinction is made in the Convention on International Liability for Damage Caused by Space Objects.[70] In some bilateral treaties, reference is made to liability rather than to responsibility of the states parties.[71]

In contrast, the Institut de Droit International adopted a resolution on September 4, 1997, clearly distinguishing responsibility and liability under international law for environmental damage. It maintains state responsibility as the consequence of breach of an international law obligation, while liability is identified as the duty to re-establish the original position or to pay compensation on the basis of harm alone. It calls for the development

---

[69] L.F.E. Goldie, *Transfrontier Pollution—From Concepts of Liability to Administrative Conciliation*, 12 Syr. J. Int'l L. & Com. 185, 185–86. (1985).

[70] Arts. 1 and 12, Convention on International Liability for Damage Caused by Space Objects (Mar. 29, 1972).

[71] *See, e.g.*, Art. 63(1), Frontier Treaty between Germany and the Netherlands (Apr. 8, 1960).

of specific rules on responsibility and liability in order to ensure effective prevention of environmental harm and provide restoration and compensation if harm occurs. Strict responsibility should result from the definition of environmentally hazardous activities that demand such result, taking into account the nature of the risk involved and the financial implications of such definition. In general environmental law should assign primary liability to operators, without prejudice to the question of international responsibility should the state concerned fail to establish and implement civil liability mechanisms or adequate insurance schemes, compensation funds or other safeguards.

1. Overview

According to international law, its subjects are responsible for international law violations that can be attributed to them.[72] In 2001 the UN International Law Commission completed work on its articles on the law of state responsibility and presented its work to the General Assembly,[73] reaffirming that as a matter of customary international law, breach of an international obligation gives rise to an independent and automatic duty to cease the wrongful act and to make reparation.

Although traditional norms of state responsibility mainly concern the treatment of aliens and their property, the *Trail Smelter* arbitration recognized that principles of state responsibility are applicable in the field of transfrontier pollution, and consequently states may be held liable to private parties or other states for pollution that causes significant damage to persons or property.[74] The principle of state responsibility for environmental harm is contained in numerous international texts. Principle 21 of the Stockholm Declaration declares that states have the responsibility to ensure that activities under their jurisdiction or control do not cause damage to the environment of other states or to areas beyond national jurisdiction and refers to responsibility for transfrontier pollution in Principle 22. Principle 13 of the Rio Declaration calls on states to develop national law regarding liability and compensation for victims of pollution and other environmental damage, providing that "[s]tates shall also cooperate in an

---

[72]   *Chorzow Factory (Indemnity) Case* (1928) P.C.I.J. Ser. A No 17, at 29.

[73]   Draft Articles on Responsibility of States for Internationally Wrongful Acts, in Report of the International Law Commission on the Work of Its 53d Session, U.N. GAOR, 56th Sess., Supp. No. 10, at 45, U.N. Doc. A/56/10 (2001), approved by the General Assembly in G.A. Res. 56/83 (Dec. 12, 2001). For a history of the ILC's work and commentary on the articles, *see* JAMES CRAWFORD, THE ILC'S ARTICLES ON STATE RESPONSIBILITY (2002).

[74]   *See supra* Chapter 5 in the text beginning at note 22, for discussion of the *Trail Smelter* case.

expeditious and more determined manner to develop further international law regarding liability and compensation for adverse effects of environmental damage caused by activities within their jurisdiction or control to areas beyond their jurisdiction." Article 13 of the Helsinki Convention on the Transboundary Effects of Industrial Accidents of March 17, 1992, also contains only a vague call to the parties to "support appropriate international efforts to elaborate rules, criteria and procedures in the field of responsibility and liability." The 1979 Convention on Long-Range Transboundary Air Pollution utilizes a procedure virtually unknown in international law to go further and exclude the issue of responsibility from its coverage: a footnote to Article 8(f) on the exchange of information on the effects of long-range transboundary air pollution and the extent of damage which can be attributed to such pollution provides that "the present Convention does not contain a rule of State liability as to damage."

The principle of state responsibility is recognized more widely than it is detailed or applied. Article 63(1) of the Boundary Treaty between the Netherlands and the Federal Republic of Germany (April 8, 1960), proclaims that if one of the contracting parties violates its obligation concerning the protection of boundary waters against pollution, it will be responsible for damage subsequently caused to the other contracting party. Conventions concerning regional seas make the same proclamation and provide that more precise rules shall be elaborated, without, however, always making a distinction between damages to be awarded to states and damages for harm to individuals.[75] A positive example is found in Art. 13 of the 1978 Kuwait Regional Convention for Cooperation on the Protection of the Marine Environment from Pollution:

> The Contracting States undertake to cooperate in the formulation and adoption of appropriate rules and procedure for the determination of:
> a) civil liability and compensation for damage resulting from pollution of the marine environment, bearing in mind applicable international rules and procedures relating to those matters; and
> b) liability and compensation for damage resulting from violation of obligations under the present Convention and its protocols.

---

[75] *See* Art. 17, Convention on the Protection of the Baltic Sea Area (Mar. 22, 1974); Art. 12, Convention for the Protection of the Mediterranean Sea Against Pollution (Feb. 16, 1976); Art. 15, Convention for Cooperation in the Protection and Development of the Marine and Coastal Environment of the West and Central African Region (Mar. 23, 1981); Art 14, Convention for the Protection and Development of the Marine Environment of the Wider Caribbean Region (Mar. 23, 1983).

Invocation of the principle of responsibility in international texts and agreements since 1972 led the International Court of Justice to assert in the *Advisory Opinion on the Legality of the Use by a State of Nuclear Weapons in Armed Conflict and in the Gabçikovo Case* that it now forms part of the corpus of customary international law. It also is included in the Restatement (Third) of the Foreign Relations Law of the United States, where state responsibility for environmental harm is found to be "rooted in customary international law."[76]

2. *Implementation of State Responsibility*

Discussions of state responsibility and liability far outstrip the actual number of cases. One major handicap is time; the *Trail Smelter* case began with the first claims presented by pollution victims in 1926, claims taken up by the government a year later. Only in 1941 was the final arbitral award rendered, in spite of the readily identifiable and attributable international harm. In addition to time, there often are special problems of defining the author and the cause of the injury, especially in complex situations such as acid rain. Perhaps for this reason, most of the precedents are bilateral cases. In addition to the time and cost involved in any type of litigation, aggravated in an international case, there are disadvantages to an adversary system in which the environment is the victim but never a party.

In order to successfully impose an obligation to cease a harmful activity or repair harm caused, the legal basis or degree of fault on which the obligation is premised must be determined. In general, international responsibility is founded on fault imputable to the acting state. Fault should not be confused with intent; it is not necessary that a state intentionally or maliciously violate an international obligation. It is necessary, however, to show that an obligation was violated and that harm resulted from the violation. Fault exists if the actor fails to perform a duty or observe a standard. Generally, the applicable international rules and standards do not hold a

---

[76]   Introductory Note, Part VI: The Law of the Environment, Restatement (Third) Foreign Relations Law of the United States (1986). Section 601, Restatement (Third) of the Foreign Relations Law of the United States (1986). Section 601 maintains that a state is responsible for any significant injury resulting from a violation of its obligations (1) to conform to generally accepted international environmental rules; and (2) to conduct its activities so as not to cause significant injury to the environment of another state or of the commons. Section 602 adds that the responsible state must afford general interstate remedies to prevent, reduce, or terminate the activity threatening or causing the violation, and to pay reparation for injury caused. Where private individuals are injured, the state of origin is obligated to accord to the person injured or exposed to significant risk of injury access to the same judicial or administrative remedies as are available in similar circumstances to persons within the state.

state responsible when it has taken necessary and practicable measures, *i.e.,* exercised due diligence.

a. Causation

The link of causality between a culpable act and the damage suffered must be established and the damage must not be too remote or too speculative. Pollution poses specific problems for several reasons. First, the distance separating the source from the place of damage may be dozens or even hundreds of miles, creating doubts about the causal link even where polluting activities can be identified. Second, the noxious effects of a pollutant may not be felt until years or decades after the act. Increase in the rate of cancers as a consequence of radioactive fallout, for example, can be substantially removed in time from the polluting incident. This problem was highlighted by the 1986 Chernobyl accident, which immediately caused 29 deaths, but which directly or indirectly may have produced thousands of cases of cancer over the long term. Intervening factors may play a role as well.

Third, some types of damage occur only if the pollution continues over time. This is true of the deterioration of buildings and monuments, for example, or, in certain circumstances, vegetation. Proof of causation also is made difficult by the fact that some substances cause little harm in isolation but are toxic in combination. Imputing responsibility to one source rather than another is difficult.

Finally, the same pollutant does not always produce the same effects due to the important role played by physical circumstances. Thus, dumping polluting substances in a river will not cause the same damage during times of drought as it will during periods where water levels are high. Similarly, wind or the lack of it, fog or sunlight can modify the impact of air pollution or even the nature of pollution. For example, urban smog, a harmful combination of persistent fog and pollutants, is exacerbated by atmospheric inversions (layers of warm, still air held below a cold air mass) that block elimination of the air pollutants. The latter derive from several sources, including industry, domestic heating, and motor vehicles. In such a situation it appears impossible to impute injury to a single precise cause in order to impose responsibility. Long-distance pollution, especially long-range air pollution, poses unique problems in identifying the author of the harm and precludes relying on state responsibility in the traditional sense of the term.

b. Attributing the Pollution

Even at a short distance, proving the identity of the polluter can pose problems. For example, gas emissions from motor vehicles are harmful, including the fumes of each individual automobile. Yet it is difficult to apply rules of responsibility and demand reparations from each driver because the numbers are too great and the effects produced by each unit are relatively limited. Nonetheless the cumulative effects are significant due to the part played by nitrous oxide (NO_2) and burned hydrocarbons (HC) in the formation of ozone at medium altitudes during sunny periods; they are factors in the depletion of forests.

The extent to which states are accountable for the actions of private parties under their jurisdiction or control is another issue of state responsibility. Many, if not most, of the activities causing environmental harm are those of private persons, in particular multinational corporations. Although the International Law Commission articles on state responsibility provide that in general states are not responsible for private activities,[77] this view does not appear to be accepted for environmental matters. The rule seems rather to be that the state whose territory serves to support the activities causing environmental damage elsewhere or under whose control it occurs is responsible for the resulting harm. This is the sense of the *Trail Smelter* decision and of Stockholm Principle 21/Rio Principle 2. Even under traditional principles, the necessary element of an act or omission by state agents is generally present, because the large majority of domestic activities capable of causing serious environmental harm outside the country now require prior approval or licensing under domestic legislation. Such approval normally will suffice to engage the responsibility of the competent territorial authority.

c. Reparations

The issue of reparations is also difficult. In the *Chorzow Factory* case, the Permanent Court of International Justice, finding the obligation to make reparations to be a principle of international law and even resulting from a general conception of law, indicated the scope and purpose of reparations:

> reparation must, in so far as possible, wipe out all the consequences of the illegal act and re-establish the situation which would, in all probability, have existed, if that act had not been committed. Restitution in kind, or, if that is not possible, payment of a sum corresponding to the value which a restitution in kind would bear, the award, if need be, of damages for loss sustained which would not be covered by restitution in kind or payment in place of it . . .[78]

---

[77]   Art. 11 of the 1980 draft rules provides that "the conduct of a person or a group of persons not acting on behalf of the State shall not be considered as an act of the State under international law." 2 Y.B. I.L.C. pt. 2, at 31 (1980).

[78]   *Chorzow Factory (Indemnity) Case* P.C.I.J. (Judgment of Sept. 13, 1928) Ser. A No 17, at 29.

Of course, damage suffered must be measurable in the absence of restitution in kind, application of which is more problematic in environmental matters than in other domains. In international practice, various conventions and drafts state that harm to the environment requires that the state of origin restore the environment to its *status quo ante* and that anyone who carries out the necessary work is entitled to reimbursement if the operation is reasonable. If it is impossible to fully restore the prior conditions, the parties must agree on compensation. However, while restitution in kind might involve restoring living resources to a polluted river or cleaning up a toxic site, often the damage may not be easily remediable, if at all. There is no restitution in kind for a species made extinct. In evaluating or measuring damages a great deal of uncertainty exists because the elements of the environment often are not viewed as having economic value when they remain outside the marketplace. For example, there may be wide divergence in valuing seabirds killed by an oil spill or the aesthetic value of a clean coastline. In other cases, damages may be estimated according to accepted case law from other fields, including such items as lowered property values due to pollution or lost business due to smoke or noise.

d. Procedural Issues

A final issue in state responsibility is to obtain diplomatic protection when an individual suffers harm due to activities taking place in another state. The victim of such pollution can seek local remedies to obtain satisfaction, and if this does not succeed, can subsequently request his or her national government to take up the case. If the complaint is taken, the complainant's government will present an international claim to the government on whose territory the activities have taken place. According to international law, diplomatic protection is exercised by states in order to ensure respect for international law vis-a-vis their nationals.[79] However, it is arguable whether the traditional conditions for the exercise of diplomatic protection must be fulfilled and whether the usual procedures must be followed in order to obtain reparation for damage caused by acts of transfrontier pollution.

The exercise of diplomatic protection generally requires the presence of two conditions: the claimant must have the nationality of the state taking up the claim[80] and local remedies must be exhausted. Recourse to any international procedure, from a simple protest through negotiations to submission of the case to an international tribunal, normally depends upon fulfillment of these prerequisites. It is not clear, however, that the victim of extraterritorial environmental injury must be a national of the state from

---

[79] *Mavrommatis Case*, P.C.I.J. (Judgment of Aug. 30, 1924), Ser. A, No. 2, p. 12.

[80] *See Nottebohm Case* (Liechtenstein v. Guatemala), 1955 I.C.J. Rep. at 4.

which he claims protection. Basically, although the quality of "victim" derives from the fact that the person or his goods have suffered measurable harm, on the international plane this quality is not dominant. According to the accepted formula of the International Court of Justice, states demand reparation by exercising diplomatic protection in order to obtain respect for international law towards their subjects.[81] In the typical case, the wrongful act is directed at the victim and occurs within the territory of the acting state. However, in cases of environmental injury, usually the acts of pollution attack the individuals incidentally or fortuitously outside the boundaries of the acting state. All who are situated on the territory or territories where the injury occurs, including human beings and their movable and immovable goods, whether private property or public domain of the state, are similarly situated. Moreover, even if no individual complains, even if there is no victim among the inhabitants of the territory of the state, the latter suffers damage because of acts of pollution originating in the other state. It is clear that the injured state has the right to assert the responsibility of the state under whose jurisdiction or control the polluter is found. The claimant state will proceed in order to protect its territorial sovereignty violated by the acts of pollution and not its personal competence exercised in favor of one of its subjects. Thus, an injured individual may be an alien in the state presenting the claim or even have the nationality of the accused state. In demanding reparations, the state enforces international law respecting its territory rather than in regard to its subjects.

With territory rather than nationality the usual basis for claims of state responsibility for environmental harm, diplomatic protection will maintain its traditional function only when the victims of polluting activities are found in places where the sole link between them and their state is personal: the high seas and air space above, Antarctica, outer space.

If these conclusions are valid, it is not necessary to examine whether the second condition for the exercise of diplomatic protection, that of exhaustion of domestic remedies, is fulfilled or not. Nonetheless, when a state exercises its right of diplomatic protection to intervene on behalf of victims of transfrontier pollution within its territory, the latter need not exhaust internal remedies offered by the polluting state. Without entering into detailed considerations concerning private international law, it is useful to look at the basis of the rule of exhaustion of domestic remedies. The requirement is justified largely because there exists a link between the individual claiming reparations and the state to whom the claim is addressed. This link may be tenuous or temporary: the individual visited the territory

---

[81]   ". . . by taking up a case on behalf of its nationals before an international tribunal, a State is asserting its own right—that is to say, its right to ensure in the person of its subject, respect for the rules of international law," *Serbian Loans*, P.C.I.J. Ser. A, Nos. 20/21, at 17.

of the state or concluded a contract with it or implicitly accepted its jurisdiction in a contract with another private persons. In all these cases, a voluntary act on the part of the claimant establishes willing contact with the legal system of the foreign state and submission to it, at least to some extent. In these conditions it is to be expected that the foreign state's legal system will provide a remedy for violations of the law of which the alien found itself victim. The rule of prior exhaustion of domestic remedies is thus justified on consensual individual links with the wrong-doing state.

A completely different situation is presented when an individual has suffered damages without manifesting any willingness to enter into contact with the foreign state or to submit to its legal system. The acting state is extending its reach into the territory of another sovereign to cause harm to those with whom it has no links. Persons remaining within the boundaries of their country are entitled to feel secure from outside intervention. Due to the burden the pollution would impose on the victim who has sought no benefit from the polluting state, nor availed himself of its jurisdiction, exhaustion of domestic remedies in the polluting state should not be required in order to claim damages for harm caused.

e. Harm to the Global Commons

The problem of harm to the global commons, including the environment itself, presents particular legal problems. First, harm to the environment *per se* is a developing legal concept and meets resistance in application, as demonstrated by the *Amoco Cadiz* damages award. The difficulties are exacerbated where it cannot be established with certainty that harm to the global commons would result in identifiable harm to human beings. Second, the threshold of harm impacting the global commons cannot easily be measured with sufficient precision to enable a liability regime to be established. Finally, attribution of the harm is extremely difficult because the effects are dispersed generally and there are multiple contributors.

In the case of transfrontier pollution, the injured state will be able to claim reparations for damages suffered by it. On the contrary, when the damage is caused to the environment of an area outside territorial jurisdiction, such as the high seas and deep sea-bed, international air space, outer space and Antarctica, no state may be able to present a claim on behalf of all humanity, which is the true victim of environmental damage. UNCLOS provides a solution for the deep sea-bed. Article 145 confers on the Authority the duty to assure protection of the ocean environment in regard to activities taking place in the Zone. This would seem to encompass the ability to present claims of state responsibility for violations of the treaty, the more so as Article 139 declares that a state party or an international organization is responsible for damages resulting from a breach of the obligations imposed on it by the Convention. It also may be claimed that norms protecting the global commons constitute obligations *erga omnes* that may be enforced by any state.[82]

Outside of conferred representation of the general interests of humanity, responsibility for damage caused to the *res communis* or common heritage of humanity can only be engaged in an indirect manner, in the case where there exist conventional rules protecting a given sector. Under general rules of international law, each contracting party to a treaty has the right to supervise application of the treaty by other contracting parties. Thus, a contracting party that discovers a violation by another treaty party can make a claim in this respect, whether or not the claimant state directly suffered damage. One example would be the dumping of wastes in the ocean in violation of conventional obligations. It is not clear, however, that a state intervening to uphold the treaty can demand damages when it has not suffered any direct injury but instead represents the common interest. Its intervention may be limited to a protest or declaration of non-compliance.

f.   Jurisprudence

In general, international practice has not shown enthusiasm for remedying environmental damage through use of traditional rules of state responsibility, but the law seems to be developing. Some examples may be found of inter-state claims presented even prior to the ecological era. Most of the claims arose from nuclear testing. First, following a 1954 United States nuclear test off the Marshall Islands, the Japanese fishing boat *Fukuryu Maru*, its crew and equipment were exposed to nuclear fallout, seriously injuring several people. The Japanese government demanded reparations of nearly $6 million. In the end, the U.S. government agreed to pay $2 million, without formally admitting its responsibility. It was a matter of a "sovereign act" leaving aside the question of state responsibility.[83] It should be noted, however, that the domestic legal authority under which the U.S. executive branch may settle foreign claims generally limits the settlement power to "meritorious" claims.[84]

---

[82]   *See Barcelona Traction, Light and Power Co. Case* (Belgium v. Spain), 1970 I.C.J. Rep. at 3, paras. 33–34. *See also* Restatement (Third) Foreign Relations Law of the United States, § 601.

[83]   J. BALLENEGGER, LA POLLUTION EN DROIT INTERNATIONAL 213.

[84]   10 U.S.C. § 2734 (1964); 22 U.S.C. § 2669(f) (Supp. 1989), 28 U.S.C. §§ 2672, 2674 (1964). *See* L. Malone, *The Chernobyl Accident: A Case Study in International Law Regulating State Responsibility for Transboundary Nuclear Pollution,* 12 COLO. J. ENVTL L. 203, 222 (1987).

Environmental damage measurement was a key issue in the later Marshall Islands Nuclear Claims Tribunal.[85] The People of Enewetak filed a class action on July 16, 1990, for damages to land resulting from the U.S. nuclear testing program conducted between 1946 and 1958. The territory is a low-lying coral atoll in the Marshall Islands, consisting of about 40 islands surrounding a lagoon of about 3,888 square miles. After the U.S. captured the area from the Japanese during World War II, the U.S. began conducting nuclear testing. The people of the atoll were relocated in December 1947, being told that it was for a period of three to five years. Instead they returned only in 1980 to find that the approximate acreage of the atoll had declined from 1919.40 to 815.33 useable acres. In the Compact of Free Association that concluded the United Nations Strategic Trust administered by the U.S., the U.S. government and the government of the Marshall Islands agreed to settle claims resulting from the nuclear testing program. A separate agreement required the establishment of a Claims Tribunal to make a final determination of all claims based on the nuclear testing program, applying the laws of the Marshall Islands, including traditional law, and international law, and in the absence of domestic or international law, the law of the United States. The agreement specified a goal of full compensation for loss or damage to person or property.

The damage award included amounts for loss of use for a specific period of years, using as a measure "the rental that probably could have been obtained" during the period. Appraisers agreed to by both sides offered a joint appraisal report that sought to measure the value of the loss by multiplying the relevant annual rental value times the affected acreage times the period of years use of the land was lost. The period of loss included past loss and future loss, from the date of valuation until return of the property in usable condition. The parties agreed that the latter period would be 30 years from the date of valuation or May 17, 2026. Adjustment was also made for the deferred nature of the compensation for past loss and a discount for future loss.

Annual rental value proved difficult because of the customary system of collective land tenure that does not include the concept of market value. Ownership of land by foreigners is forbidden by law. Instead, the relationship to the land is close to that of other traditional or indigenous peoples who "have always maintained a deep emotional attachment to their home islands and ancestral land."[86] In this society, every member of the community is born with a collective right to the lagoon and its resources and this right is passed from generation to generation. Land is regarded as sacred. Despite this context, the appraisers developed a database of comparable

---

[85] *In the Matter of the People of Enewetak*, NCT No. 23-0902, decided Apr. 13, 2000.

[86] *Id.* at 1216.

transactions, viewing the highest and best use of the islands as agricultural and residential. They found that rates did not vary according to size of parcel or location. The total amount for past lost use adjusted for prior compensation came to $140,000,000, while the value for lost future use was set at $50,154,811.

A key issue in the case was whether the damages should be set according to the difference in the value of land before and after the harm occurred, or at the cost of restoration. The Tribunal held that the cost of restoration, rather than the difference in value before and after the injury, is the appropriate measure of damage in the case. In part, the Tribunal returned to the lack of market value in finding it not an appropriate measure of damage. In addition, the Tribunal relied upon earlier cases where restoration was deemed appropriate if "there is a personal reason for the cost of repair." Relying on an expert, the Tribunal found that land is a part of the identity of the people in question and deeply embedded in a particular parcel of land on a particular atoll.

Land is valued because it is scarce, but also because it represents ancestral collective labor over generations.

The Tribunal gave attention to the question of what radiation standard should apply to restoration with reference to the position of the IAEA calling for non-discrimination: "As a basic principle, policies and criteria for radiation protection of populations outside national borders from releases of radioactive substances should be at least as stringent as those for the population within the country of release."[87] Using this standard, the Tribunal adopted the U.S. Environmental Protection Agency standard of 15 millirem per year effective dose equivalent as the maximum dose limit for humans. It then analyzed the soil and food intake of the area. The parties were in relatively close agreement on the results, but presented alternative approaches on how to meet the standard, ranging from removal of contaminated soil, application of potassium to the soil to reduce plant uptake, to phytoremediation (using plants to strip radioactive contaminants from the soil). The Tribunal rejected the last because its application to cleanup radioactive contaminants has not been demonstrated in the environment of a coral atoll and no basis exists for estimating the costs. While potassium works to limit cesium uptake, it does not work at higher concentrations. In the end, the Tribunal found soil removal, despite the attendant ecological disruption, a necessary component of the cleanup. Taking these two elements together, as well as the material costs of radiological surveys, contaminated soil disposal through causeway construction,[88] and soil rehabilitation and revegetation,

---

[87]   *Id.* at 1220.

[88]   The Tribunal considered other alternatives, including dumping in the Marianas Trench and shipping the soil to Nevada for storage. It chose the causeway alternative as one that would enhance the productivity of the community

the Tribunal came to a total restoration cost of $101,710,000, from which was deducted $10,000,000 as the amount in the Enjebi Trust Fund.

A final element in the damages claim concerned the hardship of relocation in especially bleak conditions, particularly from the early 1950s to the 1970s. Testimony reported famine, near starvation and death from illness, including polio and measles epidemics, food shortages and environmental limitations, including a rat infestation. The Tribunal took into account the maximum award for a claimant under its personal injury program, determined the appropriate annual amount for the period of greatest suffering ($4,500) and for the later period ($3,000), acknowledging both to be somewhat arbitrary and inadequate. Based upon the annual population figures for the 33 years between 1947 and 1980, the damages for the relocation hardships were deemed to total $34,084, 500. In all, the Tribunal determined the amount of compensation due the people of Enewetak to be $324,949,311.

Finally, through Security Council action, the United Nations created the United Nations Compensation Commission (UNCC) to provide reparations for environmental and other harm caused by Iraq's invasion of Kuwait in 1991. The Security Council made clear Iraq's state responsibility for the environmental harm. The work of the UNCC is discussed in Chapter 16.

Thus, despite the reluctance of states generally to demand or accept statements of responsibility, they clearly do pay compensation for damage caused, although they avoid or sometimes deliberately exclude admissions of responsibility, at least on the inter-state level. A much more common technique in international environmental law is for states to agree to transfer the problem of compensation to the private international law realm of civil actions. In other words, international state responsibility is replaced by direct compensation between polluter and victim. UNCLOS Article 235 characterizes this approach:

1.   States are responsible for the fulfillment of their international obligations concerning the protection and preservation of the marine environment. They shall be liable in accordance with international law.

2.   States shall ensure that recourse is available in accordance with their legal systems for prompt and adequate compensation or other relief in respect of damage caused by pollution of the marine environment by natural or juridical persons under their jurisdiction.

3.   With the objective of assuring prompt and adequate compensation in respect of all damage caused by pollution of the marine

---

and more fully protect the residents than other local disposal alternatives. Offsite dumping was rejected for legal and political reasons.

environment, States shall cooperate in the implementation of existing international law and the further development of international law relating to responsibility and liability for the assessment of and compensation for damage and the settlement of related disputes, as well as, where appropriate, development of criteria and procedures for payment of adequate compensation, such as compulsory insurance or compensation funds.

After affirming the principle of responsibility, this provision orients states towards civil liability in private international law, while encouraging them to find the means to assure compensation for victims.

3. *State Liability for Injurious Consequences of Lawful Acts*

The 1972 Convention on International Liability for Damage Caused by Space Objects is one of the few treaties to establish a clear rule of state liability without fault. Subject to exceptions set out in Arts. VI and VII, a state which launches a space object is "absolutely liable to pay compensation for damage caused by its space object on the surface of the earth or to aircraft in flight." Damage is defined as "loss of life, personal injury or other impairment of health; or loss of or damage to property of states or of persons, natural or judicial, or property of international intergovernmental organizations." The definition is broad enough to include claims for harm to the environment. Canada presented a claim under the Convention in 1979 to the former USSR for damage caused by the crash of Cosmos 954, a nuclear-powered satellite which disintegrated over Canada. Canada claimed that

> the principle of absolute liability applies to fields of activities having in common a high degree of risk. It is repeated in numerous international agreements and is one of the general principles of international law recognized by civilized nations. . . . Accordingly, this principle has been accepted as a general principle of international law."[89]

The claim exceeded $6 million, covering costs of restoring Canadian territory, to the extent possible, to the condition which would have existed if the intrusion had not occurred. The matter was settled in 1981 when the USSR agreed to pay $3 million in full and final compensation.

Since 1978 the International Law Commission has considered the topic of international liability for injurious consequences arising out of acts not

---

[89]   18 I.L.M. 907, para. 22.

prohibited by international law.[90] It originated in the discussions on state responsibility. In 1994–95, the Commission provisionally adopted several articles on first reading. In 1996 a new Working Group submitted draft articles containing a complete discussion on prevention and liability for compensation or other relief. In 1997, the ILC decided to divide the matter into two topics, prevention and liability, and to first concentrate on prevention. The Third Report of the Special Rapporteur, delivered in May 2000, contained revised draft articles on prevention. In 2001, the ILC adopted the revised draft articles on second reading and recommended that the entire topic could be drafted in the form of a Framework Convention. The ILC submitted the articles and recommendation to the General Assembly for consideration.

The ILC's articles on prevention describe prevention as an obligation of due diligence, conduct that is appropriate and proportional to the degree of risk of transboundary harm in any particular instance (Art. 3). The state must inform itself of factual and legal elements that relate in a foreseeable manner to the contemplated procedure and must take appropriate responsive measures in a timely fashion. While economic capacity may be taken into account in determining the level of diligence that is due, it cannot exempt a state from its obligations entirely. Activities within the territory of a state must be monitored and a necessary degree of vigilance and infrastructure must obtain. The operator of an activity is expected to bear the cost of prevention to the extent that he is responsible for the operation.

The obligations of the state of operation are set forth in Articles 6–11. First, the state must authorize any hazardous activity prior to its commencement. The authorization should be based on a prior assessment of the risk involved. If the consequences could involve significant transboundary harm, the state of origin is required to provide notification and information to states likely to be affected. Articles 9–13 provide for discussions between the state of origin and the states likely to be affected. The result could be conditions imposed on the activity or joint management of the risk and the project itself. Article 13 provides for an obligation to inform

---

90   *International Liability for Injurious Consequences Arising from Activities Not Prohibited by International Law, First Report on a Legal Regime for Allocation of Loss in Case of Transboundary Harm Arising out of Hazardous Activities,* by Mr. Pemmaraju Sreenivasa Rao, Special Rapporteur, A/CN.4/531, Mar. 21, 2003, Int'l L. Commn, 55th Sess 2003 [hereafter the *Rao Report*]. The first special rapporteur saw the issue as one of developing principles of prevention as part of due diligence, but also of providing for a regime of compensation based on equitable principles. *See Preliminary Report on Liability,* 2 Y.B. I.L.C. Part I (1980); U.N. Doc. A/CN.4/334 (1980); *Second Report on Liability,* Y.B. I.L.C. Part I (1981); U.N. Doc. A/CN.4/346; *Third Report on Liability,* Y.B. I.L.C. Part I (1982); U.N. Doc. A/CN.4/360.

the population likely to be exposed to the risk involved and to ascertain their views, without regard to boundaries. Article 15 requires protection or other appropriate redress to all persons in accordance with the judicial or other procedures and the legal system of the state of origin, without discrimination on the basis of nationality or residence or place of injury. Article 19 provides for compulsory fact-finding in case of a dispute between the states concerned, in the absence of another applicable mechanism of peaceful dispute settlement. For the most part, the articles are considered progressive development of international law rather than a codification of existing norms.

On the issue of liability, the approach approved by the ILC Working Group in 2002 proceeds on the basis that the issue is one of allocation of loss, not liability in the sense of state responsibility for wrongdoing. It thus separates the issue of compensation from the fields of torts and strict liability. To delimit the scope of the topic, the ILC has agreed to define transboundary damage as involving three criteria: (1) activities must take place in the territory or control or jurisdiction of the source state (thus leaving out the global commons); (2) they must have a risk of causing significant transboundary harm; (3) harm must be caused by the "physical consequences" of such activities or be determinable by clear direct physical effect and causal connection between the activity and the harm or injury suffered (leaves aside pollution not attributable to any one source or that emerges gradually). The requirement of significant harm was seen by the ILC as reflecting state practice; because the activities are lawful, they are not subject to the requirement in the law of state responsibility of cessation or restitution. "Significant" harm is seen as being more than detectable and appreciable, but less than serious or substantial. Such harm must be measurable by factual and objective standards.[91]

The ILC 1996 Working Group agreed on three broad policy considerations for liability: (a) each state must have as much freedom of choice within its territory as is compatible with the rights and interests of other states; (b) the protection of such rights and interests requires the adoption of measures of prevention and if injury nevertheless occurs, measures of reparations; and (c) the innocent victim should not be left to bear his or her loss or injury.[92] On the third point, the ILC recognizes that full and complete compensation may not be possible in every case because of lack of proof of loss, limits to the definition of damage or other limitations. The major objectives are to provide incentives to prevent harm through requiring the operator to bear the loss in case of harm resulting from hazardous activities, to compensate damage caused to a victim, and to internalize all the environmental costs. Treaties so far reflect the view that the direct

---

91   *Rao Report*, para. 31.
92   *Id.*, para. 43.

accountability of the polluter in national law is the best means of compensating for loss.

Finally it is necessary to mention the problem of abatement. One of the requirements arising from breach of a rule of international environmental law is that the activity causing environmental harm should cease. Lawful activities may continue, however, even if they cause harm, because their benefits outweigh the risks of harm.[93] In such a case, compensation still must be provided the victims of any substantial harm that occurs.[94] The risk-creating conduct is permitted, but the victim does not bear the burden of the injury which results. Instead, a social responsibility is imposed upon the actor to compensate the victims for harm which occurs even though the activity is legal.

D. International Dispute Settlement Procedures

Disputes over alleged breaches of international environmental norms may be settled through a variety of mechanisms, including mediation, arbitration, and judicial proceedings. Although recourse to formal procedures is not common, it appears to be increasing, perhaps reflecting a maturation of the normative framework.

1. Arbitration

While there are some early arbitrations involving environmental questions, most notably the *Trail Smelter* case, there are few modern arbitrations. In 1986 France and New Zealand asked the Secretary-General of the United Nations to act as an arbitrator in the *Rainbow Warrior Case*,[95] but the case concerned the French sinking of the Greenpeace vessel in Auckland Harbor

---

[93]   *See, e.g.*, Agreement Concerning Frontier Rivers between Finland and Sweden (Sept. 16, 1971); 825 U.N.T.S. 191, 282: "Where the construction would result in a substantial deterioration in the living conditions of the population or cause a permanent change in natural conditions such as might entail substantially diminished comfort for people living in the vicinity or a significant nature conservancy loss or where significant public interests would be otherwise prejudiced, the construction shall be permitted only if it is of particular importance for the economy or for the locality or from some other public standpoint." Chapter III, Art. 3(2).

[94]   *See* Art. 11, *Environmental Protection and Sustainable Development: Legal Principles and Recommendations* (1986).

[95]   *See Ruling Pertaining to the Differences between France and New Zealand Arising from the Rainbow Warrior Affair* (1986).

and the future of the two French intelligence agents who were serving prison sentences in New Zealand for carrying out the action. Underlying issues about the environmental consequences of French nuclear testing was not in issue.

In 2001, the Permanent Court of Arbitration (PCA) adopted by consensus Optional Rules for Arbitration of Disputes Relating to Natural Resources and/or the Environment.[96] The rules were adopted at an Extraordinary Meeting of the 94 member states of the PCA, based upon the UNCITRAL Arbitration Rules. The participants identified as a problem the absence of a unified forum where states, international organizations, nongovernmental organizations, businesses, and other private parties could seek resolution of disputes over environmental protection or conservation of natural resources. According to the PCA, over half the inquiries made in 2001–2 concerned these issues. The Rules are intended to govern disputes between all actors and to provide rapid expertise to resolve the dispute, because time may be of the essence. In order to provide both scientific and legal expertise, the Rules provide for the optional use of a panel of expert arbitrators with legal background (Art. 8) and a panel of environmental scientists who can provide technical assistance to the parties and the arbitral tribunal (Art. 27).

2. The International Court of Justice

Agenda 21, Chapter 39.10 encourages states to have recourse to the ICJ to resolve environmental disputes. The UN Charter gives the Court the power to decide cases that states submit to it, which could include environmental disputes.[97] Article 36(1) of the Statute of the Court confirms that the jurisdiction of the Court comprises, *inter alia*, all cases that the parties refer to it and all matters specially provided for in treaties and conventions in force. Several dozen multilateral environmental agreements contain provisions providing for the submission of disputes arising from their interpretation or application to the I.C.J.[98]

The Court has indicated its readiness to accept environmental cases. In a statement to UNCED, Sir Robert Jennings, then President of the Court, declared that "[t]he function of the established 'principal judicial organ of the United Nations' must include not only the settlement of disputes but also the scientific development of general international law." He noted that

---

[96]   June 19, 2001; 40 I.L.M. 202 (2001); *available at* <http://www.pca-cpa.org>.

[97]   Arts. 33(1) and 36(3).

[98]   For the list of 38 such agreements, *see* CESARE ROMANO, THE PEACEFUL SETTLEMENT OF INTERNATIONAL ENVIRONMENTAL DISPUTES, at 105 n. 78 (2000).

international environmental law constitutes a new field of law and "that new international law for the protection of the environment needs urgently to be developed cannot be a matter of doubt." Another expression of the Court's willingness to address the environmental aspects of international law was its decision to establish a seven-member chamber for environmental matters, whose first members were elected in July 1993.

While the environmental chamber has not been used to date, the International Court of Justice received five submissions in the past decade concerning environmental protection. The first three matters concerned the impact of nuclear weapons or weapons testing on the environment and are discussed in Chapter XIV. Two subsequent cases raised more general issues of environmental harm.

In the *Case of Certain Phosphate Lands in Nauru (Nauru v. Australia)*, Nauru filed its application in 1989 asserting Australian governmental liability for environmental damages permitted to occur while Australia governed the island of Nauru. The application requested that Australia be directed to pay compensation for the rehabilitation of lands which were severely degraded through phosphate mining prior to Nauru's independence in 1968, for the artificially low royalties paid by the mining consortium, and for "aggravated or moral damages." Nauru asserted that a general principle of international law obligates a state administering a territory to not bring about changes in the condition of the territory that will cause irreparable damage to, or substantially prejudice, the existing or contingent interest of another state in respect to that territory. In a judgment of June 26, 1992, the Court accepted jurisdiction over the case even though the environmental damages claimed in the case occurred over a period of 70 years prior to 1968. The case was subsequently settled by the parties, with the payment of substantial damages by Australia, and removed from the Court's docket.

The most significant environmental matter, the *Gabçikovo-Nagymaros Project Case*, is summarized in Chapter 10. In it and the previously-cited cases, the ICJ developed important environmental concepts and norms. In particular, the Court recognized the fundamental importance of environmental protection in the modern world. In both the Nuclear Weapons Advisory Opinion and in the Gabçikovo case the Court declared that the environment is not an abstraction but represents the living space, the quality of life and the very health of human beings. As a consequence, the Court found that states have the obligation to respect and protect the natural environment.[99] In this regard, the Court recognized the temporal dimension inherent in environmental protection:

---

[99]   ICJ, Legality of the Threat or Use of Nuclear Weapons in Armed Conflict, July 8, 1996, para. 63.

Throughout the ages, mankind has, for economic and other reasons, constantly interfered with nature. In the past, this was often
done without consideration of the effects upon the environment.
Owing to new scientific awareness and a growing awareness of the
risks for mankind—for present and future generations—of pursuit
of such interventions at an unconsidered and unabated pace, new
norms and standards have been developed, set forth in a great
number of instruments during the last two decades. Such new
norms have to be taken into consideration, and such new standards
given proper weight, not only when States contemplated new activities but also when continuing with activities in the past."[100]

This statement articulates the guiding principle that past and present
activities should be governed by evolving international legal norms.[101]
Among the norms and principles that the Court applied are the needs or
rights of future generations.[102] Judge Weeramantry reminds readers in his
separate opinion in the Gabçikovo case that the rights of future generations
have woven themselves into international law through major treaties,
through juridical opinions, and through general principles of law recognized by civilized nations.[103] The Court also makes it clear that the natural
environment constitutes an "essential interest" of each state.[104]

On these bases, the Court reiterated the basic international law rule
stemming from the Stockholm and Rio Declarations, announcing that the
existence of a general obligation of states to ensure that activities within
their jurisdiction and control respect the environment of other states or of
areas beyond national control is now part of the corpus of international law
relating to the environment.[105] Reinforcing this view, Judge Weeramantry
stresses that customary international law prohibits environmental damage[106]
and requires continuing environmental impact assessment,[107] and application of the precautionary principle.[108] The Court itself expresses its understanding that in the field of environmental protection, vigilance and
prevention are required on account of the often irreversible character of

---

[100]   *Gabçikovo Case*, para.140.

[101]   *See also* Vice-President Weeramantry's statement on the inter-temporal
aspect of all treaties dealing with projects impacting on the environment,
Separate Opinion, at 22.

[102]   *Gabçikovo Case*, para.29.

[103]   Sep. Op. at 17.

[104]   *Gabçikovo Case*, para.53.

[105]   *Id.*, para. 29.

[106]   Sep. Op. at 49–52.

[107]   *Id.*, at 20.

[108]   *Id.*, at 50–52.

damage to the environment and of the limitations inherent in reparation of this type of damage.[109]

States could more frequently avail themselves of the opportunities which they have created to submit environmental disputes to the International Court of Justice. It can be concluded that the Court has applied the terms of the declaration made by its President at the Conference of Rio de Janeiro, by contributing to the development of international environmental law, as often as it had has been given the possibility to do so.

3. The Law of the Sea Tribunal

UNCLOS proceeds from the basic principle that the states parties shall settle any dispute between them concerning its interpretation or application by peaceful means in accordance with the United Nations Charter and should proceed expeditiously to an exchange of views on the means of settlement to be adopted (Art. 283(1)). States may make a written declaration accepting to refer disputes to one or more of the following tribunals: the International Tribunal for the Law of the Sea, the International Court of Justice, an arbitral tribunal or a special arbitral tribunal, the last two constituted in accordance with the Convention. Where both parties have accepted the same procedure, that procedure is to be used, otherwise arbitration will be applied (Art. 287).

Special arbitration is one of the binding methods of dispute that can be accepted in advance by declaration and may be chosen whenever a technical issue arises for which specialist qualifications may be necessary. Annex VIII of UNCLOS establishes that this procedure may be used for fisheries, the marine environment, scientific research, vessel source pollution or dumping. Lists of experts in each of the four fields are to be maintained by the FAO, UNEP, the Inter-Governmental Oceanographic Commission and the International Maritime Organization. Each state may nominate two experts from the list "whose competence in the legal, scientific or technical aspects" is established and who enjoy the highest reputation for fairness and integrity (Annex VIII, Art. 3).

The International Tribunal for the Law of the Sea (ITLOS) is one of the judicial bodies designated by UNCLOS among the "compulsory procedures entailing binding decisions" in disputes over the interpretation or application of the Convention. The Tribunal, whose seat is in Hamburg, has 21 members elected for a nine-year term. They are "persons enjoying the highest reputation for fairness and integrity and of recognized competence in the field of the law of the sea" (Art. 2(1) of Annex VI). The Tribunal has jurisdiction where two states to a dispute have recognized its competence,

---

[109] *Gabčikovo Case*, para. 140.

when any agreement so provides, or when all the parties to any treaty in force concerning the law of the sea agree to refer. It is open to international organizations in certain circumstances (Art. 20(2)) and to states which are not parties to UNCLOS. A Sea-Bed Disputes Chamber of 11 members is established within the Tribunal. Its jurisdiction covers disputes between states, between a state and the Authority, between the Authority and a prospective contractor; and between parties to a contract, including state enterprises and natural or juridical persons.

The Law of the Sea Tribunal has broad jurisdiction. Article 288 provides for the reference of disputes concerning the interpretation or application of the Convention and any international agreement "related to the purposes" of the Convention, except that disputes involving coastal states' rights over marine research and fisheries shall be submitted to conciliation.[110] One important function of the Tribunal will be to settle disputes between states parties regarding the environmental protection provisions of UNCLOS. One of the disputes that may be submitted to the Tribunal is when "it is alleged that a coastal state has acted in contravention of specified international rules and standards for the protection or preservation of the marine environment which are applicable to the coastal state and which have been established by (or in accordance with) this Convention. . . ."

Article 289 allows the appointment of scientific or technical experts and the Tribunal may prescribe provisional measures upon request of a party to a dispute. It should be noted that Article 30(1) of the 1995 Straddling Stocks Agreement provides that the provisions of UNCLOS Part XV shall apply to all disputes concerning its interpretation or application, whether or not the states concerned are parties to UNCLOS. In addition, Article 30(2) extends its provisions to regional and other fisheries agreements. An admissibility provision allows the Tribunal to determine whether a *prima facie* case is set out or whether the case should be immediately dismissed as frivolous. Exhaustion of local remedies is a condition of admissibility for certain claims.

Several environmental claims have been submitted to ITLOS and most of them indicate the problem of overlapping jurisdictions between UNCLOS and regional marine or environmental agreements.

The *Southern Bluefin Tuna Case* between Australia and New Zealand against Japan, was brought before an Arbitral Tribunal constituted under Annex VII of UNCLOS.[111] Japan objected to the jurisdiction of ITLOS and the Arbitral Panel, but in an Order of August 27, 1999 ITLOS found that

---

[110] *See* A.O. Adede, *Settlement of Disputes arising under the Law of the Sea Convention*, 69 AJIL 798 (1975).

[111] ITLOS, *Australia and New Zealand v. Japan, (Award on Jurisdiction and Admissibility)*, Aug. 4, 2000.

the Arbitral Tribunal had *prima facie* jurisdiction and prescribed certain provisional measures.

Southern Bluefin Tuna (SBT) is a migratory species of pelagic fish listed in UNCLOS Annex I. The tuna range widely through the Southern Hemisphere primarily in the high seas but also in the waters of several states including New Zealand, South Africa, and Australia. They spawn in waters south of Indonesia. The main market is Japan where the fish is used for sashimi. By the early 1980s the fish stock was overexploited and the countries in the dispute agreed in 1982 to set a total annual catch, with national allocations. The stock continued to decline and in 1998 was estimated to be at only one-third of its 1960 level. The entry of other countries into the fishery exacerbated the problem. At the time of the dispute, there was disagreement over whether the stock had begun to recover, its current state, and how scientific uncertainty should be reduced or taken into account. In 1993, the three countries concluded the Convention for the Conservation of Southern Bluefin Tuna whose purpose was to ensure the conservation and optimum utilization of the species. Article 4 of the agreement nonetheless provided that "nothing in this Convention nor any measures adopted pursuant to it shall be deemed to prejudice the positions or views of any Party with respect to its rights and obligations under treaties and other international agreements to which it is party or its positions or views with respect to the law of the sea." The parties established a Commission in which each party had one vote. The Commission's functions included collecting information, considering regulatory matters, deciding upon a total allowable catch and an allocation of the catch among the parties, and deciding upon other measures. The parties agreed that the Commission decisions would be binding. A Scientific Committee was created to act as an advisory body to the Commission.

As early as 1994, Japan sought an increase in its part of the total allowable catch, but the other parties objected. Japan also sought to introduce an Experimental Fishing Program (EFP) whereby it would fish for SBT in areas where they were no longer fished, in order to study the status of the stock. By 1998 the Commission was unable to agree on any total allowable catch. That year, Japan announced it would adhere to its quota, but would begin a unilateral three-year EFP in the summer. It conducted a pilot program with an estimated catch of 1464 mt. Urgent consultations among the parties failed to resolve disagreements over the EFP and Japan continued its unilateral program. In 1999, Australia reaffirmed its position that the dispute involved obligations under UNCLOS as well as the 1993 agreement. Efforts to negotiate for mediation or arbitration failed and Australia announced it would submit the dispute under UNCLOS, seeking provisional measures to halt Japan's unilateral experimental fishing program.

In filing their claims under UNCLOS, Australia and New Zealand invoked UNCLOS Articles 64 and 116–119. They argued that Japan is obliged as a distant water state to cooperate with them, as coastal states, in the conservation of SBT. The 1993 Convention implements the obligations of UNCLOS, but does not override it. Japan argued that the 1993 Convention was the basis of the claim and hence the Arbitral Tribunal had no jurisdiction. ITLOS found that the provisions of UNCLOS appeared to provide a basis for jurisdiction and the existence of the 1993 Convention does not preclude recourse to UNCLOS dispute settlement procedures.

Subsequently, however, the Arbitral Tribunal found it clear that the most acute elements of the dispute between the parties turned on their inability to agree on a revised total allowable catch and the related conduct by Japan of unilateral experimental fishing in 1998 and 1999, as well as Japan's announced plans for such fishing thereafter. According to the Arbitral Tribunal, those elements of the dispute were clearly within the mandate of the Commission for the Conservation of Southern Bluefin Tuna. "It is plain that all the main elements of the dispute between the Parties had been addressed within the CCSBT and that the contentions of the parties in respect of that dispute related to the implementation of their obligations under the 1993 Convention."[112]

The Tribunal indeed found no dispute over that fact, only over whether UNCLOS also applies. The Tribunal accepted that *lex specialis* may govern general provisions of an antecedent treaty or statute, but also that more than one treaty may bear upon a particular dispute. Noting frequent parallelism, the Tribunal says that a single act may violate more than one treaty. In sum, the Tribunal found that while centered in the 1993 Convention, the dispute also arises under UNCLOS. In the end, however, UNCLOS itself returned the matter to the regional body because UNCLOS defers to other dispute settlement procedures agreed upon between parties to a dispute. Article 16 of the 1993 Convention contains such a procedure and thus removes the dispute from the reach of the UNCLOS compulsory procedures unless all parties agree. The Tribunal noted the conclusion of many treaties post-UNCLOS that exclude unilateral reference of a dispute to compulsory adjudicative or arbitral procedures. "The Tribunal is of the view that the existence of such a body of treaty practices . . . tends to confirm the conclusion that states parties to UNCLOS may, by agreement, preclude subjection of their disputes to section 2 procedures in accordance with article 281(1)."[113] Notably, the Tribunal does not exclude the possibility that there might be instances in which the conduct of a State Party to UNCLOS and to a fisheries treaty implementing it would be so egregious, and risk consequences of such gravity, that a Tribunal might find that the obligations of UNCLOS provide a basis for jurisdiction, having particular regard to the provisions of Article 300 of UNCLOS, but this was held not to be that case.

---

[112] Arbitral Tribunal, para. 31.

[113] *Id.*, para. 64.

The second environmental dispute before ITLOS resulted from UK authorization of a new facility in Sellafield to reprocess spent nuclear fuel into a new fuel, *i.e.*, mixed oxide fuel (MOX) combining reprocessed plutonium and uranium. The Irish government protested that the plant would contribute to pollution of the Irish Sea and emphasized the potential risks involved in transporting radioactive material to and from the plant. On October 5, 2001, the government of Ireland requested the UK government to agree to submit the dispute to an arbitral tribunal established under Annex VIII of UNCLOS. Ireland in turn asked the Tribunal to declare that the UK breached its obligations under Articles 192–3 and/or Article 194 and/or Article 207 and/or Articles 211 and 213 UNCLOS in relation to the MOX plant, including by failing to take the necessary measures to prevent, reduce and control pollution of the marine environment from intended or accidental discharges of radioactive materials and or wastes from the plant and/or international movements of materials and wastes associated with the MOX plant, and/or discharges resulting from a terrorist act. Part of the allegations concerned the failure to undertake risk assessment and prepare a response strategy. With regard to the marine environment, Ireland asserted that the UK failed to undertake a proper environmental impact assessment or share information, but instead proceeded with authorization while the dispute on access to information was pending. Under UNCLOS Article 206, Ireland asserted that the UK 1993 Environmental Statement failed to properly assess the effects of the operation of the MOX plant on the marine environment of the Irish Sea and the UK failed to take into consideration subsequent factual and legal developments.

On November 9, 2001, Ireland requested provisional measures from ITLOS pending constitution of the arbitral body. The ITLOS delivered its Order respecting provisional measures in the *MOX Plant Case (Ireland v. United Kingdom)* on December 3, 2001.[114] The jurisdiction of ITLOS allows it to prescribe provisional measures if it considers them appropriate to "preserve the respective rights of the parties to the dispute or to prevent serious harm to the marine environment." It should also find that the arbitral tribunal being constituted has *prima facie* jurisdiction and that the situation urgently requires the measures requested. ITLOS found that the dispute concerns the interpretation and application of UNCLOS, rejecting the British argument that the main elements of the dispute are governed by regional treaties. The Tribunal found, however, that the urgency of the situation did not require that provisional measures be issued prior to constitution of the arbitral tribunal. "It is the responsibility of the UK if it wants to commission the plant and later run the risk of it being closed down." The Tribunal did consider that the duty to cooperate is a fundamental principle in

---

[114] 41 I.L.M. 405 (2002).

the prevention of pollution of the marine environment under Part XII of the Convention and general international law and that rights arise therefrom which the Tribunal my find appropriate to preserve under article 290 of the Convention. The Tribunal indicated that prudence and caution require Ireland and the UK to cooperate in exchanging information concerning risks or effects of the MOX plant's operations. The Tribunal thus unanimously issued provisional measures mandating cooperation between the two parties to exchange further information about the environmental consequences of the MOX plant, to monitor risks, and to devise measures to prevent pollution of the marine environment. All other requests for measures were denied.[115]

Once the Arbitral Tribunal was constituted, it had to consider whether it had jurisdiction not only *prima facie* but also in a definitive sense. The United Kingdom raised two categories of objections to jurisdiction and admissibility. The first category concerned the Convention itself and other instruments invoked by Ireland such as the Convention for the Protection of the Marine Environment of the North-East Atlantic ("the OSPAR Convention," September 22, 1992). The Tribunal rejected the United Kingdom's objections in this respect, finding that the OSPAR Convention did not cover the field as to invoke Articles 281 or 282 of the Convention which would have precluded the Tribunal's jurisdiction. The second category of the United Kingdom's objections concerned certain European Community law issues. The Tribunal found it unclear whether "the provisions of the Convention on which Ireland relies are matters in relation to which competence has been transferred to the European Community and, indeed, whether the exclusive jurisdiction of the European Court of Justice, with regard to Ireland and the United Kingdom as Member States of the European Community, extends to the interpretation and application of the Convention as such and in its entirety." The Tribunal held that if this were the case, the jurisdiction of the Tribunal would be precluded by Article 282 of the Convention. The Tribunal recognized that these matters have to be determined within the institutional framework of the European Communities and therefore held that until these issues are definitely resolved, it could not firmly establish jurisdiction in respect of all or any of the claims of the dispute. The Arbitral Tribunal thus decided unanimously that further proceedings on jurisdiction and merits would be suspended until no later than December 1, 2003.

As to the additional provisional measures requested by Ireland, the Tribunal found that the harm caused by discharges was not "serious" and thus did not meet the threshold test in Article 290 paragraph 1 which governs the issuance of such measures. It further found that "there is no urgent and serious risk of irreparable harm to Ireland's claimed rights, which

---

[115] Text of the Order and opinions are *available at* <www.itlos.org>.

would justify the tribunal in prescribing provisional measures relating to discharges form the MOX plant." The Tribunal also found that no further order was required as to cooperation and the provision of information at this stage. The question of an environmental assessment was held to be a key question on the merits and thus deferred. The Tribunal however, affirmed the provisional measure on co-operation prescribed by ITLOS in its Order of December 3, 2001, and requested the parties to "take such steps as are open to them separately or jointly to expedite the resolution of the outstanding questions of European Community law."

In addition to potentially competing jurisdiction under UNCLOS and Community law, Ireland also submitted the MOX dispute under the 1992 Convention for the Protection of the Marine Environment of the North-East Atlantic (the OSPAR Convention), the first case submitted pursuant to this treaty. Ireland asserted that the Convention guaranteed it access to information about the MOX plant and claimed that the United Kingdom had breached its obligations under Article 9[116] of the OSPAR Convention by refusing to disclose information from two reports prepared as part of the approval process for the MOX plant. The United Kingdom argued that the information was deleted for reasons of commercial confidentiality. The Tribunal in its final award found by majority decision that Ireland's claim for information did not fall within Article 9(2) of the Convention.[117]

The Tribunal had to decide, *inter alia*, whether the reference of "applicable international regulations" in Article 9(3) of the OSPAR Convention would include, as contended by Ireland, the Aarhus Convention on Access to Information, Public Participation in Decision-making and Access to Justice in Environmental Matters ("the Aarhus Convention," June 25, 1998) which neither Ireland nor the United Kingdom had ratified. By a majority, the Tribunal found that it could only consider current international law and practice

---

[116]   The relevant sections of Article 9 of the OSPAR Convention read: "9.1. The Contracting Parties shall ensure that their competent authorities are required to make available the information described in paragraph 2 of this Article to any natural or legal person, in response to any reasonable request, without that person's having to prove an interest, without unreasonable charges, as soon as possible and at the latest within two month. 9.2. The information referred to in paragraph 1 of this Article is any available information in written, visual, aural or data base form on the state of the maritime area, on activities or measures adversely affecting or likely to affect it and on activities or measures introduced in accordance with the Convention. . . 9.3. The provision of this Article shall not affect the right of Contracting Parties, in accordance with their national legal systems and applicable international regulations, to provide for a request for such information to be refused where it affects: . . . (d) commercial and industrial confidentiality."

[117]   OSPAR Arbitral Tribunal: *Ireland v. United Kingdom, Dispute Concerning Access to Information Under Article 9 of the OSPAR Convention* (July 2, 2003).

insofar as such law and practice are admissible under Article 31 of the Vienna Convention on the Law of Treaties and held that it could not apply the Aarhus Convention.

On the OSPAR Convention itself, the United Kingdom argued that Article 9(1) did not establish a direct right to receive information but rather required parties to establish a domestic framework for the disclosure of information. The United Kingdom asserted that Ireland therefore only had a cause of action for breach of Article 9 if the United Kingdom had failed to provide a regulatory framework for disclosure of information. The United Kingdom maintained that it had taken the required legislative and administrative measures. The Tribunal rejected the United Kingdom's arguments and found by majority that "its proper construction Article 9(1) requires an outcome of result, namely that information falling within the meaning or Article 9(2) (and not excluded under Article 9(3)) is in fact disclosed in conformity with the Article 9 obligation imposed upon each Contracting Party."

The Tribunal rejected, however, Ireland's argument for a broad interpretation of Article 9(2) and held that information has to be related to the state of the maritime area, and, focusing on the second of the three categories of Article 9(2), further held that such information has to be on activities and measures "adversely affecting or likely to affect" the maritime area. It found that Ireland had failed to demonstrate that the 14 categories of information which it desired to obtain were "information on the state of the maritime area" or on "activities and measures adversely affecting or likely to affect it."

In a dissenting opinion Dr. Griffith QC disagreed as to the majority's decision regarding the applicable law, concluding that the Aarhus Convention fell within the definition of applicable law and Article 31 of the Vienna Convention. In addition, he disagreed with the majority's narrow interpretation of the second category of information under Article 9(2) and the majority's conclusion that Ireland bore the burden of proof to establish that the MOX fuel production is an activity "adversely affecting or likely to affect" the maritime area.

4. World Trade Organization

The Agreement Establishing the World Trade Organization came into force in January 1995 together with the Dispute Settlement Understanding (DSU) which is Annex 2 to the Agreement. The DSU is an integral part of the WTO Agreement and legally binding. It utilizes processes of consultation, good offices/conciliation/mediation, and arbitration, together with a process of panels and appellate review. Various disputes between states involving trade restrictions for environmental purposes have been heard by WTO panels. These decisions are discussed in Chapter 17.

E. International Criminal Law

In addition to its work on liability and the law of state responsibility, the ILC has undertaken to draft a code of crimes against the peace and security of mankind, international crimes committed by private actors. In 1991, the ILC adopted a new version[118] of the draft which had been sent to the UN General Assembly in 1954. The 1991 draft included two provisions concerning crimes against the environment. In one provision, war crimes include "employing methods or means of warfare which are intended or may be expected to cause widespread, long-term and severe damage to the natural environment." The other provision (Art. 26) criminalized the act of "an individual who wilfully causes or orders the causing of widespread, long-term and severe damage to the environment." Criticism by states of the expansive list of crimes led the ILC special rapporteur to propose reducing the number of crimes, in particular eliminating the provisions regarding environmental crimes. The ILC instead decided to create a working group "to examine the possibility of covering in the draft Code the issue of wilful and severe damage to the environment."[119] The working group decided the "time was not yet ripe" for declaring attacks on nature as such crimes against the peace and security of mankind[120] and it thus recommended that damage to the environment be constituted either a war crime or a crime against humanity only when it is so severe "that the health or survival of a population will be gravely prejudiced." The working group continued to view attacks on the environment "as an indispensable element" of the draft Code.[121] The plenary sent the text on war crimes to the drafting committee but in an equally divided vote the committee declined to send the draft on environmental damage as a crime against humanity. The drafting committee changed the working group text on war crimes to require an intent to cause damage to the environment with the aim of prejudicing the health or survival of a population. It will be virtually impossible to prove such double intent.

Finally, the Rome Statute of the International Criminal Court,[122] gives the court jurisdiction over war crimes, defined as grave breaches of the 1949 Geneva Conventions on the Laws of Armed Conflict or "other serious violations of the laws and customs applicable in international armed conflict,

---

[118] 2 Y.B. I.L.C. 94 (1991).

[119] I.L.C., *Report of the International Law Commission on the Work of its Forty-Seventh Session 2 May–21 July 1995*, U.N. GAOR 50th Sess., Supp. No. 10, A/50/10, at 67 para. 141.

[120] C. Tomuschat, *Crimes Against the Environment*, 26 E.P.L. 242 (1996).

[121] *Id.*

[122] United Nations, Rome Statute of the International Criminal Court, U.N. Doc. No. A/CONF.193/9 (July 17, 1998); 37 I.L.M. 999 (1998).

within the established framework of international law." Among the list of enumerated offenses is "intentionally launching an attack in the knowledge that such attack will cause incidental loss of life or injury to civilians or damage to civilian objects or widespread, long-term, and severe damage to the natural environment which would be clearly excessive in relation to the concrete and direct overall military advantage anticipated" (Art. 8(2)(b)(iv)). It applies only to international armed conflicts, as does Protocol I to the Geneva Convention which contains similar language.

BIBLIOGRAPHY

BERGKAMP, L., LIABILITY AND ENVIRONMENT: PRIVATE AND PUBLIC LAW ASPECTS OF CIVIL LIABILITY FOR ENVIRONMENTAL HARM IN AN INTERNATIONAL CONTEXT (2001).

BOWMAN, M. & BOYLE, A., ENVIRONMENTAL DAMAGE IN INTERNATIONAL AND COMPARATIVE LAW: PROBLEMS OF DEFINITION AND VALUATION (2002).

BROWN WEISS, E. & JACOBSON, H.K. eds., ENGAGING COUNTRIES—STRENGTHENING COMPLIANCE WITH INTERNATIONAL ACCORDS (1998).

EBBESSON, J., COMPATIBILITY OF INTERNATIONAL AND NATIONAL ENVIRONMENTAL LAW (1996).

ENVIRONNEMENT SANS FRONTIERE, VERS L'APPLICATION RENFORCÉE DU DROIT INTERNATIONAL DE L'ENVIRONNEMENT—TOWARDS STRENGTHENING APPLICATION OF INTERNATIONAL ENVIRONMENTAL LAW (1999).

L'EFFECTIVITÉ DU DROIT EUROPÉEN DE L'ENVIRONNEMENT, CONTROLE DE LA MISE EN OEUVRE ET SANCTION DU NON-RESPECT, (S. MALJEAN-DUBOIS ed., 2000).

FRANCIONI, F. & SCOVAZZI, T. eds., INTERNATIONAL RESPONSIBILITY FOR ENVIRONMENTAL HARM (1991).

GRUBB, M. et al., GREENHOUSE GAS EMISSIONS TRADING (Geneva: UNCTAD, 1998).

Handl, G., *Compliance Control Mechanisms and International Obligations*, 5 TUL J. INT'L & COMP. L. 29 (1997).

L'EFFECTIVITÉ DU DROIT INTERNATIONAL DE L'ENVIRONNEMENT: CONTROLE DE LA MISE EN OEUVRE DES CONVENTIONS INTERNATIONALES (CLAUDE IMPERIALI ed., 1998).

IMPROVING COMPLIANCE WITH INTERNATIONAL ENVIRONMENTAL LAW (JAMES CAMERON et. al. eds., 1996).

Institutions for the Earth: Sources of Effective International Environmental Protection (Peter M. Haas, et al. eds. 1993).

Lammers, J., *International Responsibility and Liability for Damage Caused by Environmental Interferences*, 30 E.P.L. 42 (2001)

O'Connell, M.E., *Symposium: Enforcement and the Success of International Environmental Law*, 3 IND. J. GLOBAL LEG. STUD. (1995).

OECD, DISPUTE SETTLEMENT IN ENVIRONMENTAL CONVENTIONS (1994).

Rehbinder, E., *Environmental Regulation Through Fiscal and Economic Incentives in a Federalist System*, 20 ECOL. L.Q. 57 (1993).

Rest, A., *New Legal Instruments for Environmental Prevention, Control, and Restoration in Public International Law*, 23 E.P.L. 260 (1993).

ROMANO, CESARE, THE PEACEFUL SETTLEMENT OF INTERNATIONAL ENVIRONMENTAL DISPUTES (2000)

ROSENZWEIG, R. et al., THE EMERGING INTERNATIONAL GREENHOUSE GAS MARKET (2002).

VICTOR, D.G. et al. eds., THE IMPLEMENTATION AND EFFECTIVENESS OF INTERNATIONAL ENVIRONMENTAL COMMITMENTS—THEORY AND PRACTICE (1998).

WETTERSTEIN, P. ed., HARM TO THE ENVIRONMENT: THE RIGHT TO COMPENSATION AND THE ASSESSMENT OF DAMAGES (1997).

Wolfrum, R, *Means of Ensuring Compliance with and Enforcement of International Environmental Law*, 272 RCADI 9 (1998).

WOLFRUM, R. & LANGENFELD, C., ENVIRONMENTAL PROTECTION BY MEANS OF INTERNATIONAL LIABILITY LAW (1999).

PART II

SECTORAL AND TRANS-SECTORAL REGULATION

CHAPTER 8

PROTECTION OF BIOLOGICAL DIVERSITY

The interaction of humans with other living organisms has been the subject of discussion, debate, and regulation throughout history. Belief in human dominion over the earth and all its living resources has led many to see other species as having only utilitarian value. Environmentalists generally accept that living organisms may be utilized, but argue that humans have a moral obligation of stewardship or trusteeship towards nature that implies restraint in the use of and respect for all life. Animal rights activists go further and contend that living creatures should not be exploited except where unavoidable to fulfill basic human needs.

The tension between exploitation and conservation is exemplified in international as well as national legal instruments. Sustainable harvesting has proved to be an elusive goal and in many instances populations have declined irretrievably before measures to stabilize populations have been taken or become effective. Until recently, the law on the subject was comprised largely of ad hoc approaches addressing specific commercially-valuable wildlife. Non-binding instruments such as the 1980 World Conservation Strategy of IUCN and the 1982 World Charter for Nature articulated the first broad principles that were subsequently embodied in the framework United Nations Convention on Biological Diversity (June 5, 1992). The Convention establishes guidelines for conduct towards all life on the planet, guidelines that are elaborated in national conservation strategies and plans of action, and the regulations contained in other international agreements.

This chapter examines the panoply of global and regional legal instruments that attempt to protect the earth's biological diversity, *i.e.*, all living resources and ecosystems. After discussing basic concepts and definitions, it describes some of the major threats to biological diversity and the evolution of legal approaches to the question. It then discusses the Convention on Biological Diversity and other general conventions. In the second section, it reviews legal instruments designed to regulate specific aspects of the problem, such as habitat protection and limiting trade or specific means of harvesting. The third part looks at instruments to protect specific species or other taxonomic groups. The issue of biotechnology and bio-engineering is discussed in Chapter 13.

A. Concepts and Definitions

Biological diversity, or biodiversity, has replaced nature conservation as the primary term used in regulating human actions towards other components of the living world. The new term encompasses all genes, species, habitats and ecosystems on earth, thus becoming a unifying principle that denotes all living organisms and their intricate interdependence. Biological diversity is defined in Article 2 of the Convention on Biological Diversity as

> the variability among living organisms from all sources including, inter alia, terrestrial, marine and other aquatic ecosystems and the ecological complexes of which they are part; this includes diversity within species, between species and of ecosystems.

The broad definition includes wild and domesticated animals and wild and cultivated plants found on land and seas, whether within or outside areas under national sovereignty or jurisdiction. The Convention and other sources generally distinguish three levels of biological diversity: genetic diversity, species diversity and ecosystem diversity. Between them they encompass the components of life, different life forms and the interrelationships of all of them. The first Conference of the Parties decided, however, that the definition excludes human beings, organs, and genetic material.

Genetic diversity refers to the variability of the genetic makeup within a single species. Flowering plants contain over 400,000 genes and even bacteria have more than 1,000.[1] In general, no two organisms are genetically identical. The smaller the number of individuals within a species, the less internal genetic diversity the species retains. Inbreeding may result in reduced fertility and increased susceptibility to disease or negative mutation. The threat to the future is particularly pronounced in agriculture, where food security rests on a few grain species with consequent loss of variable characteristics. Some 20 species account for more than 90 percent of the world's food.

Species diversity means the diversity between species of living organisms within a specific habitat or ecosystem; by definition species cannot breed with other species. The number of species on earth is not known. While more than one and one-half million species have been described by scientists, the total number is estimated to be at least five to ten million and some estimates are as high as 50 million. Vertebrates are the least numerous—about 4,200 mammal species and 9,000 species of birds have been described, compared to 250,000 species of higher plants—but the most

---

[1]   Katrina Brown et al., Economics and the Conservation of Global Biological Diversities 3 (1993).

studied order. Least well-known are lichens, bacteria, and fungi. New species are still being found. Nearly one-third of the 6,300 reptile, 23,000 fish, and 4,000 amphibian species have been identified in the past 20 years. The numbers of undiscovered species, especially insects, plants, and micro-organisms undoubtedly runs to the millions.

Living resources are unevenly distributed throughout the world, with the highest concentration of terrestrial species in humid tropical zones and the greatest marine diversity in coastal areas and coral reefs. Also, generally, diversity decreases with altitude on land and depth in the oceans; however, little is known about the deep sea bed species. Islands like Madagascar and Hawaii are rich in endemic species, as are the lakes of Africa, and the countries of the Amazon forest. One in five of the earth's higher plants are found in Amazonia. Freshwater diversity is also important and poorly known.[2]

Ecosystem diversity denotes the range of natural habitats, biotic communities and ecological processes within which species variety has evolved and to which they are uniquely adapted. Each species depends upon the surrounding environment for its survival and reproduction: temperature, humidity, water, soil and nutrition. Ecosystems contain a complex interrelationship of species and functions leading towards equilibrium, governed by natural rules. The diversity of ecosystems is itself an essential part of biological diversity. Some species may be identified as sentinel species, those, such as frogs and some other amphibians, that are sensitive to environmental change and thus important indicators of the health of an ecosystem.

B. Loss of Biological Diversity

The biological diversity of living organisms increasingly is threatened by exploitation, the destruction of habitats, pollution and the wide range of activities that also negatively impact the human environment. Extinction of species, although part of the natural order, has reached alarming proportions since the beginning of the industrial revolution. It is estimated that in less than two centuries, 128 species of bird and 95 species of mammals have disappeared. In some regions, over half the endemic species have become extinct since 1950. The rate of extinction is now thought to be 1,000 times the natural rate of 9 percent of species every million years.[3]

---

2   *See* WORLD RESOURCES INSTITUTE, GLOBAL BIODIVERSITY STRATEGY, Box 3, at 10–11 (1992), which notes that only 475 species of freshwater fish have been recorded in Thailand, while there are likely to be more than 1,000 species in existence. The Amazon River is estimated to contain 3,000 fish species. This diversity is highly threatened; it is estimated that one-third of the native freshwater fish species of North America are extinct or endangered. *Id.*

3   Report of the Ad Hoc Group of Experts to the Executive Director on Governing Council Decision 14/26, UNEP/Bio.Div.1 (Inf. 1), Oct. 7, 1988.

Nearly one-fifth of higher plant species are threatened with extinction or survive only in small populations. Some two-thirds of all bird species are in decline worldwide.

Extinction of species is directly linked to well-known phenomena such as industrialization, urbanization, desertification, disappearance of forests, including rainforests, and the human population explosion. Over-exploitation was the original problem to which legal regulation responded, but human activities have considerable direct and indirect impact, from fishing by-catch to destruction of habitats due to urbanization. Pollution and the introduction of alien species upset the natural balance, as does atmospheric and climate change.

Even agriculture contributes to the depletion of the genetic heritage. Cultivation, often of single products over large areas, replaces the genetic richness of the prairies, just as forests of a single type of tree displace natural woods. Moreover, agricultural techniques create varieties of plants or domestic animals that are particularly productive, to the detriment of varieties whose productivity is less and which are more "primitive," that is closer to the wild origin.

The problem of species loss is linked especially to tropical deforestation. Tropical rain forests cover only 6 percent of the earth's land surface but contain at least half the earth's species, perhaps as much as ninety percent. A U.S. National Academy of Science report estimates that four square miles of Amazonia forest typically contains 125 species of mammals, 400 species of birds, and 100 species of reptiles. At present rates of deforestation in Amazonia, 15 percent of all known plant species disappeared during the 20th century. The impoverishment this represents for humanity and the universe in general is not only biological, but also scientific, cultural and undoubtedly economic. As a result, international environmental measures of protection have taken on enormous importance.

⌈The immediate causes of biodiversity loss mask complex economic and social factors, from population growth to lack of economic incentives to conserve natural resources. The lack of land tenure for indigenous or other local communities undermines efforts to maintain traditional and sustainable land management practices. The lack of regulation permits the over-exploitation that results in the tragedy of the commons. Poverty is linked to unsustainable uses of natural resources. Markets fail to ascribe value to raw biological resources leading to unsustainable patterns of economic growth and consumption. Foreign debt and other international economic pressure similarly undermine conservation efforts.

Impoverishment of the global genetic heritage can have dangerous long-term consequences. The qualities of many wild species are unknown; only about one of every hundred plants has been investigated seriously. Genetic variability contributes billions a year in agriculture, medicine and industry; current trade in wildlife alone may amount to over $10 billion a year. Up to 80 percent of the human population relies on traditional medical systems that utilize natural plant products. A species that disappears may take with it forever a currently unknown biological process or substance of great importance. Moreover, crossing of domestic with wild species may become necessary either to halt the degeneration of overly cultivated species, adapt them to different environments or even to create new varieties. Thus, reserves of non-cultivated varieties are indispensible not only to develop species on which human life depends, but to maintain them over the long term at a high level. Conservation of wildlife is linked thereby with sustainable development and the general interests of humanity.

C. Development of Legal Norms

The use and protection of animals traditionally was considered part of state sovereignty over natural resources and laws within states often were limited to hunting and fishing limits concerning specified species. Plants, on the other hand, were generally considered free for taking and utilization without limits. Later, protected areas and protected species were designated. Treaties aimed at protecting different wild animals appeared at the end of the 19th century, for two reasons. Firstly, migratory species required cooperative efforts among range states to ensure conservation of the stocks. Secondly, commercially-harvested species or stocks on the high seas had to be protected from unsustainable exploitation. More recently, a third reason for adoption of bilateral or multilateral conservation rules has been recognized: non-migratory species whose range or habitat extends into the territory of more than one state may require cooperative efforts to ensure the species' survival.

The first multilateral conventions aimed at protecting non-exploited species reflected an undeniable utilitarianism. The Paris Convention of March 19, 1902, protected a limited list of birds "useful to agriculture"while the second annex to the Convention listed unprotected bird "pests," including most predators, grain-eating and fish-eating birds. New concepts appeared after World War II, reflecting the emergence of a global environmental consciousness. The International Convention for the Protection of Birds,[4] articulated a general principle that all birds should be protected, with limited exceptions set forth in the Convention and specific derogations permitted to states. Birds of prey became among the most protected species. In spite of new attitudes towards conservation, however, measures of protection were scattered among international rules that addressed the problem in a fragmentary fashion. The methods of protection that were adopted also were incomplete; most often they forbade taking examples of protected

---

4   Paris, Oct. 18, 1950.

species but failed to adopt measures to ensure that habitat conditions supported the survival of the species. Subsequent agreements expanded the focus to consider the role of species in the ecosystem in which they occur and the need to preserve genetic diversity in the light of new threats, including inadvertent or accidental harm from pollution due to oil spills, pesticides and other harm to wildlife habitats. An ecosystem approach that looks beyond protecting specific species has been coupled with efforts to develop improved compliance techniques and increased participation of non-governmental actors.

A fundamental change of attitude towards wildlife is reflected in Principle 4 of the 1972 Stockholm Declaration:

> Man has a special responsibility to safeguard and wisely manage the heritage of wildlife and its habitat which are now gravely imperilled by a combination of adverse factors. Nature conservation, including wildlife, must therefore receive importance in planning for economic development.

The idea that plants and animals constitute a heritage developed late, and even now the international community remains far from accepting all its implications. In 1980, the World Conservation Strategy, prepared by IUCN in cooperation with the United Nations Environment Program, the World Wide Fund for Nature, the FAO, and UNESCO, defined three major conservation goals: maintain essential ecological processes; preserve genetic diversity; and sustainably use species and ecosystems.

The World Charter for Nature of October 28, 1982, reaffirmed these goals. After proclaiming in its preamble that "every form of life is unique, warranting respect, regardless of its worth to man," the Charter declares in Principles 2 and 3:

> 2.   The genetic viability of the earth shall not be compromised; the population levels of all life forms, wild and domesticated, must be at least sufficient for their survival, and to this end necessary habitats shall be safeguarded.
>
> 3.   All areas of the earth, both land and sea, shall be subject to these principles of conservation; special protection shall be given to unique areas, to representative samples of all the different types of ecosystems and to the habitats of rare or endangered species.

These principles opened a new era in conservation policy, reflecting awareness of the planetary dimension of the issues. Thus, conservation of species and of their habitats was integrated into the broader conceptual framework of safeguarding the genetic heritage of the planet, a new, immense problem extending beyond the dimensions of conservation in its usual sense. The progression towards identification, regulation and management of processes that adversely affect biological diversity represents one aspect of a shift away from sectoral administration towards transsectoral approaches to protecting ecosystems.

All these factors and trends made the need for comprehensive norms to protect biological diversity increasingly apparent and led to the adoption of the United Nations Convention on Biological Diversity at Rio de Janeiro in June 1992. The Convention sets forth a general framework or normative umbrella that is reinforced by other legal instruments relating to particular species, areas, and means of protection. International agreements on nature protection or biological diversity can be grouped into three main categories. First, there are treaties that aim to protect biological diversity in general. Second, there are conventions that aim to protect broad categories, *e.g.*, endangered or threatened species, through use of a particular legal technique (habitat protection, restrictions on international trade). Third, a series of treaties, both multilateral and bilateral, aim at conserving a single species or higher taxonomic group: whales, bats, seals, migratory birds.

In general, the texts safeguard the individuals that comprise the species. Thus individual rhinoceros are protected, not the species as an abstraction apart from the individual animals. Nonetheless, the abstraction exists, because the characteristic genes of each species confer a range of different qualities to each of its individual members. It is this genetic fund which should be protected and transmitted to future generations to ensure the variability within each species. A major task of international environmental law is to assure the conservation and transmission of this fund, in reality the greatest material resource of the earth.[5]

International treaties for the protection of living organisms contain many common obligations, such as the duty to adopt regulatory measures for nature conservation. Older treaties promoted the creation of protected areas and several more recent ones mandate the protection of specific sites (*e.g.*, the Feb. 2, 1971, Ramsar Convention on the Conservation of Wetlands, the Nov. 23, 1972, Convention on the World Cultural and Natural Heritage, and protocols on specially protected areas of regional seas) although states remain free to nominate or remove the names of particular areas from the international lists. The Biodiversity Convention goes beyond these measures to require identification and management of destructive activities a primary obligation. The following section looks at this and other obligations in more detail.

---

[5]   *See* C. de Klemm, *Conservation of Species, the Need for a New Approach*, 9 E.P.L. 117 (1982).

D. General International Instruments

1. *Global Instruments*

a. Convention on Biological Diversity

The United Nations Conference on the Environment and Development opened for signature a Convention on Biological Diversity,[6] the first global comprehensive instrument on the earth's biological resources. The Convention entered into force on December 29, 1993. It takes an integrated rather than a sectoral approach to the conservation and sustainable use of biological diversity. The Convention has three broad purposes: (1) the conservation of biological diversity, (2) the sustainable use of its components, and (3) access to genetic resources, including the fair and equitable sharing of benefits arising from the use of genetic resources, and access to technology, including biotechnology.

The Convention primarily concerns the rights and responsibilities of states at the national level. The general obligation imposed on states parties is to take effective national action to halt the destruction of species, habitats and ecosystems, including the adoption of regulations on conservation of biological resources, legal responsibility, regulation of biotechnology, and norms on access to and compensation for use of genetic materials. The states parties are to apply the Convention requirements inside the territorial limits of their national jurisdiction, as well as to processes and activities under their jurisdiction or control wherever located.

The Convention contains several innovative features. Biological diversity is recognized for the first time in a global treaty as a common concern of humankind. Negotiators rejected proposals to label it as the common heritage of mankind because of concern for national sovereignty. The latter point is emphasized in Article 3, which repeats verbatim Principle 21 of the Stockholm Declaration—without the reference to development concerns found in the Rio Declaration—and in Article 15 on access to genetic resources. The Convention was the first international agreement to incorporate Stockholm Principle 21 into its operational provisions.

The Convention reverses a traditional principle of free access to genetic resources, making it clear that "the authority to determine access to genetic resources rests with the national governments and is subject to national legislation." Developing countries insisted on this extension of the norm of permanent sovereign over natural resources and the correlative requirement of prior informed consent by the party providing the genetic resource (Art. 15.5). It may be viewed as the counterpart to developed country efforts

---

   [6]   Convention on Biological Diversity, *adopted* May 22, 1992, *opened for signature* June 5, 1992, *in force* Dec. 29, 1993.

to ensure intellectual property rights over industrial development of products derived from biological resources, including living material itself. The Convention takes a positive stance on the flow of genetic resources, calling on states parties to facilitate access for environmentally-sound uses and not to impose restrictions that are counter to the objectives of the Convention. It also requires states parties to take measures to share "in a fair and equitable way" the results of research and development of uses of genetic resources with the state providing those resources.

The emphasis on national sovereignty is balanced by the inclusion of broad state duties. The preamble provides that states "are responsible for conserving their biological diversity and for using their biological resources in a sustainable manner." The specific requirements of the Convention impose an obligation on states parties to identify important components of biological diversity and priorities that may need special conservation measures, as well as to identify and monitor processes and activities that may have significant adverse effects on biological diversity (Art. 7). With this information, they must develop national strategies and plans, integrating conservation of biological diversity into relevant sectoral plans and programs and decision-making (Art. 6). The planning requirement is reinforced by the requirement in Article 10(a) that parties integrate consideration of the conservation and sustainable use of biological resources into national decision-making. Annex I contains indicative lists for the identification and monitoring of ecosystems and habitats, species and communities, and genomes and genes of social, scientific and economic importance.

After long debate among the negotiators, the Convention established a preference for *in situ* conservation, with *ex situ* conservation called for as a complement to *in situ* measures. *In situ* conservation is defined as "conservation of ecosystems and natural habitats and the maintenance and recovery of viable populations of species in their natural surroundings and, in the case of domesticated or cultivated species, in the surroundings where they have developed their distinctive properties" (Art. 2). Conservation measures range from establishment of protected areas to rehabilitation of degraded ecosystems, and protection of natural habitats (Art. 8). Most importantly, states parties are to protect ecosystems and to regulate or manage biological resources important for the conservation of biological diversity whether they are within or without protected areas. The Convention also contains a provision intended to counter the widespread destruction of native species that can occur through the introduction of exotic species against which local ones have little or no protection.[7]

Sustainable use is a major theme of the Convention and is defined as "the use of components of biological diversity in a way and at a rate that

---

[7]   Other recent international agreements include provisions to the same effect. *See* Chapter 8E.1.c.

does not lead to the long-term decline of biological diversity, thereby maintaining its potential to meet the needs and aspirations of present and future generations" (Art. 2). Parties agree to regulate or manage harvested biological resources, developing sustainable methods and minimizing adverse impacts on biological diversity. States must institute research, training and public education, as well as techniques like environmental impact assessment. Special emphasis is given to protecting and encouraging traditional cultural practices if compatible with sustainable use and to the adoption of incentives for the conservation and sustainable use of components of biological diversity.

As with all the documents adopted in connection with UNCED, the Biodiversity Convention contains qualifying language indicating that there are differentiated responsibilities among the states parties, depending upon their capacities. Most obligations must be fulfilled when "possible," "practicable," or "appropriate." States parties are asked to respect, preserve and maintain knowledge, innovations and practices of indigenous and local communities relevant to biological diversity, but only "subject to national legislation." Some provisions make explicit distinctions between developed and developing countries (*e.g.*, Arts. 6 and 20).

In other respects, the Convention reiterates the general principles of international environmental law, including responsibility for and redress of transfrontier damage (Arts. 3, 14), cooperation (Art. 5), access to information (Arts. 14, 17), and prevention. The development agenda of UNCED is also reflected in various articles that prescribe specific rules of identification and monitoring, access to genetic resources (Art. 15), access to and transfer of technology (Art. 16), and technical and scientific cooperation (Art. 18).

For the first time in a global conservation agreement, there is a legal relationship between the conservation obligations of developing countries and the financial obligations of developed countries. The latter group of countries is required to provide "new and additional financial resources" to a financial mechanism for the use of developing countries. The Convention specifies that the funding is to be applied to meet the full incremental costs deriving from measures needed to implement the Convention's obligations. The amount is set through bilateral negotiations between each developed country party and the institution chosen to handle the financial mechanism. There is explicit recognition that the implementation of obligations under the Convention is linked to and dependent upon adequate funding being supplied. In addition, implementation must take into account "the fact that economic and social development and eradication of poverty are the first and overriding priorities of the developing country Parties." The Conference of the Parties has designated the Global Environment Facility as the financial mechanism at each of its sessions to date. A Memorandum of Understanding was concluded between the CBD Executive Secretary and the GEF Council in 1996 to govern the financial mechanism.

By 2003 nearly all states were party to the Convention. The Conference of the Parties has held regular sessions at which it has adopted important decisions and recommendations on environmental impact assessment, introduction of alien species, transboundary cooperation and the involvement of local and indigenous communities. COP also appointed an Ad Hoc Open-Ended Working Group on Access and Benefit-Sharing which adopted the Bonn Guidelines on Access to Genetic Resources and Fair and Equitable Sharing of the Benefits Arising out of Their Utilization, discussed in Section E of this chapter. The guidelines are voluntary and intended to assist parties to develop legislative, administrative or policy measures and/or contracts. The COP delegated to the Subsidiary Body on Scientific, Technical, and Technological Advice authority to develop guidance on the ecosystem approach, environmental impact assessment, and the prevention and mitigation of impacts caused by the introduction of alien species. The ecosystem approach, discussed in Chapter 14, seeks to assess all human activities impacting on the ecosystem, whether economic, social, cultural, legal, recreational or other. It aims to integrate ecological, economic, and social factors to restore and maintain the health of ecological resources together with the communities and economies that they support.

Another COP decision, the Jakarta Mandate (Decision II/10), calls for the establishment and reinforcement of arrangements for integrated management of marine and coastal ecosystems and the integration of plans and strategies for such areas. In 1998, the COP approved a global work plan specifically recommending use of the precautionary approach to guide all activities affecting marine and coastal biological diversity. Other COP programs concern agricultural biological diversity, forest biological diversity, and sustainable tourism.

To monitor compliance with Convention obligations, Article 26 calls for the presentation of state reports on measures taken for the implementation of the provisions of the Convention and their effectiveness in meeting the objectives of the Convention. The first reports focus on Article 6, the general measures and information acquired during national studies on biological diversity. The COP guidelines suggest a structure consisting of an executive summary, an introduction, background, goals and objectives, the strategy chosen, partners involved, action for implementation, budget, monitoring and evaluation and sharing of national experience.

The Convention left for later negotiation two major issues: biosafety and liability. Article 14(2) calls on the COP to examine the question of liability and redress, including restoration and compensation for damage to biological diversity, except where purely an internal matter. Biosafety has been the priority issue, however, and the COP established an Open-Ended Ad Hoc Working Group to elaborate a protocol on biosafety, discussed in Chapter 13E in connection with the regulation of biotechnology.

b.   Convention on the Conservation of Migratory Species of Wild Animals

The Bonn Convention on the Conservation of Migratory Species of Wild
Animals (CMS)[8] is also a treaty of global scope. It was adopted as a follow-
up to Recommendation 32 of the Stockholm Action Plan[9] and constitutes
a recognition that the conservation and efficient management of migratory
species require concerted action by all states within whose national jurisdiction the species spend part of their lives and through which they transit.
Legal measures must broadly address threats to habitats, excessive hunting
along migration routes and degradation of feeding sites.

The Convention provides a framework within which range states of
migratory species take individual and cooperative action to conserve the
species and their habitats. The Preamble states that wild animals in their
innumerable forms are an irreplaceable part of the earth's natural system
which must be conserved for the good of mankind. Further, it states that
each generation holds the resources of the earth for future generations and
has an obligation to ensure that this legacy is conserved and utilized wisely.
Each party is to adopt strict protection measures for endangered migratory
species, conclude multilateral agreements for the conservation and management of migratory species that have an unfavorable conservation status
or would benefit significantly from international cooperation, and undertake joint research activities.

For purposes of the Convention, the term "migratory species" is defined
as the entire population or any geographically separate part of the population of a species of wild animals which habitually and predictably cross one
or more national jurisdictional boundaries. This obviously includes not only
birds, but both land and sea mammals, reptiles and fish. Other definitions,
given in Article 1, are rendered necessary by the complexity of the subject.
Thus, "endangered" signifies that the migratory species is in danger of
extinction throughout all or a significant portion of its "range," meaning
all the areas of land or water that a migratory species inhabits, stays in temporarily, crosses or overflies at any time on its normal migration route.
Another important element is the concept of a "conservation status," the
sum of the influences acting on a migratory species that may affect its long-
term distribution and abundance. According to Article 1(1), the conservation status is considered as favorable when:

---

[8]   June 23, 1979. For a detailed discussion of the Convention, *see* Clare
Shine, *Selected Agreements Concluded Pursuant to the Convention on the Conservation of
Migratory Species of Wild Animals, in* COMMITMENT AND COMPLIANCE: THE ROLE OF NON-
BINDING NORMS IN THE INTERNATIONAL LEGAL SYSTEM 196 (D. SHELTON ed., 2000).

[9]   Recommendation 32 called on governments to take into consideration
"the need to enact international conventions and treaties to protect species inhabiting international waters or those which migrate from one country to another."
The Federal Republic of Germany prepared a preliminary draft in 1974.

(1) population dynamics data indicate that the migratory species is maintaining itself on a long-term basis as a viable component of its ecosystems;

(2) the range of the migratory species is neither currently being reduced, nor is likely to be reduced, on a long-term basis;

(3) there is, and will be in the foreseeable future, sufficient habitat to maintain the population of the migratory species on a long-term basis; and

(4) the distribution and abundance of the migratory species approach historic coverage and levels to the extent consistent with wise wildlife management.

The favorable or unfavorable conservation status of a migratory species serves as a criterion for determining the applicable rules of the Bonn Convention. For example, one of the fundamental obligations of states is to pay special attention to migratory species whose conservation status is unfavorable and to take individually or in cooperation the necessary steps to conserve such species and their habitats.[10]

Like other conservation conventions, the Bonn treaty uses a system of lists. Immediate protection is accorded to endangered migratory species, listed in Appendix I. Range states of species listed in Appendix I are to conserve and, where possible, restore the habitats of these species; eliminate, prevent or minimize impediments to their migration; prevent, reduce, or control factors endangering them; and prohibit the taking of animals belonging to such species except under strictly defined conditions.[11]

Appendix II lists migratory species that have an unfavorable conservation status and thus require international agreements for their conservation and management. Formal agreements are encouraged in Article IV(3) and Guidelines for the content of such Agreements are provided in Article V. Formal agreements should cover the whole of the migratory range and should be open to accession by all range states of that species, whether or not they are parties to the Bonn Convention. The agreement's contents should identify the migratory species, describe the range and migration route, allow for designation of a national authority to implement the agreement, and establish institutional machinery to assist in achieving its objectives and monitoring its effectiveness. In relation to a migratory species of cetacean, it should, at a minimum, prohibit any taking of whales not permitted by whaling conventions. Where feasible, agreements also should provide for periodic reports on the conservation status of the migratory species concerned, coordinated conservation and management plans, research and

---

[10] Art. II(1).
[11] Art. III.

exchanges of information on the species, conservation and restoration of habitats, and maintenance of a network of suitable habitats along the migration routes, elimination of or compensation for activities and obstacles which hinder or impede migration, prevention of pollution in habitats of the species, coordinated action to suppress illegal taking, and, finally, measures of public awareness.[12]

In addition to concluding treaties governing migratory species listed in Appendix II, states parties are encouraged to enter into other agreements concerning one or more migratory species that are not listed in Appendix II (Art. IV.4). Any population that periodically crosses one or more national jurisdictional boundaries may be subject to such agreement. The Convention does not specify the form or content of the agreements. Some agreements have been treaties applying the Article V guidelines,[13] while others have been Memoranda of Understanding[14] that are not legally binding but are intended to coordinate short-term administrative and scientific measures between range states in collaboration with international non-governmental organizations having expertise on the subject. The MOUs concluded to date list specific conservation undertakings of each state in an annexed action plan.

The Convention provides for three organs: the Conference of States Parties, a Scientific Council, and a Secretariat. The first is the decision-making organ of the Convention, and it meets at least once every three years. It monitors the conservation status of migratory species, makes recommendations to parties for improving the conservation status of species, reviews the progress being made under agreements, and recommends convening meetings of range states of a migratory species for which there is no agreement, in order to improve its conservation status.[15] The Scientific Council, established by the Conference of the Parties, provides advice on scientific matters to the Conference, the Secretariat, any state party, or in appropriate cases any body set up under the Convention or an agreement. It can recommend research and make recommendations on migratory species listed in Appendices I and II and recommend specific conservation and management measures to be included in agreements.[16] The Secretariat's func-

---

[12]   Art. VI.

[13]   *See, e.g.,* the Agreement on the Conservation of Seals in the Wadden Sea (Oct. 16, 1990), Agreement on the Conservation of Small Cetaceans of the Baltic and North Seas (Sept. 13, 1991, *opened for signature* Mar. 17, 1992), and Agreement on the Conservation of Cetaceans of the Black Sea, Mediterranean Sea and Contiguous Atlantic Area (Nov. 24, 1996).

[14]   *E.g.,* Memorandum of Understanding concerning Conservation Measures for the Siberian Crane (July 1, 1993); Memorandum of Understanding concerning Conservation Measures for the Slender-billed Curlew (Sept. 10, 1994).

[15]   Art. VII.

[16]   Art. VIII.

tions include maintaining and publishing a list of range states of all migratory species included in the two Appendices and promoting the conclusion of agreements.[17] Article XI provides that amendments to the Appendices may be adopted at any session, ordinary or extraordinary, of the Conference of the Parties. Amendments are adopted by a two-third's majority of members present and voting and enter into force in regard to all states parties 90 days after the meeting, except for those that file a written reservation within the 90-day period.[18]

Parties to the Convention have concluded 13 agreements to July 2003, of which six are formal treaties pursuant to Article IV(3) and seven are Memoranda of Understanding. The six formal agreements concern the conservation of seals in the Wadden Sea, bats in Europe (1991), small cetaceans of the Baltic and North Seas (1990), African-Eurasian waterbirds (1995), and cetaceans of the Black Sea, Mediterranean Sea and contiguous area (1995), and the conservation of albatrosses and petrals (2001). The seven MOUs concern conservation of the Siberian crane (1993), the slender-billed curlew (1994), marine turtles of the Atlantic Coast of Africa (1999), the Middle-European population of the Great Bustard (2000), marine turtles of the Indian Ocean and South-East Asia (2001), the Bukhara deer, and the aquatic warbler. The contents of the different instruments are discussed later in the chapter in regard to the protection of specific species.

Although states parties to the Bonn agreement initially concluded more formal agreements, the MOU has become increasingly popular. One reason for this shift may be seen in the list of signatories to MOUs: all of them except the two agreements on marine turtles include inter-governmental and non-governmental organizations among the signatories. The Siberian Crane MOU has been signed by three organizations: the UNEP/CMS secretariat, the International Crane Foundation, and the Wild Bird Society of Japan. The Great Bustard MOU was signed by four entities: UNEP/CMS secretariat, IUCN, BirdLife International and the International Council for Game and Wildlife Conservation and all of these except IUCN also signed the MOU on the slender-billed curlew.

2. Regional Instruments

Regional conventions and other legal instruments regulate a large part of the planet: the Americas, Africa, Western Europe, South-East Asia and the Pacific.

---

[17]   Art. IX. The Secretariat is provided by UNEP and has its offices in Bonn, Germany along with the Secretariat of the UN Framework Convention on Climate Change. A Standing Committee provides policy and administrative guidance between regular meetings of the COP. The Standing Committee consists of representatives of the five geographic regions, the Depositary state (Germany) and the host states of the last and next meetings of the COP.

[18]   Art. XI.

a. Africa

Africa was the first region to have a convention on nature protection, signed in London on May 19, 1900, for the Preservation of Wild Animals, Birds and Fish in Africa.[19] It was adopted by those European powers having colonies in Africa: Germany, Spain, France, Italy, Portugal, and the United Kingdom. Despite characteristics that were progressive for the time, such as protecting certain species and recommending creation of protected zones, it encouraged the destruction of animals considered nuisances or harmful, such as crocodiles and venomous snakes, and the reduction in numbers of others such as lions, panthers and predatory birds.[20]

In 1933, the colonial powers and several independent African states concluded a new Convention that insisted on the creation of protected zones and eliminated reference to harmful or nuisance species.[21] The Convention relative to the Preservation of Fauna and Flora in their Natural State entered into force January 14, 1936 and led to the creation of many of the existing national parks in Africa.

As African countries achieved independence after the Second World War, it became obvious that a further convention was needed. The Organization of African Union, as the organization of general competence in the region, recommended that its members make efforts in this direction. As a result, the African Convention on the Conservation of Nature and Natural Resources,[22] the first of the major modern conservation treaties, was adopted in 1968.[23] On July 11, 2003, the General Assembly of the African Union meeting in Maputo adopted a revised Convention. Its provisions make it the most modern and comprehensive of all agreements concerning natural resources.

Like its predecessor, the 2003 instrument covers all aspects of environmental conservation and resource management. The Preamble proclaims the conservation of the global environment to be a common concern of humankind and the conservation of the African environment a primary concern of all Africans. States are responsible for protecting and conserv-

---

[19] 94 B.F.S.P. 715.

[20] Art. II(13) and (15).

[21] Convention Relative to the Preservation of Fauna and Flora in their Natural State (London, Nov. 8, 1933).

[22] Algiers, Sept. 15, 1968.

[23] It *entered into force* on May 7, 1969. Its states parties are Cameroon, Central African Republic, Comoros Island, Djibouti, Egypt, Ghana, Ivory Coast, Kenya, Liberia, Madagascar, Malawi, Mali, Morocco, Mozambique, Niger, Nigeria, Rwanda, Senegal, Sudan, Swaziland, Tanzania, Togo, Tunisia, Seychelles, Uganda, Upper Volta (Burkina Faso), Zaire and Zambia.

ing their environment and natural resources and for using them in a sustainable manner in order to satisfy human needs according to the carrying capacity of the environment. The preamble makes reference to the Stockholm Declaration, to the Rio Declaration and to Agenda 21, but not to the instruments adopted by the 2002 Johannesburg Summit on Sustainable Development.

Article III formulates the principles which should guide the action of states, beginning with the right of all peoples to a satisfactory environment favourable to the enjoyment of the right to development, using language from the African Charter of Human and Peoples Rights. Article XVI complements Article III by proclaiming procedural rights and requiring the parties to adopt legislative and regulatory measures necessary to ensure timely and appropriate dissemination of environmental information, access of the public to such information, participation in decision-making and access to justice in matters related to protection of the environment and natural resources.

The obligations of the parties are progressive and unusual. The Convention advocates preventive measures and the application of the precautionary principle, "with due regard to ethical and traditional values as well as scientific knowledge in the interest of present and future generations." Article XVII on the traditional rights of local communities and indigenous knowledge, Article XVIII on research and Article XIX on development and transfer of technology further develop such principles. It is noteworthy that Article XVII submits access to indigenous knowledge and its use to the prior informed consent of the concerned communities and to specific regulations recognizing their rights to, and appropriate economic value of, such knowledge. In this respect, the African Convention is more favorable to local communities than the Convention on Biological Diversity, which places its emphasis on the sovereign rights of states.

Due to the role played by IUCN in the preparation of the Convention, nature conservation and management form an important part of the text. Article V, paragraph 6 lists six conservation areas for which Article XII enunciates general rules with the aim of conserving the most representative ecosystems and ensuring the conservation of all species. Annex 2 contains rules for each of the specified areas. Even outside conservation areas, species and genetic diversity of plants and animals, whether terrestrial, freshwater or marine, shall be maintained and enhanced, in particular by the conservation of their habitats within the framework of land-use planning and of sustainable development (Art. IX). Parties shall also take all necessary measures for the protection, conservation, sustainable use and rehabilitation of the vegetation cover (Art.VIII). A more selective approach targets the species which must be identified and protected (Art. X and Annex I), in part by regulating trade in specimens and products thereof (Art. XI). Annex 3 lists prohibited means of taking.

Conservation measures are to be replaced in a more general approach. On the one hand, the parties shall take effective measures to prevent land degradation and to that effect adopt long-term integrated strategies for the conservation and sustainable management of land resources, including soil, vegetation and related hydrological processes (Art.VI). On the other hand, parties shall manage their water resources by maintaining, *inter alia*, water-based essential ecological processes, by adopting policies for the planning, conservation, management, utilization and development of underground and surface water. Parties sharing surface or underground water resources shall act in consultation and if the need arises, set up inter-state commissions for their rational management and equitable utilization (Art. VII).

Article XIII complements the conservation aspect by adding rules to prevent environmental harm from processes and activities affecting the environment and natural resources. It advocates the adoption of specific national standards, including for ambient environmental quality, emission and discharge limits as well as process and production methods and products quality. Economic incentives and disincentives shall also be used in this regard. Military and hostile activities should avoid harm to the environment (Art. XV).

The Convention establishes a Conference of the Parties which can consider any matter within its scope (Art. XXVI). It should develop and adopt rules, procedures and institutional mechanisms to promote and enhance compliance with the provisions of the Convention (Art. XXIII) and can adopt additional annexes to the Convention. Like the first African Convention at the beginning of the "ecological era," the new instrument can be considered a model for the necessary holistic approach to integrated protection of the environment.

Environmental agreements also have been concluded in Africa at the sub-regional level and some of these contain progressive enforcement measures. A short agreement on the Conservation of Common Natural Resources[24] entered into between Uganda, the Sudan, and Zaire, contains only four substantive articles. The contracting states agree to devote special attention to common natural resources,[25] to forbid taking of specimens of protected species on their territories,[26] and to prosecute all those who trade without permit in objects coming from protected species, in applying territorial law but restoring the objects seized to the state of origin.[27] Article 3 provides that a certificate of origin issued by one state pursuant to CITES will be accepted by the other contracting states. Institutionally, the Protocol envisages creation of a commission on the black market and contraband. This

---

24 Khartoum, Jan. 24, 1982.
25 Art. 1.
26 Art. 2.
27 Art. 4.

organ is to meet twice a year, to study the problems posed and to formulate recommendations which it deems necessary.[28] Another example, discussed in Chapter 7A, is the Protocol on Wildlife Conservation and Law Enforcement.[29]

b. The Americas

The Convention on Nature Protection and Wild Life Preservation in the Western Hemisphere[30] was adopted through efforts led by the Pan-American Union and inspired by the 1933 London Convention on Africa.[31] At the time, it was an advanced instrument containing the principal means of modern conservation, but with weak obligations. It refers to establishment of protected areas, protection of migratory and endangered species, monitoring and regulation of international trade in wild plants and animals. One interesting aspect of the Convention is the series of definitions in Art. I for different categories of protected zones and the legal regimes governing them. For example:

— *National parks* are areas placed under public control for the protection and preservation of superlative scenery and wildlife of national significance. No hunting, killing or capturing of fauna or destruction or collection of flora is permitted.

— *National reserves* are regions established for the conservation and utilization of natural resources. Under government control, protection is afforded in so far as consistent with the primary purpose of the reserves.

— *Nature monuments* benefit from strict protection. The purpose is to set aside as inviolate an area, object or species of flora or fauna, due to aesthetic, historic, or scientific interest.

— *Strict wilderness reserves* are placed under public control. In such areas, charaterized by primitive conditions, motor vehicles and all commercial developments are excluded. Only scientific investigation or government inspection is permitted.

States parties to the Convention are required only to explore the possibility of establishing such zones and to notify the Pan-American Union—

---

[28] Art. 5.

[29] Maputo, Aug. 13, 1999. *See also* the discussion of the Southern Africa Ivory agreement in Section E.2 of this chapter. ✶

[30] Washington D.C., Oct. 12, 1940.

[31] In 1933, the African states and colonial powers concluded the Convention relative to the Preservation of Fauna and Flora in their Natural State. *See*, Section D.2.a.

today the Organization of American States—of their establishment.[32] Once established, however, the resources of national parks cannot be exploited for commercial profit and boundaries can only be altered by legislation. In addition, the Convention calls upon states to adopt laws and regulations to protect and preserve all flora and fauna within their territories whether or not in protected areas, as well as natural scenery, striking geological formations, and regions and natural objects of aesthetic interest or historic or scientific value.[33] International cooperation and assistance also are foreseen.[34] Special measures must be adopted to protect migratory birds[35] and certain other species listed in an Annex to the Convention.[36] Finally, states parties must take measures to control and regulate the importation, exportation and transit of protected flora and fauna or any part thereof. A system of export certificates is established by Art. IX of the Convention.

The Convention has suffered from insufficient implementation due to lack of an institutional structure[37] although the Organization of American States has organized a few technical meetings. Of great potential, it lacks current effectiveness.

The 1978 Treaty of Amazonian Cooperation[38] aims to promote the harmonious development of Amazonian territories and to ensure that the joint actions of the parties produce equitable and mutually beneficial results and achieve "the preservation of the environment, and the conservation and rational utilization of the natural resources of those territories." Its measures are limited to research and exchange of information, but it creates institutional machinery in meetings of the Ministers of Foreign Affairs and annual meetings of the Amazonian Cooperation Council. The Treaty also creates a secretariat and envisages Permanent National Commissions and special Commissions to study specific problems or matters.

Three sub-regional treaties have been adopted in Central America: the 1992 Managua Convention on the Conservation of the Biodiversity and the Protection of Wilderness Areas in Central America,[39] the 1992 Guatemala Convention on the Management and Conservation of Natural Forest Ecosystems and Forest Plantation Development,[40] and the Agreement on the Mesoamerican Biological Corridor (1996).

---

[32] Art. II.

[33] Art. V.

[34] Art. VI.

[35] Art. VII.

[36] Art. VIII.

[37] S. Lyster, International Wildlife Law 97–99 (1985).

[38] *Entry into force* Feb. 2, 1980. The states parties are Bolivia, Brazil, Colombia, Ecuador, Guyana, Peru, Suriname, and Venezuela.

[39] June 5, 1992.

[40] Oct. 29, 1993.

c. Europe

The Bern Convention on the Conservation of European Wildlife and Natural Habitats was prepared within the Council of Europe.[41] It represents major progress compared to earlier regional efforts, if only because it establishes an institution charged with ensuring its functioning and implementation. It also creates substantive obligations for the contracting parties instead of merely expressing goals and encouraging their fulfillment.

The Preamble reflects modern concepts regarding conservation. Wild flora and fauna are said to constitute a natural heritage having intrinsic value which must be preserved and handed on to future generations. The resources also are recognized as playing an essential role in maintaining biological balances. Finally, the importance of conserving natural habitats is seen as one of the essential elements of conservation.

The fundamental purpose of the Convention is to conserve wild flora and fauna and their natural habitats, "especially those species and habitats whose conservation requires the cooperation of several States" (Art. 1). States parties have an obligation, however, to conserve wild flora and fauna in all circumstances, whether the problems posed are transfrontier or not.

Article 2 provides that the contracting parties will take requisite measures to maintain the population of wild flora and fauna at or adapt it to

> a level which corresponds in particular to ecological, scientific and cultural requirements, while taking account of economic and recreational requirements and the needs of sub-species, varieties or forms at risk locally.

This provision is undoubtedly more vague that the criterion of "optimal sustainable yield" but it may have an advantage in subordinating the economy and tourism to ecological, scientific, and cultural considerations. Contracting parties must take steps to promote national policies for the conservation of wild flora, fauna and natural habitats, with particular attention to endangered and vulnerable species, as well as endangered habitats (Art. 3). A first step is thus taken towards conserving the world genetic heritage "in vivo," that is in natural sites and not in museums and laboratories.

The inescapable links between the habitats, flora and fauna are reflected in Article 4 which calls for protecting the habitats of all wild species, whether endangered or not. It gives particular emphasis to those that are considered as needing special protection, listed in two Appendices. Similarly, attention is given to migratory species in protecting zones of

---

[41] Bern, Sept. 19, 1979.

importance for migratory routes, such as wintering, staging, feeding, breeding or moulting areas.[42]

The heart of the Convention is Chapter III, devoted to the protection of species.[43] The importance of conserving flora is underlined, a noteworthy development for something that often appears to be included as an afterthought to the protection of animals. Article 5 is entirely dedicated to this conservation and Appendix I lists those species strictly protected, for which picking, collecting, cutting, or uprooting is prohibited. Prohibition of sale or possession is left to the discretion of the contracting parties.

The provisions relative to the protection of wild animals also make use of lists. The second Appendix lists species which the Convention, Article 6, protects from deliberate capture and killing, damage to or destruction of breeding or resting sites, deliberate disturbance during particularly vulnerable times (breeding, rearing and hibernation), the deliberate destruction or taking or possession of eggs from the wild, even if empty, and the possession of and internal trade in these animals, alive or dead, and any recognizable part or derivative of them. The listed animals include the wolf, the lynx, and dolphins, as well as numerous bird species.[44] Special provisions respecting migratory species add a duty on range contracting parties to coordinate their efforts to protect these species and in particular to coordinate protective measures, such as closed seasons.[45]

A third Appendix to the Convention protects vulnerable species, whose exploitation must be regulated.[46] The measures that should be adopted include closed seasons, temporary or local prohibition of exploitation, and restrictions on trade in specimens. In all cases, indiscriminate means of capture and killing or means capable of causing local disappearance or disturbance are forbidden.[47]

The Convention generally permits contracting parties to make exceptions to its provisions, but only if there is no other satisfactory solution and the exception will not be detrimental to the survival of the population concerned.[48] Thus, exceptions can be adopted for the protection of flora and fauna, for public health and security, air safety or other overriding public interests, to prevent serious damage to crops, livestock, forests, fisheries, water and other property, for purposes of research and education, repop-

---

[42]   Art. 4(3).

[43]   Arts. 5–9.

[44]   The majority of the bird species listed in Appendix II to the Bern Convention also appear in Annex I to the EC Directive of Apr. 2, 1979 concerning conservation of wild birds. O.J. No. L 103, (4/25/79).

[45]   Art. 10.

[46]   Art. 7.

[47]   Art. 8.

[48]   Art. 9.

ulation, reintroduction and breeding, and for the taking, keeping or "judicious exploitation" of certain wild animals and plants. The number of reasons justifying exceptions is large, but the same article provides a form of international supervision because contracting parties must submit biannual reports on the exceptions they invoke.[49]

Another aspect of the conservation measures merits attention. Article 11 requires each contracting party to encourage the reintroduction of native species of wild flora and fauna and strictly control the introduction of non-native species. Finally, contracting parties may adopt stricter measures for conservation than those provided under the Convention.[50]

Currently the Bern Convention has the most complete institutional structure of all regional conservation conventions. Article 13 institutes a Standing Committee composed of representatives of the contracting parties, including the EC. Any member state of the Council of Europe that is not a contracting party may send an observer and any state which is not a Council of Europe member can be invited by unanimous vote of the Committee to send an observer. International organizations, at their request, also may participate unless one-third of the contracting parties object. The Committee meets at least every two years.[51]

The Committee is responsible for monitoring the application of the Convention. In particular, it makes recommendations to contracting parties on measures to be taken to implement the Convention, makes proposals for improving its effectiveness, including proposals for the conclusion with third states of agreements which would enhance the effective conservation of species or groups of species, and keeps under review the Convention and its Appendices, to examine whether modifications are necessary.[52]

Regarding the last function, there are two distinct procedures for modification set forth in Articles 16 and 17. The first concerns amendments to the Convention itself. Any proposal for amendment coming from a contracting party is examined by the Standing Committee. After decision by a three-quarters majority of the votes cast, the Committee submits the proposal either for acceptance by the contracting parties, or, if it is a procedural change, to the Committee of Ministers of the Council of Europe for approval. All amendments enter into force 30 days after all the contracting parties have informed the Secretary-General of the Council of Europe that they have accepted it.

In contrast to this classic amendment procedure, Article 17 provides a simplified means of amending the Appendices. The necessity to adapt the list of threatened or endangered species to changing conditions is obvious.

---

[49]   Art. 9(2).
[50]   Art. 12.
[51]   Art. 13.
[52]   Art. 14.

The Convention provides for proposals coming from either a contracting party or the Committee of Ministers to be examined by the Standing Committee, which may adopt them by a two-thirds majority. Unless one-third of the contracting parties submit objections, the amendment enters into force for the non-objecting states three months after adoption of the proposal by the Standing Committee.

d.   Asia and the Pacific

The Apia Convention on the Conservation of Nature in the South Pacific (June 12, 1976) is modest both in its content and in its geographic scope. It entered into force June 26, 1990, and has five states parties. From the out-set the Convention's undertakings have little legal content and its institutional aspect is skeletal. While referring to safeguarding representative samples of natural ecosystems and the heritage of wildlife and its habitat, its preamble also speaks of the production of essential renewable natural resources and underlines their nutritional, scientific, educational, cultural, and aesthetic importance. It also recognizes the importance of indigenous customs and traditional cultural practices.

The main focus of the Convention is the creation of protected areas. Each contracting party shall, "to the extent that it is itself involved, encourage the creation of protected areas" to safeguard, along with existing protected areas, representative samples of natural ecosystems, important natural features and regions or objects "of aesthetic interest or historic, cultural or scientific value." The contracting parties notify the South-Pacific Commission, the organ responsible for ensuring the Secretariat functions for the Convention, of the establishment of any protected area, as well as any legislative or administrative measures or methods of control it adopts.[53] The Secretariat functions of the South Pacific Commission are limited to receiving notifications and disseminating information and documents furnished by the contracting states.[54] The Convention does not provide for any meetings of the contracting parties.

Both endangered and migratory species are given special attention.[55] However, the Convention leaves it to each state party to establish and maintain a list of indigenous species threatened with extinction, and to communicate the list to the South Pacific Commission. The species included in the lists are protected, with the acts forbidden in comparable instruments also prohibited here. States parties are mandated "to consider carefully" the consequences of introducing non-indigenous species into ecosystems.[56]

---

[53]   Art. 2.
[54]   Art. 8.
[55]   Art. 5.
[56]   Art. 5.

These rather limited obligations are further weakened by Article 6 which permits a contracting party to "make appropriate provision for customary use of areas and species in accordance with traditional cultural practices."

The ASEAN Convention on the Conservation of Nature and Natural Resources[57] contains substantial obligations in every domain where environmental problems can arise. It is one of the most complete nature protection agreements in existence, but has not entered into force as of 2003. The states parties agree to adopt the measures necessary to maintain essential ecological processes and life-support systems, to preserve genetic diversity, and ensure the sustainable utilization of harvested natural resources, in order to achieve sustainable development. Article 2 of the Convention requires the contracting states to ensure that conservation and management of natural resources are treated as an integral part of development planning at all stages and at all levels.

The Convention's general framework includes provisions relating to the conservation of species and ecosystems (chapter II), to ecological processes (chapter III) and to measures of ecological planning (chapter IV). These chapters reflect a comprehensive approach to protecting living natural resources. Chapter II (Arts. 3–9) addresses genetic diversity, sustainable use of harvested species, endangered species, vegetation cover and forest resources, soil, water, and air. The Convention calls for creating protected areas, regulating the taking of species, prohibiting unselective taking methods, and regulating or prohibiting the introduction of exotic species. It further invites the states party to establish gene banks and other documented collections of animal and plant genetic resources.[58] It also requires the development and implementation of management plans for harvested species based on scientific studies.

Article 5 prohibits taking endangered species, seeks to ensure protection for their habitats and regulates trade in specimens and products derived from these species, named in Appendix I to the Convention. Article 5(3) is particularly important because, in proclaiming the special responsibility of each state towards endangered species in areas under its jurisdiction, the language comes close to announcing a trusteeship.

The Convention applies equally to plant and animal species. Article 6, devoted to vegetation cover and forest resources and their roles in the ecosystems, requires controlling clearance, preventing fires and overgrazing, regulation of mining operations, creation of reserves, reforestation and afforestation, and the conservation of forests, particularly mangroves. Similarly, the protection of the air,[59] soil, and water resources is viewed from

---

[57]   Kuala Lumpur, July 9, 1985, originally signed by Brunei, Indonesia, Malaysia, Philippines, Singapore, and Thailand.

[58]   Art. 3.

[59]   Art. 10. *See also* the Asean Agreement on Transboundary Haze Pollution (Kuala Lumpur, June 10, 2002).

the perspective of their functions in natural ecosystems.[60] The regulation and control of water utilization includes maintaining systems supporting aquatic flora and fauna.[61]

Article 14 requires the preparation of an environmental impact assessment for any proposed activity which may significantly affect the natural environment. When the activities are undertaken, efforts must be made to minimize or overcome an assessed adverse effects. The effects are also monitored in order to take appropriate remedial action.

E.   Addressing Specific Threats

Of the conventions in this category, three protect wildlife habitats and two protect species through trade restrictions. A final set of instruments restricts a method of taking living resources, the utilization of driftnets in the marine environment.

1.   Habitat Protection

While protected areas may only afford temporary relief in transitory places for a particular species, other measures may complete the protection by ensuring the conservation of conditions of life, that is the habitat of the species. The definition given by Article 1(1)(g) of the 1979 Bonn Convention on the Conservation of Migratory Species of Wild Animals is a good example:

> "Habitat" means any area in the range of a migratory species which contains suitable living conditions for that species.

Certain instruments, such as the Oslo Convention on Polar Bears (November 15, 1973), gives habitat a more concrete definition by incorporating areas of hibernation and feeding, as well as migration routes.

Conventions may be entirely oriented towards protecting the habitat of protected species. This is clearly the objective of the 1971 Ramsar Convention on Wetlands of International Importance, whose original title added, "particularly as waterfowl habitat." In other treaties, the protection of species of plants and animals can be one of the objectives in the creation of protected areas. For example, the 1982 Geneva protocol relating to the establishment of special areas in the Mediterranean provides in Article 3(2) that such areas are created with the aim of safeguarding genetic diversity of species as well as satisfactory population levels, areas of reproduction and

---

[60]   Art. 7.
[61]   Art. 8.

their habitats. The system of the 1972 UNESCO Convention concerning the World Cultural and Natural Heritage similarly permits the inscription on an international register of areas when the principal interest is to serve as the habitat of specific species. Numerous regional conventions also generally invite the contracting parties to establish protected areas, such as national parks or natural reserves in the framework of more comprehensive protective measures. In any case, the different conventions increasingly converge to protect endangered or vulnerable species by conserving their habitats, with all the consequences that this implies: prohibition of takings and certain other human activities, including pollution.

a. Convention on Wetlands of International Importance (Ramsar)[62]

The Convention was the first treaty based on the idea that the habitat of species should be the focus of protection. As a relatively early conservation treaty, it is rather simple in structure and has been amended twice to strengthen its procedural clauses. It is based on a recognition that wetlands are among the most productive sources of ecological support on earth, acting as the habitat for myriad species, as flood control regions, and as a resource of great economic, cultural, scientific and recreational value, the loss of which would be irreparable. Wetlands are defined in Convention Article 1 as being areas of marsh, fen, peatland or water, whether natural or artificial, permanent or temporary, with water that is static or flowing, fresh, brackish or salt, including areas of marine water whose depth does not exceed six meters at low tide. Waterfowl, whose protection was the original purpose of the Convention, are defined as birds ecologically dependent on wetlands.

In recent years, scientists have come to recognize the broad ecological importance of wetlands. Wetlands play a vital role in the water cycle, helping to refill water-tables and maintain water quality. They are highly productive ecosystems inhabited by large numbers of plant and animal species. In addition, many marine species depend on coastal wetlands for their reproduction, growth or nutrition during part or all of their life cycle. Unfortunately, during recent decades state-sanctioned or even mandated drainage operations, as well as drought and landfill, have considerably reduced the extent of the global wetlands. Due to their importance to the global environment, the Ramsar Convention has a significance that today transcends its original objective of protecting waterfowl.

The purpose of the Convention is to stop the loss of wetlands and to promote the conservation and wise use of wetlands by national action and international cooperation as a means to achieving sustainable development

---

[62]   Ramsar, Iran, Feb. 2, 1971.

throughout the world.[63] States parties are required to formulate and implement planning to promote as far as possible the wise use of wetlands in their territory (Art. 3.1). A more specific obligation applies to the conservation of wetlands included in a List of Wetlands of International Importance. The Convention requires each state party upon becoming such to designate at least one suitable wetland within its territory for inclusion on the List, which is maintained by the World Conservation Union (IUCN). The boundaries of each wetland are established in a precise manner; they may incorporate riparian and coastal zones adjacent to the wetland, and islands or bodies of marine water of importance as waterfowl habitats.[64]

Since 1980, the meetings of Ramsar state parties have formulated detailed criteria to help in selecting wetlands of international importance.[65] The choice of listed wetlands originally was based on their international importance to waterfowl at any season, as well as their significance for ecology, botany, zoology, limnology or hydrology.[66] The criteria today provide that a wetland should be considered to be of international importance when, *inter alia*, it is a particularly good representative example of a natural or near-natural wetland or a wetland that plays a substantial hydrological, biological or ecological role in the natural functioning of a major river basin or coastal system, or supports an appreciable assemblage of rare, vulnerable or endangered plant or animal species; or is of special value for maintaining the genetic and ecological diversity of a region, or as the habitat of plants or animals at a critical stage of their biological cycle, or for one or more endemic plant or animal species or communities. A wetland usually holding 20,000 waterfowl or 1 percent of the total population of a water bird species or sub-species should be considered to be of international importance. In 1996, efforts began to develop criteria based on the importance of the wetland to natural hydrological functions such as groundwater recharge or water quality improvement.[67]

Inclusion of a site on the list does not prejudice the sovereign rights of the territorial state, but the state must conserve, manage and use wisely the listed wetland and migratory stocks of waterfowl.[68] Promotion of conservation includes establishing nature reserves and providing adequately for their wardening.[69] The Conference of the Parties has given wide meaning to the

---

[63]   Preamble, para. 4; Ramsar Strategic Plan for 1997–2002, adopted at the Sixth Meeting of the COP (Brisbane, 1996).

[64]   Art. 2(1) and 2(4).

[65]   Recommendation 1.5 (Cagliari, 1980); Recommendation 3.1 (Regina, 1987); Recommendation 4.2 (Montreux, 1990); Recommendation VI.3 (Brisbane, 1996).

[66]   Art. 2.

[67]   Conference of the Parties, Resolution VI.3 (Brisbane,1996).

[68]   Art. 2(6).

[69]   Art. 4.

requirement of "wise use" contained in the Convention. Recommendation 3.3 (1987) defines wise use as "the sustainable use of wetlands for the benefit of mankind in a way that is compatible with maintaining the natural properties of the ecosystem," the latter being described as the physical, biological or chemical elements, such as soil, water, flora, fauna and nutrients, as well as the interactions between them. Sustainable use, in turn, is defined as the use by man of a wetland in such a way that present generations draw from it the maximum sustainable benefits while maintaining its capacity to satisfy the natural needs and aspirations of future generations. Recommendation 3.3 also sets forth guidelines for formulating and implementing wise use policies.

States parties maintain the right to add wetlands to the list, and extend the boundaries of those already included. In case of urgent national interests, a state may also delete a wetland from the list or restrict its boundaries[70] but then should compensate for the loss by creating additional nature reserves for waterfowl either in the same area or elsewhere.[71] A state without a listed wetland would cease to be a party to the Convention.

The Ramsar Convention provides for cooperation between states parties. They must consult with each other about implementing obligations arising from the Convention, especially where a wetland extends across the territories of more than one state or where there is a shared water system. At the same time, they must endeavor to coordinate and support present and future policies and regulations concerning conservation of wetlands and their flora and fauna.[72] An international register, known as the Montreux Record identifies priority sites for national and international conservation attention and is intended to guide the allocation of available funding resources. The Record is supported by a Management Guidance Procedure, adopted in 1990, to provide states parties with advice and assistance on measures to preserve threatened Ramsar sites. It usually involves an on-site visit by experts and members of the Ramsar Bureau.

The Convention contains few institutional provisions, but they are important in practice and have been supplemented by protocols and decisions of the parties. A protocol adopted in Paris on December 3, 1982 established an amendment procedure and a 1987 protocol that entered into force in 1994 formally established a Conference of the Parties (COP) as the primary Convention institution, by amendment to Article 6. The COP by majority vote may adopt general or specific recommendations to the states parties regarding the conservation, management and wise use of wetlands and their flora and fauna.[73] In its first six conferences, the states parties

---

70 Art. 2(5).
71 Art. 4(2).
72 Art. 5.
73 Art. 6.

adopted some 120 decisions to give greater precision to the definition of wetlands of international importance and standardize the information form to describe the sites. They also have produced a global classification system for all types of wetlands and guidelines on application of the concept of sustainable development and management of wetlands, established the Montreux Record, and adopted the Management Guidance Procedure. In addition the COPs produced texts on EIA, participation, public awareness, climate change, and other issues affecting wetlands.

The Secretariat of the Convention, known as the Ramsar Bureau, is financed by the parties and supervised by a nine-member Standing Committee, established in 1987, to carry out any necessary activities between meetings of the COP, provide the Bureau with guidance on implementing the Convention, and prepare COP meetings. In 1993, the states parties created a permanent Scientific and Technical Review Panel composed of seven experts to provide advice to the other Convention institutions. Finally, in 1990, the COP established a fund, now known as the Ramsar Small Grants Fund for Wetland Conservation and Wise Use. It provides developing states parties with financial support for wetlands conservation activities.

The Ramsar Convention is generally considered to be a success. By July 2003, the 136 states parties had listed 1,289 wetlands, with a total surface of more than 109 million hectares.[74] No state has withdrawn a site from the List. A large number of the sites are threatened, however, and many sites remain unprotected because they are in states that are not party to the Convention. The states parties have taken measures to address these problems and especially to encourage participation by developing countries. In 1993, the COP called on multilateral development banks and agencies to give greater priority to the formulation and adoption of coherent wetland development policies, procedures and practices directed at sustainable utilization, wise management and conservation of wetlands.[75] Other measures have been taken to develop cooperation with other treaty systems or conservation programs, including the Convention on Biological Diversity, the Convention to Combat Desertification, and the GEF. In 1997, the Bureau signed a Memorandum of Understanding with the secretariat of the Convention on Migratory Species to improve cooperation in the fields of implementation covered by both Conventions.

b. UNESCO World Heritage Convention

One of the most complete international instruments that exists in the field of conservation, UNESCO's Convention for the Protection of the World

---

[74]   For further information, *see* the Ramsar Internet site: <http://www.ramsar.org/>.

[75]   Recommendation 5.5 (1993).

Cultural and Natural Heritage[76] is based on a recognition that parts of the cultural or natural heritage of various nations are of outstanding universal interest and need to be preserved as part of the world heritage of humankind as a whole.[77] The Convention also affirms that cultural and natural heritage are increasingly threatened with destruction, not only by traditional causes of decay, but also by changing social and economic conditions. In spite of the dangers, the national protection of heritage sites often remains incomplete because of the insufficient economic, scientific, and technical resources of the country where the property is situated. Given the global interest in the world heritage, the international community must participate in its protection by granting collective assistance to complement individual state action.

For purposes of the Convention, Article 2 defines "natural heritage" to include:

— natural features consisting of physical and biological formations or groups of formations, which are of outstanding universal value from the aesthetic or scientific point of view;
— geological and physiographical formations and precisely delineated areas which constitute the habitat of threatened species of animals and plants of outstanding universal value from the point of view of science or conservation;
— natural sites or precisely delineated natural areas of outstanding universal value from the point of view of science, conservation or natural beauty.

Although it falls upon each state party to identify and delineate the different natural areas situated on its territory,[78] an international system of protection is nonetheless provided. It consists of three parts. First, cultural and natural property which forms part of the world heritage remains subject to the legislation of the state where it is located. These resources can continue to belong to public or private establishments or even to individuals as the national law provides. Thus, territorial sovereignty and property rights over elements of the world natural heritage are respected.[79]

Second, in determining the different parts of the world natural heritage, the jurisdiction of the territorial state includes both rights and obligations. Article 4 requires each state party to ensure the identification, protection, conservation, presentation and transmission to future generations of the

---

[76] Paris, Nov. 23, 1972.

[77] Significantly the Convention maintains the approach that the global heritage constitutes "property."

[78] Art. 3.

[79] Art. 6(1).

natural heritage situated in its territory.[80] The state also shall endeavor, as appropriate, to adopt a general policy to give the heritage a function in the life of the community and to integrate the protection of that heritage into comprehensive planning programs.[81] Other legal, scientific, technical, administrative and financial measures must be taken, including the creation of special services for the protection, conservation and presentation of this heritage, and research and training.[82] States parties periodically submit reports to a specially created committee on the measures which they have taken to implement the Convention.[83]

The final level of protection is international assistance. The entire international community has a duty to cooperate in the protection of the world cultural and natural heritage.[84] This duty includes an obligation not to take "any deliberate measures which might damage directly or indirectly the cultural or natural heritage."[85] The broad prohibition of indirect harm could apply to development assistance programs that affect the environment or to local activities causing transboundary pollution which results in harm to a site. Where appropriate to preserve part of the world cultural and natural heritage, a state party may have recourse to international assistance and cooperation.[86] For their part, other states parties undertake to support the requesting state in the identification, protection, conservation, and the presentation of cultural and natural heritage, recognizing that it constitutes a universal heritage. Thus, Article 7 establishes the concept of international protection of the world cultural and natural heritage, including establishment of a system of cooperation and international assistance supporting states parties in their conservation and identification efforts.

International mechanisms are established in the Convention, based on creation of an Inter-Governmental Committee for the Protection of the Cultural and Natural Heritage of Outstanding Universal Value. Better known as the World Heritage Committee, it consists of 21 members elected by the General Assembly of States Parties that meets during the General Conference of UNESCO.[87] Elected representatives must be per-

---

[80]   In the Commonwealth of Australia v. The State of Tasmania, No. C6 of 1983, 46 A.L.R. 625, 68 I.L.R. 266, the High Court of Australia considered whether these duties contained legal obligations to protect sites. In a 4–3 ruling, the Court decided the Convention obligations were legal in nature. *See* LYSTER, *supra* note 37, at 223–25.

[81]   Art. 5(a).

[82]   Art. 5.

[83]   Art. 29.

[84]   Art. 6(1).

[85]   Art. 6(3).

[86]   Art. 4.

[87]   Art. 8. The membership of the Committee was expanded from 15 to 21 in 1976.

sons qualified in the field of natural or cultural heritage.[88]

Representatives of international inter-governmental and non-governmental organizations may attend meetings of the World Heritage Committee in an advisory capacity and even public or private organizations or individuals may be invited to participate or may be consulted on particular problems.[89] The Committee also may create such consultative bodies as it deems necessary to perform its functions. According to Article 14(1), the Director General of UNESCO provides the Secretariat for the Committee.

One of the principal tasks of the Committee is the establishment, publication and dissemination of the "World Heritage List." For this purpose, every state party to the Convention must submit an inventory including documentation on the location and significance of property forming part of the cultural and natural heritage situated on its territory and which it considers of outstanding universal value.[90] Sites are listed by the Committee on the basis of criteria which it establishes, but only with the consent of the territorial state. If the listed property is claimed by more than one state, the competing rights to the property are deemed not to be prejudiced by inclusion on the list.[91] The World Heritage Committee also has the power to remove properties from the World Heritage List if they no longer meet its criteria. The possibility of de-listing acts as an incentive to compliance with the Convention's requirements.

As of 2003, 175 states are parties to the World Heritage Convention. ICOMOS (International Council on Monuments and Sites) evaluates nominations and management of cultural sites while IUCN evaluates natural heritage sites proposed for addition to the World Heritage List. The List is heavily tilted in favor of cultural heritage; of the 730 World Heritage sites listed in March 2003, only 144 are natural sites. The listed natural sites include Australia's Great Barrier Reef; the Grand Canyon, Yellowstone and the Everglades in the United States; the Galapagos Islands (Ecuador), and the Serengeti Park (Tanzania). In certain cases, like Machu Picchu in Peru, the sites qualify both as natural and as cultural heritage.

When a state party proposes a natural site for inclusion, IUCN prepares a technical report. The process can often raise the level of the site protection, by extending boundaries of those considered too small to be adequately

---

88   Art. 9.

89   Arts. 8(2) and 10(2).

90   Art. 11.

91   Art. 11. In spite of this provision, disputes arose over Jordan's nomination of the Old City of Jerusalem and its Walls and Argentina's proposal of Los Glaciares National Park. Both nominations were eventually approved. World Heritage Committee, First Extraordinary Session, UNESCO Doc. CC-81/CONF.008/2 Rev., Annex IV, para. 7; World Heritage Committee, Fifth Session, UNESCO Doc. CC-81/CONF/003/6, Annex III.

protected and therefore not eligible to be entered on the list or by recommending improved site management. To protect sites, the treaty relies in large part on the prestige associated with having sites included on the list and the enhanced international profile that results from it.

The threshold for inclusion on the World Heritage List is that the site be of Outstanding Universal Value according to criteria described in the Operational Guidelines. The criteria for natural sites require that areas be outstanding examples of:

1. Geological processes, and/or geomorphic or physiographic features;
2. On-going ecological or biological evolution for animals and/or plants of terrestrial or aquatic character;
3. Superlative natural phenomena, exceptional beauty or aesthetic importance; and/or
4. Contain significant habitats for *in situ* biodiversity conservation which have value for science or conservation.

It is possible to have a "serial nomination" that consists of two or more physically unconnected areas that are related in some manner, *e.g.*, they belong to the same geological, geomorphologic formation or the same ecosystem type. The total series should be of outstanding universal value, but not necessarily each component taken individually. Serial nominations are inscribed as a single entry on the World Heritage List, but the nominations can come in phases. Transboundary nominations are areas that span an international boundary and they also are listed as a single property. Finally, transboundary serial nominations combine both categories. They must be nominated as a single entry and should be managed jointly. Small island states in the Pacific, for example, could propose to link atolls and reefs in a larger ecosystem site.

In addition to the criteria listed above, a site must meet certain standards of integrity to be inscribed, *i.e.*, it should have a management plan or at least an operational plan describing how the site is managed pending a finalized management plan. Also the nominating state or states must submit information on available resources to ensure implementation of the plan.

Once a site is reviewed, IUCN's recommendation is given to the World Heritage Bureau, a seven-member executive body of the World Heritage Committee. The Committee itself makes the final decision to inscribe sites on the list. Periodic reporting is a part of the process after inscription and monitoring such reports can lead the state to act to avoid a site being listed as in danger. In 1994, UNESCO initiated a Global World Heritage Strategy to further protect World Heritage sites. The Strategy helps design adaptive regional action plans and themes to provide guidance on maintaining the integrity of World Heritage sites. As part of this process, in 1997, IUCN and the World Heritage Center collaborated on an inventory of all the world's wetlands, coastal and marine sites.

The World Heritage Committee also establishes and publishes a "List of World Heritage in Danger" that includes property threatened by serious and specific dangers such as the threat of disappearance caused by accelerated deterioration, large-scale public or private projects or rapid urban or tourist development projects, destruction caused by changes in the use or ownership of the land, major alterations due to unknown causes, abandonment, armed conflict, calamities and cataclysms, such as serious fires, earthquakes, landslides, volcanic eruptions, etc. (Art. 11.4). As this enumeration indicates, the territorial state itself may be the cause of the danger, or at least unable or unwilling to cope with natural or human threats, although inscription on the endangered list normally is subject to a request for assistance by the territorial state.[92] In case of urgent need, the Committee may make a new entry in the List of World Heritage in Danger and publicize such entry immediately. In 2003 there were 35 properties on the List of World Heritage in Danger.

The second principal function of the Committee is to receive and study requests for international assistance formulated by states parties to the Convention for protection, conservation, presentation or rehabilitation of any part of the world cultural or natural heritage, *i.e.*, property included or potentially suitable for inclusion on one of the Lists.[93] Requests also may be submitted for purposes of identifying cultural or natural property.[94] The Committee decides on action to be taken in response to the requests and determines an order of priorities for its operations, taking into account both the intrinsic value of the property to be protected and the ability of the state concerned to safeguard such property by its own means.[95] The Committee maintains and publicizes a list of property for which international assistance has been granted.[96]

The financial means to carry out assistance is provided through an international Trust Fund for the Protection of the World Cultural and Natural Heritage of Outstanding Universal Value, called the "World Heritage Fund."[97] The resources of the Fund derive from various sources. States parties have mandatory contributions, the amount of which is decided by the General Assembly of the States Parties to the Convention according to a uniform percentage applicable to all states, but which cannot exceed 1

---

[92] However, in 1983 the World Heritage Committee itself recommended to Senegal and Tanzania that they propose listing two sites facing dangers. World Heritage Committee, Seventh Session, UNESCO Doc. SC/83/CONF/009/8, para. 43.

[93] Art. 13(1).

[94] Art. 11(2).

[95] Art. 13(3) and (4). Quote from 3(4).

[96] Art. 13(5).

[97] Art. 15.

percent of the contribution to the regular budget of UNESCO.[98] Besides these sums, both states parties and other states can make voluntary contributions or gifts, as can international inter-governmental and non-governmental organizations, public or private bodies, and individuals.[99] The Committee may use the contributions only for defined purposes and may accept contributions limited to a particular program or project, provided no political conditions are attached.[100]

A state that seeks international assistance must submit a formal request together with information and documentation as required by the Committee. This information, supported by experts' reports whenever possible, should define the operation contemplated, the work that is necessary, the expected costs, the degree of urgency and the resources of the state.[101] Requests based upon natural disasters are given priority. Before deciding on a request, the Committee carries out such studies and consultations as it deems necessary.[102] It takes its decision by the normal majority provided for in Article 13(8), that is, two-thirds of the members present and voting.

The assistance granted can take various forms, including studies, provision of experts, technicians and skilled laborers, training of staff and specialists, supply of equipment, low-interest or interest-free loans, and, in exceptional cases and for special reasons, non-repayable grants.[103] As a general rule, only part of the cost of the necessary work is borne by the international community. The contribution of the state being assisted normally must be substantial.[104]

The project or program for which assistance is furnished is defined in an agreement between the World Heritage Committee and the recipient state. This agreement also sets forth the conditions under which the project or program operates.[105] Finally, Article 29 provides for a measure of international supervision through establishment of a state reporting system. Each state party submits reports to the General Conference of UNESCO containing information on the legislative and administrative provisions which it has adopted and other action which it has taken to apply the Convention.[106] These reports are communicated to the World Heritage Committee.[107]

---

[98]   Art. 16(1). Art. 16(2) allows a state to make a reservation to this provision at the time of ratification or accession.
[99]   Art. 15(3).
[100]   Art. 15(4).
[101]   Arts. 19 and 21.
[102]   Art. 21(3).
[103]   Art. 22.
[104]   Art. 25.
[105]   Art. 27.
[106]   Art. 29(1).
[107]   Art. 29(2).

✳As far as legal principles are concerned, the importance of the World Heritage Convention cannot be overstated. It encompasses the idea that certain property found under the sovereignty of a state has an interest beyond territorial frontiers and concerns all humanity, leading to the conclusion that such property must be conserved in the name and interest and by the care of the entire international community. As a counterpart to the responsibility of the territorial government, it is recognized that the international community itself has obligations and must assist the territorial state in the accomplishment of international objectives. The relevant legal concept which emerges is that of common heritage of mankind, a trust or a mandate exercised in the interest of present and future generations.

c. Protocols to Regional Seas Agreements

Four of the regional seas agreements have adopted protocols for the creation of marine and coastal protected areas and the protection of threatened or vulnerable species.

The 1976 Barcelona Convention for the Protection of the Mediterranean Sea against Pollution mainly concerned pollution, but the contracting parties complemented it with a Protocol Concerning Mediterranean Specially Protected Areas, adopted April 3, 1982, and replaced in 1995. The 1995 revision extended the scope of the Convention to coastal areas and modified the definition of pollution to include harm to marine flora and fauna. A new Article 10 provides for the conservation of biological diversity.

The 1995 Protocol implements the concepts and definitions of the Convention on Biological Diversity through creating specially-protected areas. They serve to safeguard representative types of coastal and marine ecosystems of adequate size to ensure their long-term viability and to maintain their biological diversity, habitats which are in danger of disappearing in their natural area of distribution, habitats critical to the survival, reproduction and recovery of endangered, threatened or endemic species of flora or fauna and sites of particular importance for their scientific, aesthetic, cultural or educational interest.[108] Each party may establish specially-protected areas in the marine and coastal zones subject to its jurisdiction and cooperation is encouraged between neighboring states.[109] The protective measures include, *inter alia*, a prohibition on dumping or discharge of wastes and other substances likely to impair directly or indirectly the integrity of the specially-protected area, regulation of the passage of ships and any stopping or anchoring, regulation of the introduction of any non-indigenous species, regulation or prohibition of the exploration of the soil or the exploitation of the subsoil, the regulation of any scientific research activity,

---

[108] Art. 4.
[109] Art. 5.

of fishing, hunting, taking of animals and harvesting of plants or their destruction. In sum, any activity or act likely to harm or disturb or which might endanger the state of conservation of the ecosystems or species is to be regulated and if necessary prohibited.[110] The parties also should use planning and management of the specially-protected areas. A list of such areas (SPAMI) exist and the party or parties concerned may submit proposals for inclusion.[111] The Protocol lists national and cooperative measures for the protection and conservation of species and prescribes the preparation of inventories of areas that contain rare or fragile ecosystems and species of fauna and flora that are endangered of threatened, preparation of guidelines and common criteria, and it imposes environmental impact assessments for planning processes concerning activities that could significantly affect protected areas.[112] The parties shall give appropriate publicity to the establishment of SPAMIs, their boundaries, applicable regulations, and to the designation of protected species and their habitats. They also are to cooperate in different fields and report on their implementation of the Protocol. The parties to the Protocol meet every two years to review implementation or management measures, make recommendations concerning scientific, administrative and legal information[113] and decide on designation of SPAMIs. The sessions also examine recommendations proposed by the meetings of national authorities, as well as the reports of state parties on application of the Protocol.

The Protocol on Protected Areas and on Wild Fauna and Flora in the East African Region supplements the Convention for the Protection, Management and Development of the Marine and Coastal Environment of the Eastern African Region. The Convention and the Protocol were both adopted in Nairobi, on June 21, 1985. Parties must take "all appropriate measures to maintain essential ecological processes and support systems, to preserve genetic diversity, and to ensure the sustainable utilization of harvested natural resources under their jurisdiction." The parties must develop national conservation strategies and may establish protected areas and marine reserves. They also must prohibit the intentional or accidental introduction of alien or new species that may cause significant or harmful changes to the region. Four Appendices list protected plant and animal species.

Similar Protocols have been adopted for the South-East Pacific (Paipa, Colombia, September 21, 1989) and for the Wider Caribbean Region (Kingston, Jamaica, January 18, 1990). Both contain provisions on the establishment of protected areas, while the latter also refers to protected species. The conservation measures required are similar to those contained in the previously-discussed Protocols.

---

110 Art. 6.
111 Arts. 8, 9.
112 Arts. 11–17.
113 Art. 14(2).

2. Regulation of Trade

Unlike the prior conventions, the Convention on International Trade in Endangered Species of Wild Fauna and Flora (CITES),[114] is not based on a spatial concept of protection, but on a given activity endangering wildlife: international trade. One of the most powerful motives for the exploitation of plant and animal species is income production, especially in poor countries lacking other major resources. Trade in wildlife is mostly from Southern to Northern countries and is estimated to have a value of up to $50 billion annually, most of it in luxury goods and products such as fur coats.[115] In Brazil alone, trade in wild animals is estimated to be worth $1 billion a year.[116] Nine of ten animals caught for sale die before reaching their destination.[117] In 1972, the record year, the exports of ivory from Kenya reached 150 tons.[118] Pharmaceutical companies also seek wild plants for the production of medicines and animals for bio-medical research. States sometimes impose quotas or duties to counter trade in animals, plants and their derivatives, but no measure of this type can be truly effective without international cooperation between exporting, transit, and importing states. The principal instrument in this regard is CITES, to which the majority of states in the world are party.

The aim of CITES is to protect endangered species by banning their trade and to regulate trade in other commercially-exploited species in order to ensure sustainable trade and economic benefits for exporting countries. CITES applies the technique of lists, in this case distinguishing three situations. Criteria for listing are reviewed periodically. In 1994, the "Everglades Criteria" affirmed the special role of range states of species in the listing process and provided specifics regarding the biological and statistical information to be taken into account.[119]

Appendix I contains all species[120] threatened with extinction that are or may be affected by trade, including such well-known animals as the tiger,

---

[114] Washington, D.C., Mar. 3, 1973. For a comprehensive discussion of the drafting history and interpretation of CITES, *see* D.S. FAVRE, INTERNATIONAL TRADE IN ENDANGERED SPECIES: A GUIDE TO CITES (1990).

[115] Peter Sand, *Commodity or Taboo? International Regulation of Trade in Endangered Species*, GREEN GLOBE YEARBOOK, 19 (1997).

[116] *Monkey Business*, THE ECONOMIST, Nov. 10, 2001, at 37.

[117] Brazil bans all trade in animals, not only endangered species, but there is problem of enforcement. Fake documents are used to get animals into neighboring countries. In 2001, representatives of Interpol, the US, CITES, Latin American governments and NGOs met to address the problem.

[118] U.S. Fish & Wildlife Service, *International Trade in Animal Products Threatens Wildlife* (1982).

[119] CITES Conference Resolution 9.24 (1994) on "Criteria for Amendment of Appendices I and II."

[120] The term "species" is not used in its scientific sense. For purposes of

leopard, whale, and many types of parrots. When the Convention entered into force on July 1, 1975, there were 450 species on the list. Since that date the number has more than doubled with the addition of many plants close to extinction. These species benefit from particularly strict regulation and states parties can authorize trade only in exceptional circumstances. The ban extends to any readily recognizable part or derivative of a specimen of listed plant or animal (Art. I(b)).[121] Convention Article III provides that the export of a specimen of any species included in Appendix I requires prior grant and presentation of an export permit issued only upon satisfaction of the following conditions:

- A Scientific Authority of the exporting state has advised that the export will not be detrimental to the survival of the species;
- A Management Authority is satisfied that the specimen was not obtained in contravention of the laws of the state for the protection of fauna and flora;
- The same Authority must be satisfied that any living specimen will be prepared and shipped in ways minimizing the risk of injury, damage to health or cruel treatment; and, finally,
- The Management Authority must be satisfied that an import permit has been granted for the specimen by the country of destination.

Importing states also bear some of the burden to ensure the effective protection of endangered species. Thus, before a state may allow the importation of any Appendix I specimen, Article III(3) requires the issuance of an import permit which may be granted only after a Scientific Authority attests that the importation is for purposes that are not detrimental to the survival of the species. The Scientific Authority also must be satisfied that the proposed recipient is suitably equipped to house and care for any living specimen. Finally, the Management Authority of the importing state must be satisfied that the specimen is not to be used for primarily commercial purposes.

The re-exportation of a specimen belonging to an Appendix I species also requires a permit confirming that the specimen was imported into the state in accordance with the provisions of the Convention, that its trans-

---

the Convention, it includes sub-species and any higher taxon, such as a genus, family or order. Some Appendix listings include entire orders of mammals, such as all primates, and all birds.

[121] The Conference of the Parties (COP) has adopted several resolutions to clarify what is meant by "readily recognizable." In particular, if a label, mark, or name indicates that a product is part of or derivative from a CITES protected species, the identification will be taken as true even if it is mistaken or intentionally misleading. Conf. 9.6.

portation will be safe, and that an import permit has been granted for any living specimen. Finally, Article III(5) provides that the introduction of any specimen of a marine species requires the authorization of the importing state, based on a finding that the introduction will not be detrimental to the species, that the recipient has the facilities to care for any living specimen and that the specimen is not to be used for primarily commercial purposes.

Each state party must designate one of more Scientific Authorities to give the required opinions, and one or more Management Authorities competent to grant permits or certificates.[122] Article IX requires the designation of the Management Authority at the time of ratification or accession, and provision of the name and address of the Authority to all other Parties.

Trade in Appendix II species, those which are not currently threatened with extinction but which may become so and species upon which they are dependent, is regulated by Article IV. The requirements are less strict than those of Article III. The conditions of export, like those for Appendix I specimens, require a permit based upon an opinion of the Scientific Authority that the export will not be detrimental to the survival of the species, proof to the Management Authority's satisfaction that the specimen was not obtained in violation of the state's laws for the protection of fauna and flora, and evidence that the specimen will be properly transported. The Scientific Authority monitors both the granting of permits and the actual exports. If this Authority determines that the export should be limited to maintain the species at a level within the ecosystem above the Appendix I level, it advises the Management Authority of suitable measures to take to limit the grant of export permits.

The import of an Appendix II specimen requires only prior presentation of either an export permit or a re-export certificate. Re-export, however, requires certification of the Management Authority that the specimen was imported in accordance with the Convention and that any living specimen will be properly transported, to minimize the risk of injury, damage to health or cruel treatment. For importation of marine species, the Management Authority can grant a permit based upon annual quotas established on advice of the Scientific Authority in consultation with other national or international scientific authorities.[123]

It is clear that for species appearing on Appendix II, strict limitations on imports do not exist and specimens can be brought in for commercial purposes. However, the aim of the Convention is to control the latter. Over time, the number of species contained in Appendix II has become extremely

---

[122] On the amount of evidence required in order to determine whether or not export of a specimen will be detrimental to the survival of the species, *see Defenders of Wildlife, Inc. v. Endangered Species Scientific Authority*, 659 F.2d 168 (D.C. Cir.), *cert. denied*, 454 U.S. 963 (1981).

[123] Art. IV(7).

high, especially after adoption of subsequent modifications to the list. There are thousands of items listed, including nearly all 330 species of parrots and 30,000 species of orchids.

Appendix III lists those species that one state party identifies as being subject to regulation within its jurisdiction in order to prevent or restrict exploitation, and for which it needs the cooperation of other parties to control trade.[124] Article V provides that export of a specimen of any species from a state that listed the species in Appendix III requires the prior grant and presentation of an export permit. Permits are subject to virtually identical conditions to those required for Appendix II specimens. Import of a specimen of an Appendix III species requires prior presentation of a certificate of origin, and, if the specimen comes from a state that listed the species, an export permit.

Appendix III thus allows each state to obtain the aid of other states, potential importers of the specimens that the exporting state seeks to protect and conserve. Canada listed the moose, signaling to other states that it is illegal to import a moose or products made from it without a permit issued by the Canadian authorities. This procedure has not been utilized widely. In the first decade of the Convention's application, only a dozen states listed approximately 150 species on Appendix III. The reason for this may lie in the extensive listings already contained in the first two appendices. Although Article VI provides for a standard export permit according to a model in Appendix IV, controlling trade in the tens of thousands of species listed by CITES is difficult at best. In addition, listing is not appropriate if domestic legislation is adequate to protect the species. Finally, states may be unwilling to lose unilaterally the income derived from trade in a particular species without similar measures being taken by other exporting states. This would be reflected in a preference for listing a species in one of the first two Appendices rather than the third.

It is clear that enforcement measures which state parties must take and exceptions to them are particularly important to achieve the purposes of the Convention. In this regard Article VII contains a series of flexible provisions and authorizes exemptions for specimens of certain species that were raised in captivity as household pets, or plants artificially propagated for commercial purposes. Exemptions also are granted for non-commercial loans, donations or exchanges of certain plants between scientists or scientific institutions, as well as for the movement of specimens which form part of a zoo, circus, menagerie, or exhibition. However, conditions are imposed, principally relating to the humane treatment of the specimens. In contrast, Article XIV specifically permits a state party to take stricter measures through domestic legislation or international regulation. To enforce the

---

[124]   Art. 2(3).

Convention, states must take measures penalizing prohibited trade and providing for confiscation or return to the state of export of any specimens illegally imported, with specified protection for living specimens.[125]

The CITES controls apply to all trade in listed specimens, even to trade conducted between CITES parties and non-parties. Article X provides that CITES states may accept "comparable documentation" on import or export issued by the competent authorities in non-party states, provided that it conforms to CITES requirements to a substantial degree. The applicability of CITES to non-parties has encouraged adherence to the treaty because non-compliance procedures have been applied to parties and non-parties alike. States therefore have sought to participate in discussions that concern them.

The Convention institutions are a Conference of States Parties[126] and a Secretariat.[127] The first meets every two years to examine progress in the restoration and conservation of protected species.[128] It receives and examines any report presented by the Secretariat or by a state party. Its role is particularly important in adapting the Convention to evolving conditions, especially in amending Appendices I and II. Amendments, which may involve transferring a species from one list to another as it becomes more or less endangered, are adopted by a two-thirds majority of parties present and voting at a Conference of the parties. The amendments enter into force 90 days after the session for all parties except those that file a reservation with respect to the amendment within 90 days from notification. In 1994, the COP adopted a system of classifying its rules as "resolutions," "revised resolutions" and "decisions." Although none of the categories of resolutions are legally binding, they are authoritative and influential.

A Standing Committee of the Conference, established in 1979, operates between meetings of the Conference. It has been instrumental in developing methods of collective action against non-compliance, based on Article XIV(1), which allows parties to take stricter domestic measures than those provided by the treaty. In a number of cases, the Committee has recommended that all parties apply the article collectively, if temporarily, against individual countries found to be in persistent non-compliance,[129] including

---

125   Art. VIII.

126   Art. XI.

127   Art. XII.

128   The meetings are open to observers from the United Nations, non-party states, specialized agencies and IAEA as well as non-governmental organizations and other intergovernmental bodies.

129   *E.g.*, United Arab Emirates, 1985–1990; Thailand, 1991–2. CITES Secretariat (1991), Notification to the Parties No. 636 (Apr. 22) (recommending the ban) and No. 673 (Apr. 2, 1992) (lifting the ban). Italy, 1992–3, CITES Secretariat (1992), Notification to the Parties No. 675 (June 30) (recommending the ban), and No. 842 (Apr. 18,1995) (lifting the ban).

non-parties.[130] Unilateral action also has been taken by states parties to enforce CITES protections.[131]

The Secretariat of the Convention, provided by the Executive Director of UNEP in Geneva, has extensive powers and functions. In addition to the normal duties of multilateral international organizations, the Secretariat undertakes scientific and technical studies, reviews the reports of states parties, and may request further information as necessary to ensure implementation of the Convention. It periodically publishes and distributes to the parties the lists contained in the Convention's Appendices and makes recommendations for implementing the aims and provisions of the Convention.[132] The role of the Secretariat is particularly important in monitoring compliance with the agreement. Each state party must maintain records of trade in specimens of species listed in the different Appendices to the Convention and must prepare periodic reports on enforcement of the Convention. When the Secretariat considers, in light of the information received, that a species listed in Appendix I or II is affected adversely by trade or that provisions of the Convention are not being effectively implemented, it communicates the information to the Management Authorities of the state or states concerned. In turn, the states must inform the Secretariat of any relevant facts and, where appropriate, propose remedial action. The Secretariat also may authorize an inquiry. The information provided or acquired by an inquiry is reviewed by the next Conference of the Parties which can make recommendations that it deems appropriate.[133]

As a whole, the Washington Convention functions well, although few states have enacted the full panoply of national measures required to give effect to all aspects of the Convention and resolutions and decisions of the Conferences. The record of national reporting also is mixed. In contrast, however, many early reservations have been withdrawn and COP interpretations have narrowed exceptions while allowing flexibility to accommodate short-term special needs. The flexibility of CITES has been demonstrated by the action of parties to CITES in adopting an innovative approach to shifting species from Appendix I to II, in part to respond to controversy over the listing of the African elephant. The use of "annotations" to the listing provides added protection by imposing specific restrictions to types of trade when a species is moved from Appendix I to Appendix II. Three well-known examples may be cited: the 1987 transfer of certain populations of vicuña included an annotation permitting only trade in wool sheared from live ani-

---

[130]   El Salvador, 1986–7, and Equatorial Guinea, 1988–92. In both cases the ban was lifted after the countries became CITES states parties.

[131]   *See* Sand, *supra* note 115, at 22 (discussing, *inter alia*, U.S. actions against Singapore and Taiwan and EU actions against Indonesia).

[132]   Art. 12.

[133]   Art. 13.

mals; the South African population of white rhinoceros appeared on Appendix II with an annotation allowing trade in live animals and sport hunted trophies. Finally, the African elephant populations of Zimbabwe, Botwana and Namibia were transferred to Appendix II subject to an annotation for trade in ivory stockpiles and skins. These measures help induce wider cooperation by tolerating a measure of deviation from strict treaty norms. The combination of incentives and disincentives helps achieve some of the Convention goals, but create major enforcement problems.[134]

As a result of concerns about annotations undermining the overall effectiveness of CITES, the 2000 CITES meeting adopted Conference Resolution 11.21 regulating their use. The resolution calls on parties to specify the conditions for import, export and re-export of species whose listing is annotated and directs the Secretariat and the Standing Committee to investigate reports of illegal trade in such species. If the Standing Committee finds illegal trade, it can request parties to suspend trade in that species and ask the depository government to submit a proposal to return the species to Appendix I.

Debate over the economics of banning trade and the rising populations of listed species have led to controversy and alternative legal arrangements, exemplified by actions in regard to the African elephant. Throughout the 1980s, elephant populations declined drastically, principally due to trade in ivory. The 1989 CITES Conference placed the elephant on Appendix I, despite the concerns of some states with significant elephant populations.[135] Elephant herds soon began to increase and beginning in 1992, Southern African states sought to remove the species from on Appendix I in order to engage in managed trade. In 1997, the CITES conference moved to Appendix II the African elephant populations of Namibia, Zimbabwe and Botswana, but kept all other populations on Appendix I. The Appendix II listing was annotated to permit only an experimental sale of one consignment to Japan and it was subject to a number of conditions. In particular, CITES required that the ivory not be the product of poaching and that revenue from the sale be used for elephant conservation.[136] South Africa's elephant

---

[134] *See, e.g.,* Holly Dublin, Tom Milliken, & Richard Barnes, *Four Years After the CITES Ban: Illegal Killing of Elephants, Ivory Trade and Stockpiles,* Report of the IUCN/SSC African Elephant Specialist Group (1995); Patty Storey, *Development vs. Conservation: The Future of the African Elephant,* 18 WILLIAM & MARY J. ENVTL. L. 375 (1994); Andrew Heimert, *How the Elephant Lost His Tusks,* 104 YALE L.J. 1473 (1995); James Barnes, *Changes in the Economic Use Value of Elephants in Botswana: The Effect of International Trade Prohibitions,* 18 ECOLOGICAL ECON. 215 (1996).

[135] Japan reserved the right to import raw ivory from African CITES parties.

[136] Tenth Meeting of the Conference of the Parties, 1997, Decisions 10.1, 10.2. The sale of the ivory produced revenues of approximately $5 million. *See* DAVID HUNTER ET AL., INTERNATIONAL ENVIRONMENTAL LAW AND POLICY 1018 (2d ed. 2002).

population was moved to Appendix II at the 2000 Conference. In exchange, all four African states agreed to a two-year zero quota in sales.

Even before CITES moved the elephant populations from Appendix I to Appendix II, Southern African states took action to resume marketing of ivory. In mid-1991, five southern cone states signed an Agreement to Establish a Southern African Center for Ivory Marketing (SACIM).[137] Although the title refers only to ivory, the preamble recognizes the advantages of controlling within the region the trade in elephant ivory and other wildlife products, in order to acquire the maximum revenues from sales of wildlife products. Moreover, Article XVIII provides that the Board of the Center may extend the agreement to other wildlife populations and products. The Center, located in Botswana, is created to establish, monitor and control a simple system for the marketing of ivory and other elephant products and a central facility to receive, store, inventory, mark and sell elephant products (Art. III). It also acts to strengthen elephant product manufacturing and processing industries and markets and facilitate the sale of elephant products. The Center is the repository for information on all aspects of elephant management and conservation, population statistics, movements and behavior, as well as relationships between elephants and their habitats. It will assist in determining the optimum elephant populations for the member countries and assist in elephant population management and conservation.

Pursuant to Article IV, elephant product sales are centralized. Each country agrees to monitor elephant populations and market ivory only through the Center, except for hunting trophies and small processing by nationals. The country will not exceed the annual ivory production determined for it by the Center. In turn, the Center remits to each member the proceeds generated by the sale of products which originated from that member, less fees for the Center (Art. III(e)). All importation of elephant products and the exportation of commercial shipments of worked ivory are prohibited until the Center decides otherwise (Art. 4(f)). Whole ivory tusks can be exported only to the Center, which shall determine the annual ivory production for each member state. The states will maintain a register and mark the ivory. No private dealing in or resale of unworked ivory is permitted. States are not only to take legislative, administrative or other measures necessary according to the Agreement or recommended by the Center, but shall consider increasing penalties for poaching and smuggling.

The Center is governed by a Board, made up of one representative of each member state selected from senior officers of the Department of Wildlife. It meets twice each year and decisions are taken by consensus. The Board appoints a director who is the chief executive of the Center. To ensure that the Center can function, each state contributes to the Capital

---

[137] June 20, 1991 (Lilongwe, Malawi). The states signing the agreement are Botswana, Malawi, Namibia, Zambia and Zimbabwe.

Fund for its establishment and operation. An Elephant Conservation Fund, generated by the sale of ivory and other elephant products, will be used for the promotion of elephant conservation and management.

3. Driftnet Fishing

Several legal measures on both global and regional levels attempt to combat large scale pelagic driftnet fishing. At the beginning of the regulatory efforts, more than 1,000 fishing vessels used large-scale pelagic driftnets of up to 48 kilometers (30 miles), nets that were often referred to as "walls of death" because they captured everything in their path. In late 1989, 21 countries adopted the International Convention for the Prohibition of Fishing with Long Driftnets in the South Pacific.[138] Open to members of the South Pacific Forum and states responsible for territories within the Convention area, it attached additional instruments for signature by distant-water fishing nations and by all Pacific rim countries who wished to express their solidarity with the objectives of the Wellington Convention (Noumea, October 20, 1990).

The Convention requires each party to take measures to prohibit the use of driftnets more than 2.5 kilometers long and the trans-shipment of driftnet catches. Each party may take more stringent measures against driftnet fishing activities, such as prohibiting the landing of driftnet catches within its territory, the processing of driftnet catches in facilities under its jurisdiction, or the importing of fish or fish products caught by means of driftnets. States parties also may restrict port access and port servicing facilities for driftnet fishing vessels and prohibit the possession of driftnets on board any fishing vessel within areas under its fisheries jurisdiction. More generally, each party agrees to take measures consistent with international law to restrict driftnet fishing in the Convention area and to take measures leading to the withdrawal of good standing of registered vessels engaging in driftnet fishing activities. All parties undertake to collaborate in surveillance and enforcement and to consult on matters relating to driftnet fishing activities.

The United Nations General Assembly, upon the entry into force of the Wellington Convention, called for a ban on driftnet fishing as of December 31, 1992,[139] and specifically called for individual and collective measures to prevent driftnet fishing operations on the high seas. On April 14, 1991, New Zealand adopted legislation to prohibit driftnet fishing activities in its EEZ and to implement the Wellington Convention. The law is more stringent than the Convention, targeting driftnets more than one kilometer in length and giving broad powers of search, arrest and seizure to enforcement

---

[138] Wellington, Nov. 24, 1989.
[139] G.A. Res. 46/215, Dec. 20, 1991.

officers. Persons convicted of an offense under the act are subject to fines. The United States adopted similar legislation, called the High Seas Driftnet Fisheries Enforcement Act, on November 2, 1992. The Act denies port privileges and establishes sanctions for high seas driftnet fishing. The President also is required to consult with the government of countries whose fishing fleets still engage in driftnet fishing. If the consultations are not satisfactorily concluded within 90 days, the President must direct the Secretary of the Treasury to prohibit the importation into the United States of fish and fish products and sport fishing equipment from that nation. The denial of port privileges and sanctions remain in effect until certification to the President and Congress that such nation has terminated driftnet fishing.

The South Pacific Forum Fisheries Agency took similar action when it adopted a Treaty on Cooperation in Fisheries Surveillance and Law Enforcement in the South Pacific Region at its 23rd session.[140] The objective of the Treaty is to promote maximum effectiveness in regional surveillance and enforcement through cooperation between countries on a reciprocal or joint basis. The Agreement, Article IV, provides for the implementation of harmonized minimum terms and conditions of fisheries access. The parties agree they will not license any fishing vessel that is not registered by the South Pacific Forum Fisheries Agency and they agree to exchange information to the extent permitted by the national laws on the location and movement of fishing vessels, licensing and fisheries surveillance and law enforcement activities (Art. V). Article VI provides for a Subsidiary Agreement on mechanisms of cooperation in surveillance and enforcement, allowing reciprocal enforcement in the territorial seas and archipelagic waters of the parties. Extradition procedures and other criminal procedure matters also may be detailed in further agreements (Arts. VII, VIII).

The Council of Fisheries Ministers of the EC in 1998 agreed to ban driftnet fishing on the high seas by all vessels flying the flags of EU states as of January 1, 2002.[141] An earlier regulation permitted driftnets of up to 2.5 km had proven impossible to enforce. A further ban is proposed for the Baltic Sea from 2007 in order to protect dolphins and porpoises. In the meantime, driftnets longer than 1.55 miles should be prohibited. As part of the proposal, fishing nets would also have to use acoustic warning devices to warn marine mammals away.

---

[140]   Niue, July 9, 1992.

[141]   Council Regulation 1239/98, June 8, 1998 amending Regulation 894/97 laying down certain technical measures for the conservation of fishery resources, O.J. L 171 (6/17/98), at 1–4.

F. Protection of Species or Groups of Species

A large number of treaties aim at protecting specific animal species, such as polar bears, or at conserving groups of species, like whales, seals, and birds.[142] The treaties often are concluded on a regional basis because of the localization of the species, but states that are not habitat states sometimes adhere to the agreements for reasons of principle. The European Community also has enacted regulations and directives on this subject, for example the EC regulation establishing a licensing scheme for the importation of products derived from whales[143] and directive 79/409 of April 2, 1979, concerning the conservation of wild birds.[144]

1. Marine Living Resources

In recent years marine biodiversity has become increasingly threatened due to pollution from land-based and other sources, over-exploitation, the introduction of alien species, coastal development, and global climate change and ozone depletion.[145] The 1958 Convention on Fishing and Conservation of the Living Resources of the High Seas addressed only a few of the problems, being focussed on commercial fishing, and it has been largely superceded by the 1982 Convention on the Law of the Sea (UNCLOS) and other agreements. At UNCED, Agenda 21 called for a commitment to conserve and sustainably use the marine living resources, to maintain biological diversity and productivity, cooperate on information exchange and data requirements, and to provide support to developing countries (Chapter 17.46).

The problem of over-fishing has received far more attention than the problem of marine biodiversity because of the global importance of fisheries and the urgency of the threat to them. More than 44 percent of the world's commercial fish stocks are estimated to have reached their yield limit.[146] The decreasing number of fish has led to conflicts between the

---

[142] To date, there are no instruments devoted to specific species of wild plant life.

[143] Regulation 348/81, Jan. 20, 1981; O.J. L 39 (2/12/81).

[144] O.J. No. L 103 (4/21/79).

[145] Endangered marine species include: Mediterranean monk seal, sea cucumber, blue whale, blue fin tuna, Stellers sea cow, Caribbean monk seal, black coral, giant clam, Northern right whale, estuarine crocodile, starlet sea anemone, Christmas frigate bird, Galapagos flightless cormorant, Spot-billed pelican, Townsend's shearwater.

[146] FAO, STATE OF THE WORLD FISHERIES AND AQUACULTURE 18 (1995).

approximately seventy coastal states and ten long-range fishing states competing for the resources. In fact, 20 countries account for 80 percent of the world marine catches, nearly all of which occurs in areas under national jurisdiction. A Report of the U.N. Secretary-General in March 2000 on Oceans and the Law of the Sea calls illegal, unregulated and unreported fishing one of the most severe problems facing global fisheries.[147]

The interdependence of over-exploited fishing resources with non-target species and ecosystems has led to the conclusion of international legal instruments of broader scope, including within them new principles, norms, decision-making procedures, and institutional arrangements to address marine biodiversity generally, from bans on driftnet fishing to codes of conduct for responsible fishing.

The United Nations Convention on the Law of the Sea (UNCLOS), adopted December 10, 1982, in Montego Bay, contains important provisions relating to conservation of marine living resources. Its general rule affirms coastal state authority to ensure the conservation of biological resources in the zones over which it exercises jurisdiction, *i.e.*, the territorial sea, the exclusive economic zone, and the continental shelf.[148] The exclusive economic zone, because of its size and above all because of its objectives, is of primary importance in conservation of the marine living resources. In this region the coastal state has sovereign rights to explore and exploit, conserve and manage the natural resources, but it also has the duty to ensure, through proper conservation and management, that the maintenance of the living resources is not endangered by over-exploitation.[149] UNCLOS Article 61 requires the coastal state to cooperate in appropriate cases with international organizations to achieve the goal of maintaining or restoring populations of harvested species at levels that can produce the maximum sustainable yield. An important innovation reflecting a broad ecological perspective is the requirement that the coastal state take into consideration the effects of its measures on species associated with or dependent upon harvested species, in order to maintain or restore these populations above levels at which their reproduction may become seriously threatened.

The extent of the zones under coastal state jurisdiction creates problems with respect to marine animals that traverse more than one nation's zones. The Convention designates five categories:

(a) Stocks of species that occur within the exclusive economic zones of several coastal states or within the economic zone of one and an area adjacent to that zone, are regulated by conservation measures

---

[147]   Report of the Secretary-General, Oceans and the Law of the Sea: G.A. 55th Sess., U.N. Doc. A/55/61 at 26 (2000).

[148]   Arts. 21(1)(d), 56(1), 61–65, 73(1) and 77.

[149]   Arts. 56(1) and 61(2).

agreed upon by the concerned states either directly or through appropriate international organizations.[150]

(b) For highly migratory species, such as tuna, whales, and sharks, the coastal states and other states whose nationals fish in the adjacent regions, shall seek agreement on the measures necessary to conserve and develop these species.[151]

(c) Marine mammals can be regulated more strictly by the coastal state or a competent international organization. Measures may include prohibition, limitation or regulation of the exploitation of such animals.[152]

(d) Anadromous species, those fish such as salmon, which reproduce in rivers and live in the sea, pose complex legal problems. Article 66 provides as its basic principle that states in whose rivers these stocks originate have the primary interest in and responsibility for them. They must ensure their conservation by establishing appropriate regulatory measures for fishing in all waters to the outer limits of the exclusive economic zone. For fishing outside the exclusive economic zone, the states concerned consult in order to establish the terms and conditions of such fishing, giving due regard to the conservation requirements and the needs of the state of origin. In effect, the treaty discourages fishing for these species on the high seas. When the stocks of anadromous species migrate into or through the waters of a state other than the state of origin, both states shall cooperate with regard to conservation and management of the species.

(e) Catadromous species, such as eels, reproduce in the sea and live in other environments. According to Article 67, the coastal state in whose waters these species spend the greater part of their life cycle has responsibility for their management and shall ensure their ingress and egress. These species may not be harvested on the high seas and fishing for them within the exclusive economic zone is regulated by the general regulations governing the zone. Where such species migrate through the waters of more than one state, rational management must be assured by agreement between the states.

The rules adopted by the coastal state to ensure the conservation and management of the marine living resources in its exclusive economic zone can be enforced through boarding, inspection, arrest and judicial proceedings. However, the measures cannot include imprisonment or any other form of corporal punishment.[153]

---

[150] Art. 63.
[151] Art. 64.
[152] Art. 65.
[153] Art. 72.

On the continental shelf, the Convention considers only the exploration and exploitation of natural resources and not their conservation. "Natural resources" includes living organisms belonging to sedentary species which are either immobile on or under the seabed or are unable to move except in constant physical contact with the seabed or subsoil.[154] However, considering the objectives of the Convention regarding marine living resources, stated in the Preamble, and the conservation measures required for all other marine zones, including the high seas, it seems that the coastal state also should take conservation measures with regard to these species.[155]

Conservation of marine living resources may be seen, therefore, as a general obligation, in particular as concerns the high seas. Since no territorial jurisdiction can be exercised on the high seas because of the freedoms which exist in this area, all states have the obligation to take measures applicable to their nationals, which may be necessary for the conservation of the living resources of the high seas, and to cooperate with each other in this regard.[156] Measures must be designed, on the best scientific evidence available, to maintain or restore populations at levels which can produce the maximum sustainable yield, qualified by relevant environmental and economic factors. The interdependence of stocks must be taken into consideration in order not to threaten associated or dependent species.[157] Finally, Article 120 affirms that measures taken to protect marine mammals in the exclusive economic zone may also apply to the high seas.[158]

a. Fisheries

In 1999, scientists estimated that fish is the primary source of protein for close to 950 million people and is the source of employment for about one quarter of that number. Fish resources are a major component of international trade. In some developing countries fish represent up to 80 percent of the total exports. From 1950 to 1970, fisheries production increased by approximately 6 percent annually, trebling from 18 to 56 million tons. During the 1970s the rate of increase declined to about 2 percent and in the 1990s fell to zero. Declining catches have led to job losses and higher prices for fish.

---

[154] Art. 77.

[155] This view is supported by Art. 5 of the 1958 Convention on the Continental Shelf, which provides that the exploration of the continental shelf and the exploitation of its natural resources must not result in any unjustifiable interference with conservation of the living resources of the sea.

[156] Arts. 117 and 118.

[157] Art. 119.

[158] On the problem of protection marine living resources, *see* C. de Klemm, *Living Resources of the Oceans, in* THE ENVIRONMENTAL LAW OF THE SEA (IUCN, 1981).

Efforts to enforce fishing limits have been undermined by the re-flag-ging of fishing vessels under the flags of states that are not parties to inter-national high seas fisheries agreements. On November 24, 1993, the 27th FAO Conference approved an Agreement to Promote Compliance with International Conservation and Management Measures by Fishing Vessels on the High Seas. The Agreement is designed to deal with re-flagging by reinforcing the responsibility of states in respect to vessels fishing on the high seas. It also aims to promote the free flow of information on high seas fishing operations. States are required to take such measures as are neces-sary to ensure that fishing vessels entitled to fly their flag do not engage in any activity that undermines the effectiveness of international conservation and management measures (Art. III), which are defined as measures to con-serve or manage one or more species of living marine resources that are adopted and applied in accordance with rules of international law reflected in UNCLOS (Art. 1(b)). States parties are required to provide the FAO with basic information on each fishing vessel entered in the record of fishing ves-sels entitled to fly its flag and authorized for use on the high seas. The FAO must circulate and provide the information to any fisheries organization. The Agreement has the potential to provide a data bank on fishing opera-tions for all vessels authorized to fish on the high seas.

The 1995 UN Straddling Stocks Agreement[159] includes the protection of marine biodiversity as one of its objectives but maintains a concern with utilization of the resources, referring specifically to maximum sustainable yield. Article 7 is characteristic, entitled "compatibility of conservation and management measures." The Agreement is concerned primarily with stocks that are beyond the limits of national jurisdiction, but several principles apply generally, including the precautionary principle, as well as the oblig-ation to coordinate conservation and management measures (Art. 7). The Agreement does not specify such measures, leaving them to be agreed at regional or sub-regional levels, but there is considerable emphasis on gath-ering and sharing scientific, technical and statistical information (Art. 14). The text also details the duties of flag states, which is understandable given the focus on high seas activities. In many respects, the text follows the prior FAO Agreement in requiring that states parties ensure that flag ships do not engage in any activity that might undermine the effectiveness of conserva-tion and management measures. States are not to authorize or license high seas fishing unless they can ensure compliance with applicable national, regional and international regulations. The Agreement foresees a system of boarding and inspections within the regional or sub-regional framework

---

159 Agreement for the Implementation of the Provisions of the United Nations Convention on the Law of the Sea of Dec. 10, 1982 relating to the Conservation and Management of Straddling Fish Stocks and Highly Migratory Fish Stocks, New York, *adopted* August 4, 1995, *opened for signature* December 14, 1995.

followed by sanctions imposed by the flag state, although it requires states parties to exercise their rights in a manner that would not constitute an abuse of right (Art. 34). Finally, Article 33 reveals a concern about the problem of "free riders," requiring states parties to encourage non-parties to join the Agreement and mandating states parties to take measures consistent with the Agreement and international law "to deter the activities of vessels flying the flag of non-parties which undermine the effective implementation of this Agreement."

Numerous regional instruments adopted throughout the 20th century aim at proper management of fish stocks.[160] Twenty-five Pacific states adopted a Convention on the Conservation and Management of Highly Migratory Fish Stocks in the Western and Central Pacific Ocean in Honolulu on September 5, 2000. Its objective is to ensure, through effective management, the long-term conservation and sustainable use of such stocks in accordance with UNCLOS and the Agreement of August 4, 1995, relating to the conservation and management of straddling fish stocks and highly migratory fish stocks. Its principles include application of the precautionary approach, the protection of biodiversity in the marine environment, prevention and elimination of over-fishing and implementation and enforcement of conservation and management measures through effective monitoring, control and surveillance. Article 9 establishes a Commission which can determine the total allowable catch or total level of fishing efforts within the Convention area, adopt conservation and management measures and establish cooperative mechanisms for effective monitoring, control, surveillance and enforcement. A Technical and Compliance Committee receives reports from each member of the Commission relating to measures taken to monitor, investigate and penalize violations. In addition, a regional observer program allows boarding by independent and impartial observers authorized by the secretariat of the Commission. The activities of observers include collecting catch and scientific data, monitoring the implementation of conservation and management measures adopted by the Commission and reporting of their findings in accordance with procedures developed by the Commission. An Annex to the Convention determines the terms and conditions for fishing.

Since 1992 the European Community has regulated fishing through Community policy on fisheries and aquaculture, which governs the conservation, management and exploitation of living aquatic resources. The common fisheries policy aims to ensure the long-term viability of the fisheries sector through sustainable exploitation of living aquatic resources based on sound scientific advice and the precautionary approach. A

---

[160]   One of the earliest agreements is the U.S.-Great Britain Convention for Preservation of the Halibut Fishery (Mar. 22, 1923). The Convention was replaced by a new agreement in 1959.

Regulation of December 20, 2002,[161] seeks to achieve sustainable exploitation in the waters under the jurisdiction of the member states through managing fisheries on a multi-annual basis within safe biological limits. Multi-annual management plans should establish targets and provide for coherent measures that include limiting the environmental impact of fishing. The EC Council is to adopt, as a priority, recovery plans for fisheries which are exploiting stocks above safe biological limits. Member states shall put in place measures to adjust the fishing capacity of their fleets in order to achieve a stable and enduring balance between fishing capacity and fishing opportunities. They also shall take the inspection and enforcement measures necessary to ensure compliance with common fishery policy norms in the waters subject to their jurisdiction as well as enforcement measures relating to ships flying their flag and their nationals relating to fishing activities outside Community waters. They shall ensure that appropriate measures are taken, including administrative action or criminal proceedings, against natural or legal persons who violate the rules of the common fisheries policy. Such measures may include fines, seizure of prohibited fishing gear and catches, sequestration or temporary immobilization of the vessel, suspension or withdrawal of the license. An annex to the Regulation determines the conditions of access to the coastal waters of different member states.

Another EC Regulation, adopted December 16, 2002,[162] establishes specific access requirements and associated conditions applicable to fishing for deep-sea stocks in specified waters. It provides for a special fishing permit to be issued to vessels fishing for deep-sea species and for limiting fishing efforts in order to secure precautionary management of the stocks in the deep sea.

As discussed in the previous chapter, most of the cases before the International Tribunal on the Law of the Sea have concerned illegal fishing and the requirement of prompt release of seized vessels. One of the more important cases, the *Case on the Conservation and Sustainable Exploitation of Swordfish Stocks in the South-Eastern Pacific Ocean* (Chile v. EC) was discontinued after the parties reached agreement. Another, *The Grand Prince Case* (Belize v. France) ended when it was discovered that Belize was not the flag state of the seized ship. In the southern oceans, 1980 CCAMLR devotes considerable efforts to protecting the Patagonian toothfish which is illegally fished throughout the area. Several ships have been arrested, while data received under the toothfish catch documentation scheme suggests that data is being misreported and the actual catch levels in CCAMLR waters may be four times higher than CCAMLR estimates.[163]

---

[161] Regulation EC No 2371/2002, O.J. L 358 (12/31/02).
[162] Regulation No 2347/2002, O.J. L 351 (12/28/02).
[163] *See* Chapter 14C.1.

Regimes for fisheries have been created rapidly in recent years with growing recognition of the threats to sustainability.[164] The conclusion of UNCLOS and the Straddling Stock Convention also stimulated action regionally and according to fish stock. In addition to the agreements discussed above, fisheries treaties include:

- Convention for the Conservation of Southern Bluefin Tuna[165]
- International Convention for the Conservation of Atlantic Tuna[166]
- Convention for the Establishment of an Inter-American Tropical Tuna Commission[167]
- Convention concerning Fishing in the Black Sea[168]
- Convention on Fishing and Conservation of the Living Resources in the Baltic Sea and Belts[169]
- Agreement for the Establishment of the Indian Ocean Tuna Commission[170]
- Convention on the Conservation and Management of Pollack Resources in the Central Bering Sea[171]
- Convention for the Conservation of Salmon in the North Atlantic[172]
- Convention for the Future Multilateral Cooperation in North-East Atlantic Fisheries[173]

---

[164] A complete list and texts of fisheries agreements is *available at* <http://www.oceanlaw.net>.

[165] Canberra, May 10, 1993.

[166] Rio de Janeiro, May 14, 1966.

[167] Washington D.C. May 31, 1949.

[168] Varna, July 7, 1959. *See also* Agreement for the Establishment of the International Organization for the Development of Fisheries in Central and Eastern Europe (Copenhagen, May 23, 2000).

[169] Gdansk, Sept. 13, 1973. The Baltic Sea Fisheries Commission focuses on more selective taking methods for cod, allowing juveniles to escape nets. It adopted a joint inspection program on an experimental basis whereby inspectors from all Baltic Sea coastal states participated in testing a uniform sea and port inspection scheme.

[170] FAO, Mar. 27, 1996. This agreement contains an inspection and control scheme with non-discriminatory at-port inspections and vessel monitoring.

[171] Washington D.C., June 16, 1994, *reprinted in* 34 I.L.M. 67 (1995).

[172] Reyjavik, Oct. 1, 1983. The Organization bases its work on scientific evidence that Atlantic salmon is in danger of extinction. It created an International Cooperative Salmon Research Program to identify and explain the causes of increased mortality and countermeasures that may be taken. It has a Plan of Action for the Application of the Precautionary Approach to Protection and Restoration of Atlantic Salmon Habitat which aims to produce a consistent, rational approach to the protection and restoration of habitat and provide a reporting procedure to monitor progress. Each contracting party was to establish a comprehensive salmon habitat protection and restoration plan and report by 2002.

[173] London, Nov. 18, 1980.

- Convention for the Conservation of Anadromous Stocks in the North Pacific Ocean[174]
- Convention on the Conservation and Management of Fishery Resources in the South-East Atlantic[175]
- Convention on the Conservation of Living Marine Resources of the High Seas of the South Pacific.[176]

The World Summit on Sustainable Development (Johannesburg, 2002) called for a representative network of marine protected areas by 2012 and restoration of depleted fish stocks by 2015. It also noted that it is critical to protect breeding and spawning sites to permit stocks to multiply. At the same meeting, Costa Rica, Panama, Colombia, and Ecuador agreed to establish such a network, by creating a marine conservation and sustainable development corridor in the marine waters of the four countries. IUCN, UNESCO, UNEP, ITTA, and NGOs like Conservation International all supported the initiative. The area, geographically known as the Panama Bight, contains four marine national parks, two of them World Heritage Sites. The initiative seeks to strengthen regional and international cooperation, capacity-building, trading and education, marine and coastal biodiversity assessments, and to create a unique cluster of marine World Heritage Sites. The Corridor is defined by its oceanography, topography of the sea-bed, and ecological interconnectedness. It is an area in which three tectonic plates merge as well as several ocean currents and various undersea mountain ranges. The Corridor also includes the Galapagos islands.

b. Marine Turtles

There are seven species of sea turtles, all of them listed on Appendix I of the Convention on International Trade in Endangered Species (CITES). The three main threats to sea turtles are incidental taking, direct hunting, and habitat loss. Like marine mammals, sea turtles must breathe at the surface, so when they are trapped in longlines, gill nets, and shrimp trawls, sea turtles drown. Since the 1970s, the incidental take of turtles in shrimp trawls has been identified as the single greatest cause of sea turtle mortality in

---

[174] Moscow, Feb. 11, 1992. Created in 1992, it has a Committee on Enforcement that uses patrols in the convention area through joint arrangements between the parties. Through the use of overflight, patrols were able to identify illegal drift-net fishing in the Russian EEZ. The ships were caught and escorted to port for further action.

[175] Windhoek, Apr. 20, 2001. All four coastal states in the region signed as well as some distant water fishing nations.

[176] Santiago, Aug. 14, 2000.

commercial fisheries.[177] Most sea turtle species also have been hunted for their carapace to be used in making jewelry and ornaments. CITES protection has reduced the turtle market for these purposes, but the consumption of sea turtles for food has increased. Efforts to revive endangered populations of sea turtles have been hampered by the loss of nesting beaches. Sea turtles lay their eggs above the high tide line of beaches. Coastal development has eliminated many traditional sites.

In the early 1980s, the U.S. National Marine Fisheries Service developed a Turtle Excluder Device (TED), a device inserted into fishing gear to provide an escape hatch allowing turtles caught in a trawl net to be released, without, at the same time, releasing a significant amount of intended catch. Slanted bars guide sea turtles and other large objects out of a net through a trap door, while smaller fish swim through the bars on the device to escape the net. Early TEDs excluded 97 percent of the entrapped sea turtles, retained most shrimp, increased trawling efficiency, and reduced fish by-catch by 50–60 percent as well. The use of TEDs has resulted in significantly fewer dead sea turtles washing up on beaches. Some foreign governments have shown an interest in acquiring TED technology and in developing national TED programs and U.S agencies have provided training and promoted the transfer of TEDs technology. A 1989 amendment to the U.S. Endangered Species Act requires the U.S. government to negotiate with other countries for agreements promoting the conservation of sea turtles and, in particular, mandating the use of TEDs by their fleets if they may endanger sea turtles species protected by U.S. legislation.[178]

In 1996, the first international treaty to address the conservation of sea turtles was signed. The Inter-American Convention for the Protection and Conservation of Sea Turtles[179] establishes national sea turtle conservation programs in the signatory countries. It applies to land and maritime zones of the parties and to vessels on the high seas which they register. Complementing the CITES prohibition on international trade, parties to the Inter-American Convention are required to prohibit the intentional capture, retention, or killing of sea turtles as well as the domestic trade in sea turtles, their eggs, parts or products. Parties are required, to the extent practicable, to restrict human activities that could seriously affect sea turtles, especially during the periods of reproduction, nesting and migration, as well as protect and restore sea turtle habitat and nesting areas. Most important, in reducing to the greatest extent practicable the incidental harm and taking of sea turtles through fishing activities, parties must require the use

---

[177] K.A. BJORNDAL ed., BIOLOGY AND CONSERVATION OF SEA TURTLES 489–95 (1982).

[178] Pub. L. No. 101–162, § 609(a)(1)(2), 103 Stat. 1037 (1989), codified at 16 U.S.C. § 1537.

[179] Caracas, Dec. 1, 1996.

of appropriate gear including the use of Turtle Excluding Devices. Shrimp trawl vessels subject to a party's jurisdiction must use TEDs or other measures that are equally effective to protect sea turtles. If a party permits measures other than the use of TEDs, it must provide scientific evidence demonstrating the lack of risk to sea turtles.

The Convention creates two bodies. The Consultative Committee reviews country reports and information relating to the protection and conservation of sea turtles and their habitats, including the environmental, socio-economic and cultural impacts of conservation measures on affected communities. It recommends changes to the Convention which may be adopted at the biennial Meeting of the Parties. All decisions must be adopted by consensus. The Scientific Committee, playing a similar role to the Whaling Scientific Committee, reviews the status of sea turtle conservation efforts and proposes recommendations for enhanced protection to the Consultative Committee based on scientific data. The Convention accepts that highly migratory species can only be protected on an international level.

In the same vein, the Protocol concerning Specially Protected Areas and Wildlife (SPAW Protocol) to the Convention for the Protection and Development of the Marine Environment of the Wider Caribbean Region complements the Inter-American Convention. All six species of Caribbean sea turtle are listed in Annex II of the SPAW Protocol. On a sub-regional level, the International Agreement for the Conservation of Caribbean Sea Turtles (Tripartite Agreement, May 8, 1998), deals specifically with the Caribbean coasts of Costa Rica, Nicaragua and Panama. Two Memoranda of Understanding adopted in the context of the Bonn Convention on Migratory Species also concern sea turtles: the Memorandum of Understanding concerning Conservation Measures for Marine Turtles on the Atlantic Coast of Africa[180] and the MOU on Conservation and Management of Marine Turtles and Their Habitats of the Indian Ocean and South East Asia.[181]

c. Cetaceans

Of all the marine species exploited by man, the 80 species of cetacean, especially large whales, were the first to be over-exploited; as early as the 13th

---

[180] Abidjan, May 29, 1999, *in force* July 1, 1999.
[181] June 23, 2001, *in force* Sept. 1, 2001. Fifteen range states have signed: Australia, Cambodia, Comores, Iran, Kenya, Madagascar, Mauritius, Myanmar, Philippines, Seychelles, Sri Lanka, United Kingdom, Tanzania, United States and Vietnam.

century they had practically disappeared from the Bay of Biscay.[182] By the 1930s it was clear that whale stocks needed international protection. The technical means placed at the disposition of whale hunters—in particular factory ships—accelerated the process and today the majority of species of whales are threatened with extinction.

The international community has made somewhat belated efforts to remedy this situation, but the measures have been opposed by those countries particularly attached to whaling for reasons of history, culture and economy. In 1931 the first Convention for the Regulation of Whaling[183] attempted to limit the destruction by protecting two particularly endangered species, right whales and bowhead whales, and in seeking to regulate hunting.[184] The Convention forbid killing young whales and nursing mothers, and required utilization of as much of the entire killed whale as possible. However, no quota was established. Even so, several leading whaling states refused to accept the Convention.

The 1946 International Convention for the Regulation of Whaling[185] represented a considerable advance in the situation. It was not drafted as a conservation convention, but as a fishing treaty regulating whaling in order to prevent over-exploitation and conserve and develop whale stocks. The goal was to safeguard whales for future generations as a "great natural resource." However, dramatic and continued depletion in the number of whales and the adherence of numerous states that have ceased whaling or have never engaged in it have combined to alter the approach of the regulatory organ which the Convention created, the International Whaling Commission (IWC). The Commission is composed of one member from each contracting government, assisted by a Technical Committee and Scientific Committee which meets prior to the meeting of the full Commission. The Commission undertakes its main activities during the annual sessions where it adopts recommendations, organizes studies and inquiries on whales and whaling, collects and analyzes statistical information on the current condition and trend of whale stocks and the effects of whaling activities on these populations.[186]

The Convention applies to all whale catchers including aircraft under the jurisdiction of states parties and to "all waters" in which whaling takes place.[187] "Whale" is not defined. Although the IWC initially regulated only larger whales, since 1976 it has taken limited steps toward including smaller

---

[182]　S. Lyster, International Wildlife Law 17 (1985).

[183]　155 L.N.T.S. 349, *in force* Jan. 16, 1935.

[184]　Indigenous whaling remained exempt from limitations.

[185]　Washington, Dec. 2, 1946.

[186]　Art. 4. The Rules of Procedure allow non-parties, international organizations and non-governmental organizations to observe under certain conditions.

[187]　Art. 1(2).

cetaceans such as killer and pilot whales.[188] An annexed Schedule to the Convention contains regulations on whaling. The Commission has the power to modify the Schedule according to Article 5 of the Convention:

> by adopting regulations with respect to the conservation and uti-
> lization of whale resources, fixing (a) protected and unprotected
> species; (b) open and closed seasons; (c) open and closed waters,
> including the designation of sanctuary areas; (d) size limits for each
> species; (e) time, methods, and intensity of whaling (including the
> maximum catch of whales to be taken in any one season); (f) types
> and specifications of gear and apparatus and appliances which may
> be used; (g) methods of measurement; and (h) catch returns and
> other statistical and biological records.

Any modification, which must be adopted by a three quarters majority of the parties, enters into force 90 days after the date on which the Commission notifies the contracting states. However, each government present can submit an objection to a modification within the 90-day period; the modification thereafter enters into force only for non-objecting states.[189] The procedure has been used by whaling states in the past to override decisions of the IWC.

Two other escape clauses exist and limit protection for whales. First, Article 8 authorizes governments of states parties to grant a special permit to any of their nationals authorizing them to kill, capture, and treat whales for purposes of scientific research. All authorizations granted must be brought to the attention of the Whaling Commission whose Scientific Committee is responsible for reviewing proposed permits before they are issued. However, the Convention establishes neither the number nor the conditions for issuance of permits, leaving this to the determination of states parties. In fact, not all states have respected the Scientific Committee recommendations. The other exemption from the Convention's obligations is the permission generally accorded to indigenous populations to continue whaling. At its July 1985 session, the Commission for the first time gave a quota to the Inuits of Alaska and Greenland which could not be exceeded.

In any case, the Commission's modifications of the regulatory scheme of the Schedule have multiplied since 1949. For many years the Commission experimented with different management schemes for whales, but failed to halt the progressive disappearance of certain species and reduction of the overall numbers. Consequently, the regulations issued at the 37th annual

---

188 Whaling Convention Schedule para. 26.
189 Whaling Convention, Art. 5.

session of the Commission, held in 1985, brought considerable changes. First, the Commission declared a definitive end to commercial whaling of certain species, notably blue and gray whales, and narwhales. Second, the Indian Ocean was declared off limits to whaling, being declared a sanctuary. Third, whaling by certain particularly cruel methods was prohibited. Finally, undoubtedly the most important decision was to institute a moratorium, a suspension of all commercial whaling, beginning with the 1985–1986 season and the following period, until the Commission reexamined the situation of whales in 1990.[190] Some whaling states remained opposed to these measures and refused to adhere to them.

The Convention and Schedule provide for both national enforcement and international supervision of the obligations they impose. National inspectors have been required on whalers since 1949 and a scheme of international observers was established in 1971. The international observers are appointed by the IWC, but nominated and paid by governments.[191] They may be placed on ships or land stations of whaling countries. In addition to these measures, states must report and prevent violations of the Convention[192] and supply information on its registered ships.[193]

Strong national measures to implement the Convention have been taken by various states including the United States, which prohibits U.S. nationals or vessels from whaling on the high seas.[194] In addition, legislation authorizes and in some cases requires the U.S. government to take economic sanctions against states which violate the IWC.[195]

In 2001 a major dispute arose over Iceland's bid to rejoin the International Whaling Commission. Iceland quit in 1992 in protest over the international whaling ban. It sought readmission while announcing that it did not intend to comply with the ban on commercial whaling. The Commission, by a vote of 19–18, with one nation abstaining, decided that it had the competence to decide on the legality of Iceland's reservation and thus determine Iceland's status. Nineteen states then voted in favor of a resolution declaring that the Commission rejected Iceland's reservation, three abstained, while 16 refused to take part on the basis that the vote was illegal. Iceland rejected the vote as illegal and announced that it would not abide by it.

---

[190]   Whaling Convention, Schedule, para. 10(e). *See* E.P.L. 8 (1985).
[191]   Schedule para. 21(c).
[192]   Art. 9.
[193]   Schedule, para. 28.
[194]   Marine Mammal Protection Act of 1972 as amended, 16 U.S.C. §§ 1361–2, 1371–84, and 1401–07.
[195]   Fisherman Protective Act of 1967, 22 U.S.C. § 1978 (Supp. V 1981) and the Fishing Convention and Management Act of 1976, 16 U.S.C. § 1821(e)(2) (Supp.V 1981).

The 2003 meeting of the International Whaling Commission produced a major change in policy. On July 19, the "Berlin Initiative" created a Conservation Committee and effectively redefined the role of the Whaling Commission away from managing stocks to addressing the multiple threats to their survival. The primary objective is now to conserve whales for present and future generations. Incidental catches of marine mammals, marine pollution, heavier and faster shipping, and rising ocean temperatures due to climate change are threats today as much as the deliberate taking of whales. Pollution is especially a problem for creatures at the top of the food chain who ingest the accumulated pollutants of the ocean. While the IWC reached agreement on the creation of the Conservation Committee, the three remaining whaling states (Japan, Norway and Iceland) announced continuation of "scientific takings" permitted by the Convention.

Apart from the Whaling Convention, the 1973 Washington Convention on International Trade in Endangered Species (CITES) prohibits trade in certain kinds of whales, such as the blue whale and the narwhale, by placing them on its Appendix I list. In addition, the Bern Convention establishes strict protection for several kinds of whale. The Agreement on the Conservation of Small Cetaceans of the Baltic and North Sea,[196] concluded in the framework of the Convention on Migratory Species, is based upon recognition "that small cetaceans are and should remain an integral part of marine ecosystems." Primarily concerned with harbor porpoises, it recognizes that by-catches, habitat deterioration and disturbance may adversely affect these populations. The parties agree to cooperate to achieve and maintain a favorable conservation status for small cetaceans, according to obligations of conservation, research and management prescribed in an Annex to the Convention. The Annex contains provisions on habitat conservation and management, surveys and research, reporting and retrieving stranded specimens, legislation to prohibit intentional taking and killing of small cetaceans, and information and education of the general public. The Treaty itself requires that each party submit an annual report on the progress made and difficulties experienced in implementing the agreement. Each party may take stricter conservation measures.

Institutional mechanisms include a Secretariat and an Advisory Committee. The Secretariat summarizes national reports and facilitates the exchange of information and monitoring, as well as organizes meetings and coordinates and circulates proposals for amendments to the agreement and its Annex. The Advisory Committee provides expert advice and information on the conservation and management of small cetaceans. Each party can appoint one member of the Advisory Committee. A Meeting of the Parties is foreseen once every three years to review progress made and difficulties encountered in implementing the agreement. A lengthy list is provided in

---

[196]   New York, *adopted* Sept. 13, 1991, *opened for signature* Mar. 17, 1992.

Article 6.2.1 of organizations entitled to sent observers to the meetings of the parties. These include representatives of Secretariats of other treaties concerned with species conservation (*e.g.*, CITES, the Bonn and Bern Conventions, the Wadden Sea agreement, the International Whaling Commission), or with marine pollution (the Baltic Sea Marine Environment Protection Commission, the London Dumping Convention), as well as non-party range states, the European Community, and various non-governmental organizations (IUCN). Any other body qualified in cetacean conservation and management may request to be represented by observers and can attend unless one-third of the states parties object.

A similar Agreement on the Conservation of Cetaceans of the Black Sea, Mediterranean Sea and Contiguous Atlantic Area (Monaco, November 24, 1996) calls on parties to cooperate in creating and maintaining a network of specially-protected areas to conserve cetaceans within the framework of the regional seas agreements, to prohibit any taking of cetaceans, to regulate fisheries activities to minimize the incidental taking of cetaceans specifically by prohibiting the use of long driftnets; to require environmental impact assessments for specific activities; and to take measures for research, monitoring, training and emergency planning.

In 1992, states continuing to whale signed the Agreement on Cooperation in Research, Conservation and Management of Marine Mammals in the North Atlantic (April 9, 1992). The Agreement created a regional organization North Atlantic Marine Mammal Conservation Organization (NAMMCO) in response to the actions of the IWC. NAMMCO consists of four organs: a plenary Council, management committees, a Scientific Committee, and a Secretariat. The Council is a forum to exchange information regarding North Atlantic marine mammals; to form, coordinate and direct the management committees and coordinate requests for scientific advice; negotiate and cooperate with other organizations and non-party states. The management committees are to propose to their members measures for conservation and management and make recommendations to the Council on scientific research. The management committees can only propose action. Decisions of the Council and the management committees are to be made by unanimous vote of those present. The Agreement provides no supervisory mechanisms for monitoring implementation or verifying compliance. As a coalition of pro-whaling states, it challenges the authority of the IWC.

d. Seals

Like whales, seals were exploited very early and on a massive scale. From the end of the 19th century conflicts arose among different states whose nationals were engaged in hunting seals. In 1893, in a case involving seals of the Bering Sea, an arbitration between the United States and British Colombia, Canada, led to a series of hunting rules helping to preserve seals from extinction. Several multilateral instruments followed, including a treaty signed in 1911 between Japan, the United States, the United Kingdom and Russia. However, these instruments were concerned with conservation of the species for strictly commercial reasons. Effective measures were taken, however, in particular the prohibition of pelagic (open sea) hunting during migration—a cause of large numbers of unretrieved dead or wounded animals—and the limitation on the taking of numerous reproducing females. Like many other wildlife treaties, this one excluded aboriginal hunting from its ban on pelagic hunting. When the 1911 Treaty was drafted, the initial numbers of three to four million seals had been reduced to 300,000 animals; by 1950 the numbers had risen again to more than two million.

The Treaty of 1911 expired in 1941 and was replaced by the Interim Convention on Conservation of North Pacific Fur Seals.[197] It entered into force in October 1957 between the signatory states of Canada, Japan, the United States and the Soviet Union. Concluded for an initial period of six years, it was renewed October 8, 1963, September 3, 1969, May 7, 1976, October 14, 1980, and October 12, 1984. Several times, the agreements renewing the Convention contained modifications, but as a whole the structure of the instrument has remained intact.

The objective is the rational exploitation of the fur seals resource. The Preamble of the Convention states clearly the states' desire:

> to take effective measures towards achieving the maximum sustainable productivity of the fur seal resources of the North Pacific Ocean so that the fur seal populations can be brought to and maintained at the levels which will provide the greatest harvest year after year, with due regard to their relation to the productivity of other living marine resources of the area.

The same language reappears in Article 2 setting forth the aims of scientific research and in particular coordination of research programs. These activities play a considerable role: they cover the size of fur seal herds, migration routes, eating habits. In spite of its strong commercial focus, the Convention also serves the cause of conservation. It forbids pelagic hunting, except for limited research purposes and by Indians, Ainu, Aleutes and Eskimo inhabiting the coasts, who hunt seals in canoes without firearms, and on condition that the furs they take not be sold.[198]

One of the interesting characteristics of the instruments concerning North Pacific fur seals is the sharing of the animals taken supplemented by

---

[197] Washington, Feb. 9, 1957.
[198] Art. VII.

a system of "royalties" among the contracting parties. This scheme is related to the ban on pelagic hunting, which results in clear benefits for states in whose territory breeding grounds are located, chiefly the U.S. and USSR. To compensate the parties suffering loss due to the ban, according to Article IX(1) at the end of each season Canada and Japan receive 15 percent each of the gross number or value thereof of the seals taken by the USSR and the United States.

Article V of the Convention establishes a North Pacific Fur Seal Commission composed of one member from each party. The Commission formulates and coordinates research programs, studies the data obtained from implementation of such programs, and above all recommends appropriate measures to the parties based on the research, including measures regarding the size and composition, by sex and age, of the seals taken, and the impact on the herd. The Protocol of May 7, 1976, adds a further element to this article in allowing the Commission to suspend the taking of seals on an island or group of islands where the number of specimens falls below the level of maximum sustainable productivity. An exception is permitted in certain cases for indigenous populations. In any case, states must report annually to the Commission the number of seals they have taken.[199]

Another unusual aspect of the Convention is that it provides for enforcement on the high seas by authorized officials of the states parties, who may board and search vessels of any other state party, if the officials have reasonable cause to believe that the prohibition on pelagic hunting has been violated. After searching, if the official continues to have reasonable cause to believe that the violation has occurred, he may seize or arrest the vessel or person. However, the vessel or individual must be delivered to the national state, which has sole prosecutorial jurisdiction.[200] Finally, each state party agrees to prohibit use of its ports or harbors for any purpose in violation of the Convention.[201] The furs acquired in violation of the Convention cannot be imported or traded, with certain limited exceptions which must be marked and certified.[202] An inter-state complaint procedure is created by Article XII, which provides that if any state considers that another party is not complying with its obligation, it may notify the other states parties and they must then meet within three months to discuss remedial measures. Seals living at the opposite end of the earth are protected by the Convention for the Conservation of Antarctic Seals within the framework of Antarctic regulation.[203]

---

[199] Art. II(4).

[200] Art. VI.

[201] Art. VIII(1).

[202] Art. VIII(2).

[203] *See* Chapter 17C.1.

Numerous treaties protect marine resources by establishing closed hunting and fishing seasons, especially those aimed at the conservation of particular species. Bilateral agreements, such as the Norwegian-USSR agreement regulating hunting of seals in the North-East Atlantic (Oslo, November 22, 1957)[204] and the Canada-Norway agreement on seal hunting and conservation of the population of the North-East Atlantic (Ottawa, July 15, 1971) often foresee closed seasons. Analogous norms are inserted also in multilateral conventions like the 1972 London Agreement for the Protection of Antarctic Seals, whose annex prohibits killing or capturing seals between March 1 and August 31.

The former EEC adopted a legal instrument specifically concerned with protecting baby seals. The massacre of young seals, in particular by Canadian hunters, was graphically exposed by photographs and provoked a strong movement of public opinion in Europe, demanding governments to act. As a result, the Council of the EEC adopted a resolution on January 5, 1983,[205] followed by a Directive[206] concerning the importation into member states of furs of young seals and derivative products. According to the Directive, member states must take or maintain all necessary measures to ensure that the white furs of young harp seals and blue furs of capuchon as well as objects made from these furs are not imported for commercial purposes into their territories. The Directive does not apply to products derived from traditional hunting practices by indigenous populations.

Also in Europe, Denmark, Germany and the Netherlands have established a treaty for the Conservation of Seals in the Wadden Sea.[207] Taking the most modern approach to conservation, the Treaty regards the seals not only as irreplaceable natural resources, but also as important indicator species of the condition of the sea. Their protection thus requires treating the sea as a single unit, and addressing various issues apart from the taking of seals, *i.e.*, habitat protection and pollution of the marine waters and coastal area. The Agreement was adopted within the context of the Bonn Convention on the Conservation of Migratory Species of Wild Animals (June 23, 1979).

The Agreement applies to the habitat of the seals, meaning any part of the seas, sandbanks, and shore areas of the North Sea coasts of the three countries, essential to the maintenance of the vital biological functions of seals, including breeding, whelping, nursing, feeding or resting. The parties agree to cooperate to achieve and maintain a favorable conservation status for the seal population, developing a conservation and management plan for the seal population on the basis of scientific knowledge. The plan

---

[204] 309 U.N.T.S. 280.

[205] O.J. C 14 (1/18/83).

[206] 83/129/EEC, O.J. L 91 (4/9/83).

[207] Bonn, Oct. 16, 1990, *in force* Oct. 1, 1991.

is to be kept under review and amended when necessary on the basis of scientific research. In addition, the parties shall coordinate their research and monitoring of the seal population.

The agreement calls for each party to prohibit the taking of seals from the Wadden Sea. Permits for takings may be granted to institutions performing scientific research into seal conservation or conservation of the sea. To avoid abuse, the agreement provides that such takings are permitted "insofar as the information required for such research cannot be obtained in any other way." Diseased, weakened or abandoned suckling seals can be taken by designated institutions for nursing and later released and representatives of such institutions may kill seals which are clearly suffering and cannot survive. Any party granting exemptions must notify the other parties as soon as possible and provide them with an opportunity for review and comment. Appropriate action must be taken to suppress illegal hunting and taking of seals.

Habitat protection includes the possibility of creating protected areas and the preservation of habitats from adverse effects of human activities within or without the area of the agreement. The parties also agree to explore the possibility of restoring degraded habitats. Pollution control measures include identifying the sources of pollution, coordinating research projects on the effects on seals of certain substances, and monitoring levels of substances affecting the conservation status of the seal population. Finally, measures to increase public awareness are foreseen, as is the possibility of stricter domestic measures for the conservation of seals.

There also exist bilateral treaties concerning seal hunting, such as the agreement between Norway and the Soviet Union[208] and another between Canada and Norway,[209] both regarding the North Atlantic region. Each treaty creates a mixed commission which provides certain limits on hunting harp and hooded seals and walrus. These measures include quotas and regulation of scientific research. The practical application of these agreements has declined with the extension of national jurisdiction over marine resources to 200 miles.

Finally, it must be recalled that seals, or at least certain kinds of them, can be protected by the general multilateral conventions concerned with endangered species, principally CITES and the Bern Convention. Similarly, as a migratory species, seals benefit from the 1979 Bonn Convention and the provisions of UNCLOS. Finally, their habitats can be protected through application of the 1972 UNESCO World Heritage Convention. The appendix to the 1972 London Convention for the Protection of Antarctic Seals also establishes areas where it is forbidden to kill or capture seals.

---

[208] Oslo, Nov. 22, 1957.
[209] Ottawa, July 15, 1971.

e. Polar Bears

Little reliable information exists on the Arctic polar bear; its population is thought to have seriously declined since the 1950s. This situation provoked the five circumpolar states—Canada, Denmark (including Greenland), Norway, the United States, and the USSR—to sign an Agreement on Conservation of Polar Bears in Oslo, November 15, 1973. The Convention entered into force on May 26, 1976, and by January 25, 1978, had been ratified by all five states.

The Preamble recalls that the states of the Arctic Region have special responsibilities and special interests in relation to the protection of the fauna and flora of the region. The polar bear is a significant resource of the region which should benefit from this protection.

The Agreement not only provides for cooperation and certain common actions, but also contains concrete and precise obligations. For example, Article I prohibits the taking of polar bears, including hunting, killing, and capturing. Nonetheless, taking may be permitted for *bona fide* scientific purposes, by local people using traditional methods in the exercise of their traditional rights and in accordance with the laws of the party,[210] to prevent serious disturbance of the management of other living resources, and for conservation purposes. However, in the last two cases, the skins and other objects of value resulting from the taking cannot be made available for commercial purposes.[211] Even when takings are authorized, it is forbidden to utilize aircraft and large motorized vessels, except where the prohibition would be inconsistent with local law.

The Agreement also forbids all international trade in polar bears taken in violation of its provisions,[212] but the Washington Convention (CITES), in force for all five parties to the Agreement, already provided this means of protection because the polar bear is listed among the threatened species in Annex II.

Article II also requires action to protect the ecosystems of which the polar bears are a part, with special attention to their habitats. The management of polar bear populations, based upon national research programs, is the obligation of states parties. According to Article VII of the Agreement, research shall be conducted on management problems and coordinated, especially concerning migratory polar bear populations. The effects of long-range pollution on polar bears is certainly one issue that deserves to be studied, in addition to problems caused by oil and gas drilling.

A 2000 U.S.-Russia bilateral Agreement on the Conservation and

---

[210] Unlike other exceptions for native use, the Polar Bear treaty does not prohibit commercial use of specimens taken.

[211] Art. III.

[212] Art. V.

Management of the Alaska-Chukotka Polar Bear Population[213] seeks to further the goals of the 1973 Agreement on the Conservation of Polar Bears. The parties agree to undertake all necessary efforts to conserve polar bear habitats, particularly denning areas and those in which bears concentrate to feed or migrate (Art. IV). The agreement prohibits all taking of polar bears inconsistent with either the 1973 treaty or this agreement. According to the bilateral treaty, bears may be taken only for scientific research, for rescuing or rehabilitating orphaned, sick or injured animals, or when human life is threatened. Bears may be put on public display if they are maintained in captivity for rehabilitation and either party determines that they cannot be released into the wild.

The Agreement takes into account the subsistence needs of native peoples while affording further protection to polar bears. Native taking excludes taking of females with cubs, as well as taking cubs less than a year old and bears entering, leaving or occupying dens. The treaty also prohibits the use of aircraft or large motorized vessels or vehicles and the use of poisons, traps or snares (Art. VI.1). The Agreement does not authorize taking polar bears for commercial purposes, but allows native people when permitted by domestic law to create, sell and use traditional articles associated with native harvest of polar bears.

A U.S.-Russia Polar Bear Commission is to coordinate measures for the conservation and study of bears, promote cooperation between the parties and with native peoples, and determine annual taking limits not to exceed the sustainable harvest level (Art. VIII). Each party must monitor polar bear harvests in its territory and may take more protective measures. The Commission further enhances the role of native peoples, by requiring that in the two sections of the Commission, one Russian and the other U.S., one of the two members of each section shall be a representative of the native people and the other a representative of the government. Each section has one vote and both sections must agree on action.

2.   *Terrestrial Species*

a.   Forests

Forests are categorized as tropical, temperate, and boreal. Temperate and boreal forests constitute about half the world's forest cover, but most international attention has been given to the rapid loss of the world's tropical forests. In all, about one quarter of the world's land area outside Greenland and Antarctica are covered in forests and forests are home to between 50 and 90 percent of all terrestrial species. Forests also serve as sinks for green-

---

[213]   Oct. 16, 2000.

house gases and produce oxygen for the planet. These ecological services of forests are difficult to value and to contrast with the revenues produced when trees are cut.

The demand for forest products has grown rapidly in recent years, from the production of lumber and paper to collection and burning for fuelwood and charcoal. About half the wood cut worldwide is used for subsistence purposes in developing countries where poverty precludes use of other fuel sources. In many tropical areas industrial logging is also a major threat to forests. One of the greatest increases in use of wood is in the production of paper, which is consumed at five times the level it was in 1950.[214] Seventy percent of this output is used in the industrialized Northern countries that account for 20 percent of the world's population.

A first Tropical Timber Agreement, adopted on November 18, 1983, established an International Organization of Tropical Woods and recognized the necessity to preserve and protect tropical rain forests in order to ensure their optimal exploitation, while maintaining ecological equilibrium in the concerned areas and the biosphere. A decade later, a new International Tropical Timber Agreement, also adopted in Geneva, on January 21, 1994, replaced the former. It gives recognition to the need to promote and apply comparable and appropriate guidelines and criteria for the management, conservation and sustainable development of all types of timber producing forests and notes the commitment of all members of the former organization, made in May 1990, to achieve exports of tropical timber products from sustainably-managed sources by the year 2000 (Preamble).

The Agreement itself has two principal characteristics. First, it is predominately institutional in that almost all its provisions concern the International Tropical Timber Organization (ITTO), its structures and its functioning. Second, sustainable development and management of forest resources have an important place in the Organization's objectives as determined in Article 1. In addition, Article 1(l) encourages the members of the Organization to develop national policies aimed at sustainable utilization and conservation of timber-producing forests and their genetic resources and at maintaining ecological balance in the regions concerned, in the context of tropical timber trade. Another provision encourages members to support and develop industrial tropical reforestation and forest management activities as well as rehabilitation of degraded forest land, with due regard for the interest of local communities dependent on forest resources. It is clear that the institutions have to find the balance between opposed interests and that the world's public opinion cannot forget the importance of tropical forests when opposed to trade interests.

The Non-Legally Binding Authoritative Statement of Principles for a Global Consensus on the Management, Conservation and Sustainable

---

[214] JANET ABRAMOVITZ, STATE OF THE WORLD 22–24 (1998).

Development of All Types of Forests, adopted by the Rio Conference in June 1992, also reveals these conflicting interests. Its title indicates the difficulties that arose during the negotiations. As controversial as it was, it represents the first global instrument on forests. Its preamble situates the discussion in the context of "the right to socio-economic development on a sustainable basis."

The Declaration's guiding objective is to contribute to the management, conservation and sustainable development of forests and to provide for their multiple and complementary functions and uses. The first principle repeats verbatim Principle 21 of the Stockholm Declaration, placing it in quotation marks to emphasize the reference. However, the first paragraph of the second principle of the forest declaration restates the beginning of Principle 21 in much stronger terms:

> States have the sovereign and inalienable right to utilize, manage and develop their forests in accordance with their development needs and level of socio-economic development and on the basis of national policies consistent with sustainable development and legislation, including the conversion of such areas for other uses within the overall socio-economic development plan and based on rational land-use policies.

This statement is somewhat balanced in the second paragraph which states that forest resources and forest lands should be sustainably managed to meet the needs of present and future generations.

The Declaration calls for integrated and comprehensive environmental protection and refers to the vital role of all types of forests in ecological processes. Each of the functions forests fulfill are described and measures recommended to sustaining those functions. All countries are recommended to take action towards reforestation, afforestation and forest conservation. In particular, national policies should include protection of ecologically viable representative or unique examples of forests, including primary or old growth forests, cultural, spiritual, historical, religious and other unique and valued forests of national importance. Access to biological resources of the forests is to be regulated with regard to the sovereign rights of the forest countries, with mutual agreements on technology and profits from biotechnology products derived from these resources. Reference is made to international financial and technical assistance and to traditional mechanisms of environmental protection such as impact assessments. The primary focus is development and poverty, including international indebtedness, but it also foresees transfer of technology, new financial resources, scientific research, education, and international exchange of information. Trade should be non-discriminatory, consistent with and facilitating open and free international trade in forest products. Trade barriers are to be removed, but environmental costs and benefits are to be incorporated into market forces. In particular, unilateral measures to restrict and/or ban international trade in timber or other forest products should be removed or avoided. Finally, Principle 15 refers to controlling pollution responsible for damage to forests. The document is far more an international timber trade agreement than an environmental protection statement.

In spite of the very timid language of the Forest Declaration, Agenda 21 calls for its effective implementation. Specific activities should include increasing cooperative actions to reduce pollutants and transboundary impacts affecting the health of trees and forests and conservation of representative ecosystems. (11.16). The timidity of the Declaration and the subordination of environmental considerations to short term economic goals are reflected in 11.25 where cooperation and assistance of the international community are requested in technology transfer, specialization and promotion of fair terms of trade, without resorting to unilateral restrictions and/or bans on forest products contrary to GATT and other multilateral trade agreements, and the application of appropriate market mechanisms and incentives.

The forest principles declaration was originally intended to be a binding treaty. The FAO first proposed in 1990 to adopt an International Convention on Conservation and Development of Forests.[215] A year later, the Japanese government proposed an International Charter for the World's Forest to the International Tropical Timber Organization. Extensive and often hostile discussions resulted only in "elements for a global consensus." Southern timber-producing countries fought hard against mandatory multilateral regulation in the field, due to perceived threats to sovereignty. This was in part a response to claims that, like Antarctica and the high seas, tropical rain forests could constitute part of the common heritage of mankind. No agreement was reached even on the need for further action other than promotion of international cooperation. Compared to the response to desertification, the "progress" has been limited.

The UN created a Forum on Forests (UNFF) in October 2000, with a five-year mandate, in order to give a higher political profile to the issue. Division remains over many questions, including financing, trade, technology transfer, underlying causes of deforestation, governance and illegal trade. Competing economic interests are pervasive in the forestry sector and movement in favor of protection is extremely slow. The 2001 FAO report on the State of the World's Forests showed deforestation and forest degradation continue to increase, especially in developing countries.

The International Tropical Timber Organization's Yokohama Action Plan for the years 2002–2006 aims to accelerate progress towards use of

---

[215] COFO-90/3/a.

sustainable managed sources of tropical timber exports. It has also initiated new activities on forest law enforcement and combating illegal trade of timber, including providing resources to countries for better law enforcement.

On a regional level, on July 23, 1992, the EC has adopted two regulations concerning forests. The first is to protect European forests against air pollution (Reg. 2157/92, amending regulation 3528/86), the second to protect them against fires (Reg. 2158/92). Outside the EC law-making process, the Alpine states negotiated a Protocol on the implementation of the 1991 Alpine Convention in the field of mountain forests.[216] The objective of the Protocol is the conservation of mountain forests as ecosystems, to develop and if necessary extend them and improve their stability (Art. 1). Parties undertake to assure the natural regeneration of the forest, repopulate forests with native plants and prevent erosion and soil compacting. They agree to incorporate these objectives in other policies, such as those on air pollution, wildlife, pasturage, recreation, and logging (Art. 2) and to give priority to the protective function of forests (Art. 6) while also recognizing their ecological and social functions (Art. 8). Where forests are exploited, it should be for the benefit of local communities (Art. 7). Specific forests should be set aside as nature reserves, sufficient in size and number to guarantee their natural dynamic and to be representative of the various ecosystems (Art. 10).

On March 17, 1999, the heads of state of six Central African states[217] signed the Yaounde Declaration on the Conservation and Sustainable Management of Tropical Forests, expressing their desire to promote the rational use and sustainable development of forest resources through the conservation of the entire biodiversity. They agreed to set up transborder protected areas, develop a forestry tax system and attendant measures to support the conservation, sustainable development of and research on forest ecosystems. They also concurred on harmonizing forestry policies and certification systems, involving the rural population and economic operators in sustainable management and conservation, and integrating forest ecosystem protection with other sectors such as transport and agriculture. They specifically mention making concerted efforts to stamp out large-scale poaching and other non-sustainable exploitation in the sub-region. Institutionally, they agreed to revive the Organization for Wildlife Conservation in Central Africa and to create lasting mechanisms for financing forest development, using revenues generated by the forestry sector and international cooperation. An East Asian Ministerial Conference on Forest Law Enforcement and Governance, held in September 2001, adopted an

---

[216] Feb. 27, 1996.
[217] Cameroon, Congo, Gabon, Equatorial Guinea, Central African Republic, and Chad.

unprecedented Declaration on combating illegal logging, associated illegal trade, and other forest crimes.

Finally, efforts to combat anthropogenic sources of climate change recognize the value of forests as sinks for greenhouse gases. The Framework Convention on Climate Change and the Kyoto Protocol specifically encourage afforestation and reforestation and permit states party to meet their obligations under the Protocol in part by such actions.[218] Pursuant to the Convention on Biological Diversity, meanwhile, the Sixth Conference of the Parties, held in the Hague, April 2002, adopted a strategic plan and action plan on forest biodiversity.

b. Vicuña

The vicuña, a native animal of the Andean range in South America, is hunted for its wool, said to be the finest in the world. It became seriously threatened with extinction during the 1960s, with its numbers said to be as low as 6,000 in 1965 from a pre-Colombian population of over one million. It is listed in Appendix I of the Washington Convention on International Trade in Endangered Species. On August 16, 1969, the five Andean countries, Argentina, Bolivia, Chile, Ecuador, and Peru, signed in La Paz a Convention for the Conservation of Vicuña. The agreement requires the contracting states to prohibit and repress vicuña hunting and trade in the wool, meat, and skins, as well as in articles made from these materials, both internally and internationally. The Convention also provided for the establishment and maintenance of reserves and breeding centers.

The results were positive. The population of vicuña recovered, so much that a second agreement permitting some exploitation replaced the La Paz Convention. Bolivia, Chile, Ecuador and Peru signed in Lima a new Convention for the Conservation and Management of the Vicuña on December 7, 1979. Argentina did not sign because it preferred to maintain the strict prohibition on taking vicuña and concluded that the new agreement was insufficiently protective. It subsequently entered into a bilateral agreement with Bolivia (February 16, 1981) on the protection and conservation of vicuña.

The Lima Convention provides for the conservation and management of vicuña taking into account the experience acquired through application of the previous agreement. It prohibited exploitation and trade in vicuña and its products until December 31, 1989. Thereafter, if the population of vicuña attains a high enough level that production of meat, bones, and transformation of skin and wool into products could be envisaged, the state party concerned may authorize trade under strict controls. Skins and

---

[218] Kyoto Protocol (Dec. 11, 1997), Art. 3(3)). *See further* Chapter 12D.

cloth must be marked in a way to be recognizable on the international market. These marks will be registered according to an agreement between the parties in coordination with CITES. Export of fertile vicuña or other reproductive material, except to other member countries, for research and/or for repopulation efforts, is forbidden.

The Convention also requires states parties to establish national parks, reserves, and other protected areas for vicuña. It is agreed to continue research undertaken on the vicuña and to exchange information concerning this subject. A Technical-Administrative Commission is established and called upon to meet annually in order to evaluate the implementation of the Convention and to recommend solutions to problems arising from its application. The Commission began meeting in 1981 and publishes reports on the state of the vicuña population and research on the species.

c. European Bats

On another more limited subject, European countries adopted an Agreement on the Conservation of Bats in Europe,[219] derived from the 1979 Bonn Convention on Migratory Species, and specifically based upon it. The fundamental obligations are similar: each party shall prohibit the deliberate capture, keeping or killing of bats except under permit and shall take action to conserve bat habitats. Research, public education, and measures to promote the conservation of bats are required. An unusual feature is the requirement that states consider the potential effects of pesticides on bats when assessing pesticides for use and must seek safer alternatives to timber treatment chemicals currently in use. The Convention is open to all European bat range states and the European Community.

d. Birds

It has been noted already that the first major multilateral convention in the field of conservation was that of birds "useful to agriculture" signed March 19, 1902. Since that date great progress has been made not only in abandoning the strictly utilitarian point of view which characterizes this first instrument, but also regarding techniques of conservation. The protection of habitats has become an essential element of conservation and those of migratory birds occupy an important place in the designation of protected areas.

Today birds are widely protected, sometimes by overlapping conventions and also by an important EC directive. The legal instruments may

---

[219] London, Dec. 4, 1991.

involve the creation of protected zones, such as foreseen in the UNESCO Convention and the Ramsar Convention, or have a more general scope, such as the regional instruments of Africa, Europe, and ASEAN. Finally, it is clear that birds are at the heart of the 1979 Bonn Convention on the Protection of Migratory Species and that their place also is marked in CITES.

Other instruments are specifically and solely concerned with the conservation of birds. The Paris Convention for the Protection of Birds Useful to Agriculture of March 19, 1902, in spite of its utilitarian character and its exclusion or condemnation of "harmful birds" contains certain precedential elements. In particular, it forbids the taking of nests and eggs and the capturing and destroying clutches.[220] It also prohibits the placing and use of traps, cages, nets, and other means designed to capture or destroy birds en masse.[221] Importing, transit, transporting, and selling nests, eggs, and the young of protected species are banned.[222] The period between March 1 and September 15 of each year is closed to hunting and capture of birds, with a prohibition on all sales.[223] However, the Convention provides numerous exceptions and derogations, for example, exempting from coverage birds whose presence may be a nuisance, and the capture and sale of birds to be kept in cages. A broad escape clause permits parties to avoid being bound by any of the Convention provisions if they wish.[224]

An International Convention for the Protection of Birds[225] was drafted nearly half a century later in order to replace the earlier Convention. However, a dozen of the contracting parties to the first Paris Convention have not adhered to the more recent instrument, so that the substitution is only partial. The second Paris Convention is more in conformity with modern ecological thinking. The narrowly utilitarian view of 1902 and the condemnation of certain species disappeared. The provisions also are more protective. The protection of nests, eggs, and the young is maintained,[226] as well as the prohibition on using means for mass destruction or capture of birds.[227] The list of other prohibited methods of killing and capture is extended, including, for example, the use of spring traps and motor vehicles during hunting.[228] One element in the evolution is that states can no longer offer rewards for the killing or capture of birds.[229] Finally, with certain

---

[220] Art. 2(1).
[221] Art. 3.
[222] Art. 2(2).
[223] Art. 5.
[224] Art. 4.
[225] Paris, Oct. 18, 1950.
[226] Art. 4.
[227] Art. 5(k).
[228] Art. 5.
[229] Art. 5(i).

exceptions all birds are protected during their breeding periods and migratory birds during their transit. The concept of endangered species also appears, although the protection is not absolute.[230]

Three other favorable aspects characterize the 1950 Convention. The states parties agree to regulate trade in protected birds;[231] they support the creation of land or water reserves;[232] and they agree to study and adopt the proper means to prevent the destruction of birds by waste oil and other water pollution, by lighthouses, electric cables, insecticides, poisons, or any other cause.[233] Finally, each state party agrees to prepare a list of birds which may be killed or captured lawfully on its own territory, providing the conditions established by the Convention are met.[234] This is an innovative attempt to introduce lists from the opposite perspective, it being understood that any bird which does not appear on the list is protected. The method has certain advantages for the identification of specimens, because obviously species which can be hunted or captured are far less numerous than those which must be protected.

One of the weak points of the Convention is its exceptions. The first category grants each state party the option of derogating. Individual authorizations can be accorded to destroy birds in case of massive damage to agriculture, game, or fish, or when one or several species whose conservation is desirable are threatened with extinction or with the simple reduction in numbers. However, buying or selling birds thus killed and transporting them out of the region where they were destroyed are illegal.[235] Similarly, an exception can be accorded in the interests of science and education, as well as to restock and reproduce game birds and falcons.[236] Finally, each state has the possibility of establishing a list of bird species permissible to be kept in captivity by individuals, while determining the methods of capture and the conditions of detention.[237]

Specific exceptions may be accorded individual states parties to the Convention, a rare phenomenon in international treaty law. The prohibition on harvesting eggs does not apply to lapwing eggs in the Netherlands.[238] Other countries are named for specific exceptions, but of them only Sweden has become party to the Convention.

---

[230]   Art. 2(b).
[231]   Art. 9.
[232]   Art. 11.
[233]   Art. 10.
[234]   Art. 8.
[235]   Art. 6.
[236]   Art. 7.
[237]   Art. 9.
[238]   Art. 4.

The Agreement on the Conservation of African-Eurasian Migratory Waterbirds[239] is the most extensive developed so far under the Convention on Migratory Species.[240] The agreement extends to 117 countries in Europe, Asia, North America, the Middle East and Africa. The AEWA covers 235 species of birds ecologically dependent on wetlands for at least part of their annual cycle, including many species of divers, grebes, pelicans, cormorants, herons, storks, rails, ibises, spoonbills, flamingos, ducks, swans, geese, cranes, waders, gulls, terns and the South African penguin. The Agreement provides for coordinated and concerted action to be taken by the range states throughout the migration system of waterbirds to which it applies. Parties to the Agreement are called upon to take conservation actions which are described in a comprehensive action plan (2003–2005) that addresses such key issues as species and habitat conservation, management of human activities, research and monitoring, education and information, and implementation.

The second Session of the Meeting of the Parties, which took place in September 2002 in Bonn, Germany, added 65 species of migratory waterbirds to the existing listed species. The relevant Resolution 2.1 was adopted because it had become clear that the list of species excluded some species with an unfavorable conservation status and included others with a favorable conservation status. In early 2000, the Global Environment Facility (GEF) decide to grant $350,000 for the drafting of a brief for a full-size African-Eurasian Flyway project. The goal of the project is to develop transboundary strategic measures necessary to conserve the network of critical wetlands on which migratory waterbirds depend throughout the Agreement area.

Several agreements and other instruments concluded pursuant to the Convention on Migratory Species protect specific species of bird. The MOU has been growing in popularity because of its flexibility and because it permits inter-governmental and non-governmental organizations to sign the understanding. An MOU on the Siberian Crane was signed by nine range states and three cooperating organizations on July 1, 1993, and revised January 1, 1999. Eighteen range states and three cooperating organizations signed an MOU which came into effect on September 10, 1994, to protect the slender-billed curlew. A treaty, the Convention on the Conservation of Albatrosses and Petrels, adopted February 2, 2001, and opened for signature in Canberra, Australia on June 19, 2002. The agreement is a cooperative framework to restore albatrosses and petrels to a favorable conservation status, support coordinated action to mitigate known threats to populations, coordinate data collection, analyze and disseminate information; assess international and regional conservation status of the species and threats

---

239 The Hague, June 16, 1995.

240 The Convention *entered into force* Nov. 1, 1999, after obtaining the required minimum ratifications by 14 range states, comprising seven from Africa and seven from Eurasia. As of Feb. 1, 2003, 38 countries have become party to AEWA.

to them, and communicate the conservation status to relevant international and regional bodies to promote action. Central and Eastern European states and four cooperating organizations signed an MOU on the Conservation and Management of Middle-European Populations of the Great Bustard.[241]

An EC Directive on the Conservation of Wild Birds[242] has an extremely large scope: it includes all species of birds living in the wild, as well as their nests, their eggs, and their habitats, when on the European territory of member states.[243] All necessary measures must be taken to maintain or adapt their populations at levels corresponding to ecological, scientific and cultural requirements, taking account of economic and recreational factors.[244] The general protective regime should include prohibitions on intentional killing or capturing, destruction or damaging nests and eggs, taking eggs, and disturbing and holding birds of species whose hunting and capture is not permitted.[245] A sufficient diversity and area of habitats must be provided, particularly through establishment of protected areas.[246]

The Bird Directive uses lists, but not without a certain complexity. The species enumerated in Annex I must be the object of special conservation measures, primarily concerning their habitats which must be classified as special protected areas.[247] Article 4(2) requires similar measures be taken for regularly occurring migratory species not listed in Annex I. Member states are to pay particular attention to the protection of wetlands of international importance, a phrase which supports the Ramsar Convention.[248] The Directive prohibits the sale, transport, keeping for sale and offering for sale of live or dead birds and of any readily recognizable parts or derivatives thereof.[249]

The Annex I list of birds contains 144 species.[250] Annex II, divided into two parts, is also lengthy. The first part names 24 species that can be hunted in the geographical area to which the Directive applies. In contrast, the 48 species listed in the second part of Annex II may only be hunted in those

---

[241]   Opened for signature Oct. 5, 2000, *in force* June 1, 2001. The signatory states are Hungary, Macedonia, Romania, Moldova, Bulgaria, Greece, Austria, Slovakia, Ukraine, Albania, Croatia and Germany.

[242]   Council Directive 79/409/EEC, O.J. L 103/1 (4/25/79).

[243]   Art. 1.

[244]   Art. 2.

[245]   Art. 5.

[246]   Art. 3.

[247]   Art. 4(1).

[248]   Art. 4(2).

[249]   Art. 6.

[250]   The original number of 74 species was increased by Directive 85/411, O.J. L 233 (8/30/85).

states that are specifically mentioned.[251] All hunting must comply with principles of "wise use and ecologically balanced control of the species of birds concerned."

Finally, a third Annex enumerates bird species for which sale, transport, holding and offering for sale are permitted or can be authorized provided that the birds have been legally killed or captured or otherwise legally acquired.[252] However, for nine of these 26 species, the Commission must study their biological status and the repercussions of commercialization.

Article 9 of the Bird Directive authorizes exceptions within its objectives and according to a precise procedure, under the control of the Commission, which ensures that the exceptions are not incompatible with the directive.[253] In no case may a state make exceptions from the provisions concerning the protection of habitat[254] or the maintenance of bird populations at required levels.[255] In the other direction, states may take stricter measures than those provided for by the Directive.[256] The Commission should receive periodic reports on the application of national measures taken to implement the Directive. In fact, a certain number of cases of non-application of the Directive have been referred to the European Court of Justice.[257]

Finally, the Directive has a procedure for its adaptation to technical and scientific progress. A special committee is provided for this purpose, composed of representatives of the member states and presided over by a Commission representative. The voting procedure is the same weighted voting practiced in the EEC Council. The Commission evaluates proposed measures according to their consistency with the special committee's opinion. When the propositions do not conform to the committee's opinion, or when there is no opinion, the matter is decided by the Council.[258]

Finally, a few states have adopted bilateral treaties protecting migratory birds, particularly in North America and the Pacific. The United States or Japan concluded a series of treaties with other states between 1916[259] and 1976.[260] The treaties reflect the same evolution from utilitarian to broader

---

251   Art. 7(3).

252   Art. 6(2) and (3).

253   Art. 9(4).

254   Arts. 3 and 4.

255   Art. 2.

256   Art. 13.

257   *See, e.g.*, Judgment of May 19, 1998, in Case C-3/96, *Commission of the European Communities v. The Netherlands*, [1998] E.C.R. I-3031.

258   Arts. 16 and 17.

259   Agreement between the United States and Great Britain (Aug. 1916); T.S. 628; 39 Stat. 1702.

260   Agreement between the U.S. and the USSR (Nov. 1976); 29 U.S.T. 4647; T.I.A.S. No. 9073; *in force* Oct. 13, 1978. The other treaties are U.S.-Mexico (Feb. 7, 1936); T.S. No 912; 178 L.T.S. 309; supplemented by an exchange of

ecological concerns, with the earlier ones referring to the great value of birds as a source of food and in protecting agriculture, while the more recent treaties note the aesthetic and scientific qualities of birds and their significance to the environment. The bilateral agreements rely upon lists to designate coverage of species and, except for the earliest treaty, contain amendment procedures. The treaties after 1916 all prohibit trade in specimens of covered species and their eggs and regulate takings.

G. Access to Biological Resources

The Convention on Biological Diversity asserts the rights of states over genetic resources in animals and plants under their jurisdiction, creating a complex relationship of rights and duties. On the one hand, authority to determine access to genetic resources rests with the national governments and is subject to national legislation (Art. 15.1). On the other hand, each state party must endeavor to create conditions to facilitate access to genetic resources for environmentally sound uses by other parties and should not impose restrictions that run counter to the Convention's objectives. When access is granted, it shall be on mutually agreed terms and be subject to prior informed consent by the party providing the genetic resource, unless that party determines otherwise. Permits may be required and it is likely that contractual access agreements will become the primary method by which public and private entities gain access and negotiate a share of the benefits upon a payment of collection fees, royalties or other form of benefit-sharing. Such arrangements will need to take into account as well the needs and rights of indigenous and local communities from whose land genetic resources or traditional technologies are acquired.

Even prior to the conclusion of the Convention on Biological Diversity, gene banks had become a means of protecting genetic diversity, particularly of plants. Institutions in several countries have collected germplasm, mostly of crops, since the 1970s. Difficult legal issues over safety of the material, ownership, development of national laws restricting availability of the germplasm, and intellectual rights over development of new strains, led the United Nations Food and Agriculture Organization to propose a Global System for the Conservation and Utilization of Plant Genetic Resources. The System, in place since 1983, aims to ensure the safe conservation, and promote the unrestricted availability and sustainable utilization of plant genetic resources for present and future generations, by providing a flexible framework for sharing the benefits and burdens. The System covers the

---

notes Mar. 10, 1972; 837 U.N.T.S. 125. U.S.-Japan (Mar. 1972); 25 U.S.T. 3329; T.I.A.S. No. 7990; U.S.S.R.-Japan, October 1973 (not in force); and Japan-Australia (Feb. 1974); A.T.S. No. 6 (1981).

conservation (*ex situ* and *in situ*) and utilization of plant genetic resources at molecular, population, species and ecosystem levels. It is based upon a framework agreement, the International Undertaking which creates an inter-governmental Commission and International Fund for Plant Genetic Resources. By the end of 1991, 128 countries were participating in the System.

The Understanding is now effectively incorporated in the November 3, 2001 FAO International Treaty on Plant Genetic Resources for Food and Agriculture. Unlike the Understanding, the Treaty recognizes the sovereign rights of states over plant genetic resources while seeking conservation and sustainable use of such resources by (1) encouraging farming systems that enhance the sustainable use of agrobiodiversity and other natural resources; (2) maximizing intra- and inter-specific variation for the benefit of farmers, especially those who apply ecological principles in maintaining soil fertility and combating diseases, weeds and pests; (3) broadening the genetic base of crops and increasing the range of genetic diversity available to farmers; and (4) promoting increased world food production in a manner compatible with sustainable development. The treaty includes provisions on access to information, public participation (Arts. 13, 17), and farmers' rights (Art. 9). The Treaty provides in Articles 10–14 a system of facilitated access to an agreed list of over 60 plant genera, including 35 crops. The list is established on the basis of the interdependence and importance of listed plants for food security. The benefits accruing from the use of the material accessed is to be shared fairly and equitably through a variety of actions. There is a conceptual breakthrough in respect to the sharing of monetary benefits: anyone who obtains a commercial profit from the use of genetic resources administered multilaterally is obliged, by a standard Material Transfer Agreement, to share these profits fairly and equitably and pay a royalty to the multilateral mechanism for use as part of the funding strategy for benefit sharing.

After lengthy preparatory studies and negotiations in an Ad Hoc Working Group,[261] the Sixth Conference of the Parties to the Convention on Biological Diversity (CBD) adopted the Bonn Guidelines on Access to Genetic Resources and Fair and Equitable Sharing of the Benefits Arising out of their Utilization as a first step in implementing the related provisions of the CBD, in particular Articles 8(j), 10(c), 15, 16, and 19. Decision VI/24 is intended to assist states in developing and drafting legislative, administrative or policy measures on access and benefit-sharing, as well as contracts and other arrangements under mutually agreed terms. While the Guidelines use terms such as "provider," "user," and "stakeholder," the text makes clear that the terms are not intended to assign any rights over genetic resources beyond those provided in accordance with the Convention, in other words, to anyone other than the states possessing such resources. Nonetheless, the Guidelines are to be read as mutually supportive of other international

---

[261] UNEP/CBD/COP/6/6.

instruments and as evolutionary, to be reviewed, revised and improved as experience is gained in access and benefit-sharing. As such, the Guidelines are without prejudice to the access and benefit-sharing provisions of the FAO International Treaty for Plant Genetic Resources for Food and Agriculture. The application of the Guidelines should also take into account existing regional legislation and agreements on access and benefit-sharing.

The major part of the Guidelines focus on roles and responsibilities in access and benefit-sharing pursuant to CBD Article 15. First, each party should designate one national focal point for access and benefit-sharing and make information about it available through the CBD's clearing-house mechanism. The national focal point should inform applicants for access to genetic resources on the procedures for obtaining prior informed consent on mutually agreed terms, including benefit-sharing, and on competent national authorities, relevant indigenous and local communities and relevant stakeholders, through the clearing-house mechanism. Second, the responsibilities set forth are based on recognition that parties and stakeholders may be both users and providers of genetic resources. States should ensure that stakeholders take into consideration the environmental consequences of their access activities. Users and seekers of access should obtain informed consent prior to access to genetic resources, in conformity with CBD Article 15(5). They should respond to requests for information from indigenous and local communities and should respect customs, traditions, values and customary practices of indigenous and local communities. They should only use genetic resources for purposes consistent with the terms and conditions under which the resources were acquired. The Guidelines also provide that users should ensure the fair and equitable sharing of benefits, including technology transfer to providing countries, arising from the commercialization or other use of genetic resources, in conformity with the mutually agreed terms they established with the indigenous and local communities or stakeholders involved.

On July 2, 1996, the Andean Pact,[262] through its Commission, decided to adopt a Common Regime on Access to Genetic Resources (Decision 391).[263] The states form an eco-region where biodiversity is shared and, because of this, cooperation through harmonized rules helps avoid competitive disadvantage. Decision 391 recognizes that the member countries are sovereign in the use and exploitation of their resources but Article 5 provides that they are to use their sovereign rights to determine access conditions to their genetic resources in conformity with the Decision, which eliminates the possibility of unrestricted access to genetic resources.

---

[262]   The member states are Bolivia, Colombia, Ecuador, Peru and Venezuela.

[263]   *See* Monica Rosell, *Access to Genetic Resources: A Critical Approach to Decision 391 'Common Regime on Access to Genetic Resources' of the Commission of the Cartagena Agreement,* 6 RECIEL 274 (1997).

Article 1 defines access as the obtaining and utilization of genetic resources conserved in *ex situ* and *in situ* conditions and their derivatives or their intangible components for research, biological prospecting, conservation, industrial application or commercial exploitation purposes. Genetic resources are defined as any material of a biological nature containing genetic information of actual or potential value. According to Article 4, human genetic resources and derivatives are excluded, an exclusion consistent with Decision II/11(2) of the Second COP of the Convention on Biological Diversity. Indigenous exchanges within communities for their own consumption and based on customary practices also are excluded.

Decision 391 extends the requirement of prior informed consent to all parties involved in an access procedure, particularly to indigenous and local communities. No access can be granted without their prior consent. In case of infringement the access contract will be deemed void and the violation could be a criminal offense.

The procedure requires an application made to a competent national authority within the Andean Pact countries. The application shall be admissible if it complies with formal requirements and shall be approved if it meets the substantive conditions in the Decision. The procedure requires an application be filed with a competent national authority within the Andean Pact countries. The application shall be admissible if it complies with formal requirements and shall be approved if it meets the substantive conditions in the Decision. The application must provide an outline of the project, its purpose and feasibility. Once approved, the national authority and applicant negotiate the terms and conditions of a contract, including payments, technology transfer, confidentiality, ownership, etc. After the contract is signed, a resolution approves it and it is registered for transparency. Information regarding patents or other intellectual property rights must be provided. Any person who conducts access activities without being authorized infringes the law. National legislation may provide for civil and criminal sanctions and contracts may be suspended or terminated for violation and compensation sought, including for damage to the environment. Article 12 also provides that member countries will not recognize any rights, including intellectual property rights over genetic resources, derivatives, synthesized or intangible assets obtained and/or developed from an access activity not in compliance with the decision. Article 6 declares that genetic resources are the national patrimony or goods of the state of the Andean countries.

H. Invasive or Alien Species

One of the long-standing but intensifying threats to biodiversity comes from the accidental or deliberate introduction of invasive or alien species into a new habitat. Some species, like the desert locust, are not alien, but periodically appear to decimate plants species, including crops. Other plants, animals or micro-organisms travel through modern means of transportation and trade, in the ballast water or on the hull of ships or in the cargo of airplanes for example, to areas where native species have little or no resistence to them or ability to compete for resources. The invasive and alien species often reproduce rapidly and lack their usual predators, allowing them to transform entire ecosystems.

Several invasive species have caused enormous damage in recent years,[264] including the zebra mussel which arrived in the Great Lakes from the Caspian or Black Sea. Lacking their usual predators, the mussels have covered piers, rocks and water supply tunnels, costing the U.S. and Canada some $100 million for clean up in the last five years. Pacific Islands have also suffered from the introduction of several alien species. The brown tree snake has caused the loss of nearly all native bird and bat species on Guam as well as half the native lizard species; officials in Hawaii have had to combat non-native fruit flies and ground termites coming from other islands. A toxic underwater plant, the caulerpa taxifolia, poses serious problems in Europe where it has invaded the Mediterranean Sea to kill native marine plants and animals. The West Nile virus arrived from the Middle East and Africa to New York in 2000, killing birds and spreading to humans and other animals through mosquitos. Within three years it was present in all 50 United States causing sickness and death each summer. According to the United States EPA, nearly half of all species listed as threatened or endangered in the U.S. are at risk due to alien invasive species and the total cost of combating the non-native species tops $137 billion annually.[265]

Several international legal instruments attempt to control invasive or alien species. Based on earlier efforts to combat locusts, the FAO Council approved in November 2000 the Agreement for the Establishment of a Commission for Controlling the Desert Locust in the Western Region.[266] Membership in the Commission is open to FAO Member Nations that constitute the Region defined under Article III (". . . the western region of the invasion area of the desert locust . . . comprises Algeria, Chad, Libya, Mali, Morocco, Mauritania, Niger, Senegal and Tunisia . . .") and that accept the Agreement. The Commission may, by a two-thirds majority of its members, admit to membership other states who submit an application to this effect.

---

[264] *See Invasive Species: Status, Impacts and Trends of Alien Species that Threaten Ecosystems, Habitats and Species,* UNEP/CBD/SBSTTA/6/INF/11, Feb. 26, 2001.

[265] In January 2001, the U.S. National Invasive Species Council issued a National Invasive Species Management Plan with recommendations to prevent, detect, control and respond to invasive species.

[266] Resolution No. 1/119.

More generally, Decision VI/23 of the Sixth Conference of the Parties to the Convention on Biological Diversity expands on Convention Article 8(h) which calls on states parties to "prevent the introduction of, control or eradicate those alien species which threaten ecosystems, habitats or species." Based on the work of the Convention's Scientific Body, Decision VI/23 urges parties, other governments and relevant organizations to promote and implement the Guiding Principles it drafted to prevent the introduction or mitigate the impact of invasive or alien species. States parties and other governments are urged to ratify the 1997 revised International Plant Protection Convention while major international organizations with relevant mandates (*e.g.*, the Office International des Epizooties, the FAO, the IMO, and the World Health Organization) should consider the problems posed by invasive alien species as these organizations elaborate further standards and agreements, or revise existing standards and agreements, including those on risk assessment/analysis.

In their past several conferences, the Ramsar Convention parties also have adopted recommendations on combating invasive species that detrimentally impact wetlands. Resolution VIII.18, adopted at the Eighth Conference of the Parties in November 2002, calls invasive species a "major threat to the ecological character of wetlands worldwide." Noting the link to global climate change, which brings with it movements of species into new areas, the Resolution urges parties to address the problem of invasive species in wetland ecosystems "in a decisive and holistic manner" including undertaking risk assessments of alien species which may pose a threat to the ecological character of wetlands. The resolution asks parties to transmit information to the Ramsar Bureau about the presence on Ramsar sites of invasive alien species, the threats they pose, the risk of invasions by species not yet present, and actions underway or planned for their prevention, eradication or control. The Bureau in turn is asked to develop its website as a source of information and to collaborate with other Secretariats to assess the impact of invasive species and make this information available. States that share wetland ecosystems, both marine and inland, are asked to cooperate in the prevention, early warning, eradication and control of invasive species.

I. Conclusions

It has several times been noted that the legal methods to ensure conservation of wildlife have evolved significantly since the first international instruments addressed this matter. From establishing closed hunting and fishing seasons, through a general prohibition on taking specimens and habitat protection, to the complete management of a population of wild animals, great progress has been made. However, the older methods of conservation have not completely disappeared. Today, a wide variety of means are at the disposal of public entities seeking to protect wild plants and animals, although many of the means concern only animals. The protection of plants, while not less important or difficult, may not necessitate the same variety of measures. In most cases, several techniques are combined.

Detailed measures are contained in some treaties favoring particular species. The 1979 Bern Convention on the Conservation of European Wildlife and Natural Habitats is one of the most explicit and most complete examples in this regard. It forbids the deliberate picking, collecting, cutting or uprooting of protected plants, and in regard to protected wild animals prohibits:

(a) all forms of deliberate capture and keeping and deliberate killing;
(b) the deliberate damage to or destruction of breeding or resting sites;
(c) the deliberate disturbance of wild fauna, particularly during the period of breeding, rearing and hibernation, insofar as disturbance would be significant in relation to the objectives of this Convention;
(d) the deliberate destruction or taking of eggs from the wild or keeping these eggs even if empty;
(e) the possession of and internal trade in these animals, alive or dead, including stuffed animals and any readily recognizable part or derivative thereof, where this would contribute to the effectiveness of the provisions of this Article (Article 6).

Exceptions can be granted to this general Article, but the cases where they can be introduced are specified and strict. States which adopted them must submit biennial reports to the permanent Committee established by the Convention.

Based upon a number of national legislative measures, some international agreements prohibit certain means of killing or capturing specimens of wildlife. Here again, the Bern Convention appears to be the most complete and reflecting most generally accepted rules. As a whole, it prohibits utilizing non-selective means of killing and capture and means capable of causing local disappearance of or serious disturbance to populations of a species. A special Appendix lists means which are prohibited for mammals (snares, live animal decoys, tape recorders, electrical devices, explosives, nets, traps, poison, etc.) and for birds (snares, limes, hooks, explosives, nets traps, poisons). Annex IV of the EC Directive of April 2, 1979, concerning Wild Birds is comparable, containing even more detail as far as the prohibited use of motor vehicles is concerned.

Increasingly, efforts to protect wild fauna and flora are using a comprehensive integrated or ecosystem approach aiming, for example, at flowing bodies of water, wetlands, dry, or unfertilized grasslands. The integrated approach to nature protection is supported by international understanding of the threats to biodiversity. In some cases, various types of property "setaside" or conservation measures are used to protect plants and animals. EC directive 92/43 on the conservation of natural habitats and of wild fauna and flora specifically aims to protect biodiversity by conserving natural habitats.[267] It calls for a coherent European ecological network of special conservation areas, called Natura 2000. Each member state must contribute to the creation of Natura 2000 in proportion to the representation within its territory of natural habitat types and the habitats of species listed in annexes to the directive.

One of the growing problems in protecting biological diversity stems from the proliferation of agreements and institutions. Specific areas or species are likely to be covered by the Convention on Biological Diversity and may also be encompassed by the World Heritage Convention, the Ramsar Convention, the Convention on Migratory Species, and a particular species agreement. If marine areas are involved, additional legal regulation may stem from UNCLOS, regional seas agreements, and fisheries bodies. The need for coordination is increasingly recognized and efforts are underway among parties to the Convention on Biological Diversity, the Convention on Migratory Species, Ramsar and the World Heritage Convention to harmonize state reporting requirements. The Convention on Migratory Species secretariat has taken the lead in establishing cooperative arrangements with other bodies concerned with biodiversity by concluding Memoranda of Understanding with UNESCO, CITES, UNFCCC, and IUCN. The Conference of the Parties of the CBD also decided to integrate its work on inland water ecosystems with the Ramsar Convention on wetlands, adopting a Work Programme on the biological diversity of such ecosystems. In this regard, parties are encouraged to adopt integrated land and watershed management approaches for the protection, use, planning and management of inland water ecosystems. Such arrangements are increasingly necessary to ensure coordination and consistency in monitoring the many legal obligations of states.

BIBLIOGRAPHY

BEER-GABEL, J. & LABAT, B., LA PROTECTION INTERNATIONALE DE LA FAUNE ET DE LA FLORE SAUVAGES (1999).

BILDERBEEEK, S. ed., BIODIVERSITY AND INTERNATIONAL LAW (1992).

Birnie, P.W., *The International Law of Migratory Species. International Legal Issues in the Management and Protection of the Whale: A Review of Four Decades of Experience*, 29 NAT. RES. J. 903–1065 (1989).

Bodansky, D., *International Law and the Protection of Biological Diversity*, 28 VAND J. TRANSNAT'L L. 623 (1995).

---

[267] Directive on the Conservation of Natural Habitats of Wild Fauna and Flora, 92/43/EEC, O.J. L 206 (5/21/92), at 7.

BOURRINET, J. & MALJEAN DUBOIS, S. eds., LE COMMERCE INTERNATIONAL DES ORGANISMES GENETIQUEMENT MODIFIES (2002).

BOWMAN, M. & REDGWELL C., INTERNATIONAL LAW AND THE CONSERVATION OF BIOLOGICAL DIVERSITY (1996).

BROWN, K., ET AL., ECONOMICS AND THE CONSERVATION OF GLOBAL BIOLOGICAL DIVERSITIES (1993).

Burns, W.C., *CITES and the Regulation of International Trade in Endangered Species of Flora: A Critical Appraisal,* 8 DICK J. INT'L L.J. 203 (1990).

Cooper, H.D., *The International Treaty on Plant Genetic Resources for Food and Agriculture,* 11 RECIEL 1 (2002).

DE FONTAUBERT, C., DOWNES, D., & AGARDY, T., BIODIVERSITY IN THE SEAS: IMPLEMENTING THE CONVENTION ON BIOLOGICAL DIVERSITY IN MARINE AND COASTAL HABITATS, IUCN Environmental Policy and Law Paper No. 32, at 38–39 (1996).

DE KLEMM, C. & SHINE, C., GUIDELINES FOR LEGISLATION TO IMPLEMENT CITES (2d ed. 1998).

de Klemm, C., *Migratory Species in International Law,* 29 NAT RES. J. 903–1065 (1989).

Doubleday, N.C., *Aboriginal Subsistence Whaling: The Right of Inuit to Hunt Whales and Implications for International Environmental Law,* 17 DEN J. INT'L L. & POL'Y 373–93 (1989).

FAVRE, D., INTERNATIONAL TRADE IN ENDANGERED SPECIES (1989).

FREESE, C., HARVESTING WILD SPECIES: IMPLICATIONS FOR BIODIVERSITY CONSERVATION (1997).

Glennon, M.J., *Has International Law Failed the Elephant?,* 84 AJIL 1–43 (1990).

GLOWKA, L., A GUIDE TO DESIGNING LEGAL FRAMEWORKS TO DETERMINE ACCESS TO GENETIC RESOURCES, IUCN Policy and Law Paper No. 34 (1998).

GRIFO, F. & ROSENTAL, J. eds, BIODIVERSITY AND HUMAN HEALTH (1997).

GURUSWAMY, L. & MCNEELY, J.A. eds., PROTECTION OF GLOBAL BIODIVERSITY—CONVERGING STRATEGIES (1998).

HANNA, S., FOLKE, C., & MALER K.-G., RIGHTS TO NATURE: ECOLOGICAL, ECONOMIC, CULTURAL, AND POLITICAL PRINCIPLES OF INSTITUTIONS FOR THE ENVIRONMENT (1996).

Houck, O., *On The Law of Biodiversity and Ecosystem Management,* 81 MINN L. REV. 869 (1997).

Kosloff L. & Trexler, T., *The Convention on International Trade in Endangered Species: No Carrot, But Where's the Stick?,* 17 ENVT'L L. REP. 10.222 (1987).

Lyster, S., *The Convention on the Conservation of Migratory Species of Wild Animals (the "Bonn Convention,")* 29 NAT. RES. J. 903–1065 (1989).

LYSTER, S., INTERNATIONAL WILDLIFE LAW (1985).

Mack, J. *International Fisheries Management: How the U.N. Conference on Straddling and Highly Migratory Fish Stocks Changes the Law of Fishing on the High Seas,* 26 CAL W. INT'L L.J. 313 (1996).

MARTIN, R., CALDWELL, J. & BERZDO, J., AFRICAN ELEPHANT, CITES, AND THE IVORY TRADE (1986).

Navid, D., *The International Law of Migratory Species: The Ramsar Convention*, 29 NAT RES. J. 903–1065 (1989).

ELLIOT A. NORSE ed., GLOBAL MARINE BIOLOGICAL DIVERSITY 115 (1993).

NORTON, B., THE PRESERVATION OF SPECIES, (1986).

NORTON, B., WHY PRESERVE NATURAL VARIETY? (1987).

RAMAKRISHNA, K. & WOODWELL, G., WORLD FORESTS FOR THE FUTURE (1993).

Ramsar Convention Bureau, *The Ramsar Convention Manual* (2d ed. 1997).

REID, W., ET AL., eds., BIODIVERSITY PROSPECTING: USING GENETIC RESOURCES FOR SUSTAINABLE DEVELOPMENT (1993).

Schiffman, H.S., *The Protection of Whales in International Law: A Perspective for the Next Century*, 22 BROOKLYN J. INT'L L. 303 (1996).

Schrijver, N., SOVEREIGNTY OVER NATURAL RESOURCES—BALANCING RIGHTS AND DUTIES (1997).

SNAPE, W., BIODIVERSITY AND THE LAW (1996).

STOKKE, OLAV, ed., GOVERNING HIGH SEAS FISHERIES: THE INTERPLAY OF GLOBAL AND REGIONAL REGIMES (2001).

VAN HEIJNSBERGEN, P. ed., INTERNATIONAL LEGAL PROTECTION OF WILD FAUNA AND FLORA (1997).

WILSON, E. ed., BIOLOGICAL DIVERSITY (1988).

INTERNET SITES

Biodiversity Convention
<http://www.biodiv.org/>

CITES
<http://www.wcmc.org.uk/CITES/english/index.html>

International Whaling Commission
<http://ourworld.compuserve.com/homepages/iwcoffice/>

Ramsar Convention
<http://www.iucn.org/themes/ramsar/>

World Heritage Convention
<http://www.unesco.org>

FAO
<http://www.fao.org>

CHAPTER 9

SOIL

Soil is the part of the earth between its surface and its bedrock. It ensures two types of functions. On the one hand, it contains the nutrients necessary for the maintenance of life and constitutes a habitat for humans as well as for flora and fauna.[1] On the other hand, it protects other sectors of the environment: it acts to filter pollutants before they reach subterranean water sources or enter the food chain and helps avoid flooding by absorbing considerable amounts of water. Only six to eight inches of topsoil stands between much of the world and starvation. Degraded soils have lowered global agricultural yields by approximately 13 percent since World War II. One soil scientist calls land degradation "the root of all socioeconomic problems" in developing nations.[2]

Soil naturally erodes and degrades and erosion is a principal threat to soil fertility. Erosion occurs naturally due to the ordinary flow of water, but is exacerbated due to flooding and strong winds. Throughout most of the earth's history, soil formation exceeded soil erosion. Now a combination of overplowing, overgrazing, and deforestation has reversed that relationship. The principal cause of erosion today is incorrect management of forests and agricultural lands, principally through intensive and environmentally-unsound cutting and farming methods. With soil erosion exceeding soil formation, many areas of the earth are slowly being drained of their inherent fertility.[3]

Soil also is degraded by excess demands on it. Overuse of soil depletes the nutrients and leads to desertification. Grazing lands cover an area that is roughly double the area of world's crop lands, supporting 1.32 billion cattle and 1.72 billion sheep and goats. As herds and flocks grow in response to increased demand for meat, milk, leather and other livestock products, overgrazing has become a widespread problem. Agriculture also has intensified.

---

[1]   A study of soil organisms in one acre of a pasture in Denmark revealed some 50,000 small earthworms, an equal number of mites and other insects, and nearly 12 million roundworms. A gram of soil contains an estimated 30,000 protozoa, 50,000 algae, 4,000,000 fungi and billions of bacteria. Gretchen Daily, *Introduction: What Are Ecosystem Services?, In* G. DAILY ED., NATURE'S SERVICES: SOCIETAL DEPENDENCE ON NATURAL ECOSYSTEMS 3–4 (1997).

[2]   *State of the Planet: A World Transformed,* NATIONAL GEOGRAPHIC (July 2002).

[3]   Lester R. Brown, *The Future of Growth, in* STATE OF THE WORLD 3, at 9 (1998).

The consumption of grain and other agricultural products has tripled since the middle of the 20th century.[4] Farmers use more fertilizers and pesticides and extend agriculture onto marginal lands, some in areas where rainfall is low and soils are vulnerable to wind erosion.[5]

Contamination by heavy metals and organic toxic substances is also a particularly serious problem, especially in industrialized countries. Industrial and agricultural—mainly animal—waste has become a major source of soil contamination. Air pollution also can affect soil quality: sulfuric acid, ammonia and nitric acid coming from atmospheric pollution increase the natural process of acidification of the soil. Finally, soil is removed for construction of houses, roads, airports and industrial settlements and this can create irreversible processes.

Legal protection for soil is rather recent, although some forestry laws protected trees at least in part to avoid erosion and consequent flooding. Part of the neglect was due to a general perception of soil as an inexhaustible resource in view of its use for food production. At the international level, cooperation started later than in other sectors of environmental protection, because it was generally considered that the soil conservation was mainly a domestic problem without international implications. In Europe, the Committee of Ministers of the Council of Europe adopted the European Soil Charter on May 30, 1972.[6] Globally, the UN Food and Agriculture Organization proclaimed a World Soil Charter on November 25, 1981.[7] The soil charters both contain non-binding guidelines for action and basic principles. They proclaim the responsibility of governments to develop land-use programs that include measures aimed at the best possible utilization of the land, ensuring long-term maintenance and improvement of its productivity, and avoiding losses of productive soil. The two charters focus on the need for land-use policies that create incentives for people to participate in soil conservation. These policies require technical, institutional and legal frameworks. In order to ensure optimum land use, a country's land resources should be assessed in terms of their suitability at different levels of inputs for different types of land use, including agriculture, grazing and forestry. Land having the potential for a wide range of uses should be employed so that future options for other potential functions are not denied. Utilization of land for non-agricultural purposes should be organized in such a way as to avoid, as much as possible, the occu-

---

[4]   "Feeding 80 million more people each year means expanding the grain harvest by 26 million tons, or 71,000 tons a day. Not only is the world now adding 80 million people annually, but it is projected to add nearly this number for the next few decades, reaching 9.4 billion in 2050." *Id.* at 14.

[5]   *Id.* at 8.

[6]   Resolution (72)19.

[7]   Weston V.G.2.

pation or permanent degradation of good quality soils. The World Charter for Nature also declares that the productivity of soils shall be maintained or enhanced through measures that safeguard their long-term fertility and the process of their organic decomposition, and prevent erosion and all other forms of degradation.[8]

In 1983, UNEP developed environmental guidelines for the formulation of national soil policies.[9] FAO contributed a partial, but important, approach to the problem of soil conservation by adopting an International Code of Conduct on the Distribution and Use of Pesticides on November 28, 1985. It was amended in 1989[10] and was in part a predecessor to the Convention on Prior Informed Consent signed in September 1998.

Several days before the opening of the Rio de Janeiro Conference, on May 18, 1992, the Council of Europe Committee of Ministers adopted Recommendation 92(8) on Soil Protection. It calls for action by governments of member states to combat soil loss, soil degradation, reduction of ecological habitats and species biodiversity, and for national surveys of soils to monitor changes. Suggested mechanisms for international cooperation include harmonization of methods for quantifying and assessing soils and implementation of a concerted research program. The recommendation stresses the need to take soil protection into consideration in all other policies such as agriculture, forestry, industry, transport, town planning and regional planning policies.

Agenda 21, adopted at the 1992 Rio Conference, echoes this approach by devoting five chapters to different aspects of soil conservation. Chapter 10 discusses an integrated approach to the planning and management of land resources, Chapter 11 addresses action to combating deforestation, Chapter 12 is devoted to the problem of desertification, Chapter 13 concerns sustainable mountain development and Chapter 14 discusses sustainable agriculture and rural development.

A. The UN Desertification Convention

Desertification is not a new phenomenon: old empires collapsed thousands of years ago as a result of severe drought that induced desert-like conditions.[11] In the past three decades, however, the rate of desertification increased dramatically in the 40 percent of land surface classified as arid or semi-arid. Some 80 percent of the agricultural land in arid regions currently

---

8   UN General Assembly on Oct. 28, 1982; WESTON, V.B. 11, para. 10(b).
9   UNEP, Environmental Management Guidelines No. 7 (1983).
10   WESTON, V.H.17.
11   Burns, W.C., *The International Convention to Combat Desertification: Drawing a Line in the Sand?*, 16 MICH. J. INT'L L. 831 (1995).

suffers from moderate to severe degrees of desertification, threatening the livelihood of hundreds of millions of people in Africa, Russia, Australia, the United States and Mexico, Central Europe and South America.

As a direct consequence of the crisis due to drought in the African Sahel in the 1970s, the UN General Assembly convened a conference on desertification in 1977, which adopted a plan of action to combat desertification calling for national and regional efforts through an integrated program of land management assessment, implementation of corrective measures, and strengthening of scientific and technological infrastructures in dryland nations.[12] Effective progress was made, however, only in the aftermath of the 1992 Rio de Janeiro Conference. An international negotiating committee was established[13] and on June 17, 1994 the UN Convention to Combat Desertification in Those Countries Experiencing Serious Drought and/or Desertification, Particularly in Africa, was adopted.[14]

The Convention defines desertification as land degradation in arid, semi-arid, and dry sub-humid areas resulting from various factors, including climatic variations and human activities (Art. 1(a)). To combat desertification and mitigate the effects of drought in the affected countries, the Convention advocates effective action in the form of action programs (Arts. 9–11). This involves long-term integrated strategies that focus simultaneously, in affected areas, on improved productivity of land and the rehabilitation, conservation and sustainable management of land and water resources (Arts. 2(2), 10). Accordingly, the parties shall adopt an integrated approach addressing the physical, biological and socio-economic aspects of the processes of desertification and drought (Arts. 4(2)(a), 10(4)).

The Convention adopts an original approach to the desertification problem, which is a global issue but with direct effects experienced differently among regions, states and local areas. Recognizing this variation, the Convention consists of a general treaty and five annexed regional agreements. It also emphasizes the principle of common but differentiated responsibilities and provides for cooperation at national, sub-regional and regional levels, including public participation, in particular during the elaboration and the implementation of action programs. Finally, it creates mechanisms, both administrative and financial, in order to monitor and ensure compliance.

The Convention's Preamble insists on the global dimensions of desertification and drought and the need for joint action by the international

---

[12]　Report of the UN Conference on Desertification, U.N. Doc. A/ CONF.74/36 (1977). *See also* Kyle W. Danish, *International Environmental Law and the "Bottom-up" Approach: a Review of the Desertification Convention*, 3 IND. J. GLOBAL LEG. STUD. 133, 141 (1995).

[13]　On the history of the negotiating process, *see* Burns *supra* note 11, at 11.

[14]　It entered into force Dec. 26, 1996.

community to combat it. At the same time, it notes the high concentration of developing countries, notably the least developed ones, among those experiencing serious drought and/or desertification. Each Annex to the Convention concerns a specific geographic region, setting out guidelines for the preparation of action programs and their exact focus (Art. 15). The first annex addresses Africa, Annex II is for Asia, while Latin America and the Caribbean are covered by Annex III. Annex IV addresses the Northern Mediterranean. A fifth annex, adopted by the Conference of the Parties in December 2000, applies to Central and Eastern Europe.[15] Annex I is more than twice the length of the other annexes, indicating the importance of the topic to Africa, where desertification is linked to poverty and subsistence agriculture. The Convention (Arts. 7, 13(2)) explicitly grants priority to Africa in the quest to halt desertification.

The Convention advocates cooperation and coordination at sub-regional, regional and international levels (Arts. 3(b), 4(2)(e)). The parties should implement their obligations individually or jointly, either through existing or prospective bilateral and multilateral arrangements (Art. 4.1) and they must strengthen sub-regional, regional and international cooperation and cooperate within relevant international organizations (Art. 4.2(e), (f)). Action programs, which constitute the main mechanism to implement the Convention, should also be elaborated at subregional and regional levels (Art. 11), when possible through relevant inter-governmental organizations (Art.14.1). Cooperation is specified in the fields of information collection, analysis and exchange (Art.16), research and development (Art.17), capacity building (Art. 19), and in the implementation of the Convention (Art.12). The Convention also calls for coordinating activities carried out under it and under other relevant international agreements, in particular under the Framework Convention on Climate Change (Art. 8.1).

The principle of common but differentiated responsibilities, proclaimed in the Rio Declaration and previously reflected in the Ozone Treaties and the Convention on Climate Change, is largely applied in the Desertification Convention. Article 5, containing the obligations of affected country parties, requires them to give due priority to combating desertification and mitigating the effects of drought, and to allocate resources in accordance with their circumstances and capabilities. According to Article 6, developed countries shall actively support such efforts and provide substantial financial resources and other forms of support to assist affected countries and promote the mobilization of new and additional funding including funding from the private sector (Arts. 6, 20). In addition, developed countries shall promote and facilitate access by affected countries to appropriate technology, knowledge and know-how (Arts. 6, 12, 18, 20,2(c)). The different

---

[15]   *See* 31 E.P.L. 14 (2001).

forms of assistance provided by developed countries shall give priority to supporting national, sub-regional and regional action programs of affected developing countries (Art. 9.2).

An additional important feature of the Convention is that its implementation involves many levels of cooperation, with an emphasis on public participation. The need for effective action at all levels of government, supported by international cooperation and partnership arrangements (Art. 2.1) is a basic requirement. Affected countries must create an enabling environment at higher levels to facilitate action at local levels (Art. 3(a)). Cooperation should be developed in a spirit of partnership between the government, communities, non-governmental organizations, and landholders, to establish a better understanding of the nature and value of land and scarce water resources in affected areas and to work towards their sustainable use (Art. 3(c)). One of the main elements of the Convention is the participation of populations and local communities in decisions concerning the design and implementation of programs to combat desertification (Art. 3(a)). National action programs should be prepared and updated through a continuing participatory process (Arts. 9.1, 10.2(f))). A necessary complement of public participation is capacity building, education and public awareness (Art. 19).

Finally, the Convention calls for the development of institutional mechanisms (Art. 4.2(g)), including operational mechanisms at the national and field levels (Art. 14.2) and promotes the use of existing bilateral and multilateral financial mechanisms and arrangements (Art. 4.2(h)). Article 22 establishes a Conference of the Parties assisted by a Permanent Secretariat (Art. 23) and a Committee on Science and Technology (Art. 24). Article 21 foresees a financial mechanism while Article 26 institutes a reporting system. According to the latter, each party shall transmit to the Conference of the Parties reports on the measures it has taken to implement the Convention. Affected countries shall provide a description of the strategies and programs established and of any relevant information on their implementation. Any group of affected countries may make a joint communication on measures taken at the sub-regional and/or regional levels in the framework of action programs. The Conference of the Parties is to facilitate the provision to affected developing countries, on request, of technical and financial support in compiling and communicating such information. Developed countries shall report on measures taken to assist in the preparation and implementation of action programs, including information on the financial resources they have provided, or are providing, under the Convention. Many of the states parties submitted their national actions plans in 2000.

The annexes describe the particular conditions of each concerned region and outline the recommended contents of national, sub-regional and regional action programs. All the annexes include provisions for coordinating the different programs. Article 9 of Annex IV relating to the Northern Mediterranean expressly precludes affected developed countries of the region from receiving financial assistance under the Convention.

Commentators on the Convention have stressed two of its characteristics. The first is its recognition of the importance of public participation at the local level in affected nations,[16] also called the"bottom-up" approach.[17] The second is the innovation of confronting problems of harmful patterns of land use, which underlies the whole instrument.[18]

B. General Norms on Soil Protection

International efforts to promote food security and conservation and sustainable use of plant genetic resources recognize that soil fertility is essential to fulfilling these goals. Land contamination, soil erosion and flawed irrigation schemes have meant, for example, that of Europe's total land area, 12 percent is affected by water erosion and 4 percent by wind erosion, generally as a consequence of unsustainable agriculture, salinization and water logging. The FAO's International Treaty on Plant Genetic Resources for Food and Agriculture (Rome, November 3, 2001) has as its objective conservation, sustainable use and equitable benefit sharing of plant resources. The obligations of the contracting parties include developing and maintaining appropriate policy and legal measures that promote sustainable use of plant genetic resources (Art. 6.1); these measures may include strengthening research to enhance and conserve biological diversity for the benefit of farmers, especially those who generate and use their own plant varieties and "apply ecological principles in maintaining soil fertility and in combating diseases, weeds and pests" (Art. 6.2(b)).

The first international treaty exclusively dedicated to soil was adopted October 16, 1998, as a protocol to the 1991 framework Convention on the Protection of the Alps. The Convention itself designates soil conservation as an objective, which it defines as "to reduce quantitative and qualitative soil damage, in particular by applying agricultural and forestry methods which do not harm the soil, through minimum interference with soil and land, control of erosion and the restriction of soil sealing" (Art.2(2)(d)). The Protocol for the Implementation of the Alpine Convention in the Field of the Protection of Soils has been ratified by three of the eight signatories and entered into force on December 18, 2002. The Preamble reiterates the Convention's objective and goes on to express the parties' recognition of the fact that soil occupies a particular place in ecosystems and that its reconstitution

---

[16]   Burns, *supra* note 11, at 877.

[17]   Danish *supra* note 12, at 161, 173.

[18]   *Id.* at 172.

and regeneration occur extremely slowly. The parties also recognize that erosion is a particular problem in the Alpine region because of the topography, and that the concentration of pollutants in the soil can thus be carried to other ecosystems and present a risk to humans, flora and fauna. The Protocol notes the need for an integrated approach because of the impacts on soil of industrialization, urbanization, mining, tourism, agriculture, forestry, and transport.

Article 1(2) acknowledges the multiple functions of soil as a vital base and space for biological diversity; a notable element of nature and the countryside; a part of ecosystem functioning, especially with water cycles and soil nutrients; a milieu to transform and regulate substances, notably through its filtration capacity in protecting underground aquifers; as a habitat; and as a source of natural and cultural history. The functions of the soil, particularly the ecological functions, should be guaranteed and preserved over the long term, both in quantity and in quality. The restoration of degraded soils is encouraged. The measures states parties should take must aim at utilizing soil appropriately according to location, economizing surface use, preventing erosion and structural damage to soil, as well as minimizing the transfer of polluting substances to soil. Special measures should be taken to preserve and promote the diversity of soil typical of the Alpine region and its characteristic places. In this context, prevention includes guaranteeing the functional capacity as well as the possibility of different utilizations of soil by future generations, with a view towards sustainable development.

The basic obligations of the parties are to take legal and administrative measures necessary to protect soil and to monitor the application of these measures. Where there is a risk of grave and persistent danger to the functional capacity of soil, protection should have priority over utilization as a general rule. The Protocol also provides that soil should be a factor in delimiting protected areas; especially characteristic formations or areas of particular interest for geology and understanding the evolution of the earth should be preserved. The parties agree to look into the application of financial and fiscal measures to protect soil. Article 3 adds an obligation to apply an integrated approach that incorporates soil protection into all aspects of land management. Assignment of responsibility to different levels of governance is encouraged as is international cooperation (Arts. 4, 5). Chapter II of the Protocol details the specific measures to be taken. One of these calls for including consideration of soil impact in environmental impact assessments for major projects. The contracting parties agree on the need for cartography to identify zones at risk from erosion, avalanches or other earth movements, earthquakes, or flooding and to delimit zones at risk. Preference is to be given to natural techniques to respond to threats (Arts. 10, 11). As for contaminated soil, the parties agree to inventory these sites and evaluate the risk they present, as well as to take further measures of waste management to prevent further contamination.

The comprehensive obligations contained in the Protocol are supplemented by requirements of permanent observation and monitoring, with state reports to be submitted to the Alpine Conference. The permanent committee of the Conference is to examine the reports to verify compliance with the Protocol. The committee may request additional information from the states parties or have recourse to other sources of information. A non-compliance procedure is also foreseen.

Finally, the 2003 revised African Convention on Conservation of Nature and Natural Resources reflects the Desertification Convention and other developments concerning protection of soil. Its Article VI provides:

1. The Parties shall take effective measures to prevent land degradation, and to that effect shall develop long-term integrated strategies for the conservation and sustainable management of land resources, including soil, vegetation and related hydrological processes.

2. They shall in particular adopt measures for the conservation and improvement of the soil, to, inter alia, combat its erosion and misuse as well as the deterioration of its physical, chemical and biological or economic properties.

3. To this end:
a) they shall establish land-use plans based on scientific investigations as well as local knowledge and experience and, in particular, classification and land-use capability;
b) they shall, when implementing agricultural practices and agrarian reforms,
    i) improve soil conservation and introduce sustainable farming and forestry practices, which ensure long-term productivity of the land,
    ii) control erosion caused by land misuse and mismanagement which may lead to longterm loss of surface soils and vegetation cover,
    iii) control pollution caused by agricultural activities, including aquaculture and animal husbandry;
c) they shall ensure that non-agricultural forms of land use, including but not limited to public works, mining and the disposal of wastes, do not result in erosion, pollution, or any other form of land degradation;
d) they shall, in areas affected by land degradation, plan and implement mitigation and rehabilitation measures.

4.   Parties shall develop and implement land tenure policies able to facilitate the above measures, inter alia by taking into account the rights of local communities.

With their detail and integrated approach to protecting soil as an essential component of ecosystems, the Alpine Convention Protocol and the African Convention provide models which could be adapted to other regions.

BIBLIOGRAPHY

Blue, W., *Problèmes de conservation du sol,*" *in* COUNCIL OF EUROPE, COLLECTION SAUVEGARDE DE LA NATURE (1988).
Burns, W.C., *The International Convention to Combat Desertification: Drawing a Line in the Sand?*, 16 MICH. J. INT'L L. 831 (1995).
Danish, K.W., *International Environmental Law and the "Bottom-up" Approach: A Review of the Desertification Convention*, 3 IND. J. GLOBAL LEG. STUD. 1 (1995).
DESERTIFICATION CONTROL BULLETIN
DREGNE, H.E., DESERTIFICATION OF ARID LANDS (1983).
FAO, LAW AND SUSTAINABLE DEVELOPMENT SINCE RIO: LEGAL TRENDS IN AGRICULTURE AND NATURAL RESOURCES MANAGEMENT (2002).
GRAINGER, A., THE THREATENING DESERT (1990).
HEATHCOTE, R.L., THE ARID LANDS: THEIR USE AND ABUSE (1983).
UNEP, *Fact Sheet 3: United Nations Convention to Combat Desertification* (1995).

INTERNET SITES

Desertification Convention Secretariat:
<http://www.unccd.ch/>

CHAPTER 10

FRESH WATERS

Inland or fresh water accounts for only 2.7 percent of the earth's water, and a large proportion of this limited quantity is frozen in glacial ice caps at the two poles and on high mountains. Humanity now uses, directly or indirectly, more than half of the world's accessible water supply and the demand for water is rising with increasing population, higher living standards, and the extension of water-utilizing industries such as mining and metal-processing, cement production, wood processing and irrigation-based agriculture. The global per capita availability of freshwater worldwide fell from 17,000 m^3 in 1950 to 7000 m^3 in 1995,[1] but the fall and usage levels are unevenly distributed. On average a European consumes about 800 m^3 of water per year, approximately 70 times more than a Ghanaian, but much less than each inhabitant of the United States, whose consumption exceeds 3000m^3 annually.

Fresh water is still abundant, but its availability varies widely. States are considered to experience chronic scarcity when water resources fall below a "benchmark" of approximately 1000 m^3 per person per year. Chronic shortages already exist in many areas where precipitation is low or unreliable and/or where withdrawals have been significantly increased to meet additional demand from irrigation, industry or urban populations. Many water-stressed areas in India, China, Mexico and the United States have been forced to turn to their groundwater reserves, which frequently are pumped faster than they can be recharged. In addition to pressure on water resources from economic development and changes in social consumption patterns, water supply increasingly is constrained by land use changes (for example forest clearance, which tends to increase run-off and reduce water availability) and contamination from human settlements, industry and agriculture.[2] The volume, timing and geography of water flow in more than one-half the world's great rivers is controlled by some 45,000 large dams built to secure water resources for food production, energy generation, flood control and domestic use. Dams irrigate some 30–40 percent of land worldwide

---

[1] Report of the United Nations Secretary General on a Comprehensive Freshwater Assessment, U.N. Doc. E/CN.1997/9.

[2] *See generally* THE SCARCITY OF WATER, EMERGING LEGAL AND POLITICAL RESPONSES (E.H.P. Brans, E.J. de Haan, A. Nollkaemper & J. Rinzema eds., 1997).

and generate nearly 20 percent of electricity.[3] At the same time, dams are very disruptive of aquatic habitats, leading to declining fish stocks and significant and irreversible losses in biological diversity. Retreating deltas result in the loss of productive land, a problem that could be compounded by climate change and rising sea levels. It is estimated that Egypt, for example, could lose up to 19 percent of its remaining habitable land over the next 60 years, displacing some 16 percent of its population, as a result of further changes in the flow of the Nile.[4] Dam construction already has led to the relocation of between 40 and 80 million persons worldwide, many of them poor and not receiving the benefits associated with large dams.

In sum, throughout the world, there is fear that within 25 years the need for fresh water of the projected eight billion inhabitants of this planet will exceed the earth's water resources. Sustainable development requires far greater attention be paid to reconciling competing needs and entitlements in the management of water resources than has been evident in the past.

Freshwater resources raise not only quantitative but also qualitative problems. Approximately 1.2 billion people in developing countries lack safe water supplies and nearly three billion lack access to sanitation services.[5] The World Health Organization estimates that almost half of the world's population is suffering from debilitating water-borne or water-related diseases which account for an estimated five million deaths each year, although good progress has been made in reducing the incidence of some diseases. The issue of access to water and sanitation proved to be a major issue at the Johannesburg World Summit on Sustainable Development held in 2002. The Plan of Implementation includes pledges to increase access to sanitation to improve human health, prioritize water and sanitation in national sustainable development strategies and provide clean drinking water and adequate sanitation, cutting in half by 2015 the proportion of people who are unable to reach or afford them.[6]

Threats to freshwater quality are varied and complex. Sewage disposal is a classic use of flowing water and has been linked to epidemics of plague and cholera. The disposal of chemicals and hazardous wastes, the use of pesticides and fertilizers, also affect water quality. Freshwater resources are threatened by deforestation as well; the very existence of China's Lijiang River is in jeopardy due to destruction of highland forests[7] and countries

---

[3]   Executive Summary, Report of the World Commission on Dams, xxix (2000).

[4]   U.N. Commission on Sustainable Development, Fifth Session, Apr. 7–27, 1997, *Global Change and Sustainable Development: Critical Trends*, Report of the Secretary General, paras. 124–128 and 136.

[5]   *Id.*, para. 132.

[6]   The human rights aspects of this issue are discussed in Chapter 15.

[7]   *China's Lijiang River Could Dry Up*, International Herald Tribune, July 24, 1990, at 2.

in Asia and Latin America have suffered major flooding as a result of upland deforestation.[8]

Most of the waters of the earth are linked, although the legal regimes applicable to them differ widely in response to geographic, economic, social and political factors. The sea receives a large part of its pollution from rivers, but specific rules are needed to resolve the latter problem. One-quarter of all freshwater is found under the soil and generally is closely connected with surface waters, but their legal regimes are often distinct.[9] Moreover, even the same type of water source may be regulated differently, according to the use to which the waters are put (*e.g.*, domestic, agricultural and industrial purposes). The different uses are a function of population density, the level of economic development and cultural traditions and they affect the economic and environmental values of water.[10]

The complexity of regulating water resources is accentuated when inland waters are divided by international boundaries. In fact, nearly half of all land and 40 percent of the world's population are found within international river basins. Rivers may constitute the border between two countries, traverse the frontier, or even combine the two characteristics, as with the Danube, the Rhine and the Rio Grande. Thirteen river basins are shared by five or more countries. International regulation thus must adapt itself to multiple situations, resulting in a variety of regulatory schemes, often influenced by factors other than environmental.

The physical unity of an integrated water network should lead naturally to addressing water problems for an entire hydrographic basin. The legislation of certain countries adopts this approach, but it is a recent development at the international level. For the most part, conventions concerning the protection of rivers traditionally have applied only to isolated rivers, or even certain portions of rivers. The Rhine, for example, is protected by conventional international provisions only between its exit from Lake Constance

---

[8]   In India, 20 million hectares are flooded annually, resulting in flood damage in excess of one billion dollars in the Ganges plain alone. World Bank, *Environment, Growth and Development* (1987). *See also* the case studies published in THE SCARCITY OF WATER, EMERGING LEGAL AND POLICY RESPONSES, *supra* note 2, concerning the Nile, the Jordan, Israel, Jordan and the Palestinians and Africa.

[9]   Few international agreements are addressed exclusively to groundwater. Relevant provisions can be found, however, in multilateral agreements applicable to a continent (*e.g.*, Art. 5 of the African Convention on the Conservation of Nature and Natural Resources, Nov. 15, 1968) or a region (*e.g.*, Art. 4 of the May 17, 1980 Protocol to the Barcelona Convention for the Protection of the Mediterranean (Feb. 16, 1976)).

[10]   *See* H.I.F. Saeijs & M.J. van Berkel, *The Global Water Crisis, the Major Issue of the Twenty-first Century, a Growing and Explosive Problem, in* THE SCARCITY OF WATER EMERGING LEGAL AND POLITICAL RESPONSES, *supra* note 2, at 3.

and its mouth, while waters in the Lake are governed by a separate treaty.[11] In addition, most instruments governing boundary waters concern only the surface waters in the zone regulated by these treaties. Care must be taken to identify the geographic scope of international instruments; some refer to watercourses, others to water systems,[12] and still others to frontier waters,[13] international basins,[14] or water resources.[15]

The 1997 UN Convention on the Law of the Non-Navigational Uses of International Watercourses made an important contribution to international environmental law by defining a "watercourse" as "a system of surface waters and groundwaters constituting by virtue of their physical relationship a unitary whole and normally flowing into a common terminus."[16] This definition reflects the approach taken by Rio Conference Agenda 21 (1992). According to Chapter 18, paragraph 36, the complex and interconnected nature of freshwater systems demands that freshwater management be holistic, taking a "catchment" approach, and must be based on a balanced consideration of the needs of people and the environment. Agenda 21 declares that three objectives need to be pursued concurrently to integrate water quality and water resource management: the maintenance of ecosystem integrity of the drainage basin, public health protection, and human resources development for implementing water quality management.[17]

The legal treatment of water pollution may be complicated by differences between identifiable "point" sources and "diffuse" pollution sources. The latter category includes emissions that individually or separately are responsible for possibly insignificant amounts of pollution, such as small, often continuous discharges of wastes and utilization of pesticides and fertilizers in agriculture. Taken together, however, they may result in considerable contamination and harm to the environment.

---

[11]   Steckborn, Oct. 27, 1960.

[12]   *E.g.*, Yugoslavia-Hungary Agreement, Aug. 8, 1955; U.N. Doc. ST/LEG/SER.B/12, at 830.

[13]   *E.g.*, Poland-Czechoslovakia Agreement, Mar. 21, 1958; 538 U.N.T.S. 108; Poland-USSR, July 17, 1964; 552 U.N.T.S. 177.

[14]   *E.g.*, the Statute of the Lake Chad Commission, Aug. 22, 1964; III I.U.W.R. 964. *See also* the ILA Helsinki Rules on the Use of the Waters of International Rivers (1966).

[15]   Recommendations 51–55 of the Stockholm Action Plan.

[16]   May 21, 1997, Art. 3(a).

[17]   Para. 18.38.

A. Overview

It is impossible in this text to analyze all the regimes that have developed concerning different types of waters, even those of a single region, but it is necessary to give a general outline of the evolution that has occurred[18] Early inter-state cooperation concerning rivers and lakes generally addressed utilization of a watercourse for navigation or irrigation, or concerned the management of risks, such as flooding. Environmental aspects began to be included toward the beginning of the 20th century, but cooperation generally was limited to neighboring states sharing all or part of a river or a lake. In addition, deterioration of water quality was not seen a matter of common concern because it did not affect all riparian states in similar manner, downstream states suffering more harm than the upstream riparians.[19]

International water law has to take into account, among other factors, the geography, meteorology, society, history, politics and economics of each region. For almost a century, local and sub-regional regulations have been tailored to a specific watercourse or an area. At first, particular water pollution problems were addressed when harmful activities originated in neighboring countries, applying general precedents and norms of transfrontier pollution. Later, the development of international environmental law led to the adoption of global rules and principles to govern the conduct of states in respect to the conservation and harmonious utilization of natural resources shared by two or more states. Fresh waters perhaps best illustrate the problems of shared natural resources which need integrated protection of their complex ecosystems.

The legal status of rules on shared resources has been debated but their regular inclusion in different global and regional conventions and in other forms of state practice leads to the conclusion that they constitute customary international law or at least emerging customary norms. The judgment of the International Court of Justice in the case concerning the Gabçikovo-Nagymaros Project on the Danube confirmed the creation of a coherent corpus of environmental principles governing shared water resources. This evolution also has been supported by principles announced in non-binding texts adopted by international organizations such as the United Nations, the Council of Europe, and the UNECE. Special attention must be given to

---

[18] For a history of the development of international law in this field, *see* J.L. Wescoat Jr., *Main Currents in Early Multilateral Water Treaties: A Historical-Geographic Perspective, 1648–1948,* 7 COLO. J. INT'L ENVTL. L & POL'Y 39 (1996).

[19] J.G. LAMMERS, POLLUTION OF INTERNATIONAL WATERCOURSES (1984); A.E. UTTON & L.A. TECLAFF, TRANSBOUNDARY RESOURCES LAW (1987). For a review of groundwater law, *see* FAO, *International Groundwater Resources Law,* FAO Legislative Study 40 (1986); A. NOLLKAEMPER, THE LEGAL REGIME FOR TRANSBOUNDARY WATER POLLUTION: BETWEEN DISCRETION AND CONSTRAINT (1993).

European Community action governing or at least harmonizing member state legislation.

The present chapter examines general global and regional rules protecting fresh waters before reviewing specific regional and sub-regional developments. Two concrete cases are included to illustrate the law of international watercourses: the case between Hungary and Slovakia concerning the Danube and the legal regime governing United States-Mexican boundary waters. The international rivers involved have economic, political, and ecological importance and are international boundaries.

B. General Rules

1. *Global Norms*

A holistic approach considers all water resources without regard to the existence of international borders. The 1966 "Helsinki Rules"[20] of the non-governmental International Law Association are among the first and most-often-cited norms related to international fresh waters. Article 4 contains the basic principle that each state within an international drainage basin has the right to a reasonable and equitable part of the beneficial use of the basin waters. Article 10 adds that, conforming to the principle of equitable utilization, each state should refrain from causing any new form of pollution of the waters or any increase in the level of actual pollution of the waters in the international drainage basin, likely to cause serious damage on the territory of another state in the basin. The state also should take all reasonable measures in order to reduce actual pollution of all kinds so that no serious damage is caused on the territory of another state in the basin.

After adoption of the Helsinki Rules, the 1972 Stockholm Action Plan called for international cooperation to protect inland waters and water resources against pollution (Recommendations 51 to 55). A United Nations water conference, held in 1977 at Mar del Plata, Argentina, recommended the study of methods that could be used for the management of shared water resources, the elaboration of common programs, and the implementation of mechanisms and institutions necessary for the coordinated utilization of water resources. The Principles of Conduct in the Field of Environment for the Guidance of States in the Conservation and Harmonious Utilization of Natural Resources Shared by Two or More States, approved

---

[20] *See* I.L.A., Report of the Committee on the Uses of the Waters of International Rivers, Report of the Fifty-Second Conference, Helsinki, 1966, at 484 (1966). In 1982, the ILA adopted the Montreal Rules on Water Pollution in an International Drainage Basin to update the Helsinki Rules "taking into account developments in theory and practice since 1966." ILA, Report of the Sixtieth Conference (Montreal, 1982), at 1–3, 13, 535 *et seq.*

on May 1979 by the Governing Council of UNEP, were modeled on the prior texts on shared water resources.[21] Agenda 21, Chapter 18, goes further, calling for "protection of the quality and supply of freshwater resources" by "application of integrated approaches to the development, management and use of water resources."[22]

The United Nations International Law Commission, within its mandate to develop and codify international law, began work on the law of non-navigational uses of international watercourses in 1971. In 1990, at its 42nd session, it adopted articles devoted to the environmental protection of international waters.[23] The United Nations General Assembly accepted the articles and adopted a Convention on the Law of the Non-Navigational Uses of International Watercourses on May 21, 1997.

The framework UN Convention includes four categories of provisions: general norms applicable to all international watercourses (Arts. 5–10), procedural rules to implement such norms (Arts. 11–19 and 29–32), substantive provisions concerning the fresh water protection, preservation and management (Arts. 20–28), and clauses concerning agreements between watercourse states (Arts. 3–4).

The Convention mandates that watercourse states, in their respective territories, utilize an international watercourse in an equitable and reasonable manner and with a view of obtaining optimal and sustainable utilization thereof consistent with adequate protection of the watercourse (Art. 5(1)). In addition, such states shall participate in the use, development and protection of the watercourse in an equitable and reasonable manner, with the duty to cooperate in the protection and development thereof (Art. 5(2)). Article 6 lists the factors relevant to deciding whether a use is equitable and reasonable: natural factors (geography, hydrology, climate, ecology); social and economic needs; dependent populations; existing and potential uses of the watercourse; conservation, protection, development and economy of use of the water resources and the costs of measures taken to that effect; and the availability of alternatives of comparable value to a particular planned or existing use. In determining what is a reasonable and equitable use, all relevant factors must be considered together. Article 10 adds somewhat contradictorily that in the absence of agreement or custom to the contrary, no use enjoys inherent priority over other uses, but in the event of a conflict special regard must be given to the requirements of human needs.

---

21   U.N. Doc. UNEP/IG 12/2 (1978); 17 I.L.M. 1097 (1978).

22   *See* Eyal Benvenisti, *Collective Action in the Utilization of Shared Freshwater: the Challenges of International Water Resources Law*, 90 AJIL 384 (1996).

23   International Law Commission, Report of the International Law Commission on the Work of its 42nd Session, May 1–July 20, 1990, U.N. GAOR Supp. 10, A/45/10 (1990).

Article 7 is important to the question of whether a use is equitable and reasonable. The text obliges states to take all appropriate measures to prevent significant harm to other watercourse states. Any state causing such harm "having due regard for the provisions of Articles 5 and 6" must consult with the affected state and eliminate or mitigate such harm and, where appropriate, discuss the question of compensation. Upstream states, whose long-standing uses may be harmful to downstream states, may argue that Article 7 is subordinate to Articles 5 and 6 according to its own terms, and thus harm to downstream states is only one factor to weigh in deciding on the equity or reasonableness of uses, to be balanced against costs, benefits, and prior uses. Downstream states may view or contend that Article 7 is an independent obligation that necessarily renders uses unreasonable if there is significant harm. The Convention does not resolve this problem clearly, and disputes are likely to arise which will require judicial interpretation or arbitration.

The Convention confirms the general rules of international environmental law by requiring transmission of information about planned measures that could have a transboundary impact (Arts.11–16), consultations and negotiation concerning such measures (Art.17) and emergency situations (Art. 25). It also affirms the duty of non-discrimination on the basis of nationality or residence in granting access to judicial or other procedures to any person who has suffered appreciable harm as a result of an activity related to an international watercourse or is exposed to a threat thereof (Art. 32). The term "appreciable" indicates that the threshold for individual remedies is lower than that prompting the preventive and other interstate obligations, which only arise if the threatened harm is "significant" or "serious."

The most innovative provisions are those particularly relevant for international environmental law. The Convention obliges watercourse states to protect, preserve and manage international watercourses and their waters (Art.1(1)) and specifically to protect and preserve watercourse ecosystems (Art. 20). The latter provision echos the duty imposed by UNCLOS Article 192 in respect of marine waters.[24] Watercourse states also must prevent the introduction of alien or new species into the watercourse if the species may have detrimental effects on the ecosystem of the watercourse resulting in significant harm to other watercourse states (Art. 22). The pollution of an international watercourse is defined broadly as "any detrimental alteration in the composition or quality of the waters . . . which results directly or indirectly from human conduct." Watercourse states shall prevent, reduce and

---

24   Interestingly, the Watercourses Convention also addresses the protection and preservation of the marine environment, requiring watercourse states to take all measures that are necessary to this effect, if appropriate in cooperation with other states, taking into account generally accepted international rules and standards (Art. 23).

control pollution, in particular by harmonizing their policies. The measures advocated include setting joint water quality objectives and criteria, establishing techniques and practices to address pollution from point and non-point sources, and establishing lists of substances whose introduction is to be prohibited, limited, investigated or monitored (Art. 21).

Albeit the entire Convention focuses on cooperation among watercourse states, Articles 3 and 4 promote formalized cooperation by encouraging the conclusion of watercourse agreements that further apply and adjust the provisions of the Convention. Even without concluding such an agreement, consultations shall be undertaken at the request of a watercourse state concerning the management of the watercourse, including the possible establishment of a joint management mechanism (Art. 24(1)). "Management," as used in this provision, "refers, in particular, to (a) planning the sustainable development of an international watercourse and providing for the implementation of any plans adopted; and (b) otherwise promoting the rational and optimal utilization, protection and control of the watercourse" (Art. 24(2)).

The UN Convention now constitutes the essential basis of international law on fresh waters, even though not in force as of 2003. As a codification convention, it generally expresses customary international law, although elements in the Convention also reflect compromises between upstream and downstream riparian interests and the progressive development of international environmental law. The International Court of Justice, in its judgment of September 25, 1997, in the *Gabçikovo-Nagymaros* case, explicitly recognized the obligatory nature of the principle of equitable utilization contained in Article 5(2) of the Convention.[25]

The requirement of equitable utilization has inevitably given rise to a trend favoring the conclusion of joint management agreements which create institutions and procedures for allocating shared water resources, establishing priorities and determining equitable use. An example of such cooperation is discussed below with respect to the U.S.-Mexican boundary waters agreements. As a related matter, the expansion of freshwater law to include the entire catchment area or watershed enlarges the participation of states in such management agreements. The Danube Agreement, for example, allows participation by all states that contain more than 2,000 square kilometers of the total catchment area.

2. Regional Regulation

Regional bodies have adopted general principles regarding fresh water. The Council of Europe announced fundamental principles in the 1968 European

---

[25]   *Gabçikovo-Nagymaros* Case, Judgment of Sept. 25, 1997, para. 147.

Water Charter,[26] a non-binding instrument adopted two years after the ILA Helsinki Rules and more broadly addressing all fresh waters. The Charter calls water an indispensable resource which is not inexhaustible. It proclaims that water quality must be preserved at the levels necessary for the use foreseen, that water is a heritage whose value must be recognized by all, that water knows no boundary, and that its regulation demands international cooperation.

Other regional instruments concern specific forms or sources of pollution. In 1968, the Council of Europe adopted the European Agreement on the Restriction of the Use of Certain Detergents in Washing and Cleaning Products.[27] The United Nations Economic Commission for Europe has made several recommendations through its Committee on Water Problems, including a 1970 recommendation on the protection of ground and surface waters against pollution by oil and oil products.[28] Paragraph 3 called on member governments to designate "protection zones" in areas needing to be preserved from pollution in view of their utilization; issue regulations concerning the storage, transport and disposal of oil, oil products and effluents from oil industries in order to avoid water pollution; and immediately report all spillage of oil and oil products likely to contaminate either ground or surface waters.

The OECD adopted a recommendation in 1989 on Water Resource Management Policies: Integration, Demand Management, and Groundwater Protection.[29] This instrument recommends review by member countries of existing institutional arrangements in the field of water resources to improve the integrated management of their policies. Comprehensive policies should exist for the efficient, sustainable development of groundwater resources and for their long-term protection from pollution and over-use. Particular attention should be paid to establishment and enforcement of pollution control programs and research to better understand pollution processes. Legislation on water should include environmental protection. The recommendation notes that the slow movement of groundwater and high cost of assessing its quality make it particularly vulnerable to long-term cumulative pollution and raise substantial uncertainties regarding its current and future condition. An important aspect of water resources management is thus to reduce pollution from diffuse and small point sources. Therefore, the production, sale and use of chemicals, emissions into the atmosphere, and dumping of wastes must be controlled. Finally, "because currently available information will rarely resolve all uncertainties in deci-

---

[26] May 6, 1968. Consultative Assembly Recomm. 493 (1967), *adopted* Apr. 28, 1967; Committee of Ministers Res. (67) 10, *adopted* May 26, 1967, *reprinted in* U.N. Doc. A/CN.4/274, para. 373.

[27] Sept. 16, 1968.

[28] E/ECE/WATER/7, annex I.

[29] Council Recommendation C(89)12(Final), Mar. 31, 1989.

sion-making for groundwater management, policies should encourage precautionary decisions."

In the decade between 1980 and 1990, the Committee on Water Problems of the UNECE drafted a series of general texts on cooperation in the field of transboundary waters.[30] They start from the accepted principle that states must take measures not to cause environmental damage outside national jurisdiction. As a consequence, the protection of transboundary waters cannot be national, but requires cooperation among riparian countries. Riparian states should conclude treaties, notably on matters concerning pollution, where they should jointly define water quality standards and objectives. Supervision, monitoring and observation of water quality and pollution should be jointly undertaken and states should exchange facts and information on pollution. This needs the creation of efficient alert systems in cases of serious accidental pollution and, in appropriate cases, the organization of mutual aid for emergency situations. Finally, institutional arrangements are deemed necessary including the creation of commissions and mixed working groups.

In 1990, the UNECE adopted a lengthy Code of Conduct on Accidental Pollution of Transboundary Inland Waters[31] applicable to hazardous activities resulting or likely to result in significant impairment of the quality of transboundary inland waters and/or significant damage to aquatic ecosystems in the territory of other countries. In the same regional framework a Convention on the Protection and Use of Transboundary Watercourses and International Lakes was drafted and adopted in Helsinki, on March 17, 1992, covering Europe, Canada and the U.S. The Convention has been the model for subsequent agreements on the Danube and other regional rivers in Europe.

The Helsinki Convention aims to protect watercourses against harmful transboundary environmental impacts. It is not formally a framework treaty because it does not provide for the conclusion of additional protocols for signature by all the contracting parties. While adopting some common solutions, it takes into account the variety of situations pertaining to different river systems: its preamble recites that cooperation between states parties shall be implemented primarily through the elaboration of agreements between countries bordering the same waters. Article 2(6) adds that such agreements should develop harmonized policies, programs and strategies covering the catchment areas or parts thereof. Article 9, entirely devoted to bilateral and multilateral cooperation, contains indications concerning the fields and the functioning of such cooperation.

---

[30]   Res. I(42), Apr. 10, 1987, E/1987/33, E/ECE/1148, at 65. *See also* the ECE Declaration of Policy on Prevention and Control of Water Pollution, Including Transboundary Pollution, Res. B(XXXV), Apr. 26, 1980; U.N. Doc. E/1980/28, E/ECE 1008, at 92.

[31]   Dec. C(45), U.N. Pub. E/ECE/1225, ECE/ENVWA/16 (1990).

Several aspects of the regional Convention are similar to those of the UN Convention, including the definition of transboundary waters as surface or ground waters and the call for ecologically sound and rational water management. The parties shall take appropriate measures to prevent, control and reduce pollution of waters causing or likely to cause transboundary impact and to ensure conservation and, where necessary, restoration of ecosystems (Art. 2(2)).

The Helsinki Convention, however, also includes additional elements such as prevention, precaution and the polluter pays principle which must guide the states parties (Art. 2(3) and (5)), and the obligation to avoid the transfer of pollution from one to another part of the environment (Art. 2(3)). Article 3 lists measures which the parties are to develop, adopt and implement. They include, *inter alia*, the prior licensing of waste-water discharges, stricter requirements when the quality of the receiving water or the ecosystem so requires, the reduction of nutrient inputs, environmental impact assessment, monitoring the state of the watercourses, and the development of contingency planning.

In implementing the agreement, states shall use the best available technology, which Annex I to the Convention defines as "the latest stage of development of processes, facilities or methods of operation which indicate the practical suitability of a particular measure for limiting discharges, emissions and waste." The text elaborates the criteria to which special consideration shall be given: comparable processes, technological advances and changes, economic feasibility, time limitations, the nature and volume of the discharges and effluents concerned, low and non-waste technology. Annex II proposes guidelines for developing "best environmental practices" including public information and education, product labeling, recycling, recovery and reuse, and licensing.

Primary obligations of the contracting parties include setting emission limits for discharges from point sources into surface waters (Art. 3(2)) and, where appropriate, defining water quality objectives and adopting water quality criteria (Art. 3(3)). Annex III to the Convention proposes guidelines for developing such objectives and criteria. Other provisions repeat and confirm more general international environmental law obligations such as monitoring (Arts. 4, 11), cooperation in the conduct of research (Arts. 5, 12), exchange of information (Arts. 6, 13), consultations (Arts. 6, 10) and public information. States parties are to set up and operate coordinated or joint alarm systems (Art. 14) and provide mutual assistance upon request in emergencies (Art. 14). A Meeting of the Parties reviews the implementation of the Convention.

The Protocol on Water and Health to the Helsinki Watercourses Convention[32] aims to promote the protection of human health and well-being

---

[32]   London, June 17, 1999, *available at* <http://www.waterlink. net/gb/who2cf99.htm>.

at all appropriate levels, nationally as well as in transboundary and international contexts. The Convention notes from the outset that water is essential to sustain life and that water quality and quantity must be assured to meet basic human needs, "a prerequisite both for improved health and for sustainable development." The general provisions oblige parties to take all appropriate measures to prevent, control and reduce water-related disease within a framework of integrated water management systems, aimed at sustainable use of water resources, ambient water quality which does not endanger human health, and protection of water ecosystems. (Art. 4(1)). In particular, parties shall take measures to ensure and protect adequate supplies of wholesome drinking water free from dangers to human health and provide sanitation (Art. 4(2)). Article 5 includes all the modern principles of international environmental law: polluter pays, precaution, prevention, duty not to cause transboundary harm, rights of future generations, and subsidiarity. Rights to information and public participation in decision-making are emphasized "in order to enhance the quality and the implementation of the decisions, to build public awareness of issues, to give the public the opportunity to express its concerns and enable public authorities to take due account of such concerns" (Art. 5(I)). Information and participation is to be supplemented by access to justice for review of relevant decisions when appropriate.

The European Community has made efforts to address the problem of water pollution in all its aspects. As a quasi-federal entity, its approach goes beyond the consideration of transboundary waters to include the internal water resources of its member states. The EC's water law was developed initially in the mid-1970s to address specific substances, sources, processes and uses of water, as well as its function in habitat protection. The measures lacked integration because of their piecemeal nature and were occasionally inconsistent or conflicting.

For 20 years the main EC instrument was Directive 76/464/ECE[33] concerning pollution caused by certain dangerous substances discharged into the aquatic environment of the Community. Separate directives set quality standards for different uses of the aquatic environment (drinking water, bathing, fish farming, etc).[34] A new directive adopted on October 23, 2000,

---

[33] May 4, 1976, O.J. L 129 (5/18/76).

[34] Directive 75/440, June 16, 1975, concerning the quality required of surface waters intended for abstraction of drinking water, O.J. L 194 (7/25/75); Directive 79/869, Oct. 9, 1979, relating to the methods of measurement and the frequency of sampling and analysis of surface waters to be used for drinking, O.J. L 271 (10/29/79); Directive 80/778, July 15, 1980, relating to the quality of water intended for human consumption, O.J. L 299 (7/30/80). Directive 76/160, Dec. 8, 1975, concerning the quality of bathing waters, O.J. L 31 (2/5/76); Directive 78/659, July 18, 1978, concerning the quality of fresh water needing protection or improvement in order to support fish life, O.J. L 222

establishes a comprehensive framework for Community action in the field of water policy.[35]

The new Water Directive aims to introduce a strategic framework, providing more holistic and integrated approaches to water management and conservation. The underlying aims are (1) to use hydrological catchments rather than political or administrative boundaries as the basis for action; (2) to set environmental objectives to ensure that all waters achieve good status and do not deteriorate; (3) to introduce a combined approach to pollution control and encourage sustainable water use; (4) to contribute to mitigating the effects of floods and droughts; and (5) to ensure active stakeholder and community involvement. Europe will be divided into a series of river basin districts, some of which will traverse international boundaries. River Basin Management Plans will establish a program of measures to meet specific environmental objectives for each river basin. Water management issues and the measures to be taken will be developed through public consultation.

The basic principle of the Directive is that water is not a commercial product like any other but, rather, a heritage which must be protected, defended and treated as such. The supply of water is a service of general interest. Further, protection and sustainable management of water must be integrated into other Community policy areas such as energy, transport, agriculture, fisheries, regional policy and tourism. The Directive itself aims to maintain and improve the aquatic environment in the Community by contributing to the progressive reduction of emissions of substances presenting a significant risk to or via the aquatic environment, including risks to waters used for the abstraction of drinking water. As minimum requirements and using a combined approach for point and diffuse pollution sources, the Community is to adopt common environmental quality standards and emission limit values for certain groups or families of pollutants, in order to prevent further deterioration of aquatic ecosystems, protect and enhance their status, and promote sustainable water use based on long-term protection of available water resources.

The Directive innovates by covering inland surface waters and groundwater, as well as by adding the categories of "transitional waters" and "coastal waters." Transitional waters are bodies of surface water in the vicinity of a river mouth which are partly saline but which are substantially influenced by freshwater flows. Coastal water means surface water on the landward side

---

(8/14/78); Directive 79/923, Oct. 30, 1979, relating to the quality required of shellfish waters, O.J. L 281 (11/10/79). The directive set quantity parameters, conditions of sampling, and methods of analysis and inspection.

[35]   Directive 2000/60/EC; O.J. L 327 (12/22/00). A decision of November 20, 2001 amended and complemented the framework directive by establishing a new list of priority substances in the field of water policy. Decision No 2455/2001/EC; O.J. L 331 (12/15/01).

of a line, every point of which is at a distance of one nautical mile on the seaward from the baseline, which means a portion of the territorial sea.

The Directive sets distinct environmental objectives for basin management plans for surface waters, for groundwater and for protected areas (Art. 4). Specific provisions apply to waters used for the abstraction of drinking water (Art. 7). Article 9 affirms the principle that the costs of water services, including environmental and resource costs, should be recovered from the user. The Directive encourages the active involvement of all interested parties in its implementation, by ensuring that each river basin district makes available or publishes information for public comment and consultation on significant water management issues (Art. 14). The 11 annexes of the Directive list detailed technical data corresponding to the different types of aquatic environment. Annex VI lists the categories of measures to be taken, including legislative, administrative and economic instruments. Annex VII provides the elements which river basin management plans shall cover, while Annex VIII contains an indicative list of the main pollutants. Annex XI maps 25 European "eco-regions for rivers and lakes," significantly including the territory of states which are not members of the European Union.

The Directive foresees classifying water quality as high, good, fair, poor or bad, based on a range of ecological, chemical and hydrological criteria. By 2015 all surface waters should be classified as "good." The challenge is to integrate ecological indicators with traditional water quality and quantity objectives. The Directive says that ecological status will be assessed through measuring biological, hydromophological and chemical elements, including pollution levels. Special protection zones may need to be established to protect special habitats, conserve drinking water or protect bathing water. States will be required to prevent or limit groundwater contamination, monitor groundwater, and impose measures to reverse significant pollution caused by human activity.

Although the Directive is comprehensive, it contains several loopholes. First, states can extend the deadline for meeting environmental objectives for up to 12 years if there are valid technical problems, cost implications or natural constraints, as long as the water does not deteriorate. Less stringent environmental objectives can be set for artificial and heavily modified water bodies. Objectives also may be set aside to benefit human health or sustainable development if the benefits outweigh the loss of the environmental objectives.

C. From Transfrontier Pollution Control to Shared Resource Management

Concern for water pollution in an international context has been expressed since the beginning of the industrial era, with legal instruments addressing

the topic concluded as early as 1868.[36] One comprehensive study produced
a list of 88 conventions containing similar provisions relating to the protection of inland waters from pollution.[37] Two categories of relevant international instruments may be distinguished. First, until the 1960s most
anti-pollution provisions were included in conventions of more general purpose, for example, those regulating boundary matters between neighboring states. Since that time, a growing number of sub-regional or regional
treaties have been concluded to combat the pollution of international watercourses or lakes. More recently, holistic agreements address all the environmental problems of managing fresh waters.

1. Europe

Although the Rhine river is not among the longest or widest rivers of the
world, it has exceptional economic, political, and cultural importance as
the principal international watercourse of Western Europe. It constitutes
the direct and essential source of water for a region of close to 50 million
inhabitants in one of the most industrialized areas of the world. As such,
the Rhine serves many purposes from drinking and industrial water supply,
navigation and the production of electricity, to a dumping ground for many
kinds of waste.

The legal status of the Rhine is regulated by a complex network or jux-
taposition of norms and institutions. Two international bodies, in particular, are concerned with the use of its waters. First, the Central Commission
for Navigation of the Rhine, created in 1868 in order to ensure free navigation, has become concerned with Rhine pollution and has taken preventive measures concerning pollution of the waters by hydrocarbons.[38] It
also has prohibited or regulated the transportation of certain hazardous
products. Although limited in scope, these measures are successful because
the regulations of the Central Commission are binding. In addition, the
Central Commission adopted, on September 9, 1996, a Convention on the
collection and disposal of wastes in the navigation of the Rhine.[39]

The International Commission for the Protection of the Rhine against
Pollution is the primary organ of international action to protect the river.
Created by an agreement signed in Bern on April 29, 1963, its member
states are France, Luxembourg, the Netherlands, the Federal Republic of

---

[36]   An agreement between France and Spain on the international frontier
of the Pyrenees provided in section I(6) that "The discharge of foul or harmful water into the bed of the said river by riparian or other proprietors shall also
be prohibited." U.N. Doc. A/CN.4/4122 add 1, at 9.

[37]   J.G. LAMMERS, POLLUTION OF INTERNATIONAL WATERCOURSES 124–47 (1984).

[38]   Art. 1.15, Réglement de police pour la navigation du Rhin.

[39]   EMuT 996:68

Germany, and Switzerland. Luxembourg, a non-riparian state, is also a member of the Commission due to the presence in its territory of the Mosel, which flows into the Rhine. In 1976, the Commission of the European Community joined the Rhine Commission. A new Convention on the Protection of the Rhine (Bern, April 12, 1999) reorganized the Commission, which became an international institution invested with legal personality. Concerned non-governmental organizations can be recognized as observers at the Commission and, as such, they can express opinions in discussions, submit information or reports, attend meetings of the Commission and be consulted (Art. 14).

The Commission prepares international programs for monitoring the ecosystem of the Rhine, makes proposals for individual actions, coordinates alarm plans and systems of the river states, and assesses the effectiveness of the measures adopted, largely on the basis of reports which the parties submit to it (Art. 8). The Commission adopts decisions by unanimous vote, addressed to member states in the form of recommendations for specific action and for broader programs (Art. 10). Recommendations can include implementation deadlines and provide for coordinated compliance procedures (Art. 11(1) and (2)).

A compliance control system is foreseen: the Commission can decide that the parties shall submit regular reports on the legislative, regulatory or other measures that they have taken in order to comply with the provisions of the Convention and the decisions adopted, on the problems they raise and on the results of such measures. If a contracting party cannot implement a Commission decision, it can report this fact within a prescribed period of time explaining the cause of the non-compliance. Any other party can ask for consultation, which then shall be held within two months. If no state requests consultations, the Commission can decide on measures to be taken on the basis of the reports of the contracting parties or whether to organize consultations in order to enhance the implementation of the decisions (Art.11(3)–(5)).

The 1999 Rhine Convention is based on a holistic vision with a view towards the sustainable development of the Rhine ecosystem, considering the river itself, its banks and its alluvial zones. It also takes into account the April 9, 1992 Helsinki Convention on the Protection and Use of Transboundary Watercourses and Lakes as well as the Convention on the Protection of the Marine Environment of the North-East Atlantic.[40] As a consequence, the new Convention has an extensive scope, in contrast to that foreseen by the prior regime. While the Rhine itself is defined as including the river as it exists from Lake Constance, and its side arms system in the Netherlands, the Convention is to be applied not only to the Rhine, but also to the underground waters which are in connection with it, the aquatic and terrestrial ecosystems which are or which could be con-

---

[40]   Paris, Sept. 22, 1992.

nected to it, and the catchment area as far as the pollution originating from it affects the Rhine or plays an important role in the prevention and protection of floods along the Rhine (Art. 2).

Between 1976 and 1999, the main legal instrument for controlling Rhine pollution was the Convention for the Protection of the Rhine against Chemical Pollution,[41] an instrument directly inspired by EEC Directive 76/464 concerning pollution caused by certain dangerous substances discharged into the aquatic environment of the Communities. It thus provided for emission standards of listed substances, including substances which should not be discharged into the water and substances which could only be discharged upon prior authorization. The 1976 Convention, which entered into force on February 1, 1979, represented a step forward in dealing with freshwater pollution when compared to former regulations. While previous instruments most often failed to include the relevant hydrographic basin, several provisions of this Convention have a larger territorial applicability. The concept of a hydrographic basin, the modern framework for water management, is found in the treaty and confirmed by the presence of Luxembourg in the International Commission. The 1999 Rhine Convention, discussed above, explicitly adopts and systematizes this concept.

The years following adoption of the Bonn Convention saw an improvement of water quality in the Rhine, until a 1986 accident in the Swiss company Sandoz located near Basel, demonstrated that accident prevention needed improvement. As a result of a fire in the Sandoz factory, chemicals entered the Rhine, causing serious damage to living organisms and endangering the water supply along the river in France and in Germany. In less than a year, the question of damages was settled by negotiations between the company and the victims. The company agreed to fund the establishment of a measuring station on the Rhine, a station to alert populations and inform border towns, and contribute to the restoration of the Rhine ecosystem. At the inter-state level, Rhine riparians decided to improve the emergency alert system, to address the problem of compensating victims by providing for strict liability, and to elaborate a program of action in three stages, aimed at improving the water quality of the Rhine to allow the reintroduction of species formerly present, such as salmon, and the utilization of the waters for drinking purposes.

The 1999 Rhine Convention further develops these concerns. Its objectives are the preservation and improvement of Rhine water quality, including underground water, protection against suspended substances and sediments, protection of living organisms and of species diversity, and the preservation and restoration of the natural functions of the river system, including its function as the habitat of fish. The Convention prescribes water resource management that respects the environment and takes into

---

[41]   Bonn, Dec. 3, 1976.

account ecological requirements when planning technical measures for flood protection, for navigation, and for the production of electricity. The Convention also aims at the production of drinking water and improvement in the quality of sediments as well as to contribute to controlling the pollution of the North Sea (Art 3).

Article 4 of the Convention lists as guidelines all the principles and norms which have emerged in international environmental law: the precautionary principle, prevention, control of polluting emissions at the source, polluter pays, nuisance abatement and compensation for unavoidable nuisances, sustainable development, use of best available technologies and best environmental practices, and non-transfer of pollution from one sector to others. The contacting parties are obliged to execute Commission decisions on programs of study and measurement and to transmit the results to the Commission, to endeavor to identify the causes of, and the responsibility for pollution of the water, to establish a system of permits for waste water, to progressively reduce the emission of hazardous substances, to monitor general regulations and permits, to reduce the risks of accidental pollution and immediately to inform other states of emergencies (Art. 5).

On the same day the treaty was concluded, the contracting parties adopted guidelines for a program of sustainable development of the Rhine. The program provides for ensuring a high level of protection, for an integrated approach to the protection of the Rhine, for the use of modern tools in the management of the river and for the systematic dissemination of information and knowledge of environmental problems and solutions.

Other European conventions create similar mechanisms for controlling the pollution of international watercourses. The political changes which started in the late 1980s in Central and Eastern Europe, where cooperation generally had been achieved through bilateral treaties between neighboring river states, made possible new, multilateral forms of cooperation. On October 8, 1990, unified Germany, Czechoslovakia and the European Community established an International Commission for the Protection of the Elbe. The aims of the agreement are to enable the river to be used, in particular for obtaining supplies of drinking water from bank-filtered waters and for agricultural purposes; to achieve as natural an ecosystem as possible with a diversity of species; and to reduce substantially the pollution of the North Sea from the Elbe area (Art. 1(2)). The Commission's mandate is to prepare surveys of pollution, to propose limit values for the discharge of effluents, and to propose specific quality objectives (Art. 2(1)).

The adoption of the Convention on Cooperation for the Protection and Sustainable Use of the Danube River[42] by 11 Central and Eastern European countries and the European Community marked a particularly important step in the development of regional approaches to environmental

---

[42]   Sofia, June 29, 1994; EMuT 994/49.

protection of inland waters. The Treaty is modeled after the 1992 Helsinki Convention on the Protection and Use of Transboundary Watercourses and International Lakes, applying it in a concrete project of cooperation. It is the most advanced treaty on environmental protection of inland waters, because of its integrated approach.

One of the innovative features of the Convention is the breadth of its territorial scope, which is the catchment area of the Danube, defined as the hydrological river basin. The target countries, called Danubian states, are defined as sovereign states having a share exceeding 2,000 km² of the total hydrological catchment area (Art. 1(a) and (b)). The impact and the significance of the Convention are enhanced by Article 2(1), which provides that the parties shall endeavor to contribute to reducing the pollution loads of the Black Sea from sources in the catchment area, thus addressing land-based marine pollution in the region. Finally, the Convention mandates specific preventive water resources measures, primarily concerning ground-water pollution caused by nitrates, plant protection agents, and pesticides, in particular, and measures to reduce the risks of accidents (Art. 6).

The objective of the Danube Convention is sustainable and equitable water management, including the conservation, improvement and the rational use of surface and ground waters in the catchment area, as far as possible. The contracting parties also are to make an effort to control the risk of accidents involving substances hazardous to water, from floods and from ice-hazards on the Danube River (Art. 2(1)). Sustainable use of water resources shall be ensured for municipal, industrial, and agricultural purposes, as well as for public health, while ecosystems shall be conserved and restored (Art. 2(3)). All measures must be guided by the polluter pays principle and the principles of prevention and precaution (Arts. 2(4) and (5)).

The Convention's general concern is with the transboundary impact of polluting activities, thus following the 1992 Helsinki Convention on the Protection and Use of Transboundary Watercourses and International Lakes. This means that national legislation and other regulatory measures must ensure efficient water quality protection and sustainable water use within national jurisdiction and control, thereby to prevent, control and reduce transboundary environmental impacts (Art. 5(1)). Article 4 explicitly mentions the necessity to control the discharge of waste waters, the input of nutrients and hazardous substances both from point and non-point sources, heat discharge, planned activities and measures in the field of water construction works, water power utilization, water transfer and withdrawal, the operation of existing hydrotechnical constructions, and the handling of substances hazardous to water.

The basic principle of the Convention is that emissions shall be limited to prevent pollution. To this end, the parties shall undertake periodic inventories of the relevant point and non-point sources of pollution which should form the basis for developing joint action programs (Art. 8). Taking into account proposals from the International Commission created by the convention, states parties must set emission limits, applicable to individual industrial sectors or industries, in terms of pollution loads and concentrations and based as much as possible on low- and non-waste technologies at source. Discharges of hazardous substances should be limited on the basis of the best available technologies for the abatement at source and/or for waste water purification (Art. 7). Convention Annex II lists, on the one hand, industrial sectors and industries that are potential sources of pollution and, on the other hand, hazardous substances and groups of substances, whose discharge from point and non-point sources shall be prevented or considerably reduced. The Convention also advocates defining water quality objectives and applying water quality criteria (Art. 7(4)) for which general guidance is given in Annex III. All the provisions are complemented by Annex I, which describes the criteria for best available techniques and the best environmental practice.

The parties to the convention shall exchange reasonably available data on the general conditions of the riverine environment, on experience gained in the application and operation of best available techniques, on emissions and monitoring, and on measures and regulations adopted concerning the protection of water (Art. 12). Parties can consult on planned activities between parties at the request of one or several of them (Art. 11). Information concerning the state or the quality of the riverine environment shall be made available to any natural or legal person, under the standard conditions of payment of charges and confidentiality (Art. 4). For critical situations, states shall provide warning and alarm systems as well as mutual assistance (Arts. 16 and 17).

The effective application of the Convention is ensured through the cooperation of the parties in monitoring implementation and by the Commission for the Protection of the Danube River. Convention Article 18 establishes the Commission and Annex IV contains its Statute. It is composed of delegates nominated by the parties and it can adopt consensus decisions and recommendations, the former becoming binding for all parties that voted for the measure (Annex IV, Art. 5). Article 10 establishes a reporting system whereby states parties shall provide information on, *inter alia*, national laws, ordinances and other general regulations relating to the protection and water management of the Danube, planned activities which are likely to cause transboundary impacts, and the manner, timeframe, and the financial expenses involved in implementing action-oriented decisions of the Commission at the domestic level.

France, the Netherlands and the three Belgian regions (Wallonia, Flanders, and Brussels-Capital regions) adopted two parallel agreements of more limited territorial scope for the Meuse and the Schedt.[43] The agree-

---

43   Charleville Mézières, France, Apr. 26, 1994.

ments are much shorter and less developed than the Danube Convention, although all are based on the 1992 Helsinki Convention on the Protection of Transboundary Watercourses and International Lakes.[44] They make a distinction between the river basin, including all the waterways and canals which directly or indirectly run into the main river, where situated on the territory of the contracting parties, and the drainage area, the waters of which run into the Meuse (Scheldt) or its tributaries (Art. 1). The second definition appears wider than the first in the sense that the "river basin" is defined as a hydrological network, while the "drainage area" refers not to the water itself, but the territorial area on which this water flows.[45] Cooperation between parties must be guided by the polluter pays and the precautionary principles, as well as by the principles of preventive action, containment, and pollution reduction. The contracting states shall act in a comparable way throughout the drainage area in order to avoid distortions of competition and shall take appropriate measures to achieve an integrated management of the drainage area (Art. 3). Article 4 provides for mutual information on and coordination of policies regarding the management of sediments and for limiting dumping and discharges of dredged material and its movement downstream. Such provisions were necessary for the areas covered by the two agreements, which are heavily industrialized and receive a large amount of polluting substances, in particular heavy metals, from sediments carried by the rivers.

Both agreements have strong institutions, international commissions composed of the delegations of the parties (Arts. 2(2), 5 and 6). They have the usually-conferred tasks of collecting and evaluating data provided by the parties, drawing up inventories and programs of action, and promoting the exchange of information. In addition, they also may issue advisory opinions and recommendations regarding cooperation under the agreements (Art. 5). They also draw up annual reports of their activities, made available to the public, and any other type of report deemed necessary.

Finally, the Czech Republic, the EU European Commission, Germany and Poland created an International Commission for the Protection of the Oder[46] by a Convention concluded April 11, 1996. Its aim is broad, to prevent pollution not only of the Oder River, but also of the Baltic Sea. The Commission, which consists of the delegates of the contracting parties, draws up joint action programs with timetables for their implementation, propose limit values and water quality objectives, and prepare surveys of point sources of pollution.

---

[44]   *See* Nicolette Bouman, *A New Regime for the Meuse,* 5 RECIEL 161, 165 (1996).

[45]   Axel Gosseries, *The 1994 Agreements Concerning the Protection of the Scheldt and Meuse Rivers,* EUROPEAN ENVTL. L. REV. 9 (Jan. 1995).

[46]   Wroclaw, Apr. 11, 1996.

2. North America

In North America two treaty regimes have been established, one for boundary waters shared by the United States and Canada and one for the United States-Mexico boundary waters. The Treaty relating to Boundary Waters and Questions Arising between the United States and Canada,[47] signed by the United Kingdom and the U.S. in Washington on January 11, 1909, contained in Article IV(2) the obligation not to pollute waters forming or crossing the U.S.-Canadian boundary. This provision had little effect, however, and the Great Lakes—which contain ten percent of the world's available fresh water—became extremely polluted, despite the investigations and recommendations of the International Joint Commission created by the treaty. In the 1960s renewed efforts were made to implement the obligation contained in Article IV(2). The Great Lakes Water Quality Agreements of 1972 and 1978[48] reaffirmed and elaborated the provisions for the Great Lakes system.

Particularly detailed regulations are found in the November 22, 1978, Agreement between the United States and Canada on Great Lakes Water Quality.[49] The purpose of the agreement is "to restore and maintain the chemical, physical, and biological integrity of the waters of the Great Lakes Basin Ecosystem" (Art. II). The parties agree to control pollutants and to comply with both general and specific objectives set forth in the treaty. General objectives are defined as broad descriptions of water quality conditions consistent with the protection of the beneficial uses and the level of environmental quality sought by the parties and which will provide overall water management guidance. Specific objectives set the precise concentration or quantity of a substance or level of effect that is allowable. Annex I to the agreement contains the specific objectives and lists chemical, physical, microbiological and radiological pollutants. While the specific objectives establish minimum water quality standards, Article IV of the agreement provides that if higher water quality exists, such quality must be maintained and improved.[50]

Concern for the Great Lakes system has also developed on issues of water quantity. Trade in water is becoming economically viable in water-rich countries and could pose problems for the future if water, which is often

---

[47] AJIL (1910) Supp. 239.

[48] J.G. LAMMERS, POLLUTION OF INTERNATIONAL WATERCOURSES 265–66 (1985).

[49] Nov. 22, 1978.

[50] The 1972 and 1978 Agreements were strengthened by a 1985 protocol. On the new trend to initiate an ecosystem approach to the management of the international river basins shared by the two countries across the entire boundary, *see* L.B. Dworsky, *News Notes from the International Joint Commission Canada-United States*, 1988 TRANSBOUNDARY RESOURCES REPORT 2.

considered a public good, is subject to private appropriation for export. In 1998 a Canadian company proposed to export 158 million gallons from Lake Superior to Asia, raising concerns about potential water loss in the Great Lakes. In 2001 U.S. state governors and Canadian provincial premiers in areas surrounding the Great Lakes agreed to negotiate a binding instrument setting forth standards for reviewing proposals to withdraw water from the region. Such standards are to be based upon the principles of (1) preventing or minimizing water loss to the Great Lakes basin through return flow and implementation of environmentally sound and economically feasible water conservation measures; (2) no significant adverse individual or cumulative impacts to the quantity or quality of the waters and water-dependent natural resources of the Great Lakes; (3) an improvement to the waters and water-dependent natural resources of the basin; and (4) compliance with applicable state, provincial, federal and international laws and treaties.[51]

The agreements between the United States and Mexico are treated later in this chapter.

3. South America

In South America, Argentina and Uruguay adopted a Statute of the Uruguay River in 1975 in order to coordinate, through a commission established by the treaty, "appropriate measures to prevent the alteration of the ecological balance, and to control impurities and other harmful elements in the river and its catchment area."[52] The parties also agreed to conserve and preserve living resources of the river and to "protect and preserve the aquatic environment."[53] Two decades later, in 1995, Argentina, Bolivia and Paraguay established a Tripartite Commission for the Development of the basin of the Rio Pilcomayo. This body is to monitor water quality and to propose emission standards for specific polluting substances. It also has the task of coordinating necessary national measures in order to avoid deterioration of the biological balance and the propagation of diseases.[54]

4. Africa

The Niger Basin Agreement of October 26, 1963, provides that the riparian states will cooperate regarding the study and execution of any project

---

[51]   Great Lakes Charter Annex: A Supplementary Agreement to the Great Lakes Charter, Directive No. 3 (June 18, 2001), *available at* <www.glu.org>.

[52]   Article 36, Statute of the Uruguay River, Uruguay, Ministerio de Relaciones Exteriores, *Actos Internacionales Uruguay-Argentina, 1830–1980* 593 (1981).

[53]   Arts. 37, 41.

[54]   Agreement of La Paz, Feb. 9, 1995.

likely to have an appreciable effect on certain features of the regime of the river, its tributaries and sub-tributaries, the sanitary conditions of their waters, and the biological characteristics of their fauna and flora.[55] The 1978 Gambia River Agreement[56] provides in Article 4 that "[n]o project which is likely to bring about serious modifications of the characteristics of the river's regime, . . . the sanitary state of the waters, the biological characteristics of its fauna and its flora. . . will be implemented without prior approval of the contracting states." The Agreement on the Preparation of a Tripartite Environmental Management Program for Lake Victoria, adopted August 5, 1994, by Kenya, Tanzania and Uganda[57] provides for the establishment of a Regional Policy and Steering Committee, to be assisted by a Regional Secretariat, and two regional Task Forces. The Management Program includes fisheries management and control of water hyacinth and other invasive weeds, as well as the management of water quality and land use, including wetlands.[58]

A Protocol on Shared Watercourse Systems was adopted on August 28, 1995,[59] in the framework of the Southern African Development Community[60] and revised by a new agreement adopted on August 7, 2000.[61] The Revised Protocol is largely based on the principles of the 1997 UN Convention. Its objective is to foster closer cooperation for judicious, sustainable and coordinated management, protection and utilization of shared watercourses. The state parties recognize the unity and coherence of each shared watercourse and undertake to respect the existing rules of customary or general international law relating to the utilization and management of shared watercourses. They agree to exchange available information and data regarding the hydrological, water quality and environmental condition of shared watercourses and utilize a shared watercourse in an equitable and reasonable manner, with a view to attaining optimal and sustainable utilization for the benefit of current and future generations (Art. 3).

---

[55] Art. 4, Act Regarding Navigation and Economic Cooperation between the States of the Niger Basin, October 26, 1963. The states parties are Burkina Faso, Cameroon, Chad, Dahomey, Guinea, Ivory Coast, Mali, Niger, Nigeria. One month later the states established the Niger River Commission, Nov. 25, 1964.

[56] Convention relating to the Status of the River Gambia (Gambia, Guinea, Senegal, June 30, 1978), *reproduced in* Natural Resources/Water Series No. 134, ST/ESA/141 (1984), at 39.

[57] EMuT 994:49.

[58] *See also* C.O. Okidi, *International Law and Water Scarcity in Africa, in* THE SCARCITY OF WATER, *supra* note 2, at 166.

[59] EMuT 992:62/A.

[60] The Community was created on Aug. 17, 1992 by the Treaty of Windhoek adopted by ten states of Southern Africa.

[61] Windhoek; 40 I.L.M. 321 (2001).

The Protocol follows the definitions and rules of the UN Convention on various points, such as the definition of equitable and reasonable utilization, the procedure to be followed for planned measures, for environmental protection and preservation and for the management of shared watercourses. The term "environmental use" is defined as the use of water for the preservation and maintenance of ecosystems, while "significant harm" is characterized as "non-trivial harm capable of being established by objective evidence without necessarily rising to the level of being substantial" (Art. 1). Using the existing framework of the Southern African Development Community, the Protocol establishes different Water Sector Organs such as a Committee of Water Ministers, and a Committee of Water Senior Officials which have the task to oversee and monitor the implementation of the Protocol and advise state parties on matters pertaining to the Protocol (Art. 5).

5. *Asia*

Several Asian treaties concerning international rivers and lakes focus on the utilization of waters rather than their conservation. The principal objective of the 1992 Treaty on Sharing of the Ganges Waters at Farakka between Bangladesh and India[62] and the February 12, 1996, Treaty Concerning the Integrated Development of the Mahakali River between India and Nepal is to determine the quantity of water to which the contracting parties are entitled. The first agreement aims to make "optimum utilization" of the waters of the region, applying the principles of "equity, fair play and no harm to either party" (Arts. I, IX and X), while the second makes only limited reference to similar principles. (Art. 9(1))

The Interim Agreement of September 28, 1995, between Israel and the Palestine Liberation Organization on the West Bank and Gaza Strip also mainly focuses on the sharing of water resources. Article 40 of Annex III speaks abstractly of preventing the deterioration of water quality, of using the water resources in a manner that will ensure sustainable use in the future, of preventing any harm to water resources as well as to water and sewage systems, and of treating, reusing or properly disposing of all domestic, urban, industrial, and agricultural sewage.[63] For the same region the Declaration on Cooperation on Water-related Matters, adopted February

---

[62]   Dec. 12, 1992, *reprinted in* 36 I.L.M. 519 (1997). *See* Salman M.A. Salman, *Sharing the Ganges Waters between India and Bangladesh: an Analysis of the 1996 Treaty, in* INTERNATIONAL WATERCOURSES, ENHANCING COOPERATION AND MANAGING CONFLICT. PROCEEDINGS OF A WORLD BANK SEMINAR (SALMAN M.A. SALMAN & L. BOISSON DE CHAZOURNES eds., 1998).

[63]   36 I.L.M., 551, at 624 (1997).

13, 1996, by Israel, Jordan, and the Palestine Liberation Organization is more explicit by stating that new and additional water resource projects will be based on environmentally-sound principles. Each party is responsible for protecting water against environmental pollution originating within its jurisdiction as well as for the preservation of water quality. The Declaration also proposes cooperation in sustainable water-related natural resources management and desertification control as well as the development of norms, standards and specifications for water devices.[64]

The most significant Asian treaty on the protection of inland waters is the 1995 Agreement on Cooperation for the Sustainable Development of the Mekong River Basin, adopted by Cambodia, Laos, Thailand and Vietnam. It adopts the river basin approach and thus has a comprehensive territorial aim, but it lacks participation by upstream state China. It defines "environment" as the conditions of water and land resources, air, flora and fauna that exist in a particular region and it aims at protecting the environment from pollution or other harmful effects resulting from any development plans and uses of water and related resources in the basin. Every effort shall be made to avoid, minimize and mitigate harmful effects that might occur to the environment, especially the water quantity and quality, the aquatic ecosystem conditions and the ecological balance of the river system. It also mentions the responsibility for damage caused by a state, without, however, going into details. A Mekong River Commission is given the mandate of ensuring the implementation of the Convention.[65]

D. Boundary Waters Case Studies

1. The Danube

The dispute over a project to construct a hydroelectric dam system on the Danube River illustrates the potential for conflicts between neighboring states raised by competing uses of water resources.[66] In 1920, the Treaty of Trianon made the Danube River part of the boundary between Hungary and the newly created state of Czechoslovakia. The 1947 Peace Treaty of Paris transferred to Czechoslovakia three Hungarian villages facing Bratislava, on the south, or Hungarian, bank of the river near the Austrian border. Since that time, the Danube has flowed through Slovak territory for

---

[64] 36 I.L.M. 761, at 768 and 769 (1997). *See also* S. McCaffrey, *Middle East Water Problems, the Jordan River, in* THE SCARCITY OF WATER, *supra* note 2, at 158.

[65] Chiang Mai, Thailand, Apr. 5, 1995, *reprinted in* 34 I.L.M. 864 (1995).

[66] *See* Georg M. Berrisch. *The Danube Dam Dispute under International Law,* 46 AUSTRIAN J. PUB. INT'L L. 231–81 (1994); Maurizio Arcari, *La controversia tra Slovacchia ed Ungheria circa la costruzione di un sistema di dighe sul Danubio,* 8 RIVISTO GIURIDICO DELL'AMBIENTE 951–64 (1993).

22.5 km. For the next 142 km the Danube forms the boundary between Slovakia and Hungary until its junction with the Ipoly river, where the boundary turns north and separates from the river. The Danube flows east within Hungary before making a sudden bend to the south to pass through Budapest and the rest of Hungary.

At the end of the 1940s both Czechoslovakia and Hungary came under Soviet domination and communist regimes. Like other states in the region, they became members of the Warsaw Pact and the Council for Mutual Economic Cooperation (COMECON). The ruling communist parties maintained close relations under the surveillance of Moscow. Negotiations began in 1951 concerning the construction of a system of hydroelectric plants, inspired by the Soviet construction of huge canals, dams, industrial sites and similar projects. In 1958 the governments decided to proceed with the system and, five years later, government committees of the two countries agreed to draw up a joint investment program. The two sides signed a treaty on the construction and operation of the system on September 16, 1977.

The Treaty envisaged a system of dams in order to serve four purposes: electricity production, navigation, flood protection, and regional development. It included provisions on the protection of the water quality (Art. 15), maintenance of navigation (Art. 18), the protection of nature (Art. 19) and protection of fishing interests (Art. 20). According to the Preamble of the Treaty, however, another of its aims was to further strengthen the fraternal relations of the two states and significantly contribute to bringing about the socialist integration of the states members of COMECON. Hungarian opinion later held that political considerations played a large part in the adoption of a project that was economically and environmentally unsound from the beginning.

The project involved the creation of a reservoir beginning at the southeast end of Bratislava, at river km 1,860, covering 60 km² and having a total capacity of 200 million cubic meters. Forty-nine million cubic meters were to be used to generate electricity at a power plant situated at Gabčikovo, 17 km downstream at the end of a canal that ran from the reservoir.[67] A large part of the reservoir, the power canal, and the Gabčikovo power plant were to be constructed entirely on Slovak territory, while the old bed of the Danube remained the boundary between the two states. The power plant was intended to operate in "peak mode," meaning it would utilize the accumulated water for several hours a day, depending on the discharge of the Danube. Except for the morning and evening peak hours of production, the flow of the Danube would have virtually stopped, with little water coming through the power plant into the 8.2 km long tail race canal[68] joining the Danube. The average discharge of the Danube, calculated on an annual

---

[67]   The canal is referred to as a "head-race" canal.
[68]   A "tail race" canal runs from the power plant back to the river.

basis, is 2,000 cubic meters per second. At river km. 1843 the major part of the water was to be channeled into the 31 km long diversion system[69] so that the water in the main riverbed would have fallen to a mere 50 cubic meters per second.

The operation of the Gabčikovo power plant in peak mode made it necessary to dam the Danube water to regulate the water flow. This was the objective of a second dam, situated 113 km downstream at Nagymaros, at river km 1,696, where the Danube flows between two mountain ranges. At this site, another, smaller hydroelectric plant was to be built.

A joint investment plan and national investments were to finance the project. The two governments, negotiating with the participation of their two communist parties, agreed to share the cost of the operation and the benefits of the electricity produced. The latter contributed only a small part—less than 3 percent—to the energy needs of the two countries. Furthermore, until 2015 Hungary would be obliged to use its share of the electricity produced to pay back the foreign loans which were necessary to finance its part of the construction.

As the planning continued, doubts emerged on the Hungarian side concerning the environmental impact. There were three main concerns: (1) the potential pollution of a large underground water reserve near the upstream reservoir by infiltration from the reservoir's sediments; (2) damage to Szigetköz, a unique wetland area south of the Danube, by the lowering of the level of the subsurface water; and (3) potential pollution of the underground water north of Budapest, due to the Nagymaros dam. In 1981, the Hungarian Academy of Sciences appointed an ad hoc interdisciplinary committee to investigate the project. It concluded that the ecological effects and consequences of the system had not been considered in any comprehensive way and it proposed postponing the construction work in order to make changes in the plans, or to cancel the construction plans. The report was ignored and the government then in power prohibited its publication.

Despite the ban, public opinion became aware of the potential problems. As a result, both Hungarian and foreign environmental movements mounted challenges. Street demonstrations took place in Budapest against the project, the first demonstrations in Hungary since the 1956 insurrection. Rapid political changes permitted the Hungarian Parliament to adopt a resolution on October 7, 1988, submitting the continuation of the construction to strict rules of environmental protection and, on May 13, 1989, the Hungarian government suspended the works at Nagymaros. It also announced its intention to suspend the execution of its part of the works near Gabçikovo until the environmental consequences of the project were fully assessed. Several days later, Hungary proposed to Czechoslovakia

---

[69] The diversion system consisted of the head race canal, the power plant, the ship locks and the tail race canal.

further studies and a joint analysis of the ecological risks arising from the operation of the system. On June 2, 1989, the Hungarian Parliament authorized the initiation of preliminary negotiations to amend the 1977 Treaty. When independent experts confirmed the ecological risks of the project, the Hungarian government proposed to amend the Treaty after a thorough scientific investigation. The Czechoslovak government rejected the doubts and scientific findings and expressed its conviction that monitoring and subsequent technical corrections would suffice to preserve the natural resources. It agreed only to begin negotiations with a view to putting the Gabçikovo part of the project into operation by 1991.

The following one and a half years were dominated by the total transformation of the political situation in both countries. On March 25, 1990, Hungary held its first free elections since 1945. The new Parliament requested the government to cease state investments in the Danube project. The international context changed as well, as Soviet troops withdrew from Hungary and both COMECON and the Warsaw Pact dissolved. While negotiations continued between Czechoslovakia and Hungary, Czechoslovak authorities began the construction of a "provisional solution" called "Variant C" which involved the completion of the Gabčikovo upstream reservoir entirely on Slovak territory. Variant C called for a diversion of almost all the water of the Danube, the construction of the head-race plant with ship locks, and of the tail race canal. Peak production was, however, abandoned, as a consequence of the suspension of the work on the Nagymaros part of the project.

Czechoslovak authorities notified Hungary of the decision to proceed with the construction of "Variant C" on July 30, 1991, one day after Czechoslovakia began pumping water from the Danube into the diversion canal. The Hungarian Ministry of Foreign Affairs protested and Parliament authorized the government to terminate the 1977 Treaty if the Czechoslovak government did not cease the construction works. The protest was rejected and, on May 19, 1992, the Hungarian government issued a declaration stating that the Treaty was terminated. On October 27, 1992, Czechoslovakia completed the closure of the Danube, after having rejected a Hungarian proposal to submit the dispute to the International Court of Justice and expressing preference for trilateral negotiation with EC involvement. Hungary sought urgently to ensure the discharge of water into the Danube. An agreement reached on October 28, 1992, provided for a discharge level not less than 95 percent of the former volume, but the agreement was not implemented by Czechoslovakia or, later Slovakia. Instead, they proposed a 50 percent flow rate. Slovakia became an independent state on January 1, 1993, and claimed that the Gabçikovo plant produced between eight and ten percent of the state's electricity.

On April 7, 1993, Hungary and Slovakia signed a Special Agreement on the submission of the dispute to the ICJ. The agreement requested the Court to decide, on the basis of the 1977 Treaty and "rules and principles of general international law, as well as such other treaties as the Court may find applicable":

1. Whether Hungary was entitled to suspend and subsequently abandon, in 1989, the works on the Nagymaros Project and on its part of the Gabçikovo Project;
2. Whether Czechoslovakia was entitled to proceed, in November 1991, to the "provisional solution" and to put this system into operation from October 1992 (this meant damming the Danube at river kilometer 1,851.7 on Czechoslovak territory); and
3. What are the legal effects of the notification of the termination of the Treaty by Hungary?

The parties also asked the Court to determine the legal consequences, including the rights and obligations for the parties, arising from its judgment. Pending the final judgment, the two states agreed to establish and implement a temporary water-management regime for the Danube. They also agreed to enter into negotiations, immediately after the transmission of the judgment, on the modalities of its execution. If the parties failed to reach agreement within six months, either party could request the Court to render an additional judgment to determine the modalities for executing its judgment.

The memorials, counter-memorials and replies submitted to the ICJ totaled some 25 volumes containing 8,500 pages and the Court held 42 hours of oral hearings. Between two sets of hearings, the entire Court made unprecedented on site visits to Slovakia and Hungary. The lengthy judgment is accompanied by two declarations, three separate opinions and seven dissenting opinions, indicating the complexity of the case and the difficulty of the Court's task, including analysis and understanding of extensive scientific documents and presentations.

The multiplicity of international legal issues in the case included questions of the suspension and abrogation of treaties, the role of new rules in the interpretation of treaties, state succession, state responsibility and the place of environmental law in the international system. Summarizing the position of the parties, it can be stated that the arguments of Slovakia affirmed the validity of the 1977 Treaty and the text which complemented it and the duty of the parties to fulfill the obligations therein, while Hungary asserted the need to protect the environment and in particular to safeguard natural resources in the context of the Treaty and in customary international law.

The judgment comprises four parts. The first part summarizes the facts and data of the case and the positions of the two parties. The second part has a declaratory character in reference to the lawfulness or unlawfulness of the conduct of the parties between 1989 and 1992, and the effect of that conduct on the continued existence of the 1977 treaty. In the third part, the Court determines, on the basis of its prior findings, the present and future legal rights and obligations of the parties. This prescriptive part of the judgment has to be implemented through an agreement on the modalities to execute the judgment. The final part consists of one paragraph in which the Court answers the questions formulated in the Special Agreement.

The Court addresses the law of international watercourses and, in particular, environmental protection of them, in several sections of the second part of the judgment. Notably, the Court accepted the duty not to cause transboundary harm as part of general international law and recognized the existence of ecological necessity as a legal excuse for an otherwise illegal act.

Hungary alleged that there was, in 1989, a state of necessity created by the threats to the environment, including pollution of the underground water resource, drying-out of an ecologically-important alluvial plain, and potential harm to the supply of drinking water to Budapest, that justified its suspension and abandonment of the works. The Court evaluated the doctrine of a state of necessity according to the criteria laid down by the International Law Commission in Article 33 of the Draft Articles on the International Responsibility of States.[70] The Court acknowledged that the concerns expressed by Hungary for its natural environment related to an essential interest in the meaning of that provision. It also recalled its advisory opinion on the *Legality of the Threat of Use of Nuclear Weapons* where it recognized the general obligation of states to ensure that activities within their jurisdiction and control respect the environment of other states or of areas beyond national control is now part of the corpus of international law relating to the environment.[71] The Court was not convinced, however, by the Hungarian argument on the state of necessity, because the government did not prove that a real grave and imminent peril existed in 1989 and that the measures taken by Hungary were the only possible response to it (paras. 49–54). Instead, the Court found that the dangers ascribed to the upstream reservoir at Nagymaros "were mostly of a long-term nature and, above all . . . they remained uncertain" (para. 55). The Court's analysis indicates the limits of juridical intervention in environmental cases, where deterioration of the environment has very often a long-term nature and cannot be proven in the present.

The second question submitted to the Court concerned the legality of Hungary's termination of the 1977 Treaty as a response to the construction and the operation of the system unilaterally by Czechoslovakia, exclusively under its own control and for its own benefit. The termination of the 1977

---

[70]   The articles were completed and presented to the U.N. General Assembly in Dec. 2002.

[71]   1996 I.C.J. Rep. 241–242, para 29.

Treaty by Hungary also was based, *inter alia*, on a state of necessity. The Court did not accept this argument, holding that necessity does not allow a treaty to be terminated, but will only exonerate the state from responsibility for not having executed the agreement.

Hungary also sought to justify terminating the 1977 Treaty on the basis that it was impossible to perform the obligations flowing from it. Hungary contended that it could not be "obliged to fulfil a practically impossible task, namely to construct a system of dams on its own territory that would have caused irreparable environmental damage." The Court held, however, that the 1977 Treaty—and in particular Articles 15, 19 and 20—actually made available to the parties the necessary means to proceed at any time, by negotiation, to the required readjustments between economic and ecological imperatives (para. 103).

Hungary further argued that it was entitled to invoke a number of events that, cumulatively, constituted a fundamental change of circumstances allowing it to escape the Treaty. One of the circumstances cited was the progress of environmental knowledge and the development of new norms and prescriptions of international environmental law. The Court answered that such new developments could not be said to have been completely unforeseen. In addition, the Treaty provisions relating to the quality of water in the Danube and the protection of nature could accommodate change, allowing the parties to take account of developments when implementing those treaty provisions.

One of the most important elements of the case was Hungary's claim that it was entitled to terminate the 1977 Treaty because new requirements of international law for the protection of the environment precluded performance of the Treaty. The Court once more referred to the Treaty's environmental provisions, Articles 15, 19 and 20, in pointing out that new environmental norms are relevant for the implementation of the Treaty and that the parties could, by agreement, incorporate them into the Treaty (para. 112). Significantly, by inserting those dynamic provisions in the Treaty, the parties recognized the potential necessity to adapt the Project. Consequently, the Treaty allows reference to emerging norms of international law. In this context, the Court recalled its statement in the Advisory Opinion on the *Legality of the Threat or Use of Nuclear Weapons* that "the environment is not an abstraction but represents the living space, the quality of life and the very health of human beings, including generations unborn." It added that awareness of the vulnerability of the environment and recognition that environmental risks have to be assessed on a continuous basis have become much stronger in the years since the Treaty's conclusion (para. 112). The result enhances the importance of Articles 15, 19 and 20.

Respecting riparian rights on the river, the Court held that Hungary's unlawful termination of the treaty did not mean that it had forfeited its basic right to an equitable and reasonable sharing of the resources of the watercourse. Czechoslovakia, by putting Variant C, the so-called "provisional solution," into operation, and appropriating between 80 and 90 percent of the Danube waters, had violated this provision (para. 78).

The third part of the judgment contains particularly important *dicta* for the protection of the environment, in particular three statements of the Court. First, after holding that the 1977 Treaty is still in force and consequently governs the relationship between the parties, the Court said it could not disregard the fact that the Treaty had not been fully implemented by either party for years and that their acts of commission and omission contributed to the present factual situation. What might have been the correct application of the law in 1989 or 1992, could be a miscarriage of the justice in 1997. The Court pointed out that the Slovak reservoir was significantly smaller than what was planned, that the plant was operated in a run-of-the-river mode and not in a peak hour mode, and that Nagymaros had not been built. As both parties appeared to have abandoned the peak operation mode, there was no longer any point in building the second dam.

Second, the Project's implementation and environmental impact were necessarily a key issue. According to the Court, the parties must take into account current standards in evaluating environmental risks, as implicitly prescribed by Treaty Articles 15 and 19 concerning water quality and nature protection. On this point, the Court proclaimed its concern for the environment:

> . . . (I)n the field of environmental protection, vigilance and prevention are required on account of the often irreversible character of damage to the environment and of the limitations inherent in the very mechanism of reparation of this type of damage.
>
> Throughout the ages, mankind has, for economic and other reasons, constantly interfered with nature. In the past, this was often done without consideration of the effects upon the environment. Owing to new scientific insights and to a growing awareness of the risks for mankind—for present and future generations—of pursuit of such intervention at an unconsidered and unabated pace, new norms and standards have been developed, set forth in a great number of instruments during the last two decades. Such new norms have to be taken into consideration, and such new standards given proper weight, not only when States contemplate new activities but also when continuing with activities begun in the past.

As a consequence, the parties should look afresh at the environmental effects of the operation of the power plant and, in particular, find a satisfactory solution regarding the volume of water to be released into the old bed of the Danube and into the side-arms on both sides of the river. Such solution should take account of the objectives of the Treaty as well as the norms of international environmental law and the principles of the law of international watercourses (para. 141). The parties should participate in the use and the benefits of the system of locks in equal measure (para. 146) and the re-establishment of the joint regime must optimally reflect the concept of common utilization of shared water resources. The Court mentions with approval Article 5(2) of the 1997 UN Convention on the Law of the Non-Navigational Uses of International Watercourses, which states "[w]atercourse states shall participate in the use, development and protection of an international watercourse in an equitable and reasonable manner. Such participation includes both the right to utilize the watercourse and the duty to cooperate in the protection and development thereof, as provided in the present Convention."

On the whole, although the International Court of Justice did not take into account several aspects of environmental protection, such as avoiding long-term effects of present activities, and did not apply the precautionary principle, its judgment will certainly be among the most quoted ones and constitutes a major development in international environmental law.

2. *United States-Mexico Boundary Waters*

The 2,000 mile border between the United States and Mexico extends from the Pacific Ocean across the Sonora Desert to the Gulf of Mexico. The border region includes the Rio Grande, Colorado, Tijuana, San Pedro, Santa Cruz and New Rivers, along which lie such "twin" cities as San Diego/Tijuana, Calexico/Mexicali, El Paso/Cuidad Juarez, Brownsville/Matamoros and Laredo/Nuevo Laredo. They fall under the jurisdiction of six Mexican and four U.S. states, although they constitute a single geographic region of shared air and water resources, both surface and groundwater.

Some environmental issues in this complex network are common to those of other international watercourses, but in other ways are vastly different. There are similar problems of industrial accidents, dumping of wastes, sewage, and other forms of pollution. Unlike the land around many other rivers, however, virtually the entire area is desert, with attendant shortage and poor quality of both underground and surface waters. Population growth, unplanned urbanization and rapid industrialization, including the enormous increase in "maquiladora,"[72] have added to the pressures on transfrontier water resources.[73]

---

[72] Maquiladora are Mexican-based border industries, largely U.S. and other foreign-owned, which take advantage of significant savings in labor, services and other operational costs, while remaining close to the United States. *See* R.A. Sanchez, *Health and Environmental Risks of the Maquiladora in Mexicali*, 30 Nat. Res. J. 63 (1990).

[73] Water scarcity also has led to internal legal and political conflicts

Historically, due to water scarcity in the arid borderlands, competition between Mexico and the United States focused on the use of the Colorado and Rio Grande River systems for agricultural irrigation. Two treaties resolved some of the allocation disputes between Mexico and the United States: the 1906 Rio Grande Irrigation Convention[74] and the 1944 Treaty Relating to the Utilization of Waters of the Colorado and Tijuana Rivers and of the Rio Grande.[75] However, many issues of water quality remained unsettled by the treaties.

Today the major surface waters are completely allocated and the border faces an imminent severe water shortage.[76] As a result, both countries are turning to groundwaters to satisfy their needs. However, these exhaustible resources can become depleted irreversibly if pumping exceeds the natural rate of renewal. Unmanaged drilling of groundwater in the El Paso/Ciudad Juarez area threatens exhaustion of the resource in the immediate future.

Apart from allocation, the most critical water issues are increased salinity of water flowing into Mexico from the United States, and the discharge of municipal sewage from Mexico into rivers and the ocean flowing towards the United States. Nearly all Mexican border cities lack adequate municipal sewage collection and treatment systems. Nuevo Laredo has no system for either domestic or industrial waste, with the result that 14 million gallons of raw sewage is discharged into the Rio Grande daily. The problem becomes more critical with burgeoning populations along the border. In addition, Mexican industries lack treatment and disposal facilities for industrial waste with the result that many toxic substances are dumped directly into river systems. Copper mines along the border are the source of heavy metal contamination of the San Pedro River which flows into Arizona, contaminating drinking and irrigation waters.

High concentrations of salt in downstream water supplies result from extensive irrigation. When water is applied to a field, salts are leached from the soil and return through drainage water to water sources. Increased salinity of Colorado River waters led to disputes between the United States and Mexico for over 30 years before a 1973 agreement set water quality standards for the downstream water supply. However, the reduced availability of fresh water for dilution and the high cost of desalinization has created renewed problems.

---

between states within the United States and between the states and the federal government. The rapid and unsustainable population growth in the southwestern United States has placed the Colorado River under enormous pressure.

[74] May 21, 1906.

[75] Feb. 3, 1944.

[76] *See* Stephen P. Mumme, *Managing Acute Water Scarcity on the U.S. Mexico Border: Institutional Issues Raised by the 1990's Drought*, 1998 TRANSBOUNDARY RESOURCES REPORT 6.

Attempts to protect the environment of U.S.-Mexican boundary waters are affected not only by the desert climate, but by the different economic and political situations of the two countries. Mexico's environmental problems, like those of other developing countries, are strongly linked to poverty. United States difficulties stem from industrialization and consumption patterns, although some parts of the U.S. border regions outside Southern California are perhaps socially and economically closer to Mexico. While both the U.S. and Mexico have strong domestic environmental legislation, enforcement along the border has been weak.

International cooperation to protect the environment of U.S.-Mexican boundary waters has been slow in coming. All the lands and rivers which now form the border region were Mexican territory until 1848. After the U.S. acquired the area, it asserted the Harmon Doctrine of absolute sovereignty for upstream states in response to Mexican objections to large water diversions from the Rio Grande River by U.S. farmers and ranchers. The United States adhered to the Harmon Doctrine with regard to the Colorado River Basin until the 1944 Water Utilization Treaty quantified each nation's share of the Tijuana, Rio Grande and Colorado Rivers.

The 1944 Agreement failed to include any guarantees of water quality, although Article 3 provided that both nations "hereby agree to give preferential attention to the solution of all border sanitation problems." The Treaty also provided a list of priority uses for the waters, with highest priority given to domestic and municipal uses, followed by agriculture and stock-raising, then electric power, other industrial uses, navigation, fishing and hunting.

An International Boundary and Water Commission (IBWC) was established by the 1944 Treaty, replacing an earlier International Boundary Commission. The IBWC, although an international agency, has specific authority to address boundary water pollution problems. The Treaty authorizes the Commission to plan, build, and manage water works; to enter into further agreements relating to international waters; and to settle disputes between the two countries involving interpretation of the Treaty. The Commission also has authority to initiate investigations and to make decisions involving utilization of the international waters. The decisions, known as Minutes, are binding on the two nations unless one of the governments objects within 30 days.[77] The jurisdiction of the IBWC is, however, limited to surface waters at the boundary.

Given the date of the 1944 Treaty, it is not surprising that it contains no substantive obligations or principles for water quality protection or regulation

---

[77]   In the United States, the Minute has the legal status of an executive agreement. *See* S. Mumme, *The U.S.-Mexican Conflict over Transboundary Groundwaters: Some Institutional and Political Considerations*, 12 Case W. Res. J. Int'l L. 505 (1980).

of border pollution problems. Perhaps because of this and because there was little pressure from the respective governments, the IWBC initially did not pay much attention to environmental protection. Later, several Minutes and Agreements expanded protection and focused attention on environmental issues.

Minute 242 was adopted in 1973 as a "Permanent and Definitive Solution to the International Problem of the Salinity of the Colorado River."[78] Beginning in the 1960s, Mexico protested that United States water deliveries included highly saline drainage waters which caused severe damage to Mexico's agriculture. For its part, Mexico began extracting large quantities of groundwater from the border near Yuma, Arizona. In Minute 242, the United States recognized an obligation to deliver good quality water to Mexico. In return, Mexico agreed to control its groundwater mining near Yuma. However, the agreement applies only to one aspect of water quality, salinity, and only to one water source, the Colorado. No comprehensive agreement on boundary groundwater or salinity exists.

The role of the IBWC was expanded in 1979 by Minute 261[79] which gave the IBWC authority to solve any water quality problems "that present a hazard to the health and well-being of the inhabitants of either side of the border or impair the beneficial uses of the waters." Emphasis was placed on the need for preventive measures. With Minute 261, the IBWC obtained the authority to determine when a water pollution problem exists.

The first major use of the IBWC expanded powers came with Minute 264 which adopted specific water quality objectives and standards for the New River.[80] The goal of Minute 264 was the complete elimination of all domestic and industrial waste waters in the New River at the boundary through action by Mexico. Mexico also agreed to improve the Mexicali sewage treatment system to achieve specific water quality standards within established time limits. The water quality standards adopted are based upon U.S. standards and act to harmonize the laws of the two countries. IBWC is responsible for monitoring Mexico's implementation of Minute 264.

In 1983, the United States and Mexico adopted a new framework agreement to cooperate on border environmental issues.[81] The two states agreed

---

[78]   IBWC Minute No. 242, Aug. 30, 1973, Mexico-United States; 24 U.S.T. 1971; T.I.A.S. No. 7708.

[79]   IBWC Minute 261, Recommendations for Solutions of Border Sanitation Problems (El Paso, Texas, Sept. 24, 1979).

[80]   IBWC, Minute 264, Recommendations for Solution of the New River Border Sanitation Problem at Calexico, California-Mexicali, Baja California Norte (Ciudad Juarez, Chihuahua, Aug. 26, 1980).

[81]   Agreement between the United States of America and the United Mexican States on Cooperation for the Protection and Improvement of the Environment in the Border Area (Aug. 14, 1983, *in force* Feb. 16, 1984).

to strengthen and expand both individual and cooperative efforts to address pollution at the border, implicitly recognizing the ecological unity of the region. In Article 2, for the first time, both countries acknowledged their obligations to prevent transborder pollution, as they agreed to adopt appropriate measures to prevent, reduce and eliminate sources of pollution that affect the border area of the other and agreed to cooperate to solve environmental problems of mutual concern. The Agreement also requires each party to monitor polluting activities, to consult on the measurement and analysis of pollution sources, and to share all information obtained from monitoring. Article 7 requires assessment of projects that may have significant impacts on the environment of the border area. Perhaps most importantly, Article 3 requires the drafting of implementing annexes to address specific issues.

The parties have adopted four annexes to the 1983 agreement, two of which directly concern boundary waters.[82] Annex I, adopted July 18, 1985, concerns solving sanitation problems in the Tijuana-San Diego border region. Annex II, adopted the same day, addresses pollution of the environment due to the discharge of hazardous substances. Annex II also establishes a Joint Contingency Plan regarding polluting incidents (a discharge or threat of discharge of any hazardous substance on one side of the boundary which causes or threatens to cause imminent and substantial adverse effects on the public health, welfare, or the environment) caused by hazardous substances. In Article III, the parties agree to develop response plans to detect sewage spills.

The Annex also concerns cooperation to expand and improve drinking water and the sewage system of Tijuana and calls on the states to determine the measures necessary to preserve environmental conditions and ecological processes. The Annex specifically anticipates U.S. assistance to Mexico in case of a breakdown or interruption in service and calls for a consideration of the existence or threat of polluting incidents and adoption of measures to eliminate the threat posed by such incidents and to minimize any adverse effects on the environment and the public health and welfare. The parties agree to consult and exchange information and to implement agreed upon joint responses to a polluting incident. Appendices establish the joint contingency plan and the joint response team that has the responsibility for determining the hazardous substances covered by the Annex. As with similar agreements, appendices may be added or amended through flexible procedures.

In the 1990s, a drought caused severe impacts in Northern Mexico. Ranching and agricultural drought-based losses were estimated at upwards of U.S. $1.1 billion. Acknowledging the evidence of serious Mexican conservation and mitigation efforts in the face of the persistent drought, the

---

[82]   All four Annexes are *reprinted in* 26 I.L.M. 18, 19, 25 and 33 (1987).

U.S. consented to loan water, up to the amount of 81,000 acre-feet over a period of 18 months, beginning in November 1995. IBWC Minute 293 expresses this arrangement. According to an author, "this agreement may be taken as *de facto* recognition by both parties, but particularly by the US, of the need, indeed the obligation, to assist its treaty partner in times of acute water scarcity"[83]

The recent agreements and activities reflect growing concern with environmental protection of U.S.-Mexican boundary waters, indeed with the entire boundary region. It remains to be seen whether effective implementation of the agreements will alleviate the enormous problems that exist.

E. Conclusions

There is general recognition that freshwater is fundamental to all forms of life and at the same time crucial to many human activities. The protection of this vital resource needs a holistic approach, taking into account the interrelationships among different forms of water resources (surface and groundwater, atmospheric water, ice) over a large geographic area (water basins, interfaces between continental waters and sea) and the multiple uses of water (basic human needs, irrigation, industrial uses, energy production). Water usage also must respect the integrated nature of resources within ecosystems. It also must be remembered that water quality and quantity cannot be separated.

The law of water resources and in particular international cooperation must be based on such complex analysis. In addition, it is necessary to recognize that while access to water is a fundamental human need, water is also an economic good whose distribution requires infrastructure that sometimes necessitates massive investment and good governance. Left as a public good, water can be subject to the "tragedy of the commons" because there are no incentives to conservation. Proper use of economic instruments with pricing reflecting the quantities of water appropriated by consumers can help to reduce waste and ensure long-term protection of water quantity and quality.

Two principles are increasingly asserted. The first is that despite the reluctance of many agreements to prioritize uses of water, the fulfillment of basic needs (drinking and sanitation) should be generally given the highest priority as a substantive element of the right to environment.[84] Such a rights-based approach to water is increasingly asserted within human rights bodies. Second, as a general framework, water should be looked upon as a heritage to be shared among all users, including different ecosystems, in a

---

[83]   S. Mumme, *supra* note 77 at 7.

[84]   *See further* Chapter 15.

reasonable and equitable way, in a spirit of solidarity and in a manner consistent with the needs of sustainable development. The Johannesburg World Summit on Sustainable Development has made a first but important step toward the recognition of such principles by establishing targets and timetables for providing safe drinking water and sanitation. The importance of this is reinforced by the fact that it is the one specific pledge contained in the WSSD texts.

BIBLIOGRAPHY

Benevisti, E., *Collective Action in the Utilization of Shared Freshwater: The Challenges of International Water Resources Law,* 90 AJIL 384 (1996).

BRUHACS, F., THE LAW OF NON-NAVIGATIONAL WATERCOURSES (1993).

CLARKE, R., WATER: THE INTERNATIONAL CRISIS (1993).

Francis, G., *Binational Cooperation for Great Lakes Water Quality: A Framework for the Groundwater Connection,* 65 CHI-KENT L. REV. 359–73 (1989).

Kiss, A., *The Protection of the Rhine Against Pollution,* 25 NAT. RES. J. 613 (1985).

LAMMERS, J., POLLUTION OF INTERNATIONAL WATERCOURSES (1984).

Leroy, P., *Troubled Waters: Population and Water Scarcity,* 6 COLO. J. INT'L L. & POL'Y 299 (1995).

McCAFFREY, S., THE LAW OF INTERNATIONAL WATERCOURSES (2002).

NOLLKAEMPER, A., THE LEGAL REGIME FOR TRANSBOUNDARY WATER POLLUTION: BETWEEN DISCRETION AND CONSTRAINT (1993).

Sette-Camara, J., *Pollution of International Rivers,* 186 RCADI 117 (1984).

SOHNLE, JOCHEN, LE DROIT INTERNATIONAL DES RESSOURCES EN EAU DOUCE: SOLIDARITÉ CONTRE SOUVERAINETÉ (2002).

TANZI, M.A., THE UNITED NATIONS CONVENTION ON THE LAW OF INTERNATIONAL WATERCOURSES: A FRAMEWORK FOR SHARING (2001).

Teclaff, L.A. & Teclaff, E., *Transboundary Toxic Pollution and the Drainage Basin Concept,* 25 NAT. RES. J. 589–612 (1985).

Trevin, J.O. & Day, J.C., *Risk Perception in International River Basin Management: The Plata Basin Example,* 30 NAT RES. J. 87–105 (1990).

Wescoat, Jr., J.L., *Main Currents in Early Multilateral Water Treaties: A Historical-Geographic Perspective, 1648–1948,* 7 COLO. J. INT'L ENVTL. L. & POL'Y 39 (1996).

CHAPTER 11

PROTECTION OF THE MARINE ENVIRONMENT

A. Overview

Maritime waters cover over 70 percent of the planet's surface area and a vast majority of the total volume that is known to sustain life. Despite the importance of the marine environment, human activities everywhere are depleting marine and coastal living resources and degrading ecosystems in sometimes irreversible ways. The oceans possess great natural capacity for self-purification, but there are limits to this process that are being reached and exceeded as the amount of harmful substances flowing directly or indirectly into the seas has increased along with growing world population and expanding industrialization. In fact, the major threats to the health, productivity, and biodiversity of the marine environment result from human activities that take place on land, in coastal areas, and even further inland.[1] Erosion of soil carrying pesticides and fertilizers has created approximately 50 marine dead zones, one of the largest being off the mouth of the Mississippi River in the Gulf of Mexico.

The marine environment is also under threat because the traditional uses of the sea have intensified and diversified. The sea has always played a particularly important role in the transport of products. This is still its principal role, and today the vast number and size of ships provokes great concern about the heightened risk of marine pollution. Another traditional use of the sea, fishing, equally has seen an unprecedented expansion. Practiced since time immemorial, ocean fishing has been transformed into an industry which today impacts upon biological resources in the farthest and most inhospitable ocean reaches. With annual total catches of many stocks decreasing,[2] it appears that the limits of sustainable exploitation of marine

---

[1]   UNEP Intergovernmental Conference to Draft a Global Program of Action for the Protection of the Marine Environment from Land-Based Sources (Washington D.C., Oct. 23, to Nov. 3, 1995), 26/1 E.P.L. 11, 37 (1996). *See* G.A. Res. 51/189 on *Institutional Arrangements for the Implementation of the Global Programme of Action for the Protection of the Marine Environment from Land-Based Activities, reproduced in* 27/2 E.P.L. 132 (1997).

[2]   World marine capture fisheries production reached a record of 87.1 million tons in 1996. Overall, as fishing pressures continue, the number of under-exploited and moderately exploited fisheries resources continues to decline slightly, the number of fully exploited stocks remains relatively stable

biological resources are close to being reached. Overfishing is not the only cause for concern about the preservation of marine living resources. Fish are increasingly showing signs of contamination and damage from pollution, including concentrations of carcinogens, tumors, wounds, and malformations, which render them unsuitable for consummation and which threaten their ability to reproduce.[3]

Besides the intensification and transformation of traditional uses of the seas, new activities increase ocean pollution. Although exploitation of the seabed for the production of oil is of relatively recent origin, today nearly one-third of all oil comes from offshore oil drilling. The discovery of polymetallic nodules on the ocean floor has not led to massive exploitation thus far, but the International Seabed Authority has now approved the first exploration contracts. Tourism also plays an important role in recent uses of the sea. Although transoceanic liners almost disappeared with the development of mass air transport, pleasure cruises are increasingly popular and create numerous sources of pollution that are difficult to control. Treasure hunters seeking ancient wrecks and marine archeologists abound in shallower waters, particularly among fragile coral reefs. Finally, massive utilization of the sea as a dumping ground for waste means thousands of tons of matter that must be disposed of can be dumped by a single ship in one voyage.

International environmental law must respond to this evolution, despite two distinct but converging problems. First, while the oceans share homogeneous characteristics such as ocean currents, salt, and contiguity, their geophysical situation differs widely in the various regions of the world. There are nearly enclosed seas, such as the Baltic and Mediterranean, which do not have the same enormous intermixing of waters from which other seas benefit.[4] They are less able to absorb and diffuse pollution, although

---

and the number of overexploited, depleted and recovering stocks is increasing slightly. An estimated 47 percent of the main stocks or species groups for which information is available are fully exploited and are therefore producing catches that have reached, or are very close to, their maximum sustainable limits. Thus, nearly half of world marine stocks offer no reasonable expectations for further expansion. Another 18 percent of stocks or species groups are reported as overexploited. Prospects for expansion or increased production from these stocks are negligible, and there is an increasing likelihood that they will decline further and catches will decrease, unless remedial management action is taken to reduce overfishing conditions. Ten percent of stocks have become significantly depleted, or are recovering from depletion and are far less productive than they used to be. *See* FAO, THE STATE OF THE WORLD'S FISHERIES AND AQUACULTURE (2002). On fisheries law, see Chapter 8F.1.a.

    [3]   *See* U. FORSTNER & G. WITTMAN, METAL POLLUTION IN THE ACQUATIC ENVIRONMENT (1977).

    [4]   Specifically, it is thought that the Mediterranean renewal is so slow that

these two seas have among the highest known densities of maritime traffic and also suffer from exceptionally concentrated population levels along their shores, with all the attendant pollution. It seems clear that the problem of maritime pollution requires measures be taken on both the regional and the global level, with local variation being resolved through appropriate specific regulations at the same time that universal norms are formulated.

Secondly, the origins of the pollutants that affect the marine environment differ greatly one from the other. They can be intentional, for example the dumping of wastes whose disposal is difficult or more expensive on land and the cleaning of oil tanker hulls on the high seas followed by discharge of the residue of oils into the ocean waters. Pollution also can be accidental, resulting from tanker grounding or loss of containers of toxic or dangerous products. It may be necessary to utilize various regulatory techniques which take into account these differences.

As a whole, international instruments concerning marine environmental pollution distinguish four categories of pollution: vessel-based pollution coming from normal utilization of the oceans; pollution arising from exploration or exploitation of the sea-bed; land-based pollution whether coming from direct discharges into the ocean or carried into it by rivers; and finally deliberate and large, mostly industrial, dumping of wastes. Pollution transported by air may be added, including that derived from incineration of wastes at sea or along the coast.

Legal norms must be flexible to deal with this diversity of situations. International legal rules affirming state responsibility for environmental damage caused by pollution are a beginning, but they lack concrete standards and means of implementation.[5] International responsibility for marine pollution is clearly recognized in principle (UNCLOS Art. 235), but the development of more precise rules is necessary. In the meantime, compensation must be assured by other means, primarily through internal legal proceedings, for damage caused by pollution of the marine environment.

International environmental law places its emphasis on prevention. Numerous standards prohibit certain deliberate or intentional acts or strictly regulate them. To minimize accidental environmental harm, other legal principles must be applied, such as strict rules governing the construction of tankers, navigation, and the training of crews. It is clear that marine environmental pollution due to accidents can only be combated through international cooperation. In this regard, a 1969 Convention permits

---

its waters are exchanged only once every century. The waters of the Baltic are also quite static, with 90 percent replacement only every 25 years. H. Velner, *Baltic Marine Environment Protection Commission, in* COMPREHENSIVE SECURITY FOR THE BALTIC: AN ENVIRONMENTAL APPROACH (A.J. WESTING ed., 1989).

5   *See* Chapter 7C.

intervention on foreign-flag vessels on the high seas in case of accidents that involve or threaten marine environmental pollution.[6] Part of the task of international law is to further develop international cooperation.

B. Historical Evolution

Marine pollution is a relatively long-standing concern, although initial efforts to regulate it were unsuccessful. A 1926 international conference, convened by the United States, elaborated a convention to limit discharges of oil and gas into the sea, but the treaty was never signed. A second draft, prepared under the auspices of the League of Nations in 1935, contained many of the same provisions but also failed to gain acceptance. Not until 1954 was an International Convention for the Prevention of Pollution of the Sea by Oil adopted to prohibit the deliberate discharge of oil in specified zones.[7]

In the meantime, two of the 1958 United Nations Conventions on the law of the sea contained prohibitions relating to pollution of the sea by oil or pipelines as well as by radioactive wastes and wastes resulting from oil drilling on the continental shelf.[8] The 1958 Convention on the High Seas obligates all states to draw up regulations to prevent pollution of the seas by the discharge of oil from ships or pipelines or resulting from the exploitation and exploration of the sea-bed and its sub-soil, "taking account of existing treaty provisions on the subject;"[9] to take measures to prevent pollution of the seas from the dumping of radioactive waste, "taking into account any standards and regulations which may be formulated by the competent international organizations;[10] and "to cooperate with the competent international organizations" in taking measures for the prevention of pollution of the seas resulting from "any activities with radioactive materials or other harmful agents."[11] Although these provisions are general, they established several important precedents. First, the goal of universality is reflected in the Preamble's statement of intent to "codify the rules of international law relating to the high seas." Second, the numerous references to existing treaty provisions and organizations emphasize that states must com-

---

[6]   International Convention Relating to Intervention on the High Seas in Cases of Oil Pollution Casualties (Brussels, Nov. 29, 1969).

[7]   London, May 12, 1954. The Convention was amended several times: in 1962, extending the protected zones; in 1969, enacting a general prohibition on oil pollution; and finally in 1971.

[8]   Arts. 24, 25, Convention on the High Seas (Geneva, Apr. 29, 1958); Art. 5, Convention on the Continental Shelf (Geneva, Apr. 29, 1958).

[9]   Art. 24, Convention on the High Seas (Geneva, Apr. 29, 1958).

[10]   Art. 25(1), Convention on the High Seas.

[11]   Art. 25(2), Convention on the High Seas.

ply with internationally-developed standards and cooperate with competent international organizations in implementing such standards.

A rise in general environmental awareness, coupled with the 1967 *Torrey Canyon* tanker accident, which spilled over 100,000 tons of crude oil into the English Channel causing black tides and damage to both the French and English coastlines, led to further serious consideration of the problem of marine environmental pollution regionally and globally. Soon after the disaster, the UN General Assembly passed Resolution 2414 (XXIII) on "international cooperation in problems related to the oceans," inviting member states and organizations to promote the adoption of effective international agreements for the prevention and control of maritime pollution.[12] Another resolution, on prevention of pollution of the marine environment by sea-bed development, requested that the Secretary-General study the problem of pollution resulting from undersea development.[13] Two years later, the General Assembly, in a recommendation concerning effective measures for the prevention and control of marine pollution, requested the Secretary-General to prepare a review concerning harmful substances affecting the ocean and activities of member nations and international agencies dealing with the prevention and control of marine pollution, and also to seek the views of member nations on the desirability and feasibility of an international treaty on this subject.[14]

During this period global efforts centered on finding a solution to the problems posed by accidents causing serious pollution. The *Torrey Canyon* spill revealed the difficulty of resolving the numerous compensation claims and liability issues under then-existing law. As a result, the International Maritime Consultative Organization (now International Maritime Organization) drafted two Conventions in 1969, one concerning civil responsibility for oil pollution damage and the other relating to intervention on the high seas in cases of oil pollution casualties.[15] These agreements were supplemented in 1971 with the adoption of a Convention creating an international fund for compensation for oil pollution damage.[16]

In 1972, the Stockholm Conference gave new impetus to the development of international environmental norms. The Conference Declaration contains a general principle regarding pollution, providing that the discharge of toxic substances or of other substances and the release of heat in quantities or concentrations that exceed the capacity of the environment to render them harmless must be halted in order to ensure that serious or

---

[12] G.A. Res. A/RES/2414 (XXIII), Dec. 17, 1968.
[13] G.A. Res. A/RES/2467 B (XXIII), Dec. 21, 1968.
[14] G.A. Res. A/RES/2566 (XXIV), Dec. 13, 1969.
[15] Brussels, Nov. 29, 1969.
[16] Brussels, Dec. 18, 1971.

irreversible damage is not inflicted upon ecosystems.[17] Following this general provision, Principle 7 specifically addresses marine pollution, declaring that states shall take all possible steps to prevent pollution of the seas by substances that are liable to create hazards to human health, harm living resources and marine life, damage amenities or interfere with other legitimate uses of the sea. In addition, Recommendations 86–94 of the Stockholm Action Plan address marine pollution. Most of the measures concern scientific research and monitoring the state of the environment, but Recommendation 86 urges states to adhere to and implement existing instruments combating marine pollution, and to develop norms, national as well as international, to prevent more effectively further deterioration of the marine environment.

Before the end of 1972, a conference in London created a new global international instrument, with the states present signing the Convention on the Prevention of Marine Pollution by Dumping of Wastes and other Matter.[18] One year later, also in London, a conference convoked by IMCO (now IMO) adopted a treaty that aimed at all pollution caused by ships.[19] The same year saw the beginning of the Third United Nations Conference on the Law of the Sea, whose work resulted in the Law of the Sea Convention (UNCLOS).[20]

UNCLOS, whose provisions generally reflect customary international law, provides the overall legal framework for ocean activities.[21] Its comprehensive regulation addresses the protection and preservation of the marine environment in Part XII.[22] In addition, Article 145 specifically aims to prevent pollution resulting from exploration and exploitation of the deep seabed. The Convention recognizes the competence of the coastal state to combat pollution in the territorial sea[23] and in the UNCLOS-created exclusive economic zone.[24] On the other hand, UNCLOS contains no new substantive rules to combat pollution of the high seas, although there are rules protecting marine living resources.

Marine environmental law is evolving towards comprehensive regulation. The 1992 Conference of Rio de Janeiro built on the norms contained

---

[17] Principle 6.

[18] Dec. 29, 1972.

[19] International Convention for the Prevention of Pollution by Ships (MARPOL) (London, Nov. 2, 1973).

[20] Montego Bay, Dec. 10, 1982, *entry into force* 1994, A/CONF.62/122. As of 2003, 173 states were party to UNCLOS.

[21] WSSD, Plan of Action, para. 38(d) (referring to UNCLOS as "the overall legal framework for ocean activities" and inviting all states to become party to and implement it).

[22] Arts. 192–237.

[23] Art. 21.

[24] UNCLOS Art. 56(1)(b)(iii).

in UNCLOS, with Chapter 17 of Agenda 21 attempting an integrated approach in its reference to all matters that concern the sea. The formulation of the title, *Protection of the oceans, all kinds of seas, including enclosed and semi-enclosed seas and coastal areas and the protection, rational use and development of their living resources*, announces the three main areas of interest: the sea itself, the coastal areas and living resources.

While protection of the marine environment against pollution and protection of the living resources of the sea against depletion are traditionally related and included within international environmental law, broad extension of international norms to coastal areas is an innovation. Until UNCED, the management of coastal areas and of waters under national jurisdiction was generally considered a national concern: the Principles Concerning Coastal Management adopted by OECD on October 12, 1976,[25] exceptionally focused on coastal land areas. Agenda 21 also linked the problem of marine pollution and of the management of coastal zones for two obvious reasons. First, coastal areas play a major role in human settlements. Half of the world's population lives within 60 kilometers of the marine shoreline and this proportion could rise to three-quarters by the year 2020. At the same time, many of the world's poor are crowded in coastal areas and the development of such areas is a problem of growing importance. Linked to the concentration of people, more than 70 percent of the pollution of the oceans results from land-based sources. There is a trend towards adopting conventions against land-based pollution, particularly for the seas around Europe.

Agenda 21, including Chapter 17, is not a treaty setting detailed rules of conduct for states. Rather, the commitment of states is to cooperate in taking action. Section 17.30 of Agenda 21 establishes a list of measures which should be taken to address degradation of the marine environment. Such measures include, *inter alia*, cooperation in monitoring marine pollution from ships, especially from illegal discharges, and enforcing MARPOL discharge provisions more rigorously; assessment of the state of pollution caused by ships in particularly sensitive areas and implementation of applicable measures; respect for areas designated by coastal states, within their exclusive economic zones, in order to protect and preserve rare or fragile ecosystems, such as coral reefs and mangroves; adoption of stricter international regulations to reduce further the risk of accidents and pollution from cargo ships and the development of an international regime governing the transportation of hazardous and noxious substances carried by ships. The present section discusses only the protection of the marine environment against pollution ; the conservation of living resources is contained in Chapter 8F.1.

---

[25]   C(76)161(Final).

Paragraph 17.22 of Agenda 21 confirms that the main rules of international law in this realm are those formulated in the United Nations Convention on the Law of the Sea, Part XII:

> States, in accordance with the provisions of the United Nations Convention on the Law of the Sea on protection and preservation of the marine environment, commit themselves, in accordance with their policies, priorities and resources, to prevent, reduce and control degradation of the marine environment so as to maintain and improve its life-support and productive capacities. . . .

The Convention for the Protection of the Marine Environment of the North-East Atlantic recognized the applicability of at least some of Part XII of UNCLOS even before the latter entered into force.[26] In fact, all international treaties concerning the oceans adopted since 1989, and even the Convention on Biological Diversity, follow the general principles set forth in UNCLOS and many specifically cite to it. The international common law of the environment thus applies to specifically protecting the marine environment.

The law of marine environmental protection also developed regionally, following the main directions of UNCLOS. First states of different maritime regions of the Northern hemisphere, *i.e.*, the Baltic Sea, North-East Atlantic and Black Sea, concluded general treaties on these waters. Second, UNEP initiated a "regional seas program" resulting in treaty systems, each consisting of a main convention, additional protocols, and, often, action plans for the development of the region.

Eight European states signed the first regional convention dedicated to the problem of marine pollution in Bonn on June 9, 1969.[27] The states parties, clearly responding to the *Torrey Canyon* accident in 1967, developed the means of cooperation to combat pollution of the North Sea by oil. Two years later, Denmark, Finland, Norway and Sweden signed another regional agreement concerning regional marine pollution.[28] In 1972, 12 European states bordering the Atlantic or the North Sea signed a convention to address the previously ignored problem of marine pollution caused by dumping of wastes from ships and aircraft.[29] The agreement only concerned

---

[26]   "Recalling the relevant provisions of customary international law reflected in Part XII of the United Nations Law of the Sea Convention and, in particular, Art. 197 on global and regional cooperation for the protection and preservation of the marine environment . . . ," Preamble, Convention for the Protection of the Marine Environment of the North-East Atlantic (Paris, Sept. 22, 1992).

[27]   Agreement of Cooperation in Dealing with Pollution of the North Sea by Oil (Bonn, June 9, 1969).

[28]   Agreement Concerning Cooperation in Taking Measures Against Pollution of the Sea by Oil (Copenhagen, Sept. 16, 1971).

[29]   Oslo, Feb. 15, 1972.

a part of the Atlantic and the Arctic oceans, however, to the exclusion of the Baltic and Mediterranean Seas. The same maritime zone was the subject of another convention, signed by the same European countries on June 4, 1974, aimed at preventing marine pollution from land-based sources.[30]

In 1974, the Helsinki Convention on the Protection of the Marine Environment of the Baltic Sea Area initiated another advance in international legal mechanisms to protect the marine environment.[31] For the first time, the seven littoral states (Denmark, Finland, the then-two Germanies, Poland, Sweden and the USSR) agreed to comprehensively address all forms of marine pollution. A 1992 Convention for the Baltic Sea replaced the 1974 Helsinki Convention.[32] Similarly, a 1992 Paris Convention comprehensively regulates all sources of marine pollution that may affect the North Sea and the North-East Atlantic, replacing both the 1972 Oslo Convention to prevent the dumping of wastes and the 1974 Paris Convention regulating the prevention of land-based pollution.[33] A third convention, equally adopted in 1992 although somewhat less developed, concerns the Black Sea.[34] Given the importance of the three instruments, they will be analyzed later in detail.

The United Nations Environment Program launched its program for "regional seas" aiming to create a treaty system for each targeted area. The systems consist of a plan and a framework convention for the protection of the marine environment, accompanied by special protocols devoted to problems such as the dumping of wastes and cooperation in case of accident or land-based pollution. The earliest of these treaty systems concerns the Protection of the Mediterranean Sea against Pollution.[35] The main treaty is accompanied by two protocols signed the same day, one concerning dumping from ships and aircraft,[36] the other concerning cooperation in combating pollution by oil and other harmful substances in cases of emergency.[37] Five additional protocols, subsequently concluded, relate to

---

[30] Convention for the Prevention of Marine Pollution from Land-Based Sources (Paris).

[31] Mar. 22, 1974.

[32] Convention on the Protection of the Marine Environment of the Baltic Sea Area (Helsinki, Apr. 9, 1992). *See* S. Mahmoudi, *The Baltic and the North Sea*, *in* MANUAL OF EUROPEAN ENVIRONMENTAL LAW 360 (A. Kiss & D. Shelton eds., 2d ed. 1997).

[33] Convention for the Protection of the Marine Environment of the North-East Atlantic (Paris, Sept. 22, 1992). *See also* Mahmoudi, *id.*

[34] Convention on the Protection of the Black Sea against Pollution (Bucharest, Apr. 21, 1992).

[35] Barcelona, Feb. 16, 1976.

[36] Protocol for the Prevention of Pollution of the Mediterranean Sea by Dumping from Ships and Aircraft (Barcelona, Feb. 16, 1976).

[37] Protocol concerning Co-operation in Combating Pollution of the Mediterranean Sea by Oil and other Harmful Substances in Cases of Emergency (Barcelona, Feb. 16, 1976).

land-based pollution,[38] to Mediterranean specially protected areas[39]—replaced by a more recent instrument[40]—to pollution resulting from exploration and exploitation of the sea-bed,[41] and to pollution by transboundary movements of hazardous wastes.[42] The Protocol on land-based pollution was amended March 7, 1996 (Syracuse) and its title changed significantly into Protocol for the Protection of the Mediterranean Sea against Pollution from Land-Based Sources and Activities. The modified text notes the increasing environmental pressures resulting from human activities in the Mediterranean Sea Area, particularly from industrialization and urbanization, as well as the seasonal increase in the coastal population due to tourism.

The original Barcelona Convention was revised and amended by an agreement of June 10, 1996,[43] which expands its scope to coastal areas, integrates into it principles such as the precautionary principle, the polluter pays principle, and public information and introduces into it the obligation to prepare environmental impact assessments as well as to adopt integrated management for coastal areas. The amendments also oblige the contracting parties to submit reports on the implementation of the Convention. In sum, the Barcelona Convention was revised substantially, taking into account recent developments in international environmental law.

Other regional seas are similarly regulated by UNEP-sponsored treaty systems: the Persian Gulf,[44] West and Central Africa,[45] the South-East

---

[38]   Protocol for the Protection of the Mediterranean Sea against Pollution from Land-Based Sources (Athens, May 17, 1980).

[39]   Protocol concerning Mediterranean Specially Protected Areas (Geneva, Apr. 3, 1982).

[40]   Protocol concerning Specially Protected Areas and Biological Diversity in the Mediterranean (Barcelona, June 10, 1995).

[41]   Protocol for the Protection of the Mediterranean Sea against Pollution resulting from Exploration and Exploitation of the Continental Shelf and the Seabed and its Subsoil (Madrid, Oct. 14, 1994).

[42]   Protocol on the Prevention of Pollution of the Mediterranean Sea by Transboundary Movements of Hazardous Wastes and their Disposal (Izmir, Oct. 1, 1996) UNEP(OCA)/MED/IG.4/4, Oct. 11, 1996.

[43]   Doc. UNEP(OCA)/Med.IG.6/7.

[44]   Kuwait Regional Convention for Cooperation on the Protection of the Marine Environment from Pollution (Apr. 24, 1978); Protocol Concerning Regional Cooperation in Combating Pollution by Oil and other Harmful Substances in Cases of Emergency (Kuwait, Apr. 24, 1978); Protocol Concerning Marine Pollution Resulting from Exploration and Exploitation of the Continental Shelf (Kuwait, Mar. 29, 1989); Protocol for the Protection of the Marine Environment against Pollution from Land-Based Sources (Kuwait, Feb. 21, 1990).

[45]   Convention for Cooperation in the Protection and Development of the Marine and Coastal Environment of the West and Central African Region (Abidjan, Mar. 23, 1981); Protocol Concerning Cooperation in Combating

Pacific,[46] the Gulf of Aden and the Red Sea,[47] the Caribbean,[48] the Indian Ocean and East Africa,[49] and the South Pacific.[50]

In early 2002, eight countries of Central and Western America adopted the latest treaty for a regional sea. The Antigua Convention for Cooperation in the Protection and Sustainable Development of the Marine and Coastal

---

Pollution in Cases of Emergency (Abidjan, Mar. 23, 1981).

[46] Convention for the Protection of the Marine Environment and Coastal Area of the South-East Pacific (Lima, Nov. 20, 1981); Agreement on Regional Cooperation in Combating Pollution of the South-East Pacific by Hydrocarbons or Other Harmful Substances in Cases of Emergency (Lima, Nov. 12, 1981); Protocol for the Protection of the South-East Pacific against Pollution from Land-Based Sources (Quito, July 22, 1983); Supplementary Protocol to the Agreement on Regional Cooperation in Combating Pollution of the South-Pacific by Hydrocarbons or Other Harmful Substances (Quito, July 22, 1983); Protocol for the Protection of the South-East Pacific against Radioactive Pollution (Paipa, Sept. 21, 1989); Protocol for the Conservation and Management of Protected Marine and Coastal Areas of the South-East Pacific (Paipa, Sept. 21, 1989).

[47] Regional Convention for the Conservation of the Red Sea and of the Gulf of Aden Environment (Jeddah, Feb. 14, 1982); Protocol Relating to Regional Cooperation to Combat Pollution by Oil and Other Harmful Substances in Case of Emergency (Jeddah, Feb. 14, 1982).

[48] Convention for the Protection and Development of the Marine Environment of the Wider Caribbean Region (Cartagena de Indias, Mar. 24, 1983); Protocol Concerning Cooperation in Combating Oil Spills in the Wider Caribbean Region (Cartagena de Indias, Mar. 24, 1983); Protocol concerning Specially Protected Areas and Wildlife to the Convention for the Protection and Development of the Wider Caribbean Region (Kingston, Jan. 18, 1990); Protocol concerning Pollution from Land-Based Sources and Activities (Oranjestad, Aruba, Oct. 6, 1999).

[49] Convention for the Protection, Management and Development of the Marine and Coastal Environment of the Eastern African Region (Nairobi, June 21, 1985); Protocol concerning Co-operation in Combating Marine Pollution in cases of Emergency in the Eastern African Region (Nairobi, June 21, 1985); Protocol concerning Protected Areas and Wild Fauna and Flora in the Eastern African Region (Nairobi, June 21, 1985.

[50] Convention for the Protection of the Natural Resources and Environment of the South Pacific Region (Noumea, Nov. 24, 1986); Protocol for the Prevention of Pollution of the South Pacific by Dumping (Noumea, Nov. 25, 1986); Protocol concerning Co-operation in Combating Pollution Emergencies in the South Pacific Region (Noumea, Nov. 25, 1986).

Environment of the Northeast Pacific[51] contains several innovations in responding to the main problems that arise in protecting the marine environment. It also foresees the adoption of other agreements by meetings of the contracting parties. The Convention includes the precautionary principle, the polluter pays principle, environmental impact assessment procedures, participation of local authorities and civil society in decisions that affect the marine environment, and provision of information to civil society and local authorities on the status of the marine environment of the region.[52] Its new elements include providing for integrated development and management of coastal areas and shared water basins and adopting an ecosystem approach to fisheries management.[53] Also, the core of the Convention not only advocates measures to prevent, reduce, control and remedy different forms of pollution, but also measures to counter biophysical modifications of the marine environment, including alteration and destruction of habitats. It expresses the need to identify and protect endangered species of flora and fauna and contains a special provision on the erosion of coastal areas. Detailed measures also are foreseen for emergency situations.

Taken together, more than 130 states today cooperate in UNEP's regional seas program. The details of the regional conventions diverge although there are commonalities. All the systems address emergency situations due to their importance. The Barcelona system has seven protocols, making it the most detailed regulatory system, while the regional convention for the South-East Pacific provides the most precise rules concerning land-based pollution.

As international environmental law has expanded, it is increasingly recognized that treaties have overlapping mandates and may apply to regulate the same geographic area. Coastal areas, for example, may be regulated not only according to the provisions of UNCLOS and a regional sea agreement, but also the Convention on Biological Diversity, the Ramsar Convention on Wetlands, the UNESCO World Heritage Convention, and treaties and other rules governing freshwaters. The consequence is a considerable network of law and institutions that are not always coordinated. The Convention on Biological Diversity is one of the few to specifically mention and give deference to UNCLOS (Art. 22). For the rest, it is unclear how competing rules will be reconciled.

C.   Rights and Duties of States in Maritime Areas

The environmental provisions of UNCLOS have a dynamic character, not only building on prior instruments, but adding structure and establishing

---

[51]   Feb. 18, 2002.
[52]   Art. 3(6).
[53]   Art. 10(2)(e).

the means for incorporating future developments. The Convention covers the three major sources of marine pollution: land-based sources, vessel source pollution, and atmospheric pollution. The provisions apply to all ocean surfaces, not only the high seas, but also to areas under the jurisdiction of coastal states. They also seek to combat marine pollution by various preventive measures, including the duty to notify states of any imminent danger of pollution, to develop contingency plans for responding to incidents, to monitor the risks of pollution, and to assess potential effects of planned activities that may cause substantial pollution or significant changes in the marine environment and communicate such assessments.

As previously noted, UNCLOS Article 192 proclaims that states have a general obligation to protect and preserve the marine environment. The primary concern seems to be the prevention of pollution, given that Article 192 figures first among a series of provisions relating to marine pollution. In contrast, clauses relating to the preservation of marine biological resources are contained in the sections of the Convention regulating each of the established marine zones.[54]

The Convention enunciates only broad principles respecting pollution prevention, such as the requirement in Article 194(1) that states take, individually or jointly as appropriate, all measures consistent with the Convention that are necessary to prevent, reduce, and control pollution of the marine environment from any source. The Convention reaffirms several principles of the Stockholm Declaration. For example, Art. 191, like Principle 21, confirms the sovereign right of each state to exploit natural resources pursuant to its environmental policies. Similarly, Convention Art. 194 reaffirms the duty expressed in Principle 21 for states to respect the environment of others. More precisely, states must combat pollution of the marine environment from all sources.[55] At the same time, they must take care to avoid cross-media pollution, *i.e.*, transfer, directly or indirectly, of damage or hazards from one area to another or one type of pollution into another.[56]

The Convention uses a now classic definition of pollution by stating that it means "the introduction by man, directly or indirectly, of substances or energy into the marine environment, including estuaries, which results or is likely to result in such deleterious effects as harm to living resources and marine life, hazards to human health, hindrance to marine activities, including fishing and other legitimate uses of the sea, impairment of quality for use of sea water and reduction of amenities."[57]

---

[54] The protection of marine living resources is treated in Chapter 8.
[55] Art. 194(3).
[56] UNCLOS Art. 195,
[57] Art. 1(4). Compare the OECD definition of pollution in Chapter 5A.1.

Article 196 expands the scope of the definition in an unexpected way by calling for preventing, reducing and controlling pollution of the marine environment resulting from the "use of technologies," without specifying what technologies are envisaged. It additionally prohibits "the intentional or accidental introduction of species, alien or new, to a particular part of the marine environment, which may cause significant and harmful changes thereto."

International cooperation both regionally and globally is presented as an obligation, explicitly with the aim of formulating and elaborating international rules and standards and "recommended practices and procedures."[58] Specific provisions govern cooperation in emergency situations.[59] States also are required to continuously monitor the risks or effects of pollution. In particular, they must "keep under surveillance" the effects of any activities that they permit or in which they engage, in order to determine whether these activities are likely to pollute the marine environment.[60] The results obtained from such surveillance must be communicated to international organizations who should make them available to all states.[61] In addition, states should assess the potential effects of any activities that may cause substantial pollution and communicate the results of such assessments.[62] As a final element in the framework of international cooperation, the Convention foresees assistance to developing states in the fields of science and technology and preferential treatment for these states by international organizations.[63]

The Convention identifies three states competent to exercise jurisdiction over matters of marine pollution: flag states, port states, and coastal states. One aspect common to the jurisdiction of all is the repeated obligation to take into account or enact and enforce internationally agreed rules and standards. In some cases, UNCLOS requires that national laws and measures "shall be no less effective than international rules, standards and recommended practices and procedures"[64] whether the international rules, standards and recommended practices have been established before or after the adoption or entry into force of UNCLOS. Finally, states "shall adopt laws and regulations and take other measures necessary to implement applicable international rules and standards established through competent international organizations or diplomatic conference to prevent and control pollution of the marine environment" from various sources.[65] The unusual

---

58 Art. 197.
59 Arts. 198–99.
60 Art. 204.
61 Art. 205.
62 Art. 206.
63 Arts. 202–03.
64 Arts. 207(4), 208(5), 210(4), 211(1), 212(3).
65 Arts. 213–14, 216–20, 222.

feature of these obligations is that the state's duty to adopt laws and regulations conforming to the international rules and standards does not depend on its ratification of a particular agreement or its actual participation in the adoption of a rule or standard; it is enough that the international rules and standards be "generally accepted."[66] The process is thus one of elaboration and incorporation under the umbrella of UNCLOS, of a veritable code of rules and standards for the protection of the marine environment.

1. Flag State Jurisdiction

Pursuant to the detailed provisions of UNCLOS Article 217, states must ensure that ships under their jurisdiction and control comply with applicable international rules and standards and with flag state laws and regulations adopted in accordance with the Convention. They also shall take appropriate measures to ensure that ships they register or which fly their flag are prohibited from sailing unless they are in compliance with international rules and standards. Ships shall carry any certificates required by international law and be periodically inspected. In case of any violation, the flag state shall investigate and where appropriate institute proceedings regardless of where the violation or pollution occurred. Penalties must be adequate in severity to discourage violations wherever they occur. The 1993 Agreement to Promote Compliance with International Conservation and Management Measures by Fishing Vessels on the High Seas approved by the FAO Conference on November 24, 1993[67] reinforces the obligation of flag states to take such measures as may be necessary to ensure that fishing vessels entitled to fly their flag do not engage in any activity that undermines the effectiveness of international conservation measures (Art. III (1)(a)). In particular, no state shall allow any fishing vessel entitled to fly its flag to be used for fishing on the high seas unless it has been authorized to do so by the appropriate authority of that state (Art. III(2)).

2. Port State Jurisdiction

Port states have jurisdiction, confirmed in Article 218, in cases where ships voluntarily enter a port or off-shore terminal. The state may undertake investigations and, where the evidence warrants, institute proceedings against the ship for any discharge on the high seas in violation of applicable international rules and standards. For discharges in the internal waters, territorial sea or exclusive economic zone of another state, the port state

---

66 Art. 211(2).
67 33 I.L.M. 968 (1994).

may open a proceeding only if requested by the other state or if the violation has caused or is likely to cause pollution of its own waters. Port states should respond also to requests from any state for investigation of pollution caused in its waters as well as requests from the flag state. Finally, the port state may prevent from sailing any foreign ships in violation of international rules and standards relating to seaworthiness that could thereby threaten damage to the environment, until the violations have been cured.

Port state exercise of this jurisdiction (port state control) is a crucial step towards the reinforcement of flag state responsibilities to comply with international rules and standards and the elimination of sub-standard ships. In effect, allowing the inspection of foreign-flagged vessels can act as a safety net when shipowners, classification societies, insurers, or flag state administrators have in one way or another failed to comply with legal and technical regulations. As noted above, all countries have the right to inspect ships visiting their ports to ensure that they meet IMO requirements regarding safety and marine pollution prevention standards. Port authorities of different countries have concluded Memoranda of Understanding (MOUs) to improve and harmonize port state inspections and avoid distorting competition among ports. Such agreements also preempt unilateral approaches that could lead to international conflict.[68] IMO has been fully involved in encouraging the establishment of these agreements.

Experience has shown that port state control works best when it is organized on a regional basis. MOUs generally require each maritime authority which is a signatory to the agreement to establish and maintain an effective system of port state control and set an annual required total of inspections of at least 10 percent of the estimated total number of foreign merchant ships entering the ports during the year. MOUs encourage exchange of information so that ships that have been inspected by one port state and found to be in compliance with all safety and marine pollution prevention rules are not subject to too frequent inspections, while ships presenting a hazard and those ships which have been reported by another port state as having deficiencies which need to be rectified will be targeted.

Western European national port authorities adopted the first Memorandum of Understanding on the Surveillance of Ships by Port States[69] in 1982, covering Europe and the North Atlantic. The primary objective of the 14 signatories was to dissuade dangerous ships that could pollute the marine environment from frequenting European ports and adjacent waters. The contracting authorities agreed to enforce within their

---

68   *See* Lee Kimball, Introductory Note, *Memorandum of Understanding on Port State Control in the Caribbean Region*, 36 I.L.M. 231(1997).

69   This agreement, known as the "Paris MOU" was signed on January 26, 1982 between national port authorities. It is thus not considered as an international treaty, but as a soft law instrument.

ports a body of international conventions regarding the security of ships and the prevention of pollution[70] even if the flag state was not a contracting party. The parties harmonized their supervisory mechanisms both as to the means of control and the number of regulated ships, the target being 25 percent of the ships frequenting European ports. In addition, the contracting maritime authorities agreed to exchange information and evidence regarding breaches of maritime rules and of pollution.

The first results from application of the Memorandum were very encouraging. During the initial four years following its entry into force, authorities inspected 38,000 ships or 21.5 percent of those entering European ports. Of these, they held 1,500 in port because of infractions. Nearly one quarter (23.6 percent) were held for violation of norms concerning pollution and 13 percent for irregular documents, more than half of which related to the "international certificate" on oil pollution.[71]

The system of port state control expanded to other parts of the world and since 1992 the inspections cover not only technical requirements but also operational requirements. At present ships may be subject to a review of relevant certificates and documents on board the vessel, a cursory survey that may lead to more detailed inspection if clear grounds exist for doing so, and possible detention of the vessel until serious deficiencies are rectified. If the defects cannot be remedied in the port of inspection, the ship may proceed to another port, subject to appropriate conditions determined by the inspecting state's authorities to ensure that the vessel does not pose unreasonable danger to safety, health or the environment.[72]

Since the beginning of the 1990s many regions have adopted MOUs on port state control. A Latin American Agreement (Acuerdo de Viña del Mar) was signed in 1992; an Asia-Pacific Memorandum of Understanding (Tokyo) in 1993; a Caribbean Memorandum of Understanding in 1996; a Mediterranean Memorandum of Understanding in 1997; an Indian Ocean Memorandum of Understanding on Port State Control in 1998; a Memorandum of Understanding for West and Central Africa in 1999, and an MOU on Port State Control in the Black Sea (Istanbul, 2000).

The process of elaborating an MOU can be illustrated by the process followed in West and Central Africa. In 1997, 19 nations in the region agreed to work towards establishing a Port State Control (PSC) regime in the shortest possible time in order to eradicate sub-standard ships from the region. They agreed on a preliminary draft text of a Memorandum of Understanding (MOU) and a draft Training Program. They also agreed to

---

[70]   For example the Nov. 1, 1974 International Convention for the Safety of Human Life at Sea (SOLAS) and the Nov. 2, 1973 MARPOL Convention.

[71]   J.-L. Prat, *Le système spécifique de l'Europe du Nord-Ouest, in* DROIT DE L'ENVIRONNEMENT MARIN 83, at 92 (S.F.D.E., 1988).

[72]   Lee Kimball, *supra* note 68, at 232.

make every effort to put in place or strengthen competent maritime administrations in order to implement an effective PSC regime. International bodies such as IMO, the International Labor Organization (ILO), the United Nations Development Program (UNDP), the Economic Commission for Africa (ECA), the International Association of Classification Societies (IACS), the International Transport Workers Federation (ITF), the Communauté Economique et Monétaire de l'Afrique Centrale (CEMAC) and other regional organizations supported this initiative which resulted in final agreement on the MOU in 1999.

The adoption of an MOU for the Gulf region will complete the coverage of all areas of the world. Countries in the region have agreed informally on the need to establish a regime of port state control.

3. *Coastal State Jurisdiction*

Coastal states are granted extensive jurisdiction by Article 220 to combat pollution of the marine environment in their territorial seas and exclusive economic zones, supplementing the general grant of coastal state jurisdiction over these zones proclaimed by Article 21(1) and Article 56(1)(b)(iii). The legislative power of the coastal state to combat pollution by ships is affirmed for the territorial sea by Article 211(4) and for the exclusive economic zone by Article 211(5). The scope of authority over the two zones differs. For the more distant exclusive economic zone, the coastal state must adopt laws and regulations that conform to and give effect to generally accepted international rules and standards. No such limitation appears on the jurisdiction of the coastal state for the more proximate twelve mile territorial sea, except that laws and regulations governing the territorial sea must not hamper innocent passage of foreign vessels (Art. 211(4)).

The interplay between coastal state regulation of environmental protection and innocent passage is not entirely clear. Article 19(2)(h) provides that any act of wilful and serious pollution contrary to the Convention shall be considered prejudicial to the peace, good order, or security of the coastal state and therefore is not innocent passage. It thus seems that the coastal state may enact the strictest possible measures against ships which engage in wilful and serious pollution and may enact other stringent local rules and regulations to prevent, reduce and control pollution, preventing non-innocent passage or taking other enforcement measures. It is less clear what measures a coastal state may take to reduce the risk of pollution by ships passing through the territorial sea. The Convention allows the coastal state to require use of sea lanes and traffic separation schemes by tankers, nuclear-powered ships and ships carrying nuclear or other inherently dangerous or noxious substances or materials. The implication is that the coastal state cannot bar such ships from the passage through the territorial sea regardless of the hazardous nature of the cargo being carried, provided there is no wilful pollution. On the other hand, passage is defined as innocent if it is not prejudicial to, *inter alia*, the security of the coastal state. With the emergence of the concept of environmental security, coastal states may find objectionable the passage of ships carrying ultra-hazardous cargos.

Article 220 distinguishes several possibilities respecting the enforcement of norms against pollution. These follow the general approach in UNCLOS of diminishing coastal state competence the further the maritime zone is from the coast,[73] while other rules in the Convention are common to the exercise of jurisdiction by any of the interested states. Article 224 provides that the powers of enforcement against foreign vessels is a governmental function, to be exercised by officials or by warships, military aircraft, or other government ships or aircraft. Moreover, the exercise of enforcement powers must not endanger the safety or navigation.[74]

When the ship is voluntarily within a port of a state whose territorial waters or exclusive economic zone it is suspected of having polluted in violation of laws and regulations adopted in accordance with the Convention or applicable international rules and standards, the state may institute proceedings.[75] If the ship is navigating in the territorial sea and there are clear grounds to believe that it has violated applicable norms against pollution, the coastal state may subject it to physical inspection, detention, and proceedings, where the evidence so warrants.[76]

Where the offense concerns the exclusive economic zone and the ship is navigating in the territorial sea or in the exclusive economic zone of the coastal state, the state may require the vessel to give information regarding its identity and port of registry, its last and its next port of call and other relevant information required to establish whether a violation has occurred. The laws, regulations and other measures adopted by all states shall require their registered ships to comply with requests from other states for information regarding suspected violations.[77]

If the coastal state has clear grounds for believing that a violation has resulted in a substantial discharge causing or threatening significant pollution to the marine environment, Article 220(5) permits the state to undertake physical inspection of the vessel. The following paragraph provides that if the discharge causes major damage or threat of major damage to the coastline or related interests of the coastal state, the state may institute proceedings, including detention of the vessel, in accordance with its laws. The

---

[73] *See* D. Shelton & G. Rose, *Freedom of Navigation* 17 SANTA CLARA L. REV. 523 (1977).

[74] Art. 225.

[75] Art. 220(1).

[76] Art. 220(2).

[77] Art. 220(3) and (4).

vessel can be authorized to proceed, however, if there exist procedures foreseen in advance to assure compliance by a bond or other appropriate financial security.[78]

The provisions of Article 226 also apply where foreign vessels are the object of an investigation or an enforcement action, whether these occur in ports or on the sea. Physical inspection of a foreign vessel is limited to an examination of such certificates, records or other documents as the vessel is required to carry; further inspection may be undertaken only when there are clear irregularities or omissions. Even in case of a violation, a vessel cannot be detained unless it presents an unreasonable threat of damage to the marine environment. In such case, the flag state must be promptly notified. In no case may states discriminate in form or in fact against the vessels of any other state.[79]

The Convention also seeks to guarantee the interests of the flag state in cases where the coastal state institutes proceedings. Article 231 requires that the measures taken must be reported to the flag state. If the flag state itself institutes proceedings to impose penalties, the coastal state must suspend its proceedings, unless the violation took place within the territorial sea or relates to a case of major damage to the coastal state or, finally, if the flag state has failed repeatedly to enforce applicable international rules and standards.[80]

As regards the rules of liability, the Convention distinguishes between civil, criminal, and international liability. States are liable for damage or loss attributable to them arising from unlawful or excessive measures taken to apply the provisions of the Convention relating to protection of the marine environment. This liability falls within the internal legal order; it is explicitly provided that states shall allow recourse to their courts for actions in respect of such damage or loss.[81] While this provision aims to deter overreaching by the coastal state, its interests are also protected: nothing in the Convention may affect the ability to institute civil proceedings in respect of any claim for loss or damage resulting from pollution of the marine environment.[82] Criminal liability is foreseen in rules that distinguish the place of the harm: only monetary penalties may be imposed on foreign vessels for violations outside the territorial sea, but within the territorial sea criminal sanctions are permitted for willful and serious acts of pollution.[83]

International responsibility is governed by Article 235, which affirms that states shall be liable in accordance with international law for failure to

---

[78]   Art. 220(7).

[79]   Art. 227.

[80]   Art. 228.

[81]   Art. 232.

[82]   Art. 229.

[83]   Art. 230.

fulfill their international obligations concerning the protection and preservation of the marine environment. States also must ensure the availability within their legal systems of procedures for prompt and adequate compensation or other relief in respect of damage caused by pollution by natural or juridical persons under their jurisdiction, being understood that states are to cooperate in the implementation and further development of international law in this field.

Finally, UNCLOS contains concessions to state sovereignty. By the terms of Art. 236, the provisions of the Convention regarding the protection and preservation of the marine environment do not apply to any warship, naval auxiliary, or other vessels or aircraft being used by the government in non-commercial service. This serious derogation is not only irreconcilable with the rest of the Convention, it is incompatible with the usual principles of immunity which provide only for exemption from enforcement procedures, not from applicability of the law. Logically and according to general international law, there is no reason why government ships and aircraft should be exempt from marine pollution rules, even though they may be immune from otherwise applicable enforcement procedures. Undoubtedly, the drafters of the Convention sought to remedy this loophole by inserting the final sentence of Article 236 which requires states to take "appropriate measures not impairing operations or operational capabilities of such vessels or aircraft owned or operated by it, that such vessels or aircraft act in a manner consistent, so far as is reasonable and practicable, with this Convention." It is difficult to see in this tortured phraseology anything other than a reaffirmation of state sovereignty and an invitation to military or other state actors to ignore environmental norms.

D. Comprehensive Regional Treaties

Several important regional agreements were concluded after 1990. The Convention for the Protection of the Marine Environment in the North-East Atlantic replaced both the 1972 Oslo Convention on dumping and the 1974 Paris Convention on land-based pollution, following a 1990 decision of the states parties.[84] The earlier agreements had a similar geographic coverage, an established commission that met annually, and a joint Secretariat based in London. The other significant new conventions protect the Baltic Sea against pollution, replacing a 1974 instrument, and the Black Sea. The first of the three Conventions is of particular importance, however, not only because of the large area covered, but also because it incorporates many modern trends of international environmental law.

---

[84] Between 1984 and 1990, the North Sea coastal states organized three ministerial conferences to update the two instruments (Bremen, 1984; London 1987; and The Hague, 1990). Not all states parties participated in the meetings.

The Convention on the North-East Atlantic, adopted in Paris on September 22, 1992, proclaims in its Preamble two important principles. The first recognizes the inherent value of the marine environment of the North-East Atlantic; this implies that it should be protected independently of all direct utility for the contracting states. The second principle, already mentioned, recognizes that UNCLOS Part XII contains norms of customary international law.

Several environmental principles are incorporated in the body of the Convention, including the polluter pays principle (Art. 2(2)(b)) and the precautionary principle. As previously noted, the 1990 Declaration of the International North Sea Conference contained the first international formulation of the precautionary principle. Article 2(2)(a) of the Paris Convention defines it.[85]

The Convention definition, like that of the Rio Declaration, focuses on the uncertainty of a causal relationship between inputs and effects, establishing a test of "reasonable grounds for concern" as the basis for action. "Reasonableness" may require some objective evidence, but no conclusive proof is required. The latter would be particularly difficult to obtain where an area as vast as the marine environment is involved, or when new products or substances are being dumped in a river far upstream.

The Convention defines two other widely used terms. The first, "best available techniques" is "the latest stage of development (state of the art) of processes, of facilities or of methods of operation which indicate the practical suitability of a particular measure for limiting discharges, emissions and waste." Special consideration is given to comparable processes, facilities, or methods, to technological advances and changes in scientific knowledge and understanding, to the economic feasibility, to the characteristics of plants and to the nature and volume of the discharges and emissions (Appendix I).

The term "best environmental practice" is defined as the application of the most appropriate combination of environmental control measures and strategies ranging from education and information to establishing a system of licensing. Here again, particular consideration should be given to specific criteria such as the environmental hazard of the product or activity and its ultimate disposal, the scale of use, the substitution of less polluting activities or substances, benefit to the environment and social and economic implications (Appendix I).

The body of the Convention outlines the obligations of contracting parties regarding pollution from land-based and offshore sources, dumping, incineration, installations and pipelines from which substances or energy reach the maritime area. Two land-locked countries, Luxembourg and Switzerland, have become parties to the new Convention, taking into

---

[85]   *See* Chapter 5B.2.

account their contribution to the pollution carried by the Rhine River to the North Sea.

Detailed regulations are found in four annexes. Annex I, related to the prevention and elimination of pollution from land-based sources, provides that the parties shall adopt programs and measures using best available techniques for point sources and best environmental practices for point and diffuse sources. Point source discharges into the maritime area and releases into water or air which reach and may affect the maritime area, shall be strictly subject to authorization or regulation by the competent national authorities, implementing relevant decisions of the Commission. The Commission also draws up plans for the reduction and phasing out of hazardous substances and for the reduction of inputs of nutrients from urban, municipal, industrial and other sources.

Annex II concerns the prevention and elimination of pollution by dumping or incineration. When compared to the Oslo Convention, the main innovation is the prohibition on the dumping of all wastes or other matter, with specified exceptions (dredged material, inert materials of natural origin, fish waste, etc.). Permitted dumping is subject to prior authorization or regulation by the competent authorities, in accordance with the relevant rules of the Commission. The dumping of low and intermediate level radioactive substances, including wastes, is prohibited.

Annex III prohibits any dumping of wastes or other matter from offshore installations. The use of substances on offshore sources or any discharge or emission which may reach and affect the maritime area are strictly subject to authorization or regulation by the competent national authorities in conformity with the Convention and the rules which may be adopted under it.

Each of the two former Conventions created a commission (OSCOM for the convention on dumping and PARCOM for that on land-based pollution). The 1992 Paris Convention sets up a new Commission to supervise the implementation of the Convention and generally review the condition of the maritime area, the effectiveness of the measures being adopted, the priorities and the need for any additional or different measures (Art. 10). It can adopt amendments to the Convention and its Annexes and Appendices. The contracting parties report to it at regular intervals on the measures they have taken to implement the Convention, including, in particular, measures taken to prevent and punish conduct in contravention of its provisions (Art. 22). The Commission assesses compliance by contracting parties on the basis of their periodic reports. When appropriate, it decides upon and calls for steps to bring about full compliance with the Convention and the decisions adopted thereunder, and promotes the implementation of recommendations, including measures to assist a contracting party to carry out its obligations (Art. 23).

The Convention on the Protection of the Marine Environment of the Baltic Sea Area (Helsinki, April 9, 1992) is the second instrument to replace a former one. The earlier Convention was considered as particularly advanced when adopted in March 1974. Nevertheless, progress in knowledge concerning marine pollution made it necessary to adopt a replacement treaty. Initially, the states adopted a Baltic Sea Declaration (1990) with a Joint Comprehensive Program aiming to restore the Baltic Sea Area to a sound ecological balance.

The Convention is similar to the treaty on the North-East Atlantic: it concerns all forms of pollution; it announces the principles of precaution (Art. 3(2)) and polluter pays (Art. 3(4)) in comparable terms; it prescribes the use of the Best Environmental Technology and of the Best Environmental Practice (Art. 3(3)) defining them as well as the criteria for their use (Annex II). It also provides that information shall be made available to the public, but limits accessible information to permits issued, the conditions required to be met, the results of water and effluent sampling, and water quality objectives. The means of obtaining such information also are restricted to all reasonable times, with reasonable facilities, on payment of reasonable charges (Art. 17). Information related to intellectual property including industrial and commercial secrecy or national security and confidential personal data may be withheld (Art. 18).

The 1992 Baltic Sea Convention contains several innovations. It stresses the need to prevent and eliminate pollution in order "to promote the ecological restoration of the Baltic Sea Area and the preservation of its ecological balance" (Art. 3(1)). It reflects the importance of the catchment area of this sea: measures relevant to combating the pollution from land-based sources shall be taken by each contracting party in the catchment area (Art. 6) and in particular, they are obliged to ban listed substances or groups of substances not only from the sea, but also from its catchment area. The use of such substances, including pesticides, must be minimized and, whenever possible, banned in the same zone (Annex I, parts 2 and 3). Permits for industrial plants also are determined for the entire catchment area (Annex II), as is the scope of information to be made available to the public (Art. 17(1)).

Article 24 is noteworthy as a step forward in the definition of international law rules for environmental responsibility. The contracting parties undertake jointly to develop and accept rules concerning responsibility for damage resulting from acts or omissions in contravention of the Convention including, *inter alia*, limits of responsibility, criteria and procedures for the determination of liability, and available remedies (Art. 25). This approach is useful in identifying the source of responsibility as duties owed under the Convention. Damage caused by the breach of Convention obligations gives rise to responsibility.

In its remaining provisions, the Convention regulates the usual sources of marine environmental harm, although its approach is often different from that of the other treaties concerning regional seas. In addition to rules concerning vessel-source pollution (Art. 8 and Annex IV), it foresees special measures to combat harm caused by pleasure craft (Art. 9). It prohibits incineration in general, not specifying wastes and dumping of wastes and other matter in the sea (Art. 11). Disposal of dredged materials at sea is permitted if a prior special permit has been obtained in accordance with specified conditions (Annex V).

The Baltic Marine Environment Protection Commission (HELCOM), established by the 1974 Convention, is maintained. It meets at least once a year, and its functions follow the pattern of international bodies rather than the more innovative North-East Atlantic Commission. The Baltic Commission continuously observes the implementation of the Convention, makes recommendations, and promotes cooperation (Arts. 19–20). The contracting parties report to it at regular intervals on the legal, regulatory and other measures taken for the implementation of the Convention and of recommendations adopted thereunder, on their effectiveness and on the problems encountered in their implementation (Art. 16). No specific review of the reports is foreseen, however, except that the Commission can ask the parties to provide information on discharge permits, emission data or data on environmental quality, as far as available (Art. 16(2)). The most important task of the Commission is to define pollution control criteria, objectives for the reduction of pollution, and objectives concerning measures taken (Art. 29(1) and Annex III).

Six coastal states adopted the Convention on the Protection of the Black Sea against Pollution at Bucharest on April 21, 1992. It follows the pattern established by the UNEP regional seas program—consisting of a framework convention completed by three protocols—without being integrated into that program. The general undertaking is to prevent, reduce and control pollution in order to protect and preserve the marine environment of the Black Sea. The area of application includes the territorial sea and the exclusive economic zone of each contracting party in the Black Sea (Art. 1), but the adverse effects of pollution within the internal waters on the marine environment also must be taken into account (Art. 5(1)).

The Convention's principles to protect the Black Sea marine environment against pollution and polluting activities derive in large part from the rules of UNCLOS and comparable regional sea treaties (Arts. 6–12), but two original provisions are added. The first concerns pollution by hazardous substances and matter: each contracting party shall prevent in the Black Sea any introduction of substances or matter listed in the annex to the Convention (mercury, cadmium, persistent carcinogenic substances, organohalogen compounds) (Art. 6). Secondly, states parties must combat pollution by wastes in transboundary movement (Art. 14).

Some of the terminology used by formerly communist regimes appears in the Convention: Article 3 speaks of full equality in rights and duties, respect for national sovereignty and independence, non-interference in internal affairs and mutual benefit. The weak institutional mechanisms set up by the Convention may be another heritage of the previous era. The Convention defines the functions of the Commission and of the Meeting of the Parties only vaguely and provides no real supervision of implementation. In addition, decisions and recommendations of the Commission must be adopted unanimously (Art. 18).

The first of the three Protocols, adopted on the same day, concerns the protection of the Black Sea marine environment against pollution from land-based sources. It aims to prevent, reduce and control pollution caused by discharges from rivers, canals, coastal establishments, other artificial structures, outfalls or run-off, as well as pollution transported by the atmosphere (Art. 1). It applies to the waters landward of the baseline and in the case of fresh-water courses, to the fresh-water limit.

The protocol uses the technique of lists: the parties undertake to prevent and eliminate pollution caused by hazardous substances and matter listed in Annex I, while reducing and, whenever possible eliminating, pollution from land-based sources by substances listed in Annex II. Annex III determines the conditions under which states parties may issue permits for the discharge of wastes containing substances and matter included in both lists. Thus, the Protocol contains no prohibitions on discharges: it only submits them to authorization. Uniform emission standards and timetables for the implementation of the programs and measures will be fixed by the contracting parties, who also will define pollution prevention criteria (Art. 6).

The second additional instrument to the Black Sea Convention is the Protocol on Cooperation in Combating Pollution of the Black Sea Marine Environment by Oil and Other Harmful Substances in Emergency Situations. Like other earlier agreements, it provides for the preparation of contingency plans, the reporting of accidents and the notification of other states. Its Annex contains detailed prescriptions, to be given to the masters of vessels and the pilots of aircraft, concerning the reports to be made.

The third Protocol, on the Protection of the Black Sea Marine Environment Against Pollution and Dumping, is also similar to earlier international instruments. It prohibits dumping of wastes or other matter listed in Annex I and mandates that national authorities issue a prior special permit for dumping of wastes or other matter listed in Annex II and a prior general permit for the dumping of all other wastes or matter. Annex III adds prescriptions which should be applied in issuing permits for dumping at sea, relating to the characteristics and composition of the matter and those of the dumping site and disposal method.

In sum, maritime pollution agreements increasingly show uniform patterns based upon UNCLOS. The primary concerns, revealed by a comparison of their provisions, are accidental pollution and prevention of pollution at source, including land-locked states through which watercourses flow that may carry pollution to maritime areas. The result is a holistic approach to maritime pollution linked to a more general integrated approach to environmental protection.

E. Combating Different Forms of Pollution

1. Vessel Source Pollution

Certain longstanding and formerly accepted practices on the part of maritime vessels are among the main sources of marine pollution: dumping of wastes in the ocean, the discharge of various forms of oil, including used oil, rinsing of tanker containers, and the release of sea water serving as ballast in empty tankers. When accidental pollution is added, coming from grounded oil tankers or the loss of cargoes containing dangerous substances, the result is an estimated annual discharge of roughly 1.6 million tons of oil by shipping.

The general framework of international norms concerning this problem is outlined by UNCLOS Articles 194(3)(b), 211, and 217–221. The provision first cited summarizes the problem, providing that the measures taken to enforce the Convention should include those designed to minimize to the fullest possible extent "pollution from vessels, in particular measures for preventing accidents and dealing with emergencies, ensuring the safety of operations at sea, preventing intentional and unintentional discharges, and regulating the design, construction, equipment, operation and manning of vessels."

Article 211 entirely concerns vessel-source pollution. It reaffirms the legislative mandate and obligation of states to prevent, reduce, and control pollution of the marine environment. Paragraph 1 emphasizes the role of international rules and standards which states shall establish, "acting through the competent international organization or general diplomatic conference." States also should promote the adoption, as appropriate, of routing systems designed to minimize the threat of accidents which might cause pollution.

The remaining parts of Article 211 mandate state laws and regulations to combat pollution by vessels registered by them or flying their flag. The same rules can be imposed on foreign vessels entering coastal state ports or internal waters. Similarly, coastal states can adopt laws and regulations to prevent, reduce and control pollution of the marine environment by foreign vessels within their territorial sea and their exclusive economic zone. However, for the exclusive economic zone these norms shall conform to and give effect to generally accepted international rules and standards.

Those applicable to their flag ships may be stricter, but they shall "at least have the same effect" as international rules. When the international rules and standards are inadequate to meet special circumstances in an exclusive economic zone or part of it, the coastal state that exercises jurisdiction over the zone may enact special measures to prevent pollution from vessels. In such case, the competent international organization shall be consulted and may decide if the situation in the zone corresponds to the claimed oceanographic and ecological conditions. Local laws and regulations do not become applicable to foreign vessels until 15 months after submission of the communication to the organization.[86]

The various provisions of UNCLOS relating to jurisdiction over vessel violations of environmental norms have been supplemented by a global convention and by several conventions applying to regional seas. The general instrument, the International Convention for the Prevention of Pollution by Ships (MARPOL) has as its objective "the complete elimination of intentional pollution of the marine environment by oil and other harmful substances and the minimization of accidental discharge of such substances."[87] MARPOL and its 1978 protocol replaced an earlier 1954 Convention which also has been amended several times. Together, the current law consists of the principal convention, three protocols, five annexes—themselves accompanied by nine appendices—as well as 26 resolutions adopted by the 1973 London Conference. Several of the resolutions contain important recommendations directed at the International Maritime Organization and its participating states.

MARPOL applies to ships, the term being defined in Article 2(4) as a vessel of any type whatsoever operating in the marine environment, including hydrofoil boats, air-cushion vehicles, submersibles, floating craft and fixed or floating platforms. Pollution itself is not defined, but its elements are found in the definition of discharge. This term means any release from a ship, whatever its cause, including escape, disposal, spilling, leaking, pumping, emitting or emptying.[88] Dumping[89] is excluded, however, as is the release of harmful substances directly arising from the exploration, exploitation and processing of sea-bed mineral resources or legitimate scientific research into pollution abatement or control.[90] Article 3(3) of the Convention also excludes government, non-commercial vessels from its coverage, in language identical to that found in the later-adopted UNCLOS.

---

[86]   Art. 211(6)(a).

[87]   Nov. 2, 1973, *amended by* Protocol adopted Feb. 17, 1978.

[88]   Art. 2(3).

[89]   Art. 2(3)(a), adding in subparagraph (b) that ". . . discharge does not include (i) dumping within the meaning of the Convention on the Prevention of Marine Pollution by Dumping of Wastes and Other Matter. . . ."

[90]   Art. 2(3)(b).

The principal obligation of states parties to the MARPOL Convention, contained in Article 1, is to give effect to its provisions and its annexes, an obligation which exists under general international law even without an explicit statement to that effect. Article 4 adds that any violation of the requirements of the Convention shall be prohibited and sanctioned by legislation enacted by the authority over the ship, that is, the flag state. This competence is exclusive on the high seas; in other zones either the flag state or the coastal state may exercise jurisdiction. In case the coastal state chooses not to institute proceedings, it must furnish the flag state with the information and evidence in its possession regarding the violation. In all cases, the sanctions specified by local law shall be adequate in severity to remedy violations of the Convention and equally severe irrespective of where the violations occur.

MARPOL also reaffirms the police powers of the port state where a ship is found: its authorities can inspect the ship not only to verify its documentation, but to determine whether it discharged harmful substances in violation of the Convention. If a violation is uncovered, a report is forwarded to the flag state in order for appropriate action to be instituted pursuant to Article 4.[91] Whenever an incident occurs involving the actual or probable discharge into the sea of a harmful substance or containing such a substance, MARPOL requires the master of the ship which is involved or other person having charge of the ship to prepare a report for the state administering the vessel as well as any other state that could be affected by the incident.[92] Other rules are deferred for inclusion in the Annexes, no doubt because of their highly technical nature and because there is a simplified procedure for their modification.[93]

The governing scheme of MARPOL is the use of Annexes containing regulations according to the type of pollutant. Thus, Annex I governs oil, Annex II concerns control of pollution by noxious liquid in bulk (*e.g.*, acetone, acrylic acid, ammonia, benzene, formaldehyde), Annex III applies to "harmful substances carried by sea in packaged forms or in freight containers, portable tanks or road and rail tank wagons," Annex IV controls sewage, and Annex V regulates garbage. Annexes III, IV and V are optional.

Annex I is by far the most complex and detailed. The general principle established is that discharge into the sea of oil or oily mixtures is prohibited except under strictly controlled conditions. The conditions vary depending upon whether the vessel is or is not an oil tanker; if it is not, its size is determinative. Discharges are prohibited in specially threatened areas (the Mediterranean, the Baltic, the Black, and the Red Seas, and Gulf areas) but all prohibitions may be suspended when necessary to secure the safety

---

[91]   Art. 6(2).

[92]   Art. 8 and Protocol I.

[93]   Art. 16(2)(f)(ii) and (iii).

of a ship or save life at sea. Furthermore, numerous provisions that have been modified by an Amendment to the Annex,[94] concern the construction of oil tankers, the construction of facilities for loading and discharge of oil, and the retention of oil on board ships.

The regulations of Annex II regarding transportation of noxious liquid in bulk divide the approximately 425 substances into four categories. Those found in category A present a major hazard to either marine resources or human health or could cause serious harm to amenities or other legitimate uses of the sea. In principle they should not be discharged. Annex II establishes specific conditions for the discharge of substances classified in categories B, C and D and particularly severe conditions are imposed to protect the Baltic and Black Seas. The appendices to this Annex list the noxious liquid substances and the category for each. A revised Annex on Bulk Liquids and Gas (2003) incorporates all amendments that have been adopted on this topic since the MARPOL Convention entered into force in 1983 and deletes outdated requirements.

The optional Annexes III to V, concerning container cargo, sewage and garbage, contain technical prescriptions for combating pollution from these sources; special zones also are established where discharge of garbage is not permitted and the discharge of sewage and plastics generally is prohibited.

Amendments to MARPOL 73/78 adopted in 1992 require the application of the double hull or equivalent design standards to existing single hull oil tankers when they reach a certain age. New rules, adopted April 27, 2001, provide for an accelerated phasing-out scheme for single hull oil tankers.[95] Seriously concerned by shipping accidents involving oil tankers and the associated pollution of its coastlines, the EC decided to support the IMO actions by upgrading and/or phasing out existing ships.[96]

In the context of MARPOL, the IMO Assembly has adopted Guidelines for the Designation of Special Areas. A "Particularly Sensitive Sea Area" is one that needs special protection through the IMO because of its significance for ecological, socio-economic, or scientific reasons and that may be vulnerable to damage by shipping activities. Two areas have been identified since the first guidelines were adopted in 1991: the Great Barrier Reef and the Sabana-Camaguey (Cuba). In 2001 the Marine Environmental Protection Committee proposed adding Malpelo Island (Cuba) and the Florida Keys.

Further measures to combat vessel source pollution were adopted by the IMO on October 5, 2001, when it adopted the International Convention on the Control of Harmful Anti-Fouling Systems. This convention aims to

---

[94] Sept. 7, 1984.

[95] Adopted by the 46th Session of the Marine Environment Protection Committee of the International Maritime Organization by Res. MEPC 95(46), *in force* Sept. 1, 2002.

[96] Regulation No 417/2002, Feb. 18, 2002, O.J. L 64 (3/7/02).

protect the marine environment from toxic paint or other harmful means of preventing marine organisms from attaching to ships' hulls. Preventing the encrustation of ship's hulls with marine life, such as barnacles, is necessary to ensure that ships can move smoothly and quickly through the water. Such encrustation or fouling will slow down the ship and cause it to use more fuel, thereby causing both commercial and environmental problems. The primary obligation of states parties to the Convention is to prohibit or restrict the use of the harmful anti-fouling systems listed in Annex I, which were leaching into the water and causing serious harm to marine life and possibly to humans eating affected seafood. The only item on the initial list was fouling systems with organotins acting as biocides, banned in systems as of January 1, 2003.

The Convention on the Protection of the Marine Environment of the Baltic Sea, March 22, 1974, was the first regional marine treaty to be adopted. A large part of its regulations concern pollution from vessels. The 1992 Convention on the Protection of the Marine Environment of the Baltic Sea Area[97] which replaced it, includes special provisions (Art. 8 and Annex IV) relating to vessel pollution. Article 8 provides that the contracting parties shall develop and apply uniform requirements for the provision of reception facilities for ship-generated wastes. Annex IV invites the parties to promote the development of international rules including the promotion of the use of Best Available Technology and Best Environmental Practice. The Convention refers to the annexes of MARPOL 73/78, with the exception of specific provisions concerning sewage which are included in Regulation 5.

Safety at sea, especially with regard to ships carrying hazardous cargoes, has become a major topic within the IMO. In January 2001, amendments to the IMO SOLAS Convention[98] made mandatory an International Code for the Safe Carriage of Packaged Irradiated Nuclear Fuel, Plutonium, High-Level Radioactive Waste on Board Ships. Its provisions include shipboard emergency plans, notification in the event of an incident, training, cargo securing arrangements, and damage stability. Shortly thereafter, the *Castor*, a fully laden oil tanker, discovered structural damage while in the Mediterranean Sea and sought shelter to transfer its cargo and conduct repairs. Fear of potential harm caused states to refuse entry into various ports and waters. IMO has thus placed the issue of providing shelter for stricken vessels on its agenda as a priority matter.

In contrast to the Baltic Sea Convention, the regional sea conventions drafted under the auspices of UNEP do not contain rules additional to those set out in MARPOL 73/78. Instead, they generally declare that the states parties shall take all appropriate measures conforming to

---

[97] Helsinki, Apr. 9, 1992.

[98] International Convention for the Safety of Human Life at Sea, Nov. 1, 1974.

international law to prevent, abate, combat and control pollution caused by ships and ensure effective implementation for the zones in question of applicable international rules relating to this type of pollution.[99] The 1981 Lima Convention for the Protection of the Marine Environment and Coastal Area of the South-East Pacific contains this obligation in Article 4(b), although formulated differently. It adds that the measures to be taken by the states parties shall aim, in particular, at preventing accidents, managing emergency situations, and assuring the safety of operations at sea by preventing intentional discharges, as well as by regulating the design, construction, crew, utilization and equipment of ships in conformity with international rules and standards.

2. Marine Pollution Transported by Air

This form of pollution appears to have received relatively little attention, perhaps because the basic rules relative to air pollution generally apply to the marine environment as well as to land. Nonetheless, UNCLOS contains two provisions directed towards combating air-borne pollution. According to Article 212, states shall take the measures necessary to prevent, reduce and control atmospheric pollution. These measures shall include the adoption of laws and regulations applicable to the air space under their sovereignty and to vessels flying their flag or vessels or aircraft of their registry. Internationally, they shall act to establish global and regional rules, standards and recommended practices and procedures. Article 222 provides that states shall enforce within their air space or with regard to flag state or registered ships or aircraft the laws and regulations they adopt, including applicable international rules and standards.

Certain regional seas treaties also provide that states should take all appropriate measures to prevent, abate and control atmospheric pollution. The obligation is contained in Article 9 of the 1981 Abidjan Convention for West and Central Africa, Article 4(a)(ii) of the 1981 Lima Convention for the South-East Pacific, Article 9 of the 1983 Cartagena Convention for the Caribbean, and Article 9 of the 1986 Noumea Convention for the South Pacific. Atmospheric pollution is assimilated to land-based pollution in instruments relating to the Mediterranean and to the Gulf.[100] This solution

---

[99]   Such provisions are found in:
— Art. 6 of the 1976 Barcelona Convention for the Mediterranean Sea;
— Art. 4 of the 1978 Kuwait Convention for the Gulf;
— Art. 5 of the 1981 Abidjan Convention for West and Central Africa;
— Art. 4 of the 1982 Jeddah Convention for the Red Sea;
— Art. 5 of the 1983 Cartagena Convention for the Caribbean;
— Art. 6 of the 1986 Noumea Convention for the South Pacific Region.
[100]   *See* 1978 Kuwait Convention for the Gulf and the Protocol of Athens

also appears in the Montreal Guidelines on the Protection of the Marine Environment against Land-Based Pollution (April 19, 1985), adopted by a group of experts under the auspices of UNEP.[101] The same idea is contained in the 1992 Convention for the Protection of the Marine Environment of the North-East Atlantic,[102] Article 1(e) of which defines land-based sources of pollution as point and diffuse sources on land from which substances or energy reach the maritime area by water, through the air, or directly from the coast.

Another form of marine pollution transported by air, even if only for short distances, stems from the incineration of wastes on board ships. Incineration with the aid of special vessels was used, primarily by the Netherlands in the North Sea, to eliminate chemical substances, especially organohalogen compounds. UNCLOS did not include incineration in the issue of dumping of wastes and until relatively recently, no international text directly addressed the question, although basic regulations that could apply to incineration were included in the Convention for the Prevention of Marine Pollution by Dumping from Ships and Aircraft.[103] A Protocol, opened for signature March 2, 1983, added to the Convention a fourth annex setting forth "rules on incineration at sea."[104] In addition, other recent treaties have developed specific norms on this topic. The 1992 Conventions relating to the Baltic Sea Area (Art. 10) and to the North-East Atlantic (Art. 4 and Annex II) formally prohibit incineration, defined by the former as "the deliberate combustion of wastes or other matter at sea for the purpose of their thermal destruction. Activities incidental to the normal operation of ships or other man-made structures are excluded from the scope of this definition." (Art. 2(5)). On the global level, a 1996 Protocol to the London Dumping Convention bans all incineration of wastes at sea (Art. 5).

3. *Dumping of Wastes*

According to the definition given by UNCLOS, dumping means any deliberate disposal of wastes or other matter from vessels, aircraft, platforms or

---

(May 17, 1980) supplementing the Barcelona Convention for the Protection of the Mediterranean, Art. 6. Art. 4(1)(b) of the March 7, 1996 Amendments to the Athens Protocol applies to inputs of polluting substances transported in the Mediterranean Sea Area from land-based activities within the territories of the Contracting Parties under conditions defined in Annex III to the Protocol.

[101]   *See* the text in 14 E.P.L. 77 (1985).

[102]   Paris, Sept. 22, 1992.

[103]   Oslo, Feb. 15, 1972.

[104]   Protocol Amending the Oslo Convention for the Prevention of Marine Pollution by Dumping from Ships and Aircraft (March 2, 1983).

other man-made structures at sea. Dumping does not include the disposal of wastes or other matter arising from the normal operations of vessels, aircraft, platforms or other man-made structures at sea or placement of matter for a purpose other than disposal.[105]

Use of the sea as a universal waste disposal site is tempting for those who seek to avoid or reduce the sometimes high costs of eliminating industrial wastes. Dumping of radioactive wastes has been widespread in the past and poses serious problems. In some cases, dumping of toxic wastes at sea has given rise to strong protests. The incident of the "boues rouges," where specially-constructed ships dumped waste off the island of Corsica in the early 1970s, is one example.[106] The dumping was followed by a judgment holding the director of the company liable.

States began to take measures to reduce or resolve the problem of dumping rather rapidly after the beginning of the ecological era. UNCLOS declares at the beginning of Part XII that among the measures states should take, individually or jointly, are those which are designed to minimize to the fullest possible extent the release by dumping of toxic, harmful or noxious substances, especially those which are persistent.[107] Article 210 provides that states shall adopt laws and regulations to prevent, reduce and control pollution of the marine environment by dumping. In particular, no dumping shall take place without the permission of the competent authorities of the state. For the territorial sea, the exclusive economic zone and the continental shelf, the coastal state should deliver an authorization and regulate and control dumping, taking due consideration of the matter with other states which by reason of their geographical situation could be adversely affected. It is also necessary to adopt global and regional rules, standards and recommended practices and procedures to prevent, reduce, and control such pollution. National laws, regulations and measures must be no less effective than the global rules and standards. Article 216 relating to enforcement of laws and regulations with respect to pollution by dumping, reaffirms the jurisdiction of the coastal state within its territorial sea, exclusive economic zone, or continental shelf. It adds that the flag state also has jurisdiction with regard to its vessels and aircraft. Finally, any state may exercise jurisdiction in response to acts of loading of wastes or other matter occurring within its territory or at its off-shore terminals.

International law concerning dumping of wastes at sea was already in place well before the adoption of UNCLOS. Like vessel-source pollution, the regulatory scheme consisted of a global instrument and several treaties or conventional instruments of a regional nature. The first global treaty on

---

[105]   UNCLOS, Art. 1(5).

[106]   *See* A. Kiss, *Un Cas de pollution internationale: L'Affaire des boues rouges,* 102 JOURNAL DU DROIT INTERNATIONAL 207 1975).

[107]   Art. 194(3).

this subject, the Convention on the Prevention of Marine Pollution by Dumping of Wastes and other Matter was opened for signature simultaneously in London, Mexico, City, Moscow and Washington on December 29, 1972. It clearly has a preventive purpose, underlined both in its preamble and in its first two articles: the states parties shall take all practicable steps to prevent the pollution of the sea by dumping of wastes and other matter that is liable to create hazards to human health, to harm living resources and marine life, to damage amenities or to interfere with other legitimate uses of the sea. The Convention initially permitted the dumping of wastes except those on the "black list" contained in Annex I, which included such substances as organohalogenic compounds, mercury and its compounds, and persistent plastics. Annex II established a "gray list," those products containing significant amounts of, *inter alia*, lead, arsenic, copper, zinc, cyanides, fluorides, pesticides and their by-products.

Following developments at the regional level, a 1996 Protocol to the Convention[108] reversed the listing process to prohibit all dumping except for those substances specified in Annex I, which may be dumped, but only with a permit delivered by the appropriate authority of the contracting party in accordance with Annex II. The Protocol prohibits the incineration at sea of waste and other matter and the export of waste or other matter to other countries for dumping or incineration at sea. Each state must designate one or several authorities competent to issue the required permits in respect of matter intended for dumping and loaded in its territory as well as that loaded by a vessel or aircraft registered in its territory or flying its flag if the loading occurs in the territory of a state not party to the Convention.[109] The nature and the quantities of all matter to be dumped as well as the location, time and method of dumping must be recorded and communicated to other parties.

The Convention and the Protocol require each state party to enforce the Convention by ensuring that the measures are applied by vessels and aircraft registered in its territory or flying its flag, as well as by those who are found under its jurisdiction, notably in its territorial waters, and those who load matter which is to be dumped.[110] International measures are only outlined: states agree to cooperate in the development of procedures for the effective application of the Convention, particularly on the high seas, including procedures for the reporting of vessels and aircraft observed dumping in contravention of the Convention. Vessels and aircraft entitled to sovereign immunity are excepted from coverage of the rules.[111]

---

[108] Protocol to the Convention on the Prevention of Marine Pollution by Dumping of Wastes and Other Matter, Nov. 7, 1996.

[109] Art. 6.

[110] Convention, Art. 7; Protocol, Art. 10.

[111] *Id.*

The London Dumping Convention also invites the conclusion of regional accords addressing the same problem. One such agreement, the Oslo Convention for the Prevention of Marine Pollution by Dumping from Ships and Aircraft[112] was in fact adopted before the London Conference and may have provided a model for the authors of the London Convention ten months later. The "reverse listing" procedure was first introduced in another regional agreement, the 1974 Helsinki Convention on the Protection of the Marine Environment of the Baltic Sea[113] which forbids all dumping except as specified in Annex 5. The 1992 Convention on the Protection of the Marine Environment of the Baltic Sea Area[114] applies the same principle: dumping is prohibited in the Baltic Sea Area, subject to exemptions which can be given for dredged material when a prior special permit is issued by the appropriate national authority (Art. 11). Annex V to the Convention specifies the conditions under which such permits can be delivered. Compliance with the provisions of Article 11 shall be ensured by each contracting state respecting ships and aircraft registered in its territory or flying its flag, loading within its territory or territorial sea matter which is to be dumped, or believed to be engaged in dumping within its internal waters and territorial sea.

The 1992 Paris Convention for the Protection of the Marine Environment of the North-East Atlantic[115] follows the same method by prohibiting the dumping of all wastes or other matter, but admits the dumping of dredged material and inert materials of natural origin, *i.e.*, solid, chemically-unprocessed, geological material, the chemical constituents of which are unlikely to be released into the marine environment. Fish waste from industrial fish processing operations also can be dumped as can scuttled vessels and aircraft, until the end of 2004 and under specified conditions. (Art. 3(1) and (2)). In each case the competent authorities must authorize the dumping (Art. 4). Each contracting party shall keep, and transmit to the Commission of the Convention, records of the nature and quantities of wastes or other matter dumped in accordance with the Convention's provisions, and of the dates, places and methods of dumping (Art. 4).

The regional treaties elaborated under the auspices of UNEP call on states parties to take all appropriate measures to prevent and reduce in the relevant areas pollution of the sea due to dumping carried out by their vessels and aircraft.[116] More detailed regulation of this problem appeared first

---

[112]   Oslo, Feb. 15, 1972.
[113]   Mar. 22, 1974.
[114]   Apr. 9, 1992.
[115]   Sept. 22, 1992.
[116]   These include:
—   Art. 6 of the Barcelona Convention for the Mediterranean (Feb. 16, 1976).

in the framework of the Barcelona Convention, followed by the Noumea Convention. A special protocol to the former, signed at the same time as the principal Convention, relates to "the prevention of pollution of the Mediterranean Sea by dumping by vessels and aircraft," Its contents are similar to those of the model 1972 London Convention. A permit regime based on three categories is set out: matter on a black list cannot be dumped (Art. 4); substances or matters appearing on the gray list can only be dumped after receiving in advance a special permit (Art. 5); any other dumping requires a prior general permit (Art. 6). Annex III sets out the factors which must be considered before a permit is authorized. UNEP, designated as the Secretariat for the Convention, receives information relating to the permits delivered. A Protocol for the Prevention of Pollution in the South Pacific by Dumping, signed the same day as the general Noumea Convention contains provisions comparable to the Barcelona treaty.

The pressure of public opinion has led to significant progress in restricting the dumping of radioactive wastes. During the 1958 effort to codify the international law of the sea, the question of dumping, primarily the dumping of radioactive wastes on the high seas was raised. At the time, states accepted that coastal states could take the measures they deemed necessary to take in their territorial seas. Agreement was reached on including a specific provision respecting the commons area in the 1958 Convention on the High Seas: "Every state shall take measures to prevent pollution of the seas from the dumping of radioactive waste, taking into account any standards and regulations which may be formulated by the competent international organizations."[117]

Over time, a norm emerged forbidding the dumping of radioactive wastes. The 1972 London Convention, Annex I, enumerates those substances for which dumping is prohibited and includes "high-level radioactive wastes or other high-level radio-active matter, defined on public health, biological or other grounds, by the competent international body in this field, at present the International Atomic Energy Agency, as unsuitable for dumping at sea."[118] In 1977, the International Atomic Energy Agency itself established a multilateral mechanism for consultation and

---

— Art. 5 of the Kuwait Convention for the Gulf (Apr. 24, 1978).
— Art. 6 of the Abidjan Convention for West Africa (Mar. 23, 1981).
— Art. 4(a)(iii) of the Lima South-East Pacific Convention (Nov. 20, 1981).
— Art. 5 of the Jeddah Convention for the Red Sea (Feb. 14, 1982).
— Art. 6 of Cartagena Convention for the Caribbean (Mar. 24, 1983).
— Art. 5(3) of the Noumea Convention for the South Pacific (Nov. 24, 1986).
117 Art. 25(1).
118 Annex I(6).

monitoring of dumping of radioactive wastes at sea. The European Agency of Nuclear Energy established technical criteria and procedures on the topic.

Further progress led towards the eventual prohibition on dumping all radioactive wastes. First, 20 member states of the OECD unilaterally renounced any dumping of such wastes. Subsequently, the contracting parties to the London Dumping Convention adopted a ten-year moratorium on the dumping of nuclear waste at sea. Finally, the moratorium was replaced by a permanent ban approved November 12, 1993, by a vote of 37–0 with five abstentions (Britain, France, Russia, China and Belgium). Each state had 100 days to file an objection refusing to be bound by the ban. The same meeting also banned dumping industrial waste and outlawed incineration of industrial waste at sea.[119]

Regionally, strong provisions were placed in the 1974 Baltic Sea Convention which forbid any dumping not authorized by Annex V. The Annex enumerated limited exceptions to the general prohibition on dumping and did not include radioactive wastes among them. The 1976 Protocol Additional to the Barcelona Convention relating to the Mediterranean Sea also forbids dumping of "wastes and other matters highly, partly, or slightly radioactive."[120] Finally, Article 3(3) of the Convention for the Protection of the North-East Atlantic explicitly prohibits the dumping of low and intermediate level radioactive substances, including wastes.

4.   Exploration and Exploitation of the Sea-Bed

Paralleling other provisions relating to marine pollution, UNCLOS provides that states should take measures individually or jointly to minimize to the fullest possible extent:

> pollution from installations and devices used in exploration or exploitation of the natural resources of the sea-bed and subsoil, in particular measures for preventing accidents and dealing with emergencies, ensuring the safety of operations at sea, and regulating the design, construction, equipment, operation and manning of such installations or devices.[121]

Other provisions of the Convention distinguish between pollution resulting from activities taking place in the Area—*i.e.*, the sea-bed declared to be the common heritage of mankind—and those resulting from activities relating to underwater areas falling under national jurisdiction. The rel-

---

[119]   By the end of the 100 days, only Russia had opted out.
[120]   Art. IV and Annex I, no. 7.
[121]   Art. 194(3)(c).

evant principles for the Area are contained in Article 145, located in UNCLOS Part VI rather than in the section devoted to protection of the marine environment. Article 145 reads:

> Necessary measures shall be taken in accordance with this Convention with respect to activities in the Area to ensure effective protection for the marine environment from harmful effects which may arise from such activities. To this end the Authority shall adopt appropriate rules, regulations and procedures for, inter alia:
>
> (a) the prevention, reduction and control of pollution and other hazards to the marine environment, including the coastline, and of interference with the ecological balance of the marine environment, particular attention being paid to the need for protection from harmful effects of such activities as drilling, dredging, excavation, disposal of waste, construction and operation or maintenance of installations, pipelines and other devices related to such activities;
>
> (b) the protection and conservation of the natural resources of the Area and the prevention of damage to the flora and fauna of the marine environment.

Article 209, containing the environmental protection measures of Part XII, supplements Article 145 to affirm that international rules, regulations and procedures shall be established to prevent, reduce and control pollution of the marine environment from activities in the Area. Article 215 confers responsibility for implementation of this obligation on the Authority. Nonetheless, all states must adopt laws and regulations governing activities in the Area by their vessels, installations, structures and other devices flying their flag or of their registry or operating under their authority. National laws and regulations shall not be less effective than the international rules.[122]

In 2000 the International Seabed Authority (ISA) drafted and adopted Regulations on Prospecting and Exploration for Polymetallic Nodules in the Area.[123] Part V of the Regulations, adopted by the Council and approved by the Assembly on July 13, 2000, concerns protection and preservation of the marine environment. Both the Authority and holders of contracts for exploration are to ensure effective protection of the marine environment from harmful effects which may arise from activities in the Area. The term "marine environment" is defined in an inclusive way as "the physical, chemical, geological and biological components, conditions and factors which interact and determine the productivity, state, condition and quality of the

---

[122] Art. 209(2).
[123] *See* 30 E.P.L. 174–77 (2000).

marine ecosystem, the waters of the seas and oceans and the airspace above those waters as well as the seabed and ocean floor and subsoil thereof."

The Regulations mandate the Authority to establish and keep under periodic review environmental rules, regulations and procedures to ensure effective protection of the marine environment. The regulations will have to be supplemented and revised regularly by the Authority as more knowledge and experience is gained. The Authority, sponsoring states and, indirectly, the contractors are required to apply the precautionary approach.

Under the Regulations, contractors applying for exploitation rights must propose areas to be set aside and used exclusively as impact reference zones (areas used to assess the effects of mining activities on the marine environment and which are representative of the environmental characteristics of the Area) and preservation reference zones (areas in which no mining shall occur to ensure representative and stable biota of the seabed in order to assess any changes in the flora and fauna of the marine environment). Contractors also must submit contingency plans and promptly report to the Authority any incident arising from activities that has caused or is likely to cause serious harm to the marine environment.

On July 4, 2001, the Legal and Technical Commission of the International Seabed Authority approved the Recommendations for the Guidance of Contractors for the Assessment of Possible Environmental Impacts Arising from the Exploration for Polymetallic Nodules in the Area.[124] These recommendations were adopted pursuant to Regulation 38 of the Mining Code. The recommendations specify the data the contractor should gather on natural conditions before exploration begins (baseline data), what information should be provided by the contractor to the ISA, and what observations and measurements should be made by the contractor while performing a specific activity as well as following its performance. Baseline data fall into six groups: physical oceanography, chemical oceanography, sediment properties, biological communities, bioturbation, and sedimentation. The information is required to allow the Legal and Technical Commission to carry out its responsibilities to ensure the protection of the marine environment.

Under the Regulations and Recommendations, EIAs are not required for: gravity and magnetometric observations and measurements; bottom and sub-bottom acoustic or electromagnetic profiling or imaging without the use of explosives; water and biotic sampling and mineral samplings of a limited nature such as those obtained using core, grab, or basket samplers to determine sea-bed geological or geotechnical properties; meteorological observations and measurements, including the setting of instruments; oceanographic, including hydrographic, observations and measurements, including the setting of instruments; television and still photographic obser-

---

[124]   Doc. ISBA/7/LTC/1/Rev.1, July 10, 2001.

vation and measurements; shipboard mineral assaying and analysis; and positioning systems, including bottom transponders and surface and sub-surface buoys filed in notices to mariners.

List 2 includes activities that require an EIA and monitoring: dredging to collect nodules for on-land studies for mining and/or processing; the use of special equipment to study the reaction of the sediment to disturbances made by collecting devices or running gears; and testing of collection systems and equipment.

The Legal and Technical Commission admitted that while "current knowledge of the deep-sea environment is insufficient to predict the real impacts of tests of [actual technology yet to be developed], the environmental disturbances, based on the experience and knowledge gathered from previous activities carried out by the registered pioneer investors and by the scientific community, may be forecast to some extent. The main impacts are expected to occur at the seafloor, with minor impacts expected at the tailings-discharge depth. The nodule collector will disturb the semi-liquid sediment-surface layer and will create a near-bottom plume. The nodule collector will compress, breakup and squeeze the harder underlying sediment layer."[125]

The adoption of the Mining Code and recommendations allowed the ISA to proceed with signing contracts for exploration with six initial investors: the French Research Institute for Exploitation of the Sea; the Deep Ocean Resources Development Company (Japan); Yuzhmorgeologiya (Russia); China Ocean Mineral Resources Research and Development; the InterOceanMetal Joint Organization (Bulgaria, Cuba, Czech Republic, Poland, Russia and Slovakia) and the Republic of Korea.[126]

While the earlier known sources of minerals are thus regulated, recent scientific explorations have revealed other sources of metals in the deep sea: polymetallic sulphides and cobalt-rich crusts. The former are linked to vents from underwater volcanos where the tectonic plates meet. They contain copper, lead, zinc, silver and gold in varying amounts. Cobalt crusts usually occur as hard encrustations on the sides of islands and on seamounts. They are widely distributed in the Pacific Ocean. The characteristics of these new sources make application of the rules developed for nodules inappropriate and work is underway to develop a separate set of regulations. For the future, there is also a need to consider the legal relationship between the Biodiversity Convention and UNCLOS because of bio-prospecting of genetic resources on seabed, especially surrounding the thermal vents.

Pollution from sea-bed activities subject to national jurisdiction is governed by UNCLOS Article 208. It requires coastal states to adopt laws and regulations, no less effective than international rules, for activities subject

---

[125] Doc. ISBA/7/C/7, July 12, 2001, para. 9.
[126] *See* Doc. ISBA/7/C/4, June 22, 2001.

to their jurisdiction, while endeavoring to harmonize their policies in this connection at the regional level. States shall also act through international organizations or conferences to establish global or regional rules which they shall then implement.[127]

The 2001 UNESCO Convention on the Protection of the Underwater Cultural Heritage[128] aims to protect the historical and archaeological resources represented by shipwrecks and other human artifacts on the sea floor. In general, the Convention requires that activities directed at underwater cultural heritage are conducted in conformity with an Annex containing rules and standards for underwater archaeology. Parties to the Convention must regulate the activities of their nationals and flagged vessels. When a find is made, the coastal state becomes the "coordinating state" for activities on its continental shelf, controlling access in conformity with the Convention. The Convention itself has a strong preference for *in situ* conservation and requires efforts to prevent trade in illegally taken artifacts. Many states, including France, Germany, the Netherlands, Norway, Russia, the U.S. and the UK, opposed the treaty or withheld approval, contending that the Convention fails to adequately protect flag states of warships and extends coastal state jurisdiction beyond the provisions of UNCLOS, despite the "without prejudice" clause of Article 3, which requires the Convention be interpreted and applied consistent with UNCLOS. Although many shipwrecks are associated with fragile coral reefs, the environment is not mentioned in the Convention itself, but is included in the Rules annexed to the treaty. Part II of the Rules requires a project design be developed and submitted to the appropriate authorities prior to any activity directed at underwater cultural heritage and mandates that all activities be conducted in conformity with the project design. Rule 10 specifies that the project design include, *inter alia*, an environmental policy while Rule 29 adds the rather weak statement that the environmental policy shall be adequate "to ensure that the seabed and marine life are not unduly disturbed."

All the regional seas treaties reaffirm the UNCLOS principles,[129] but two regional seas agreements include specific rules in additional protocols,

---

[127] Arts. 208, 214.

[128] UNESCO, Nov. 6, 2001.

[129] See:

— Art. 10, Helsinki Convention for the Baltic Sea (Mar. 22, 1974);

— Art. 7, Barcelona Convention for the Mediterranean (Feb. 16, 1976);

— Art. 7, Kuwait Convention for the Gulf (Apr. 24, 1978);

— Art. 8, Abidjan Convention for West Africa (Mar. 23, 1981);

— Art. 4(c), Lima Convention for South-East Pacific (Nov. 20, 1981);

— Art. 7, Jeddah Convention for the Red Sea (Feb. 14, 1982);

— Art. 8, Cartagena Convention for the Caribbean (Mar. 24, 1983);

— Art. 9, Noumea Convention for the South-Pacific (Nov. 24, 1986).

due to the potential for harm from this source in their regions. The Kuwaiti system added a Protocol Concerning Marine Pollution Resulting from Exploration and Exploitation of the Continental Shelf.[130] Article II requires contracting states to take all appropriate measures to prevent, abate and control marine pollution from offshore operations in those areas within their jurisdiction, as well as to take action individually and jointly to combat such pollution. According to the Protocol, any offshore operation must be licensed. Article IV requires a prior assessment of the potential environmental effects before the licensing of any offshore operation which could cause significant risks of pollution in the Protocol Area. Moreover, no license shall be granted until the competent state authority is satisfied that the operation will entail no unacceptable risk of environmental damage in the Area. The regional organization establishes guidelines for the environmental impact statements and states must transmit to the organization a summary of the environmental effects reported in the assessments submitted to them. Within four days of receiving the assessment summaries, the organization sends them to all other contracting states who are allowed to submit representations through the organization within a stated reasonable time. States must consider any such representations before licensing an operation.

Once an operation is licensed, Article IX prohibits most discharges from any offshore installation and establishes limits for the oil content of permitted discharges. Dumping of plastics and garbage are prohibited or regulated by Article X. In one of the most advanced measures, Article XI requires that each operator of an offshore installation prepare a "Chemical Use Plan" for approval by the competent state authority. Except in case of emergency, the operator must amend the plan any time he wishes to use a chemical outside the approved plan and that chemical may escape into the marine environment. The state authority has the power to prohibit, limit or regulate the use of a chemical or product and to impose conditions on its storage and its use, for the protection of the marine environment. In exercising its power, the authority shall have regard to any guidelines issued by the regional organization. Remaining articles establish stringent requirements for the disposal of all other wastes.

The treaty system founded in Barcelona in 1976 also has been enriched by a Protocol for the Protection of the Mediterranean Sea against Pollution resulting from Exploration and Exploitation of the Continental Shelf and the Seabed and its Subsoil[131] which similarly introduces an authorization system for exploration or exploitation. Article 5 lists the requirements for such authorization, including an environmental impact assessment,

---

[130]   ROME, Fourth Legal/Technical Expert Meeting, Kuwait, Dec. 11–12, 1988 reprinted in 19/1 ENVTL. POL'Y & L. 32 (1989).

[131]   Madrid, Oct. 14, 1994.

evidence of the qualification of the candidate operator and personnel of the installation, safety measures, a contingency plan, plans for the removal of installations, precautions for specially-protected areas and insurance or other financial security to cover liability. Each country is obliged to prescribe sanctions for breach of obligations arising out of the Protocol. (Art. 7) The parties also must impose a general obligation upon operators to use the best available, environmentally-effective and economically-appropriate techniques and to observe internationally-accepted standards regarding wastes, as well as the use, storage and discharge of harmful or noxious substances and materials. (Arts. 8 and 9) Common standards shall be adopted for the disposal of oil and oily mixtures from installations (Art. 10) and the discharge of sewage shall be prohibited from installations permanently manned by ten or more persons. (Art. 11) The disposal in the Protocol area of specified products and materials is also prohibited (Art. 12). The contracting parties agree to cooperate in promoting studies and research, in establishing common rules, standards and recommended practices and procedures (Arts. 22 and 23) and also in formulating and adopting appropriate rules and procedures for the determination of liability and compensation for damage resulting from activities dealt with in the Protocol (Art. 27).

At a global level, UNEP has contributed to this field by formulating a certain number of "conclusions" addressed to states. A group of experts in environmental law adopted 42 principles which should govern operations relating to the sea-bed and subsoil within the limits of national jurisdiction. These principles generally establish permit systems based on prior impact assessments and statements concerning the ecological consequences of exploitation, a monitoring system in the interest of the environment, procedures of information and consultation between states when damage could result from operations outside the limits of national jurisdiction, security measures to apply to the operations, prior measures to take to remedy emergency situations and, finally, international responsibility and in particular compensation for victims.[132] In fact, most states having a maritime zone or where activities relating to the deep sea-bed and its sub-soil can be envisaged have enacted legislation requiring prior authorization.

The only detailed global treaty in this field concerns civil responsibility for damage from pollution by oil resulting from the research and exploitation of mineral resources of the sea-bed. The Convention (London, May 1, 1977) establishes a regime parallel to that of the 1969 Brussels Convention, to permit compensation for damage caused by an installation at sea placed

---

[132] *See Aspects concerning the Environment Related to Offshore Drilling and Mining within the Limits of National Jurisdiction,* adopted by the Working Group of Experts on Environmental Law (Feb. 1981), published in English in 7 E.P.L. 50–52 (1981).

under the jurisdiction of a state party, for damage suffered on the territory or in the waters of a state party, as well as safeguard measures designed to prevent or to limit such damage by pollution, wherever it might be (Art. 2). The owner of the installation at the moment of the accident is strictly liable (Art. 3), but has the right to limit responsibility if he has established a fund (Art. 6). A state party can set a liability limit higher that provided by the Convention or even abolish limits, on condition that no discrimination based on nationality is exercised (Art. 15). The competent courts are those of the state where the damage has been suffered (Art. 11) and their decisions must be executed in the other states parties (Art. 12).

5. Land-Based Pollution

Land-based pollution can be defined as pollution of maritime zones due to discharges by coastal establishments or coming from any other source situated on land or artificial structures, including pollution transported by rivers into the sea. Approximately 70 percent of marine pollution comes directly from land-based sources. Land-based pollution is particularly severe in heavily-populated regions, such as along the Mediterranean and the Baltic Sea coastlines, as well as in regions where seasonal tourism may greatly increase the number of inhabitants.

The diversity of origins of land-based pollution makes it difficult to combat. Such pollution can occur directly, by dumping or discharges along the coast, or indirectly, by the intermediary of rivers or streams or subterranean waters. Applicable rules should in principle include all waters that flow into the sea, thus governing the entire aquatic environment in certain regions. As such, in addition to the "traditional" techniques of forbidding discharge or requiring prior authorization of certain discharges, cooperation between states plays a great role, notably in establishing programs to progressively reduce pollution throughout an entire water basin.

UNCLOS regulates land-based pollution by the methods it applies to other pollution sources. Article 194 provides that states should take the necessary measures tending to limit as much as possible "the release of toxic, harmful or noxious substances, especially those which are persistent, from land-based sources, from or through the atmosphere or by dumping."[133] Article 207 provides that states shall adopt laws and regulations as well as all other measures that may be necessary to prevent, reduce and control this pollution. Article 213 requires states to ensure their application.

Apart from UNCLOS, existing conventional sources regulating land-based pollution are exclusively regional. The United Nations Environment Program studied the problem during 1984–85 and a group of experts

---

[133] Art. 194(3)(a).

adopted guidelines to combat it.[134] However, the legal effect of the guidelines remains limited because they are not contained in a treaty or government document. Regionally, all regional seas treaties proclaim the principle of combating land-based pollution. The most precise regulations are those for the North-East Atlantic, the Baltic, the Mediterranean and the South-East Pacific. There are also several European Community directives that concern, in one manner or another, pollutants originating on land.

The first convention to address land-based pollution was adopted in 1974[135] and replaced in 1992 by the Convention for the Protection of the Marine Environment of the North-East Atlantic.[136] According to Article 3 of the 1992 treaty, the contracting parties shall take, individually and jointly, all possible steps to prevent and eliminate pollution from land-based sources as provided in Annex I, in particular by adopting programs and measures for the prevention and elimination of this type of pollution. The large number of recommendations[137] and agreements adopted under the former Convention continue to be applicable, unaltered in their legal nature, according to Article 31.

The 1992 Convention obliges the contracting parties to set priorities and assess the nature and extent of the programs and measures and their time scales, using the criteria given in Appendix 2 to the Convention. These criteria are, *inter alia*, persistency, toxicity or other noxious properties, tendency to bioaccumulation, radioactivity, risk of eutrophication, risk of undesirable changes in the marine ecosystem and irreversibility or durability of effects, and non-fulfillment of environmental quality objectives. The criteria identify substances that must be subject to programs and measures, including heavy metals and their compounds, organohalogen compounds, biocides, and radioactive substances. Point source discharges to the maritime area, and releases into water or air which reach and may affect the maritime area are strictly subject to authorization or regulation by the competent authorities of the contracting parties, taking into account relevant decisions of the Commission. The states parties also are to establish systems of regular monitoring and inspection to assess compliance with such authorizations and regulations. The new system seems more flexible than the former one which also required the use of best available techniques for point sources and best environmental practice for point and diffuse sources.

The 1992 Convention on the Protection of the Marine Environment of

---

[134]   Montreal, Apr. 19, 1985. For the text, *see* E.P.L. 77 (1985).
[135]   Convention for the Prevention of Marine Pollution from Land-Based Sources, Paris, June 4, 1974.
[136]   Paris, Sept. 22, 1992.
[137]   *See* P. SANDS, PRINCIPLES OF INTERNATIONAL ENVIRONMENTAL LAW 321–23 (1994).

the Baltic Sea Area[138] includes detailed rules relating to land-base pollution (Art. 6 and Annex III). The main principle is that harmful substances from point sources originating from the catchment area of the Baltic Sea shall not, except in negligible quantities, be introduced directly or indirectly into the marine environment of the Baltic Sea Area, without a prior special permit, subject to periodic review and issued by the appropriate national authority (Art. 6). Convention Annex III describes detailed criteria and measures to prevent pollution from land-based sources. It also refers to the best environmental practice, recommended for eliminating pollution from diffuse sources including agriculture, and the best available technology, described in Annex II. Like the Convention for the North-East Atlantic, the Baltic Sea treaty shows the same trend toward flexibility in efforts to control land-based pollution.

All the regional marine pollution conventions elaborated under the auspices of UNEP contain agreement in principle to combat land-based pollution. Three of them, the Barcelona Convention for the Mediterranean,[139] the Lima Convention for the South-East Pacific,[140] and the Convention for the Protection and Development of the Marine Environment of the Wider Caribbean Region[141] have adopted more precise measures which are contained in Protocols additional to the Conventions. The Barcelona Convention is supplemented by the Protocol for the Protection of the Mediterranean Sea against Pollution from Land-Based Sources and Activities.[142] The text notes the increasing environmental pressures resulting from human activities in the Mediterranean Sea Area, particularly from industrialization and urbanization, as well as the seasonal increases in coastal population due to tourism. The general obligations of the parties include controlling discharges from rivers, coastal establishments or outfalls, and pollution emanating from any other land-based sources and activities, giving priority to the phasing out of inputs from substances that are toxic, persistent and liable to bioaccumulate. Reflecting developments in the law of international watercourses, the Protocol covers the hydrologic basin of the contracting parties, defined as the entire watershed area within their territories

---

[138]   Helsinki, Apr. 9, 1992; EMuT 992:28. The treaty replaced the Convention for the Protection of the Marine Environment of the Baltic Sea, Mar. 22, 1974.

[139]   Barcelona, Feb. 16, 1976.

[140]   Lima, Nov. 20, 1981.

[141]   Cartagena de Indias, Mar. 24, 1983. The parties adopted the Protocol concerning Pollution from Land-Based Sources and Activities in Oranjestad, Aruba on Oct. 6, 1999.

[142]   The Protocol was originally adopted in Athens in 1980 as the Protocol for the Protection of the Mediterranean Sea against Pollution from Land-Based Sources. It was amended and its titled changed in Syracuse, Mar. 7, 1996.

and draining into the Mediterranean Sea Area.[143] Non-party states whose territories include part of the hydrologic basin of the Mediterranean Sea are invited to cooperate in the implementation of the Protocol.[144] The Protocol also applies to discharges originating from land-based and point sources and activities within the territories of the contracting parties that may affect directly or indirectly the Mediterranean Sea Area.[145]

The parties generally undertake to eliminate pollution deriving from land-based sources and activities, in particular to phase out inputs of the substances listed in Annex I that are toxic, persistent and liable to bioaccumulate. The Annex lists 30 sectors of activities, including energy production, petroleum refining, animal husbandry, and tourism, as well as thirteen characteristics of polluting substances (*e.g.*, persistence, health effects and risks, effects on the smell, colour, transparency or other characteristics of sea water) and categories of hazardous substances such as organohalogen compounds and substances, heavy metal, and biocides. Article 4 (1)(b) and Annex III add concern for atmospheric pollution from land-based sources or activities within the territories of the parties, taking into account prevailing meteorological conditions.

Article 6 of the amended Protocol provides for an authorization or regulation system: the competent authorities of the parties are to strictly regulate point source discharges into the Protocol area and releases into water or air that reach and may affect the Mediterranean area. A revised Annex II lists the elements to be taken into account in issuing of the authorizations for discharges of wastes. It distinguishes the characteristics and composition of the discharges according to their harmfulness and the characteristics and composition of discharge site and the receiving environment. According to Article 8, the parties shall carry out monitoring activities and give public access to the findings in order to systematically assess the levels of pollution along their coasts and to evaluate the effectiveness of action plans, programmes and measures implemented to eliminate to the fullest possible extent pollution of the marine environment.

The Protocol establishes a reporting system providing for bi-annual reports from the parties about measures taken, results achieved and difficulties encountered in the application of the Protocol (Art. 13). Meetings of the Parties shall take place in conjunction with ordinary Meetings of the Parties to the Barcelona Convention. Such meetings shall adopt the short-term and medium-term regional action plans and programs containing measures and timetables for their implementation (Art.15).

---

[143] Art. 2(d).

[144] Art. 4(3).

[145] Art.4(1)(a).

The Quito Protocol relating to Protection of the South-East Pacific against Pollution from Land-Based Sources,[146] supplements the Lima Convention. Article 3 of the Protocol, indicating the general obligations of the states parties, is directly inspired by UNCLOS. Two methods are used to combat land-based pollution: a system of lists and a program to eliminate or reduce pollution. The agreement has two annexed lists that are the same as those attached to the Athens Protocol but the legal obligations respecting them differ because the Quito Protocol states agreed only to endeavor to eliminate discharge of substances contained in Annex I[147] and to endeavor progressively to reduce those contained in Annex II.[148] States parties also are obliged to cooperate in application of the provisions of the instrument and their meetings monitor implementation of the rules adopted.

The 16 states parties to the Convention for the Protection and the Development of the Marine Environment of the Wider Caribbean Region[149] adopted a Protocol Concerning Pollution from Land-Based Sources and Activities on October 6, 1999, at Oranjestad, Aruba. It calls for the preparation of environmental impact assessments for planned land-based activities or planned modifications to such activities which are subject to regulatory control and which are likely to cause substantial pollution of or significant harmful changes to the Convention area (Art. VII). The parties are to promote public access to relevant information concerning pollution of the Convention area as well as public participation in decision-making processes concerning the implementation of the Protocol (Art. XI). Annexes to the Protocol list source categories, activities and associated pollutants of concern, but also factors to be used in determining effluent and emission source controls and management factors. A very detailed Annex relates to domestic wastewater and the last Annex proposes plans for the prevention, reduction and control of agricultural non-point pollution sources. Finally, the Protocol calls for reporting by the parties on measures adopted and results obtained, as well as on the state of the environment of the Convention area (Art. XII).

The EC also has adopted several directives in this field. In particular, the directive of May 4, 1976,[150] relating to the protection of the aquatic environment explicitly applies to the territorial seas of member states. This text contains a system of prohibition and authorization based on lists of harmful discharges, but it also envisages quality standards. Programs to reduce pollution and improve water quality had to be implemented within time

---

[146] July 22, 1983.

[147] Art. 4.

[148] Art. 5.

[149] Cartagena de Indias, Mar. 24, 1983.

[150] 76/464/EEC, O.J L 129 (5/18/76).

limits fixed by the European Commission. A series of EC directives to preserve the water quality of the Community applies to inland waters as well as
to the marine environment. Although they primarily aim at protecting fresh
waters from pollution, their effect can lessen marine pollution from land-
based sources. Similarly, a Directive of October 30, 1979,[151] which applies
to coastal waters and brackish waters designated by the states members as
needing protection or improvement in order to support shellfish, sets the
applicable limits which member states should take into account in fixing
the standards for the designated waters.

Many rivers carry pollution into the sea and it is thus useful to add
international treaties protecting watercourses against pollution to this summary. Review of the developments concerning inland waters is necessary to
give a complete picture of international regulation concerning land-based
pollution.[152] The 1997 UN Convention on the Law of the Non- Navigational
Uses of International Watercourses, confirms in Article 23 that:

> Watercourse States shall, individually and, where appropriate, in
> cooperation with other States, take all measures with respect to an
> international watercourse that are necessary to protect and preserve
> the marine environment, including estuaries, taking into account
> generally accepted international rules and standards.[153]

6. Emergencies

Emergencies can be defined as those where the presence or danger of
hydrocarbons or other dangerous polluting substances constitute a serious
and imminent danger for the coasts or related interests of a state. In part
due to the harm caused by the tankers *Torrey Canyon, Amoco Cadiz, Exxon
Valdez,* and *Erica* this is one of the most developed parts of international law
relating to marine pollution. On the global level it is governed by general
principles set out in UNCLOS,[154] and by the International Convention on
Oil Pollution Preparedness, Response and Cooperation, elaborated in the
framework of the International Maritime Organization.[155] Before its conclusion, only regional instruments handled this matter, such as the 1969
Bonn Agreement which concerned pollution only by oil and was
replaced, by the Bonn Agreement for Cooperation in Dealing with
Pollution of the North Sea by Oil and Other Harmful Substances.[156]
Several additional protocols to regional seas conventions also provide for
cooperation in emergencies.

---

[151]   79/923/EEC, O.J. L 281 (11/10/79).
[152]   *See* Chapter 10.
[153]   New York, May 21, 1997.
[154]   Arts. 189, 204 and 211(7).
[155]   London, Nov. 30, 1990.
[156]   Bonn, Sept. 13, 1983.

The main obligations of the parties to the 1990 London Convention are to take, individually or jointly, all appropriate measures to prepare for and respond to an oil pollution incident (Art. 1). The Convention provides for measures in two stages. Preparedness includes setting up national and regional systems. This means designating competent authorities with responsibility for oil pollution response and operational contact points as well as establishing authorities entitled to act on behalf of the state to request assistance or to render any requested assistance. National contingency plans shall be prepared and adequate oil spill control equipment made available. Relevant personnel shall be trained and detailed plans and communication capabilities established (Art. 6). Each ship entitled to fly the flag of a contracting party must have a shipboard oil pollution emergency plan, which can be inspected while in a port or at an offshore terminal under the jurisdiction of a party. All offshore units, sea ports and oil handling facilities must also have such plans (Art. 3). The parties shall cooperate by providing advisory services, technical support and equipment, administrative and other facilities and by promoting research and relevant technical activities (Arts. 8 and 9).

The Convention regulates the reporting procedures in case of an oil pollution incident (Art. 4) and establishes rules concerning the action required on receiving an oil pollution report (Arts. 4 and 5). Upon the request of any party affected or likely to be affected, the parties will cooperate according to their capabilities and the availability of relevant resources, by providing advisory services, technical support and equipment, for the purpose of responding to the incident. An Annex to the Convention concerns the reimbursement of costs of assistance. If the action was taken at the express request of another state, the latter state shall reimburse the assisting state the costs of its action. A state which acts on its own initiative will bear the costs of the its action.

The London Convention was complemented on March 15, 2000, by a Protocol on Preparedness, Response and Cooperation to Pollution by Hazardous and Noxious Substances.[157] The Protocol expands the scope of cooperation between the parties to include spills of hazardous and noxious substances, defined in the Protocol as "any substance other than oil which, if introduced into the marine environment is likely to create hazards to human health, to harm living resources and marine life, to damage amenities or to interfere with other legitimate uses of the sea." Incidents covered include those causing fire and explosion, as well as discharges, releases or emissions which pose or may pose a threat to the marine environment, to the coastline or related interests of a state and which require emergency action or immediate response.

---

[157] *See* 31 E.P.L. 145(2001).

The Protocol contains the same provisions as those of the London Convention on reporting of spills, contingency planning and positioning of equipment and emergency response. States parties are required to establish national and regional systems for emergency response, including the preparation of contingency plans, the institution of the necessary administrative infrastructure, the pre-positioning of emergency equipment, and the establishment of a mechanism to coordinate response at the bilateral or regional level, as appropriate. Ships are required to report incidents involving hazardous and noxious substances in accordance with requirements in other conventions and to have emergency plans on board to guide response to such incidents. Sea ports and handling facilities where such substances are loaded and unloaded are also required to have appropriate plans for emergency response.

A more limited regional treaty related to accidental pollution is the Accord of Cooperation for the Protection of the Coasts and Waters of the North-East Atlantic against Pollution Due to Hydrocarbons and Other Harmful Substances. Adopted by the representatives of France, Morocco, Portugal, Spain and the European Community,[158] it aims at combating accidental pollution in the North-East Atlantic exclusive economic zones of the contracting states (Art. 3(1)). This agreement corresponds to the global London Convention.

The major obligation imposed by the agreement is to cooperate in preparedness and joint action for accidental pollution. The measures foreseen are rather like those prescribed by other regional instruments. Contracting parties must establish national systems for preventing and combating incidents of pollution at sea and prepare a minimum volume of material to cope with accidental discharges (Art. 4). An interesting feature of the treaty is the division of the North-East Atlantic region into zones: the party in whose zone an incident of pollution takes place shall undertake the necessary evaluations of its nature, importance, and probable consequences (Art. 8). The governments must give corresponding instructions to competent officials, captains of ships and pilots of aircraft (Art. 7). Unless bilateral agreements decide otherwise, the zones correspond to the exclusive economic zones of the contracting states (Annex I). The parties may designate zones of joint interest.

If pollution occurs individual or joint action is initiated by the party in whose zone the incident occurs. Detailed rules regulate cooperation in combating the pollution. An International Center is established for the purpose of aiding the states parties to react rapidly and effectively to incidents of pollution (Arts. 18–19 and Annex 2).

In the regional context, eight protocols additional are attached to UNEP-sponsored regional seas conventions.[159] Each Convention contains

---

[158]   Lisbon, Oct. 17, 1990.

[159]   The applicable instruments are:

a provision envisaging adoption of the protocol. All except the Caribbean instrument are directed towards oil pollution as well as other harmful substances. In fact, it is surprising that even one of the agreements is limited to oil, because the general trend has been to extend these instruments to regulate all polluting substances.

Generally speaking, the provisions relating to emergencies caused by oil pollution fall into three categories. One part aims at organizing advance cooperation, before the existence of an emergency situation. A second part becomes applicable when an emergency arises and concerns the actions which must be taken. Finally, most of the instruments contain institutional clauses, providing either for the creation of a mutual aid center among the states parties or for periodic meetings of the states parties, or for both.

a. Preventive Actions

The fundamental requirement is that states maintain the ability to react efficiently to emergency situations. Article 2(2) of the Kuwait Protocol provides a good example:

The Contracting States shall endeavor to maintain and promote, either individually or through bilateral or multilateral cooperation,

---

— Protocol Concerning Cooperation in Combating Pollution of the Mediterranean Sea by Oil and Other Harmful Substances in Cases of Emergency (Feb. 16, 1976), supplementing the Barcelona Convention on the Mediterranean;

— Protocol Concerning Regional Cooperation in Combating Pollution by Oil and other Harmful Substances in Cases of Emergency (Apr. 24, 1978), supplementing the Kuwait Convention on the Gulf;

— Protocol Concerning Cooperation in Combating Pollution in Cases of Emergency (Mar. 23, 1981), supplementing the Abidjan Convention on West-Africa;.

— Agreement on Regional Cooperation in Combating Pollution of the South-East Pacific by Hydrocarbons or Other Harmful Substances in Cases of Emergency (Nov. 12, 1981), supplementing the Lima Convention on the South-East Pacific;

— Protocol Concerning Regional Cooperation in Combating Pollution by Hydrocarbons or Other Harmful Substances in Cases of Emergency (Feb. 14, 1982), supplementing the Jeddah Convention on the Red Sea;

— Protocol Concerning Cooperation in Combating Oil Spills in the Wider Caribbean Region (Mar. 24, 1983), supplementing the Cartagena Convention on the Caribbean.;

— Protocol Concerning Cooperation in Combating Pollution Emergencies in the South Pacific Region (Nov. 25, 1986), supplementing the Noumea Convention on the South Pacific.

their contingency plans and means for combating pollution in the Sea Area by oil and other harmful substances. These means shall include, in particular, available equipment, ships, aircraft and man-power prepared for operations in cases of emergency.[160]

One of the initial obligations is to transmit to other states parties information necessary to respond to any potential action: information regarding national authorities responsible for combating pollution, including their structure and operation, and designating the authorities who should receive information concerning marine pollution and implement measures of assistance between parties.[161] Often the instruments additionally require that states parties provide each other with their laws, regulations, and other legal instruments relating generally to combating pollution of the sea by hydrocarbons and other harmful substances.[162] Some also request transmission of information on the existing national methods of responding to pollution, which could be useful in international emergencies.[163] A few provisions require that new techniques to combat, prevent and limit the effects of pollution be shared. This is especially the case in regional instruments whose states parties include both industrialized and developing countries.[164] Finally, in certain cases it is required that states transmit and centralize a list of experts who can be called upon in case of emergency.[165]

One of the most important tasks among the anticipatory measures is to assure that communications will function at the moment an emergency arises. Article 7 of the Barcelona Protocol codifies this need: "The Parties undertake to coordinate the utilization of the means of communication at their disposal in order to ensure, with the necessary speed and reliability, the reception, transmission and dissemination of all reports and urgent information which relate to the occurrences and situations referred to in Article 1...."[166]

It is obvious that the most reliable means of alerting states in case of major marine environmental pollution is to exercise systematic monitoring. Article 204 of UNCLOS summarizes this:

---

[160] *See also* Art. 2, Helsinki Convention; Art. 4, Protocol of Barcelona; Art. 9, Protocol of Abidjan; Art. 2(2), Protocol of Jeddah.

[161] Art. 9(1), Helsinki; Art. 6(a), Barcelona; Art. 5, Kuwait; Art. 5(a) Abidjan; Art. 7, Lima; Art. 5, Jeddah; Art. 4, Cartagena; Art. 4(a),(b), Bonn.

[162] Art. 1(b), Helsinki; art. 3(3), 5, Kuwait; Art. 5(b), Abidjan; Art. 5(b), Jeddah; and Art. 4, Cartagena.

[163] Art. 4(c), Bonn; Arts. 3(3)(iii), 12, Kuwait; Art. 1(a), Quito.

[164] Art. 6(1)(c), Barcelona; Arts. 3(3)(ii), 6, Kuwait; Art. 6(a) Jeddah.

[165] *E.g.*, Art. 3(3)(iii), Kuwait.

[166] See also Art. 5, Helsinki; Art. 9, Abidjan; Art. 8, Lima; Art. 5(3), Bonn.

1.   States shall, consistent with the rights of other States, endeavor, as far as practicable, directly or through the competent international organizations, to observe, measure, evaluate and analyze, by recognized scientific methods, the risks or effects of pollution of the marine environment.

2.   In particular, States shall keep under surveillance the effects of any activities which they permit or in which they engage in order to determine whether these activities are likely to pollute the marine environment.

Article 205 adds that states shall publish reports of the results obtained in applying Article 204 or provide such reports, at appropriate intervals, to the competent international organizations.

A number of regional treaties provide for the organization of ocean monitoring to detect pollution.[167] The Bonn agreement on the North and Baltic Seas[168] best accomplishes this in an Annex which divides the North Sea region into zones. The Convention designates one or several states to be responsible for each zone. In case of emergency, the responsible state evaluates the nature and importance of the accident or, if appropriate, the type and approximate quantity of hydrocarbons or other dangerous substances, as well as the direction and speed of its movement. The state is to immediately inform all other states parties, transmitting to them its evaluations. It also must maintain its surveillance of the pollution for as long as it remains within the zone.[169]

UNCLOS Article 199 invites states to jointly develop and promote contingency plans for responding to pollution incidents in the marine environment. Several protocols concerning regional seas provide for the preparation on the national level of such contingency plans,[170] and some require that these plans be communicated to other states parties.[171]

Another anticipatory measure on the international level is the establishment of mutual aid centers in case of emergency at sea as provided for in several regional protocols.[172] The Malta Center, established within the framework of the Barcelona Convention for the Mediterranean Sea, serves as a model for other comparable initiatives. Article 3 of the Kuwait Protocol has the most complete provision in this regard, granting numerous functions to its regional Marine Emergency Mutual Aid Center: gathering and

---

[167]   Art. 3, Helsinki; Art. 4, Barcelona; Art. 5, Lima.

[168]   Sept. 13, 1983.

[169]   Art. 6.

[170]   Art. 4, Lima; Art. 2, Quito.

[171]   Art. 5, Kuwait; Art. 5(c), Abidjan.

[172]   Arts. 6–11, Barcelona; Arts. 3, 8 Kuwait; Art. 3, Jeddah; Art. 9, Cartegena.

disseminating information, assisting states parties in developing laws and regulations, preparing marine emergency contingency plans, establishing procedures for transport of personnel, equipment and materials, transmitting reports concerning marine emergencies, and promoting and developing training programs for combating pollution. In addition, in emergency situations, the Center must be immediately informed and transmit this information to states parties as soon as possible.

b. Responsive Actions

Obviously, the first task of states who learn of an emergency at sea is to inform the states exposed to it as well any competent international organizations.[173] This general obligation is reaffirmed and detailed in all the instruments specially concerned with international cooperation in case of emergencies. Thus, information should be addressed without delay to the competent authorities of any state which could be affected by the pollution. Moreover, according to the terms of the Barcelona Protocol, the maritime authorities of the states parties should instruct the captains of vessels flying their flag and aircraft pilots registered on their territory to signal a state participating in the regional center, by the most rapid and adequate means, information regarding all accidents causing or likely to cause pollution of the sea by oil or other harmful substances. They must also notify of the presence, characteristics and extent of spillage of such substances observed at sea which are likely to present a serious and imminent threat to the marine environment or to the coast or related interests of one or more states parties.[174] The information thus received is communicated to other states susceptible of being affected by the pollution, either directly by the state which received the information or by the regional center.[175]

An Annex to the Protocol sets out the precise contents of the report to be made pursuant to Article 8. Each report must contain, as far as possible, the identification of the source of pollution, the geographic position, time and date of the occurrence, the prevailing wind and sea conditions, relevant details concerning the ship, and a clear indication or description of the harmful substances involved. Supplementary information should be furnished where appropriate. Several other protocols contain similarly detailed provisions,[176] while other instruments contain the same principles, but are less detailed.[177]

---

[173]   Arts. 198, 211(7), UNCLOS.

[174]   Art. 8(1).

[175]   Art. 8 (2).

[176]   Art. 7 and Annex A, Kuwait; Art. 7 and Annex, Abidjan; Art. 9 and Annex, Lima.

[177]   Art. 5(2)–(5), Helsinki; Art. 7, Jeddah; Art. 5, Cartagena; Art. 5(2) and (3), Bonn.

The states parties to such treaties also have financial or material obligations. They must not only observe and evaluate polluting incidents, but intervene. In case of a release or loss overboard of harmful substances in packages, freight containers, portable tanks or road and rail tank wagons, they shall cooperate to salvage and recover such substances in order to reduce the danger of pollution of the marine environment.[178] The principal types of assistance required by the different regional instruments are, first, furnishing of personnel, material, and equipment, as well as means of monitoring and control; and second, facilitating the transfer of personnel, material, and equipment into, out of, and through the territories of the contracting states.[179]

A complete picture of obligations in emergency situations is found in Article 7 of the Cartagena Protocol, titled *Operational Measures:*

Each contracting party shall, within its capabilities, take steps including those outlined below in responding to an oil spill incident:

(a) make a preliminary assessment of the incident, including the type and extent of existing or likely pollution effects;

(b) promptly communicate information concerning the incident pursuant to Article 5;

(c) promptly determine its ability to take effective measures to respond to the incident and the assistance that might be required;

(d) consult as appropriate with other contracting parties concerned in the process of determining the necessary response to the incident;

(e) take the measures necessary to prevent, reduce or eliminate the effects of the incident, including monitoring of the situation.

Financing assistance is explicitly discussed only in the Protocol of Quito[180] and the 1983 Bonn Accord. Article 9 of the latter states the principle that unless otherwise agreed between the interested states, when action is undertaken by a state at the express request of another state party, the latter should reimburse the first for the costs incurred because of its assistance. When the action is undertaken at the sole initiative of a state, it accepts the costs incurred by reason of its action. Finally, when the state having solicited the assistance terminates its request—which can occur at any time—it pays the expenses already incurred by the assisting state party. In all cases, unless otherwise agreed, the costs incurred by an action undertaken by a state at the demand of another are calculated according to the legislation and practices in force in the assisting country.[181]

---

[178] Art. 5, Barcelona; Art. 4, Helsinki; Art. 6, Lima.

[179] Art. 10, Abidjan and Art. 11(2), Kuwait. *See also* Art. 8, Helsinki; Art. 10, Barcelona; Art. 11, Lima; Art. 1(b), Quito, Art. 11, Jeddah; Art. 6, Cartagena; Art. 7, Bonn.

[180] Art. 1(c).

[181] Art. 10.

The use of regional centers has already been discussed.[182] It must be added that the same regional instruments frequently provide for regular meetings of the states parties to exercise a general monitoring of the implementation of the treaty obligations, to examine regularly the efficiency of the measures taken by virtue of the agreement, and to exercise any other function which might be necessary.[183]

7. *Intervention on the High Seas*

According to one of the most universally recognized norms of international law, the high seas are free and vessels on it are under the sole jurisdiction of the state whose flag they fly. The result is that in case of an accident causing pollution, only the flag state can intervene, even if it is a question of taking absolutely indispensable measures to stop the pollution. Following the 1967 *Torrey Canyon* catastrophe, the necessity to modify this rule became apparent. Soon after IMO adopted the International Convention Relating to Intervention on the High Seas in Cases of Oil Pollution Casualties.[184] It establishes that each of the states parties can take such measures on the high seas as may be necessary "to prevent, mitigate or eliminate grave and imminent danger to their coastline or related interests from pollution or threat of pollution of the sea by oil, following a casualty or acts related to such a casualty, which may reasonably be expected to result in major harmful consequences."

"Related interests" is defined to include the interests of a coastal state directly affected or threatened by the casualty, such as maritime coastal, port or estuarine activities including fisheries activities, tourism, the health of the coastal population and the well-being of the area concerned, including conservation of living marine resources and of wildlife. The coastal state thus has the right to take measures with regard to the vessel involved in or causing the accident, which could extend to the towing of the vessel or the sealing off of tears in the hull to the destruction of the wreck. However, before taking any measures the state shall consult with other states affected, particularly with the flag state. It should also notify those who might be affected by its actions, and it shall avoid any risk to human life.[185] Above all, the measures taken shall be proportionate to the damage actually suffered or threatened and not go beyond what is reasonably necessary.[186] Measures taken in contravention of the Convention causing damage to others shall

---

[182]   *See supra* note 172.
[183]   Art. 12, 14 Bonn; Art. 12, Barcelona; Art. 13, Kuwait; Art. 11, Abidjan; Art. 12, Lima; Art. 10, Cartagena.
[184]   Brussels, Nov. 29, 1969.
[185]   Art. 3.
[186]   Art. 5.

be compensable[187] and no measures may be taken against any warship or other state-owned ship used for government non-commercial service.

In 1973, the provisions of this Convention were extended by a protocol[188] to cover substances other than oil. The substances referred to are those designated by the International Maritime Organization and those which are liable to create hazards to human health, harm living resources and marine life, damage amenities or interfere with other legitimate uses of the sea.[189] Each time that a state takes measures regarding one of these substances which has not been listed by the Organization, it has the burden of establishing that the substances, under the circumstances present at the time of the intervention, could reasonably pose a grave and imminent danger analogous to that posed by any of the enumerated substances (Art. 1(3)).

Since the adoption of the two conventions concerning intervention on the high seas, the applicable area has considerably shrunk and the distance which separates the high seas from the coasts has greatly enlarged. In effect, in applying UNCLOS, even before its entry into force, most coastal states have extended their jurisdiction by establishing exclusive economic zones where they may intervene with regard to vessels causing or threatening to cause serious pollution. Thus, the practical consequences of the two conventions on intervention on the high seas have lessened.

8. *Responsibility and Damages for Harm*

This question is treated in detail in Chapter 7A.2, but there may be cited here the 1969 Brussels Convention from Oil Pollution Damage with its 1971 treaty creating a compensation fund, later amended; the 1977 London Convention on Civil Liability for Oil Pollution Damage Resulting from Exploration for and Exploitation of Seabed Mineral Resources; certain principles of the 1982 Law of the Sea Convention and, most recently the International Convention on Civil Liability for Bunker Oil Pollution Damage (March 23, 2001).

F. Conclusions

Increasing recognition of the mutual impacts of land and marine areas and the activities on them has produced a trend towards integrated ecosystem management, including integrated management of coastal areas, coral reefs and their associated mangroves and sea grasses, wetlands, and freshwater systems. Chapter 14C.3 addresses integrated environmental management of coastal and marine ecosystems.

---

[187]   Art. 6.
[188]   London, Nov. 2, 1973.
[189]   Art. 1(2).

BIBLIOGRAPHY

BROWN, E.D., THE INTERNATIONAL LAW OF THE SEA (1994).

BRUBAKER, D., MARINE POLLUTION AND INTERNATIONAL LAW (1993).

BEURIER, J-P, KISS, A. & MAHMOUDI, S., NOUVELLES TECHNOLOGIES ET DROIT DE L'ENVIRONNEMENT MARIN (2000).

CHURCHILL R.R. & LOWE, A.V., THE LAW OF THE SEA (1988).

KASOULIDES, G.C., PORT STATE CONTROL AND JURISDICTION: EVOLUTION OF THE PORT STATE REGIME (1993).

KHODJET EL KHIL, L., LA POLLUTION DE LA MER MEDITERRANEE DU FAIT DU TRANSPORT MARITIME DE MARCHANDISES (2003).

KURIBAYASHI, T., AND MILES, E.L. eds., THE LAW OF THE SEA IN THE 1990s: A FRAMEWORK FOR FURTHER INTERNATIONAL COOPERATION (1992).

MITCHELL, R.B., INTENTIONAL OIL POLLUTION AT SEA: ENVIRONMENTAL POLICY AND TREATY COMPLIANCE (1994).

MOLENAAR, E.J., COASTAL STATE JURISDICTION OVER VESSEL-SOURCE POLLUTION (Kluwer, 1998).

NANDAN, S. & ROSENNE, B. eds., UNITED NATIONS CONVENTION ON THE LAW OF THE SEA 1982: A COMMENTARY (1995).

Peet, G., *The MARPOL Convention: Implementation and Effectiveness*, 7 J. ESTUARINE & COASTAL L. 290 (1992).

VAN DYKE, J., ET AL., FREEDOM FOR THE SEAS IN THE 21ST CENTURY (1993).

INTERNET SITES

UNCLOS secretariat
<http://www.un.org/Depts/los/>

CHAPTER 12

ATMOSPHERE, STRATOSPHERE AND CLIMATE

The earth is surrounded by a cover of gases that condition life, protect all living things from harmful solar radiation, and regulate the global climate. The chemical composition of the atmosphere has been quite stable for 600 million years, with four gases comprising 99.99 percent of dry air: nitrogen (78.08 percent), oxygen (20.95 percent), argon (0.93 percent) and carbon dioxide (0.03 percent).[1] The proportion of these gases remains almost identical up to an altitude of approximately 50 miles (80 kilometers).

The atmosphere is also composed of several layers where inputs of pollutants may have very different impacts. The lowest level is the troposphere, whose upper boundary lies at the point at which temperatures level off at minus 75–80 centigrade. The troposphere contains about 85 percent of the gases and is where most weather occurs, in part due to the water vapor that mixes with air in a convection process. It is also where many trace gases (methane, helium, ozone, hydrogen, neon) are found that are critical to biological diversity. The next level is the stratosphere followed by the thermosphere, which comprises only 0.0001 percent of the atmosphere's gases and extends upward to approximately 500 km.

The introduction of pollutants into the atmosphere creates multiple effects, because the air is essentially a place of transit: gases or particles remain there temporarily and manifest many of their impacts only after returning to the soil, plants, marine waters, lakes or rivers. Poisonous air also directly damages living creatures and objects. The three most serious known ecological catastrophes—Bhopal, India; Chernobyl, Ukraine; and the Indonesian forest fires—produced most of their victims as a result of direct contact with polluting elements in the atmosphere. Pollutants often undergo modifications in their composition once they enter the atmosphere. Finally and significantly, air pollutants move quickly and cover greater distances than do pollutants in watercourses or the marine environment. The atmosphere is in fact the planet's largest single shared resource consisting of several large air basins.

Numerous sources emit pollution into the atmosphere, including energy-production facilities, industrial processes, waste incinerators, transportation vehicles, and even animal farms. The amount of pollutants varies

---

[1]   M. Soroos, The Endangered Atmosphere: Preserving a Global Commons 24 (1997).

from one area to another, depending on the type and concentration of human activities and on the measures taken to reduce emissions. According to estimates, the countries of OECD account for about half of the total annual global polluting emissions.[2]

Legal regulation of other environmental issues can have an impact on air pollution. Efforts to clean up water or soil, for example, including the tendency to incinerate wastes instead of depositing them on the ground or dumping them into the sea or into inland waters, can aggravate air pollution. Similarly, the siting of industrial facilities is important, because when pollutants are emitted into the atmosphere, the amount and direction of their dispersion plays a significant role in determining the extent of damage they cause. Efforts to reduce atmospheric pollution must not only set emission and air quality standards, but should address the use of fuels that are rich in sulfur, lead or other pollutants, and control combustion processes. With 60 to 70 percent of all acid rain estimated to be due to sulfur oxide emissions, with nitrous oxides responsible for the rest, reducing acid rains means reducing the sulfur content of combustion gases, either by using low-sulfur fuels or by removing sulfur before or during the combustion process.

This chapter, like Agenda 21, Chapter 9, addresses the three main international legal issues concerning the atmosphere: transfrontier pollution, protection of the ozone layer, and climate change. The three problems first will be described, then the legal aspects of each of them will be analyzed separately.

A. Overview

Air pollution has been defined as

> the introduction by man, directly or indirectly, of substances or energy into the air, resulting in deleterious effects of such a nature as to endanger human health, harm living resources and ecosystems and material property, and impair or interfere with amenities and other legitimate uses of the environment.[3]

---

[2]   According to the World Resources Institute, the United States leads in both total (25 percent) and per capita (19.4 metric tons annually) emissions of greenhouse gases. With its increasing industrialization, China's emissions significantly grew during the past decade and are expected to continue to rise. See World Resources Institute, *Historic CO2 Emissions by Fossil Fuels, available at* <http://www.wri.org (Sept. 2001).

[3]   Art. 1(a), Convention on Long-Range Transboundary Air Pollution (Geneva, Nov. 13, 1979).

This definition adapts the general concept of pollution, focusing on risk or harm resulting from changes in the environment.

Atmospheric pollution appears in multiple forms, some only recently understood. Domestic and international regulation has evolved as the impacts of each form of pollution have become known. First, sulfuric gas of industrial origin, in part converted into sulfate in the troposphere and lower stratosphere, becomes sulfuric acid.[4] In addition to its impact on fresh waters, the acid is returned to the soil in rain, where it attacks the roots of trees.[5] Other pollutants, principally nitrous oxides (NO_x)[6] and hydrocarbon emissions such as carbon dioxide[7] combine with sulfuric gases to produce ozone (O_3) or smog during sunny periods. Ozone harms the needles of conifers, particularly the membrane which supports photosynthesis. These lie at the source of the serious damage caused above all on Western and Southern slopes at an altitude near 800 meters. Ground level ozone[8] is also particularly harmful to those who have vulnerable respiratory systems, including children, the elderly and the sick. The major sources of ozone pollution are motor vehicles, power stations, and industries utilizing fossil fuels. Particulates are larger than a single molecule and consist of matter such as ash and bits of heavy metal. Particulates corrode buildings, monuments, and other objects and harm vegetation. Among the other substances entering the atmosphere, the impact of persistent organic pollutants (POPs)[9] and chloroflourocarbons (CFCs)[10] in the atmosphere has become a major concern.

---

[4] Also known as sulfur dioxide (SO_2), it is a primary cause of acid rain. The major sources are coal and oil combustion and the major effects are acidification of water and soil.

[5] Acid rain has no uniform definition, but most scientists regard pH readings below 4.5 to be highly acidic. This level is ten times that of normal rain. Some areas of Europe and North America regularly receive precipitation that is 40 times the normal level.

[6] Nitrous oxides, emitted by many industrial processes, are a precursor to smog. They are also a source of acid rain.

[7] Carbon dioxide (CO_2) is the largest contributor to anthropogenic climate change. Carbon dioxide is released by the combustion of fossil fuels, largely by automobiles and other motor vehicles.

[8] In contrast, stratospheric ozone is a necessary component of the atmosphere because it acts to filter harmful ultraviolet radiation.

[9] POPs are organochlorides that are released as chemical byproducts of industrial production. They do not decompose easily and can travel great distances, and bioaccumulate, resulting in high concentrations in animals at the top of the food chain. Some of them have been linked to cancer, immune difficiencies and loss of fertility.

[10] CFCs deplete stratospheric ozone. *See* below in this chapter.

Air pollution led to international disputes relatively early. From the end of the 19th century, fumes emitted by a zinc and lead smelter situated in Trail, Canada, some dozen kilometers from the United States border, posed the problem of transfrontier pollution and reparation for the harm it caused. Slightly more than 40 years later, an arbitral decision rendered in the *Trail Smelter* case became the first major decision of international jurisprudence announcing the obligation of each state not to cause or allow to be caused transfrontier pollution damage to other states.

To combat deterioration in air quality, initial measures sought to disperse the pollutants through increasing the height of factory smokestacks. The "solution" created new environmental problems: emissions taken to higher atmospheric levels traveled considerable distances on air currents, causing long-range pollution damage. As a result, air pollution was no longer solely a local phenomenon concerning large cities and industrial zones, but by the 1970s was a matter that affected non-industrial countries and agricultural areas often far from the source of the emissions. The effects were particularly felt in Scandinavian countries, even though their air quality was not considered unacceptable. The rivers and lakes of Scandinavia showed disquieting symptoms, due to the increase in sulfuric substances, transformed into sulfuric acid. The increased presence of acid in freshwaters reached a point where it endangered fish, micro-decomposers, algae, and other aquatic life.[11]

While acidification of Scandinavian lakes by sulfuric rain originating from afar was at the heart of discussions during the 1970s, by 1980 public opinion in Central and Eastern Europe and in Canada turned to the disappearance of forests due to pollution. In 1995–1997, a survey of European forests taking in 116,000 hectares in 29 countries revealed that one in every four trees was suffering from abnormal thinning of the crown, with only slight differences between conifers and broad-leaved trees.[12] Multiple causes for the destruction have been suggested, including successive drought years, viral diseases, and fungi; atmospheric pollution is still considered the primary factor, either as principal agent or as contributing to the weakening of trees, making them less resistant to the lack of water or disease.

In the 1980s scientists discovered two other problems related to the emission of substances into the atmosphere: the depletion of the stratospheric ozone layer and the threat of a major, anthropogenic change of the global climate.

---

[11]   G.P. Smith, *Acid Rain: Transnational Perspectives*, 4 N.Y.U. INT'L & COMP. L. 459, 463 (1983).

[12]   The surveys were carried out by the UN Economic Commission for Europe and the European Union. *See Forest Conditions in Europe, Results of the 1996 Crown Conditions Survey: 1997 Technical Report*, ACID NEWS (Dec. 4–5, 1997), 14–15.

Ozone is a form of oxygen, containing one more atom than the oxygen breathed in the atmosphere. While ground-level ozone in the form of "smog" produces harmful consequences, especially to plants, stratospheric ozone, whose strongest concentrations are found between 20 and 25 kilometers above earth, filters a part of the sun's ultraviolet radiation which otherwise would injure life forms on earth. The absorption of ultraviolet rays by stratospheric ozone is also a source of climatic energy. According to a study prepared under the aegis of UNEP, a reduction in ozone risks not only an increase in the number of human skin cancers and harm to the eyes but also unforeseen biological effects, because all living beings have evolved under the protection of the ozone layer.[13]

The anthropogenic source of ozone depletion[14] was clear by the late 1970s. The utilization of chlorofluorocarbons (CFCs), contained in aerosol sprays and to a lesser extent in solvents and refrigeration, was identifid as a major contributing cause. When first developed CFCs were viewed favorably because they are nontoxic, non-flammable, non-corrosive and stable. It is the very stability of CFCs that is the source of the problem because they migrate over long distances and survive for many years. When they reach the stratosphere intact, solar radiation breaks the molecules apart to free reactive chlorine atoms, catalyzing chain reactions that destroy ozone; even if CFC production and use are phased out, ozone depletion will remain for some time, because of the substances already released. By 1985 it was understood that most depletion of the ozone layer occurs on a seasonal basis above Antarctica and, increasingly, over the Arctic region.[15] The Antarctic ozone hole has expanded to a size greater than North America and scientists expect it to begin shrinking only in 30 to 50 years as ozone-depleting substances are removed from the atmosphere.

The third major problem of the atmosphere is "climate change," meaning a change of climate attributed directly or indirectly to human activity that alters the composition of the global atmosphere and is in addition to natural climate variation observed over a comparable time period.[16] The adverse effects from this change have been characterized as changes in the

---

13   Asik K. Biswas, The Ozone Layer (1979).

14   The first publication linking CFCs and their role in the destruction of the ozone layer appeared in 1974. *See* F. Sherwood Rowland & Mario Molina, *Stratospheric Sink for Chlorofluoromethanes: Chlorine Atoms-Catalyzed Destruction of Ozone*, 239 Nature 810 (1974).

15   The European Commission reported that the Arctic stratosphere may have lost up to 60 percent of its ozone during the 1999–2000 winter and that average ozone concentrations over Europe were 15 percent less than those of the early 1970s. *See* D. Hunter, J. Salzman & D. Zaelke, International Environmental Law and Policy 530 (2d ed. 2002).

16   U.N. Framework Convention on Climate Change (New York, May 9, 1992), Art. 1(2).

physical environment or biota which have significant deleterious effects on the composition, resilience or productivity of natural and managed ecosystems or on the operation or socio-economic systems or on human health and welfare.[17]

Since the 1960s scientists have expressed concern that a generalized warming of the planet's atmosphere might lead to changes in the global climate. The global average temperature between 1866 and 1996 increased by more than one degree.[18] The 1990s were the warmest decade on record and included the seven warmest years ever recorded. The accumulation of gases such as carbon dioxide, nitrous oxide, methane, chlorofluorocarbons and tropospheric ozone is viewed as at least partly responsible for the warming. There is evidence that the carbon dioxide concentration in the atmosphere today is 25 to 30 percent higher than what it was in the pre-industrial times. In 2001, the Intergovernmental Panel on Climate Change, a network of more than 2,000 scientists and policy experts advising governments on climate policy, concluded that most of the warming observed in the last 50 years has been due to the increase in greenhouse gas concentrations attributable to human activity.[19]

Carbon dioxide is a basic by-product of the combustion of fossil and other natural fuels such as wood, coal, oil and gasoline. Other significant greenhouse gases are chlorofluorocarbons, which also contribute to the depletion of the ozone layer, methane and nitrous oxide. Methane is a metabolic by-product of animals (including humans) and is produced in significant quantities by domestic cattle. It is also a byproduct of petroleum production and, when burned as a fuel (*i.e.,* "natural gas), is actually one of the most benign or environmentally "friendly" fuels, in terms of both its global warming potential and its less severe contribution to more "traditional" forms of air pollution. Nitrous oxide has various industrial applications as an aerosol propellant, and is used as an anesthetic gas. The accumulation of these gases acts as an insulating blanket that traps the energy of sunlight and prevents it from radiating back into outer space. The accumulation of solar energy causes a gradual increase in the average temperature of the earth's surface.

The trend towards increasing temperatures is likely to result in rising sea levels from the melting of the Greenland ice sheet and from the thermal expansion of sea water. A rise in the world's sea levels of approximately 50 centimeters, which is possible during the coming decades, would wreak havoc with the low-lying coastal areas that are home to a substantial proportion of the world's population. According to some projections, many

---

[17]   *Id.,* Art. 1(1).

[18]   *See* STATE OF THE WORLD 2001, 168 (L. BROWN ET AL. eds. 2001).

[19]   IPCC, Third Assessment Review: Climate Change 2001, Impacts, Adaptation, and Vulnerability (2001).

small islands would be submerged or become unsafe[20] and huge areas of heavily-populated countries such as Bangladesh or Indonesia could become partly uninhabitable. Louisiana has already lost significant amounts of coastal land because of a recent rise in the Gulf of Mexico, with New Orleans itself at risk for the future. According to one estimate, approximately five million square kilometers may be threatened by the year 2075, an area that represents three percent of the world's land mass, one-third of global cropland and home to a billion people.

Climate change also would modify the world's agriculture: some areas would become arid, while other regions that are presently too cold would become able to grow cereals, corn or fruit and other products needing a warmer climate. Increased water temperatures would disrupt aquatic ecosystems and further burden already distressed fisheries. A particularly sinister consequence of global climate change is the multiplication of violent weather patterns, including severe drought, tropical storms, hurricanes, unusually heavy rainfalls, and the consequential floods and landslides. In addition, a slight rise in average annual air temperature could greatly increase the risk of insect outbreaks. Insects represent more than half of the nearly two million identified living species on earth. Warmer weather speeds up insect metabolism, making them grow more quickly, breed more frequently and migrate sooner and further. Tropical diseases carried by pests and micro-organisms, including malaria and dengue fever, may become widely endemic throughout new areas.

The global warming issue exemplifies the ecological principle that all activity in an ecosystem is interrelated and interdependent. In addition to industrial and motor vehicle emissions from developed countries, a large part of global warming results from agricultural and resource activities in developing countries. Tropical deforestation is a serious problem that concerns more than loss of renewable resources and biological diversity; two aspects of deforestation contribute significantly to global warming. First, much of the deforestation that occurs in tropical countries results from land-clearing for agriculture. Soils in most tropical countries are so poor that they cannot sustain crops for more than one or two seasons. The farmers then move and clear still more forest, typically by means of the "slash and burn" technique. The trees are chopped down or bulldozed, followed by the burning of all the native vegetation and the unuseable wood that remains. Industrialized logging practices increase the destruction through burning large areas to clear roads; in 1997 and 2001, forest fires in Indonesia created a thick layer of smoke that covered a large part of South-East Asia. The problem and its aftermath are discussed later in Section B.2.

Unsustainable exploitation of tropical forests also contributes to the greenhouse effects. Forests and oceans are natural "sinks" that remove

---

[20]   *See* 27 E.P.L. 58 (1997).

greenhouse gases by absorbing carbon dioxide, although it is difficult to know the exact proportion of such absorption. Deforestation hinders the process and thus enhances global warming. The greenhouse effect can also be slowed down by the storage of greenhouse gases by components of the climate system which then constitute "reservoirs."

B. International Efforts to Control Air Pollution

1. Initial Legal Approaches

Although air pollution was traditionally considered as a local problem, the leading early case in international environmental law concerns transfrontier pollution caused by fumes. The pollution resulted from the activities of a smelter, located in Trail, Canada, and the resulting dispute was decided by an arbitral award, 1941.[21] Fumes from the smelter damaged agricultural lands in the United States by releasing into the air up to 350 tons daily of sulfurous smoke beginning in 1896. Some victims were indemnified, but in 1925 it became necessary to undertake a collective action. Two years later, the United States government officially began negotiations with Canada, resulting in an agreement to submit the dispute to an international arbitral tribunal. The latter delivered its final judgment on March 11, 1941, concluding that

> under the principles of international law . . . no State has the right to use or permit the use of its territory in such a manner as to cause injury by fumes in or to the territory of another or the properties or persons therein, when the case is of serious consequence and the injury is established by clear and convincing evidence.[22]

The first international regulations addressing air pollution were aimed at resolving a different problem. In 1958 the Economic Commission for Europe of the United Nations sought to facilitate international trade by establishing uniform standards for automobile equipment and parts, today accepted in all European countries. Several of the measures adopted aimed at creating "cleaner" exhaust by imposing engine standards concerning carbon monoxide (CO), nitrous oxides, and unburned gasoline emissions.[23]

---

21   3 U.N. RIAA 1938, 1965 (1949).

22   *Id.* at 1965.

23   Regulations 15, 24, 47, and 49 annexed to the Geneva Accord of March 20, 1958; affirmed by EC Directive 70/220, Mar. 20, 1970, O.J. L 76 (4/6/70). Regulation 15 concerns the Approval of Vehicle Equipment with a Positive-Ignition Engine with regard to Emission of Gaseous Pollutants by the Engine; Regulation 20 concerns the Approval of Vehicles Equipped with Diesel Engines

The Council of Europe took a major step forward when it adopted a regional Declaration of Principles on Air Pollution Control, on March 8, 1968.[24] The text sets forth very general but still relevant principles such as the demand that national legislation should require contributors to air pollution to reduce the pollution. Regulations applying one or more methods should be based on the principle of prevention, which may differ according to the nature of the source of pollution. In the first method, fixed installations capable of causing a significant increase in air pollution should be subject to individual authorization specifying the conditions of construction and operations in order to limit emissions. Installations not presenting a risk of significantly increasing air pollution may be the object of general operational specifications if the density of such operations may provoke a significant concentration of pollutants in the neighborhood. Finally, motor vehicles and mass-produced fuel-burning appliances should be subject to general provisions. The Declaration takes into account urbanization and regional growth: planning for urban and industrial development should consider the effect of development on air pollution.

During the same year, WMO established a global network to monitor atmospheric chemical components related to climate change and environmental issues. Today, the Background Air Pollution Monitoring Network (BAPMON) comprises more than 200 stations measuring the atmospheric content of a variety of chemical pollutants including carbon dioxide, sulfate, and nitrogen oxides. It receives support from UNEP through the Global Environment Monitoring System (GEMS).

OECD first adopted a strategy of proposing rules for controlling the emission of specified pollutants, then in 1974 recommended measures for "further air pollution control."[25] It simultaneously adopted guidelines for action to reduce emission of sulfur oxides and particulates from stationary fuel combustion sources. The following step was the adoption of a recommendation on the control of air pollution from fossil fuel combustion.[26] The annex to this recommendation proposed guiding principles such as the development of innovative regulatory schemes to improve efficiency or flexibility of compliance while achieving existing emission control regulations; regulations to ensure availability and use of clean fuels or against use of polluting fuels where emission controls are not usually feasible (*e.g.*, small central heating boilers); the implementation of emission standards by an effective program of control measures for large stationary installations; and

---

with regard to the Emission of Pollutants by the Engine; Regulation 47 the Approval of Mopeds Equipped with a Positive Ignition Engine with regard to the Emission of Gaseous Pollutants by the Engine.

[24] Resolution (68)4.
[25] OECD Resolution of Nov. 14,1974, C(74)219.
[26] OECD Guidelines, adopted June 20, 1985, C(85)101.

incentives (tax, investment, loan or grant) for timely retirement of modernization of older, more polluting installations.

2. International Treaties to Combat Air Pollution

There are few global rules concerning air quality. The first binding rules of a global nature concerning atmospheric pollution are found, perhaps unexpectedly, in UNCLOS (December 10, 1982). According to Article 212, states must adopt laws and regulations to prevent, reduce and control pollution of the marine environment from or through the atmosphere. The laws and regulations should apply to the states' airspace, and to vessels and aircraft flying their flag or under their registry. States also must take other measures as necessary to prevent, reduce and control such pollution. On the international level, they must endeavor to establish global and regional rules and procedures. Within the limits of their jurisdiction, they must enforce the laws and regulations they adopt.[27]

Significant progress in air pollution control has been achieved at the regional level, primarily within Europe. The Final Act of the Helsinki Conference on Security and Cooperation in Europe (August 1, 1975) gave the UNECE the task of preparing an international treaty concerning air pollution, which became the Geneva Convention on Long-Range Transboundary Air Pollution (LRTAP).[28] Adopted on November 13, 1979, by all European states as well as U.S. and Canada, the Geneva Convention is a framework treaty. It is primarily concerned with cooperation and its character is essentially programmatic; it contains almost no precise rule aimed at reducing air pollution which could be implemented as such. The definition given to long-range transboundary air pollution suggests why there are difficulties in developing legal techniques to achieve results in this field:

> Long-range transboundary air pollution means air pollution whose physical origin is situated wholly or in part within the area under the national jurisdiction of one State and which has adverse effects in the area under the jurisdiction of another State at such a distance that it is not generally possible to distinguish the contribution of individual emission sources or groups of sources.

Obviously, this definition excludes any idea of individual responsibility of the polluter because that person or entity cannot be identified.

---

[27]   Art. 222.
[28]   Geneva, Nov. 13, 1979.

The general obligation of the states parties is to protect humans and the environment against air pollution, and to endeavor to limit and, as far as possible, gradually reduce and prevent it (Art. 2). The article is cautiously drafted and includes no duty to limit pollution to a given level. The parties are to develop policies and strategies to serve as a means of combating the discharge of air pollutants, using the best available, economically feasible technology. They are also to exchange information concerning national policies, scientific activities, and technical measures aimed at combating the risks of pollution. The principle of consultation is an important element of the Convention. According to the terms of Article 5, consultations shall be held at an early stage between contracting parties that are affected by or exposed to a significant risk of long-range transboundary air pollution and parties within which and subject to whose jurisdiction a significant contribution to this pollution originates or could originate in connection with activities carried on or contemplated therein.

More systematic cooperation is called for in Article 7 of the Convention, primarily concerning the conduct of research and/or development in areas of science and nature, but also with regard to economic, social and ecological assessment of measures that might be envisaged and the elaboration of teaching and training programs concerning pollution. Article 9 provides for implementing a cooperative program for monitoring and evaluating long-range transmission of air pollutants in Europe, including continuous monitoring of sulfur dioxide and related substances not only in the air, but in other media such as water, soil and vegetation, utilizing comparable or standardized procedures, and establishing a monitoring program and exchange of data on emissions.

The main organ of the Convention, called the Executive Body, consists of representatives of the contracting states, within the framework of the Senior Advisers to the ECE Governments on Environmental Problems. This organ meets at least once annually to review the implementation of the Convention. By decision 1997/2 the Executive Body established an Implementation Committee to carry out such reviews and report to the parties. The Executive Secretary of UNECE provides the Secretariat.

A cooperative program for monitoring and evaluating the long-range transmission of air pollutants in Europe (EMEP)[29] provides a framework for fulfilling the Convention's obligations. Notably, when the Convention was signed, EC member states participating in the conference adopted a resolution deciding to provisionally apply the Convention and to execute

---

[29]   Protocol to the 1979 Convention on Long-Range Transboundary Air Pollution on Long-Term Financing of the Cooperative Programme for Monitoring and Evaluation of the Long-Range Transport of Air Pollutants in Europe (EMEP) (Geneva, Sept. 28, 1984).

as fully as possible the obligations it contained.[30] Thus, EMEP was initiated rather rapidly for the observation and study of long-range air pollution. In a relatively short time, a bank of more than 90 monitoring stations was set up in 24 countries. States parties submitted documents to the UNECE indicating numerous other national measures as well, including the establishment of licensing systems for polluting activities, adoption of stricter emission and quality standards, energy conservation, and controls on lead and nitrous oxide emissions from motor vehicles.

Regulatory priority has been given to the reduction of sulfur emissions. In 1984, ten states, meeting at a ministerial conference in Ottawa, agreed to reduce the 1980 emission levels of sulfurous substances by at least 30 percent by 1990. A protocol to this effect was adopted by 21 countries July 8, 1985, in Helsinki,[31] becoming the first international treaty to contain precise and verifiable objectives to combat air pollution. It entered into force on September 2, 1987. The Protocol required states to reduce their national sulfur emissions by at least 30 percent as soon as possible and at the latest by 1993, using 1980 levels as the basis for calculation. Implementation is controlled by EMEP utilizing its monitoring system and by state reporting on national annual sulfur emissions and the basis on which they have been calculated.

By 1986, ten countries had already achieved the 30-percent reduction. It appeared, however, that the reductions were counterbalanced by sulfur increases in countries not party to the Protocol. Rio Conference Agenda 21 included as a topic for future action the control of transboundary atmospheric pollution.[32] Conforming to this aim and drawing upon the principles of the Rio Declaration, the parties to the Geneva Convention adopted a new Protocol on Further Reduction on Sulfur Emissions.[33] The preamble of the instrument refers to the precautionary principle and expresses a new preoccupation in stating that measures to control emissions of sulfur and other air pollutants should also contribute to protecting the sensitive Arctic environment.

The main obligation of the parties is to ensure, as far as possible without entailing excessive costs, that the presence or deposition of oxidized sulfur compounds in the long term do not exceed critical loads for sulfur represented on a map of Europe in Annex I (Art. 2(1)). This new approach is more flexible, but also more technical, than attacking the problem by limiting emissions. Article 1 of the Protocol defines critical sulfur deposition and critical load. The first is a quantitative estimate of the exposure to oxidized sulfur compounds, below which significant harmful effects on speci-

---

[30]   For the text of the resolution, *see* O.J. L 171 (6/27/81).
[31]   July 8, 1985.
[32]   U.N. Doc. A/CONF.151/26 Nr. 9.1–9.35.
[33]   Oslo, June 14, 1994.

fied sensitive elements of the environment do not occur, according to present knowledge. Critical load is a quantitative estimate of an exposure to one or more pollutants below which significant harmful effects on specified sensitive elements of the environment do not occur, according to present knowledge. Annex I presents a table that shows the critical sulfur depositions for different zones of Europe.

Emissions limits have not been abandoned, however. As a first and minimum step, the parties agreed to reduce and maintain their annual sulfur emissions in accordance with the timing and levels specified in Annex II. The Annex specifies the obligations of each of the 29 contracting states and the European Union, with a table determining the emission levels in 1980 and in 1990, the sulfur emission ceilings per year in 2000, in 2005 and in 2010 and the percentage emission reductions in 2000, 2005 and 2010 taking as a base year 1980. The greatest burden is imposed on the United Kingdom which must reduce its emissions calculated on the base year of 1980 by 50 percent by 2000, 70 percent by 2005 and 80 percent by 2010. In contrast, Greece could keep the level of its 1980 emissions to 2000 and should reduce it only by 3 percent in 2005 and 4 percent by 2010. Annex III designates Southeast Canada a Sulfur Oxides Management Area (SOMA), where annual sulfur emissions at a minimum shall be reduced and maintained according to the timing and levels specified in Annex II. This means that different sulfur emission ceilings were fixed for Canada in general and for the SOMA which is a part of its territory.

Article 2(4) lists the most effective measures for the reduction of sulfur emissions, for new and existing sources. The measures include increasing energy efficiency, utilizing renewable energy, reducing the sulfur content of particular fuels, and applying the best available technology not entailing excessive cost. Annex V lists emission limit values for major stationary sources, while Annex IV proposes control technologies for sulfur emissions from stationary sources.

Several articles of the Protocol show the evolution of the treaty system to more developed regulation, in particular those provisions that apply new legal techniques aimed at ensuring compliance with environmental treaty obligations. The provisions stress the importance of the Executive Body established by the Geneva Convention. In particular, the Protocol requires that each party periodically report to this body on its implementation measures to control and reduce sulfur emissions and on the levels of national annual sulfur emissions. Moreover, the Implementation Committee reports to the parties at sessions of the Executive Body and may make recommendations. The parties, after considering the report and any recommendations made by the Implementation Committee, may decide upon and call for action to bring about full compliance with the Protocol, including measures to assist a party's compliance with the Protocol.

The problem of nitrogen oxides has been more difficult to solve, not only because, as Russia has pointed out, these substances originally were not mentioned by the Convention, but also because a principal source of this pollution is motor vehicles, a politically-sensitive issue in many countries as the Kyoto Protocol has further evidenced. Nonetheless, in the wake of Community directives and alarming reports by EMEP, the parties signed a Protocol on October 31, 1988[34] calling for the reduction of emissions and transboundary fluxes of nitrogen oxides (NO_x) from fixed or mobile sources, with the aim of stabilizing them at the 1987 level by the year 1995. The agreement entered into force on February 14, 1991. Twelve of the 25 signatory states also made a Declaration undertaking to reduce NO_x emissions by at least 30 percent by 1998, as compared with any year between 1980 and 1986.

A fourth Protocol Concerning the Control of Emissions of Volatile Organic Compounds (VOC) or their Transboundary Fluxes was signed in Geneva on November 18, 1991.[35] In the presence of sunlight, VOCs react with nitrogen oxides to form ground-level ozone, which is harmful to health and the environment. The Protocol generally obliges the parties to control and reduce their emissions of VOCs in order to reduce their transboundary fluxes and the fluxes of the resulting secondary photochemical oxidant products (Art. 2(1)). The aim can be achieved in two ways. The first option is to reduce national annual emissions of VOCs by at least 30 percent by the year 1999, using 1988 levels as a baseline or any annual level during the period 1984 to 1990. The second method can be used by countries whose VOC emissions causing transfrontier pollution originate only from specified areas. These areas, called Tropospheric Ozone Management areas (TOMAS), are designated in Annex I to the Protocol. Two are found in Canada and one exists in Norway. Annual emissions in TOMAS also must be reduced by at least 30 percent but, in addition, the total national annual emissions of the countries who designate TOMAS were not to exceed the 1988 levels by the year 1999. An exception was foreseen for Central and Eastern European countries with economies in transition: no reduction of their emissions of VOCs was required immediately, but they had to ensure that their emissions did not exceed the 1988 levels by the end of 1999 (Art. 2(2)(c)).

The Protocol specifies incremental obligations. No less than two years after the entry into force of the instrument, the parties were to apply emission standards to new stationary sources and to new mobile sources, in each

---

[34]   Protocol Concerning Control of Emissions of Nitrogen Oxides or their Transboundary Fluxes (Sofia, Oct. 31, 1988).

[35]   Protocol to the 1979 Convention on Long-Range Transboundary Air Pollution Concerning the Control of Emissions of Volatile Organic Compounds or Their Transboundary Fluxes (Geneva, Nov. 18, 1991).

case using control measures foreseen in Protocol Annex II (Art. 2(3)). The same techniques should apply in those areas in which national or international tropospheric ozone standards were exceeded or where transboundary flux originated.

Each party has to foster public participation in emission control programs through public announcements, encouraging the best use of all modes of transportation, and promoting traffic management schemes (Art. 2(3)(a)(iv)). A mechanism for monitoring compliance is foreseen (Art. 3(3)) and the parties must report annually on national programs, policies and strategies, and on progress in applying national or international emission standards and control techniques (Art. 8). Finally, the Protocol foresees negotiations on further steps to reduce VOC emissions and proposes a work program in this regard (respectively Art. 2(6) and (7)).

A Meeting of the European Ministers for Environment held in Aarhus in June 1998 adopted two further protocols to the 1979 Geneva Convention. First, the Protocol on Persistent Organic Pollutants[36] (POPs) addresses pollutants that resist degradation under natural conditions and have been associated with adverse effects on human health and the environment. POPs can biomagnify in upper trophic levels to concentrations that could affect the health of exposed wildlife and humans. The Arctic ecosystems and especially its indigenous people, who subsist on Arctic fish and mammals, are particularly at risk. Article 3 lists the basic obligations of the contracting parties: eliminate the production and use of the substances listed in Annex I and ensure that the destruction or disposal is undertaken domestically in an environmentally sound manner.[37] Each party also shall reduce its total emissions of each of the substances listed in Annex III, shall adopt limit values at least as stringent as those specified in Annex IV for each existing stationary source,[38] and shall take effective measures to control emissions from mobile sources. Eight highly technical Annexes treat in detail the substances scheduled for elimination, substances scheduled for restrictions on use, limit values for emissions from stationary sources, and the best available techniques to control emissions of persistent organic pollutants from such sources.

A parallel Protocol to the Convention on Long-Range Transboundary Air Pollution on Heavy Metals,[39] adopted the same day as the POPs Protocol,

---

[36] Aarhus, June 24, 1998.

[37] The terms waste, waste disposal, and environmentally sound are to be interpreted in a manner consistent with the use of those terms in the 1989 Convention on the Control of Transboundary Movements of Hazardous Wastes and their Disposal (Basel, Mar. 22, 1989). *See* Chapter 13B.2.

[38] A fixed stationary source, according to Art. 1(10) is "any fixed building, structure, facility, installation or equipment that emits or may emit any persistent organic pollutant directly or indirectly into the atmosphere."

[39] Aarhus, June 24, 1998.

contains many corresponding provisions. Each party commits itself to reduce its total annual emissions into the atmosphere of each of the heavy metals listed in Annex I, applying the best available techniques (Annex III). Limit values are specified for the listed stationary sources of emission (Annexes V and II). Other regulations provide for product control measures and product management measures (Annexes VI and VII).

The parties to the 1979 Convention adopted a further Protocol in Gothenburg on November 30, 1999 in order to apply a multi-effect, multi-pollutant approach to prevent or minimize exceeding critical loads and levels.[40] This Protocol is the first agreement under the Convention to deal specifically with reducing nitrogen compounds. According to Article 2, the objective of the Protocol is to control and reduce emissions of sulphur, nitrogen oxides, ammonia and volatile organic compounds that are caused by anthropogenic activities and are likely to cause adverse effects on human health, natural ecosystems, materials and crops. For most parties the critical loads of acidity, nutrient nitrogen, and ozone are described in Annex I to the Protocol. Article 3 specifies that each party having an emission ceiling in a table in Annex I shall reduce and maintain the reduction in its annual emissions in accordance with that ceiling and the timetable specified in that Annex. Specific limit values are applied to stationary sources under specified conditions (Annexes IV to VII). Annex VIII establishes the limit values for fuels and new mobile sources while Annex IX foresees ammonia control measures. States parties are to promote public awareness by giving information to the general public on annual emissions, deposits and concentrations of the relevant pollutants, as well as strategies and measures applied or to be applied and means to minimize emissions.[41] Each party shall report on a periodic basis information on the measures that it has taken to implement the Protocol as well as on levels of emissions of the substances to be controlled.[42] The Implementation Committee established by a 1997 decision of the Executive Body for the 1979 Convention reviews the information supplied by the parties, the data on the effects of concentrations and depositions of specifical pollutants. Reviews shall take into account the best scientific information on the effects of such pollutants (Art. 10).

The protocols demonstrate the aptitude of the treaty system established by the 1979 LRTAP Convention to evolve and develop new techniques. They are also a good example of the permanent negotiations carried on through the conferences of the parties, which have become a necessary part of inter-

---

[40] Protocol to Abate Acidification, Eutrophication and Ground-Level Ozone (Gothenburg, Nov. 30, 1999).

[41] Art. 5.

[42] Art. 7.

national environmental law. Finally, they show the increasing place of detailed technical approaches to international environmental protection.

Outside the region of the LRTAP Convention system, in the closing years of the 20th century, forest fires devastated Brunei and Indonesia, producing a heavy haze that polluted the atmosphere and caused serious health problems not only in the originating countries but also in Malaysia, Myanmar, Singapore and Thailand. In 1997, in response to the problem, ASEAN adopted a Regional Haze Action Plan followed in 2002 by an Agreement on Transboundary Haze Pollution.[43]

The Agreement defines haze pollution as smoke resulting from land and/or forest fire which causes deleterious effects of such a nature as to endanger human health, harm living resources, ecosystems and material property, and impair or interfere with amenities and other legitimate uses of the environment. The Agreement aims at preventing and monitoring such pollution which should be mitigated through concerted national efforts and intensified regional and international cooperation.[44] To that effect, precautionary and preventive measures should be taken, when necessary by developing and implementing international measures aiming at controlling sources of fires, identifying fires, creating monitoring, assessment and early warning systems, exchanging information and technology and providing mutual assistance.[45] The parties shall take appropriate measures to monitor all fire prone areas, land and/or forest fires, the environmental conditions conducive to such fires and haze pollution arising from them[46] as well as the necessary preventive measures.[47] Technical cooperation should include relevant training, education and awareness-raising campaigns, in particular relating to the promotion of zero-burning practices and raising awareness of the impact of haze pollution on human health and the environment. Markets should be developed for the utilization of biomass and appropriate methods developed to treat agricultural wastes.[48]

An ASEAN Coordinating Center for Transboundary Haze Pollution Control works on the basis that the national authorities will act first to put out the fires. If a party needs assistance in the event of land and/or forest fires or haze pollution arising from such fires within its territory, it may request such assistance from any other party, directly or through the ASEAN Center.[49] Unless otherwise agreed, the requesting party shall exercise the overall direction, control, coordination and supervision of the assistance

---

[43]   Kuala Lumpur, June 10, 2002.
[44]   Art. 2.
[45]   Art. 4.
[46]   Art. 7.
[47]   Art. 9.
[48]   Art. 16.
[49]   Art. 12.

within its territory. It shall provide, to the extent possible, local facilities and services for the proper and effective administration of the assistance and ensure the protection of personnel, equipment and materials brought into its territory by or on behalf of the assisting party for such purposes.[50] The requesting or receiving party shall accord to personnel of the assisting Party the necessary exemptions and facilities for the performance of their functions.

In bilateral relations, systematic cooperation between Canada and the United States has existed since the January 11, 1909, Treaty Respecting Boundary Waters Between the United States and Canada[51] which created the International Joint Commission for the protection of boundary waters. The Commission has been invoked in several instances of air pollution, notably in the *Trail Smelter* case. In 1978, the two states established a bilateral research group on the long-range transport of atmospheric pollutants. On August 5, 1980, a memorandum of intent was signed in Washington,[52] establishing joint working groups to prepare a formal agreement. At the same time the memorandum called for national measures and a procedure for notification and consultation in regard to projected activities which could cause significant increases in air pollution. The two countries concluded a special agreement in Ottawa, August 23, 1983, concerning research into the effects of weather on long-range transboundary air pollution.[53] Subsequently, the Great Lakes Water Quality Agreement was amended to include air pollution among the regulated subjects. Finally, on March 13, 1991, the two countries signed an Agreement on Air Quality[54] whose general objective is to control transboundary air pollution. They commit themselves to establish specific objectives for emission limitations or reductions of specific air pollutants (Art. 4). Annex I sets such objectives for sulfur dioxide and nitrogen oxides separately and differently for the U.S. and for Canada.

The Agreement applies customary environmental law rules, such as the prior assessment of proposed actions, activities, and projects if they are likely to cause significant transboundary air pollution, the duty to notify the other state concerning such activities or projects as well as those that create a potential risk of significant transboundary harm, and to consult on request of the other party. Consultation also can be sought if changes to laws, reg-

---

[50]   Art. 13.

[51]   36 Stat. 2448, T.S. No 548; U.N. Doc. ST/LEG/SER.B12.261.

[52]   Memorandum of Intent between Canada and the United States Concerning Transboundary Air Pollution (Aug. 5, 1980).

[53]   Memorandum of Understanding between Canada and the United States on the Cross Appalachian Tracer Experiment (Aug. 23, 1983), 22 I.L.M. 1017 (1983).

[54]   30 I.L.M. 676 (1991).

ulations, or policies of a party are foreseen. Pursuant to the agreement, the International Joint Commission has oversight of a permanent bilateral Air Quality Committee which is to report on the progress of the parties in meeting the specific objectives of the agreement. The process involves soliciting public comments on the report and recommendations to the parties.[55]

3. Legislation of the European Union

The European Union, as it has evolved from the Common Market and the European Community, adopted three types of legislation concerning air pollution. Several directives have a general scope, others concern specific forms and sources of pollution, and the third establishes ambient air quality objectives.

Following the "discovery" at the beginning of the 1980s of damage to the forests of Central Europe, the EC adopted a general directive relating to air pollution produced by industrial installations.[56] This directive introduced the obligation to obtain specific authorization for new industrial installations that emit pollutants into the air, including energy (mines, oil refineries), production and working of metals and minerals, chemical industries, waste treatment, and certain paper mills. Authorities may not deliver licenses unless the enterprise has adopted appropriate measures to prevent air pollution and respects the limit values for emissions and air quality. The license should require utilization of the best available technology not involving excessive costs and, in addition, take into account existing value limits. Member states also are required to develop strategies and programs to progressively adapt existing industrial facilities to the requirements of the best available technology. Specially protected zones can be established. Demands for authorization and decisions of competent authorities should be placed before the affected public and environmental impact statements can be required. When pollution is capable of affecting other EC states, they should be informed and may request consultations.

Following the lead of this directive, the Council adopted, in 1988, a directive on installations of combustion of 50 megawatt or more.[57] Each new installation must respect the emission norms fixed by the directive for sulfur dioxide, particulates and nitrogen oxides. For existing plants, member states create and implement programs aimed at progressively reducing their annual emissions of these elements. The reductions in relation to 1980 and

---

[55]   The progress reports are publicly available. *See* <http://www.epa.gov/airmarkets>. In the 2000 report, both states reported emissions well below the allowable limits. See U.S.-Ca.

[56]   Directive 84/360, June 28, 1984, O.J. 1984 L 188 (7/16/84).

[57]   Directive 88/609, June 12, 1988, O.J. L 336 (7/12/88). *See also* Directive 2001/80, Oct. 23, 2001.

up to the year 2003 are indicated in absolute quantities and in percentages. Parallel directives provide for emission limit values for municipal waste-incineration plants[58] and for the incineration of hazardous wastes.[59] General EC directives, such as directive 85/337/EEC of June 27, 1985[60] concerning assessment of the effects of certain public and private projects, and the *Seveso* directive,[61] relating to the risks of major accidents of certain industrial activities, apply to activities that risk causing major air pollution.

In addition to efforts to reduce air pollution by directives of general scope, EC measures aim to reduce emissions from specific sources. Directive 70/220,[62] modified several times, concerns polluting emissions from automobiles; a 1975 directive fixed the limit of sulfur in diesel fuel;[63] another directive limited the amount of lead in gasoline.[64] These laws began by establishing uniform rules, but the directive relating to the sulfur content of diesel fuel introduced flexibility by providing that states should establish zones in which the permissible amount of sulfur differs according to local conditions.

Other environmental directives aimed at air pollution control establish quality objectives for the entire Community. Such objectives are fixed for sulfur dioxide and particulates,[65] lead,[66] and nitrogen dioxide.[67] Community legislation has evolved away from quality objectives, however, because adequate environmental protection is difficult to attain by this method. Recent directives show a preference for an "at source" approach that limits polluting emissions. This technique also has its limits, given that the notion of the "best available technology not involving excessive costs" is viewed in a different manner from one member state to another, so that a permanent coordination at the Community level is required to assure harmonized implementation.

Also within Europe, Directive 2002/3/EC of the European Parliament and of the Council of February 12, 2002[68] aims at controlling concentrations of ozone in ambient air in order to avoid, prevent or reduce harmful

---

[58]   Directives 89/369 and 89/429, O.J. L 163, at 32 (1989) and O.J. L 203, at 50 (1989), amended by Directive 2000/69 of Dec. 16, 2000.

[59]   Directive 94/67, O.J. L 365, at 34 (1994).

[60]   O.J. L 175 (7/5/85).

[61]   82/501/EEC June 24, 1982, O.J. L 230 (8/5/82), *modified by* Directive 87/216, Mar. 19, 1987, O.J. L. 85 (3/28/87).

[62]   Directive 70/220, O.J. L 76, at 1 (1970).

[63]   Directive 75/116, O.J. L 307, at 22 (1975).

[64]   Directive 78/611, Feb. 20, 1978, O.J. L 197, at 19 (1978).

[65]   Directive 80/779, O.J. L 229, at 30 (1980).

[66]   Directive 82/884, O.J. L 378, at 15 (1980).

[67]   Directive 85/203, O.J. L 87, at 1 (1985).

[68]   O.J. L 67 (3/9/02).

effects on human health and the environment. It sets target values for 2010 in respect to such concentrations, invites states to draw up a list of zones and regions in which ozone levels meet the long-term objectives. Where ozone concentrations exceeding target values or long-term objectives are due to precursor emissions in other states, joint plans and programs shall be drawn up in order to attain the target values or long-term objectives. If appropriate, member states shall prepare and implement short-term joint action plans covering transboundary neighbouring zones.

C. Protection of the Ozone Layer

The discovery that widely-used chemical substances were destroying stratospheric ozone induced a number of countries in the early 1980s to ban the use of CFCs for aerosol sprays. At the same time, their general use made it obvious that the problem could not be solved unilaterally or even regionally. Thus, UNEP made protection of stratospheric ozone a priority item in its legal action plan and after several years of effort, succeeded in negotiating the Convention for the Protection of the Ozone Layer.[69]

The treaty is a framework convention, providing the basis for systematic cooperation among the states parties respecting protection of stratospheric ozone. The general obligation of states parties is to take appropriate measures to protect human health and the environment against adverse effects resulting or likely to result from human activities that modify or are likely to modify the ozone layer (Art. 2). Annex I of the Convention details the duty to cooperate in research and scientific assessments, set out in Article 3. Article 4 and Annex II require cooperation in the legal, scientific and technical fields, including the exchange of information. The parties define the information to exchange through their regular meetings in conferences (Art. 6 and Annex II) within the boundaries of the Convention, which recognizes the need to protect intellectual property rights. States parties generally are to make known their laws, their national administrative measures and legal research relevant to protection of the ozone layer, as well as relevant methods and terms of licensing and availability of patents.

According to Convention Article 8, the Conference of the Parties may adopt protocols to the Convention. Two months after the conclusion of the Vienna Convention, a British Antarctic Survey team published its findings indicating a 40 percent loss of stratospheric ozone over Antarctica. This ozone "hole" stimulated UNEP and the World Meteorological Organization to issue a comprehensive international assessment, which concluded that CFC production trends would lead to dangerous ozone depletion. A subsequent meeting of the parties to the Vienna Convention adopted the

---

[69]   Vienna, Mar. 22, 1985.

Montreal Protocol on Substances that Deplete the Ozone Layer.[70] At the time the Protocol was adopted, scientific uncertainty remained about global ozone loss and increases in UV radiation reaching the earth. The action taken in adopting the Protocol thus represents the first significant application of the precautionary principle.

The Montreal Protocol foresees the control of various forms of chlorofluorocarbons and halons, and their progressive elimination. Industrial countries agreed to cut production and use of CFCs in half by 1998, and by 1992 to freeze production and use of halons.[71] Countries with an annual consumption of CFCs under 0.3 kilograms per capita, which were mainly developing countries, were given a ten-year period to comply. The Protocol also restricted trade between states parties and non-parties, addressing the "free rider" problem.

The Montreal Protocol came into force on January 1, 1989. The parties to it have met regularly, as foreseen by the agreement. At the first meeting, (Helsinki, May 1989), new information indicated that ozone losses were two to three times more severe than had been predicted. Participating states thus adopted a declaration that called for accelerating the phase-out of substances that destroy stratospheric ozone. The meeting also initiated a major revision of the Montreal Protocol.[72]

The second meeting (London, June 1990) considerably tightened the reduction schedule, again in light of scientific findings: it decided on new and shorter deadlines for the complete phaseout of substances. This made even more necessary the effective participation of all significant producers and consumers of ozone depleting substances, in particular countries like China, Brazil and India. In a breakthrough, the London amendments endorsed a financial mechanism and an interim international fund consisting of voluntary contributions from the industrialized nations in order to assist developing countries in meeting the costs of compliance with the Convention and Protocols. For the first time an international environmental treaty called for financial transfers from industrialized to developing countries.[73]

The Fourth Meeting of the Parties (Copenhagen, November 1992) completed the task of adapting the Montreal Protocol and of making it operational.[74] The meeting advanced the phase-out dates for industrial countries to 1994 for halons and to 1996 for CFCs, methyl chloroform, and carbon tetrachloride. It also took up the question of hydrochlorofluorocarbons (HCFCs), a proposed substitute for CFCs that is still ozone-deplet-

---

[70]   Montreal, Sept. 16, 1987.
[71]   Halons are a bromine-containing chemical used in fire-fighting.
[72]   WESTON V.E.14.
[73]   WESTON V.E.17.
[74]   WESTON V.E.20.

ing but less so than CFCs. The agreement called for their complete phase-out by 2030. A 1995 meeting in Vienna[75] added a phase-out for methyl bromide, to the year 2010 for industrial countries. The meeting also strengthened requirements for industrialized country use of HCFCs, and added a complete phase-out by 2040 for developing countries. Subsequently in the San José, Costa Rica, meeting held from November 18–27, 1996,[76] the states parties adopted new reduction schedules for a number of ozone-depleting substances as well as decisions on illegal trade in such substances and on financial issues.

With the various actions taken by the states parties, the 1985 Vienna Convention for the Protection of the Ozone Layer has grown into an international treaty system composed of the Convention itself, the Montreal Protocol, and its amendments (London 1990, Copenhagen 1992, Vienna, 1995, San Jose 1996, Beijing, 1999). It is managed by the Conference of the Parties to the Vienna Convention, the Meeting of the Parties to the Montreal Protocol, a Financial Mechanism,[77] and a secretariat. The Ninth Meeting of the Parties (Montreal, September 15–17, 1997) further strengthened control measures and dealt with improving treaty implementation compliance.[78]

The control measures on ozone depleting substances applying to industrialized countries adopted until 2002 are the following:

— CFCs 11,12,113,114,115 which originally were to be reduced by 50 percent in 1998 were phased out in 1996;
— Halons 1211, 1301, 2402 were phased out in 1994 (instead of 2000);
— Ten other CFCs were phased out in 1996 (instead of 2000);
— Carbon tetrachloride was phased out in 1996 (instead of 2000);
— Methyl chloroform was phased out in 1996 (instead of 2005);
— HCFC: in 2004 -35 percent; in 2010 -65 percent, in 2015 -90 percent; phased out in 2020;
— H-BCFCs were phased out in 1996;
— Methyl bromide use was frozen in 1995 and will be phased out in 2005.
— Bromochloromethane was banned as of 2002, except to the extent the parties decide to permit the level of production or consumption that is necessary to satisfy uses agreed by them to be essential.

An agreement reached in November 1998 provides for new reporting and use requirements for ozone-depleting chemicals used as inert solvents

---

[75]   26 E.P.L. 66 (1996).
[76]   27 E.P.L 86 (1997).
[77]   *See* Chapter 4.
[78]   27 E.P.L. 432 (1997).

in chemical manufacturing processes. The 10th COP to the Montreal Protocol held in Cairo adopted Decision X/14 which establishes a list of 25 applications (*e.g.*, use of CFC 12 for the manufacture of vaccine bottles) in which ozone-depleting substances may be used as process agents in the framework of emission limits determined on a country-by-country basis.[79] In addition to banning a new substance, the Beijing Amendments of 1999[80] strengthened compliance measures, in particular by requiring that as of January 1, 2004, each party prohibit the import and export of certain controlled substances listed in Annex C from any state not party to the Protocol. The Colombo annual meeting in 2001 emphasized compliance, with one-third of all decisions taken concerning the topic.[81] In addition, Decision XIII/5 concerns procedures for assessing the ozone-depleting potential of new substances. Parties are required to request private industry to pay the cost of a preliminary calculation of the ozone-depleting potential for new substances, a strong signal to industry.

The ozone regime is administered, in principle, by three Secretariats: one for the Vienna Convention, one for the Montreal Protocol and one for the Multilateral Fund. In fact, the two first are joined in a small body and all of them are affiliated with UNEP. The core of the international structure is the annual Meeting of the Parties to the Montreal Protocol which allows the participating states to decide collectively when there is a conflict concerning the interpretation of or the compliance with the treaty obligations accepted. The main organ of the Fund is an Executive Committee of 14 members of whom seven are selected by the group of developing country states parties to the Protocol and seven others by the industrialized states. It develops and monitors the implementation of specific operational policies, guidelines, and administrative arrangements, including the disbursement of resources; develops the plan and the budget for the Fund, as well as criteria for project eligibility; and approves, where appropriate, country programs for compliance with the Protocol. Decisions are taken by consensus; a two-third majority of the parties present and voting, including majority of both groups is needed. One of the most interesting features of the Financial Mechanism is the non-compliance procedure, established by annex IV of Decision IV/18, and discussed in detail in Chapter 4F.

---

[79]   21 INT'L ENVTL. REP. 1153 and 1210 (1998).

[80]   The Beijing Amendment, in force Feb. 2002, is contained in Annex V of the Report of the Eleventh Meeting of the Parties to the Montreal Protocol on Substances that Deplete the Ozone Layer.

[81]   In conformity with the objectives of the ozone treaty system, a European Community regulation aimed at protecting the stratospheric ozone layer progressively reduces the production and consumption of CFCs in the Community. Regulation 3322/88, O.J. L 297, at 1 (1988).

Unless effectively halted, illegal trade in ozone-depleting substances could undermine the Montreal Protocol's key achievements. While the consumption of ozone-depleting substances has been greatest in Europe and in North America in the past, the fastest growing use has been in developing countries. Estimates of the amount of the illegal trade vary, but the chemical industry suggests that as much as 20 percent of the CFCs in use worldwide are illegally traded.[82] In the United States, more than 450 tons of illegal CFCs have been seized.[83] NGOs have recommended that developing countries be given greater funding to assist with the accelerated phase-out of harmful substances. An amendment to the Montreal Protocol[84] aims at remedying the situation, at least in part. It requires that when, after the phase-out date applicable to it for a controlled substance, a party is unable, despite having taken all practicable steps to comply with its obligation under the Montreal Protocol, to cease production of that substance for domestic consumption, other than for uses agreed by the parties to be essential, it shall ban the export of used, recycled and reclaimed quantities of that substance, other than for the purpose of destruction. As a complementary measure, by January 1, 2000, each party had to establish and implement a system for licensing the import and export of new, used, recycled and reclaimed controlled substances.

In spite of the problems, international efforts to protect the ozone layer have had substantial impact. By 1995, global production of the most significant ozone-depleting substances, the CFCs, was down 76 percent from the peak year of 1988. Several countries and regions advanced beyond the agreements. The EU announced that it will phase out HCFCs by 2015, 15 years before it is legally required to do so. The U.S. Clean Air Act mandates phase-out of methyl bromide nine years ahead of the Protocol requirements. Other countries similarly have accelerated their compliance. Although the task is not complete, the international community has responded clearly to the issue. What may be important for the future is to ensure compatibility between the ozone and climate change regimes, as several substitutes for ozone depleting substances are greenhouse gases.

The Implementation Plan of the 2002 WSSD in Johannesburg, paragraph 37, agreed to enhance cooperation in the field of air pollution and ozone depletion. States agreed to take actions to facilitate implementation of the Montreal Protocol by ensuring adequate replenishment of the Multilateral Fund by 2003/2005 and to further support the regime for

---

[82] J. Vallette, *Deadly Complacency: US CFC Production, the Black Market, and Ozone Depletion*, OZONE ACTION (Sept. 1995); D. BRACK, INTERNATIONAL TRADE AND THE MONTREAL PROTOCOL n. 17 (1996).

[83] H. French, *Learning from the Ozone Experience*, STATE OF THE WORLD 1997, at 151 (1997).

[84] *Adopted* Sept. 17, 1997. EMuT 985:22/D.

protection of the ozone layer established by the convention system. They pledged to improve access by developing countries to alternatives to ozone-depleting substances by 2010 and assist them in complying with the phase-out schedule under the Montreal Protocol. In a significant phrase, the WSSD text recognizes the scientific and technical interrelationship between ozone depletion and climate change. Finally, participating states agreed to take measures to address illegal traffic in ozone-depleting substances.

D. Anthropogenic Climate Change

The first signs of international concern over climate change emerged in a series of international conferences on CO_2 between 1985 and 1987.[85] The rather disappointing results of these meetings led to an international Conference on the Atmosphere in Evolution and its Implications for the Safety of the Globe, held in Toronto from June 27 to 30, 1988.[86] At that time, UNEP joined its efforts with those of WMO and ICSU in order to study the scientific aspects of the problem. In November 1988, an Inter-governmental Panel on Climate Change (IPCC) was created, made up of scientific and political experts, and given the task of exploring possible measures to be taken in order to protect the atmosphere.

On December 6, 1988, the UN General Assembly adopted Resolution 43/53 on the conservation of the global climate for present and future generations of mankind.[87] It stated that climate change is a "common concern of mankind" and that it was necessary to adopt promptly the necessary measures to deal with it within a global framework. It approved a World Climatological Program to be set up by UNEP in collaboration with WMO and ICSU, and it supported the work of the Intergovernmental Panel on Climate Change (IPCC). It requested the institutions to carry out an overall study on the matter and to examine in particular those aspects that might be addressed in a possible international convention on the climate.

Two months later, an International Assembly of Political and Legal Experts met in Ottawa, charged with working out elements for an international agreement for the protection of the atmosphere. The Hague Conference of March 10 and 11, 1989, convened by France, Norway and the Netherlands, went still further; its Final Declaration, adopted by 24 states, proclaimed the fundamental duty to do all that can be done in order to preserve the quality of the atmosphere for present and future generations. It also called for the development of new principles of international

---

[85]   Villach Conference (PNUE/OMM/ICSU) 1985, Brussels Symposium (CEE) 1986, Bellagio and Villach Seminars 1987.

[86]   *See* WMO/OMM, No. 70 (1989).

[87]   28 I.L.M 1326 (1989).

law and new and more effective decision-making and enforcement mechanisms, including a new institutional authority within the framework of the United Nations which would be responsible for defining protection standards, the respect for which would be under the control of the International Court of Justice.[88]

Resolution 15/36, adopted by the UNEP Executive Council on May 25, 1989, reaffirmed the idea of a framework convention on the climate.[89] The Council of the European Communities adopted a June 21, 1989, resolution on the greenhouse effect and the Community, declaring the need to conclude an international agreement on climate change, to promote action with a view to reducing emissions of other greenhouse gases (CO_2 in particular), to protect forests and engage in reforestation.[90] On December 22, 1989, the UN General Assembly adopted a new resolution on the subject, emphasizing the urgent need to work out a general convention on climate change issues as well as the to set up international mechanisms for financing and to guarantee access of developing countries to the technologies required.

The Second World Climate Conference, held in Geneva from October 29 to November 7, 1990, was attended by delegations from more than 100 states, in some cases led by their Heads of State or Government. The Conference had before it the IPCC report which, although less dramatic than some had imagined, was explicit regarding the need to adopt immediate precautionary measures in order to reduce emissions of gases having a greenhouse effect, as well as other measures aimed at stabilizing the climate such as reforestation. The Final Declaration of the Conference contained a compromise solution requesting developed countries to establish either reduction objectives by specific dates, or "feasible national programs and strategies," which should have a significant effect on the limitation of emissions of CO_2 and other gases having a greenhouse effect.

On December 21, 1990, the UN General Assembly adopted another Resolution on the protection of the world climate for present and future generations.[91] The Resolution reflected a desire for an Intergovernmental Negotiating Committee (INC) to prepare a general and effective convention on climate change.[92]

The UN Framework Convention on Climate Change was adopted on May 8, 1992, in New York and opened for signature during the Rio de

---

[88] 28 I.L.M. 1308 (1989).

[89] 28 I.L.M. 1330 (1989).

[90] 28 I.L.M. 1306 (1989).

[91] 21 E.P.L. 76 (1991).

[92] *See* José Juste, *Protection of the Atmospheric Environment by International Law, in* A. KISS & D. SHELTON, MANUAL OF EUROPEAN ENVIRONMENTAL LAW 394, 403–404 (1997).

Janeiro Conference. It defines climate change as a modification of the climate which is attributed directly or indirectly to human activity that alters the composition of the global atmosphere, and which is in addition to natural climate variability observed over comparable time periods (Art. 1(2)). The stated objective is to stabilize the concentrations of all greenhouse gases in the atmosphere at a level that will prevent dangerous anthropogenic interference with the climate system (Art. 2). In this regard, precautionary measures must be taken to anticipate, prevent, or minimize the causes of climate change and mitigate its adverse effects (Art. 3(3)).

The obligations of all parties are mainly contained in Articles 4 and 12: developing, periodically updating, publishing, and making available national inventories of anthropogenic emissions and sinks; formulating and implementing national and regional programs containing measures to mitigate climate change; promoting the application of processes that control emissions including transfer of technologies; promoting sustainable management of sinks and reservoirs of all greenhouse gases; elaborating integrated plans for coastal zone management and cooperation in research (Art. 4(1)).

The Convention recognizes the necessity of returning to earlier levels of anthropogenic emissions of carbon dioxide and other greenhouse gases (Art. 4(2)(a)), but sets no specific timetables and targets for limiting such emissions, establishing only that the parties' obligations differ. Applying the principle of common but differentiated responsibilities and capabilities, the treaty provides that its developed country parties should take the lead in combating climate change and its adverse effects (Art. 3(1)). Annex I to the Convention lists as developed 36 countries and the European Community; they pledge to adopt national and regional policies and take corresponding measures to mitigate climate change by limiting their emissions of greenhouse gases and protecting and enhancing their greenhouse sinks and reservoirs. They recognize the need for equitable and appropriate contributions to the global effort. To this end, each is obliged to communicate, within six months of the entry into force of the Convention for it, and periodically thereafter, detailed information on its policies and measures. This information is reviewed by the Conference of the Parties. Each of the developed parties shall coordinate with other such parties, as appropriate, relevant economic and administrative instruments developed to achieve the objective of the Convention (Art. 4(2)).

Ten of the 36 identified developed states are former communist countries, considered as undergoing the process of transition to a market economy. They have a special status under the Convention which grants them some flexibility to enhance their ability to address climate change (Art. 4(6)). The remaining developed country parties include all the members of OECD and the European Community. They are to provide new and additional financial resources to meet the agreed full costs incurred by developing countries in complying with their obligations relating to the communication of national inventories and the measures taken or envisaged to implement the convention. The most developed states also must assist developing countries that are particularly vulnerable to adverse effects of climate change in meeting costs of adaptation to those adverse effects (Art. 4(3)(4)). The transfer of environmentally-sound technologies is particularly stressed, but the development and enhancement of endogenous capacities and technologies should also be supported (Art. 4(5)). The Convention explicitly provides that the extent to which developing countries will implement their commitments depends on the effective implementation by developed countries of their commitments related to financial resources and transfer of technology (Art. 4(7)).

The instrument deserves its title: it constitutes a framework for which concrete and specific obligations must be elaborated. This is the task of the institutions established by it: the Conference of the Parties (Art. 7), the Secretariat (Art. 8), and two subsidiary bodies—one for scientific and technological advice (Art. 9), the other for implementation (Art. 10). A Financial Mechanism is also defined (Art. 11).

The Conference of the Parties (COP) is the supreme body of the Convention. In addition to duties comparable to those of bodies created by other treaties—facilitation of information exchanges, coordination of measures adopted to address climate change, elaboration of recommendations, organization of its own work—it has three broad categories of functions:

(a) Adoption of protocols to the Convention. Article 17, which foresees such instruments, is not very developed, but it is clear that these instruments are intended to inject substance into the framework convention.

(b) Supervision of the implementation. According to Article 12(1), information concerning national inventories of emissions and sinks and steps taken or envisaged to implement the Convention should be communicated by all states parties. Developed states also should furnish a detailed description of their policies and measures on the mitigation of climate change and on the assistance they grant developing countries (Art. 12(2)). Such information shall be considered by a subsidiary body on implementation in order to assess the overall aggregated effects of the steps taken by the parties (Art. 10). The COP then assesses the implementation of the Convention by the parties, taking into account the environmental, economic, and social effects of the measures taken, as well as their cumulative impacts (Art. 7(2)).

(c) The COP must mobilize financial resources (Art. 7(2)(h)), the amount of which should be determined in a predictable and identifiable manner. The COP also decides on the policies, program priorities, and eligibility criteria related to financial assistance to developing countries. Under its guidance, the Financial Mechanism, established following the principle of an equitable and balanced representation of all parties, has the task of providing financial resources on a grant or concessional basis (Art. 11(1)(2)). Arrangements must be agreed upon, including modalities, to ensure that the funded projects are in conformity with the policies, program priorities and eligibility criteria established by the COP. The weakness of the commitments contained in the Convention thus had to be balanced by the strength of the institutions established. The rules agreed upon primarily served as the basis of future negotiations both inside and outside these institutions.

The parties to the UNFCCC could choose from a range of policy options to counter anthropogenic climate change, some of the policies having important impacts on national economies. Measures could include improving energy efficiency, forest management, air pollution control, fuel switching and restructuring transportation. Many environmental economists support carbon taxes as a way to establish appropriate incentives away from polluting fuels. Reforestation and other measures to expand carbon sinks are also possible. The debates that have taken place since adoption of the Climate Change Convention have largely centered on determining the appropriate measures to be taken.

At its first session, held in Berlin from March 28 to April 7, 1995,[93] the COP had to consider the establishment of a multilateral consultative process regarding questions on the implementation of the Convention (Art. 13). It was decided that any body or agency, whether national or international, governmental or non-governmental, qualified in matters covered by the Convention, may be represented at a session of the COP. Such presence can be very useful when the implementation of the Convention is discussed on the basis of national reports. The importance of the meeting was enhanced by an interim report released by the Intergovernmental Panel on Climate Change (IPCC) at the end of 1994, which pointed out that even with a stabilization of current global CO_2 emissions, atmospheric concentrations of this most important greenhouse gas would continue to rise for at least two centuries. The presence of around 4,000 participants, including 2,000 journalists at this "Berlin Summit" demonstrated the interest raised by the problem of climate change.

---

[93]   For the full texts of decisions adopted by the Conference of the Parties at its first through fifth sessions, *see* documents FCCC/CP/1995/7/Add.1, FCCC/CP/1996/15/Add.1, FCCC/CP/1997/7/Add.1, FCCC/CP/1998/16/Add.1 and FCCC/CP/1999/6/Add.1. *See also* Sebastian Oberthür and Hermann Ott, *UN/Convention on Climate Change, the First Conference of the Parties*, 25 E.P.L. 144–56 (1995).

Taking into account the rising emission trends of industrialized countries and of developing countries, it appeared that the commitments in the UNFCCC were too weak. Several mainly oil-exporting countries opposed negotiating further commitments, however. As a compromise, the COP adopted the "Berlin Mandate" in which the parties agreed to begin a process that could lead to the conclusion of a "protocol or another legal instrument" based on an analysis and assessment identifying appropriate policies and measures. It was also to aim at setting "quantified limitation and reduction objectives within specified time-frames" for greenhouse gas emissions.

The first COP also adopted institutional arrangements. The restructured Global Environmental Facility continued to be the international entity entrusted with the operation of the Convention on an interim basis. The two subsidiary organs foreseen by Articles 9 and 10 were established,[94] both as plenary organs open for all parties and observers from other states, international organizations and NGOs. Finally, the Berlin COP decided to install the Secretariat of the Convention in Bonn.[95]

The Second COP, convened in July 1996 in Geneva, adopted a Declaration recording the belief of the ministers representing more than 100 states that "the findings of the IPCC's second assessment report indicate dangerous interference with the climate system." They also stressed the need for accelerating negotiations on a legally binding protocol and outlined the directions of future action. The Third COP, held in Kyoto on December 1–10, 1997, concluded the negotiations by adopting the Kyoto Protocol, moving forward in the development of precise rules to mitigate the greenhouse effect.

The Kyoto Protocol to the UN Framework Convention specifies different goals and commitments for developed and developing countries concerning future emission of greenhouse gases. The complexity of the text increases the risk of disagreement over interpretation and thus of implementation. The main features of the protocol are the reduction targets accepted by the industrialized countries, without corresponding obligations for developing countries; acknowledgment of the role of sinks of greenhouse gases (seas, forests) and their inclusion in the targets; the possible creation of "bubbles" and trading emissions as means for reducing their aggregate emissions and joint implementation agreements with countries that only emit small amounts of greenhouse gases, in principle developing countries.

Articles 2 to 8 of the Protocol concern the 36 industrialized and "economy in transition"[96] states listed in Annex I of the Framework Convention.

---

[94] The two organs are called the "Subsidiary Body for Scientific and Technological Advice" (SBSTA) and the "Subsidiary Body for Implementation" (SBI).

[95] On the aftermath of the Berlin Conference, *see* 26 E.P.L. 158 (1996).

[96] Bulgaria, Croatia, Czech Republic, Estonia, Hungary, Latvia, Poland Romania, Russia, Slovakia, Slovenia and Ukraine. Croatia and Slovenia were not originally listed in Annex I to the UNFCCC (see p. 582), but were added when they later signed.

Article 3(1) adopts a "big bubble approach:" these countries must, individually or jointly, cut their aggregate anthropogenic carbon dioxide equivalent emissions of greenhouse gases listed in Annex A by at least 5 percent (averaging 5.2 percent) below 1990 levels by the first commitment period of 2008–2012. These reductions cover six greenhouse gases: carbon dioxide, methane, nitrous oxide, hydrofluorocarbons (HFCs), perfluorocarbons (PFCs) and sulfur hexafluoride (SF6). Thus, if a state party is able to limit emissions of greenhouse gases other than carbon dioxide, restrictions on the use of fossil fuels may be correspondingly relaxed. Each state of this group shall, by 2005, have made demonstrable progress in achieving its commitments under the Protocol. Countries in transition benefit from a certain degree of flexibility in the implementation of their commitments (Art. 3(6)). They may use, for example, a different base year to determine the reduction of their emission (Art. 3(5)).

Article 2 lists methods that may be used in order to achieve quantified emission limitation and reduction: enhancement of energy efficiency, protection and enhancement of sinks and reservoirs of greenhouse gases, promotion of sustainable forms of agriculture, increased use of new and renewable forms of energy and of environmentally-sound technologies, reduction or phasing out of market imperfections, the use of economic instruments, limitation and reduction of emissions of greenhouse gases in the transport sector and limitation and/or reduction of methane through recovery and use in waste management.

Annex I parties are allowed to join together in the establishment of "bubbles" and thereby attain their emission reduction commitments jointly. Countries doing this will be deemed to have met their reduction requirements provided that their total aggregate emissions do not exceed the total of their combined amounts set out in Annex II. In the event of failure to achieve the aggregated target, each of the countries concerned will still be held responsible for its respective individual commitment in Annex B (Art. 4).[97]

Another specific form of cooperation in the reduction of the emission of greenhouse gases is emission trading. According to Article 6(1), any developed country, for the purpose of meeting its commitments, may transfer to or acquire from, any other Annex I party emission reduction units resulting from projects aimed at reducing emissions. It also can enhance anthropogenic removals by sinks of greenhouse gases in any sector of the economy. The condition is that any such project provides a reduction in emission by sources or an enhancement of removal by sinks, that is additional to any that would otherwise occur. The acquisition of emission reduction units thus shall be supplemental to domestic actions for the purposes

---

[97] James H. Searles, *Analysis of the Kyoto Protocol to the U.N. Framework Convention on Climate Change*, 21 INT'L ENVTL. REP. 132 (1998).

of meeting commitments under Article 3. A developed country may also authorize legal entities to participate, under its responsibility, in actions leading to the generation, transfer or acquisition of emission reduction units (Art. 6(3)). The COP defines the relevant principles, modalities, rules and guidelines, in particular for verification, reporting and accountability for emission trading (Art. 16bis).

Any emission reduction units, or any part of an assigned amount, that a party acquires from another party shall be added to the assigned amount for that party (Art. 3(10)). Parallel to this provision, Art. 3(11) foresees that any emission reduction units, or any part of an assigned amount, that a party transfers to another party shall be subtracted from the assigned amount for that party.

Article 12 outlines a "clean development mechanism" the task of which is to assist developing countries in achieving sustainable development and in contributing to the ultimate objective of the convention and also to assist developed countries in achieving compliance with their quantified emission limitation and reduction commitments. Emission reductions resulting from each project activity shall be certified on a voluntary basis approved by each party involved, by operational entities to be designated by the COP (Art. 12(5)). Developing countries will benefit from project activities resulting in certified emission reductions while developed countries may use the certified emission reductions accruing from such project activities to contribute to compliance with part of their quantified emission limitation and reduction commitments (Art. 12(3)(b)). The clean development mechanism will assist in arranging funding of certified project activities as necessary. Certified emission reductions obtained during the period 2000 to 2008 can be used by developed countries to assist in achieving compliance in the commitment period 2008 to 2012.

Monitoring of greenhouse gases plays an important role in the Kyoto Protocol. Developed countries must establish national systems to estimate anthropocentric emissions by sources and removals by sinks (Art. 5) as well as annual inventories to incorporate the supplementary information necessary to demonstrate compliance with the commitments accepted under the Protocol (Art. 7). Such information will be reviewed by teams composed of experts nominated by parties to the Framework Convention and, as appropriate, by inter-governmental organizations, and coordinated by the Secretariat. The information submitted by the parties and the reports of the expert reviews shall be considered by the COP which can take decisions on any matter required for the implementation of the Protocol (Art. 8).

Articles 10 and 11 of the Protocol concern in particular developing countries. Their emissions are not limited, but they should formulate, where relevant, cost-effective national and where appropriate regional programs to improve the quality of local emission factors, formulate, implement, publish and regularly update national or regional programs to mitigate climate change, taking into account all relevant economic activities. Cooperation with developing countries shall include the transfer of, or access to, environmentally-sound technologies, know-how, practices and processes pertinent to climate change as well as capacity building. Article 11 foresees that new and additional financial resources should be provided to meet the agreed full costs incurred by developing country parties in advancing the implementation of existing commitments.

The COP of the Convention serves as the Meeting of the Parties to the Protocol. It keeps under regular review the implementation of the Protocol and shall make the decisions necessary to promote its effective implementation. It assesses, on the basis of the information made available to it, the overall effects of the measures taken and makes recommendations on any matters necessary for the implementation of the Protocol (Art. 13). The COP approves appropriate and effective procedures and mechanisms to determine and to address cases of non-compliance with the provisions of the Protocol (Art. 17). Any body or agency, whether national or international, governmental or non-governmental that is qualified in matters covered by the Protocol may be admitted as an observer, unless at least one-third of the parties present at the meeting objects (Art. 13). The Secretariat and the subsidiary bodies established by the Framework Convention shall be used for the Protocol (Arts. 14 and 15).

The Fourth Conference of Parties to the UNFCCC was held in Buenos Aires from November 2–14, 1998, and adopted the Buenos Aires Mandate. Its results were modest. In spite of the insistence of the U.S. delegation, the developing countries did not accept any obligation to reduce their emissions of greenhouse gases, which would have been necessary to satisfy the U.S. private sector demand for the rapid creation of a pollution trading market. European countries stressed the need for industrialized countries to reduce their emissions within the limits of their jurisdiction, while the developing countries asked for the transfer of clean technologies. In the end, the 161 countries present adopted an action plan listing issues for future discussion including the elaboration of rules on emission trading, the Clean Development Mechanism (CDM) and joint implementation.

In 2000 the Sixth Conference of the Parties to the UNFCCC met at the Hague and failed to reach agreement on implementing the Kyoto Protocol. Soon thereafter, the United States administration announced it would not proceed to ratify the Kyoto Protocol which it had signed, following which Europe, Japan and other countries resumed COP-6 in Bonn. At Bonn, they established an international regulatory framework to make Kyoto operational; this was translated into the Marrakech Accords at COP-VII at the end of 2001. The Marrakech Accords, at 218 pages, represent the detailed legal framework for implementing the Kyoto Protocol. (See Chapter 5.)

The most important controversy at Marrakesh was over whether or not there should be an absolute cap to the use of emissions trading, Joint

Implementation and the Clean Development Mechanism (CDM) to fulfil Kyoto commitments, thus keeping the pressure on states to reduce national emissions. The final agreement, contained in Decision 15 of COP-VII is that "the use of the mechanisms shall be supplemental to domestic action and domestic action shall thus constitute a significant element" of implementing Article 3.1 of the protocol." Nuclear power is banned from the CDM and Joint Implementation. In Article 12 of the Kyoto Protocol, the parties agreed on a prompt start to the CDM. According to Decision 17/CP.7, projects that started from 2000 onwards may be credited retroactively. The determination of whether a CDM project is sustainable lies with the host country. Parties also may use afforestation and reforestation activities in the CDM up to a ceiling of 1 percent of a party's 1990 emissions.[98] An Executive Board of ten members will oversee the CDM. Five of them will come from the five regional groups, one from a small island state, and two each from Annex I and non-Annex I countries. Since the Executive Board may taken decisions only with a three-quarters majority, the four Annex I countries could block action. Joint implementation has its own supervisory committee to be elected immediately after the entry into force of the protocol, also composed of ten members: three from countries in transition, three from other annex I countries, three from developing countries and one from a small island developing country. In this body, the four developing countries could potentially block action.

From 1990 to 1995, the European Union decreased its carbon dioxide emissions by about one percent, while the other OECD countries together increased emissions by about 8 percent. Of these, Australia, Canada, Japan and the U.S. all increased their emissions by 7 to 9 percent. Annex I countries undergoing a transition to market economy, on the other hand, decreased their emissions by almost 30 percent. This means that total emissions of CO_2 by all Annex I parties decreased by about 5 percent from 1990 to 1995. According to the targets agreed to in Kyoto for Annex I parties, the European Union should achieve a further reduction from 1 to 8 percent below 1990 levels and the other OECD countries should move from a 7 percent increase to a 7 percent reduction.

The EC adopted Directive 2001/77 on the Promotion of Electricity from Renewable Sources in the Internal Electricity Market in order to contribute towards meeting EC commitments under the Kyoto Protocol and to achieve the target of doubling renewable energy's contribution to Europe's consumption from 6 percent to 12 percent by 2010. States are to pursue this development in accordance with energy and environmental objectives set at national and EC levels. Future national energy targets are to be met from renewable energy sources and states are to set up a system to guarantee the origin of renewable electricity. The directive also contains measures to create

---

[98]   Dec. 17/7, para. 7.

fair conditions and facilitate market entry of renewables in accordance with the rules on competition. The Directive provides that member states will set national targets to be reviewed by the commission for consistency with the global indicative target of 12 percent of gross national energy consumption. Considerable discretion is left to states to develop methods to support the generation of electricity from renewable energy sources. After four years the Commission will review the national experiences to try and develop a more harmonized support system.

Countries in economic transition are allowed to increase their present emissions by 22 percent to 30 percent. The Russian Federation and Ukraine are particularly favored. Other special allowances are given to Australia, Iceland, New Zealand and Norway.[99] The net changes in greenhouse gas emissions from sources and removals by sinks resulting from direct human-induced land use and forestry activities, limited to afforestation, reforestation and deforestation since 1990, can be used to meet the commitments of each party (Art. 3 (3)).

The United States policy on global climate change has itself changed significantly. Voluntary measures to stabilize carbon dioxide emissions by the year 2000 were first developed by the first Bush Administration as it entered the 1992 Framework Convention on Climate Change.[100] The Bush Administration's "no regrets" early action policy laid the foundation for President Clinton's 1993 Climate Change Action Plan. The Clinton administration actively participated in negotiations for the existing international agreements, serving as a principal architect of the emissions trading scheme, a major innovation of the Kyoto Protocol. The relatively positive views of the Clinton administration encountered considerable hostility in the Congress. A July 1997 Senate resolution[101] sought to restrict the administration's policy choices towards climate change agreements. The U.S. Senate

---

[99]   B. Bolin, *The Kyoto Negotiations on Climate Change: A Science Perspective*, 279 Science 330 (1998).

[100]   For a critique of the environmental benefits of voluntary emissions trading, *see* Richard Toshiyuki Drury et al., *Pollution Trading And Environmental Injustice: Los Angeles' Failed Experiment in Air Quality Policy*, 9 Duke Envtl L. & Pol'y F. 231 (1999) (pollution trading makes for ineffective air quality policy in at least four ways: (1) it does not significantly reduce air pollution; (2) it does not spur technological innovation; (3) it decreases public participation in environmental decision-making; and (4) it increases the difficulty of monitoring and enforcing emission reductions.)

[101]   *See* S. Res. 98, 105th Cong., 143 Cong. Rec. S8138 (1997) (adopted by vote of 95-0). The resolution specifies that "the United States should not be a signatory to any protocol to, or other agreement regarding, the United Nations Framework Convention on Climate Change of 1992, at negotiations in Kyoto in December 1997, or thereafter, which would . . . mandate new commitments to limit or reduce greenhouse gas emissions for the Annex I Parties [to the Convention, consisting of industrialized states], unless the protocol or other

passed the so-called Byrd-Hagel Resolution, expressing disagreement with the approach that developed countries with the largest share of GHG emissions should take the first steps to reduce such emissions. Congressional and other opponents not only opposed the absence of commitments by developing countries, but also argued that: (1) insufficient evidence exists to prove the existence or effects of anthropogenic global warming; (2) carbon emissions in the United States are rising less rapidly than the GDP; and (3) reducing carbon emissions will hurt the U.S. economy. During the 2000 presidential election, candidate George W. Bush spoke in favor of action to curb greenhouse gases, but after the election he formally announced in March 2001 that the United States would not proceed to ratification of the Kyoto Protocol, calling it "fatally flawed" and harmful to the U.S. economy.[102]

Despite the views of the United States administration, the Plan of Implementation of the World Summit on Sustainable Development strongly urged states that have not done so to ratify the Kyoto Protocol in a timely manner and recalled the UN Millennium Declaration in which heads of state and government resolved to embark on the required reduction of emissions of greenhouse gases in conformity to the Framework Convention on Climate Change. The Plan of Implementation calls the Convention "the key instrument for addressing climate change, which is a global concern."

BIBLIOGRAPHY

ANDERSON, D. & GRUBB, M. eds., CONTROLLING CARBON AND SULPHUR: JOINT IMPLEMENTATION AND TRADING INITIATIVES (1997).

BENEDICT, R.E., OZONE DIPLOMACY: NEW DIRECTIONS IN SAFEGUARDING THE PLANET (1991).

FERMANN, G. ed., INTERNATIONAL POLITICS OF CLIMATE CHANGE: KEY ISSUES AND CRITICAL ACTORS (1997).

FLINTERMAN, C. ET AL., TRANSBOUNDARY AIR POLLUTION (1986).

French, H., *Learning from the Ozone Experience, in* LESTER R. BROWN, ET AL., STATE OF THE WORLD (1997).

---

agreement also mandates new specific scheduled commitments to limit or reduce greenhouse gas emissions for Developing Country Parties within the same compliance period."

[102] *See Cooler Heads on Kyoto*, N.Y. TIMES, June 12, 2001, at A18 (commenting that one study estimates that implementing the Kyoto Protocol would cost the United States $400 billion in lost productivity over the next decade); Press Release, *White House, President Bush Announces Clear Skies & Global Climate Change Initiative* (Feb. 14, 2002) (announcing a new plan for climate change mitigation, which would involve transferable emission credits and emission reductions tied to GDP), *available at* <http://whitehouse.gov/news/releases/2002/02/print/20020214.html>.

Goldberg, D., *A Legal Analysis of the Kyoto Protocol*, CIEL (1998).

Goldberg, D.M., *As the World Burns: Negotiating the Framework Convention on Climate Change*, 5 GEO. ENVTL. L. REV. 239 (1993);

IPPC, CLIMATE CHANGE 2001: IMPACTS, ADAPTATION, AND VULNERABILITY (2001).

Lang, W., *Trade Restrictions as a Means of Enforcing Compliance with International Environmental Law: Montreal Protocol on Substances that Deplete the Ozone Layer, in* R. WOLFRUM ed. ENFORCING INTERNATIONAL STANDARDS: ECONOMIC MECHANISMS AS VIABLE MEANS? 265–83 (1996).

MACKENZIE J. & EL-ASHRY, M., AIR POLLUTION'S TOLL ON FORESTS AND CROPS (1989).

MAKHIJANI, A. & GURNEY, K., MENDING THE OZONE HOLE (1995).

Mintz, J. A., *Keeping Pandora's Box Shut: A Critical Assessment of the Montreal Protocol on Substances that Deplete the Ozone Layer*, 20 U. MIAMI INTER-AM. L. REV. 565–78 (1989).

Nagle, O.E., *Stratospheric Ozone: United States Regulation of Chlorofluorocarbons*, 16 B.C. ENVTL. AFF. L. REV. 531–80 (1989).

Nanda, V., *Stratospheric Ozone Depletion: A Challenge for International Environmental Law and Policy*, 10 MICH. J. INT'L L. 482 (1989).

Ott, H.E., *The Kyoto Protocol, Unfinished Business*, 40 ENVIRONMENT No. 6, 17–45.

PETERS, R. & LOVEJOY, T., GLOBAL WARMING AND BIOLOGICAL DIVERSITY (1993).

Read, J., *The Trail Smelter Dispute*, CAN. Y.B. INT'L L. 213 (1963).

Sarma, K.M., *The Montreal Protocol's First 10 years: The United Nations Environment Program's Perspective*, INT'L ENVTL. REP. Sept. 3, 1997, 853.

Smelofff, E.A., *Global Warming : The Kyoto Protocol and Beyond*, 28 E.P.L. 63 (1998).

SOROOS, M., THE ENDANGERED ATMOSPHERE: PRESERVING A GLOBAL COMMONS (1997).

UNEP, ENVIRONMENTAL EFFECTS OF OZONE DEPLETION (1994).

VELLINGA, P. & GRUBB, M. eds., THE CLIMATE CHANGE POLICY IN THE EUROPEAN COMMUNITY (1993).

Wexler, P., *Protecting the Global Atmosphere: Beyond the Montreal Protocol*, 14 MD. J. INT'L L. & TRADE 1–19 (1990).

INTERNET SITES

Framework Convention on Climate Control
<http://www.unfccc.int>

Convention and Protocol on Protection of the Ozone Layer
<http://www.unep.org/ozone/index.html>

United Nations Economic Commission for Europe
<http://www.unece.org>

CHAPTER 13

REGULATING THREATS TO THE ENVIRONMENT

Human activities introducing hazardous or toxic substances into the environment may cause irremediable harm to natural, cyclical phenomena such as the life cycle (birth, life, death, decomposition and environmental fertilization assisting birth), the water cycle or the carbon cycle. Non-cyclical phenomena are exceptional and often arise in catastrophic circumstances such as volcanic eruptions, earthquakes, landslides. Toxic substances similarly introduce a non-cyclical element because these substances do not return, at least in the short term, to their original state, and thus may accumulate and produce synergistic effects with other substances leading to irreversible harm. Radioactive matter provides an example: the longevity of some radioactive substances is measured in thousands or millions of years. The environmental impacts of utilizing radioactive materials are thus practically irreversible.

Since the end of the 1970s, rules increasingly have regulated the substances and human activities that produce or can produce harmful environmental consequences and that transfer from one sector to another. Such "beginning of the pipeline" regulation addresses hazardous and toxic products and wastes, radioactivity and nuclear wastes, and dangerous industrial and other activities. Their consequences in producing long-term or irreversible harm were taken into account by international environmental law from the beginning of the 1990s with the formulation of the precautionary principle.[1]

Non-industrialized countries often willingly import chemical products without local authorities knowing or having the means to know their nature and what effects they can have on human health and on the environment. In order to remedy this situation, if only partially, UNEP established an International Register of Potentially Toxic Chemicals (IRPTC) in 1976. A legal catalogue in the Register contains important information on the national and international regulations concerning more than 6,000 chemical substances. Similarly, in response to General Assembly Resolution 37/137 of December 17, 1982, the United Nations Secretariat initiated periodic listing of products whose consumption and/or sale have been banned,

---

[1]   The precautionary principle is discussed in detail in Chapter 5B.2.

withdrawn, severely restricted or not approved by governments.[2] A year later, the General Assembly began publishing the list annually. In 1985, in cooperation with the World Health Organization and UNEP/IRPTC, the UN Secretariat carried out the first review of the list to determine criteria for inclusion and the treatment of commercial data. The three entities entered into a memorandum of understanding, still in effect, to allocate responsibilities. In 1997 the agencies decided to divide the reports into two parts to be published in alternate years, one part concerning pharmaceuticals and the other part chemicals. By the fifth and last combined report, more than 700 products were reported by 94 governments. The List is the only document that presents in a unified manner information on restrictive regulatory decisions taken by governments on a range of pharmaceuticals and agricultural and industrial chemicals. It is available to governments, NGOs, institutions and consumer groups. Each issue of the List is sent to major NGOs active in the field, such as the Pesticide Action Network.

A. Toxic and Hazardous Products

The production and utilization of chemical substances in the world have undergone unprecedented growth in the course of the past half century. At least 75,000 different chemicals are used in pesticides, pharmaceuticals, plastics and other products.[3] Although it is difficult to obtain exact figures, chemical substances including pesticides and fertilizers represent about 10 percent of world trade, amounting to approximately $18 billion in annual sales. Over 10,000 organochlorines are currently in commerce, used to make plastics, solvents, and disinfectants, refine petroleum, bleach pulp and paper, to treat wastewater, and for dry cleaning.[4] Each year 1000 to 2000 new products arrive on the market, without, in all cases, being tested or evaluated for their potentially harmful effects. Of some 75,000 chemical substances currently utilized in the United States, the facts concerning their effects on human health are available for only about 10 percent of the pesticides and 18 percent of the medicines.

According to one source, the human body on average contains some 500 anthropogenic chemicals that did not exist before 1920, many of them persistent organic pollutants and endocrine disruptors.[5] Although some scientific testing has been done on the direct effects on human health, little

---

2   *See* Report of the UN Secretary General on Products Harmful to Health and the Environment, A/53/156, June 29, 1998.

3   LESTER BROWN et al., VITAL SIGNS 130 (2000).

4   On the impact of chlorine on the U.S. economy, *see* the information of the Chlorine Chemistry Council, *available at* <http://c3.org/chlorine>.

5   *Id.*

research exists on the impact on plant life, soil or other environmental sectors. The long-term consequences of many of the substances, alone or in combination, are unknown but short-term harm is increasing: incidents of pesticide poisonings have doubled approximately every decade since the 1940s.[6] Some substances travel long distances and affect populations who have never sought access to or used the products containing them. The Inuit of the Canadian Arctic, for example, have the highest known concentrations of PCBs in their bodies.[7]

International instruments devoted to hazardous substances have been adopted mostly since the second half of the 1980s, although the regulation of toxic or dangerous products appeared earlier and continues to appear in instruments addressing sectoral problems, such as rules relating to discharges into the marine environment and inland waters. All regulation of hazardous products must take into account their production, trade (including transportation), use, and elimination. The last aspect presents particular problems and thus normally is treated separately. The same is true for nuclear activities, which are specially regulated, particularly with respect to the increasing problem of disposal of radioactive wastes.

1. Production and Use

The potential effects of chemical substances on humans and the environment, including the long-term risks, should be evaluated before and during production. Reliable testing and sharing of resulting data was an early concern of OECD, which adopted a 1974 recommendation on assessing the potential environmental effects of chemical compounds (eco-toxicity)[8] supplemented by a 1977 resolution[9] recommending a procedure for anticipating the potential effects of chemical products on man and the environment. A series of decisions from 1981[10] to 1983 set forth guidelines for good laboratory practices and testing, the mutual recognition of data and the minimum pre-marketing data requirements.

A major step in the control of hazardous chemicals occurred when 154 states and the European Union adopted the Stockholm Convention on Persistent Organic Pollutants (POPs).[11] POPs possess toxic properties, resist

---

6   World Health Organization, Public Helath Impact of Pesticides Used in Agriculture 28–29 (1990).

7   David Hunter et al., International Environmental Law and Policy 881 (2d ed. 2002).

8   OECD Res. C(74)215, Nov. 14, 1974.

9   OECD Res. C(77)97, July 7, 1977.

10   OECD Res. C(81)30, May 12, 1981; OECD Res. C(82)196, Dec. 8, 1982; OECD Res. C(83)95, July 26, 1983.

11   May 22, 2001.

decay, bioaccumulate and are transported through air, water and with migratory species across international boundaries, where they accumulate in terrestrial and aquatic ecosystems. They create risks to health, especially in developing countries and the polar ecosystems. Using the precautionary approach and advocating the polluter pays principle, the Convention insists on the responsibility of POPs' manufacturers to reduce adverse effects caused by their products and to provide information to users, governments and the public at large on the hazardous properties of these chemicals.

The Convention makes a distinction between releases from intentional production and use (Arts. 3 and 4) and from unintentional production (Art. 5). The first category of chemicals, listed in Annex A, includes certain insecticides and PCBs. Each party shall prohibit and/or take the legal and administrative measures to eliminate their production and use and regulate their import and export. Each party also shall take measures concerning the unintentional production of the chemicals listed in Annex C (primarily PCBs and dioxins), such as developing and implementing an action plan designed to identify, characterize and address their release by using the best available techniques and best environmental practices. Parties may make proposals for listing a chemical in one of the Annexes (Art. 8). Article 6 suggests measures to reduce or eliminate releases from stockpiles and wastes, such as identification of stockpiles and the adoption of appropriate measures so that such wastes, including products and articles becoming wastes, are handled, collected, transported and stored in an environmentally sound manner and finally disposed in such a way that the POP content is destroyed or irreversibly transformed so that it represents no environmental danger. Cooperation with the appropriate bodies of the Basel Convention on the Control of Transboundary Movements of Hazardous Wastes and their Disposal is foreseen. Article 10 of the Convention invites the parties to promote and facilitate public information, awareness and education.

The Convention seeks to promote and facilitate compliance by foreseeing technical and financial assistance mainly to developing countries (Arts. 12 and 13) and also by imposing reporting obligations on the states parties concerning the measures they have taken to implement the provisions of the Convention and on their effectiveness (Art. 15). A Conference of the Parties (Art. 19) assisted by a Secretariat (Art. 20) is charged with evaluating the effectiveness of the Convention (Art. 16) and developing procedures and institutional mechanisms to determine and respond to noncompliance with the provisions of the Convention (Art.17).

The importance of the POPs Convention lies in the fact that most other international instruments respecting chemicals or dangerous wastes concern international trade or transfrontier movements of such substances. The exceptions are the Chemical Weapons Convention and the Montreal Protocol which prohibits the production and use of ozone-depleting substances. The Stockholm Convention now imposes a global ban on a wider range of toxic and environmentally-hazardous chemicals, a ban that could be extended to other materials.

ILO Convention No. 184 (Safety and Health in Agriculture)[12] adopted one month after the POPs Convention covers agricultural and forestry activities including crop production, forestry activities, animal husbandry and insect raising, the primary processing of agricultural and animal products by or on behalf of the operator of the undertaking as well as the use and maintenance of machinery, equipment, appliances, tools, and agricultural installations, including any process, storage, operation or transportation in an agricultural undertaking, which are directly related to agricultural production. The Convention does not cover subsistence farming, industrial processes that use agricultural products as raw material and the related services, or the industrial exploitation of forests.

The aim of the Convention is to have ILO members formulate, carry out and periodically review a coherent national policy on safety and health in agriculture with the aim of preventing accidents and injury to health by eliminating, minimizing or controlling hazards in the agricultural working environment. National laws and regulations should designate a competent authority responsible for implementing and enforcing relevant national laws and regulations. A specific section of the Convention governs chemicals. Article 12 requires the competent authority to take measures to ensure that (a) there is an appropriate system establishing specific criteria for the importation, classification, packaging and labeling of chemicals used in agriculture and for their banning or restriction; (b) those who produce, import, provide, sell, transfer, store or dispose of chemicals used in agriculture comply with national or other recognized safety and health standards, and provide adequate and appropriate information to the users in the appropriate official language or languages of the country and, on request, to the competent authority; and (c) there is a suitable system for the safe collection, recycling and disposal of chemical waste, obsolete chemicals and empty containers of chemicals so as to avoid their use for other purposes and to eliminate or minimize the risks to safety and health and to the environment. Article 13 adds that there must be preventive and protective measures for the use of chemicals and handling of chemical waste at the level of the undertaking. The measures must cover, *inter alia*, the preparation, handling, application, storage and transportation of chemicals; agricultural activities leading to the dispersion of chemicals; the maintenance, repair and cleaning of equipment and containers for chemicals; and the disposal of empty containers and the treatment and disposal of chemical waste and obsolete chemicals.

---

[12]   June 21, 2001.

2. Trade and Transport

Specific international conventions regulate the transport of hazardous substances according to the different means of transport.[13] The requirements
of these agreements are often highly technical and focus on packaging, handling, insurance, and liability.

The marketing of chemical products in particular, has been regulated
by the EC since the end of the 1960s, as a response to the necessities of the
common market. One directive,[14] of June 27, 1967, which has been modified many times, aims at harmonizing the legislative, regulatory and administrative measures in force in the member states as far as the classification,
packaging and handling of dangerous substances is concerned. It establishes
methods for determining the physico-chemical properties as well as the toxicity and eco-toxicity of substances and preparations and the characteristics
which should be taken into account in evaluating the danger, real or potential, which the substances can pose to the environment. It also establishes a
notification system. Three other directives contain specific regulations for
particular products: solvents,[15] paints, varnishes, printing inks, glues and
related products,[16] and pesticides.[17] The EC as well as OECD have also
adopted special rules for phytopharmaceutical products,[18] polychlorinated
biphenyls (PCBs),[19] polychlorinated terphenyls (PCTs)[20] and mercury.[21]

---

[13]   *See, e.g.,* European Agreement Concerning the International Carriage
of Dangerous Goods by Road (1957); Convention Concerning International
Carriage by Rail (1924) and its annex; the Regulations Concerning the
International Carriage of Dangerous Goods by Rail, 1924/1985; International
Convention for Safety at of Human Life at Sea (SOLAS, Nov. 1, 1974);
Convention on Liability and Compensation, for Damage in Connection with
the Carriage of Hazardous and Noxious Substances by Sea (May 3, 1996);
Convention on International Civil Aviation (1944), Annex 18; and Technical
Instructions for the Safe Transport of Dangerous Goods by Air; International
Convention for the Prevention of Pollution by Ships (MARPOL Nov. 2, 1973,
Feb., 17, 1978); Regulation of the Carriage of Dangerous Substances on the
Rhine (1970).

[14]   67/548/EEC, O.J. L 196 (8/16/67).

[15]   73/173/EEC, June 4, 1973, O.J. L 189 (7/11/73); most recent modification June 10, 1982 by Directive 82/473/EEC, O.J. L 213 (7/21/82).

[16]   77/728/EEC, Nov. 7, 1977, O.J. L 303 (11/28/77), modified by
Directive 82/265/EEC, May 16, 1983, O.J. L 147 (6/6/83).

[17]   78/631/EEC, June 26 1978, O.J. L 206 (7/29/78), modified by directive 81/187/EEC, Mar. 26, 1981, O.J. L 88 (4/2/81).

[18]   Directive 79/117/EEC, Dec. 21, 1978, O.J. L 33 (2/8/79).

[19]   OECD decisions C(73)1, Feb. 13, 1973 and C(87)2, Feb. 13, 1987.

[20]   Directive 76/769/EEC, July 27, 1976, O.J. L 262 (9/27/76) and L 197
(8/3/79).

[21]   OECD Res. C(73)172, Sept. 19, 1973.

The safe use of chemicals supposes that the user knows their characteristics and their potential danger. For this reason, international instruments put the accent on notification and consultation, and detail the modalities of trade. OECD was one of the first to take action concerning trade, and largely to protect commerce, by suggesting advance notification and consultation about proposed measures concerning hazardous substances, when those measures could have significant impact on the economies of other countries.[22]

In 1985, the FAO adopted the first International Code of Conduct on the Distribution and Use of Pesticides to reduce the hazards associated with the use of pesticides.[23] The Code established voluntary standards for use by countries without existing pesticide regulation. It allocated shared responsibility among government, industry and the public. In November 1989, the FAO amended the Code to adopt the principle of prior informed consent (PIC) and subsequently produced operational procedures for PIC and guidelines on its process. Under the PIC provision, a pesticide that is banned or severely restricted in an exporting country because of its threat to human health or the environment should not be shipped to an importing country over that country's objection. It requires relevant information be provided each country so that it can determine the risks and benefits associated with the chemical. The Pesticide Code had limited success. One hundred fifteen countries responded to an FAO questionnaire in 1993 and over half of them, mostly developing countries, lacked adequate legislation, while four out of five were unable to enforce international standards.

UNEP also adopted guidelines to address trade in hazardous chemicals, including but not limited to pesticides. The 1987 London Guidelines for the Exchange of Information on Chemicals in International Trade[24] aimed to provide access to information on hazardous chemicals in order to facilitate informed choices on importation, handling and use. The London Guidelines on Prior Informed Consent Procedure was added in 1989 as a voluntary procedure implemented through the FAO/UNEP Joint Program for the Operation of the PIC.

Prior informed consent became increasingly required for trade in hazardous substances and products. In 1983, the United Nations General Assembly declared that

> products that have been banned from domestic consumption and/or sale because they have been judged to endanger health and the environment should be sold abroad by companies, corporations

---

[22]   OECD Res. C(71)73, May 18, 1971.

[23]   FAO Code of Conduct on the Distribution and Use of Pesticides, U.N. Doc. M/R8130, E/8.86/1/5000 (1986).

[24]   London Guidelines for the Exchange of Information on Chemicals in International Trade, U.N. Doc. UNEP/GC, 14/17, Annex IV (1987).

or individuals only when a request for such products is received from an importing country or when the consumption of such products is officially permitted in the importing country.[25]

Finally, in 1998, the FAO sponsored adoption of the Rotterdam Convention on the Prior Informed Consent Procedure for Certain Hazardous Chemicals and Pesticides in International Trade (PIC Convention),[26] incorporating the various voluntary arrangements into a legally binding instrument. The preamble expresses the desire of the states parties to ensure that hazardous chemicals that are exported from their territory are packaged and labeled in a manner that is adequately protective of human health and the environment. Similarly, the objective of the Convention expressed in Article 1 is

> to promote shared responsibility and cooperative efforts among Parties in the international trade of certain hazardous chemicals in order to protect human health and the environment from potential harm and to contribute to their environmentally sound use, by facilitating information exchange about their characteristics, by providing for a national decision-making process on their import and export and by disseminating these decisions to Parties.

The PIC Convention relies in large part on private actors to ensure that information on chemical and pesticide hazards is made available to the public. Each party is to require that exported Annex III chemicals as well as chemicals banned or severely restricted in its territory are subject to labeling requirements that ensure the provision of information about risks and/or hazards to human health or the environment, taking into account relevant international standards. The Convention thus implicitly places the primary duty to provide information on the manufacturer or packager of the export. Whenever a customs code has been assigned to a chemical by the World Customs Organization, each state party also must require that the shipping document for that chemical bears the code when exported.[27]

---

[25]   G.A. Res. 37/137 (1983), para. 1

[26]   Sept. 10, 1998.

[27]   Article 13(1)(a) calls on the Conference of the Parties to encourage the World Customs Organization to assign specific Harmonized System Customs Codes to the individual chemicals or groups of chemicals listed in Annex III, as appropriate. At UNCED in 1992, a group of participating states launched an initiative to develop a common set of chemical hazard symbols, terms, data sheets and classification techniques. The proposed Globally Harmonized System (GHS) has been coordinated by the UN Inter-Organizational Program for Sound Management of Chemical with the cooperation of OECD and the par-

Article 13 requires that exporting parties include for the importer a safety data sheet following an internationally-accepted format with the most up-to-date information available on the listed chemicals. Article 15, which concerns implementation, requires each state party to ensure, to the extent practicable, that the public has appropriate access to information on chemical handling and accident management and on safer alternatives to the chemicals listed in Annex III to the Convention.

B. Wastes

The problem of wastes changed and increased with the industrial age and the growth and concentration of human populations. In pre-industrial Europe and in China there was little waste product, other than human sewage, because the bulk of substances and objects were reutilized in some way. Domestic animals consumed some waste, another part was used as agricultural fertilizer, and most metal was recycled. Today, the constant increase of waste has become a major concern. The activities of mass production in agriculture and in industry have created an accumulation of garbage. Moreover, the current economic system is based upon obsolescence and a "throw-away" culture designed to sell a larger number of products. All these factors accelerate waste accumulation. UNEP estimates that more than 400 million tons of hazardous waste is generated annually throughout the world, representing about 16 percent of total industrial waste.[28] Most of this amount is treated within the country that produces it; only about 4 percent of the hazardous waste generated by OECD countries is shipped across an international border.[29] In total amount, however, this still represents a considerable hazard to human health and the environment, because OECD countries generate the largest amount of waste in the world. In addition, transfrontier movements have increased because of the economic advantages involved in shipping wastes for disposal to poorer countries where the costs are much lower.[30]

---

ticipation of companies, labor representatives and environmental groups. Harmonized criteria were completed at the end of 1998 for classifying chemicals for their various physical, environmental, and health hazards, coordinated by the United Nations and the OECD at the Intergovernmental Forum on Chemical Safety. Industry strongly favors harmonization because wide variation in classification and labeling requirements have negative impacts on trade.

[28] UNEP, THE WORLD ENVIRONMENT 1972–1992 264 (1997).

[29] OECD, PRACTICAL INFORMATION FOR THE IMPLEMENTATION OF THE OECD CONTROL SYSTEM: TRANSFRONTIER MOVEMENTS OF WASTES DESTINED FOR RECOVERY OPERATIONS (1997).

[30] Disposal of hazardous waste may cost $2000 per ton in a developed country compared to $40 per ton in Africa. *See* Jennifer Kitt, *Waste Exports to the Developing World: A Global Response*, 7 GEO. INT'L ENVTL. L. REV. 485 (1995).

There is general agreement that the best means to control wastes is the reduction of the quantity of wastes produced. Those that are produced can be eliminated by different methods: discharge into surface dumps, burial in the earth, submersion into the oceans or lakes, and incineration. More ecological methods consider wastes as much as possible as primary derived material which should be reutilized or recycled. This concept is badly expressed in legal instruments, however, which generally are based upon the notion of waste as *res derelicta* (abandoned property).

The problem of toxic or dangerous wastes is becoming an increasingly serious concern. Growing numbers of dump sites are found to contain toxic products. Sometimes these sites are clandestine and result in severe consequences. As a result, the Council of Europe's Convention on Civil Liability for Damage Resulting from Activities Dangerous to the Environment (June 21, 1993) includes in its definition of dangerous activity "(c) the operation of an installation or site for the incineration, treatment, handling or recycling of waste . . . provided that the quantities involved pose a significant risk for man, the environment or property; and (d) the operation of a site for the permanent deposit of waste."

One of the legal problems raised by this topic results from the difficulty of defining "wastes." The initial tendency in international regulation was to turn to national legislation for the definition of wastes. Thus, the OECD defined waste as "any material considered as waste or legally defined as waste in the country where it is situated or through or to which it is conveyed."[31] The Governing Council of UNEP[32] approved a decision utilizing the same terms. The framework EC directive[33] of July 15, 1975, declares that "waste" is any substance or object which the holder disposes of or is required to dispose of pursuant to the provisions of legislation. It unfortunately failed to take into account recycling.

In two cases, the European Court of Justice attempted to clarify the EC definition of waste and to establish criteria to determine whether waste is destined for recovery or disposal.[34] Also at issue in the first case was the question of who determines whether waste is shipped for disposal or recovery, a significant issue because the rules governing waste vary according to whether it is for disposal or recovery.[35] The Court permitted the authorities

---

[31]   OECD Rec. C(83)180, Feb. 1, 1984.

[32]   Art. 1(a), Decision 14/30, June 17, 1987.

[33]   75/442/EEC, O.J. L 194/39 (7/25/75).

[34]   *See* Case C-6/00, Abfall Service AG (ASA) v. Bundeminister für Umwelt, Jugend und Familie (2002) and Case C-9/00, Palin Granit OY and Vehmassalon kansanterveystyon huntayhtyman hallitus (2002).

[35]   The most important difference concerns the grounds on which various competent authorities concerned may oppose the proposed shipment. Waste for recovery is subject to less stringent rules.

of the destination to scrutinize the initial classification of the shipping state, but also held that the decision in favor of "recovery" must be based on whether the operation serves a "useful purpose" in replacing other materials which would have been used for that purpose. Waste might be bound for recovery if "its principal objective is that the waste serve a useful purpose in replacing other materials which would have had to be used for that purpose."[36] In the second case, the issue of stone as waste arose. The Court held that the test of waste is whether a substance constitutes a production residue not sought for subsequent use and whether it is likely that the substance will be reused without any further processing prior to its reuse. Where, as here, the stone was likely to be stored for an indefinite period of time to await possible reuse, it was considered discarded and therefore waste.

The problem of toxic or dangerous wastes involves other legal problems. There is considerable overlap in regulation; *e.g.*, specific rules regulate wastes and rules aimed at protecting the seas and continental waters from pollution indirectly regulate them as well. There are also general rules concerning chemical products and norms for the protection of workers that affect waste policies.[37] Transport regulations, norms of transfrontier pollution, rules relating to territorial management, regimes of prior authorization, and environmental impact procedures also are relevant. Two particular aspects are of special concern and have led to direct international regulation of toxic or dangerous wastes: their management and transfrontier shipments of them.

1. Waste Management

Three international institutions have addressed the problem waste management: OECD, UNEP, and the EC. The first two have elaborated texts which for the most part are not obligatory. Those of the EC are in the form of mandatory directives.

On the global level, UNEP has taken measures to avoid environmental harm from toxic or dangerous wastes. Following discussions within the Governing Council, UNEP added to its legal program the question of limiting production and international transport of toxic or dangerous wastes as a priority matter[38] leading to the adoption of the Cairo Guidelines of December 10, 1985, which were endorsed by the Governing Council of UNEP.[39] The Cairo Guidelines inspired the Basel Convention on the Control of Transboundary Movements of Hazardous Wastes and their

---

36   ASA, *supra* note 34, at para. 71.

37   *See, e.g.*, ILO Convention No. 170 Concerning Safety in the Use of Chemicals at Work (June 1990), and Convention No. 162 on Asbestos (1986).

38   Conference of Montevideo, 1981.

39   Decision 14/30, June 17, 1987.

Disposal, discussed below, but are broader in their focus on management.

The Cairo Guidelines recognize that differences exist among countries of the world in their ability to safely manage toxic and hazardous wastes and they seek to establish a general framework for administrative action aimed at the good management of dangerous wastes, especially in developing countries. The text is very general, perhaps because it primarily aims at countries that have not yet regulated the problem of dangerous wastes. It calls on states to take legislative or other measures to assure the protection of health and the environment against dangers posed by the production and management of dangerous wastes. States should cooperate to attain this objective, notably in elaborating and implementing technologies that produce the least wastes and, where appropriate, in transferring applicable technology.

Principle 7 of the Cairo Guidelines insists on prevention and contributes an important principle: the production of wastes should be reduced to a minimum and even the pollution that is permitted by the Guidelines should be avoided as much as possible. Each state should designate a special authority to plan, authorize and monitor the management of dangerous wastes. This authority should ensure that hazardous wastes are collected, transported and separately eliminated from other garbage. Lists of international waste treatment and elimination installations are foreseen. As for the effects that these installations may produce in other countries, the state which grants the authorization for a plant should furnish to any state potentially affected by such a facility all necessary information and enter into consultation with it as needed. In the granting of authorizations and in all administrative or judicial procedures relative to these grants, states must ensure equality of access and treatment of nationals and those from states that could be affected by nuisances coming from treatment plants or other discharges.

The Guidelines also announce principles related to monitoring of activities concerning dangerous wastes. They emphasize that appropriate authorities should maintain registers of operating permits and that the public should have free access to information relating to the number and the type of authorizations delivered as well as to details of the measures which accompany them. Several principles are devoted to the training of personnel employed in operations relating to dangerous wastes, to emergency plans and to the provision of information to other states in case of emergency. The problem of transport is addressed only in recalling applicable international rules on the subject and in foreseeing systems to assure that dangerous wastes will be accompanied by appropriate documents from the place of their production until they are eliminated. The final principle concerns responsibility for damage caused by dangerous wastes, inviting states to adopt domestic rules concerning liability, insurance and compensation for damage caused by dangerous wastes. These rules should be harmonized with international norms.

The texts adopted by OECD in this field are very different and are more numerous. There is one general recommendation and specific instruments concerning particular products, *e.g.*, beverage containers and waste paper. The general Recommendation envisages state development and implementation of a comprehensive waste management policy.[40] Such a policy involves a coherent system of measures concerning the design, manufacture and use of products as well as the reclamation and disposal of wastes aiming at the most efficient and economic reduction of the nuisances and costs generated by waste. Protection of the environment should be one objective of this policy.

The principles of a comprehensive waste management program should include reduction at the source of waste, especially measures concerning the design and marketing of products, their rational use and, where appropriate, the extension of product life. Changes in manufacturing processes, the reuse of products or their reclamation and recycling and, eventually, the use of alternative products are also addressed. The operations should not increase the risk of pollution transfer, however. Application of the "polluter pays" principle should encourage waste prevention and recycling. Appropriate measures should be taken in order to permit the appropriate authorities to receive all necessary information to assure that waste disposal or reclamation is realized in the most economic and judicious way with regard to environmental protection. Finally, the Recommendation foresees the adoption of administrative arrangements designed to organize waste management: reducing the types and quantities of wastes to be disposed of, the promotion of research on minimal-waste technology, and encouraging the creation of markets for recycled products.

Recommendations relative to the reuse and recycling of beverage containers[41] and to waste paper recovery[42] provide the most detailed indications on practical implementation of the principles envisaging a general policy of waste management. OECD also has adopted a classification scheme for hazardous wastes based on chemical components of the wastes, reasons why the materials are intended for disposal operations.[43]

The EC legal framework for waste management includes two approaches: general regulation and specific measures focused on particular types of wastes or on methods of disposal. General regulations are found in Directive 91/689[44] which prescribes measures of adequate waste management based on a twofold objective: to protect human health against noxious influences caused by the collection, transport, treatment, storage and disposal of waste and to promote the recovery, recycling and reuse of waste in order to

---

[40] Recommendation C(76)155, Sept. 28, 1976.
[41] Recommendation C(78)8, Feb. 3, 1978.
[42] Recommendation C(79)218, Jan. 30, 1980.
[43] C(88)90(Final), May 27, 1988.
[44] Dec. 20, 1991, O.J. L 377 (12/31/91).

preserve natural resources. Both objectives establish a permit system to ensure the coherence of waste management, using waste disposal plans, and to control all establishments or undertakings that carry out the main waste operations.

The general framework has been complemented by Regulation 259/93 on the Supervision and Control of Shipments of Waste Within, Into and Out of the EC[45] which established a notification and control procedure for all shipments of waste. The competent authorities may object to certain movements of waste or impose special requirements for environmental, safety, public policy or health protection.

Other international organizations have become involved in the question of toxic or hazardous wastes, although they are not generally concerned with environmental protection. The International Labor Organization (ILO) adopted a Convention Concerning Safety in the Use of Chemicals at Work in June 1990.[46] Over the objections of the employer members, this Convention includes a provision that hazardous chemicals and contaminated empty containers "shall be handled or disposed of in a manner which eliminates or minimizes the risk to safety and health and to the environment, in accordance with national law and practice." The worker members insisted that this language be retained, and also insisted on the inclusion of other provisions in the Convention that were not directly applicable to worker health and safety, but rather to public health and environmental protection.

The Protocol on Environmental Protection to the Antarctic Treaty[47] contains a general obligation for the states parties to reduce as much as possible the amount of wastes produced or disposed of in the Antarctic Treaty Area. Annex III includes provisions on waste disposal by removal from the area, by incineration, by disposal on land and in the sea. It also provides for waste management planning and recommends management practices. Even before the adoption of the Protocol, the 1989 Basel Convention on the Control of Transboundary Movements of Hazardous Wastes and Their Disposal, discussed in the next section, prohibited the export of hazardous wastes or other wastes for disposal within the area south of 60 degrees South latitude, (Art. 4(6)).

2.   *Transfrontier Movements*

The transport of toxic or dangerous substances from one country to another in order to eliminate, recycle or dispose of them is one of the most

---

[45]   Feb. 1, 1993, O.J. L 30 (6/2/93).

[46]   Seventy-seventh Session of the International Labor Conference, Geneva, June 1990.

[47]   Madrid, Oct. 4, 1991.

common forms of exporting pollution. Several reasons may motivate the producer of waste to seek to dispose of it in another country. First, the regulations of the producing country may make disposal there difficult. The wastes will thus be sent towards a country where regulation is less strict or the monitoring of compliance is less effective. The most targeted countries obviously are those that offer protection against claims and accept the wastes without always being concerned with the dangers they pose.

A second reason that could motivate a producer to export waste is lower disposal costs, even if the operation conforms to the law. The "importing" country could offer inexpensive possibilities of storage, for example in abandoned mines, or waste treatment plants less costly than those in the producing country. It is also evident that installations capable of treating certain types of waste do not exist in all countries. Radioactive wastes, for example, can be disposed of in only a few countries adequately equipped for re-treatment and disposal. Finally, a multinational enterprise might have a foreign subsidiary specialized in the elimination of certain types of dangerous wastes. The enterprise will transport its wastes to the foreign subsidiary to be treated and disposed of, even if borders must be crossed.

These factors led to an increasing movement of hazardous wastes across boundaries in the 1980s. According to OECD estimates for European countries, the volume of dangerous wastes crossing boundaries in 1983 was approximately 2.2 million tons.[48] As of July 1990, more than ten percent of the wastes generated in OECD countries was being transported across national borders for disposal. The content of the waste being transported and the attendant hazards became as much a concern as the rising quantity of the transfrontier movement.

The transport of hazardous wastes from developed countries to developing countries, which acquired the title "garbage imperialism," led at least 39 states to adopt and implement national legislation entirely prohibiting the importation into or trans-shipment through their territories of all foreign wastes.[49] In addition, by the end of the 1980s a general opposition to transboundary movements of hazardous wastes led to international regulation, first at a global level, then regionally. Transfrontier disposal of waste also may be controlled by norms dealing with chemicals or transfrontier pollution.[50]

---

[48] United Nations Environment Program, *1989 The State of the World Environment*, UNEP/GC.15/7/Add.2, 1989.

[49] States that have adopted such prohibitions include, *e.g.*, Algeria, Barbados, Belize, Benin, Burundi, Comoros, Congo, Dominican Republic, Gabon, Gambia, Ghana, Guatemala, Guinea, Guinea-Bissau, Guyana, Haiti, Indonesia, Ivory Coast, Jamaica, Kenya, Liberia, Libya, Niger, Nigeria, Peru, Philippines, Saint Lucia, Senegal, Sierra Leone, Solomon Islands, Tanzania, Togo, Trinidad & Tobago, Turkey, Vanuatu, Venezuela, Yugoslavia, Zambia, and Zimbabwe.

[50] In addition to the measures discussed in this chapter, see the work of the United Nations Human Rights Commission discussed in Chapter 15.

At the global level, UNEP first developed the Cairo Guidelines and Principles for the Environmentally Sound Management of Hazardous Wastes, adopted by the Governing Council.[51] The Guidelines aimed to assist states in preparing appropriate bilateral, regional and multilateral agreements and national legislation for the environmentally sound management of hazardous wastes. They were followed by the Basel Convention on the Control of Transboundary Movements of Hazardous Wastes and their Disposal,[52] adopted on March 22, 1989, by 116 states. This instrument establishes a global framework for international regulation, although it has been criticized as not going far enough. Indeed, it does not ban all transboundary movements of hazardous waste. One of its objectives is to make the movements of hazardous waste so costly and difficult that industry will find it more profitable to cut down on waste production.

The Convention defines wastes as substances or objects that are disposed of or are intended to be disposed of or are required to be disposed of by the provisions of national law. The hazardous character of wastes is defined by combined approaches of Annexes I, II and III. Annex I lists categories of wastes to be controlled (*e.g.*, chemical wastes from medical care in hospitals, and waste from different products such as pharmaceuticals, or production of specified substances such as biocides, organic solvents). Annex II contains two categories of wastes that require special consideration: wastes collected from households and residues arising from the incineration of household wastes. Annex III adds a list of hazardous characteristics of wastes, such as explosive, flammable, oxidizing, poisonous, infectious, corrosive, toxic and eco-toxic. This combined method is now increasingly used in international regulation, since the simple listing of polluting substances is inadequate.

Some of the important provisions in the Basel Convention are:

- the generation of hazardous wastes and other wastes and their transboundary movement should be reduced to a minimum consistent with the environmentally sound and efficient management of such wastes (Art. 4(2)(a) and (d));
- a signatory state cannot send hazardous waste to another signatory state that bans importation of it (Art. 4(1)(b)), to another signatory state if the importing country does not have the facilities to dispose of the waste in an environmentally-sound manner (Art. 4(2)(b)(e) and (g)), or to any non-party state (Art. 4(5));
- every country has the sovereign right to refuse to accept a shipment of hazardous wastes (Art. 4(1)(a)) and (12);
- before an exporting country can start a shipment on its way, it must have the importing country's consent in writing (Art. 4(1)(c));

51　　Decision 14/30, June 17, 1987.
52　　28 I.L.M. 657 (1989).

- when an importing country proves unable to dispose of legally imported waste in an environmentally sound way, then the exporting state has a duty either to take it back or to find some other way of disposing of it in an environmentally sound manner (Art. 8);
- the parties consider that "illegal traffic in hazardous wastes is criminal" (Art. 4(3));
- shipments of hazardous waste must be packaged, labeled, and transported in conformity with generally accepted and recognized international rules and standards (Art. 4(7)(b) and accompanied by a movement document from the point at which a transboundary movement commences to the point of disposal (Art. 4(7));
- bilateral agreements may be made, but they must conform to the terms of the Basel Convention and be no less environmentally sound (Art. 11);
- parties should cooperate in the training of technicians, exchange of information and transfer of technology (Arts.10 and 13).

The Convention established a Conference of the Parties and a Secretariat to supervise and facilitate its implementation. The Secretariat plays, in particular, an important role in receiving and conveying information to and from the parties and in handling the notification system provided for by the convention.

Decision II/12 adopted by the Conference of Parties to the Basel Convention in September 1995[53] phased out and prohibited by December 31, 1997, all transboundary movements of waste for disposal, recovery and recycling from OECD member states, the European Community and Liechtenstein to all other states. However, because the decision was not incorporated in the text of the Convention itself, the question arose as to whether or not it was legally binding. Therefore, at COP-3, it was proposed that the ban be formally incorporated in the Basel Convention as an amendment.[54] Decision III/1 bans hazardous wastes exports for final disposal and recycling from Annex VII countries (EU and OECD member states plus Liechtenstein) to non-Annex VII countries (all other parties to the Convention). In order to enter into force, the Ban Amendment required ratification by three-fourths of the Parties who were present at the time of the adoption of the Amendment (62 parties).

The Fourth Conference of the Parties, meeting in February 1998, adopted lists of hazardous (List A) and non-hazardous (List B) wastes. The first list comprises wastes that may not be sent by Annex VII countries to other states. List B, contained in Annex IX, includes materials that are not subject to the shipment ban unless they contain constituents at a level that causes them exhibit hazardous characteristics, such as flammability or

---

53 Decision III/I.
54 Decision III/1, Sept. 22, 1995.

toxicity. Even prior to the entry into force of the annexes, the European Union adopted a regulation giving effect to it.[55]

Since 1998, parties to the Basel Convention have turned their attention to elaborating a liability protocol, adopted December 10, 1999, and discussed in Chapter 7A.2, and to drafting guidelines on environmentally sound management of particular categories of hazardous wastes, *e.g.*, lead acid batteries, plastic wastes, decommissioned ships to be dismantled. These guidelines may include technical specifications for recycling and reclamation and specific strategies for implementation. In January 2002, a working group of the Basel Convention adopted a set of technical guidelines to protect human health and the environment from the improper management and disposal of plastic wastes.[56] The guidelines address a range of waste management issues such as sorting for mechanical recycling, health and safety mechanisms, shipping and transport services, feedstock recycling, compaction, energy recovery, and final disposal.

In June 2001, the OECD revised its texts on transboundary movement of wastes to harmonize its work with the Basel Convention. It adopted Council Decision C(2001)107 on Control of Transboundary Movements of Wastes Destined for Recovery Operations.

Several regional conventions and EU rules also have been adopted in order to regulate transboundary movements of hazardous wastes. African states generally did not consider the original Basel Convention satisfactory and wanted to ban the importation of all hazardous wastes onto their continent. They concluded, in the framework of the Organization of African Unity, a Convention on the Ban of the Import of Hazardous Wastes into Africa and on the Control of their Transboundary Movements within Africa.[57] The Convention, which advocates inter-African cooperation (Art. 10), is based on two principles: (1) states have the sovereign right to ban, for human health and environmental reasons, the transportation of hazardous wastes and substances into and across their territory; and (2) hazardous wastes should, as far as is compatible with environmentally sound and efficient management, be disposed of in the country where they were generated.

Most of the provisions of the Bamako Convention correspond to those of the Basel Convention, but the regional Convention differs in some important respects from the global instrument. First, the definition of waste is broader and includes those radioactive wastes that are subject to any international control system (Art. 2(3)). Second, the parties must strive to apply

---

55   Regulation 2408/98, O.J. Nov. 7, 1998.
56   Technical Guidelines for the Identification and Environmentally Sound Management of Plastic Wastes and for their Disposal, *adopted by* the Technical Working Group, Jan. 18, 2002.
57   Bamako, Jan. 29, 1991.

the precautionary approach (Art. 4(3)(f)). Most importantly, it prohibits the import of hazardous wastes for any reason into Africa from outside the continent and from non-contracting states and declares such movement a criminal act (Art. 4(1)). It prohibits dumping hazardous waste at sea, including incineration. Finally, the Convention requires the parties to impose unlimited and joint and several liability on hazardous waste generators in Africa (Art. 4(3)(b)). Like the Basel Convention, the Bamako Convention establishes a Conference of the Parties and a Secretariat.

In conformity with the Bamako Convention, the Treaty Establishing the African Economic Community[58] declares that member states undertake, individually or collectively, every appropriate step to ban the importation and dumping of hazardous wastes in their respective territories and to cooperate in the transboundary movement, management and processing of such wastes produced in Africa (Art. 59)

The Bamako Convention also corresponded to Article 39 of the Fourth Lomé Convention between the EC and African, Caribbean and Pacific (ACP) countries.[59] According to this text the contracting parties undertake to make every effort to ensure that international movements of hazardous waste and radioactive waste are generally controlled, with the Community agreeing to prohibit all direct or indirect export of such waste to the ACP states while the ACP states undertake to prohibit the direct or indirect import into their territory of such waste from the Community or from any other country. On June 23, 2000, the EC-ACP states signed a new Partnership Agreement in Cotonou, Benin. In Article 32(1)(d) the parties agree to cooperate on questions relating to the transport and elimination of hazardous wastes.

Even before the Basel Convention, the problem of the transboundary movements of hazardous wastes was envisaged in the Convention for the Protection of the Natural Resources and Environment of the South Pacific Region,[60] a convention of large scope containing general obligations. Articles 10 and 11 of this instrument speak of measures that the states in the region should take to prevent, reduce and monitor, in the area covered by the Convention, pollution which could be caused by the immersion in the sea or by dumping of toxic or hazardous wastes.

Other regional treaties were adopted after the Basel Convention and are inspired by it. The Regional Agreement on the Transboundary Movement of Hazardous Wastes[61] adopted in 1992 by six Central-American countries prohibits the transboundary transport as well as the import and transit of hazardous wastes. A 1995 Convention to Ban the Importation into Forum

---

58 Abuja, June 3, 1991.
59 Fourth ACP-CEE Convention, Dec. 15, 1989.
60 Noumea, Nov. 24, 1986.
61 Panama, Dec. 11, 1992.

Island Countries of Hazardous Wastes and Radioactive Wastes and to Control the Transboundary Movement and Management of Hazardous Wastes within the South Pacific,[62] further expanded the geographic area where movements of hazardous waste should be controlled. Within the Convention area, developing Pacific Island states shall ban the import of all hazardous wastes and radioactive wastes from outside that Area. Any other party—in fact Australia and New Zealand—shall ban the export of all hazardous wastes and radioactive wastes to all Forum Island countries. Finally, in 1996 the treaty system elaborated for the protection of the Mediterranean Sea was supplemented by a specific Protocol for the Prevention of the Pollution of the Mediterranean Sea by Transboundary Movements of Hazardous Wastes and their Disposal.[63] It is framed on the principles and approaches of the Basel Convention, but is integrated in the structures of the Mediterranean treaty system.

Examples of bilateral agreements are the agreement between Canada and the United States on Transfrontier Movements of Hazardous Wastes[64] and Annex III to the Agreement of Cooperation for the Protection and Amelioration of the Environment in the Frontier Region Between Mexico and the United States.[65] The American-Canadian agreement provides that the two countries are obliged not only to promulgate all the necessary regulations to apply the agreement, but they should also transmit them to the other party by diplomatic note when they enter into force.[66] Annex III to the United States-Mexico agreement insists on the obligation of the contracting states to apply their own legislation regarding hazardous wastes to shipments which leave their territory.[67] It adds to this the obligation to inform the other contracting party of any measure prohibiting a pesticide or other chemical substance or restraining its utilization.[68]

Several points deserve particular attention in the problem of transporting hazardous wastes beyond national frontiers. The obligation of states relating to the transboundary movement of hazardous wastes is based on the rule of international law formulated first in Principle 21 of the Stockholm Declaration, now recognized as customary law: States have the obligation to ensure that activities carried out within the limits of their jurisdiction—in this case the production and export of hazardous wastes—do not cause damage to the environment of other states.[69] Equally in the spirit

---

[62] Waigani, Sept. 16, 1995.

[63] Izmir, Oct. 1, 1996.

[64] Ottawa, Oct. 28, 1986.

[65] Washington, Nov. 12, 1986.

[66] Art. 5, para. 3.

[67] Art. 2, para. 2.

[68] Art. 5.

[69] Declaration on the Human Environment, Stockholm, June 16, 1972. *See* G.A. Res. 2994/XXVII, 2995/XXVII and 2996/XXVII, Dec. 15, 1972.

of Principle 21 of the Stockholm Declaration and respectful of the sovereignty of states, the Preamble of the Basel Convention on the Control of Transboundary Movements of Hazardous Wastes and their Disposal reaffirms the right of states to refuse to accept on their territory hazardous wastes produced elsewhere. The fundamental principle in the field is that a state should only permit the export of hazardous wastes to a receiving state if that state consents to the importation by an explicit act in writing.[70] Similarly, Article 9 of the Basel Convention provides that the exporting country will accept the return of any transport of hazardous waste that was not legally imported into the other country.

C. Regulating Hazardous Industries

On a general basis, the regulation of hazardous industrial activity is carried out through risk assessment and environmental impact assessment procedures, as well as licensing and permitting. These subjects are dealt with in Chapter 5 above. Industrial activities involving hazardous substances, particularly those like radioactive substances and biological agents that could be diverted into weapons or used in terrorist activities, must also be subject to strict security measures.

The risk of major accident hazards involving certain industrial activities was the subject of a well-known EC Directive[71] of June 24, 1982. The text, known as the "Seveso directive," is named for the Italian town where the most serious industrial accident in European history occurred on July 10, 1976. The Directive requires EC member states to take measures necessary to ensure that all manufacturers engaged in certain listed activities prove to the competent authority that they have identified the existing major accident hazards, adopted the appropriate safety measures, and provided persons working on the site with sufficient information, training and equipment in order to ensure their safety. The manufacturers should notify the appropriate authorities of information relating to dangerous substances contained in a list annexed to the Directive, which are employed or produced in one form or another at some stage during the manufacturing process. Emergency plans and assistance relating to events outside the concerned installation should be established and persons potentially victims of a major accident must be informed of the emergency measures to be taken in case of accident. Should such an accident occur, the manufacturer must inform the appropriate authorities, providing them with all the necessary information. States in turn are obliged to inform the Commission of the

---

[70] Art. 4, Convention on the Control of Transboundary Movements of Hazardous Wastes and their Disposal, Basel, Mar. 22, 1989.

[71] 82/501/EEC, O.J. L 230 (8/5/82).

EEC of all major accidents. The Commission may advise the appropriate authorities of other states members which may need to act.

The Seveso Directive was modified by Directive 96/82 which widened its scope and simplified it with no distinction between production and storage. The list of named substances has been substantially shortened, a safety management system is now required for the larger sites, and emergency response plans must be tested. Major accident hazards must be taken into account in member states' land-use planning policies and there are formal requirements for member states' inspection systems. Safety reports and other information received under the Directive are to be made available to the public.

D. Radioactivity

The use of radioactive substances constitutes one of the most urgent but technically and politically difficult areas of environmental protection. In addition to the problem of nuclear weapons, which nuclear states jealously guard,[72] nuclear energy production has become a major industry. At the end of 2000 a total of 438 nuclear power plants were operating around the world. Twenty-nine new units were under construction, many of them in Eastern Europe. These power plants supply 16 percent of the worlds electricity, but over three-quarters of the power to France and nearly that much to Lithuania. Seventeen countries rely upon nuclear energy for at least one-quarter of their total electricity demand. To these issues must be added the growing problem of illicit trafficking in nuclear materials. The IAEA identified 213 such incidents between 1993 and 1998,[73] most of them involving security breakdowns in former Warsaw Pact states.

The International Atomic Energy Agency (IAEA), headquartered in Vienna, has been given broadest responsibility in the field.[74] The IAEA negotiates international treaties providing the structure of the nuclear safety system, supplemented by recommendations that set forth the detail of protective measures. The IAEA Statute was adopted in 1956, authorizing the

---

[72] In addition to the acknowledged nuclear powers, (U.S., France, UK, Russia, China, India, Pakistan), approximately another dozen possess or control separated plutonium for military or commercial use. *See* Barry Kellman, *Protection of Nuclear Materials, in* COMMITMENT AND COMPLIANCE: THE ROLE OF NON-BINDING NORMS IN THE INTERNATIONAL LEGAL SYSTEM 486, 488 (D. Shelton, ed., 2000).

[73] IAEA, Incidents in the IAEA Database on Illicit Trafficking Confirmed by States, Mar. 2, 1998.

[74] Two regional organizations also work on the topic: the European Agency for Nuclear Energy, created in 1957 within the OECD framework; and Euratom, also created in 1957 by the European Community.

organization to sponsor atomic energy research and development[75] and to have international regulatory authority over nuclear materials and technologies. In addition, states parties to the Nuclear Non-Proliferation Treaty accept IAEA verification of their non-proliferation commitments. The structure and functioning of the IAEA are described in Chapter 4.

International regulations on radiation aim to safeguard human health and life. For nuclear weapons, the most general international text is the Treaty Banning Nuclear Weapons Tests in the Atmosphere, in Outer Space, and Underwater.[76] Nearly all states of the world are parties to it. Five years later, the Nuclear Non-Proliferation Treaty (NPT)[77] obliged each non-nuclear weapon state to ensure that nuclear materials, equipment, facilities, and information are not used to advance military purposes. The Treaty requires these states to accept international safeguards under IAEA supervision, including reporting requirements, installation of monitoring equipment, and on-site inspections. (NPT Art. III). More than 180 states have entered into bilateral safeguards agreements with the IAEA pursuant to the NPT and according to an IAEA internal guidance document, INFCIRC/153.[78] These agreements are themselves supplemented by subsidiary agreements containing more detailed operating procedures. The package of commitments allows the IAEA to verify through state reporting and on-site inspections the security of nuclear materials and the features of nuclear facilities. In 1997, the IAEA Board of Governors proposed a new model Additional Protocol to safeguards agreements (INFCIRC/540) which aims at obtaining more information about nuclear facilities, including the collection of environmental samples.

The Antarctic Treaty goes further in forbidding not only nuclear explosions, but also eliminating all weapons and radioactive wastes in the Antarctic region.[79] Placing objects carrying nuclear arms on the moon or in orbit around the moon is equally forbidden by the Agreement Governing

---

[75]   Statute of the International Atomic Energy Agency, Oct. 26, 1956; 8 U.S.T. 1093; 276 U.N.T.S. 3.

[76]   Moscow, August 5, 1963.

[77]   Treaty on the Non-Proliferation of Nuclear Weapons, July 1, 1968. The treaty has over 175 states parties.

[78]   The Structure and Content of Agreements Between the Agency and States Required in Connection with the Treaty on the Non-Proliferation of Nuclear Weapons, IAEA Doc. INFCIRC/153 (May 1971).

[79]   Washington, Dec. 1, 1959, Art. 5. Several regions of the world have similarly declared themselves nuclear weapons free zones. *See* the Treaty of Tlatelolco for the Prohibition of Nuclear Weapons in Latin America, Feb. 14, 1967; South Pacific Nuclear Free Zone Treaty, Aug. 6, 1985; African Nuclear Weapon Free Zone Treaty, Apr. 11, 1996; South-East Asia Nuclear Free Zone Treaty, Dec. 15, 1995.

the Activities of States on the Moon and Other Celestial Bodies.[80] Finally, in 1996 the Nuclear Test Ban Treaty of 1963 was expanded to ban all categories of nuclear tests by a Comprehensive Nuclear Ban Treaty and a Protocol which complements it.[81]

1. *Security of Nuclear Materials*

In addition to the IAEA Statute and the NPT, several other treaties address the protection of nuclear materials. The most important is the 1980 Convention on the Physical Protection of Nuclear Material, but other agreements also add protective norms, especially the 1994 Convention on Nuclear Safety and the 1997 Convention on the Safety of Spent Fuel Management and on the Safety of Radioactive Waste Management. To these must be added the IAEA Recommendations which are linked to the treaties and provide specifications and details of necessary measures. The Recommendations can be incorporated into a binding treaty, but even without this they are widely followed.

Separate instruments govern matters of transport and radiological emergencies. Regulations on the transport of nuclear material are contained within general conventional norms concerning transport by road, rail, sea[82] and air, supplemented at the request of the United Nations Economic and Social Council (ECOSOC), by an IAEA Regulation on the safe transport of radioactive materials, drafted in 1961 and periodically updated since that time. A separate Code of Practice governs the transboundary movement of radioactive waste and is discussed later in this chapter.[83] The general IAEA Transport Code contains Recommendations formulated so that they can be easily incorporated into the domestic legislative provisions of member states. The Recommendations set appropriate technical criteria (packaging, handling, and other aspects of transport) but also contain provisions relating to the institution of administrative procedures (*e.g.*, verifications, procedures in case of accident).

In 1972 the IAEA issued its first recommendations for the physical protection of nuclear materials, aimed at avoiding theft or sabotage. To strengthen the normative base on this issue, the member states subsequently negotiated the Convention on the Physical Protection of Nuclear Material

---

[80]   December 5, 1979, Art. 3, para 3.

[81]   Sept. 24, 1996.

[82]   *See, e.g.*, the IMO Code for the Safe Carriage of Irradiated Nuclear Fuel, Plutonium, and High-Level Radioactive Waste in Flasks on Board Ships, IMO Assembly Res. A. 748(18), Nov. 4, 1993.

[83]   *See* IAEA Code of Practice on the International Transboundary Movement of Radioactive Waste (Dec. 11, 1991), 30 I.L.M. 556.

(March 3, 1980). The Treaty establishes a framework for international cooperation to protect civilian nuclear material while in storage and transport. Its aims are to avert the potential dangers of unlawful taking and use of nuclear materials; adopt appropriate and effective measures to ensure the prevention, detention and punishment of such offenses; establish effective measures for the physical protection of nuclear material; and facilitate its safe transfer. The provisions focus on the obligations of states during transport of nuclear material to ensure a minimum level of physical protection.

With the dissolution of the Soviet Union and rising threat of terrorist attacks, the IAEA revised its Recommendations based an expert proposal entitled "Physical Protection Objectives and Fundamental Principles."[84] The objectives are to (1) protect against unauthorized removal of nuclear material in use and storage, and during transport, (2) implement rapid and comprehensive measures to locate and recover missing or stolen nuclear material, (3) protect against sabotage of nuclear facilities or of nuclear material in use and storage and during transport, and (4) mitigate or minimize the radiological consequences of sabotage. Each state is responsible for the establishment, implementation and maintenance of its own effective physical protection regime, which should be based upon a legislative and regulatory framework, designate a competent authority, establish the responsibility of the licence holders and elaborate contingency plans.

As for operations using nuclear materials, the IAEA has carried out a program aimed at establishing codes of good practices and guidelines relating to safety of nuclear facilities. These texts form a body of regulation in five chapters concerning governance, siting of facilities, construction, operation and quality controls[85] and are designed to lead to the elaboration of consistent national regulations. Each chapter is introduced by a "code of good practice" and contains a number of safety standards. Current recommendations for strengthening physical protection systems include making standards mandatory for domestic uses, rasing standards, and requiring international inspections or enforcement mechanisms to provide verification of compliance.

IAEA further developed the law by sponsoring the adoption in Vienna, on September 20, 1994, of a Convention on Nuclear Safety. It entered into force after only two years on October 24, 1996, probably due to awareness of the danger posed by some unsafe conditions in nuclear installations in former parts of the Soviet Union. Its objective is to achieve and maintain a high level of nuclear safety worldwide through enhancement of national measures and international cooperation including safety-related technical cooperation (Art. 1(i)). The Convention reaffirms that responsibility for

---

[84] IAEA, GOV/2001/41, Aug. 15, 2001; 41 I.L.M. 737 (2002).

[85] International Atomic Energy Agency, Regulation of Nuclear Activities, Legal Collection No. 13, Vienna, 1986, at 13–19.

nuclear safety rests with the state having jurisdiction over a nuclear installation. It entails a commitment to apply fundamental safety principles for
such installations (Preamble).

The general obligation of the contracting parties is to establish and
maintain effective defenses in nuclear installations against potential radiological hazards (Art.1(ii)), in particular by reviewing as soon as possible the
safety of existing nuclear installations (Art. 6). The Convention stresses the
importance of the legislative and regulatory framework which each party
shall establish and maintain to govern the safety of nuclear installations,
including a system of licensing and inspection and assessment to ascertain
compliance with applicable regulations and the term of licenses (Art. 7).
The license holder has primary responsibility for the safety of the installation (Art. 9). A regulatory body shall be established or designated in each
contracting party (Art. 8) and adequate financial resources made available
to support the safety of each nuclear installation throughout its life (Art.
11(1)). States parties must establish and implement quality assurance programs for satisfying specified requirements for all activities important to
nuclear safety throughout the life of a nuclear installation (Art. 11).

In addition to the general safety norms the Convention includes specific prescriptions concerning the siting (Art. 17), the design and construction (Art. 18), and the operation (Art. 19) of nuclear installations.
States parties must periodically report (Art. 5) and hold meetings for reviewing the reports that are filed (Art. 20). IAEA provides the secretariat for the
meetings (Art. 28).

2. Nuclear Accidents

IAEA first elaborated directives concerning the procedures to be followed
in case of nuclear accident. These directives were published in 1969; they
were further developed in 1981 and in 1985, but were not implemented as
they should have been, as the Chernobyl accident demonstrated.

On April 26, 1986, at 1:23 in the morning, an explosion occurred in
reactor Number 4 of the Chernobyl nuclear power plant, near Prypiat, a
town of 25,000 inhabitants situated 130 km north of Kiev, Ukraine, in the
Soviet Union. An investigation which took place after the accident established that negligence led to the explosion. The procedure to stop the reactor for routine maintenance had begun at the time of the accident, but
before it was completed management at the plant had decided to proceed
with tests without obtaining the authorization of the responsible authority.
They also declined to wait for the properly prepared team which would have
been present the following night. The tests were insufficiently monitored
and the necessary safety measures were not taken, with the result that over-
heating caused a chemical explosion. The resulting fire melted a portion

of the uranium fuel. Although there was no nuclear explosion and the core of the reactor did not melt, the fire which engulfed the reactor was serious and released a large quantity of radioactive material into the air.

Large amounts of fallout occurred near the plant and spread beyond. Between April 27 and May 8, nearly 50,000 persons were evacuated from towns located within a 30 kilometer radius of the plant. Two persons were immediately killed by the explosion, 29 died shortly after, and 203 were afflicted with radiation poisoning. The foreign consequences were also severe, even though no deaths were immediately attributed to the accident. Following rapid changes in the wind direction, the radioactive cloud which had formed crossed the airspace of a series of countries beginning with those of Scandinavia. Four days after the incident, radiation measurements along the Swedish coast were ten times higher than normal.

The radioactive cloud moved south, crossing Germany, Austria, Switzerland, Yugoslavia and Italy. Preliminary studies showed that about half the radioactive material consisted of iodine, but other more persistent elements, like cesium, were detected. On May 4, unusually high levels of radioactivity were found in the milk on farms in Austria, Hungary, Italy, Sweden and Yugoslavia, and relatively high values of Cesium-137 in milk on farms in Switzerland, the United Kingdom, Austria and Germany. The radioactive half-life of Iodine-131 is only about eight days, while the half-life of Cesium-137 is approximately 30 years, meaning the latter could persist in the environment at significant levels for well over a century after the Chernobyl release.

No conventional international regulation applied at the time the accident occurred in the Soviet Union. The interpretation then given to the Convention on Long-Range Transboundary Air Pollution[86] excluded pollution by radioactive elements. The USSR was not a contracting party to the Vienna Convention on Civil Liability for Nuclear Damage.[87] Indeed, among the states that suffered effects from the radioactive cloud, only Yugoslavia had signed and ratified the Convention. There remained, therefore, only the recourse to general rules of international environmental law.

The IAEA that took action after being requested to assist in fact-finding concerning the circumstances of the accident and to prepare a text transforming certain principles of international environmental law into obligatory rules applicable in cases of nuclear accidents of international scope. The Governing Council of the Agency decided, in an extraordinary session held May 21, to convoke a group of governmental experts in order to elaborate measures to reinforce international cooperation in the field of nuclear security and radioactive protection. This meeting took place in

---

[86] Geneva, Nov. 13, 1979.
[87] May 21, 1963.

Vienna from July 21 to August 15, 1986, and drafted two conventions which were subsequently adopted by the IAEA General Conference, meeting in extraordinary session from September 24 to 26. The Convention on Early Notification of a Nuclear Accident, signed September 26, entered into force on October 27; the Convention on Assistance in the Case of a Nuclear Accident or Radiological Emergency was signed the same day and also rapidly ratified by the signatories.

The first of the two conventions, relating to rapid notification of nuclear accidents, expresses and gives concrete application to the duty to inform other states that may be affected by a accident causing environmental harm. While making this obligation explicit, the Convention remains a cautious text. It does not speak to the problems of liability and reparation for damage, but instead of the necessity for states to furnish pertinent information on nuclear accidents as soon as possible. The drafters rejected Germany's proposal for an explicit proclamation that all states have a responsibility to see that their nuclear activities are carried out in such a manner as to protect the health and security of the public and the environment.

The essential obligation of states parties is to notify without delay of any nuclear accident and to rapidly furnish pertinent available information in order to limit as much as possible the radioactive consequences in other countries.[88] The types of information to be furnished are detailed in Article 5. They should include, to the extent the notifying state knows: the exact time, location and the nature of the accident, the installation or activity concerned, the presumed or known cause, the likely evolution of the accident, and the general characteristics of the radioactive discharge. The state should also provide information on the current meteorological conditions, and protective measures taken or projected outside the site. This information should be supplemented as new data become available. The states affected can demand further information or consultations in order to limit as much as possible the radioactive consequences within the limits of their jurisdictions.[89] Information furnished confidentially should not be released to the public.[90] Each state should indicate to the Agency in Vienna—which should also receive the information and transmit it to each state which requests it—the responsible authorities and the points of contact capable of furnishing and receiving the notification.[91]

Contrary to other provisions of the Convention adopted without great difficulty, Article 1, which determines when notification is required, gave rise to serious disagreement. Its first paragraph was finally approved as follows:

---

[88] Convention on Early Notification of a Nuclear Accident, Art. 2.
[89] *Id.*
[90] Art. 5, para. 3.
[91] Arts. 4, 7.

This Convention shall apply in the event of any accident involving facilities or activities of a state party or of persons or legal entities under its jurisdiction or control, referred to in paragraph 2 below, from which a release of radioactive material occurs or is likely to occur and which has resulted or may result in an international transboundary release that could be of radiological safety significance for another state.

According to paragraph 2, the obligation to notify applies to all accidents from any nuclear reactor, to any nuclear fuel cycle facility, radioactive waste management facility, the transport and storage of nuclear fuels, as well as any operation involving the manufacture, use, storage, disposal or transport of radioisotopes, including the use of nuclear-powered spacecraft. Nuclear arms are not mentioned, and from the *travaux préparatoires*, as well as from the terms of Article 3, this omission is in fact an exclusion. Article 3 envisages that "other nuclear accidents" may be the subject of notification on a voluntary basis, but notification in these situations is not required by the Convention. In actual fact, all nuclear powers have declared themselves ready to notify of such accidents.

The Convention on Assistance in the Case of a Nuclear Accident or Radiological Emergency, also adopted on September 26, 1986, similarly corresponds to rules already existing in international law. However, even if customary international law imposes on states a general obligation to cooperate, it does not indicate the means and methods of the assistance, which must be explicitly detailed by conventional law. The Vienna Convention on Assistance reinforces the duty to aid states that are victims of catastrophes, and expands it in particular to radiological catastrophes, developing the implications of this expanded norm. The Convention still remains, however, a framework treaty which explicitly calls for the conclusion of bilateral or multilateral arrangements and action of the Agency to promote, facilitate and encourage cooperation between the states parties.

The instrument on assistance traces a general framework for cooperation between states on the one hand, and between the states and the IAEA on the other, in the case of nuclear accident or other radiological emergency. It seems that the last term can be interpreted as covering any danger caused by radiation, whatever the cause, and includes nuclear arms testing. Any state which is exposed can claim assistance, whether or not the origin of the accident or emergency is found within its territory, under its jurisdiction or under its control.[92] Thus, in the case of the Chernobyl accident, the states affected by the radioactive cloud could have demanded the aid of other states or of the IAEA. It is clear, however, that states parties do not

---

[92]   Art. 2, para. 1.

accept any obligation other than cooperating between themselves and with the Agency in order to facilitate early response.[93]

As always when there is a question of mutual assistance in response to an emergency, two types of measures are foreseen by the Convention: preventive measures and those to be undertaken when the situation is actually presented. In the first category, the Convention provides for identifying and notifying the IAEA of experts, equipment and materials which could be made available to provide assistance, as well as the terms, notably financial, under which such assistance could be furnished,[94] the authorities competent to intervene and points of contact,[95] the emergency plans and implementation of programs of assistance and monitoring of radioactivity.[96] When a crisis arises, the state party to the Convention who requires assistance should indicate the scope and type of assistance required and should furnish all information which could be necessary.[97] Each state may request assistance relating to medical treatment or the temporary relocation of persons involved in a nuclear accident or radiological emergency into the territory of another state.[98]

The state requiring assistance has direction, control, coordination and supervision of all assistance on its territory. Within possible limits, it should furnish the equipment and local services necessary for the proper and effective administration of assistance. On the other hand, measures which occur on the territory of the state which furnishes the assistance are under the latter's control.[99]

The Convention also addresses the issue of reimbursement of costs. If the state which furnishes the assistance does not offer its services freely, the state having requested the assistance should reimburse the assisting state, as well as any persons or organizations acting on its behalf, for all costs incurred for the services rendered and for any other costs of assistance.[100] Article 8 provides that privileges and immunities are accorded to personnel who furnish assistance to a foreign state—immunity from arrest, detention, and legal process in the jurisdiction—and also exemption from taxation, duties, or other charges.

Finally, the Convention grants a large role to IAEA in the organization and coordination of assistance operations. The Agency should facilitate

---

[93]   Art. 1, para. 1.
[94]   Art. 2, para. 4.
[95]   Art. 4.
[96]   Art. 5b.
[97]   Art. 2, para. 2.
[98]   Art. 2, para. 5.
[99]   Art. 3.
[100] Art. 7.

cooperation with and between states;[101] it receives information relating to the capacities of intervention of different states;[102] it should itself respond to certain requests for assistance;[103] it centralizes information concerning the responsible authorities and the points of contact different states;[104] it collects and disseminates all information regarding available resources and emergency situations, helps with the elaboration of emergency plans, etc.[105]

On the whole, it can be said that the Chernobyl accident had positive effects on the development of international environmental law. It also demonstrated the inevitable character of international institutions at a moment when these organizations were the object of serious criticism. States recognized the gravity of the accident and above all, that similar situations that could arise in the future.

Finally, it is interesting to note that it seems no government pushed to conclude rules on state responsibility for accidental environmental harm. Negotiations would no doubt have been lengthy and perhaps unsuccessful over such matters as standard of care (strict liability or negligence), proximate harm, and mitigation of damages. The difficulty of evaluating the cost of the consequences of the Chernobyl accident, especially the precautionary measures taken by the affected countries, also may have been a determinant factor in avoiding the issue of state responsibility. It also seems, however, to be consistent with the general reticence displayed towards rules imposing international responsibility or liability on states for damages caused by that state or its citizens. The emphatic preference remains measures of prevention rather than cure.

3. Radioactive Wastes

One of the principal problems posed by nuclear activities is the disposal of radioactive wastes. It is therefore important to regulate the discharge of nuclear matter into the environment. In many cases the disposal of radioactive wastes is accomplished within a state's borders, but the level of international shipments appears to be rising. The principal questions in international law thus concern transport and the immersion of radioactive waste in areas beyond national jurisdiction.

Several international conventions contain provisions aimed at the dumping of radioactive wastes. The most important of them is the London Convention on the Prevention of Pollution by Dumping of Wastes and

---

[101] Art. 1, para. 1.
[102] Art. 2, para. 4.
[103] Art. 2, para. 6(a).
[104] Art. 4.
[105] Art. 5.

Other Matter ("London Dumping Convention") of December 29, 1972. Article IV of this convention, combined with Annex I, forbids the immersion of "high-level radioactive wastes or other high level radioactive matter,[106] . . . as unsuitable for dumping at sea." In 1983, the Seventh Consultative Meeting adopted a non-binding resolution establishing a moratorium on all dumping at sea of radioactive materials pending scientific studies. Several states publicly opted not to comply, including many of the nuclear weapons states. In 1994, the IMO made the ban mandatory and this was accepted by all states parties except Russia. Annex I, paragraph 3 now provides that materials containing more than *de minimis* levels of radioactivity shall not be considered eligible for dumping; the ban is subject to a 25-year scientific review. An international evaluation process approved by the 21st Consultative Meeting of the London Convention defines the *de minimis* level of radioactivity.[107]

As to transport, the IAEA adopted a Code of Practice on the International Movement of Radioactive Waste in 1991. These recommendations have been adopted by the UN and all other international organizations concerned with the transport of hazardous goods, as well as by a large number of states. In general, the regulations hold the shipper responsible for design safety and for the correct assembly of the package, as well as for labeling and marking. The carrier is responsible for providing the necessary control measures during transport and storage in transit. Access to packages should be restricted. As noted above, the 1997 Spent Fuel Management treaty also contains safety measures for the transport. States parties must develop programs to ensure that transboundary movement is properly authorized and transpires with prior notification and consent of the receiving state. The latter may consent only if it has the technical and administrative capacity as well as regulatory structure to manage the spent fuel or radioactive waste.

E. Biotechnology

Throughout history, farmers have used selective breeding to alter their livestock and crops for qualities sought by the farmers or consumers. They have also applied biological fermentation to produce new products and increase the period of conserving food. These techniques rely on genetic variation, including mutations, already present in species and populations of flora and fauna. All major crops and farm animals are the product of some degree of human intervention.

---

[106] Defined on public health, biological or other grounds by the competent international body in this field (at present the International Atomic Energy Agency).

[107] U.N., Report of the Secretary-General, Mar. 2000, U.N. Doc. A/55/61.

Genetic modification or biotechnology differs from the directed but natural processes of selective breeding. Genetic engineering isolates single genes from an organism and transfers one or more to another organism, across populations and across species or phyla. Animal genes may be inserted into plants and vice versa. Once inserted, the genes may be transmitted to subsequent generations.

The 1992 UN Convention on Biological Diversity defines biotechnology to include any technological application that utilizes biological systems, living organisms, or derivations of them, to create or modify products or processes to a specific use. One of the most controversial subjects concerning this science is the scope of potential risks associated with the handling and introduction into the environment of living modified organisms (LMOs) or, as they were first referred to, genetically-modified organisms. The need to promote biosafety has centered on two related issues: first, the handling of LMOs at the laboratory level, in order to protect workers and prevent the accidental liberation of such organisms into the surrounding ecosystem ("contained use"); second, the need for regulatory systems to govern the deliberate release of LMOs into the environment, either for testing or commercial purposes.

Genetic engineering has reached the point where living organisms can be adapted and created in the laboratory. Many of these LMOs are not intended to stay in the laboratory, however. Genetically altered corn and soybean seeds are already in use, perhaps as many as 20 million acres planted with them in the United States alone. Research is being carried out to introduce herbicide resistance into virtually all major crops as a means of making it easier to control weeds. In addition, because of the noxious effects of long-term pesticide use, genetic engineering of micro-organisms has developed as an alternative strategy to improve pest control. Some 100 fungus species and many bacteria species are known to have insecticidal effects. The use of biotechnology to raise crop yields has received the most publicity and been the most controversial, including efforts to broaden the germplasm basis from which new genetic combinations can be created and improving and speeding up the propagation of plants. The most widely-used and commercially-successful application of plant biotechnology is the rapid and large-scale multiplication of plants through clones produced in tissue culture. The technique is currently used to mass-produce ornamental, fruit, vegetable, medicinal plant and tree species.

Many scientists see biotechnology as permitting them to pursue plant breeding efforts, with favorable impact on food supplies, international trade in agricultural products, the environment and existing plant resources. The commercial nature of many of these potential benefits is another source of conflict, however, particularly between developed and developing countries who disagree over access to, control of, and benefits from primary and modified genetic resources.

Aware of possible benefits, a substantial number of scientists nonetheless urge caution in releasing genetically engineered organisms, because of the possibility that such organisms might have an unfavorable impact upon the environment and because considerable scientific uncertainty exists about the scope and degree of the environmental risks. There is fear that the LMOs, as living organisms, could evolve into destructive pathogens. Moreover, genetically-altered genes may naturally transfer to wild-grown relatives, with unforeseeable consequences. Thus far, the major negative impact that has been identified and studied is the harm to monarch butterflies caused by the protein used in genetically-altered corn to repel certain pests.[108]

Particular concerns arise over the release of LMOs in or close to a center of genetic diversity of that crop. Mass production of identical plant materials introduces greater danger of genetic destruction because all specimens are equally vulnerable to a single disease or pest. No resistant varieties remain as alternative sources. The widespread use of cloned crops or artificial seeds to replace sexually reproducing crops will thus likely increase crop vulnerability. Finally, the release of genetically modified micro-organisms (bacteria and fungi) could pose particular problems. Very little is known about microbial communities; few have been named or studied. However, current research indicates that natural genetic transfer between different micro-organisms is relatively frequent, making it conceivable that engineered species could transfer throughout the microbial world in unpredictable ways.

OECD was one of the first organizations to act on genetic modifications. In 1986, OECD published an extensive report identifying safety considerations associated with LMOs, but finding that the development of international guidelines was premature.[109] A new report in 1992, Safety Considerations for Biotechnology, contained general principles for the design and safety assessment of small scale-field testing of LMOs that have low or negligible risk. Two sets of "Good Development Principles," one for plants and one for microorganisms, assume that low or negligible risk in field testing can be identified.

Uncertainty surrounding the environmental impacts of LMOs is recognized in the Convention on Biological Diversity (CBD) which does not define the term "living modified organism" but calls on the contracting parties to consider the need for and modalities of a protocol setting out procedures for the safe transfer, handling and use of any living modified organism

---

[108] *See Monarch Larvae Killed by Bt-Dusted Leaves, Iowa State University Researchers Report*, BNA INT'L. EVNTL. REP., Aug. 30, 2000, 682.

[109] OECD, Recombinant DNA Safety Considerations—Safety Considerations for Industrial, Agricultural and Environmental Applications of Organisms Derived by Recombinant DNA Techniques (1986).

resulting from biotechnology that may have adverse effect on the environment (Art. 19(3)). The Convention itself obligates parties to "provide any available information about the use and safety regulations required by th[e] contracting party in handling such organisms, as well as any available information on the potential adverse impact of the specified organisms to concerned" to any party into which those organisms are introduced.

In respect to *in situ* conservation, the CBD requires the parties to establish or maintain means to regulate, manage or control the risks associated with the use and release of living modified organisms resulting from biotechnology which are likely to have adverse environmental impacts that could affect the conservation and sustainable use of biological diversity, taking into account the risks to human health. The Convention also calls for implementing the rights of countries of origin of genetic resources or countries providing genetic resources, particularly developing countries, to benefit from the biotechnological development and the commercial utilization of products derived from such resources (Art. 15.4(j)).

While thus expressing some concerns over the risks of biotechnology, both the CBD and UNCED's Agenda 21 encourage such technology in order to increase benefits from biological resources. Agenda 21, chapter 16, "Environmentally Sound Management of Biotechnology" states that its goal is to foster international principles for the environmental management of biotechnology, as well as to promote sustainable applications of biotechnology.[110] In addition to increasing the availability of food and improving human health, the program calls for enhancing protection of the environment and "establishing enabling mechanisms for the development and the environmentally sound application of biotechnology." States are to consider the need for and feasibility of internationally agreed guidelines on safety in biotechnology releases, including risk assessment and risk management, and consider studying the feasibility of guidelines which could facilitate national legislation on liability and compensation. In national legislation governments are encouraged to promote rights associated with intellectual property and informal innovations, including farmer's and breeder's rights.

Decision II/5, adopted by the Conference of the Parties in 1995, expressed concern about the significant gaps that remain in knowledge about LMOs and the environment and called for application of the precautionary principle pending further scientific findings.[111] The same meet-

---

[110] Agenda 21, chapter 16, at 218. Other sections of Agenda 21 containing references to biotechnology are chapter 14 on sharing of research and plant genetic resources; chapter 19, risk management of hazardous products; and chapter 15, conservation of biological diversity.

[111] A Call to Action: Decisions and Ministerial Statement from the Second Meeting of the Conference of the Parties to the Convention on Biological Diversity, Jakarta, Indonesia, Nov. 6–17, 1995, UNEP/CBD, 1996, at 17.

ing authorized an Ad Hoc Working Group to begin negotiations on a biosafety protocol to the Convention.

After extensive negotiations, the parties to the Convention on Biological Diversity adopted a Protocol on Biosafety on January 29, 2000.[112] The objective of the Protocol is to contribute to ensuring an adequate level of protection in the safe transfer, handling and use of living biotechnology-modified organisms that may have adverse effects on the conservation and sustainable use of biological diversity, taking into account risks to human health and specifically focusing on transboundary movements.[113] The Protocol does not apply to the transboundary movement of living modified organisms which are pharmaceuticals for human use and that are addressed by relevant international agreements or organizations, nor to the transit and contained use of living modified organisms. These exceptions do not preclude a party from subjecting such actions to prior risk assessment.[114]

The Protocol institutes an "advance informed agreement" procedure which mirrors prior informed consent procedures contained in other international treaties. Thus, the state of export must notify or require the exporter to notify, in writing, the competent national authority of the state of import prior to the intentional transboundary movement of a living modified organism. Annex I of the Protocol specifies the information which must be transmitted. It requires technical data and a risk assessment report consistent with the conditions set forth in Annex III. The party of import is to acknowledge the notification in writing, but failure to do so does not imply consent to the shipment.[115] The importing state has 270 days from the date of notification to make a decision on permitting or denying the importation and must transmit the decision to the notifying party and to a Biosafety Clearing House established by the Protocol (Arts. 10 and 20). A special procedure is foreseen for domestic use of LMOs, including marketing a living modified organism that may be subject to transboundary movement for direct use as food or feed or for processing (Art. 11). Annex II lists the information required for such use, which may include a risk assessment report.

Apart from the intentional movements of LMOs, each party shall take appropriate measures to notify affected or potentially affected states, the Biodiversity Clearing House and, when appropriate, relevant international organizations, when it knows of a release that leads or may lead to an unintentional transboundary movement of a living modified organism that is

---

[112]   Although the Protocol was adopted in Montreal, it is known as the Cartagena Protocol because of the importance of the prior negotiations which took place in Cartagena, Columbia.

[113]   Preamble, Arts. 1 and 4.

[114]   Arts. 5, 6.

[115]   Art. 9.

likely to have significant adverse effects on the conservation and sustainable use of biological diversity or creates risks to human health.[116] States parties also must prevent and, if appropriate, penalize illegal transboundary movements of living modified organisms.[117] Generally states parties are to promote and facilitate public awareness, education, consultation and participation, encompassing access to information on living modified organisms that may be imported, but the notifier is permitted to identify information to be treated as confidential.[118] Finally, compliance monitoring procedures are foreseen. Parties to the Protocol shall, at intervals to be determined by the Conference of the Parties to the Biodiversity Convention, report to that Conference on measures that they have taken to implement the Protocol and the states parties should develop additional cooperative procedures and institutional mechanisms to promote compliance and address cases of non-compliance.[119]

Although the body of the CBD does not contain a reference to the precautionary principle it was a focus of debate during negotiations for the Biosafety Protocol, especially on the extent to which measures could be taken by states to exclude LMOs either on scientific or socio-economic grounds. In the end, it was agreed that parties must undertake a process of scientific risk assessment that conforms to the Protocol's requirements (carried out "in a scientifically sound and transparent manner," on a case-by-case basis, according to the provisions of Annex III, Article 15). Perhaps best reflecting the divergence of views, Annex III(4) provides that "lack of scientific knowledge or scientific consensus should not necessarily be interpreted as indicating a particular level of risk, an absence of risk, or an acceptable risk."

Another area of disagreement centered on the inclusion of products made of LMOs or processed materials of LMO origin. In the end, such products and materials were not included, although they are encompassed in the risk assessment procedures of Article 23(3)(c), Annex I(i) and Annex III(5). Any state actions in regard to such products probably must conform to WTO rules (discussed in Chapter 17). In fact, the relationship between the Protocol and the WTO remains unresolved. The preambular language is accompanied by an explanatory statement stating that it "is not intended to subordinate this Protocol to other international agreements."

The Protocol is open for signature only by states that are party to the CBD. As is increasingly common in regard to international environmental agreements, the CBD Conference of the Parties decided to establish an Inter-Governmental Committee for the Cartagena Protocol on Biosafety to take action pending entry into force of the protocol. In particular it was

---

[116] Art. 17.
[117] Art. 25.
[118] Arts. 21, 23.
[119] Arts. 33, 34.

charged with preparing decisions to be adopted at the first meeting of the parties to the Protocol.[120] The Committee met in three sessions between 2001–2003.

On the regional level, the European Community issued directives in 1990 creating a lengthy series of control procedures both for laboratory research and for release of LMOs. The first Directive,[121] on Contained Use of Genetically Modified Microorganisms (GMM), was amended in 1998 to establish four classes of contained uses and the restrictions that apply to each.[122] The four classes are: Class 1, activities of "no or negligible risk" to human health or the environment; Class 2, "low risk" activities; Class 3, "moderate risk" activities; and Class 4, "high risk" activities. Any user of a GMM in a contained use must follow procedures set forth in Annex III of the predecessor Directive and its future amendments for determining the class to which a particular activity belongs. This includes an assessment of the risks to human health and the environment that the contained uses may incur, including the question of waste disposal. The directive requires the users to maintain a record of the assessment and make it available to the competent national authority.

The precautionary principle has been incorporated by requiring that "where there is a doubt as to which class is appropriate for the proposed contained use, the more stringent protective measures shall be applied" unless there is sufficient evidence according to the competent authority that less stringent measures are justified. Any use in Classes 2–4 requires prior notification of the competent authority and prior written authorization of the authority if the use is in Class 3 or 4. Further notification is required for any relevant new information or modifications that could have significant consequences for the risks posed. Users must develop and make available to the public contingency plan for emergencies. Member states are required to notify annually the European Commission of all Class 3 and 4 uses.

Directive 2001/18/EC, replacing Directive 90/220/EEC,[123] concerns the voluntary release of genetically modified organisms into the environment. The precautionary principle is explicitly incorporated into several provisions. In particular, Article 4 provides that member states, "in accordance with the precautionary principle, shall ensure that all appropriate measures are taken to avoid adverse effects on human health and the environment which might arise from the deliberate release or the placing on the market of GMOs." Applicants for release must carry out an environ-

---

[120]   Decision EM-I/3, UNEP/CBD/ExCOP/1/3, Annex.

[121]   Community Directive 90/219/EEC, Apr. 23, 1990, O.J. L 117 (8/5/90).

[122]   Directive 98/81/EC, O.J. L. 330 (12/12/98), amends and substantially revises Directive 90/212/EEC on the Contained Use of Genetically Modified Microorganisms.

[123]   Council directive 90/220/EEC, Apr. 23, 1990, O.J. L 117, (5/8/90).

mental risk assessment of the GMO being proposed for authorization. Environmental risk assessment means that "direct or indirect, immediate or delayed risks" shall be evaluated by the national authorities. Assessors may not discount any potential adverse effect on the basis that it is unlikely to occur. (Annex II, C(2)(1)). The authorization system has a ten year limit and renewal is only permitted if monitoring carried out during the period shows no negative results. Labelling of products is also required.

Finally, it should be recalled that the 1993 Council of Europe Convention on Civil Responsibility for Damage Resulting from the Exercise of Activities Dangerous for the Environment specifically covers damage caused by genetically modified organisms.[124] GMOs are defined in the Convention as an organism in which the genetic material has been altered in a way which does not occur naturally by mating and/or natural combination.

F. Noise

In recent years, society has increasingly recognized excessive noise as a form of pollution. It is both a nuisance and a threat to health. In Europe about ten million people are exposed to noise levels in the environment that may cause hearing loss.[125] The non-binding Stockholm Action Plan addressed the elaboration of norms to combat noise as early as 1972. In addition, as discussed in Chapter 15C.3, several cases submitted to the European Court of Human Rights have alleged that levels of airport noise constitute a violation of their right to privacy and home life guaranteed in the European Convention on Human Rights, Article 8.

International environmental law primarily regulates two forms of noise pollution: airport noise and urban noise. In 1983, the International Civil Aviation Organization (ICAO) established a Committee on Environmental Protection, a technical committee reporting to the ICAO Council, charged with addressing the main environmental problems of civil aviation: pollution caused by aircraft engine emissions and aircraft noise. The main approaches to controlling or reducing aircraft noise seek to reduce the noise at source, use noise abatement operating measures, and adopt land use planning for the siting of airports. The ICAO has also established a noise certification standard in Annex 16 to the Convention on International Civil Aviation.[126]

EC legislation also regulates noise generated by air traffic. An EC Directive adopted in 2002 established rules and procedures with regard to the introduction of noise-related operating restrictions at Community

---

[124]   *See supra* Chapter 7A.2.
[125]   UNEP, GLOBAL ENVIRONMENTAL OUTLOOK 116 (2000).
[126]   Vol.1, Pt II, Ch. 4. *See further* the discussion of ICAO in Chapter 4C.9.

airports in order to limit or reduce the number of people significantly affected by the harmful effects of noise.[127]

A growing number of international and regional rules aim to reduce noise from other sources. A general EC Directive[128] aims to define a common approach to prevent or reduce the harmful effects of exposure to noise. "Environmental noise" is defined as unwanted or harmful outdoor sound created by human activities, including noise emitted by means of transport, road, rail or air traffic and from sites of industrial activity. Noise indicators are proposed and states should make and approve noise maps and action plans for urban areas and major roads, railways and airports. The Directive applies to noise emitted by road and rail vehicles and infrastructure, aircraft, outdoor and industrial equipment and mobile machinery. It applies in noise-sensitive areas such as in public parks and near schools and hospitals. Specific categories of noise emissions are also regulated by EC legislation: motor vehicles,[129] agricultural or forestry tractors[130] two- or three-wheel motor vehicles.[131]

G. Conclusion

The shift from regulating each sector of the environment to addressing the sources of harm has led to recognition of the interrelated impacts of various human activities. Combining concern over sources of harm and resulting impacts has given rise to broader integrated or ecosystem approaches to environmental protection. These approaches are discussed in the following chapter.

BIBLIOGRAPHY

Baender, M., *Pesticides and Precaution: The Bamako Convention as a Model for an International Convention on Pesticides Regulation*, 24 N.Y.U. J. INT'L L. & POL'Y. 557 (1991).

COLBORN, T., DUMANOSKI, D., & MYERS, J., OUR STOLEN FUTURE (1996).

Colopy, J., *Poisoning the Developing World: The Exportation of Unregistered and Severely Restricted Pesticides from the United States*, 13 UCLA J. ENVTL. L. & POL'Y 167 (1995).

---

[127]   Directive 2002/30/EC, Mar. 26, 2002, O.J. L 85/40 (3/28/02). The member states had to implement the Directive by Sept. 28, 2003.

[128]   Directive 2002/49/EC, O.J. L. 189/12 (7/18/02).

[129]   Directive 70/157/EEC, Feb. 6, 1970, O.J. L 42 (2/23/70).

[130]   Directive 77/311/EEC, Mar. 29, 1977, O.J. L 105 (4/28/77).

[131]   Directive 92/61/EEC, June 30, 1992, O.J. L 225 (8/10/92) and 2002/51/EC, July 19, 2002, O.J. L 252 (9/20/02).

Donald, J., *The Bamako Convention as a Solution to the Problem of Hazardous Waste Exports to Less Developed Countries*, 17 COLUM. J. ENVTL. L. 419 (1992).

HILZ, C., THE INTERNATIONAL TOXIC WASTE TRADE (1992).

Kiss, A., *The International Control of Transboundary Movement of Hazardous Waste*, 26 TEXAS INT'L L.J. 521 (1991).

KUMMER, K. & RUMMEL-BULSKA, I., THE BASEL CONVENTION ON THE CONTROL OF TRANSBOUNDARY MOVEMENT OF HAZARDOUS WASTES AND THEIR DISPOSAL (1990).

KWIATOWSKA, B., & SOONS, A. eds., TRANSBOUNDARY MOVEMENTS AND DISPOSALS OF HAZARDOUS WASTE IN INTERNATIONAL LAW: BASIC DOCUMENTS (1993).

LE DROIT EUROPEEN DES CONSOMMATEURS ET LA GESTION DES DECHETS— EUROPEAN CONSUMER LAW AND WASTE MANAGEMENT (BOUCQEY, N. ed., 1999).

LOUKA, E., OVERCOMING NATIONAL BARRIERS TO INTERNATIONAL WASTE TRADE (1995).

MACKENZIE, R., ET AL., AN EXPLANATORY GUIDE TO THE CARTAGENA PROTOCOL ON BIOSAFETY (IUCN, 2003).

OECD, PRACTICAL INFORMATION FOR THE IMPLEMENTATION OF THE OECD CONTROL SYSTEM: TRANSFRONTIER MOVEMENTS OF WASTES DESTINED FOR RECOVERY OPERATIONS (1997).

PEREZ MARTIN, M.T., QUE FAIT LE VILLAGE PLANETAIRE DE SES DECHETS DANGEREUX? (2001).

Shearer, C., *Comparative Analysis of the Basel and Bamako Conventions on Hazardous Waste*, 23 ENVTL. L. 141 (1993).

Uram, C., *International Regulation of the Sale and Use of Pesticides*, 10 NW. J. INT'L L. & BUS. 460 (1990).

INTERNET SITES

Basel Convention
<http://www.unep.ch/basel/>

IAEA
<http://www.iaea.org/>

PART III

INCLUSIVE ENVIRONMENTAL PROTECTION

CHAPTER 14

INTEGRATED ENVIRONMENTAL PROTECTION

New approaches to achieving effective environmental protection derive from greater knowledge and understanding of the biosphere and its components. Some changes may also be attributed to a greater involvement of non-state actors in the international legal system and a stronger role for international institutions, particularly financial institutions, in developing and applying international environmental law. Increased recognition of the global and multidimensional character of environmental problems and potential remedies is clear. Most states now accept that holistic international efforts are required to address many aspects of environmental deterioration, such as ocean pollution, depletion of stratospheric ozone, the greenhouse effect, and threats to biodiversity.

Concern for ecosystems has been broadened due to integrated approaches to safeguarding the planet's environment. The aim of protecting wild fauna and flora is now incorporated in the larger goal of maintaining biological diversity. This means that domesticated species in all their varieties also must survive, as well as insects, moss and microbes. The expanded vision includes efforts to reverse the trend towards monocultural agriculture and stock-breeding, and devotes increased attention to the potential contributions of and threats posed by biotechnology.

The evolution of international environmental law has thus led to emphasizing the integration of environmental considerations into policies and institutions concerned with a wide range of human activities. The integrated approach is being applied to activities through "mainstreaming" environmental protection.[1] Tourism, for example, has risen in the last 40 years from 25 million persons a year to 800 million.[2] More than 212 million persons around the world are employed in tourism-related activities. The impact of tourism on the environment can be enormous. On the one hand, tourism raises awareness of the beauty of wilderness areas and landscapes and of the need to protect the environment. On the other hand, it puts pressure on the environment due to the massive utilization of resources needed (water, energy, land) and the emissions produced (waste, used

---

[1]   Some of the major activities are discussed in the following chapters: human rights, armed conflict, trade and investment.

[2]   See Hanna B. Hoffmann, *Les défis du tourisme pour le prochain siècle: de l'intérêt d'un tourisme durable, in* The IPTS Report, No. 28, Oct. 1998, at 29.

water, noise, air pollution). In many areas, there are too many visitors for the carrying capacity of the area. The need for a holistic approach involving a partnership between tourism, local populations and the environment has led to a new theory of Integrated Total Quality Tourism Management which integrates socio-cultural, economic and environmental aspects in a global fashion.[3]

The Hague Declaration on Tourism (1989), Principle III notes the intrinsic interrelationship between tourism and the environment and sets out measures to ensure an unspoiled natural, cultural and human environment as a condition for the development of tourism. Since the Manila Declaration on World Tourism (1982), the World Tourism Organization has adopted a series of measures concerning relationships. The most recent WTO Declaration is the 1997 Maldives Declaration on Sustainable Tourism adopted by tourism and environment ministers of the Asia Pacific region. Essential requirements for sustainable tourism are promotion of ethics in tourism, reduction of unsustainable patterns of consumption of resources and reduction of wastes; conservation of natural, social and cultural diversity; integration of tourism planning; promotion of the local economy and the participation of the local population, the groups of tourists affected and the general public; the development of responsible tourism marketing; assessment of the impacts of tourism on natural and cultural heritage; and the special role of the private sector. Similar principles are contained in the Manila Declaration on the Social Impact of Tourism (May 22, 1997). UNEP also has adopted draft principles on sustainable tourism, endorsed in February 1999 by the UNEP Governing Council. The Global Code of Ethics for Tourism, adopted by the WTO Summit October 1, 1999, is the most recent and perhaps the most important of these declarations. It consolidates and reinforces previous recommendations on sustainable tourism with the aim of preserving the world's natural resources and cultural heritage from disruptive tourist activities and ensuring a fair and equitable sharing of benefits. Article 3 of the Code refers specifically to sustainable development and includes the most progressive legal principles and environmental methods. The World Committee on Tourism Ethics enforces the mechanism which involves private and inter-governmental conciliation. The Committee of 12 independent experts is able to consider disputes between states and other entities involved in tourist development. The Committee does fact-finding, hears the parties and renders a recommendation to resolve the dispute.

On the regional level, the Parliamentary Assembly of the Council of Europe in Recommendation 810 (1977) called for European Cooperation in the Field of Tourism. It recommended that the member states make an

---

[3]   Proposed by Hoffman, *id.*, in cooperation with the World Travel & Tourism Environment Research Centre (Oxford 1995).

appropriate and detailed analysis of the effects on the environment and the socio-cultural situation before developing tourist facilities.

In a different sphere of activity, the Baltic Marine Environment Protection Commission (HELCOM)[4] has taken measures to ensure integrated action to protect the Baltic. Its actions indicate the potentially broad reach of regulation to protect the marine environment, discussed in more detail below in "coastal and marine ecosystems." Recommendation 22/4 of March 2001 on the Proper Handling of Solid Waste/Landfill, relating to Article 13(b) of the Convention, applies to all landfill sites built after January 1, 2001. It has a large geographic scope, appling to existing sites within ten kilometers of the Baltic sea or five kilometers from a river bank zone where the zone is within 50 kilometers of the mouth of the river and the river discharges into the Baltic sea and has a catchment area of more than 200 square kilometers. All sites will be covered as of July 16, 2009. Parties are to reduce the quantities of waste going into landfill and to decrease the hazardousness of disposed waste. Environmental risks posed by existing closed landfills should be assessed and pollution prevention measures implemented. The recommendation also indicates what constitutes a proper landfill over the life-cycle of the site, taking into account the location, design, and construction of the site and its operation, closure, aftercare. The operational techniques and management practices are at the same level as EC Directive 1999/31 on the Landfill of Waste.

The 1996 EC Directive Concerning Integrated Prevention of Environmental Pollution lays down measures designed to prevent or, where that is not practicable, to reduce emissions in the air, water, and land from activities listed in an Annex to the Directive. The Directive is, however, limited to pollution prevention and control.

An ecosystem approach to environmental protection is integrated and considers the totality of environmental impacts on the functioning of an entire ecosystem, even when it crosses international boundaries. Both integrated protection and an ecosystem approach are stressed in the current work of international bodies concerned with environmental protection. Early legal measures for the joint or common management of shared resources are thus being extended to ecosystem management.

A. Shared Resource Management

The concept of joint management of shared resources began with commercially exploited species and international watercourses.[5] Establishment

---

4   HELCOM is established by the Convention on the Protection of the Marine Environment of the Baltic Sea Area (Helsinki, Apr. 9, 1992).

5   *See* UNEP, the Principles of Conduct in the Field of the Environment

of permanent institutions or rules for joint management allows treating the resource as an integrated whole, reflecting the ecological reality. Common or joint management is not a new technique—it was utilized as early as the last century in Convention for the Navigation of the Rhine River and later in the 1911 Treaty for the Preservation and Protection of Fur Seals—but it is increasingly applied to international watercourses and to shared ecosystems such as the Alps and the Arctic. Almost half the earth's land surface lies within 263 international river basins, *i.e.*, those that traverse political boundaries.[6] The Congo, Niger, Nile, Rhine, and Zambesi, for example, are each shared by more than nine countries. The essential need for water and potential conflicts that can arise from competition over it makes it important that countries reach agreement on sharing water resources. State practice demonstrates awareness of this fact: the first known international water agreement dates back to the settlement of a water dispute over the Tigris River between the Sumerian city-states of Lagash and Umma (2500 B.C.).[7] The FAO has identified more than 3,600 international water treaties concluded between 805 and 1984. Since 1948, states have adopted some 295 international water agreements.[8]

Early agreements mostly aimed to regulate navigation and demarcate boundaries, but the development of hydropower and large-scale irrigation development in the 20th century shifted the focus to reconciling non-navigational uses. Now better knowledge and understanding of ecosystems and their natural processes lead states to conclude more comprehensive agreements protecting freshwater resources as hydrographic units rather than as individual watercourses. These agreements recognize the difficult problem of balancing competing demands and differences between upstream and downstream states and their varied interests, including agriculture, industry, recreation, flood control, hydropower, environmental protection and human health. The physical, economic and social disparities between riparian nations can make management complex. An integrated approach offers a legal framework to reconcile differences and make choices. When coupled with joint or shared management and monitoring, water basin agree-

---

for the Guidance of States in the Conservation and Harmonious Utilization of Nature Resources Shared by Two or More States, May 19, 1978; and A. Kiss, *Can We Speak of the Protection and Management of Shared Natural Resources?* JURIDISK TIDSKRIFT 1997–1998, at IV 1.

    [6]   A "river basin" is the area which contributes hydrologically to surface and groundwater of a first order stream. The latter discharges into the ocean or a closed lake or inland sea. River basin is thus similar in concept to watershed or catchment area.

    [7]   A. T. WOLF, *Conflict and Cooperation Along International Waterways*, 1 WATER POL'Y 251 (1998)

    [8]   UNEP, ATLAS OF INTERNATIONAL FRESHWATER AGREEMENTS (2002), UNEP/DEWA/DPDL/RS.02/4, at 3.

ments may provide the structure for effective environmental protection in the context of sustainable development.

The 1987 Agreement on the Action Plan for the Environmentally Sound Management of the Common Zambezi River System was one of the first to adopt a holistic approach to water resources management through the entire river system. Although the action plan is not legally binding, it provides the framework for action by the riparian states. The use of a "soft law" instrument may reflect the fact that basin conditions and priorities may change considerably over time, necessitating flexibility in provisions and institutions. Water allocation, in particular, may vary according to availability, changing needs and values. In contrast to the approach of the Zambezi states, the newly independent countries around the Aral Sea adopted a series of binding agreements between 1993 and 1999 on water-related activities, improving the environment and economic development of the region.[9] Similarly, the SACD countries adopted a Protocol on shared water systems in the Southern African Development Community on August 28, 1995, and revised it on August 7, 2000.

Despite the large number of positive developments, more than half the international water basins lack a cooperative management framework.[10] In addition, many of the older agreements lack provisions on water quality management, monitoring, public participation, flexible allocation and dispute resolution. Future agreements may be developed within the legal framework of the 1997 UN Convention on the Non-Navigational Uses of International Watercourses, which adopts the principles of "equitable and reasonable utilization" and the "obligation not to cause significant harm." These principles, together with an adaptable management structure and flexible criteria for maintaining water quality and quantity, can promote holistic water management.

In the context of international agreements, the environmental unity of international watercourses has led to a recognition of the need for common management with the active participation of all concerned states. Article 24 of the 1997 UN Convention on International Watercourses stops short of mandating the establishment of joint management, but provides that water-

---

[9] *E.g.,* Agreement on Joint Activities in Addressing the Aral Sea and the Zone around the Sea Crisis, Improving the Environment, and Ensuring the Social and Economic Development of the Aral Sea Region (Mar. 26, 1993); Agreement between the Government of the Republic of Kazakhstan, the Government of the Kyrgyz Republic, and the Government of the Republic of Uzbekistan on Cooperation in the Area of the Environment and Rational Nature Use (Mar. 17, 1998); Agreement on the Use of Water and Energy Resources of the Syr Darya Basin (Mar. 17, 1998); Protocol to the Agreement on the Use of Water and Energy Resources of the Syr Darya Basin (May 7, 1999).

[10] UNEP, ATLAS, *supra* note 8, at 7.

course states must enter into consultations concerning management, including possible creation of a joint management mechanism, at the request of any of the concerned states. In this regard, management means planning the sustainable development of the watercourse and implementation of any plans adopted. It also means promoting the rational and optimal utilization, protection, and control of the watercourse. Such joint management has been adopted in many regions of the world. The Great Lakes, which contain one-fifth of the world's freshwaters, are jointly managed by the United States and Canada pursuant to a 1909 Boundary Waters Treaty through the International Joint Commission, an independent bilateral agency. The Commission today also addresses transboundary air pollution. Namibia and South Africa also have created a permanent water commission.

Agreements among interested states call for common management of the Niger, the Mekong, the Danube, the Meuse, the Scheldt, the Zambezi, the Mosel, the Mahakali (Nepal-India), the Ganges (India-Bangladesh) and La Plata Rivers, and the Lake Chad basin. A declaration of principles between Jordan, the Palestine Liberation Organization and the state of Israel seeks cooperation in regard to the Jordan River. The Agreements on the rivers Meuse and Scheldt, signed in 1994, call for integrated management of the drainage area of the two rivers and agree on the need for measures of management and cooperation in regard to the sediments in the bed of the rivers. The agreements create an international commission to facilitate international cooperation.

The Convention on Cooperation for the Protection and Sustainable Use of the Danube River (Sofia, June 29, 1994) establishes an International Commission to coordinate consultation and joint activities for the sustainable and equitable management of surface and ground waters in the Danube catchment area. It looks to joint or harmonized programs in part because its aim is regional and includes the reduction of the pollution loads of the Black Sea from sources in the catchment area. According to Article 4a, the states parties should engage in consultations and joint activities in the framework of the International Commission. Other provisions call for harmonized domestic regulations for emission limits and standards (Art. 7(5)(a)), harmonized monitoring and assessment methods (Art. 9(1)), joint monitoring systems and programs (Art. 9), joint research (Art. 15) and joint warning systems (Art. 16).

B. Transboundary Protected Areas and Landscapes

On a bilateral or even multilateral basis, transboundary protected areas are being created. Recently, the governments of Argentina, Paraguay and Brazil agreed to link state and private reserves in the Parana jungle region, thus creating a green corridor. Since 1972, the Gran Paradiso National Park in the Italian Alps has been paired with the Vanoise National Park in France, nearly tripling the protected area and providing year round protection to the ibex. On the regional level, the Waddenzee National Park covers all the natural range of seals along the tidal flats of Denmark, Germany and the Netherlands. In 1987, the three coastal states entered into an administrative agreement on a common Secretariat to set out their duties to cooperate in research and management of the Waddenzee ecosystem as a whole. Similarly, Spain and France coordinate signposts, visitor centers and tourist information for the French Pyrenees Occidentales National Park and the Spanish Ordesa National Park. On November 30, 1999, Kenya, Tanzania and Uganda signed in Arusha a Treaty for the Establishment of the Eastern African Community. Chapter 19 of the treaty provides for cooperation in environment and natural resources management providing, in this framework *inter alia*, for irrigation and water catchment management, food security, and wildlife management (Arts. 109, 110 and 116). It also advocates the integration of environmental management and conservation measures in all development activities such as trade, transport, agriculture, industrial development, mining and tourism in the Community (Art. 112, paragraph 1(e)).

The Council of Europe member states adopted the European Landscape Convention on October 20, 2000, with the objective of promoting landscape protection, management and planning and to organize European cooperation on landscape issues. "Landscape" is defined in the Convention as an area, as perceived by people, whose character is the result of the action and interaction of natural and/or human factors. Landscape protection means action to conserve and maintain the significant or characteristic features of a landscape justified by its heritage value derived from its natural configuration and/or from human activity. These definitions place the Convention fully in the approach of integrated protection, reinforced by Article 2 which provides an extensive scope of application including the entire territory—land, inland waters and marine areas—of the parties and covers natural, rural, urban and peri-urban areas.

The general measures parties should take include recognition of landscapes in law as an essential component of peoples' surroundings, an expression of the diversity of their shared cultural and natural heritage and a foundation of their identity. This formulation indicates an understanding that humans throughout the world have altered the natural environment in diverse ways, that today are part of the cultural identity of the group. This is expressed in the Preamble which notes that developments in agriculture, forestry, industrial and mineral production techniques and the regional planning, town planning, transport, infrastructure, tourism and recreation and, at a more general level, changes in the world economy are in many cases accelerating the transformation of landscapes.

Specific obligations include identifying, assessing and developing quality objectives for landscapes, with public participation. There should also be education and awareness-raising of the general public. Article 9 calls on parties to encourage transfrontier cooperation on local and regional levels and whenever necessary to prepare and implement joint landscape programs.

C. Ecosystem Protection and Management

The integrated approach plays a particularly important and growing role in protecting large ecosystems of the planet: the polar regions, mountains, and marine ecosystems.

1. The Polar Regions

Antarctica, while almost entirely ice and snow covered, nonetheless supports abundant wildlife. It is also plays critical if not entirely understood roles in the global climate, ocean currents, the marine food chain, and sea temperatures and levels. Approximately 70 percent of all freshwater is located in Antarctica. It is increasingly popular as a tourist site and its waters have been the target of considerable illegal and unreported fishing.

The foundations of the Antarctica Treaty System (ATS) emerged from the International Geophysical Year 1957–1958, proclaimed by the International Council of Scientific Unions, a non-governmental organization supporting open scientific research. The 1959 Antarctic Treaty, concluded outside the auspices of the United Nations, de-militarized the continent and established that it be set aside for peaceful purposes in the interest of all humanity. The Treaty guarantees freedom of scientific investigation and promotes the exchange of scientific information. All issues respecting state claims to portions of Antarctica are frozen for the period the Treaty is in force.[11] State compliance with treaty obligations is ensured through a system of mutual inspections. The Antarctic Treaty parties are also, according to Article X to "exert appropriate efforts consistent with the Charter of the United Nations, to the end that no one engages in any activity in Antarctica contrary to the principles or purposes of the . . . Treaty." The language of Article X has given rise to many debates over whether or not it is intended to ensure that the activities of non-parties conform to the treaty within

---

[11]　Seven nations had made sometimes overlapping territorial claims on Antarctica by 1950: Argentina, Australia, Chile, France, New Zealand, Norway, and the United Kingdom. The United States and Russia, among others, have rejected these territorial claims.

Antarctica and its surrounding waters.[12] Article IX foresees regular meetings of the contracting parties[13] who are given authority to adopt measures regarding, *inter alia*, the preservation and conservation of living resources in Antarctica. Thus, although the word "environment" does not appear in the Treaty, there is a juridical base for considering and acting on environmental issues. The Scientific Committee on Antarctic Research regularly attends meetings of the parties and has considerably influence.

The Antarctic Treaty (December 1, 1959) has been progressively complemented by conservation measures and by two conventions, one adopted June 1, 1972 on the Conservation of Antarctic Seals, the second May 20, 1980, on the Conservation of Antarctic Marine Living Resources (CCAMLR) in the area. While CCAMLR was negotiated largely in response to over-fishing in the waters off Antarctica, the treaty is one of the first international agreements to adopt an ecosystem approach because it considers the interrelationship between all species and their particular physical environment. Its coverage is uniquely based upon a biological boundary, because it extends to ocean waters that are south of the "Antarctic convergence," the cold waters favorable to nutrients and phytoplankton growth and to the proliferation of krill, one of the bases of the marine food chain. The parties to CCAMLR meet regularly to adopt conservation measures, including maximum sustainable yield for target species, which they do by consensus on the basis of recommendations by the scientific advisory committee and regulatory commission.

CCAMLR envisages the creation of a system to observe and supervise compliance with the Convention, including procedures relating to on-site visits to and inspections of ships operating within the Treaty area. These inspections are undertaken by observers and inspectors designated by members of an international Commission established by the Convention.[14] The major problem has been unreported and illegal catches, most of them made by non-parties to the agreement.[15] In order to strengthen its effectiveness,

---

[12] The provisions of the Antarctic Treaty and the Environmental Protocol apply to the area south of 60 deg. South Latitude, including all ice shelves (Art. VI). The CCAMLR applies to the area within the "Antarctic convergence," an area of marine waters that changes with the seasons.

[13] The parties to the treaty do not all have the same rights of participation. Fully participating states are those which demonstrate their interest in Antarctica "by conducting substantial scientific research activity there, such as the establishment of a scientific station or the dispatch of a scientific expedition." These are the Antarctic Treaty Consultative Parties (ATCP) who meet in the Consultative Meeting (ACTM).

[14] May 20, 1980.

[15] Greenpeace estimates that over half of the Patagonian toothfish catch is taken by illegal fishing conducted from countries that are not party to CCAMLR. *See* <http://www.greenpeace.org/>.

the CCAMLR Commission created a documentation scheme[16] in 1999 and a monitoring system at the end of 2000.

In 1991, the parties to the Antarctic Treaty negotiated a Protocol to the Antarctic Treaty on Environmental Protection that includes principles and rules concerning all activities in the Antarctic Treaty area. The Madrid Protocol designates Antarctica as "a natural reserve, devoted to peace and science" (Art. 2). It invests the Antarctic Treaty System Consultative Meetings with the task of defining the general policy for the comprehensive protection of the Antarctic environment (Art. 10) and creates a Committee for Environmental Protection to assist it in this task (Art. 11). The Committee provides advice and formulates recommendations to the parties in connection with the implementation of the Protocol. In particular, it provides advice on the effectiveness of implementation measures, on the state of the Antarctic environment and on the need for scientific research and on procedures for situations requiring urgent action (Art. 12). The Treaty foresees opening all areas of Antarctica, including stations, installations and equipment and all ships and aircraft within this area, to inspection by observers designated by the consultative parties (Art. 7). Article 12 of the Madrid Protocol mandates that the Committee for Environmental Protection provide advice on inspection measures, including formats for inspection reports and checklists for the conduct of inspections in application of Article 7 of the 1959 Treaty. Article 14 adds more details on the inspection.

Activities shall be planned and conducted so as to

- limit adverse impacts on the Antarctic environment and dependent and associated ecosystems, in particular on climate and weather patterns, on air or water quality,
- avoid significant changes in the atmospheric, terrestrial, glacial or marine environment,
- avoid detrimental changes in the distribution, abundance or productivity of species or populations of species of fauna and flora,
- avoid jeopardy to endangered or threatened species or degradation of, or substantial risk to, areas of biological, scientific, historic, aesthetic or wilderness significance (Art. 3).

Unless an activity is determined to have less than a minor or transitory impact, a Comprehensive Environmental Evaluation shall be prepared and procedures shall be put in place to assess and verify the impact of any activity that proceeds following the completion of the evaluation (Art. 6 and Annex I).

---

[16] Although the Catch Documentation Scheme is intended to ensure that all toothfish are legally procured, in practice the captain of a vessel need only state that the fish were caught outside the Convention area to circumvent the restrictions.

As of the end of 2001, 27 states conducted activities in Antarctica sufficient to be recognized as Antarctic Treaty Consultative Parties. Eighteen more states are non-consultative parties. Also in 2001, a permanent Secretariat was established in Buenos Aires after years of traveling according to the site of the bi-annual meeting. Most recently, the Committee on Environmental Protection has begun to designate historic sites.

At the northern extreme of the earth, eight Arctic countries adopted in 1991 a detailed instrument on environmental protection. Called the Arctic Environmental Protection Strategy, it is based on the principle that management, planning and development activities shall provide for the conservation, sustainable utilization and protection of Arctic ecosystems and natural resources for the benefit and enjoyment of present and future generations, including indigenous peoples. Use and management of natural resources shall be based on an approach which considers the value and interdependent nature of ecosystem components. Management, planning and development activities which may significantly affect the Arctic ecosystems shall

— be based on informed assessments of their impact, including cumulative impact, on the Arctic environment,
— provide for the maintenance of the region's ecological system and biodiversity,
— respect the Arctic's significance for and influence on the global climate,
— be compatible with the sustainable utilization of Arctic ecosystems,
— take into account the results of scientific investigations and the traditional knowledge of indigenous peoples, and
— develop a network of protected areas.

The Arctic Strategy identifies six specific pollution issues that require attention: persistent organic contaminants, oil pollution, heavy metals, noise, radioactivity and acidification. Potential disturbance from noise also is taken into account, which is quite exceptional in the field of international cooperation. The Strategy identifies existing international mechanisms and proposes actions for each identified nuisance. Separate chapters relate to the protection of the Arctic marine environment, to emergency prevention, preparedness and response and to the conservation of Arctic fauna and flora.

In order to implement the Arctic Environmental Strategy, the eight Arctic countries agreed to hold regular meetings. A 1996 Declaration, also a legally non-binding text, created the Arctic Council as a multilateral forum in order to serve as a permanent high-level inter-governmental framework in which the eight Arctic nations can oversee existing Arctic multilateral activities, as well as develop new initiatives. In addition to the eight member states, three organizations representing the majority of indigenous peoples in the circumpolar Arctic are Permanent Participants in the Council. The Council meets on a biennial basis, with meetings of senior officials taking place more frequently. Responsibility for hosting meetings of the Arctic Council, including provision of Secretariat support functions, rotates sequentially among the Arctic states.

The Arctic Council oversees and coordinates programs originally established under different instruments: the Arctic Environmental Protection Strategy, the Arctic Monitoring and Assessment Program, the Conservation of Arctic Flora and Fauna, the Protection of the Arctic Marine Environment, and Emergency Prevention, Preparedness and Response. Other developments include the adoption of an International Code of Safety for Ships in Polar Waters and a Circumpolar Protected Areas network.

The Arctic Council has established a number of working groups: Arctic Monitoring and Assessment Program (scientific assessments of POPs, heavy metals, radioactivity, human health); Conservation of Arctic Flora and Fauna (overview completed on June 11, 2001); the Circumpolar Seabird Working Group which has published several technical reports on management and harvesting, and the group on Emergency Prevention, Preparedness and Response, a forum for information exchange in regard to national activities relating to contingency planning and emergency response. In 2001 the working group agreed to a timetable for completing a circumpolar map of resources at risk from oil spills in the Arctic, and continued to develop a standarized approach to shoreline cleanup assessment technology. The Protection of the Arctic Marine Environment Working Group has prepared amendments and additions to the 1997 Offshore Oil and Gas Guidelines. The Sustainable Development Working Group has given special attention to Arctic Council health initiatives, the future of children in the region, culture and eco-tourism, and prevention and control of infectious disease.

2. *Mountain Ecosystems*

Mountains and uplands constitute about half of the terrestrial landmass of the earth and exist in over three-quarters of the world's countries. Mountain areas contain all the environmental milieu and human activities that have been part of international environmental regulation. They are places of unique and rich biodiversity, cultural diversity within largely traditional lifestyles, freshwater, pristine landscapes, tourism (eco- and industrial) and forest and mineral resources. They are also areas of poverty, erosion, natural disasters, desertification, and industrial development. They have a significant impact on other ecosystems and areas, being important water towers and sensitive indicators of global climatic and environmental change. Some of the activities most destructive to mountain areas, such as extractive mining and large-scale dams, have few or no international norms governing them. Further, it has been argued that

> [a]pplying laws and policies that were enacted with lowland environments in mind to mountain areas can have disastrous effects. Developing mountain-specific approaches requires an understanding of what characteristics of mountains are unique. These characteristics include economic and legal marginalization, isolation, transboundary location, diversity of livelihood strategies, cultural diversity, and environmental sensitivity and diversity.[17]

On the global level no single treaty for mountain areas exists; only Chapter 13 of Agenda 21 offers a blueprint for mountain resources. Chapter 13, together with CSD progress reports, ECOSOC Resolution 1997/45, and a 1997 FAO report on Chapter 13 of Agenda 21, identify the importance of law in the promotion of mountain conservation and development.[18] A study by the Mountain Institute found that legal, regulatory and enforcement structures are perhaps the most important contributing factors to promoting conservation and sustainable development, particularly when utilizing the principle of subsidiarity to enhance local participation.[19]

The UN exercised efforts in connection with the International Year of the Mountains and International Year of Eco-Tourism in 2002. Other institutions also took action during this period, including the program Environment for Europe and the Work Program on mountain ecosystems adopted by the states parties to the Convention on Biological Diversity. Indeed, most treaties for the protection of nature developed projects on mountain ecosystems during 2002.

The Convention on the Protection of the World Cultural and Natural Heritage (November 23, 1972) has more than 40 mountain areas around the world on the World Heritage List, including Virunga National Park (DRC), Mount Kenya, Simen National Park (Ethiopia), Prinin National Park (Bulgaria) and Yosemite National Park (USA). In New Zealand, the

---

[17] Owen J. Lynch & Gregory F. Maggio, *Mountain Laws and Peoples: Moving Towards Sustainable Development and Recognition of Community-Based Property Rights* 6 CIEL (2002).

[18] FAO, Task Manager's Report on Chapter 13, Agenda 21, Report of the Secretary-General, E/CN.17/1997/2/Add.12, Jan. 22, 1997. The report refers to the need for new or reinforced legal mechanisms (charters, conventions, national legislation etc.) to protect fragile mountain ecosystems and promote sustainable development in mountain regions.

[19] LYNELLE PRESTON, ed., INVESTING IN MOUNTAINS: INNOVATIVE PRACTICES AND PROMISING EXAMPLES FOR FINANCING CONSERVATION AND SUSTAINABLE DEVELOPMENT (The Mountain Institute, 1997).

sacred peaks of Tongariro National Park became the first national park to be created from a gift of land by an indigenous people and a World Heritage Site in 1992, the first to be granted that status on both landscape and cultural grounds. Listing increases international recognition for the importance of the sites, but measures are largely left to national authorities.

The treaty system established for the protection of the Alps is the most extensive and explicit corpus concerning mountain areas. It aims at protecting one of the largest continuous and relatively unspoilt natural regions in Europe. A Convention Concerning the Protection of the Alps adopted November 7, 1991 by seven countries of the region and the EU,[20] proclaimed a set of principles covering virtually every aspect of human activities which produce direct or indirect impacts on the environment. The Convention is a framework treaty which lists the main fields where specific protocols are to be drafted (Art. 2). It also establishes the foundations of legal, scientific, economic and technical cooperation and creates a Conference of Contracting Parties, called the Alpine Conference, charged with elaborating the Protocols. The Conference also has established a Compliance Mechanism providing for reporting procedures.

The first Protocol, adopted in 1994, aims to implement the Alpine Convention in the Field of Town and Country Planning and Sustainable Development.[21] Its specific objectives are to ensure the rational use of land and the harmonious development of the whole region, to avoid under- and over-use and the conservation and rehabilitation of natural habitats by means of a clarification and evaluation of land-use requirements, and to develop farsighted integral planning and coordination of the measures taken. The protocol stresses both international cooperation and the importance of the participation of local communities.

A second instrument, the Protocol for the Implementation of the Alpine Convention in the Field of Mountain Agriculture,[22] insists on the use of agricultural methods of production which are respectful of nature and the environment. It also advocates the integration of agricultural considerations into other policies and has a particular importance for land conservation and management. The aim of the Protocol on Nature Protection and Landscape Conservation[23] is not only to protect, but also to manage and, if necessary, to restore landscapes and nature in the Alpine region. It recommends cooperation, in particular transboundary cooperation, in the preparation of inventories, the creation and monitoring of protected areas. Here again, local communities should participate in the action.

---

20   Salzburg, Nov. 7, 1991.
21   Chambéry, Dec. 20, 1994.
22   Chambéry, Dec. 20, 1994.
23   Chambéry, Dec. 20, 1994.

After this first series of Protocols, the Alpine states adopted a further instrument in 1996, related to mountain forests.[24] It insists on the main functions of the forests and on protecting them as well as urban areas and agricultural land, on maintaining the productivity of forests and their social and ecological functions.

On October 16, 1998, parties to the Alpine Convention adopted three more Protocols. The first of them, on the protection of soils,[25] is analyzed in Chapter 9B. The Protocol concerning Energy[26] invites the parties to harmonize their plans related to energy with their general management scheme for the Alpine region, to optimize energy production, transport and distribution taking into account the needs of environmental protection, and to limit the impact of the uses of energy on the environment including negative effects on landscapes. The Protocol also advocates energy-saving and the use of renewable sources of energy. Parties shall exchange information on the use and surveillance of nuclear energy sources. All new projects related to energy and all modification of existing installations should be submitted to an environmental impact assessment. The third Protocol adopted on the same day[27] is no less creative: its objective is to ensure sustainable development of the Alpine region through tourism which respects the environment. The influx of tourists should be controlled within the natural limits of the development of the region. This principle should be applied to different aspects of tourism: housing, transport, sports, use of aircraft, coordination of the dates of vacation, and cooperation with agriculture, forestry and local handcraft. Quiet areas should be created and the use of ski-lifts and of ski-slopes should be in conformity with environmental requirements.

The two last Protocols were adopted on October 31, 2000. The objective of the first, related to transport,[28] is to adopt a sustainable policy in this field by reducing nuisances and risks, avoiding or minimizing danger for biodiversity and using means of transport which respect as much as possible the environment and natural resources. Such objectives should also be taken into account in other policies. As with all the Protocols, participation of the local population is encouraged. The last Protocol concerns dispute settlement[29] and aims to reach such settlement by consultation and by arbitration.

---

[24] Protocol for the Implementation of the Alpine Convention in the Field of Mountain Forests, Brdo, Feb. 27, 1996.

[25] Protocol for the Implementation of the Alpine Convention in the Field of Protection of Soil, Bled, Oct. 16, 1998.

[26] Bled, Oct. 16, 1998.

[27] Protocol for the Implementation of the Alpine Convention in the Field of Tourism, Oct. 16, 1998.

[28] Protocol for the Implementation of the Alpine Convention of 1991 in the Field of Transport, Lausanne, Oct. 31, 2000.

[29] Lausanne, Oct. 31, 2000.

On November 19, 2002 the seventh Alpine Conference meeting in Merano passed a resolution establishing a compliance mechanism called the Reviewing Committee. Each party is to provide the Committee every four years with a country report concerning compliance, which will be sent to the other Alpine Convention contracting parties and to observers. The Secretariat is to make the reports public, except information that the relevant party has classified as confidential. The report is to include information on compliance with protocol-specific obligations: measures of compliance taken and an assessment of the effectiveness of the measures; problem areas, such as divergent interests concerning the use of natural resources, as well as measures which relate to these areas; measures taken in cooperation with other contracting parties, implementation of resolutions and recommendations of the Alpine Conference. Each relevant contracting party has the right to participate in the entire proceedings, to seek all relevant documentation and to comment on the work of the Reviewing Committee. As regards matters dealt with by a specific protocol, only contracting parties to that protocol are entitled to vote. With the agreement of the relevant contracting party, the Reviewing Committee can undertake enquiries on that party's territory. Information that has been described as confidential is to be treated as confidential and discussions during the entire mechanism are confidential. In certain situations observers can be excluded from discussion during the proceedings.

Based on the reports adopted by the Reviewing Committee, the Alpine Conference can pass resolutions or recommendations by consensus. These resolutions and recommendations encompass advice and support of contracting parties; support in the setting up of a compliance strategy; assistance of experts to assist the relevant party, enquiries on the spot if the party agrees, in order to identify compliance problems and possible solutions; demands that the concerned party set up a compliance strategy; requirement of a timetable for compliance. The reports of the Reviewing Committee as well as the resolutions of the Alpine Conference are published.[30]

Finally, the Framework Convention on the Protection and Sustainable Development of the Carpathians was adopted in Kiev on May 23, 2003, by the fifth ministerial conference "Environment for Europe" and signed by five countries: Hungary, Romania, Serbia and Montenegro, Slovakia and Ukraine. It follows the model of the Alpine Conventional system but so far no protocol has been adopted, although the possibility of protocols is foreseen by its Article 18. The Convention itself includes all the aspects of protecting the environment of mountain areas. Detailed provisions concern the conservation, sustainable use and restoration of biological and landscape diversity including the protection of endangered species, endemic species and large carnivores. It also aims at preventing the introduction of

---

[30]   33 E.P.L. 179 (2003).

alien invasive species and release of genetically modified organisms threatening ecosystems, habitats or species, and their control or eradication. Article 6 also has a particular importance in the light of serious pollution accidents which caused major environmental effects. The provision invites states parties to ensure sustainable and integrated water/river management, including land-use planning. It also calls on them to adopt policies aimed at conserving natural watercourses, springs, lakes and groundwater resources, recognizing the importance of pollution and flood management, prevention and control. States parties should also preserve and protect wetlands and wetland ecosystems. An early warning system for transboundary impacts on the water regime or flooding and accidental water pollution should also be further developed. Other provisions concern an integrated approach to land resource management, spatial planning, sustainable agriculture and forestry, sustainable transport and infrastructure, sustainable tourism, cultural heritage and traditional knowledge. The parties shall apply, where necessary, risk assessments, environmental impact assessments and shall consult on projects of a transboundary character. Awareness raising, education and public information and participation are also imposed by the Convention.[31] All the obligations of the Convention are to be applied on the basis of general principles listed in Article 2(2): precaution and prevention, polluter pays, public participation and stakeholder involvement, transboundary cooperation, integrated planning and management of land and water resources, a programatic approach and the ecosystem approach.

The Convention establishes a Conference of Parties which also should define the geographic scope of the Carpathian region, and which can adopt protocols to the Convention. It is assisted by a Secretariat. This first result of the UN General Assembly declaring 2002 International Year of Mountains is likely to be followed by other developments concerning different mountain areas in the world.

3. Coastal and Marine Ecosystems

Efforts to protect the marine environment increasingly take an ecosystem approach, recognizing that coastal areas, mangroves, sea grasses, coral reefs and other marine living and non-living resources combine to produce complex ecosystems demanding integrated management. There are several definitions of what integrated coastal and marine management means. Agenda 21, chapter 17 defines integrated coastal management as a system that: (a) provides for an integrated policy and decision-making process, including

---

[31] Parties to this agreement are also parties to the June 24, 1998 Aarhus Convention on information, participation and access to remedies in environmental matters.

all involved sectors, to promote compatibility and a balance of uses; (b) identifies existing and projected uses of coastal areas and their interactions; (c) concentrates on well-defined issues concerning coastal management; (d) applies preventive and precautionary approaches in project planning and implementation, including prior assessment and systematic observation of the impacts of major projects; (e) promotes the development and application of methods, such as national resource and environmental accounting, that reflect changes in value resulting from uses of coastal and marine areas, including pollution, marine erosion, loss of resources and habitat destruction; and (f) provides access, as far as possible, for concerned individuals, groups and organizations to relevant information and opportunities for consultation and participation in planning and decision-making at appropriate levels.

The Ramsar states parties also have defined integrated coastal zone management in adopting principles and guidelines for incorporating wetland issues into Integrated Coastal Zone Management (ICZM).[32] According to Appendix I of the Recommendation VIII.4, integrated coastal zone management is a mechanism for bringing together the multiplicity of users, stakeholders, and decision-makers in the coastal zone in order to secure more effective ecosystem management while achieving economic development and equity within and between generations through the application of sustainability principles. This, like most other definitions, recognizes that ICZM is a continuous, pro-active and adaptive process of resource management for sustainable development of coastal zones. Its goals must be achieved within the constraints of physical, social, economic and environmental conditions.

The purposes of integrated management are generally recognized to be to guide uses so as not to exceed the carrying capacity of the resource base; respect natural dynamic processes; reduce risks to valuable resources; ensure ecosystem biodiversity; encourage complementary activities; ensure that environmental, social and economic objectives are achieved at an acceptable cost; protect traditional uses and rights and equitable access to resources; and resolve sectoral issues and conflicts. All of these goals require full participation of local communities based upon a "bottom-up" approach.

The Jakarta Mandate on Marine and Coastal Biological Diversity adopted by the second Conference of the Parties to the Convention on Biological Diversity in 1995 and supplemented by a program of work adopted in 1998[33] also has a focus on integrated marine and coastal area management, sustainable use of living resources, protected areas, maricul-

---

[32]	Resolution VIII.4, Principles and Guidelines for Incorporating Wetland Issues into Integrated Coastal Zone Management, Eighth Meeting of the Conference of the Parties, Valencia, Spain, Nov. 18–26, 2002.

[33]	Decision IV/5.

ture and alien species. The five key program areas are chemical pollution and eutrophication, fisheries operations, global climate change, alterations of physical habitat, and invasion of exotic species.

The Jakarta Mandate identifies key operational objectives and priority activities within the five areas and as a general element looks to coordinate and collaborate with other organizations and experts. It also solicits from states a list of experts from scientific, technical, technological, social, management, economic, policy, legal and indigenous and traditional knowledge.

The Mandate calls integrated marine and coastal area management "the most suitable framework" for addressing human impacts and promoting conservation and sustainable use of biodiversity. The basic principle of the Program of Work is that "The ecosystem approach should be promoted at global, regional, national and local levels." In addition, "protected areas should be integrated into wider strategies for preventing adverse effects to marine and coastal ecosystems from external activities and take into consideration, inter alia, the provisions of Article 8 of the Convention [on Biological Diversity]." The precautionary approach should be used as a guidance for all activities, with science providing knowledge on key processes and influences in the marine and coastal ecosystems which are critical for structure, function and productivity of biological diversity.

The Jakarta Mandate supports the involvement of relevant stakeholders in protecting marine ecosystems. "The primary basis for this program of work is action at national and local levels." Regional bodies should be invited to coordinate activities when relevant, while global organizations should be encouraged to implement the CBD.

Coral reefs exemplify the need for integrated coastal zone management. Reefs are animals that evolved some 200 million years ago.[34] They cover a tiny fraction of the ocean floor (less than 0.1 percent) but healthy reefs are the most biologically diverse of all known ecosystems, containing more species than tropical rainforests, perhaps as many as two million species.[35] Coral reef ecosystems are highly integrated with sea grasses and

---

[34]   While the simplest may consist of a single tube-like polyp, with a mouth surrounded by a ring of tentacles, the polyps may form colonies. Other corals lay down a "skeleton"; soft corals and fan corals have protein skeletons, while reef-builders lay down skeletons of calcium carbonate or limestone. Most corals obtain their food in a unique symbiosis with thousands of microscopic algae (zooxanthellae), which derive their energy from photosynthesis. Corals get most of their energy and oxygen from the zooxanthellae, while the latter utilize the carbon dioxide produced by the corals in their metabolic processes.

[35]   Coral reefs are distributed off the coasts of 101 countries, where they provide habitat for up to 10 percent of the global fisheries and up to 20–25 percent of the fish catch of developing countries. There are some 800 known species of sclereactinian (reef-building) corals alone, more than three-fourths of which are located in the Asia-Pacific region.

mangroves. The latter bind soft sediments and help keep waters clear enough for corals to grow. Corals in turn buffer the impacts of waves and storms, allowing grasses and mangroves to flourish and thus protect the coastal areas from erosion and flooding.

Many human communities, especially in the tropics, live near reefs, because they depend upon them for food and livelihood. In addition, coral reefs are a focus of medical research.[36] Some 10 percent of the world's reefs are already seriously degraded and 30 percent are seriously threatened.[37] Scientists estimate that without preventive action up to 70 percent of the world's coral reefs will disappear within 40 years. The slow growth rate of coral reefs compounds the severity of these many threats. Coral reefs grow no more than 12 meters every 1,000 years, provided the waters remain at the appropriate temperature, are clean and allow light to pass through.

The environmental threats to coral reef ecosystems are numerous. Corals are sensitive to water quality that is often affected by marine pollution, including land-based agricultural run-off and untreated sewage. This type of pollution causes eutrophication that stimulates algae growth, covering the coral and blocking light. The movement of topsoil into coastal waters due to erosion linked to coastal development also blocks sunlight from reaching the corals. When the algae die, covered by sediment, so do the corals. Coral also is extremely sensitive to changes in water temperature and clarity, making global warming and climate change a potential threat. Overheated corals release their algae, exposing the white of the coral skeletons. Many "bleached" reefs can return to their previous state over time if the water cools down, but die if the stress is not relieved. During the 1998 "El Nino" phenomenon, some 40 percent of the world's coral reefs suffered bleaching. Some reefs are damaged by destructive fishing methods such as those that rely on dynamite blasts or poison. Over-fishing of herbivores such as parrot fish causes damage because no protection is left against fast-growing seaweed that can engulf reefs. The complexity of a reef ecosystem makes it particularly vulnerable to over-exploitation of individual species. Vessel anchoring, marine archaeology, the use of coral for souvenirs and jewelry, and sports diving also threaten reefs.

Few international instruments mention coral reefs, although the general protection of regional seas agreements can apply to them. Recent international activity has focused on raising awareness of the issues and promoting local and regional initiatives. One reason for the lack of regulation to date may be the mistaken view that coral reefs present no trans-

---

[36]   AZT, a treatment for HIV/AIDS, is derived from a Caribbean reef sponge.
[37]   The rate of loss varies widely. Eighty-five to ninety percent of the reefs of Indonesia and the Philippines are threatened with destruction despite their economic value of approximatley $1.1 billion and $1.6 billion, respectively.

boundary issues, being located for the most part within coastal state juris-diction. In fact, coral reefs have a juvenile stage when larvae migrate on ocean currents to rebuild and replenish existing reefs. Restoring degraded reefs and maintaining existing ones depends upon the genetic flow and repopulation that comes from migration of the larvae. Thus coral reefs pre-sent issues of regional, if not global, concern.

Coral reefs received some attention at the 1992 Earth Summit, partic-ularly in Chapter 17 of Agenda 21. Chapter 17.30 calls on states, acting indi-vidually or internationally and within the framework of IMO and other relevant international organizations to assess the need for additional mea-sures to address degradation of the marine environment. In particular they should take action to ensure respect of areas designated by coastal states, within their exclusive economic zones "in order to protect and preserve rare or fragile ecosystems, such as coral reefs and mangroves." Section 17.85 rec-ommended that states identify

> marine ecosystems exhibiting high levels of biodiversity and pro-ductivity and other critical habitat areas and should provide necessary limitations on use in these areas, through, inter alia, designation of protected areas. Priority should be accorded, as appropriate, to:
> (a) Coral reef ecosystems;
> (b) Estuaries;
> (c) Temperate and tropical wetlands, including mangroves;
> (d) Seagrass beds;
> (e) Other spawning and nursery areas.

In 1994, Australia, France, Jamaica, Japan, the Philippines, Sweden, the U.K. and the U.S. created the International Coral Reef Initiative (ICRI), in cooperation with the UNDP, UNEP, and UNESCO, regional organizations (*e.g.*, the South Pacific Regional Environment Program), the World Bank, the Inter-American Development Bank and IUCN as well as other NGOs. The aims of the group are to strengthen the commitment of governments and international organizations and to implement programs at the local, national, regional, and international levels to conserve, restore and pro-mote sustainable use of coral reefs and associated environments. In addi-tion, each country and region should incorporate into existing local, regional, and national development plans, management and provisions for protection, restoration, and sustainable use of the structure, processes and biodiversity of coral reefs and associated environments. ICRI also seeks to strengthen capacity for development and implementation of policies, man-agement, research and monitoring of coral reefs and associated environ-ments; and establish and maintain coordination of international, regional and national research and monitoring programs, including the Global

Coral Reef Monitoring Network, in association with the Global Ocean Observing System, to ensure efficient use of scarce resources and a flow of information relevant to management of coral reefs and associated environments. ICRI has developed a Framework for Action to provide governments and other interested parties a framework for effective measures to protect coral reef ecosystems. A Global Coral Reef Monitoring Network aims to survey the earth's estimated 400,000 square miles of reef.

Eight reefs have been listed as World Heritage Sites under the UNESCO World Heritage Convention, including the Great Barrier Reef in Australia and Tubbataha Reefs Ocean National Park in the Philippines. UNESCO's Man and the Biosphere program also lists ten biosphere areas that have coral reefs under local community control. In total, some 8 percent of all reefs are within protected areas. Finally, GEF and the EU financed a regional monitoring group with Indian Island states following the 1998 coral bleaching due to El Niño. The network assists the Comoros, Madagascar, Mauritius, Reunion and Seychelles to manage their reef resources within the Regional Environment Program of the Indian Ocean Commission. Some 43 stations provide continuous monitoring to strengthen national capacity for resource management.

D. Conclusions

The three developments described in this chapter represent the emergence of a holistic approach to environmental protection that corresponds to the nature of the environment, but which also pose considerable legal difficulties. Concrete integrated action is effective, but more difficult to achieve than the narrower sectoral or source-based approach that was seen in prior decades. Many international instruments contain vague directives calling for integrated participatory action, but the provisions lack specificity. This may be partly responsible for the proliferation of "case studies" to illustrate best practices as a starting point for action. Such studies are increasingly published by treaty bodies to accompany guidelines and action plans.

The concept of adaptive management has become central to an ecosystem approach to conservation of living resources. An ecosystem approach is defined as the "strategy for the integrated management of land, water and living resources that promote conservation and sustainable use in an equitable way." CBD Decision V/6 emphasizes the role of adaptive management and stresses the necessity of flexibility of management systems of biological resources. The lack of knowledge about ecosystems requires that "management must be adaptive in order to be able to respond to such uncertainties and contain elements of 'learning-by-doing' or research feedback." The Decision recognizes the necessity of measures based on the precautionary principle. The latter is described as measures needed "even when some cause-and-effect relationships are not yet fully established scientifically." Monitoring is in fact key to adaptive management because it helps reduce uncertainties and allows quick response to changes in the ecosystem.

An ecosystem approach to environmental protection still requires incorporation and balance with other societal goals, including economic and social development. The WSSD refers to the "three pillars" of sustainable development: economic development, social development and environmental protection. The participating states called for a collective responsibility to advance and strengthen these three interdependent and mutually reinforcing social goals, at local, national, regional and global levels. The problem remains to determine the bases and procedures for balancing the sometimes competing, although interdependent aspects.

BIBLIOGRAPHY

FRANCIONI, F. & SCOVAZZI, T. eds., INTERNATIONAL LAW FOR ANTARCTICA (1987).

JOYNER, C. & CHOPRA, S., eds., THE ANTARCTIC LEGAL REGIME (1988).

MCCAFFREY, S., THE LAW OF INTERNATIONAL WATERCOURSES (2002).

Rothwell, D., *The Antarctic Treaty: 1961–1991 and Beyond,* 14 SYDNEY L. REV. 62 (1992).

SOHNLE, J., LE DROIT INTERNATIONAL DES RESSOURCES EN EAU: SOLIDARITE CONTRE SOUVERAINETE (2002).

TRIGGS, C. ed., THE ANTARCTIC TREATY REGIME (1987).

WOUTERS, P. CODIFICATION AND PROGRESSIVE DEVELOPMENT OF INTERNATIONAL WATER LAW (2000).

Zang, D., *Frozen in Time: The Antarctic Minerals Convention,* 76 CORNELL L. REV. 722 (1991).

INTERNET SITES

FAOLEX (online database of the FAO) offers the full text of post-1980 water treaties.

Transboundary Freshwater Dispute Database
<http://www.transboundarywaters.orst.edu>

CHAPTER 15

HUMAN RIGHTS AND THE ENVIRONMENT

Protecting human rights and safeguarding the environment, along with achieving peace and security, are fundamental values of modern international society. The first two topics emerged as matters of international concern several decades apart and the earlier development of human rights law[1] encouraged international lawyers and activists as early as the 1972 Stockholm Conference on the Human Environment to explore and attempt to understand the inter-relationship human rights and environmental protection. As this understanding has grown, the two fields have increasingly interacted. At the same time, differences in goals and priorities have demonstrated the obstacles to merging them or integrating either subject entirely into the framework of the other.

Human rights emerged fully as an international concern at the close of the Second World War, although specific human rights issues, *e.g.*, slavery, labor rights, and the protection of religious minorities, were addressed far earlier.[2] The primary objective of human rights law is to protect individuals from abuse of power by state agents, including legislative representatives of the democratic majority. Each state is also obliged to exercise due diligence to ensure that human rights are not violated by non-state actors. Due diligence requires action to prevent abuses where possible, investigate violations that occur, prosecute the perpetrators as appropriate, and provide redress for victims.

The first stage in modern international human rights law consisted of enumerating the fundamental human rights which are internationally guaranteed and protected, along with the state duties to respect and ensure them. After the United Nations adopted the International Covenants on Economic, Social and Cultural Rights and Civil and Political Rights in 1966, many human rights activists turned their attention to developing effective

---

[1]   The United Nations and the Organization of American States both adopted international declarations of human rights in 1948. Universal Declaration of Human Rights, Dec. 10, 1948, and American Declaration of the Rights and Duties of Man, Apr. 30, 1948. Most of the major global and regional human rights treaties, discussed in this chapter, were adopted before the emergence of environmental protection as an international issue.

[2]   *See* Paul Gordon Lauren, Visions Seen: The Evolution of Human Rights (1998).

compliance and enforcement procedures to supervise state implementation of human rights. Other individuals and groups have continued to devote their attention to the articulation of new norms or the further elaboration of existing ones in response to new problems that detrimentally impact human dignity and well-being. The issue of environmental degradation impairing or undermining human rights emerged in this context.

From the environmental perspective, human rights law initially provided the only international legal recourse available to individuals seeking to remedy environmental harm. At the time of the 1972 Stockholm Conference, international environmental law was undeveloped, although environmental issues had clearly emerged on the international agenda. Significantly, preparations for the Stockholm Conference coincided with the United Nations convening the 1968[3] Teheran Conference on Human Rights, the first international conference organized by the United Nations and marking the 20th anniversary of the adoption of the Universal Declaration of Human Rights. The Teheran Conference, overcoming a long-standing political debate that led to the adoption of two human rights covenants[4] rather than a single instrument, proclaimed that all human rights are interdependent and indivisible, opening the door for consideration of complex issues like environmental rights. Human rights language also provided an inducement to developing countries to participate in the emerging environmental movement. While developing states largely viewed environmental degradation as a problem of rich, industrialized countries, they were vitally concerned with human rights, particularly decolonization, self-determination and economic development. The Teheran Conference addressed concerns about economic development and human rights, proclaiming the interdependence of peace, development and human rights. Resource depletion fit within this agenda and stimulated interest among developing states in the forthcoming Stockholm Conference. Nonetheless, from Stockholm to the present, most advances in considering the relationship between human rights and environmental protection have occurred first, if not only at the regional level.

---

[3]   Also in 1968, a wave of student-led demonstrations throughout Europe and North America represented a rejection of many then-dominant social values, including conspicuous consumption. Public awareness of environmental threats expanded considerably after the Torrey Canyon oil spill in 1967. *See further* Chapter 2.

[4]   The two Covenants divide human rights into categories of civil and political rights, on one hand, and economic, social and cultural rights, on the other hand. *See* International Covenant on Civil and Political Rights, Dec. 16, 1966; International Covenant on Economic, Social and Cultural Rights, Dec. 16, 1966.

A. Introduction: Inter-Relating Human Rights and Environmental Protection

Four principal and complementary approaches have emerged to characterize the relationship between human rights and the environment. The approaches are outlined below, before a detailed analysis of the international instruments and state practice that reflect the first three approaches:

- International environmental laws incorporates and utilizes those human rights guarantees deemed necessary or important to ensuring effective environmental protection. *Procedural rights*
- Human rights law re-casts or interprets internationally-guaranteed human rights to include an environmental dimension when environmental degradation prevents full enjoyment of the guaranteed rights. *greening*
- International environmental law and international human rights law elaborate a new substantive right to a safe and healthy environment.
- International environmental law articulates ethical and legal duties of individuals that include environmental protection and human rights.

The first approach selects from among the catalogue of human rights those rights most relevant to the aims of environmental protection, independent of the utility of environmental protection to the enjoyment of the full human rights catalogue. The approach thus emphasizes procedural rights such as freedom of association, which permits the existence and activities of non-governmental environmental organizations, and the right of access to information concerning potential threats to the environment, which may be used for nature protection not necessarily related to human health and well-being. The potential for improving environmental protection through effective guarantees of procedural rights is solid, but the absence of complaint mechanisms or other recourse in international environmental agreements is a limiting aspect.[5]

The second approach, which uses existing human rights norms and institutions, is unreservedly anthropocentric and supported by indications of the public health impacts of environmental deterioration: a 1998 study estimated that 40 percent of the world's deaths can be attributed to environmental factors.[6] Some 1.2 billion people in developing countries lack

---

[5]   Note, however, that procedural rights, such freedom of association and access to information also appear in human rights instruments and thus in appropriate instances complaints of their violation may be filed with human rights bodies. *See infra* Sections C.4 and C.6.

[6]   D. Pimental, *Ecology of Increasing Diseases: Population Growth and Environmental Degradation*, BIOSCIENCE (Oct. 1998).

clean and safe drinking water, with the result that waterborne infections account for 80 percent of all infectious diseases worldwide. In many areas industrial and household wastes are dumped directly into rivers and lakes. Air pollution adversely affects the health of 4 billion people. With some 2.5 billion kg of pesticides used worldwide each year—a 50-fold increase over the past 50 years—about 3 million cases of human pesticide poisonings are reported annually.

Human rights law seeks to ensure that environmental conditions do not deteriorate to the point where the right to life, the right to health, the right to a family and private life, the right to culture, and other human rights are seriously impaired. As Judge Weeremantry of the International Court of Justice expressed it:

> The protection of the environment is . . . a vital part of contemporary human rights doctrine, for it is a *sine qua non* for numerous human rights such as the right to health and the right to life itself. It is scarcely necessary to elaborate on this, as damage to the environment can impair and undermine all the human rights spoken of in the Universal Declaration and other human rights instruments.[7]

Klaus Toepfer, Executive Director of the United Nations Environment Program, also reflected this approach in his statement to the 57th Session of the UN Commission on Human Rights in 2001:

> Human rights cannot be secured in a degraded or polluted environment. The fundamental right to life is threatened by soil degradation and deforestation and by exposures to toxic chemicals, hazardous wastes and contaminated drinking water. . . . Environmental conditions clearly help to determine the extent to which people enjoy their basic rights to life, health, adequate food and housing, and traditional livelihood and culture. It is time to recognize that those who pollute or destroy the natural environment are not just committing a crime against nature, but are violating human rights as well.

The General Assembly has called the preservation of nature "a prerequisite for the normal life of man."[8]

With a focus on the consequences of environmental harm to existing human rights, this approach serves to address most serious cases of actual

---

[7]   Gabçikovo-Nagymaros Case (Hungary-Slovakia), I.C.J., Judgment of Sept. 25, 1997 (Sep. Op. Judge Weermantry), at 4.

[8]   G.A. Res. 35/48 of 30 Oct. 1980.

or imminently-threatened pollution. The primary advantage over the first approach is that existing human rights complaint procedures may be employed against those states whose level of environmental protection falls below that necessary to maintain any of the guaranteed human rights. Using existing human rights law has its own limits, however, because its anthropocentric nature means it cannot easily resolve threats to other species or to ecological processes.

The third possibility is to formulate a new human right to an environment that is not defined in purely anthropocentric terms, an environment that is safe not only for humans, but one that is ecologically-balanced and sustainable in the long term. Some international success has attended the various efforts undertaken in this direction, as discussed below.[9] More than a few environmentalists, however, object to the anthropocentrism inherent in taking any human rights approach to environmental protection. The notion of a right to environment has also met resistance from those who claim that the concept cannot be given content and who assert that no justiciable standards can be developed to enforce the right, because of the inherent variability of environmental conditions.[10]

Finally, the fourth approach prefers to address environmental protection as a matter of human responsibilities rather than rights. Draft declarations of human responsibilities such as the Earth Charter focus on duties towards the environment. Many proponents of this approach posit ecological rights or rights of nature as a construct to balance human rights, attempting to reconcile human rights and ecology by introducing ecological limitations on human rights. "The objective of these limitations is to implement an eco-centric ethic in a manner which imposes responsibilities and duties upon humankind to take intrinsic values and the interests of the natural community into account when exercising its human rights."[11]

The concept of nature's rights has been proposed in a variety of formulations, from legally enforceable rights, to "biotic rights" as moral imperatives, to human responsibilities and duties. Some suggest giving legal

---

[9]   Far more success has been achieved among national constitutions. As discussed in part C, more than 100 constitutions presently proclaim a right to an environment of a specified quality or impose duties on the government to protect the environment.

[10]   *See, e.g.*, Gunther Handl, *Human Rights and Protection of the Environment: A Mildly 'Revisionist' View, in* A.A. CANCADO-TRINDADE ed., HUMAN RIGHTS AND ENVIRONMENTAL PROTECTION (1992); ALAN BOYLE AND MICHAEL ANDERSON eds., HUMAN RIGHTS APPROACHES TO ENVIRONMENTAL PROTECTION (1996).

[11]   Prudence Taylor, *From Environmental to Ecological Human Rights: A New Dynamic in International Law*, 10 GEORGETOWN INT'L ENVTL. L. REV. 309, 310 (1998). *See also* Catherine Redgwell, *Life, the Universe and Everything: A Critique of Anthropocentric Rights*, in HUMAN RIGHTS APPROACHES TO ENVIRONMENTAL PROTECTION 71 (ALAN E. BOYLE & M. ANDERSON eds., 1996).

recognition to the intrinsic value of nature, by adding new "subjects" of law: "[i]f it is possible to grant rights to people [in international law], and to future generations, then it is arguably possible to grant rights to animals and to the environment itself, and thus confer upon them limited subject status."[12] Others argue that this has already occurred[13] while some object that the ascription of rights to nature anthropomorphizes it to its detriment.[14] Still others view rights-conferring as one tool to enhance the value of nature.

A legal system in which the environment is said to have rights will evolve differently from one in which such rights do not exist. A system of biotic rights for nature had been described as "morally justified claims or demands on behalf of nonhuman organisms, either individuals or aggregates (populations and species), against all moral agents for the vital interests or imperative conditions of well-being for nonhumankind."[15] The same author posits a Bill of Biotic Rights that includes claims or demands for participation in the natural competition for existence; healthy and whole habitats; reproduction without artificial distortions; no human-induced extinctions; freedom from human cruelty, flagrant abuse or frivolous use; restoration of natural conditions disrupted by human abuse and the right to a fair share of the goods necessary for sustainability. At present, no international legal instrument takes this approach, albeit the World Charter for Nature proclaimed the intrinsic value of nature.

The remainder of this chapter addresses the interface between the international protection of human rights and international environmental law from the perspective of the first three approaches. It looks at the efforts in environmental law to articulate the human rights aspects of environmental protection, especially in the realm of procedural rights. It then discusses how human rights law recognizes the consequences of environmental degradation on the enjoyment of human rights. The merger of the two fields through elaborating a human right to the environment is then considered, as well as the special recognition given the rights of indigenous peoples and farmers.

B. Human Rights in International Environmental Law

States and non-state actors participating in the Stockholm Conference initiated the enduring process of appraising the relationship between environmental protection and human rights. The United States delegation submitted the most far-reaching proposal at Stockholm, seeking to proclaim:

---

12   Taylor, *id.* at 373.

13   *See* Anthony D'Amato & Sudhir K. Chopra, *Whales: Their Emerging Right to Life*, 85 AJIL 21 (1991).

14   *See* Cynthia Giagnocavo & Howard Goldstein, *Laws Reform or World Reform*, 35 McGILL L.J. 346 (1990).

15   James A. Nash, *The Case for Biotic Rights*, 18 YALE J. INT'L L. 235 (1993).

Every human being has a right to a healthful and safe environment, including air, water and earth, and to food and other material necessities, all of which should be sufficiently free of contamination and other elements which detract from the health or well-being of man.

The proposal was supported by non-governmental organizations, but participating states preferred the formulation of what became the oft-quoted Principle 1 of the Final Declaration:

Man has the fundamental right to freedom, equality and adequate conditions of life, in an environment of a quality that permits a life of dignity and well-being, and he bears a solemn responsibility to protect and improve the environment for present and future generations.

This complex sentence stops short of proclaiming a right to environment, but it clearly links human rights and environmental protection. It sees human rights as a fundamental goal and environmental protection as instrumental to achieve the "adequate conditions" for the guaranteed "life of dignity and well-being."

The lack of state support for a substantive right to environment like that proposed by the United States led scholars[16] and activists during the following decade to consider human rights in a more instrumental fashion, to give content to environmental rights by identifying those rights whose enjoyment could be considered a prerequisite to effective environmental protection. They focused in particular on the procedural rights to environmental information, public participation in decision-making and remedies in the event of environmental harm. Various international instruments, particularly in Europe, built upon this concept to give content to Stockholm Principle I.

Almost 20 years later, in Resolution 45/94, the UN General Assembly recalled the language of Stockholm, stating that it:

Recognizes that all individuals are entitled to live in an environment adequate for their health and well-being; and calls upon Member States and intergovernmental and non-governmental organizations to enhance their efforts towards ensuring a better and healthier environment.[17]

---

16   *See, e.g.,* A. Kiss, *Peut-on définir le droit de l'homme à l'environnement?*, 1976 Rev. Juridique de L'environnement 15; A. Kiss, *Le droit à la conservation de l'environnement*, 2 Rev. Univ. Des Droits de L'homme 445 (1990); A. Kiss, *An Introductory Note on a Human Right to Environment, in* E. Brown Weiss ed., Environmental Change and International Law 551 (1992).

17   *Need to Ensure a Healthy Environment for the Well-Being of Individuals*, G.A. Res. 45/94, U.N. GAOR, 45th Sess.; U.N. Doc. A/RES/45/94 (1990).

The texts adopted in connection with UNCED contain few references to human rights. No right to environment is declared and there is almost no discussion of the inter-relationship of human rights and environmental protection. Working Group III of the UNCED Preparatory Committee considered numerous proposals to include a right to environment in the Rio Declaration. The consolidated draft Declaration contained several provisions referring to a human right to a healthy environment. In the final meetings prior to Rio, however, the participants failed to reach consensus on including such a right.

The resulting text changes the formulation of the Stockholm Declaration. The Rio Declaration states that human beings are "entitled to a healthy and productive life in harmony with nature." Unlike the Stockholm Declaration, the Rio Declaration proclaims only the sovereign right of states to exploit their resources (Principle 2) and the right to development (Principle 3). The Rio Declaration accepts the importance of a role for the public, but—consistent with its avoidance of rights language—calls for including it on the ground of efficiency: "Environmental issues are best handled with the participation of all concerned citizens at the relevant level" (Principle 10). Principle 10 adds that individuals

> shall have appropriate access to information concerning the environment that is held by public authorities, including information on hazardous materials and activities in their communities, and the opportunity to participate in decision-making processes. States shall facilitate and encourage public awareness and participation by making information widely available. Effective access to judicial and administrative proceedings, including redress and remedy, shall be provided.

Numerous environmental instruments now contain the three procedural rights, discussed in turn in the following materials.

1. *The Right to Environmental Information*

Access to environmental information is a prerequisite to public participation in decision-making and to monitoring governmental and private sector activities. It also can assist enterprises in planning for and utilizing the best available techniques and technology. The nature of environmental deterioration, which often arises only long after a project is completed and can be irreversible, compels early and complete data to make informed choices. Transboundary impacts also produce significant demands for information across borders.

A "right to information" can mean, narrowly, freedom to seek information, or, more broadly, a right of access to information, or even a right to receive it. Corresponding duties of the state can be limited to abstention from interfering with public efforts to obtain information from the state or from private entities, or expanded to require the state to obtain and disseminate all relevant information concerning both public and private projects that might affect the environment. If the government duty is limited to abstention from interfering with the ability of individuals or associations to seek information from those willing to share it then little may actually be obtained. A governmental obligation to release information about its own projects can increase public knowledge, but fails to provide access to the numerous private-sector activities that can affect the environment. Information about the latter may be obtained by the government through licensing or environmental impact requirements. Imposing upon the state a duty to disseminate this information in addition to details of its own projects provides the public with the broadest basis for informed decision-making.

As noted above, Rio Principle 10 calls for states to provide environmental information. Similarly, Chapter 23 of Agenda 21, on strengthening the role of major groups, proclaims that individuals, groups and organizations should have access to information relevant to the environment and development, held by national authorities, including information on products and activities that have or are likely to have a significant impact on the environment, and information on environmental protection matters.

Informational rights are widely found in environmental treaties, in weak and strong versions.[18] The Framework Convention on Climate Change,

---

[18] *E.g.*, Convention for the Protection of the Marine Environment of the North-East Atlantic (Paris, Sept. 22, 1992) Art. 9; Convention on Civil Liability for Damage Resulting from Activities Dangerous to the Environment (Lugano, June 21, 1993), Arts. 13–16; North-American Agreement on Environmental Co-operation (Sept. 13, 1993), Art. 2(1)(a); International Convention to Combat Desertification in those Countries Experiencing Serious Drought and/or Desertification, particularly in Africa (Paris, June 17, 1994), Preamble, Arts. 10(2)(e), 13(1)(b), 14(2), 19 and 25; Convention on Co-operation and Sustainable Use of the Danube River (Sofia, June 29, 1994), Art.14; Energy Charter Treaty, Lisbon (Dec. 17, 1994), Arts. 19(1)(i) and 20; Amendments to the 1976 Barcelona Convention for the Protection of the Mediterranean Sea against Pollution (Barcelona, June 10, 1995), Arts. 15 and 17; Protocol concerning Specially Protected Areas and Biological Diversity in the Mediterranean (Barcelona, June 10, 1995), Art.19; Rotterdam Convention on the Prior Informed Consent Procedure for Certain Hazardous Chemicals and Pesticides in International Trade (Sept. 10, 1998), Art.15(2); Protocol on Water and Health to the 1992 Convention on the Protection and Use of Transboundary Watercourses and International Lakes (London, June 17, 1999), Art. 5(i); Cartagena Protocol on Biosafety to the Convention on Biological Diversity

Article 6, exemplifies the weak approach. It provides that its parties "shall promote and facilitate at the national and, as appropriate, sub-regional and regional levels, and in accordance with national laws and regulations, and within their respective capacities, public access to information and public participation." The Convention on Biological Diversity similarly does not oblige states parties to provide information, but refers in its preamble to the general lack of information and knowledge regarding biological diversity and affirms the need for the full participation of women at all levels of policy-making and implementation. Article 13 calls for education to promote and encourage understanding of the importance of conservation of biological diversity. Article 14 provides that each contracting party, "as far as possible and as appropriate," shall introduce "appropriate" environmental impact assessment procedures and "where appropriate" allow for public participation in such procedures. Broader guarantees of public information are found in regional agreements, including the 1992 Helsinki Convention on the Protection and Use of Transboundary Watercourses and International Lakes (Art. 16), the 1992 Espoo Convention on Environmental Impact Assessment in a Transboundary Context (Art. 3[8]), and the 1992 Paris Convention on the North-East Atlantic (Art. 9). The last mentioned obliges the contracting parties to ensure that their competent authorities are required to make available relevant information to any natural or legal person, in response to any reasonable request, without the person having to prove an interest, without unreasonable charges and within two months of the request.

The provisions of the Rotterdam Convention on the Prior Informed Consent Procedure for Certain Hazardous Chemicals and Pesticides in International Trade (September 10, 1998) vaguely encourage parties to ensure that information on chemical and pesticide hazards is made available to the public. The prior informed consent referred to in the title is that of the government of the importing state; there are few direct references to the duty to inform. The only provision imposing a direct duty on states parties to make information available to the public is Article 15 on implementation. Paragraph 2 requires each state party to ensure, "to the extent practicable" that the public has "appropriate" access to information on chemical handling and accident management and on alternatives that are safer for human health or the environment than the chemicals listed in Annex III to the Convention. Nonetheless, the objectives of the Convention cannot be carried out in the absence of informed persons.

Other treaties require states parties to inform the public of specific environmental hazards. The IAEA Joint Convention on the Safety of Spent Fuel

---

(Montreal, Jan. 29, 2000), Art. 23; International Treaty on Plant Genetic Resources for Food and Agriculture (Nov. 3, 2001).

Management and on the Safety of Radioactive Waste Management[19] is based to a large extent on the principles contained in the IAEA document "The Principles of Radioactive Waste Management." The Preamble of the treaty recognizes the importance of informing the public on issues regarding the safety of spent fuel and radioactive waste management. This is reinforced in Articles 6 and 13, on siting of proposed facilities, which require each state party to take the appropriate steps to ensure that procedures are established and implemented to make information available to members of the public on the safety of any proposed spent fuel management facility or radioactive waste management facility. Similarly, Article 10(1) of the Convention on Persistent Organic Pollutants[20] specifies that each party shall, within its capabilities, promote and facilitate provision to the public of all available information on persistent organic pollutants and ensure that the public has access to public information and that the information is kept up-to-date (Art. 10 (1)(b) and(2)).

Regionally, the European Community generally guarantees the right of the individual to be informed about the environmental compatibility of products, manufacturing processes and their effects on the environment, and industrial installations.[21] Directives vary respecting public rights to information. Some air pollution directives, for example, make no reference to public information[22] while others[23] provide that information shall be made available to the public concerned in accordance with the national legal procedures.

The Community also requires that information be provided to those who may be particularly at risk from certain activities or products. For example, Framework Directive 89/391[24] on the protection of workers against risks in the workplace, calls for employee information and consultation. Other

---

[19]   Vienna, Sept. 5, 1997, *reprinted in* 36 I.L.M. 1431 (1997).

[20]   Stockholm, May 22, 2001.

[21]   *See, e.g.*, Directive 76/160, on bathing water quality, which states that "public interest in the environment and in the improvement of its quality is increasing; the public should therefore receive objective information on the quality of bathing water." Article 13 requires member states to submit regularly to the Commission a "comprehensive report on the bathing water and most significant characteristics thereof." The Commission publishes the information "after prior consent from the Member State concerned." However, the consent may limit the information provided, undermining its "objective" nature. Directive 76/160, O.J. L 31/1 (2/5/76).

[22]   Directives: 80/778/EEC, O.J. L 229 (8/30/80); 82/884/EEC, O.J. L 378/15 (12/31/82); 85/203/EEC, Mar. 7, 1985, O.J. L 87/1 (3/27/85).

[23]   *E.g.*, Directive on Combating Air Pollution from Industrial Plants, 84/360/EEC, O.J. L 188 (7/16/84).

[24]   89/391/EEC, O.J. L 183 (6/29/89); 90/394/EEC, O.J. L 196 (7/26/90).

directives applicable to specific industries, such as mining and fishing, or to specific hazards, such as asbestos[25] require information be given to workers about the risks they face.

Two general directives address rights of information. First, Council Directive 85/337 Concerning the Assessment of the Effects of Certain Public and Private Projects on the Environment[26] makes explicit the duty to provide information in connection with mandatory environmental assessment projects. Second, the EC adopted in 1990 a Directive on Freedom of Access to Information on the Environment,[27] replaced in January 2003[28] as a consequence of the adoption of the 1998 Aarhus Convention on Access to Information, Public Participation in Decision-Making and Access to Justice in Environmental Matters. The new Directive insists that the disclosure of information should be the general rule, making information more accessible than was required under the 1990 Directive. Public authorities should be authorized to refuse requests for environmental information only in specific and clearly defined cases. Environmental information means any information in written, visual, aural, electronic or any other material form on the state of the elements of the environment; factors affecting or likely to affect those elements; measures, including administrative ones; policies, legislation, plans, programs, environmental agreements and activities affecting or likely to affect the environment; reports on the implementation of environmental legislation; relevant economic analyses and the state of human health and safety. "Public authority" means government or other public administration, at the national, regional or local level, any natural or legal person performing public administrative functions or having public responsibilities, excluding bodies or institutions acting in a judicial or legislative capacity.

Public authorities shall make available environmental information held by or for them to the public. The latter means one or more natural or legal persons and, in accordance with national legislation or practice, their associations, organizations or groups. Environmental information shall be made available to the applicant as soon as possible. Article 7 of the Directive provides for the dissemination of environmental information, in particular by means of computer telecommunication and/or electronic technology. The information shall include texts of international treaties and of Community, national, regional or local legislation on the environment or relating to it as well as progress reports on the implementation of such texts. Public

---

[25]   *E.g.*, 83/477/EEC, O.J. L 263 (9/24/83).

[26]   Council Directive 85/337/EEC June 27, 1985, O.J. L 175/40 (7/5/85).

[27]   Council Directive 90/313/EEC June 7, 1990, on the freedom of access to information on the environment, O.J. L 158 (6/23/90).

[28]   Directive 2003/4/EC Jan. 28, 2003 on public access to environmental information and repealing Council Directive 90/313/EEC.

authorities may charge a reasonable amount for supplying such information, while access to any public registers or lists and examination in situ of
the information requested shall be free of charge. Authorities may refuse a
request for environmental information in conditions similar to those foreseen by the Aarhus Convention.

The Directive does not mention public participation. The scope of its
Article 6 on access to justice is limited to situations where a request for information has been ignored, wrongfully refused, inadequately or not dealt with
in accordance with the provisions related to the access to information.

Other organizations have issued non-binding declarations proclaiming
a right to environmental information. The World Health Organization's
European Charter on the Environment and Health states that "every individual is entitled to information and consultation on the state of the environment."[29] The states participating in the OSCE have confirmed the right
of individuals, groups, and organizations to obtain, publish and distribute
information on environmental issues.[30] The Bangkok Declaration, adopted
October 16, 1990, affirms similar rights in Asia and the Pacific[31] while the
Arab Declaration on Environment and Development and Future Perspectives of September 1991 speaks of the right of individuals and non-governmental organizations to acquire information about environmental issues
relevant to them.[32]

2. *Public Participation in Environmental Decision-Making*

The process by which rules emerge, how proposed rules become norms and
norms become law, is highly important to the legitimacy of the law and legitimacy in turn affects compliance. To a large extent, legitimacy is a matter

---

[29]   European Charter on Environment and Health, adopted 8 December
1989 by the First Conference of Ministers of the Environment and of Health of
the Member States of the European Region of the World Health Organization.

[30]   Conference on Security and Cooperation in Europe, Sofia Meeting on
Protection of the Environment (Oct.–Nov. 1989), (CSCE/SEM.36, Nov. 2,
1989).

[31]   Ministerial Declaration on Environmentally Sound and Sustainable
Development in Asia and the Pacific (Bangkok, Oct. 16, 1990), A/CONF.151/
PC/38. Paragraph 27 affirms "the right of individuals and non-governmental
organizations to be informed of environmental problems relevant to them, to
have the necessary access to information, and to participate in the formulation
and implementation of decisions likely to affect their environment."

[32]   Arab Declaration on Environment and Development and Future
Perspectives, adopted by the Arab Ministerial Conference on Environment and
Development (Cairo, Sept. 1991), A/46/632, *cited in* U.N. Doc. E/CN.4/Sub.2/
1992/7, 20.

of participation: the governed must have and perceive that they have a voice in governance through representation, deliberation or some other form of action. Participation may take place through elections, grass roots action, lobbying, public speaking, hearings, and other forms of governance whereby various interests and communities participate in shaping the laws and decisions that affect them.

The major role played by the public in environmental protection is participation in decision-making, especially in environmental impact or other permitting procedures. Public participation is based on the right of those who may be affected, including foreign citizens and residents, to have a say in the determination of their environmental future.

The preparation of the Rio Conference was itself an important step in encouraging the participation of non-governmental organizations and the representatives of economic interests. The Global Forum of Rio, a meeting of non-governmental organizations parallel to the official conference, represented world public opinion in favor of conserving the world's ecosystems. The Rio Declaration reflects and confirms the importance of this opinion. In addition to Principle 10, the Declaration includes provisions on the participation of different components of the population: women (Principle 20), youth (Principle 21), and indigenous peoples and local communities (Principle 22).

Public participation is also emphasized in Agenda 21. The Preamble to Chapter 23 states:

> One of the fundamental prerequisites for the achievement of sustainable development is broad public participation in decision-making. Furthermore, in the more specific context of environment and development, the need for new forms of participation has emerged. This includes the need of individuals, groups, and organizations to participate in environmental impact assessment procedures and to know about and participate in decisions, particularly those that potentially affect the communities in which they live and work. Individuals, groups and organizations should have access to information relevant to environment and development held by national authorities, including information on products and activities that have or are likely to have a significant impact on the environment, and information on environmental protection measures.

Section III identifies major groups whose participation is needed: women, youth, indigenous and local populations, non-governmental organizations, local authorities, workers, business and industry, scientists, and farmers.

The right to participate has two components: the right to be heard and the right to affect decisions. Principle 23 of the 1982 World Charter for Nature provides most explicitly:

All persons, in accordance with their national legislation, shall have the opportunity to participate, individually or with others, in the formulation of decisions of direct concern to their environment, and shall have access to means of redress when their environment has suffered damage or degradation.

Most recent multilateral and many bilateral agreements contain references to or guarantees of public participation.[33] The Climate Change Convention, Article 4l(i) obliges parties to promote public awareness and to "encourage the widest participation in this process including that of non-governmental organizations." The Convention on Biological Diversity allows for public participation in environmental impact assessment procedures in Article 14(1)(a). Outside the UNCED context, the 1991 Espoo Convention on Environmental Impact Assessment in a Transboundary Context requires states parties to notify the public and to provide an opportunity for public participation in relevant environmental impact assessment procedures regarding proposed activities in any area likely to be affected by transboundary environmental harm. In a final decision on the proposed activities, the state must take due account of the environmental impact assessment, including the opinions of the individuals in the affected area. The Desertification Convention goes furthest in calling for public participation, embedding the issue throughout the agreement. Article 3(a) and (c) begins by recognizing that there is a need to associate civil society with the actions

---

33 In addition to the treaties discussed in the text, other agreements referring to public participation are the: Protocol to the 1979 Convention on Long-Range Transboundary Air Pollution Concerning the Control of Emissions of Volatile Organic Compounds or Their Transboundary Fluxes (Geneva, Nov. 18, 1991), Art. 2(3)(a)(4); Convention on the Protection and Utilization of Transboundary Rivers and Lakes (Helsinki, Mar. 17, 1992), Art. 16; Convention on the Transboundary Effects of Industrial Accidents (Helsinki, Mar. 17, 1992), Art. 9; Convention for the Protection of the Marine Environment of the Baltic Sea (Helsinki, Apr. 9, 1992), Art. 17; Convention for the Prevention of Marine Pollution of the North-East Atlantic (Paris, Sept. 22, 1992), Art. 9; Convention on Civil Responsibility for Damage resulting from Activities Dangerous to the Environment (Lugano, June 21, 1993), Arts. 13–16; North American Convention on Cooperation in the Field of the Environment (Washington, D.C., Sept. 14, 1993), Arts. 2(1)(a), 14; Convention on Cooperation and Sustainable Development of the Waters of the Danube (Sofia, June 29, 1994), Art. 14; Protocol to the 1975 Barcelona Convention on Specially Protected Zones and Biological Diversity in the Mediterranean (Barcelona, June 10, 1995), Art. 19; Joint Communique and Declaration on the Establishment of the Arctic Council (Ottawa, Sept. 19, 1996), Preamble and Arts. 1(a), 2, 3(c); Kyoto Protocol to the United Nations Framework Convention on Climate Change (Dec. 11, 1997), Art. 6(3); Convention on Persistent Organic Pollutants (Sept. 22, 2001), Art. 10(1)(d); 40 I.L.M. 532 (2001).

of the state. The treaty calls for an integrated commitment of all actors—national governments, scientific institutions, local communities and authorities, and non-governmental organizations, as well as international partners, both bilateral and multilateral.[34]

The trend towards including rights of public participation is not followed in all multilateral environmental agreements. The United Nations Convention on the Law of the Non-Navigational Uses of International Watercourses[35] and recent regional agreements for water management provide for interstate cooperation, but do not refer to public participation in decisions regarding the uses and management of international watercourses.[36]

In contrast, the 1993 North American Agreement on Environmental Cooperation (NAAEC), also known as the NAFTA side agreement, contains institutional arrangements for public participation. It creates a permanent trilateral body, the Commission for Environmental Cooperation, composed of a Council, a Secretariat and a Joint Public Advisory Committee (Art. 8). The Joint Public Advisory Committee includes 15 members from the public, five from each member country, and advises the Council as well as provides technical, scientific, or other information to the Secretariat. The Committee also may advise on the annual program and budget as well as reports that are issued. NAAEC is also the first environmental agreement to establish a procedure which allows individuals, environmental organizations and business entities to complain about a state's failure to enforce its environmental law, including those deriving from international obligations.

Recent bilateral agreements also provide for public participation. The 1991 Canada-United States Agreement on Air Quality[37] provides that the International Joint Commission established pursuant to an earlier agreement, shall invite comments, including through public hearings as appropriate, on each progress report prepared by the Air Quality Committee established to assist in implementing the agreement. A synthesis of public views and, if requested, a record of such views shall be submitted to the parties. After submission to the parties, the synthesis shall be released to the public. The parties agree to consult on the contents of the progress report based in part on the views presented to the Commission. Further, in Art.

---

[34]   *See also* Arts.s 10(2)(e), 13(1)(b), 14(2), 19, and 25.

[35]   New York, May 21, 1997.

[36]   *See, e.g.*, Kenya-Tanzania-Uganda, Final Act of the Conference of Plenipotentiaries on the Establishment of the Lake Victoria Fisheries Organization (Kisumu, Kenya, June 30, 1994); Bangladesh-India Treaty on Sharing of the Ganges Waters at Farakka (New Delhi, Dec. 12, 1996); India-Nepal, Treaty Concerning the Integrated Development of the Mahakai River (New Delhi, Feb. 12, 1996).

[37]   Ottawa, Mar. 13, 1991.

XIV, the parties shall consult with state or provincial governments, interested organizations, and the public, in implementing the Agreement.

The Agreement on Environmental Cooperation between Canada and Chile[38] lists among its objectives to promote transparency and public participation in the development of environmental law, regulations and policies. The obligations of the parties include periodically preparing and making publicly available reports on the state of the environment. In more detail, Article 4 provides that each party shall ensure that its laws, regulations, procedures and administrative rulings of general application respecting any matter governed by the agreement are promptly published or otherwise made available to enable interested persons and the other party to become acquainted with them. To the extent possible, each party is to publish in advance any such measure that it proposes to adopt and provide interested persons and the other party a reasonable opportunity to comment on the proposed measures.

3. The Right to a Remedy for Environmental Harm

Principle 10 of the Rio Declaration provides that "effective access to judicial and administrative proceedings, including redress and remedy, shall be provided." Agenda 21 calls on governments and legislators to establish judicial and administrative procedures for legal redress in order to remedy actions affecting the environment that may be unlawful or infringe on rights under the law. They should provide such access to justice to individuals, groups and organizations with a recognized legal interest. UNCLOS also provides that states shall ensure that recourse is available for prompt and adequate compensation or other relief in respect of damage caused by pollution of the marine environment by natural or juridical persons under their jurisdiction (Art. 235(2)).

Some instruments make explicit that the right to a remedy is not limited to nationals of a state, *e.g.*, the OECD Recommendation on Equal Right of Access in Relation to Transfrontier Pollution.[39] International agreements may contain obligations to grant a potential or *de facto* injured person a right of access to any administrative or judicial procedure equal to that of nationals or residents. Equal access to national remedies has been considered one way of implementing the polluter pays principle. Implementing the right of equal access to national remedies requires that states remove jurisdictional barriers to civil proceedings for damages and other remedies in respect to environmental injury. Both the February 25, 1991 Espoo Convention and the March 17, 1992, Helsinki Convention on

---

[38] Ottawa, Feb. 6, 1997, *reprinted in* 26 I.L.M. 1193 (1997).
[39] May 11, 1976, C(76)55(Final).

the Transboundary Effects of Industrial Accidents call for equality of access. The 1997 UN Convention on the Non-Navigational Uses of International Watercourses, Article 32, formulates the same principle under the title "nondiscrimination."

4. The Aarhus Convention

The various international efforts to promote procedural rights in environmental instruments produced a landmark agreement on June 25, 1998, when 35 states and the European Community signed a Convention on Access to Information, Public Participation and Access to Justice in Environmental Matters.[40] The Convention builds on prior texts, especially Principle 1 of the Stockholm Declaration. Indeed, it is the first environmental treaty to incorporate and strengthen the language of Principle 1. The Preamble expressly states that "every person has the right to live in an environment adequate to his or her health and well-being, and the duty, both individually and in association with others, to protect and improve the environment for the benefit of present and future generations." The following paragraph adds that to be able to assert the right and observe the duty, citizens must have access to information, be entitled to participate in decision-making and have access to justice in environmental matters. These provisions are repeated in Article 1 where states parties agree to guarantee the rights of access to information, public participation, and access to justice. The Convention acknowledges its broader implications, expressing a conviction that its implementation will "contribute to strengthening democracy in the region of the UNECE."

The Convention obliges states parties to collect and publicly disseminate information, and respond to specific requests. (Arts. 4–5) Each party is to prepare and disseminate a national report on the state of the environment at three to four year intervals. In addition, it must disseminate legislative and policy documents, treaties, and other international instruments relating to the environment. Each party must ensure that public authorities, upon request, provide environmental information to a requesting person without the latter having to state an interest. Public authorities means, in addition to government bodies, any natural or legal person having public responsibilities or functions or providing public services. The information has to be made available within one month, or in exceptional cases up

---

[40] The Convention was sponsored by the United Nations Economic Commission for Europe and is open for signature by the 55 members of the UNECE, which includes all of Europe as well as the United States, Canada, and states of the former Soviet Union. States having consultative status with the UNECE may also participate.

to three months. In addition to providing information on request, each state party must be pro-active, ensuring that public authorities collect and update environmental information relevant to their functions. This requires that each state party establish mandatory systems to obtain information on proposed and existing activities which could significantly affect the environment. This provision is clearly aimed at the private sector and is supplemented by Article 5(6) which requires states parties to encourage operators whose activities have a significant impact on the environment to inform the public regularly of the environmental impact of their activities and products, through eco-labeling, eco-auditing or similar means. States parties are also to ensure that consumer information on products is made available.

To enhance the effectiveness of the Convention, the states parties must provide information about information, *i.e.*, the type and scope of information held by public authorities, the basic terms and conditions under which it is made available and the procedure by which it could be obtained. The Convention also foresees the establishment of publicly-accessible electronic sites that should contain reports on the state of the environment, texts of environmental legislation, environmental plans, programs and policies, and other information that could facilitate the application of national law.

The treaty provides numerous exceptions to the duty to inform in Article 4(4), reflecting other political, economic and legal interests. A state may refuse to provide the information if the information is not in its possession; the request is manifestly unreasonable or too general; concerns material not completed or internal communications of a public authority; or if the disclosure would adversely affect:

- the confidentiality of public proceedings;
- international relations, national defense or public security;
- criminal investigations or trials;
- commercial and industrial secrets (however, information on emissions relevant to the protection of the environment shall be disclosed);
- intellectual property rights;
- privacy;
- the interests of a third party;
- the environment, such as the breeding sites of rare species.

The Convention demands that all exceptions be read restrictively and provides that the state may provide broader information rights. In addition, where non-exempt information can be separated from that not subject to disclosure, the non-restricted information must be provided. Despite these interpretive provisions, some environmental groups expressed concern that the exceptions could result in state officials withholding extensive or crucial information.

Any refusal to provide information must be in writing and with reasons given for the refusal. Reasonable fees may be charged for supplying information. The government has special disclosure obligations in case of any imminent threat to human health or the environment.

Public participation, guaranteed in Articles 6–8, is required for all decisions on whether to permit or renew permission for industrial, agricultural and construction activities listed in an Annex to the Convention, as well as other activities which may have a significant impact on the environment. The public must be informed in detail about the proposed activity early in the decision-making process and given time to prepare and participate in the decision-making. During the process, the public must have access to all relevant information on the proposal including the site, description of environmental impacts, measures to prevent and/or reduce the effects, a non-technical summary, an outline of the main alternatives, and any reports or advice given. Public participation can be through writing, hearings or inquiry. All public comments, information, analyses or opinions shall be taken into account by the party in making its decision. All decisions shall be made public, along with the reasons and considerations on which the decision is based.

In addition to providing for public participation regarding decisions on specific projects, the Convention calls for public participation in the preparation of environmental plans, programs, policies, laws and regulations. Further, states parties are to promote environmental education and to recognize and support environmental associations and groups.

The provisions of Article 9 on access to justice mirror many human rights texts in requiring proceedings before an independent and impartial body established by law. Each state party must provide judicial review for any denial of requested information, and a remedy for any act or omission concerning the permitting of activities and "acts and omissions by private persons and public authorities which contravene provisions of its national law relating to the environment." Standing to challenge permitting procedures or results is limited to members of the public having a sufficient interest or maintaining impairment of a right; however, the Convention provides that environmental non-governmental organizations "shall be deemed" to have sufficient interest for this purpose. The public has standing to challenge violations of environmental law as do NGOs, "where they meet the criteria, if any, laid down in national law" (Art. 9(3)).

The Convention's topic induced the drafters to take steps towards creating compliance procedures and public participation on the international level. Primary review of implementation is conferred on the Meeting of the Parties (MOP), at which non-governmental organizations "qualified in the fields to which this Convention relates" may participate as observers if they have made a request and not more than one-third of the parties present at the meeting raise objections. (Art. 10). The Convention adds a provision on compliance review (Art. 15) which directs the MOP to create a "non-confrontational, non-judicial and consultative" optional arrangement for compliance review, which "shall allow for appropriate public involvement and may include the option of considering communications from members of the public on matters related to this Convention." This tentative language marks the first time an open compliance procedure has been contemplated in an international environmental agreement. The compliance procedure foreseen marks an important step in enhancing the effectiveness of international environmental agreements. At present, nearly all environmental agreements vest jurisdiction over issues of implementation and compliance in the Conference or Meeting of the Parties, a plenary and political body.

A Protocol to the Aarhus Convention[41] requires each party to establish a publicly accessible and user-friendly Pollutant Release and Transfer Register, based on a mandatory scheme of annual reporting. The Register covers information on 86 pollutants including greenhouse gases, acid rain pollutants, heavy metals and cancer-causing chemicals such as dioxins. States must report on any significant levels of a wide range of activities, including refineries, thermal power stations, chemical and mining industries, waste incinerators, wood and paper production and processing and intensive agriculture and aquaculture. The Protocol also provides a framework for reporting on pollution from diffuse sources such as traffic, agriculture and small and medium-sized enterprises. Some of the reported information may be kept confidential, for example, where disclosure could affect commercial confidentiality, national defense or public security, but such examples should be interpreted in a restrictive way, taking into account the public interest served by disclosure. The public should be able to find out about the annual pollution of a given source when it is covered by the Protocol. In what will probably become common in future agreements on public information, the Protocol provides that the Register should be accessible by Internet.

C. Environmental Protection in International Human Rights Law

The above section described the human rights provisions contained in environmental instruments. This section reviews environmental protection in human rights law and practice. In general, the human rights community now views environmental protection as an appropriate part of the human rights agenda and the legal protection of human rights through international complaints procedures as an accepted means to achieve the ends of

---

[41] Kiev, May 23, 2003, *available at* <www.unece.org>. The Protocol was developed under the auspices of the UN Economic Commission for Europe, but is open to access to non-members of the UNECE.

environmental protection. An applicant normally cannot choose between bringing an international human rights complaint or an international environmental case because almost no forum exists for the latter. Human rights tribunals thus currently provide the main international avenues to challenge government action or inaction on environmental protection.

The rights to life, health, adequate standard of living, association, expression, information, political participation, personal liberty, equality and legal redress, all contained in international legal instruments, can and have been invoked to further environmental goals. The right of minorities to maintain their traditional cultures is also pursued. International courts and other treaty bodies[42] have expanded or reinterpreted these guarantees in light of environmental concerns, despite the lack of explicit reference to environmental rights in most human rights instruments. The UN Commission on Human Rights, the UN Human Rights Committee, the Inter-American Commission on Human Rights, the European Commission and Court of Human Rights, and the African Commission on Human Rights, have developed a jurisprudence that recognizes and enforces rights linked to environmental protection. Members of the Committee on the Elimination of Racial Discrimination and the Committee on the Rights of the Child have questioned states parties on environmental matters related to the guarantees of the treaties they monitor. The UN Committee on the Rights of the Child has called for better compliance with Article 24(2)(c), which concerns safe drinking water, sanitation, and nutrition, in its concluding observations on the reports of states parties.

1. Right to Life and Right to Health

The 18 independent experts on the UN Human Rights Committee supervise state implementation of and compliance with the International Covenant on Civil and Political Rights, primarily through a system of state reporting. Each state party submits periodic reports on the measures taken to give effect to the rights in the Covenant, then sends a representative to answer questions of the Committee members.[43] The Committee may make

---

[42]   International human rights courts exist in the European and Inter-American regional systems and such a court is foreseen for the African regional system. The main global treaty bodies are the Human Rights Committee, Committee on Economic, Social and Cultural Rights, Committee on the Elimination of All Forms of Racial Discrimination, Committee on the Elimination of Discrimination against Women, Committee on the Rights of the Child, and Committee against Torture.

[43]   A study published in 1990 surveyed 36 states whose periodic reports had been considered by the Committee. Of these 32 reported changes in their laws or practices in response to the review procedure. *See* C. Cohn, *Human Rights Quarterly* (1990).

comments and recommendations to the state individually or issue General Comments to all states parties. In the latter context, the Committee has indicated that state obligations to protect the right to life can require positive measures designed to reduce infant mortality and protect against malnutrition and epidemics, which clearly implicate environmental protection.[44]

The Human Rights Committee may hear individual complaints against a state party to the International Covenant on Civil and Political Rights if the state has also accepted the first Optional Protocol to the Covenant that creates the procedure. The Committee has received several complaints concerning environmental damage as a violation of one or more civil and political rights. First, a group of Canadian citizens alleged that the storage of radioactive waste near their homes threatened the right to life of present and future generations. The Committee found that the case raised "serious issues with regard to the obligation of states parties to protect human life," but declared the case inadmissible due to failure to exhaust local remedies.[45]

The Committee on Economic, Social and Cultural Rights supervises implementation of the Covenant guaranteeing these rights, also by means of periodic reporting. In this context, states often report on environmental issues as they affect guaranteed rights. The Ukraine reported in 1995 on the environmental situation consequent to the explosion at Chernobyl, in regard to the right to life. Committee members sometimes request specific information about environmental harm that threatens human rights. Poland, for example, was asked to provide information in 1989 about measures to combat pollution, especially in upper Silesia.[46] The Committee may pose questions and make recommendations in response to state reports.

On November 8, 2000, the Committee on Economic, Social and Cultural Rights issued General Comment No. 14 on "Substantive Issues Arising in the Implementation of the International Covenant on Economic, Social and Cultural Rights" (Art. 12).[47] The Comment states in paragraph 4 that "the right to health embraces a wide range of socio-economic factors that promote conditions in which people can lead a healthy life, and extends to the underlying determinates of health, such as . . . a healthy environment." General Comment 14 adds that "[a]ny person or group victim of a violation of the right to health should have access to effective judicial or other appro-

---

[44] *See* the General Comment on Art. 6 of the Civil and Political Covenant, issued by the United Nations Human Rights Committee, in *Compilation of General Comments and General Recommendations adopted by Human Rights Treaty Bodies*, U.N. Doc. HRI/GEN/1/Rev.3 (1997), at 6–7 [hereinafter *Compilation*].

[45] Communication No. 67/1980, *EHP v. Canada*, 2 Selected Decisions of the Human Rights Committee (1990), 20.

[46] E/1989/4/Add.12.

[47] U.N. CESCR, General Comment 14, U.N. Doc. E/C.12/2000/4 (2000).

priate remedies at both national and international levels and should be entitled to adequate reparation."[48]

Among UN Charter-based organs, the UN Commission on Human Rights decided in 1995 to appoint a special rapporteur to study the adverse effects of the illicit movement and dumping of toxic and dangerous products and wastes on the enjoyment of human rights.[49] In addition to investigating the human rights effects of illegal dumping of toxic and dangerous products and wastes in developing countries, the special rapporteur was given authority to receive and examine communications and undertake fact-finding concerning illicit traffic and dumping, in effect creating an individual complaints procedure. The rapporteur may make recommendations to states on measures to be taken and must produce an annual list of the countries and transnational corporations engaged in illicit dumping, as well as a census of persons killed, maimed or otherwise injured in the developing countries due to the practice.

The 1998 report[50] of the special rapporteur contained information on specific cases and incidents. Most of them involved chemical companies in Europe exporting contaminated wastes to Asia and the Middle East. In many cases, the government replies indicated prosecutions were initiated and the waste returned to the place of origin. The special rapporteur found that the communications showed the right to life and security of person, health, an adequate standard of living, adequate food and housing, work and non-discrimination, were implicated by the acts denounced. In certain cases the reported incidents had led to sickness, disorders, physical or mental disability and death. In other instances, the rights of association and access to information were ignored or curtailed, hampering the ability of individuals or groups to prevent dumping or obtain a remedy. Most communications mentioned violation of the right to information which led to often irreversible consequences to the environment and rights of individuals. Information had been withheld not only prior to but after incidents. According to the special rapporteur, the most vulnerable groups are the main targets of illegal dumping, with discrimination often occurring.

---

[48] *Id.*, para. 59.

[49] Res. 1995/81. The vote was 32 to 15, with six abstentions. The division was geographic, with all developing countries of the South voting in favor of the proposal and all Northern states expressing opposition. France, on behalf of the European Union, argued that the question could be dealt with much more effectively through instruments such as the Basel Convention on the Control of Transboundary Movements of Hazardous Wastes and their Disposal. Consequently, the study "would lead to needless duplication of international mechanisms and to dissipation or wastage of resources."

[50] Adverse effects of the illicit movement and dumping of toxic and dangerous products and wastes on the enjoyment of human rights, E/CN.4/1998/10/Add 1 (1998). For a summary of the annual reports, *see Human Rights and the Environment*, Y.B. INT'L ENVTL. L. 1994–2003.

Unlike many international human rights procedures, the mechanism appears to have generated complaints or communications from states as well as NGOs and individuals. In the 1998 report, for example, the government of Paraguay informed the special rapporteur of its investigation of a possible serious case of illicit movement and dumping of toxic wastes in its territory. The government asked the special rapporteur for assistance in the investigation. Similarly, the government of Thailand informed the special rapporteur of a 1991 fire in warehouses in the port of Bangkok that caused loss of life and property in the surrounding areas.

The UN Commission on Human Rights has appointed other special rapporteurs whose mandates extend to environmental matters. In 2002, for example, it named a special rapporteur on the right of everyone to the enjoyment of the highest attainable standard of physical and mental health. This will certainly involve consideration of environmental conditions and how they impact the right to health. The World Health Organization, whose constitution proclaims a right to health, has already begun to consider this issue.

International human rights bodies in Europe, the Americas and Africa have all examined cases alleging violations of the right to life due to environmental harm. In the Inter-American system, the Commission established a link between environmental quality and the right to life in response to a petition brought on behalf of the Yanomani Indians of Brazil. The petition alleged that the government violated the American Declaration of the Rights and Duties of Man[51] by constructing a highway through Yanomani territory and authorizing the exploitation of the territory's resources. These actions led to the influx of non-indigenous who brought contagious diseases which remained untreated due to lack of medical care. The Commission found that the government had violated the Yanomani rights to life, liberty and personal security guaranteed by Article 1 of the Declaration, as well as the right to residence and movement (Art. VIII) and the right to the preservation of health and well-being (Art. XI).[52]

Apart from receiving and examining individual complaints, the Inter-American Commission on Human Rights has the authority to study the human rights situation generally or in regard to specific issues within an OAS member state. The Commission devoted particular attention to environmental rights in reports on Ecuador[53] and Brazil.[54] In regard to Ecuador,

---

[51]   Pan American Union, Final Act of the Ninth Conference of American States, Res. XXX, at 38 (1948), *reprinted in* OAS, BASIC DOCUMENTS PERTAINING TO HUMAN RIGHTS IN THE INTER-AMERICAN SYSTEM (1996).

[52]   Case 7615 (Brazil), INTER-AM.C.H.R., 1984–1985 ANNUAL REPORT 24, OEA/Ser.L/V/II.66, Doc. 10, rev. 1 (1985).

[53]   Inter-Am.C.H.R., *Report on the Situation of Human Rights in Ecuador*, OEA/Ser.L/V/II.96, Doc. 10 rev. 1 (1997).

[54]   Inter-Am.C.H.R., *Report on the Situation of Human Rights in Brazil*, OEA/Ser.L/V/II.97, Doc. 29, rev. 1 (1997). Among the problems discussed are

the Commission noted that the human rights situation in the Oriente region had been under study for several years, in response to claims that oil exploitation activities were contaminating the water, air and soil, thereby causing the people of the region to become sick and to have a greatly increased risk of serious illness.[55] After an on-site visit, it found that both the government and inhabitants agreed that the environment was contaminated, with inhabitants exposed to toxic byproducts of oil exploitation in their drinking and bathing water, in the air, and in the soil. The inhabitants were unanimous in claiming that oil operations, especially the disposal of toxic wastes, jeopardized their lives and health. Many suffered skin diseases, rashes, chronic infections, and gastrointestinal problems. In addition, many claimed that pollution of local waters contaminated fish and drove away wildlife, threatening food supplies.

The Commission identified relevant human rights law and emphasized the right to life and physical security. It stated that

> [t]he realization of the right to life, and to physical security and integrity is necessarily related to and in some ways dependent upon one's physical environment. Accordingly, where environmental contamination and degradation pose a persistent threat to human life and health, the foregoing rights are implicated.[56]

States parties may be required therefore to take positive measures to safeguard the fundamental and non-derogable rights to life and physical integrity, in particular to prevent the risk of severe environmental pollution that could threaten human life and health, or to respond when persons have suffered injury.

The Commission also directly addressed concerns for economic development, noting that the Convention does not prevent or discourage it, but rather requires that it take place under conditions of respect for the rights of affected individuals. Thus, while the right to development implies that

---

those of environmental destruction leading to severe health and cultural consequences. In particular indigenous cultural and physical integrity are said to be under constant threat and attack from invading prospectors and the environmental pollution they create. State protection against the invasions is called "irregular and feeble" leading to constant danger and environmental deterioration.

[55] *Report on Ecuador, supra* note 53, at v. The Commission first became aware of the situation in the Oriente through a petition filed on behalf of the indigenous Huaorani people in 1990. The Commission decided that the problem was more widespread and thus should be treated within the framework of the general country report.

[56] *Report on Ecuador, id.* at 88.

each state may exploit its natural resources, "the absence of regulation, inappropriate regulation, or a lack of supervision in the application of extant norms may create serious problems with respect to the environment which translate into violations of human rights protected by the American Convention."[57] The Commission returned to the procedural dimension, concluding that

> [c]onditions of severe environmental pollution, which may cause serious physical illness, impairment and suffering on the part of the local populace, are inconsistent with the right to be respected as a human being. . . . The quest to guard against environmental conditions which threaten human health requires that individuals have access to: information, participation in relevant decision-making processes, and judicial recourse.[58]

The Commission called on the government to implement legislation enacted to strengthen protection against pollution, clean up activities by private licensee companies, and take further action to remedy existing contamination and prevent future recurrences. In particular it recommended that the state take measures to improve systems to disseminate information about environmental issues, enhance the transparency of and opportunities for public input into processes affecting the inhabitants of development sectors.

The cases submitted in the African system initially invoked the right to health, protected by Article 16 of the African Charter, rather than the right to environment contained in the same document. In *Communications 25/89, 47/90, 56/91 and 100/93 against Zaire* the Commission held that failure by the Government to provide basic services such as safe drinking water constitutes a violation of Article 16. More recently, applicants successfully alleged a violation of the right to environment by Nigeria, as described below.

---

57   *Id.* at 89.

58   *Id.* at 92, 93. The Commission also stated that the right to seek, receive and impart information and ideas of all kinds is protected by Art. 13 of the American Convention. According to the Commission, information that domestic law requires be submitted as part of environmental impact assessment procedures must be "readily accessible" to potentially affected individuals. Public participation is viewed as linked to Art. 23 of the American Convention, which provides that every citizen shall enjoy the right "to take part in the conduct of public affairs, directly or through freely chosen representatives." Finally, the right of access to judicial remedies is called "the fundamental guarantor of rights at the national level." The Commission quotes Art. 25 of the American Convention that provides everyone "the right to simple and prompt recourse, or any other effective recourse, to a competent court or tribunal for protection against acts that violate his fundamental rights recognized by the constitution or laws of the state concerned or by th[e] Convention."

2. Right to an Adequate Standard of Living and the Fulfillment of Basic Needs

UN human rights treaty bodies and the UN Charter-based Human Rights Commission and Sub-Commission have taken up the relationship between environmental protection and the enjoyment of human rights in the context of economic, social and cultural rights. The Human Rights Commission has appointed a special rapporteur on the right to food. In considering his initial report, the Commission asked that the study continue with specific attention given to the issue of safe drinking water.[59] The Commission specifically linked implementation of the right to food with sound environmental policies and noted that problems related to food shortages "can generate additional pressures upon the environment in ecologically fragile areas."

The Committee on Economic, Social and Cultural Rights has pursued such questions in monitoring state reports. In 1986, Tunisia reported to the Commission on Economic, Social and Cultural Rights, in the context of Article 11 on the right to an adequate standard of living, on measures taken to prevent degradation of natural resources, particularly erosion, and about measures to prevent contamination of food.[60] The Committee has referred to environmental issues in its General Comment on the Right to Adequate Food[61] and its General Comment on the Right to Adequate Housing. In the first, the Committee interpreted the phrase "free from adverse substances" in Article 11 of the Covenant to mean that the state must adopt food safety and other protective measures to prevent contamination through "bad environmental hygiene." The Comment on housing states that "housing should not be built on polluted sites nor in proximity to pollution sources that threaten the right to health of the inhabitants."[62]

The right to water has been recognized in a wide range of international documents, including treaties, declarations and other international normative instruments. Article 14(2) of the Convention on the Elimination of All Forms of Discrimination Against Women (1979) stipulates that states parties shall ensure to women the right to "enjoy adequate living conditions, particularly in relation to . . . water supply." Article 24(2) of the Convention on the Rights of the Child (1989) requires states parties to combat disease and malnutrition "through the provision of adequate nutritious foods and clean drinking-water."

---

[59]   Res. 2001/25, The Right to Food, E/CN.4/RES/2001/25, Apr. 20, 2001.

[60]   E/1986/3/Add.9.

[61]   General Comment 12, E/C.12/1999/5.

[62]   General Comment 4, Dec. 13, 1991, United Nations, *Compilation, supra* note 44, HRI/GEN/1/Rev.3, 63, para. 5.

In late 2002, the Committee on Economic, Social and Cultural Rights adopted General Comment No. 15 (2002) on the right to water.[63] The Committee, noting that water is a limited natural resource and a public good fundamental for life and health, calls it "a prerequisite for the realization of other human rights." It points out that the continuing contamination, depletion and unequal distribution of water is exacerbating existing poverty and makes clear that "[s]tates parties have to adopt effective measures to realize, without discrimination, the right to water, as set out in this General Comment." According to the Committee, the human right to water entitles everyone to sufficient, safe, acceptable, physically accessible and affordable water for personal and domestic uses. An adequate amount of safe water is necessary to prevent death from dehydration, reduce the risk of water-related disease and provide for consumption, cooking, personal and domestic hygiene requirements. The Committee finds that while Covenant Article 11(1) does not specifically mention water, it specifies a number of rights emanating from, and indispensable for, the realization of the right to an adequate standard of living "including adequate food, clothing and housing." The use of the word "including" indicates that this catalogue of rights is not exhaustive. The right to water clearly falls within the category of guarantees essential for securing an adequate standard of living, particularly since it is one of the most fundamental conditions for survival. The right to water is also inextricably related to the right to the highest attainable standard of health (Art. 12(1) and the rights to adequate housing and adequate food (Art. 11(1)). The right should also be seen in conjunction with other rights enshrined in the International Bill of Human Rights, foremost amongst them the right to life and human dignity.

The Committee specifies that priority in the allocation of water must be given to the right to water for personal and domestic uses. These uses ordinarily include drinking, personal sanitation, washing of clothes, food preparation, personal and household hygiene. The quantity of water available for each person should correspond to World Health Organization (WHO) guidelines. The water required for each personal or domestic use must also be safe, therefore free from micro-organisms, chemical substances and radiological hazards that constitute a threat to a person's health. Furthermore, water should be of an acceptable colour, odor and taste for each personal or domestic use. Priority should be given to the water resources required to prevent starvation and disease, as well as water required to meet the core obligations of each of the Covenant rights.

---

[63]   ICESCR, Arts. 11 and 12, E/C.12/2002/11, Nov. 26, 2002. The Committee had previously recognized that Art. 11 contains a right to water in its General Comment No. 6.

The Committee notes the importance of ensuring sustainable access to water resources for agriculture to realize the right to adequate food. Attention should be given to ensuring that disadvantaged and marginalized farmers, including women farmers, have equitable access to water and water management systems, including sustainable rain harvesting and irrigation technology. States parties should ensure that there is adequate access to water for subsistence farming and for securing the livelihoods of indigenous peoples. The adequacy of water should not be interpreted narrowly, by mere reference to volumetric quantities and technologies, but instead water should be treated as a social and cultural good. The manner of realizing the right to water must also be sustainable, ensuring that the right can be realized for present and future generations.

According to the Committee, the right to water contains both freedoms and entitlements. The freedoms include the right to maintain access to existing water supplies necessary for the right to water, and the right to be free from interference such as the arbitrary disconnections or contamination of water supplies. In contrast, entitlements include the right to a system of water supply and management that provides equality of opportunity for people to enjoy the right to water. States parties have a special obligation to provide those who do not have sufficient means with the necessary water and water facilities and to prevent any discrimination on internationally prohibited grounds in the provision of water and water services.

The Committee distinguishes between immediate obligations and those which states must progressively realize. According to the Committee, states parties have immediate obligations in relation to the right to water, such as to guarantee that the right will be exercised without discrimination of any kind (Art. 2(2)) and the obligation to take steps (Art. 2(1)) towards the full realization of Articles 11(1) and 12. Such steps must be deliberate, concrete and targeted towards the full realization of the right to water. There is a strong presumption that retrogressive measures are prohibited under the Covenant.

The Committee specifies that there are three types of legal obligations imposed on states parties: obligations to *respect*, to *protect* and to *fulfill*. The obligation to *respect* requires that states parties refrain from interfering directly or indirectly with the enjoyment of the right to water. The obligation includes, *inter alia*, refraining from engaging in any practice or activity that denies or limits equal access to adequate water; arbitrarily interfering with customary or traditional arrangements for water allocation; unlawfully diminishing or polluting water, for example through waste from state-owned facilities or through use and testing of weapons; and limiting access to, or destroying, water services and infrastructure as a punitive measure, for example, during armed conflicts in violation of international humanitarian law.

The obligation to *protect* requires states parties to prevent third parties from interfering in any way with the enjoyment of the right to water. Third parties include individuals, groups, corporations and other entities as well as agents acting under their authority. The obligation includes, *inter alia*, adopting the necessary and effective legislative and other measures to restrain third parties from denying equal access to adequate water, or from polluting and inequitably extracting water.

The obligation to *fulfill* is disaggregated into the obligations to *facilitate, promote* and *provide*. The obligation to *facilitate* requires the state to take positive measures to assist individuals and communities to enjoy the right. To *promote*, the state party must take steps to ensure that there is appropriate education concerning the hygienic use of water, protection of water sources and methods to minimize water wastage. States parties are also obliged to *fulfill (provide)* the right when individuals or a group are unable, for reasons beyond their control, to realize that right themselves by the means at their disposal. The obligation to *fulfill* includes, *inter alia*, according sufficient recognition to the right to water within the national political and legal systems, preferably by way of legislative implementation; adopting a national water strategy and plan of action to realize the right; ensuring that water is affordable for everyone; and facilitating improved and sustainable access to water, particularly in rural and deprived urban areas.

States parties are asked to adopt comprehensive and integrated strategies and programs to ensure that there is sufficient and safe water for present and future generations. Such strategies and programs may include: (a) reducing depletion of water resources through unsustainable extraction, diversion and damming; (b) reducing and eliminating contamination of watersheds and water-related eco-systems by substances such as radiation, harmful chemicals and human excreta; (c) monitoring water reserves; (d) ensuring that proposed developments do not interfere with access to adequate water; (e) assessing the impacts of actions that may impinge upon water availability and natural ecosystems, such as climate changes, desertification and increased soil salinity, deforestation and loss of biodiversity; (f) increasing the efficient use of water by end-users; (g) reducing water wastage in its distribution; (h) developing response mechanisms for emergency situations; and (i) establishing competent institutions and appropriate institutional arrangements to carry out the strategies and programs.

To comply with their international obligations in relation to the right to water, states parties also have to respect the enjoyment of the right in other countries. International cooperation requires states parties to refrain from actions that interfere, directly or indirectly, with the enjoyment of the right to water in other countries. Any activities undertaken within the state party's jurisdiction should not deprive another country of the ability to realize the right to water for persons in its jurisdiction. States parties should refrain at all times from imposing embargoes or similar measures, that prevent the supply of water, as well as goods and services essential for securing the right to water. Water should never be used as an instrument of political and economic pressure.

States parties should ensure that the right to water is given due attention in international agreements and, to that end, should consider the development of further legal instruments. With regard to the conclusion and implementation of other international and regional agreements, states parties should take steps to ensure that these instruments do not adversely impact upon the right to water. Agreements concerning trade liberalization should not curtail or inhibit a country's capacity to ensure the full realization of the right to water. States parties should ensure that their actions as members of international organizations take due account of the right to water. Accordingly, states parties that are members of international financial institutions, notably the International Monetary Fund, the World Bank, and regional development banks should take steps to ensure that the right to water is taken into account in their lending policies, credit agreements and other international measures.

The lengthy General Comment goes on to discuss "core obligations" and the state acts and omissions that may be deemed to violate the Covenant's guaranteed right to water. The text sets a precedent for future actions on the substantive aspects of environmental rights.

3. Right to Privacy, Home and Family Life

In Europe, those who have suffered from environmental harm have often complained that the resulting conditions violate the right to privacy and home guaranteed by the 1950 European Convention on Human Rights and Fundamental Freedoms. Article 8(1) provides that "everyone has the right to respect for his privacy, his home and his correspondence." The second paragraph of Article 8 sets forth the permissible grounds for limiting the exercise of the right.[64]

The former European Commission on Human Rights[65] and the European Court have held that environmental harm attributable to state action or inaction which has significant injurious effect on a person's home or private and family life constitutes a breach of Article 8(1). The harm may be excused, however, under Article 8(2) if it results from an authorized activ-

---

[64] Paragraph 2 provides: "There shall be no interference by a public authority with the exercise of this right except such as is in accordance with the law and is necessary in a democratic society in the interests of national security, public safety or the economic well-being of the country, for the prevention of disorder or crime, for the protection of health and morals, or for the protection of the rights and freedoms of others."

[65] With the entry into force of Protocol 11 to the European Convention on Human Rights, the former Commission and the European Court were merged into a new permanent European Court which was inaugurated on November 1, 1998.

ity of economic benefit to the community in general, as long as there is no disproportionate burden on any particular individual; *i.e.*, the measures must have a legitimate aim, be lawfully enacted, and be proportional. States enjoy a margin of appreciation in determining the legitimacy of the aim pursued. Recent decisions of the court overtly balance the competing interests of the individual and the community with considerable deference to the state's decisions.

Many of the European privacy and home cases involve noise pollution. In *Arrondelle v. United Kingdom*,[66] the applicant complained of noise from Gatwick Airport and a nearby motorway. The application was declared admissible and eventually settled with the payment of 7,500 pounds. *Baggs v. United Kingdom*, a similar case, also was resolved by friendly settlement.[67] Settlement of the cases left unresolved numerous issues, some of which were addressed by the Court in *Powell & Raynor v. United Kingdom*[68] in which the Court found that aircraft noise from Heathrow Airport constituted a violation of Article 8, but was justified under Article 8(2) as "necessary in a democratic society" for the economic well-being of the country. Noise was acceptable under the principle of proportionality, if it did not "create an unreasonable burden for the person concerned," a test that could be met by the state if the individual had "the possibility of moving elsewhere without substantial difficulties and losses."[69]

The Court later revisited the question of noise at Heathrow because of changes in flight patterns, in *Hatton and Others v. The United Kingdom*. The initial Chamber judgment of October 2, 2001, found that the noise from increased flights at Heathrow airport between 4 a.m. and 6 a.m. violated the rights of the applicants to respect for their home and family life. This judgment was overturned by a Grand Chamber decision (12–5) on July 8, 2003. Both judgments considered that as neither Heathrow airport nor the airlines that use it are owned, controlled or operated by the government, the case raised an issue of the scope of a government's positive obligations to secure respect for rights by non-state actors. Both panels found that the applicable principles are broadly similar to those applied when analyzing a direct state interference with a right. The two opinions differ primarily on the degree of deference to be given the government on the question of

---

66 Application 7889/77, *Arrondelle v. United Kingdom*, 19 D. & R. 186 (1980) and 26 D. & R. 5 (1982).

67 Application 9310/81, *Baggs v. United Kingdom*, 44 D. & R. 13 (1985); 52 D. & R. 29 (1987).

68 *Powell and Rayner v. United Kingdom*, 172 Eur.Ct.H.R. (ser.A) (1990).

69 In a subsequent case, the Commission found that the level and frequency of the noise did not reach the point where a violation of Art. 8 could be made out and the application was therefore inadmissible Application 1281/87, *Vearncombe et al. v. United Kingdom and Federal Republic of Germany*, 59 D. & R. 186 (1989).

striking the appropriate balance between the competing interests of the individual and of the community as a whole. The Chamber held that the state cannot simply refer to the economic well-being of the country[70] "in the particularly sensitive field of environmental protection." Instead, the state is required to minimize the interference with rights by trying to find alternative solutions and by generally seeking to achieve their aims in the way least burdensome to human rights. The Grand Chamber held this to be a new and inappropriate test that failed to respect the subsidiary role of the Court and the wide margin of appreciation (discretion) afforded the state.

The Grand Chamber's lengthy decision provides guidance and a somewhat higher threshold for applicants to cross in future pollution cases. The Court clearly continues to accept that "where an individual is directly and seriously affected by noise or other pollution, an issue may arise under Article 8."[71] Moreover, the Court will assess the government's actions on the substantive merits, to ensure that it is compatible with Article 8, and procedurally, "it may scrutinize the decision-making process to ensure that due weight has been accorded to the interests of the individual."[72] It apparently will give some weight to the compatibility of the state's actions or inactions with domestic law.[73]

According to the Court, the government was acting to balance economic interests of the country with the rights of the affected persons. The Court agreed that states should take into consideration environmental protection in acting within their margin of appreciation. The Court will review the state's exercise of its discretion, "but it would not be appropriate for the Court to adopt a special approach in this respect by reference to a special status of environmental human rights."[74] Applying its "fair balance" test with deference to the government, the Court assessed the economic contribution of the flights and the harm to the individuals. It noted as an additional "significant" factor that the 2–3 percent of the population specially affected can "if they choose, move elsewhere without financial loss."[75] It is not clear from the judgment that such an assumption was warranted in this case, or would be warranted in any pollution case, because the pollution is likely to have significant impact on property values.

---

[70]   Notably, British Airways filed comments in the case about the economic impact on it of banning night flights.

[71]   Judgment of July 8, 2003, para. 96.

[72]   *Id.*, para. 99.

[73]   The Grand Chamber noted that the Hatton case is unlike either *Lopez Ostra* or *Maria Guerra*, discussed *infra*, because in the latter two cases the government's actions were irregular or incompatible with domestic law or procedures. *Id.*, para. 120.

[74]   *Id.*, para. 122.

[75]   *Id.*, para. 127. As several applicants in the case had moved away from Heathrow by the time the Court heard the case, the record may have included information on the economic impact of the moves.

On the procedural side, the Court agreed that the government must undertake appropriate investigations and studies in order to allow them to strike a fair balance between the various conflicting interests,[76] but this does not require "comprehensive and measurable data . . . in relation to each and every aspect of the matter to be decided."[77] Looking at the studies done, the Court found that the government did not exceed its margin of appreciation in striking the balance and following the procedures it did to allow more night flights at Heathrow. Thus there was no violation of Article 8. The Grand Chamber (with one dissenting vote) upheld the Chamber's judgment finding a violation of Article 13 (right to a remedy) and awarded some costs and fees to the applicants.

It is worth noting the dissenting opinion of five judges who reflected on "the close connection between human rights protection and the urgent need for a decontamination of the environment" and who thus saw "health as the most basic human need and as pre-eminent." Citing both the Stockholm Declaration, Principle 1, and the European Union's Charter of Fundamental Rights, they concluded that states have indicated their choice for a high level of environmental protection. Further, the transboundary aspects of the environment, shown by the Kyoto Protocol, make this as "an issue par excellence for international law" and less grounded in national sovereignty. They saw environmental protection as sharing "common ground" with the general concern for human rights and in the context of the European Convention as part of the rising level of protection afforded in progressively interpreting its provisions. The dissent viewed the majority opinion as inconsistent with prior judgments and as a step backwards, giving precedence to economic considerations over basic health conditions. Notably, the dissent recalled that the Court earlier held sleep deprivation to be an element of inhuman and degrading treatment in the case of *Ireland v. United Kingdom*.[78] The dissent also gave greater weight to the World Health Organization Guidelines on noise levels, which were discounted by the majority. Like the original Chamber, the dissent would have applied a narrower version of the margin of appreciation to test the government's actions, found a violation, and compensated the applicants.

Lopez-Ostra v. Spain[79] is the major decision of the Court on pollution as a breach of the right to private life and the home. The applicant and her daughter suffered serious health problems from the fumes of a tannery

---

[76]   The dissent points out that the report on the economic well-being of the country were prepared for the government by the aviation industry and no attempt was made to assess the impact of the aircraft noise on the applicants' sleep.

[77]   *Id.*, para. 128.

[78]   25 Eur. Ct. H.R. (ser. A), judgment of Jan. 18, 1978, para. 96. The dissent also notes the findings of the Committee against Torture concerning excessive noise.

[79]   *Lopez-Ostra v. Spain*, 303C Eur. Ct. H.R. (ser. A) (1994).

waste treatment plant which operated alongside the apartment building where they lived. The plant opened in July 1988 without a required license and without having followed the procedure for obtaining such a license. The plant malfunctioned when it began operations, releasing gas fumes and contamination, which immediately caused health problems and nuisance to people living in the district. The town council evacuated the local residents and rehoused them free of charge in the town center during the summer. Despite this, the authorities allowed the plant to resume partial operation. In October the applicant and her family returned to their flat where there were continuing problems. The applicant finally sold her house and moved in 1992.

The decision is significant for several reasons. First, the Court did not require the applicant to exhaust administrative remedies to challenge operation of the plant under the environmental protection laws, but only to complete remedies applicable to enforcement of basic rights. Mrs. Lopez exhausted the latter remedies after the Supreme Court of Spain denied her appeal on a suit for infringement of her fundamental rights and the Constitutional Court dismissed her complaint as manifestly ill-founded. Two sisters-in-law of Mrs López Ostra, who lived in the same building, followed the procedures concerning environmental law. They brought administrative proceedings alleging that the plant was operating unlawfully. On September 18, 1991 the local court, noting a continuing nuisance and that the plant did not have the licenses required by law, ordered that it should be closed until they were obtained. However, enforcement of this order was stayed following an appeal. The case was still pending in the Supreme Court in 1995 when the European Court issued its judgment. The two sisters-in-law also lodged a complaint, as a result of which a local judge instituted criminal proceedings against the plant for an environmental health offence. The two complainants joined the proceedings as civil parties.

The European Human Rights Court noted that severe environmental pollution may affect individuals' well-being and prevent them from enjoying their homes in such a way as to affect their private and family life adversely, without, however, seriously endangering their health. As in the noise cases, it found that the determination of whether this violation had occurred should be tested by striking a fair balance between the interest of the town's economic well-being and the applicant's effective enjoyment of her right to respect for her home and her private and family life. In doing this, the Court applied its "margin of appreciation" doctrine, allowing the state a "certain" discretion in determining the appropriate balance, but finding in this case that the margin of appreciation had been exceeded. It awarded Mrs. Lopez damages, court costs, and attorneys fees.

In *Maria Guerra v. Italy*[80] the Court reaffirmed that Article 8 can impose

---

[80]   *Guerra and Others v. Italy*, Judgment of February 19, 1998, 1998-I Eur. Ct. H.R.

positive obligations on states to ensure respect for private or family life. Citing the *Lopez Ostra* case, the Court reiterated that "severe environmental pollution may affect individuals' well-being and prevent them from enjoying their homes in such a way as to affect their private and family life."[81] The Court found a violation of Article 8, noting that the individuals waited throughout the operation of fertilizer production at the company for essential information "that would have enabled them to assess the risks they and their families might run if they continued to live at Manfredonia, a town particularly exposed to danger in the event of an accident at the factory." The Court's decision is strained and seemingly due to reluctance to extend Article 10 on freedom of information to impose positive obligations on the state. The actual basis of the complaint, as discussed below, was the government's failure to provide environmental information, not pollution. The Court also declined to consider whether the right to life guaranteed by Article 2 had been violated, considering it unnecessary in light of its decision on Article 8. The decision seems unwarranted, given that deaths from cancer had occurred in the factory and this would have a clear bearing on damages.

In *Chapman v. The United Kingdom*, a judgment delivered January 18, 2001, the European Court of Human Rights considered a conflict between Article 8 and planning restrictions imposed to preserve natural areas. A Grand Chamber of the Court decided 10–7 that prohibiting a gypsy family from occupying its own land in its caravans did not violate Article 8 of the European Convention on Human Rights. The applicant bought land in 1985 after suffering harassment when staying at temporary or unofficial sites in England. Her request for planning permission to live on the site in three caravans was denied, however, because the land lies in the Metropolitan Green Belt. She was given an extended period of time to move because there is no official gypsy site in the region. At the end of the period she still had no place to go and consequently filed another request for planning permission, this time for a bungalow. This was refused and the refusal upheld on appeal. She and her family subsequently were twice fined for failing to move. They finally returned to nomadic life, having no permanent place to live.

The parties and the Court agreed that there had been an interference with applicant's family and home life and that this was in accordance with the law and pursued a legitimate aim (environmental protection). The disagreement centered on whether or not the interference was "necessary in a democratic society" as required by the Convention. The applicant submitted that there must exist "particularly compelling reasons" to justify evicting her from her land and thus interfering with her home and her traditional lifestyle. She also claimed that legal developments in the Council of Europe demonstrated concern for the particular plight of the gypsies that should weigh in the Court's balancing of her rights and the community's interest.

---

[81]   *Id.*, para. 60.

The Court gave considerable deference to the government, finding that "the judgment in any particular case by the national authorities that there are legitimate planning objections to a particular use of a site is one which the Court is not well equipped to challenge. It cannot visit each site to assess the impact of a particular proposal on a particular area in terms of impact on beauty, traffic conditions, sewage and water facilities, educational facilities, medical facilities, employment opportunities and so on." Consequently, the Court will look for "a manifest error of appreciation by the national authorities" and will be especially cognizant of the procedural safeguards available to the individual applicant. The Court was unwilling to afford any particular weight to the fact that the applicant is a gypsy, finding only "an emerging consensus" that is insufficiently concrete about the special needs of minorities. Finally, the majority of the Court spoke to the appropriate balance between individual rights and the protection of the environment, using the term "environmental rights" for the first time in its jurisprudence:

> Where a dwelling has been established without the planning permission which is needed under the national law, there is a conflict of interest between the right of the individual under Art. 8 of the Convention to respect for his or her home and the right of others in the community to environmental protection (. . .). When considering whether a requirement that the individual leave his or her home is proportionate to the legitimate aim pursued, it is highly relevant whether or not the home was established unlawfully. If the home was lawfully established, this factor would self-evidently be something which would weigh against the legitimacy of requiring the individual to move. Conversely, if the establishment of a home in a particular place was unlawful, the position of the individual objecting to an order to move is less strong. The Court will be slow to grant protection to those who, in conscious defiance of the prohibitions of the law, establish a home on an environmentally protected site. For the court to do otherwise would be to encourage illegal action to the detriment of the protection of the environmental rights of other people in the community.

The Court showed little sympathy for the applicant's situation, saying that the individual's preference as to her place of residence cannot override the general interest, adding "if the applicant's problem arises through lack of money, then she is in the same unfortunate position as many others who are not able to afford to continue to reside on sites or in houses attractive to them." The minority expressed more sensitivity to the impact of planning and enforcement measures on gypsies and would require either that the planning authorities find that there is available alternative housing or "there must exist compelling reasons for the measures concerned." In this instance, the minority did not find a "pressing social need" to outweigh what was at stake for the applicant. The options open to the applicant were "severely limited, if existing at all."

Finally, Article 8 has been useful primarily when the environmental harm consists of pollution. Issues of resource management and nature conservation or biological diversity are more difficult to bring under this rubric. A 1974 opinion of the European Commission on Human Rights indicates an early attitude of some human rights bodies and the limits of the human rights approach. In rejecting an application alleging a violation of the right of privacy and family life because authorities refused to allow an Icelandic resident to have a dog, the Commission stated:

> The Commission cannot however accept that the protection afforded by Art. 8 of the Convention extends to relationships of the individual with his entire immediate surroundings, in so far as they do not involve human relationships and notwithstanding the desire of the individual to keep such relationships within the private sphere. No doubt the dog has had close ties with man since time immemorial. However, given the above considerations this alone is not sufficient to bring the keeping of a dog into the sphere of the private life of the owner.[82]

4. *Freedom of Association*

Several recent cases in the European human rights system mark the first efforts to address issues of nature protection through human rights. All of the cases were brought against France and concerned a French law requiring certain owners of small areas of land to belong to the local hunting association and to permit hunting on their property. The applicants oppose hunting and complained that the French legal obligations violated their right to peaceful enjoyment of their possessions, their right to freedom of association, and the right to freedom of conscience. They also maintained that the obligations are discriminatory.

The Court joined and decided, *Marie-Jeanne Chassagnou, René Petit and Simone Lasgrezas v. France, Leon Dumont and others v. France,* and *Josephine Montion v. France* on April 29, 1999.[83] It found a violation of all the rights except freedom of conscience, which it decided it need not address because

---

[82] Eur. Comm'n H.R., Case 68/25/74, 5 D. & R. 86.
[83] Eur. Ct. H.R., 1999-III Reports of Judgments and Decisions

of the other findings. The report was submitted to the Committee of Ministers.

5. Right to Property

Article 1 of Protocol 1, ensures that "every natural or legal person is entitled to the peaceful enjoyment of his possessions." The former European Commission accepted that pollution or other environmental harm may result in a breach of Article 1 of Protocol 1, but only where such harm results in a substantial reduction in the value of the property and that reduction is not compensated by the state,[84] in effect the matter is treated as an issue of expropriation.

The *Case of Pialopoulos and Others v. Greece*, judgment of February 15, 2001, concerned planning restrictions that prevented applicants from building a shopping center on their land. The case was filed after ten years of delays and, according to the applicants, amount to expropriation without compensation. The Court accepted that the impugned measures aimed at environmental protection, but held that the applicants were entitled to compensation and that their property rights had been violated.

6. Freedom of Information and Expression

Human rights texts generally contain a right to freedom of information or a corresponding state duty to inform. The right to information is included in the Universal Declaration of Human Rights (Art. 19), the International Covenant on Civil and Political Rights (Art. 19(2)), the Inter-American Declaration of the Rights and Duties of Man (Art. 10), the American Convention on Human Rights (Art. 13), and the African Charter on the Rights and Duties of Peoples (Art. 9). European states are bound by Article 10 of the European Convention on Human Rights, which guarantees "the freedom to receive information." In the case of *Leander v. Sweden*, the applicant alleged violation of Art. 10 after he was refused access to a file that was used to deny him employment. The Court unanimously stated:

> the right to receive information basically prohibits a Government
> from restricting a person from receiving information that others
> wish or may be willing to impart to him. Article 10 does not, in cir-
> cumstances such as those of the present case, confer on the indi-
> vidual a right to access to a register containing information on his

---

[84]   *See* R. Desgagne, *Integrating Environmental Values into the European Convention on Human Rights*, 89 AJIL 263 (1995).

personal position, nor does it embody an obligation on the Government to impart such information to the individual.[85]

The Court has applied its restrictive approach to Article 10 in environmental cases.[86] In *Anna Maria Guerra and 39 Others against Italy*[87] the applicants complained about the chemical factory "ENICHEM Agricoltura," situated near the town of Manfredonia; pollution and the risk of major accidents at the plant; and the absence of regulation by the public authorities. Invoking Article 10 of the European Convention on Human Rights, the applicants asserted the government's failure to inform the public of the risks and the measures to be taken in case of a major accident, prescribed by the domestic law transposing the EC "Seveso" directive.[88]

The European Commission on Human Rights admitted the complaint insofar as it alleged a violation of the right to information. It did not accept the claim of pollution damage. Most of the facts were uncontested. The Commission found that the government had classified the factory as a "high risk" facility in applying the criteria established by the directive and Italian law and that there had been accidents at the factory, including an explosion that sent more than 150 persons to the hospital. According to the factory's own study, the treatment of emissions was inadequate and the environmental impact study incomplete. The government had instigated several inquiries and the residents of the town had filed civil actions. The government failed, however, to take any measure between the adoption of the "Seveso" law and the cessation of chemical production by the factory in 1994 to inform the population of the situation or to make operational a contingency plan.

By a large majority, the Commission concluded that Article 10 imposes on states an obligation not only to disclose to the public available information on the environment, but also the positive duty to collect, collate, and disseminate information which would otherwise not be directly accessible

---

85   *Leander v. Sweden*, 116 Eur.Ct. H.R. (ser.A) (1987), para. 74. *See also Gaskin v. United Kingdom*, 160 Eur. Ct. H.R. (ser.A) (1987) (government did not breach Convention in failing to allow access to a personal file of former foster child).

86   *See* Stefan Weber, *Environmental Information and the European Convention on Human Rights*, 12 HUM. RTS. L.J. 177 (1991). Contrast the views of the former Commission which found that the right to receive information envisages not only access to general sources of information, which may not be restricted by state authorities, but also the right to receive information not generally accessible that is of particular importance to the individual. *X v. Federal Republic of Germany*, App. No. 8383/78, 17 D. & R. 227, 228–29 (1980).

87   Case 14967/89.

88   Directive on the Major Accident Hazards of Certain Industrial Activities, 82/501/EEC, 1982 O.J. 230. Amended by 87/216/EEC, Mar. 19, 1987. *See infra* Chapter 13C.

to the public or brought to the public's attention. In arriving at its conclusion, the Commission relied upon "the present state of European law"
which it said confirmed that public information represents one of the essential instruments for protecting the well-being and health of the populace in
situations of environmental danger. The Commission referred specifically
to a resolution of the Parliamentary Assembly of the Council of Europe,
relating to the Chernobyl nuclear accident, which the Commission said recognized, at least in Europe, a fundamental right to information concerning activities that are dangerous for the environment or human well-being.

A Grand Chamber of the European Court of Human Rights, in a judgment of February 19, 1998, reversed the Commission on its expanded reading of Article 10, but unanimously found a violation of Article 8, the right
to family, home and private life.[89] The Court reaffirmed its earlier case law
holding that Article 10 generally only prohibits a government from interfering with the ability of a person to receive information that others wish or
may be willing to impart. According to the Court, "[t]hat freedom cannot
be construed as imposing on a State, in circumstances such as those of the
present case, positive obligations to collect and disseminate information of
its own motion."[90] Although Article 10 was found to be not applicable to
the case, eight of the 20 judges indicated through separate opinions a willingness to consider positive obligations to collect and disseminate information in some circumstances.

The Court has also considered the applicability of Article 10 to prosecutions for defamation in the dissemination of environmental information.
In a 1999 decision, the European Court held that the state may not extend
defamation laws to restrict dissemination of environmental information of
public interest. In the case of *Bladet Tromsø and Stensaas v. Norway*,[91] a Grand
Chamber of the European Court held 13–4 that Norway had violated the
rights of a newspaper and its editor by fining them both for defamation
after they published extracts of a report by a governmental seal hunting
inspector.[92] The report claimed among other things that seals had been
flayed alive and that there were other violations of seal hunting regulations.
The names of the crew were deleted from the publication but they successfully sued for defamation. The European Court held that the judgment
was an unjustified interference with Article 10 of the Convention. The Court
found that the reporting should have been considered in the wider context
of the newspaper's coverage of the controversial seal hunting issue, a matter of public interest. Its reporting conveyed an overall picture of balanced

---

[89]   *See supra* note 80.

[90]   *Guerra and Others v. Italy*, Judgment of February 19, 1998, para. 53.

[91]   *Bladet Tromsø and Stensaas v. Norway*, Judgment of May 20, 1999.

[92]   The government decided, based on Norwegian law, to not publish the
report because the contents alleged violations of law.

reporting. The Court also was influenced by the fact that the report was an official one that the Ministry of Fisheries had not questioned or disavowed. In the view of the Court the press should normally be entitled, when contributing to public debate on matters of legitimate concern, to rely on the contents of official reports without having to undertake independent research. Otherwise its public-watchdog role could be undermined.

In the subsequent judgment *Thoma v. Luxembourg* (March 29, 2001), the Court again considered the question of a conviction of defamation for reporting on environmental matters. In this case, a radio journalist presented a weekly program dealing with nature and the environment. During one of his programs he discussed a written article suggesting bribery in reforesting woodlands. He was convicted of defamation in civil actions brought by 54 forest wardens and nine forestry engineers. He appealed and then challenged his conviction at the European Court as a violation of freedom of expression. The court noted the fact that the criticisms were of public officials, not of private individuals and that journalistic freedom allows recourse to a degree of exaggeration or even provocation. Thus, while the state can limit speech by law to protect the rights and reputation of others, this particular interference was not "necessary in a democratic society" *i.e.*, meeting a pressing social need, proportionate to the legitimate aim pursued and with relevant and sufficient reasons given. The Court noted in particular that restrictions on freedom of expression are to be strictly construed when they are directed at debate over a problem of general interest.

7. The Right of Public Participation in Governance

As with the right to information, the right to public participation is widely expressed in human rights instruments. Article 21 of the Universal Declaration of Human Rights affirms the right of everyone to take part in governance of his or her country, as does the American Declaration of the Rights and Duties of Man (Art. 20) and the African Charter (Art. 13). Article 25 of the International Covenant on Civil and Political Rights provides that citizens have the right, without unreasonable restrictions "to take part in the conduct of public affairs, directly or though freely chosen representatives. . . ." The American Convention contains identical language in Article 23.

8. The Right to a Remedy

The right to a remedy when a right is violated is itself a right expressly guaranteed by universal and regional human rights instruments. The Universal Declaration of Human Rights affirms that "[e]veryone has the right to an effective remedy by the competent national tribunals for acts violating the fundamental rights granted him by the constitution or laws."[93] The International Covenant on Civil and Political Rights also obliges states to provide remedies.[94] The Human Rights Committee, established pursuant to the Covenant, has identified the kinds of remedies required, depending on the type of violation and the victim's condition. The Committee has indicated that the state which has engaged in human rights violations, in addition to treating and financially compensating the victim, must undertake to investigate the facts, take appropriate action, and bring those found responsible for the violations to justice. The ILO Convention concerning Indigenous and Tribal Peoples in Independent Countries[95] specifically refers to "fair compensation for damages" (Art. 15(2)), "compensation in money" (Art. 16(4)) and full compensation for "any loss or injury" (Art. 16(5)). Several other treaties refer to the right to legal protection for attacks on privacy, family, home or correspondence, or attacks on honor and reputation.[96]

Declarations, resolutions and other non-treaty texts also proclaim or discuss the right to a remedy. In some instances, the issue is raised by human rights organs as part of the mechanism of issuing General Comments. The third General Comment of the Committee on Economic, Social

---

[93]   Universal Declaration of Human Rights, Art. 8.

[94]   According to Art. 2(3),

Each State Party to the . . . Covenant undertakes:

(a) To ensure that any person whose rights or freedoms as . . . recognized [in the Covenant] are violated shall have an effective remedy notwithstanding that the violation has been committed by persons acting in an official capacity.

(b) To ensure that any person claiming such a remedy shall have the right thereto determined by competent judicial, administrative or legislative authorities, or by any other competent authority provided for by the legal system of the State, and to develop the possibilities of judicial remedy;

(c) To ensure that the competent authorities shall enforce such remedies when granted.

[95]   Convention Concerning Indigenous and Tribal Peoples in Independent Countries, I.L.O. No. 169, June 27, 1989, *in force* Sept. 5, 1991.

[96]   *See* Universal Declaration on Human Rights, *supra* note 1, Art. 12; International Covenant on Civil and Political Rights, *supra* note 4, Art. 17; Convention on the Rights of the Child, Nov. 20, 1989, Art. 16; American Declaration of the Rights and Duties of Man, *supra* note 1, Art. v; American Convention on Human Rights, Nov. 22, 1969, Art. 11(3), *entered into force* July 18, 1978; European Convention for the Protection of Human Rights and Fundamental Freedoms, Nov. 4, 1950, Art. 8; African Charter on Human and Peoples Rights, Banjul, June, 27, 1981, Art. 5.

and Cultural Rights, concerning the nature of state obligations pursuant to Article 2(1) of the Covenant, states that appropriate measures to implement the Covenant might include the provision of judicial remedies with respect to rights which may be considered justiciable. It specifically points to the non-discrimination requirement of the treaty and cross-references to the right to a remedy in the Covenant on Civil and Political Rights. A number of other rights are cited as "capable of immediate application by judicial and other organs."[97]

Regional instruments also contain provisions regarding legal remedies for violations of rights. Article XVII of the American Declaration of the Rights and Duties of Man guarantees every person the right to resort to the courts to ensure respect for legal rights and protection from acts of authority that violate any fundamental constitutional rights. The American Convention entitles everyone to effective recourse for protection against acts that violate the fundamental rights recognized by the constitution "or laws of the state or by the Convention," even where the act was committed by persons acting in the course of their official duties (Art. 25).[98] The states parties are to ensure that the competent authorities enforce remedies that are granted.

Article 6 of the European Convention on Human Rights[99] guarantees a fair and public hearing before an international tribunal for the determination of rights and duties.[100] Applicability of Article 6 depends upon the existence of a dispute concerning a right recognized in the law of the state concerned, including those created by licenses, authorizations and permits that affect the use of property or commercial activities.[101] In *Oerlemans v. Netherlands*[102] Article 6 was deemed to apply to a case where a Dutch citizen could not challenge a ministerial order designating his land as a protected site.

In *Zander v. Sweden*,[103] the applicants claimed they had been denied a remedy for threatened environmental harm. The applicants owned property next to a waste treatment and storage area. Local well water showed contamination by cyanide from the dump site. The municipality prohibited use of the water and furnished temporary water supplies. Subsequently, the

---

[97] *Compilation, supr* note 44, HRI/GEN/1/Rev.3, 63, para. 5.

[98] American Convention on Human Rights (Nov. 22, 1969), Art. 25.

[99] Art. 6, para. 1 states: "In the determination of his civil rights and obligations or of any criminal charge against him, everyone is entitled to a fair and public hearing within a reasonable time by an independent and impartial tribunal established by law."

[100] *Golder v. United Kingdom*, 18 Eur. Ct. H.R. (ser.A) (1975); *Klass v. Germany*, 28 Eur. Ct. H.R. (ser.A) (1978).

[101] *Benthem v. Netherlands*, 97 Eur. Ct. H.R. (ser.A) (1985).

[102] *Oerlemans v. Netherlands*, 219 Eur. Ct. H.R. (ser.A) (1991).

[103] *Zander v. Sweden*, 279B Eur. Ct. H.R. (ser.A) (1993).

permissible level of cyanide was raised and the city supply was halted. When the company maintaining the dump site sought a renewed and expanded permit, the applicants argued that the threat to their water supply would be sufficiently high that the company should be obliged to provide free drinking water if pollution occurred. The licensing board granted the permit, but denied the applicants' request. They sought but could not obtain judicial review of the decision. The European Court held that Article 6 applied and was violated. The applicability of Article 6 was based on the Court's finding that the applicants' claim concerned the environmental conditions of the property and they "could arguably maintain that they were entitled under Swedish law to protection against the water in their well being polluted as a result of the company's activities on the dump."[104]

The right to a remedy extends to compensation for pollution. In *Zimmerman and Steiner v. Switzerland*,[105] the Court found Article 6 applicable to a complaint about the length of proceedings for compensation for injury caused by noise and air pollution from a nearby airport. Article 6 does not, however, encompass a right to judicial review of legislative enactments. In *Braunerheilm v. Sweden*,[106] the Commission denied a claim that Article 6 was violated when the applicant could not challenge in court a new law that granted fishing licenses to the general public in waters where the applicant previously had exclusive rights.

The 1981 African Charter contains a broad right to a remedy in Article 7, supplemented by "the right to adequate compensation for the spoliation of resources of a dispossessed people."[107] Article 26 also imposes a duty on states parties to the Charter to guarantee the independence of the courts and to allow the establishment and improvement of appropriate national institutions entrusted with the promotion and protection of rights and freedoms guaranteed by the Charter.

9. Cultural and Minority Rights

Indigenous groups have invoked provisions of the Covenant on Civil and Political Rights to protect their land and culture from environmental degradation.[108] The United Nations Human Rights Committee has interpreted

---

[104] *Id.*, para. 24.

[105] *Zimmerman and Steiner v. Switzerland*, 66 Eur. Ct. H.R. (ser.A) (1983).

[106] *Braunerheilm v. Sweden*, App. No. 11764/85 (Mar. 9, 1989). *See* Maguelonne Déjeant-Pons, *Le Droit de l'homme à l'environnement, droit fondamental au niveau européen dans le cadre du Conseil de l'Europe et la Convention européenne de sauvegarde des droit de l'homme et des libertes fondamentales*, 4 REV. JUR. DE L'ENVIRONNEMENT (1994).

[107] African Charter on Human and Peoples Rights, Art. 21(2).

[108] For specific recognition of indigenous rights apart from the recogni-

Article 27[109] of the Covenant on Civil and Political Rights (CCPR) in a broad manner to encompass resource and land rights:

> With regard to the exercise of the cultural rights protected under Art. 27, the Committee observes that culture manifests itself in many forms, including a particular way of life associated with the use of land resources, especially in the case of indigenous peoples. That right may include such traditional activities as fishing or hunting and the right to live in reserves protected by law. The enjoyment of those rights may require positive legal measures of protection and measures to ensure the effective participation of members of minority communities in decisions which affect them. . . . The protection of these rights is directed towards ensuring the survival and continued development of the cultural, religious and social identity of the minorities concerned, thus enriching the fabric of society as a whole[110]

The invocation of Article 27 presents the matter under the rubric of the right to cultural life rather than the right to physical life, even though the survival of members of the group, may be at stake. In a rare case decided on the merits, the Committee decided that Article 27 was not violated by the extent of stone-quarrying permitted by Finland in traditional lands of the Sami.[111] The Committee explicitly rejected the European doctrine of margin of appreciation, holding that measures whose impact amounts to a denial of the right to culture will not be compatible with the Covenant, although those which simply have a "certain limited impact on the way of life of persons belonging to a minority" will not necessary violate the treaty.

---

tion of indigenous peoples as minority groups under CCPR Art. 27, *see* section E of this Chapter.

[109] CCPR Art. 27 provides that members of minority groups "shall not be denied the right, in community with other members of their group, to enjoy their own culture, to profess and practice their own religion, or to use their own language." CCPR Art. 27.

[110] General Comment 23 paras. 7, 9 in *Compilation, supra* note 44, at 41. *See Kitok v. Sweden,* Comm. 197/1985, *II Official Records of the Human Rights Committee 1987/88,* U.N. Doc. CCPR/7/Add.1, at 442 (Swedish 1971 Reindeer Husbandry Act held not to violate rights of an individual Sami as a reasonable and objective measure necessary for the continued viability and welfare of the minority as a whole); Bernard Ominayak and the *Lubicon Band v. Canada,* Communication No. 167/1984, Decisions of the Human Rights Committee, U.N. Doc. CCPR/C/38/D/167/1984 (1990) (oil and gas exploitation threaten the way of life and culture of the Band and thus violate Art. 27).

[111] Communication No. 511/1992, *Ilmari Lansman et al. v. Finland,* Human Rights Committee, Final Decisions, 74, CCPR/C/57/1 (1996).

The Committee concluded that the amount of quarrying which had taken place did not constitute a denial of the applicants' right to culture. It noted that they were consulted and their views taken into account in the government's decision. Moreover, the Committee determined that measures were taken to minimize the impact on reindeer herding activity and on the environment. In regard to future activities, "if mining activities in the Angeli area were to be approved on a large scale and significantly expanded" then it might constitute a violation of Article 27. According to the Committee, "[t]he State party is under a duty to bear this in mind when either extending existing contracts or granting new ones."[112]

The balance between minority rights and protection of marine living resources was at stake in *Apirana Mahuika et al. v. New Zealand*.[113] The petitioners claimed violations of the rights of self-determination, right to a remedy, freedom of association, freedom of conscience, non-discrimination, and minority rights as a result of New Zealand's efforts to regulate commercial and non-commercial fishing after a dramatic growth of the fishing industry. The government and the Maori, whose rights are guaranteed by the Treaty of Waitangi, executed a Deed of Settlement in 1992 to regulate all fisheries issues between the parties. The authors of the communication represented tribes and sub-tribes that objected to the Settlement, contending that they had not been adequately informed and that the negotiators did not represent them. The government acknowledged its duty to ensure recognition of the right to culture, including the right to engage in fishing activities, but argued that the Settlement met the obligation because the system of fishing quotas reflected the need for effective measures to conserve the depleted inshore fishery, carrying out the government's "duty to all New Zealanders to conserve and manage the resource for future generations" "based on the reasonable and objective needs of overall sustainable management." The Human Rights Committee held for the government and emphasized "that the acceptability of measures that affect or interfere with the culturally significant economic activities of a minority depends on whether the members of the minority in question have had the opportunity to participate in the decision-making process in relation to these measures and whether they will continue to benefit from their traditional economy." The process of consultation undertaken by the government complied with this requirement, because the government paid special attention to the cultural and religious significance of fishing for the Maori.

---

[112]   Other cases involving Sami reindeer breeders include Communication No. 431/1990, *O.S. et al. v. Finland*, decision of Mar. 23, 1994, and Communication No. 671/1995, *Jouni E. Lansmann et al. v. Finland*, decision of Oct. 30, 1996.

[113]   *Communication No. 547/1992, Apirana Mahuika et al. v. New Zealand*, CCPR/C/70/D/547/1993, views issued Nov. 16, 2000.

D. The Right to a Safe and Healthy Environment

The concept of a right to a healthy and safe environment has generated debate and contradictory developments since the first efforts were made to use international human rights law and procedures to enhance environmental protection. Clearly, not every social problem must result in a claim becoming expressed as a human right and there remains disagreement even about some of the human rights already enunciated. The volume of the debate increases when further claims are formally proposed for addition to the list of guaranteed human rights. Nonetheless, the recognition that human survival depends upon a safe and healthy environment places the claim of a right to environment fully on the human rights agenda. Moreover, recognizing a right to environment could encompass elements of nature protection and ecological balance, substantive areas not generally protected under human rights law because of its anthropocentric focus.

An immediate, practical objective of international human rights law is to gain international recognition of specific human rights. Successfully placing personal entitlements within the category of individual human rights preserves them from the ordinary political process.[114] Individual rights thus significantly limit the political will of a democratic majority, as well as a dictatorial minority. In attempting to attain a widely accepted policy goal, even a representative democracy may not produce legislation that, *e.g.*, limits or abolishes the individual right to be free from cruel, inhuman, or degrading treatment or punishment. This absolute limitation on domestic political decisions is potentially an important consequence of elaborating a right to environment, particularly given the high short-term costs involved in many environmental protection measures and the resulting political disfavor they experience.

The issue of a right to an environment of a certain quality is complicated by both temporal and geographic elements absent from other human rights protections. While most human rights violations affect only specific and identifiable victims in the present, environmental degradation harms not only those currently living, but future generations of humanity as well. The harm can take various forms. First, an extinct species and whatever benefits it would have brought to the global ecosystem are lost forever. Second, economic, social, and cultural rights cannot be enjoyed in a world where resources are inadequate due to the waste of prior generations. Third, the very survival of future generations may be jeopardized by sufficiently serious environmental problems. A right to environment thus implies significant, constant duties toward persons not yet born.

---

[114] In most legal systems, human rights are of constitutional status and override ordinary legislative or executive acts.

The other unusual aspect of a right to environment is the potentially vast expansion of the territorial scope of state obligations. Presently, human rights instruments require each state to respect and ensure guaranteed rights "to all individuals within its territory and subject to its jurisdiction." This geographic limitation reflects the reality that a state normally will have the power to protect or the possibility to violate human rights only of those within its territory and jurisdiction. Nature recognizes no political boundaries, however. A state polluting its coastal waters or the atmosphere may cause significant harm to individuals thousands of miles away. States that permit or encourage depletion of the tropical rain forest can contribute to global warming that threatens the entire biosphere.

Ultimately, the definition of a right to environment would have to include substantive environmental standards to restrict harmful air pollution and other types of emissions. Although establishing quality standards requires extensive international regulation of environmental sectors based upon impact studies, such regulation is by no means impossible. Adoption of quality standards demands extensive research and debate involving public participation, but substantive minima are a necessary complement to the procedural rights leading to informed consent. Otherwise, a human rights approach to environmental protection would be ineffective in preventing serious environmental harm.

Establishing the content of a right through reference to independent and variable standards is often used in human rights, especially with regard to economic entitlements, and need not be a barrier to recognition of the right to a specific environmental quality. Rights to an adequate standard of living and to social security are sometimes defined in international accords such as the European Social Charter or conventions and recommendations of the International Labor Organization. States implement these often flexible obligations according to changing economic indicators, needs, and resources. The human rights treaties provide a "framework" containing the basic guarantees on which international, national and local laws and policies are elaborated.

A similar approach can be utilized to give meaning to a right to environment. Both the threats to humanity and the resulting necessary measures are subject to constant change based on advances in scientific knowledge and conditions of the environment. Thus, it is impossible for a human rights instrument to specify precisely what measures should be taken, *i.e.*, the products which should not be used or the chemical composition of air which must be maintained. These technical requirements can be negotiated and regulated through international environmental norms and standards, giving content to the right to environment by reference to independent environmental findings and regulations capable of rapid amendment. The variability of implementation demands imposed by the right to environment in response to different threats over time and place does not undermine the concept of the right, but merely takes into consideration its dynamic character.

More than 100 constitutions throughout the world guarantee a right to a clean and healthy environment, impose a duty on the state to prevent environmental harm, or mention the protection of the environment or natural resources.[115] Over half of the constitutions, including nearly all adopted since 1992, explicitly recognize the right to a clean and healthy environment.[116] Ninety-two constitutions impose a duty on the government to prevent harm to the environment. Within federal systems, including those whose federal constitution lacks mention of the environment, state or provincial constitutions contain environmental rights.[117]

The constitutional rights granted are increasingly being enforced by courts.[118] In India, for example, a series of judgments between 1996 and 2000

---

[115] Examples include: Angola ("all citizens shall have the right to live in a healthy and unpolluted environment." Art. 24–1); Argentina ("all residents enjoy the right to a healthy, balanced environment which is fit for human development . . ." Art. 41); Azerbaijan ("everyone has the right to live in a healthy environment."); Brazil ("everyone has the right to an ecologically balanced environment, which is a public good for the people's use and is essential for a healthy life." Art. 225).

[116] Angola, Argentina, Azerbaijan, Belarus, Belgium, Benin, Brazil, Bulgaria, Burkina Faso, Cameroon, Cape Verde, Chad, Chechnya, Chile, China, Colombia, Congo, Costa Rica, Croatia, Cuba, Ecuador, El Salvador, Equatorial Guinea, Eritrea (draft), Finland, Georgia, Germany, Ghana, Greece, Guatemala, Guyana, Haiti, Honduras, Hungary, India, Iran, Kazakhstan, Kuwait, Laos, Latvia, Lithuania, Macedonia, Madagascar, Malawi, Mali, Malta, Mexico, Micronesia, Mongolia, Mozambique, Namibia, Nepal, Netherlands, Nicaragua, Niger, Palau, Panama, Papua New Guinea, Paraguay, Peru, Philippines, Poland, Portugal, Romania, Russia, Sao Tome and Principe, Saudi Arabia, Seychelles, Slovakia, Slovenia, South Africa, South Korea, Spain, Sri Lanka, Suriname, Switzerland, Taiwan, Tajikistan, Tanzania, Thailand, Togo, Turkey, Turkmenistan, Uganda, Ukraine, Uzbekistan, Venezuela, Vietnam, Yugoslavia, Zambia.

[117] The Constitution of the State of Pennsylvania, for example, in art. I, sec. 27 provides: "The people have a right to clean air, pure water, and to the preservation of the natural, scenic, historic and esthetic values of the environment. Pennsylvania's public natural resources are the common property of all the people, including generations yet to come. As trustee of these resources, the Commonwealth shall conserve and maintain them for the benefit of all the people." For a commentary, *see* John C. Dernbach, *Taking the Pennsylvania Constitution Seriously When it Protects the Environment: Part II: Environmental Rights and Public Trust*, 104 DICKENSON L. REV. 97 (1999); *Part I An Interpretative Framework for Art. I, Section 227,* 103 DICKENSON L. REV. 693 (1999).

[118] For a discussion of African cases, *see* Carl Bruch et al., *Constitutional Environmental Law: Giving Force to Fundamental Principles in Africa,* 26 COLUM. J. ENVTL. L. 131 (2001).

responded to health concerns caused by industrial pollution in Delhi.[119] In some instances, the courts issued orders to cease operations.[120] The Indian Supreme Court has based the closure orders on the principle that health is of primary importance and that residents are suffering health problems due to pollution. South African courts also have deemed the right to environment to be justiciable. In Argentina, the right is deemed a subjective right entitling any person to initiate an action for environmental protection.[121] Colombia also recognizes the enforceability of the right to environment.[122] In Costa Rica, a court stated that the right to health and to the environment are necessary to ensure that the right to life is fully enjoyed.[123]

Most international human rights instruments were drafted before the emergence of environmental law as a common concern and, as a result, do not mention the environment. On the global level, the UN Convention on the Rights of the Child, Article 24, is unique in speaking of the provision of clean drinking water and the dangers and risks of pollution.[124] At present no global human rights treaty proclaims a general right to environment.

On the regional level, the African Charter on Human and Peoples Rights was the first international human rights instrument to contain an explicit guarantee of environmental quality (Art. 24). Subsequently, the Protocol on Economic, Social and Cultural Rights to the American Convention on Human Rights included the right of everyone to live in a

---

[119]   As early as 1991, the Supreme Court interpreted the right to life guaranteed by Art. 21 of the Constitution to include the right to a wholesome environment. *See Charan Lal Sahu v. Union of India*, AIR 1990 SC 1480 (1991). In a subsequent case, the Court observed that the "right to life guaranteed by Art. 21 includes the right of enjoyment of pollution-free water and air for full enjoyment of life." Subhash *Kumar v. State of Bihar*, AIR 1991 SC 420, 1991 (1) SCC 598.

[120]   *See, e.g., M.C. Mehta v. Union of India & Others,* JT 1996, *reprinted in* 1 ENVTL. ACTIVISTS' HANDBOOK, at 631.

[121]   *Kattan, Alberto and Others v. National Government,* Juzgado Nacional de la Instancia en lo Contencioso administrativo Federal. No. 2, ruling of May 10, 1983, La Ley, 1983-D, 576; *Irazu Margarita v. Copetro S.A.*, Camara Civil y Comercial de la Plata, ruling of May 10, 1993, *available at* <www.eldial.com> (the right to live in a healthy and balanced environment is a fundamental attribute of people. Any aggression to the environment ends up becoming a threat to life itself and to the psychological and physical integrity of the person . . .).

[122]   *Funde publico v. Mayor of Bugalagrande and Others,* Juzgado Primero superior, Interlocutorio # 032, Tulua, Dec. 19, 1991 ("It should be recognized that a healthy environment is a *sina qua non* condition for life itself and that no right could be exercised in a deeply altered environment.").

[123]   *Presidente de la Sociedad Marlene S.A. v. Municipalidad de Tibas*, Sala Constitucional de la Corte Supreme de Justicia. Decision No. 6918/94, Nov. 25, 1994.

[124]   United Nations Convention on the Rights of the Child, *supra* note 96, art. 24.

healthy environment (Art. 11).[125] In Europe, neither the European Convention for the Protection of Human Rights and Fundamental Freedoms[126] nor the European Social Charter[127] contains a right to environmental quality and the former European Commission on Human Rights held that such a right cannot be directly inferred from the Convention. Also within Europe, the Convention for the Protection of Human Rights and Dignity of the Human Being with Regard to the Application of Biology and Medicine[128] takes a human rights approach to biotechnology, but does not mention environmental protection. Concerned with human dignity and respect for the human being, the Convention requires prior informed consent before there is any intervention in the health field.

On a sub-regional level, according to the terms of the Memorandum of Understanding between Kenya, Tanzania and Uganda for Cooperation on Environment Management of October 22, 1998, the three states agree to cooperate in developing, enacting and harmonizing their national environmental laws on the rights of their peoples to a clean, decent and healthy environment.

Given the innovations in Africa, it is probably appropriate that the African Commission on Human and Peoples' Rights should be the first international human rights body to decide a contentious case involving violation of the right to a general satisfactory environment. The case is a landmark not only in this respect, but also in the Commission's articulation of the duties of governments in Africa to monitor and control the activities of multinational corporations. Acting on a petition filed by two non-governmental organizations on behalf of the people of Ogoniland, Nigeria, the African Commission on Human and Peoples Rights found Nigeria had breached its obligations to respect, protect, promote, and fulfill rights guaranteed by the African Charter on Human and Peoples Rights.[129] The

---

[125]   As an extension of the American Convention on Human Rights, *supra* note 96, the Organization of American States adopted the Additional Protocol to the American Convention on Human Rights in the Area of Economic, Social and Cultural Rights, Nov. 17, 1988, *entered into force* Nov. 16, 1999. The Protocol guarantees the right to a healthy environment in Art. 11 ("(1) Everyone shall have the right to live in a healthy environment and to have access to basic public services. (2) The States Parties shall promote the protection, preservation, and improvement of the environment."). Art. 11 is not, however, one of the rights in the Protocol that is subject to the petition procedure established by the American Convention. *See* Dinah Shelton, *Environmental Rights, in* PEOPLES' RIGHTS 185 (PHILIP ALSTON ed., 2001).

[126]   European Convention for the Protection of Human Rights and Fundamental Freedoms, *supra* note 96.

[127]   European Social Charter, (Oct. 18, 1961); E.T.S. No. 35; 529 U.N.T.S. 89.

[128]   Oviedo, Spain, Apr. 4, 1997; 36 I.L.M. 817 (1997).

[129]   Decision regarding Communication 155/96 (*Social and Economic Rights*

Commission held that Nigeria had violated the right to enjoy Charter-guaranteed rights and freedoms without discrimination (Art. 2), the right to life (Art. 4), the right to property (Art. 14), the right to health (Art. 16), the right to housing (implied in the duty to protect the family (Art. 18(1)), the right to food (implicit in Arts. 4, 16, and 22), the right of peoples to freely dispose of their wealth and natural resources (Art. 21), and the right of peoples to a "general satisfactory environment favorable to their development" (Art. 24). Most of the violations stemmed from actions taken by or involving the Nigerian National Petroleum Development Company (NNPC) in a consortium with Shell Petroleum Development Corporation (SPDC).[130]

The Communication alleged that the military government of Nigeria was involved in oil production through NNPC in consortium with SPDC and that the operations produced contamination causing environmental degradation and health problems; that the consortium disposed of toxic wastes in violation of applicable international environmental standards and caused numerous avoidable spills near villages, consequently poisoning much of the region's soil and water; that the government aided these violations by placing the state's legal and military powers at the disposal of the oil companies; and that the government executed Ogoni leaders and, through its security forces, killed innocent civilians and attacked, burned, and destroyed villages, homes, crops, and farm animals. The Communication also alleged that the government failed to monitor the activities of the oil companies, provided no information to local communities, conducted no environmental impact studies, and prevented scientists from undertaking independent assessments.

After finding the petition admissible, the Commission analyzed what is generally expected of governments under the Charter. It acknowledged four separate but overlapping duties with respect to guaranteed rights: to respect, protect, promote, and fulfill them. According to the Commission these obligations universally apply to all rights and entail a combination of negative and positive duties.[131] Respect entails refraining from interference with the "enjoyment of all fundamental rights."[132] With regard to socioeconomic rights, in particular, respect means that "[t]he State is obliged to respect the

---

Action Center/Center for Economic and Social Rights v. Nigeria), Case No. ACHPR/COMM/A044/1 (Afr. Comm'n Hum. & Peoples' Rts. May 27, 2002), *at* <http://www.umn.edu/humanrts/africa/comcases/allcases.html>.

130 For a lawsuit directed against Shell for its involvement in these activities, *see Wiwa v. Royal Dutch Petroleum*, 226 F.3d 88 (2d Cir. 2000), *cert. Denied*, 121 S. Ct. 1402 (2001) and the discussion in Chapter 6, *supra*.

131 *See supra* note 129, at para. 44 (citing Asbjørn Eide, *Economic, Social and Cultural Rights as Human Rights, in* ECONOMIC, SOCIAL AND CULTURAL RIGHTS: A TEXTBOOK 21 (ASBJØRN EIDE, CATARINA KRAUSE & ALLAN ROSAS eds., 1995).

132 *Id.*, para. 45.

free use of resources owned or at the disposal of the individual alone or in any form of association with others, including the household or the family, for the purpose of rights-related needs. And with regard to a collective group, the resources belonging to it should be respected, as it has to use the same resources to satisfy its needs."[133]

Protection of rights requires legislation and provision of effective remedies to ensure that rights-holders are protected against other subjects and political, economic, and social interferences.[134] Promotion involves such actions as promoting tolerance, raising awareness, and building infrastructures.[135] Finally, fulfillment of rights and freedoms requires the state to move its "machinery" toward the actual realization of rights—for example, by directly providing, as necessary, "basic needs such as food or resources that can be used for food (direct food aid or social security)."[136] Since states are "generally burdened" with the four above duties in committing themselves to human rights instruments,[137] it was incumbent on the Commission to take these duties into account in assessing the Communication's allegations in relation to the African Charter and "the relevant international and regional human rights instruments and principles."[138]

Assessing the claimed violations of the rights to health (Art. 16) and to a general satisfactory environment (Art. 24), the Commission found that the right to a general satisfactory environment imposes clear obligations upon a government, requiring the state to take reasonable and other measures to prevent pollution and ecological degradation, to promote conservation, and to secure an ecologically sustainable development and use of natural resources.[139] Moreover, "[g]overnment compliance with the spirit of Arts. 16 and 24 of the African Charter must also include ordering or at least permitting independent scientific monitoring of threatened environments, requiring and publicizing environmental and social impact studies prior to any major industrial development, undertaking appropriate monitoring and providing information to those communities exposed to

---

[133] *Id.*

[134] *Id.*, para. 46.

[135] *Id.*

[136] *Id.*, para. 47 (citing Eide, *supra* note 131, at 38).

[137] *Id.*, para. 48.

[138] *Id.*, para. 49. The African Charter provides that the Commission shall draw inspiration from international law on human and peoples' rights, including the Universal Declaration of Human Rights and other UN instruments, the instruments of specialized agencies, and, as subsidiary measures to determine the principles of law, other general or special international conventions, African practices consistent with international norms on human and peoples' rights, general principles of law, and legal precedents and doctrine. African Charter on Human and Peoples Rights, *supra* note 96, Arts. 60, 61.

[139] *Id.*, para. 52.

hazardous materials and activities and providing meaningful opportunities for individuals to be heard and to participate in the development decisions affecting their communities."[140] Applying these obligations to the facts of the case, the Commission concluded that although Nigeria had the right to produce oil, it had not protected the Article 16 and Article 24 rights of those in the Ogoni region.

The Commission found numerous other rights violated, as well, and concluded its analysis by emphasizing that collective rights, environmental rights, and economic and social rights are essential elements of human rights in Africa, that the Commission intended to apply them, and that here is no right in the African Charter that cannot be made effective.[141] While governments may labor under difficult circumstances in trying to improve the lives of their peoples, they must reconsider their relationships with multinational corporations if these relationships fail to be mindful of the common good and of the rights of individuals and communities. The Commission called on the Nigerian government to stop all attacks on Ogoni communities; to allow independent investigators free access to the territory to conduct an investigation into the human rights violations that occurred; to prosecute those responsible for any such violations; to ensure adequate compensation for victims of violations, including a comprehensive cleanup of lands and rivers damaged by oil operations; to ensure that appropriate environmental and social assessments are prepared for future oil operations and that effective and independent oversight bodies exist for the petroleum industry; and, for communities likely to be affected by oil operations, to provide information on health and environmental risks, and meaningful access to regulatory and decision-making bodies.

The suggestion of a broadly justiciable right to environment is reinforced by the Commission's final comment that all rights in the Charter may be applied and enforced. The Commission gives the right to environment meaningful content by requiring the state to adopt various techniques of environmental protection, such as environmental impact assessment, public information and participation, access to justice for environmental harm, and monitoring of potentially harmful activities. The result offers a blueprint for merging environmental protection, economic development, and guarantees of human rights.[142]

---

[140]   *Id.*, para. 53.

[141]   *Id.*, para. 68.

[142]   The Inter-American Commission on Human Rights has adopted a similar approach in the context of countrywide studies of the human rights performance of OAS member states. *See* Inter-Am. Comm'n on Hum. Rts., *Report on the Situation of Human Rights in Ecuador*, OAS Doc. OEA/Ser.L/V/II.96, Doc. 10, rev. 1 (1997); Inter-Am. Comm'n on Hum. Rts., *Report on the Situation of Human Rights in Brazil*, OAS Doc. OEA/Ser.L/V/II.97, Doc. 29, rev. 1 (1997).

On the global level, a number of non-binding instruments include references to environmental rights or a right to an environment of a specified quality. In 1988, the UN Sub-Commission on Prevention of Discrimination and Protection of Minorities, considering the question of the movement of toxic and dangerous products and wastes, adopted Resolution 1988/26 which refers to the right of all peoples to life and the right of future generations to enjoy their environmental heritage. It notes that the movement and dumping of toxic and dangerous products endangers basic human rights, including the right to live in a sound and healthy environment.

During its 1989 session, the Sub-Commission added the topic of human rights and the environment to its agenda, adopting a resolution to undertake a study of the environment and its relation to human rights. The Human Rights Commission, influenced in part by preparations for UNCED, approved the Sub-Commission decision on March 15, 1990.[143] The Sub-Commission thereupon appointed a special rapporteur who presented reports on the subject between 1991–1994.[144] In her 1993 report, the special rapporteur left open the question of the preparation of a new international instrument on the right to a satisfactory environment or environmental rights. However, the report acknowledged such a right in its discussion, integrating it with a right to development, with action to ensure the enjoyment of all human rights, and with a right to prevention of environmental harm.

The special rapporteur annexed a set of Draft Principles on Human Rights and the Environment to her final report in 1994. The Human Rights Commission decided to request a report of the Secretary-General on the issues raised by the report and Draft Principles, based on the comments of states, intergovernmental and non-governmental organizations. The Secretary-General submitted reports in 1996, 1997 and 1998. At its 1998 session, the Commission decided to appoint a review committee to submit a revised version of the Draft Declaration. More recently, in Resolution 2001/65, the UN Human Rights Commission affirmed that "a democratic and equitable international order requires, inter alia, the realization of . . . [t]he right to a healthy environment for everyone."[145] The Commission's resolutions on toxic and dangerous wastes similarly refer consistently to "the human rights to life, health and a sound environment for every individual" and affirm that illicit traffic in and dumping of toxic and dangerous products and wastes is a serious threat to these rights.

---

[143] The United States and Japan both abstained on the resolution, stating that environmental issues should be dealt with exclusively by environmental bodies.

[144] Human Rights and the Environment: Preliminary Report, U.N. Doc. E/CN.4/Sub.2/1991/8, Aug. 2, 1992; First Progress Report, U.N. Doc. E/CN.4/Sub.2/1992/7, July 2, 1992; Second Progress Report, U.N. Doc. E/CN.4/Sub.2/1993/7, July 26, 1993.

[145] Res. 2001/65, U.N. Comm'n on Hum. Rts., 57th Sess., at para. 3k.

E. Indigenous Populations

There are over 200 million indigenous people in the world and many of them live in some of the world's most vulnerable ecosystems: the Arctic and tundra, the tropical rainforests, the boreal forests, riverine and coastal zones, mountains and semi-arid rangelands. In the last 40 years or so, these lands have come under pressure as governments, development banks, transnational corporations and entrepreneurs search out resources to supply a growing demand. The territories used and occupied by indigenous peoples often are seen as important repositories of unexploited riches. Once largely inaccessible, these regions and their mineral deposits, hydroelectric potential, hardwoods, old and new farm and pasture lands have been put within reach by modern technology.

Indigenous peoples[146] are particularly affected by environmental harm. As found by the special rapporteur on human rights and the environment:

> indigenous peoples have a special relationship with the land and the environment in which they live. In nearly all indigenous cultures, the land is revered; "Mother Earth" is the core of their culture. The land is the home of the ancestors, the provider of everyday material needs, and the future held in trust for coming generations. According to the indigenous view, land should not be torn open and exploited—this is a violation of the Earth—nor can it be bought, sold or bartered. Furthermore, indigenous peoples have, over a long period of time, developed successful systems of land use and resource management. These systems, including nomadic pastoralism, shifting cultivation, various forms of agroforestry, terrace agriculture, hunting, herding and fishing, were for a long time considered inefficient, unproductive and primitive. However, as world opinion grows more conscious of the environment and particularly of the damage being done to fragile habitats, there has been a corresponding interest in indigenous land-use practices. The notion of sustainability is the essence of both indigenous economies and their cultures.

---

[146] Although there is no clear definition of the term "indigenous peoples," a certain number of criteria have emerged in the course of discussions in the Working Group on Indigenous Populations. Indigenous peoples are the descendants of the original inhabitants of territories since colonized by foreigners; they have distinct cultures which set them apart from the dominant society; many have, until comparatively recently, had a high degree of control over their development; indigenous peoples have a strong sense of self-identity.

Where there is unrestrained deforestation, forest-dwelling indigenous peoples may be forced from their traditional homelands, may thereby be denied a means of livelihood, may be driven to take refuge among strangers and, in the most extreme cases, may fall victim to diseases against which they have no immunity. Similarly, desertification, a phenomenon which is as much man-made as it is an act of nature, has led many self-sufficient pastoralists to an impoverished existence in refugee camps. Even smaller scale environmental sacrifices—the inundation cased by dam-building, mining, prospecting and so on—have affected indigenous peoples all over the world, causing them to leave lands they have occupied for generations, often without their willing consent or any compensation.

The chapter of Agenda 21 on indigenous populations mentions existing treaties[147] and the draft universal declaration on indigenous rights. It provides that indigenous people and their communities "may require, in accordance with national legislation, greater control over their lands, self-management of their resources, participation in development decisions affecting them, including, where appropriate, participation in the establishment or management of protected areas." It makes no reference to the fact that the ILO Indigenous and Tribal Peoples Convention (No. 169) contains environmental rights for the indigenous, requiring states parties to take special measures to safeguard the environment of indigenous peoples (Art. 4). In particular, governments must provide for environmental impact studies of planned development activities and take measures, in cooperation with the peoples concerned, to protect and preserve the environment of the territories they inhabit.

United Nations and OAS organs have drafted Declarations on the Rights of Indigenous Peoples that contain environmental and resource rights.[148] The United Nations Sub-Commission on Prevention of Discrimination and

---

[147] It should be noted that traditional hunting rights of Arctic indigenous peoples are regularly accorded in international conventions on whaling and fishing. *See* Chapter 8.

[148] Part VI of the UN draft includes the right of indigenous peoples "to maintain and strengthen their distinctive spiritual and material relationship with the lands, territories, waters and coastal seas and other resources which they have traditionally owned or otherwise occupied or used, and to uphold their responsibilities to future generations in this regard" (Art. 25). Specific protection is also afforded to medicinal plants, animals and minerals. Indigenous peoples have the right to special measures to control, develop and protect their genetic resources, including seeds, medicines, and knowledge of the properties of fauna and flora. Indigenous are given the right to own, develop control and use the total environment of the lands, air, waters, coastal seas, sea-ice, flora and fauna and other resources which they have traditionally owned or otherwise occupied or used. Restitution of or compensation for lands taken without free and informed consent is required. Art. 28 provides that indigenous peoples

Protection of Minorities adopted a draft on August 26, 1994, which it sub-mitted to the Commission on Human Rights for further action.[149] The Commission decided on March 3, 1995, to establish an intergovernmental working group to review the draft. The Inter-American Commission on Human Rights drafted the OAS Declaration which it transmitted to the OAS General Assembly in 1997.[150]

The UN General Assembly, in the context of the International Decade of the World's Indigenous Peoples (1994–2004), has noted that the goal of the decade is to strengthen international cooperation for the solution of problems faced by indigenous peoples in various areas, including the envi-ronment. It has called for increased participation of indigenous peoples in activities for the decade, affirming its conviction of their contribution to environmental advancement of all countries of the world.[151] In 2001, the UN Human Right Commission appointed a special rapporteur on the situ-ation of human rights and fundamental freedoms of indigenous peoples.[152] The rapporteur's mandate includes receiving communications on violations of human rights.

The case law of the Inter-American human rights system has con-tributed considerably to recognizing the rights of indigenous peoples in respect to their environmental and natural resources. The case of *Awas Tingni Mayagna (Sumo) Indigenous Community v. Nicaragua*, decided by the Inter-American Court of Human Rights, involved the protection of Nicara-guan forests in lands traditionally owned by the Awas Tingni. The case orig-inated as an action against government-sponsored logging of timber on native lands by Sol del Caribe, S.A. (SOLCARSA), a subsidiary of the Korean company Kumkyung Co. Ltd. The government granted SOLCARSA a log-

---

have the right to the conservation, restoration and protection of the total envi-ronment and the productive capacity of their lands, territories and resources. Part IV of the UN draft contains procedural rights, including the right of indige-nous peoples to participate fully at all levels of decision-making in matters which may affect them.

[149]   Res. 1994/45, Sub-Commission on Prevention of Discrimination and Protection of Minorities, 46th Sess. (1994), *reprinted in* 34 I.L.M. 541 (1995). The chair of the Working Group on Indigenous Peoples also prepared a spe-cial study on the protection of the cultural and intellectual property of indige-nous peoples. *See* E.-I. Daes, *Discrimination against Indigenous Peoples: Protection of the Heritage of Indigenous People*, E/CN.4/Sub.2/1994/31.

[150]   *See* IACHR, *The Human Rights Situation of the Indigenous Peoples in the Americas*, OEA/Ser.L/V/II.108, Doc. 62 (Oct. 20, 2000).

[151]   G.A. Res. 52/108, Dec. 12, 1997, A/52/641.

[152]   Res. 2001/57, Apr. 24, 2001. For the work of the Sub-Commission, *see Indigenous Peoples and Their Relationship to Land*, E/CN.4/Sub.2/2001/21, June 11, 2001.

ging concession without consulting the Awas Tingni community, although the government had agreed to consult them subsequent to granting an earlier concession. The Awas Tingi filed a case at the Inter-American Commission, alleging that the government violated their rights to cultural integrity, religion, equal protection and participation in government. The Commission found in 1998 that the government had violated the human rights of the Awas Tingni and brought the case before the Court on June 4, 1998, alleging violation by Nicaragua of Articles 1, 2, 21 and 15 of the American Convention, due to the state's failure to demarcate and to grant official recognition to the territory of the community. The Commission requested that the Court determine award compensation.

On August 31, 2001, the Court issued its judgment on the merits and reparations. The Court decided by seven votes to one to declare that the state violated the Convention right to judicial protection (Art. 25) and the right to property (Art. 21). It unanimously declared that the state must adopt domestic laws, administrative regulations, and other necessary means to create effective surveying, demarcating and title mechanisms for the properties of the indigenous communities, in accordance with customary law and indigenous values, uses and customs. Pending the demarcation of the indigenous lands, the state must abstain from realizing acts or allowing the realization of acts by its agents or third parties that could affect the existence, value, use or enjoyment of those properties located in the Awas Tingni lands. By a vote of seven to one, the Court also declared that the state must invest U.S. $50,000 in public works and services of collective benefit to the Awas Tingni as a form of reparations for non-material injury and U.S. $30,000 for legal fees and expenses.

The *Maya Indigenous Communities and their Members v. Belize (Case 12.053)* petition was presented to the Inter-American Commission on Human Rights by the Indian Law Resource Center on behalf of the Toledo Maya Cultural Council of Belize, claiming that the state has violated the rights of Mayan communities in relation to their lands and natural resources by granting numerous concessions for logging and oil development. The petition alleged that the state's actions violate rights guaranteed by the American Declaration on the Rights and Duties of Man: the right to life, the right to equality before the law, the right to religious freedom and worship, the right to a family and protection thereof, the right to the preservation of health and to well-being, the right to judicial protection, the right to vote and to participate in government, and the right to property. Although a case had been filed in Belize to stop the logging and to affirm Mayan rights to the land and resources, no judgment had issued after more than three and a half years. Negotiations aiming at a friendly settlement were unsuccessful and on October 5, 2000, the Commission found the case admissible and asked the state to respond on the merits.

The Inter-American Commission's *Third Report on the Situation in Paraguay*,[153] addresses environmental protection in Chapter V on Economic, Social and Cultural Rights and in Chapter IX, on the rights of indigenous peoples. The Commission expresses concern about lack of protection for the habitats of indigenous groups, specifically referring to deforestation and ecological degradation, contrary to the provisions of Article 64 of the Paraguayan Constitution. According to complaints received "[t]he environment is being destroyed by ranching, farming, and logging concerns, who reduce the [indigenous people's] traditional capacities and strategies for food and economic activity." In addition to pointing to the deforestation, the Commission noted that the waters have been polluted and hydro-electric projects have flooded traditional lands and destroyed a unique system of islands that contained invaluable biodiversity. The Commission recommended that the state adopt the necessary measures to protect the habitat of the indigenous communities from environmental degradation, with special emphasis on protecting the forests and waters, "which are fundamental for their health and survival as communities."

Among environmental agreements, the most innovative in regard to indigenous rights and responsibilities is the Declaration on the Establishment of the Arctic Council.[154] A major feature of the Council is the involvement of indigenous peoples as Permanent Participants, based on "recognition of the special relationship and unique contributions to the Arctic of indigenous peoples and their communities" (Preamble). Three organizations, the Inuit Circumpolar Conference, the Sami Council and the Association of Indigenous Minorities of the North, Siberia and the Far East of the Russian Federation, are specifically included in the Declaration. Other groups may participate, up to one less than the number of member states, if they meet the criteria set forth in Article 2 of the Declaration including having a majority Arctic indigenous constituency. The category of Permanent Participation is created, according to the Declaration "to provide for active participation and full consultation with the Arctic indigenous representatives within the Arctic Council."

The Conference of the Parties to the Convention on Biological Diversity (CBD) addressed indigenous rights in the context of implementing Article 8 of the Convention, which calls for protecting traditional knowledge and practices consistent with sustainable development. Decision VI/1 of the Sixth Conference of the Parties emphasizes the need for dialogue with representatives of indigenous and local communities, particularly women, for the conservation and sustainable use of biological diversity, and recognizes

---

[153]   OEA/Ser.L/V/II.110, Doc. 52, Mar. 9, 2001.

[154]   Canada-Denmark-Finland-Iceland-Norway-the Russian Federation-Sweden-United States, Declaration on the Establishment of the Arctic Council, Ottawa, Sept. 19, 1996, *reprinted in* 35 I.L.M. 1382 (1996).

the need to explore additional ways and means to enhance the full and effective participation of indigenous and local communities in the Convention process.

The Decision asserts that the Convention on Biological Diversity is the primary international instrument with a mandate to address issues regarding the traditional knowledge, innovations and practices of indigenous and local communities relevant to the conservation and sustainable use of biological diversity. It acknowledges that indigenous and local communities have their own systems for the protection and transmission of traditional knowledge as part of their customary law but notes the need to strengthen national laws, policies and other measures, where necessary, along with measures at the international level, to protect traditional knowledge, innovations and practices of indigenous and local communities.

The Decision specifically recommends that cultural, environmental and social impact assessments be done for developments proposed to take place on, or which are likely to impact sacred sites, lands and waters traditionally occupied or used by indigenous and local communities. International funding and development agencies should facilitate the incorporation of this recommendation into policies and processes for the assessment of proposed developments. States should provide information on any operational links between national intellectual-property authorities and indigenous and local communities to aid in protecting traditional knowledge. At the same time, states parties should encourage disclosure of the origin of relevant indigenous and local traditional knowledge, innovations and practices in applications for intellectual property rights, where the subject matter of the application concerns or makes use of such knowledge in its development.

Annex II of the decision contains "Recommendations for the Conduct of Cultural, Environmental and Social Impact Assessments Regarding Developments Proposed to Take Place on, or Which Are Likely to Impact on, Sacred Sites and on Lands and Waters Traditionally Occupied or Used by Indigenous and Local Communities." The Recommendations allow for integrated consideration of the cultural, environmental, and social impacts of a proposal as a single process. Possible impacts on all aspects of culture, including sacred sites should be taken into consideration while developing cultural impact assessments. Effective environmental impact assessment should include areas of significant conservation value, environmental constraints, geographical aspects and potential synergistic impacts. The direct and indirect impacts of the development proposal on local biological diversity at the ecosystem, species and genetic levels should be assessed, and particularly in terms of those components of biological diversity that the relevant community and its members rely upon for their subsistence, livelihood, and other needs. Development proposals should be rigorously assessed for their potential to introduce alien invasive species into local ecosystems.

The socio-economic impact assessment should analyze demographic factors, housing and accommodation, employment, infrastructures and services, income and asset distribution, traditional systems of production as well as educational needs, technical skills and financial implications. Proposed developments should be evaluated in relation to tangible benefits to such communities, such as job creation, viable revenue from the levying of appropriate fees, access to markets and diversification of income-generating (economic) opportunities for small and medium-sized enterprises. Developments involving changes to traditional practices for food production, or involving the introduction of commercial cultivation and harvesting of a particular wild species should assess those changes and introductions. Social development indicators consistent with the views of indigenous and local communities should be developed and give consideration to gender, generational considerations, health, safety, food and livelihood security aspects and the possible effects on social cohesion and mobilization.

Indigenous and local communities should be fully and effectively involved in the assessment process. The traditional biodiversity-related knowledge of involved indigenous and local communities should be applied along with modern scientific assessment methodologies and procedures. Consultation should allow for sufficient time and should take place in the appropriate language and in a culturally appropriate manner. Where the national legal regime requires prior informed consent of indigenous and local communities, the assessment process shall consider whether such prior informed consent has been obtained. The vital role of women, particularly indigenous women, in the conservation and sustainable use of biological diversity and the need for the full and effective participation of women in policy-making and implementation for biological diversity conservation should be fully taken into consideration, in accordance with the Convention.

On a regional level, in the context of the North American Agreement on Environmental Cooperation, on November 6, 2001, the Secretariat decided to accept and transmit to Mexico a case alleging that Mexico has denied indigenous communities of the Sierra Tarahumara access to environmental justice by failing to enforce its environmental laws regarding citizen complaints, environmental crimes and forest resources. As part of its case, the applicants invoked ILO Convention 169 concerning indigenous peoples. The regional body indicated that it would have jurisdiction over the Convention if it forms part of the domestic law of a state party, but that proper procedures had not been followed in the case to allow it to be considered. On August 29, 2002, following Mexico's reply, the Secretariat notified the Council that development of a factual record is warranted (A14/SEM/00-28/ADV).

F. Farmers' Rights

The issue of protecting traditional knowledge and local resources is one that goes beyond indigenous peoples to encompass local communities in general, particularly farmers that have been instrumental in conserving, improving and contributing to plant genetic resources. Farmers' rights are crucial to food security in providing an incentive for the conservation and development of plant genetic resources.

The international community was initially very divided over whether intellectual property rights or other equitable considerations should apply to farmers' developments of plant genetic resources or whether plant genetic resources constitute part of the common heritage of mankind or the natural resources of sovereign states. The FAO Global System for the Conservation and Utilization of Plant Genetic Resources attempted to reconcile competing interests by providing in an International Undertaking that such resources are the common heritage, but subject to the overriding sovereign rights of nations over their genetic resources. FAO Resolution 5/89 also accepted the concept of farmers' rights arising from their contributions, rights it sees as vested in the international community as trustee for present and future generations of farmers, for the purpose of ensuring full benefits to farmers and supporting the continuation of their contributions.

The FAO's International Treaty on Plant Genetic Resources for Food and Agriculture concluded in 2002 provides for access to information (Arts. 13 and 17) and public participation. Farmers' rights are formally endorsed by this legally-binding instrument at the global level, for the first time (Art. 9). The treaty provides in Articles 10–14 a system of facilitated access to an agreed list of over 60 plant genera, including 35 crops, chosen on the basis of interdependence and importance of those listed for food security. The benefits accruing from the use of the material accessed is to be shared fairly and equitably through a variety of actions. There is a conceptual breakthrough in respect to the sharing of monetary benefits: anyone who obtains a commercial profit from the use of genetic resources administered multilaterally is obliged, by a standard Material Transfer Agreement, to share these profits fairly and equitably and pay a royalty to the multilateral mechanism for use as part of the funding strategy for benefit sharing.

India was one of the first countries to pass legislation specifically protecting plant breeders' rights.[155] The Organization of African Unity (now the African Union) also drafted a model law on biological resources in 2000.

G. Conclusions

The interrelationship between human rights and environmental protection is undeniable. Human rights depend upon environmental protection, and environmental protection depends upon the exercise of existing human

---

[155] The Protection of Plant Varieties and Farmer's Rights Act No. 53, Aug. 31, 2001.

rights such as the right to information and the right to political participation. Despite this common core, the two topics remain distinct. Environmental protection probably cannot be wholly incorporated into the human
rights agenda without deforming the concept of human rights and distorting its program. Also, some human rights are not directly affected by environmental considerations, *e.g.*, the right to a name or to be free from *ex post
facto* laws. Moreover, without the link of property or privacy, health, conscience or association, it is difficult to see human rights tribunals moving
more broadly into nature protection, given the current human rights catalogue. Neither scenic areas, flora and fauna, nor ecological balance are
viewed as part of the rights to which humans are entitled, absent explicit
recognition of the right to a specific environment. No doubt debate will
continue over whether such a recognition serves to enhance environmental protection or simply to further the anthropocentric, utilitarian view that
the world's resources exist solely to further human well-being.

If a right to environment becomes widely accepted as part of the human
rights catalogue, there remains the problem of balancing it with other
human rights. The General Assembly has pronounced itself many times on
the indivisibility, interdependence, interrelatedness, and universality of all
human rights.[156] In December 1997 it reiterated its conviction of this reality and emphasized that transparent and accountable governance in all sectors of society, as well as effective participation by civil society, are an essential
part of the necessary foundations for the realization of sustainable development.[157] Yet, the possibility of collision or conflict between rights cannot
be avoided. For example, among the human rights guaranteed by international law is the right of each family to decide on the number and spacing
of their children. Demographic pressures have been recognized as a threat
to environmental quality and economic development, leading to demands
that national birthrates be lowered to achieve sustainable development.[158]
The possibility that some human rights may be limited to achieve the right
to environment is seen in the Constitution of Ecuador where Article 19
establishes "the right to live in an environment free from contamination."
The Constitution invests the state with responsibility for ensuring the enjoyment of this right and "for establishing by law such restrictions on other
rights and freedoms as are necessary to protect the environment." As noted
by the Inter-American Commission on Human Rights, the Constitution thus

---

[156] *See* the Vienna Declaration and Program of Action, adopted by the
World Conference on Human Rights, June 25, 1993, U.N. Doc. A/CONF.157/
24 (Part I).

[157] G.A. Res. 52/136, Dec. 12, 1997, U.N. Doc. A/52/644/Add.2.

[158] *See* Report of the International Conference on Population and
Development, Cairo, Sept. 5–13, 1994, U.N. Pub. E.95.XIII.18.

establishes a hierarchy according to which environmental protection may have priority over other entitlements.[159]

International organizations continue to express interest in the relationship between human rights and environmental protection. On September 11, 2001, the General Assembly of the Organization of American States, meeting in Lima, adopted an Inter-American Democratic Charter which recognizes in its preamble that a safe environment is essential to the integral development of the human being, which contributes to democracy and political stability. Article 15 proclaims that the exercise of democracy promotes the preservation and good stewardship of the environment, and finds it essential that the states of the Hemisphere implement policies and strategies to protect the environment, including application of various treaties and conventions, to achieve sustainable development for the benefit of future generations. Article 6 proclaims the right and the responsibility of all citizens to participate in decisions relating to their own development, also a necessary condition for the full and effective exercise of democracy.[160]

At its 2001 session, the OAS General Assembly adopted its first, rather cautious resolution on human rights and the environment.[161] The Resolution underscores the importance of studying the link that "may exist" between the environment and human rights. It speaks of the need to promote environmental protection and the effective enjoyment of all human rights. It requests the General Secretariat to conduct a study of the "possible interrelationship of environmental protection and the effective enjoyment of human rights." A subsequent Resolution of the same session recalls Principle 10 of the Rio Declaration, seeing human rights as instrumental to better environmental protection, stating:

> [T]he effective enjoyment of all human rights, including the right to education and the rights of assembly and freedom of expression, as well as full enjoyment of economic, social, and cultural rights, could foster better environmental protection by creating conditions conducive to modification of behavior patterns that lead to environmental degradation, reduction of the environmental impact of poverty and of patterns of unsustainable development, more effective dissemination of information on this issue, and more active participation in political processes by groups affected by the problem. . . .[162]

---

[159] Inter-Am.Comm'n Hum. Rts., *Report on the Situation of Human Rights in Ecuador* 87.

[160] The Declaration is reprinted at 40 I.L.M. 1289 (2001).

[161] *Human Rights and the Environment*, Resolution adopted at the third plenary session, June 5, 2001, OEA/Ser.G, AG/RES.1219 (XXXI-O/01).

[162] AG/RES. 1819 (XXXI-O/01), Human Rights and the Environment.

A year later, the Permanent Council adopted a resolution on human rights and the environment at a meeting on May 22, 2002.[163] The resolution calls for paying special attention to the work being carried out by the pertinent multilateral forums in this area and for encouraging institutional cooperation in the area of human rights and the environment in the framework of the Organization, in particular between the IACHR and the OAS Unit for Sustainable Development and Environment. One month after the Summit, the Inter-American Commission on Human Rights held hearings on the relationship between human rights and the environment.

A similar restrained approach was taken by the European Union at its Nice Summit. The Charter of Fundamental Rights of the European Union, adopted during the Summit on December 7, 2000, omits environmental protection from its listed rights of persons and duties of member states. Instead, the Charter simply provides that "[a] high level of environmental protection and the improvement of the quality of the environment must be integrated into the policies of the Union and ensured in accordance with the principle of sustainable development."

The 2002 World Summit on Sustainable Development, held in Johannesburg, South Africa expressed a very different view. It conspicuously avoided any rights-based approach to sustainable development. Indeed, the Johannesburg Declaration on Sustainable Development omits entirely the word "rights," albeit it includes reference to "the need for human dignity for all" and lists "social development" as one of the three pillars of sustainable development. Paragraph 19, which lists the worldwide conditions that pose severe threats to sustainable development includes, *inter alia*, hunger and malnutrition, armed conflict, organized crime and illicit drugs, terrorism, intolerance and xenophobia, but does not include violations of human rights among those conditions that threaten sustainable development. The participating states do express a commitment to "ensuring that women's empowerment, emancipation and gender equality," but not their rights, are integrated in Agenda 21 activities. Similarly, the "vital role" but not the rights of indigenous peoples is mentioned in paragraph 25. Principle 10 of the Rio Declaration is weakly echoed in paragraph 26, which recognizes that sustainable development requires "a long-term perspective and broad based participation in policy formulation, decision-making and implementation at all levels." The rights to information and a remedy for harm caused do not appear in the Declaration.[164]

---

163   *Human Rights and the Environment in the Americas*, OEA/Ser.P, June 2, 2002, AG/doc.4118/02, Bridgetown, Barbados, May 22, 2002.

164   The two rights appear in para. 128 of the Plan of Implementation which provides for states to "Ensure access, at the national level, to environmental information and judicial and administrative proceedings in environmental matters, as well as public participation in decision-making, so as to further princi-

The Johannesburg meeting clearly emphasized poverty eradication, globalization, and international trade, rather than environmental protection or human rights. This emphasis is particularly apparent in the Plan of Implementation adopted at the Summit, which is primarily devoted to poverty eradication—called the greatest global challenge facing the world today—and economic development. The Plan of Implementation, unlike the Declaration, includes an affirmation of the importance of human rights, but couples it with reference to the need to respect cultural diversity, suggesting the revival of cultural relativism that was rejected at the 1993 Vienna World Conference on Human Rights. Paragraph 5 in the Introduction to the Plan of Implementation reads:

> Peace, security, stability and respect for human rights and fundamental freedoms, including the right to development, as well as respect for cultural diversity, are essential for achieving sustainable development and ensuring that sustainable development benefits all.

Chapter VI of the Plan of Implementation, addressing health and sustainable development, is one of two substantive chapters to refer to human rights, but is similarly deferential to national authorities. It calls for strengthening health care systems to combat diseases and reduce environmental health threats "in conformity with human rights and fundamental freedoms and consistent with national laws and cultural and religious values." The other reference to human rights is found in the chapter on Sustainable Development for Africa, Chapter VIII, which calls for creation of "an enabling environment" to achieve, *inter alia*, respect for human rights and fundamental freedoms, including the right to development and gender equality.

The crucial Chapter X, addressing Means of Implementation, considers the transboundary context of human rights, in calling on states to avoid unilateral measures that impede the development of populations in other countries or "that hinders their well-being or that creates obstacles to the full enjoyment of their human rights, including the right of everyone to a standard of living adequate for their health and well-being and their right to food, medical care and the necessary social services." No reference is made to the duty of the population's own government to avoid impeding human rights.

On a more theoretical level, human health is the bridge between human rights and environmental protection, being a primary objective of both areas of regulation. Human rights exist to promote and protect human

---

ple 10 of the Rio Declaration on Environmental and Development, taking into full account principles 5, 7 and 11 of the Declaration."

well-being, to allow the full development of each person and the maxi-
mization of the persons goals and interests, individually and in community
with others. This cannot occur without basic conditions of health, which
the state is to promote and protect. Among the prerequisites for health are
safe environmental milieu, *i.e.*, air, water, and soil. Pollution destroys health
and kills and thus not only destroys the environment, but infringes human
rights as well. From the perspective of the law of state responsibility, there
may be little difference between a state that arbitrarily executes persons and
a state that knowingly allows drinking water to be poisoned by contaminants. In both instances, the state can be responsible for depriving individuals of their life in violation of human rights law; in the second case,
international environmental law is also implicated. Implementing and
enforcing the latter will also help protect the former. Thus, the goal of
human health provides the basis for reinforcing both areas of law.

The view that mankind is part of a global system may reconcile the aims
of human rights and environmental protection, since both ultimately seek
to achieve the highest quality of sustainable life for humanity within the
existing global ecosystem. Potentially conflicting differences of emphasis
still exist, however: the essential concern of human rights law is to protect
individuals and groups alive today within a given society, while the purpose
of environmental law is to sustain life globally by balancing the needs and
capacities of present generations of all species with those of the future. The
broad protection of nature at times may conflict with preservation of individual rights. It is not surprising, then, that international environmental law
and international human rights law have placed emphasis on different components of environmental protection.

BIBLIOGRAPHY

Alfredson, G. & A. Ovsiouk, *Human Rights and the Environment*, 60 NORDIC
      J. INT'L L. 19 (1991).
Anaya, S.J, *Indigenous Rights Norms in Contemporary International Law*, 8 ARIZ
      J. INT'L & COMP. L. 1 (1991).
Cullet, P. *Definition of an Environmental Right in a Human Rights Context*, 13
      NETH. Q. HUM. RTS. 25 (1995).
Dejeant-Pons, M., *The Right to Environment in Regional Human Rights Systems*,
      in HUMAN RIGHTS IN THE TWENTY-FIRST CENTURY 595 (MAHONEY, P. &
      MAHONEY, K. eds., 1993).
DEJEANT-PONS, M. & PALLEMAERTS, M., DROITS DE L'HOMME ET ENVIRON-
      NEMENT (2002).
Desgagne, R., *Integrating Environmental Values into the European Convention on
      Human Rights*, 89 AJIL 263 (1995).
Eaton, J.P., *The Nigerian Tragedy, Environmental Regulation of Transnational
      Corporations and the Human Right to a Healthy Environment*, 15 B.U. INT'L
      L.J. 261 (1997).

Handl, G., *Human Rights and Protection of the Environment: A Mildly 'Revisionist' View, in* HUMAN RIGHTS AND ENVIRONMENTAL PROTECTION (A.A. CANCADO TRINDADE ed., 1992).

Hitchcock, R., *International Human Rights, the Environment, and Indigenous Peoples,* 1 COLO. J. INT'L L. & POL'Y 1 (1994).

HUMAN RIGHTS APPROACHES TO ENVIRONMENTAL PROTECTION (BOYLE, A. & ANDERSON, M. eds., 1996).

Kane, M.J., *Promoting Political Rights to Protect the Environment,* 18 YALE J. INT'L L. 389.

Kiss, A., *Le droit á la conservation de l'environnement,* 1 REV. UNIVERSELLE DES DROITS DE L'HOMME 445 (1990).

McClymonds, J.T., *The Human Right to a Healthy Environment: An International Legal Perspective,* 37 N.Y.L.S. L. REV. 583 (1992).

Popovic, N., *In Pursuit of Environmental Human Rights: Commentary on the Draft Declaration of Principles on Human Rights and the Environment,* 27 COL. HUM. RTS. REV. 487 (1996).

POSEY, D., TRADITIONAL RESOURCE RIGHTS: INTERNATIONAL INSTRUMENTS FOR PROTECTION AND COMPENSATION FOR INDIGENOUS PEOPLES AND LOCAL COMMUNITIES (1996).

Shelton, D., *Human Rights, Environmental Rights, and the Right to Environment,* 28 STAN. J. INT'L L. 103 (1991).

Shelton, D., *What Happened in Rio to Human Rights?* 4 Y.B. INT'L ENVTL. L. 75 (1994).

Shelton, D., *Environmental Rights* in PEOPLES RIGHTS (Philip Alston, ed., 2001).

Shelton, D., *Fair Play, Fair Pay: Protecting the Traditional Knowledge and Resources of Indigenous Peoples,* 1993 Y.B. INT'L ENVTL. L. (1994).

Shutkin, W., *International Human Rights Law and the Earth: The Protection of Indigenous Peoples and the Environment,* 31 VA. J. INT'L L. 479 (1991).

Swepston, L., *A New Step in the International Law on Indigenous and Tribal Peoples: ILO Convention 169 of 1989,* 15 OKLA CITY U. L. REV. 677 (1990).

Symonides, J., *The Human Right to a Clean, Balanced and Protected Environment,* in DIRITTI DELL'UOMO.

Thorme, M., *Establishing Environment as a Human Right,* 19 DENV. J. INT'L L. & POL'Y 302 (1991).

van Dyke, B., *A Proposal to Introduce the Right to a Healthy Environment into the European Convention Regime,* 13 VA. ENVT'L L.J. 323 (1993);

Weber, S., *Environmental Information and the European Convention on Human Rights,* 12 HUM. RTS. L.J. 177 (1991).

Wiggins, A., *Indian Rights and the Environment,* 18 YALE J. INT'L L. 345 (1993).

CHAPTER 16

ENVIRONMENTAL PROTECTION AND ARMED CONFLICT

Throughout history, militaries have deliberately harmed the environment as a wartime strategy. From the Roman salting of lands around Carthage during the Third Punic War to Iraqi-set oil fires during the 1991 Gulf War, nature and its resources have been targets of attack or turned into weapons. Throughout the 20th century, the scope for destruction increased with the development of weapons of mass destruction. The potential for harm was evidenced during the Vietnam War when widespread use of chemical defoliants destroyed entire ecosystems and led to public health concerns in the United States and Vietnam due to the exposure of individuals to the chemicals used. To many observers, the severity of the environmental impacts in Vietnam revealed a need for new international law to mitigate the ecological consequences of armed conflict.[1]

Environmental damage during war threatens harm to present and future living organisms. Those who live in or near a combat zone may ingest persistent toxins or be exposed to radiation or other carcinogenic or mutagenic substances. Military action may contaminate air, water and soil or disrupt ecological processes, generating streams of refugees who flee the damage only to find new forms of environmental degradation associated with large refugee camps. Ecological damage also can hamper or prevent the rebuilding of communities after cessation of the conflict.

Effectively summing up these consequences, Principle 24 of the Rio Declaration affirms that warfare is inherently destructive of sustainable development. The Declaration calls on states to respect international law concerning the environment in times of armed conflict and cooperate in its further development, as necessary. The International Committee of the Red Cross has asserted its view that environmental law remains generally applicable during armed hostilities.[2] Agenda 21 delegated to the Sixth

---

[1]   Peacetime military activities, including weapons testing, pollution from military vessels, and contamination of land around military bases, also give rise to environmental concerns. Yet most environmental agreements and national laws exclude the military from their scope.

[2]   *See infra*, text at note 29. Some commentators disagree, concluding that environmental agreements may be suspended during wartime. *See* Arthur

Committee of the United Nations General Assembly authority to consider action on the issue of environmental protection in times of armed conflict, taking into account the specific competence and role of the International Committee of the Red Cross.[3]

The current law of war contains principles that can apply to protect the environment. They are found in customary international law and codified in the Hague Conventions of 1899 and October 18, 1907, and the Geneva Conventions of August 12, 1949. In 1976, states adopted the first treaty specifically aimed at protecting the environment against military assault: the Environmental Modification Convention (ENMOD, December 10, 1976).[4] The following year, Additional Protocol I to the 1949 Geneva Conventions made further progress. Despite these developments, some claim that existing law is inadequate and further legal measures are needed to ensure environmental protection during armed conflicts.

A. Customary and Treaty Law of Armed Conflict

State practice and religious traditions have long prohibited deliberate attacks on certain features of the environment. Jewish and Muslim texts, for example, enjoin the destruction of trees during war.[5] Grotius, in his classic *On the Law of War and Peace*, contended that the law of nations forbid the poisoning of water[6] and in a chapter on "moderation in laying waste" promoted the principle of military necessity.[7] Until the United States Civil War (1861–1864), however, states had not approved any agreement defining the laws of war. During that conflict the U.S. army adopted the Lieber Code of 1863 which imposed rules on the treatment of civilians and prisoners of war and limits on the means and methods of warfare. Four principles emerged from the Lieber Code to become generally accepted in state practice and international agreements: the principle barring unnecessary and unlawful damage (the principle of military necessity); proportionality (actions should not cause excessive or indiscriminate damage in relation to the military

---

Westing, *Environmental Protection from Wartime Damage: The Role of International Law, in* N.P. GLEDITSCH, ed., CONFLICT AND THE ENVIRONMENT 535, 538 (1997).

    [3]   Agenda 21, para. 39.6.

    [4]   G.A. Res. 31/72, Dec. 10, 1976 approved the ENMOD Convention and opened it for signature on May 18, 1977. The text is reprinted at 16 I.L.M. 90 (1977).

    [5]   Deuteronomy 20:19–20 prohibits during a siege the cutting of trees that yield food, while the Qur'an contains a prohibition on harming trees or other plants during war, except in case of grave military necessity.

    [6]   Hugo Grotius, ON THE LAW OF WAR AND PEACE Bk. III, ch. XI (F.W. Kelsey, trans., 1925).

    [7]   *Id.*, Bk. III, ch. XII.

advantage); prevention of unnecessary suffering; and discrimination between civilian and military targets. These principles have been elaborated in many treaties establishing the law of armed conflict, including agreements on treatment of wounded and prisoners of war, bans on certain weapons, the duties of occupying powers, and specific rules for different theaters of conflict (land, air, sea).

Among the disparate legal instruments governing armed conflict are several that contain provisions relevant to environmental protection:

- St. Petersburg Declaration Renouncing the Use, in Time of War, of Explosive Projectiles under 400 Grammes in Weight;[8]
- Hague Convention (No. IV) Respecting the Laws and Customs of War on Land (1907);[9]
- Geneva Protocol for the Prohibition of the Use in War of Asphyxiating, Poisonous or other Gases and of Bacteriological Methods of Warfare (1925);[10]
- Geneva Convention (IV) of August 12, 1949[11] and Additional Protocol I Relating to the Protection of Victims of International Armed Conflicts;[12]
- Nuclear Test Ban Treaty (1963)[13] and Comprehensive Test Ban Treaty (1996);[14]
- Convention on Military or Any Other Hostile Use of Environmental Modification Techniques ("ENMOD");
- Protocols II and III to the 1980 UN Convention on Certain Conventional Weapons, restricting mines and incendiary weapons;[15]
- Convention on the Prohibition of the Development, Production, Stockpiling and Use of Chemical Weapons and on their Destruction.[16]

---

[8] St. Petersburg, Nov. 29, 1868.

[9] The Hague, Oct. 18, 1907.

[10] Geneva, June 17, 1925.

[11] Convention Relative to the Protection of Civilian Persons in Time of War (Geneva, Aug. 12, 1949).

[12] June 8, 1977.

[13] Treaty Banning Nuclear Weapon Tests in the Atmosphere, in Outer Space and Under Water (Moscow, Aug. 5, 1963).

[14] Comprehensive Nuclear Test Ban Treaty (Sept. 24, 1996).

[15] Art. 2(4) of Protocol III rather weakly prohibits making forests or other kinds of plant cover the object of attack by such weapons except "when such natural elements are used to cover, conceal or camouflage combatants or other military objectives, or are themselves military objectives."

[16] Paris, Jan. 13, 1993.

Most of these texts do not explicitly mention the environment, but they contain general principles and provisions that may be applied in order to promote environmental protection. The St. Petersburg Declaration on explosive projectiles, for example, proclaims that "[t]he only legitimate object which States should endeavour to accomplish during war is to weaken the military forces of the enemy." Thus, any action lacking a military purpose would be unlawful.

The 1907 Hague Convention with its detailed and annexed regulations prohibits the use of poison or poisoned weapons and requires occupying states to refrain from over-exploiting resources such as forests.[17] These rules emerged from a general agreement of the parties that "the right of belligerents to adopt means of injuring the enemy is not unlimited."[18] Several customary international norms enshrined in the Hague Convention could provide potentially far-reaching environmental protection, including the fundamental principles of necessity, proportionality and discrimination between military and civilian targets.

Perhaps most importantly, the Preamble to the Convention recites the well-known Martens Clause. That clause proclaims:

> [u]ntil a more complete code of the laws of war has been issued, the High Contracting Parties deem it expedient to declare that, in cases not included in the Regulations adopted by them, the inhabitants and the belligerents remain under the protection and the rule of the principles of the law of nations, as they result from the usages established among civilized peoples, from the laws of humanity, and the dictates of the public conscience.

The wording of the clause has been echoed in a number of subsequent treaties, including the 1949 Geneva Conventions, the 1977 Additional Protocols I and II, and the 1980 Convention on Certain Conventional Weapons. In the aftermath of the 1991 Gulf War, the ICRC and the General Assembly asserted the relevance of the Martens Clause to environmental protection. The IUCN's Amman Congress also recommended that states apply the clause.[19]

---

[17]   Convention (No. IV) Respecting the Laws and Customs of War on Land, with Annex of Regulations (The Hague, Oct. 18, 1907), Arts. 23(a), 55; 36 Stat. 2277 (1911).

[18]   Hague Convention (IV) Respecting the Laws and Customs of War on Land, Art. 22 Annex, sec. 2, ch. I.

[19]   At its Second World Conservation Congress (Amman, Oct. 4–11, 2000), IUCN urged UN member states to endorse the following policy: "Until a more complete international code of environmental protection has been adopted, in cases not covered by international agreements and regulations, the biosphere

Although the 1925 Geneva Protocol on gas and bacteriological warfare does not mention the environment, the UN General Assembly invoked it in 1969 during the conflict in Vietnam. The General Assembly declared that the Protocol prohibits the use of any chemical agents of warfare which might be employed because of their direct toxic effects on man, animals or plants and any biological agents intended to cause disease and death in man, animals or plants.[20]

The Geneva Conventions of 1949 built on the provisions of the 1907 Hague Regulations and like them protects property, including property owned collectively or by the state or other public authorities. Article 147 of Geneva Convention (IV) on the protection of civilians includes among "grave breaches" of the Convention any extensive destruction and appropriation of property not justified by military necessity and carried out unlawfully and wantonly. One unresolved question is whether or not the term "property" includes public goods such as water resources, public lands, and air.

Other treaties include specific measures relating to the environment, *inter alia,* Article I of the ENMOD Convention; Articles 35(3) and 55(1) of the 1977 Additional Protocol I to the Geneva Convention; and Article 2 of Protocol III to the United Nations Conventional Weapons Convention. ENMOD is primarily concerned with the use of nature as a weapon of war. Article 1 prohibits all "hostile use of environmental modification techniques having widespread, long-lasting or severe effects as the means of destruction, damage or injury" to the opposing side. Environmental modification, defined in Article II, means "any technique for changing—through the deliberate manipulation of natural processes—the dynamics, composition or structure of the Earth, including its biota, lithosphere, hydrosphere and atmosphere, or of outer space." A contemporaneous understanding of the Conference of the UN Committee on Disarmament defined widespread to mean an area on the scale of several hundred square kilometers. Long-lasting means a period of months, approximately a season, while severe is defined as "involving serious or significant disruption or harm to human life, natural and economic resources or other assets."

Additional Protocol I to the 1949 Geneva Convention significantly advanced environmental protection during warfare. It reflects two aims of

---

and all its constituent elements and processes remain under the protection and authority of the principles of international law derived from established custom, from dictates of the public conscience, and from the principles and fundamental values of humanity acting as steward for present and future generations." While inspired by the Martens Clause, this formulation is not limited to the context of armed conflict, but applies as an overarching principle to all human activities. *See* 30 E.P.L. 285 and 313(2000); Alexandre Kiss, *International Humanitarian Law and the Environment,* 31 E.P.L. 223 (2001).

[20] G.A. Res. 2603A(XXIV), Dec. 16, 1969 (80 in favor, three against, 36 abstentions).

environmental protection: protection of the environment itself, which is contained in Article 35(3) of the Protocol, and protection of the human population from environmental harm, which is contained in Article 55. Article 35(3) prohibits employing methods or means of warfare "which are intended, or may be expected, to cause widespread, long-term and severe damage to the natural environment" without mentioning potential impacts on humans. Article 55(1) repeats that care should be taken to avoid such harm, but adds that "this protection includes a prohibition of the use of methods or means of warfare which are intended or may be expected to cause such damage to the natural environment and thereby to prejudice the health or survival of the population." Article 55(2) further specifies that attacks against the natural environment by way of reprisals are prohibited.

Without mentioning the environment specifically, other provisions of Protocol I may provide additional protection. Article 52, which concerns the general protection of civilian objects, prohibits attacks on objects indispensable to the survival of the civilian population, such as food, agricultural areas, crops, livestock, drinking water installations and supplies and irrigation works. Article 56 affords protection to works and installations containing dangerous forces, namely dams, dykes and nuclear electrical generating stations. These protections were notably referred to in the 1997 UN Convention on International Watercourses,[21] whose Article 29 refers to the protection afforded international watercourses and related installations, facilities and other works during international and non-international armed conflicts.

Protocol I applies only to land warfare and to sea or air warfare that affects the land. The Protocol does not protect the atmosphere generally or the air above the land if the land below is not affected. In addition, Article 35(3) and Article 55 set a high threshold for prohibited acts, only banning those which cause "widespread, long-term and severe damage." Protocol I defines "long-term" to be a period of decades, in contrast to ENMOD, and uses the conjunctive "and" instead of ENMOD's "or." The Conference Committee clearly stated that the terms of Protocol I must be interpreted in accordance with the meaning specified in the Protocol, and not in the light of similar terms contained in other instruments, such as ENMOD. On the other hand, as noted by the U.S. Army's Operational Law Handbook, "once the degree of damage to the environment reaches a certain level, Geneva Protocol I does not employ the traditional balancing of military necessity against the quantum of expected destruction. Instead, it establishes this level as an absolute ceiling of permissible destruction."[22]

---

[21] May 21, 1997.

[22] U.S. Army, Operational Law Handbook, 2st rev. ed. JA 422 (1997) at 5. The 1998 Rome Statute of the International Criminal Court, Art. 8 concerns war crimes within the jurisdiction of the ICC and appears to reintroduce a pro-

The majority of states are parties to Protocol I, but it has not attracted support among several key states. The rules embodied in the Protocol can only be binding on non-signatories if the rules constitute or become customary international law. A further limiting factor arises from the fact that Protocol I applies only to international armed conflicts. Additional Protocol II to the Geneva Conventions specifically applies to non-international armed conflicts and contains no provision concerning the environment.

The Convention on the Prohibition of the Development, Production, Stockpiling and Use of Chemical Weapons and on their Destruction[23] contains far-reaching provisions on control of national chemical production facilities and international verification of state obligations. Contracting states must destroy all chemical weapons and all production facilities within ten years of the agreement's entry into force. Each state party must provide access to any chemical weapons destruction facility for the purpose of on-site systematic verification and monitoring.

The treaty covers all toxic chemicals and their precursors, listed in three schedules or annexes. Schedule 1 chemicals, including all nerve and mustard gases now in existence, cannot be produced in excess of 10 kilograms per year, and production must be done at a single specially designated facility. Schedules 2 and 3 list chemicals which can be used for both civilian and military purposes. States may produce these chemicals without production limits, but production above a range from one kilogram to one ton triggers a reporting obligation in regard to the producing facility. In addition, there may be on-site inspections. For Schedule 3 chemicals, states are required to submit reports for each facility that produces amounts over limits ranging from 30 to 200 tons per year.

Within 30 days of the entry into force of the agreement on April 29, 1997, each state party had to submit to the Organization for the Prohibition of Chemical Weapons (OPCW), a treaty monitoring group based in the Hague, a declaration on its ownership or possession of chemical weapons, the precise location, quantity and detailed inventory of such weapons, and information on the import or export after January 1, 1946, of weapons-producing equipment. Each state also had to provide a general plan for destruction, closure, or conversion of any chemical weapons production facility it owns or possesses or is within its jurisdiction or control. Contracting states must also forward annual data on the national production, import and export of listed chemicals and provide to the Technical Secretariat, for each of its chemical weapons destruction facilities, plant operations manuals, safety and medical plans, laboratory operations and

---

portionality analysis by referring to "widespread, long-term and severe damage to the natural environment which would be clearly excessive in relation to the concrete and direct overall military advantage anticipated."

23   Paris, Jan. 13, 1993.

quality assurance and control manuals, and the environmental permits that have been obtained.

The Convention is the first agreement to apply verification procedures to the civilian chemicals industry. All locations at which chemical weapons are stored or destroyed are subject to systematic verification through on-site inspection and monitoring with on-site instruments. The procedures allow international inspectors to examine chemical facilities on request of another signatory state. More detailed measures concerning the elimination and disposal of chemical reserves are dealt with by the Organization.

Implementation of the agreement raises significant environmental problems due to the number of weapons and technical difficulties involved. Environmentally-sound implementation of the Convention is costly. Article IV, paragraph 12, obligates states parties to cooperate and provide information and assistance regarding methods for the safe and efficient destruction of chemical weapons. The Convention includes some specific obligations regarding the environmental implications of the destruction of chemical weapons. Article VII(3) provides that each state party shall assign the highest priority to ensuring the safety of people and to protecting the environment as the treaty is implemented. Thus, a state party may not refuse to implement the Convention on environmental grounds, but must reconcile environmental protection with the goals of the Convention to the fullest extent possible. A similar provision is included in the Convention on the Prohibition of the Development, Production and Stockpiling of Biological and Toxic Weapons and Their Destruction.[24] It provides that "in implementing the provisions of this Article all necessary safety precautions shall be observed to protect populations and the environment" (Art. II(2)).

The Chemical Weapons Convention refers to national standards for safety and emissions in regard to the destruction of chemical weapons (Art. IV(10)). In principle each state party may decide how it shall destroy chemical weapons consistent with its obligation to place safety and environmental protection at the forefront. The weapons must be destroyed, however, in designated facilities suited for the task and states may not eliminate agents through dumping in water, land burial or open-air burning. Old chemical weapons, *i.e.*, those produced before 1925 and those produced between 1925 and 1946 which have deteriorated to such extent that they can no longer be used as chemical weapons are to be treated as toxic waste under national and international regulation according to paragraph B.6 of Part IV(B) of the Verification Annex.

Finally, the Convention indicates that a state party bears responsibility for all chemical weapons it abandoned on the territory of another state party. The explicit obligations are, however, limited. Paragraph C.15 of Part

---

[24]   April 10, 1972.

IV(B) of the Verification Annex provides that for the purpose of destroying abandoned chemical weapons, the abandoning state party shall provide all necessary financial, technical, expert, facility, as well as other resources. The territorial state on which the abandoned weapons are located must provide appropriate cooperation. The Convention specifies that the weapons are to be destroyed in accordance with Article IV of the Convention and Part IV(A) of the Verification Annex. This means that destruction of the weapons has to be carried out in conditions that do not result in significant damage to the environment. The interplay with environmental conventions such as the Basel and Bamako Conventions dealing with the transboundary transport of hazardous wastes means that in general the transboundary shipment of war materials in order to destroy them is permitted only in very limited circumstances. Other conventions such as the Geneva Convention on Long-Range Transboundary Air Pollution may limit the disposal of weapons inland and abroad.

Several bilateral agreements have been concluded that also may contribute to the environmentally sound destruction of chemical weapons. In the United States-Russia Agreement Concerning the Safe, Secure and Ecologically Sound Destruction of Chemical Weapons (July 30, 1992), the United States agreed to provide up to $55 million to assist Russian chemical weapons destruction. An agreement of December 1992 between Russia and Germany enabled the construction of a plant to destroy specific materials. Similarly, Sweden agreed to assist Russia by examining the risks associated with the storage and destruction of the Russian chemical stockpile.

Other specific weapons systems have been restricted because of their indiscriminate effects or the excessive injuries they cause. In particular, nuclear weapons and anti-personnel land mines have been targeted by the international community. In 1996, the conference of state parties to the Convention on Prohibitions or Restrictions on the Use of Certain Conventional Weapons adopted a protocol on the use of mines, booby-traps and other devices.[25] The Protocol applies to international and to internal armed conflicts. It limits the types of weapons that can be used and calls on each contracting party to clear, remove, or destroy all mines, booby-traps and similar devices.

Another weapons treaty, the Convention on the Prohibition of the Use, Stockpiling, Production and Transfer of Anti-Personnel Mines and on Their Destruction,[26] mentions the environment, although its purpose is to end the casualties caused by land mines. According to Article 5 of the Convention, each state party must clear all mines in areas under its jurisdiction

---

25 Protocol II to the Convention on Prohibitions on the Use of Certain Conventional Weapons which may be Deemed to be Excessively Injurious or to have Indiscriminate Effects, Geneva, May 3, 1996, *reprinted in* 35 I.L.M. 1206 (1996).

26 Oslo, Sept. 18, 1997.

or control at the latest within ten years following the entry into force of the Convention. Within that time, if a state party believes it cannot destroy or ensure the destruction of all anti-personnel mines by the end of ten years, it may submit a request for an extension to a meeting of the states parties or a review conference. The request must contain, *inter alia*, a reference to the environmental implications of the extension (Art. 5(4)(c)). The meeting of the states parties or the review conference decides by majority vote whether to grant the request, taking into consideration the factors mentioned in the agreement, including the environmental implications. The Convention does not require an environmental impact assessment prior to mine clearance activities, although this may be necessary pursuant to other international agreements or national law. Each state party is required to report to the Secretary-General of the United Nations within 180 days of the entry into force of the Convention for that party on numerous matters related to mines and mined areas. Included in the reporting obligation is information regarding the status of programs for the destruction of anti-personnel mines, including details of the methods which will be used in destruction, the location of all destruction sites and the applicable safety and environmental standards to be observed (Art. 7(1)(f)).

Throughout the 1990s, various international organizations attempted to consider the impacts of armed conflict on the environment and to propose new rules. The IAEA General Conference adopted a resolution on September 21, 1990, recognizing that attacks or threats of attack on nuclear facilities devoted to peaceful purposes could jeopardize the development of nuclear energy, affirmed the importance and reliability of its safeguard procedures, and emphasized the need for the Security Council to act immediately should such a threat or attack occur.[27]

The UN General Assembly supported the IAEA with its own Resolution 45/581 of December 4, 1990, in which it referred to the IAEA Resolution and expressed its conviction of the need to prohibit armed attacks on nuclear installations. It expressed its awareness of the danger that such an attack could result in radioactive releases with grave transboundary consequences. On November 25, 1992, the General Assembly again adopted a resolution on the protection of the environment in times of armed conflict,[28] affirming that environmental considerations constitute one of the elements to be taken into account in implementing the principles of law applicable in armed conflict. In referring to the Iraqi occupation of Kuwait, it condemned the destruction of hundreds of oil-well heads and the release and waste of crude oil into the sea and noted that existing provisions of international law prohibit such acts. It stressed that destruction of the environment, not justified by military necessity and carried out wantonly, is clearly

---

[27]   IAEA GC (XXXIV)RES/533 (Sept. 21, 1990).
[28]   G.A. Res. 47/37, Nov. 25, 1992.

contrary to existing international law. The Resolution invited the International Committee of the Red Cross to report on activities undertaken by the Committee and other relevant bodies with regard to the protection of the environment in times of armed conflict.

In a report to the Secretary-General in 1992, the ICRC contended that existing law is sufficient to protect the environment adequately and that deficiencies are due to improper implementation.[29] The ICRC report discusses the major international legal rules relevant to the protection of the environment in time of armed conflicts, including the rules concerning the protection of property and those concerning the protection of the environment as such, embodied in Additional Protocol I to the Geneva Conventions (Arts. 35, 36, 55). It also mentions the May 14, 1954, Convention for the Protection of Cultural Property in the Event of Armed Conflict and the November 23, 1972, UNESCO Convention concerning the Protection of the World Cultural and Natural Heritage. The report recommends that mechanisms provided by Protocol I, such as the designation of Protecting Powers and of an International Fact-Finding Commission, be used for protection of the environment. The ICRC calls for application of the Martens clause which it finds indisputably valid in the context of environmental protection during times of armed conflict. In addition, the ICRC advocates applying the precautionary principle to the protection of the environment and the protection of nature reserves. It suggests drafting guidelines for military manuals and instructions and stresses that the law of armed conflict must take technical developments of weapons into account and contain their effects. As a result of further discussions, the ICRC produced a second report that included model guidelines for military manuals.[30] The General Assembly did not formally approve the guidelines, but invited states to disseminate them widely.[31]

In 1994, UNEP established a Working Group on Liability and Compensation for Environmental Damage Arising From Military Activities as part of its Montevideo Program for the Development and Periodic Review of Environmental Law (II-1993). According to the Report, a state which has committed an act of aggression cannot rely on the rules of international law allowing for exclusions or exemptions of responsibility and liability, but will be fully liable for damage to the environment.[32] The Working Group also

---

[29]   U.N. Doc.A/47/328.

[30]   "Protection of the Environment in Time of Armed Conflict," submitted by the UN Secretary-General to the 48th session of the General Assembly, U.N. Doc. A/48/269 (July 29, 1993).

[31]   The Guidelines for Military Manuals and Instructions on the Protection of the Environment in Times of Armed Conflict appear as an Annex to U.N. Doc. A/49/323 (Aug. 19, 1994). *See also* G.A. Res. 49/50 (Dec. 9, 1994), para. 11 (inviting states to disseminate the guidelines).

[32]   UNEP/ENV.LAW/3/info.1, Oct. 15, 1996, *reprinted in* 27 E.P.L. 134 (1997).

proposed a comprehensive definition of environmental damage and methods of valuation.

B. Environmental Claims and Damages in Armed Conflicts

The Gulf War raised numerous questions about the law applicable to environmental protection during armed conflicts. In January, 1991, the Iraqi military occupying Kuwait detonated more than 700 Kuwaiti oil wells, igniting more than 600 of them. Smoke from the fires affected not only Kuwait, but Iran, Turkey, Jordan and Saudi Arabia, while oil that spilled into the desert seeped into the underground aquifer. Iraq also opened valves at several oil terminals and pumped large quantities of crude oil into the Gulf, perhaps as much as 11 million barrels. Subsequent allied bombing of the terminals halted the flow of oil. Other oil slicks appeared, apparently caused by damage to tankers and oil-storage facilities. Oil refineries, oil gathering stations and power and water desalination plants were all damaged or destroyed.[33]

The United Nations Security Council reacted to the Iraqi destruction in Resolution 687 which affirmed that Iraq:

> is liable under international law for any direct loss, damage, including environmental damage and the depletion of natural resources, or injury to foreign Governments, nationals and corporations, as a result of Iraq's unlawful invasion and occupation of Kuwait (para. 16).

Paragraph 18 of the Resolution created a fund for the payment of claims and established a commission to administer the fund. A portion of the export sales of Iraqi oil is used for the fund. This action represented the first time that an international body has been charged with compensating for wartime environmental damage.

The United Nations Compensation Commission (UNCC) established its procedures regarding claims in a series of decisions taken by its Governing Council. Council Decision 7 provides that payments are to be made available with respect to direct environmental damage and the depletion of natural resources, including losses or expenses resulting from:

> (a) Abatement and prevention of environmental damage, including expenses directly relating to fighting oil fires and stemming the flow of oil in coastal and international waters;

---

[33] Letter of July 12, 1991 from the Chargé d'affaires of the Permanent Mission of Kuwait to the United Nations to the Secretary-General, July 15, 1991; U.N. Doc. A/45/1035, S/22787, at 2.

(b) Reasonable measures already taken to clean and restore the environment or future measures which can be documented as reasonably necessary for that purpose;

(c) Reasonable monitoring and assessment of environmental damage for the purpose of evaluating and abating harm and restoring the environment;

(d) Reasonable monitoring of public health and performing medical screening for the purposes of investigation and combating increased health risks as a result of the environmental damage; and

(e) Depletion of or damage to natural resources.[34]

The list is not exhaustive. The word "direct" limits the extent of liability for environmental damage, excluding indirect and remote harm. It appears that the two terms "environmental damage" and "depletion of or damage to natural resources" were included to provide comprehensive relief, in order to ensure that components of the natural environment having no commercial value as well as those primarily commercial in nature would be encompassed in the claims process. Given the potentially large claims, Decision 7 requires documentary and other appropriate evidence sufficient to demonstrate the circumstances and the amount of the claimed loss.

Following completion of earlier categories of cases, such as those concerned with individual personal injuries, the UNCC turned to the question of environmental claims. In 1996, the UNCC approved a payout of U.S. $610,048,547 to the Kuwait Oil Company on behalf of the public oil sector as a whole for the well blowout.[35] In December 1998, the Governing Council of the UNCC appointed a three-member panel to review other claims for losses resulting from environmental damage and the depletion of natural resources submitted by governments and by public sector enterprises. Before the Panel began consideration of the environmental claims, the Governing Council decided to "consider the special circumstances pertaining to successful environmental monitoring and assessment claims and, in this context, to consider addressing the level and priority of payments to be made in respect of such claims."[36] Two years after establishing a template for claims, the UNCC decided to provide technical assistance to Iraq in defending the environmental claims.[37] The Governing Council, observing the complexity and limited amount of international practice relevant to environmental losses, noted

---

[34]   UNCC, Governing Council Decision 7, para. 35, revised Mar. 16, 1992, S/AC.26/1991/7/Rev.1.

[35]   *See* Decision Concerning the Well Blowout Control Claim, Governing Council of the UNCC, 66th meeting, Dec. 17, 1996, S/AC.26/Dec. 40 (1996), Dec. 18, 1996.

[36]   Dec. 73, S/AC.26/Dec. 73 (1999), June 25, 1999.

[37]   S/AC.26/Dec. 124 (2001), June 22, 2001.

that this category of claims, unlike the others, would be conducted through written and oral proceedings. As a result, pursuant to the decision, Iraq was permitted to select experts to assist in developing the facts and technical issues, with the UNCC compensating the experts.

On June 22, 2001, the UNCC delivered its first set of awards[38] on 107 claims for monitoring and assessment of environmental damage, depletion of natural resources, monitoring of public health, and performing medical screenings for the purposes of investigation and combating increased health risks (the "monitoring and assessment claims"). The total amount of the claims exceeded U.S. $1 billion ($1,007,412,574), with Kuwait and Saudi Arabia each claiming close to $500 million.

In its report, the Commission notes that its mandate requires it to apply Security Council Resolution 687 and other relevant Security Council resolutions, Governing Council criteria and decisions, and "where necessary, . . . other relevant rules of international law."[39] The Commission reaffirmed its status as a fact-finding body whose function is to examine claims, verify their validity, evaluate losses, assess payments and resolve disputed claims.

The environmental claims reported in the first installment concerned monitoring and assessment related to damage from air pollution; depletion of water resources and damage to groundwater; damage to "cultural heritage resources;" oil pollution to the Persian Gulf; damage to coastlines; damage to fisheries; damage to wetlands and rangelands; damage to forestry, agriculture and livestock; and damage or risk of damage to public health. In addition to the claims that were expected to be filed related to oil fires and released oil from destroyed wells, claims were filed over disruption of desert and coastal ecosystems due to the movement of military vehicles, personnel, and ordnance, as well as adverse impacts on the environment resulting from the transit and settlement of persons who departed Iraq and Kuwait as a result of the invasion.

The claims for monitoring and assessment presented special problems because they were heard before any substantive claims were considered, although the latter were needed to demonstrate that environmental damage or depletion of nature resources occurred. The Panel accepted that the claims for monitoring and assessment should be determined first, however, because the results of the monitoring and assessment could be critical in enabling claimants to establish the existence of damage and evaluate the quantum of compensation to be claimed. The claims for monitoring and assessment were thus permitted in order to generate evidence of substantive harm. At the same time, the Panel sought to avoid accepting claims for

---

[38] *See* UNCC, *Report and Recommendations Made by the Panel of Commissioners Concerning the First Instalment of "F4" Claims,* U.N. Doc. S/AC.26/2001/16, June 22, 2001.

[39] *Id.,* para. 6.

monitoring and assessment activities of a purely theoretical nature. It sought a "nexus between the activity and environmental damage or risk of damage that may be attributed directly to Iraq's invasion and occupation of Kuwait."[40]

In assessing the nexus and reasonableness of the monitoring and assessment activity, the Panel considered:

- the possibility of causality, *i.e.*, the plausibility that pollutants released during the invasion and occupation could have impacted the territories of the claimants;
- whether the areas or resources in question could have been affected by pollutants resulting from the conflict.
- whether there is evidence of environmental damage or risk of damage; and
- whether the monitoring and assessment might produce results that could assist the panel in determining substantive claims.

The mere fact that monitoring and assessment activity does not establish conclusively that environmental damage has been caused does not necessarily supply a valid reason for rejecting a claim for expenses of the monitoring activity, because it could be of benefit even if no evidence of war-caused damage is found. The same is true if the results show that damage has occurred but no restoration or remediation is possible or feasible.

To be within the UNCC mandate, any proven damage has to be attributable to Iraq's invasion and occupation. As in other liability proceedings, separating out the causation has been a difficult matter, particularly in the absence of baseline information. Monitoring and assessment to determine causality would be compensable even if the results ultimately demonstrate the cause was other than Iraq.

In assessing each claim, the Panel considered the circumstances of the claim, including the nature of the damage to be assessed and the location and purpose of the monitoring and assessment activity and the appropriateness of the activity by reference to generally accepted scientific criteria and methodologies. Where supporting evidence and documentation was lacking, the Panel rejected claims.[41] On June 21, 2001, the Governing Council rejected the claim of Turkey and awarded compensation to Iran, Jordan, Kuwait, Saudi Arabia, and Syria, but with a lower assessment of damages than asserted. The lower amounts and rejected claims appear to have been based on lack of evidence. The successful claimant states must submit

---

[40]   *Id.*, para 31.

[41]   *See, e.g.*, Iran's claim for a preliminary monitoring study to evaluate possible damage to cultural relics by pollutants from the oil fires. The claim was rejected because no reports or other evidence were submitted to show that any work had been undertaken. Claim No. 5000331, paras. 79–83.

periodic progress reports on environmental monitoring and assessment.

The Panel reported a second installment of environmental claims in late 2002.[42] In addition to receiving 11 new claims from Iran, Kuwait and Saudi Arabia, the Panel received 19 claims from states outside the region (Australia, Canada, Germany, the Netherlands, United Kingdom, and United States). The 30 claims totaled some U.S. $872,760,534 for expenses incurred for measures to abate and prevent environmental damage, to clean and restore the environment, to monitor and assess environmental damage, and to monitor public health risks alleged to have resulted from Iraq's invasion and occupation of Kuwait.

Iran, Kuwait and Saudi Arabia sought compensation in the amount of U.S. $829,458,298 for measures to respond to environmental damage and human health risks from:

(a) mines, unexploded ordnance and other remnants of war;

(b) oil lakes formed by oil released from damaged wells in Kuwait;

(c) oil spills in the Persian Gulf caused by oil released from pipelines, offshore terminals and tankers; and

(d) pollutants released from oil well fires in Kuwait.

Australia, Canada, Germany, the Netherlands, the United Kingdom and the United States asked U.S. $43,302,236 for expenses incurred in providing assistance to countries in the Persian Gulf region to respond to environmental damage, or threat of damage to the environment or public health, resulting from Iraq's invasion and occupation of Kuwait.

The second installment claims involved some novel issues and by Procedural Order Nos. 7 and 8, both dated February 1, 2002, the Panel informed Iraq and the Regional Claimants that oral proceedings would be held to focus on:

(a) whether compensation be awarded for environmental damage or depletion of natural resources even if such damage or depletion may not have been caused solely as a result of Iraq's invasion and occupation of Kuwait;

(b) where environmental damage or depletion of natural resources may not have resulted solely from Iraq's invasion and occupation of Kuwait, what factors should the Panel take into account in determining that:

(i)   a portion of the damage or depletion is compensable, or

(ii) no portion of the damage or depletion is compensable;

---

[42]   UNCC, *Report and Recommendations Made by the Panel of Commissioners Concerning the Second Instalment of "F4" Claims*, U.N. Doc. S/AC.26/2002/26, Oct. 3, 2002.

(c) whether the phrase "environmental damage and the depletion of natural resources" under Security Council Resolution 687 (1991) and Governing Council Decision 7 include loss or damage to elements such as cultural property, human health, aesthetic values of landscapes, etc.; and

(d) to what extent, if any, should the procedure and criteria used for selecting contractors to undertake the removal of mines and ordnance affect compensability of expenses arising from these activities?

After oral and written proceedings, the Panel gave an expansive reading to Governing Council Decision 7 on the meaning of environmental damage. As the Panel noted, some of the losses or expenses for which compensation was sought were not included in the list of specific losses or expenses in paragraph 35 of Governing Council Decision 7. The Panel noted, however, that paragraph 35 of Governing Council decision 7 did not purport to give an exhaustive list of the activities and events that could give rise to compensable losses or expenses and thus should be considered as providing guidance regarding the types of activities and events that can result in compensable losses or expenses, rather than as a limitative enumeration of such activities or events. In the view of the Panel, the term "environmental damage" in paragraph 16 of Security Council Resolution 687 (1991) similarly is not limited to losses or expenses resulting from the activities and events listed in paragraph 35 of Governing Council Decision 7, but can also cover direct losses or expenses resulting from other activities and events. A loss or expense may be compensable even if it does not arise under any of the specific subparagraphs of paragraph 35 of Governing Council Decision 7. For example, expenses incurred due to measures undertaken to prevent or abate harmful impacts of airborne contaminants on property or human health could qualify as environmental damage, provided that the losses or expenses are a direct result of Iraq's invasion and occupation of Kuwait.

On the second issue, the Panel found that the question of Iraq's liability for environmental damage resulting from parallel or concurrent causes was not an issue that needed to be addressed in relation to the claims being made, because the claims were principally for losses or expenses allegedly incurred by the Claimants in undertaking measures to respond to the oil spills and oil fires or to remove and dispose of mines, unexploded ordnance and other remnants of war. According to the Claimants, these measures were all the direct result of Iraq's invasion and occupation of Kuwait. The Panel agreed, finding that there was well-documented evidence showing that massive quantities of oil were released into the marine environment of the Persian Gulf and onto the territories of Kuwait and other countries of the region as a result of Iraq's invasion and occupation of Kuwait. The evidence also showed that numerous oil fires which were deliberately caused by Iraqi forces in Kuwait resulted in the release of large volumes of contaminants into the atmosphere of the entire region. Finally, the Panel found it "undeniable" that a large number of mines and unexploded ordnance remained in the territory of Kuwait as a result of Iraq's invasion and occupation of Kuwait. On compensable losses, the Panel also agreed with the claimants that expenses resulting from activities undertaken by military personnel are compensable if there is sufficient evidence to demonstrate that the predominant purpose of the activities was to respond to environmental damage or threat of damage to the environment or to public health in the interest of the general population. For other government employees, salaries and related expenses were not compensable if such expenses would have been incurred regardless of Iraq's invasion and occupation of Kuwait.

Regarding the prevention and abatement claims of states from outside the region, the Panel found that neither Security Council Resolution 687 nor Governing Council Decision 7 restricted eligibility for compensation to losses or expenses incurred by the countries in which the environmental damage occurred or by countries located in the Persian Gulf region. In the view of the Panel, expenses resulting from assistance rendered to countries in the Persian Gulf region to respond to environmental damage, or threat of damage to the environment or public health, qualified for compensation. The Panel found that its conclusion on this point was reinforced by the fact that the United Nations had made specific appeals for assistance in dealing with the environmental damage caused by Iraq's invasion and occupation of Kuwait, as did other organizations and bodies of the United Nations system and the affected countries. The Panel cautioned, however, that compensation paid to an assisting country should not duplicate any compensation paid or to be paid to any country in the Persian Gulf region.

The Panel awarded less than claimed in all instances and denied the claim of the Netherlands in its entirety. The Panel found that the latter claim was for services rendered in the military campaign and not for prevention or abatement of environmental harm. In total, the Panel awarded U.S. $711,087,737 in the second installment.

Other institutions also stepped in to assess environmental damage resulting from the Gulf War. At the beginning of the conflict, UNEP's Governing Council expressed concern over destruction of the environment. The Global Resources Information Database of UNEP and IMO conducted an extensive preliminary assessment of the impact of the oil spill on the coastal waters of Kuwait and Saudi Arabia. IMO responded to a request of Saudi Arabia and other governments in the region, pursuant to the International Convention on Oil Pollution, Preparedness and Cooperation of 1990, and took action to facilitate and coordinate international assistance.

The UNEP Governing Council decided in May 1991 to recommend:

> that governments consider identifying weapons, hostile devices and ways of using such techniques that would cause particularly serious effects on the environment and consider efforts in appropriate forms to strengthen international law prohibiting such weapons, hostile devices and ways of using such techniques.

It invited the General Assembly to review the 1977 Convention on the Prohibition of Military or Any Other Hostile Use of Environmental Modification Techniques with a view to strengthening and encouraging accession to it and establishing concrete means of verification of its implementation.[43]

The conflicts that marked the breakup of the former Yugoslavia also involved environmental damage, and the precedent of the Gulf War stimulated international organizations and civil society to monitor and document the damage.[44] The 1999 Kosovo conflict allegedly included poisoning of wells, scorched earth tactics and indiscriminate bombing, leading UNEP to establish an expert task force that included NGO representatives to assess the environmental damage.

Other consequences followed the air campaign conducted by members of the North Atlantic Treaty Organization (NATO) against Yugoslavia during the Kosovo conflict. Allegations that the environmental and other impacts of the bombing made the attacks illegal under international humanitarian law persuaded the prosecutor for the International Tribunal for the Former Yugoslavia to appoint a committee to advise on whether or not to conduct a formal investigation. The June 14, 2000, Final Report of the Committee Established to Review the NATO Bombing Campaign against the Federal Republic of Yugoslavia,[45] recommended against an investigation. In so doing, the Committee assessed both the law and the available evidence that were relevant to its mandate.

On the first matter, the Committee considered Additional Protocol I's Articles 35(3) and 55 to state the "basic" legal provisions applicable to envi-

---

43   UNEP/GC.16/L.53, Part B, "Environmental Effects of Warfare" (May 1991).

44   *See, e.g.*, Regional Environmental Center for Central and Eastern Europe, *Assessment of the Environmental Impact of Military Activities during the Yugoslavia Conflict: Preliminary Findings* (June 1999), *available at* <http://www.rec.org/REC/Announcemen>.

45   Final Report of the Committee Established to Review the NATO Bombing Campaign against the Federal Republic of Yugoslavia, *available at* <http://www.un.org/icty/pressreal/nato/061300.htm>.

ronmental protection during armed conflict. Significantly, the Committee asserted that article 55 "may . . . reflect current customary law,"[46] despite a suggestion from the International Court of Justice four years earlier that it does not.[47]

Turning to the facts, the Committee found that the bombing campaign did cause some environmental damage through attacks on industrial facilities such as chemical plants and oil installations which released pollutants.[48] But, given the duty to find cumulative conditions fulfilled (long-term, widespread and severe damage) and acknowledging the high threshold set by those conditions, the Committee concluded that it would be difficult to assess whether such a threshold was reached in this case "even if reliable environmental assessments were to give rise to legitimate concern concerning the impact of the NATO bombing campaign."[49] The Committee referred to UNEP's Balkan Task Force, established to consider the environmental impacts of the Kosovo conflict and noted that the UNEP assessment was hampered by "a lack of alternative and corroborated sources regarding the extent of the environmental contamination caused by the NATO bombing campaign."[50] It also noted that reliable assessment of long-term effects of such contamination may not yet be practicable. The Committee concluded by expressing its opinion that, according to the information in its possession, "the environmental damage caused during the NATO bombing campaign does not reach the Additional Protocol I threshold."[51]

The conclusion did not end the matter because the Committee estimated that the legality of the attacks also had to be tested in light of the principles of military necessity and proportionality. It would appear that there was little debate over the issue of military necessity, because most of the discussion in the report concerns proportionality. The Committee states that in applying this principle "it is necessary to assess the importance of the target in relation to the incidental damage expected: if the target is sufficiently important, a greater degree of risk to the environment may be justified."[52] Regretting the lack of concrete guidelines on what constitutes excessive damage, the Committee said that "at a minimum, actions resulting in massive environmental destruction, especially when they do not serve a clear and important military purpose, would be questionable."[53] While

---

[46] *Id.*, para. 15.
[47] *See Advisory Opinion on the Threat or Use of Nuclear Weapons*, 1996 ICJ Rep. at 242, para. 31.
[48] Final Report, *supra* note 45, para. 14.
[49] *Id.*, para. 15.
[50] *Id.*, para. 17.
[51] *Id.*
[52] *Id.*
[53] *Id.*, para. 22.

recommending that no investigation proceed, the Committee considered that independently of the principle of proportionality, there is a duty to take precautionary measures to minimize collateral damage to the environment. "If there is a choice of weapons or methods of attack available, a commander should select those which are most likely to avoid, or at least minimize incidental damage. In doing so, however, he is entitled to take account of factors such as stocks of different weapons and likely future demands, the timeliness of attack and risks to his own forces."[54] Thus, the general principles of international humanitarian law play as great a role as do the more recent provisions that specifically mention environmental protection.

C. Advisory Opinions of the International Court of Justice

In a general effort to determine the scope of legal obligations towards the environment during armed conflict or in weapons testing, the International Court of Justice was asked on three occasions after 1993 to consider the legality of nuclear weapons and weapons testing. First, on September 6, 1993, the World Health Organization (WHO) requested an advisory opinion of the International Court of Justice on whether the use of nuclear weapons is a violation of international law, including the WHO Constitution, "in view of the health and environmental effects" such use would have. The Court decided in 1996 that the request exceeded the competence of the WHO. It viewed the question as being one within the purview of those organs of the United Nations expressly conferred the responsibility to regulate the use of force and armaments.[55] Perhaps anticipating this result, the United Nations General Assembly presented its own request asking a series of similar questions in 1995.[56] In fact, transnational civil society, in the form of a coalition of non-governmental organizations and individuals calling themselves "the World Court Project," was behind both requests, having successfully exerted pressure on both the WHO and the General Assembly to make the request of the Court. The Court decided it had jurisdiction to answer the General Assembly's questions and did so on July 8, 1996,[57] the same date it rejected the WHO request. A third proceeding before the

---

[54] *Id.*, para. 21. *See also* para. 17.

[55] *Request for an Advisory Opinion from the International Court of Justice on the Legality of the Threat or Use of Nuclear Weapons*, G.A. Res. 49/75K U.N. GAOR, 49th Sess., Supp. No. 49, at 71; U.N. Doc. A/4949 (1995). Advisory Op., 1996 I.C.J. 226. For a critical analysis of the Court's opinion, *see* Burns Weston, *Nuclear Weapons and the World Court: Ambiguity's Consensus*, 7 Trans. Nat'l L. & Contemp. Prob. 371 (1997).

[56] *Legality of the Use by a State of Nuclear Weapons in Armed Conflict, supra* note 55.

[57] *Legality of the Threat or Use of Nuclear Weapons, supra* note 55. The Court decided to comply with the request by a vote of 13-1, Judge Oda dissenting.

Court was an effort to reopen a contentious case filed by Australia and New Zealand against France, challenging the legality of nuclear testing in the South Pacific.[58] The Court held that the proceedings were definitively terminated but noted that its conclusion was "without prejudice to the obligations of states to respect and protect the natural environment."[59]

The Court was intensely divided on some issues and unanimous in regard to others in the advisory opinion on the legality of nuclear weapons. Given the complexity of the matter, it is perhaps not surprising that for the first time in its history, every judge sitting in the matter issued a separate declaration or opinion. Several holdings were closely linked to international environmental law. First, the Court found by a vote of 11-3 that neither customary nor conventional international law—including international environmental law—prohibits nuclear weapons *as such*.[60] The three dissenting judges found that nuclear weapons in all their probable uses are so devastating that they would be likely to breach human rights and environmental standards and thus are prohibited as such. The Court unanimously agreed that "[a] threat or use of nuclear weapons should . . . be compatible with . . . the principles and rules of international humanitarian law, as well as with specific obligations under treaties and other undertakings which expressly deal with nuclear weapons."[61] The Court noted that certain treaties prohibit the use of nuclear weapons in specific geographic areas,[62] but none of them prohibit the threat of use of nuclear weapons.

The Court's final holdings were the most divided. The Court's vote was 7-7, necessitating a deciding vote of the president, in holding that "the threat or use of nuclear weapons would generally be contrary to the rules of international law applicable in armed conflict and, in particular, the principles and rules of humanitarian law."[63] The Court went on, however, to say that it could not conclude definitively whether or not extreme self-defense

---

[58] *See* Request for an Examination of the Situation in Accordance with Paragraph 63 of the Court's Judgment of Dec. 20, 1974 in the Nuclear Tests (New Zealand v. France) Case, Order of Sept. 22, 1995, 1995 I.C.J. Rep. 288.

[59] *Id.* at 306, para. 64.

[60] *Legality of the Threat or Use of Nuclear Weapons, supra* note 55, at 36, para. 105(2)(B).

[61] *Id.* at 36, para. 105(2)(D).

[62] *E.g.*, the Antarctic Treaty (Dec. 1, 1959); the Partial Test-Ban Treaty (Aug. 5, 1963); the Outer Space Treaty (Jan. 27, 1967); the Treaty of Tlatelolco (Feb. 14, 1967); the 1971 Sea-Bed Arms Control Treaty, the Moon Treaty (Dec. 5, 1979); the South Pacific Nuclear Free Zone Treaty (Aug. 6, 1985); the Treaty on an African Nuclear-Weapon-Free Zone (Apr. 11, 1996); and the Treaty on the Southeast Asia Nuclear-Weapon-Free Zone (Dec. 15, 1995).

[63] *Legality of the Threat or Use of Nuclear Weapons, supra* note 55, at 36, para. 105(2)(E).

in which the life of the state would be at stake, would allow the threat or use of nuclear weapons.[64]

Some of the 28 states participating in the proceedings argued that any use of nuclear weapons would be unlawful according to international environmental law, making reference to various international treaties,[65] Principle 1 of the Stockholm Declaration and Principle 2 of the Rio Declaration. Other states contended that international environmental law principally applies in times of peace. The Court itself recognized that "the use of nuclear weapons could constitute a catastrophe for the environment," the latter representing "not an abstraction but . . . the living space, the quality of life and the very health of human beings, including generations unborn." Given this, the Court held that states must take environmental considerations into account in assessing what is necessary and proportionate in the pursuit of military objectives. The Court noted that the provisions of Additional Protocol I to the 1949 Geneva Conventions embody a general obligation to protect the natural environment against widespread, long-term and severe environmental damage; the prohibition of methods and means of warfare which are intended, or may be expected to cause such damage; and the prohibition of attacks against the natural environment by way of reprisals. Thus, while no specific provision prohibits the use of nuclear weapons, humanitarian law indicates that important environmental factors should be taken into account in the use of such weaponry in armed conflicts.

D. Environmental Security and Conflict Prevention

War is inimical to sustainable development and can lay the seeds for future violence. The aftermath of war can place additional pressures on natural resources as governments struggle for reconstruction and can be as harmful to the environment as war itself.[66] If it is now generally recognized that

---

64   Note that the three dissenters from the earlier holding also dissented on this point, finding the Court's pronouncement too weak, not too strong. Only four judges, three of them from nuclear power states, felt the Court had gone too far in questioning the legality of the threat or use of nuclear weapons pursuant to international humanitarian law. On the other hand, some of those concurring with the majority clearly seemed to approve mutual deterrence, *i.e.*, the threat of use of nuclear weapons, disagreeing with the view that all threats of use of nuclear weapons are illegal.

65   The instruments referred to included Additional Protocol I of 1977 to the Geneva Conventions of 1949 and the Convention on the Prohibition of Military or Any Other Hostile Use of Environmental Modification Techniques (Dec. 10, 1976), Art. 1.

66   J. McNeely, *War and Biodiversity*, in R. Matthew, M. Halle, J. Switzer . & A. Hammill, Conserving the Peace: Resources, Livelihoods and Security, IISD/IUCN, 2002.

war causes environmental harm, it is increasingly recognized that environmental degradation has the potential to produce internal and interstate conflict by undermining stability and producing mass migrations. Given the integrated nature of the environment it is impossible for a state to protect itself entirely against intentional or accidental environmental harm originating in another state. The consequences of that harm may be severe and long-lasting to the receiving state.

An additional concern is the problem of "environmental refugees," many fleeing water scarcity and no longer fertile soil. Their numbers are increasing to the point where they may outnumber refugees displaced by wars and persecution.[67] The number of refugees may double by the year 2010 if soil and water degradation continues at current rates. If predictions of rising sea levels due to global climate change are accurate, a staggering number of refugees from low-lying areas could join them. The rapid movement of refugees and the sudden increase in local demand for food, fuelwood and goods for barter can lead to significant degradation of ecosystems and natural spaces.

Given these concerns, traditional visions of state security are expanding to include environmental security. National security law and policy have traditionally focused on protecting the territorial integrity and political sovereignty of the state from military aggression from other states, but now place increasing emphasis on the growing array of non-military and non-conventional threats, including economic change, terrorism, population growth and migration. Key environmental threats that have received scrutiny include: resource scarcity, outbreaks of infectious disease, toxic contamination, ozone depletion, global warming, water pollution, soil degradation and loss of biodiversity.

Both "environment" and "security" are abstract concepts whose meaning has been extensively debated.[68] In its 1994 Human Development Report, the UNDP described security as an "integrative" rather than merely a "defensive" concept. The UNDP definition of human security includes seven categories of threats, ranging from economic and food security to protection of human rights and access to clean water, air and land.

In addition to recognizing that environmental harm can be a threat to state security, an emerging consensus accepts that the object of security pol-

---

[67] L. Brown, Vital Signs 83 (1997). Brown estimates the number of environmental refugees at 25 million, some two million more than "traditional" refugees.

[68] *See, for example,* J.T. Matthews, *Redefining Security,* Foreign Aff. (Spring 1989), R.H. Ullman, *Redefining Security,* International Security (Summer 1983), and Daniel Deudney & Richard Matthew eds., Contested Grounds: Security and Conflict in the New Environmental Politics (1999).

icy can no longer be confined to the state, but must range to governance levels above (*e.g.*, regional and international) and below (*e.g.*, sub-regions and individuals) the state. The 1986 nuclear meltdown at Chernobyl and its attendant devastation of neighboring human populations and ecosystems, and the global recognition of the common threat to humanity posed by the declining ozone layer, placed individual health and international environmental governance within the domain of security institutions.

There is also growing agreement that environmental degradation, inequitable access to resources and predation of valuable plants, animals and minerals are among the most important sources of human insecurity. They can, in many instances, trigger or fuel violence, and increase vulnerability to natural disasters.[69] More sustainable and equitable management of the environment can be a cost-effective means for building social cohesion and reinforce mechanisms for collaboration across social and political boundaries. In sum, environmental protection has become an essential part of conflict prevention.

There are few legal instruments addressing this issue. None of the refugee treaties, for example, defines refugee to include those fleeing environmental harm or devastation. Such individuals do not, therefore, qualify for asylum within the territory of another state. Despite the absence of legal measures, the issue of environmental security has emerged in national policies and international discussions. In 1996 the United States created a high level position to focus on international environmental issues that bear on national security.

As an example of conflict prevention, the governments of Colombia and Panama suggested that establishing a series of nature parks along their common border could reduce tension there. Earlier, the United States and Mexico established Chamizal National Memorial in 1963 as a key part of the agreement that resolved 100-year-old border dispute along the Rio Grande. Another combined environmental/security action can be seen in the Arctic Military Environmental Cooperation (AMEC) Program, a forum for dialogue and joint activities among U.S., Russian, and Norwegian military and environmental officials to ensure that the militaries of the respective nations help assess, preserve, and repair the Arctic environment. The program addresses Arctic environmental issues that are related to the militaries' capabilities and unique activities. Currently, six projects fall under the AMEC, including four radioactive waste projects and projects dealing with military base cleanup and the treatment of shipboard wastes.

---

69   STATE OF THE ART REVIEW OF ENVIRONMENT, SECURITY AND DEVELOPMENT COOPERATION (IUCN/OECD, 1999); M. BERDAL, & D. MALONE, GREED AND GRIEVANCE: ECONOMIC AGENDAS IN CIVIL WAR (IPA, 2000); and J. ABRAMOVITZ, UNNATURAL DISASTERS (Worldwatch Institute, 2001).

UNEP began an initiative for South-Eastern European and Central Asian states for presentation to the Kiev Summit in May 2003.[70] UNEP's report maps out the environmental concerns with likely security implications and outlines the environmental policy tools best suited for promoting peace in the regions. A subsequent phase of activities will commission and verify, through multi-stakeholder consultations, environmental security priorities and promote appropriate remedies and implementation strategies.

According to UNEP, principal environmental issues with implications for regional security include:

- Environmentally-induced migration as a consequence of natural resources degradation and exclusion from resources, or transboundary air pollution.
- Increasing water scarcity. Poor water quality as a consequence of pollution and lack of infrastructure is among the major causes of infant mortality in the two regions. Many of the major cities are dependent on and are over-exploiting their groundwater resources. Water pollution and scarcity may worsen in the near term as a consequence of economic recovery.
- Aging and obsolete hydropower and nuclear energy generation facilities, chemical production facilities and infrastructure.
- Land contamination, soil erosion and flawed irrigation schemes creating food insecurity. Of Europe's total land area, 12 percent is affected by water erosion and 4 percent by wind erosion, generally as a consequence of unsustainable agriculture, salinization and water logging.
- Severe over-harvesting of forest resources in Armenia, Georgia and Central Asia, triggering avalanches and diminishing water quality.
- Over-fishing of transboundary marine and coastal areas, including the North Sea, Baltic Sea, Mediterranean, Black Sea and Azov Sea. The Caspian Sea, for example., possesses 85 percent of the world's sturgeon and 90 percent of its black caviar. Shared between five states, it is increasingly threatened by extensive hydromodifications, growing oil exploration, and overfishing (including illegal traffic in caviar).

---

[70]   As UNEP reports, "Regional inequalities figure prominently in local tensions—per capita GDP in Western Europe is ten times that of the rest of Europe, whereas GDP in many countries of Eastern Europe and Central Asia fell (for some by as much as 40%) after 1990 as a consequence of the economic collapse of the East Bloc. Internal economic fragility place great pressure on newly-democratic transition states. Ensuring economic development and responding to governance challenges in the context of deepening regional integration will intensify pressure on natural resources unless mechanisms are put in place in advance to manage the transition."

- Coupling of environmental and ethnic grievances to fuel political insurgencies.

In sum, environmental degradation and scarcities of resources threaten to undermine the way of life of populations around the world and the stability of internal governance structures. Environmental security calls for action to prevent the degradation and scarcity from leading to internal and international conflict. The concept also implies and requires the maintenance or reestablishment of ecological balance because an emphasis on conflict prevention alone is not effective to secure long-term security. Emphasis on protecting the environment attacks some of the root causes of conflict and at the same time highlights the common concern of humanity in this issue.

BIBLIOGRAPHY

ARKIN, W.M. ET AL., MODERN WARFARE AND THE ENVIRONMENT: A CASE STUDY OF THE GULF WAR (1991).

AUSTIN, JAY E. & BRUCH, CARL E. eds., THE ENVIRONMENTAL CONSEQUENCES OF WAR: LEGAL, ECONOMIC, AND SCIENTIFIC PERSPECTIVES (2000).

Bostian, Ida, *The Environmental Consequences of the Kosovo Conflict and the NATO Bombing of Serbia,* 1999 COLO. J. INT'L ENVTL. L. & POL'Y 230 (2000).

Brunnee, J. & Toope, S., *Environmental Security and Freshwater Resources: Ecosystem Regime Building,* 91 AJIL 26 (1997).

N. P. GLEDITSCH ed., CONFLICT AND THE ENVIRONMENT (1997).

Green, L., *The Environment and the Law of Conventional Warfare,* 29 CAN. YB INT'L L. 222 (1991).

Liebler, A., *Deliberate Wartime Environmental Damage: New Challenges for International Law,* 23 CAL. W. INT'L L.J. 67 (1992).

MEYERS, N. & KENT, J., ENVIRONMENTAL EXODUS (1995).

MOLLARD-BANNELIER, LA PROTECTION DE L'ENVIRONNEMENT EN TEMPS DE CONFLIT ARME (2001).

Plant, G., ENVIRONMENTAL PROTECTION AND THE LAWS OF WAR (1993).

Schafer, B., *The Relationship Between the International Law of Armed Conflict and Environmental Protection: The Need to Reevaluate What Types of Conduct are Permissible During Hostilities,* 19 CAL. W. INT'L L.J. 287 (1989).

Roberts, A., *Environmental Destruction in the 1991 Gulf War,* 291 INT'L REV. RED CROSS 538 (1992);

Schmidt, Michael, *Green War: An Assessment of the Environmental Law of International Armed Conflict,* YALE J. INT'L L. 22 (1997).

Seacor, J.E., *Environmental Terrorism: Lessons from the Oil Fires of Kuwait,* 10 AM U.J. INT'L L. & POL'Y 481 (1994).

WESTING, A. ed., ENVIRONMENTAL HAZARDS OF WAR (1990).

WESTING, A. ed., ENVIRONMENTAL WARFARE: A TECHNICAL, LEGAL AND POL-
ICY APPRAISAL (1984).

Weston, B., *Nuclear Weapons and the World Court: Ambiguity's Consensus*, 7
TRANSNAT'L L. & CONTEMP. PROBS. 371 (1997).

CHAPTER 17

ENVIRONMENTAL PROTECTION AND ECONOMIC ACTIVITIES

International environmental law does not and cannot develop in isolation, because all human activities have an impact on the environment. Many organized and common endeavors have their own laws and procedures with goals specific to them. Previous chapters have discussed some of the problems that arise in interrelating or reconciling environmental protection with, *e.g.*, human rights, armed conflict, and various uses of the earth's waters. The present chapter presents an overview of economic activities, especially those that have an international dimension, and the relationship of the laws and institutions governing them with those seeking to protect the environment. The chapter looks first at efforts to address poverty and how this has coalesced with environmental and social concerns to give content to the concept of sustainable development. A second and related problem is external or international debt. Third, the role of foreign investment and the conduct of multinational companies is presented followed by some examples of unilateral national laws given extraterritorial effect and the difficulties they pose. Finally, the chapter offers an overview of international trade law, with its emphasis on eliminating barriers to trade, and the conflicts that have emerged between its aims and those of environmental protection.

A. Poverty Reduction and Environmental Protection

Developing countries contain more than three-quarters of the world's population[1] and one-quarter of them, or over a billion individuals, live in absolute poverty, defined as surviving on less than $1 a day.[2] For middle income countries, the figure of under $2 per day is an equivalent measure and it applies to some 2.8 billion people, or half the population of developing countries.[3] These numbers have not changed substantially in the past decade. In its preamble the Stockholm Declaration recognized that

---

[1]   ILO, *Environment and the World of Work*, Report of the Director-General 7 (1990).

[2]   UNDP, Choices for the Poor (2001).

[3]   World Bank, World Development Indicators 2003.

[i]n the developing countries most of the environmental problems are caused by underdevelopment. Millions continue to live far below the minimum levels required for health and sanitation. Therefore, the developing countries must direct their efforts to development, bearing in mind their priorities and the need to safeguard and improve the environment. For the same purpose, the industrialized countries should make efforts to reduce the gap between themselves and the developing countries . . .

Prior to the Stockholm Conference many poor countries did not accept the necessity of global cooperation to protect the environment,[4] because such problems were considered predominately an ailment of rich, industrialized countries. At Stockholm, developing countries seeking to become industrialized chose to ignore the environmental costs of industrialization. The same countries also suspected that wealthy nations of the North subordinated foreign economic development to environmental protection, considering the former less urgent than pollution and nature protection. Some feared that funds previously dedicated to development would be diverted to fight environmental deterioration. These fears seemed to be borne out several days before the Stockholm meeting, when the Third United Nations Conference on Trade and Development produced particularly disappointing results on development aid.[5]

This background explains the parts of the Stockholm Declaration and Action Plan that are dedicated to economic and social development as a condition of environmental protection. Various principles promote transfer of financial and technical aid, stability of prices and adequate remuneration for basic commodities and raw materials, enhancement of the potential for progress of developing countries, and international assistance to help developing countries face costs which can delay incorporation of environmental safeguards in development planning. Principle 23 first expressed the now widely-recognized notion that a distinction may be necessary in applying envi-

---

    [4]   In fact, prior to Stockholm, a General Assembly Resolution on development and the environment stated that standards to preserve the environment "as a general rule will have to be defined at the national level and, in all cases, will have to reflect conditions and systems of values prevailing in each country." Furthermore "each country has the right to formulate, in accordance with its own particular situation and in full enjoyment of its national sovereignty, its own national policies on the human environment, including criteria for the evaluation of projects . . . ," G.A. Res. 2849, *adopted* Dec. 20, 1971; U.N. Doc. A/Res. 2849 (XXVI) (1972); 11 I.L.M. 422. (The vote was 85-2-34, the United States and the United Kingdom opposed.)

    [5]   A. Kiss, & J.-D. Sicault, *La Conférence des Nations Unies sur l'environnement,* A.F.D.I. 603, 624 (1972).

ronmental norms according to the state of development of different countries, a concept now incorporated in many environmental agreements as the principle of "common but differentiated responsibilities."

In the aftermath of Stockholm, consensus emerged about the need for global cooperation to safeguard the planet. The December 12, 1974, Charter of Economic Rights and Duties of States, adopted by the United Nations General Assembly, proclaims that protection, preservation and management of the environment for present and future generations is the responsibility of all states and that they should strive to halt detrimental policies in environmental matters and develop programs conforming to this responsibility. The appointment of the Brundtland Commission in 1983 can be seen as a further confirmation of the need to integrate development and environment; it was the Commission that first articulated and defined the concept of "sustainable development."

Following the report of the Brundtland Commission, developing countries manifested greater concern with environmental issues. In 1989, the neighboring states of the Amazon basin adopted the Amazon Declaration,[6] expressing support for the newly created Amazon Special Environmental Commission, established to foster development and conserve natural resources and the environment. While reaffirming the sovereign right of each country to manage freely its natural resources, the Declaration expressed the willingness of the signatories to cooperate and to carry out protection and conservation of the environment in the region for the benefit of present and future generations. Environmental protection was linked, however, to resolution of the foreign debt crisis, economic development and growth, "an essential condition for the protection, conservation, exploitation and rational utilization" of the region.

In June 1989, the OAU convened a Ministerial meeting in Kampala to assess environmental problems affecting the African region and evolve a common strategy for environmental management and sustainable development. The study undertook an overall evaluation of progress made on implementation of the recommendations contained in the Brundtland Report. The result was adoption of the Kampala Declaration, which identified several priority areas for achieving environmentally-sound sustainable development: managing demographic change and pressures, achieving food self-sufficiency and food security, ensuring efficient and equitable use of water resources, securing greater energy self-sufficiency, optimizing industrial production, maintaining species and ecosystems, and halting and reversing desertification.

In a more widespread initiative, the EC and some 70 African, Caribbean and Pacific states (ACP) signed the Lome IV agreement on December 15,

---

6   May 6, 1989; U.N. Doc. A/44/275, E/1989/79, Annex, May 15, 1989; 28 I.L.M. 1303 (1989).

1989,[7] which included a chapter, Title I, specifically devoted to protection of the environment and conservation of natural resources, deemed to be fundamental objectives sought by the ACP states with the support of the EC.[8] The Lome agreement was reaffirmed in a revised form November 4, 1995, in Mauritius. The EC-ACP states replaced Lome IV by an Agreement on Partnership between ACP and EU states, signed in Cotonou on June 23, 2000. The agreement calls on the states to take into account questions related to the transport and disposal of hazardous waste (Art. 32.1.d), but otherwise does not discuss environmental matters.

The OECD also adopted measures to link environmental protection to development assistance. It recommended an environmental checklist for development assistance, calling on member countries to ensure that bilateral and multilateral development assistance takes into account environmental considerations in the identification, planning, implementation and evaluation of those development projects which are proposed for funding.[9] Despite generalized concern with environmental protection, some developing countries continue to view such conditions as constraints on development opportunities and national sovereignty as well as attempts to protect markets rather than the environment.

During the 1980s, several developing countries began to take a leadership role in environmental matters, especially on the issue of transfer of hazardous substances and wastes. They also ratified most global environmental instruments.[10] Zaire initiated the World Charter for Nature in the United Nations General Assembly while Brazil agreed to host the 1992 United Nations Conference on Environment and Development. The title of the Rio Conference reflects the importance given to addressing both topics equally.

The texts adopted at Rio affirm the central concept of sustainable development, referring to the right to development, but stating that it must be fulfilled so as to equitably meet developmental and environmental needs of present and future generations (Principle 3). Principle 4 of the Rio Declaration emphasizes the merger of environmental and developmental concerns, stating that in order to achieve sustainable development, envi-

---

7   *Le Courrier*, ACP-CEE, No. 120 (Mar.–Apr. 1990); 29 I.L.M. 783 (1990).

8   Art. 33, Lome IV.

9   OECD, Doc. C(89)2(Final), Mar. 2, 1989; 28 I.L.M. 1314 (1989).

10   On the whole, the participation of Third World countries in global instruments is comparable to that of industrialized states. Among the contracting parties to the UNESCO World Heritage Convention are 31 of the 51 African states, 15 of 20 Latin American states and 22 of 38 Asian states. Still more comprehensive is participation in CITES: 36 African states have ratified or signed it, while all but one Latin American and half the Asian states (19 out of 38) are parties to it. Most of the UNEP regional seas conventions also include developing countries.

ronmental protection shall constitute an integral part of the development process and cannot be considered in isolation from it. The Rio Declaration contains several other principles that reflect the concerns of the developing countries: Principle 7 proclaims common but differentiated responsibilities, and the special responsibility of developed countries "in view of the pressures their societies place on the global environment;" Principle 8 adds that states should reduce and eliminate unsustainable patterns of production and consumption and promote demographic policies; Principle 12 advocates a "supportive and open economic system," avoiding "arbitrary or unjustifiable discrimination or a disguised restriction on international trade" in the use of trade measures for environmental purposes and calling for measures to be adopted on the basis of "international consensus." One of the four main parts of Agenda 21, the Rio program of action, concerns the socio-economic dimensions of sustainable development.

During and after the Rio Conference, commentators expressed contrasting views on the impact of environmental measures on economic development. One view called measures to control pollution inflationary, leading to increased production costs, and in part responsible for raising levels of unemployment. A contrasting perspective claimed that effective environmental policies can stimulate technological progress and create new forms of enterprise and economic development, resulting in growth of job opportunities. An ILO study on the relationship between environmental protection and economic development concluded that neither of these viewpoints can be held to be generally valid. The "relationship is empirical rather than theoretical. It is extremely difficult to draw conclusions or generalize about the relationship between environmental policies and employment."[11]

There are several reasons why many developing countries have given enhanced attention to environmental protection. First, the link between environmental deterioration and poverty and its consequences became obvious, including the fact that pollution from urban growth, lack of water quality and quantity, and desertification, harm developing countries more than industrialized nations. Second, the natural resources of poor countries overwhelmingly bear the cost of unregulated development. Third, health, nutrition, and general well-being of the peoples of developing countries depend on the integrity and productivity of the environment and the compatibility of the development process with the imperatives of conservation. These principles were strictly formulated in the development strategy elaborated for the Third United Nations Development Decade.[12]

Fourth, Third World countries increasingly realized the dangers of the "exportation of pollution" by companies or individuals seeking to profit

---

[11]　ILO, *Environment and the World of Work*, Report of the Director-General 42 (1990).

[12]　G.A. Res. 35/36, Jan. 20, 1981.

from the weakness of protective legislation or enforcement mechanisms in developing countries. Especially acute problems have arisen from exports of dangerous products prohibited or regulated in industrialized states, the dumping of industrial waste products, and the installation of dangerous industrial operations. The accident at an American-owned chemical factory in Bhopal, India, which caused 2,500 deaths in December 1984, emphasized the problem.

Perhaps most importantly, the long-held assumption that conditions for reconciling growth and the attainment of environmental quality involved a tradeoff, with environmental quality reached only at the expense of higher incomes and improved levels of welfare, began to give way to the idea that the development process could be compatible with or even enhanced by environmental protection, as reflected in the notion of "sustainable development."

Serious issues remain about how to implement and integrate environmental protection and economic development, many centering on the problem of environmental costs. Developing countries often see increased efforts to implement stringent environmental safeguards across boundaries as creating new non-tariff trade barriers or at least as imposing significant costs and constraints on production processes or products, resulting in a loss of competitive advantage.

At the same time, efforts since UNCED have tried to address poverty reduction and environmental protection through various programs. The United Nations Development Program and the European Commission, for example, are engaged in a joint initiative on poverty and the environment aimed at identifying concrete policy recommendations and practical measures that address the environmental concerns of the poor in developing countries. The programs seek more localized, community-based approaches to natural resource management and sustainable development, informed by an understanding that the various groups in a society often experience environmental problems in very different ways. The goal of the Poverty and Environment Initiative is to provide a forum for practitioners, policy-makers and researchers working in this area to share their experiences and identify solutions.

In September 2000, 147 heads of state and government, and 189 nations in total, endorsed the United Nations Millennium Declaration,[13] expressing their committment to making the right to development a reality for everyone and to freeing the entire human race from want. They acknowledged that progress is based on sustainable economic growth, which must focus on the poor, with human rights at the center. The objective of the Declaration is to promote "a comprehensive approach and a coordinated strategy, tackling many problems simultaneously across a broad front." The

---

[13]　　United Nations Millennium Declaration, A/RES/55/2.

Declaration calls for halving by the year 2015, the number of people who live on less than one dollar a day. This effort also involves supporting the Agenda 21 principles of sustainable development. Direct support from the richer countries, in the form of aid, trade, debt relief and investment is to be provided to help the developing countries. To help track progress, the United Nations Secretariat and the specialized agencies of the UN system, as well as representatives of IMF, the World Bank and OECD defined a set of time-bound and measurable goals and targets for combating poverty, environmental degradation and other goals of the program. International experts also selected relevant indicators to be used to assess progress over the period from 1990 to 2015, when targets are expected to be met. Each year, the Secretary-General prepares a report on progress achieved towards implementing the Declaration, based on data on the 48 selected indicators, aggregated at global and regional levels. The political framework for achieving the Millennium Development Goals was provided by an agreement between North and South reached in 2002 in Monterrey, Mexico. This global compact, "Financing for Development" was reaffirmed at the World Summit for Sustainable Development held in Johannesburg, South Africa, in August 2002, which determined that "poverty eradication, changing consumption and production patterns and protecting and managing the natural resource base for economic and social development are overarching objectives of and essential requirements for sustainable development."[14]

B. International Debt

The environmental damage that results from conditions of poverty is most evident in the case of developing countries burdened with severe foreign debt and dependent on a narrow range of exports to earn the foreign exchange to meet their debt obligations. Policy-makers tend to take less account of environmental consequences when they are faced with short-term financial pressures. This pressure is increased by the fact that the developing countries lack the capacity of the industrialized countries to undertake research on more environmentally desirable technologies and processes.

World indebtedness of states increased dramatically between 1982 and 1999, growing from U.S. $838 billion to over $2 trillion.[15] Half the debtor countries are in sub-Saharan Africa, but their total debt is about one-third that owed by Latin America. The debt amounts to roughly one-half of the combined GNP of developing countries or approximately ten times the debt

---

[14] Johannesburg Declaration on Sustainable Development, A/CONF. 199/20, para. 11.

[15] A. van Trotsenburg, & A. MacArthur, *The HIPC Initiative: Delivering Debt Relief to Poor Countries* 2 (IMF, 1999).

outstanding during the worst years of the Great Depression. The debt of the 40 poorest countries is $170 billion, on average more than four times their annual export earnings and in excess of their annual GNPs. Thirty-three African countries have unsustainable debt levels. One-half of export earnings of Africa goes to service debt and thirty African countries had to reschedule their debt in the late 1980s. The declining exchange rate of developing countries—during the 1980s there was a 40 percent loss involving more than 80 developing countries—also had an inflationary impact making imports more expensive and often reducing investment and output.

Structural adjustment loans (SALs) became popular after 1980 when the first such loan was made by the World Bank. More than 50 countries received such loans in the 1980s and they became a major part of the Bank's development assistance program during this period. They allowed the Bank to play an active role, in theory, in helping developing countries overcome structural weaknesses in their programs for rapid development. SALs often introduced severe conditionality in clauses that allowed the lender to directly influence policy and institutions in the debtor states. A study undertaken by the World Bank[16] found, however, that the high degree of compliance with conditions set down in SALs had been coupled with a worsening of the mal-distribution of incomes.

The problem for debtor countries is that debt servicing hampers the achievement of other important objectives, including eradication of poverty, combating global environmental damage, and establishing global conditions for trade and capital flows conducive to overall growth with a narrowing of income/welfare gap between rich and poor. In 1996, the World Bank and the IMF launched the Highly Indebted Poor Country Initiative agreed to by governments around the world. It was a comprehensive approach to reduce the external debt of the world's poorest, most heavily indebted countries, and represented an important step forward in placing debt relief within an overall framework of poverty reduction. A major review in 1999 resulted in a significant enhancement of the original framework to produce even greater relief.

An innovative program that emerged from non-governmental organizations allows developing countries to pay off part of their external debt by committing themselves to invest funds in environmental protection.[17] These "debt for nature swaps" have been undertaken by private foundations, commercial banks and a few national governments. In October 1990 the United States included debt-for-nature swaps in the "Enterprise for the Americas" initiative. Congress also approved conversion of debt into nature conser-

---

[16]   *Id.* at 70, *citing* R. Faini & J. de Melo, *Adjustment, Investment and the Real Exchange in Developing Countries,* ECONOMIC POLICY (World Bank, 1990).

[17]   *See* E.B. WEISS, IN FAIRNESS TO FUTURE GENERATIONS, at 157–59 (1996).

vancy projects. Scandinavian states have also used debt-for-nature exchanges to promote environmental protection by the Baltic States that were formerly part of the Soviet Union.

C. Private Economic Enterprises

Business associations, like other NGOs, have long been active and have expanded their international presence in recent years. The International Chamber of Commerce participated in League of Nations proceedings and even signed some legal instruments.[18] Today, many multinational corporations have an enormous influence on the global economy and environmental protection, being linked with foreign affiliates throughout the world.

Organized business groups participate in the international arena as NGOs, subject to the same requirements and enjoying the same rights as other NGOs. Like other NGOs, business entities often are excluded from international dispute settlement procedures, even when they are the real parties in interest.[19] Some groups organize for specific issues, such as the World Business Council on Sustainable Development that participates in multilateral forums relating to the environment and was particularly effective in climate change negotiations. The Global Climate Coalition is a national industry group that represents the interests of fossil fuel and transportation companies in the U.S.

The role of business entities is particularly important in international environmental law, where regulation most often is aimed at private economic activities, although it is states that sign the agreements. The Energy Charter Treaty,[20] for example, requires state parties to ensure that state enterprises and other "privileged" entities conduct their operations in a manner consistent with the Treaty. Each state party is also required to take reasonable measures to ensure observance by regional and local governments and authorities within its area. These obligations likely will bring in private entities acting under governmental authority.

---

[18] The ICC delegate signed League instruments relating to import/export restrictions and customs formalities. *See* LYMAN C. WHITE, INTERNATIONAL NON-GOVERNMENTAL ORGANIZATIONS: THEIR PURPOSES, METHODS AND ACCOMPLISHMENTS, at 22 (1951).

[19] *See* G. Richard Shell, *Participation of Nongovernmental Parties in the World Trade Organization: The Trade Stakeholders Model and Participation by Nonstate Parties in the World Trade Organization*, 17 U. PA. J. INT'L ECON. L. 359, 368 (1996).

[20] The Energy Charter Treaty (Dec. 17 1994).

Since the 1980s, two major developments have increased the role of private enterprise and brought it under increased scrutiny. These developments are globalization and privatization or deregulation. Together they have shifted state power to the private sector in many areas of the world. In Central and Eastern Europe, the transition to market economies has dismantled many state structures, but many other regions have seen a less dramatic but equally profound direction favoring private investment and freeing of markets. Additional impetus to the growing power of the private sector has come from globalization, the integration of markets, communications, and national economies. Policies and laws are being redrafted in many countries in order to provide investment incentives.

With growing power comes growing responsibility. International efforts are being made to ensure socially-responsible investment and business conduct, including in respect to the environment. In addition to corporate codes of conduct for self-regulation, described in Chapter 6, international norms are developing through various institutions and transnational litigation is increasingly attempting to hold business enterprises accountable for their environmental and social policies.

In accordance with its general approach, OECD has drafted voluntary principles and standards for responsible business conduct, jointly addressed by its member governments to multinational enterprises.[21] Section V of the Guidelines affirms that enterprises should take due account of the need to protect the environment, within the framework of laws, regulations and administrative practices in the countries in which they operate and in consideration of relevant international agreements, principles, objectives and standards. In particular, enterprises should establish and maintain a system of environmental management appropriate to the enterprise, including collection and evaluation of adequate and timely information regarding the environmental impacts of their activities, the establishment of measurable objectives and where appropriate, targets for improved environmental performance and regular monitoring and verification of progress toward such objectives or targets. They should provide the public and employees with adequate and timely information on the potential environmental impacts of the activities of the enterprise and engage in consultation with the communities directly affected by their environmental policies and by their implementation, as far as this is compatible with concerns about cost, business confidentiality and protection of intellectual property rights. They should assess and address in decision-making the foreseeable environmental impacts associated with the processes, goods and services of the enterprise over their full life cycle and if necessary they should prepare an appropriate environmental impact assessment. They should use a precau-

---

21   OECD, Guidelines for Multinational Enterprises (June 27, 2000), 40 I.L.M. 237 (2000).

tionary approach where there are threats of serious damage to the environment and maintain contingency plans for preventing serious environmental damage. They also should seek to improve corporate environmental performance by adopting adequate technologies and operating procedures, by developing products or services that have no undue environmental impact, by promoting higher levels of awareness among customers of the environmental implications of using the products and services of the enterprise and by providing adequate education and training to employees in environmental matters. Finally, enterprises are encouraged to contribute to the development of environmentally meaningful and economically efficient public policy, for example, by means of partnerships.

For its part, the UN Sub-Commission on Human Rights drafted Fundamental Human Rights Principles for Business Enterprises in 2002.[22] Article 24 of the draft states that businesses must respect the rights of local communities by avoiding endangerment of "the health, environment, culture and institutions of indigenous peoples and communities. . . ."[23] Businesses are also "to respect international agreements and standards with regard to the environment as well as human rights; . . . take due account of the need to protect the environment, public health, and safety, and shall generally conduct their activities in a manner contributing to the wider goal of sustainable development."[24] In its commentary to the draft, the Sub-Commission states "businesses shall respect the right to a clean and healthy environment in light of the relationship between the environment and human rights."[25]

Within NAFTA, Chapter 11 contains investment rules that operate in parallel with trade rules to regulate investors and foreign investment activities in host countries. Article 1114(1) provides: "Nothing in this Chapter shall be construed to prevent a Party from adopting, maintaining or enforcing any measure otherwise consistent with this Chapter that it considers appropriate to ensure that investment activity is undertaken in a manner sensitive to environmental concerns." The second paragraph of the same article recognizes that it is "inappropriate to encourage investment by relaxing domestic health, safety or environmental measures." Accordingly a party should not "waive or otherwise derogate from, or offer to waive or otherwise derogate from, such measures as an encouragement for the establishment, acquisition, expansion or retention in its territory of an investment of an investor." At the same time, Chapter 11 seeks to protect the security of foreign investment.

In the event of a breach of Chapter 11, an investor may bring a claim for damages to himself or his company within three years of the harm alleged

---

[22] U.N. Doc. E/CN.4/Sub.2/2002/WG.2/WP.1/Add.1.

[23] *Id.*, art. 24.

[24] *Id.*, art. 12.

[25] *Id.*, art. 12, Comment m.

to arise out of the breach. A Notice of Intent to Submit a Claim to Arbitration must be filed at least 90 days before the actual claim is filed (NAFTA Art. 1119). Investors must waive their right to initiate any other dispute settlement procedure. It appears from the practice of the tribunals that the rule of exhaustion of local remedies applies. Procedures are governed by the rules of ICSID or UNCITRAL which are less transparent than other international procedures. Hearings before a NAFTA tribunal generally have not been open to the public, but the U.S. and Canada have sought to make available submissions to and decisions from the arbitral panels through official government websites. Awards may be contested in domestic courts.

Most of the complaints under Chapter 11 have concerned the requirement of non-discrimination, that each party treat an investor no less favorably than it treats a domestic investor "in like circumstances."[26] In these cases the NAFTA tribunals have stated that the phrase "like circumstances" must take into account NAFTA's concern with the environment as well as the need to avoid trade distortions that are not justified by environmental concerns. A few matters have found direct conflict between investment activities and environmental protection. The *Metalclad* case, for example, arose from a complaint of alleged indirect expropriation because of government environmental regulation. The Tribunal agreed that Metalclad's investment in a hazardous waste facility was expropriated by the denial of a construction and operating permit contrary to Mexican law and the issuance of an "Ecological Decree" declaring the site a nature reserve in order to preserve a rare cactus.[27] Other Chapter 11 cases have similarly alleged expropriation due to environmental regulations.[28] Efforts on the global level to draft a multilateral agreement on investment have not succeeded, in part due to opposition from environmental groups about early drafts that appeared to omit environmental protection from their scope.

---

[26]   *See Pope and Talbot v. Canada, Award on the Merits of Phase 2* (Apr. 10, 2001) (imposition of fees by Canada on lumber exports to the U.S. found non-discriminatory); *S.D. Myers v. Canada* (Nov. 13, 2000) (Canadian prohibition on export of PCB wastes to U.S. found discriminatory); *In the Matter of Cross-border Trucking Services* (Feb. 6, 2001) (finding Mexican and U.S. trucking companies to be in like circumstances and U.S. ban on Mexican trucks to be unjustified).

[27]   *In the Matter of an Arbitration Pursuant to Chapter 11 of NAFTA between Metalclad and the United Mexican States*, ICSID Case No. ARB(AF)/97/1. A Canadian Court reviewed the Tribunal's decision and agreed that there had been an expropriation, but only on the second assertion.

[28]   *See Ethyl Corp. v. Canada; S.D. Meyers v. Canada, Partial Award* (Nov. 13, 2000); *Pope and Talbot v. Canada* (Interim Award, June 26, 2000); *Azinian;* ICSID Case No. ARB(AF)97/2; Methanex: (UNCITRAL), (Aug. 7, 2002), *available at* <http://www.naftaclaims.com>; *Methanex v. United States; Waste Management Inc. v. United Mexican States*, ICSID Case No. ARB(AF)98/2.

Independently of efforts to set international standards for corporate conduct, companies engaged in multinational business operations are finding themselves the subject of litigation over their practices. Bhopal was an early instance where the conduct of a company gave rise to litigation in the home state of the company, Union Carbide,[29] as well as in the state where the event took place. More recently, plaintiffs alleging injuries due to pollution—usually linked to human rights violations—have invoked broad jurisdictional provisions to file lawsuits in the country where the company is registered or has its home office. Most of these cases have been filed in the United States pursuant to the federal Alien Tort Claim Act.[30]

D. Extraterritorial Application of National Laws

With increasing awareness of environmental interdependence, states may enact national laws that are intended to promote environmental protection in other countries, promote environmental protection of the global commons, or stimulate the adoption of multilateral agreements by seeking to influence a foreign government to refrain from acting or to compel it to act, either in its domestic policies or towards third states. As reflected in Principle 12 of the Rio Declaration, there is intense debate over unilateral measures applied extraterritorially to raise or enforce environmental standards.

States often enact trade restrictions to ensure that domestic environmental goals, such as consumer safety, are attained. A state's ban on the sale of locally-produced products containing a hazardous substance will be ineffective if the same or similar goods can be imported. In other circumstances, local laws may seek to induce or coerce another country to change or better enforce its own national environmental laws or policies. Finally, domestic laws may seek to contribute to international aims such as preservation of the global climate.

Generally, a state has authority to apply its laws with respect to: (1) conduct that takes place within its territory; (2) the status of persons or things within its territory; (3) conduct outside its territory that has a substantial effect within its territory; (4) activities of its nationals both outside and inside its territory; and (5) certain conduct outside its territory by persons other than nationals that is directed against the security of the state. Some

---

[29]   In fact, some 145 lawsuits were filed against Union Carbide in the U.S. seeking over $250 billion in damages on behalf of more than 400,000 injured persons. *See In re Union Carbide Corp. Gas Plant Disaster*, 809 F.2d 195 (2d Cir. 1987) (affirming dismissal for *forum non conveniens* conditioned upon defendant consenting to personal jurisdiction in India).

[30]   28 U.S.C. § 1350. *See, e.g., Jota v. Texaco Inc.*, 157 F.2d 153 (2d Cir. 1998); *Wiwa v. Royal Dutch Petroleum*, 226 F.3d 88 (2d Cir. 2000); *Doe v. Unocal*, 110 F. Supp. 2d 1294 (C.D. Cal. 2000).

environmental agreements require that domestic laws apply to the full range of a state's jurisdiction, *e.g.*, the Biodiversity Convention.[31] Many states now apply all or some of their environmental laws broadly to activities of their nationals wherever they take place.

The U.S. National Environmental Protection Act (NEPA) applies to require an environmental impact assessment when extraterritorial actions have direct or indirect impacts in the United States.[32] When the environmental impact occurs *only* in foreign countries, NEPA does not apply. However, U.S. Executive Order 12114, signed in January 1979, requires analysis of environmental impacts from any major federal action significantly affecting the environment of the global commons or the environment of a foreign nation, and major actions outside the United States which significantly affect protected natural or ecological resources of global importance. Exceptions are provided for, *inter alia*, armed conflicts, intelligence activities, arms transfers, disaster and emergency relief action.

Another U.S. domestic law seeking to enhance environmental protection is the so-called "Pelosi Amendment."[33] It requires the United States Executive Director for each multilateral development bank (including the World Bank), to refrain from voting in favor of any proposed action by the bank that would have a significant effect on the human environment unless an environmental assessment has been prepared and circulated to the bank and other interested organizations at least 120 days before the date of the vote. The assessment analyzing the environmental impacts of the proposed action and its alternatives can be prepared by the borrowing country or the lending institution and must be made available to the board of directors of the institution. Absent compelling circumstances, the assessment must also be made available to the bank, affected groups and local non-governmental organizations. In practice, the Pelosi Amendment extends NEPA's broad coverage to multilateral development bank operations.

In a related development, the U.S. Export-Import Bank, a 60-year-old independent agency that finances overseas sales of U.S. goods and services, has incorporated environmental considerations into its lending policies. The Bank guarantees loans for U.S. exporters and repayment of loans by foreign purchasers of U.S. goods and services and often provides credit for risks commercial banks will not accept. In 1995, as required by statute, the Bank adopted a detailed set of Environmental Guidelines to consider the

---

[31]   Article 4 provides that the jurisdictional scope of the Convention applies, in relation to each contracting party, to areas within the limits of national jurisdiction, *i.e.*, land and maritime zones, and to processes and activities carried out under its jurisdiction or control, whether within or beyond the limits of its national jurisdiction.

[32]   *See Sierra Club v. Adams*, 578 F.2d 389 (D.C. Cir. 1978).

[33]   22 U.S.C.A. § 262m-7.

environmental consequences of proposed transactions prior to approving export finance.[34] Applicants are required to submit for evaluation information about the project's environmental impacts. The Guidelines establish standards for air quality, water quality, waste management and noise for projects in specific industry sectors (*e.g.*, mining, pulp and paper, energy). Certain transactions that do not raise significant environmental issues are exempt from review procedures. Projects that do not meet all the environmental guidelines are reviewed on a case-by-case basis by the Bank's Board of Directors, taking into account mitigating effects and circumstances. Financing may be conditioned on the implementation of mitigating measures.

The U.S. Congress also directed the United States Overseas Investment Corporation (OPIC) to take account of the environmental effects of projects in determining whether to provide insurance, financing, or reinsurance for a development project. OPIC provides insurance for American investments in new ventures and expansions of existing enterprises, including protection against limits on repatriation of local currency, expropriation, and political violence. Congress has directed OPIC "to the maximum degree possible," consistent with its development purposes, to refuse to "insure, reinsure, guarantee or finance any investment in connection with a project which the Corporation determines will pose an unreasonable or major environmental, health, or safety hazard, or will result in the significant degradation of national parks or similar protected areas."[35] OPIC screens all investment requests to determine whether they meet the environmental standards. Major projects will require preparation of an environmental impact assessment.

Other national measures are directed specifically at international trade, including the EC enforcement of CITES trade bans, Austria's brief effort to regulate trade in tropical hardwoods, and the U.S. restrictions on dolphin-unsafe tuna. Agenda 21, based almost entirely on earlier work at UNCTAD, calls for reversing unilateral trade barriers that restrict access to markets, as well as for reducing external debt. It insists upon improved access for exports of developing countries, an open, non-discriminatory and equitable multilateral trading system. It provides that in particular states should avoid use of trade restrictions or distortions to offset differences in cost arising from differences in environmental standards and regulations, and should ensure that environmental regulations or standards do not constitute a means of arbitrary or unjustifiable discrimination or disguised restriction on trade. Even when based upon the required international consensus, trade measures necessary to render effective environmental objectives

---

[34] 12 U.S.C. §635i-5; Export-Import Bank of the United States Environmental Procedures and Guidelines, effective Feb. 1, 1995.

[35] 22 U.S.C.A. § 2191(n).

should be non-discriminatory and the least restrictive necessary to achieve the objectives. Transparency and notification are required, as well as public input in the formation, negotiation and implementation of trade policies. Although setting out general guidelines, the difficult issues involved in reconciling free trade and environmental protection were not settled at Rio nor have they been resolved by later developments.

E.   Trade and the Environment

International trade law is dominated by the desire to eliminate protectionism and promote free trade. The theory underpinning this system is that free trade and investment can increase consumer choice, reduce the expense of manufacturing consumer goods, thus lowering the price of products, and produce economy of scale resulting in potentially higher returns on investment for producers of goods and services. In addition, advocates of globalization claim that technological advances are rapidly diffused, with social progress stimulated due to sharing of ideas and policies, leading to an enhanced prospect of international harmony and peace. Skeptics of the open market express doubts that free trade will lead to environmental protection, based on the conviction that the economic/financial system today operates with an overwhelming reliance on business decisions driven by short-term financial gains, without regard to social costs, unless the latter are imposed through regulation.

The goal of free trade and that of environmental protection may collide, first, because national environmental laws increase production costs for domestic industries. States may seek to avoid the competitive disadvantage that would result for domestic companies if they were forced to implement expensive environmental protection measures. Many fear a race to the bottom in environmental standard setting if the free market approach dominates. This was the original basis for European Community regional action. Without harmonized regional or global norms, domestic countervailing action may be sought against imports not bearing the burden of environmental costs.

Second, states may impose trade restrictions to enforce compliance with international environmental agreements. International environmental treaties have used quantitative restrictions at least since the 1940 Convention on Nature Protection and Wildlife Preservation in the Western Hemisphere. Agreements for the protection of wildlife typically use restrictions on export or import between parties based on a permit system. CITES and the Basel Convention on the Control of Transboundary Movements of Hazardous Wastes and Their Disposal address trade issues directly and as the primary means to achieve the objectives of the agreements.

The Montreal Protocol on Substances that Deplete the Ozone Layer was the first global environmental agreement containing trade restrictions as a subsidiary but necessary measure. The Protocol addresses trade as part of the effort to ensure that non-parties do not benefit from the advantages of the Protocol without accepting its obligations. Its provisions also limit the possibility that parties can circumvent their obligations by ensuring that the production of controlled substances cannot be transferred to the territory of non-parties.[36]

Trade and the environment began separately, with different aims, but have increasingly converged or collided. Free traders fear that environmental regulations will become pretexts to close markets. Environmentalists fear that free trade will eliminate or restrict environmental protection. Both international and unilateral measures have been taken to try and reconcile the differences. Unilaterally, in November 1999, U.S. President Clinton announced Executive Order 13141, requiring the Office of the United States Trade Representative and the Council on Environmental Quality within the White House to carry out environmental reviews of all international trade negotiations. The aim is to identify environmental threats and opportunities posed by trade arrangements. The multilateral responses are described in the following sections.

1. GATT/WTO

The General Agreement on Tariffs and Trade (GATT) of 1947, revised in 1969, provides the legal framework for the use of trade restrictions. GATT was intended to be the normative framework for an international trade organization, a goal that was only achieved in 1994 with the creation of the World Trade Organization.

GATT generally treats environmental protection measures as undesirable trade restrictions. It accepts customs duties and other charges applied in a non-discriminatory fashion, but Article III requires that imported products be treated no less favorably than "like" products of national origin with respect to all "regulations and requirements affecting the internal sale" of such products. Thus, a regulation on product safety or quality, such as auto emission standards, applied neutrally to domestic and imported products is permissible under GATT.

Article XIII requires that import or export restrictions be non-discriminatory. It provides that no prohibition or restriction shall be applied by any contracting party on the importation of any product from the territory of any other contracting party or on the exportation of any product destined for the territory of any contracting party, unless the importation of the like product of all third countries or the exportation of the product to all third

---

[36]   *See* the GATT Secretariat Note of Sept. 18, 1991, Doc. L/6899.

countries is similarly prohibited or restricted. Article XI of GATT prohibits quantitative restrictions (quotas or bans) on imports and exports. There are no rules regarding trade restrictions on products that are deemed environmentally harmful. Thus, massive importation of products that have a low price due to cheap and highly polluting production methods is not considered dumping by GATT and therefore may not be countered by countervailing duties, nor may the imports be limited. Further, environmental taxes for goods in transit, such as road use fees to clean up increased air pollution, may run afoul of GATT Article V(3) which guarantees freedom of transit.

A major issue in many trade disputes is the classification of a state's action as a regulation affecting "processes and production methods" (PPMs) rather than the physical attributes of the traded product. It has been held that PPM measures do not fall under GATT Article III governing the domestic sale of a product, but under Article XI, quantitative restrictions on importation. As such, they violate GATT unless the state can fall within an exception in Article XX, discussed below. While some commentators argue that Article III should apply,[37] others disagree and contend that the relevant issue is trade discrimination.[38] The WTO has continued to analyze PPMs under Article XI.

PPMs are important to environmental protection, as recognized by the OECD.[39] PPM regulations set standards on pollution emissions or manufacturing techniques and substances used in making products (*e.g.*, CFCs). Product regulations, in contrast, concern the design, characteristics, and uses of particular products. GATT grants governments broad discretion to set product standards and even ban their sale. The characteristics of fuel economy of automobiles, for example, is accepted as a legitimate product standard, so long as it is non-discriminatory in application.[40] Access restric-

---

[37]   *See* Robert Howse & Donald Regan, *The Product/Process Distinction an Illusory Basis for Disciplining 'Unilateralism' in Trade Policy*, 11 Eur. J. Int'l L. 249 (2000) (arguing that PPM measures are regulations affecting the internal sale of products).

[38]   David M. Driesen, *What is Free Trade?: The Real Issue Lurking Behind the Trade and Environment Debate*, 41 Va. J. Int'l L. 279 (2001); Dale Arthur Oesterle, *The WTO Reaches Out to the Environmentalists: Is It Too Little, Too Late?* Colo. J. Int'l Envtl. L. & Pol'y 1, 19 (1999).

[39]   OECD, *Processes and Production Methods (PPMs): Conceptual Framework and Considerations on Use of PPM-based Trade Measures*, OECD/GD (97) 137 (Aug. 11, 1997), *available at* <http://www.oecd.org>. *See also* Richard Parker, *The Use and Abuse of Trade Leverage to Protect the Global Commons: What We Can Learn from the Tuna-Dolphin Conflict*, 12 Geo. Int'l Envtl. L. Rev. 1 (1999) (demonstrating the utility of trade measures for environmental protection).

[40]   The issue most often debated is whether products are "like" products which must be treated identically. The Report of the Appellate Body in the case

tions to limited resources, such as fish, also may be permitted provided foreign nationals are not treated unfairly.[41] PPM trade measures may concern transboundary pollution; management of transboundary living resources; global environmental concerns, like greenhouse gases; or conditions in the affected country or countries. The fourth is the most likely to fail under GATT, because it attempts to impose environmental laws extraterritorially on foreign sovereigns without an international dimension to the issue.

Many common PPMs seek to enforce resource conservation agreements or alleviate global problems like depletion of the ozone layer or climate change. Given their beneficial aim, but recognizing their harmful impacts on trade, PPM measures have been the most difficult trade/environment disputes in GATT and WTO. The early refusal to liberally apply Article XX exceptions led to many concerns about the WTO. With more environmentally-conscious application of the exceptions, many restrictions can be upheld.[42]

An impermissible trade restriction under GATT may still be justified if it falls within the exception allowing measures "necessary" to protect human, animal or plant life or health (Art. XX(b)) or measures relating to the conservation of exhaustible natural resources if such measures are made effective in conjunction with restrictions on domestic production or consumption (Art. XX(g)).

GATT fundamentally changed in 1994 with adoption of the Marrakech Agreement establishing the World Trade Organization.[43] Environmental concerns appear in the Preamble where the parties recognize that their relations should be conducted so as to allow for the optimal use of the world's resources in accordance with the objective of sustainable development, seeking both to protect and preserve the environment and to enhance the means for doing so in a manner consistent with their respective needs and concerns at different levels of economic development.

Article XIV of Annex IB entitled General Agreement on Trade in Services provides for the possibility of general exceptions for specific environmental purposes: ". . . nothing in this Agreement shall be construed to

---

involving France's regulations severely limiting the use of certain kinds of asbestos, found that the dangers associated with the particular type of asbestos made it a different product than less hazardous forms of the product or competing materials. *See* European Communities, Measures Affecting Asbestos and Asbestos-Containing Products, Report of the Appellate Body, WT/DS135/AB/R (Mar. 12, 2001), para. 192.

[41] *See* Sanford E. Gaines, *Process and Production Methods: How to Produce Sound Policy for Environmental PPM-Based Trade Measures?*, 27 COLUM. J. ENVTL. L. 383, 393 (2002).

[42] *See* Sanford Gaines, *The WTO's Reading of the GATT Article XX Chapeau: A Disguised Restriction on Environmental Measures*, 22 U. PENN. J. INT'L ECON. L. 739 (2001).

[43] Apr. 14, 1994; 33 I.L.M. 15 (1994).

prevent the adoption or enforcement by any Member of measures . . . b) necessary to protect human, animal or plant life or health"[44] Similarly, Annex 1C, the Agreement on Trade-Related Aspects of Intellectual Property Rights (TRIPS) states that members may, in formulating or amending their laws and regulations, adopt measures necessary to protect human health and nutrition, and to promote the public interest in sectors of vital importance in their socio-economic and technological development, provided that such measures are consistent with the provisions of the Agreement (Art. 8). They also may exclude from patentability those inventions whose commercial exploitation must be prevented in order to protect *ordre public*, morality, human, animal or plant life or health or to avoid serious prejudice to the environment, provided that such exclusion is not made merely because the exploitation is prohibited by their law (Art. 27(2)). Members also may exclude from patentability plants and animals other than microorganisms and biological processes for the production of plants and animals other than non-biological and microbiological processes (Art. 27(3)(b)).[45]

The WTO Sanitary and Phytosantiary Agreement (SPS) allows countries to apply sanitary and phytosanitary measures to ensure that plants and animals are protected from pests and diseases and that food is safe for consumers. By their nature, such measures act to restrict trade. The purpose of the Agreement is not to limit the right of states to set their own levels of health protection, but to require transparent decision-making to avoid disguised barriers to trade. The Agreement encourages the harmonization of sanitary and phytosanitary measures through the adoption of international standards such as those provided by the Codex Alimentarius Commission. Countries may adopt higher standards provided they are based on a risk assessment consistent with the requirements of the SPS Agreement. To be consistent, they must be applied only to the extent necessary to protect human, animal or plant life or health, be based on scientific principles, and not be maintained without sufficient scientific evidence. A measure also must not arbitrarily or unjustifiably discriminate between WTO member states or constitute a disguised restriction on international trade. Measures should be based on an appropriate risk assessment process, taking into account available scientific evidence as well as relevant economic, ecological and environmental conditions. Finally, any measure which a party does impose should not be more trade restrictive than required to achieve the appropriate level of sanitary or phytosanitary protection.[46]

---

[44]   33 I.L.M. 58, 81 (1994).

[45]   33 I.L.M. 94 (1994).

[46]   SPS Agreement, arts. 3, 5.

The Declaration on the Contribution of the Multilateral Trading Order to Achieving Greater Coherence in Global Economic Policymaking[47] proclaims that successful cooperation in each area of economic policy should contribute towards the expansion of trade, sustainable growth and development. Two of the four Declarations adopted at Marrakech have a particular importance for the environment. The Decision on Trade in Services and the Environment acknowledges that measures necessary to protect the environment may conflict with the provisions of the General Agreement on Trade in Services (Annex 1 B), but adds that because such measures typically have as their objective the protection of human, animal or plant life or health "it is not clear that there is a need to provide for more than is contained in Art. XIV(b)."

The most important text concerning the environment is a Decision of the Ministers on Trade and Environment. It refers to the relevant paragraph of the preamble of the Agreement establishing the WTO and to other texts adopted at the Conference, but also to the Rio Declaration, to Agenda 21 and to its follow-up in GATT. It declares that there should not be, nor need be, any policy contradiction between the trading system as it should result from the new structures and rules on one hand, and the protection of the environment and the promotion of sustainable development on the other hand. In deciding that the policies in the two fields should be coordinated, the Decision directs the General Council of WTO to establish a Committee on Trade and Environment at its first meeting. The terms of reference of the Committee include identification of the relationship between trade measures and environmental measures, enhancement of the positive interaction between trade and environmental measures for the promotion of sustainable development, avoidance of protectionist measures, and the surveillance of trade measures used for environmental purposes as well as environmental measures which have significant trade effects. A list of issues for the Committee to address initially was included, particularly the relationship between the multilateral trading system and trade measures and policies for environmental purposes. The environmental measures that had to be scrutinized were: charges and taxes, requirements relating to products such as standards and technical regulations, packaging, labeling and recycling, exports of domestically prohibited goods, effects on market access. The problem of the relationship between the dispute settlement mechanisms provided for in the multilateral trading system on the one hand and in environmental treaties on the other hand also was mentioned.

Throughout its history, GATT and now the WTO have faced questions about reconciling the demands of free trade with concerns for environmental protection. Several cases have been brought against states to

---

[47]   33 I.L.M. 138 (1994).

challenge their trade restrictions. The GATT exceptions to free trade contained in Article XX cover only human or animal health and the conservation of exhaustible natural resources. They do not mention protection of non-living environmental sectors such as water or air or renewable resources. The case law has established several criteria for permissible trade-related environmental measures.

First, the state seeking to justify a trade restriction under Article 20(b) (protection of human, animal or plant life or health) is tested under a three-part analysis:

1. Is the substance of the policy or the measure in question the protection of human, animal, or plant life or health;
2. Is the measure for which the exception being invoked necessary to protect that aim;
3. Is the measure applied consistently with the chapeau, avoiding arbitrary or unjustifiable discrimination and/or a disguised restriction on international trade?

A GATT panel has found that Article XX(b) can only be used for a measure that is necessary and that "entails the least degree of inconsistency with other GATT provisions." The necessity requirement is the primary problem because it has been interpreted to mean least inconsistent with free trade. The approach appears to misread the exception which requires only that the measure be necessary to protect the resource, not that the trade restriction is necessary.

Second, for the exception contained in Article 20(g) (protection of exhaustible natural resources), dolphins, gasoline and clean air have been held to be exhaustible natural resources. GATT dispute settlement panels have assumed that animals are capable of falling within this category[48] while in the case concerning reformulated gasoline,[49] a WTO appellate body concluded that clean air is an exhaustible natural resource within the meaning of Article XX(g). The legality of environmental measures that restrict trade has been tested by asking:

(1) Does the law and policy relate to the conservation of exhaustible natural resources;
(2) Are the measures made effective in conjunction with restrictions on domestic production or consumption; and
(3) Do the measures constitute arbitrary discrimination, unjustifiable discrimination or a disguised restriction on international trade, in violation of the heading of Article 20?

---

[48]   *See for example*, the *Final Report of the Panel in the Matter of Canada's Landing Requirement for Pacific Coast Salmon and Herring*, Oct. 16, 1989, para. 7.02.
[49]   WTO, *United States—Standards for Reformulated and Conventional Gasoline*, WT/DS2/AB/R, Apr. 20, 1996.

In the Reformulated Gasoline Case, the plaintiff states argued against the United States that a measure could only be "related to" or "primarily aimed at" conservation if the measure both primarily was intended to achieve a conservation goal and had a positive conservation effect. The original panel found no direct connection between less favorable treatment of imported gasoline that was chemically identical to domestic gasoline and the U.S. objective of improving domestic air quality and thus concluded that the measure was not primarily aimed at the conservation of natural resources. The Appellate Panel disagreed with this conclusion, finding that it was the purpose of the measure as a whole that had to be tested. A GATT Panel stated that Article XX(g) can only be used for a measure that is "primarily aimed at" rendering domestic conservation restrictions effective.[50] It relied on an earlier case in which it "acknowledged that the conservation of natural resources encompasses broader environmental concerns reflecting both economic and non-economic [ecological] interests."[51] Even if justified, however, an Article 20 exception cannot be applied if it constitutes arbitrary discrimination, unjustifiable discrimination or a disguised restriction on international trade. A measure may be considered to be the last mentioned if less burdensome alternatives were available.

The GATT tuna/dolphin cases[52] were first heard after a Mexican complaint concerning the U.S. Marine Mammals Act. The Act forbid importation of tuna caught with nets which also catch and kill dolphins. The objective of the U.S. law was the protection of cetaceans, in particularly dolphins, from indiscriminate forms of fishing which led to large loss of marine mammal life without regard to the place of the fishing. The action was not pursuant to treaty, but involved unilateral sanctions imposed by the U.S.

The Panel held that the import ban imposed on Mexico violated Article XI of GATT and was not a permissible exception under Article XX. The Panel refused to accept process standards related to products as exceptions under Article XX(b) and (g) because then

> each contracting party could unilaterally determine the life or health protection policies from which other contracting parties could not deviate without jeopardizing their rights under the General Agreement. The General Agreement would then no longer constitute a multilateral framework for trade among all contracting parties but would provide legal security only in respect of

---

[50]   *Report of the Panel, Canada—Measures Affecting Exports of Unprocessed Herring and Salmon*, Nov. 20, 1987, para. 4.6

[51]   *In the Matter of Canada's Landing Requirement for Pacific Coast Salmon and Herring*, U.S.-Canada FTA Panel Report, applying GATT provisions incorporated into the Free Trade Agreement, Oct. 16, 1989.

[52]   Panel Report of Sept. 3, 1991, sub. 5.27.

trade between a limited number of contracting parties with identical internal regulations.

The Panel also declared that the exceptions cannot be used for extraterritorial measures, *i.e.*, protection of dolphins outside the jurisdictional limits of the state taking the measure.[53] The Panel added that the appropriate way to protect such resources is through multilateral negotiation of an environmental agreement, not through unilateral measures threatening market access; however it is not clear that the Panel would approve measures taken pursuant to CITES against a non-party state. The GATT Council was not asked to adopt the Panel Report, because Mexico and the United States attempted to negotiate an environmental agreement to ensure proper dolphin protection.

Tuna II, a 1994 case brought by the EC against the U.S., also found U.S. actions improper, but partly modified Tuna I. The U.S. said that the law prohibiting imports of European processed tuna that had been harvested in violation of U.S. law by non-European countries was necessary to protect the environment and especially the global commons. The Panel said that in the ordinary meaning of "necessary," a member could not justify a GATT inconsistent measure if an alternative GATT-consistent measure was available that the member could reasonably be expected to employ. Significantly, Tuna II did accept the permissibility of extraterritorial laws affecting the international commons. The U.S. policy to conserve dolphins in the eastern tropical Pacific Ocean was deemed within the range of policies covered by GATT Article 20(g).

A 1998 dispute again involved U.S. trade restrictions, this time measures designed to protect endangered sea turtles. As discussed in Chapter 8, all seven species of sea turtles are listed in Appendix I of CITES and on the IUCN Red List.[54] The challenged law was intended to counter the costs for U.S. shrimpers of complying with U.S. environmental regulations when foreign shrimpers were not. To export shrimp to the U.S., as of May 1996, all countries in whose waters shrimp and sea turtles coexist had to be certified by the U.S. State Department as having and enforcing legislation requiring

---

[53]	This could affect the implementation of the Montreal Protocol. The import prohibitions on chloroflourocarbons violate GATT requirements if the exporting country is not a party to the Montreal Protocol.

[54]	All of the parties to the dispute are signatories to CITES. In the U.S., CITES is implemented by the Endangered Species Act of 1973, Public Law No. 93-205, 87 Stat. 884 (codified as amended at 16 U.S.C. §§ 1531–1543 (1988)). The Sea Turtle Conservation Act, or § 609 of Public Law No. 101–162, requires the U.S. to negotiate with countries whose fleets appear to threaten sea turtle populations after which it may restrict the importation of shrimp harvested with commercial fishing technology which may adversely affect sea turtles.

turtle excluder devices on commercial shrimp trawlers. The shrimp/ turtle case was brought to the WTO by India, Malaysia, Pakistan and Thailand, who objected to the measures as extra-territorial and unilateral.[55] Sixteen countries and the EU joined as third parties. On April 6 a Panel ruled that the U.S. violated its obligations under GATT and on July 23, 1998, the U.S. appealed.

The Appellate Body on October 12, 1998, upheld the shrimp ban decision against the United States, but overturned several aspects of the Panel's decision.[56] Most importantly, the Appellate Body agreed with the U.S. that it had a right to adopt its restrictions for environmental purposes. In looking at the contemporary context, it affirmed that the term "exhaustible natural resources" is not static in its content but is rather "by definition, evolutionary." The words "must be read . . . in the light of contemporary concerns of the community of nations about the protection and conservation of the environment." In this and other respects, the ruling indicated greater sensitivity to environmental concerns:

> We have not decided that the protection and preservation of the environment is of no significance to the WTO. Clearly it is. We have not decided that the sovereign nations that are members of the WTO cannot adopt effective measures to protect endangered species, such as sea turtles. Clearly, they can and should. And we have not decided that sovereign states should not act together bilaterally, plurilaterally, or multilaterally, either within the WTO or in other international fora, to protect endangered species or otherwise protect the environment. Clearly they should and do.

The U.S. failed, however, to ensure that the ban was imposed in a non-discriminatory manner. The ruling set down a number of criteria to ensure that environmental trade measures do not discriminate between WTO members.[57]

On October 23, 2000, Malaysia invoked Article 21.5 to assert US non-compliance with the decision in the Shrimp/Turtle case. Malaysia requested the Dispute Settlement Body (DSB) to decide whether the U.S. had complied with the recommendations and rulings of the DSB's earlier decision adopting the reports of the original panel and the Appellate Body. The DSB had recommended that the U.S. bring its import prohibition into conformity

---

[55]   *United States—Import Prohibition of Certain Shrimp and Shrimp Products*, WTO Panel established Feb. 25, 1997, WT/DS58/R and Corr.1, as modified by the AB Report, WT/DS58/AB/R, *adopted* Nov. 6, 1998.

[56]   Appellate Body Report, WT/DS58/AB/R *adopted* Nov. 6, 1998.

[57]   The Dispute Settlement Body adopted the decision, WT/DS58/15, July 15, 1999.

with its obligations under the WTO. At the DSB meeting held October 23, 2000, Malaysia said it was not satisfied with U.S. compliance. The matter went back to the original panel.[58] In fact, the U.S. did not amend its import prohibition to protect and conserve certain species of sea turtles considered to be an endangered species.[59] It did, however, issue Revised Guidelines for the Implementation of Section 609 of Public Law 101-162 Relating to the Protection of Sea Turtles in Shrimp Trawl Fishing Operations. The Revised Guidelines do not prohibit imports of shrimp that come from harvesting nations "certified" by the U.S. The main change is to allow certification of governments whose harvesting programs require commercial shrimp trawlers to have devices that are "comparable in effectiveness" to those used in the U.S. and to have a credible enforcement program that includes monitoring for compliance. The Revised Guidelines allow countries to apply for certification even if they do not require Turtle Excluder Devices (TEDs) provided they have a comparably effective regulatory program to protect sea turtles. The Department of State is required "to take fully into account any demonstrated differences between the shrimp fishing conditions in the United States and those in other nations, as well as information available from other sources." A nation may also be certified if its shrimp fishing environment does not pose a threat of incidental capture of sea turtles because (1) the relevant species of sea turtles do not occur in waters subject to that country's jurisdiction; (2) shrimp is harvested in that country's waters exclusively by means that do not pose a threat to sea turtles, such as by artisanal means; or commercial shrimp trawling operations take place exclusively in waters in which sea turtles do not occur.

In a report of June 15, 2001, the Panel found the measure to be in violation Article XI.1, but justified by Article XX "as long as" there are ongoing serious good faith efforts to reach a multilateral agreement on the matter. The Panel urged the two parties to conclude as soon as possible an agreement "which will permit the protection and conservation of sea turtles to the satisfaction of all interests involved and taking into account the principle that States have common but differentiated responsibilities to conserve and protect the environment" (para. 9). Malaysia appealed, contending that the Panel did not adequately scrutinize the Revised Guidelines for conformity with the WTO agreement, that in effect it is "a new and different measure" that must be subject to *de novo* consideration. It argued that the Panel erred by relying solely on the reasoning of the earlier Appellate Body decision. It argued that the proper result would be to consider the obligation of the United States as one to conclude an agreement, not to negotiate towards one. In its view, negotiations could not insulate a unilat-

---

58   Panel Report WT/DS58/RW, June 15, 2001.
59   Public Law No. 101–162, § 609.

eral measure from constituting unjustifiable discrimination; otherwise a member could effectively incorporate its unilateral standards in an agreement and circumvent WTO standards or could even claim that its measure is valid in the absence of reaching agreement, provided it negotiated in good faith. Other parties in the case took conflicting positions.[60]

In the DSB review,[61] jurisdiction was a major issue: should the Panel and Appellate Body look at the new U.S. measure for consistency with GATT 1994 or only at the consistency of the measure with recommendations and rulings of the prior DSB? The Appellate Body found the U.S. measure to be new and different measure and thus the Panel had to consider the new measure "in its totality" according to the complaint filed, but neither the Panel nor the Appellate Body would reopen issues that were previously decided and thus *res judicata*. The issue was the application of the U.S. statute and whether it was being applied through the new measure in a way that constituted unjustified discrimination. According to the Appellate Body, in the first case, the U.S. was found in violation of GATT in part because it treated WTO members differently, cooperating with Caribbean and Western Atlantic states to conclude an agreement, while failing to negotiate with other states. The differential treatment was held "plainly discriminatory." To comply, all exporting countries had to be given similar opportunities to negotiate an international agreement. Requiring an agreement to be concluded would not be justified, because it would give any country a veto over U.S. measures. "The protection and conservation of highly migratory species of sea turtles . . . demands concerted and cooperative efforts on the part of the many countries whose waters are traversed in the course of recurrent sea turtle migrations."[62] The "need for, and the appropriateness of, such efforts have been recognized in the WTO itself, as

---

[60] Australia and India agreed with Malaysia that the panel should conduct a fresh factual and legal analysis on the inconsistency of the new measure with Article XX. They also agreed that good faith negotiations were insufficient to validate the unilateral measure. They further claimed that the burden of proof was on U.S. to demonstrate its serious good faith efforts to obviate or eliminate the unjustifiably discriminatory nature of the ban, including the design, extent and implementation of the measure. The EC agreed with the U.S. position that Malaysia's request limited itself to the earlier findings of the Appellate Body and made no new claim. It also called the claim premature because Malaysia had not applied for certification under new U.S. guidelines, which are more flexible.

[61] DSB Appellate Body decision on appeal from panel, Decision of Oct. 22, 2001, *United States—Import Prohibition of Certain Shrimp and Shrimp Products, Report of the Appellate Body*, WT/DS58/AB/RW, Oct. 22, 2001; 41 I.L.M. 149 (2002). Also *available at* <www.wto.org.

[62] Para. 124.

well as in a significant number of other international instruments and declarations."[63] Yet, while a multilateral approach "is strongly preferred . . . it
is one thing to *prefer* a multilateral approach in the application of a measure
that is provisionally justified under one of the subparagraphs of Article XX
of the GATT 1994; it is another to require the *conclusion* of a multilateral
agreement as a condition of avoiding 'arbitrary or unjustifiable discrimination' under the chapeau of Article XX. We see, in this case no such
requirement."[64] Both the Panel and Appellate Body contrast the conditionality of the original measure with the flexibility of the new measures,
because "comparable in effectiveness" is less rigid than "essentially the
same." The Appellate Body finds this flexibility sufficient to avoid the measure being arbitrary or unjustifiable discrimination. Further the new U.S.
Guidelines at issue note that sea turtles require protection throughout their
life-cycle, not only when they are threatened by commercial shrimp trawl
harvesting. So, in making certification decisions, the Department is to take
fully into account other measures such as protection of nesting beaches and
other habitat, prohibitions on taking sea turtles, national enforcement and
compliance programs and participation in any international agreement for
the protection and conservation of sea turtles.

More generally, because GATT's emphasis is on reducing trade barriers, a state imposing a restriction for environmental protection bears the
burden of proving that the measure is necessary, non-discriminatory and
not a disguised restriction on trade. Action based on the precautionary principle or even preventive measures may be condemned in this regard; "necessity" demands that the measures be "consistent with sound scientific
evidence." The difficulties are evident in regard to wildlife conservation
measures where some countries claim that measures are not necessary
because the animals in question are not endangered. Numerous wildlife
conventions, some adopted prior to GATT, tie trade restrictions to manufacturing or harvesting methods. This was understood during drafting of
GATT. The major concern today is that process standards have a disproportionate impact on developing countries.

Others challenging environmental regulations argue that Article XX(g)
can be invoked only when the conservation benefits are large enough, compared to the commercial cost, to make a credible case that the government
acts "primarily" for conservation reasons, using a cost/benefit analysis. In
the beef hormone dispute, the WHO panel directed detailed scientific questions to six experts on the issues raised by the dispute. The scientific evidence submitted by the EU was deemed insufficient to justify the ban[65] in

---

63   *Id.* at n. 24, citing Principle 12 of the Rio Declaration.

64   *Id.*, para. 124.

65   *United States-EC Measures Concerning Meat and Meat Products (Hormones)*,
WTO Doc. WT/DS26/R/USA (Aug. 18, 1997); *Canada-EC Measures Concerning*

part because in 1995, the Codex Commission adopted maximum residue limitations for the hormones in question, thus approving their use. Despite the consequential presumption of validity, the WHO panel sought information from the Commission and requested the nomination of experts from the secretariat. Finding that there was no scientific evidence in support of the action, the Panel rejected the precautionary principle as inapplicable, instead holding that members must base their actions on a risk assessment adopting the criteria laid down by the SPS Agreement. According to the Panel, unilateral restrictions should be allowed as long as there is a scientific justification, but if there is no scientific evidence, the ban could not be "based on" science. The Panel rejected the EU scientific interpretations as being "minority views" in the scientific community."

As long as measures are applied equally to domestically-produced and imported products (national treatment rule) and do not discriminate against imports from whatever sources (most-favored nation rule), many environmental measures will avoid any challenge under GATT. The difficult issue is that one country's environmental protection measure may be seen by another as disguised protectionism. GATT has been notified of some 300 environmental regulations concerning hazardous products, environmental packaging, marking and labeling requirements, waste disposal regulations and requirements. Any or all of these could be challenged.

The WTO has been criticized for its emphasis on trade and lack of expertise in and understanding of environmental problems. Its panel decisions have been hostile in general to environmental measures. The Committee on Trade and Environment has produced few results of any substance. Its primary recommendation has been the extension of its mandate, something that was approved in 1996 at the Ministerial Meeting held in Singapore. The WTO has improved its transparency, however, agreeing to release more documents to the public and to set up an internet site to provide greater access. The Secretariat has instituted symposia for NGOs and granted observer status at the 1996 and 1998 Ministerial Conferences. An Appellate Body approved the acceptance of NGO amicus briefs in disputes. Finally, the 2002 Doha Ministerial Meeting adopted a Declaration that contains a renewed commitment to sustainable development, sets goals for the WTO Committee on Trade and Environment and specifically agrees to address fisheries subsidies and to reduce or eliminate tariff and non-tariff barriers to environmental goods and services.

Meat and Meet Products (Hormones), WTO Doc. WT/DS48/R/CAN (Aug. 18, 1997).

2. NAFTA

The North American Free Trade Agreement between Canada, Mexico and the United States, signed at three different places at four different dates in December 1992 mentions in its preamble the will of the three contracting governments to promote sustainable development and to strengthen the development and enforcement of environmental laws and regulations. Article 104 and Annex 104.1 state that in the event of any inconsistency between the Agreement and the specific obligations set out in three multilateral and two bilateral treaties,[66] the latter obligations prevail to the extent of the inconsistency. The same provision requires, however, that parties implementing these agreements adopt the implementing alternative that is the least inconsistent with other provisions of the Agreement. (NAFTA Art. 104).

NAFTA Chapter 7B on sanitary and phytosanitary standards (SPS) and Chapter 9 which concerns other technical barriers to trade, including environmental product standards, attempt to balance environmental and free trade concerns, in the process creating some contradictions in the text. On the one hand, each party has the right to set and maintain environmental health and safety standards consistent with the level of protection it alone deems appropriate (Art. 712). On the other hand, the measures must be based on scientific principles (Art. 712.3). NAFTA Article 715(4) encompasses the precautionary approach by allowing provisional measures to be adopted where relevant scientific evidence is insufficient. The Agreement on Technical Barriers to Trade allows each party to establish levels of health and environmental protection that it considers appropriate in accordance with risk assessment (Arts. 904(2) and 907(2)). Standards-related measures concerning the environment may include import prohibitions (Art. 904(1)), but parties need to avoid arbitrary or unjustifiable distinctions.

The SPS agreement also provides that national measures that conform to international standards, such as those established by the Codex Alimentarius Commission, are presumptively valid.[67] More stringent measures may

---

[66]   Respectively: CITES, the Montreal Protocol, the Basel Convention on Wastes, a 1986 agreement between Canada and U.S. on hazardous wastes, and a 1983 agreement between Mexico and U.S. for the Protection and Improvement of the Environment in the Border Area.

[67]   The Codex Alimentarius Commission was created in 1962 as a joint undertaking of the FAO and the WHO. Membership in the Commission is open to all FAO and WHO member states. It has a dual function: "protecting the health of the consumers and ensuring fair practices in the food trade." Statutes, art. 1, para. a, *reprinted in* Codex Alimentarius Commission, Procedural Manual 5 (Joint FAO/WHO Food Standards Programme 9th ed. 1993). The Commission is specifically charged with adopting advisory multilateral "good prac-

be approved. NAFTA Article 712.5 requires that SPS standards be "necessary for the protection of human, animal or plant life or health" and can be applied only to the extent "necessary" to achieve the chosen level of protection, echoing the language of GATT Article XX. Other limitations require that the measures not be maintained where there is no longer a scientific basis for them, not be arbitrarily or unjustifiably discriminatory against imported products, and not create a disguised restriction on trade. The party challenging a regulation has the burden of proof, creating a soft presumption that regulation is valid. Either of the parties or the panel may convene a panel of technical experts to render advisory opinions on the scientific issues involved. Article 1114 addresses the concern about a "race to the bottom." It provides:

> The parties recognize that it is inappropriate to encourage investment by relaxing domestic health, safety or environmental measures. Accordingly, a Party should not waive or otherwise derogate from, or offer to waive or otherwise derogate from, such measures as an encouragement for the establishment, acquisition, expansion or retention in its territory of an investment of an investor. If a Party considers that another Party has offered such an encouragement, it may request consultations with the other Party and the two Parties shall consult with a view to avoiding any such encouragement.

Due to concerns about the lack of specificity in NAFTA, an environmental side accord was signed September 13, 1993, by the three governments. The NAFTA Side Agreement[68] addresses environmental concerns in more detail. It is highly likely that the agreement would not have been approved without its protections. It establishes a trilateral North American Commission for Environmental Cooperation (NACEC) designed to (1) facilitate cooperation between NAFTA countries on environmental issues; (2) serve as a forum for regular ministerial-level meetings; (3) provide an independent secretariat to report regularly on significant environmental issues confronting NAFTA parties; (4) ensure that environmental enforcement remains a priority in all three countries, including provision for an annual enforcement activity report; (5) coordinate with trade officials in all three countries on any NAFTA-related environment issues; and (6) ensure that there are opportunities for public participation in the development and implementation of environmental laws and programs in all three NAFTA countries.

---

tice" standards on such matters as the composition of food products, food additives, labeling, food processing techniques, and inspection of foodstuffs and processing facilities.

[68] Sept. 13, 1993, Can.-Mex.-U.S. (formally the North American Agreement on Environmental Cooperation).

The agreement requires each NAFTA country to prepare periodic reports on the state of the environment and make these reports available to the public. Each state party must assess environmental impacts "as appropriate" and consider stopping exports to NAFTA partners of any pesticide or toxic substance whose use is banned within the exporting nation's borders.[69] In addition, the NAFTA parties commit themselves to guarantee their citizens access to national courts to undertake enforcement actions and to seek redress of harm. They also agree to ensure the openness of judicial and administrative proceedings and transparent procedures for the creation of environmental laws and regulations. They further seek to limit trade in toxic substances that they have banned domestically.

The side agreement, the first environmental agreement negotiated to accompany a trade agreement, created a Commission on Environmental Cooperation (CEC). The three countries' top environmental officials comprise the Commission's Council. A Joint Advisory Committee made up of non-governmental organizations from all three countries will advise the Council in its deliberations. The Commission acts to consider the environmental implications of process and production methods and to promote greater public access to information about hazardous substances. It also considers ways to promote the assessment and mitigation of transboundary environmental problems and is an avenue for NAFTA dispute settlement panels to obtain environmental expertise. As described in Chapter 7, citizens of all three countries may make submissions to the Commission on their concerns related to the full range of environmental issues, including any "persistent pattern of failure . . . to effectively enforce" environmental laws or regulations."

The CEC has a number of programs and activities related to environmental protection: the North American Bird Conservation Initiative (a trinational coalition of over 250 government agencies and NGOs); North American Marine Protected Areas Network to enhance and strengthen the conservation of marine biodiversity in critical habitats throughout North America by creating functional linkages and information exchanges; Global Program of Action for the Protection of the Marine Environment from Land-based Activities in North America; and the North American Pollutant Release and Transfer Register Project. The last-mentioned aims to ensure citizen access to accurate information about the release and transfer of toxic chemicals from facilities in their communities. Other programs include the Air Quality Program, Sound Management of Chemicals Program; and Children's Health and the Environment.

---

[69]　　On September 21, the United States government proposed banning the export of pesticides that are prohibited in the United States. It also would ban the export of a pesticide if the manufacturer withdrew an application for approval.

On a bilateral basis, one of the side agreements between the U.S. and Mexico establishes the Border Environment Cooperation Commission to help states, localities and the private sector develop and find financing for environmental infrastructure projects along the U.S.-Mexico border. Other elaborate cooperative environmental programs and an action agenda of collaborative projects have been established pursuant to the joint U.S.-Mexican Integrated Border Environmental Plan.

3. Other Regional Economic Institutions

Despite questions about the short-term economic impact of environmental protection, developing countries began expressing concern for environmental protection in their economic relations. Taking a cue from the European Community, which began its environmental programs after the Stockholm Conference, other legal instruments of economic integration began to proclaim the need to protect the environment. In Africa, the Treaty of the Southern African Development Community[70] proclaimed among its objectives the promotion of self-sustaining development and the achievement of sustainable utilization of natural resources and effective protection of the environment (Art. 5(d), (g)). More widely, the Constitutive Act of the African Union was adopted July 2000 and came into force 26 May 2001. The objectives identified in Article 3 include the promotion of sustainable development and cooperation in order to raise the living standards of African peoples; cooperation towards the eradication of disease and the promotion of good health, and the development of common African positions on issues of interest to the continent. Environment is not specifically mentioned, but the Executive Council is given authority to make decisions on a range of issues that include mineral resources, agriculture and forestry; water resources; and environmental protection.

The Treaty Establishing the Common Market for Eastern and Southern Africa[71] provides for cooperation of the contracting parties in the joint and efficient management and sustainable utilization of natural resources within the Common Market, especially in the management of fresh water resources, fisheries resources (Art. 122) and in general in the management of natural resources (Art. 123) and of the environment (Art. 124). The parties also undertake to develop a collective and coordinated approach to sustainable development and management, rational exploitation and utilization and the protection of wildlife in the Common Market (Art. 125). These principles are developed in detail so as to provide the states members of the Common Market with precise instructions. The treaty also integrates environmental protection in agricultural development policy (Art. 130).

---

[70]   Windhoek, Aug. 17, 1992.
[71]   Kampala, Nov. 5, 1993.

In the Western Hemisphere, apart from the North American Free Trade Agreement (NAFTA),[72] which recognizes the superiority of specified environmental treaties on the rules of free trade, thus established (Arts. 104 and 105) and should be read together with the North American Agreement on Environmental Cooperation,[73] the Caribbean Common Market (CARICOM), established in 1973,[74] and the Mercado Commun del Sur (MERCOSUR),[75] which also seek to eliminate trade barriers in their regions in order to stimulate economic development and have expressed interest in environmental matters. MERCOSUR was established January 1, 1995, between Brazil, Argentina, Paraguay and Uruguay based on the Treaty of Asuncion in 1991. Bolivia and Chile are associate members. MERCOSUR aims to establish a common market of free movement of goods, services, labor and capital. The Preamble of the MERCOSUR Agreement recognizes that the objective of establishing a common market "must be achieved by making optimum use of available resources, preserving the environment, improving physical links, coordinating macroeconomic policies and ensuring complementarity between the different sectors of the economy, based on the principles of gradualism, flexibility and balance." Prior to UNCED, the parties adopted the Declaration of Canela (February 1992) adopting a common political position on biological diversity, global climate change, water resources, human settlements, forests, soils, international trade, maritime ocean protection, hazardous wastes, and institutional mechanisms for sustainable development. A Special Meeting on Environmental Issues has worked to analyze environmental legislation in the member states and recommend action to assure adequate environmental protection and harmonization of environmental legislation within MERCOSUR. In 1995 a Working Sub-Group on environmental issues was assigned the task of developing common policies for the region.

---

[72]   Washington, Dec. 8 and 17, 1992, Ottawa, Dec. 11 and 17, 1992, and Mexico City, Dec. 14 and 17, 1992. NAFTA is discussed further in this chapter, Section D.

[73]   Washington, Sept. 9 and 13, 1993, Ottawa, September 12 and 14, 1993 and Mexico City, Sept. 8 and 14, 1993.

[74]   The member states are Antigua and Barbuda, the Bahamas, Barbados, Belize, Dominica, Grenada, Guyana, Jamaica, Montserrat, St. Kitts and Nevis, St. Lucia, St. Vincent and the Grenadines, and Trinidad and Tobago. Treaty Establishing the Caribbean Community, July 4, 1973.

[75]   Treaty of Asuncion, South American Quadripartite Common Market, Argentina, Brazil, Paraguay and Uruguay, Mar. 26, 1991. *See* Daniel Esty & Damien Geradin, *Market Access, Competitiveness, and Harmonization: Environmental Protection in Regional Trade Agreements*, 21 HARV. ENVTL. L. REV. 265 (1997).

In Asia, the six member states of the Association of Southeast Asian Nations (ASEAN)[76] adopted the Singapore Declaration on political and economic cooperation on January 28, 1992. The Declaration provides that ASEAN member countries shall continue to play an active part in protecting the environment by further cooperating to promote the principle of sustainable development and integrate it into all aspects of development. The Declaration calls for enhanced environmental cooperation, particularly on issues of transboundary pollution, natural disasters, forest fires and "in addressing the anti-tropical timber campaign." The Declaration also asks developed countries to commit to assisting developing countries by providing new and additional financial resources as well as the transfer of and access to environmentally sound technology on concessional and preferential terms. The framework Agreement on Enhancing ASEAN Economic Cooperation, signed the same day, makes no reference to the environment, however.

Finally, the Central European Free Trade Agreement (CEFTA)[77] provides that its implementation shall not preclude prohibitions or restrictions on imports, exports or goods in transit justified by the conservation of exhaustible natural resources if such measures are made effective in conjunction with restrictions on domestic production or consumption (Art. 18).

Other treaties concerning economic cooperation also stress the importance of environmental protection and of its integration into economic policies. The International Tropical Timber Agreement[78] which tends to promote the expansion and diversification of international trade in tropical timber affirms the will of the contracting parties to contribute to the process of sustainable development (Art. 1(c)) and encourages states members of the International Tropical Timber Organization to support and develop not only industrial tropical timber reforestation but also rehabilitation of degraded forest land and to develop national policies aimed at sustainable utilization and conservation of timber-producing forests and their genetic resources and at maintaining the ecological balance in the regions concerned, in the context of tropical timber trade (Art. 1(j) and (l)).

The European Energy Charter Treaty of December 17, 1994,[79] which intends to establish long-term cooperation in the energy field, includes detailed provisions concerning environmental aspects of such cooperation (Art. 19). Each contracting party shall strive to minimize, in an economically efficient manner, harmful environmental impacts occurring either within or outside its area from all operations within the energy cycle in its

---

[76]   Brunei Darussalam, Indonesia, Malaysia, Philippines, Singapore, Thailand.

[77]   Czech Republic, Hungary, Poland and Slovak Republic, Krakow, Dec. 21, 1992. CEFTA will end when the parties join the EU.

[78]   Geneva, Jan. 26, 1994.

[79]   Lisbon; 33 I.L.M. 360 (1995).

area, striving to take precautionary measures to prevent or minimize environmental degradation. The polluter should, in principle, bear the cost of pollution, including transboundary pollution, with due regard to public interest and without distorting investment in the energy cycle or international trade. Parties should have particular regard to energy efficiency and develop and use renewable energy sources. They also should promote the transparent assessment at any early stage and prior to decision, and subsequent monitoring, of environmental impacts of environmentally significant energy investment projects.

From the experience of the regional economic institutions, it seems clear that attention to environmental concerns improves the performance and political attractiveness of multilateral trade agreements because of the need to ensure internal coherence in managing the world's economic relations. The absence of environmental considerations limits the potential for obtaining the full benefits of trade liberalization because it fails to require internalization of environmental externalities and to prevent the over-exploitation of common resources. Allocative inefficiencies and environmental degradation result from omitting the environment, thereby diminishing the trade-derived gains in social welfare. The greater the degree of economic integration in a trading system, the greater the level of policy coordination and integration required in other realms; otherwise conflicts inevitably arise.

F. Conclusions

The key to making trade and environmental policies compatible and mutually supportive in a market economy lies in pricing environmental resources properly to reflect their real scarcity and true social value. Undervalued resources pose a particularly difficult case for trade restrictions. Part of the reason for the destruction of tropical rain forests is the undervaluing of them as an international environmental resource. Unilateral restrictions on imports of tropical timber or other reduction of demand, reduces the value of the trees at the source. As a result, exploitation may be accelerated in order to maintain income levels or the trees may be cleared to obtain higher income levels from mining or cattle ranching. Restrictions on production and sale need to be taken at the source, as well as at the market, in order to work. GATT will not impede some trade measures, but will question whether they are necessary trade restrictions or create distortion.

While trade negotiations are becoming more ecologically conscious, states parties to environmental agreements based on trade restrictions, like CITES, are questioning the economic and environmental consequences of their policies. There is evidence that strict prohibition of trade can be counterproductive in discouraging conservation efforts and undervaluing the resource, while encouraging black market activities.

In the meantime, treaty law does not entirely resolve the problem of conflicting norms in trade agreements and environmental instruments. GATT Article XXV allows the its parties acting together to waive any and all obligations under GATT for any specified measures of a contracting party, by a two-thirds majority of those voting, including a majority of contracting parties. Potentially, this could resolve some of the conflicts. General treaty law provides that later treaties take priority over earlier ones, between the same parties; more specific treaties take priority over general ones. Where a treaty says it is subject to another, the other will prevail. The rules set out in Article 30 of the Vienna Convention on the Law of Treaties apply in the absence of express treaty provisions regulating the issue of priority. One problem is that GATT and environmental treaties deal with different subject matters while the Vienna Convention rules are designed to cope with the problem of successive treaties governing the same subject matter.

While many continue to view trade and environment as hostile and competing policies, there is evidence that they are complementary; increasing world welfare can lead to demands for greater environmental protection. The basic policy underlying GATT is to liberalize trade across national boundaries and to pursue the benefits of comparative advantage and economies of scale. The theoretical foundation of free trade assumes that when nations specialize, they become more efficient in producing a product or service and can trade with other nations specializing in other goods and services, with the result that everyone is better off. The question is whether the theory is always correct in practice because externalities can distort the picture: a producer who pollutes the air imposes a cost on the world which is not recouped unless the polluter pays principle requires internalizing the environmental costs. Much of the debate about trade and the environment concerns how much the cost of environmental protection should be internalized.

BIBLIOGRAPHY

CAMERON, J., et al., TRADE AND THE ENVIRONMENT: THE SEARCH FOR BALANCE (1994).

Charnovitz, S., *Critical Guide to the WTO's Report on Trade and Environment*, 14 ARIZ. J. INT'L & COMP. L. 341 (1997).

ESTY, D., GREENING THE GATT (1994).

Esty, D. & Geradin, D., *Market Access, Competitiveness, and Harmonization: Environmental Protection in Regional Trade Agreements*, 21 HARV. ENVTL. L. REV. 265 (1997).

GLOBAL ENVIRONMENTAL GOVERNANCE, OPTIONS AND OPPORTUNITIES (ESTY, D., IVANOVA, M., eds., 2002).

Housman, R., *The North American Free Trade Agreement's Lessons for Reconciling Trade and the Environment*, 30 STAN. J. INT'L L. 379 (1994).

JACKSON, J., WORLD TRADE AND THE LAW OF THE GATT (1969).

JOHNSON, P.-M., & BEAULIEU, A., THE ENVIRONMENT AND NAFTA (1996).

Meier, M., *Gatt, WTO, and the Environment: To What Extent Do GATT/WTO Rules Permit Member Nations to Protect the Environment When Doing So Adversely Affects Trade*, 8 COLO. J. INT'L L. & POL'Y 241 (1997).

Petersmann, E.-U., *International Trade Law and International Environmental Law*, 27 J. WORLD TRADE L. 43 (1993).

Safrin, Sabrina, *Treaties in Collision? The Biosafety Protocol and the WTO Agreements*, 96 AJIL 606 (2002).

Schoenbaum, T.J., *International Trade and Protection of the Environment: The Continuing Search for Reconciliation*, 91 AJIL 268 (1997).

UNEP, THE USE OF TRADE MEASURES IN SELECT MULTILATERAL ENVIRONMENTAL AGREEMENTS (1995).

ZAELKE, D., ET AL., TRADE AND THE ENVIRONMENT: LAW, ECONOMICS AND POLICY (2d ed. 2002).

INTERNET SITES

OPIC
<http://www.OPIC.gov/SUBDOCS/ENVIRON.HTM>

HIPC Initiative
<http://www.worldbank.org/hipc>

IMF
<http://www.imf.org>

Free trade agreements
<http://www.sice.oas.org/root/tradee.stm>

WTO
<http://www.wto.org/>

CONCLUSIONS

International environmental law is complex and ever-increasing, progressively moving towards a holistic approach to environmental, social and economic problems. Its development during the past three decades has led to the emergence of an increasing number of concepts, principles and norms. At the same time, more technical concepts and rules have appeared and been repeated in different treaties or non-binding instruments. The importance of frequent reference in international legal instruments to the principles proclaimed by the Rio Declaration concerning public participation, environmental impact assessment, transboundary relations, environmental emergencies, prevention, precaution and the polluter pays principle is evident. Norms proposed by UNEP, FAO and OECD have also had a significant impact on the development of environmental law. The repetition of norms along with other state practice very much contributed and will continue to contribute to the creation of a global framework for international environmental law.

Concepts, principles and rules appear in numerous treaties, largely following their general formulation in international instruments of fundamental importance but non-binding character, such as the Declarations of the 1972 Stockholm and the 1992 Rio Conference. Another general characteristic of present international environmental law is the increased utilization of non-binding international instruments. Such texts are often easier to negotiate and amend in the light of new problems where scientific knowledge and public awareness can be the major factors pressing for international action. Principles in non-binding texts help develop international environmental law and directly or indirectly give birth to new legal rules.

The previous examination of the profusion of rules reveals some general trends and emerging issues in the field. Many principles and norms of international environmental law are being given more legal content and greater uniformity by treaties and other texts that now often contain detailed definitions of concepts and statements of obligations. In a way, one can speak of a certain harmonization of international environmental law due to the horizontal expansion of such principles, which means their inclusion in different legal instruments. Increasingly, international instruments cross-reference each other, such as the UNCLOS reference to MARPOL standards. International environmental law is also characterized by the proliferation and inter-penetration of legal rules at all levels of governance from the global to the municipal. Laws and policies adopted at each level influence the others and initiatives begun at one level of governance often lead to similar approaches being adopted in other legal orders.

As environmental instruments proliferate, coordination of overlapping or even conflicting obligations becomes a problem. Adherence to global and regional instruments can create problems of rationalization and choice in implementation. The regional seas obligations concerning specially-protected areas and their coordination with the Convention on Biological Diversity is a case in point. UNEP views the former as giving greater specificity to the general requirements of the latter, but it is not clear that the obligations are identical. The problem of overlapping treaties is becoming widespread as the number of instruments grows.

The proliferation of international environmental agreements also has resulted in a corresponding increase in the number and variety of international mechanisms to supervise national implementation of and compliance with international environmental obligations. International environmental agreements increasingly include detailed provisions for monitoring, implementation review, compliance verification, and non-compliance mechanisms. One of the issues for the future will be evaluating the effectiveness of such institutions, their possible reform, and harmonization. Another is evaluating the underlying normative framework to understand whether, if fully implemented, it is capable of producing the desired improvement in the status of the environment. Good compliance with rules that do not go beyond existing practice or that represent an inadequate goal are unlikely to suffice to avoid further environmental deterioration. A technique to respond to treaty-proliferation is cooperation between secretariats, often through concluding a Memorandum of Understanding or Cooperation. Such an agreement was concluded in 1997 between the secretariats of the Caribbean regional seas treaty and the Convention on Biological Diversity. The MOU recognized the problem of overlapping obligations and the need for rationalization and called for institutional cooperation, including exploration of the possibility of observer status of each secretariat in meetings of the others. Each secretariat is to develop means to regularly inform the other about work in their respective fields of action and for exchange of data on biodiversity. They are also to seek to coordinate respective work plans and possibly harmonize the reporting requirements under both conventions. While they are trying to coordinate national conservation plans, there is no real attempt to reconcile obligations.

On a vertical axis, many environmental policies and instruments now respond to emerging problems by calling for application of the principle of subsidiarity or for decentralized implementation of environmental norms. The principle of subsidiarity, which is a general organizing principle of governance, expresses a libertarian value in favor of making decisions and implementing them at the lowest effective level of government or other organization. In this differentiated approach towards state regulation, subsidiarity establishes a rebuttable presumption in favor of local control. It is based on an assumption that decentralized decision-making will enhance personal autonomy and public participation and facilitate choices based on the particularities of local conditions, especially where the local population will bear the highest environmental and developmental costs. At the international level, it reflects traditional notions of state sovereignty, while at the local and national levels it introduces non-state actors and stakeholders in the functioning of environmental protection.

Problems that transcend the community and/or cannot be effectively resolved locally will continue to necessitate solutions at the national, regional or global level. In some cases, political obstacles to local action must be overcome by regulation at the national level. Similarly, international environmental law may be required to surmount national political reluctance to adopt sound environmental policies, which is especially likely when environmental damage may be exported at relatively low cost. This is one basis of international watercourse agreements that control the emissions of upstream states and marine environment conventions regulating land-based pollution of the seas. Shared resources, transboundary ecosystems that form a physical unit, and international commons obviously require international regulation by the states concerned.

The enormous expansion of concern for environmental deterioration has had important consequences for international law generally. Every human activity affects the environment and raises questions of the need for regulation. Areas of international law that developed during earlier periods are now evolving in new directions because of insistence that they take into account environmental considerations. The result is an infusion of environmental norms into nearly every branch of international law. Treaties and other international texts now almost routinely include provisions related to the environment, even if only to mention the need to protect natural resources. In some regards this can be considered a parallel to the development of integrated environmental protection in national and regional legal systems.

One of the principal problems of the coming decades will be to ensure that contracting states comply with their international commitments. Implementation of, and compliance with, such obligations may involve action at the international level, such as the notification of other states of activities which may harm their environment. In most cases, however, the major obligations will require a response within the domestic sphere, especially the adoption of legal measures. International control mechanisms and assistance can help states that lack the capacity to comply immediately with the full panoply of their obligations. This assistance may require international cooperation in institutional frameworks, including financial assistance and training.

Economic instruments are used with growing frequency and can enhance environmental protection, especially in economic systems based on free markets, existing within an underlying, adequate legal framework. Such norms can be adopted by national authorities or private actors—e.g. associations of industrialists—either within a country or at the regional or global level. International, regional or domestic *public* authorities are the only ones that can create legally-binding rules of general application, however, although norms established by non-state actors can be as effective as law or even enforceable by law if they are contained in contracts among the relevant actors.

Financial incentives and disincentives, which are used in national law to affect the behavior of individuals and groups towards the environment, are also a growing part of international environmental law and policy. Financial mechanisms are incorporated in international environmental agreements and in the policies of financial institutions. They are also used by individual states and non-governmental organizations through debt-for-nature exchanges. Although conditionality is sometimes criticized as coercive, it is used extensively, both by financial institutions that condition loans on compliance with environmental norms, and by states that condition compliance on the provision of financial and technical assistance.

The integrated approach that generally seeks to address and monitor all activities potentially endangering the environment is an important contribution to the development of international environmental law. Regulations to protect individual sectors or to restrict the impact of given substances and materials such as chemicals or wastes are increasingly complemented or even superseded by this larger approach, based on ecological needs and considering the impact of all human action. Clearly, such activities as industrial or agricultural production, urban or rural development, scientific research or tourism, and, of course, the combination of them, are at the origin of most environmental degradation. It is thus justified to adopt an integrated approach in norms and rules which are necessary to plan and conduct human activities in the appropriate way in order to save the environment. The key method for future development of international environmental law seems to be to foresee as fully as possible the impact of future activities and to avoid or mitigate their impact, most often by planning and management, including broader use of risk assessment.

With the enormous growth in international environmental law, the opportunity missed at the Rio Conference on Environment and Development to develop a single comprehensive treaty of fundamental environmental norms may be seized in the future. Such an overarching agreement could provide the legal framework to support the further integration of various aspects of environment and development, reinforcing the consensus on basic legal norms both nationally and internationally. It would thus create a single set of fundamental principles to guide states, international organizations and individuals. Perhaps most importantly, it would consolidate and codify many widely-accepted, but disparate, principles and norms contained in non-binding texts on environment and development and fill in gaps in existing law. Additionally, it could facilitate institutional and other linkages among existing treaties and their implementation. Finally, it could establish a common basis for future law-making if needed.

Institutions are essential to environmental protection. They can provide incentives, contribute to developing a consensus on environmental threats and the appropriate responses thereto, and contribute to national policy responses to control the sources of environmental harm. Where there are multiple institutions each with specific and sometimes competing agendas, their contribution becomes diffuse and less effective. It is appropriate, therefore, to consider the possible development of a specialized agency or institution with comprehensive authority over environmental matters. A single institution can enhance public attention to environmental problems and to failures by states to comply with international obligations, in the same way that single environmental agencies within states can be effective in directing general policy in response to threats to the environment. A single institution may better coordinate the collection and dissemination of environmental information and be a focal point of cooperation among states and between states and other international actors.

The necessary two-fold approach to environmental protection, normative and institutional, raises the issue of international environmental governance. There is a need for overall policy coordination that is currently lacking. States appear to prefer a case-by case approach to international environmental policy making, but there is still a need for coherence. Multilateral environmental agreements could be clustered to allow coordination, but this will require political impetus and direction. In addition, there are problems of linking different international legal regimes, including environment, trade, finance, health, human rights, and peace. Substantively, the differences between developed and developing countries should be reduced in order to create an effective and equitable system. This is particularly the case when financing of environmental protection is in question.

In sum, legal developments in the field of environmental protection can be seen as an aspect of globalization, a step toward the creation of a unified or harmonized system for the protection of the planet's environment. The trend seems clearly toward the creation and application of common norms and rules at the different governance levels: global, regional and national.

INDEX